W9-CEH-494

Marketing Research
Methodological Foundations
9th Edition

Gilbert A. Churchill, Jr.
University of Wisconsin-Madison

Dawn Iacobucci
The Wharton School
University of Pennsylvania

THOMSON
SOUTH-WESTERN

Australia · Canada · Mexico · Singapore · Spain · United Kingdom · United States

THOMSON
★
SOUTH-WESTERN

Marketing Research: Methodological Foundations, 9e
Gilbert A. Churchill, Jr. and Dawn Iacobucci

VP/Editorial Director:
Jack W. Calhoun

VP/Editor-in-Chief:
Michael P. Roche

Publisher:
Melissa S. Acuña

Sr. Developmental Editor:
Susanna C. Smart

Marketing Manager:
Nicole C. Moore

Sr. Production Editor:
Elizabeth A. Shipp

Manufacturing Coordinator:
Diane Lohman

Technology Project Editor:
Peggy Buskey

Media Editor:
Pam Wallace

Design Project Manager:
Stacy Jenkins Shirley

Internal and Cover Designer:
Craig Lagesse Ramsdell,
http://www.ramsdelldesign.com

Cover Image:
Karl Weatherly/Getty Images

Production House:
Stratford Publishing Services

Printer:
QuebecorWorld
Versailles, KY

For permission to use material
from this text or product, submit a
request online at http://www.thomson
rights.com. Any additional questions
about permissions can be submitted
by email to thomsonrights@
thomson.com.

For more information contact
South-Western,
5191 Natorp Boulevard,
Mason, Ohio, 45040.
Or you can visit our Internet site at:
http://www.swlearning.com

To my wife and children;

and in memory of my grandmother,
dad, mother, and our son, John.

GAC

Brief Contents

Contents

Part 2: Determine Research Design   71

Part 3: Design Data-Collection Methods and Forms   165

Part 4: Sample Design for Data Collection and Sample Size   319

Part 5: Data Analysis and Interpretation   403

Part 6: The Research Report   637

Preface

Marketing research is complicated—it requires answers to many questions and tough decisions are made at each step in the process, for example, techniques to be used to solve the research problem. In *Marketing Research: Methodological Foundations,* we provide an overarching framework so that students won't become overwhelmed by the bits and pieces, but instead will be able to see the interrelationships of the parts to the whole. This appreciation is important because decisions made at one stage in the marketing research process have consequences at other stages. Managers must be aware of the subtle and pervasive interactions among the parts of the research process in order to be appropriately confident about a particular research result.

Marketing Research: Methodological Foundations attempts to serve both the marketing manager and marketing researchers by its basic organization through the stages of the research process. These stages form the structure of the book:

1. Formulate the problem.
2. Determine the research design.
3. Design the data-collection methods and forms.
4. Design the sample and collect the data.
5. Analyze and interpret the data.
6. Prepare the research report.

Breaking down the steps allows students to see the forest from the trees, and also provides instructors a great deal of latitude in what is covered. An instructor's decision about what to cover will depend, of course, on the background, interests, and preparation of the students, and on the time provided in the curriculum for marketing research. Given the flexibility in the structure of this book, *Marketing Research: Methodological Foundations* can be used in a variety of marketing research course sequences: one- or two-quarter sequences, semester courses, and so on. The first eight editions of the book have been used at all levels: undergraduate, graduate, and executive courses.

Intended Market

This book introduces marketing research to MBA students, executive MBA students, and advanced undergraduates. It is also designed to serve as a reference for marketers seeking to better understand marketing research.

Organization

Part 1, *Marketing Research, the Research Process, and Problem Definition,* consists of three chapters. Chapter 1 provides an overview of marketing research, including who is doing the research and the kinds of problems for which it is used. Chapter 2 provides an overview of the various ways of gathering marketing intelligence. It emphasizes the increasingly important role played by marketing intelligence systems in providing business and competitive information. Chapter 3 provides an overview of the research process in terms of the kinds of decisions to be made at each stage, and then discusses in greater detail the problem formulation stage of the research process.

Part 2, *Determine Research Design,* consists of three chapters and emphasizes ensuring that the research addresses the appropriate questions and treats them in an efficient manner. Chapter 4 presents the varieties of research designs and proceeds to exploratory research and qualitative data. Chapter 5 presents aspects of descriptive designs. Chapter 6 discusses the role of experiments.

Part 3, *Design Data-Collection Methods and Forms,* gets into data. Chapter 7 focuses on secondary data as an information resource and includes a discussion of commercial marketing information services. The prime sources of secondary data are just a click away on our Web site. Chapter 8 discusses the kinds of information we can gather, for example attitudes and behaviors, and the means by which we can gather that information—via observation or techniques that rely on forms of communication (e.g., interviews, surveys). Chapter 9 covers the construction of questionnaires. Chapter 10 explains the general topic of attitude measurement using scales, and discusses some of the more common types of attitude scales. The important topic of developing measures for marketing constructs is discussed in the appendix to Chapter 10.

Part 4, *Sample Design for Data Collection and Sample Size,* consists of three chapters and is concerned with the actual data that are needed to answer questions. Chapter 11 discusses the various types of sampling plans that can be used to determine the population elements from which data should be collected. Chapter 12 considers how many of these elements are needed, so that the problem can be answered with the required precision and confidence in the results. Chapter 13 discusses the types of errors that can arise in completing this data collection task, so that managers can assess the quality of the information they receive from research.

Part 5, *Data Analysis and Interpretation,* emphasizes the search for meaning in the collected information. The five chapters and several appendices attempt to overview the steps and questions. Chapter 14 reviews the preliminary analysis steps of editing, coding, and tabulating the data. The appendix covers chi-squares and related approaches to analyzing categorical data. Chapter 15 provides a framework of basic questions that must be resolved before statistical examination of the data can begin. Next, Chapters 16, 17, and 18 review the statistical techniques most useful in the analysis of marketing data. Chapter 16 discusses the procedures appropriate for examining the differences between groups; Chapter 17 covers the assessment of association—namely, correlation and regression, including conjoint analysis; and Chapter 18 examines the multivariate techniques of discriminant analysis, factor analysis, cluster analysis, and multidimensional scaling. The appendix to Chapter 18 introduces several additional multivariate techniques: correspondence analysis, structural equations modeling, neural network models, and social networks.

Part 6 consists of one chapter and an epilogue. Chapter 19, *The Research Report,* discusses a critical part of the research process, which often becomes the standard by which the research effort is assessed. Chapter 19 discusses the criteria a research report should satisfy, and the form it should follow in order to contribute positively to the research effort. This chapter also discusses some of the graphical means that can be used to communicate the important findings more forcefully. The epilogue ties together the elements of the research process by demonstrating an overview of their interrelationships.

Organizational Flexibility

The organization of the book by the stages in the research process produces several significant benefits. First, it demonstrates and continually reinforces how the "bits" of research technique fit into a larger whole. Students can see readily, for example, the relationship between statistics and marketing research, or where they might pursue additional study to become research specialists.

Second, the organization permits great flexibility. For example, instructors with only a single, brief, one-quarter introductory course in marketing research who are faced with the need to develop some appreciation for the basic questions addressed in research might choose to overview the research process at an elementary level. One way to accomplish this would be to omit Chapter 6 on causal research designs, Chapter 10 on attitude measurement, and Chapter 12 on sample size, and to cover only Chapter 14 from among the five analysis chapters. This approach would serve to present the process and at the same time avoid some of the more technical questions of research design, measurement, sampling, and the statistical analysis of the collected data.

In contrast, instructors who wish to emphasize, say, data analysis would have ample materials to do so. There are data sets available for download at the textbook support web site (**http://churchill.swlearning.com**) that instructors can have students analyze. The "buying through catalogs" database in the book can be used to demonstrate everything from the coding of data to the most involved statistical techniques. The appendices to various chapters provide students with a direct connection between statistical concepts and the application of these concepts. Students can perform their own analyses, thereby increasing their comfort level with the statistical techniques discussed. More suggestions about structuring courses based on selections of chapters are provided in the instructor's manual.

Each part of the book offers cases that illustrate many of the major issues raised in the section. The cases present actual situations, although many of them have disguised names and locations to protect the identity of the sponsors. Students can apply what they have learned by critically evaluating what others have done, thereby increasing their analytical skills.

Changes to the Ninth Edition

This ninth edition contains some major changes:

1. The material has been condensed where appropriate to "tighten up" the text and make it more student friendly.
2. Learning objectives now launch each chapter, so students know why they're reading it.
3. Margin boxes succinctly summarize central points.

4. More examples draw from international marketing research settings and others are about the Internet.
5. 25 percent of the cases are new.
6. Given their popularity with instructors, we've retained

- the Thorndike Sports Video Case discussion questions, which appear on our Web site (http://churchill.swlearning.com), as do the former Avery Sporting Goods appendices);
- the Ethical Dilemmas presented in each chapter to take class discussion beyond techniques; and
- the nearly 100 Research Realities to demonstrate to students "how they do it in the *real world*."

Special Features

The level and difficulty of the material varies across the chapters. Certain parts, such as the discussion of secondary data, are purely descriptive. Others, such as the concept of measurement, are by their nature abstract and often difficult for students. This range of difficulty is characteristic of marketing research, and the book does not shy away from topics simply because they are challenging. Rather, it includes topics vital to understanding marketing research, while attempting to simplify complex ideas into their basic elements. Throughout, the emphasis is on a student's conceptual understanding of the material rather than on the mathematical niceties or discussions of interesting but unimportant tangents. We didn't want to produce a marketing research text that is fluff, one that provides an overview but not sufficient detail about some topic in research. We also didn't want to provide a book decipherable only by highly motivated technophiles. *Marketing Research: Methodological Foundations,* 9th edition, is designed to avoid such extremes through a thorough treatment of the important concepts, both simple and complex.

Our philosophy is to provide the student with the pros and cons of the various methods, and to help them appreciate why the advantages and disadvantages arise. Then students will be better able to creatively apply and critically evaluate the procedures of marketing research.

Some of the features we've designed to help students develop their marketing research skills include:

- *Cases.* The cases at the end of each part are included to assist students in developing their evaluation and analytical skills. They are also diverse, and therefore are useful in demonstrating the universal application of marketing research techniques beyond distributors of products, nonprofits, e-commerce, banking services, and international arenas. Moreover, raw data for the cases are available to let students try their hand at analyses by answering the questions posed, and in the process, to develop their data analysis skills.
- *The Thorndike Video Case.* The video case, by Ronald M. Weiers of Indiana University of Pennsylvania, is available to adopting instructors and allows for an interactive learning environment. Students can be shown segments of the video, and class discussion can then be structured to identify the issues and determine what should be done next. In this sense, the video case parallels the type of situation students are likely to encounter in the workplace. It also helps show how decisions made at one stage of the research process affect decisions made at later stages.

- *Ethical Dilemmas*. The ethical dilemmas present students with possible scenarios for making marketing research choices. They are presented along with discussion of the technical choices, so students can see not only the advantages and disadvantages of proceeding in particular ways, but also the social consequences of doing so.
- *Research Realities*. Numerous research realities throughout the text illustrate what is happening in the world of marketing research today, both generally and with regard to specific companies.
- *Problems*. The problems at the end of each chapter allow students to apply the chapter concepts to specific situations, thereby developing firsthand knowledge of the strengths and weaknesses of the various techniques.
- *NFO Coffee Study*. The questionnaire, coding form, and raw data from a study on ground coffee conducted by NFO are available on the Web site (**http://churchill. swlearning.com**), and are used to frame a number of application problems. The study gives students an opportunity to work with "live" data and to hone their skills in translating research problems into data analysis issues and in interpreting computer output. Moreover, the database is rich enough for instructors to design their own application problems/exercises, thereby allowing even more opportunity for hands-on learning.
- *Exercises*. There are exercises in the instructor's manual for each chapter that include small-scale projects using particular techniques. The exercises develop students' in-depth understanding of the techniques, including their proper application.

Supplements

A majority of the supplements to the text are now available on the text Web site at **http://churchill.swlearning.com** and on the Instructor's Resource CD-ROM. Both contain the Instructor's Manual, Test Bank, Computerized Test Bank, PowerPoint slides, and Data Sets. The electronic access allows better customization for instructors, allowing them to extract whatever they need for their course, as they need it. The supplements include the following:

- *Instructor's Manual*. The Instructor's Manual begins the comprehensive teaching package. It includes a preface that offers suggestions on how the book can be used most effectively. The preface is followed by suggestions on how to teach the course to achieve desired emphases within different time frames. Next are the chapter-by-chapter resource materials, which include the following for each chapter:

  1. Learning objectives
  2. List of key terms
  3. Detailed outline
  4. Lecture and discussion suggestions
  5. Suggested supplementary readings
  6. Answers to the application questions and/or problems in the book
  7. Student exercises and answers
  8. Suggested cases for the chapter

The individual chapter materials are followed by a section containing the analyses for the cases included in the book. A number of the cases ask students to perform their own analyses to answer the questions posed. The Thorndike Case Script is also available as part of the Instructor's Manual, for classroom use and as a reference for the video.

- *Test Bank*. There are more than 1,100 multiple-choice objective examination questions in the test bank, many of which are new for this edition. The Web site includes the test bank in Microsoft Word files for instructors only, if they prefer these to the computerized testing program, ExamView.
- *Computerized Test Bank*. ExamView Computerized Testing Software contains all of the questions in the printed test bank. This program is an easy-to-use test creation software compatible with Microsoft Windows. Instructors can add or edit questions, instructions, and answers, and select questions by previewing them on the screen, selecting them randomly, or selecting them by number. Instructors can also create and administer quizzes online, whether over the Internet, a local area network (LAN), or a wide area network (WAN). ExamView is available on the Instructor's Resource CD-ROM.
- *PowerPoint slides*. More than 200 PowerPoint slides were created to facilitate classroom discussion and to serve as a lecture and study aid. Many slides are drawn from the book and others are new additions.
- *Data Sets*. The raw data for the cases allows instructors and students to use them for analysis. The data are also available in SPSS format.
- *Cases*. Thirty-four additional cases not in the text are also provided.

Available separately are:

- The *Video Collection to Accompany Marketing Research: Methodological Foundations*. In addition to the Thorndike Video Case, there are other videos in the series. Companies such as Fossil watches, Hard Candy, Upjohn's Rogaine, and more, focus on the concepts presented throughout the text.
- *South-Western's Marketing Resources Web site*. South-Western offers a suite of content-rich dynamic Web features developed specifically for marketing students at **http://marketing.swlearning.com**. These features include summaries of the latest marketing news stories, a number of marketing resource links organized by topics, and valuable information regarding marketing careers and job opportunities. In addition, cases from Harvard Business School Cases have been selected to accompany *Marketing Research: Methodological Foundations* and can be accessed through the text Web site (**http://churchill.swlearning.com**).

Acknowledgments

Writing a book is never the work of a single person, and when attempting to acknowledge the contributions of others, one always runs the risk of omitting some important contributions. Nonetheless, the attempt must be made, because this book has benefited immensely from the many helpful comments I have received along the way from users and interested colleagues. I especially wish to acknowledge those people who reviewed the manuscript for this or for one of the earlier editions of the book. While much of the credit for the strengths of the book is theirs, the blame for any weaknesses is strictly mine. Thank you one and all for your most perceptive and helpful comments.

My colleagues at the University of Wisconsin have my thanks for the intellectual stimulation they have always provided. Dr. B. Venkatesh was particularly instrumental in getting the first edition off the ground. My discussions with him were important in determining the scope and structure of the book.

I wish to thank the many assistants at the University of Wisconsin, especially Janet Christopher, who helped in the preparation of one or more versions of the manuscript. I also wish to thank students Tom Brown, Sara Evans, Margaret Friedman, Diana Haytko, Jacqueline Hitchon, Larry Hogue, Joseph Kuester, Jayashree Mahajan, Jennifer Markanen, Sara Pitterle, Kay Powers, and Frank Wadsworth for their help with many of the miscellaneous tasks on either this edition or one of the earlier ones.

I would like to thank Melissa Acuña, publisher, as well as the entire production staff at Thomson Business and Professional Publishing for their professional effort. I also want to thank P. J. Ward of NFO for contributing the questionnaire, coding form, database, and the compatible problems and exercises using the database regarding coffee consumption that illustrate so nicely the statistical ideas discussed in the text.

Finally, I owe a special debt of thanks to my wife, Helen, and our four children, Carol, Elizabeth, David, and Thomas. Their understanding, cooperation, and support through all editions of this book are sincerely appreciated.

Gilbert A. Churchill, Jr.
Madison, Wisconsin

I'd like to add my thanks, first and foremost, to Gil Churchill, and also to Bill Schoof for giving me the opportunity to participate in this text. Anyone who knows Gil will not be surprised by my comment that I couldn't have hoped for a more gracious and encouraging coauthor and mentor. I also thank the reviewers I have e-mailed for suggestions about various elements of the text, including Neeraj Arora, CB Bhattacharya, Ruth Bolton, Ray Burke, Peter Danaher, Paul Dholakia, Bill Dillon, Fred Feinberg, Sachin Gupta, Jackie Kacen, John Lastovicka, Bob Leone, Michael Lewis, David Mick, Tom Miller, Reza Moinpour, Vicki Morwitz, Priya Raghubir, Marsha Richins, Raj Sethuraman, Sharon Shavitt, Donald Stem, Dave Stewart, and Madhu Viswanathan.

Dawn Iacobucci
Evanston, Illinois

Reviewers

Mark I. Alpert,
University of Texas–Austin

Robert L. Anderson,
University of South Florida

Gary M. Armstrong,
University of North Carolina

Emin Babakus,
University of Memphis

Sri Beldona,
University of Dallas

Frank J. Carmone, Jr.,
Drexel University

Joseph Chasin,
St. John's University

Imran S. Currim,
University of California–Irvine

Michael R. Czinkota,
Georgetown University

Albert J. DellaBitta,
University of Rhode Island

John Dickinson,
University of Windsor

James F. Engel,
Eastern College

Peter Faynzilberg,
Carnegie Mellon University

Claes Fornell,
University of Michigan

Margot Griffin,
California Lutheran University

Sachin Gupta,
Northwestern University

James W. Harvey,
George Mason University

Vince Howe,
University of North Carolina–
Wilmington

Roy Howell,
Texas Tech University

G. David Hughes,
University of North Carolina

Dipak C. Jain,
Northwestern University

Robert Krapfel,
University of Maryland

Patrick Kurby,
Rutgers University

H. Bruce Lammers,
California State University–
Northridge

Peter La Placa,
University of Connecticut

Charles L. Martin,
Wichita State University

M. Dean Martin,
Western Carolina University

David Mick,
University of Virginia

Carlos W. Moore,
Baylor University

About the Authors

Gilbert A. Churchill, Jr., received his DBA from Indiana University and joined the University of Wisconsin faculty in 1966. Professor Churchill was named Distinguished Marketing Educator by the American Marketing Association in 1986—only the second individual so honored. This lifetime achievement award recognizes and honors a living marketing educator for distinguished service and outstanding contributions in the field of marketing education. Professor Churchill was also awarded the Academy of Marketing Science's lifetime achievement award in 1993 for his significant scholarly contributions. In 1996, he received the Paul D. Converse Award, which is given to the most influential marketing scholars, as judged by a national jury drawn from universities, businesses, and government. Also in 1996, the Marketing Research Group of the American Marketing Association established the Gilbert A. Churchill, Jr., lifetime achievement award, which is to be given each year to a person judged to have made significant lifetime contributions to marketing research. In 2002, he received the Charles Coolidge Parlin lifetime achievement award for his substantial contributions to the ongoing advancement of marketing research practice.

Professor Churchill is a past recipient of the William O'Dell Award for his outstanding article appearing in the *Journal of Marketing Research*. He has also been a finalist for the award five other times. He is coauthor of the most and third most influential articles of the past century in sales managements as judged by a panel of experts in the field. He was named Marketer of the Year by the South Central Wisconsin chapter of the American Marketing Association in 1981. He is a member of the American Marketing Association and has served as consultant to a number of companies, including Oscar Mayer, Western Publishing Company, and Parker Pen.

Professor Churchill's articles have appeared in such publications as the *Journal of Marketing Research, Journal of Marketing, Journal of Consumer Research, Journal of Retailing, Journal of Business Research, Decision Sciences, Technometrics,* and *Organizational Behavior and Human Performance,* among others. He is coauthor of several books, including *Basic Marketing Research,* 5th ed. (Mason, OH: South-Western, 2004), *Marketing: Creating Value for Customers,* 2nd ed. (Burr Ridge, IL: McGraw-Hill, 1998), *Sales Force Management: Planning, Implementation, and Control,* 6th ed. (Burr Ridge, IL: Irwin/McGraw-Hill, 2000), and *Salesforce Performance* (Lexington, MA: Lexington Books, 1984), in addition to his coauthorship of *Marketing Research: Methodological Foundations,* 9th ed. (Mason, OH: South-Western, 2005). He is a former editor of the *Journal of Marketing Research* and has served on the editorial boards of the *Journal of Marketing Research, Journal of Marketing, Journal of Business Research, Journal of Health Care Marketing,* and the *Asian Journal of Marketing.* Professor Churchill is a past recipient of the Lawrence J. Larson Excellence in Teaching Award.

Dawn Iacobucci joined the marketing department at The Wharton School of the University of Pennsylvania in 2004. Previously she was professor of marketing at Kellogg, Northwestern University, from 1987, when she received her Ph.D. in quantitative psychology from the University of Illinois at Urbana-Champaign. During 2001–2002, she was the Coca-Cola Distinguished Professor of Marketing and Psychology, and head of the marketing department at the University of Arizona. She is currently editor of the *Journal of Consumer Research,* and past editor of the *Journal of Consumer Psychology.* She edited the volumes *Kellogg on Marketing, Kellogg on Integrated Marketing, Networks in Marketing,* and coedited the *Handbook of Services Marketing and Management* with Teresa Swartz.

Professor Iacobucci's articles have appeared in the *Journal of Marketing Research, Journal of Marketing, Journal of Consumer Psychology, Harvard Business Review, Sloan Management Review, Journal of Interactive Marketing, Journal of Service Marketing, Psychometrika, Psychological Bulletin, Multivariate Behavioral Research, Journal of Personality and Social Psychology,* and more. She teaches marketing research and services marketing courses to MBA students and analysis of variance and multivariate statistics seminars to doctoral students.

## PART 1

Marketing Research, the Research Process, and Problem Definition

We begin with an overview, addressing two basic questions: What is marketing research? Why is it important?

- Chapter 1 illustrates the enormous variety of problems that marketing research can be used to address and the types of businesspeople who require a working knowledge of marketing research—marketing researchers and marketing managers, as well as consultants, entrepreneurs, financial analysts, Internet moguls—anybody who seeks an edge in understanding customers in competitive market environments.

- Chapter 2 discusses alternative ways of providing marketing intelligence, namely, projects designed to investigate specific issues, or information technologies for ongoing data collection and analytical systems.

- Chapter 3 presents the research process that forms the backbone of this book and discusses in detail the problem formulation stage of that process.

## CHAPTER 1

Marketing Research: It's Everywhere!

Questions to Guide Your Learning:

Q1: What is marketing research?

Q2: What kinds of questions can marketing research answer?

Q3: Why is marketing research important?

Q4: What is the relationship among marketing, marketing research, and the other activities of a firm?

Q5: Who does marketing research?

Many people have a mistaken impression about marketing research—that it's only about asking consumers what they think about a brand or ad. Although marketing research does use consumer surveys, it involves much more than that. Consider the following examples.

Example   After watching countless hours of videotapes of consumers entering various retail outlets such as department stores, grocery stores, and banks, marketing researchers have advised against investing in elaborate store displays for the first 30 feet from the entrance, the so-called "decompression zone" in which shoppers are merely getting oriented to the store layout and are not inclined to pick up merchandise for purchase. Similarly, researchers noted that most consumers are likely to veer right as they proceed into the store, not because most are right-handed, but because we drive on the right—British and Australian consumers veer left.[1]

---

[1] Paco Underhill, *Why We Buy: The Science of Shopping* (Touchstone Books, 2000).

Example You know the stories about Amazon.com, but did you know how much its executives like marketing research data? They want to know "average customer contacts per order, average time per contact, the breakdown of e-mail vs. telephone contacts, and the total cost to the company of each." One exec says he looks at "about 300 charts a week for his division alone." They *love* data and state, "The trouble with most corporations is that they make judgment-based decisions when data-based decisions could be made."[2]

Example Gillette develops new products (e.g., laser hair removal) by watching consumers shave—not by standing in their bathrooms, but by watching video from microcameras that have been attached to razors that the consumers were using to shave. This close-up view shows clearly what the blades do to the whiskers and surrounding skin, enabling Gillette to create more effective shaving instruments, to make superior product claims, and to charge premium prices.[3]

Example Marketing researchers are increasingly combining sources of data to get a fuller understanding of their customers and their competitive marketplace. For example, customer relationship management databases and models can identify the customers' behaviors, e.g., a customer who "contacted the call center on Jan. 5 at 12:31 P.M. to order product Y based on promotional offer Z," etc., but it's marketing research that allows marketing managers to understand *why;* why did the customer order through the call center and not the retail outlet or the Web site? Why that product and not one similar to it? Why that style, size, shape, color? Why did that promotional offer trigger a response, when others, similar in incentive structure, had failed?[4]

Example Many organizations are supplementing customer satisfaction surveys by deploying "secret shoppers" to conduct discreet tests of the moments-of-truth between customers and service providers. The secret shopper engages in a normal purchase transaction and reports back to the firm his or her experience, answering questions such as: Was the merchandise easy to find and of high quality? Were the service people helpful? Could you get through to a knowledgeable person when calling the company's 800 customer service center number? Did the Web site function properly or were there dysfunctional links?[5]

Example When Audi executives started listening to their customers, their sales grew 60% in 5 years, and they retained some 40% repeat loyal customers. Five years ago, Audi ranked last in luxury autos in U.K. surveys of customer satisfaction. Though the owners liked the cars, they identified serious service flaws: nonstandard hours of operation, inconsistent and idiosyncratic service availability, etc. Audi used this marketing research to redesign its network to provide at least these basics: easy appointment access, courtesy cars, free car wash, and itemized invoices with no charge for unauthorized work. In just two years, 87% of the U.K. customers reported perfect delivery of these basic services by their service center.[6]

Example Researchers are intrigued by the potential of online chat-rooms as a focus group forum. They cite large savings in travel expenses, because the participants can log in from all over the world. They also say that new products or advertisements

---

[2] Fred Vogelstein, "Mighty Amazon," *Fortune* (May 26, 2003), p. 64, pp. 60–74.

[3] Charles Forelle, "Razors to Lasers," *Wall Street Journal* (Feb. 20, 2003), p. D4.

[4] Doug Grisaffe, "See About Linking CRM and MR Systems," *Marketing News* (Jan. 21, 2002), p.13.

[5] Bob Donath, "It's Time for You to Be a 'Mystery Inquirer,'" *Marketing News* (Jan. 17, 2000), p. 6.

[6] Susan Suffes, "Audi's Drive to Service Excellence," *Gallup Management Journal* (April 10, 2003), http://gmj.gallup.com.

can be shown online just as easily as in person, and they point out that the time-consuming and expensive step of transcribing focus group tapes is unnecessary, because the online focus group is already conducted in text, which may simply be downloaded and saved. Critics of online focus groups say that important cues and reactions such as nonverbal body language are lost in the online environment, but supporters respond that they encourage online focus group participants to use emoticons, such as the smiley faces [:)], and note that soon, video capabilities will allow all participants to see each other, simulating more closely a traditional focus group.[7]

Example When Wrigley found sales and market share for its Juicy Fruit gum declining, the company asked teens who were frequent gum-chewers to find pictures that reminded them of the gum and to write a short story about them. Marketing researchers studied each montage and noted a common theme of "sweet tasting." Advertising was created with the tag line "Gotta Have Sweet," which proved memorable, and sales rose 5% after the campaign.[8]

Example Frequent-shopper programs get customers to provide personal information (e.g., name, address), in exchange for a card that the company uses to track buying habits. In exchange, club members get price discounts and direct-mail promotions customized to reflect the individual's shopping habits. The cards also help logistics—because the stores know which products are selling and how fast, they can order just what they need, when they need it, from their suppliers.

Example Arby's Inc. opened an Allentown, PA prototype store called The Pinnacle, based on consumer feedback. Consumer research identified problems such as the easily measured "speed of service," as well as more subjective issues regarding "food variety and quality," and even the truly intangible issue of "ambience." The innovations include a single-line customer service system, computers and wireless integrated systems, redesigned kitchen and counter layout, better bun toasting equipment, and beef steamer scales and temperature probes. These changes have collectively led to more efficient traffic flow, reduced operational equipment needs, and greater customer satisfaction. The store has been so successful, there are of course plans to roll out the prototype throughout the 3300-unit franchise.[9]

These examples only scratch the surface regarding the scope of marketing research activities. This book will show you what marketing research is and how it can be used. The choice of marketing research tools depends on the problem to be solved. Marketing research is a pervasive activity that can take many forms. The basic purpose of marketing research is to help managers make better decisions in any of their areas of responsibility.

> Marketing research turns *data* into *information.*

Role of Marketing Research

Anyone planning a career in business should understand what marketing research can do. Every day, marketing managers are called upon to make *decisions,* sometimes minor, sometimes far-reaching, each of which will be better-informed and likely to produce better results with the intelligent use of marketing research. Effective decision

[7] Steve Jarvis and Deborah Szynal, "Show and Tell," *Marketing News* (Nov. 19, 2001), pp. 1, 13.

[8] Jennifer Lach, "How Sweet It Is," *American Demographics* (March 2000), pp. s4–s21.

[9] Howard Riell, "Arbys Poised at the Pinnacle," *Foodservice Equipment & Supplies* (Feb. 2003), pp. 36–40.

making depends on quality input, and marketing research plays an essential role in translating data into useful information. Any business seeking an edge in attracting and retaining customers in competitive market environments turns to marketing. In turn, marketing can create strategies to work toward these goals of attraction and retention, if the business understands its customers. This understanding comes through marketing research, using both periodic projects directed toward specific problems at hand, and continuing, ongoing measurement of the marketplace.

Beyond marketing researchers and marketers, the success of one's career in many related fields is enhanced by a working knowledge of marketing research. For example, much of management consulting is fundamentally marketing research. Entrepreneurs enhance their likelihood of staying in business by understanding their growing customer base. Financial analysts need to understand the perceptions of their customers to sell their products. Those Internet service providers who invest the time to understand what their customers value will be around long after their less knowledgeable upstarts crash.

People beyond traditional business boundaries also benefit from research. For example, land planners use marketing research to understand the desires of their constituents—from shopping mall site location to where a new neighborhood park might be built. Politicians use marketing research to plan campaign strategies; e.g., as much as citizens protest negative ad campaigns, such ads continue because they are memorable and advertising agencies measure success in part through short-term memory measures. Clergy and congregations use marketing research to determine when to hold services, what genre of worship music to play, and how to serve the different segments in the congregation.

The principal task of marketing is to create value for customers, where customer value is the comparison between customer perceptions of the benefits they receive from purchasing and using products and services, and their perceptions of the costs they incur in exchange for them. Customers who are willing and able to make exchanges do so when (1) the benefits of exchanges exceed the costs of exchanges, and (2) the products or services offer superior value compared to alternatives. In their attempts to create customer value, marketing managers generally focus their efforts on the elements of the marketing mix, i.e., the four Ps—the product or service, its price, its placement or the channels in which it is distributed, and its promotion or communications mix.

The marketing manager develops a marketing strategy combining the marketing mix elements in a complementary way to positively influence customers' value perceptions and behaviors. This task would be much simpler if all the elements that affect customers' perceptions of value were under the manager's control and if customer reaction to any contemplated change could be predicted with certainty. Usually, however, a number of factors affecting the success of the marketing effort, including economic, political and legal, social, natural, technological, and competitive environments, are beyond the marketing manager's control, and the behavior of individual customers is largely unpredictable.

Figure 1.1 summarizes the task of marketing management. Customers are the focus of the firm's activities. Their satisfaction is achieved through simultaneous adjustments in the elements of the marketing mix, but the results of these adjustments are uncertain because the marketing task takes place within an uncontrollable environment (see Figure 1.2). Consequently, as director of the firm's marketing activities, the marketing manager has an urgent, continuous need for information—and marketing research is responsible for providing it. Marketing research is the firm's formal communication link with the customer and environment. It is the means by

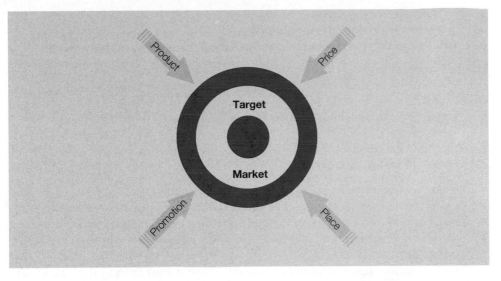

FIGURE 1.1
The Task of Marketing
Management

which the firm generates, transmits, and interprets information from the customer and environment about or relating to the success of the firm's marketing plans.

The American Marketing Association's (AMA) definition of marketing research emphasizes its information-linkage role (marketingpower.org):

Marketing research is the function which links the consumer, customer, and public to the marketer through information—information used to identify and define marketing opportunities and problems; generate, refine, and evaluate marketing actions; monitor marketing performance; and improve our understanding of marketing as a process.

Note that this definition indicates that marketing research provides information to the marketer for use in at least four areas:

1. Generate ideas for marketing action, including identifying marketing problems and opportunities

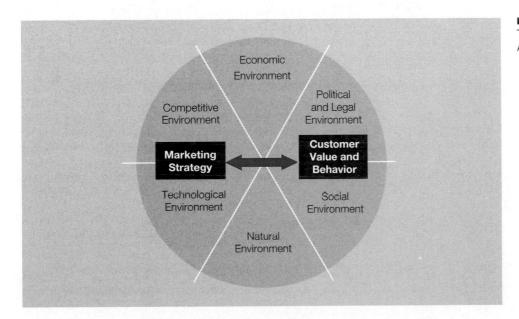

FIGURE 1.2
The Environments That
Affect Marketing

2. Evaluate marketing actions
3. Compare performance versus objectives
4. Develop a general understanding of marketing phenomena and processes

Further, marketing research is involved with all phases of the information management process, including: (1) the specification of what information is needed; (2) the collection and analysis of the information; and (3) the interpretation of that information with respect to the objectives that motivated the study in the first place.

Overseers of the marketing research industry, e.g., the American Marketing Association, regularly detail how organizations use marketing research. The research topics span all aspects of marketing, for example:

- Product (concept testing, brand name development, test markets, packaging designs)
- Pricing (cost, price, elasticities, market demand, sales potential and forecasting)
- Distribution (Web site testing, channel performance, coverage, exports)
- Promotion (media and ad copy effectiveness, image, sales force compensation and territory structure)
- Buyer behavior (segmentation, awareness, satisfaction, brand preferences, attitudes and behavior)
- General corporate research (market trends, diversification opportunities)

Of course, some topics are more popular than others. Figure 1.3 shows the frequency of different kinds of marketing research applications, as measured by the research firms' revenues per market activity.

Another way of looking at the function of marketing research is to consider how management uses it (see Table 1.1). Some marketing research is used for planning, some for problem solving, and some for control. When used for planning, it deals largely with determining which marketing opportunities are viable and which are not promising for the firm. When workable opportunities are uncovered, marketing research provides estimates of their size and scope, so that marketing management can better assess the resources needed to develop them. Problem-solving marketing research focuses on the short- or long-term decisions regarding the marketing mix. Control-oriented marketing research helps management isolate trouble spots and monitor current operations.

FIGURE 1.3
Where Marketing
Research Dollars Are
Concentrated

Source: From *American Demographics,* June 2001. Copyright 2001 PRIMEDIA Business Magazines & Media, Inc. All rights reserved.

TABLE 1.1
Kinds of Questions
Marketing Research
Can Help Answer

A. Planning

1. Segmentation: What kinds of people buy our products? Where do they live? How much do they earn? How many of them are there?

2. Demand estimation: Are the markets for our products increasing or decreasing? Are there promising markets that we have not yet reached?

3. Environmental assessment: Are the channels of distribution for our products changing? What should our presence on the Internet be?

B. Problem Solving

1. Product
   a. In testing new products and product-line extensions, which product design is likely to be the most successful? What features do consumers value most?
   b. What kind of packaging should we use?
   c. What are the forecasts for the product? How might we reenergize its life cycle?

2. Price
   a. What price should we charge for our products?
   b. How sensitive to price changes are our target segments?
   c. Given the life-time value assessments of our segments, should we be discounting or charging a premium to our most valued customers?
   d. As production costs decline, should we lower our prices or try to develop higher quality products?
   e. Do consumers use price as a cue to value or a cue to quality in our industry?

3. Place
   a. Where, and by whom, are our products being sold? Where, and by whom, should our products be sold?
   b. What kinds of incentives should we offer the trade to push our products?
   c. Are our relationships with our suppliers and distributors satisfactory and cooperative?

4. Promotion
   a. How much should we spend on promotion? How should it be allocated to products and to geographic areas?
   b. Which ad copy should we run in our markets? With what frequency and media expenditures?
   c. What combination of media—newspapers, radio, television, magazines, Internet ad banners—should we use?
   d. What is our consumer coupon redemption rate?

C. Control

1. What is our market share overall? In each geographic area? By each customer type?

2. Are customers satisfied with our products? How is our record for service? Are there many returns? Do levels of customer satisfaction vary with market? With segment?

3. Are our employees satisfied? Do they feel well-trained and empowered to assist our customers?

4. How does the public perceive our company? What is our reputation with the trade?

It is important to highlight the key role of marketing research in the decision-making process. Marketing research is an essential element of marketing. Consider the lessons learned, and exhortations offered, from industry:

- "Marketing research departments must involve themselves in marketing programs as early as possible. . . . Researchers . . . [should] initiate involvement at the strategic level before emotional commitments are made to particular courses of action. . . . if research waits to be asked, the department is missing the boat."[10]

- ". . . how many of the dot-com business ventures were based on solid marketing research? Virtually none. How many of the high-profile telecommunications ventures were based on sound marketing research? Very few. . . . [H]ow many companies use marketing research to refine their business concepts and tweak their processes after new ventures were launched? Fewer still." What kinds of marketing research are most important? Strategy research is "critical"; product testing is the "single most important research you'll ever do"; advertising pretesting is also "important"; operations research is an "important type of research for all businesses"; and "Not one in a hundred companies does a good job of analyzing its own sales data."[11] Ouch! (With the marketing research training you've initiated, you'll do better!)

- The management bible, the *Harvard Business Review,* concedes that "The choices facing managers and the data requiring analysis have multiplied even as the time for analyzing them has shrunk." But it advises the use of marketing research analytical tools, and urges managers to rely on more than instinct![12]

- CFOs understand that marketing research may be useful, but they want it to be "cost-effective." For example, don't start from scratch with each project, but build on existing in-house company information; use research to keep existing customers; factor in time and scheduling when budgeting and planning research.[13] Marketing research is increasingly being used to determine ROI for various marketing mix tactics, ultimately also justifying its own value to the firm.[14]

- Usually all it takes for marketing research to be useful and actionable is communication! Research is better received and more likely acted upon if the researcher-client relationship begins with an agreement on the objectives of the research and a commitment to take action upon learning the results.[15]

- Marketing research gives a voice to your customers. It "represents a philosophy that everyone's voice must be heard and those in power should listen to everyone's opinions. Product development is a key . . . to the industrial world's economies, and a key aspect of product development is designing products that meet and exceed customers' needs."[16] Marketing research . . . brings the customer's voice into the corporate boardroom. . . . [R]esearchers are the lifeline to

Do executives think marketing research is important? Yes!

---

[10] Brett Hagins, "Introduce Research Role Early in Programs," *Marketing News* (Aug. 18, 2003), p. H31; Dana James, "Establish Your Place at the Table," *Marketing News* (Sept. 16, 2002), pp. 1, 19.

[11] Jerry Thomas, "Skipping MR a Major Error," *Marketing News* (March 4, 2002), p. 50.

[12] Eric Bonabeau, "Don't Trust Your Gut," *Harvard Business Review* (May 2003), pp. 116–123.

[13] Deborah Colby, "Using Marketing Research," *Quirk's Marketing Research Review* (http://www.quirks.com).

[14] Steve Jarvis, "MR Adds Value to Shows: Surveys, Customer Sponsorships Help Improve ROI," *Marketing News* (June 24, 2002), p. 11; Debra Goldman "Planning Gets Domesticated," *Adweek* (March 31, 2003), pp. 22–24.

[15] Catherine Arnold, "Seven Steps to Better Research," *Marketing News* (Jan. 20, 2003), p. 13.

[16] John Hauser, "Marketing Makes a Difference," *Marketing Management* (Feb. 2002), pp. 46–47.

the customer . . . and often end up being the translator between the jargon of the marketplace and the jargon of the organization."[17]

In addition, the communication link that marketing research serves between the firm and its customers and environment has become critical and difficult as we've moved to a highly competitive global economy (Table 1.2). Globalization of marketing research naturally follows the globalization of large, multinational clients, and just as products are adapted and tailored for local cultures and tastes, it is also important to recognize that for research too, what works in one environment does not necessarily work in another. Marketing researchers point to international business as one of three key influences on changes in how they conduct their business— the other two factors being the Internet and one-to-one marketing:

The Internet, globalization, and one-to-one marketing are expected to be the primary influences on marketing research, says a survey of marketing research professionals. Interactive research and virtual reality are expected to flourish over the Internet and future broadband electronic communications technologies. The globalization of business will drive more cross-cultural research, to recognize increasing diversity and changing demographic bases. And as companies build relationships with their customers as unique individuals, they will need marketing and marketing research like never before—just who is this customer and what does he or she want? "Marketing research in the 21st century may be barely recognizable by a 20th century researcher" and the marketing research industry will be under more pressure to attract top talent.[18]

TABLE 1.2
Marketing Research Questions About International Markets

- What is the nature of competition in the international market? Who are the major direct and indirect competitors? What are their characteristics?
- What are our firm's competitive strengths and weaknesses in reference to such factors as product quality, product lines, warranties, services, brands, packaging, distribution, sales force, customer service, advertising, prices, experience, technology, capital and human resources, and market share?
- What are the trade incentives and barriers in the country under consideration? What specific requirements (e.g., import or export licenses) must be met to conduct international trade?
- Are we likely to encounter any prejudice against imports or exports among the country's customers? Its government?
- What are different governments doing specifically to encourage or discourage international trade? How difficult are the government regulations for our firm?
- How well developed are the international mass communication media? Are the print and electronics media abroad efficient and effective?
- Are there adequate transportation and storage or warehouse facilities in the foreign market? What is the state of the retailing institutions?

---

[17] William Neal, "Getting Serious About Marketing Research," *Marketing Research* (Summer 2002), pp. 24–28.

[18] Doss Struse, "Marketing Research's Top 25 Influences," *Marketing Research* 11 (Spring 2000), pp. 5–9.

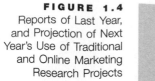

FIGURE 1.4
Reports of Last Year,
and Projection of Next
Year's Use of Traditional
and Online Marketing
Research Projects

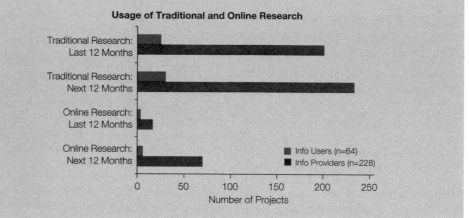

Source: Thomas W. Miller and Abhilasha Gupta (2001), "Studies of Information, Research, and Consulting Services (SRICS): Fall 2000 Survey of Organizations." Technical report published by the A.C. Nielsen Center for Marketing Research, University of Wisconsin-Madison, retrieved from the World Wide Web January 29, 2004 at: http://www. uwisc.edu/nielsencenter.

We say more about these factors in the next chapter. It's important to see these trends in perspective. For example, though Internet-based marketing research is on the rise, as Figure 1.4 depicts, it is still peanuts compared to the bread-and-butter marketing research studies that firms require.

Who Does Marketing Research?

Research Realities 1.1 identifies the historical origins of marketing research, but the industry really began to grow after WWII, when firms found they could no longer sell all they could produce but rather had to gauge market needs and produce accordingly. Marketing research was called upon to estimate these needs. As consumer discretion became more important, there was a shift in the orientation of many firms. Marketing began to assume a more dominant role, and production a less important one. The marketing concept emerged, and along with it came a reorganization of the marketing effort. Many marketing research departments were born in these reorganizations. The growth of these departments was stimulated by a number of factors, including past successes, increased management sophistication, and the data revolution created by computers.

Currently, most firms have a formal marketing research department, or at least a person assigned specifically to the marketing research activity.[19] Marketing research departments are prevalent among industrial and consumer manufacturing companies, as well as other types of companies. Publishers and broadcasters, for example, do

---

[19] At least 75% of recently surveyed firms, whether a manufacturer of consumer or industrial products, a provider of financial services, a broadcaster or advertising agency, retailers and wholesalers, nonprofits or utilities, etc. have an actual department. Perhaps the only industry collectively lagging is the health services industry, which is as likely to have only a single person as an entire (albeit small) department, assigned the responsibilities of marketing research. However, even that industry is trying to catch up, recognizing the importance of marketing research to understand customers and competitors; cf., Jerry Spicer, "How to Measure Patient Satisfaction," *Quality Progress* (Feb. 2002), pp. 97–98; Milton Liebman, "Competitive Edge," *Medical Marketing and Media* (Feb. 2003), pp. 36–41.

Research Realities

1.1 Marketing Research History

Marketing research, as a significant business activity, largely owes its existence to the shift from a production-oriented to a consumption-oriented economy that occurred in the U.S. at the end of World War II. However, some marketing research was conducted before the war, and the origins of formal marketing research predate the war by a good number of years:

More by accident than foresight, N. W. Ayer & Son applied marketing research to marketing and advertising problems. In 1879, in attempting to fit a proposed advertising schedule to the needs of the Nichols-Shepard Company, manufacturers of agricultural machinery, the agency wired state officials and publishers throughout the country requesting information on expected grain production. As a result, the agency was able to construct a crude but formal market survey by states and counties. This attempt to construct a market survey is probably the first real instance of marketing research in the United States (Lockley, pp.1–4).

There were certainly a few formal marketing research departments and marketing research firms before World War II. The Curtis Publishing Company is generally conceded to have formed the first formal marketing research department with the appointment of Charles Parlin as manager of the Commercial Research Division of the Advertising Department in 1911. The A. C. Nielsen Company, the largest marketing research firm in the world, began operation in 1934. But the boom in marketing research growth accompanied the marketplace surge after WWII.

Sources: Lawrence C. Lockley, "History and Development of Marketing Research," in Robert Ferber, ed., *Handbook of Marketing Research*, pp. 1–4. For a detailed treatment of the development of marketing research, see Robert Bartels, *The Development of Marketing Thought* (Irwin, 1962), pp. 106–124, or Jack J. Honomichl, *Marketing Research People* (Crain Books, 1984), pp. 95–184. Also see the article "Notes on the History of Marketing Research," published in the *Journal of Marketing*, accessible online at: http://www.marketingpower.com.

research to generate audience statistics to measure market averages and demographic profiles. These data are then used to sell advertising space and time. Financial service companies also use marketing research to forecast, measure market potentials, and analyze sales and locations.

Most advertising agencies have research departments. They are devoted to studying the effectiveness of alternative ad copy and optimizing the frequency of exposures of customers to ads.

The entire spectrum of marketing research activity also includes specialized marketing research and consulting firms, government agencies, and universities. Research Realities 1.2 shows the revenues of the largest U.S. marketing research firms and the proportion of their revenues generated outside the U.S. Some firms provide syndicated research—they collect certain information on a regular basis, which they then sell to interested clients. The syndicated services include such operations as ACNielsen, which provides product movement data for grocery stores and drugstores, and the NPD Group, which operates a consumer panel. The syndicated services are distinguished by the fact that their research is not custom designed (except that the firm will perform special analyses for the client on the data it regularly collects). Other research firms specialize in custom-designed research. Some of these provide only field service—collecting data for the research sponsor. Some limited-service firms collect the data and also analyze the data for the client. And some research suppliers are full-service, helping the client in the design of the research as well as in collecting and analyzing data.

Other organizations also provide marketing information, e.g., the U.S. federal government is the largest producer of marketing facts through its various censuses and other publications (see the chapter on secondary data). Marketing faculty at business schools report their research in marketing journals, and their counterparts in marketing research firms similarly produce in-house "white papers."

Figure 1.5 shows a glimpse of the industry worldwide. The first panel shows the big spenders on marketing research in Europe. The U.K. dominates, along with

Research Realities

1.2 Top 20 Global Research Organizations

Top 20 U.S. Research Organizations

Source: Reprinted with permission from *Marketing News,* published by the American Marketing Association (June 9, 2003), Chicago: American Marketing Association.

FIGURE 1.5
Who's Conducting
Marketing Research?

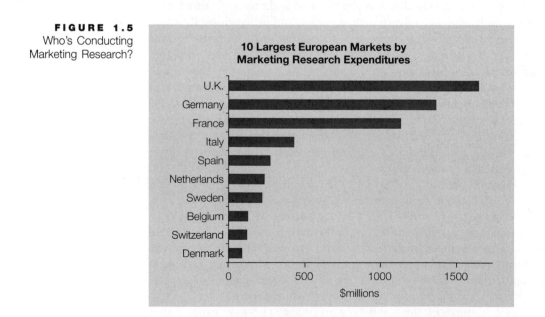

(continued)

FIGURE 1.5
(*continued*)

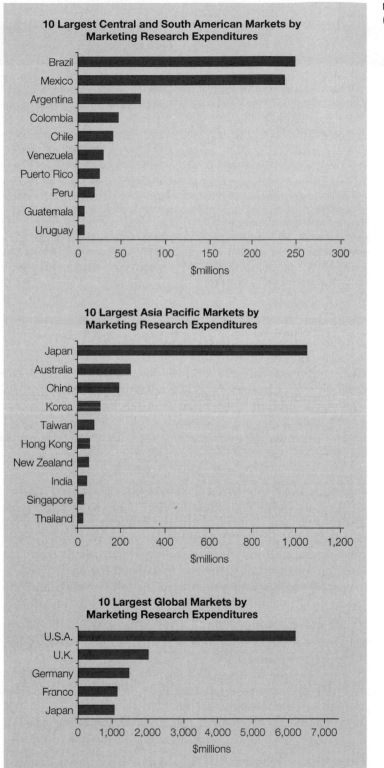

Source: Reprinted with permission from *Marketing News* published by the American Marketing Association, Top 20 U.S. Research Organizations from June 9, 2003 *Marketing News*. All others from July 7, 2003 issue of *Marketing News, Marketing Fact Book*.

Research Realities

1.3 Marketing Research in China

- As China moves toward a free market system, the marketing industry is trying to service managers hungry for information on its customers. You'd think these firms would be busy, since there are only some 400 firms in all of China, but half have revenues of only $10,000 to $50,000.
- Where are most of the MR firms? Guangzhou. Why? Closest to Hong Kong (good template for business success, and cha-ching$). Privately owned firms, systems we take for granted, are forming to provide marketing research.
- Procter & Gamble is widely acclaimed as the company that single-handedly jump-started marketing research in China. It provided hardware, software, and professional training in sampling and research methodologies. It is still a primary client of Guangzhou Market Research Co., the first professional marketing research company formed in China.

- Other marketing research providers are entering the market: Gallup, Nielsen, Taylor Nelson Sofres, NPD Group, Millward Brown. The emphasis of research expenditures is currently on advertising, contributing to stimulating consumer demand and pulling the country toward a market economy.
- How are customers contacted? Not by phone (only 6% of surveys are done via phone, due to penetration low enough to be inefficient and not representative). Internet is growing rapidly but the base is still small (9% of surveys done online). Face-to-face, either door-to-door or in a central location, is the most popular access point (85% of all surveys). Funny, yes? A means of contacting customers that would never work "back home" is the best way to reach the Chinese customer.

Source: Barton Lee, Soumya Saklani and David Tatterson " 'Top Prospects,' State of the MR Industry in China," *Marketing News* 36 (June 10, 2002), pp. 12–13.

Germany and France. The second panel illustrates the relatively large marketing research efforts by Brazil and Mexico. In Asia, the volumes of research are largely conducted in Japan (though see Research Realities 1.3 for some facts on China). Finally, reflecting trade or perhaps our obsession with information, the U.S. marketing research numbers dominate even the largest international players.

Organization of Marketing Research

The organizational form of marketing research depends largely on the size and organizational structure of the individual company. In small firms, where one person often handles all the organization's research needs, there are few organizational questions other than determining to whom the research director reports. Most often, the marketing researcher reports to the sales or marketing manager, though some report directly to the president or the executive vice president. Larger research units can take a variety of organizational forms.

1. Organization by areas of application, e.g., by product line, brand, market segment, geographic area.
2. Organization by marketing function performed, e.g., field sales analysis, advertising research, product planning, e-commerce and electronic forms of research (see Research Realities 1.4).
3. Organization by research technique or approach, e.g., sales models, statistical analysis, field interviewing, questionnaire design.

Firms with very large marketing research departments combine these organizational structures.

The centralization of the firm also affects the organization of the marketing research function. In decentralized companies, the fundamental question is whether

Research Realities

1.4 Marketing Research, E-Commerce, and the Internet

Electronic marketing research takes one of two forms:

1. **Research on the Internet:** These studies use the Internet to study any consumer or market behavior. The Internet is another modality for communicating with customers, like paper-pencil surveys, telephone interviews, and so on.
2. **Research about the Internet:** These studies focus on e-commerce or consumer and market behavior on the Internet. They often also use the Internet as a means of collecting data, for example, through e-mail contacts, Web-based surveys, or surreptitious observation and measurement of Web page visitations.

Electronic marketing research companies come in one of two forms:

1. **Full-service established marketing research firms** are extending their menu of services to include the Internet as another means of gathering information to help their clients. For example:
   a. **ACNielsen:** best known for media and retail measurement, formed a subsidiary, eRatings.com as a global service to track audiences, advertising, and user activity on the Internet. Already in multiple countries, this group measures Web site traffic, audience exposure and response to banner advertising, and user demographics. ACNielsen also uses the medium in its e-Panel services, an electronic variant of its traditional ongoing consumer panels, which are used to assess reaction to new product concepts and movie previews, for example.
   b. **The NPD Group:** traditionally strong in consumer diaries, conducts both research about the Internet (e.g., audience measurement, chats with Web site visitors, competitor site analysis, online purchase tracking, quick polls, and so on) and research for which the Internet is the means for studying other consumer behaviors (e.g., online focus groups, mystery shoppers, general surveys). SiteSelect is an NPD tool that randomly samples Web users to invite them to participate in a survey. The ongoing NPD Online Panel is occasionally contacted via e-mail that an online NPD survey awaits them. NPD Online Focus Groups gather international participants in virtual rooms for speedy qualitative consumer insights.
   c. **Information Resources Inc.:** the powerhouse of consumer packaged goods data, combined with Media Metrix Inc. (described in the next section) in e-SCAN, to let clients (e.g., manufacturers of consumer packaged goods) mea-

sure the value of their online marketing investments. Clients can track known users of their brands to see which Web sites interest them, and in turn follow the Web site visitation data with subsequent purchase data (online or offline). Software is installed on the PCs of IRI's panel members who already use a ScanKey to record all their take-home purchases. The two sources of data are integrated to allow the Internet activities (sites visited, ad exposures, surfing patterns) to be correlated with purchase data (volume, purchase cycles, promotional effectiveness, brand loyalty).

2. **Internet specialists** are newly formed or spun-off marketing research firms that concentrate their research efforts on the Internet and e-commerce. These firms use the Internet both as a means (research "on" the Internet) and as an end (research "about" the Internet) to studying customers and marketing. Examples follow:
   a. **Media Metrix Inc.** is the pioneer and leader in the field of Internet and other digital media measurement services. Consisting of a panel of more than 50,000 individuals in homes and in the workplace, they measure which of their computer applications are open, which Web pages are loaded on their browsers, which ads drew clicks, and so on. Results on frequencies of unique visitors can be reported per Internet or media industry, or per consumer usage segment.
   b. **i-tracks** specializes in Web-based surveys. Computer-assisted interviews allow clients to formulate quantitative surveys (rating scales) and qualitative surveys (open-ended questions) tailored for the survey-taker by programming skip patterns (e.g., if yes, go to question 3; if no, go to question 4). Images, audio, and video can be included. Surveys can be addressed to customers or employees for in-house assessments.
   c. **eMarketer** provides statistics and demographic data about Internet users, their usage patterns, advertising, electronic commerce and market size, growth, and geography. It offers reports on measured Internet activities and provides online weekly newsletters for business professionals.
   d. **Jupiter Communications** is a research, consulting, and publishing firm that focuses on consumer online behaviors and interactive technologies for business-to-business and business-to-consumer clients. It uses population measures and user demographics to enhance market-size forecasts.

each division or operating unit should have its own marketing research department, whether a single department in central headquarters should serve all operating divisions, or both. The primary advantages of a corporate-level location are greater coordination and control of corporate research activity, economy, increased capability from an information system perspective, and greater usefulness to corporate management in planning. The primary advantage of a division or group-level location is that it allows research personnel to acquire valuable knowledge about divisional markets, products, practices, and problems. Even though shifting between the corporate and divisional structures occurs quite frequently, the recent trend is toward a mixed arrangement in an attempt to secure the advantages of each.

For example, Kodak has a combination centralized/decentralized marketing research function. The people in the divisions work directly with managers of those business units. The centralized group is responsible for staying on top of industry trends and changing technology, because changes here could affect numerous business units. Researchers assigned to corporate marketing research are also responsible for competitive analysis to ensure the most objective view. Finally, the centralized group serves as a quality control center for the research activity. Division-initiated projects are passed before this group for feedback.

The Japanese are more likely to view research as a "line" function performed by all involved in the decision process rather than as a "staff" function performed by professional marketing researchers. Those involved in the decision team may play a role in gathering and interpreting information. For example, along with product quality and inventory control, it is still marketing research that is acclaimed as the secret to the success of Japanese car sales (and reciprocally of course, marketing research helps inform about product quality and inventory). Reliability and perceptions of fair-valued prices matter particularly during tough economies, and when fuel prices rise. A reputation for reliability also enhances resale prices, which is a benefit that accrues in the same time span as the decision to purchase another car, hence likely to further increase the probability of a repeat purchase. These varied benefits are not all under the purview of, say, engineering or the R&D department, but represent different competitive advantages of the product and consumption experience as a whole. A more integrated organizational structure enhances the overall view of the customer experience, rather than a more focused assessment of some feature in isolation.[20]

The organization of the marketing research function is dynamic and ever changing. It depends on the importance of the marketing research function within the firm, the scale and complexity of the research activities to be conducted, and the firm's philosophy as to how marketing research should interface with the firm's decision making. For example, the data indicate that large firms are likely to spend a larger proportion of their marketing budgets on research than do small firms. As the firm's size and market position change, the emphasis and organization of the marketing research function must also change so that it continues to suit the firm's information needs.

In the next chapter, we look at the information technologies and storage of massive customer databases, which allow for marketing information systems, decision support systems, customer relationship management, and the like. Increasingly, firms are conducting both discrete marketing research projects, as well as analyzing continually incoming streams of data. Both means of marketing research are playing ever more important roles in the management and marketing roles in the firm.

---

[20] Anon., "Twenty Years Down the Road: Japanese Car Makers in America," *The Economist* (Sept. 14, 2002), pp. 62–63.

Employment Opportunities in Marketing Research

In addition to marketing managers, brand managers, advertising VPs, etc., many types of businesspeople (e.g., consultants, entrepreneurs, Internet marketers) frequently find themselves conducting and using marketing research to enhance their business efforts. Thus, if your heart is set on one of these career paths, you must think creatively about how to incorporate marketing research into your corporate responsibilities. Even if you're not going to be a marketing researcher, or even a marketing manager, it is important to be a knowledgeable and discerning consumer of marketing research. Thus, whether you conduct the research or commission it, it is important to be able to evaluate the quality of the research and its implications or caveats. The best CEOs do not forget that marketing research helps them understand their customers. Marketing research is the premier means to find and sustain competitive advantages.

Marketing research opportunities abound and in this section, we describe the traditional kinds of job opportunities in the field. The responsibilities depend upon the type, size, organizational structure, and philosophy of the firm. They also depend upon whether the person works for a research supplier or for a consumer of research information.

The responsibilities of a marketing researcher could range from the simple tabulation of questionnaire responses to the management of a large research department. Research Realities 1.5 lists some common job titles and the functions typically performed by occupants of these positions. The requisite skills vary depending on whether

Research Realities

1.5 Marketing Research Job Titles and Responsibilities

1. Research Director/Vice President of Marketing Research: The senior position in research. Responsible for the entire research program in the company. Accepts assignments from superiors, clients, and may take initiative to develop research. Employs personnel, supervises research department. Presents research findings to clients, company executives.

2. Analytically Skilled Methodologists
   A. Statistician/Data Processing Specialist: Expert consultant on theory and application of statistical technique to specific research problems. Usually responsible for experimental design and data processing.
   B. Qualitative Specialist: Some firms have a person specifically assigned to oversee interview techniques and focus groups.

3. Analysts
   A. Senior Analyst: Participates in planning research projects and directs execution of projects assigned. Minimum supervision. Prepares or works with analysts in preparing questionnaires. Selects research and analytical techniques,

and writes final report. Responsible for budgetary control and meeting time schedules.
   B. Analyst: Handles the bulk of the work of research projects. Assists in survey preparation, pretests questionnaires, and makes preliminary analyses of results.
   C. Junior Analyst: Handles routine assignments, editing and coding of questionnaires, statistical calculations above the clerical level, and library research.

4. Data-Collection Specialists
   A. Field Work Director: Hires, trains, and supervises field interviewers.
   B. Full-Time Interviewer: Conducts personal interviews. Often outsourced.

5. Support Staff
   A. Clerical Help: Tabulates results.
   B. Clerical Supervisor: Central handling and processing of surveys and data.
   C. Librarian: Builds and maintains reference sources.

one is pursuing a career as a technical specialist, a statistician, or a research generalist managing others, such as a research director.

The typical entry-level position in consumer goods companies (e.g., Kraft, General Motors, Procter & Gamble) is a Brand Analyst. While learning the characteristics and details of the industry, the analyst receives on-the-job training from a research manager. The usual progression of responsibilities is to Senior Analyst, Research Supervisor, and Research Manager for a specific brand, after which time the researcher's responsibilities broaden to include a group of brands.

The typical entry-level position among research suppliers (e.g., ACNielsen, Information Resources, Market Facts, and NPD) is that of Research Trainee, a position that offers exposure to the types of studies in which the supplier specializes and the procedures that are followed in completing them. Trainees may spend some time actually conducting interviews, coding completed data-collection forms, or assisting with the analysis. The training provides exposure to the processes and philosophies followed in the firm so that when the trainees become Account Reps, they are sufficiently familiar with the firm's capabilities to be able to develop intelligent responses to client needs for research information. Research Realities 1.6 presents recent job listings, in both marketing research supplier and buyer firms, that give some representation of the variety of employment possibilities.

In particular, there is a need for technically skilled marketing researchers—high-level data analysts and methodologists. Their skills are crucial to the excellence of a marketing research firm, and these talented people are in short supply. Usually these researchers have training in several of the following areas: probability and statistics, multivariate statistics and modeling, psychology, psychometric measurement, marketing research, sociology, consumer buying behavior, microeconomics, marketing management, and business communications. They stay current in methodologies by subscribing to academic journals and by attending professional development conferences such as the American Marketing Association meetings, the Advanced Research Techniques Forum, and those sponsored by the Advertising Research Foundation. Without these talented professionals, a great deal of analyses would be implemented by people with no understanding of models or consumers, yielding erroneous results detrimental to the research buyer, and ultimately impacting the marketing research supplier.

A successful marketing researcher needs human relations, communication, conceptual, and analytical skills. Marketing researchers must be able to interact effectively with others, because they rarely work in isolation. They should be able to communicate well both orally and in writing. If researchers cannot communicate the results and discuss what the results mean, it makes little difference what they know or how good the research is. They need to understand business in general and marketing in particular. When dealing with brand, advertising, sales, or other managers, they must understand the issues of these managers and the types of mental models they use to make sense of situations. Marketing researchers also should have some basic numerical and statistical skills, or be capable of developing those skills.

An increasingly common career path for those working in divisional structures is to switch from the research department to product or brand management. One advantage these people possess is that after working intimately with marketing intelligence, they often know a great deal about customers, the industry, and competitors. Researchers who desire to make this switch need more substantive knowledge about marketing phenomena and greater business acumen in general than those who plan on staying in marketing research, although all researchers need a good foundation of business and marketing knowledge if they are going to succeed.

Research Realities

1.6 A Sampling of Marketing Research Job Advertisements

1. *Blockbuster Inc.:* Rapid store growth, launching new business units, and passion to understand our consumers has created several exciting opportunities in our worldwide headquarters.
   A. Manager of E-Commerce Marketing Research: Design and manage the research function for online retailing. Candidates must have strong research skills, a creative outlook, and insatiable desire to understand the consumer.
   B. Manager of Database Analysis: Provide information about Blockbuster's different market tests and the home entertainment preferences of our consumers.

2. *The Gallup Organization:* Cutting-edge, data-based *Fortune* 500 consulting. Gallup hires consultants to work with executives, implementing data-based management and client systems. Our work includes employee selection and development; and attitude, customer, and brand research.

3. *NFO Research Inc.:* Insight is what NFO Research Inc. delivers. An NFO Worldwide company, we are an exciting, growing marketing information company and the world's leading provider of insight into the opinions, attitudes, and needs of consumers. Marketing Project Director: We'll rely on your expert communication ability and analytical problem-solving skills to coordinate and monitor all phases of marketing projects with Account Executives and our Marketing Manager.

4. *ACNielsen*
   A. Positions in Systems: Senior Technical Analyst, Software Engineer and Senior Software Engineer, Project Manager and Senior Project Manager, Software Quality Assurance Analyst.
   B. Positions in Finance: Pricing Manager.

5. *NBC:* Must-see TV and a must-take job!: Research Director, this highly organized person will provide support for a growing Sales staff, as well as the News and Programming/Promotion departments. Requires proficiency in evaluating NSI+ studies and rating trends. Will use Stowell research, TV Works, Nielsen Galaxy Navigator, CMR, Audience Analyst. Must be detail-oriented and proficient in analyzing statistical data.

6. *Reeve & Associates:* Manager, Hispanic Research: Full-service custom research supplier is looking for a researcher with Moderating, Primary Research, Business Development and Client Service background. Requirements: Ideal candidate will have 7+ years of supplier experience; Speak, read, and write Spanish and English; Must have moderated Hispanic focus groups.

7. *NY Importer/Distributor* seeks market research analyst to estimate potential sales of our products in U.S. and International Markets; research and keep a database on market conditions; design, organize, coordinate surveys and questionnaires on customer preferences, predict market trends to make decisions on the promotion, design, distribution, pricing of company products, Min. 3 years in job/job-related experience.

8. *Data-Pro* Project Director, Requirements: 3 years market research Project Direction experience with a research supplier. Must have supplier experience. 3 years working in the Pharmaceutical arena, either supplier or client side.

9. *Maritz Research:* Account Manager—Financial Services Research: We are seeking an Account Manager for our financial services research group. Position requires executive-level sales of marketing research resources as solutions to client challenges and opportunities, focusing on the financial services sector.

Sources: Excerpts taken from *Marketing News* (April 10, 2000), p. 23 and (Aug. 18, 2003), p. 19; *American Demographics* (July 2003), pp. 61, 63; http://acnielsen.com.

It is important to recognize that marketing research is a profession and that marketing researchers are professionals. Marketing researchers report that they generally feel that they can do much of their work fairly autonomously, they enjoy a good variety in their responsibilities, and generally proceed without too much bureaucracy or rules, all of which contribute to their employment satisfaction.[21]

Successful marketing researchers tend to be proactive rather than reactive—they identify and lead the direction for studies and programs rather than simply respond to explicit requests for information. Successful marketing researchers realize that marketing research is conducted for one reason—to help make better marketing decisions.

---

[21] Cf., Terry Grapentine, "Overshadowing the Black Box Debate," *Marketing Research* (Fall 2002), p. 39.

Summary

This chapter presented an overview of the nature of marketing research, its usefulness in marketing decision making, a sense of how marketing research gets used and by what types of companies. Marketing research is *the function that links the consumer, customer, and public to the marketer through information, which is used to identify and define marketing opportunities and problems; to generate, refine, and evaluate marketing actions; to monitor marketing performance; and to improve understanding of marketing as a process.*

Marketing research is a pervasive activity. Marketing research is used in every domain of marketing management.

The form of the marketing research function is organized to reflect the specific organization's unique needs. Two factors that are important are the firm's size and the degree of centralization of its operations.

Job opportunities in marketing research are good and are getting better. There is great variety in the positions available and in the skills needed for them. Most positions require analytical, communication, and human relations skills. Marketing researchers must be comfortable working with numbers and statistical techniques and must be familiar with a great variety of marketing research methods and techniques.

Review Questions

1. What is marketing management's task? What is marketing research's task? What is the relation between the two tasks?

2. How is marketing research defined? What are the key elements of this definition?

3. Who does marketing research? What are the primary kinds of research done by each type of enterprise?

4. What factors influence the internal organization of the marketing research department and its reporting location within the company?

5. What are the necessary skills for employment in a junior or entry-level marketing research position? Do the skills change as one changes job levels? If so, what new skills are necessary at these higher levels?

6. How might your responsibilities vary if you conducted marketing research at the following places?

   a. A marketing research firm

   b. An ad agency

   c. A large consumer packaged goods manufacturer

   d. An Internet startup company

Applications and Problems

1. Discuss whether marketing research would be valuable for the types of organizations that follow. If you believe that marketing research would be valuable, describe in detail how it would be used to aid in decision making.

   a. A bank

   b. A multinational oil company

   c. A retail shoe store with only one outlet

   d. A Mercedes dealership in LA? In NY?

   e. A candidate for the U.S. Congress, representing a district in Chicago

   f. The L.A. Lakers

   g. A distributor of large-screen televisions operating in Mexico City

   h. The English Department at your university

   i. A wheat farmer in Nebraska with 850 acres

2. What do the two following research situations have in common?

   Situation I: The SprayIt Company marketed a successful insect repellent. The product was effective and a leader in the market. The product was available in blue aerosol cans with red caps. The instructions were clearly specified on the container, in addition to a warning to keep the product away from children. Most of the company's products were also produced by competitors in similar containers. The CEO was worried because of declining sales and shrinking profit margins. In addition, companies such as his were being criticized by government and consumer groups for their use of aerosol cans. The CEO contacted the company's advertising agency and asked it to do the necessary research to find out what was happening.

   Situation II: This past April, the directors of a nearby university were considering expanding the business school because of increasing enrollment during the past 10 years. Their plans included constructing a new wing, hiring new faculty members, and increasing the number of scholarships from 100 to 120. The funding for this project was to be provided by private sources, internally generated funds, and the state and federal governments. However, a previous research study completed five years earlier, using a sophisticated forecasting method, indicated that student enrollment would have peaked last year, and that universities could expect gradual declining enrollments for the near future. A decision to conduct another study was made to determine likely student enrollment.

3. What do the two following research situations have in common?

   Situation I: The sales manager of CanAl, an aluminum can manufacturing company, was wondering whether the company's new cans, which would be on the market in two months, should be priced higher than the traditional products. He confidently commented to the VP of marketing, "Nobody in the market is selling aluminum cans with screw-on tops; we can get a small portion of the market and yet make substantial profits." The product manager disagreed with this strategy. In fact, she was opposed to marketing these new cans. The cans might present problems in preserving the contents. She thought, "Aluminum cans are recycled, so nobody is going to keep them as containers." There was little she could do formally because these cans were the company president's own idea. She strongly recommended to the VP that the cans should be priced in line with the other products. The VP thought a marketing research study would resolve this issue.

   Situation II: A large toy manufacturer was in the process of developing a tool kit for children from 5 to 10 years old. The tool kit included a small saw, screwdriver, hammer, chisel, and drill. This tool kit was different from the competitors', in that it included an instruction manual, "101 Things to Do." The product manager was concerned about the safety of the kit and recommended the inclusion of a separate booklet for parents. The sales manager recommended that the tool kit be made available in a small case, as this would increase its marketability. The advertising manager recommended a special promotional campaign be launched to distinguish this tool kit from the competition. The vice president thought that all the recommendations were worthwhile but the costs would increase drastically. She consulted the marketing research manager, who further recommended that a study be conducted.

4. Evaluate the research in the following example:

   The HiFlyer Airline company was interested in altering the interior layout of its aircraft to suit the tastes and needs of business travelers. Management was considering reducing the number of seats and installing small tables to enable people to work during long flights. Prior to the renovation, management decided to do some research to ensure that these changes would suit the needs of the passengers. To keep expenses to a minimum, the following strategy was employed.

   Questionnaires were completed by passengers during a flight. Because they were easy to administer and collect, the questionnaires were distributed only on the short flights (those less than one hour). The study was conducted during the 2nd and 3rd weeks of December, because that was when flights were full. To increase the response rate, each flight attendant was responsible for a certain number of questionnaires. The management thought this was a good time to acquire as much information as possible, so the questionnaire included issues apart from the new seating arrangement. As a result, the questionnaire took 20 minutes to complete. After the study, management decided that the study would not be repeated, because the information was insightful enough.

5. Specify some useful sources of marketing research information for the following situation:

   Dissatisfied with the availability of ingredients for his favorite dishes, Albert Lai would like to open his own retail ethnic grocery store. Based on the difficulty of finding many specialty ingredients, Albert realizes the need for a local wholesale distributor specializing in hard-to-find ethnic foodstuffs. He envisions carrying items commonly used in Asian and Middle-Eastern recipes.

   With the help of a local accountant, Albert prepared a financial proposal that revealed the need for

$150,000 in start-up capital for Lai's Asian Foods. The proposal was presented to a local bank for review by its commercial loan committee, and Albert subsequently received the following letter from the bank:

Dear Mr. Lai:
We have received and considered your request for start-up financing for your proposed business. Though the basic idea is sound, we find that your sales projections are based solely on your own experience and do not include any hard documentation concerning the market potential for the products you propose to carry. Until such information is made available for our consideration, we have no choice but to reject your loan application.

Albert does not wish to give up on his business idea because he truly believes that there is a market for these ethnic food products. Given his extremely limited financial resources, what types of information might be useful? Where and how might he obtain the needed information?

6. Suppose that you have decided to pursue a career in the field of marketing research. In general, what types of courses should you take in order to help achieve your goal? Why? What types of part-time jobs, internships, and volunteer work would look good on your résumé? Why?

CHAPTER 2

Alternative Approaches to Marketing Intelligence

Questions to Guide Your Learning:

Q1: What are the roles of "projects" and "information systems" in marketing research?

Q2: What are the basic operations of marketing information systems (MIS) and decision support systems (DSS)?

Q3: What is data mining?

We stated in Chapter 1 that the fundamental purpose of marketing research is to help marketing managers and other businesspeople make the decisions they face each day. As directors of their firms' marketing activities, marketing managers have an urgent need for marketing intelligence, e.g., changes that might be expected in customer purchasing patterns, types of marketing intermediaries that might evolve, optimal choices among alternative product designs, etc. Many issues can affect the way they plan, solve problems, or evaluate and control the marketing effort. Marketing research is traditionally responsible for this intelligence function. As the formal link with the environment, marketing research generates, interprets, and transmits feedback regarding the success of the firm's marketing plans and the strategies and tactics employed to implement those plans.

There is a natural complementarity in marketing research between *projects* executed to *address specific problems* and ongoing, overall marketing intelligence systems perspectives. The emphasis in this book is on marketing research projects. A project is composed of steps to be taken to solve a specific problem faced by a marketing manager. The next chapter gives an overview of these steps, and the remainder of the book discusses each step in detail.

In contrast, the emphasis in a **marketing information system (MIS)** or **decision support system (DSS)**[1] is on the information needs of each marketing decision-maker so that these people have the kinds of information they need, when they need it, to make good decisions. These systems are intended for *continuous monitoring* of consumer and market behavior, and they're the focus of this chapter. These systems can be designed to be narrow in focus, to address well-defined, predictable issues, e.g., scanner data from groceries may be checked by manufacturers to obtain hourly market shares. Alternatively, they can be broader in scope, developed to reflect much of consumer behavior. Once developed, these systems are popular because they allow a manager to answer simple questions to a user-friendly interface. Then the computer takes the input to a model and produces some numbers and answers, such as sales forecasts for a new product launch.

The philosophical difference between a project approach to marketing research and an emphasis on information systems is analogous to the difference between taking a snapshot vs. getting a continual read on the pulse of the marketplace. Thoughtful marketing managers recognize the value in conducting marketing research and commission such projects recurrently. Myopic managers devise a marketing research project only in times of crisis to be carried out with urgency, which often leads to an emphasis on data collection and analysis instead of the development of pertinent, actionable information. One suggestion for making research information more actionable is to think of management in terms of an ongoing process of decision making that requires a regular flow of input. Increasingly popular are the large consumer databases (e.g., from loyalty programs) that provide continual monitoring (of purchases and reactions to promotions, that may be optimally blended with available data from periodic projects). MISs and DSSs represent ongoing efforts to provide pertinent decision-making information to marketing managers on a regular basis. Marketing research projects provide the regular input and can discretely fine-tune these more continuous systems.

In the remainder of this chapter, we discuss the essential nature of MISs and the components of DSSs. A critical element to any marketing research project, MIS, or DSS is the data set. Finally, because these data sets are increasingly becoming huge, we discuss issues of "data mining."

> **Marketing Research as a Project →**
> **Snapshot**
> **Marketing Research to inform Intelligence Systems →**
> **Streaming Video**

Marketing Information Systems and Decision Support Systems

Marketing information systems (MIS) and decision support systems (DSS) monitor and provide a steady flow of information. They involve procedures and methods for the regular collection and analysis of information for the marketing researcher and managers to use in making marketing decisions. The information is needed and produced for decision making on a recurring rather than periodic basis.

---

[1] When discussing corporate information systems, MIS stands for management information system, and DSS refers to the structure of the decision support system for the whole company. Our interest is marketing intelligence, so we use the term MIS to refer to the marketing information system and DSS to refer to the structure of the information system to support marketing decision making. Sometimes MRIS is used to distinguish the marketing information system from MIS, the management information system. The generic label "IT" (Information Technology) has been popular for some time now, but the collective "BI" (for Business Intelligence) is the current buzzword.

The design of these systems begins with a detailed analysis of the decision-maker roles who will be using the system and the types of decisions to be made, and therefore, the types of information required to make those decisions. Systems designers need to understand the types of information the individual receives regularly as well as the special studies that are needed periodically. They need to know how the input data are obtained, which pieces of data are stored in which data banks, which analyses would be helpful, and what report formats would be useful. The system is then programmed. When the procedures are debugged so that the system is operating correctly, it is put online. Once online, managers access the reports through their company's intranet. Finally, the system designers also seek feedback from the decision makers for improvements to the current information system.

When first proposed, these information systems were held up as a panacea. Reality, however, tends to fall short of promise. The primary reasons are as much human as technical. For example, different managers emphasize different things and consequently have different data needs; few report formats can be optimal for different users. Either the developers have to design "compromise" reports that are satisfactory but not ideal for any single user, or they have to engage in the laborious task of programming to meet each user's needs.

Moreover, the costs and times required to establish such systems are often underestimated, due to underestimating the size of the task, changes in organizational structure or key personnel, and the electronic data processing systems they require. By the time these systems are developed, the personnel for which they are designed often have different responsibilities, or the economic and competitive environments have changed. Thus, soon after being put online, these systems intended for continual monitoring tend to need continual updating.

Another fundamental problem is that it is difficult to create a thoughtful, rigorous system that lends itself to solutions for the kinds of problems managers typically face. Many of the activities performed by managers cannot be programmed, nor can they be performed routinely or delegated to someone else, because they involve personal choices. Because a manager's decision making is often *ad hoc* and addresses unexpected events and choices, standardized reporting systems lack the necessary scope and flexibility to be useful. In addition, some decision making and planning are exploratory, so managers, even if they are willing to, may not be able to specify in advance what they want from programmers and model builders. Furthermore, decision making often involves exceptions to rules and qualitative issues that are not easily programmed.[2]

Components of MISs and DSSs

As depicted in Figure 2.1, an intelligence system comprises data, a model, and dialog systems that can be used interactively by managers. We discuss each system component in turn.

Data. The **data system** includes the processes used to capture data as well as the methods used to store data coming from marketing, finance, the sales force, and manufacturing, as well as any other external or internal sources. The typical data

---

[2] Quentin Hardy, "The Biggest Damn Opportunity," *Forbes* 170 (Dec. 23, 2002), pp. 342–344; Maximilian von Zedwitz and Oliver Gassmann, "Market vs. Technology Drive in R&D Internationalization," *Research Policy* 31 (May 2002), pp. 569–588.

FIGURE 2.1
Components of a
Decision Support
System

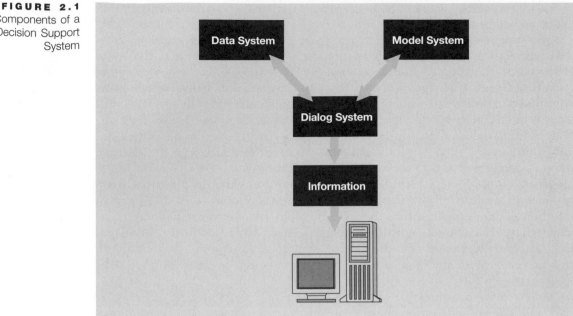

system has different modules containing customer information, general economic and demographic information, competitor information, and industry information, including market trends.

The customer information module typically contains information on who buys and who uses the product, where they buy and use it, when, in what situations and quantities, and how often. It could also include information on how the purchase decision is made, the most important factors in making that decision, the influence of advertising or some sales promotion activity on the decision, the price paid, and so on. Marketing research projects would typically supply some of the information input to the customer information module of the data system. Other input might come from the purchase of syndicated commercial marketing information. In the section that follows on data mining, we see how several firms use their customer information databases.

The data module that contains general economic and demographic information attempts to capture some of the most relevant facts about what is happening in the external environment, such as national or international economic activity and trends, interest rates, unemployment, or changes in GNP. The demographic facts concern changes in population, household composition, or any of the other factors that could potentially affect the future success of the firm. Much of this input comes from government data, primarily from the various censuses.

Another data module could contain information on specific competitors. This information would address questions such as: Who are the competitors and what are their market shares? In which market niches do they operate? What is their percentage of sales by product? What are their distribution methods? Where are their production facilities located? How big are they? What are their goals? What are their unique capabilities?

The industry information and market trend data module contains general information on what is happening in the industry, including financial information about margins, costs, R&D activities, and capital expenditures. It could represent trends in manufacturing or technology, with respect to raw materials or processes, e.g., new technologies.

A popular application of marketing information systems that incorporates many of these different data modules is the forecasting of sales for new products. Data input to these systems includes factors such as developmental resources (the number of R&D hours behind the prototype), concept testing (percentage of consumers checking the "very likely" box on a scale of likelihood to purchase), prototype testing (comparable percentages of consumers "very satisfied" with product usage), and marketplace promotion expenditures (advertising budget allocated in millions of dollars).[3]

One important trend in information technology is the explosion in the past few years of databases that provide information on customers, competitors, industries, or general economic and demographic conditions. Several thousand databases can now be accessed online via computer, compared to fewer than 900 twenty years ago. Several hundred of these apply to the information needs of business. In addition, following the globalization of business, marketing information systems are increasingly becoming part of international competitive intelligence data systems. The insights that marketing managers can gather from commercially available databases are mind-boggling.

As the number of databases has expanded, managers have also come to realize that sometimes, more is not necessarily better. For example, just because information may be available, it is important to ask whether a particular variable should be included in the data bank, that is, whether it will be useful for marketing decision making. Variables that are included "just in case" tend to collect dust (take up storage space and overwhelm and confuse the decision maker). We want to capture *relevant* marketing data in reasonable detail and organize those data in a truly accessible form. It is crucial that the database management system logically organize the data the same way a manager does.

Models. When managers look at data, they have a preconceived idea of how something works and, therefore, what is interesting and worthwhile in the data. These ideas are called *models*.[4] Most managers also want to manipulate data to gain a better understanding of a marketing issue. The procedures for analyzing the data run the gamut from summing a set of numbers, to conducting a complex statistical analysis, to finding an optimization strategy using some kind of nonlinear programming routine. In the real world, the most frequent tools for analyzing marketing research data are the simplest: frequencies, percentages, cross-tabs, comparing different groups, and making plots and tables. (We'll cover these techniques and far more throughout the book.) Sometimes all a manager really means by a "model" is a basic assumption (see Research Realities 2.1 for an example).

The explosion in recent years in the number and size of the databases available has triggered a need for ways to analyze them efficiently. Analyzing these large databases has become known as *data mining,* which we discuss in the next section. For example, brand managers of consumer packaged goods receive huge quantities of scanner data every week and even an astute analyst requires a great amount of time to extract simple summaries to see the major trends. In response, a number of firms

Components of MISs & DSSs:
• *Data* (what information do you need?)
• *Models* (how does the marketplace work?)
• *Interface* (how does the manager input and extract information?)

[3] Glen L. Urban, "An Autobiographical Essay: When I Stop Learning, I Will Leave," *Journal of Marketing* 66 (Oct. 2002), pp. 118–124.

[4] Efraim Turban and Jay E. Aronson, *Decision Support Systems and Intelligent Systems,* 6th ed. (Prentice Hall, 2000); Nikolaos Matsatsinis and Yannis Siskos, *Intelligent Support Systems for Marketing Decisions* (Kluwer, 2002).

Research Realities

2.1 Global Youth

Sometimes a "model" is just a fancy word for an "assumption." If you're a brand manager for anything trendy, such as music, fast foods, blue jeans, funky fashion accessories, or other elements of pop culture, one of your most important target markets is teens and young adults. Yet getting this group to adopt any product is nearly impossible, and even once you've got their attention, the group is known to have an attention span of a fruit fly, so loyalty and extensive repeat purchasing is iffy.

So, if you come upon a successful product, how might you leverage it while it's still hot? Go global!

One commonly held assumption (model!) is that the pre-teens, teens, and 20-somethings are surprisingly homogeneous globally, due to satellite television, the Internet, and other media. Thus, once you have the recipe for success with the youth of one country, find the youth in another!

- Kids become brand-conscious at about 2 years of age, and by 3 years old, they're evaluating brands as "cool" or not.
- Kids in the U.S. between 4–12 years of age spent about $30 billion of their own money, requested another $310 billion from mom, and indirectly influenced still another $340 billion of parental spending. Don't ignore these powerful rugrat consumers!

- Fisher-Price's Play Lab is the only full-time, on-site facility of its kind at an American toy company.
- Since 1961, children have tested toy concepts and prototypes, and product reliability.

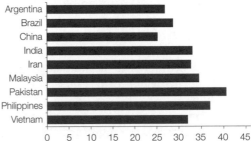

Percentage Population Aged 14 Years or Younger

Sources: Arundhati Parmar, "Global Youth United," *Marketing News* 36 (Oct. 28, 2002), pp. 1, 49; Jennifer Comiteau, "First Impressions" *Adweek* 44 (March 24, 2003), pp. 26–27; Douglas McGray "Babes in R&D Toyland," *Fast Company* 65 (Dec. 2002), p. 46.

have been developing expert systems, computer-based artificial intelligence (AI) systems that attempt to model how experts solve problems. These systems sort through all the data, comparing current results with past results, by brand, by category, by markets, regions, or key accounts.

The Interface. The **dialog system** is the interface that permits managers who are not programmers themselves to explore the databases, using the system models to produce reports that satisfy their particular information needs. The reports can be tables or graphs, and the report formats can be specified by the manager. The interfaces are often menu-driven to facilitate user-friendliness, reduce errors, and increase usage. Instead of funneling their data requests through a team of programmers, managers can conduct their analyses themselves, which has the side benefit of allowing them to target the information they want rather than being overwhelmed by irrelevant data. Managers can ask a question and, on the basis of the answer, follow it with a subsequent question, and thus proceed interactively and quickly.

As the availability of online databases has increased, so too has the need for better dialog systems. The dialog systems are what put data at the managers' fingertips. That sounds simple, but it is a difficult task because of the large amounts of data that are available, the speed with which data hit a company, and the fact that data come from various sources. To compound matters, the geographic boundaries used by the data suppliers differ from each other and most often from the firm's own geographic territories. Further, the services typically collect data on different time cycles. Some might provide it weekly; others might provide it once or twice a month. The discrepancies must be reconciled if the various data are going to be combined in a way that enables effective decision making.

Increasingly common is distributed network computing—a user taps into a network of computers that are linked so as to integrate otherwise disparate information storage. This structure is likely to continue because firms are finding that decentralization has additional benefits, such as greater protection from hackers.[5] The Internet facilitates this linking of marketing intelligence sources, with usage across more than 150 countries, and 150 million users in the U.S. alone. The use of the Web to capture and provide access to information on customers, competitors, industries, or general economic and demographic conditions clearly will continue to grow rapidly (the number of Web sites is no longer estimable).

Huge amounts of data can easily overwhelm the user. Many companies are exploring graphical interfaces as a means to express more intuitively the core findings in their databases. Merrill Lynch uses visualization displays for real-time stock updates and mutual funds data, as well as company financial reports and customer profile data. When the initial screen pops up with the aggregate picture, the user can click on an area in the figure to drill down (or pop up) more detailed information about that microcosm of the marketplace.[6]

Using the Data, Model, and Interface

Information technology systems allow managers to play "what-if" scenarios. Managers can simulate real-world conditions to learn about the relationships among different marketing actions and likely competitive response in a virtual marketplace, without the risk that such experimentation would cause in the real marketplace. Simulations can be programmed to be as complex and realistic as there are variables, data, experience, and assumptions to help support the interrelationships among the elements of the simulation. Input can include data and estimates on market characteristics (such as seasonality), customer preferences (attributes sought per segment, price sensitivity), customer loyalty (switching costs, trends over time), competitors' positions (consumers' judgments of their known product attributes, their prices and perceived prices), and competitors' access to customers (their distribution channels). Good simulations allow users to modify the input assumptions and parameters to see the range of possible outcomes, so as to make predictions with some degree of confidence.

AI models begin with the kind of information that marketing research projects can provide, including customers' historical behavior (purchase transactions, reactions to past promotional efforts) and perceptual data (from surveys and internal databases). Banks use decision tree AI tools to analyze a database of loan applicants to predict who will pay back a loan and who will not. Such systems usually begin by making classifications on current customers for whom the outcome is known (that is, whether they paid back the loan or not). Decision tree analysis detects which customer characteristics are most diagnostic in distinguishing the good bets from the deadbeats. In developing decision tree rules, the model iterates toward better prediction, and the iteration gives the appearance that the machine is "learning," hence the label "artificial intelligence."

---

[5] Perry Trunick, "Weapons of Mass Confusion," *Transportation & Distribution* 44 (2003), pp. 59–61; Thomas Davenport, Jeanne Harris and Ajay Kohli, "How Do They Know Their Customers So Well?" *Sloan Management Review* 42 (2001), pp. 63–73; Darrell Rigby, Frederick Reichheld and Phil Schefter, "Avoid the Four Perils of CRM," *Harvard Business Review* 80 (2002), pp. 101–109.

[6] Jack McCarthy, "Envisioning Enterprise Data," *InfoWorld* 24 (Nov. 18, 2002), pp. 53–54.

Comparing Marketing Information Technologies and Marketing Research Projects

The explosion in databases and information technology has only increased the need for traditional marketing research projects and for understanding their strengths and weaknesses in gathering marketing intelligence. Decision support systems and projects are not competitive, but are complementary and function best if they are well integrated. For one thing, many of the project-oriented techniques discussed in this book are used to generate the information that goes into the large databases. In addition, although a DSS allows managers to stay in tune with their external environments, and thus serves as an excellent early warning system, it sometimes does not provide enough information about what to do in specific instances; e.g., when the firm is faced with a new product, a change in distribution channels, or a new promotion campaign. When actionable information is required to address specific marketing problems or opportunities, the research project continues to play a major role.

In sum, both kinds of marketing research, shorter-term, focused projects and longer-term monitoring systems, are important approaches to marketing intelligence. In an increasingly competitive world, information is vital, and a company's ability to obtain and analyze information will largely determine the company's future.

Data Mining

Analyzing large databases has become known as *data mining*. Businesses hope it will allow them to boost sales and profits by better understanding their customers. The analysis of databases is not new—what is new and challenging is the extraordinary size of these databases.

The availability of huge databases began with scanner purchase data. Estimates suggest that marketing managers in packaged goods companies are inundated with 100 to 1,000 times more bits of data than even a few years ago because of the adoption of scanner technology in their channels of distribution. Some data mining techniques also arose in response to "database marketing" or "direct marketing" (by catalog vendors or coupon distribution providers) in which a company tries to form relationships with its individual customers, as marketing attempts to proceed from "mass" (one media message for all potential buyers), to "segments" (some targeting and positioning differences), to "one-to-one" marketing, e.g., via customized promotions and dynamic pricing.[7] In order to achieve such tailored market offerings, a company has to know a lot about its customers—hence the data contain many pieces of information on each of the company's many customers.

Traditionally, a company's database contained only current business information, but many now contain historical information as well. These "data warehouses" literally dwarf those available even a few years ago. For example, in an alliance with NCR Corporation, Wal-Mart has built the world's largest retailer data warehouse, with 285 terabytes[8] of data storage. The system provides information about each of

---

[7] Cf. Fred Feinberg, Aradhna Krishna and John Zhang, "Do We Care What Others Get? A Behaviorist Approach to Targeted Promotions," *Journal of Marketing Research* 39 (2002), pp. 277–291.

[8] 1 terabyte = 1,000 gigabytes = 1,000,000 megabytes. We're talkin' BIG.

Research Realities

2.2 Size and Impact of Customer Information Databases

- Compared to Wal-Mart's giant 285 terabytes (285 million megabytes), consider these middling (!) databases:
  - Aetna's health care insurance information on customers takes up 200 terabytes
  - Boeing's 150 terabytes are hosted in data stores over 27 states and some locations overseas
  - Unilever has 106 terabytes (for North America)
  - Kmart has 90 terabytes
  - Sears has 70 terabytes
- Staples, the $11 billion a year office supply store, has created huge databases of store location potential indicators (sales taxes per zip codes, location of competitors) to project ideal new retail sites, and has acted upon the projections, building 1000 new stores during the past ten years using the models. Store inventory is similarly scrutinized; as a function of sales analyses, the office furniture sections have been dramatically downsized, requiring less square footage to carry the basic, profitable SKUs such as labels and pens.
- Ben & Jerry's tracks every one of 190,000 pints of ice cream each day, to and fro, in 50,000 grocery stores in the U.S. and 12 other countries.
- AT&T's 650 GB database is devoted solely to work orders and billing data. Its larger database stores every phone call you place (!).
- Fingerhut is the $2 billion mailer of 400 million catalogs a year to 65 million customers, approximately 10 million of whom are considered "active" customers. Fingerhut stores data representing transactions, demographics, and psychographics on these customers. A data mining expedition identified increased purchasing by households that had recently moved, and in response, Fingerhut created a special "mover's" catalog to address these special consumers' needs. They estimate their tailoring of their direct marketing efforts saves the company more than $3 million a year.
- American Century Investments, a provider of mutual funds, stores 800 pieces of information for each of 25 million customers. Segmentation of their customers allows a more refined direct mailing effort, which tripled their customer response to a recent promotional effort.
- Vermont Country Store sends out 3 million catalogs annually, for yearly sales around $50 million. More effective targeting based on a segmentation of their 10 years of accumulated marketing data enhanced recent sales of different target products from 2% to 12%.
- Pillsbury's internal network allows its employees in over 70 countries access to data of several kinds, including consumer feedback that has been logged into a massive database (based on 3,500 calls a day to the 800 number printed on every Pillsbury product), manufacturing (testing equipment at new plants, statistics on production quality, packaging), and so on. Any employee, at a plant or at a sales call pitching new products to a grocer, can access the company's data.
- Business Intelligence (BI) software tops companies' technology spending ($7.5 billion).
- Consumer privacy is expected to all but disappear.

Sources: Julie Schlosser, "Looking for Intelligence in Ice Cream," *Fortune* (March 17, 2003), pp. 114–120; Barry Nance, "Managing Tons of Data," *Computerworld* 35 (April 23, 2001), pp. 62–63; Jennifer Lach, "Data Mining Digs In," *American Demographics* (http://www.demographics.com); Roger O. Crockett, "A Digital Doughboy," *Business Week E.Biz* (April 3, 2000), pp. EB78–86; Roland Rust, P. K. Kannan and Na Peng, "The Customer Economics of Internet Privacy," *Journal of the Academy of Marketing Science* 30 (2002), pp. 455–464.

Wal-Mart's over 3,000 stores in multiple countries. Wal-Mart plans to use the information to select products that need replenishment, analyze seasonal buying patterns, examine customer buying trends, select markdowns, and react to merchandise volume and movement.[9] Research Realities 2.2 gives you a better sense of the size of companies' customer information databases.

In response to the increasingly massive data sets, firms have been working to create increasingly sophisticated data mining technologies (hardware and software) to analyze the data. Data mining uses massively parallel processing (MPP) and symmetric multiprocessing (SMP) supercomputer technologies.[10] These huge machines support "relational" database programs that can slice massive amounts of data into dozens of smaller, more manageable pools of information.

---

[9] Julie Schlosser, "Looking for Intelligence in Ice Cream," *Fortune* (March 17, 2003), pp. 114–120.

[10] In the parallel processing of "supercomputers," multiple data points and subroutines are processed simultaneously, compared with old-fashioned "serial" processing, in which one datum is processed after another.

Sometimes these intensive approaches are applied to databases that are being analyzed with fairly traditional statistical techniques. For example, regression is still a premier analytical tool, because many predictors can be used to capture complex consumer decision-making and market behavior—forecasting sales as a function of season, price, promotions, sales force, and competitor factors. Other popular techniques of data mining include cluster analysis for segmentation and neural networks to supplement forecasting (e.g., nonlinear models instead of linear regressions).[11] Businesses regularly use data mining analytical tools to mathematically model customers who respond to their promotional campaigns versus those who do not. The effects of direct mailing efforts are easily measured and compared as a function of customer information (demographics such as age, household size, income) and purchase behavior (past buying history, cross-sales). Data mining can also be used to measure incremental business (additional traffic, sales, profits) that may be directly attributed to a recent promotion by deliberately withholding the promotional mailing from a "control" group (in experiments).

In addition to standard techniques being applied to these huge data sets, marketing research methodologists are creating techniques and software especially for data mining analyses on large data sets. Sales of such customer management software are currently growing at five times the rate of the overall software market, as managers struggle to track every encounter with each customer, to facilitate call-center interactions between customers and customer service representatives, and to manage internal customers, such as one's sales force. Some of these relational database systems include NCR's Teradata system, IBM's Intelligent Miner, and SAS's Enterprise Miner. Other software companies offer "content aggregator" services that synthesize multiple databases—company financial information, histories, executive profiles, and the like.[12]

There are analogous techniques being developed for the goal of "text mining." That is, just as there are huge databases of quantitative data, increasingly there are large storages of qualitative data. For example, companies such as General Motors need to know whether there are recurrent problems with its products, which can only be determined from studying mechanics' reports of customers' car repairs. These text files are so numerous and unsystematic, that without the assistance of a computer seeking various structures in the data, the task would be impossible. "Pattern recognition" is the class of analytics being developed and explored for the analysis of qualitative data.[13]

As an illustration of a data mining exercise, Farmers Insurance used IBM's Decision-Edge software to look at the 200 pieces of information the company maintained on its database of 10 million automobile insurance policyholders. Think of a sports car owner and "you probably imagine a twenty-something single guy flaming down the highway in his hot rod." This profile fit many of its customers, but the data mining exercise identified another segment of sports car owner—married baby boomers with kids and more than one car. These customers produced fewer claims, yet had

---

[11] We discuss these techniques in the chapters that follow, also see Otis Port, "Smart Tools," *The Business Week 50* (Spring 2003), pp. 154–155; Richard De Veaux "Data Mining," *Stats* 34 (2002), pp. 3–10; James Drew, D. R. Mani, Andrew Betz and Piew Datta, "Targeting Customers with Statistical and Data-Mining Techniques," *Journal of Service Research* 3 (2001), pp. 205–219.

[12] Susan Avery, "IT Sourcing Strategies," http://*www.purchasing.com*; and see http://www.sas.com "Finding the Solution to Data Mining," *White Paper* series.

[13] Mitchell Waldrop, "Data Mining," *Technology Review* 104 (2001), pp. 101–102; Dan Sullivan, *Document Warehousing and Text Mining: Techniques for Improving Business Operations, Marketing, and Sales* (Wiley, 2001).

Research Realities

2.3 Consumer Insights Gained from Data Mining

Loyalty programs, such as those offered at supermarkets, offer consumers discounted prices and coupon incentives. In the past 10 years, more than 100 million loyalty cards and key tags have been issued: 30% of supermarket customers have them; of those, 70% use them. Companies know that all customers are not equal, and loyalty cards enable one-to-one marketing, customizing the shopping experience for households with different purchasing profiles (sensitivities to price, value, brand, and quality). Due to their success, loyalty programs have expanded to other industries, yielding consumer insights and marketing actions such as these:

- CLICK, a product from the CleverIdeas company, stands for *Customer Loyalty Increased through Consumer Knowledge.* This operation produces, mails, and tracks direct marketing efforts for small chain restaurants, which enables them to assess the effectiveness of their "bonus points" and "birthday specials" promotions. They supplement guest history data with guest preferences, and can thereby provide better quality and customized service. Implementers of such data systems find greater customer satisfaction and loyalty, and increased revenue per customer.

- Harrah's Entertainment has loyal customers in the casino industry, known for variety-seeking customers. They distinguish themselves on excellent service, tailored to their special customers on the basis of their transactions database. Customers inserted their "Total Gold" cards into slot machines, earned "frequent gambler" points, and were rewarded with hotel rooms, dinners, and show tickets. So far, no different. But Harrah's analyzed its data to find their 26% of customers responsible for 82% of their revenues, and studied their habits (e.g., not staying in town but visiting casinos en route to other travels), and the promotions to which they were most sensitive (not rooms or meals but extra casino chips). How would you have guessed these characteristics without seeing the data? Customer service representatives are empowered to go to greater lengths to satisfy customers who have been segmented as more profitable. This customer-relationship management effectively creates a profit-and-loss statement per customer and customer segment.

- SAS, one of the largest statistical computing suppliers, assists companies in their information management and manipulation needs. SAS helps companies in many phases of marketing:
  - Planning: Which of my 10 million customers are my "best"? What do these attractive customers want?
  - Targeting: Which of my 200+ variables tell me the most important information about my customers? For example, which customers are at risk for leaving versus which customers show potential for being responsive to attempts at cross-selling?
  - One of SAS's biggest challenges is helping the client firm coordinate the data sets across the firm's multiple "customer touch points" (call centers, direct mail, e-mail, trade shows, etc.). In its Customer Relationship Management architecture, SAS facilitates a client's integration of internal data, purchased external data, front line records, data analytics, and rules modeling the content management of the data.
  - For example, in the insurance industry, data mining is used to predict a company's profits, and its expected customers' claims and losses. By studying current customer profiles in profitability, the policies can be targeted more precisely than "potential customer" to "potential customer who: meets policy criteria, is likely to purchase policy, is likely to retain policy for ten years or more."

- SPSS, the other large statistical computing supplier has its own success stories:
  - A leading telecommunications company analyzed its repairs data, found a frequently occurring glitch, fixed the system, and saved $1 million last year.
  - A bath-and-beauty supplies chain analyzed its data, "found" its customers, and has been reaping the rewards: growing its direct mail response rates by 250%, and its number of retail stores from 18 to 165.

Sources: Shari Weiss, "More Customers, More Visits, More Profits," *Nation's Restaurant News* 36 (Oct. 28, 2002), pp. T12–T18; Gary Loveman, "Diamonds in the Data Mine," *Harvard Business Review* 81 (2003), pp. 109–113; http://www.sas.com "Advanced Marketing Automation" and "Taming the CRM Information Explosion," *White Paper* series; http://www.spss.com "Gain a Competitive Advantage," *White Paper* series.

been paying the same sports car surcharge. With this information in hand, Farmers could charge them less, providing greater value and customer satisfaction.[14] For additional examples of the kinds of consumer insights gained from data mining, see Research Realities 2.3.

There is no question that the explosion in databases, computer hardware and software for accessing those databases, and the World Wide Web are all changing the

---

[14] Jennifer Lach, "Data Mining Digs In," *American Demographics*, http://www.demographics.com.

way marketing intelligence is obtained. Companies are becoming more sophisticated in using them for general business and competitive intelligence. This, in turn, has produced some changes in the organization of the marketing intelligence function, including the emergence of the Chief Information Officer (CIO).

The CIO's major role is to run the company's information and computer systems like a business. The CIO serves as the liaison between the firm's top management and its information systems department. CIOs typically know more about the business in general than do the managers of the information systems department, who are often more technically knowledgeable and report to the CIO. Information systems are not intended to be simply data warehouses—the management of information is ideally designed as an electronic library that allows all employees access to the firm's "collective wisdom."

Summary

This book takes a project-based approach to the provision of marketing intelligence. The difference between a project emphasis to research or the alternative marketing information system or decision support system emphasis is that the latter relies on the continual monitoring of the firm's activities, its competitors, and its environment, whereas the former emphasizes the in-depth study of some specific problem or environmental condition.

An MIS or DSS was defined as a set of procedures and methods for the regular, planned collection, analysis, and presentation of information for use in making marketing decisions. They provide more regular marketing intelligence than periodic, pointed marketing research projects.

A DSS is a coordinated collection of data systems, model systems, and dialog systems. The data systems include the processes used to capture and store information useful for marketing decision making. A marketing research project might be one input to a data system. The model system includes all the routines that allow users to manipulate data to conduct the kinds of analyses they desire. The dialog systems allow managers to conduct their own analyses by logging onto the company's intranet, even from their PDAs.

Data mining is the term used to describe the analysis of huge consumer databases—scanner purchase data, or investigations in database marketing or direct marketing—tasks for which companies can have hundreds of pieces of information on each of its millions of customers. Large databases require special storage and increasingly sophisticated hardware and software to enable massively parallel processing and symmetric multiprocessing. Traditional statistical techniques (regression, cluster analysis) are used, as is special customer management software.

Review Questions

1. What is a marketing information system? How does a project emphasis to marketing research differ from an information systems emphasis?

2. What are the steps in MIS analysis? In developing an MIS system?

3. In a DSS, what is a data system? A model system? A dialog system? Which of these is most important? Why?

4. What is (are) the likely future approach(es) to marketing intelligence? Will there be a change in the relative importance of traditional research vs. MISs or DSSs?

5. What is data mining? How does it differ from traditional data analysis?

Applications and Problems

1. You are responsible for deciding whether to adopt a DSS for the following situations. How would you design the system?

   a. Production of profit-and-loss statements to estimate customer lifetime values for segments of video renters.

   b. Introduction of a new product line extension for Smucker's preserves and jellies.

   c. Determination of seasonal pricing schedules for Johnson outboard motors.

   d. Identification of the amount of time spent on hold by consumers on a toll-free, customer-service assistance telephone line.

2. Consider the industries of health care management, consulting, or financial investments. What specific capabilities of a DSS would enable greater customer satisfaction and profitability? What kinds of input should the company seek? Who should use the system, and to address what specific needs and questions?

3. You are the vice president of international marketing for a consumer packaged goods company. In a recent board of directors meeting, it was decided that you would head the development of a competitive information system (CIS) for your organization. You have been asked to write a brief description of the types of data to be stored in the CIS along with possible uses of the data by employees within your company. Write a clear and concise paragraph describing your recommendations.

## CHAPTER 3

The Research Process and Problem Formulation

Questions to Guide Your Learning:

Q1: What is the difference between a *program strategy* and a *project strategy* to research?

Q2: How does the *research process* unfold? What are the steps and how are they interrelated?

Q3: What is the first stage in the research process: *problem formulation*?

Q4: What does a *research proposal* look like and how do I choose among *research suppliers*?

Chapter 1 highlighted the many kinds of problems that marketing research can be used to solve. It emphasized that marketing research is the firm's communication link with the environment and that it can help the marketing manager in planning, problem solving, and control. Different companies use marketing research for different subsets of these activities.

A company's philosophy of how marketing research fits into its marketing plan determines its program strategy for marketing research. Some companies may use marketing research on a continuous basis, such as via decision support systems, described in Chapter 2, to track sales or to monitor the firm's market share. Other companies may use marketing research only when a problem arises or an important decision like the launching of a new product needs to be made.

Research Realities

3.1 Marketing Research at Gillette

Gillette is the global leader in male toiletries products. Its cutting-edge products are offered at premium prices. It is also among the most financially stable of firms. It has achieved these positions through a strong belief in marketing research and the development of innovative products, such as its MACH 3 razors, which outperform all other shaving instruments, and sell at a 2:1 ratio over the next razor, which is also a Gillette product. Gillette also creates special products for women, including laser-based technologies. In recent years, Gillette has been introducing more than 20 new products per year, and approximately half of its sales come from brands that are no older than five years. What follows is a sample of the marketing research methods Gillette uses:

1. **Annual National Consumer Studies.** The objectives of these studies are to determine what brand of razor and blade was used for the respondents' last shave, to collect demographic data, and to examine consumer attitudes toward the various blade and razor manufacturers. These studies rely on personal interviews with national panels of men and women who are selected by using probability sampling methods.

2. **National Brand Tracking Studies.** These studies track the use of razors and blades to monitor brand loyalty and brand switching tendencies over time. Mail questionnaires are issued annually to panels of male and female shavers.

3. **Annual Brand Awareness Studies.** These studies are aimed at determining the "share of mind" Gillette products have. Telephone surveys employ aided and unaided recall of brand names and advertising campaigns.

4. **Consumer Use Tests.** The key objectives of the use-testing studies are to ensure that Gillette remains competitive, with products performing up to desired standards, and to substantiate claims in advertising and packaging. At least two consumer use tests are conducted each month by Gillette. In these tests, consumers are asked to use a single variation of a product for an extended period of time, at the end of which their evaluation of the product is obtained.

5. **Radio Frequency Identification (RFI) and Electronic Product Codes (EPC).** Retailers track sales of individual Gillette products through electronic microchip tags. These data allow for timely market share data, but are thought to be especially useful as a source of information along the supply chain, e.g., informing choices regarding distribution, out-of-stock, and inventory levels.

6. **Laboratory Research Studies.** These studies are designed to test the performance of existing Gillette products and to help in the design of new products. They include having people shave with Gillette and competing products and measuring the results, as well as determining the number of whiskers on a man's face, how fast whiskers grow, and how many shaves a man can get from a single blade.

Sources: Charles Forelle, "Razors to Lasers," *Wall Street Journal* (Feb. 20, 2003), p. D4; Chris Murphy and Mary Hayes, "Tag Line," *Information Week* (June 16, 2003), p. 18; Tim Hammonds, "EPC No Longer a Fantasy," *Chain Store Age* 79 (May 2003), p. 30; Anon., "Men's Market Leads the Way," *Retail World* 56 (May 9, 2003), p. 29. Also see Gerry Khermouch and Heather Green, "Bar Codes Better Watch Their Backs," *Business Week* (July 14, 2003), p. 42.

A program strategy specifies the types of studies to be conducted and their purposes. Research Realities 3.1 outlines the types and purposes of the various studies conducted by Gillette Company in its constant endeavor to maintain its dominant share of the blade and razor market. The design of the individual studies themselves defines the firm's project strategy: You'll see the use of personal interviews in national consumer studies, mail questionnaires in brand-tracking studies, and telephone interviews when measuring brand awareness. Thus, a *program strategy* addresses the question of what types of studies the firm should conduct and for what purposes, whereas a *project strategy* deals with how a study should be conducted.

Every marketing research problem is unique in some way, requiring some custom tailoring for its own special emphases and approaches. Still, there is a sequence of steps, called the **research process** (see Figure 3.1), that can be followed when designing any research project.

Program Strategy:

What studies should we conduct?

Project Strategy:

How should we conduct this study?

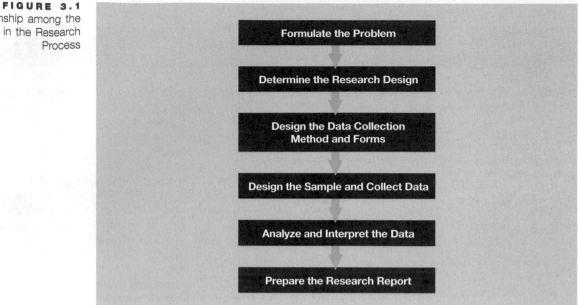

Marketing Research—Sequence of Steps

I. Formulate the Problem

The first valuable role marketing research plays is to help define the problem to be solved. Only when the problem is defined carefully and precisely can research be designed to provide pertinent information. Part of this process includes specifying the objectives of the research projects that might be undertaken. Each project should have one or more clear objectives, and the next step in the process should not be taken until these goals can be explicitly stated.

II. Determine the Research Design

The sources of information for a study and the research design go hand in hand. They both depend on how much is known about the problem. If relatively little is known about the phenomenon to be investigated, exploratory research is warranted. Exploratory research begins with a review of **secondary data**, such as published or syndicated data, or trade literature that discusses similar cases. Exploratory research may then involve interviewing knowledgeable people or conducting focus groups. One of the most important characteristics of exploratory research is its flexibility. Researchers know little about the problem at this point, so they must be ready to follow their experience and intuition about possible areas of investigation.

If, on the other hand, the problem is precisely and unambiguously formulated, descriptive or causal research is needed. In these research designs, data collection is not flexible—it is rigidly specified with respect to both the data collection and the sample design to obtain precise results and conclusions, with implications that yield actionable results.

III. Design the Data-Collection Method and Forms

Given the dynamic nature of business and customers, it is often the case that the information needed is not found in the firm's own sales data, nor, say in census reports or industry sales trends. The research then must depend on **primary data**, which are collected specifically for the new research needs. But how? Should the data be collected by observation or questionnaire? Should the form be structured with a fixed set of alternative answers, or should the responses be open-ended? Should the purpose be made clear to the respondent, or should the study objectives be disguised? These questions illustrate some basic concerns of the research process.

IV. Design the Sample and Collect Data

In designing the sample, the researcher must specify: (1) the sampling frame, (2) the sample selection process, and (3) the size of the sample. The **sampling frame** is the list of population elements from which the sample will be drawn. We also need to think carefully of whom we (marketers) are targeting and whose opinions we (marketing researchers) are soliciting.

- For example, we may appeal to *pet owners* with advertisements and pricing, but if the product doesn't pass muster with the pets, there will be no repeat purchase.
- Similarly, we might solicit *parents* about buying educational toys, but if their children find the toys boring, or worse, un-cool, word-of-mouth will ensure no further growth in sales.
- Suppliers might offer discount to *buyers*, who are often rewarded for finding such deals, but if the in-house end-user isn't satisfied, the long-term satisfaction of the buying firm is affected, and they'll go elsewhere in the future.

Sampling the purchasing agents (pet owners, adults, business marketing buyers) is clearly important, but so is the testing on the ultimate customer. In these examples, the dog population, children population, and corporate user need to be part of the sampling frame for at least part of the marketing research study, not just the buyers. The careless specification of population elements can have dire consequences. Similarly, we need to realize that when we sample from a phone book or a CD-ROM mailing list, we are not sampling from the population as a whole but only from people whose names appear in these sources.

The sample selection process requires specification about such things as whether it will be a probability or nonprobability sample (these terms are defined in the chapter on sampling plans). The decision on *sample size* involves determining how many people, households, business firms, or other entities must be studied to get sufficiently accurate and reliable answers that will allow a decision to be made regarding this problem, without exceeding the time and money budgeted for the project.

Once the dimensions of the sample design are specified, data collection can begin. Data collection requires field personnel of some type, and the methods themselves are dictated by the kinds of information to be obtained and the sampling requirements. The use of a field staff to collect data raises a host of questions with respect to their selection, training, and control—questions that must be anticipated in designing the research.

V. Analyze and Interpret the Data

Researchers may amass a mountain of data, but these data are useless unless the findings are analyzed and the results interpreted in light of the problem at hand. Data analysis involves several steps. First, the data-collection forms must be **edited**—scanned to be sure that they are complete and consistent and that the instructions were followed. Once the forms have been edited, they must be coded. **Coding** involves assigning numbers to the answers so they can be analyzed. The final step is **tabulation**, the orderly arrangement of data in a table or other summary format achieved by counting the frequency of responses to each question. It is common also to cross-classify the data against other variables. For example, if researchers ask women if they liked a certain kind of new cosmetic, their responses would be analyzed by age group, income level, etc.

The coding, editing, and tabulation functions are common to most research studies. The statistical tests applied to the data are specific to the sampling procedures chosen and the data-collection instruments used in the research. These tests should be anticipated before data collection has begun to assure that the data and analyses will be appropriate and answer the specified problem.

VI. Prepare the Research Report

The research report is the document submitted to management that summarizes the research results, with conclusions and recommendations. It is all that many executives see of the research effort, and it becomes the standard by which that research is judged. Thus, it is imperative that the research report be clear and accurate, because no matter how well all previous steps have been completed, the project will be no more successful than the report. It is one of the most important factors affecting whether the research will be used to implement change.

Additional Comments

Each step is more complex than this overview suggests. Each involves numerous issues rather than a single decision or even a few decisions (see Table 3.1).

In addition, we have presented the stages rather simply, as if you proceed through them in a lockstep fashion when designing a research project. Not true—Figure 3.1 (shown earlier) could include feedback loops, suggesting a possible need to rethink

> The stages of the research process are linked—choices made at one stage impact another.

TABLE 3.1
Questions to be Addressed Throughout the Research Process

Stage in the Process	Typical Questions
Formulate the Problem	• What is the purpose of the study: solve a problem, identify an opportunity?
	• Is additional background information necessary?
	• What information is needed to make the decision?
	• How will the information be used?
	• Should research be conducted?
Determine the Research Design	• How much is already known?
	• Can a hypothesis be formulated?

(continued)

TABLE 3.1
(*continued*)

Stage in the Process	Typical Questions
	• What types of questions need to be answered? • What type of study will best address the research questions?
Determine the Data-Collection Method and Forms	• Can existing data be used to advantage? • What is to be measured? How? • What is the source of the data? • Are there any cultural factors that need to be taken into account in designing the data-collection method? • Are there any legal restrictions on the collection methods? What are they? • Can objective answers be obtained by asking people? • How should people be questioned? • Should the questionnaires be administered in person, over the phone, through the mail, via fax, on the Internet, or through e-mail? • Should electronic or mechanical means be used to make the observations? • What specific behaviors should the observers record? • Should rating scales be used in the questionnaires?
Design the Sample and Collect Data	• What is the target population? • Is a list of population elements available? • Is a sample necessary? • Is a probability sample desirable? • How large should the sample be? • How should the sample be selected? • Who will gather the data? • How long will the data gathering take? • How much supervision is needed? • What operational procedures will be followed? • What methods will be used to ensure the quality of the data collected?
Analyze and Interpret the Data	• Who will handle the editing of the data? • How will the data be coded? • Who will supervise the coding? • Will computer or hand tabulation be used? • What tabulations are called for? • What analysis techniques will be used?
Prepare the Research Report	• Who will read the report? • What is their technical level of sophistication? • Are managerial recommendations called for? • What will the format of the written report be? • Is an oral report necessary? • How should the oral report be structured?

and revise the various elements in the process as the study proceeds. The process begins with problem formulation, but after that, anything could happen. The problem might not be specified explicitly enough to allow the development of the research design, in which case the researcher would need to return to stage 1 to delineate the research objectives more clearly. Alternatively, the process may proceed smoothly to the design of the data-collection forms, the pretest of which may require a revision of the research objectives or the research design. Or the sample necessary to answer the problem as specified may be cost prohibitive, requiring a revision of the earlier steps.

Once the data are collected, no revision of the procedure is possible. It is possible, though, to revise the earlier steps on the basis of the *anticipated* analysis. It is imperative, therefore, that the methods used to analyze the data be determined before the data are collected. It is sometimes difficult for beginning marketing researchers to understand, but the steps in the research process are highly interrelated. A decision made at one stage affects decisions at each of the other stages, and a revision of the procedure at any stage often requires modifications of procedures at each of the other stages. Unfortunately, it seems that this lesson is understood only by those who have experienced the frustrations (and satisfactions!) of being involved in an actual research project.

All the steps in the research process are necessary and vital. It is true that errors can arise during any stage, but it is dangerous to worry about one kind of error to the exclusion of others. The "total error" associated with a project cumulates the errors at each stage. For example, you might think that a large sample size will help reduce sampling error, but sometimes other errors may increase more than proportionately with sample size, e.g., larger samples typically mean using more interviewers, who need to be trained so they all handle the interviews in a standard way. Otherwise, the different responses can be as much a function of the interviewers collecting the data as they are differences in respondents.

Thus, researchers frequently face a dilemma because of budget and time constraints. Should they select a large sample to minimize sampling error, or should they select a smaller sample, thereby ensuring better interviewer controls, more accurate responses, and a higher response rate among those contacted? These latter "nonsampling errors" are often underestimated.

The stages in the research process serve as a structure for this book. The remainder of this chapter, for example, deals with stage 1, problem formulation, and each of the remaining stages is addressed in its own section in the book.

Problem Formulation

An old adage says, "A problem well defined is half-solved." This is especially true in marketing research. It's only when the problem has been clearly defined and the objectives of the research precisely stated that research can be designed properly. "Properly" here means not only that the research will generate the kinds of answers needed but that it will do so efficiently.

Problem definition is being used in the broadest sense of the term here. It refers to those situations that might indeed represent real *problems* to the marketing decision maker as well as those situations that might be better described as *opportunities*. Let's look at both.

Marketing research problems or opportunities arise from three fundamental sources: (1) unanticipated change, (2) planned change, and (3) serendipity in the form of new ideas. Change in one form or another is by far the most important source.

One of the great sources of *unanticipated change* is the environment in which firms operate. Demographic, economic, technological, competitive, political, and legal changes often have significant effects on the marketing function. How the firm responds to new technology, or a competitor's new product, or changes in the lifestyles of their key customers, etc. largely determines whether the change turns out to be a problem or an opportunity.

For example, Apple's Newton was the first hand-held digital assistant to the market, but Palm responded with its Pilot and soon dominated Apple. An example of a political or legal change is the deregulation of the financial services industry. Firms such as Fidelity capitalized on this environmental change by introducing enhanced services packages, including a discount brokerage service.

Unanticipated change can also arise from within the firm's internal environment. The firm may be losing market share or sales might not be as high as forecast. The firm may find itself losing key salespeople or its best distributors to competitors. In situations of unanticipated change, a key issue is finding exactly what is happening and why. Marketing research plays a role in answering all these questions.

Not all change is unanticipated; much of it is *planned*. Most firms want business to grow and contemplate marketing actions for facilitating that growth, e.g., with the introduction of new products, improved customer service, and more effective pricing and advertising strategies. Planned change is oriented more toward the future, whereas unanticipated change is oriented more toward the present and past. The basic question surrounding planned change is how the firm may bring about the desired change. The role of marketing research in this scenario involves investigating the feasibility of alternatives under consideration.

A third source of marketing problems or opportunities is *serendipity*, or chance ideas. The new idea might be generated internally, from R&D or one's sales force, or it might even come from a customer via a complaint letter. For example, Rubbermaid makes it a practice for its executives to read customer letters to find out how people like the company's products. These letters often lead to new product ideas. Tracking trends and interacting with consumers also yield ideas. Customers complain of time famine and the need for convenience, so Rubbermaid's larger products, such as closet storage units and outdoor tool sheds, are built to be assembled quickly and without tools. Attention to detail and suggestions like this allow the company to introduce hundreds of new products a year, from auto accessories to pet products to luggage.[1] Not only are they innovative, but the company claims a success rate of 80–90%.

"Serendipity" can also ironically be the result of planning. Procter & Gamble relies on the National Food Lab (NFL) to help develop new products. For example, continually monitoring consumers' tastes and desire for variety seeking in beverages, the NFL helps with chemical analysis and sensory consumer research. P&G isn't

Ethical Dilemma 3.1

A manufacturer of bolts and screws approaches you and outlines the following problem: "My friend owns a hardware store, and you used a technique called multidimensional scaling to produce what I think he called a perceptual map, which positioned his operation in relation to his competitors and showed him where there was space in the market to expand his business. I don't understand the details of it, but I was very impressed with the map and I want you to do the same for me."

- What have you learned about the manufacturer's research problem?
- Is it likely that the development of a perceptual map will be useful to the manufacturer of bolts and screws?
- Is it ethical to agree to her proposal?

---

[1] Sandra O'Loughlin, "Rubbermaid, Graco Set to Grow," *Brandweek* (June 9, 2003), p. 16.

likely to miss a "trend" and the partnership suggests it can move quickly to market upon its identification.[2]

Regardless of how decision problems or opportunities arise, most of them require additional information for resolution. The manager must determine what information is necessary and how it can be obtained. Good communication between the marketing manager (the decision maker) and the marketing researcher is imperative. The decision makers need to understand what research can and cannot accomplish. The researchers need to understand the nature of the decision the managers face and what they hope to learn from research—the project objectives.

Researchers must avoid simply responding to requests for information. To do so is akin to allowing a patient who is seeing a doctor to make his or her own diagnosis and prescribe the treatment as well. Rather, the researcher needs to work with the manager much like a patient works with a doctor; both need to be open in their communication as they translate symptoms into underlying causal factors.

There are still other issues in problem formation. For example, sometimes marketers confuse problems with symptoms. A problem is a situation requiring some type of action, whereas a symptom is merely evidence that a problem exists. For example, when Xerox became concerned that it was rapidly losing photocopier sales to Japanese competitors, that was the symptom. An investigation revealed that whereas Xerox was focusing on features to add, the problem was one of product quality. Customers wanted copiers that would break down less often.

Consultants face this issue of clarifying problem definitions all the time; clients think they know what is wrong and they hire consultants to fix it. Often as not, consultants must assess what is "really" wrong before they hope to fix it. Marketing researchers are the consultants in this case—they are the keepers and procurers of useful marketplace information.

There is a tendency to assume that managers have a clear understanding of the problems they face and that the only difficulty lies in communicating that understanding. This assumption is false. To many managers, the research problem is seen primarily as a lack of important facts. They count on preliminary research to clarify what they know and what they do not know, thinking that with the research, they will be able to confidently decide how to proceed (including commissioning more research). A steady income of such exploratory research is important to the firm because it keeps the company close to the customer and helps reduce uncertainty in decisions throughout the organization. However, research results based on such a mode of operation most often turn out to be "interesting" but not very actionable. With marketing researchers increasingly expected to answer in-house for their own ROI, "interesting" doesn't cut it. Although exploratory research is not particularly well-suited for addressing specific decision problems, it can comprise inputs to decision support systems to inform more realistic forecasts.[3]

Even with a more precisely defined research question and impeccably executed research, both managers and researchers need to recognize that marketing research does not produce answers or strategies. It produces data—data that must be interpreted and converted into action plans by management. To be sure that the research

[2] Andrew Kaplan, "Case Study: Test-Driving Beverages," *Beverage World* (Oct. 15, 2002), p. 54.

[3] Catherine Arnold, "Seven Steps to Better Research," *Marketing News* 37 (2003), p. 13; Warren Hersch, "Market Pulse: Actionable Analytics," *Call Center Magazine* 15 (2002), p. 12; Sanjay Rao, "A Marketing Decision Support System for Pricing New Pharmaceutical Products," *Marketing Research* 12 (2000), pp. 22–29.

reflects management's needs, managers must play an active role in communicating their information needs to researchers, and they need to stay in touch during the research process itself to ensure that they'll be getting the information they truly need to help them make the decisions they face.

In other cases, managers need to get directly involved in the research process. For example, one factor that plays an important part in Japan's new-product development is that the Japanese consider marketing research a line function requiring involvement by all participants in the product development process rather than a staff function performed only by marketing researchers. An advantage of this perspective is a more hands-on approach that looks at the broader context and an emphasis on softer, less-formal data-collection methods. For example, Sony knows what appeals to children by watching them play video games, including their own PlayStation games. The "Aibo" dog-robot was a runaway success and its third generation is already in development.[4]

A proper understanding of the basic structure of *decision making* can help researchers interact with management to better specify research issues. Decision situations can be characterized by the following conditions:

1. A decision maker is operating in some environment in which there is a problem.
2. There are at least two courses of action (A_1 and A_2) that the decision maker can follow (e.g., "go" and "no go" on a new-product launch).
3. Once the decision maker chooses an action, at least two outcomes of that choice (O_1 and O_2) are possible (product is "successful" or "not"), and one outcome is preferred.
4. There is an unequal chance that each course of action will lead to the desired outcome. (If the chances are equal, the choice does not matter.)

Thus, a person faces a decision situation if he or she (1) has a problem, (2) has several good (but not equally good) ways of solving it, and (3) is unsure about which course of action to select. Research can assist in clarifying any of these characteristics of the decision situation. Let's see how.

The Decision Maker and the Environment

A critical element for the researcher in defining the problem is understanding the decision maker and the environment in which that person is operating: What is the background of the business? What factors have led to the manager's concerns with the issues? What information would help the decision maker in dealing with these issues? What would the decision maker do with the information?

If the decision maker's original posture will not change regardless of what is found, the research will be wasted. Surprisingly, research is sometimes simply "conscience money"—the results are readily accepted when they are consistent with the decision the individual wants to make, but when the results conflict with the decision maker's original position, the results are questioned or discarded as somehow being inaccurate. The reason, of course, is that the individual's view of the decision problem is so strongly held that research will do little to change it. To avoid wasting resources because of the "I know better" or "don't bother me with the facts" traps, researchers need to assess the situation before doing the research, not after. This

---

[4] Anon., "How Sony, Samsung, and Merck Cope with the R&D Dilemma," *Strategic Direction* 19 (2003), pp. 6–8.

means determining the decision maker's objectives and finding out how the decision might change if certain results were found. Understanding these implications is a difficult task, made more complicated when the researcher's contact is not the final decision maker but a liaison. Yet this determination must be made if the researcher is to design a cost-effective attack on the problem.

The researcher also needs to understand the environment in which the decision maker operates. What are the constraints on that person's actions? What are the resources at the decision maker's disposal? What is the time frame in which the manager is operating? It does little good to design a study, however accurate, that costs $50,000 and takes six months to complete when the decision maker needs the results within one month and has only $15,000 for the research. Obviously, some compromises must be made, and it is the researcher's responsibility to anticipate them by carefully examining the decision environment.

Researchers also need to be aware that the corporate culture can affect decision making—does the "process" or "management personality" dominate? At General Mills, for example, the emphasis is on research that evaluates alternatives, and the culture tries to force all information requests into action alternatives. Instead of focusing on one descriptive question, "What proportion of potato chips are eaten at meals?" the emphasis would be on translating the question into options with actionable implications: "How can I advertise my potato chips for meal consumption?" vs. "Will a 'meal commercial' sell more chips than my present commercial?"

Alternative Courses of Action

Research can be properly designed only when the alternative courses of action being considered are known. The obvious options are given to the researcher by the decision maker, and the researcher must determine whether that list exhausts the possibilities. If the research is to be germane to all the alternatives, implicit options must be made explicit. Thus, it is important that the decision maker and the researcher work together to come up with a complete list of the alternative courses of action being considered.

For example, as part of the ongoing research at the Campbell Soup Company, product managers keep an eye on consumer and technological trends, probing for openings in the market. Campbell's monitors the traditional family market, as well as the eating habits and flavor preferences of career women, Hispanics, consumers over age 55, and owners of microwave ovens. As for alternative courses of action, the company has considered: lowering prices, advertising heavily, positioning their soups against General Mill's Progresso, extending their dry soup mix offerings, etc.[5]

Researchers must be like detectives to uncover the hidden agendas and alternatives lurking beneath the surface in any decision situation. If a critical piece of information remains undiscovered, even the most sophisticated research techniques cannot solve the problem. In a classic example, researchers at Pillsbury discovered this fact belatedly.

The late Bob Keith, then president of the Pillsbury Company, was once persuaded by Pillsbury's operations researchers to review one of his major marketing decisions using a formal decision model. He agreed to the outcomes, their values, and their probabilities, and chose the decision rule he felt most appropriate. The computer

---

[5] Sarah Ellison and Betsy McKay, "Campbell Hires Coke Aid to Push Pepperidge Lines," *Wall Street Journal* (Dec. 4, 2002), p. B11.

then calculated the expectations, compared them, and reported the alternative that should be chosen according to that rule. Mr. Keith disagreed, noting that another alternative was obviously the only correct choice—indeed, it was the choice that had been made not long before. "How can that be?" the researchers asked. "You accepted all the values and probabilities and chose the decision rule yourself. The rest is just arithmetic." "That's fine," Keith replied, "but you forgot to ask me about a few other things that were more important."[6]

Objectives of the Decision Maker

One of the more basic facts of decision making is that individuals differ in their attitudes toward risk, and these differences influence their choices. Some people are risk takers, willing to assume a good deal of risk for the chance of a big gain. Some are risk averse, not wanting to assume much risk at all, even when the size of the potential gain is large, if the chance of loss also exists. A person's attitude toward risk can change with the situation and the magnitude of the potential consequences. The researcher can often discover the decision maker's comfort with risk from intensive probing, using "what-if" hypothetical outcomes of the research.

It is also important to determine the decision maker's specific objectives. Despite what one might expect, the decision maker's objectives are rarely explicitly stated to the researcher, or they might not have been formulated accurately or precisely. For example, the decision maker might state that the firm wants customers to perceive their brand as "high quality," without elaborating—what does that *mean*? A clarification of goals is often among the most useful services the marketing researcher provides to the marketing manager.

The researcher must transform the vague platitudes ("high quality") into specific, operational objectives for the research. The marketing researcher can engage the decision maker in a discussion to explore possible solutions to the problem, to see whether the firm would follow the prescribed course of action. If not, the conversation may probe further until the real objectives are revealed.

Once the objectives for the research are finally determined, they should be committed to writing. Doing so often produces additional clarity in communication and thinking. The decision maker and researcher should then agree formally on their written expression (by each initialing each statement of purpose, seriously!) to prevent later misunderstandings (we provide a template in Figure 3.3 on page 55). The formal endorsement of objectives also helps ensure that the research will not treat symptoms, but the problem that produced the symptoms.

Consequences of Alternative Courses of Action

A lot of marketing research is intended to determine the consequences of various courses of action. The marketing manager wants to know the effect of manipulating an element in the marketing mix to achieve customer satisfaction. It is natural for much of marketing research to seek answers to questions such as: What will be the change in sales produced by a change in the product's package? If we change the sales compensation plan, what will be the effect on the sales representatives' performance and on their attitudes toward the job and company? Which advertisement is likely to generate the most favorable customer response?

---

[6] Charles Raymond, *The Art of Using Science in Marketing* (Harper & Row, 1974), p. 17.

Researchers are primarily responsible for designing research that accurately assesses the outcomes of past or future contemplated marketing actions. In this capacity, they must gauge the actions against all the outcomes management deems relevant. For example, if management wants to know the impact of some proposed change on both sales and consumer attitudes, but the research addresses only one, management will most assuredly ask for the other, and won't be too happy with an "I don't know." Embarrassing questions of this nature can be avoided only if researchers painstakingly probe for all relevant outcomes before designing the research.

Translating Decision Problem to Research Problem

A detailed understanding of the total decision situation should enable researchers working in consort with managers to translate the decision problem into a research problem. Suppose a new product is introduced and sales are below target. The marketing manager has to decide what to do about the shortfall. Should the target be revised? Was the forecast too optimistic? Should the product be withdrawn? Should an element in the marketing mix, such as advertising, be altered? Suppose the manager suspects that the advertising campaign supporting the new product has been ineffective. The product manager would want evidence that either confirmed or denied that suspicion before changing the advertising program. The research problem would then become the assessment of product awareness among potential customers.

Some of the distinctions between decision problems and research problems are illustrated in Table 3.2. The decision problem involves what needs to be done. Research can provide the necessary information to make an informed choice, and the research problem involves determining what information is needed and how to obtain it.

In making this determination, the researcher must make certain the real decision problem (not just the symptoms) is being addressed. Poor problem definition leads to unfortunate, sometimes dire, consequences. The debacle with Coca-Cola Classic is well-known. A less well-known example is that Miller did not invent Lite Beer. It was first developed by Meister Brau and taste tests went well, but when the product was introduced, it failed. Meister Brau sold Lite Beer to Miller, who defined the decision problem and the research problem as something *more* than having a preferred taste. Miller's research suggested that big (er, "frequent") beer drinkers tried to project macho images, and the concept of a diet beer connoted "wimp." Miller's emphasis thus became one of changing the image of the brand through its use of famous sports personalities (presumably perceived as non-wimps).

Sometimes the difficulty in problem definition involves cultural differences. A U.S. manager was trying to interest investors in Southeast Asia in a bagel restaurant franchise. The manager described the entire system, including the corporate support, local marketing, the menu, and products. After the four-hour meeting concluded, the investors politely thanked the presenter and voiced their first question, "What is a bagel?"[7] The manager had been focusing on solving implementation issues, but neglected simple marketing research on the investors.

---

[7] Christopher Brady, "How to Integrate Your Company into the Global Market," *Foodservice Equipment & Supplies* 52 (Oct. 1999), pp. 29–30.

Decision Problems	Research Problems
1. Develop package for a new product	1. Evaluate effectiveness of alternative package designs
2. Increase market penetration by opening new stores	2. Evaluate prospective locations
3. Increase store traffic	3. Measure current image of the store
4. Increase amount of repeat purchasing behavior	4. Assess current amount of repeat purchasing behavior
5. Develop more equitable sales territories	5. Assess current and proposed territories with respect to their potential and workload
6. Allocate advertising budget geographically	6. Determine current level of market penetration in the respective areas
7. Introduce new product	7. Design a test market through which the likely acceptance of the new product can be assessed
8. Expand into other countries	8. Assess market potential for firm's products in each of the countries being considered
9. Select international distribution channels	9. Evaluate current channel structures and channel members in each of the countries being considered
10. Decide which merchandise will be made available for purchase over the Internet	10. Determine consumers' confidence in purchasing, unseen, different categories of products

How does one avoid the trap of researching the wrong problem? The primary way is by refusing to respond to requests for information without developing a proper appreciation for the decision problem. The difference in response perspectives is highlighted in the Minute Maid example in Research Realities 3.2. There is an old saying: "If you do not know where you want to go, any road will get you there." Same goes for decision making—if you don't know what you want to accomplish, any alternative will be equally (un)satisfactory. If the decision maker doesn't know what he or she wants to achieve, the research study will not accomplish it. Instead of preparing a research proposal outlining the methods to be used when a research request first comes in, researchers should take the time to probe the situation carefully until they have acquired the necessary appreciation for: (1) the decision maker and the environment, (2) the alternative courses of action, (3) the decision maker's objectives, and (4) the consequences of alternative actions. As Figure 3.2 indicates, even marketing managers concur that researchers should take an active role defining the decision problem and in specifying the information that will be useful for solving it.

Research Realities

3.2 Alternative Approaches to an Information Request and their Likely Effects

Kevin is a research analyst who has been with The Minute Maid Company for a little more than two years now. He is well regarded by the marketing team he works with, and is responsive to its research requests.

One morning, Kevin receives a phone call from the marketing manager on Minute Maid fruit punches. The marketing manager tells him that R&D has come up with a new, improved flavor. Before authorizing full production of the new formula, it would be prudent to conduct a taste test to determine if consumers will react favorably to the new flavor. He is calling Kevin to find out how much product would be required for such a test. He adds that it is very important that this research be initiated quickly because a competitor, Tropicana, has just come out with a new, improved version of its product.

Kevin says he needs more information. Will this new flavor be available in both chilled and frozen? When will the product be available for the test? After getting those questions answered, Kevin decides to conduct blind taste tests with 600 respondents in a mall. He'll first find out if respondents can detect differences between the products. Then each product will be rated for preference.

You might be thinking this design sounds pretty good—sequential approach so time and money aren't wasted if the new flavor is not as good as everyone thinks; adequate sample sizes for both the chilled and frozen forms; and two parts to the evaluation.

Now let me introduce you to Joan. She has the same credentials as Kevin and is faced with the same initial phone call. The marketing manager asks her how much product she will need in order to conduct a taste test for him.

Joan responds (like Kevin had) that she needs more information. Joan suggests a meeting with the manager to discuss the situation. She reviews the information she has been given by the marketing manager and she develops a list of questions she wants to ask the marketing manager when they get together. First, she goes to her computer and pulls up the most recent Nielsen Scantrack information she has on the Punches segment of the Juice and Juice Drink category. She checks both to see if any change has occurred in the marketplace since the introduction of the new Tropicana Fruit Punch, and to see if Minute Maid Fruit Punch sales have been affected by this introduction. Next, she checks on the Nielsen household scanner panel information to see if any changes have occurred in key household purchase behavior—specifically, household penetration, buying rate, and loyalty rates for both Minute Maid and Tropicana. Finally, she reviews the historical project files to understand the previous research on the brand.

Joan meets with the marketing manager, and asks the following questions:

1. Why are we considering a new formula? Tropicana doesn't seem to have hurt our franchise with the new flavor.
2. If we do use a new formula, what do we hope to accomplish? Do we expect to pull in new users or do we want to minimize the chances of our consumers shifting over to Tropicana?

3. How will we announce the new flavor? Will it be advertised or will we just use a notice on the package?
4. Does the new formula perform the same in both chilled and frozen forms? Are the sensory profiles identical?
5. Can we obtain product from a regular production location? Often R&D's controls are much more stringent than those of our production plants. We would rather use product for this test that most closely resembles the product that consumers would be buying from grocery stores.

After getting answers to her questions, Joan then works out her research objectives and specific design. She recommends a two-phase study, with objectives to determine Minute Maid users' response to the new flavor in terms of taste and overall preference and to determine competitive users' response to the new flavor versus the new Tropicana flavor.

Joan will also interview 600 respondents who are female heads of household, primary grocery shoppers, between 18 and 60, and who have used Minute Maid fruit punch in the past month. Respondents in the first phase of the research must be regular, loyal users of Minute Maid. In the second phase, respondents must be users of the competitive product.

The research will involve in-home placements over a two-week period. In the first phase, 300 respondents will evaluate Minute Maid's new formula versus the current formula to understand how the current franchise will react to the formulation change. In the second phase, 300 respondents will compare the new Minute Maid formula to the new Tropicana formula to determine if the new flavor would attract competitive users. In both phases, half the sample will evaluate the chilled formula, while the other half will evaluate the frozen formula.

There are several clear differences between this research design and the first example, all dependent on the approach used to define the problem.

Kevin is what I would call a "research order taker" or "research technician." He basically responded to the marketing manager's request for a taste test without considering the marketing situation that prompted the request. His research design was sound, at least on the surface, given the information he had. He would have obtained answers to his questionnaire and those answers would probably be correct. Unfortunately, both he and the marketing manager would be wondering why the company was receiving so many consumer calls on the company's 800 number from longtime Minute Maid users complaining about the new flavor.

Joan, on the other hand, is an internal *marketing consultant*—a true *marketing information professional*. Her approach was to understand the marketplace situation and potential marketing actions that could be taken based on this research. Her research design was more costly and time-consuming because she understood the risks involved as well as the potential gains that could accrue to the company based on this formula change.

(continued)

In both instances, the marketing manager could make a decision based on the data obtained from a research study. The difference is that in one case, the manager might feel suspect about marketing research because it failed to predict some Minute Maid users' negative response to the formula change, whereas in the other case, the manager may be more confident in using marketing research.

Marketing information professionals must strive to go beyond simple problem solving. They must be internal marketing consult-

ants. That is the only way to assure that research designs, techniques, and statistical analyses will be valid. It is the only way that marketing management will become more confident in its use of marketing research. It is the only way senior management can be assured that the company is receiving full value for its investment in resources and spending for marketing research.

Source: Personal correspondence with Larry P. Stanek, Marketing Information, The Minute Maid Company.

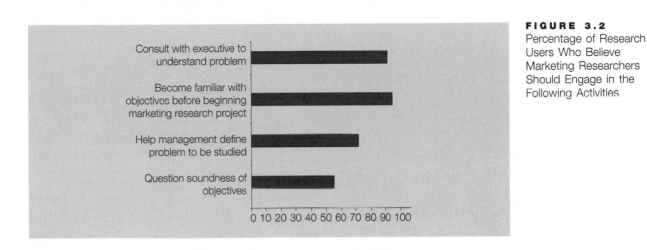

FIGURE 3.2
Percentage of Research Users Who Believe Marketing Researchers Should Engage in the Following Activities

Several mechanisms are available for making sure that the true decision problem will be addressed by the research. One way is to execute a "research request step," which requires that the decision maker and researcher have a meeting in which the decision maker describes the problem and the information that is needed. The researcher then drafts a statement describing his or her understanding of the problem. A template for such a statement would include, but is not limited to, the following items:

1. **Origin:** the events that led to a need for the decision to act. Even though the events may not directly affect the research to be conducted, they help the researcher understand more thoroughly the nature of the research problem.

2. **Action:** the actions that are contemplated on the basis of the research.

3. **Information:** the questions that the decision maker needs to have answered in order to take a course of action.

4. **Use:** a section that explains how each piece of information will be used to help make the action decision; supplying logical reasons for each piece of the research ensures that the questions make sense in light of the action to be taken.

5. **Targets and subgroups:** a section that describes the customer bases from whom the information must be gathered; specifying the target groups helps the researcher design an appropriate sample for the research project.

6. **Logistics:** a section that gives approximate estimates of the time and money available to conduct the research—both will affect the techniques finally chosen.

Another way of ensuring that the research will address the true decision problem is to use scenarios that anticipate the results. Based on his or her understanding of the total decision situation, the researcher tries to anticipate what the final report could look like and prepares approximate templates. The researcher then confronts the decision maker with tough questions, such as, "If I come up with this cross-tabulation with these numbers in it, what would you do?" This communication can clarify the parameters of the study. For example, one large electronics company wanted to determine the knowledge of and preferences for stereo components among young consumers. It was only after the researchers prepared mock tables showing preference by age and gender that the client's wishes became truly clear. Based on their prior discussions, the researchers specified the age breakdowns for the tables as 13 to 16 and 17 to 20. Only after presenting this scenario to the company's managers did the researchers learn that to the client, young meant children age 10 or older. The client further believed that preteens are very volatile, undergoing radical changes from year to year as they approach puberty. Thus, not only was the contemplated research wrong from the standpoint of the age groups not starting young enough, but the planned categories were not fine enough to capture the client's concerns about the dynamic nature of preferences. Without the scenarios, the client's expectations may not have surfaced until the research was too far underway to change it.

The Research Proposal

Once the purpose and scope of the research are agreed on, researchers can turn their attention to choosing the techniques to conduct the research. These techniques should also be communicated to the decision maker before the research begins through a formal research proposal, which allows another opportunity to make sure that the research being planned will provide the information necessary to answer the decision maker's problem.

Research proposals can take many forms. Some are very long and detailed, running 20 pages or more. Others are short and to the point. The length depends on the detail describing each part. Figure 3.3 contains a template that can be followed in preparing a research proposal.

Research Realities 3.3 contains portions of an actual research plan (with some authorization and budget information removed) that was prepared by the research department at General Mills. Note the clearly stated criteria that will be used to interpret the results and the carefully crafted action standards, specifying what will be done depending on what the research results indicate. The effort expended by the marketing research department in translating information requests into specific, action-oriented statements like this helps account for the wide acceptance of and enthusiastic support for the research function at General Mills.

Is Marketing Research Justified?

The benefits of marketing research are many, but it is not without its drawbacks. The question of whether the research costs are likely to exceed the research benefits always needs to be asked. There is no denying that the research process is often time-consuming and expensive. One might first ask, "Is there enough time to conduct a thoughtful research investigation?" In today's fast-paced marketplace, it might seem

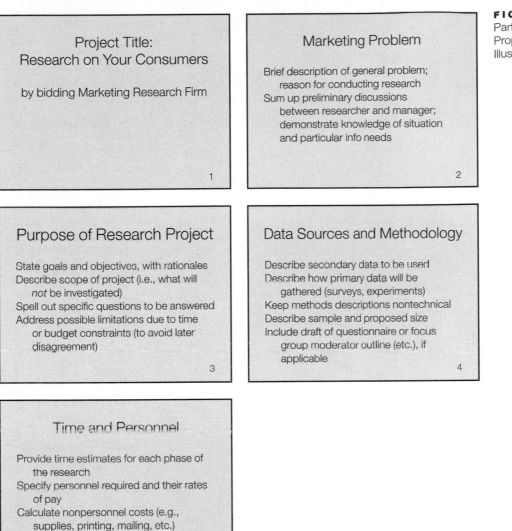

FIGURE 3.3
Parts of a Research Proposal, with an Illustrative Example

that the answer is frequently no. However, a negative answer neglects three important resources:

1. Informal queries of in-house experts can be made quickly to yield at least preliminary insights.
2. Secondary data, including free published and relatively inexpensive syndicated databases, may be tapped instantaneously for detailed and comprehensive results.
3. Ongoing, continual data collection and mining efforts, which are increasingly pervasive across companies in the guise of customer relationship databases, can be accessed to understand customers' attitudes and behaviors.

If the manager is pressed for time, therefore, and cannot conduct a new marketing research project, there is likely to be relevant information around the organization already.

FIGURE 3.3
(continued)

**Eau de Internet:
Selling Fragrances
Online**

by Marketing Researchers R Us

1

Marketing Opportunity

$27 billion U.S. beauty market
45% U.S. population Internet access
Related Internet site (fashion) up, possible
    profitable link?
Manager concern fragrances cannot be
    sampled electronically
Past research: trial is important
Can image and brand dominate?

2

Purpose of Research Project

Objective: determine if consumers will buy
    perfumes online
Focus on women's attitudes (buying for
    self or gift), not yet purchased
Concerns women have re: buying
    fragrances online?
What factors lower resistance
    (brand, price, return policy?)
Client desires results in 3 months . . .

3

Data Sources and Methodology

Secondary data: sales in beauty, perfumes,
    online apparel
Primary data: e-mail contact directed to
    Internet surveys
Analysis: averages, cross-tabs
Sample size goal of 300 women, given
    time constraints, target those with
    Internet access, modify questions for
    gift purchases

4

Time and Personnel

Preliminary phase, 3 weeks
Survey pre-test, debug, 2 weeks
Sample select & solicitation, 2 weeks
Administer survey, follow-up, 1 week
Analyses, 1 month
Discuss required staff (and salaries)
Other costs minimal (given format of
    electronic contact and survey
    execution)

5

One might then ask, "Is there a budget to conduct the requisite marketing research?" Myopic managers often look to marketing research as a luxury, a budget line some are quick to trim. We may of course be biased, but we would suggest an alternative question: "Will you have any budget to spend in the future if you do not understand your customers?" Ouch!

If conducted and interpreted properly, marketing research can be very illuminating and therefore, absolutely (more than) worth the time and cost. However, if it is done incorrectly, it can be misleading. Or it might pose risks that outweigh its possible advantages, e.g., the benefits of testing a new product must be weighed against the risk of tipping off a competitor, who might rush to market with a similar product at perhaps a better price. The best strategy is to examine the potential benefits from the research and to make sure they exceed the anticipated costs, both financial and otherwise.

Research Realities

3.3 A Sample Proposal at General Mills for Research on Protein Plus Cereal

1. **Problem and Background.** Protein Plus has performed below expectation in its test market. New product and copy alternatives are being readied for testing. Three alternative formulations—Hi Graham, Nut, and Cinnamon, which retain the basic identity of current Protein Plus, but which have been judged to be sufficiently different and of sufficient potential—have been developed for testing against the current formula.

2. **Decision Involved.** Which product formulations should be carried into the concept fulfillment test?

3. **Method and Design.** In-home product tests will be conducted. Each of the four test products will be tested by a separate panel of 150 households. Each household will have purchased adult ready-to-eat (RTE) cereal within the past month and will be interested in the test product as measured by the selection of Protein Plus as one or more of their next 10 cereal packages they would like to buy. They will be exposed to Protein Plus in a booklet that also contains an ad for several competitive products, such as Product 19, Special K, Nature Valley, and Grape Nuts. A Protein Plus ad will be constructed for each of the four test products, differing primarily in the kind of taste reassurance provided. Exposure to these various executions will be rotated so that each of the four test panels are matched on RTE cereal usage.

   The study will be conducted in eight markets. Product will be packaged in current Protein Plus package flagged with the particular flavor reassurance for that product.

   The criterion measure will be the homemakers' weighted post-study brand-share, adjusted to reflect the breadth of interest in the various Protein Plus communications strategies.

   Rather than trust a random sampling procedure to represent the population at large, a quota will be established to ensure that the sample of people initially contacted for each panel will conform as closely as possible to the division of female heads of households under 45 (56%) and over 45 (44%) in the U.S. population.

4. **Criteria for Interpretation.** Each formulation generating a higher weighted homemaker share than standard will be considered for subsequent testing. If more than one formulation beats standard, each will be placed in a concept fulfillment test unless one is better than the other(s) at odds of 21 or more.

5. **Estimated Project Expense.** $15,000 to $65,000.

6. Individual who must finally approve recommended action: _____

7. Report to be delivered by _____ if authorized by _____ and test materials shipped by _____.

Source: Used with permission of General Mills, Inc.

Choosing and Using a Research Supplier

There are lots of reasons to hire marketing research suppliers, e.g., your research department might be small. Even large consumer products companies with large marketing research departments use outside suppliers, e.g., outsourcing to manage variable workloads, bringing in vendors with special skills and expertise (say, in "focus groups," or "youth"), hiring suppliers so the sponsoring company can remain anonymous, and finally to avoid problems regarding internal politics. Don't pretend to have expertise you don't have—buy it![8]

Though it is common to buy marketing research, many managers are uncertain as to how to select a research supplier. The first step is to know what you want. Before contacting research suppliers, it is important to identify the most critical areas of uncertainty and the issues that would benefit most from research.

---

[8] Deborah Vence, "Leave It to the Experts," *Marketing News* (April 28, 2003), p. 37.

Ethical Dilemma 3.2

The president of a small bank approaches you with plans to launch a special program of financial counseling and support for women and asks you to establish whether sufficient public interest exists to justify starting the program. No other bank in the city caters specifically to women, and you think that professional women, in particular, might be enthusiastic. If news of the plan leaks out, the president believes that competitors may try to preempt him, so he asks you to keep the bank's identity secret from respondents and to inquire only into general levels of interest in increased financial services for women. However, as you read through the literature that he has left on your desk, you notice that the bank is located in the most depressed area of the city, where women might be harassed and feel unsafe.

- Would it be unethical to research the general problem of how much demand exists for a women's banking program, when the bank in question will interpret the demand as encouragement to launch such a program itself?
- What might be the costs to the researcher in voicing misgivings about the suitability of this particular bank's launching of the program? Would you voice your misgivings?
- Does it violate respondents' rights if you do not reveal the identity of the research sponsor? If so, is it a serious violation in this case? Is there a conflict of interest here with respect to respondents' right to be informed versus the client's right to confidentiality?

Selecting the right supplier is not easy. There are thousands of qualified marketing research companies in the U.S. alone. Some are full-service, generalist companies; others specialize in marketing areas like advertising-copy testing or concept testing; while others specialize in research approaches such as interviews, data processing, or statistical analyses.

An excellent source that describes the larger and medium-sized providers is the *Marketing News* newsletter published by the American Marketing Association (http:// www.marketing power.org). Periodically, it also publishes directories that highlight specialists, e.g., firms that focus on customer satisfaction measurement, focus groups, or international marketing research firms. These directories are superior to an Internet search of "marketing research companies," because the AMA is a long-established association and the newsletter objectively describes the different marketing research suppliers. Search engines find the providers, but the descriptions of the providers are made up of their own sales pitches, making a comparison across suppliers more difficult.

Once you have a short list of candidate suppliers, their capabilities must be evaluated in light of your company's research needs. Sometimes a small-scale qualitative study may be most appropriate, and at other times, a large-scale quantitative research project would be optimal. It is essential that the vendor selected understand the firm's information needs and have the expertise required to conduct the research.

Experts suggest that managers should seek proposals from at least three companies. Don't cut corners. Spend the time investigating your potential research suppliers, not so much comparison shopping on cost as on more important qualifications, like the firm's expertise, and your comfort level with their style and the attention they would devote to your project.[9] Talk with the people at the research supplier company who will be processing and analyzing the data, writing the report, supervising the interviewers, and making presentations to your management.

Marketing research is still a bit of an art, not entirely a science. It benefits from heavy involvement of senior research professionals who provide insights that come only from years of training and experience. A research firm's most important asset is the qualification of the research professionals who are involved in the design, day-to-day supervision, and interpretation of the research.

The research user's responsibility is to communicate effectively with the prospective vendor and provide the necessary background and objectives for the study. It is also a good idea to ask about the supplier's quality-control standards. Most research firms are pleased when clients show concern about quality and will gladly explain their quality-control steps in the areas of fieldwork, coding, and data processing.

---

[9] Cam Davis, "Research Your Researcher," *CMA Management* 76 (2003), pp. 14–15.

After reading the proposals and meeting key personnel, the manager should perform a comparative analysis. He or she should use the proposals to evaluate each vendor's understanding of the problem, how each will address it, and the cost and timing estimate of each. In making this evaluation, the manager needs to keep in mind that the value of the information is determined by its use, not its mere presence. Thus, the manager must be forthright in addressing how he or she would use the information provided by executing the various proposals.

Many firms have formal evaluation systems with specified criteria for evaluating suppliers, especially if they use suppliers on a regular basis. Land O'Lakes, the dairy producer, uses the criteria shown in Table 3.3. Top suppliers will seem equally competent, so a manager must rely on judgment regarding the soundness of the research design proposed, the supplier's responsiveness to questions, and the vendor's understanding of the subtler aspects of the marketing problem.

An increasingly popular way for firms to work with marketing research suppliers is to form long-term partnering relationships with a few select firms. Doing so helps the research buyer feel that the research supplier is going to act more collaboratively, in a manner holding the research supplier more accountable.[10] In a typical collaborative partnership, the client and research firm work together on an ongoing basis on those projects where the research firm has expertise, instead of the client relying on project-by-project bids to select suppliers for each of those projects. In some situations, the

Useful resource:

American Marketing Association

http://www. marketingpower.com

- **General Attitude, Responsiveness** (enthusiastic, helpful, provides prompt replies on cost estimates, proposals)

- **Marketing Insight** (informative, understands study objectives, ability to analyze data, provides recommendations)

- **Fundamental Design** (questionnaire is well designed, instructions are clear to consumers)

- **Questionnaire Construction** (format is sensible and easy to follow, order and wording of questions are clear, scales are suited to research questions)

- **Tabulation Design** (format is easy to understand, calculations are accurate)

- **Day-to-Day Service** (responsive and informative on study progress)

- **Analysis** (thorough, accurate, relates to objectives)

- **Quality of Report Writing** (concise, clear, accurate, provides executive summary)

- **Presentation** (well-planned, concise, materials organized to enhance clear communication, presenter is verbally skilled, smooth presentation)

- **Delivery Time** (topline, tables, report)

- **Cost** (over, under, justified)

Source: Courtesy of Stephen Lauring, Marketing Research Manager, Land O'Lakes, Inc.

TABLE 3.3
Criteria Used to Evaluate Research Suppliers

---

[10] Scott Young, "Packaging Design, Consumer Research, and Business Strategy: The March Toward Accountability," *Design Management Journal* 13 (2002), pp. 10–14.

research firm's staff may actually work at the client's premises on a regular basis. For example, many ACNielsen employees work directly at the offices of firms purchasing its scanner data, performing data analysis tasks that might have been done formerly by the client. The net result of partnering relationships is that both sides work with fewer companies, and the research firm becomes a resource that extends the client's information-gathering and analysis capabilities. Over time, the research firm becomes more familiar with the client's business and issues, which then allows the client firms to spend more time on managerial functions, including problem definition, interpretation, and recommendations, and less time on the nuts-and-bolts of a typical study.

Finally, most marketing research providers are comfortable and familiar with online surveys. And many firms enthusiastically embrace Internet versions of marketing research as exciting compared to traditional surveys (in the mall, on the phone, hardcopy in the mail). There are advantages of course, but Internet research is no panacea. See Research Realities 3.4.

Summary

A company's philosophy of how marketing research fits into its marketing plan determines its program strategy for marketing research. A program strategy specifies the types of studies that will be conducted and determines their purposes. The design of the individual studies defines the firm's project strategy.

Although each research problem imposes its own special requirements, a marketing research project can be viewed as a sequence of steps—the research process—that includes the following:

1. Formulate the problem.
2. Determine the research design.
3. Design the data-collection method and forms.
4. Design the sample and collect data.
5. Analyze and interpret the data.
6. Prepare the research report.

These steps are highly interrelated and are usually performed not simply consecutively, but with a good deal of iteration between the various steps.

The first stage in the research process is problem formulation. In defining the decision problem, the researcher and the manager need to be honest in their communications with each other. Decision problems or opportunities can arise from three sources: unplanned change, planned change, and serendipity, or chance ideas. The simplest decision problem is characterized by an individual who wants something, has alternative ways of pursuing it, and is in doubt about which course of action to take because the available options will not be equally efficient. The decision problem is what to do in this situation. To determine whether research can assist the decision maker in making the choice, it is necessary to translate the decision problem into a research problem that addresses the questions of what information to provide and how to obtain it.

It is imperative that the research address the "real" decision problem and not some visible, but incorrect, aspect of it. For this to happen, the researcher working on the problem must develop sufficient understanding of the decision maker and the environment, the alternative courses of action being considered, the decision maker's objectives (including the person's attitude toward risk), and the potential consequences of the alternative courses of action. One useful mechanism for ensuring that

Research Realities
3.4 Online, Pros and Cons

No question: online marketing research is very cool. But if it were perfect, suppliers would have closed down focus group facilities, canceled subscriptions to scanner databases, and moth-balled their call centers. So, what are the techniques' strengths, and what are the issues to watch out for? (We'll elaborate on these issues throughout the book.)

- **Fast.** Definitely. It's easy to program and post a survey on the Web. Turnaround times are quick. (We'll say more about "methods of administering surveys" in later chapters.)
- **Cheap.** Not free, but definitely inexpensive relative to many other forms of research.
- **Flexible, Convenient.** The mantra is "at my own pace, in my own place." Telephone marketing research calls are the most inconvenient to the user because call recipients have no control over when the call comes in, and the survey-taker naturally expects them to answer immediately, though of course a call-back may be arranged. Similarly, mall-intercepts expect immediate participation (who would want to come back just for the interview?), but if one is goal-directed in shopping, pausing to complete a survey is time taken out of a busy schedule. Online surveys, via e-mail or the Web, may be done at the respondent's convenience, more like a hardcopy mail survey.
- **Accurate?**
  - There are concerns of samples being not representative. Some 40% of the U.S. households are still not wired, and they are likely different from the 60% who do have Internet access. Does this matter? Depends on the product category you're investigating. (We'll say more about sampling later in the book.)
  - Accuracy used to be considered strong because of relatively high response rates, but online surveys are no longer novel, response rates have dropped, and now Internet marketing researchers are scrambling to enhance response rates analogous to traditional media. Nevertheless, online surveys are still considered more "fun" than traditional surveys.
- More thorough and thoughtful responses? Possibly. Consider these indices:
  - Reading rate (faster!)
    - by respondent, on Web survey: 325 words per minute
    - by survey-taker, to respondent, in interview: 200 wpm
  - Writing rate (more!)
    - by respondent, in open-ended question on hard-copy survey: 32 wpm

- by respondent, typing in answer to open-ended question on Web: 48 wpm
  - Number unique thoughts coded from verbal/text protocol (equal content!)
    - when respondents wrote answers to open-ended question: 4
    - when respondents type in answers on Web: 4
    - Yet, is "thoughtful" a trade-off with "spontaneity"?
- There are technology issues. Your programmers may want to add many bells and whistles, but you have to have empathy for the consumer who is online at home with a slow connection. Similarly, some branching (programming conditional upon previous responses) is great for keeping attention (respondents don't have to see questions irrelevant to them) and for keeping the pace of the survey quick. Yet often surveys are programmed without the capacity for consumers to go back and change their answers (which is sometimes intentional), but it is often frustrating.
- Promising potential: virtual reality and 3D presentations could help customers really "see" the product. Reality? Not there yet.
- **Weird developments:**
  - **Lurking.** Analogous to going to a grocery store and surreptitiously watching a consumer choosing among laundry detergents, marketing researchers are lurking online. They're reading the exchanges between members of various online communities, to see what these highly involved users are saying of products in their category. If you're curious, go to cabelas.com to be a voyeur of discussions among users of camping equipment, bakingcircle.com for bakers, palm.com /community for palm users, scea.com/underground for video game enthusiasts, and so forth.
  - Hershey Foods Corp. has enthusiastically embraced Internet research, moving its historical product testing databases online, okay, but also its entire new product testing online. Hmm, see any problems with that?

Sources: Nina Ray and Sharon Tabor, "Cybersurveys," *Marketing Research* (2003), pp. 32–37; Theo Downes-LeGuin, Ted Kendall and Ruchira Gupta, "Respondents Share Their Thoughts on Participating in Online Bulletin Board Research," *Quirk's Marketing Research Review* (http://www.quirks.com); Eric Lesser and Michael Fontaine, "What Are Your Customers Saying?" *Marketing Management* (2002), pp. 22–26; Catherine Arnold, "Hershey Research Sees Net Gain," *Marketing News* (Nov. 25, 2002), p. 17.

the actual decision problem will be addressed by the research is for the researcher to prepare a written statement of the problem after meeting with the decision maker. Another way is by preparing scenarios that anticipate the contents of the final report, including the planned cross-tabulations, and asking the decision maker what he or she would do with the results. In either case, it is useful to secure a signed agreement from the decision maker that the written statement correctly captures the situation. After such agreement is obtained, the researcher should prepare a research proposal that describes the techniques that will be used to address the problem. The research proposal should include some perspective on how each stage in the research process will be handled, as well as the time and cost estimates.

Before proceeding with the research, the potential gains to be derived should always be specified explicitly and compared with the costs to ensure that the research is likely to be worthwhile.

Review Questions

1. What is the difference between a program strategy for research and a project strategy?

2. What is the research process?

3. What is the most serious error in research? Explain.

4. What are the sources of marketing problems or opportunities? Does a source change typically trigger a change in research emphasis? Explain.

5. What are the fundamental characteristics of decision problems?

6. What is involved in a research request step? What is included in the written statement?

7. What is involved in using scenarios to help define the decision problem?

8. What is the purpose of a research proposal? What goes into the various parts?

9. Why would firms want to use outside suppliers for their research? How should decision makers go about choosing an outside supplier for some research?

Applications and Problems

1. Given the following decision problems, identify the research problems:

   a. What pricing strategy to follow for a new product

   b. Whether to increase the level of advertising expenditures on print or online

   c. Whether to increase in-store promotion of existing products

   d. Whether to increase training for frontline service providers

   e. Whether to change the sales force compensation package

   f. Whether to change the combination of ticket price, entertainers, and security at the Indiana State Fair

   g. Whether to revise a bank's electronic payment service

2. Given the following research problems, identify corresponding decision problems for which they might provide useful information.

   a. Design a test market to assess the effect on sales volume of a particular discount scheme.

   b. Evaluate inventory for retail and e-tail warehouses.

   c. Evaluate the sales and market share of grocery stores in a metropolitan area.

   d. Develop sales forecasts for a new product.

   e. Assess the level of awareness of the benefits of a new generation of mobile phones.

   f. Assess attitudes and opinions of customers toward existing theme restaurants.

3. Briefly discuss the difference between a decision problem and a research problem.

4. In each of the following situations, identify the fundamental source of the marketing problem or opportunity, a decision problem arising from the marketing problem or opportunity, and a possible research problem.

   a. Cool Pool Supply is a manufacturer of swimming pool maintenance chemicals. Recently, a malfunction of the equipment that mixes anti-algae compound resulted in a batch of the product that not only inhibits algae growth but also causes the pool water to turn a beautiful shade of light blue (with no undesirable side effects).

   b. The MBA director of a local college recently extended offers to 20 promising students. Only 5 offers were accepted. In the past, acceptance rates have averaged 90 percent. A survey of nonacceptors conducted by the director revealed that the primary reason students declined the offer was their perception that the college's course requirements are too "restrictive."

   c. Chocoholic Candy Company has enjoyed great success in its small regional market. Management attributes much of this success to Chocoholic's unique distribution system, which ensures twice-weekly delivery of fresh product to retail outlets. The directors of the company have instructed management to expand Chocoholic's geographical market if it can be done without altering the twice-weekly delivery policy.

5. You are the marketing manager of a two- year-old Internet company. Recently you solicited proposals for an upcoming research project from three outside marketing research suppliers. You have the formal proposals in hand and must choose which supplier to use. In general, what criteria should you use in making your decision?

6. This chapter discussed the research problem and the problem formulation step in research design. Take a step back for a moment and consider the following question: In the absence of company problems, is there any need to conduct marketing research?

Cases

CASE 1.1

Big Brothers of Fairfax County

Big Brothers of America is a social-service program designed to meet the needs of boys ages 6 to 18 from single-parent homes. Most of the boys served by the program live with their mothers and rarely see or hear from their fathers. The purpose of the program is to give these boys the chance to establish a friendship with an interested adult male. Big Brothers of America was founded on the belief that an association with a responsible adult can help program participants become more responsible citizens and better adjusted young men.

The program was started in Cincinnati in 1903. Two years later, the organization was granted its first charter in New York state through the efforts of Mrs. Cornelius Vanderbilt. By the end of World War II, there were 30 Big Brothers agencies. Today there are more than 300 agencies across the United States, and more than 120,000 boys are matched with Big Brothers. The Fairfax County chapter of Big Brothers of America was founded in Fairfax in 1966. In 1971, United Way of Fairfax County accepted the program as part of its umbrella organization and now provides about 85% of its funding. The remaining 15% is raised by the local Big Brothers agency.

Information about the Big Brothers program in Fairfax County reaches the public primarily through newspapers (feature stories and classified advertisements), radio, public-service announcements, posters (on buses and in windows of local establishments), and word-of-mouth advertising. The need for volunteers is a key message emanating from these sources. The agency phone number is always included so that people who want to know more about the program can call for information. Those calling in are given basic information over the telephone and are invited to attend one of the monthly orientation sessions organized by the Big Brothers program staff. At these meetings, men get the chance to talk to other volunteers and to find out what will be expected of them should they decide to join the program. At the end of the session, prospective volunteers are asked to complete two forms. One is an application form and the other is a questionnaire in which the person is asked to describe the type of boy he would prefer to be matched with, as well as his own interests.

The files on potential Little Brothers are then reviewed in an attempt to match boys with the volunteers. A match is made only if both partners agree. The agency stays in close contact with the pair and monitors its progress. The three counselors for the Big Brothers program serve as resources for the volunteer.

The majority of the inquiry calls received by the Fairfax County agency are from women who are interested in becoming Big Sisters (in the Big Brothers program) or from people desiring information on the Couples Program. Both programs are similar to the Big Brothers program and are administered by it. In fact, of 55 calls concerning a recent orientation meeting, only 5 were from males. Only three of the five callers actually attended the meeting, a typical response.

Although the informational campaigns and personal appeals thus seemed to have some effect, the results were also generally disappointing and did little to alleviate the shortage of volunteer Big Brothers. Currently, 250 boys are waiting to be matched with Big Brothers, and the shortage increases weekly.

Big Brothers of Fairfax County believed that a lack of awareness and accurate knowledge could be the cause of the shortage of volunteers. Are there men who would volunteer if only they were made aware of the program and its needs? Or is the difficulty a negative program image? Do people think of Little Brothers as problem children, boys who have been in trouble with the law or who have severe behavioral problems? Or could there be a misconception of the type of man who would make a good Big Brother? Do people have stereotypes with respect to the volunteers, for example, that the typical volunteer is a young, single, professional male?

Questions

1. What is (are) the marketing decision problem(s)?
2. What is (are) the marketing research problem(s)?
3. What types of information would be useful to answer these questions?
4. How would you go about securing this information?

CASE 1.2

Hand-to-Hand Against Palm (A)

An electronics and personal computing firm has been watching closely the success of the Palm Pilot and seeks to introduce a competitive device, beta-named "Organize My Life!" or OML for short. The OML marketing manager has gathered some intelligence on the Palm Inc. sales and believes that, for all its success, some potential markets are being underserved.

Hand-held personal digital assistants (PDAs) were introduced unsuccessfully at first by Apple in 1993. Some analysts argue that the Newton, Apple's market offering, was not clearly positioned to the consumers; others argue that it was simply ahead of its time. 3Com's Palm Computing focused the PDA, limiting its functionality to calendars and appointments, contact directory information, and to-do lists, so as to convey its technological benefits more clearly to the potential user. In only five years, Palm achieved more than two-thirds of the global market to support this claim.

Over 5.5 million devices have been sold, and sales continue to show strong growth (sales are expected to reach 13 million in the next two years).

Competitors offer Internet access, including wireless variants, but the OML group has data that indicate only 17% of PDA users would pay extra for this feature—these users already have PC Internet access and view the PDA's access version as redundant, and worse, likely to be slow. OML is considering conducting research to investigate whether other features, such as voice recognition capabilities, stereo quality sound systems for downloading music, video and digital photographic abilities, and global positioning mapping ("u r here") software would be valued.

In addition to seeking data on features, OML is considering the attractiveness of this technology to another segment. Its data indicate the typical Palm Pilot user is a male, in his early 40s, college-educated, and a white-collar professional with a relatively high income. OML is interested in serving the university student market. An important concern is that the typical student has fewer discretionary funds than the current PDA purchaser profile. Thus, OML marketing discussions revolve around questions like these: What is the price point beyond which students would be less inclined to purchase this device? If the device were priced at, say, $299 or less, which features would be prohibitive to continue to offer? What are students' priorities in terms of the functions and features they would like to see bundled into the PDA? Would the benefits sought depend on whether this device were targeted to undergraduates "in general" compared with engineering and computer science students and compared with MBA graduate students? How do we choose the features to offer and the segments to target?

Questions

1. What is the decision problem?
2. What is (are) the research problem(s)?
3. What recommendations would you make to the OML marketing manager to address the research problem(s)? That is, what data would you collect and how might those data be used to answer the research question(s) posed?

CASE 1.3
E-Food and the Online Grocery Competition (A)

When everybody's busy, something's got to give. The relatively new service industry of online groceries (that is, grocery shopping online and the home delivery of the purchased items) has grown to address today's consumer demands of convenience and time savings. Perhaps the best-known provider in the industry is Peapod.com, an operation that began outside Chicago.

Since its founding in 1989, it has expanded to nearly a dozen metropolitan markets, serving over 100,000 households. Other competitors sense the market potential, and many firms share space in the marketplace, including groceronline.com (which uses UPS and Federal Express rather than local delivery operators); or netgrocer.com (which covers towns and rural areas, with no annual fee and makes available merchandise such as books and CDs); as well as many as-yet-local providers. Industry experts predict continued strong growth. (Though their numbers vary wildly, home food shopping is expected to grow to anywhere from $5 billion to $80 billion in the next three to five years.)

These online grocery services provide virtual stores through which the electronic visitor navigates, as if pushing a shopping cart in a traditional market. The user clicks on items to purchase, which are placed in the user's cart. When complete, the user is "checked out," specifying a delivery date and time (paying a premium for narrower windows of delivery time precision, such as from 1 to 1:30 P.M. compared to 1 to 4 P.M.). Users pay annual dues and delivery costs proportionate to each shopping bill.

The software allows the user to store his or her preferences in a personal shopping list, which may be altered, adding or deleting items as deemed necessary with each e-visit. Across the various providers, the software also usually allows facile consumer comparison; for example, the SKUs in a particular category may be sorted by brand name, by price, by value (price per ounce, for example), by what is on "feature" (sale and point of purchase promotions), by various dietetic goals ("healthy," "low fat"), and so on. The user may write in "notes," to specify in more detail, for example, "Please pick up green (unripe) bananas, not yellow ones," or, "If Fancy Feast is out of beef, please get turkey instead," which instruct the professional shopper as to the user's particular preferences. Categories of items that can be purchased are continually expanding, from foods to drugstore items and other merchandise.

Most users are women, employed full-time, and married, with household incomes that exceed $100,000. Online grocery providers tend to conduct the online business very well, if customers' satisfaction, repeat visits, and word-of-mouth are any indicators. That is, the software provided, the merchandise selected, the delivery reliability, and so on, are valued by the customer, with few complaints. However, home delivery of food is not a particularly profitable industry. One of the major paths to profit is in selling the data that result from the visitors' trips to the Web site.

Ashley Sims is an MBA student, taking her last term of classes, and thinking about starting up a local competitor online grocer. She's certain that by learning from the templates of the current providers in other markets, that she too can run the logistics of the business. However, she hopes that given her computer expert contacts, she can create a competitive advantage in the software setup, if she understands the consumers' mindset as they travel through the e-grocery stores. She wants to know just what a user is thinking from the first click onto the Web site to the last "Done Shopping" click off the site. This knowledge would allow her to offer better advice to her software developers in terms of what features would facilitate the visitors' traversal of the grocery store. Data like these would help improve the system, and it would also lend great insight to the consumers' decision processes.

Questions

1. What is the decision problem?
2. What is (are) the research problem(s)?
3. Prepare a research proposal to submit to an online grocer on behalf of your research team.

CASE 1.4

Choosing a Brand Name

The choice of a brand name is very important. It is a single word with a great deal of responsibility. The word must convey what the product is, what it is not, why it's great, or at least better than the others, and why you should buy it.

New brand names are required in a number of marketing settings. A new product course requires a new name. A line extension for a brand may be created to help stimulate sales.

Oddly enough, one arena that is seeing a frequent need to generate and test a "brand name" is in the health services sector. Increasingly, two or more offices of physicians are merging to meet some mutual goal more effectively (serve more patients, service more needs of their patients, share management and overhead costs, etc.). When this occurs, the groups have a decision to make: shall they go by the first group's name? The second group's name? Or pick a new name?

Most frequently, the groups choose to pick a new name. The reasons are usually two. First, there are politics. Specifically, the management of group 1 (or 2) likes its name better and doesn't want group 2 (or 1) to think they're going to run the show. But the better reason for our purposes is the "marketing" reason. Specifically, given that the groups are combining so as to achieve a new goal, the new brand name is the opportunity to communicate to the new potential customers how the merger could be good for them.

Usually a brand name choice study runs something like this: (1) many names are generated. These names can come from the marketing research and advertising team, top management, the employees (e.g., in a contest), etc.

(2) All the names are collected and the list is pruned, in house, by a number of criteria, including, for example, deleting names that are too close to the competition or that are already legally registered, deleting names that are difficult to pronounce or spell, deleting names that have negative or lame connotations, and in international applications, names that don't translate well, etc.

(3) Then the remaining short list of candidate names are pretested with "real" customers. Usually a number of con-

stituencies are polled. Internal customers are asked for their reactions to the list of potential names. In this example, the employees would be the physicians. Multiple external customers would also be queried (by interview or survey). These include business partners, such as representatives of nearby hospitals and medical centers, and the insurance payers. These external customers also include patients of various sorts. "Current" customers would be asked, as would patients who are the kind the new group hopes to serve more often. It would be relatively easy to find members of all but the last of these groups to include in your study.

The results of just this process produced, for one health group merger, the following names:

- Mid-Central Hospital
- Downtown Medical Center
- Airus Group
- Health Protection Facilities
- Wellness Consultants
- Health and Life
- Touchpoint

The attributes that were tested for each of these proposed names, in each of the constituency samples, included:

- general positivity or negativity toward the name
- connotations of excellence and quality
- affiliation with a particular geographic focus
- a traditional vs. contemporary image
- a formal vs. friendly image
- distinctiveness
- easily understood
- perceptions of convenience and accessibility

Questions

1. Which of these attributes do you think are more important than others? With regard to achieving what goals?
2. Which name(s) do you think scored best on which attributes? From which segment's perspective?
3. How would you modify the names? Why?

CASE 1.5

Moving Consumers from Awareness to Loyalty

Marketers talk about the phases that consumers go through in terms of their relationships with products. There needs to be awareness before trial. If there is trial, there can be repeat purchasing. If there is predictable repeat purchasing, we might call that loyalty, etc.

Marketing strategies, such as goals to find segments of customers to target who will be profitable for the firm are translated into marketing tactics. The marketing tactics involve decisions about the product features, the price level that's right for the product and segment, the promotions

FIGURE 1.5.1
Diagnosing Marketing
Issues: Awareness,
Trial, Repeat

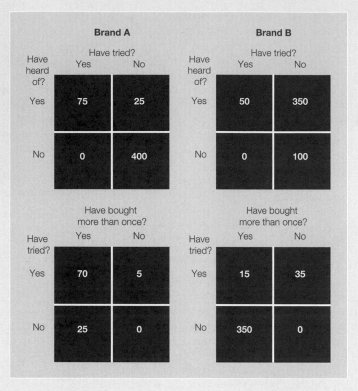

used to convey the competitive advantages of this product vs. its competitors, and the place or distribution points of availability for the product's purchase. Sometimes even very simple data can shed light on the successfulness of the marketing campaign at the different stages.

Figure 1.5.1 contains two sets of data, one for the brand offered by firm A (brand A), and one for another firm's offering, brand B. Each brand was tested in the marketplace for awareness, trial, and repeat purchasing.

The data are simple to collect and easy to represent, and they communicate very clearly the marketing challenges at the two companies. Discuss these scenarios either in class or with a group of fellow students. Use the data and the following questions to structure your discussion.

1. Which brand is better known in the marketplace?
   a. How can you enhance awareness for the other brand?
   b. If there is low awareness, what is the most likely reason? Product? Price? Promotion? Place?

2. Which brand, once there is awareness, is more likely to induce people to try it?
   a. If there is awareness but not trial, what's the problem? Perception? Price? Availability?
   b. For the brand with lower awareness, how would you entice more people to try the product?
   c. If there is low trial, what is the most likely reason? Product? Price? Promotion? Place?

3. Which brand enjoys the most repeat purchasing?
   a. If the brand with lesser repeat wanted to improve on this aspect, what should it do?
   b. When repeat is strong, what does that mean the company has done well? Product? Price? Promotion? Place?

4. If you could request more marketing research for either of the brands, what would you request and why?

CASE 1.6

Qualitative Data from Open-Ended Survey Items: A Service Quality Example

In order to understand how customers think about service quality, people were asked to reflect on examples in their recent experiences in the marketplace of good service and poor service. We then asked the sample to elaborate and tell us the extended story about the bad service encounters in particular. People are quite willing to do this—it's an opportunity to vent and it feels good, so the marketing researcher can get high response rates.

We asked the following questions of all respondents in an attempt to identify the features of service encounters that make them satisfactory or unsatisfactory:

FIGURE 1.6.1
Service Quality Open-Ended Survey Question

Think back to the last time you had a bad encounter with a service provider (e.g., airline, hotel, bank, restaurant, retail shop, etc.). Think about what made the experience so dissatisfying, and why you thought the service quality was so poor. Describe the situation and your feelings—what about the situation went wrong?

_____

_____

_____

_____

- Think of a time when, as a customer, you had a particularly dissatisfying interaction with an employee of an airline, hotel, or restaurant, etc.
- When did the incident happen?
- What specific circumstances led up to this situation?
- Exactly what did the employee say or do?
- What resulted that made you feel the interaction was dissatisfying?

The part of the qualitative data we'll focus on was gathered through the survey item in Figure 1.6.1. People were free to write as little or as much as they wished, about anything they wanted that was related to their disappointing service interaction.

The surveys were collected, and administration assistance was hired to type in the verbatim responses (sometimes online surveys are used, and then respondents type in their reactions, so the data are already entered in text form). Pay your staff well, because this work is challenging: it is tedious, it is difficult to decipher many people's handwriting, and finally, you need high quality control on data entry if you're going to be interpreting the data shortly.

Figure 1.6.2 depicts the beginning of the qualitative database. (You can get the rest of these data online.) The first column is simply an arbitrary label for the survey respondent. The second column is the verbatim response from the customer about what upset them about the service encounter.

FIGURE 1.6.2
Service Quality Open-Ended Survey Verbata: A Sampling of the Data

ID#	Typed Verbatim Consumer Response
002b	It was too expensive.
001c	It was slow.
006a	The waitress didn't acknowledge our presence when we sat down.
005f	I felt it was low quality.
007a	The attitude of the employees.
009a	All she did was bring me a grilled cheese.
010a	Timeliness.
011b	Individuals at the service desk appear to not know their jobs.
012b	The service provider completed the process quickly.
013a	They did nothing to calm my anger.
003c	They did not apologize. They made excuses.
004g	I knew they could do better.
014a	The service throughout the flight by the attendants was very good.
015c	I was able to get an omelet that met my vegetarian needs without egg yolk (no fat/low cholesterol).

Figure 1.6.3 offers the beginnings of a coding scheme. These schema are developed iteratively, beginning with the marketing manager's "hunches" about the qualities that people are sensitive to and therefore are likely to mention, integrated with a perusal of the comments themselves.

FIGURE 1.6.3
Service Quality Open-Ended Survey Coding Scheme

A.   Cost, price, value

B.   Speed of service (usually too slow, but note if too fast)

C.   (Not) treated like a valuable customer

D.   Employee related

E.   Equipment or technology failure

F.   Fell short of my customer expectations

G.   Were they empowered to meet my specific requests

Figure 1.6.4 shows how the data in Figure 1.6.2 would be coded. So, for example, for survey 002b, the customer's comment was pretty clearly about cost, so the category label of "A" seems appropriate. Note, however, that some survey responses are less easily categorized, making the task of coding overall nontrivial. A number of decisions must always be made.

When coders have difficulty applying the coding scheme to the data, it is always the fault of the coding scheme. For example, there isn't really a code that may be applied to respondent 005f, "I felt it was low quality," so the coding scheme needs to be expanded.

Sometimes a customer can offer a comment that needs multiple codes, and the marketing researcher has to think about how to treat that observation, e.g., expand the variable into two variables and allow for multiple thought units? The survey labeled 012b is such an example. The respondent said, "The service provider completed the process

FIGURE 1.6.4
Using the Coding Scheme

The datafile would resemble:

002b	A
001c	B
006a	D
005f	
007a	D
009a	
010a	B
011b	D
012b	B, D
013a	
003c	
004g	F
014a	
015c	G

quickly." Is this thought predominately about the service provider, hence warranting the code "D" for employee, or is the comment more about speed, for which "B" would be the appropriate code.

Questions

1.   Go online, get the rest of the data.
2.   Develop a coding scheme you believe in. What is it based on?
3.   Apply the coding scheme to the data. There are almost 70 responses in the database. Try to code at least half. Estimate how long it would take you to do them all!
4.   What can you do with the data? An easy quantitative assessment would be to calculate frequencies for the occurrence of the different codes in your database. What do those summary statistics tell you? What don't they tell you? Qualitative marketing researchers wouldn't perform such counts—they'd assess the data by reading through and forming a judgment about what customers are saying. If you were to do this, how could you substantiate your claims to convince others (e.g., your boss)?

PART 2

Determine Research Design

Part 2 deals with the general nature of designing research so that it addresses the appropriate questions effectively.

- Chapter 4 provides an overview of the role of various research designs: exploratory, descriptive, and causal research designs. The chapter continues with a discussion of exploratory research and qualitative data.

- Chapter 5 discusses descriptive research, the most popular kind of marketing research.

- Chapter 6 discusses the role of causal experiments in marketing research.

Research Design, Exploratory Research, and Qualitative Data

Questions to Guide Your Learning:

Q1: What is *exploratory research*? How does it relate to *qualitative data*?

Q2: What can a literature search, experience survey, or case study do for me?

Q3: What makes for a good *focus group* or *interview*?

Q4: What is a *projective test*?

Q5: What kinds of *observational methods* are there?

Q6: What is an *ethnography*?

Part 1 presented some of the kinds of problems that marketing research can help solve. You saw that there can be great variation in the nature of marketing research questions. Some can be very specific: "If we change the advertising mix, what might happen to sales?" Others are more general: "Why have sales fallen below target?" Or, "How do customers feel about the product?" Different formulations of a problem lead to different research approaches to finding answers.

This chapter introduces types of research designs. We then proceed to the topics of exploratory designs and qualitative data.

Plan of Action

A **research design** is the framework or plan for a study, used as a guide to collect and analyze data. It is the blueprint that is followed to complete a study. It is analogous to an architect's blueprint for a house—even though it is possible to build a house without a detailed blueprint, doing so will more than likely produce a final product that is different from what was originally envisioned by the buyer, e.g., a certain room is too small, the traffic pattern is poor, some features really wanted are omitted, other less important details are included, and so on.

Research can also be conducted without a detailed blueprint, but these findings, too, will probably differ greatly from what the user of the research wanted, e.g., "These results are interesting, but they do not solve the basic problem," is a common lament. Further, just as the house built without a blueprint is likely to cost more because of midstream alterations, research conducted without a design is likely to cost more than that executed using a proper design.

Thus, a research design ensures that the study (1) will be relevant to the problem and (2) will use economical procedures. There are many research design frameworks, but they can be classified into three basic types: exploratory, descriptive, or causal.[1]

Types of Research Design

The major emphasis in **exploratory research** is on the discovery of *ideas and insights*. For example, a soft-drink manufacturer faced with decreased sales might conduct an exploratory study to generate possible explanations. Or, an electronics firm looking to launch a new-to-the-world product needs to begin with exploratory research to assess consumers' reactions.

The **descriptive research** study is typically concerned with determining the *frequency* with which something occurs or the *relationship* between two variables. The descriptive study is typically guided by an initial hypothesis. An investigation of trends in the consumption of soft drinks with respect to such characteristics as age, gender, and geographic location would be a descriptive study. Or, a segmentation study that tied propensity to try the new-to-the-world technology to user characteristics, such as average daily time spent online, would be a descriptive study.

A **causal research** design is concerned with determining *cause-and-effect* relationships, and these are studied via experiments. For instance, a typical advertising experiment would be one designed to ascertain the effectiveness of different ad appeals, where the different ads would be used in different geographic areas to investigate which ad generated the highest sales. If the experiment is designed properly, the company is in a position to conclude that one specific appeal caused the higher rate of sales. An electronics firm might put a new product to market at different price points in different test markets to assess price sensitivity.

Having stated the basic general purpose of each major type of research design, three important caveats are in order:

1. The distinctions are not absolute. Any study will likely serve several purposes. Still, certain types of research designs are better suited to some purposes than

Research Designs

- **Exploratory**
- **Descriptive**
- **Causal**

---

[1] Fred N. Kerlinger and Howard B. Lee, *Foundations of Behavioral Research*, 4th ed. (Wadsworth, 2000).

others. The crucial tenet of research is that *the design of the investigation should stem from the problem*. Each design is appropriate to specific kinds of problems.

2. As we present more detail on each of the types of design, we'll emphasize their basic characteristics. But it is often the case that there is no single best way to proceed, so depending on the particular marketing problem, the marketing researcher may modify the basic design.

3. Figure 4.1 shows how the three basic designs are interrelated as stages in a continuous process. Exploratory studies are often seen as the initial step. When researchers begin an investigation, it stands to reason that they lack a great deal of knowledge about the problem. The question, "Why is our brand share slipping?" is too broad to serve as a guide for research. Exploratory research will help narrow and refine the question. The possible explanations, or hypotheses, for the sales decrease then serve as specific guides for the subsequent descriptive or causal studies.

Suppose the tentative explanation that emerged was that "Brand X is economy-priced, originally designed to compete with low-cost store brands. Families have more money today than when the brand was first introduced and are willing to pay more for higher quality products. It stands to reason that our market share would decrease." The hypotheses that families have more real income to spend and that a larger proportion of that money is going toward products in this category could be examined in a descriptive study of trends in the industry.

Suppose that the descriptive study did support the hypotheses. The company might then want to determine whether parents were, in fact, willing to pay more for higher quality products and, if so, what features were most important to them. This might be accomplished partially through a test marketing study, a causal design.

Each stage in the process thus represents the investigation of a more detailed statement of the problem. Although we have described the sequence as one that progresses from exploratory → descriptive → causal research, alternative sequences might occur. The "families have more money to spend on these products" hypothesis might be so generally accepted that the sequence would go from exploratory directly to causal. The potential also exists for conducting research in the reverse direction. If a hypothesis is disproved by causal research (the product bombs in the test market), the analyst may then decide that another descriptive study, or even another exploratory study, is needed. Not every research problem begins with an exploratory study. It depends on how specific researchers can be in formulating the problem

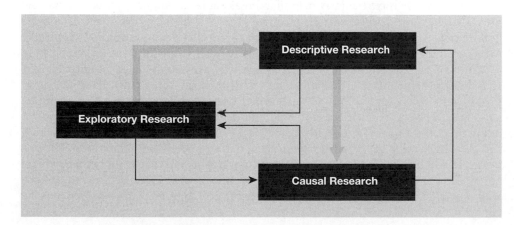

FIGURE 4.1
Relationship among
Research Designs

FIGURE 4.2
Types of Research Designs

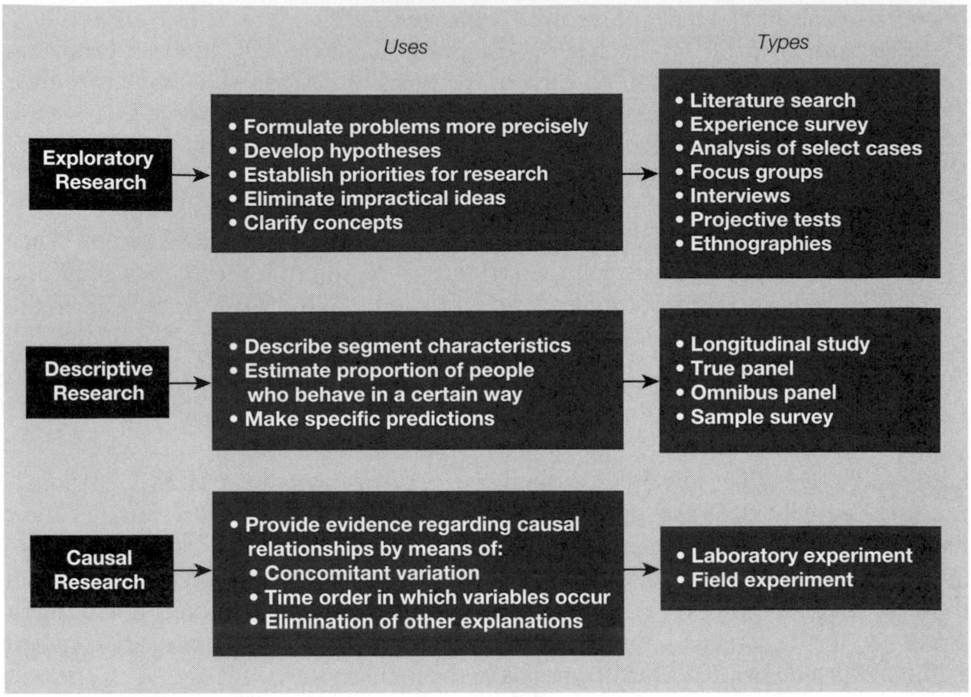

before them. A general, vague statement leads naturally to exploratory work, whereas a specific cause-effect hypothesis lends itself to experimental work.

Figure 4.2 provides an overview of the three kinds of research—exploratory, descriptive, and causal. In this chapter, we continue elaborating on exploratory research. Descriptive and causal designs are treated in more detail in the next two chapters.

Exploratory Research

The general objective in exploratory research is to gain insights and ideas. The exploratory study is particularly helpful in breaking large, vague problem statements into smaller, more precise sub-problem statements, ideally in the form of specific hypotheses. A **hypothesis** is a statement that specifies how two or more measurable variables are related. A good hypothesis also carries clear implications for testing stated relationships. In the early stages of research, we usually lack sufficient understanding of the problem to formulate a specific hypothesis. Further, there are often several tentative explanations for a given marketing phenomenon. For example: Sales are off because our price is too high, our dealers or sales representatives are not doing the job they should, our advertising is weak, and so on. Exploratory research can be used to establish priorities in studying these competing explanations. The priorities would be established because a particular hypothesis discovered in the exploratory study appears to be promising. They might also arise because the exploratory study generates information about the practical possibilities of researching specific conjectures.

Exploratory studies are also used to increase the marketer's familiarity with the problem. This is particularly true when the marketing manager or marketing researcher is new to the problem area.

The exploratory study may be used to clarify concepts. Say management is considering a change in a service policy that should result in improved dealer satisfaction. An exploratory study could be used to clarify the notion of "dealer satisfaction" and to develop such a measure.

When Congress discusses revising the tax code in order to make it "more fair" (so as to increase taxpayer compliance), a problem that often surfaces is how to determine what fairness means. Is it tax enforcement that bothers people? Tax avoidance by other people? The complexity of tax laws? Tax rates? That tax dollars are poorly spent? Exploratory research could clarify this concept.

In sum, an exploratory study is used for any or all of the following purposes:

- Formulating a problem for more precise investigation or for developing hypotheses
- Establishing priorities for further research
- Gathering information about the practical problems of carrying out relevant research
- Increasing the marketer's familiarity with the problem
- Clarifying concepts

In general, exploratory research is appropriate for any problem about which little is known. Exploratory research is the foundation for a good study.

Exploratory studies are characterized by *flexibility* with respect to the research methods used. They rarely use detailed questionnaires or complex sampling plans. Rather, investigators frequently change the research procedure as the vaguely defined initial problem is transformed into one with more precise meaning. Researchers follow where their noses lead them in an exploratory study. Ingenuity, judgment, and good luck inevitably play a part in leading to the one or two key hypotheses that may ultimately account for the phenomenon.

With the preceding discussion serving as an overview to the goals of exploratory research, we turn next to the relationship between exploratory research and qualitative data. We then present a number of marketing research techniques that may be characterized as exploratory and qualitative.

Relationship Between Exploratory Research and Qualitative Data

In long-standing tradition, qualitative research methods are considered to be exploratory in nature. The tradition holds that, say, in a new product launch, early in a product's life cycle, exploratory research is conducted (some focus groups are run), followed by some descriptive research to "get the numbers" (surveys are conducted), perhaps followed up with some causal research as the product and category matures (experiments are run to tweak pricing issues).

This characterization is not unfounded. It is difficult to create an exploratory survey (it would require many open-ended questions, and respondents quickly tire of writing or typing long answers). Similarly, it would seem impossible to conduct an exploratory experiment (it would require knowledge of which factors are relevant to the purchasing decision in order to vary them systematically in the causal design), and so forth.

Still, qualitative methodologists bristle at the techniques being referred to as "exploratory" as if that status makes the methods and the studies' findings more tentative and somehow of lesser import. In fact, one might argue instead that research conducted at the earliest stages is the most critical, because if it is not executed well, the entire marketing research program goes down the wrong path, eventually to answer questions about which no manager cares.

In a way, though, the results of a focus group are usually more tentative. For example, it's the rare focus group where, say, every participant thinks the concept being discussed is an absolute dud. First, by the time an idea reaches the focus group stage, it's been considered in-house by numerous personnel, and presumably the idea hadn't encountered uniform resistance. Second, we marketers know about segments, so although some participants might hate an idea, others may be intrigued. Most focus groups result in such mixed opinion compositions. Third, even if all focus group participants hated the idea, we would probably question whether there was "groupthink," or whether the sample of 8–10 individuals was perhaps not representative of the broader customer population.

Marketing managers and those higher-up love focus groups. They're interesting and there is nothing more compelling than a customer verbatim. A good quote from a person who looks like he or she could be your neighbor brings to life customer opinions in a way that number crunching reams of scanner data cannot do. However, those same higher-ups are usually reluctant to spend vast amounts of resources to take the next marketing tactical steps (a product launch, the rollout of a new ad campaign) on the basis of those same focus groups. After all, the results of even three focus groups (say $24,000–$45,000), yields the opinions of a maximum of 24–30 persons. Given that product launches and advertising campaigns are expensive ($mm), and jobs rest on such decisions, the decisions usually require the more conservative approach of gathering even more intelligence.

Finally, we might also note that sometimes qualitative techniques are used later in the research process, where their role is more "confirmatory" than exploratory. For example, if in a study of a national retailer, overall customer satisfaction scores seemed to be correlated with a factor called "pleasantness of store layout," such a result would necessitate follow-up to understand just what about a retail layout makes it pleasant. This sort of follow-up is frequently conducted via interviews, hence the interviews are being used to clarify the descriptive research.

Qualitative research methods can be used prior to quantitative studies, e.g., in identifying the issues that should be surveyed subsequently. Sometimes a qualitative study is run to get some "quick and dirty" data, because a focus group, say, is less expensive ($10,000–$25,000) than a large scale survey ($20,000–$100,000). Qualitative methods can be also used after quantitative studies to find greater depth of meaning to the numbers that the surveys yield. Nevertheless, with all those caveats aside, usually when someone in industry (marketing or marketing research) says "qualitative" they usually mean "exploratory," and vice versa.

Some Basic Types of Exploratory Research

Initial tools for exploratory research include literature searches, experience surveys, and the analysis of selected cases. We'll discuss each in turn. When people speak of qualitative marketing research methods, however, they're usually referring to focus groups, interviews, or ethnographies, and we'll discuss these techniques later in the chapter.

Literature Search

One of the quickest and cheapest ways to discover hypotheses is in the work of others, through a literature search. The search may involve *conceptual literature, trade literature,* or *published statistics,* depending on the problem being addressed. *Conceptual literature* would pop up from a search using Proquest or the Web of Science for articles in marketing journals, or those in psychology, sociology, or economics journals. Even such search engines as Google now yield surprising amounts of information from these basic disciplines (the quality of which of course varies, but see, e.g., faculty Web sites). Most industries have *trade publications* to keep track of competition and common customer concerns. The information in these databases is usually extensive and may be accessed with membership to affiliated associations. *Published data* on many industries are so vast that we devote a large section to them in our chapter on secondary data, and many of those sources are linked on our Web site.

When these sources of information are combined, a firm's problem might be diagnosed fairly clearly. For example, if "sales are down," we need to know whether the problem was an industry problem or a firm problem. Different research is in order if the firm's sales are down but (1) the company's market share is up, because industry sales are down farther; (2) the company's market share has remained stable; or (3) the company's market share has declined. The last situation would trigger an investigation of the firm's marketing mix variables, whereas the first condition would suggest an analysis to determine why industry sales are off. The great danger in omitting exploratory research is obvious from the preceding example—without the analysis of these existing data sources as a guide, there is a great danger of researching the wrong "why."

> **Basic Explorations**
> - Literature search
> - Experience surveys
> - Case analyses

Experience Survey

The experience survey, sometimes called the key informant survey, taps the knowledge of those familiar with the general subject being investigated. In studies concerned with the marketing of a product, anyone who has any association with the marketing effort is a potential source of information. This would include the top executives of the company, the sales manager, the product manager, and sales representatives. It would also include wholesalers and retailers who handle the product as well as consumers who use the product. It might even include individuals who are not part of the chain of distribution but who might, nevertheless, possess some insight into the phenomenon. For example, a publisher of children's books investigating a sales decrease talked with librarians and schoolteachers. It turned out that the product's sales decline coincided with an increased use of library facilities. The library holdings of children's books had increased as a result of recent federal funding.

Usually, a great many people know something about the general subject of any given problem. One does not use a probability sample in an experience survey because it is a waste of time to interview people who have little experience or competence in the area. It is important to include people with differing points of view, e.g., company executives, key people in the product group, sales representatives, managers of retail outlets, etc.

Analysis of Cases

The analysis of selected cases involves the intensive study of selected cases of the phenomenon under investigation (e.g., business school cases).[2] Cases comprise several sources of input data: existing records, observations of the phenomenon, interviews, etc. "Best Practices" studies (good leaders, financially sound companies, etc.) are also case analyses.

In the analysis of a case, the researcher records all relevant data, not just those that support initial hypotheses. In exploratory research, the goal is to gain insights, not to test explanations. By remaining neutral, it is easier for the researcher to be flexible as new information emerges. The researcher must also be able to sort through all the data and see the "big picture," insights that should apply across multiple cases, not just details that apply only to individual cases.

Some approaches to case studies that are particularly productive (help generate hypotheses) include:

- Cases reflecting (abrupt) changes, e.g., the adjustment of a market to the entrance of a new competitor can be quite revealing of the structure of an industry.
- Cases reflecting extremes of behavior, e.g., insights about sales reps may result from comparing the best and worst performers.
- Cases reflecting sequences of events, e.g., in diagnosing differential sales across territories, it would be important to log personnel replacements, such as a manufacturer's agent or an industrial distributor replacing a branch office salesperson.

Cases that have striking features are most useful because subtle differences are difficult to discern.

A frequently used example of the use of selected cases to develop insights is **benchmarking**. One or more organizations are identified that excel at some function, and those companies' best practices are used as a source of ideas for improvement. Xerox is synonymous with benchmarking, beginning the practice in the U.S. 25 years ago. Xerox studied Japanese competitors to learn how they could sell mid-sized copiers for less than what it cost Xerox to make them. Today many companies, including AT&T, Eastman Kodak, and Motorola, use benchmarking as a standard research tool. It's not unusual for a company to look to a leader in a different industry, e.g., a consumer packaged goods company may study the efficiency of a catalog retailer to redesign its call center.[3]

Standard Qualitative Marketing Research Methods

Literature searches, experience surveys, and the analysis of cases are important in exploratory research, but when people talk about "qualitative" methods, they usually mean one or more of the following techniques:

- Focus group
- Depth interview

---

[2] Robert K. Yin, *Case Study Research*, 3rd ed. (Sage, 2002).

[3] Mohamed Zairi and John Whymark, "The Transfer of Best Practices: How to Build a Culture of Benchmarking and Continuous Learning," *Benchmarking* 7 (2000), pp. 146–167.

- Projective technique
- Ethnography
- Observational techniques, including those assisted by mechanical devices (e.g., galvanometers, eye cameras, EEGs, voice pitch analyses)

We'll discuss each in turn.

Focus Groups

Focus groups are one of the most popular tools in marketing research, and the most frequently used qualitative technique.[4] In a focus group, a small number of individuals are brought together in a room to sit and talk about some topic of interest to the focus group sponsor. The discussion is directed by a moderator. The *moderator* attempts to follow a rough outline of the issues under consideration, while at the same time making sure that the comments made by each person present are included in the group's discussion. The group discussion should be dynamic, much like a conversation. Each individual hears the ideas of the others and also voices his or her own opinions to the group for consideration.

Focus groups are an extremely useful method for gathering ideas and insights. They are used for a variety of purposes, including the following:

- Generate hypotheses that can be further tested quantitatively
- Generate information helpful in structuring consumer questionnaires
- Provide background information on a product category
- Obtain customer impressions on new product concepts or ad copy.

As an example, BMW conducted focus groups in which it asked for customer feedback to some 25 different sounds and pitches, to select just the right sounds and noises for the instrument warning panel. BMW wants its customers to say that a BMW even sounds like a BMW.[5] Instead of some harsh buzz, the BMW managers sought a warning signal that fit the luxurious brand essence of a Beamer. They "wanted something that would say, 'Excuse me sir or madam, if you wouldn't mind, please turn your attention briefly to the dashboard. There is something I would like to tell you about the operation of the car.'" They selected a "low, slowly pulsating tone based on the sound of a vibraphone" for the top-of-the-line 7-Series models. If you want to know what "low, slowly pulsating . . ." sounds like, go to your BMW dealership and have a listen. For more examples of companies that have benefited from focus group research, see Research Realities 4.1.

NUMBER OF PARTICIPANTS?

Although focus groups vary in size, most consist of 8 to 12 members. Smaller groups are too easily dominated by one or two members; and with larger groups, frustration and boredom can set in, because members have to wait their turn to respond or get involved. Respondents are generally screened in selection so that the groups are relatively homogeneous, minimizing differences in experience in the category, as well as conflicts among group members on irrelevant attributes. Differences that are too great with respect to any of these characteristics can intimidate some of the group participants and stifle discussion.

Focus Group Rules of Thumb:

- 8–12 participants
- Each compensated $60–$75
- Tues., Wed., Thurs. best
- Small, cool room
- Comfortable chairs
- Soft drinks, cookies
- Approx. 4 groups
- 1½–2 hours
- One-way mirror (observers)
- Taped
- Approx. 6 week turnaround (from planning to report)

---

[4] Edward Fern, *Advanced Focus Group Research* (Sage, 2001).

[5] Scott Miller, "Why BMW Obsesses Over Every Whir and Thunk," *Wall Street Journal* (Jan. 24, 2002), p. B1.

Research Realities

4.1 Examples of Focus Groups

- A focus group of affluent homeowners in Las Vegas discussed the features they most wanted in their next homes. Convenience was important (easy access, no extra steps, everything within reach). A luxury custom home builder took their comments and designed single-story homes, with ergonomically efficient designs in the kitchen and bathrooms. The focus group participants also associated "luxury communities" with golf course access and gates between neighbors.

- Corporate Apparel was getting 1500 clicks a month on its Web site, indicating what they thought was a high level of interest, yet these clicks translated into only 20–50 sales per month. Customers complained that the ordering process was too complicated, having to call the 800 number to complete the sale. A focus group of business executives who hadn't seen the site previously were recruited to try the site, fill out a survey about the site, and then discuss the site in the group. The result—a better site, with fewer clicks required to purchase.

- Focus groups were conducted with affluent consumers to determine whether the rich are different. Yes, they have more money, but that's about it. Life goals, needs, and concerns are the same as less affluent consumers. They worked hard, learned if they made bad investments, and did not live beyond their means or become burdened with debt. The groups didn't differ in investment experience, life stages, gender, tolerance for risk, or their entrepreneurship. The focus groups were spon-sored by investment agencies and the characterization of the affluent was intended to help shape their advertising appeals.

- CPA firms have used focus groups to understand their clients' views of the firms and the services they provide. Focus groups have also been used to get clients' reactions to proposals of new practice niches.

- Marketing researchers have used focus groups to study consumers' perceptions of travel destinations and the brand equity of locations, for the purposes of enhancing consumer tourism and attracting more businesses. Researchers studying perceptions of Scotland found that the country's core industries were incorrectly perceived to be whisky, wool, and salmon, when in fact, information technology (IT) is its greatest export. Ad copies were tested for consumer reaction: themes of tenacity played well (especially to the Japanese consumers), and an ad that emphasized Scotland's spirit with bright and dramatic tartan colors played especially well to younger consumers. (The project's name, "Galore," comes from the fact that galore is supposedly one of only two words to come out of Gaelic to enter into the English language. The other word is whisky.)

Sources: Christina Farnsworth, "Calling the Affluent Home," *Builder* (Nov. 2002), pp. 152–158; Deborah Vence, "How One Company Listened Its Way to Success," *Marketing News* (May 13, 2002), p. 4; Kent Jamison and Cheryl Retzloff, "The Affluent Market," *LIMRA's MarketFacts Quarterly* (Spring 2002), pp. 86–95; Roslyn Myers, "CPAs Get into Focus," *Journal of Accountancy* 193 (Feb. 2002), pp. 28–30; Kate Hamilton, "Project Galore," *Journal of Advertising Research* 40 (2000), pp. 107–111.

Screening interviews determine who will be allowed to participate in a focus group. One type of person usually screened out is the individual who has participated in focus groups before, since these people tend to behave as "experts." Their presence can cause the group to behave in dysfunctional ways as they continually try to make their presence felt. Participants are also screened to be sure friends or relatives aren't already included in the group, because this tends to inhibit spontaneity in the discussion as the acquaintances talk to each other.

NUMBER OF GROUPS?

Given that the participants in a group are reasonably homogeneous, a firm ensures that it gets a wide spectrum of insights by having multiple groups. The characteristics of the participants can vary across groups, as can the moderator's guide regarding the issues to be covered in each group. For example, ideas discovered in one group can certainly be followed up in a subsequent group for reaction.

A typical project has 4 groups, but some may have up to 12. The guiding criterion is whether the later groups are generating additional insight into the phenomenon under study. When they show diminishing returns, the groups are stopped.

The typical focus group session lasts from 1½ to 2 hours. Most focus groups are held at specially designed focus group facilities:[6] they are centrally located, for easy access by the participants; they have one-way mirrors with room behind the mirror to accommodate 6–10 observers (e.g., the marketing research and brand management team); they have audio- and videotaping technologies, etc. Increasingly, there are also video-conferencing capabilities, and Internet chat-room set-ups to facilitate participants at different locations to interact with one another.

QUALITIES OF MODERATORS

The moderator in the focus group has a key role.[7] A good moderator begins the job long before the actual focus group. The moderator needs to understand the marketing problem and the most important information the client hopes to obtain from the research. The moderator takes this background information and translates the study objectives into a discussion guide that serves as an outline for the focus group session. The moderator also needs to understand the parameters of the groups (size, number, and composition), to make suggestions about how they might be structured to build on one another. In the focus group itself, the moderator must lead the discussion so that all objectives of the study are met, encouraging interaction among the group members. In successful focus groups, participants talk to each other, rather than to the moderator, about the issues raised.

The moderator's role is extremely delicate. It requires someone who is familiar with the objectives of the research and someone who possesses good interpersonal communication skills. Other key qualifications are described in Table 4.1 (to set your expectations realistically, moderators who possess all these desired skills are

TABLE 4.1
Traits of Effective Focus Group Moderators

- **Personable:** A moderator must put people at ease quickly and develop rapport with participants so they will "open up" during the discussion. Must not be overbearing or pretend to know it all.
- **Superior Listening Ability:** A moderator must pay close attention to what the participants are saying. Comments cannot be missed due to lack of attention or misunderstanding. Is often silent so as to encourage others to speak. Doesn't answer the question "What do you think?" but turns the question around to get the focus group participants to do so.
- **A Quick Learner:** An effective moderator learns about a topic quickly to be effective in guiding successful group sessions. Knows topic so well, moderator outline is rarely consulted.
- **High Energy Level:** When a group gets laid back and lifeless, it dramatically lowers the quality of the information that the participants generate. The best moderators find a way to inject energy and enthusiasm into the group so the participants are energized throughout the session. The moderator must be able to keep his or her own energy level high so the discussion can continue to be very productive to the end.

---

[6] See the annual (March) issues of *Marketing News,* available from the American Marketing Association (http://www.marketingpower.com) "Directory of Focus Group Facilities and Moderators."

[7] Edward F. Fern, *Advanced Focus Group Research* (Sage, 2001); Edward F. McQuarrie, *The Mirrored Window: Focus Groups from a Moderator's Point of View* (American Marketing Association, 2001); Shay Sayre, *Qualitative Methods for Marketplace Research* (Sage, 2001).

extremely rare).[8] Prepping a moderator for a focus group on consumer products is fairly straightforward, but business-to-business and technical topics usually require more extensive briefings. For some topics, the group participants know more about the product than the moderator, and it's fine for a moderator to ask for more information, e.g., "Well, what is the problem when you use that company's drill bit in your patient's mouth?"

Many benefits can accrue from properly conducted focus groups. Often as not, ideas simply drop "out of the blue" during a discussion. This serendipity is often a result of the group dynamics—the comment by one individual can trigger a chain of responses from the others until the discussion has snowballed into something unanticipated.

A TYPICAL SESSION

Usually focus groups start with a brief introductory warm-up period (often just 5–10 minutes covering background material and setting a context), to simply begin building rapport and trust. For example, participants often begin by writing their first names on placards to be placed in front of them, to facilitate reference from the moderator and the other participants, all strangers. The moderator begins by saying a few introductory words. For example, if the focus group is about vitamins, the moderator might say, "As you're probably aware from the questions you were asked when you were invited to come here, we're going to talk about health-related behaviors—eating, drinking, exercising, vitamin supplements, etc. So tonight we're going to talk about all those kinds of things. There are no right or wrong answers here, so please just talk freely about your opinions. Just so you know, I have some colleagues observing us and taking notes in that room behind the mirror, and we're taping the session so that we can remember all the issues that you folks raise. You'll see on the other side of the room there are soft drinks and snacks—feel free to help yourself at any time during the evening." To get the participants warmed up and get them all to talk, the moderator continues by asking a general question, such as, "What sorts of things do you do to try to stay healthy?"

After this initial roundtable, the moderator, participants, and observers already have a sense of the group—Joe is a bodybuilder, uh-oh watch out that he doesn't dominate the discussion, Jerry is a beer and pizza-nut, uh-oh watch that he doesn't slip out of a conversation on vitamins, etc. Then the moderator poses another, slightly more specific question, but calls upon a few participants in a mixed-up order. The moderator begins to studiously not look at the speaker, so the speaker must look to the other group members for affirmation. The participants soon begin speaking to each other and the moderator knows to fade into the background.

Usually, that's all it takes. At this point, the group is going. Soon respondents become sufficiently involved that they want to express their ideas and feelings. Many people actually feel more secure in a group environment than if they were being interviewed alone, in part because it is nearly inevitable that someone else in the group will feel the same way you do about something. Consequently, responses are often more spontaneous than they might be in an interview. The moderator's job as the discussion progresses is to know when to allow the discussion to follow some unanticipated path versus when to reign the members back in and move on to the next talking point on the moderator's guide. See Table 4.2 for guidelines.

---

[8] Occasionally to cut costs, marketing managers think they can run a focus group themselves. This is the height of stupidity. First, they will not be objective. Second, there are real skills that moderators have. Pay for that expertise!

TABLE 4.2
Tips for Successful
Focus Groups

- **Keep the Moderator Guide Simple:** In an attempt to "get their money's worth," sometimes clients put too many topics and discussion points on the moderator's guide. Unfortunately, then the topics are covered superficially. Prioritize the "need to know" items from the "nice to know" ones.

- **Begin by Bonding:** A simple, nonthreatening warm-up exercise is a great ice-breaker.

- **Behind the Scenes:** Clients often watch the focus group sessions in the room behind the one-way mirror at focus group facilities. These rooms are difficult to soundproof entirely, so turn off cell phones, and don't laugh too loudly.

- **Don't Look to Project Findings:** These data are small samples, not representative; the data are qualitative, gathered in an artificial environment. Findings are more suited to "suggesting" (e.g., lines of follow-up research), than predicting (e.g., sales or market shares).

- **Do a Focus Group When:** you want feedback on new product concepts, advertising copy or proposed marketing promotions, product and service positioning, and product usability tests.

- **Don't Conduct a Focus Group When:** you want answers to numerical questions ("How many customers . . . ?" "What percentage . . . ?"), you cannot afford a survey, you're trying to set prices, or you need to make a "go/no go" decision.

Source: Mary Gadbois, "What I Wish I Had Known: Tips for Clients Conducting Qualitative Research," and Tom Greenbaum, "The Gold Standard," both in *Quirk's Marketing Research Review* (http://www.quirks.com); Naomi Henderson, "Enjoy the View: Ground Rules for Observing Focus Groups," *Marketing Research* (Spring 2003), pp. 38–39; Dennis Rook, "Out-of-Focus Groups," *Marketing Research* (Summer 2003), pp. 10–15; Arundhati Parmar, "Table Matters: Strange, But True, Tales from the Moderator's Chair," *Marketing News* (March 3, 2003), pp. 1, 15–16; R. Kenneth Wade, "Focus Groups' Research Role Is Shifting," *Marketing News* (March 4, 2002), p. 47.

AFTER THE FOCUS GROUP

Finally, moderators' responsibilities do not end when the group sessions end. They supervise the preparation of a transcript of each session and use the transcripts to develop a report for the client detailing the key insights the focus groups generated. They've also seen zillions more focus groups than the shiny new marketing VP who was an observer behind the one-way mirror, who might attach undue weight to a single comment when the moderator knows to wait until all the groups have been run to determine whether such a comment was a theme, even by a minority-sized segment, or just a random idiosyncrasy.

It is important to remember that the focus group results are a direct function of the group dynamics, including the directions the moderator provided as well as the unpredictable, creative process of the group interactions. Accordingly, the results are not "representative" of what would be found in the general population, and thus are not projectable. Further, the unstructured nature of the responses makes coding, tabulation, and analysis difficult; thus focus groups shouldn't be used to develop head counts of the proportion of people who feel a particular way. Focus groups are better for generating ideas and insights than for systematically examining them.

Focus groups have many benefits, but they are not without their weaknesses. For example, the results can be difficult to interpret—it's easy to find evidence in one or more of the group discussions that supports almost any position. And, because executives can observe the discussions through one-way mirrors or watch tapes of the sessions, focus groups are even more susceptible to executive biases than other data-collection techniques.

WHAT'S NEW IN FOCUS GROUPS?

There are two main new trends in focus groups. First, given the increasingly global presence of companies, U.S. companies need to use focus groups to research their targeted global markets. Be prepared for some startling differences:

• Focus groups in the States are composed of 8–12 members, but that's large compared with European or Asian focus groups, which are more likely to have 4–6 participants.
• Focus groups in the U.S. run 1½–2 hours, but in Europe and Asia, they tend to run 4 hours.
• The overall project length is also much longer in Europe and Asia. In the U.S., the project will run 2–6 weeks from planning to running to the report, depending on the difficulty in recruiting target customers and the number of groups run. In Europe, double that length; in Asia, it can be still longer.

Second, focus group service providers are still exploring the pros and cons of focus groups run via chat-rooms on the Internet. The cited advantages include: (1) convenient access for participants (no travel required, more flexibility in scheduling throughout the day); (2) transcripts are immediately available, since participants are typing in their responses; and (3) costs are lower (travel need not be reimbursed, no transcription is required). But there are disadvantages also: (1) expressions are completely verbal—there are no body language or emotional cues. An emoticon smiley :) isn't quite the same thing as one person looking another in the eye; (2) conversation is more stilted when participants are writing and the posting is sequential, than when people are excited and interrupting each other with a good free-flowing conversation. See Research Realities 4.2 for more developments.

Depth Interviews

An interview with a customer is much like a focus group. (Well, without the group.) See Figure 4.3 for an overview of the commonalities and differences. Focus groups used to be called "group interviews." In a one-on-one interview, the interviewer also tries to build rapport quickly and then proceeds through a set of questions, from the general to the more specific, with the list of questions intended more as a guide than a structured survey.

Any given respondent will answer some questions in greater depth and others in a more perfunctory manner. The former usually indicate greater knowledge and involvement, and are worth pursuing. The latter usually indicate lack of interest or expertise and may be worth pursuing to be sure the interviewer is communicating clearly with the interviewee.

This flexibility, as you've come to see, is the critical quality of exploratory research methods. Thus, after presenting a few initial questions, an interview becomes very unstructured as the interviewer probes more deeply, asking follow-up questions. Hence, interviews are often termed (the rather redundant), "depth interviews."[9]

[9] Margaret Morrison, Eric Haley, Kim Sheehan and Ronald Taylor, *Using Qualitative Research in Advertising* (Sage, 2002).

Research Realities

4.2 Developments in Focus Groups

1. **Technology:** Web casting and Internet video streaming are getting smoother now and better than the technology that provides the still herky-jerky video-conferencing. More people can be hooked up to simultaneously view a common Web stream, but propensities for hiding and not participating in the group discussion are also greater, given that none of the other participants can see you. In addition, critics say that this technology still does not match face-to-face human interaction, so that one of the greatest strengths of focus groups, the dynamic group interplay, will never be as fully achieved with the techno-focus group. Critics are also concerned that body language is not captured and the setting is artificial. Yet supporters say the discussion is more efficient (less babble due to participants having to type, not talk), inhibitions are reduced, and flexibility in recruiting is enhanced. E-focus group agnostics say, "Let's wait and see how this new technology compares and develops."

2. **Psychology:** Some marketing researchers are experimenting with the rather weird—hypnosis focus group. The underpinnings are theoretical—a psychoanalytic freeing of the sub-sconscious via hypnosis, and then a group discussion to "truly" get at motives and complex emotions. Hmm. Again, stay tuned (cf. http://www.hypnosisinsights.com).

3. **Virtual Communities:** Many highly involved consumers like to share their opinions about their favorite brands and increasingly are doing so in chat-rooms. The focus group industry is looking to this vehicle as both an active and passive tool. In its active form, a marketing research company can recruit some participants and ask them to participate in a chat-room, e.g., in which every day for 2 weeks, a new question is posted. Members state their reaction, and their reactions to the others' reactions, etc. In its passive form, marketing research companies are lifting the textual exchange and content analyzing it for themes about its clients' brands and their competitors.

Sources: Steve Jarvis, "Two Technologies Vie for Piece of Growing Focus Group Market," *Marketing News* (May 27, 2002), p. 4; Yardena Rand, "Reviving Online Focus Groups," *Quirk's Marketing Research Review* (http://www.quirks.com), Yaniv Poria and Alex Taylor, "Wrestling with MUDs," *International Journal of Wine Marketing* 13 (2001), pp. 5–17; Dana James, "This Bulletin Just In," *Marketing News* (March 4, 2002), pp. 45–46.

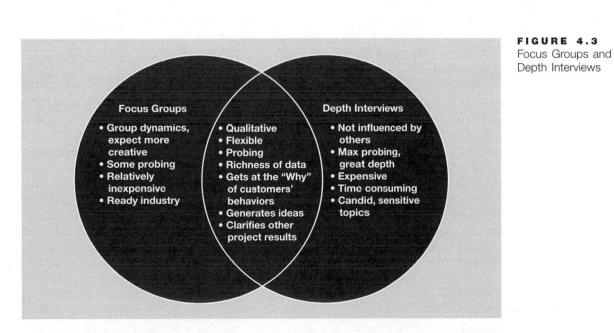

FIGURE 4.3
Focus Groups and Depth Interviews

Focus Groups
- Group dynamics, expect more creative
- Some probing
- Relatively inexpensive
- Ready industry

- Qualitative
- Flexible
- Probing
- Richness of data
- Gets at the "Why" of customers' behaviors
- Generates ideas
- Clarifies other project results

Depth Interviews
- Not influenced by others
- Max probing, great depth
- Expensive
- Time consuming
- Candid, sensitive topics

The respondent's answers determine the direction the interviewer takes next. The interviewer may attempt to follow a rough outline, but the order and the specific framing of the questions will vary from interview to interview, as will the specific content resulting from each interview.

The freedom permitted the interviewer in conducting interviews reveals the major advantages and disadvantages of the method. Proponents of interviews (or qualitative techniques generally) say these methods enable the researcher to obtain deeper, richer, "thicker" descriptions than, say, surveys with fixed-alternative responses. By careful probing and by not constraining the respondent to a fixed set of replies, an experienced interviewer derives a fairly accurate picture of the respondent's true position on some issue, particularly for sensitive matters where there is social pressure to conform and offer a "socially acceptable" response.

Note the caveats: "experienced interviewer" and "careful probing" . . . depth interviews require highly skilled interviewers. Good interviewers are hard to find and expensive to hire. Further, the lack of structure allows the interviewer to influence the result; that is, the interviewer's judgment about when to probe and how to word the probes affects the response.

Good depth interviews can take a long time to complete (an hour or more), which makes it difficult (and expensive) to obtain the cooperation of respondents. Studies using depth interviews tend to involve fewer respondents, or require more interviewers. The more interviewers there are, the more likely responses will be partly interviewer-induced because of differences in administering the questionnaire.[10]

Qualitative
Techniques
• Focus Groups
• Depth Interviews
• Projective Tasks
• Ethnographies

The interview can also be problematic to analyze. The services of a skilled psychologist are typically required to interpret the responses. These consultants are expensive, and their own background will affect the interpretation. This subjectivity raises questions about both the reliability and validity of interview results. It also causes difficulty in determining what the correct interpretation is and presents problems when tabulating the replies.

However, with these caveats in mind, the depth interview is well suited to exploratory research. It allows the flexibility to pursue whatever the consumers wish to talk about—topics that the marketing researcher is unlikely to anticipate fully enough to write questions for a survey.

A currently popular use of the depth interview is called "laddering," which seeks to discover the relationship between product attributes and consumer benefits.[11] The ladder metaphor implies that the researcher is going from specific attributes as a means to achieve the more abstract values.

For example, in one study, consumers identified values important to them, e.g., good health, family security, happiness. Each of those goals, in turn, is sought through different routes. Good health may be achieved via relaxation, exercise, low-sugar diets, low-cholesterol diets, and cleanliness. These intermediary goals are achieved by even more specific means. For example, relaxation is achieved through the use of products as diverse as red wine and hot tubs. Low-sugar diets are achieved through eating dietetic foodstuffs, and low cholesterol through eating fish and chicken. Cleanliness is achieved through the use of dishwashers, which kill germs;

---

[10] Another source of possible interviewer bias is the interviewer and respondent match on demographics such as gender or ethnicity; usually the matching is unnecessary unless the topic is culturally sensitive; see Naomi Henderson, "Right Ways to Conduct Qualitative Research," *Marketing News* (Sept. 16, 2002), pp. 26–29.

[11] Brian Wansink, "Using Laddering to Understand and Leverage a Brand's Equity," *Qualitative Market Research* 6 (2003), pp. 111–118.

soaps and deodorants, which make one feel clean; and bottled water, which contains no sediment. These value chains are then often reflected in advertising appeals, e.g., "These disposable paper towels do not pick up the bacteria that kitchen cloths do, and keep your family safer from germs," and "The purity of this bottled water helps to keep your body clean and healthy."

Projective Techniques

A projective technique involves the use of a vague stimulus (the proverbial inkblot) that an individual is asked to describe, expand on, or build a story around. Three common types of projective methods are: word association, sentence completion, and storytelling.[12]

WORD ASSOCIATION

With word association projective methods, consumers respond to a list of words, reacting to them with the first word that comes to mind. The test words are interspersed throughout the list with some neutral words to conceal the purpose of the study. In a study on pollution, the list of keywords might be traffic, lakes, smoke stacks, and city, mixed in with words such as margarine, blue jeans, and government.

The responses to each of the keywords are recorded verbatim and analyzed. The key analysis is the examination of the content of the responses to see what themes may be derived from these respondents' word choices.

Although the analysis of the responses is subjective, some common responses often emerge. These common responses are classified and grouped, and tend to reveal patterns of underlying motivations. It is often possible to categorize the associations as favorable–unfavorable, pleasant–unpleasant, modern–old-fashioned, etc., depending on the research question.

For example, for each of the following words, very often only two or three common descriptor words emerge (try it among your friends!): Coca-Cola, Exxon, McDonald's, Microsoft, Nordstrom's, Sears, Verizon, Madonna, Sammy Sosa, Michael Jackson, Chicago, Mexico, Japan, lawyers, accountants, marketers, and consultants. This list also illustrates the flexibility of the method—one can obtain consumer perceptions of firms and brand equity, celebrity endorsers, tourist destinations, career objectives, or anything else. When a word elicits a greater variety of associations across respondents, it is thought that the stimulus may be less familiar (e.g., lacrosse, Swedish royal family) or more complex (e.g., California, carbohydrates, Supreme Court), or for other reasons yields greater individual differences.

Ethical Dilemma 4.1

Prompted by an increasing incidence of homes for sale by owner, the president of a local real estate company asks you to undertake exploratory research to determine the image of realtors in the community. Unbeknownst to your current client, you undertook a similar research study for a competitor two years ago and, based on your findings, have formed specific hypotheses about why some homeowners are reluctant to sell their houses through realtors.

- Is it ethical to give information obtained while working for one client to another client who is a competitor? What might you tell or not tell your current client about the earlier project?
- Is it ethical to undertake a research project when you think that you already know what the findings will be?
- Can you generalize findings from two years ago to today?
- Should you help this company define its problem, and, if so, how?

---

[12] Sidney J. Levy, *Brands, Consumers, Symbols, and Research* (Sage, 1999); Paul E. Meehl, "The Dynamics of 'Structured' Personality Tests," *Journal of Clinical Psychology* 56 (2000), pp. 367–373; Marvin Leibowitz, *Interpreting Projective Drawings* (Brunner/Mazel, 1999).

The word association responses are also judged in three more objective, easily measured ways:

- By the frequency with which any word is given as a response
- By the amount of time that elapses before a response is given (easily measured in milliseconds if the words are administered via computer)
- By the number of respondents who do not respond at all to a test word after a reasonable period of time

A trained psychologist can also lend insight by interpreting nonverbal cues, such as body language. Respondents who hesitate (operationally defined as taking longer than three seconds to reply) are judged to be sufficiently emotionally involved in the word that they do not provide their immediate reaction but an acceptable response. If they do not respond at all, their emotional involvement is judged to be so high as to block a response. An individual's pattern of responses, along with the details of the response to each question, are then used to assess the person's attitudes or feelings on the subject.

SENTENCE COMPLETION

This method is much like the word association task except that more words are offered as the stimulus to which the respondent is expected to react. As the name implies, the method requires the respondent to complete a number of sentences. Respondents are instructed to reply with the first thoughts that come to mind. The responses are recorded verbatim and then analyzed.

Once again, though the analysis of qualitative responses is subjective, the results are nevertheless often clear and there would be good agreement in their interpretation. For example, imagine one person completing sentences about the environment as follows:

- People who are concerned about ecology *care about the future.*
- A person who does not use our lakes for recreation is *being thoughtful about the ecosystem.*
- When I think of living in a city, I *can't help but think of smog.*

Compare those responses to these of another person:

- People who are concerned about ecology *are just tree-huggers who want to run up my taxes.*
- A person who does not use our lakes for recreation is *a person who doesn't enjoy water sports.*
- When I think of living in a city, I *think about cruising my car downtown on Saturday night!*

Presumably, these two respondents could easily be characterized as belonging to segments of consumers who are more and less ecologically concerned.

Sometimes the disguised nature of sentence completion questions can shed light on a topic that a more direct rating scale might not. For example, when consumers are asked, "Do you think it is important to give blood?" most say yes, due to pressures for social desirability and conformity. And we might indeed be convinced that a person regularly gives blood who completes sentences like:

- "I always give blood during blood drives at work, unless . . . *I'm sick.*"
- "People who don't give blood . . . *are pretty selfish, in my opinion.*"

Contrast the values of that person with someone who completed the sentences as follows:

- "I always give blood during blood drives at work, unless . . . *I'm in a hurry.*"
- "People who don't give blood . . . *just don't like needles.*"

From this second person's sentences, a picture emerges of someone who will resist donating blood in the presence of only minor hurdles, suggesting that their actual compliance will be low.

A particular form of association tests that is gaining some popularity is to have consumers draw metaphors and analogies in the sentence completions, "An X is like a Y." For example, one recent study took place in a competitive HMO market in a major U.S. city. Participants were asked to talk about their HMO and their perceptions of the other HMO brands. Then they were asked to draw comparisons between the HMOs and brands of cars. Weird, yes? But watch this: One consumer said, "[HMO A] is a Cadillac. . . . If I were to get into an accident, the car would absorb most of my injuries, [HMO A] would absorb my financial aspects. [HMO B] is a GMC or Chevy truck . . . it has the cushion in case I ever did need it . . . a truck might be pretty big but . . . it's got a lot of metal to take care of you. You can be injured a lot worse."

Again, the responses are open, and it may seem that the interpretation would be subjective, but the consumers help interpret their own metaphors when they say, "HMO A is like a Lincoln Town Car *in that it is* comfortable, nice, all-American," or "HMO A is like a Lexus or Infiniti *in providing* a very good product, and very good service." In comparison, in this study, HMO B was likened to a station wagon (low-key transportation, not flashy), Ford Escort (comparably small and inexpensive), and Hyundai (unproven, unfamiliar, comparably small). These researchers didn't care about cars, per se, but that the cars metaphor allowed consumers to talk about their HMOs in unrestricted and creative ways.[13]

STORYTELLING

The storytelling approach often relies on pictorial material, such as cartoons, photographs, or drawings.[14] These pictorial devices are descendants of the psychologists' Thematic Apperception Test (TAT), which in turn descended from the famous Rorschach inkblot tests. Respondents are shown a picture and asked to tell a story about the picture. The responses are used to assess attitudes toward the consumer behavior phenomenon.

For the environmental pollution example, the stimulus might be a picture of a city, and the respondent might be asked to describe what it would be like to live there. The analysis of the individual's response would then focus on the emphasis given to pollution in its various forms. If no mention were made of traffic congestion, dirty air, noise, and so on, the person would be classified as displaying little concern for pollution and its control.

Sometimes the participant is asked to create a collage of photos cut out of magazines that remind them of a brand. Research Realities 4.3 describes a study in which participants were asked to draw pictures themselves. In this study, people are interviewed about flowers, and they are asked to draw pictures of flowers. Their pictures

---

[13] Russell Lacey, "Dimensions of the Ideal HMO Brand," *Marketing Health Services* 20 (2000), pp. 32–35.

[14] Gwendolyn Castello, "The Zmet Alternative," *Marketing Research* 12 (Summer 2000), pp. 6–12.

Research Realities

4.3 Customers Drawing Pictures for a Study Sponsored by a Large Florist Retail Chain*

Interviewee #1:

Woman, 30–39 years old.

Describe yourself:

I am a quiet person, I keep mostly to myself and keep out of trouble that way.

When do you buy flowers?

I love flowers because they beautify the surroundings. They give me a special calm feeling of enjoyment. I give flowers to let someone know I am thinking about them.

Describe a dream involving flowers:

I would send flowers to the ladies at work with a note attached and they would all start crying at one time.

How are flowers and funerals related?

All the funerals I've been to have flowers. I guess when you die, you will be in paradise and paradise is full of flowers.

Her drawing:

Interviewee #2:

Woman, 20–29 years old.

Husband sends her flowers because:

I am sweet.

Three words associated with flowers?

I love you.

Compared to other gifts, flowers are:

Warmest, most romantic, highest class, sexiest, most fun.

Flowers remind me of:

Love!

Describe a dream involving flowers:

Someone gets married, they are happy and I am pleased for them and I send flowers to congratulate them. Everyone likes it and they live happily ever after.

How are flowers and funerals related?

I'm opposed to the idea of flowers at funerals. Flowers at funerals are sad. The tradition of sending flowers to a funeral may have come about in order to cover the smell of the body.

Her drawing:

Interviewee #3:

Man, 40–49 years old.

Describes himself as:

. . . a loving and generous man. He celebrates all occasions with lavish and often costly gifts. He is enthusiastic about giving flowers and says they make him think about happiness and warmth.

He also says:

The main reason to send flowers is to apologize for having a fight. They lift the spirits, women would be happy about the flowers.

Describe a dream involving flowers:

I had a dream that I sent some flowers and as the person bent down to smell the flowers, a thorn cut her lips. Even though she was bleeding she called to thank me for sending her the lovely roses.

His drawing:

*A million thank you's to Sidney Levy for sharing these stories and pictures.

and stories are remarkably consistent. The first woman remarks on themes of beauty and thoughtfulness, and she drew soft, fluffy looking flowers. The second woman associates flowers with love, and her flower petals are drawn in the shape of hearts. The third respondent was a man who reports a common male theme, that flowers are associated with ambivalence. The man describes a dream and draws flowers that also express his mix of positive and negative feelings.

A quality that focus groups, interviews, and projective tests share is that they rely on some form of communication between the researcher and the respondent. There are also research methods that do not require such interactions. Instead, the researcher observes the respondents' behaviors. We discuss those methods next.

Ethical Dilemma 4.2

A national department store chain with a relatively sophisticated image is planning to open a store in an area inhabited by wealthy professionals. The marketing research director of the company wants a detailed profile of the residents' characteristics and lifestyles to tailor the new store to the tastes of this lucrative new market. He suggests that you, a member of his staff, contribute to the research effort by spending a month observing the residents going about their daily affairs, such as eating in restaurants, attending church, shopping in other stores, socializing with one another, and so on. You are then expected to prepare a report on what types of expenditures support their lifestyles.

- Are there ethical problems involved in observing people in public places?
- Are there ethical problems if you socialize with your informants?
- Who has ethical responsibility for your behavior: The marketing research director? You? Both?

Observational Methods

Here are some examples of observations on consumer behaviors that have been used over the years:

- Researchers watching consumers buying dog food found that adults bought the dog food, but that senior citizens and children bought dog treats. The elderly want to treat their pets like their kids, and children may not appreciate the responsibility of feeding the dog, but they can understand giving the dog a treat, just as they might want a cookie. Unfortunately for these no-longer-flexible adults and the vertically challenged children, the treats were usually stocked on the top-most shelf. These researchers' cameras "witnessed one elderly woman using a box of aluminum foil to knock down her brand of dog biscuits." When the retail grocer moved the treats to where children and older people could reach more easily, sales soared overnight.[15]
- A car dealer in Chicago checked the position of the radio dial of each car brought in for service. The dealer then used this as a proxy for share of listening audience in deciding upon the stations on which to advertise.
- The number of different fingerprints on a page has been used to assess the readership of various ads in a magazine, and the age and condition of the cars in the parking lot has been used to gauge the affluence of the group patronizing the outlet.
- Scuff marks on museum floor tile have long been used as a means of measuring the popularity of the display.
- Consumers have been watched through one-way mirrors trying to assemble a PC from right out of the box to surfing on the Net (and no, we don't tend to read the instructions).

---

[15] Paco Underhill, *Why We Buy: The Science of Shopping* (Touchstone, 2000), p. 18.

- By peering from catwalks built above the stores, researchers for a large supermarket chain discovered (to their dismay) that people shopped heavily the periphery of the store—the produce, dairy, and meat sections—but often bypassed the central dry-goods section that accounted for the bulk of the store space.

Observations like these may be made either in the field or in the lab. The field study may be a completely natural setting or we may induce an experimental manipulation. For example, if we want to understand customers' brand choices for soups, we might simply snoop around the soup aisle of a grocery store, watching shoppers as they deliberate before they toss a can of soup into their carts. Alternatively, we may introduce a point-of-purchase display and measure its effectiveness, namely, how much more frequently does the focal brand get chosen in the stores in which we've set up the display compared with the stores whose shelf facings we left alone. Both of these studies would take place in a supermarket, which would be the natural setting. Alternatively, we could bring consumers into a controlled lab environment, where they could engage in some simulated shopping behavior. We'll say more about field studies, and then we'll turn to lab observations. First, we consider some strengths of the observational methods for marketing researchers.

WHY OBSERVATIONAL TECHNIQUES?

Observation is often more useful than surveys in sorting fact from fiction with respect to behaviors, particularly "desirable" behaviors. For example, most people would not want to acknowledge that they spend more on cat food than on baby food, but consumers can be observed doing so. In another study, asking parents whether the color of a new toy would matter, the parents uniformly said no, yet at the end of the study, as a token of their participation, the parents were offered a toy to take home to their child, and all the parents clamored for the purple and blue toys.

Observation can help us see consumer behaviors that the consumers themselves probably aren't aware of or couldn't articulate.[16] For example, to try to understand why a new frozen baby food was underperforming relative to expectations, a researcher hung out where that product was sold and noticed that children got fidgety in the frozen-food sections because they were cold, so mothers would rush down that aisle. The researcher was able to persuade managers to place smaller freezer units in the regular (warmer climate) baby food aisles. Sales were then quite successful. Or consider that over 90% of furniture shoppers are couples, and potential purchases are most likely if one of the parties is in the store at least ten minutes. The woman may be looking over the "fluffed pillows and floral duvets," but if the spouse pulls her away, the sale is lost. As a result, some furniture stores are being retrofit with entertainment centers where sports fans can watch live events via cable.[17] Thus, observations can also be helpful in designing store layout and operations.

In this multicultural world, observation methods are useful for marketers to learn about tastes and preferences of different ethnic groups. Rather than creating a survey that might not be in the respondent's first language, or worrying about translations and back-translations, researchers can simply watch what consumers do.

[16] Maria Letelier, Charles Spinosa and Bobby Calder, "Taking an Expanded View of Customers' Needs: Qualitative Research for Aiding Innovation," *Marketing Research* 12 (Winter 2000), pp. 4–11.

[17] Bill Abrams, *The Observational Research Handbook* (American Marketing Association, 2000); also see *Quirk's Marketing Research Review* "Mystery Shopping Directory" (http://www.quirks.com).

Like the language barrier issue, observational techniques can also be useful in studying children as consumers. For example, the appeal of new toy offerings can be assessed readily by simply watching children play. In a natural play setting, children can behave naturally, rather than struggling with an interview or offering opinions on a 9-point scale. For examples of observational methods on children, see Research Realities 4.4.

Observational data comprise the heart of a currently very popular form of research, the "mystery shopper." In this technique, firms use paid observers disguised as shoppers to evaluate sales service and the attitudes and courtesy of employees. Hotels supplement guest and employee surveys with reports from secret shoppers to diagnose which features of the customer experience at the hotel (e.g., the check-in process or the cleanliness of the bathrooms) should be high priority for redesign and improvement.

Research Realities

4.4 Using Observational Primary Data Collection Techniques to Study Children as Consumers

1. Ethnography involves observation techniques, depth interviews, and perhaps audio- and videotaping technology to record people, typically in their natural settings. It is a technique that has gained credibility and is quite popular in marketing research. For example, General Mills' researchers watch children and their eating habits. To allow children to eat on the run, while simultaneously assuring mothers that they were providing healthy food snacks, General Mills created "Go-Gurt," yogurt packaged in a tube, to be eaten "on the go," without a spoon.

2. Researchers find that, like adults, children have less free playtime—toy manufacturers find themselves competing with the Internet, children's time with their friends, TV shows, and soccer practice. Today's kids are sophisticated, having outgrown dolls and action figures by age 8, instead preferring complex software. It is difficult to capture their attention and advertise toys to them. It is equally challenging to cut through the clutter to capture parents' attention. Parents trust brand names (Hot Wheels, Barbie, Crayola) and if they perceive a toy to be of high quality, price is not an issue (e.g., Lego's $200 Mindstorms robot-building toys sold much better than had been projected). Marketing researchers have found it to be much more effective to get children to try toys (and then parents to buy toys) through demo testing and sampling the products and brands. Researchers then observe the children in play, noting what toys are popular, what features might be troublesome, and so forth. Observational research provides feedback about the products, which researchers expect, but it also functions as a sales vehicle, because these play sessions generate big word-of-mouth among the pint-size consumers.

3. Observational techniques can be used on older children also. For example, MTV tries to understand the youth market, to be on the leading edge in trendsetting. It's easier to project an image of "cool" if the music station knows what teens care about. So, researchers for MTV regularly reconnaissance young teen consumers' CD collections, their closets, and the places they hang out. All these venues give the adult researchers insights into youth values, enabling them to design more relevant programming and to advertise in a way that communicates more authentically to these rather affluent young people. Teens are a substantial segment, spending a good $150 billion annually.

4. Some marketing researchers seek to capture teens surfing the Internet (e.g., through online focus groups and surveys) to collect product-specific information from teens as well as general information about their interests and life issues. Some researchers are so aggressively pursuing these young Internet users that policies and guidelines are already being established to protect young people. For example, in accordance with the Children's Online Privacy Protection Act, researchers are required to obtain a parent's permission prior to the child's participation in the research.

Sources: T. L. Stanley and Becky Ebenkamp, "In Search of the Magic Formula," *Brandweek* 41 (Feb. 14, 2000), pp. 28–34; Margaret Littman, "How Marketers Track Underage Consumers," *Marketing News* 34 (May 8, 2000), pp. 4, 7; Lisa Holton, "The Surfer in the Family," *American Demographics* 22 (2000), pp. 34–36; Sally Beatty and Carol Hymowitz, "How MTV Stays Tuned in to Teens," *Wall Street Journal* (March 21, 2000), pp. B1, B4.

Finally, such research can also help determine who the appropriate customer is to target. For example, when observing patterns of interactions between spouses in making decisions on large household expenditures (e.g., large-screen TVs or washers and dryers at electronics and appliances stores), observers record verbatim the verbal exchanges and perhaps codes for body language and facial expressions. The coders assess which person initiated the selection, the response of the spouse, and the content and tone of the communication, including the occurrence of arguments. Such studies determine who dominates the purchase choice in a given category and whether both parties appear to be satisfied.

OBSERVATIONS IN THE FIELD

A popular form of field consumer study is the simple *audit*. Instead of asking people, "What's your favorite brand?" with the question's inherent subjectivity in recollection and reporting, the researcher can conduct a pantry audit. With permission, the marketer visits respondents' homes and opens cupboards. An audit can be focused on a single brand or product category, but for cost efficiency purposes is often used to assess the consumption of a pre-specified set of products. For example, part of understanding how consumers use a particular product (e.g., peanut butter) can be determined by the other products they buy and use with it (jelly, chocolate, bananas, crackers). The inventory of kitchen cabinets and refrigerators would demonstrate the co-ownership of complementary products.

Researchers have inventoried or photographed the contents of consumers' medicine cabinets, closets, garages, students' lockers, etc. Photos of a medicine cabinet indicate not only what products it contains, and what brands and sizes, but also their arrangement—what is stored front and center is probably used most frequently.

Researchers for *Gourmet* magazine have moved right into their readers' homes to "look into their cabinets," "pore over their Visa bills," or "snip labels out of their clothes." Gourmet is especially trying to understand its younger readers—readers who are affluent, knowledgeable about food trends, and know hot restaurants and fine wines. A sample of readers were given disposable cameras and asked to take photos of cherished household belongings. Knowing what customers treasure can yield insight into cross-selling opportunities, or even subtle messages in ads to appeal to this target group by indicating an understanding of their values.[18]

Another popular form of field consumer study is the *ethnography*.[19] Ethnographic methods are increasingly being used by marketers, as another example of an in-depth case approach to develop insights. These procedures, which have been adapted from anthropology, involve the prolonged observation of consumers' behaviors, emotional responses, and cognitions during their ordinary daily lives. Unlike anthropologists, though, who might live in an exotic culture for a year, marketing researchers ethnographers use a combination of direct observations, interviews, and video and audio recordings to make their observations on consumers far more quickly, as business demands.[20]

Ethnographic research can employ a number of methods, but a hallmark of the technique is a combination of observation and interviews. The marketing researcher

---

[18] Tony Case, "Getting Personal," *Brandweek* 41 (2000), pp. M52–M54.

[19] Alex Stewart, *The Ethnographer's Method* (Sage, 1998).

[20] Shorter excursions into the field have been termed "ethno-dunking."

observes consumers in their natural settings. This direct observation offers a number of advantages, e.g., actual consumer behavior is observed, so there is no need to rely on self-reported intentions of future behavior or faulty recollections of past behaviors. In addition, this holistic approach to research gives the ethnographer an environment and context that helps explain the observations they make, the consumers' behaviors, and the consumers' comments offered in their interviews.

In the field, researchers take notes on the observations they make

Ethical Dilemma 4.3

A leading manufacturer of breakfast cereals was interested in learning more about the decision processes involved in buying a particular brand of cereal. To gather this information, an observational study was conducted in the major food chains of several large cities. The observers were instructed to assume a position well out of the shoppers' way, because it was thought that the individuals would change their behavior if they were aware they were being observed.

- Is it ethical to observe another person's behavior systematically without that person's knowledge? What if the behavior had been more private in nature? What if the behavior had been recorded on videotape?
- Does use of this method of data collection invade an individual's privacy?
- Even if no harm is done to the individual, is harm done to society?
- Is the use of such a method a form of "Big Brother-ism"?
- Can you suggest alternative methods for gathering the same information?

and the interviews they conduct. One or more individuals are trained to systematically observe a phenomenon and record specific events. Methods include the written field notes, wherein researchers make their initial on-site observational impressions. Audio and video recorders assist the capture of observations, and they're surprisingly unobtrusive during the research and interactions with the consumers at the field site. Increasingly, field researchers bring laptops with them to take note, supplementing their observations, to minimize memory error later.

Researchers also interview consumers and may ask them to provide tangible artifacts. For example, to understand the context of consumers and their uses of brands, consumers might be asked to take photos or show favorite possessions to express their individualities ("This tie is special to me because I wore it at my first job interview," or "I know this vase is chipped, but it was my grandmother's, from the old country, and it always adds warmth to the flowers I pick up at the market," or "This picture shows me and my kid brother on our trip to Vegas—our first trip without our parents—it was cool that the hotel treated us like adults"). Later, off-site, all these sources of data are reviewed by the researcher who reflects, integrates, and provides a theoretical summary. For more examples of observational techniques in marketing research, see Research Realities 4.5.

Although the marketing manager's observations can be valuable for self-edification, for the serious data-collection effort, as with any marketing research, it is best to hire an expert (e.g., a marketing researcher trained in anthropology), to minimize the biases that a brand manager is likely to have that the objective, neutral party would not. Most of what you pay for in hiring marketing research experts is neither their time nor even the logistics of sending them to the field to observe. Their added value comes from their training, their experience, and their ability to yield insights from observational data.

OBSERVATIONS IN THE LAB

An increasingly popular method for assessing customer reactions in a controlled environment is using computer simulations, even virtual reality, which enable marketers to display potential new products or product displays without going to the expense of physically building them. For example, automobile manufacturers like General Motors use virtual reality technology to test consumers' reactions to the

Research Realities

4.5 Examples of Observational and Ethnographical Marketing Research

1. **New Product Concept Testing:** To enhance the accuracy of projections, new product testers say marketing research must move beyond an understanding of the who (the target user group of prospective end-users, business partners, retailers, or suppliers) and the what (the new concept) to also incorporate the how (with regard to "observable behavior") and the where (with regard to the "natural environment"). The "behavior" in the "natural environment" begs for an ethnography, or some variant. If the firm cannot follow, say, tweens around to see their typical school days, they can equip the kids with disposable cameras and ask them to capture all the details of their days—friends, clothes, their bedrooms, the snacks they consume, etc.

2. **"Hanging Out with Your Customers":** The official, technical term is "participant observation," when the ethnographic marketing researchers immerses themselves into the customers' culture. Sometimes it's easier to fit in than others . . . BBDO West in San Francisco wanted to understand young male car enthusiasts, so they cruised around with them. Their client was an electronics firm that produces audio equipment for cars. When they saw the passion of the boys for their cars in the contexts of their lifestyles, the ad agency created ads not about the audio equipment, but how the equipment fit into the young men's lives, with tag lines like, "My car gets 37 songs per gallon."

3. **Wireless Technology in the Field:** Instead of hauling paper and pencil, ethnographers are free to choose among a number of media, including wireless surveys, in text-based or voice-based formats, executable via cell phones or laptops. Any new technology enjoys some boosted participation rates due to the respondents' curiosity about the novel approach. The wireless tools are clearly mobile, so the research can be done anywhere. In addition, the research can be conducted at any time, allowing for both a dynamic study, as well as a longitudinal one.

4. **Into the Privacy of the Consumers' Homes:** Oil of Olay sponsored an ethnography that involved photographing women in their showers using bath products (participants in the study wore swimsuits). They learned that a soft soap can be more than a cleanser, rather a de-stressor and a luxurious brief spa treatment. Using similar methods, Moen redesigned showerheads to accommodate women shaving their legs while trying to balance the hand-held shower jet.

Sources: Larry Zaback, "Alternative Qualitative Approaches in New Product Research," *Quirk's Marketing Research Review* (http://www.quirks.com); Sarah Heim, "BBDO Riding in Cars with Boys," *Adweek* 52 (April 1, 2002), p. 4; Anon., "Wireless Technology Ideal to Study Behavior," *Marketing News* (Jan. 20, 2003), pp. 19–20; Lawrence Osborne, "Consuming Rituals of the Suburban Tribe," *New York Times Magazine* (Jan. 13, 2002), pp. 28–31; Gerry Khermouch, "Consumers in the Mist," *Business Week* (Feb. 26, 2001), pp. 92–94.

---

view from the front seat of a new car without having to go through the expense of building even a single prototype car. Programming simulations for flight instruction has been used for decades; it's even easier to simulate a car's interior and ride.

The technology has also been used in consumer shopping experiments. The computer screen simulates the retail environment, beginning with, say, static pictures of grocery store shelf facings, and including an ability to "lift" an icon of a box of cereal, rotate it to see the side of the box and list of nutrients, etc. Similarly, in studies on retail department store layouts, user interfaces allow respondents to simulate mobility throughout the store. The customer can comment on the appearance of the displays as well as the merchandise itself. This technique can also be used in concept testing prototypes, such as interactive accounting or tax preparation software.

These interactive interviews are vivid and often intrinsically interesting and fun for the respondent—it feels like a video game. Thus, data quality is thought to be good and response rates can be relatively high. These multimedia interviews often strike clients of marketing researchers as having high face validity (they seem "believable"), which should therefore enhance forecasting consumer reactions to new product concepts.

In addition, you can imagine how easy it would be to program an experiment. The system could have both test and control conditions simulated for different marketing mix variables; e.g., change the price points to gauge customers' levels of interest.

The advantage of the laboratory environment over the field is that we are better able to control extraneous influences that might affect the interpretation of what happened, thus creating greater internal validity.[21] For example, shoppers in a natural setting might see a friend shopping and stop to chat about their kids, while standing in front of the display of soups, deliberating over which to buy. If we were measuring the time spent in deliberation, this interruption could raise havoc with the accuracy of the measurement. The disadvantage of the laboratory setting is that the contrived setting itself may cause differences in behavior and thus raise real questions about the external validity (generalizability) of the findings. Yet the vividness of these virtual reality shopping "games" makes progress toward a testing scenario that is high on both internal validity (due to the lab control) and external validity (due to the seeming realness of the simulation).

OBSERVATIONS VIA HI-TECH MECHANICAL MEASURES

Technology carries with it the advantage of precision in measurement, but the drawback of the contrived nature of the process. A **galvanometer** records changes in the electrical resistance of the skin associated with the (slight) sweating that accompanies emotional arousal. A consumer is fitted with small electrodes to monitor electrical resistance and then is shown some ad copy. The instrument measures autonomic reactions, that is, reactions not under an individual's voluntary control. Because these responses are not controlled, consumers cannot hide their "true" reactions to a stimulus. The strength of the current induced is used to infer a person's interest or attitude toward the copy.

The **eye camera** is used to study eye movements while a respondent views some stimulus, again, often reading ad copy. Tiny cameras are positioned to strike the cornea of the respondent's eye, and eye movements are traced on videotape and analyzed by computer. Watching where people look allows the marketer to answer questions such as: Where do people look first? How long did they linger on any particular place? Did they read the whole ad or just part of it? Following eye paths has also been used to analyze package designs, billboards, and displays in the aisles of supermarkets.[22] Similar technology measures pupil dilation, which is assumed to indicate a person's interest in the stimulus being viewed. *Pupilometrics* have been used to evaluate color schemes in packaging and optimal advertisement placement in magazines.

Two measures, response latency and voice pitch analysis, began to be implemented as the industry of telephone surveying matured. Response latency is also easily measured during Web surveys. **Response latency** is the amount of time a respondent deliberates before answering a question. Response time is assumed to be related to a consumer's uncertainty, thereby indicating the consumer's strength of preference when choosing among alternatives. Once a survey question appears on the computer

---

[21] We say more about extraneous factors, and internal and external validity in the chapter on causal research.

[22] Rik Pieters, Edward Rosbergen and Michel Wedel, "Visual Attention to Repeated Print Advertising," *Journal of Marketing Research* 36 (Nov. 1999), pp. 424–438; Arthur F. Kramer et al., "Age Differences in the Control of Looking Behavior," *Psychological Science* 11 (2000), pp. 210–217.

screen, a stopwatch function internal to the computer gets reset to zero and counts time (in milliseconds!) until a response is entered into the keyboard. The method provides an accurate measure without respondents even being aware that this aspect of their behavior is being recorded.[23]

Voice pitch analysis relies on the same premise as the galvanometer in that involuntary physiological reactions, such as changes in blood pressure, rate of perspiration, or heart rate, accompany emotional arousal by external or internal stimuli. Voice pitch analysis examines changes in the relative vibration frequency of the human voice. A baseline is established by recording the respondent during an unemotional conversation. Deviations from the baseline indicate that the respondent has reacted to the stimulus question (whether or not the changes were discernible to the human ear).

Perhaps most exotic of all, marketing researchers are exploring the use of high-tech headsets based on electroencephalogram (*EEG*) technology developed at NASA to monitor astronauts' alertness. Five times per second, electrodes monitor the electrical impulses emitted by the brain as the consumer is exposed to various stimuli (e.g., again, often advertising). The two hemispheres of the brain respond to different stimuli, with the right hemisphere responding more to emotional stimuli and the left to rational stimuli.[24] Critics argue that the technique is too new to have benchmarking data to interpret results. Supporters argue that brain waves indicate more objectively than consumers' self-reports which ads they find more interesting. Consumers may shade answers on a survey to appear more socially acceptable, but they cannot mask their emotions as indicated by brain waves.

Coding

We close this chapter by discussing **coding**, the task of translating qualitative observations into quantitative measures. Coding is actually an anathema to qualitative researchers who argue that the "analysis" of qualitative data (whether interview transcripts, focus group interactions, observations in the field or lab) needs to be done holistically and qualitatively, namely, verbally—that the inferences about consumer behavior come from identifying the themes elicited from the respondents and the manner in which the themes are interwoven in the context of the consumers' lives.

SHOULD WE CODE?

Qualitative marketing research methodologists vary in their regard for, or disdain of numbers.[25] Some would argue that if even only one consumer informant talked about, say, how taking the family car in for an oil change is a way to express care for his family, then there is a segment, however large, of consumers who feel similarly, and whose sentiments this informant represents. Others urge that reports, e.g., from

---

[23] I. Koch and J. Hoffmann, "Patterns, Chunks, and Hierarchies in Serial Reaction-Time Tasks," *Psychological Research* 63 (2000), pp. 22–35.

[24] Rebecca Gardyn, "What's on Your Mind?" *American Demographics* (April 2000), pp. 31–33; Jennifer Gilbert, "Capita Taps Brain Waves to Study Web Ads' Potency," *Advertising Age* (Feb. 14, 2000), p. 55.

[25] Avi Shankar and Christina Goulding, "Interpretive Consumer Research," *Qualitative Market Research* 4 (2001), pp. 7–16.

focus group studies, not include numbers, such as "2 of the 8 focus group members liked the layout of the Web site, and 4 of the 8 found the merchandise available online limited," because it is too tempting to generalize (to 25% and 50% of the population). Instead, reports include cautious language, e.g., "some respondents . . ." or "a few participants . . ." mentioned their desire to try the new flavor of coffee.

Yet, fair or not, there is a perception that such statements (with the modifiers "some," "a few," etc.) and summaries of qualitative studies in general, are soft and somehow not as rigorous as numbers, so there is a desire to quantify the qualitative data.[26] Hence, there is coding.

Ethical Dilemma 4.4

You are running a laboratory experiment for the promotion manager of a soft drink company. The promotion manager read a journal article indicating that viewers' responses to upbeat commercials are more favorable if the commercials follow very arousing film clips, and he is interested in testing this proposition with respect to his firm's commercials. You have the commercials, but you need to pre-test a sample of film clips for their capacity to arouse. To do this, you are recording respondents' blood pressure levels as they watch various film clips. The equipment is not very intrusive, consisting of a finger cuff attached to a recording device. You are satisfied that the procedure does not threaten the participants' physical safety in any way. In addition, you have made the participants familiar with the equipment, with the result that they are relaxed and comfortable and absorbed in the film clips. On getting up to leave at the end of the session, one person turns to you and asks, "Is my blood pressure normal then?"

- Is it ethical to give respondents information about their physiological responses that they can interpret as an informed comment on the state of their health?
- What might be the result if you do not tell that person the function of the equipment?

As an example of coding, let's return to our "spying on soup purchasers" example. Say you've posted yourself mid-way down the grocery's soup aisle, pretending to be shopping for the nearby Ragu, but instead are surreptitiously studying the consumer who is checking out Campbell's and Progresso. A coding form looks like an Excel spreadsheet, where each new shopper is a row, and the columns might be structured for you to enter:

length of time standing in front of soups, number of cans picked up, number of can labels read, number of cans placed in cart, brands of cans (picked up, read, placed in cart), whether any brands were on sale, gender of shopper, approximate age, shopping alone or with children, was shopper reading from a grocery list or not (i.e., did this appear to be a planned purchase), day of week, time of day, etc.

The number of categories of information requested of each observation can be extensive, and if the coding form is too elaborate, mistakes are more easily made.

In this example, the structured observational form (i.e., specific things to look for) implies that the marketing manager and researcher decided precisely what was to be observed and the specific categories and units that would be used to record the observations. These decisions presuppose specific hypotheses (based on secondary data, account manager experience, or intelligent guesswork). Thus, the odd thing is that such structured coding forms require the research to be more descriptive or causal in nature. For exploratory research, it would be difficult to create a coding scheme with such precision. Exploratory research, as this chapter has been illustrating, is ideally suited to generating insights into the relevant dimensions of the soup purchaser's deliberation and search behavior.

---

[26] But just wait till we start talking about errors of measurement in survey numbers!

HOW TO CODE

Coding open-ended questions can be challenging, and it is nearly always more time-consuming than entering rating scale data and computing means. However, the information obtained from consumers "in their own words" through interviews and open-ended questions on surveys can also be extremely rewarding and insightful. Further, some of the problems with coding open-ended questions may be changing with new technology. Researchers are increasingly feeding respondents' answers into computers programmed to recognize a large vocabulary of words in their search for regularities in the replies. Consumers' responses are usually first broken into *thought units*. For example, if a consumer is asked, "Tell me about the last time you had poor service at a restaurant," and answers, "Well, the service was slow and the waiter was rude," the sentence would be parsed into "service was slow" and "waiter was rude," because they express different characteristics of the encounter and would need to be coded differently. Each word is ranked by the frequency of usage across respondents so researchers can see recurring themes.[27] These systems automate the coding, but they still leave the interpretation to the analyst. Nevertheless, the systems achieve in hours what would take a person weeks to accomplish.

Once the codes are obtained, remember again that this is not a numbers game. If "service is slow" is clearly the most popular complaint, then subsequent research (descriptive surveys) would be required to obtain more precise estimates as to this attitude's prevalence relative to the other issues that customers raised. It would not be appropriate to test hypotheses on the coded behavior, partly due to the difficulty of coding and quantifying the data in a consistent manner. For example, a rough coding scheme might not have differentiated "it was difficult to get a reservation" (i.e., "service" prior to entering the premises) vs. "service at the bar was slow" vs. "food came slowly," etc.[28] One way to develop consistency in coding is to train multiple coders. Inter-rater agreement is judged, e.g., percentage codes assigned in common to the observed behaviors or the interview verbata.

Summary

A research design is the blueprint for a study that guides the collection and analysis of data. The three classes of research designs are: exploratory research, descriptive research, and causal research.

---

[27] A popular program for content analysis goes by the acronym NUD*IST (for Non-numerical Unstructured Data Indexing Searching and Theorizing) and is easily found online (http://www.qsr.com.au). In addition, just as there are statistical computing programs to help with "data mining" there are also programs to assist "text mining," e.g., streams of documents, customer complaint e-mails, virtual community discussion groups, open-ended questions on customer satisfaction surveys, call center staff notes, etc. (SAS Text Miner, sas.com; SPSS Ascribe, spss.com). A document taxonomy or dictionary searches for common themes, and these themes are then easily tabulated and clustered.

[28] To be fair, a survey might also have just a single item, "speed of service," which would be equally non-diagnostic for the restaurateur in suggesting means of improvement. The point of exploratory research is to break down what "speed of service" means to inform the survey design, to include items about reservations, bar, food, etc.

Exploratory research is basically "general picture" research. It is very useful for becoming familiar with a phenomenon, for clarifying concepts, for developing but not testing "if-then" statements of causality, and for establishing priorities for further research. Exploratory methods are characterized by their flexibility. Literature searches, experience surveys, and case studies are all useful means for gaining insight into a phenomenon.

Qualitative techniques also include the popular methods of focus groups, depth interviews, projective testing, and observational ethnographic studies. A focus group is the most popular qualitative marketing research tool. They are thought to be creative in generating ideas to follow up in subsequent research because the group members interact dynamically, playing off each other's remarks. Interviews are more labor intensive, given that they are conducted one-on-one, but have the advantage that the researcher understands this particular consumer's attitudes in their idiosyncratic life context richly and in depth. Projective tests are indirect means of getting at consumers' underlying motivations and wants and needs. They can include word association tasks, sentence completions, storytelling, and picture drawing.

Most observations in marketing research are conducted in a completely natural setting, some observational studies are conducted in the lab using computers and other mechanical equipment. The lab allows greater control of extraneous influences and thus may be more internally valid, although less externally valid. Electrical and mechanical measuring instruments permit more objective, reliable measurements by eliminating possible human observers' biases such as selective attention. However, the human researcher must still provide the overall interpretation and understanding of the data.

Ethnographies are typically a combination of observations and interviews, in which the researcher is embedded in the natural setting. Observations of the field site are made, and interactions with the other participants in the setting form the basis of these qualitative studies. Finally, the coding of qualitative data is somewhat controversial, and is difficult to do well until the researchers have some basic questions to form the structure of the coding schema.

Review Questions

1. What is a research design? Is a research design necessary to conduct a study?

2. What are the different types of research designs? What is the basic purpose of each?

3. What is the crucial tenet of research?

4. What are the basic uses for exploratory research?

5. What is the key characteristic of exploratory research?

6. What are some of the more productive types of exploratory research? What are the characteristics of each type?

7. What is a word association test? A sentence completion test? A storytelling test?

8. What is the difference between an observational study conducted in the field vs. the lab?

9. What is an ethnography?

10. What principle underlies the use of a galvanometer? What is an eye camera? What does response latency assess? What is voice pitch analysis?

Applications and Problems

1. Industrial Health Technologies, Ltd. (IHT), located on the East Coast, is a manufacturer of industrial respirators. The R&D department designed a prototype respirator that is battery powered and would extend the operating life of current models from 8 to 30 hours without recharging. A similar model introduced by Deep Mine Safety Apparatus (DMSA) four months earlier was marginally successful. However, both IHT's and DMSA's models suffered from a technical flaw (using the respirators for 30 hours without recharging required 18 hours of recharging the batteries). Still, IHT's management team, headed by Chuck Montford, was excited about the product's potential. He, with Carl Corydon, IHT's marketing manager, decided to do a sample survey to gauge customer reactions. A random sample of 100 firms was chosen from a list of East Coast firms. Mail questionnaires were designed to determine respondents' attitudes and opinions toward this new respirator. In this situation, is the research design appropriate? If yes, why? If no, why not?

2. Gettings & Gettings, a father-and-son insurance agency in Lafayette, Indiana, was concerned with improving its service. In particular, the firm wanted to assess whether customers were dissatisfied with current service and, if so, the nature of this dissatisfaction. What research design would you recommend? Justify your choice.

3. Greg Martin is the owner of a pizza restaurant that caters to college students. Through informal conversations with his customers, Greg has begun to suspect that a video-rental store specifically targeting college students would do quite well in the local market. Though his informal conversations with students have revealed an overall sense of dissatisfaction with existing rental outlets, he hasn't been able to isolate specific areas of concern. Thinking back to a marketing research course he took in school, Greg has decided that focus group research would be an appropriate method to gather information that might be useful in deciding whether to pursue further development of his idea (developing a formal business plan, store policies, etc.).

   a. What is the decision problem and resulting research problem in this situation?

   b. Whom should Greg select as participants in the focus group?

   c. Where should the focus group session be conducted?

   d. Who should be the moderator of the focus group?

   e. Develop a discussion outline for the focus group.

4. Airways Luggage is a producer of lightweight cloth-covered luggage. The company distributes its luggage through major department stores, mail-order houses, clothing retailers, and other retail outlets, such as stationery stores and leather-goods stores. The company advertises rather heavily, and supplements this promotional effort with a large field staff of sales reps, numbering around 400. Sales rep turnover is high (10–20% per year). Because the cost of training a new person is estimated at $5,000 to $10,000, not including the lost sales that might result because of a personnel switch, Ms. Brooks has been conducting exit interviews with each departing sales rep. On the basis of these interviews, she has formed the opinion that the major reason is dissatisfaction with promotional opportunities and pay. But top management has not been sympathetic to Ms. Brooks's pleas regarding the changes needed in these areas of corporate policy, saying her suggestions are based on intuition and little hard data. Ms. Brooks has decided to call on their in-house Marketing Research Department.

   a. Identify the general hypothesis that would guide your research efforts.

   b. What type of research design would you recommend to Ms. Brooks? Why?

5. Fred Spears, director of advertising for ScubaYou, is responsible for selling advertising space in the magazine. The magazine deals primarily with vacation spots and the marketing of the hospitality industry, and is distributed solely by subscription.

   The size and composition of the target audience for ScubaYou are key concerns for prospective advertisers, so Mr. Spears wants more detailed data on the magazine's readership. He has total circulation figures, but these typically understate the real readership and thereby the potential exposure of an ad in ScubaYou. In particular, he thinks that for every subscriber, the magazine is read by several friends. Fred wishes to determine how large this secondary audience is, and also wishes to develop more detailed data on readers.

   a. Does Fred have a specific hypothesis? If yes, state the hypothesis.

   b. What type of research design would you recommend? Justify your answer.

6. Investment Services, Inc. (IS) is a real estate developer headquartered in Florida but operating throughout the southeastern U.S. One of the military bases located in one of the cities within IS's market area recently closed, and the 40 housing units for military people located at the base were put up for public sale. The housing units, which were all duplexes, were somewhat rundown. IS's management thinks that these units will command only a very low price at the public sale because of their dilapidated condition. The developers believe that because of this low price, the units could be repaired and sold at a nice profit. Before bidding on the contract, though, IS's management is interested in determining what kind of demand there might be for these units. It has asked you to assist in determining this reaction. What kind of research design would you suggest? Why?

## CHAPTER 5

Descriptive Research

Questions to Guide Your Learning:

Q1: What is *descriptive research*?

Q2: When is it used? When in the product life cycle? When in the *research program*?

Q3: What *hypotheses* may be tested using descriptive techniques?

Q4: What marketing questions would require a *longitudinal* study vs. a *cross-sectional* one?

Q5: What are: dummy tables? marketing research panels? brand switching tables?

This chapter covers descriptive research designs in detail. The vast majority of marketing research studies are descriptive in nature—the marketing manager has moved beyond the "What's going on?" stage of exploratory research, but either hasn't progressed to, or isn't for the moment interested in the "If I tweak this marketing mix variable, what will happen to sales?" sort of question that may be answered using the causal designs in the next chapter. In this chapter, we distinguish between longitudinal and cross-sectional descriptive designs.

When to Use Descriptive Research

Descriptive research is used when the purpose is to:

- Describe characteristics of certain groups, e.g., we might attempt to *profile users* of our brand with respect to income, gender, age, educational level, etc.
- Estimate the proportion of people who behave in a certain way, e.g., the proportion of *people who live or work within a specified radius* of a proposed shopping complex who would shop there.
- Make specific predictions, e.g., if we could *predict the level of sales* we should expect over the next five years, we could plan for the hiring and training of new sales representatives.

Descriptive research encompasses an array of research objectives. The fact that a study is descriptive doesn't mean that it is simply a fact-gathering expedition. There are tons of facts out there—just surf the Internet. What makes facts useful is an understanding, a theory, an explanation of the facts and how they relate to each other.

> **Descriptive studies require a clear specification of the who, what, when, where, why, and how of the research.**

We shouldn't submit to the temptation of designing a descriptive research study with the vague thought that the data collected should be interesting. A good descriptive study presupposes much prior knowledge about the phenomenon studied. It rests on one or more specific hypotheses. These conjectural statements guide the research in specific directions. Thus, a descriptive study design is very different from an exploratory study design—whereas an exploratory study is characterized by its flexibility, descriptive studies are more rigid. Consider a chain of convenience stores planning to open a new outlet. The company wants to determine how people would patronize the new outlet. Sounds easy, but consider these questions:

Who is to be considered a patron? Anyone who enters the store? What if they do not buy anything but just participate in the grand-opening prize giveaway? Perhaps a patron should be defined as anyone who purchases anything from the store. Should patrons be defined on the basis of the family unit, or should they be defined as individuals, even though the individuals come from the same family? What characteristics of these patrons should be measured? Are we interested in their age and gender, or perhaps in where they live and how they came to know about our store? When shall we measure them—while they are shopping, or later? Should the study take place during the first weeks of operation of the store, or should the study be delayed until the situation has stabilized somewhat and word-of-mouth has had a chance to operate. Where shall we measure the patrons? Should it be in the store, or immediately outside of the store, or should we attempt to contact them at home? Why do we want to measure them? Are we going to use these measurements to plan promotional strategy? In that case the emphasis might be on measuring how people become aware of the store. Or are we going to use them as a basis for locating other stores? In that case the emphasis might shift more to determining the trading area of the store. How shall we measure them? Shall we use a questionnaire, or shall we observe their purchasing behavior? If we use a questionnaire, what form will it take? Will it be highly structured? Will it be in the form of a scale? How will it be administered? By telephone? By mail? Perhaps by personal interview?

Yikes.

Sometimes we can answer some of these questions after some labored thought or after a small pilot or exploratory study. It's best to delay the fuller data collection until we know what hypotheses we're going after, and how the data will be analyzed. Ideally,

TABLE 5.1
Dummy Table—Store
Preference by Age

Age	Prefer A	Prefer B	Prefer C
<30 yrs			
30–39			
40+			

we would mock up a set of "dummy tables" before beginning the collection process to make explicit how the data will be structured and the analyses conducted. The dummy tables would be complete in that they contain titles, headings, and specific categories for the variables making up the tables. They just don't yet have any data in them.

Table 5.1 illustrates a table used by a women's specialty store investigating whether it is serving a particular age segment better than its competitors. The table lists the particular age segments. The variables and categories are specified before data collection begins. The tables also help us see which statistical tests should be used to study the relationship between age and store preference, again, determined prior to data collection. Inexperienced researchers often question the need for such detailed decisions before collecting the data. They assume that delaying these decisions until after the data are collected will somehow make the decisions easier. They'll only make that mistake once.

Once the data have been collected and analysis is begun, it is too late to lament, "If only we had collected information on X" or "If only we had measured Y using a finer scale." Rectifying such mistakes at this time is impossible. Rather, we must account for such contingencies when planning the study. Structuring the tables used to analyze the data makes such planning easier. To ensure that we'll be getting the data we need, we should specify in advance the objective each question addresses, the reason it's included, and the analysis in which it will be used.

Figure 5.1 is an overview of the various types of descriptive studies. The basic division is between longitudinal and cross-sectional designs. The cross-sectional study is the most common and most familiar. We measure various characteristics on a sample from the population of interest. The measures are taken one time only. Longitudinal studies, on the other hand, involve panels. A panel is a sample (stores, individuals, etc.) that remains relatively constant over time, although periodic additions are made to replace dropouts or to keep it representative. The sample members in a panel are measured repeatedly. Both cross-sectional and longitudinal studies are frequently used, and both have weaknesses and strengths.

Longitudinal Analysis

There are two types of panels: true panels and omnibus panels. *True panels* rely on repeated measurements of the same variables. Nielsen maintains an international panel of households as a basis of its Homescan service. The panel households use a hand-held scanner to record every UPC-coded item they purchase. They pass the scanner across the UPCs on the packages of the purchased items when they return from shopping and then answer a programmed set of questions (e.g., store where purchased, price paid) by responding to a series of prompts from the machine. Similarly, National Purchase Diary (NPD) maintains a consumer panel of families who

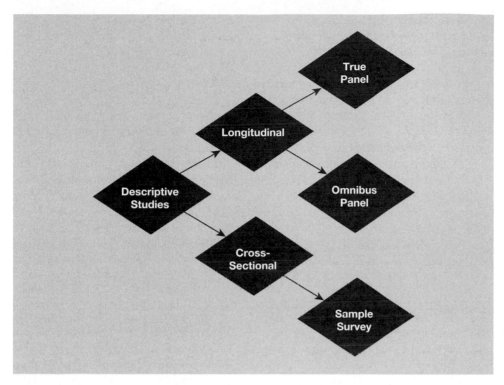

FIGURE 5.1
Classification of
Descriptive Studies

record their purchases in a paper diary when they return from shopping. Handscanning (and diaries) supplement grocery and drug store scanner data sets, because even items of clothing, office supplies, furniture, etc. have codes on them, but their manufacturers and retail distributors do not participate in aggregate scanner data services. These panels yield the secondary sources of information we'll discuss later in the book.

Measuring the same variables over time allows the marketer to ask questions such as:[1]

- What is the long-term effect of the price promotions that occur in our category?
- Is the brand equity cheapened?
- Do consumers stockpile, creating domestic inventories; hence only purchase when another sale is in effect? That is, have we in essence taught our consumers to be price sensitive?

If the same variables were not measured at multiple points in time, data patterns might vary not as a result of promotions on brand equity, say, but perhaps simply due to different households providing the data, or because the data obtained represent different selections of brands in the category, etc.

In an **omnibus panel,** a sample is maintained, but the information collected from the members varies over time. At one time, we might ask the sample about attitudes toward a new product. At another time, the panel members might be asked to evaluate alternative ad copy. In each case, a sample is selected from the panel (which is, of

---

[1] Koen Pauwels, Dominique Hanssens and S. Siddarth, "The Long-Term Effects of Price Promotions on Category Incidence, Brand Choice, and Purchase Quantity," *Journal of Marketing Research* 39 (2002), pp. 421–439.

course, a sample of the population). The subsample might be drawn randomly, or participants may be chosen who meet a screener; i.e., they have some desired characteristics. For example, the Parker Pen Company maintains a panel of 1,100 individuals who were chosen because they expressed some interest in writing instruments. If Parker wishes to evaluate a new fountain pen, they would choose individuals who prefer fountain pens to test the products.

Nickelodeon, the children's cable television network, uses a panel of children to help it evaluate its programming and magazine ideas. It uses online computer connections to gather their reactions (see Research Realities 5.1).

The distinction between the true panel and the omnibus panel is important. True longitudinal analysis, or time series analysis, can be performed only on the first type of data, with repeated measurements of the same variables and the same respondents over time. Omnibus panels mostly offer the advantage of easy access—the panelists are a relatively random sample who are readily available to participate in research. But the studies are usually very different, for different clients, and rarely are the responses from one study compared to another.

Brand Loyalty and Brand Switching

The single most important advantage of panel data is analytical and perhaps the most important longitudinal question that these data can address is the question of brand loyalty and brand switching. Suppose we are currently subscribing to the type of service that generates consumer purchase data from a panel of 1,000 families. Suppose further that we are interested in determining the effect of a recent package design for our Brand A and that our brand has two main competitors, B and C, and a number of other smaller competitors. Let's lump all the smaller, miscellaneous brands into a single miscellaneous category, labeled Brand D. We'll look at our brand at time t_1, before the change, and time t_2, after the package change.

We could perform several types of analyses on these data.[2] We could look at the proportion of those in the panel who bought our brand in period t_1 and period t_2. Table 5.2 shows a scenario where the package change was successful. Brand A's market share increased from 20% to 25%, and it seemed to make its gains at the expense of its two major competitors, whose market shares decreased.

But that is not the whole story. Given that we have repeated measures of the same individuals, when we maintain the identity of the sample members, we can count the number of families who bought Brand A in both periods, those who bought B in both periods, and those who switched brands between the two periods.

	TABLE 5.2

TABLE 5.2
Number of Families in Panel Purchasing Each Brand

Brand Purchased	During First Time Period, t_1	During Second Time Period, t_2
A	200	250
B	300	270
C	350	330
D	150	150
Total	1000	1000

[2] Cheng Hsiao, *Analysis of Panel Data* (Cambridge University Press, 2002).

Research Realities

5.1 Nickelodeon Marketing Research

Nickelodeon has been the highest-rated basic cable television network in the U.S. for the past 10 years. Critics complain that even poor shows get good ratings just due to the popularity and brand equity of the network.

Nickelodeon has a lock on the 2-to-11 year old market, and it is attributable to their "obsession with research." They run 300 focus groups a year to test shows and identify trends among kids. They also set up one of the first online consumer product testing panels. They argue that the kids' market is notoriously fickle, hence must be continually monitored. The focus groups show the children in action, and the online panel allows convenient access, both due to the immediacy of the online technology as well as the availability of the established panel.

The children in the panel are in households that are wired and that have cable. They try to represent diverse ethnic groups, and have equal gender representation. Household income is also wide ranging, to further enhance the likely generalizability of the findings to the eventual market placements of shows, ads, and products.

Online isn't perfect for the youngest among this target, who are expected to type in answers, or point to a face that says "cool" or "ick" so the online panel is supplemented with traditional research, including the focus groups or interviews at schools.

Source: Diane Brady and Gerry Khermouch, "How to Tickle a Child: Nickelodeon Keeps the Hits—and the Revenue—Coming," *Business Week* (July 7, 2003).

Table 5.3 is a **brand-switching matrix** (also called a "turnover table"), containing the same basic information as Table 5.2 (e.g., we see that 20% of the families bought Brand A in period t_1).

Table 5.3 also shows that Brand A did not make its market share gains at the expense of Brands B and C, as originally suggested, but rather captured some of the families who previously bought one of the brands in D: 75 families switched from D in t_1, to Brand A in period t_2. And, Brand A lost some of its previous users to Brand B: 25 families switched from A at t_1 to B at t_2.

Table 5.3 also allows the calculation of brand loyalty. For Brand A, 175, or 87.5% of the 200 who bought Brand A in period t_1, remained "loyal" to it (bought it again) in period t_2. Table 5.4 contains the row percentages, which suggest that among the three major brands, Brand A elicited the greatest loyalty and Brand B the least. This is important to know because it indicates whether families like the brand when they try it.[3]

TABLE 5.3
Number of Families in Panel Buying Each Brand in Each Period

		During Second Time Period, t_2				
		Bought A	**Bought B**	**Bought C**	**Bought D**	**Total**
During First Time Period, t_1	Bought A	175	25	0	0	200
	Bought B	0	225	50	25	300
	Bought C	0	0	280	70	350
	Bought D	75	20	0	55	150
	Total	250	270	330	150	1000

[3] The table is also called a "transition matrix," because it depicts the brand-buying changes or transitions occurring from period to period. Knowing the proportion of switching allows early prediction of the ultimate success of some new product or some change in market strategy.

		During Second Time Period, t_2				
		Bought A	**Bought B**	**Bought C**	**Bought D**	**Total**
During	Bought A	.875	.125	.000	.000	1.000
First	Bought B	.000	.750	.167	.083	1.000
Time	Bought C	.000	.000	.800	.200	1.000
Period, t_1	Bought D	.500	.133	.000	.367	1.000

Whether those who switched from D to Brand A were induced to do so by the package change is open to question for reasons that we discuss in the next chapter. The point is that turnover or brand-switching analysis can be performed only when repeated measures are made over time, for the same variables on the same respondents. It is not possible on omnibus panel data, in which the variables being measured are constantly changing, nor is it appropriate for cross-sectional studies.

These tables enable us to look at changes in consumers' behavior and relate those changes to our marketing tactics—advertising copy changes, package changes, price changes, etc. Further, because the same respondents are measured before and after changes in marketing variables, small changes in the criterion variable are more easily identified than if separate studies were made using two or more independent samples. The turnover table is the heart of panel analysis.

Additional Advantages of Panels

Although the major advantage of a panel is analytical, panels also have some advantages in terms of the information collected in a study. In many studies, we'd like to have a great deal of demographic information to conduct more sophisticated analysis of the results. Unfortunately, cross-sectional studies are limited in this respect. Respondents being contacted for the first and only time typically do not tolerate lengthy interviews. The situation is different in panels because panel members are compensated for their participation, so the interviews can be longer and more exacting, or there can be several interviews. In addition, when soliciting the person or household to join the panel, the demographic classification information is obtained at that time (partly to maintain a "representative" panel composition).

Panel data can also be more accurate than cross-sectional data, because panel data tend to be freer from the errors associated with reporting past behavior. Errors arise in reporting past behavior because humans tend to forget, partly because time has elapsed, or for other reasons. In particular, research has shown that events and experiences are forgotten more readily if they are inconsistent with attitudes or beliefs that are important to the person or threaten the person's self-esteem. Because behavior is recorded as it occurs in a panel, we don't need to rely on a respondent's memory. When diaries are used to record purchases, the problems should be virtually eliminated because the respondent is instructed to record the purchases immediately upon returning home.

When other behaviors are of interest, respondents are asked to record those behaviors as they occur, again thereby minimizing the possibility that they will be forgotten or distorted when they are eventually asked. Figure 5.2 shows a page out of an Arbitron radio listening diary. These diaries are used to determine radio station listening audiences, and they're used by stations to make programming decisions and

FIGURE 5.2 Arbitron Radio Listening Diary

THURSDAY									
	Time		Station				Place		
	Start	Stop	Call letters or station name. Don't know? Use program name or dial setting.	Check one		Check one			
				AM	FM	at home	in car	at work	other
→ Early morning from 5AM									
→ Midday									
→ Late afternoon									
→ Night to 5AM Friday									

If you didn't hear a radio today, please check here: _____

by advertisers to figure out when to buy air. The diary is portable and can be filled out anywhere, which tends to increase its accuracy.

The panel design also helps reduce bias due to the interaction between an interviewer and the respondent. First, respondents come to trust the interviewer to a greater degree because of repetitive contact. Second, more frequent contact creates rapport.

Concerns About Panels

The main disadvantage of panels is that they are probably somewhat nonrepresentative. The agreement to participate involves a commitment on the part of the designated sample member. Some individuals refuse this commitment—they don't want to be bothered with filling out consumer diaries, testing products, evaluating ad copy or whatever. Marketing research firms that provide the service of a panel are clearly motivated to be sure their panels are as "representative" as possible for their clients.[4] Consumer panels that require households to keep a record of their purchases generally have cooperation rates of about 60% when participants are contacted in person and lower participation rates if telephone or mail is used for the initial contact.

---

[4] Brian Wansink and Seymour Sudman, "Building a Successful Convenience Panel," *Marketing Research* 14 (2002), pp. 23–27; Sudman and Wansink, *Consumer Panels*, 2nd ed., (American Marketing Association, 2002).

The better ongoing panel operations select prospective participants systematically. The sponsoring organization attempts to generate and maintain panels that are representative of the total population of interest with respect to such characteristics as age, occupation, education, and so on. The organization usually uses quota samples so that the proportion of those in the sample with a particular characteristic (such as gender) equals the proportion in the population.

All the research organization can do, though, is designate the families or respondents that are to be included in the sample. It cannot force individuals to participate, nor can it require continued participation from those who initially choose to cooperate. It often encourages participation by offering some premium or by paying panel members for their cooperation. Nevertheless, a significant percentage of individuals designated for inclusion refuse to cooperate initially or quickly drop from the panel. Depending on the type of cooperation needed, the refusal and attrition rates might run over 50%.

Of course, not all panel attrition is due to quitting. Some individuals move away and others die. In any case, the question arises whether the panel is then indeed representative of the population, since those designated to participate are not participating. Further, the payment of a reward for cooperation raises the question of whether particular types of people are attracted to such panels.

It is generally understood that panel samples underrepresent African Americans, people with poor English-language skills, and those at the extremes of the socioeconomic spectrum.[5] Whether these characteristics of the panel are problematic depends on the purpose of the study and the particular variables of interest. Such concerns may be further exaggerated in the composition of "online" panels, wherein convenience is even greater, but sampling self-selection may be even more biased. Again, though, the value-added of this service provision heightens the concerns by these research suppliers to recruit a balanced panel.[6]

In a series of studies investigating the "representativeness" of a continuing household panel, Market Facts compared survey results on specific issues when the data were gathered using their mail panel against the data gathered from randomly selected telephone samples. Research Realities 5.2 displays some of the findings with respect to selected product ownership, lifestyle, and leisure activity characteristics. As the sample of comparisons suggests, the evidence indicates that mail panel samples are similar to the population with regard to these, and probably many more, dimensions of leisure activity and lifestyle. However, the studies also revealed instances of significant differences between the data that were generated by mail panel and data that were generated through telephone interviewing, leading the company to conclude that caution must be exercised when using mail panels because of their potential to not be representative. The trouble with bias, of course, is that we never know in advance whether it will affect the results, much less how.

Cross-Sectional Analysis

The cross-sectional study is the best known, most frequently employed, and therefore most important type of descriptive design. The cross-sectional study has two

---

[5] "Mail Panels vs. General Samples," *Research on Research* 59 (MarketFacts.com).

[6] Cf., GreenfieldOnline.com; and Paul McDevitt and Michael Small, "Proprietary Market Research: Are Online Panels Appropriate?" *Marketing Intelligence & Planning* (20, 2002), pp. 285–296.

Research Realities

5.2 Comparison of Responses of the Market Facts Mail Panel and a Randomly Selected Telephone Sample

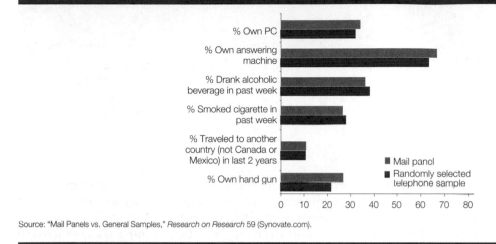

Source: "Mail Panels vs. General Samples," *Research on Research* 59 (Synovate.com).

distinguishing features. First, it provides a snapshot of the variables of interest at a single point in time. Second, the sample is typically selected to be representative of some known universe. Therefore, a great deal of emphasis is placed on selecting sample members, usually with a probability sampling plan. That is one reason that the technique is often called a sample survey. The large number of cases usually resulting from a sample survey also allows for cross-classification of the variables.

The objective of cross-classification is to establish categories so that classification in one category implies classification in one or more other categories. We detail the methods later, in the discussion of tabulation. For the moment, simply note that it involves counting the simultaneous occurrence of the variables of interest.

For example, suppose you're a brand manager and you believe that a consumer's occupation is an important factor in determining the consumption of your product; say you expect white-collar workers to be more likely to use the product than blue-collar workers. In a cross-sectional study, you'd measure a representative sample of the population with respect to occupation and use of the product. In cross-tabulation, you'd count the number of cases that fell in each of the following classes:

- White-collar and use the product
- Blue-collar and use the product
- White-collar and do not use the product
- Blue-collar and do not use the product

That is, the emphasis would be on the relative frequency of occurrence of the joint phenomenon—white-collar occupation *and* user of the product. According to your hypothesis, the proportion of white-collar workers using the product should exceed the proportion of blue-collar workers using the product.

The chapters on analysis illustrate that cross-classification analysis is an important technique that marketing researchers use to make sense out of all survey data. One particular type of cross-tabs in descriptive research arises when there is a series of "properly spaced" surveys, because this allows cohort analysis of the data. A **cohort**

Cross-sectional studies are the bread-and-butter of marketing research.

TABLE 5.5
Set-up of Cohorts

Age	1970	1980	1990	2000
10–19	C5	C6	C7	C8
20–29	C4	C5	C6	C7
30–39	C3	C4	C5	C6
40–49	C2	C3	C4	C5
50+	C1	C2	C3	C4

C1-cohort born before 1920   C5-born 1951–1960
C2-born 1921–1930   C6-born 1961–1970
C3-born 1931–1940   C7-born 1971–1980
C4-born 1941–1950   C8-born 1981–1990

is the group of individuals who experience the same event within the same interval, and it serves as the basic comparison unit of analysis. A common analysis is on birth cohorts; i.e., groups of people born within the same time interval.

In Table 5.5 we see such a cohort structure. Note that the table is constructed so that the interval between any two survey periods corresponds approximately to the age-class interval that is used to define the age cohorts used in the study (10 years in this case). Because of this, the consumption of the various age cohorts over time can be determined by reading down the diagonal. For example, in 1970, cohort 5 (C5) comprised people born between 1951 and 1960, that is, they were between 10 and 19 years old. In 1980, they had matured to 20–29 years old, by 1990 they were 30–39 years of age, etc. We might ask marketing questions about their changing needs, e.g., comparing the data of the C5 group from 1970 to 2000. We might ask different questions comparing this group when they were in their 30s (hence, data collected on them in 1990) to people in their 30s today (i.e., people born between 1961 and 1970, C6).[7]

Table 5.6 illustrates one use of cohort analysis. Life insurance is a product that tends to be bought as we get older, when we carry financial obligations that might burden loved ones, when we have discretionary monies to buy the product, etc. Insurance agents might have been pleased with growth in sales during the 1980s and 1990s, but all that was happening was the aging of the baby boomers. Table 5.6 indicates fairly stable percentages in purchasing over the life cycle. As people hit the 30–39 year old bracket, more purchase, and that percentage increases more in the

TABLE 5.6
Percentage Purchasing
Life Insurance

Age	1970	1980	1990	2000
10–19	0.0	0.5	1.0	0.5
20–29	2.5	3.7	4.0	4.5
30–39	25.0	26.5	32.0	27.0
40–49	35.5	41.0	42.0	45.0
50+	37.0	40.5	45.0	49.0

---

[7] In a regression analysis, cohort is defined as the time period minus age.

40s and seems to level off in the 50s. There does seem to be a slight increase from 1970 to 2000, e.g., among 50 year olds, with percentages increasing from 37.0% to 49.0%, or 40 year olds, with percentages increasing from 35.5 to 45.0. However, large volumes of unit increases would be attributable to the expansion of the population base as the boomers (C4 and C5) aged.

In an extensive study, the population of the U.S. has been mapped into cohorts, ranging in age from the Depression Cohort to Generation X and beyond.[8] Cohort analysts provide the marketers a snapshot of the contextual experience of being a member of the cohorts, by noting what events shaped their lives (e.g., good economies or bad, which wars and what political events they lived through), as well as consumption items (e.g., what music and television shows were popular). Understanding the mind set of a cohort group can help the marketer communicate through advertising with more resonance.

Marketing research studies don't have to be cohort designs in order to examine differences between age groups. Figure 5.3 depicts television viewing habits of children for three age groups: 6–8, 9–11, and 12–14 years of age. For many genres of television entertainment, there are discernible maturing patterns. Cartoon shows are popular with both boys and girls, especially among the youngest viewers, but this preference falls off with age, declining at a faster rate for girls than boys. Comedies and sitcoms show the reverse trends (though neither quite achieves the early popularity of cartoons). Specifically, preferences for these shows increase with age, with the rate of increase faster for girls than for boys. There are predictable gender differences as well. Action shows and sports programs are preferred by boys, at any age. (We'll talk more later in the book about how to test where all these differences are significant.)

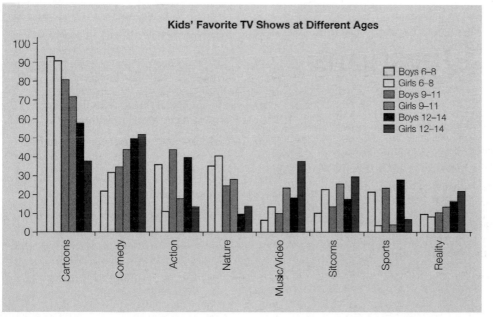

Source: quirks.com

FIGURE 5.3
Television Viewing
Habits of Children

---

[8] Geoffrey Meredith, Charles Schewe and Janice Karlovich, *Defining Markets, Defining Moments* (Hungry Minds, 2002).

Summary

Descriptive studies are systematic, and fixed in format and structure. They require a precise specification of the who, what, when, where, why, and how of the research. Descriptive studies rest on one or more specific hypotheses. They are used when the research is intended to describe the characteristics of certain groups, to estimate the proportion of people who behave in a certain way, or to make predictions.

Descriptive studies are of two types: longitudinal and cross-sectional. Longitudinal studies rely on panel data. A panel is simply a fixed sample of individuals or some other entities from whom repeated measurements are taken. There are two different kinds of panels—panels in which the same measurements are taken in each measurement period (true panels) and those in which different measurements are taken in each measurement period (omnibus panels). The turnover table, a most informative method of analysis that is unique to panel data, is applicable only to the first.

Cross-sectional studies, or sample surveys, rely on a sample of elements from the population of interest that are measured at a single point in time. A great deal of emphasis is placed on the scientific generation of the sample so that the members are representative of the population of interest. A typical sample survey involves summarizing and generalizing the data collected. The analysis of sample survey results rests heavily on the cross-classification table, which is used to report the joint occurrence of the variables of interest.

Cohort analysis is a special type of cross-classification analysis that can be used when there is a series of surveys and the spacing between them corresponds to a natural, or cohort, division of the population, where a cohort refers to the aggregate of individuals who experience the same event within the same time interval.

Review Questions

1. What are the basic uses of descriptive research?

2. What is the key characteristic of descriptive research?

3. What are the main types of descriptive studies, and what do their differences mean?

4. What are the basic types of panels, and how important are the differences?

5. What is the turnover table? How is it read? What kinds of analyses does a turnover table allow that cannot be done with other types of studies?

6. What is the fundamental thrust of a sample survey? What are its advantages and disadvantages?

7. What are the basic types of cross-sectional studies? What are their relative advantages and disadvantages?

8. What is a cross-tabulation table? What is the objective of cross-classification analysis?

9. What is a cohort? What is cohort analysis?

Applications and Problems

1. Emilie Malti, president of Jamaican Specialties, a specialty food marketing firm, was convinced that the target audience for her line of Caribbean conserves in mango, lime, passion fruit, and papaya consisted of women, ages 25 to 44, with household incomes of $30,000 and up. Jamaican Specialties' major competitor's (Pacific Flavor) market segment appeared to be more widely dispersed with respect to both age and income. Emilie and her marketing vice president, Ruth Marion, attributed this difference to the type of magazines in which Pacific Flavor advertised. Emilie and Ruth decided to conduct a study to determine the socioeconomic characteristics of their firm's market segment. They formed a panel of 800 women ages 18 and up. Mail questionnaires would be sent to all panel members. One month after receiving all questionnaires, the company would send similar questionnaires to all panel members again. In this situation, is the research design appropriate? If yes, why? If no, why not?

2. A medium-sized manufacturer of high-speed copiers and duplicators was introducing a new desktop model. The vice president of communications had to decide between two advertising programs for this product. He preferred advertising program gamma and was sure it would generate more sales than its counterpart, advertising program beta. The next day he was to meet with the senior vice president of marketing and planning to decide on an appropriate research design for a study that would aid in the final decision about which advertising program to implement. What research design would you recommend? Justify your choice.

3. The Federal Reserve (the Fed) controls currency in the U.S. Recently, the Fed has been considering some changes in the currency design. One change involves paper money, which is currently all the same size and shape (no matter what the bill's denomination). Some members of the Fed believe that money would be easier to use if it came in different colors, e.g., $1 on green paper, $5 on blue paper, $10 on red, etc. In addition to color, the Fed is considering changing the size of the bills, so that the five-dollar bill would be larger than the one, the ten would be larger than the five, and so on.

   Before making these changes, the Fed believes that it might be useful to conduct some marketing research. Thus, La Jolla Marketing Research Inc. (LJMR) is contacted by the Fed and asked to collect some information to help forecast whether these changes will be successful and popular with consumers. What research should La Jolla Marketing Research propose? Be specific when describing alternative research designs.

4. The leadership of the Boy Scouts of America (BSA) is concerned about several issues related to their membership. These issues include low retention rates among members (many scouts quit after only one or two years); high turnover rates among leaders; and declining membership in some regions (such as in large urban areas). Design a marketing research program to assist BSA in assessing and reversing these trends.

5. The Pen-Lite Company is a manufacturer of writing instruments such as fountain pens, ballpoint pens, soft-top pens, and mechanical pencils. Typically, these products have been retailed through small and large chains, drugstores, and grocery stores. The company recently diversified into the manufacture of disposable cigarette lighters. Distribution of this product was to be restricted to drugstores and grocery stores because management believed that its target market of low- and middle-income consumers would use these outlets. Your expertise is required to decide on an appropriate research design to determine if this would indeed be the case. What research design would you recommend? Justify your choice.

6. The Wisconsin Ice Cream Co. of Mount Horeb, Wisconsin, a regional manufacturer of gourmet ice cream and frozen novelties, conducted a study in 2001 to assess how its brand of gourmet ice cream was faring in the market. Mail questionnaires were sent to a panel of 1,575 households. Wisconsin Ice Cream has three major competitors: Baumgardt's Food Co. of State College, Pennsylvania; Doug's Ice Cream of Michigan City, Indiana; and Guyer Foods of Charlevoix, Michigan. A similar study conducted in 2000 had indicated the following market shares: Wisconsin, 29.84% (470 families); Baumgardt's, 22.54% (355 families); Doug's, 26.03% (410 families); and Guyer's, 21.59% (340 families). The current study indicated that Wisconsin's market share had not changed during the one-year period. Results of the study indicated that Baumgardt's market share had decreased to 20% (315 families), Doug's market share had decreased to 20.32% (320 families), and Guyer's market share had increased to 29.84% (470 families). Wisconsin Ice Cream Co. managers decided that they had little to worry about.

The 2001 study revealed some additional facts. Over the one-year period, 80 families had switched from Doug's and 50 families had switched from Guyer's to Wisconsin Ice Cream. Ten families had switched from Wisconsin and 15 families had switched from Doug's to Baumgardt's Ice Cream. Results also indicated that although none of Baumgardt's families had switched to Doug's Ice Cream, 40 of the Wisconsin and 5 of Guyer's families now purchased Doug's Ice Cream. It was revealed that Guyer's current customers comprise 80 families formerly purchasing Wisconsin Ice Cream, 65 families formerly purchasing Baumgardt's Ice Cream, and 40 families formerly purchasing Doug's Ice Cream.

a. Do you think that Wisconsin's management team is accurate in analyzing the situation? Justify your answer.

b. You are called on to do some analysis. From the preceding data, construct the brand-switching matrix. (Hint: Begin by filling in the row and column totals.)

c. Indicate what this matrix reveals for each of the brands over the one-year period.

d. Complete the brand loyalty and switching possibilities matrix on the next page.

e. What can be said about the degree of brand loyalty for each of the four products?

		At Time t_2				
		Bought Wisconsin	Bought Baumgardt's	Bought Doug's	Bought Guyer's	Total
At Time t_1	Bought Wisconsin					
	Bought Baumgardt's					
	Bought Doug's					
	Bought Guyer's					
	Total					

7. Peppy Pet Company, a large manufacturer of pet food products, conducted a study in 2001 in order to assess how its brand of dog food was faring in the market. Questionnaires were mailed to a panel of 1,260 families with a dog. The Peppy Pet brand had three major competitors: Brand A, Brand B, and Brand C. A similar study conducted in 2000 had indicated the following market shares: Peppy Pet, 31.75% (400 families); Brand A, 25% (315 families); Brand B, 32.54% (410 families); and Brand C, 10.71% (135 families). The present study indicated that Peppy Pet's market share had not changed during the one-year period. However, Brand B increased its market share to 36.5% (460 families). This increase could be accounted for by a decrease in Brand A's and Brand C's market shares (Brand A now had a share of 22.23%, or 280 families; Brand C now had a share of 9.52%, or 120 families). The management of the Peppy Pet Company decided it had little to worry about.

The 2001 study also revealed some additional facts. Over the one-year period, 70 families from Brand A and 30 families from Brand C had switched to Peppy Pet. Five families from Brand B and 30 families from Brand C had switched to Brand A, while none of the Peppy Pet users had switched to Brand A. These facts further reassured management. Finally, 45 families switched from Brand B to Brand C, but none of the families using Peppy Pet or Brand A had switched to Brand C. Brand C's loyalty was estimated to be .556.

a. Do you think that the management of the Peppy Pet Company was accurate in its analysis of the situation? Justify your answer.

b. You are called upon to do some analysis. From the preceding data, construct the brand-switching matrix.

c. Indicate what this matrix reveals for each of the brands over the one-year period.

d. Complete the following table and compute brand loyalties.

e. What can be said about the degree of brand loyalty for each of the four products?

| | At Time t_2 | | | | |
	Bought Peppy Pet	Bought A	Bought B	Bought C	Total
At Time t_1 Bought Peppy Pet					
Bought A					
Bought B					
Bought C					
Total					

8. The LoCalor Company is a medium-sized manufacturer of highly nutritional food products. The products have been marketed as diet foods with high nutritional content. Recently, the company was considering marketing these products as snack foods but was concerned about their present customers' reaction to the change in the products' images. The company has decided to assess customers' reaction by conducting a study using one of the established consumer panels.

What type of panel would you recommend in the preceding situation? Why?

## CHAPTER 6

Causal Designs

Questions to Guide Your Learning:

Q1: What is *causality*?

Q2: What are the *types of evidence* necessary to infer causal relationships?

Q3: What is an experiment, and what's the difference between *lab* and *field* experiments?

Q4: What are the *extraneous factors* that can affect the interpretation of research results?

Q5: In marketing, what are: standard test markets, controlled test markets, electronic test markets, and simulated test marketing, and what are the advantages and disadvantages of each?

Marketing managers frequently wish to answer the question, "Does X cause Y?" For example, "Will a 5% increase in price have an impact on the quantity demanded by customers?" "Will a cereal package that's been redesigned for kids, to be shorter and less likely to tip over, improve families' attitudes toward the product?" Research Realities 6.1 shows the lessons learned through an e-mail experiment for Crayola.com. These research questions are best answered via experimentation and causal analysis. We look at the meaning of causality, the types of evidence that establish causality, and the effect of extraneous variables in a research setting. We explain these concepts in the context of experimental designs.

Research Realities

6.1 Experiments Are More Than Kids' Play

Crayola.com was trying to encourage more potential users to go to their site to see arts-and-crafts projects ideas, and buy the requisite art supplies. E-mails were sent to parents and teachers, in which various elements of the e-mail itself were manipulated, to assess the impact on the e-mail's attraction and subsequent Web site draw.

For example, half of the e-mails were sent out with the "subject line" reading "Help Us Help You." This appeal was lame. In comparison, the subject line of "Crayola.com Survey" increased responses 7.5%. (It pays to be informative and honest that the purpose of the e-mail was a survey.)

Customization helps. The first line of the e-mail was either the generic "Greetings!" (resulting in a low base-rate response rate), "Hi <user name> :-)" (boosting response relative to the first salutation by 2.7%), or simply "<user name>" (which enhanced responses 3.4%).

To motivate participation and completion of the survey, some respondents were offered incentives. Compared to the one-third of respondents to whom no promotion was offered, those who were offered a $25 gift certificate at amazon.com responded more frequently (5.2%) and those offered a chance at a $100 product drawing responded even more frequently (8.4%).

These results are crystal clear, and immediately implemented—a clear instance of marketing research being worthwhile and paying for itself. The results are also likely to generalize to other e-mail survey appeals (though of course that hypothesis should be tested—luckily it would be easy to do so).

Source: Eric Almquist and Gordon Wyner, "Boost Your Marketing ROI with Experimental Design," *Harvard Business Review* (Oct. 2001), pp. 135–141.

Concept of Causality

The concept of causality is actually rather complex, but we can at least understand the essentials. Then we can see the role of experiments in establishing the validity of a statement of the form, "X causes Y."

The scientific concept of causality is different from the commonsense, everyday notion. First, the commonsense notion suggests that there is a single cause of an event. The everyday interpretation of the statement "X causes Y" implies that X is the only cause, whereas the scientific statement holds that X is only one of a number of determining conditions. In addition, whereas the everyday interpretation implies a completely deterministic relationship (i.e., X must always lead to Y), the scientific understanding of causality implies a probabilistic relationship (i.e., the occurrence of X makes Y more likely). Finally, the scientific concept implies that we can never *prove* that X is a cause of Y. We *infer* that a relationship exists—an inference typically based on data, perhaps acquired in a controlled experimental setting—but the scientific approach recognizes the fallibility of any procedure.

Thus, the question becomes, "What kinds of evidence can be used to support scientific inferences?" There are three basic kinds of evidence: concomitant variation, time order of occurrence of variables, and elimination of other possible causal factors.

Concomitant Variation

Consider the statement "X is a cause of Y." Evidence of *concomitant variation* is the extent to which X and Y occur together (or vary together) in the way predicted by the hypothesis. There are two cases—the qualitative and the quantitative.

Consider the qualitative case first. Suppose we were interested in testing the statement, "The quality of our dealers (X) drives our company's market share (Y)." We believe that where we have good dealers, we have good market penetration, and where we have poor dealers, we have less of the market. If X is to be considered a

Evidence supporting causality:

- concomitant variation
- time order of variables
- elimination of alternative explanations

cause of Y, we should expect to find the following: In those territories with good dealers, we would expect to have satisfactory market shares, and in those territories where poor dealers are located, we would expect to have unsatisfactory market shares. However, if we found that the proportion of territories with unsatisfactory market shares was higher where the good dealers were located, we would conclude that the hypothesis was untenable.

In Table 6.1, the 100 dealers in each of the company's sales territories have been classified as good or poor. Suppose that the research department has also investigated the firm's market penetration in each sales territory and has categorized these market shares using some criteria supplied by management as being either satisfactory or not. This table provides evidence of concomitant variation. Where we find the presence of X, a good dealer, we also find the presence of Y, good market share. In fact, 67% of the good dealers are found in territories where our market share is satisfactory. A perfect relationship would yield data where all good dealers were located in territories with satisfactory market shares and all poor dealers were located in territories with unsatisfactory market shares. The "pure" case will rarely be found in practice, because other causal factors will produce some deviation from this one-to-one correspondence between X and Y. So we search for the proportion of cases having X that also possess Y.

When the cause and effect factors are continuous variables, the approach is similar, e.g., a firm's advertising dollar expenditure is logically considered a cause (X), and sales, the effect (Y). The hypothesis would be stated, "The higher the level of advertising expenditure, the greater the sales." We would expect to find a positive relationship between the variables, but again, we wouldn't expect the relationship to be perfect, because there are likely other sales-determining factors.

If we analyze the relationship between X and Y and find supporting evidence of concomitant variation, we can say that the association makes the hypothesis, "X causes Y" more tenable, but it does not "prove" it.[1] Similarly, the absence of an association between X and Y cannot be taken in and of itself as evidence that there is no causal relationship between X and Y, because we are always inferring, rather than proving, that a causal relationship exists.

Consider first the case in which there is positive evidence of concomitant variation. Table 6.2 suggests that candy consumption is affected by marital status.[2] Single people are more likely than married people to eat candy regularly: 75% of the single people in the sample ate candy regularly, whereas only 63% of the married people were regular consumers. The evidence is not to be taken lightly, because it was obtained from a rather large sample of 3,009 cases. On the basis of this evidence, can

TABLE 6.1
Evidence of Concomitant Variation: Qualitative Case

	Market Share—Y		
Dealer Quality—X	Satisfactory	Unsatisfactory	Total
Good	40 (67%)	20 (33%)	60 (100%)
Poor	10 (25%)	30 (75%)	40 (100%)

---

[1] We'll discuss in subsequent chapters how to test for concomitant variation. Note that association or correlation between X and Y does not mean there is causality between X and Y.

[2] Adapted from Hans Zeisel, *Say It with Figures,* 5th ed. (Harper & Row, 1968), pp. 137–139. An oldie but a goodie.

TABLE 6.2
Evidence of Concomitant
Variation between Marital
Status and Candy
Consumption

Marital Status—X	Candy Consumption—Y		
	Eat Candy Regularly	Do Not Eat Candy Regularly	Total
Single	750 (75%)	249 (25%)	999 (100%)
Married	1265 (63%)	745 (37%)	2010 (100%)

we safely conclude that marriage causes a decrease in candy consumption? Or are there other possible explanations? What about the effects of age? Married people are usually older than single people, and perhaps older people eat less candy. Table 6.3 shows the relationship between candy consumption and marital status for different age segments of the population—younger than vs. older than 25 years. In this table, we are essentially holding the effect of age constant, and now we see there is little difference in the candy-eating habits of married and single people: Up to 25 years of age, 79% of the singles and 81% of the marrieds eat candy regularly. For those over 25 years of age, 60% of the singles and 58% of the marrieds eat candy regularly. The data suggest that a person's candy consumption is unaffected by the individual's marital state. The original association suggested by Table 6.2 was spurious.

Consider now the absence of initial evidence of concomitant variation and let's see why that does not imply that there is no causation between X and Y. Table 6.4 implies that there is no relationship between a person's listening to classical music and the individual's age: In a sample of 1,279, 64% of those under 40 and 64% of those over 40 listen to classical music.[3] Is that result what you'd have expected?

TABLE 6.3
Candy Consumption by
Age and Marital Status

	<25 Yrs			25 Years +		
	Eat Candy Regularly	Do Not Eat Candy Regularly	Total	Eat Candy Regularly	Do Not Eat Candy Regularly	Total
Single	632 (79%)	167 (21%)	799 (100%)	120 (60%)	80 (40%)	200 (100%)
Married	407 (81%)	96 (19%)	503 (100%)	873 (58%)	634 (42%)	1507 (100%)

TABLE 6.4
Lack of Evidence of
Concomitant Variation
between Age and
Listening to Classical
Music

Age—X	Listening to Classical Music—Y		
	Listen	Do Not Listen	Total
Below 40	390 (64%)	213 (36%)	603 (100%)
40+	433 (64%)	243 (36%)	676 (100%)

---

[3] Zeisel, *Say It with Figures,* pp. 123–125.

TABLE 6.5
Listening to Classical
Music by Age and
Education

Age	College			Less than College		
---	Listen	Do Not Listen	Total	Listen	Do Not Listen	Total
<40	162 (73%)	62 (27%)	224 (100%)	228 (61%)	151 (39%)	379 (100%)
40+	195 (78%)	56 (22%)	251 (100%)	238 (56%)	187 (44%)	425 (100%)

Consider what happens when educational level is introduced as an additional explanatory variable. Table 6.5 reveals that an association exists between age and listening to classical music. As college-educated people get older, they display a higher propensity to listen to classical music: 78% of those 40 and over listen, whereas only 73% of the under-40 listen. The reverse occurs among those who do not have a college education: 61% of the under-40 age group listen to classical music, and only 56% of the 40-plus age group do so. The relationship between age and listening to classical music was originally obscured by the effect of education. When education was held constant, the relationship became visible.

Though the concept of concomitant variation may seem straightforward, you can see it's actually somewhat complex. Further evidence of the existence of a causal relationship can be provided by looking at both the order of occurrence of variables and also by eliminating other possible sources of explanation.

Time Order of Occurrence of Variables

The *sequential ordering* of the occurrence of variables X and Y helps provide evidence of a causal relationship between the two. If X causes Y, typically X precedes Y. X and Y may occur nearly simultaneously, but we cannot claim X to be a cause of Y if Y precedes X.

Although conceptually simple, this type of evidence requires an intimate understanding of the time sequence governing the phenomenon. For example, we usually think of X (advertising) causing Y (sales), but a portion of this year's sales (Y) is usually budgeted for the subsequent year's advertising (X). So, which way does the relationship run: does advertising lead to higher sales, or do higher sales lead to an increased ad budget? Again we see the lesson that we need to understand something about the phenomenon before we can interpret the data.

Elimination of Other Possible Causal Factors

The *elimination of other possible causal factors* is very much like playing Sherlock Holmes, "When you have eliminated the impossible, whatever remains, however improbable, must be the truth."[4] To eliminate other possible explanations, we might physically hold other factors constant, or we might need to "adjust" our results to remove the effects of other factors.

---

[4] Arthur Conan Doyle's Sherlock Holmes: *The Sign of the Four.*

Say you're advising the divisional manager of a chain of supermarkets who is interested in the effects of end-of-aisle displays on munchy apple sales. Suppose the per-store sales increased during the past week and that a number of stores were using the displays. To reasonably conclude that the displays (X) were responsible for the sales increase (Y), we'd need to eliminate other explanatory variables such as price, size of store, apple type and quality, etc. We'd need to compare apple sales for stores of approximately the same size. We'd check to see if the prices were the same in stores having an increase in sales and stores with no increase, and we'd check to determine if the type and quality of apples were consistent with those of the previous week.

Or consider the testing of new products, where manufacturers usually want to determine whether the new product has any differential advantages in consumers' minds (e.g., superior quality, better features, etc.). Yet when consumers are given a product to test, their responses can be affected by awareness of the manufacturer of the product. Respondents might rate the product higher or lower because of their attitudes toward the manufacturer, which makes it difficult to determine whether respondents liked the product itself. To overcome such bias, letters rather than brand names are often used to label the products presented to respondents. You might think, "Oh good, problem solved," but no . . . that, in turn, raises the issue of whether the evaluations might be affected by the letters that are used. Research Realities 6.2 describes an extensive investigation of whether respondents systematically favor particular letters.

The figure displays the mean rating of each letter across the sample. The findings were that:

With a few notable exceptions, letters near the beginning of the alphabet tended to be rated higher than those near the end. Letters A and B were rated the highest in all versions, and letters U through Z were among the lowest. However, the letters M and S (and, to a lesser extent, L, R, and T) were rated high, and letters F and Q were rated low in all versions.

Because some letters were consistently perceived as being more favorable than others, care should be exercised in the selection of letters as brand labels. Choosing letters that are relatively similar with respect to their ratings may help minimize bias caused by the product labels. Letters G through P (except L and M) were relatively homogeneous in their ratings. Of course, the letters used should not suggest or appear to be abbreviations for the actual brand names.[5]

Role of the Evidence

We shall see shortly that the controlled experiment provides all three types of evidence of causality. It allows us to check for concomitant variation, time order of occurrence, and if the experiment has been designed correctly, many alternative explanations will have been eliminated. However, even in an experiment, it's difficult to eliminate all other explanations. For example, we might conclude that X caused Y, when in fact we had neglected another factor that is associated with X but was the true cause of Y. Or, we might conclude that X did not cause Y, but be wrong because we neglected some condition under which X is indeed a determiner of Y.

The correct philosophy toward these three types of evidence is that they provide a reasonable basis for believing that X is (or is not) a cause of Y. We can never be

---

[5] "Using Letters to Identify Products or Brands," *Research on Research* (MarketFacts.com).

Research Realities
6.2 Using Letters to Identify Products or Brands

To determine if some letters are perceived more favorably than others, Market Facts sent questionnaires to 4,000 households in its Consumer Mail Panel. Each subsample of 1,000 was balanced to be nationally representative with respect to geographic region, population density, age, and income. Approximately 3,000 questionnaires were returned. The instructions given to the respondents were as follows:

When some people look at different letters of the alphabet, they may feel that certain letters have a more favorable meaning than other letters. For each letter shown below, please check the response that best describes how you feel about any meaning of the letter.

The 26 letters were then listed in one of four sequences:

1. Alphabetical order
2. Reverse alphabetical order
3. Random order: TJENXBFHZOGPACRWLQKDSIVYMU
4. Reverse random order

The responses available to the respondents were as follows:

Very Favorable	(200)
Somewhat Favorable	(100)
No Meaning	(0)
Somewhat Unfavorable	(−100)
Very Unfavorable	(−200)

The numbers in parentheses are the values assigned to the responses for the analysis of the data (and were not shown to the respondents).

Source:"Using Letters to Identify Products or Brands," *Research on Research* 16 (Synovate.com).

absolutely sure that the relationship has been conclusively demonstrated. But we gain confidence in the result as an accumulation of studies point to the same conclusion. Further, an intimate knowledge of the phenomenon helps us interpret research results with more clarity than would a person untrained in the subject matter. Method knowledge is not a substitute for conceptual knowledge.

Experimentation

An **experiment** can provide more convincing evidence of causal relationships than exploratory or descriptive designs. In fact, experiments are often called "causal research." An experiment can provide evidence of causality because of the *control* it affords researchers.

An experiment *is taken to mean a scientific investigation in which an investigator manipulates and controls one or more independent variables and observes the dependent variable or variables for variation concomitant to the manipulation of the independent variables. An* experimental design, *then, is one in which the investigator* manipulates *at least one independent variable.*[6]

Because we control a manipulation of the presumed causal factor, we can be more confident that the relationships discovered are "true" relationships. Figure 6.1a displays the design of a classic scientific study. Participants are randomly sampled (to enhance external validity, discussed shortly), and then randomly assigned (to enhance internal validity, again, discussed shortly) to get a new drug or a placebo. The measure of success of the new treatment is whether there are fewer sick people among the group that received the new drug, compared to the group that didn't get medical treatment. Analogously, we run marketing research experiments. They can of course be more complex, but Figure 6.1b shows the same design for a market test of two package designs for perfume boxes ("contemporary and abstract" or "flowering and romantic"). The consumers are randomly sampled (so they should resemble all our potential customers), randomly assigned, and we measure estimates of the two groups' preferences between the abstract vs. flowering packages.

Both exploratory and descriptive designs are distinguished from **experimental designs** in that they are examples of *ex post facto* research. Ex post facto literally means "from what is done afterward." In *ex post facto* research, the criterion variable Y is observed. The analyst then attempts to find one or more causal variables, Xs, that offer plausible explanations as to why Y occurred. This kind of retrospective analysis allows little control of the Xs and therefore contains great potential for error—the occurrence of Y may be attributable to some other Xs than the ones being investigated.

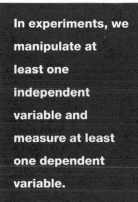

In experiments, we manipulate at least one independent variable and measure at least one dependent variable.

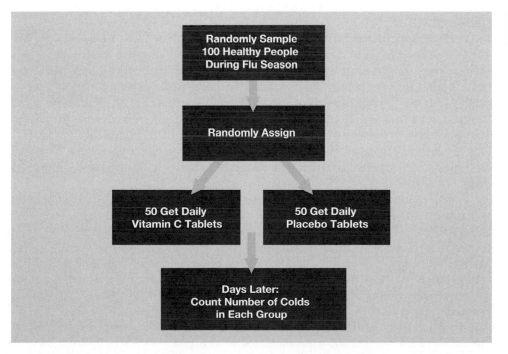

FIGURE 6.1A
Example of a Classic
Scientific Experiment

---

[6] Fred N. Kerlinger and Lee, *Foundations of Behavioral Research,* 4th ed. (Harcourt, 2000).

FIGURE 6.1B
Example of a Marketing
Research Experiment

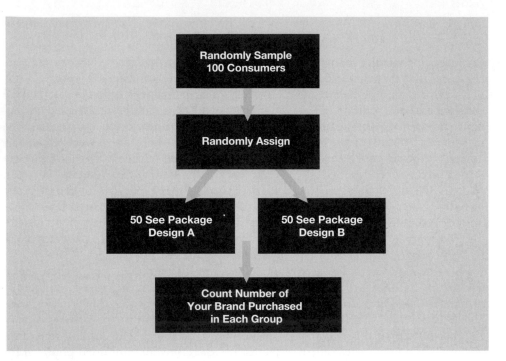

Laboratory and Field Experiments

There are two types of experiments—the laboratory experiment and the field experiment. Each has its own advantages and disadvantages, so you need to be familiar with both.

A **laboratory experiment** is one in which the researcher creates a situation with the desired conditions and then manipulates some variables while controlling others. The investigator is thus able to observe and measure the effect of the manipulation of the independent variables on the dependent variable holding the other variables constant (or at least minimizing their effect). A **field experiment** is a research study in a realistic or natural situation, and involves the manipulation of independent variables under conditions that are as carefully controlled as the field situation will permit.

The laboratory experiment is distinguished from the field experiment, then, primarily in terms of environment. The researcher creates a setting for a lab experiment, whereas a field experiment is conducted in a natural setting.

For example, a popular marketing question is to study the relationship between price and demand. We might wonder how close the price-demand estimates from a lab experiment correspond to those generated from a field experiment. First, a lab experiment was run to simulate shopping trips. Respondents chose the brand they wished to purchase from a full assortment of pre-priced brands of cola and coffee. The relative prices of the different brands were changed for each of the simulated purchase trips. This study was administered in a systematic sample of 135 homes in a small town in Illinois.

The prices of brands of cola and coffee were also manipulated in a field experiment. The field experiment was conducted in two small towns in Illinois, 10 miles apart. Four supermarkets were used in all, two from each town. The stores in one town were designated as control stores, where the price of each brand was maintained at its regular level throughout the experiment. In the experimental town, the prices were systematically varied during the experiment. The effect of the price changes was monitored by recording weekly sales for each brand so that brand market shares for each price condition could be determined. All other controllable factors were also held as constant as possible (no displays, special packaging, etc. were used to draw consumer attention to the fact that the relative prices of the brands had been altered).

Note the distinction between the two studies. In the field experiment, no attempt was made to set up special conditions. The manipulation of the experimental variable—price—was imposed in the natural environment. The laboratory experiment, on the other hand, was contrived. People were told to behave *as if* they were actively shopping for the product. Though the simulated shopping trips generated reasonably valid estimates of consumers' reactions to "real life" (field study) price changes for cola, they produced relatively invalid estimates for brands of coffee (the lab study overstated the effects of the price changes). Is there something about cola vs. coffee (e.g., frequency of purchasing)? Possibly. Do we have to be careful in drawing conclusive statements from the lab *or* the field (for different reasons)? Of course.

Ethical Dilemma 6.1

The promotions manager of a soft-drink company asks you to help her run an experiment to determine whether she should start advertising in cinemas showing X-rated movies. She explains that she has read a journal article indicating that viewers' responses to upbeat commercials are more favorable if the commercials follow arousing film clips, so she believes that her soft-drink commercial will stimulate more sales of the drink in the cinema if it follows previews of very violent or erotic films.

- If you ran a laboratory experiment for this client, what kinds of manipulations would you use, and what are the ethical issues involved in their use?
- Is it feasible to run a field experiment, and would the ethical issues change if a field experiment were run rather than a laboratory experiment?
- If you found that increasing viewers' arousal levels did indeed make them more favorably disposed toward products advertised through upbeat commercials, what are the ultimate ethical implications for influencing television programming?

Internal and External Validity

The two types of experiments have different advantages and disadvantages. The lab experiment typically has greater internal validity because of the greater control. We are better able to eliminate the effects of other factors that may obscure or confound the relationships, either by physically holding the factors constant or by controlling for them statistically. Thus, we may conclude that the observed effect was due to the manipulation of the experimental variable. **Internal validity** is this ability to attribute the effect that was observed to the experimental variable, and not to other factors. In the pricing experiment, the question is whether demand is due to price, rather than other factors, e.g., advertising, display space, store traffic. In the study, we couldn't have attributed demand differences to, say advertising, because this factor didn't exist in the simulated shopping trip.

The field experiment is considered to exhibit greater externally validity. **External validity** is the extent to which the effect can be generalized. Lab experiments are more artificial than field experiments, so it's questionable whether the results can be generalized to other populations and settings. In the simulated shopping trip, no real purchase takes place. Further, the experimenter called attention to the price, which may induce people to be more price conscious than they would be in a supermarket. Further, people who agreed to participate in the lab study may not be representative of the larger population of shoppers, and this too would jeopardize the external validity, or generalizability, of the findings.

The distinction between internal and external validity is important, and what's even trickier is that the goals usually conflict. Optimizing one means suboptimizing the other, as we'll soon demonstrate.

Internal validity: Is the effect due to our hypothesized cause?

External validity: Can we generalize to other samples/stimuli?

Experimental Design

There are a number of types of experimental design and a common notation is used to describe them.[7] Let "X" refer to the exposure of an individual or group to an experimental treatment, the effects of which are to be measured and compared. The marketing mix elements are all frequently used as experimental treatments (e.g., alternative prices, package designs, advertising themes). We'll let "O" refer to the process of observation or measurement of the test units. The test units could be individuals, groups, stores, sales reps, etc.

Time is represented by a horizontal arrangement of Xs and Os. Thus:

$$X \ O_1 \ O_2$$

indicates that a test unit was exposed to an experimental variable and then its response was measured at two different points in time. Different test units are arranged vertically. Within a "column," different groups are simultaneously treated. The symbolic arrangement

$$X_1 \ O_1$$
$$X_2 \ O_2$$

indicates two different groups of test units (one per row); and each group was exposed to a different experimental treatment at the first point in time (and at the same time); and then the responses of the two groups were subsequently measured (again, simultaneously).

Extraneous Variables

Extraneous variables are alternative explanations.

We need to design experiments carefully, because we want to be able to conclude that the observed response was due to our experimental manipulations. In particular, we need to rule out extraneous factors as possible causes. Extraneous factors fall into several categories.

History refers to the specific events, external to the experiment but occurring at the same time, that may affect the criterion variable. Suppose a major appliance manufacturer was interested in consumers' price sensitivity for refrigerators. Say they proposed the following experiment to take place in Detroit.[8] Sales (at regular prices) would be monitored for a 4-week period, then prices would be cut 10%, and sales monitored for 4 more weeks. We'd compare weekly sales at the lower price with those at the higher price. The experiment is a pretest, intervention, post-test design:

$$O_1 \ X \ O_2$$

What if, soon after the price reduction, the union contract with the auto industry expired and there was a strike. The purchase of refrigerators and other major appliances would likely be postponed, so we might see fewer sales at the lower price than at the higher one. Would we therefore conclude that higher prices induce the sales of more units? No, because we know there were extenuating circumstances that caused the aberration.

---

[7] This symbolism is pervasive, so it's worth your knowing, following the classic, Donald T. Campbell and Julian C. Stanley, *Experimental and Quasi-Experimental Designs for Research* (Rand McNally, 1966).

[8] The experiment is admittedly poor, but it demonstrates the history effect vividly.

Unfortunately, the effects of history on a research conclusion are rarely so obvious. There are always many variables that can affect what we observe, and whose effect is subtle or hidden. We need a way of isolating the effect, given that we're rarely in a position to physically control it.

Seasonality is a related phenomenon. Literal seasons are obvious (e.g., sales of snow shovels in the north will be greater in the late fall and winter). But many products have purchasing cycles, so whether you're testing price changes, in-store ads, product placement, etc., seasonality can confound your results. The best solution is to be sure to run the experiment (particularly in a field vs. lab study) for a sufficient duration so as to give the "season" a chance to cycle through.[9]

Maturation specifically refers to changes occurring within the test units (consumers) that are not due to the effect of the experimental variable but result from the passage of time. For example, people get older, become tired, or hungry and distracted. Measured changes in attitude toward a product may occur simply because people have become bored and disinterested while using the product, and not because of the reinforcement advertising to which they were exposed. Similarly, individuals in a consumer panel may change brands over time not because of any changes in marketing strategies, but perhaps their marital or family status changed.

Maturation effects can occur in test units other than people. Organizations also change. Dealers grow, become more successful, diversify, etc. Stores change—traffic increases, its composition changes, the store's physical makeup decays and then is renovated, etc.

Of course, the type of maturation depends on the duration of the experiment. We wouldn't worry about maturation of people in an experiment that lasted only a week. On the other hand, if they were participating in an interview, and the questioning lasted a couple of hours, they could very well grow tired or feel pressed for time. Thus, responses to later questions may be affected because their personal situation has changed, and for no other reason.

Testing is concerned with the fact that the experiment itself may affect the responses. There are two kinds: the *main testing effect* is the effect of a prior observation O_t on a later observation O_{t+1}. For example, students taking achievement tests for the second time usually do better than their first time, even though there is no feedback about the items missed the first time.[10] The first administration in and of itself is responsible for the improvement.

In many situations, the main testing effect is a result of respondents' desire to be consistent. Thus, in successive administrations of an attitude questionnaire, respondents reply in a consistent manner even though there has been some change in their attitudes. Or even in a single survey administration, they answer later questions to be similar to their early replies, as best they can recall them. That is, the responses to the latter part of the questionnaire are not independent of, but conditioned by, responses to the early questions.

The main testing effect may also be *reactive*; there are very few things in social science that can be measured so that the process of measurement itself doesn't change what's being measured. The very fact that people report their attitudes to someone else may make them start thinking more about those attitudes, and they even might change. Or, the very fact that a person is a member of a consumer panel

[9] Daryl Wehmeyer, "In-Store Marketing Needs Careful Evaluation," *Marketing News* (Nov. 11, 2002), pp. 14–16.

[10] Campbell and Stanley, *Experimental and Quasi-Experimental Designs*, p. 9.

that reports purchasing behavior may change that person's purchasing behavior (e.g., people might edit their behaviors, buying more vegetables, fewer chocolates).

There is also an *interactive testing effect,* which means that a prior measurement affects perceptions of the experimental variable. For example, people who are asked to indicate their attitudes toward Chevrolet may become more aware of the Chevrolet ads than those who are not queried. Yet if we are interested in the attitude impact of the ads, we are interested in their effect on the population as a whole and not simply on those individuals in our sample.

The results of the two testing effects are different. The main testing effect manifests itself in the relation between observations and can be depicted as:

$$O_1 \quad X \quad O_2$$

That is, the process of measurement O_1 in turn affects the measurement O_1 or the latter measurement O_2. The interactive testing effect, on the other hand, can be diagrammed as:

$$O_1 \quad X \quad O_2$$

The process of measurement O_1 results in a change in the reaction to the experimental stimulus. The main testing effect usually exerts its greatest impact on the internal validity of an experiment, whereas the interactive testing effect most typically affects the external validity.

Instrument variation includes any and all changes in measuring instruments that might account for differences. The change may occur in the instrument itself, or it may result from variations in its administration. When many interviewers participate, significant instrument variation can occur because it is difficult to ensure that all the interviewers will ask the same questions with the same voice inflections, the same probes, with the same rapport, and so on. As a result, the recorded differences between, say, the awareness level of two respondents may not reflect a true difference but rather a difference that arose because each interviewer handled the interview slightly differently. The same thing can occur with interviews conducted by the same interviewer—it's unlikely that each situation will be handled in exactly the same way. Interviewers may become more adept at eliciting the desired responses, or they may become bored with the project and tired of interviewing.

We might modify the measuring instrument during the course of the research project. If the changes are big (e.g., a new set of attitude statements), the responses to each questionnaire would probably be analyzed separately. Sometimes, though, a minor modification is needed, such as a slight change in wording of a specific question that makes it more understandable without changing its meaning. Although slight, this kind of change should be checked for variations in the reported answers.

Statistical regression is the tendency of "extreme" cases to move closer to the average during the course of an experiment. For example, people may be *chosen* for investigation because they exhibit extreme behavior, say, in their alcohol consumption. If a consumer panel is formed of such people, it is likely that in subsequent monitoring, their reported alcohol intake would appear closer to the average.

Alternatively, a study investigating the use of a brand of orange juice might *reveal* several families who consumed 10 cartons in a week. If they had had house guests, it wouldn't be surprising if subsequent consumption would be less.

Extraneous factors

- **history**
- **maturation**
- **testing**
  - ○ **main**
  - ○ **interactive**
- **instrument variation**
- **statistical regression**
- **selection bias**
- **experimental mortality**

Selection bias arises from the way in which test units are selected and assigned in an experiment. It's said to be present when there is no way of certifying that groups of test units were equivalent before being tested.

As an example, consider the standard news reaction to a presidential address, "Many say the president has convinced them that the X (pick your topic) crisis is real. In an Associated Press–CNN poll last week, 60% of those who heard the president's speech agreed that there is a worldwide crisis, whereas 40% of

Ethical Dilemma 6.2

The regional sales manager for a large chain of men's clothing stores asks you to establish whether increasing his salespeople's commission will result in better sales performance. Specifically, he wants to know whether increasing the commission on limited lines of clothing will result in better sales on those lines, along with the penalty of fewer sales on the remaining lines, or even whether raising the commission on all lines will produce greater sales on all lines. Suppose that you think that the best way to investigate the issue is through a field experiment in which some salespeople receive increased commission on a single line, others receive increased commission across the board, and still others make up a control group whose members receive no increase in commission.

- Are there ethical problems inherent in such a design?
- Is the control group being deprived any benefits?

those who didn't hear the speech believe the crisis is real." The results, 60:40, make it appear that the president is persuasive, but the fallacy in the argument is that there is no way of determining if those who saw the president's speech had similar attitudes toward X, before viewing, to those who did not see it. Exposure to some mass communication is voluntary, and thus the exposed and unexposed groups inevitably possess a systematic difference on the factors determining the choice. Republicans listen to the speeches of Republican candidates, Democrats listen to Democrats, people with a favorable attitude toward a product pay more attention to the product's ads, and so on. If we are to conclude that exposure to the experimental stimulus (TV special, speech, ad, whatever) was responsible for the observed effect, we must ensure that the groups were equal before exposure.

The equality of groups is established in two ways: *matching* or *randomization*. Say we have 20 stores, 10 of which will comprise an experimental group and the other 10, a control. Sales of anything in the stores are likely to be correlated with the store's traffic, so to make the groups as similar as possible before introducing an intervention into the experimental group, we'd try to match the stores according to some external criterion, such as annual sales or square feet of floor space. Then we'd assign one store from each matched pair to the experimental group and one to the control.

Matching isn't perfect. It's hard to match test units on any but a few characteristics, so the test units may be equal in terms of the variables chosen but unequal in terms of others. In addition, if the matched characteristic turns out not to be an important determinant of the response, the researcher has wasted time and money in matching the test units.

Randomization doesn't have these problems and is generally the preferred procedure. We would assign the 20 stores at random to each of the groups, using a table of random digits. Randomization produces groups that are "equal on the average" when the sample is large enough to allow the positive and negative deviations about the average to balance. With small samples, matching complements the randomization, e.g., matched test units would be randomly assigned to treatment conditions.[11]

---

[11] Cook and Campbell suggest that "perhaps the best way of reducing the error due to differences between persons is to match before random assignment to treatments" with the best matching variables being those "that are most highly correlated with post-test scores" Thomas D. Cook and Donald T. Campbell, *Quasi-Experimentation* (Rand McNally, 1979), p. 47.

Experimental mortality is the loss of test units during the course of an experiment. The problem is that there is no way of knowing if the lost test units would have responded to the experiment in the same way as those that were retained. In the example of testing a special display in a grocery store, suppose that in the middle of the experiment, the managers of two of the stores in the experimental group got nervous—they thought the display wasn't working, so they used the display for another product. This would reduce the number of experimental stores to eight. Our interest is in the average store sales in the experimental group vs. those in the control group, and we'd have no way of knowing if the experimental group average would have been higher or lower if the two dropout stores had continued participating. We can't simply assume that the sales would have been like those in the other experimental stores. They might have been, but they might not have been. We need to design studies so that this issue is eliminated.

Specific Designs

Three types of experimental designs are commonly distinguished: *pre-experimental designs, true experimental designs,* and *quasi-experimental designs.* True experimental designs provide the most control over extraneous factors, so they are the most effective in helping us confidently interpret research results. Not all marketing problems allow the use of true experimental designs, but knowledge of their features allows a more rigorous scientific interpretation of results. Then we can better understand the necessary caveats when pre-experimental or quasi-experimental designs are used.

Pre-Experimental Designs

In a *pre-experimental design,* the researcher has very little control over when participants are exposed to the experimental stimuli, or even who the participants are. Similarly, there is little control of the measurement, the timing, or the respondents.

THE ONE-SHOT CASE STUDY

Let's start simply. The one-shot case study is diagrammed:

X O

A single group of test units is exposed to an experimental variable, and then that group's response is observed. There is no random allocation of test units; rather, the group is self-selected or is selected arbitrarily by the experimenter. For example, we might interview (O) a convenience sample of readers of a particular trade journal (X) for their reaction to our ad.

The one-shot case study is of little value in establishing the validity of hypothesized causal relationships because it provides too little control over extraneous influences. It provides no basis for comparing what happened in the presence of X with what happened when X was absent. The minimum demands of scientific inquiry require that such comparisons be made. Thus, the one-shot case study is more appropriate for exploratory than conclusive research; that is, suggesting hypotheses, but not testing their validity.

THE ONE-GROUP PRETEST–POSTTEST DESIGN

The one-group pretest–posttest design is diagrammed as follows:

$$O_1 \; X \; O_2$$

It adds a pretest to the one-shot case study design. The convenience sample of respondents is interviewed for their attitudes toward our product before the ad is placed. They are also interviewed after the ad is run, and the effectiveness of the ad is taken as the difference (d) in their attitudes before and after exposure to the ad: $d = O_2 - O_1$.

This design is widely used to argue the effectiveness of marketing strategies, but the design's failure to control extraneous error nullifies its conclusions. Consider some of the factors that might be responsible for the $O_2 - O_1$ difference, aside from the experimental variable X. First, history is uncontrolled. Other ads, trade journal articles, some firsthand experience with the product, or any of a host of other factors may have occurred simultaneously with the experiment that caused the attitude change observed in a particular respondent. The respondents may have been more responsive to the product at O_2 than at O_1 (maturation). Both the interactive and main testing effects might be at work—respondents were interviewed at O_1, which might make them pay more attention to the ad than the normal reader might (interactive testing effect), so the $O_2 - O_1$ difference cannot be generalized to the population. In addition, respondents might attempt to appear consistent with their O_1 score (main testing effect). Perhaps the respondents' initial responses created an extreme attitude score in either a positive or negative direction; then statistical regression is likely to have occurred with the O_2 scores. Suppose there is some experimental mortality. Would the $O_2 - O_1$ difference have been larger or smaller if the lost participants were included? We don't know. Further, the sample was a convenience sample, and the result probably could not be generalized to the larger population. What a mess!

THE STATIC GROUP COMPARISON

The static-group comparison is a design using two groups, one that has experienced X and another that has not. A key feature is that the groups have not been created by randomization. The static-group comparison is diagrammed:

$$
\begin{aligned}
&\text{EG:} \quad X \;\; O_1 \\
&\text{CG:} \qquad\;\; O_2
\end{aligned}
$$

To continue with our previous example of the effectiveness of a particular ad, this design would be conducted as follows: After the ad is run, interviews would be conducted among a sample of readers. Those who remembered seeing the ad would be considered the "experimental group," EG. Those who did not recall seeing the ad would be considered the "control group," CG. The attitudes of each group toward the product would be measured, and the effectiveness of the ad would be taken to be $d = O_1 - O_2$. The equation states the difference in attitudes between those who saw the ad and those who didn't.

There are sources of extraneous error in this design. For example, there is no way of ensuring that the groups were equivalent prior to the comparison, e.g., people with favorable attitudes toward a product often pay more attention to ads for the product than people with unfavorable attitudes. The $O_1 - O_2$ difference may reflect a difference in the initial attitude of the two groups, and might not be in any way attributable to the ad.

True Experimental Designs

Randomization makes the data from true experimental designs more valid than data from any pre-experimental design. The true experimental design is distinguished by the fact that the experimenter can *randomly assign* treatments to randomly selected test units. The experimenter can control who gets the experimental condition and who doesn't, and when the intervention (X) and measurement (O) occur. To distinguish the true experiment, we denote a random assignment of test units to treatments by (R).

BEFORE–AFTER WITH CONTROL GROUP DESIGN

The before–after with control group design was considered ideal for a number of years. The design is:

EG: (R) O_1 X O_2
CG: (R) O_3 O_4

This design diagrams simply, but it imposes a number of requirements on the researcher. The researcher decides which test units receive the experimental stimulus and which do not. (It is not up to the test units to self-select whether they will be members of the control or experimental groups, as they did in the pre-experimental designs.) Further, the experimenter must assign test units to the experimental and control groups randomly. (The experimenter may first match the test units on some external criterion and then assign one member from each of the matched pairs to the experimental and control groups, but this final assignment is made randomly.) Finally, each of the test units in both groups is measured before and after the introduction of the experimental stimulus.

Consider the problem faced by an in-house credit union in promoting the credit union idea among the company's workers. Suppose that the company is considering the effectiveness of a rather expensive brochure, "Know Your Credit Union," in creating awareness and understanding of the functioning of the credit union. The brochure is the experimental stimulus, X. The use of the "before–after with control group" design to investigate the effectiveness of the brochure would proceed along the following lines.

1. A sample of the firm's employees would be selected at random.
2. Half of these employees would be randomly assigned to the experimental group (to receive the brochure), and the other half would form the control group.
3. Each respondent would fill out a questionnaire to assess the employee's knowledge of the credit union.
4. The brochure would be mailed (or somehow distributed) to the respondents in the experimental group.
5. After the lapse of some appropriate time interval (say, 1–2 weeks), the questionnaire would again be administered to the sample to assess their current knowledge.

Now consider this design in terms of the various sources of extraneous error. The difference O_4 minus O_3 reflects effects of extraneous influences. For instance, it's possibile that during the course of the experiment, there may be a change in the bank prime lending rate and credit might become more expensive. This history effect would be partially responsible for any differences in O_4 and O_3. However, it would also exert a similar influence on those belonging to the experimental group. Thus, if we were to consider the effect of the experimental variable to be E and the effect of these extraneous or uncontrolled sources of variation to be U, the impact of the experimental stimulus X could be:

$$O_2 - O_1 \qquad\qquad = E + U$$
$$O_4 - O_3 \qquad\qquad = \quad U$$
$$\overline{(O_2 - O_1) - (O_4 - O_3) = E}$$

But note that this calculation applies to the following sources of extraneous variation: history, maturation, main testing effect, statistical regression, and instrument variation. All these influences should affect both groups approximately equally. Selection bias was eliminated by random assignment. The design can suffer from experimental mortality, however, if some of the employees designated for the study refuse to participate.

This design is nearly ideal, however, it may not control for the interactive testing effect (defined previously). The pretest can make the experimental subjects respond to X partly because they have been sensitized. Yet the key question for credit union management is how employees in general, not just those pretested, respond to the brochure.

If there is an interactive testing effect, the calculation does not isolate the experimental effect, E, as cleanly as we've just seen. Instead, the situation becomes:

$$O_2 - O_1 \qquad\qquad = E + U + I$$
$$O_4 - O_3 \qquad\qquad = \quad U$$
$$\overline{(O_2 - O_1) - (O_4 - O_3) = E + I}$$

where "I" measures the interactive effect of testing. We're basically unable to determine the impact of the experimental stimulus because it's confounded with the interactive testing effect. Our calculation of the net difference among the Os provides a result, but the result has two components—one due to the E and another due to I.

FOUR-GROUP SIX-STUDY DESIGN

When an interactive testing effect is likely to be present, the four-group six-study design is a good choice.

EG#1:	(R)	O_1	X	O_2
CG#1:	(R)	O_3		O_4
EG#2:	(R)		X	O_5
CG#2:	(R)			O_6

Let's use this design to make the credit union brochure example more elaborate. We'd first select a random sample of the firm's employees. Then we'd randomly divide the sample into four groups. Those designated for the first experimental and control groups would be measured for their knowledge of the credit union. The brochure would then be mailed to those designated as belonging to the first and second experimental groups. Finally, all four groups would be measured on their knowledge of the credit union. Six measurements are made in all, per the name of the design.

This design offers the researcher much control. Selection bias is handled by the random assignment of test units to groups. The other extraneous sources of error are handled as they were in the previous design; i.e., by making the logical assumption that factors such as history or maturation should affect all groups. By looking at the "difference in differences," the impact of these extraneous factors should be netted out. Further, whereas there might be an interactive testing effect with the first experimental group, there couldn't be any with the second experimental group, because there is no prior measurement to sensitize the respondents.

As with the other designs, let's see how to calculate the effect of X. When we randomly assign test units to groups, we can assume that, except for sampling variation, the four groups were equal *a priori* in their knowledge of the credit union. Thus, the best estimate of the "before measurement" for EG#2 and CG#2 (where there hadn't been pretest measures), would be the average of the before measurements that were taken: $\frac{1}{2}(O_1 + O_3)$.

Substituting in this estimate, the differences between before and after measurements are as follows:

EG#1: $\quad O_2 - O_1 \qquad\qquad = E + U + I$

CG#1: $\quad O_4 - O_3 \qquad\qquad = \quad\ \ U$

EG#2: $\quad O_5 - \frac{1}{2}(O_1 + O_3) \quad = E + U$

CG#2: $\quad O_6 - \frac{1}{2}(O_1 + O_3) \quad = \quad\ \ U$

What is the impact of the experimental stimulus? It is determined by comparing the second experimental and control groups and is given specifically by the calculation

$$[O_5 - \tfrac{1}{2}(O_1 + O_3)] - [O_6 - \tfrac{1}{2}(O_1 + O_3)] = [E + U] - [U] = E$$

This design also allows us to estimate the effect of the uncontrolled extraneous factors, U, by looking at each of the control groups. In addition, an estimate of the interactive testing effect is provided by comparing Experimental Groups I and II through the calculation:

$$[O_2 - O_1] - [O_5 - \tfrac{1}{2}(O_1 + O_3)] = [E + U + I] - [E + U] = I$$

Given that this design allows us to estimate the experimental effect so cleanly, it's become a conceptual ideal. Its practical application in marketing is somewhat limited, though, because the design is expensive—marketing samples aren't always so large that we have the luxury of dividing the sample into four groups. Nevertheless, this design enables the isolation of various effects, which makes it a standard against which other designs may be compared.

AFTER-ONLY WITH CONTROL GROUP DESIGN

You might have noticed that we can estimate the impact of the experimental stimulus in the four-group six-study design simply by comparing Experimental Group #2 to Control Group #2, which raises the question of why Experimental Group #1 and Control Group #1 are included. They aren't needed to estimate a "before" measure for Experimental Group #2 and Control Group #2, because regardless of what this measurement is, it cancels in the basic calculation of the effect of the experimental variable:

$$[O_5 - \tfrac{1}{2}(O_1 + O_3)] - [O_6 - \tfrac{1}{2}(O_1 + O_3)] = O_5 - O_6$$

The before measurements are helpful if we wish to study individual cases of change, but if the sole interest is in estimating the impact of the experimental variable, as is often the case, this estimate can be provided by studying the last two groups of the four-group six-study design in an after-only with control group design:

EG: (R) X O_5

CG: (R) O_6

The observations have been subscripted with a 5 and 6 to indicate that these groups have not been pretested in the four-group six-study design. Returning to our "Know Your Credit Union" brochure example, the researcher would again begin by selecting a random sample of employees. One-half would be randomly assigned to the experimental group, and the other half would form the control group. Neither group would be premeasured, and the brochure would be mailed to all those in the experimental group. After some appropriate time lapse, both groups would be measured for their knowledge, and the estimated effect of the brochure would be provided by the difference O_5 minus O_6.

Many extraneous sources of error are eliminated even in this fairly simply designed experiment. The main extraneous factors are assumed to affect both groups, so their influence is eliminated by calculating the difference between O_5 and O_6. No interactive testing effect occurs since no pretest has taken place. The experimental test units should behave much like the larger population of employees, in that some might read the brochure carefully, some might read it casually, and some might simply throw it away without reading it. This is as it should be, so the results can be generalized to the population of employees. For all these reasons, this design is probably the most frequently used form of experiment conducted in marketing research. With only two groups and two measures, it offers sample-size, cost, and time advantages.

There are two very important caveats, though, with respect to this design. First, it is very sensitive to problems of selection bias. The prior equality of the groups is assumed because of the random assignment of test units to groups. No pre-measure is made, so this assumption cannot be checked. Further, the design is highly sensitive to experimental mortality. There is no way of determining whether those who refuse to cooperate or who drop out of the experimental group are similar to those dropping out of the control group. Experimental mortality would call into question the assumption that the groups are equal except for the impact of the experimental stimulus.

Quasi-Experimental Designs

We have just seen that the true experimental design is distinguished by the control it imposes in the research. The researcher is able to determine who will be exposed to the experimental stimulus, when the exposure will occur, who will be measured, and where that measurement will take place. In a *quasi-experimental design*, the investigator is not able to schedule the experimental stimuli, and perhaps more problematic is that the researcher isn't able to randomly assign test units to groups.

TIME-SERIES EXPERIMENT

There are a number of quasi-experimental designs, though we discuss only the time-series experiment, a methodology well-suited to some types of routine marketing data.[12] The time-series experiment can be diagrammed as:

O_1 O_2 O_3 O_4 X O_5 O_6 O_7 O_8

---

[12] See Campbell and Stanley, *Experimental and Quasi-Experimental Designs*, pp. 36–64 for more.

This diagram indicates that a group of test units is observed over time, that an experimental stimulus is introduced, and that the test units are again observed for their reaction. A change in the previous pattern of observations is taken as the effect of the experimental stimulus.

The time-series experiment requires that researchers have repeated access to the same test units. Further, though researchers cannot schedule the exposure of the experimental stimulus, they can control when the respondents are surveyed. Panel data are a popular sort of marketing research time-series experiment.

The goal of establishing that the observed effect is due to the experimental variable requires that we eliminate other plausible hypotheses for the occurrence of the phenomenon. Consider some of the possible patterns of responses that may result, as illustrated in Figure 6.2.

Note first of all that the *pattern* of responses, rather than any single observation, is key in interpreting the data from a time-series experiment. Consider the impact of a package change, X, on the firm's market share. On the basis of the plot of the data points in Figure 6.2, it would seem logical to conclude that the package change:

1. Exerted a positive impact in situation A (it raised the firm's market share).
2. Had a positive impact in situation B (it halted a decline in market share).
3. Had no long-run impact in situation C (sales in Period 5 seem to be borrowed from sales in Periods 6 and 7).
4. Had no impact in situation D (the firm's market share growth remained steady).
5. Had no impact in situation E (the observed fluctuation after the introduction of the experimental variable is no greater than what was previously observed).

(And of course, we would be interested in testing the statistical significance of these changes.)

In the time-series experiment, maturation can be partially ruled out as causing the difference in O_5 and O_4 because it is unlikely that it would operate only in this one instance. Rather, it would logically have an effect on a number of other observations. Instrument variation, statistical regression, and the main testing effect would be similarly avoided. Selection bias can be reduced by the random selection of test

FIGURE 6.2
Some Possible Outcomes in a Time-Series Experiment When Introducing an Experimental Variable X

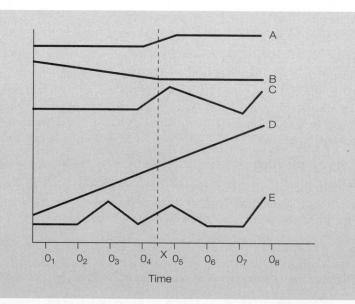

units. Experimental mortality can be controlled by paying some premium to maintain cooperation.

The failure to control for history is the critical weakness of the time-series experiment. Despite this, a carefully executed time-series experiment can provide some useful insight. If the careful examination of consumer panel data before, during, and after introducing the experimental variable fails to turn up any unusual competitive reaction, and if researchers also record other environmental changes as they occur, the researchers are in a position to make a valid assessment of the effect of the experimental stimulus. Of course, researchers can never be as sure that the impact of history has been ruled out entirely in a quasi-experimental design as they can in a true experimental design. However, a repeatable stimulus, such as a cents-off coupon program, allows greater certainty, because the history wouldn't be the same each time.

Another weakness of the time-series experiment is that it may be influenced by the interactive testing effect. There may be some peculiarity in the experimental stimulus so that it affects only those sampling units subjected to repeated testing.

Experimental versus Nonexperimental Designs

By now you should appreciate that exploratory and descriptive designs are not particularly useful in establishing the existence of causal relationships. They don't provide the control necessary to infer that a causal relationship does indeed exist. Exploratory studies are less of a problem in this regard, since they are rarely used to make causal statements. Unfortunately, the same cannot be said about descriptive studies. Frequently, the evidence of a cross-sectional survey is used to argue that X caused Y or the evidence from some time-series data is analyzed using, say, regression analysis to establish X as causing Y.

The error in such arguments can be appreciated by dissecting the typical descriptive study: A random sample of respondents is selected. The respondents are measured with respect to some response variable Y. Next they are queried about the hypothesized causal factor X. If it is found that those who possess X also possess Y and those who lack X also lack Y, the truth of the assertion that "X causes Y" is established. The research is *ex post facto*, because the researcher is starting with the observation of a dependent variable and is retrospectively searching for plausible explanations.

A problem arises in descriptive studies with respect to all three types of evidence used to support causality. *Concomitant* variation is observed, but there is no way of knowing that those who did and did not possess Y were at some prior time equivalent with respect to both Y and X. In the experiment, the researcher is able to establish this equivalence by the random assignment. The researcher also knows who was exposed to X and doesn't have to rely on a respondent's memory. The researcher is also better able to establish the *time order* of occurrence of variables in an experiment. Due to random assignment, the experimental and control groups should not differ in terms of the response variable before exposure to the experimental stimulus, and with some experimental designs, the pre-measures can be verified to be roughly similar. The descriptive study affords little control in *eliminating other possible explanations*. All the extraneous factors that affect experimental results also operate in descriptive research, but there is no way of removing their effects. The result is the awkward position of asserting it is "this X" and no other X that is causing Y—an assertion resting on a great deal of faith.

Internal validity:

Need random assignment

External validity:

Need random sampling

This is not to deny the important role descriptive designs play in marketing research. They are, after all, the dominant type of marketing research. But you need to be aware of the dangers of using descriptive designs to establish causal linkages between variables.

Experimentation in Marketing Research

The growth of experiments in marketing has been steady over the past 40 years. One of the most important growth areas has been in market testing, or test marketing. Some marketers make a distinction between the terms, but the essential feature of the **market test** is that it is an experiment, done in a small section of the marketplace, with the goal of predicting the sales results of some proposed marketing action.[13] Very often the action in question is the marketing of a new or improved product or service. Test markets aren't infallible, but they help. New product success, including survival three years post-launch, is enhanced with large samples in test markets.[14] Test marketing is not just for new products; it's been used to examine the sales impact of almost every element of the marketing mix. Consider these examples of test marketing:

- To compete with Quiznos' heated sub sandwiches, Togo's launched tests in 45 Chicago and New York locations, including testing the effectiveness of the small toasters, given the typically constrained Togo's retail square footage.[15]
- Sometimes employees are the first guinea pigs, er, test market. Before Mastercard even approached retailers in Orlando to test its contactless smart card, PayPass, among consumers, the card was tested among employees. Results were encouraging. Transaction times were cut by two-thirds, and amounts purchased increased by 10%.[16]
- With each progressive success, rollout becomes closer. Kodak tested photo developing kiosks in Atlanta, found positive results, and soon began plans for 500 such photo developing stations.[17]
- As pharmaceuticals gain direct access to consumers, test marketing is increasing. Pfizer has used Canada as a test for the U.S. (sorry northern neighbor!) to test Viagra ads, Listerine Pocket Paks, and medicated freezer pops for children.[18]

Problems of Experimentation

Marketing experiments have many strengths, particularly that of determining the precise effect of a marketing intervention. Still, no methodology is perfect. Three of

[13] See "Some Methodological Issues in Product Testing," *Research on Research* 41 (MarketFacts.com).

[14] Kevin Clancy and Peter Krieg, "Surviving Innovation," *Marketing Management* 12 (April 2003), pp. 14–20.

[15] Lori Lohmeyer, "Sub Shops Launch Toasted Sandwich in Bid to Warm Up Sales," *Nation's Restaurant News* 37 (March 17, 2003), pp. 4, 115.

[16] Marie Lingblom, "Mastercard Puts Contactless Smart Card to the Test," *CRN* 1035 (March 3, 2003), p. 55.

[17] Todd Wasserman, "Moms in Kodak's Focus," *Brandweek* 44 (Feb. 17, 2003), p. 10.

[18] Jim McElgunn, "The Ultimate Test Market," *Marketing Magazine* 108 (Feb. 10, 2003), p. 30.

the more critical problems with experimentation in general and test marketing in particular are cost, time, and control.

Cost

A major consideration in test marketing has always been cost. There are the normal research costs (designing the data-collection instruments, wages paid to the data-collection field staff, etc.); the direct research costs are often substantial; and other costs must be borne as well. Moreover, if the test market is to reflect the marketing strategy intended for rollout, the test also includes marketing costs (advertising, personal selling, etc.). With new-product introductions, there are also the costs associated with producing the merchandise. To produce the product on a small scale is typically inefficient. Yet to gear up immediately for large-scale production can be wasteful if the test market indicates that the product is a failure.

Test markets are so helpful as diagnostic marketing research tools, however, that companies are getting creative in executing large tests, but doing so cost effectively. For example, American West and Southwest are testing concepts such as paying for meals on board, and new snack foods such as mint Oreos. They have captive audiences, which can cut sampling costs by $2–3 million.[19]

Time

The time required for an adequate test market can be substantial. The accuracy of a test market increases with its duration; experiments conducted over short periods do not allow for the cumulative effect of the marketing actions. Consequently, a year is often recommended as a minimum period before any kind of go/no-go decision is made, to account for seasonal sales variations and repeat purchasing behavior.

Time is of the essence particularly in today's fast-paced global environment, where competitive reaction can be so swift that many firms have committed themselves to speeding product introductions worldwide.

Control

The problems associated with control manifest themselves in several ways. In the experiment itself, the issues include: choice of specific test markets; product distribution in those markets; soliciting cooperation from wholesalers and retailers, etc. Often, simply because the product is being test marketed, it receives more attention than it would as a regular product on a national scale, e.g., in the test market, store shelves may be better stocked, the sales force more diligent, and the advertising more prominent than would normally be the case.

Control problems are associated with competitive reaction, too. Although the test marketing firm can control its own marketing actions, competitors can, and do, sabotage experiments by cutting the prices of their own products, gobbling up quantities of the test marketer's product (thereby creating false results for the test marketer), etc.

---

[19] Anon., "In-Flight Meals Get Air Checks," *Restaurants & Institutions* 113 (Feb. 1, 2003), p. 14; Stephanie Thompson, "Snacks Take Flight," *Advertising Age* 73 (Nov. 11, 2002), p. 6.

Sometimes a seeming "misfire" in a test market is a good outcome. It's better to find out about possible problems in a test market than after a product is introduced nationally. There is loss in company prestige and simple embarrassment when mistakes are made such as Apple Computer's introduction of the Newton.[20]

Types of Test Markets

Figure 6.3 shows some of the most commonly used *standard test markets*.[21] A standard test market is one in which companies sell the product through their normal distribution channels. The results are typically monitored by a standard distribution service (discussed in the next chapter). Research Realities 6.3 walks you through other logical questions for choosing markets to compare.

An alternative is the *controlled test market* (or the "forced-distribution test market"), in which the entire experiment is conducted by an outside service (e.g., Audits & Surveys, Burgoyne). The service pays retailers for shelf space and therefore can guarantee distribution to those stores, which represent a predetermined percentage of the marketer's total food store sales volume. The service also positions the product in the best location in the store with the right number of shelf facings; it stocks the store shelves and coordinates any trade promotion programs.

An increasingly popular variation of the controlled test market is the *electronic test market*. A panel of households in the test market area are recruited, and we get their demographic information. People in these households are given ID cards, which they show when checking out at grocery stores. Everything they purchase is automatically recorded and associated with the household through scanners found in all supermarkets in the area. Suppliers of these services are also capable of moni-

FIGURE 6.3
Some Popular Standard Test Markets

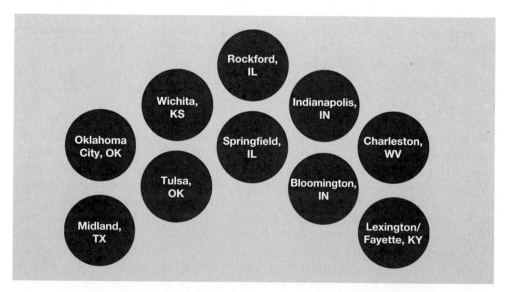

---

[20] Jim Carlton, "Apple Drops Newton, an Idea Ahead of Its Time," *Wall Street Journal* (March 2, 1998), p. B1.

[21] These locations are generally "middle America," chosen to be representative. Still, it makes sense to alter the locations when appropriate, e.g., when a medical supply company tested its arthritic knee solutions, it ran test markets in Miami and Phoenix. Cinda Becker, "Skipping the Hospital," *Modern Healthcare* 33 (April 28, 2003), p. 16.

Research Realities

6.3 Factors to Consider when Choosing Test Cities

You don't have to use only the tried-and-true test markets, known for being "average America." Other cities could be used, providing knowledge of those marketplaces is available and sensible for the particular test. Figure A shows data that were used to argue that Portland has managed its metropolitan growth more effectively than Atlanta has, as indicated by property taxes, and commuting factors like number of miles and time spent in the commute, as well as environmentally related effects like measures of ozone and energy consumption. Depending on the product category or service sector you were studying, you might say the cities were similar (e.g., both urban areas are enjoying strong growth rates, job growths, incomes) so one market could serve as a proxy for the other. Or you could argue the cities were so different (e.g., the aforementioned commute) that comparing data on them would be apples-to-oranges; that is, you wouldn't know whether differences in sales were due to the different products you've made available to those markets' consumers, or to the natural differences among those markets.

You don't only have to worry about matching cities. If you were conducting advertising tests where the experiment involved showing one version of the ad during one television show and another version of the ad during another time slot or show, you better be confident the time slots or shows are comparable, to defend your conclusion that a difference in the memorability of the ads was due to the ads themselves, rather than some by-product of one show being more popular, or a better context in which to show one of the versions of the ads.

Figure B gives you a sense of the media coverage for some of the highest-rated shows, by category of music or acting awards shows, and the top sports programming.

Could you compare the Grammys to the Golden Globes—even with similar ratings, might those audiences differ? Could you compare performances of ads run during the AFC and NFC championships?

Ad testing requires ratings information!

Increases for Two Cities During Last Decade

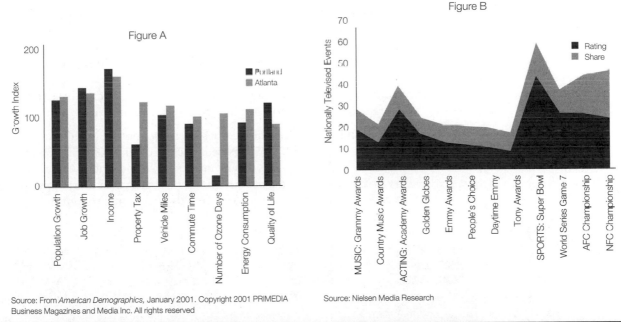

toring each household's television-viewing behavior. They then correlate exposure to commercials with purchase behavior, which in turn allows testing of the consumer acceptance of a new or modified product and other marketing elements.

Another variation is to use a *simulated test market* (STM) as a prelude to a full-scale market test. Most STMs operate similarly: consumers are interviewed in shopping malls, exposed to the new product, and asked to rate its features. They are then shown commercials for it and for competitors' products. In a simulated store environment, they are given the opportunity to buy the product using seed money or cents-off coupons to make the purchase.[22] Those not purchasing the test product are typically given free samples. After a usage period, follow-up phone interviews are conducted with the participants to assess their reactions to the product and their repeat-purchase intentions. All the information is fed into a computer model, which has equations for the repeat purchase and market share likely to be achieved by the test model. The key to the simulation is the equations built into the computer model. Validation studies indicate that most STM models can come within +3% of actual sales in two-thirds of the cases.[23]

A prime advantage of STMs is the protection from competitors. They can be used to assess trial- and repeat-purchasing behavior. They're faster and cheaper than full-scale tests and good for spotting weak products. The Achilles' heel of STMs is that, by definition, given their simulated nature, they don't provide information about trade support or competitive reaction. Thus, they're more suited for evaluating product extensions than for examining the likely success of new-to-the-world products.

The controlled test market provides a useful laboratory for testing acceptance of the product and for fine-tuning the marketing program. When the product is novel or represents a radical departure for the manufacturer, the question of trade support is much more problematic, and the controlled test is less useful under these circumstances.

The traditional test market provides a more natural environment than either STMs or controlled test markets. The standard test market plays a more vital role when the following situations apply:

1. It is important for the firm to test its ability to actually sell to the trade and get distribution for the product.
2. The capital investment is substantial, and the firm needs a prolonged test market to accurately assess its capital needs or its technical ability to manufacture the product.
3. The firm is entering new territory and needs to build its experience base so that it can play for real, but it wants to learn how to do so on a limited scale.

In the choice among types of test market, it's useful to look at the alternatives as stages in a sequential process, with STMs preceding controlled test markets, which in turn come before standard test markets (see Figure 6.4). The sequence is not always as pictured. A very promising STM or controlled market test can cause a firm to skip one or more intermediate stages and perhaps move directly to national rollout.

FIGURE 6.4
A Perspective on Various
Types of Test Markets

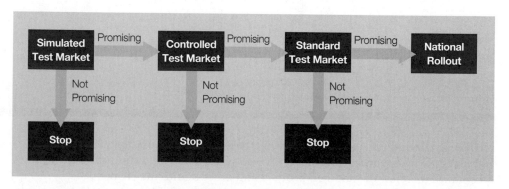

---

[22] Klaus Wertenbroch and Bernd Skiera, "Measuring Consumers' Willingness to Pay at the Point of Purchase," *Journal of Marketing Research* 39 (2002), pp. 228–241.

[23] Kevin J. Clancy, Robert S. Schulman and Marianne Wolf, *Simulated Test Marketing* (Lexington Books, 1994).

Summary

The emphasis in this chapter was on the third basic type of research design—causal design. The notion of causality was reviewed, and, according to the scientific interpretation of the statement "X causes Y," it was found that (1) we could never prove that X caused Y, and (2) if the inference that it did was supported by the evidence, X was one factor that made the occurrence of Y more probable, but it did not make it certain.

Three types of evidence support the establishment of causal linkages. Concomitant variation implies that X and Y must vary together in the way predicted by the hypothesis. The time order of occurrence of variables suggests that X must precede Y. The elimination of other factors requires the analyst to design the investigation so that the results do not lend themselves to a number of conflicting interpretations.

Experiments provide the most convincing evidence of causal linkages. An experiment is a scientific study in which an investigator manipulates and controls one or more predictor variables and observes the response of a criterion variable. There are two general types of experiments: the laboratory experiment, in which an investigator creates an artificial situation for the manipulation of the predictor variables; and the field experiment, which allows these manipulations to take place in a natural setting. The greater control of a lab experiment allows more precise determination of the effect of the experimental stimulus, but there is a greater danger of generalizing the results because of its artificial nature.

In either type of experiment, we must be on guard against extraneous sources of error that may confound interpretation: history, maturation, testing (both main and interactive), instrument variation, statistical regression, selection bias, and experimental mortality. True experimental designs are useful in minimizing the impact of these errors. They are distinguished from pre-experimental and quasi-experimental designs by the fact that the researcher decides who is to be exposed to the experimental stimulus and when the exposure is to occur.

The growth of experiments in marketing has been steady. The market test has become standard practice for some companies to establish the sales potential of new products, and increasingly to determine the effectiveness of contemplated changes of any elements of the marketing mix. Two popular variations are the controlled test, in which the distribution of the product is guaranteed by the service provider, and the simulated test market (STM), in which reactions from users of the product are used in a series of equations to predict the repeat-purchase behavior and market share likely to be realized by the test product. Despite causal designs' growing use, descriptive designs are still the dominant form of marketing research investigations. This is partly due to tradition, but it also reflects the cost, time, and control problems associated with experimental research.

Review Questions

1. How do the scientific notions and commonsense notions of causality differ?

2. What types of evidence can be employed to support an inference of causality?

3. What is an experiment?

4. What is the distinction between a laboratory and a field experiment?

5. What is the difference between internal and external validity?

6. What are the extraneous variables that can affect the outcome of a research investigation?

7. What is the difference between the main testing effect and the interactive testing effect? Why is the distinction important?

8. What are the main ways of establishing the prior equality of groups? Which method is preferred, and why?

9. What are the distinctions among pre-experimental, true experimental, and quasi-experimental designs?

10. What are the basic types of pre-experimental designs?

11. What are the main types of true experimental designs? What are the key issues or problems associated with each of these designs?

12. How is the effect of the experimental stimulus determined in a before–after with control group design? In a four-group six-study design? In an after-only with control group design?

13. How does the true experimental, after-only with control group design differ from the pre-experimental, static-group comparison research design?

14. When would one want to employ a four-group six-study design instead of a before–after with control group design, and vice versa?

15. When would one want to employ a before–after with control group design or a four-group six-study design in lieu of an after-only with control group design, and vice versa?

16. What is the nature of the time-series experiment? How does the time-series experiment differ from the pre-experimental, one-group pretest–posttest design? What is the importance of this difference?

17. Compare descriptive research and true experimental design with respect to the ability of each to control or allow for extraneous factors.

18. How would you explain marketing's infrequent use of experimental research before 1960 and its steadily increasing use since then?

19. What is a test market? For what kinds of investigations can test markets be used? What are the problems associated with test markets?

20. What is the primary difference between a standard test market and a controlled test market?

21. How does an electronic test market work? What are its advantages compared to a traditional test market?

22. How does a simulated test market (STM) work? What are its main advantages and disadvantages compared to full market tests?

23. Under what conditions is a standard test market a better choice than either an STM or a controlled test market?

Applications and Problems

1. Charlie Sharp is the national sales manager of Hitech Inc. Charlie recently hypothesized that "Hitech's increase in sales is due to the new sales personnel that we recruited from the vocational school over the last several years. Sales of the new salespeople are up substantially, whereas sales for longer-term salespeople have not increased." Identify the causal factor X and the effect factor Y in the preceding statement.

2. To gather support for his conclusion, Charlie asked the research department of Hitech to investigate the sales of each of the company's salespeople. Using criteria supplied by management, the department categorized territory sales changes as increased substantially, increased marginally, or no increase. Consider the following table, in which 260 sales personnel have been classified as old or new:

   a. Does this table provide evidence of concomitant variation? Justify your answer.

   b. What conclusions can be drawn about the relationship between X and Y on the basis of the table?

Salesperson Assigned	Territory Sales Change			
	Increased Substantially	Increased Marginally	No Increase	Total
New	75	30	5	110
Old	50	40	60	150

3. Consider the following statement: "The increase in repeat-purchase frequency is due to retailers' decisions to stock our product in the gourmet food section of supermarkets during the last nine months. Repeat purchases from the gourmet section are up as much as 50% from our previous store location." Identify the causal factor X and the effect factor Y in the preceding statement.

4. The research department of the company in Question 3 investigated the change in repeat-purchase frequency for each store location. Using criteria supplied by management, the department categorized repeat-purchase frequency changes as increased substantially, increased marginally, or no increase. Consider the following table, in which 624 store locations have been classified as old or gourmet:

   a. Does this table provide evidence of concomitant variation? Justify your answer.

   b. What conclusions can be drawn about the relationship between X and Y on the basis of the preceding table?

In-Store Location	Repeat-Purchase Frequency			
	Increased Substantially	Increased Marginally	No Increase	Total
Gourmet	180	72	12	264
Old	120	96	144	360

5. Six months later, the research department in Question 4 investigated the situation once again. However, a new variable was considered in the analysis—the size of the package. More specifically, it considered if repeat-purchase frequency was affected depending on whether the package was a 14- or 18-ounce size. The following tables summarize the research department's findings:

   a. If the size of package is ignored, does this table provide evidence of concomitant variation between a change in repeat purchases and in-store location? Justify your answer.

   b. If the size of package is considered, does the table provide evidence of concomitant variation between repeat purchases and in-store location? Justify your answer.

Salesperson Assigned	14-ounce Package			
	Increased Substantially	Increased Marginally	No Increase	Total
New	84	24	—	108
Old	65	19	—	84

| Salesperson | 18-ounce Package | | | |
Assigned	Increased Substantially	Increased Marginally	No Increase	Total
New	6	12	6	24
Old	24	48	24	96

Several experimental designs are described in Questions 6–10. For each design, complete the following tasks:

    a. Determine what type of design is being used. Explain.

    b. Diagrammatically represent the design.

    c. Discuss the threats to internal and external validity for the design.

6. A leading manufacturer of frozen food products decided to test the effectiveness of an in-store display. Four large supermarkets, located near the company's main office, were selected for the experiment. The display was set up in two of the stores, and sales were monitored for a period of two weeks. The sales of the other two stores were also recorded, but no displays were used. Sales volume for the frozen food products increased 2% more in the stores that used the in-store displays than in the stores that did not use the displays.

7. A branch of Alcoholics Anonymous wanted to test consumer attitudes toward an anti-drinking advertisement. Two random samples of respondents in Piscataway, New Jersey, were selected for the experiment. Personal interviews relating to consumer attitudes toward alcoholism were conducted with both samples. One of the samples was shown the anti-drinking advertisement, and, following this, personal interviews were conducted with both samples in order to examine consumer attitudes toward alcoholism.

8. A manufacturer of a line of office equipment, based in Houston, Texas, marketed its products in the southwest United States. The region consisted of 30 geographic divisions, each headed by a divisional manager who had a staff of salespeople. The firm's management wanted to test the effectiveness of a new sales training program in which the sales personnel in five of the divisions typically participated. The divisional managers of these five divisions were instructed to monitor sales for each salesperson for each of the five months before and after the training program. The results were to be sent to the vice president of sales in Houston, who planned to compare them against sales changes in the other divisions.

9. A new manufacturer of women's cosmetics was planning to retail the firm's products through mail order. The firm's management was considering the use of direct-mail advertisements to stimulate sales of their products. Prior to committing themselves to advertising through direct mail, management conducted an experiment. A random sample of 1,000 consumers was selected from Memphis, Tennessee. The sample was divided into two groups, with each subject being randomly assigned to one of the two groups. Direct-mail advertisements were sent twice over a period of one month to respondents of one of the groups. Two weeks later, respondents of both groups were mailed the company's catalog of cosmetics. Sales to each group were monitored.

10. Milbar Corporation, a specialty hand-tool company located in Chagrin Falls, Ohio, was considering introducing a new style of snap ring pliers. Before it went ahead with production of the pliers, Jack Bares, CEO, decided that the company should test the effectiveness of its sales promotion campaign. Jack chose four disparate cities in which to run the experiment. In two of the randomly chosen cities, Binghamton, New York, and Manderville, Louisiana, Milbar first questioned mechanics and parts people on their attitudes toward snap ring pliers. Next, Milbar ran the new pliers sales promotion campaign in the randomly chosen Binghamton and Medford, Oregon. Then Milbar went back to all four cities—Binghamton, Manderville, Medford, and Omaha, Nebraska—and measured mechanics' and parts people's attitudes toward the new and old snap ring pliers.

11. The product development team at Flameglo Log Company has been working on several modifications of Flameglo's highly successful line of fireplace logs. The most promising development is a new log that burns in several different colors. Based on favorable feedback from a few employees who have tested the product in their homes, management feels that the new log has the potential to become a major seller.

At a recent strategy meeting, the vice president of marketing suggested a test-marketing program before committing to introduction of the new log. He pointed out that a test market would be a good way to evaluate the effectiveness of two alternative advertising and promotional campaigns that have been proposed by Flameglo's ad agency. He feels that effectiveness should be evaluated in terms of the trial- and repeat-purchasing behavior engendered by each program. He also wants to gauge Flameglo's current distributors' acceptance of the new product.

The CEO of Flameglo, however, is not very enthusiastic about the idea of test-marketing. She is concerned that Flameglo's competitors could easily duplicate the new log, that the company is nearing the limit of its budgeted costs for developing the new log, and that the seasonal nature of log sales makes it imperative to reach a go/no-go decision on the new log by early April, only four months away.

The director of marketing research stated that she felt a test-marketing plan could be devised that would satisfy both the vice president of marketing and the CEO. She was instructed to submit a preliminary proposal at the next strategy meeting.

a. What information should be obtained from the test market in order to satisfy the vice president of marketing?

b. Under what constraints must the test-marketing plan operate in order to satisfy the CEO?

c. Given your answers to the Questions a and b, what method of test-marketing should the director recommend? Why?

Cases

CASE 2.1
Riverside County Humane Society (A)

The demands on the Riverside County Humane Society (RCHS) had increased rather dramatically over the past several years, while the tax dollars the society received to provide services had remained relatively unchanged. In an effort to halt further decline in the quality of its services and to provide better care for the pets at the center, the membership committee of the board of directors began making plans for a member/contributor drive. The organized drive was to be the first of its kind for the local chapter and the committee members wanted it to be as productive as possible.

As the plans began to evolve, the committee realized that the organization had only scattered bits and pieces of information about its current members. It did have a list of members and contributors for the last five years that had been compiled by the RCHS staff. In addition, it had access to the results of a survey done by a staff member several years earlier that focused on member usage of shelter facilities and their opinions of shelter services and programs. However, the organization had only sparse knowledge of the profile of its typical member and contributor, why they belonged or contributed, how long they had been associated with the Humane Society, how the services of the Humane Society could be improved, and so on. The committee members believed information on these issues was important to the conduct of a successful membership drive, and thus they commissioned some research to secure it.

One of the first things the researchers did was to contact other Humane Society chapters to determine what kinds of research they had done, particularly with respect to identifying the characteristics of their members. The researchers also interviewed key Riverside County Humane Society staff members and several board members for their thoughts and ideas regarding RCHS membership. The researchers held a focus group among members of the membership committee. These research activities produced the following general ideas about membership and contributions:

1. The people who use the center's facilities are not necessarily the same people who would become members. Members love their own pets, take good care of them, and want other animals to be treated humanely.
2. Most contributors do not care about being a "member" because membership does not confer any rights or privileges, except a newsletter. Members are very different from contributors.
3. The female member of the household is probably making the decision regarding membership or contribution to the RCHS.

4. The majority of members in the RCHS are female and are at least 35 years old.
5. Many retired or elderly people contribute to or are members of the RCHS.
6. The average contribution is about $15 to $25.
7. People in the community have a generally positive perception of the RCHS.
8. An emotional appeal in a membership drive is likely to have the best chance for success.
9. Most people have heard about the RCHS primarily through education programs conducted by the society.
10. The greatest benefit associated with membership is the warm feeling that people get from belonging to the RCHS.

The research firm planned to select a sample of names from the current lists of members and contributors and to send them mail questionnaires to explore these ideas further.

Questions
1. What kind of research design is being used?
2. Is it a good choice?
3. Design a questionnaire that addresses the issues raised and that also gathers helpful demographic information on members and contributors.

CASE 2.2
Hotstuff Computer Software (A)[1]

Simpson, Edwards and Associates has had considerable success with a computer software package that it designed to enable government agencies to manage their database systems. The firm is currently developing a second product, a more specialized version of its first endeavor. Called HotStuff, its latest computer software concept targets the firefighting industry. Researchers at Simpson, Edwards and Associates have a hunch that fire departments are a prime market for database software because of their extensive information-handling responsibilities—equipment inventories, building layouts, hazardous materials data, budget records, personnel files, and so on.

At this embryonic stage in the new product's development, the company is following the same game plan that helped it launch its previous success. Responsibilities have been broadly divided: Jean Edwards has assumed command of the production side and Craig Simpson has taken charge of marketing and promotion. Craig's first move was to reassemble the original team of staff members who had

[1] The contributions of Jacqueline C. Hitchon to the development of this case are gratefully acknowledged.

154

researched the market for government agency software. At their first orientation meeting, he submitted the following objectives for their deliberation:

1. Determine market potential.
2. Identify important product attributes.
3. Develop an effective promotional strategy.
4. Identify competitors in the market.

By the close of discussion, the group had decided that its first task would be exploratory research. Specifically, it decided to conduct experience surveys involving local fire chiefs, informal telephone interviews with state and national fire officials, and a literature search. Based on findings from the exploratory research effort, the group hoped to pursue descriptive research to fulfill the four objectives.

EXPLORATORY RESEARCH

The first finding to emerge from the exploratory research affected the target market for HotStuff. Fire departments are made up of two broad categories: municipal departments with full staffs of paid firefighters, and volunteer departments consisting of a paid chief and remaining members who may or may not be paid firefighters. The team quickly discovered that the two kinds of departments differ in two important ways. First, from the point of view of funding, municipal departments receive the majority of their funds from taxes, so the money is tightly controlled and tends to be earmarked for specific uses. Volunteer fire departments, on the other hand, rely heavily on donors and special events as sources of income, to the extent that fundraising may account for more than 50% of their total receipts. Since money obtained through fundraising is not technically part of the budget, it is not subject to budgetary controls per se.

The second key difference between municipal and volunteer departments concerned purchasing procedures. Local municipal departments tended to route all purchases through a central purchasing agent, who would then apply for approval from the data-processing center at city hall before acquiring computer hardware and software. Fire chiefs interviewed in volunteer departments, however, reported that they had sole authority to purchase any hardware or software required.

Telephone calls to out-of-state fire officials indicated that these differences were consistent across the nation. As a result, Simpson, Edwards and Associates decided to restrict its target market to volunteer fire departments.

A second finding uncovered in the exploratory research concerned the extent to which the needs of the target market were already being met. Inquiries within the state revealed that only a few volunteer departments had already purchased computers. Further, those with computers had not possessed them for long and were still in the process of automating manual databases. The general feeling among fire officials was that computerization would be an inevitable development in the industry in the near future. Indeed, four specialized software packages were already being advertised in fire prevention journals: Chief's Helper, Fire Organizer, Spread Systems, and JLT Software. Spread Systems differed from the others in that it consisted of separate programs, each of which sold individually and covered a particular information type, such as inventory records or hazardous materials. The strategy followed by Spread Systems allowed fire departments to reduce their expenditure on software because they could select only those programs that they needed. It was conjectured at Simpson, Edwards and Associates that specific programs for specific functions may help overcome initial consumer caution toward spending several thousand dollars for computer software, because the expenditure would not be made all at one time. It was also believed that some makers of generic software packages that perform spreadsheet or database management analysis should be included in the list of competitors, although users of generic software packages needed some proficiency with computers to tailor these basic packages to their specific applications.

A third finding of interest from the exploratory research was that the term volunteer was offensive to departments officially classified as volunteer because they thought that it implied a lack of professionalism. In fact, their staffs were as well trained as members of municipal departments. This sentiment led the researchers to conclude that the label volunteer should not be used in the future promotion of HotStuff.

Based on what it learned from the exploratory research, Simpson, Edwards and Associates decided to conduct a more formal investigation to address the following objectives:

1. Determine the market potential for its new software by
   a. establishing the incidence of computer use and planned computer purchases in volunteer fire departments, and
   b. obtaining more information about volunteer fire departments' funding and authority structures.

2. Identify important product attributes—that is, the types of information that need to be handled by volunteer fire departments and that therefore need to be incorporated into the software.

3. Secure ideas for promotional strategy by
   a. determining which fire publications are read by the target market, and
   b. determining which association conventions are most well attended by the target market.

4. Identify competitors in the market by
   a. establishing which brands of software are currently used in volunteer fire departments, and
   b. establishing how satisfactory existing software packages are perceived to be.

STUDY DESIGN

Simpson, Edwards and Associates' researchers believed that the best way to address these objectives was through a national survey of volunteer fire departments. They decided on a structured-disguised telephone survey using team members as interviewers. The state fire marshall informed the group that most volunteer fire departments were located in communities with populations under 25,000. Consequently, it was decided to sample towns with populations under 25,000 that were situated within a 20-mile radius of cities of at least 100,000 people. Volunteer fire departments within those towns could then be contacted by telephone by means of directory assistance. Two large cities were randomly selected from each state in the United States, excluding Alaska and Hawaii, and then a town located near each city was randomly selected. An atlas and the most recent Current Population Reports were used to identify cities and towns of the right specification.

A questionnaire was devised and pretested twice. The first pretest was conducted through personal interviews and was meant to test the questionnaire; the second pretest was performed by telephone and was meant to test the mode of administration.

In each case, inquiries were directed to the fire chiefs as representatives of the departments. The actual survey was conducted between April 13 and April 24. It would have taken less time to administer the survey had there not been a national fire convention the week that the phone survey began. Because the national fire convention coincided with Easter week, many fire chiefs were not at their departments; because their children were not in school, they attended the convention with their families. Nonetheless, the interviewer team was able to increase the response rate to 85% by numerous callbacks.

Questions

1. Evaluate Simpson, Edwards and Associates' decision to focus on volunteer fire departments as its target market, based on the exploratory research.
2. Do you think the exploratory research was productive in this case? Could further useful insights have been gained without significantly greater expenditure of resources? If so, what and how?
3. Comment on the differences among the four objectives as originally formulated and as reformulated after exploratory research.
4. Was the choice of phone interviews a good one?

CASE 2.3

Hand-to-Hand Against Palm (B)

The marketing manager for the "Organize My Life!" (OML) personal digital assistant (PDA) competitor to Palm Computing's Palm Pilot device is evaluating a number of proposals for research to be commissioned to investigate what kinds of features users of these devices might like to see in competitive and next-generation models (for example, sound, video, and so on), and to understand the particular needs of the university student segment (such as price sensitivities, special needs of different groups of students, and so on). The manager is choosing from among three proposals, each of which has been presented by different members of the brand management team.

Proposal 1 advocates exploratory research. It argues that insufficient knowledge about the PDA category is known, so it would not be useful to go out and execute some large-scale survey. Rather, this proposal suggests that students come to a central point on campus (the campuses and the meeting places on each campus to be determined), at which place the students will be asked to do a "backpack dump." In addition to the usual textbooks and notebooks, the researchers will see in a clear manner, using this observational technique, just what electronic equipment the student carries (for example, laptop computer, CD player, tape recorder, and so on), along with what kind of appointment book (such as electronic PDA or paper calendar) the student uses to keep track of homework assignments, friends and social events, and the like.

Proposal 2 recommends that since plenty of secondary data are available on the Palm Pilot and extant competitors, exploratory data would be a waste of time. If the OML team wants to know what the students want, the team should simply ask them. A survey has been designed which is composed largely of lists of potential features for the OML PDA. The respondent would be asked to indicate the importance of each feature. For example, the features would be rated on a 10-point scale, where "0" means "I don't care about this; I would never use this feature," to "10," which means "This feature would be very important to me; I would use it several times a day." The list of features to be rated includes a calendar, to-do list, calculator, video games, hot sync capability, digital photography storage, infrared e-mailing ability, and so on. Pricing could be assessed similarly, for example, "How much would you be willing to pay for this PDA? less than $100, $101 to $199, $200 to $299," and so on. The proponent of this research proposal reasons that the attributes that are most valued would appear as the features with the highest means on the rating scales, and that the OML developers would focus on offering the resulting combination of these important features.

Proposal 3 recommends a causal design. The idea would be to set up a "mock" store, featuring the OML with its list of attributes and price, side-by-side with the Palm and competitors (with the lists of their features and prices) and ask the student participants which PDA they would buy, how likely it is that they would buy the OML, and so on. The next group of students would see the OML with a different list of attributes and price point, with the competitors' information held constant, and they would be asked to make the same kind of choices. At the end, having cycled through different variations of the OML features, the team would know which properties were most attractive to the students, and the devices could be developed for market on this basis.

Questions

1. What are the trade-offs among the research designs being proposed? What information can each technique obtain that the others cannot?

2. Imagine role-playing one of the OML team members and defending one of the three proposals. What strengths does your approach offer? What shortcomings must you acknowledge? What action could be taken as a result of obtaining the information in the form you seek it?

CASE 2.4
Bakhill Foods

Michelle Gill, the marketing manager for Bakhill Foods, was discussing the future advertising strategy for Bakhill Coffee with the firm's advertising agency when the discussion turned to magazine ads and the copy for those ads.

Gill had recently been to a conference on psychological perception. At that conference, it was pointed out that in spite of the old adage "you can't judge a book by its cover," we do just that in our interpersonal relations; an individual's initial perception of and reaction to another individual is affected by the physical attractiveness of the other person. Further, a fair summary statement of that research is "what is beautiful is good." The evidence cited at the conference supporting this proposition was impressive. What particularly impressed Gill, though, was that the positive attributes one associates with a physically attractive person do not depend on actual contact with that person. They arise when the judge is simply shown photographs of physically attractive and unattractive individuals but is otherwise unaware of the subjects' traits.

Gill thought that this knowledge could be used to advantage in the advertising copy for Bakhill Coffee. She proposed that the product be shown with a physically attractive female. The advertising agency countered with the argument that it would be better to employ physically unattractive people in the ads to make the ads more believable and effective by making them less "romantic," since coffee is not a romantic product. Further, the agency suggested it might be better to employ males in the ads rather than females. After considerable discussion, the advertising agency proposed and conducted the following research to answer two questions: Should physically attractive or unattractive individuals be used in the ads? Should male or female models be employed?

THE DESIGN

Four different advertisements were prepared. The copy was the same in each ad; only the person holding the coffee was changed. The four ads included an attractive male, an attractive female, an unattractive male, and an unattractive female. The attractiveness of each model was determined by having a convenience sample of subjects view photographs of 20 different models (10 men and 10 women) and rate each model on a seven-point scale where "1" was unattractive and "7" was attractive. The male and female models with the highest and the lowest mean scores were then selected as the stimulus persons for the experiment.

A color ad with each of the four models and the planned copy was then developed. A sample of subjects for the experiment was developed by random sampling from the New York City telephone book. Contacted subjects were asked to participate in a marketing research experiment. The subjects were paid for their participation, and they were also reimbursed for their travel to the agency's headquarters.

On their arrival at the ad agency, the 96 recruits who had agreed to participate were randomly assigned to one of the advertisements. The 48 men and 48 women were first divided randomly into 12 groups of four persons each. One member of each group was then assigned to one of the four ads. Each saw one, and only one, test ad. However, three other "filler" ads were also used to disguise the particular ad of interest. The "fillers" were the same for each participant. Each participant was introduced to the experiment with the following instructions:

> We are interested in obtaining your opinions concerning particular test advertisements. You will be shown four ads, one at a time, and after each showing, you will be asked several questions about your reaction to the ad and the particular product depicted in the ad. You should note that this is not a contest to see which ad is better, so please do not compare the four ads in making your evaluations. Each ad should be judged by itself, without reference to the other ads.

After answering any questions, the experimenter presented the first ad. When the respondent had read the advertisement, it was taken away, and the experimenter then handed the respondent a copy of the data-collection sheet (see Figure 2.4.1). After completion of this form, the experimenter presented the second ad, and the process was repeated. At no time were the participants allowed to look back at the advertisements once they had surrendered them to the researcher. To allow the respondents time to warm up to the task, the experimenter always placed the test ad third in the sequence of four.

FIGURE 2.4.1 Sample Questionnaire for Bakhill Coffee Study

On each of the scales below, please check the space that you feel best describes the advertisement you just read.

Interesting	⌊⌋⌊⌋⌊⌋⌊⌋	Dull
Unappealing	⌊⌋⌊⌋⌊⌋⌊⌋	Appealing
Unbelievable	⌊⌋⌊⌋⌊⌋⌊⌋	Believable
Impressive	⌊⌋⌊⌋⌊⌋⌊⌋	Unimpressive
Attractive	⌊⌋⌊⌋⌊⌋⌊⌋	Unattractive
Uninformative	⌊⌋⌊⌋⌊⌋⌊⌋	Informative
Clear	⌊⌋⌊⌋⌊⌋⌊⌋	Confusing
Not eye-catching	⌊⌋⌊⌋⌊⌋⌊⌋	Eye-catching

What is your overall reaction to this ad?

Unfavorable ⌊⌋⌊⌋⌊⌋⌊⌋ Favorable

With regard to the product itself, how do you feel this product compares to similar products put out by other manufacturers?

Distinctive ⌊⌋⌊⌋⌊⌋⌊⌋ Ordinary

Would you like to try this product?

No, Definitely Not ⌊⌋⌊⌋⌊⌋⌊⌋ Yes, Definitely

Would you buy this product if you happened to see it in a store?

Yes, Definitely ⌊⌋⌊⌋⌊⌋⌊⌋ No, Definitely Not

Would you actively seek out this product in a store in order to purchase it?

No, Definitely Not ⌊⌋⌊⌋⌊⌋⌊⌋ Yes, Definitely

THE SCALE

The items in the scale were chosen in order to tap all three components (cognitive, affective, and conative) of attitude. *A priori*, it was thought that the cognitive component would be measured by the terms believable, informative, and clear; that the affective or liking component would be effectively tapped by the terms interesting, appealing, impressive, attractive, and eye-catching; and that the conative component would be captured by the three behavioral-intention items at the bottom of the questionnaire.

These *a priori* expectations were not strictly confirmed. A basic item analysis suggested that the term "interesting" was not related to any of the three components, and it was dropped from the analysis. Responses to the remaining items in each component were summed to produce a total score for each component. The analysis of these scale scores indicated the following:

1. The attractive male model produced the highest cognition scores for the ad among females and males.

2. The attractive male model produced the highest affective scores among female subjects, whereas the attractive female model produced the highest affective scores among males.

3. The attractive male model produced the highest conative scores toward the product for female subjects, whereas the unattractive male model produced the highest conative scores among male subjects.

On the basis of these results, the advertising agency suggested that the attractive male model be employed in the advertisement.

Questions

1. What kind of design is being employed in this investigation?
2. Evaluate the design.

CASE 2.5

Internet Advertising and Your Brain (A)

Enough Internet startups have failed that they (or at least the venture capitalists) have finally come to recognize that their business is no different from any other business, in that success depends on marketing—understanding one's customers, and hence, using marketing research. Imagine that your first job after business school is as the main marketing person for the six-month-old Internet company started by a friend of a friend.

This particular startup is a travel site that specializes in "extreme sports" (skiing off cliffs, riding mountain bikes from great heights into large air bags, as well as the more "traditional" bungee jumping and skydiving). The target audience is the current profile of users, that is, men in their 20s (though the percentages of women and older thrill-seekers are growing). This group of customers is coincidentally also highly likely to be "wired"; thus, advertising on the Internet is expected to be effective at reaching this audience.

It is your responsibility as the Extreme Marketer to conduct tests to assess the effectiveness of your company's advertisements on the Internet. At the moment, you've created two variations of a banner ad inviting browsers to your Web site and you're trying to choose between the two—which is most likely to attract these guys to click onto your Web site to learn more about your vacation packages and then possibly purchase one?

One of the ad banners your creative staff has developed is depicted in vivid colors, with captivating graphics that attempt to illustrate the possible thrills, for example, a photo with a view of skiers at the top of a mountain shot from their delivery helicopter, or a photo of a skydiver in mid-air taken by a skydiving photographer. This ad format offers very little by way of informative content, such as details about the logistics of the trips, locations, lengths of stay, price, and so on. This ad is analogous to what is traditionally called the "beauty" shot in advertising production (a televised or still photo shot that shows the car or the jar of peanut butter without mentioning miles per gallon or caloric content). Thus, we call this version of the possible banner ad "beauty."

Another banner ad has been prepared that appears somewhat less colorful and less pictorial in style, but which contains more detailed information about the extreme sports outings you are hoping to encourage the viewers to purchase. Given its greater information content, we call this version of the banner ad "info."

You could just run a little study at this point. You could purchase banner ad space on your usual business relationship Web sites, randomly assigning half of those sites your beauty ad, and half your info ad. Then you would sit back and count over some duration (such as the next two weeks) the number of click-throughs you achieved with the one ad format versus the other, and conclude that the banner ad with the greater draw should be the one with which your firm proceeds.

However, you have done your homework and are aware of some secondary data from eye-tracking studies. These studies insert small cameras into PC screens that monitor where the PC user is looking. The results suggest that placing the banner ad on some locations on the screen may be more effective than others. For example, one theory is that the brain processes whatever is in the right of a person's visual field in the left half of the brain, and stimuli in the left part of a person's visual field is processed in the right-brain hemisphere. Research conducted by physiological psychologists suggests that the left brain processes analytical features and verbal descriptions most effectively, whereas the right brain processes pictures and holistic impressions better.

The info ad is verbal and offers many facts that readers could use to analyze and assess their interest, and the beauty ad is mostly graphics and leaves a holistic impression of the thrill-seeking vacation. Thus, you're beginning to think that perhaps the info ad would be best understood and most persuasive if it were processed by a viewer's left brain, which would dictate placing it on the right side of a Web page. In contrast, the beauty ad might be better understood and more persuasive if it were processed by a viewer's right brain, which means placing the banner ad on the left side of the viewer's screen. See Figure 2.5.1.

So now the Internet advertising study you've created is somewhat more complicated. There are two factors, rather than just one: the advertising type (beauty or info) and the banner placement (left or right). Your expectations are that the ad is most likely to be effective (measured for the moment by the number of click-throughs it achieves) if the beauty ad is placed to the left or the info ad is placed to the right. However, you create all possible combinations because, after all, your hypothesis about "which ad should do better where" is in fact just a hypothesis. Thus, although each Web traveler sees only one ad, there are four ad variations: beauty on the left, beauty on the right, info on the left, and info on the right. You buy your ad space at your usual supplier Web sites, and you randomly assign one of the four ads to each of those locations. You determine how long you will wait (for example, two weeks) before counting the results.

Questions

1. What kind of design has been described?
2. How might you improve upon what has been proposed?
3. What are the (null) hypotheses that will be tested using this design?
4. What method(s) will you use to analyze the resulting data that you obtain?
5. What strategic questions might supplement your approach to investigating these issues?

FIGURE 2.5.1 Internet Advertising and Your Brain

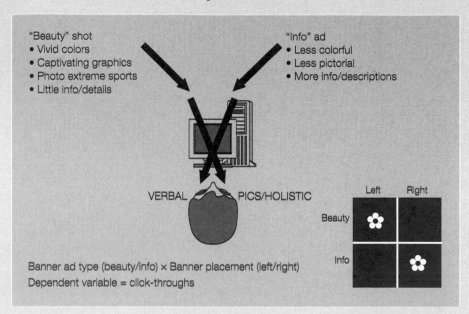

CASE 2.6

Customer Relationship Management

A long time ago, when a customer thought of a "relationship" in the marketplace, he or she might have thought of the neighborhood butcher, baker, tailor, grocer, newspaper boy, milkman, door-to-door encyclopedia salesman (ask your grandparents), etc. Now of course, the word is used a little more loosely to mean, a company knows something about your past purchases and some of your preferences, and it tries to use that information to figure out how to get you to buy some of their other products. This knowledge is stored in huge databases, and marketing researchers and direct marketing managers try to "mine" the data to find nuggets of insight that they can implement to get you to buy more.

Table 2.6.1 shows the beginning of what an example database looks like. This particular data set is captured from Web visits, but catalog data look similar. You'd have access to the household/customer's electronic contact information, which is important of course, because once you understand the data, you want to take advantage of the new-found marketing knowledge by sending more announcements, ads, pdf catalogs, etc. to the people in your database whom you think are the best prospects for more purchases.

TABLE 2.6.1 Customer Relationship Management (CRM) Data

Contact E-mail	On Page	Past Purchase	Bought Now	$
jack@v.com	10.15:08:15:34	0	0	0
bert@x.gov	10.12:14:35:22	3	0	0
elena@swim.com	09.01:22:23:09	1	1	49.99
chris@ggk.net	10.14:03:46:13	1	0	0
craig@ledg.com	08.04:10:13:19	1	0	0
nanc@wash.gov	09.29:13:09:54	0	0	0
marina@agon.com	10.14:09:04:44	2	1	12.99
more1@erb.edu	09.15:16:40:11	0	0	0
. . .				
Etc.				

TABLE 2.6.2 CRM Aggregated Data

Most Recent Week of Visit	Bought before	Bought this time
T=0 (this week)	693	22
T-1 (last week)	772	31
T-2 (2 weeks ago)	501	62
T-3 (3 weeks ago)	596	109
T-4 (last month of previous)	7438	233

Of those who bought this time, value of purchase:	Bought before?	
	Yes ("Loyals")	No ("Acquisitions")
$5–25	5	5
$26–50	50	23
$51–100	45	54
$101–200	36	36
$200–350	99	15
$351+	74	15

The variables in this data set are as follows. First, the company has captured the time of the most recent Web visit (the units are month.day:hour:minutes:second); the total number of purchases this customer has made from the company's Web site in the past (since the beginning of the Web site database); a 0/1 variable indicating whether they bought during this particular Web visit. Finally, the last variable is the information about the purchase, if they made one, and what the dollar value was of purchases they made this time.

Customer Relationship Management databases (and direct marketing databases) have several distinctive properties: (1) they have gobs of observations, in our example, tens of thousands of Web visiting potential customers; (2) yet they often have very few variables; and (3) even stranger, these databases are mostly full of zeroes (this property of these large databases would be more obvious if you saw the entire data set, but it is clearer in the table that follows). But this makes sense . . . think about your own Web site visits— what proportion of them translate into sales for the company? Some do, but we "browse" a lot too, or we might look several times before actually buying, etc.

Table 2.6.2 gives a picture of the aggregated data. Use the information in the tables to answer the following.

Questions

1. How many people are in this database? How is the database defined, i.e., what single criterion is required, that, once the customer does it, the customer is entered into the database?

2. Is there any way to test whether the 80:20 rule, where 20% of your customers are responsible for 80% of the purchases, applies here? If so, what's the answer? If not, what's an analogous question that might be answered?

3. Is there a marketing problem with the products being sold? If you were showing these numbers to your company's CEO, the CEO might say that the response rates look low, but how do you know what's low? Go online and search for statistics on direct marketing rates of conversion to make comparisons and evaluate these proportions.

4. What are some of the descriptive questions the marketing manager could pose that the marketing research could answer? What additional variables do you think the database manager should begin capturing? What new marketing questions would that information allow you to address?

5. What are some questions that a marketer might pose that could be answered if you designed an experiment? What would your experimental group be? Who would compose your control group? What would you do to the experimental group? What response would you measure in the experimental and control groups to make comparisons?

6. In general, how could you use databases like these to think about segmentation studies? How could you study price sensitivities? How could you compute lifetime customer values? How might you pretest an ad? How would you select the segments you would target?

7. If you were to implement any of the marketing research procedures you've just proposed, how would you measure the effectiveness of the marketing change? How would you demonstrate the value of the marketing information in leading to that marketing decision?

CASE 2.7

Ethnography in Practice: The Case of ESPN Zone, Chicago[2]

ESPN—THE BRAND

ESPN was founded in 1979 and bought by Disney in 1996. It is the first network to own the rights to broadcast all major pro sports leagues (NFL, MLB, NBA, NHL) as well as college basketball and college football. ESPN is a highly successful brand: awareness is strong (97% among Americans, comparable to Coca-Cola); 87 million Americans rely on ESPN for their sports, the channel is #1 in local cable advertising sales ($500 million last year). ESPN Zone is essentially an elaborate sports bar brand extension.

---

[2] The authors are grateful to Adam Duhachek for writing this case.

FIELD SITE BACKGROUND AND PROJECT MISSION

ESPN Zone, Chicago embodies recent retail trends toward enhancing brand image through the creation of flagship brand stores. The site inhabits a stretch of E. Ohio St. in Chicago's Magnificent Mile retail corridor, with neighboring stores for Sony, Nike, Disney, and Harley-Davidson. ESPN Zone, Chicago is a 35,000 square-foot retail complex that includes a 10,000 square-foot sports video and skill game arena, as well as a large sports screening room and two separate dining areas (see Figure 2.7.1).

THE RESEARCH

The research team, consisting of two faculty and four doctoral students, set out to understand this retail servicescape, extracting themes emergent from consumers' experiences at ESPN Zone and meanings consumers associate with the ESPN brand. To illustrate the evolutionary nature of ethnography, the discussion proceeds chronologically. We divide the research into three, six-week stages and discuss critical aspects associated with each stage.

STAGE 1 (WEEKS 1–6)

First, permission to conduct the observations and interviews on-site was procured from the store's managers. This took several meetings with several managers requesting additional detail.

The research team then organized a plan for on-site coverage, for each day of the week, all times of the day. The team also convened bi-weekly strategy meetings to share field notes, compare observations and preliminary interpretations, and adjust field immersion and interviewing strategies as necessary.

Very early on it became clear that the highly brand loyal ESPN customers considered the heart of ESPN Zone to be the "Screening Room." This room houses dozens of

FIGURE 2.7.1 Topographic Map of ESPN Zone, Chicago

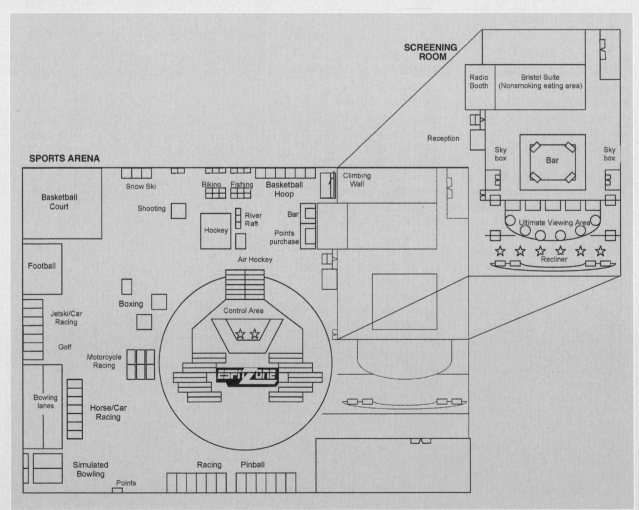

TV screens at various points in the room such that multiple screens are plainly visible no matter one's position in the room. The focal point of the room is an electronic monolith consisting of digital boards reminiscent of a Las Vegas sportsbook displaying sports statistics, and 12 medium-sized TV screens outlining an enormous 16' × 12' television.

In this room, we were struck by the ways in which gender was made salient. For instance, the best seats in the room, a row of leather recliners (called the "Throne Zone") equipped with stereo sound speakers, a tray table for food and drink, and remote controls to tune in particular games, were disproportionately occupied by men. Women in this room rarely sat in these highly visible chairs. In preliminary on-site interviews, we elicited widely contrasting views from men and women about their experiences "in the chair." Women referred to their experience in the chair as one marked by sensations of conspicuousness and discomfort, and isolation stemming from the difficulty in maintaining conversation with friends directly to their right or left in adjacent recliners. Men, however, seemed to relish this sense of isolation. Men consistently remarked that their experience in the chair was sports nirvana, a transcendental couch potato episode of extreme comfort and luxury that allowed them to experience games without distraction.

STAGE 2 (WEEKS 7–12)

In this stage of the research, we began to delve deeper into the emerging themes. For example, consumer experiences throughout the Zone seem to be distinguished by varying levels of personal control and interactions with technology (see Table 2.7.1). To test or validate these thematic interpretations, the focus of the research tools turn to interviews,

TABLE 2.7.1 Games and Arenas Catalogued by Perceptions of Control and Technology/Media

	Low Technology	High Technology / Interactive Media
High Perceived Control	*Example Games:* • Armchair Quarterback • 3-Point Basketball Game	*Example Games:* • Car Racing
	Representative Activity: • Walking around game arena floor • Watching others participate in games	*Representative Activity:* • Sitting in Throne Zone • Viewing across multiple sound and television feeds
	Consumer Sensations/Themes: • Competition • Skill • Athleticism • Confidence	*Consumer Sensations/Themes:* • Mind/body dissociation • Unaware of passage of time
Low Perceived Control	*Example Games:* • Skeet Shooting	*Example Games:* • 3-D Bowling • 3-D Boxing
	Representative Activity: • Standing in lower level bar when Screening Room is closed (for private parties or at capacity)	*Representative Activity:* • Standing in rear of Screening Room, reacting viscerally to large screen in front
	Consumer Sensations/Themes: • Frustration • Envy • Isolation	*Consumer Sensations/Themes:* • Passivity • Increased effort • Embarrassment

conducted to see if the resulting consumer verbatim responses would concur or refute our initial impressions.

At this point, we began to encounter an unanticipated methodological difficulty. The site often prohibited elaborate conversations with consumers because the atmosphere is noisy, and the people we wished to interview were engaged in sports games as participants (we couldn't interrupt their video game) or as spectators (they were watching a game and we were distracting them). Thus, we ran print ads in the *Trib* to recruit informants for longer interviews off-site that allowed us to probe deeper in an interview session ($50 for 2 hours).

From these longer interviews, we began to converge on another critical Zone consumer theme, one related to consumers' sense of reality in different areas within ESPN Zone. For example, in the game arena, consumers formulated strong opinions about which games were "really real." The entertainment ranged from sophisticated virtual reality games (like the virtual reality boxing game where players actually don gloves to battle digitally created foes, or the skydiver game where virtual reality headsets cast the illusion that consumers were "really" falling toward a target landing site), to more traditional, "real" skill games such as the armchair quarterback game where consumers must throw "real" footballs through "real" cardboard cutout receivers to earn points before the timeclock expires.

Consumer interpretations of these experiences ran counter to our team's preconceived notions. Many consumers told us that the computer-mediated reality games felt more "real" than those where there was no digital interface. In probing deeper, we found that consumers thought the computers enhanced the feelings that they were "really playing the game."

STAGE 3 (WEEKS 13–18)

In the final stages of the research, the focus of the field immersion became more precise. We sought further consumer insight into such themes as: the meaning and importance of sport, consumers' associations and images of the ESPN brand, consumer fantasy, the phenomenology of television viewing, etc. These themes were explored in greater depth by asking consumers specific questions around these topics, rather than conducting completely consumer-driven, unstructured interviews as was done earlier in the project. At this point in the research, we also employed projective techniques by having consumers view photographs and other artifacts collected on-site to improve the sharpness of their expositions.

CONCLUSION

Although this brief synopsis omits a number of insights emergent from this extended field research project, the sampling of ethnographic findings and summary of the research trajectory taken were meant to illustrate ethnographic techniques. Market researchers are frequently asked to procure relevant, consumer-driven insights to guide managerial practice. Ever increasingly, researchers are finding that such insights are practically obtained via ethnography.

Questions

1. What kind of information have these researchers discovered?
2. How is the nature of this information related to the research methodology?
3. How might these findings be communicated back to "management"?
4. What kinds of marketing decisions can be made on the basis of this kind of study?

PART 3

Design Data-Collection Methods and Forms

Part 3 covers the third stage in the research process—designing the methods of data collection and the data-collection forms.

- Chapter 7 focuses on secondary data as an information resource.

- Chapter 8 presents the main methods of data collection.

- In Chapter 9, you learn how to construct questionnaires.

- Chapter 10 discusses the general topic of attitude measurement and reviews the many types of attitude scales. The appendix to Chapter 10 presents the criteria for assessing the quality of questionnaires—reliability and validity.

## CHAPTER 7

Data Collection: Secondary Data

Questions to Guide Your Learning:

Q1: What are *secondary data*? What are the advantages and disadvantages of these sources of information?

Q2: What are some of the key sources of *internal* and *external* secondary data?

Q3: What kind of free data does the *government* compile?

Q4: What kinds of data are available from *commercial* providers?

Once the research problem is defined and clearly specified, the research effort logically turns to data collection. The natural temptation for inexperienced researchers is to advocate some sort of survey among appropriate respondent groups. However, surveys shouldn't be conducted until other possibilities have been exhausted. First attempts at data collection should logically focus on secondary data. We'll show you why.

Secondary data are statistics that already exist; they had been gathered for a previous purpose, not your particular study. **Primary data,** in contrast, are originated by the researcher for the purpose of the immediate investigation at hand. The purpose of the research defines the distinction of the data. For example, if GE collected information on the demographic characteristics of refrigerator purchasers to determine who buys various refrigerators, this information would be primary data. If the company looked up this same information from internal records gathered previously for other purposes (e.g., warranty information) or from published statistics, the information would be considered secondary data.

Using Secondary Data

Inexperienced researchers usually underestimate the amount of secondary data available. Table 7.1 lists just some of the information on people and households that is available, even down to the refined level of small geographic areas, due to the government's population census. Secondary data possess important advantages over primary data, so the researcher should always start with secondary data, particularly given the "information explosion" and the enormous volume of existing data. If you go online and conclude, "There are no data on this out there," you haven't looked hard enough.

Advantages of Secondary Data

The most significant advantages of secondary data are the *cost* and *time* economies they offer. If the required information is available as secondary data, the researcher simply needs to get online or go to the library, locate the appropriate sources, and extract and record the information desired. Doing so takes little time and involves little cost. If the information was collected in a field survey, the following steps would have been executed: (1) data-collection form designed and pretested, (2) field interview staff selected and trained, (3) sampling plan devised, (4) data gathered and checked for accuracy and omissions, and (5) data coded and tabulated.

As a conservative estimate, the survey process would take 2–3 months and could cost $1000s, because it would include expenses and wages for field and office personnel. With secondary data, these expenses have been incurred by the original source of the information and don't need to be borne again by the current user. Expenses are shared by the users of commercial sources of secondary data, but even so, the user's costs will be much less than had the firm collected the same information itself.

These time and cost economies prompt the general admonition: *Do not bypass secondary data.* Begin with secondary data, and only when the secondary data are exhausted or show diminishing returns, proceed to primary data. Sometimes secondary data may provide enough insight that there is no need to collect primary data on

TABLE 7.1
Information from the
Population Census

	Population	Housing
All households report on:	• Household relationships • Gender • Race • Age • Marital status • Hispanic origin	• Number of units in structure • Number of rooms in unit • Tenure owned or rented • Value of owned unit, or rent paid
Some households report on:	• Education • Place of birth, citizenship • Language spoken at home • Disability • Veteran status • Occupation • Commute	• Source of water • Autos, light tricks, vans • Year structure built • Year moved into residence

the topic. This scenario is true when all the analyst needs is a ballpark estimate (and this is often the case). For example, a common question that confronts marketing research analysts is, "What is the market potential for the product or service?" Secondary data may be used to begin to answer parts of the question, such as:

- What are the estimates of proportions of potential customers in the target markets?
- How might the marketplace be segmented?
- What are the recent sales histories in the industry?
- Who are the major competitors, and what are their approximate relative market shares?
- What are the existing environmental influences that will impact the success of this venture?[1]

To use secondary data effectively, it is often necessary to make some assumptions. One practical way to do this is to vary your assumptions in "what-if" scenarios to determine how much the conclusion changes. If you alter an assumption and your forecasts don't change much, additional information on this aspect of the marketing problem probably isn't that beneficial.

Rarely do secondary data completely answer all your questions, but they typically will:

1. Help clarify the problem under investigation
2. Suggest improved methods or data for investigating the problem
3. Provide comparative benchmarks against which primary data can be more insightfully interpreted

Thus, *any good marketing research study should begin with secondary data!*

> **A good marketing research study should *always* start with secondary data.**

Disadvantages of Secondary Data

Two problems commonly arise when secondary data are used: (1) they typically do not completely fit the problem, and (2) there may be problems with their accuracy.

PROBLEMS OF FIT

Because secondary data were collected for someone else's purposes, it is rare when they fit your problem perfectly. In some cases, the fit is so poor as to render the data completely inappropriate. Secondary data may be ill-suited to problems for three reasons: (1) units of measurement, (2) class definitions, or (3) publication currency.

It is common for secondary data to be expressed in units different from those required for the project. Size of retail establishment, for instance, can be expressed in terms of gross sales, profits, square feet, and number of employees. Consumer income can be expressed by individual, family, household, and spending unit. So it is with many variables, and it is a recurring source of frustration in using secondary data.

Even if the units are consistent, the classification boundaries are often different from those needed. For example, the census data aggregates people by age into the

---

[1] Stephen Castelberry, "Using Secondary Data in Marketing Research," *Journal of Marketing Education* (Dec. 2001), pp. 195–203; even more technical questions may be addressed, such as, What are the current retail shelving slotting fees for this product category?, cf., William Wilkie, Debra Descrochers and Gregory Gundlach, "Marketing Research and Public Policy," *Journal of Public Policy and Marketing* (Fall 2002), pp. 275–288.

following categories: <18 years old, 18 to 24, 25 to 34, 35 to 44, and so on. If FirstMortgage.com sought to learn more about potential home buyers who were "30-something," to tailor its services and position its Internet banners, it would not be able to identify this age group cleanly. The firm could access data on people who were 25 to 34 and 35 to 44 years old. That imprecision may be acceptable for some purposes, but not others. Research Realities 7.1 provides another example.

Finally, secondary data quite often lack publication currency. The time from data collection to dissemination is often long—2–3 years with government census data. Census data have great value while they're current, but this value diminishes with time, given that many marketing decisions require current, rather than historical, information.

PROBLEMS OF ACCURACY

The accuracy of much secondary data is also questionable. As we discuss throughout this book, numerous sources of error are possible in the collection, analysis, and presentation of marketing information. Researchers collecting the information can assess its accuracy better than subsequent users of that information. Knowledge of the data's shortcomings can be critical for marketing decisions. When using secondary data, the researcher is not relieved from assessing accuracy, although the task is indeed more difficult.[2] The following criteria, though, should help the researcher judge the accuracy of any secondary data: (1) the *source*, (2) the *purpose of publication*, and (3) *general evidence regarding quality*.

Secondary data can be obtained from either a *primary source* or a *secondary source*. A primary source is the source that originated the data. A secondary source is a source that, in turn, obtained the data from the original source. The *Statistical Abstract of the United States*, which is published each year, contains a great deal of useful information for many research projects. The *Statistical Abstract* is a secondary source (of secondary data), because none of what is published in the *Statistical Abstract* originates there. Rather, all of it is compiled from other government and trade sources. The researcher who terminated the search for secondary data with the *Statistical Abstract* would violate the most fundamental rule in using secondary data—*always use the primary source of secondary data*.

Why? Two reasons. First, the researcher needs to look for general evidence of quality. The primary source is typically the only source that describes the methods of data collection and analysis, thus it is the only source by which this judgment can be made. Second, a primary source is usually more accurate and complete than a secondary source. Secondary sources typically do not include the caveats and qualifications included as disclaimers by the primary source. Errors in transcription can even occur in copying the data from a primary source.

A second criterion by which the accuracy of secondary data can be assessed is the purpose of publication. If CNN announced, "Studies show that pizza can be the mainstay in a healthy diet," wouldn't it matter if the research were sponsored by the American Heart Association versus a pizza restaurant franchise? In which case might you believe the claims? In which case might you have confidence in the objectivity of the results? The objectivity of data is generally suspect when the findings are used as propaganda; that is, to promote sales or to advance the causes of a political party or special industry.

---

[2] Ernest Ackermann and Karen Hartmann, *Searching and Researching on the Internet and the World Wide Web* (Franklin Beedle and Associates, 2003); Paula Berinstein and Charles Cotton, *Business Statistics on the Web: Find Them Fast—At Little or No Cost* (Cyberage Books, 2003).

Research Realities

7.1 Challenges in Categorizing Ethnicity in the Census

The most recent census survey was modified with regard to categories for reporting race or ethnicity. To recognize the increasing diversity of the U.S. population, citizens were offered the opportunity to check multiple affiliations to identify their ethnic origin more precisely. In addition, the ethnicity categories were refined, offering more distinct options.

Of particular interest was the attempt to clarify the meaning of the "Latino" or "Hispanic" category. This concern was addressed by providing more subcategories.

Take a look at the form. One person in the household answers this question for everyone in the household, hence the odd wording:

Regardless of the good intentions (for political correctness and greater measurement accuracy), census administrators were disappointed with the "confusion of the results," and are working to clarify the categories and instructions for the next census. They said the results were confusing because 43% of the Hispanic/Latino citizens marked "Some other race" in question 6. The instructions said to complete both questions 5 and 6, so if you were Hispanic, what would you have marked? (Who's writing these surveys anyway? Not someone who has read this book! Election results anyone?)

---

5) **Is this person Spanish / Hispanic / Latino**? Mark the "**No**" box if **not** Spanish / Hispanic / Latino:

☐ No, not Spanish / Hispanic / Latino   ☐ Yes, Puerto Rican

☐ Yes, Mexican, Mexican American, Chicano   ☐ Yes, Cuban

☐ Yes, other Spanish / Hispanic / Latino—print group:

— — — — — — — — — — — — — — — —

6) **What is this person's race? Mark one or more races** to indicate what this person considers himself/herself to be:

☐ White

☐ Black, African American, or Negro

☐ American Indian or Alaska Native— print name of principal tribe:

— — — — — — — — — — — — — — — —

☐ Asian Indian   ☐ Japanese   ☐ Native Hawaiian

☐ Chinese   ☐ Korean   ☐ Guamanian or Chamorro

☐ Filipino   ☐ Vietnamese   ☐ Samoan

☐ Other Asian—print race: ☐ Other Pacific Islander—print race:

— — — — — — — — — — — — — — — —

☐ Some other race—print race:

— — — — — — — — — — — — — — — —

Fun census facts

1. U.S. population is estimated at 281,421,906 (906? Sure not 907?)
2. 97.6 of us claimed "one race" (marked only one box); 2.3% claimed 2 races, .1% claimed 3.
3. About 43% of Hispanics/Latinos classified themselves as "Some other race" and 97% of the people reporting themselves as "Some other race" were Hispanic or Latino.
4. Hispanic or Latino is considered an ethnicity; people may be of any race (e.g., Mexican, Cuban, Puerto Rican)
5. There were 28 Hispanic or Latino categories: Mexican, Puerto Rican, Cuban, Dominican Republic, Central American (Costa Rican, Guatemalan, Honduran, Nicaraguan, Panamanian, Sal-

vadoran, Other Central American), South American (Argentinean, Bolivian, Chilean, Colombian, Ecuadorian, Paraguayan, Peruvian, Uruguayan, Venezuelan, Other South American), Other Hispanic or Latino (Spaniard, Spanish, Spanish American, All other Hispanic or Latino)

6. 66.1% of the U.S. Hispanic population is composed of people of Mexican origin; 14.5% from Central and South America, 9.0% Puerto Rican, 4.0% Cuban, 6.4% all other
7. Five Alaska Native categories: Alaska Athabaskan, Aleut, Eskimo, Tlingit-Haida, All other tribes
8. 36 American Indian categories: Apache, Blackfeet, Cherokee, Cheyenne, Chickaswa, Chippewa, Choctaw, Colville, Comanche,

(continued)

Cree, Creek, Crow, Delaware, Houma, Iroquois, Kiowa, Latin American (Aztec, Inca, Mayan, etc.), Lumbee, Menominee, Navajo, Osage, Ottawa, Palute, Pima, Potawatomi, Pueblo, Puget Sound Salish, Seminole, Sioux, Tohomo O'Odham, Ute, Yakama, Yaqui, Yuman, All other categories

9. 17 detailed Asian categories: Asian Indian, Bangladeshi, Cambodian, Chinese except Taiwanese, Filipino, Hmong, Indonesian, Japanese, Korean, Laotian, Malaysian, Pakistani, Sri Lankan, Taiwanese, Thai, Vietnamese, Other Asian

10. 12 detailed Native Hawaiian and Pacific Islander categories: Polynesian (Native Hawaiian, Samoan, Tongan, Other Polynesian), Micronesian (Guamanian or Chamorro, Other Micronesian), Melanesian (Fijian, Other Melanesian), Other Pacific Islander.

An important direct use of shifting populations is the allocation of the number of seats each state is entitled to in the House of Representatives according to the Constitution. Federal programs that address Affirmative Action, Community Reinvestments, and Public Health Services also use this information. Beyond politics and civics, there are commercial implications; e.g., the multicultural Hispanic market comprises 13% of the U.S. population, resulting from a 58% growth in the previous decade. Clearly these numbers represent huge opportunities. Companies as varied as Hanes, Enterprise Rent-a-Car, Sears, H&R Block, and ESPN are paying attention, introducing tailored market offerings, and bilingual advertising appeals.

Sources: Eduardo Porter, "Census Forms Work Hard to Find Proper Way to Identify Hispanics," *Wall Street Journal* (Jan. 21, 2003), p. A.12; John Kavaliunas, "Get Ready to Use Census Data" *Marketing Research* 12 (Fall 2000), pp. 42–43; Paul Miller, "The Overlooked Hispanic Market," *Catalog Age* 20 (Jan. 2003), p. 23; Eduardo Porter, "Buying Power of Hispanics Is Set to Soar," *Wall Street Journal* (April 18, 2003), p. B1; Laurel Wentz, "Hispanic Market Stays Hot," *Advertising Age* 74 (Feb. 3, 2003), p. 26. See http://www.census.gov.

You can be most confident in a source that has no ax to grind but, rather, publishes secondary data as its primary business function. If data publication is a source's *raison d'être,* high quality must be maintained to ensure its own long-term sustenance. Inaccurate data offer a firm no competitive advantage, and poor quality data would eventually lead to its demise. The success of any organization supplying data as its primary purpose depends on the long-term satisfaction of its users that the information supplied is indeed accurate.[3]

The third criterion by which the accuracy of secondary data can be assessed is the general evidence of quality. One item of evidence here is the ability of the supplying organization to collect the data. The Internal Revenue Service, for example, has greater leverage in securing income data than does an independent marketing research firm. Related to this issue, though, is the question of whether the additional leverage introduces bias. Would a respondent be more likely to hedge in estimating income in completing a tax return or in responding to a consumer survey? In addition, the user needs to ascertain how the data were collected. A primary source should provide a detailed description of the methodology, including definitions, data-collection forms, methods of sampling, and so forth. If it does not, researcher beware! Such omissions are usually indicative of sloppy methods.

When the details of data collection are provided, the user of secondary data should examine them thoroughly. Was the sampling plan sound? Was this type of data best collected through questionnaire or by observational methods? What about the quality of the field force—what kind of training was provided, what kinds of checks of the fieldwork were employed? What was the extent of nonresponse due to refusals, to respondents not at home, and by item? Is the information presented in a well-organized manner? Are the tables properly labeled, and are the data within them internally consistent? Are the conclusions supported by the data? As these questions suggest, the user of secondary data must be familiar with the research process and the potential sources of error, and we address all these elements throughout the book.

---

[3] Robert Granader, "Choose Off-the-Shelf Studies Carefully," *Marketing News* (Sept. 24, 2001), pp. 25–26; also see the National Council on Public Polls' words on the matter, e.g., "Who paid for the poll and why was it done?" (http://www.ncpp.org).

Types of Secondary Data

Secondary data can be classified in several ways. One of the most useful is by source: **internal data** are those found within one's own organization, whereas **external data** are those obtained from outside sources. The external sources can be further classified into those that regularly publish statistics and make them available to the user at no charge (such as the United States government) and the commercial organizations that sell their services to various users (e.g., Information Resources, ACNielsen). Together they represent the most commonly used sources of secondary data, the places where researchers begin (see Figure 7.1).

Internal Secondary Data

Data that originate within the firm are internal data. The sales and cost data compiled in the normal accounting cycle represent promising internal secondary data for many research problems, such as evaluating past marketing strategy or assessing the firm's competitive position in the industry. In future-directed decisions, such as evaluating a new product or a new advertising campaign, internal sales data are more helpful simply as a foundation for planning the research.

The sales invoice alone is a very productive source document. From it, information can be extracted such as:

- Customer name and location
- Products and services sold
- Volume and dollar amount of the transaction
- Salesperson or agent responsible for the sale
- Location of customer facility where product is to be shipped and/or used
- Customer's industry, class of trade, and/or channel of distribution
- Applicable discount
- Transportation used in shipment, etc.

For answers and data, start in-house.

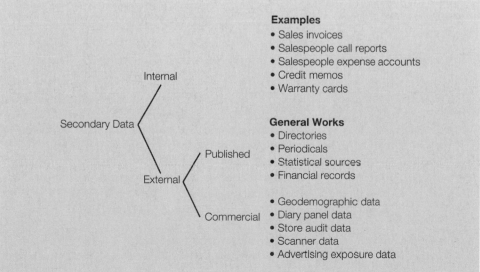

FIGURE 7.1
Types of Secondary Data

Loyalty programs, membership clubs, and Internet shopping allow companies to accumulate the details of each sale for each transaction over time with each customer. The marketing orientation is changing toward a longer-term relational database approach—a stored and continually updated sequence of sales transactions. Ideally, such detailed data also enable the firm to offer customized market offerings to the consumer, with the presumed goal of greater customer satisfaction. In reality, many companies are overwhelmed with the enormous size of the databases, and are only beginning to learn how to sort through the masses of information (see Research Realities 7.2).

Other internal documents provide more specialized input (see Table 7.2). Most companies are likely to use only two or three of these sources of sales information in addition to the sales invoice. The selections depend on the company and the types of analyses used to plan and evaluate the marketing effort.

TABLE 7.2
Sources of Internal
Secondary Data

Document	Info Provided
Cash register receipts	• Type (cash or credit) and dollar amount of transaction by department by salesperson
Salesperson's call reports	• Customers and prospects called on (company and individual seen; planned or unplanned calls) • Products discussed • Orders obtained • Customers' product needs and usage • Other significant information about customers • Distribution of salesperson's time among customer calls, travel, and office work • Sales-related activities: meetings, conventions
Salesperson's expense reports	• Expenses by day, by item (hotels, meals, travel, accounts)
Individual customer (and prospect) records	• Name and location and customer • Number of calls by company salesperson (agents) • Sales by company (in dollars and/or units, by product or service, by location of customer facility) • Customer's industry, class of trade, and/or trade channel • Estimated total annual usage of each product or service sold by the company • Estimated annual purchases from the company of each such product or service • Location (in terms of company sales territory)
Financial records	• Sales revenue (by product, geographic market, customer, class of trade, unit of sales organization) • Direct sales expenses (similarly classified) • Overhead sales costs (similarly classified) • Profits (similarly classified)
Credit memos	•Returns and allowances
Warranty cards	• Indirect measures of dealer sales • Customer service

Research Realities

7.2 Data Mining

Data mining is the term applied to the exercise of digging through a lot of "coal"—seemingly uninteresting data—to find the golden nugget of useful marketing information. The analogy is continued when researchers speak of "drilling down" into the data. Database technology, statistics, and business acumen are all brought to bear in data mining. The phenomenon of making sense out of data is not new, but what is new is the enormous size of the databases on which the analytics are applied, due in part to the reduction in the expense of data storage technology (>$10 per megabyte 10 years ago to pennies today).

The databases are also extensive due to the pervasiveness of loyalty programs, which allow a company to accumulate a great deal of knowledge about consumer purchase histories and expenditures, preferences, and demographics. However, data mining assisted database marketers and direct marketers even before loyalty programs; e.g., if a magazine can communicate its readership profile clearly, it can generate more advertising revenue and do so more efficiently, facilitating the support of the magazine, and in turn, enhancing a more relevant fit of ads for the readers. As an example, Conde Nast, after analyzing its data on its 10 million subscribers across 17 magazines, noted a subscriber segment that owned Lexus automobiles and also had an affinity to Coach leather products. This ultimately resulted in a Lexus partnership with Coach leather interiors.

Data mining can enrich relationship management. The benefit to the company is the discovery and understanding of one's best (most profitable) customers, and an ability to experiment with market offerings because it can track customers' sales responses to various promotions. The benefit to business customers can be direct store delivery (the replenishment of inventory as stock is electronically counted down) and the coordination of invoices and ven-

dors. The benefit to end-user consumers is usually a product tailored more specifically to their particular needs.

For the portions of customer databases that are quantitative, sample sizes are typically huge, so most inferential statistics (t-tests) are generally significant. Thus, analysts often rely on simple descriptive statistics, such as means and correlations. Regressions and predictions are also common, as are cluster analyses to form customer segments. The goals of all these analyses are standard marketing fare: customer acquisition (responses to offers), retention (targeting valuable customers who may be tempted to leave to competitors), and even customer abandonment (identifying where to minimize service to costly customers).

For the qualitative data on customers, such as click-stream data, stored e-mail communications, or histories of Web page traversals, analysts use "text mining" techniques. These methods are comparable to standard descriptive statistics, but are applied to alphabetic strings rather than numeric strings of data.

Recommendation technologies (RTs) such as those on books and CD e-tail vendors can be applied to the large quantitative or qualitative databases. These algorithms are the fastest-growing models among data mining tools. The models use "collaborative filtering," which is a form of cluster analysis to identify similar users, who, due to their similarity, help (collaborate) in creating overlapping lists of products that form the basis of the recommendations. (We say more about the models underlying these recommendations in the chapter on multivariate statistics, in the section on cluster analysis.)

Sources: Maggie Biggs, "Resurgent Text-Mining Technology Can Greatly Increase Your Firm's 'Intelligence' Factor," *InfoWorld* 22 (Jan. 10, 2000), p. 52; Barbara Depompa Reimers, "Getting Personal," *Informationweek* (Jan. 3, 2000), pp. 51–55.

Another useful but often overlooked source of internal secondary data is previous marketing research studies on related topics. Even though each study typically addresses a number of specific questions, great synergy can result when the key learnings are studied and combined. Many marketing research and consulting firms have built internal video libraries in which key personnel describe a study they had recently executed for a client. These video clips are cross-referenced by keywords such as industry, segment, marketing issue, and the study's purpose, etc., and they can be accessed over the firm's intranet. Managers at these firms are convinced that such aggregations of knowledge are yielding a competitive advantage as their researchers collectively move further and more quickly up the learning curve, compared to their counterparts at competitor firms.

Two of the most important advantages associated with internal secondary data are their ready availability and low cost. Internal secondary data are the least costly of any type of marketing research. Internal sales data can be used to analyze the company's sales performance by product, geographic location, customer, channel of distribution, and so on. Cost data allow the further determination of the profitability of these segments of the business.

Searching for Published External Secondary Data

Such a wealth of external data exists that beginning researchers typically underestimate what is available. Some relevant external secondary data are available on almost any problem a marketer might confront. The fundamental problem is not availability; it is identifying and accessing what is there. See Figure 7.2 for some guidelines to get started on a search of secondary data.

STEP 1

Identify what you already know and what you wish to know about your topic, including relevant facts, names of researchers or organizations associated with the topic, and key papers and other familiar publications.

STEP 2

Develop a list of keywords and names. These terms will provide access to secondary sources. Unless you have a very specific topic of interest, it is better to keep this initial list long and general.

FIGURE 7.2
How to Search
Published Sources
of Secondary Data

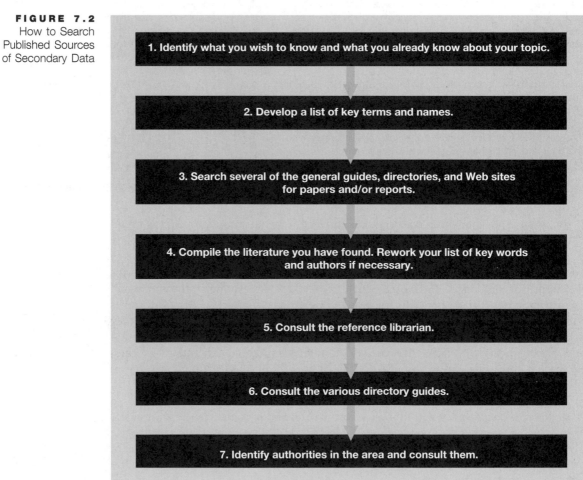

1. Identify what you wish to know and what you already know about your topic.

2. Develop a list of key terms and names.

3. Search several of the general guides, directories, and Web sites for papers and/or reports.

4. Compile the literature you have found. Rework your list of key words and authors if necessary.

5. Consult the reference librarian.

6. Consult the various directory guides.

7. Identify authorities in the area and consult them.

STEP 3

You are ready to use the Internet or the library. Begin with the directories listed throughout this chapter and on our Web site. Look at only the previous 2–3 years of work in the area, using 3–4 general guides. Some directories and indexes use a specialized list of keywords or descriptors. Such indexes often have thesauri that can help you map your keywords onto the directory's terms.

STEP 4

Compile the literature you have found. Is it relevant to your needs? You may be overwhelmed by information, or you may have found little that is relevant (if so, rework your list of keywords and expand the search to include a few more years and a few additional sources). By the end of step 4, you should have a clear idea of the nature of the information you are seeking and sufficient background to use more specialized sources.

STEP 5

One very useful specialized source is a reference librarian. These people are specialists who have been trained to know the contents of many of the key information sources in a library and on the Web, as well as how to search those sources most effectively. (Don't think that just because you know Yahoo or Google that these people can't help you.)

STEP 6

If you have had little success or your topic is highly specialized, consult more general guides to information. These are really directories of directories, which means the search will be very general. You first need to identify potentially useful primary directories, which will then lead you to other sources.

STEP 7

If you are still unhappy with what you have found, use an authority. Identify some individual or organization that might know something about the topic. The *Consultants and Consulting Organizations Directory, Encyclopedia of Associations,* or *Research Centers Directory* should help you identify sources. The Bureau of the Census puts out a list of department specialists whom users can contact for information on any of the bureau's studies. These people are knowledgeable about related studies in their areas of expertise. Faculty at universities, government officials, and business executives can also be useful sources of information.

> **Some sources of *secondary data* are free. Others, you have to pay for, but it's still usually *less expensive* and *faster* than collecting primary data.**

Key General Sources of External Secondary Data

Additional important sources of external secondary data are associations, general guides to useful marketing information, and online computer searches.

ASSOCIATIONS

Most associations gather detailed information on such matters as industry sales, growth patterns, environmental factors affecting the industry, etc. Trade associations are often able to get information from members that other research organizations cannot because of the working relationships that exist between the association and its member firms. Two useful sources for locating associations serving a particular industry are *Directories in Print* and the *Encyclopedia of Associations* (described online).

GENERAL GUIDES TO BUSINESS INFORMATION

There are many useful sources for locating information on any given topic. Table 7.3 lists what the *Encyclopedia of Business Information Sources* has to say about data sources on just one single industry. It is important also to acquaint yourself with the general sources of marketing information so that you know what statistics are available and where they can be found.

Online Computer Searches

Online computer searches are the state of the art, having become increasingly popular, more comprehensive, and user-friendly for locating published information and data via computer-readable storage systems and databases. Many public and university libraries have invested in the equipment and personnel necessary to make database searching available to their patrons. There are several thousand databases to pick from, with several hundred of them applying to business.

One huge, free, accessible database that should never be overlooked is the census data. The census data contain information on population characteristics as well as economic and business conditions. The directory begins at http://www.census.gov. See Research Realities 7.3 for an overview of this amazing resource.

An online service involves three main components: a database producer, a database vendor, and a data user. The database producer collects the information and edits it according to the organization's criteria, compiles it, and sells it to the vendor. The vendor mounts the data onto a computer, or e.g., sells the information on a CD. The vendor might combine or split the information to fit its own needs, thus, the same database from different vendors might have different subsets of information. The vendor pays a fee every time the database is used online and pays a fee for all citations from it. Public libraries and university access are often free, but some sources charge for accessing the database, and sometimes for printing charges. Some useful databases for marketers contain the following information (for an overview of resources accessible through our Web site, see Research Realities 7.4):

- *Specific company or industry information:* This information comes primarily from reports filed with the Securities and Exchange Commission, stockholder reports, and stock market information. The databases cover financial, marketing, and product information, some company profiles, and the usual directory information, such as the name of the organization and its address and phone number. For example, both Moody's and Standard and Poor's provide both U.S. and international corporate profiles (see http://moodys.com and http://www.computstat.com or http://www2.standardandpoors.com). And of course, Internet search engines (e.g., the business category at Yahoo.com) are extremely useful in locating information about companies.
- *Mergers, affiliations, ownership information:* These databases list the institutions and people that own a stock by name, ownership changes, including the mergers and acquisitions that have taken place in the recent past or are pending. Examples include Disclosure/Spectrum Ownership (http://www.dialogweb.com), the Insider Trading Monitor (http://library.dialog.com) and World Trade Resources (http://www.worldtraderesources.com).
- *Company directory information:* Numerous directories are available that differ in the types of companies they cover (such as public or private), the size of the companies covered, and their geographic coverage. In addition to the name,

TABLE 7.3
Sources of Data on the
Music Industry

Abstracts and Indexes

- *Music Index*. Subject-Author Guide to 300+ International Periodicals. Harmonic Park Press. Monthly.

Bibliographies

- *Information Sources in Music*. Lewis Foreman, ed. Bowker-Saur. Evaluates information on range of topics, including copyright, music publishing, reprographics, and the use of computers in music publishing.

- *Mix Bookshelf: Information Resources for Music Professionals*. Cardinal Business Media, Inc. Annotated catalog of about 600 publications relating to music, electronic music technology, musical instruments, and the music business.

Biographical Sources

- *Celebrity Register*. The Gale Group. Profiles 1,300 famous individuals in the performing arts, sports, politics, business, and other fields.

Directories

- *Billboard's International Buyer's Guide of the Music-Record-Tape Industry*. BPI Communications. Record companies; music publishers; record and tape wholesalers; services and supplies for the music-record-tape-video industry; record and tape dealer accessories, fixtures, merchandising products; U.S. and over 65 countries.

- *Music Address Book: How to Reach Anyone Who's Anyone in the Music Business*. Michael Levine. Harper & Collins.

- *Recording Industry Sourcebook*. Cardinal Business Media, Inc. More than 12,000 listings in 57 categories of record/tape/compact disc labels, producers, distributors, managers, equipment suppliers.

Handbooks and Manuals

- *All You Need to Know About the Music Business*. Donald S. Passman. Simon & Schuster. Covers the practical and legal aspects of record contracts, music publishing, management agreements, touring, and other music business topics.

- *Entertainment Law*. Howard Siegel, ed. New York State Bar Assn. Covers legal aspects of television, motion pictures, theatre, music, phonograph records, and related topics.

Statistics Sources

- *U.S. Industry and Trade Outlook*. McGraw-Hill. Provides basic data, outlook for the current year, and Long-Term Prospects (5-year projections) for a wide variety of products and services. Includes high-technology industries.

Trade/Professional Associations

- *American Society of Composers, Authors, and Publishers*. One Lincoln Plaza, New York, NY 10023.

Source: Adapted from James Wov (ed.), *Encyclopedia of Business Information Sources*, 14th ed. (Gale, 2000), pp. 587–588.

Research Realities

7.3 Data Available from http://www.census.gov

The Bureau of the Census of the United States Department of Commerce is the largest gatherer of statistical information in the country. There are some two dozen population and economic industry censuses, all of which are of interest to the marketing researcher. Here are a few:

- **Census of Finance, Insurance, and Real Estate:** collects statistics on commercial banks, savings institutions, credit unions; life insurance providers; hospital and medical service planners; fire, marine, and casualty insurance providers; and real estate land developers. Information includes location, revenue, and payroll.
- **Census of Government:** presents information on the general characteristics of state and local governments, including employment, size of payroll, amount of indebtedness, and operating revenues and costs.
- **Census of Housing:** lists type of structure, size, building condition, occupancy, water and sewage facilities, monthly rent, average value, and equipment, including stoves, dishwashers, air conditioners. For large metropolitan areas, it provides detailed statistics by city block.
- **Census of Manufacturers:** categorizes 450 types of manufacturing establishments and contains detailed industry and geographic statistics for such items as the number of establishments, quantity of output, value added in manufacture, capital

expenditures, employment, wages, inventories, sales by customer class, and energy consumption.

- **Census of Population:** reports the population by geographic region. It also provides detailed breakdowns on such characteristics as gender, marital status, age, education, race, national origin, family size, employment and unemployment, income, and other demographic characteristics.
- **Census of Retail Trade:** classifies retail stores by type of business, presenting statistics on the number of stores, total sales, employment, and payroll. The statistics are broken down by small geographic areas, such as counties, cities, and standard metropolitan statistical areas.
- **Census of Service Industries:** provides data on receipts, employment, type of business (e.g., hotels), and number of units by small geographic areas.
- **Census of Transportation, Communications, and Utilities:** covers passenger travel, truck and bus inventory and use, and the transport of commodities by the various classes of carriers, telephone and telegraph communications, and electric, gas, steam, water, and sanitary services. Indices cover expenses, revenues, and output measures per state.

Also see Thomas Kemp, *The American Census Handbook* (Scholarly Resources, 2000).

---

address, and telephone number, many directories list the NAICS (formerly SIC) codes for the business. Examples include Dun's Business Locator (http://www.dnb.com), and Standard and Poor's Corporate Register.

- *U.S. government contract information:* These databases are particularly useful to businesses dealing with the government. They contain information on whether a specific company has any government contracts and any recent contract awards; an example is Commerce Business Daily (http://www.cbd.savvy.com).
- *Economic information:* These databases contain general economic and demographic information from U.S. census materials and from the private sector. Many even contain forecasts of future economic activity; an example is Cendata (http://www.agnic.org).
- *General business information:* These databases cover companies, industries, people, and products. Increasingly these sources locate global, not just U.S., information. The sources are primarily trade and business-oriented journals, selected newspapers, and various reports. Examples are ABI/Inform (libraries and universities have access) and Harvard Business Review (http://www.hbsp.harvard.edu/products/hbr). Lexis/Nexis facilitates searches by organizing information into categories: news, business, statistics, general reference, and legal, which are further subcategorized; e.g., the business category covers business news, financials, company comparisons, industry information, and so on.

Research Realities

7.4 Noncommercial Sources of Secondary Data

- **Census**
  - Economic
  - Population

- **Industry and Company Information**
  - Dun & Bradstreet
  - Knight-Ridder
  - Gale Research
  - Moody's Industry Review
  - Standard & Poor
  - Yahoo
  - *Fortune*
  - Dun & Bradstreet and other industry resources listed above

- **Market and Consumer Information**
  - *A Guide to Consumer Markets*
  - *Aging America—Trends and Projections* (U.S. Senate Special Committee)
  - *Marketing Economics Guide*
  - *Rand-McNally Commercial Atlas and Marketing Guide*
  - http://www.statistics.com (crime, environment, opinion surveys, sports, etc.)
  - http://www.SecondaryData.com (company annual reports, business wire, Dow Jones)
  - http://www.ojp.usdoj.gov/bjs/ Bureau of Justice Statistics

- **General Economic and Statistical Information**
  - *Economic Report of the President*
  - *The Economic Policy Institute*
  - *Federal Reserve Bulletin*
  - *The Handbook of Basic Economic Statistics*
  - *Handbook of Cyclical Indicators*
  - *Monthly Labor Review*
  - *Statistical Abstract of the United States*
  - stats.bls.gov U.S. Department of Labor statistics (consumer spending, wages, productivity, safety, etc.)

- **Indexes**
  - *ABI/Inform*
  - *The Wall Street Journal Index*

- **Academic Indexes**
  - *Social Sciences Citation Index*

- **International and Cross-Cultural Information**
  - *Country Information Kits* (http://www.opic.gov)
  - *Foreign Trade of the U.S. Statistics*
  - *Hispanic and Asian Marketing Communication Research, Inc.* (http://www.hamcr.com)
  - *Global Trade Information Services* http://www.gtis.com (world trade, state exports, atlases)
  - *Greenbook: International Directory of Marketing Research Companies and Services*
  - *United Nations Statistical Yearbook*
  - *World Almanac and Book of Facts*
  - *World Factbook*

- **Marketing Research Industry Information** providers
  - Marketing Research Association (MRA)'s *Blue Book Research Services Directory* (http://www.mra-net.org)
  - American Demographic's (http://www.demographics.com) *Marketing Tools SourceBook* (information on business services, demographics, direct marketing, ethnic marketing, Internet, mapping, media, psychographics, telemarketing, etc.)
  - American Marketing Association (http://www.marketing power.org) *Marketing News* supplements, such as the "Directory of Marketing Analysis / Software Suppliers"; "Focus Group Services"; etc. In April 23, 2003, the featured supplement was "Directory of International Marketing Research Firms" and in the Sept. 1, 2003 issue, the supplement was "Directory of Multicultural Marketing Firms."

Links to these sites at http://churchill.swlearning.com.

- *Brand name/trade name information:* These databases contain information on specific products, including what competitors might be doing with respect to new-product introductions or expenditures on advertising, and which company owns a specific trademark; e.g., Thomas Register Online (http://www.thomas register.com).

As the preceding list indicates, companies use online databases to search for marketing data, economic trends, legislation, inventions, reports, speeches, journal articles, and many other types of information on a particular topic (see Table 7.4).

In addition to using online databases, researchers can use the Internet to execute general searches to locate secondary data on a subject. Search engines compile and

TABLE 7.4
How to Conduct a
Database Search

Step 1: Specify the information to be sought and develop a "search strategy," a set of words that will be entered into the computer for the actual search.

Step 2: Log onto the host and specify the name of the database to be searched.

Step 3: Input the search strategy, e.g., keywords. When the search strategy has been entered, the computer will begin the search and will report the number of matches. If the number of matches is large, add qualifiers to the search terms to find the specific information.

Step 4: If the results are satisfactory, the user must decide the level of detail sought for each match made. The choices of published articles may include a simple bibliography, an annotated bibliography, a bibliography with abstracts, or the full text. If the system is not free (e.g., public libraries, universities for affiliated personnel), greater detail usually induces greater costs.

index an electronic catalog of Web contents, then provide the software needed to search through the index for keywords or concepts specified by the user. The indices may be directory- or word-based or a combination of the two (see Research Realities 7.5).

Standardized Marketing Information Services

Many standardized marketing information services provide another important source of secondary data. These services are available at some cost to the user and thus are more expensive than published secondary data. However, they are still typically much less expensive than primary data, because purchasers share the costs incurred in collecting, editing, coding, and tabulating these data. Because the databases must be suitable for a number of users, though, what is collected and how the data are gathered must be uniform. Thus, the data may not always fit the needs of the user, which is still their main disadvantage. Here are some of the types of standardized marketing information service data.

Customer Profiles

Market segmentation demands that firms classify their customers into relatively homogeneous groups, to tailor marketing programs for each group. A common segmentation base starts with the industry designations of its customers, by means of the North American Industry Classification System (NAICS) codes. Figure 7.3 displays an example, the categorization for marketing consultants.

One of the popular commercial services is Dun's Business Locator, an index that provides data on over 10 million U.S. businesses, including the industry code of each establishment (see dnb.com). These records allow sales management to construct B-to-B sales prospect files, define sales territories and measure territory potentials, and isolate potential new customers with particular characteristics. They allow advertising management to select prospects by size and location; to analyze market prospects and select the media to reach them; to build, maintain, and structure current mailing lists; to generate sales leads qualified by size, location, and quality; and to locate new markets for testing. They allow marketing researchers to assess market potential by

7.5 Searching the World Wide Web

Yahoo! is frequently cited as the best all-around starting point for conducting research on the Web. Fans say it's the fastest way to find Web sites dedicated to any topic.

Unlike search engines, which use computers to automatically index every word at a Web site, Yahoo is a directory with sites sorted by Yahoo's staff into subject categories (e.g., "Business and Economy"), subcategories (e.g., "Employment," "Finance and Investment"), etc.

If you need to find the Web site for General Motors quickly, but you aren't sure of the address, typing "General Motors" into Yahoo's search comes back immediately with a category listing all of GM's sites. Searching the same phrase at a search engine would call up a list of Web pages that merely contain the words "General Motors," forcing a user to sift through dozens of pages before finding the actual GM corporate site.

Yahoo's directory-style guide is speedy, but search engines are thorough—almost unbelievably so. For that reason, experts suggest that searches also include at least one of these massive indexes.

To avoid overload, don't forget to narrow your results by placing words within quotation marks; usually search engines treat these strings as one phrase (e.g., "jet ski").

Source: For more information, see Eric Bradlow and David Schmittlein, "The Little Engines That Could," *Marketing Science* 19 (2000), pp. 43–62.

FIGURE 7.3   Excerpts of NAICS Codes For *Marketing Consultant*

The NAICS codes have replaced the former SIC (Standard Industrial Classification) codes to reflect the changing economic base, and particularly to reflect more detail the growing services sectors. For example, the former SIC category of "Services" is refined into seven new categories: Information; Professional, Scientific, and Technical; Administrative Support, Waste Management and Remediation; Education; Health Care and Social Assistance; Arts, Entertainment, and Recreation; and Other Services. Newly recognized industries include: software, convenience stores, pet supply stores, HMOs, and casinos. The U.S. Census Bureau provides tables showing the correspondence between the former SIC codes and the new NAICS.

51: Information

52–53: Finance, Insurance, Real Estate

54: *Professional, Scientific, Technical Services* →

55: Management of Companies

54:15: Computer System Design

54:16: *Management, Scientific, Technical Consulting* →

54:17: Scientific R&D

54:18: Advertising and Related Services

54:16:1.1: Administrative Management, General Management Consulting

54:16:1.2: Human Resources and Executive Search Consulting

54:16:1.3: *Marketing Consulting Service*

54:16:1.4: Process, Physical Distribution, Logistics Consulting

54:16:1.8: Other Management Consulting

54:16:2: Environmental Consulting Services

---

territory; to measure market penetration in terms of numbers of prospects and numbers of customers; and to make comparative analyses of overall performance by districts and sales territories and in individual industries.

Analogously, firms selling consumer goods cannot afford to target individual customers, because no single customer is likely to buy much of any product or service. Rather, firms need to target groups of customers. Their ability to do this has increased substantially with the electronic census. The Census Bureau makes available computer files of the facts that have been gathered that make the data usable from your laptop. Having the data available in electronic form allows their tabulation by geographic boundaries, and other cuts of the data. "Geodemographers" combine census data with survey data or other data (e.g., motor vehicle registrations, credit card transactions), to produce customized products for their clients.

For example, R. L. Polk has a product for retailers called the Vehicle Origin Survey (http://www.stratmap.com and http://www.polk.com). Polk gathers license-plate numbers from cars parked in shopping centers and matches them against Polk's National Vehicle Registration Database to find out where these retail customers live.[4] The shopping center can then use plots of its customers' residences to determine its trading area. Moreover, the locations can be matched with the Census Bureau's data, thereby providing a demographic profile of the people who shop there.

Geodemographic Data

If you're in retailing, and you live by the mantra, "Location, location, location," you've probably heard of, and used, geomarketing data. Geographic information systems (GIS) combine demographic data with geographic information on maps. The user draws a map showing average income levels of a county or zip code (to the 9th zip code digit), then zooms in closer to look at particular towns in more detail. GIS programs show information as detailed as a single block, and some programs can show individual buildings. Seeing the information on a map can be more illustrative than reading tables of numbers.[5]

Geodemographic data can be clustered to derive homogeneous groups to help marketers understand their segments. For example, Claritas, Inc., the pioneer and a leader in the industry (claritas.com), used over 500 demographic variables in its PRIZM (Potential Ratings for Zip Markets) system when classifying residential neighborhoods. This system breaks the 250,000 neighborhood areas in the U.S. into 40 types based on consumer behavior and lifestyle. Each of the types has a label that describes the type of people living there, such as *Urban Gold Coast, Shotguns and Pickups, Pools and Patios,* etc. (e.g., see Figure 7.4). Claritas, Inc. or other suppliers of geomarketing data will do a customized analysis for whatever geographic boundaries a client specifies. A client can submit an electronic list of the zip code addresses of its customer database, and the geodemographer will attach the cluster codes.[6]

---

[4] The U.S. Department of Motor Vehicles is also directly involved as a supplier of data to marketing researchers, providing driver information (age, gender, marital status, household income, number of children, homeownership, etc.), automobile information (car make, model, year, purchase date, engine size, fuel type, bought new or used, etc.), along with the geographic details (state, county, zip, area code, etc.), to research suppliers such as Survey Sampling International (see http://www.ssi.com and http://www.world opinion.com/the_ frame).

[5] Programs designed specifically for use as GISs include Maptitude (Caliper Corporation; see http://www. caliper.com) and MapInfo (see http://www.mapinfo.com).

[6] For more information, see David Grimshaw, *Bringing Geographical Information Systems into Business* (Wiley, 2000); Michael Weiss, *The Clustered World* (Little Brown & Co., 2000); Kerry Hucker-Brown, "Estimating the Potential of your Chosen Market," *Direct Response* 33 (2003) p. 33. Most issues of the monthly journal *American Demographics* contain a feature column called "The Grid," which uses such data to map phenomena as varied as where high consumer demand exists for digital cameras (Aug. 2003); which U.S. destinations are most popular with tourists (Nov. 2002); where new or used car buyers live (Jan. 2000); and so on. Another useful keyword is TIGER, for Topologically Integrated Geographic Encoding and Referencing, in the U.S. Government's Census Bureau's database. Claritas now oversees operation of NRB, which compiles the Shopping Center Database, covering 40,000 shopping centers, with 500,000 tenants, and this acquisition should further refine the level of detail available through the geomarketing approach.

FIGURE 7.4
Sample Cluster Profile

The **Towns and Gowns** cluster describes most of our college towns and university campus neighborhoods. With a typical mix of half locals (Towns) and half students (Gowns), it is wholly unique, with thousands of penniless 18–24 year-olds, plus highly educated professionals, all with a taste for prestige products beyond their evident means.

Predominant Characteristics:

- 1,290,200 (1.4% of U.S. households)
- College Town Singles
- Ethnicities: Dominant White, High Asian
- Single marital status
- Age ranges: under 24, 25–34
- Education: College Grads
- Employment level: White-collar/Service
- Housing: Renters/Multi-Unit 10+

Descriptors: More Likely To:

Lifestyle

- Go to college football games
- Go skiing
- Play pool
- Use cigarette rolling paper

TV/Radio

- Listen to rock
- Watch MTV, VH1
- Watch *Jeopardy*
- Watch *The Simpsons*

Products and Services

- Have student loans
- Use ATM cards
- Own a Honda
- Buy 3+ pairs jeans annually
- Drink Coca-Cola Classic
- Eat Kraft Macaroni and Cheese

Print

- Read newspaper comics section
- Read *Rolling Stone*
- Read *GQ, Cosmo*

Source: http://Claritas.com

Measuring Product Sales and Market Share

Firms use market share to assess their status in the marketplace. Firms selling B-to-B goods or services typically track their own sales and market shares through analyses of their sales invoices. They also obtain feedback from the sales force in terms of how they did in various product or system proposal competitions. Often online data sources publish market share statistics.

Manufacturers of consumer packaged goods (CPGs) also monitor sales by account through the examination of sales invoices. For CPGs, though, more information is required. Using factory shipments as a sales barometer neglects the filling or depleting of distribution pipelines that may be occurring. The other part of the equation involves the measurement of sales to final consumers. Historically, such measurements have been handled several ways, including the use of diary panels of households and the measurement of sales scanned at the store level.

DIARY PANELS

The NPD Group, the largest national paper diary panel in the U.S., samples continually from its panel of more than half a million households, which report their purchases and consumption using a preprinted diary to document their monthly purchases in approximately 50 product categories (4,000 food products alone). Figure 7.5 illustrates a sample diary for food purchases. Note that the diary asks for

FIGURE 7.5 Sample Food Diary

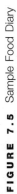

DAILY MEAL DIARY

QUESTIONS OR PROBLEMS?

If you have any questions or problems concerning this diary, give us a call at our toll-free number 800-645-1900 Monday through Friday between 9:15AM and 4PM Eastern Time. In New York State call 800-632-1911.

SPECIAL LABEL CODES
1. Light, "Lite", Diet
2. Low Fat
3. Fat free/Non Fat
4. Low Cholesterol
5. Cholesterol Free
6. Low Salt/Low Sodium
7. No Salt, Salt Free
8. Low Sugar/Sugar Free
9. Contains Nutra-Sweet
10. Caffeine Free/Decaffeinated
11. All Natural
12. Other

TYPE OF PACKAGE CODES
1. Can
2. Bottle/Jar
3. Box/Carton
4. Tube
5. Bag
6. Pouch
7. Tray/Tub/Bowl
8. Wrapped
9. Loose/Not Pkg.
10. All Other

ORIGINAL FORM CODES
1. Liquid
2. Dried/Dehydrated
3. Powdered/Dry Mix
4. Freeze Dried
5. Concentrate/Condensed
6. Cubes/Tablets
7. Paste
8. Shredded/Grated
9. Chunk/Loaf
10. Bar/Stick/Squares
11. Sliced
12. Ready to Eat (From Pkg.)
13. Other

NOW SERVED CODES
1. Appetizer
2. Main Dish
3. Side Dish
4. Dessert
5. Beverage

HOUSEHOLD MEMBERS
Write in names of any household members now shown below. Also, include their year of birth and sex (M or F) in the boxes below each member's name

METHOD USED CODES
1. Warmed, Heated
2. Uncooked, Raw
3. Chilled, Frozen
4. Unheated
5. Fried, Pan Broiled
6. Boiled, Stewed, Simmered, Perked
7. Broiled, Barbecued
8. Baked, Roasted
9. Braised, Steamed
10. Toasted, Browned
11. Added Hot Water
12. Deep Fried
If Other, Write In

APPLIANCE CODES
1. Stove Top
2. Oven
3. Broiler
4. Microwave Oven
5. Toaster, Toaster Oven
6. Grill, Barbecue
7. Pressure Cooker
8. Blender
9. Percolator
10. Crock Pot
11. Hot Plate, Elec. Fry Pan
12. Deep Fryer
If Other, Write In

PAGE 1 — IN-HOME MORNING

WHAT WAS THE FOOD ITEM SERVED? Write in the name of each food, dish, drink, etc. served at this meal. ALSO If the item had toppings or other foods "added-to" it when served, please enter. Such as: ketchup on french fries, milk in coffee, gravy on potatoes, lemon on fish, dressing on salad, butter on toast, etc. Enter each one on a separate line.		COMPLETE DESCRIPTION OF FOOD ITEM Write in the KIND, TYPE, FLAVOR, STYLE to help us identify it exactly. Examples: Vanilla for instant pudding, ham for sandwich, scrambled for eggs, breasts for chicken, etc.	DID LABEL SHOW ITEM TO BE: See list above. Enter up to 4 codes below.	BRAND NAME Write in the brand name as it appears on the label. If there is no brand, tell us if you bought it at a bakery, butcher, fruit stand, etc. If the item was made from more than one product, skip to ingredients section.	WHERE WAS ITEM OBTAINED? If purchased, was it: 1. Fresh 2. Frozen 3. Refrigerated 4. From Shelf 5. From Restaurant Or was it: 6. Homemade/ Homegrown Enter code below.	HOW WAS ITEM PACKAGED? (outer package) See list above. Enter code below.	WHAT WAS OUTER PACKAGE MADE OF? 1. Glass 2. Plastic 3. Paper/ Cardboard 4. Aluminum/ Tin/Other Metal 5. Other 6. No Package Enter code below.	WHAT WAS ORIGINAL FORM OF ITEM? See list above. Enter code below.	HOW WAS ITEM SERVED? See list above. Enter code below	HOW MUCH WAS SERVED? ENTER THE AMOUNT AND UNIT OF MEASURE Food Examples: 5 lbs., 16 oz., 2 cups, 1 tbsp. Beverage Examples: 8 oz., 1 mug, 2 glasses	OF WHAT WAS SERVED, HOW MUCH WAS ACTUALLY EATEN? (✓) One ALL	3/4	1/2	1/4	1 Year of Birth SEX	2 Year of Birth SEX	3 Year of Birth SEX	4 Year of Birth SEX	5 Year of Birth SEX	6 Year of Birth SEX	7 Year of Birth SEX	8	WAS THIS A LEFT-OVER? (✓) One YES	NO	PARTIALLY	HOW WAS ITEM PREPARED? If no preparation used, put in a dash (-). WHAT METHOD DID YOU USE?	WHAT APPLI-ANCE DID YOU USE?
															For each food item below, write the number of helpings (0, 1, 2, etc.) for each household member.											See Lists Above. Enter Codes Below.	
MENU ITEM 1																											
Topping or Additive										X																	
MENU ITEM 2																											
Topping or Additive										X																	
MENU ITEM 3																											
Topping or Additive										X																	
MENU ITEM 4																											
Topping or Additive										X																	
MENU ITEM 5																											
Topping or Additive										X																	
MENU ITEM 6																											

considerable detail about the food consumed at each meal. Was the food bought fresh or frozen? Was the packaging glass, plastic, cardboard? How much of the food item was served? What was served with it? Were toppings or side orders added? How much of the food remained after the meal?

The households composing NPD panels are geographically dispersed but demographically balanced so they can be projected to total U.S. purchasing. The panel is balanced with respect to size, age of female head of household, household income, and geography. Panel members are recruited quarterly and added to the active panel after they have satisfactorily met NPD's reporting standards. Panel members are compensated for their participation with small gifts, and households are dropped from the panel at their request or if they fail to return three of their last six diaries.

The diaries are returned to NPD monthly, the purchase histories are aggregated, and reports are prepared. Using these reports, the subscribing company is able to assess the following:

- Size of the market, % of households buying over time, and amount purchased per buyer
- Manufacturer and brand shares over time
- Brand loyalty and brand-switching behavior
- Frequency of purchase and amount purchased per transaction
- Influence of price and special price deals, as well as average price paid
- Characteristics of heavy buyers
- Impact of a new manufacturer or brand on the established brands
- Effect of a change in advertising or distribution strategy[7]

If you see the media reporting trends in food consumption, the data probably originated with NPD. Its food guru, Mr. Harry Balzer, points to trends such as the growth in take-out foods, or the concern by the industry—but not consumers—of healthy meals.[8] Regarding the latter, the beauty of the NPD diaries is that actual behaviors are recorded rather than attitudes, which are likely biased in the direction of social desirability (e.g., "Yes, I would like to eat more healthily. . . . Say, are you going to finish your fries?").

Ethical Dilemma 7.1

An independent marketing research firm was hired by a Los Angeles clothing designer to study the Denver ski resort market for upscale, *après* ski-wear. The manufacturer wanted to determine (1) whether sufficient market potential existed to warrant opening a retail store there, and (2) if so, where precisely the store should be located in the metropolitan area. The research firm went about the task by examining secondary data on the Denver market, particularly statistics published by the Census Bureau. In less than two months, the research firm was able to develop a well-documented recommendation as to what the clothing designer should do.

Approximately six months after completing this study, the firm was approached by an outdoor sporting goods designer and manufacturer to do a similar study concerning the location of a store through which it could more effectively serve its Denver customers.

- Is it ethical for the research firm to use the information it had collected in the first study to reduce its cost quote to the client in the second?
- Does it make any difference if the sporting goods firm also designs and distributes ski-wear?
- Would your answers change if some of the data were collected through personal interviews that the first client paid for?

---

[7] See Insights (http://www.npd.com) for discussion of these and other analyses using diary panel data.

[8] See http://www.npd.com/press/releases.

STORE AUDITS

A historically popular way of measuring sales is at the store level, using store audits.[9] The basic concept of a store audit is a simple inventory. The research firm sends field workers to a select group of retail stores at fixed intervals. On each visit, the auditor takes a complete inventory of all designated products. The auditor also notes the merchandise moving into the store by checking wholesale invoices, warehouse withdrawal records, and direct shipments from manufacturers. Sales are determined by the following calculation:

Sales = Beginning inventory + Net purchases (wholesalers and manufacturers) – Ending inventory.

The store audit was pioneered by ACNielsen and served as the backbone of their Retail Index for many years. The company takes the auditing records and generates the following information for each of the brands audited: sales to consumers, retail inventories, out-of-stocks, prices, dealer support (displays, local advertising, coupon redemption), etc.

SCANNERS

Since the late 1970s, ACNielsen has been replacing its Retail Index service with its SCANTRACK service. The SCANTRACK service was made possible by the grocery industry's installation of scanning equipment to read Universal Product Codes (UPCs), the 11-digit numbers imprinted on each product sold in a supermarket (see Figure 7.6).

FIGURE 7.6
Universal Product Codes (UPCs)

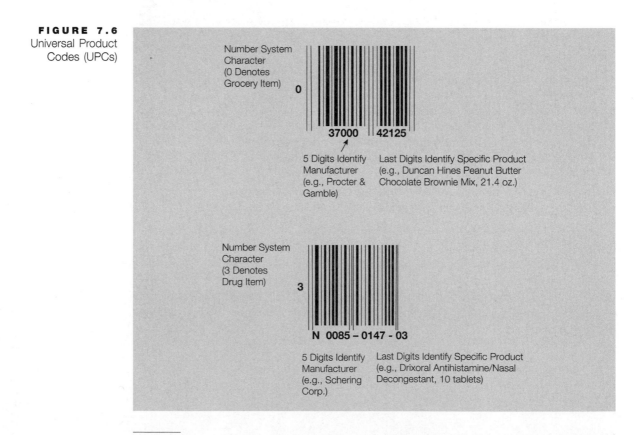

---

[9] Store audits are still used in some types of stores, primarily because the products they sell do not lend themselves to scanner processing or because the stores have not made the investment in scanner equipment.

As each product, with its unique 11-digit code, is pulled across the scanner, the scanner identifies the 11-digit number, looks up the price in the attached computer, and immediately prints the description and price of the item on the cash register receipt. At the same time, the computer can keep track of the movement of every item that is scanned.

Scanners' effects on the collection of sales and market share data have been profound. Scanners are so pervasive that the majority of information supplied today is based on scanning data. Using either a sample of stores to represent a channel or a census of all stores to represent a retail organization, scanning data are available across multiple outlets, including grocery, mass merchant, drug, selected warehouse club, and selected convenience stores.

By combining the retail sales and marketing mix factors (TV and local newspaper ad exposure data, coupon usage), the effectiveness of various marketing actions can be assessed, e.g., by estimating what sales would have been without the presence of the action. These databases allow marketing researchers to investigate the "causes" of sales fluctuations, such as:

- Display information—stores are audited and items on display are recorded
- Feature information—features are collected and coded to identify items being advertised
- Price decreases—the system identifies decreases via comparisons to historical prices (see Table 7.5 for more ideas)

Several firms have developed systems to further link purchase behavior with household demographic information, including Information Resources (IRI) and ACNielsen.[10] When these large marketing research suppliers link household demographics, TV-viewing behavior, and product-purchasing behavior, the results are called *single-source data*.[11]

The basics of single-source research are straightforward. In IRI's BehaviorScan system, their panel of more than 55,000 households presents an ID card at each of the grocery or drugstores every time they make a purchase. Almost all the supermarkets and drugstores in each area are provided scanners by IRI.[12] The household member presents the family's ID card when checking out. The card is scanned along with the purchases, allowing IRI to relate that family's purchases (by brand, size, and price, etc.) to the family's demographic characteristics and the household's known exposure to coupons, newspaper ads, free samples, and point-of-purchase displays. (Cool, huh?)

IRI also is able to direct different TV advertising spots to different households through the "black boxes" that have been attached to the television sets in each test household, in cooperation with the cable television systems serving the markets. Doing so allows IRI to monitor the buying reactions to different ads or to the same ad in different types of households (e.g., whether the buying reactions to a particular ad are the same or different among past users and nonusers of the product). This targeted-TV capability allows IRI to balance the panel of members for each ad test

---

[10] Diaries can link purchase behavior with demographic information, but their accuracy depends on the conscientiousness of those in the panel to record their purchases as they occur.

[11] Henry Assael and David Poltrack, "Consumer Surveys vs. Electronic Measures for Single-Source Data," *Journal of Advertising Research* (Oct. 2002), pp. 19–25; Chris Powell, "NMR Service Links Viewers to Usage," *Marketing Magazine* (Dec. 9, 2002), p. 4.

[12] IRI now also offers BehaviorScan for testing in mass merchandisers, such as Wal-Mart and Target, in addition to grocery stores and drugstores. See http://www.infores.com. Nielsen has begun its BookScan service, to measure flow through Barnes & Noble, Borders, etc.

TABLE 7.5
Sample Scanner Data

Scanner data are the grocery- and retail-scanned purchases made by consumers. Variables include store number, brand purchased, quantity purchased, number of ounces or size purchased, whether any of the brands in the category were on sale or otherwise featured (e.g., end-of-aisle displays), whether a coupon was used, etc. Any random grocery shopper's purchases are captured in scanner data. Scanner panel data are those that further integrate a household's purchases with information on its family's demographics, TV viewing behavior, etc. These additional data are known only for the participating panel members (families agree to participate, presenting their membership card to be scanned to flag their data in the database for later analyses, in exchange for moderate compensation). In this data set, the variables are interpreted as follows:

X_1 = observation number
X_2 = household identification number
X_3 = brand bought during this purchase
X_4 = brand bought last purchase
X_5 = price per ounce of brand A
X_6 = price per ounce of brand B
X_7 = price per ounce of brand C
X_8 = price per ounce of brand D
X_9 = 1 if brand bought was advertised on television last week
X_{10} = 1 if brand bought was on display or otherwise featured in the grocer
X_{11} = 1 if a coupon was used to buy the brand
X_{12} = number of total purchases by this household through the duration of this data set

X_1	X_2	X_3	X_4	X_5	X_6	X_7	X_8	X_9	X_{10}	X_{11}	X_{12}
109	2212251	A	—	.53	.59	.62	.51	1	0	0	5
110	2212251	C	A	.63	.51	.66	.50	0	0	0	5
111	2212251	B	C	.57	.60	.56	.45	0	1	0	5
112	2212251	A	B	.55	.54	.42	.41	1	0	0	5
113	2212251	A	A	.56	.54	.56	.49	0	0	0	5
114	4412319	D	—	.55	.53	.51	.48	0	0	0	9
115	4412319	B	D	.53	.55	.52	.50	0	1	0	9
116	4412319	C	B	.44	.50	.46	.51	0	0	0	9
117	4412319	B	C	.61	.40	.65	.50	0	1	0	9
118	4412319	C	B	.54	.59	.60	.51	0	1	0	9
119	4412319	C	C	.56	.56	.46	.50	0	0	0	9
120	4412319	B	C	.56	.54	.41	.49	0	1	0	9
121	4412319	A	B	.55	.55	.52	.48	1	0	0	9
122	4412319	C	A	.55	.54	.71	.50	0	0	0	9
123	4142957	C	—	.55	.53	.45	.50	0	1	1	4
124	4142957	B	C	.53	.53	.52	.50	0	1	0	4
125	4142957	C	B	.54	.50	.55	.51	0	0	1	4
126	4142957	B	C	.51	.51	.53	.49	0	1	1	4
127	5281115	B	—	.55	.50	.64	.48	0	1	0	5
128	5281115	A	B	.49	.54	.46	.45	1	0	0	5
129	5281115	B	A	.60	.48	.61	.52	0	1	0	5
130	5281115	B	B	.56	.52	.42	.50	0	1	1	5
131	5281115	B	B	.55	.52	.56	.50	0	0	0	5
132	2143377	A	—	.53	.52	.51	.51	1	0	1	7

(continued)

TABLE 7.5
(continued)

X_1	X_2	X_3	X_4	X_5	X_6	X_7	X_8	X_9	X_{10}	X_{11}	X_{12}
133	2143377	C	A	.52	.51	.42	.52	0	1	1	7
134	2143377	B	C	.55	.50	.46	.48	0	0	0	7
135	2143377	C	B	.50	.54	.51	.47	0	1	0	7
136	2143377	B	C	.51	.50	.62	.44	0	1	1	7
137	2143377	A	B	.55	.50	.56	.45	0	0	1	7
138	2143377	A	A	.56	.50	.61	.48	0	0	1	7
139	3301329	A	—	.56	.55	.62	.51	1	0	0	3
140	3301329	A	A	.54	.54	.66	.50	0	0	1	3
141	3301329	A	A	.55	.53	.61	.51	1	0	0	3

within each market according to the criteria the sponsor chooses (such as past purchasers of the product), thereby enhancing the comparability of experimental and control groups.

ACNielsen's Homescan Service maintains a panel of 55,000 participating households whose purchases are measured through an electronic wand they manually pass over the UPCs on products they've bought. The Homescan Panel does not depend on retailer cooperation or retailer scanning abilities, so it is not outlet-dependent and provides a total market perspective regarding sales of a product. The electronic unit then queries panel members with respect to where the purchase was made, age and gender of the shopper, price paid, deal type, etc. (see Table 7.6).[13]

The impact of single-source measurement on the conduct of marketing activities has been tremendous. All the large marketing research providers try to persuade clients that they add the most value analytically to these immense marketing databases. Clients encourage the competition between providers to get their money's worth.[14]

A different kind of integrated data source is on the horizon through TiVo. Television service is becoming personalized, and marketers are exploring the utility of experimenting with long-form advertising (TV ads that run for four minutes!), e.g., for Porsche and Acura. The consumer is completely in charge and can end the ad with a button click, or can request more information on the products featured (e.g., a Web address, or information on a local dealership). Experimentation with incentives is also in its infancy. Just as with early Web surveys, the novelty draws many, but only for a while. In the TiVo experiments, participation is currently promoted by entering the participant in a contest.[15]

Measuring Advertising Exposure and Effectiveness

A great deal of commercial information is available for marketers that relates to the assessment of exposure to and effectiveness of advertising. Most suppliers of B-to-B goods advertise most heavily in trade publications. To sell space more effectively, the various trade publications typically sponsor readership studies, which they then make available to potential advertisers. Suppliers of consumer goods and services also have access to media-sponsored readership studies. In addition, a number of services have evolved to measure consumer exposure to the various media.

---

[13] See http://www.acnielsen.com.

[14] Jack Neff, "P&G Pits Rivals in Data Review," *Advertising Age* 73 (Nov. 11, 2002), pp. 3, 44.

[15] Tobi Elkin, "Porsche, Acura Latest to Try out TiVo Showcases," *Advertising Age* (Feb. 24, 2003), p. 4.

TABLE 7.6　Analyses Possible Using ACNielsen's Homescan Service, Scantrack

Type	Purpose	Key Measures
Market Overview, Trend Analysis	To provide a general overview of consumer purchasing for a particular product category, its major segments, and major brands. Measures are compared between brands and over time to identify changes in the marketplace. Data can be analyzed for any time period, across or within outlet types, even for specific consumer groups (e.g., heavy buyers, microwave owners).	Volume and market share % households purchasing category (penetration) Volume per buyer (buying rate) Volume per purchase Purchase occasion per buyer (frequency) Pricing (total, deal, nondeal) % volume on deal (coupon vs. store special) Distribution of volume by outlet (e.g., grocery, drug, club warehouse)
Demographic Analysis	To target advertising and promotional efforts most effectively by determining the demographic profile of particular buyer groups (e.g., brand buyers, heavy buyers, frequent commercial viewers). By evaluating one demographic segment versus another, along with the importance of each demographic segment relative to the general population, the overall profile of each buyer group can be identified.	Across all demographic characteristics, the following measures are produced: 　Distribution of buyers 　Distribution of volume 　Market share 　% volume on deal 　Buyer index (distribution of buyers and population) 　Volume index (distribution of volume and population)
Loyalty, Combination Purchase	To understand the extent to which buyers are loyal to a brand or store; to determine the competitive set in which brands or stores operate; and to identify size, flavor, form preference, and the importance of price when buyers purchase competitive items.	% brand buyers purchasing competitive items % brand volume by buyers who purchase competitive brands % competitive brand volume purchased on deal
Brand-Shifting	To identify the sources of growth or decline in a brand's sales. By looking at changes from period to period on a household-by-household basis, we can see if volume changes were attributed to consumers switching to or from other brands, increasing or decreasing their overall category purchasing.	Brand-shifting volume Change in category purchasing New or lost category buyers % shifting gains and losses Gain/loss index
Trial and Repeat	Trial measures consumer interest in a new product by evaluating the percentage of households making at least one purchase of the product. Trial also measures the ability of a marketing plan to translate interest into purchasing. Repeat purchasing evaluates product satisfaction by determining the percentage of triers repurchasing the brand—the ability of a product to deliver on its promise.	Cumulative trial Cumulative repeat Depth of repeat Package rate (volume on trial, on repeat) % volume on deal (total on trial, on repeat) Market share (total from trial vs. repeat)

Source: ACNielsen.

TELEVISION AND RADIO

The Nielsen Television Index is probably the most generally familiar commercial information service. Even the most casual television watcher has probably heard of the Nielsen ratings and the impact they have on which TV shows are canceled by the networks and which are allowed to continue. The index itself is designed to provide estimates of the size and nature of the audience for individual television programs. For a long time, the basic data were gathered through the use of audimeter instruments, which are electronic devices attached to the TV sets in cooperating households. Each audimeter was connected to a central computer, which re-

corded when the set was on and what channel was on. In the late 1980s, Nielsen started measuring TV audiences through the use of "people meters." These devices attempt to measure not only the channel to which a set is tuned, but who in the household is watching. Each member of the family has his or her own viewing number. Whoever turns on the set, sits down to watch, or changes the channel is supposed to enter his or her number into the people meter. All this information is transmitted immediately to Nielsen for processing.

Nielsen estimates the number and percentage of all TV households viewing a given TV show. Ratings are tabulated per 10 socioeconomic and demographic characteristics, including location, education and occupation of head of household, time zones, household income, age of female head of house, Internet service subscription, number of children, and household size. These classifications assist the network in selling advertising on particular programs, while they assist the advertiser in choosing programs to sponsor that reach households with the desired characteristics.[16]

Advertisers buying radio time are also interested in the size and demographic composition of the audiences they will be reaching. Radio-listening statistics are typically gathered using household panel diaries. Arbitron, for example, calls households (telephone numbers generated randomly, to ensure reaching households with unlisted numbers). Those household members who agree to participate are sent diaries, in which they record their radio-listening behavior for a short period. Most radio markets are rated only once or twice a year, although some of the larger ones are rated four times a year. The April/May survey is conducted in every Arbitron market and consequently is known as the "sweeps" period. Radio ratings are broken down by audience age and gender and focus more on individual than household behavior, in contrast to television ratings.

PRINT MEDIA

Several services measure exposure and readership to print media. For example, the Roper Starch Readership Service measures the reading of ads in magazines and

[16] Greater detail about the Nielsen television rating can be found at http://www.acnielsen.com.

newspapers. They maintain the world's largest database of some 10,000s of print ads in more than 1,000 issues of consumer magazines, business publications, and newspapers, which are assessed each year, using over 50,000 personal interviews in more than 35 countries. Starch measures recognition—with the magazine open, the respondent is asked to indicate whether he or she has read each ad. Three degrees of reading are recorded:

1. Noted—a person who remembered seeing any part of the ad in that particular issue
2. Associated—a person who not only "noted" the ad but also saw or read some part of it that clearly indicates the brand or advertiser
3. Read most—a person who read 50% or more of the written material in the ad[17]

During the course of the interview, data are also collected on the observation and reading of the component parts of each ad, such as the headlines, subheadings, pictures, copy blocks, etc.

Interviewing begins a short time after the issue of the magazine is placed on sale. For weekly and biweekly consumer magazines, interviewing begins 3–6 days after the on-sale date and continues for 1–2 weeks. For monthly magazines, interviewing begins two weeks after the on-sale date and continues for two weeks. The size of the sample varies by publication. Most Starch studies are based on a minimum of 100 issue readers.

Starch readership reports are compiled issue by issue and include three features: (1) labeled issue, (2) summary report, and (3) adnorm tables. The target ads in each issue are labeled to indicate overall readership level as well as the noting or reading of the major components of the ads. The summary report lists all the ads that were measured in the issue. The ads are arranged by product category and show the percentages for the three degrees of ad readership: noted, associated, and read most, allowing the comparison of the readership of each ad versus the other target ads in the issue. The adnorm tables enable one to compare the readership of an ad in a given issue with the norm for ads of the same size and color that are for the same product category for that publication.

Starch readership data allow advertisers to compare their ads with competitors' ads, current ads with previous ads, current ads against competitors' previous ads, and current ads against Starch adnorm tables. This process can be effective in assessing changes in theme, copy, layout, use of color, etc.[18]

MULTIMEDIA SERVICES

The Simmons Media/Marketing Service uses a national probability sample of more than 19,000 respondents and serves as a comprehensive data source allowing the cross-referencing of product usage and media exposure. Four different interviews are conducted with each respondent so that magazine, TV, newspaper, and radio can all be covered by the Simmons Service.[19]

---

[17] See the Starch Readership Report: Methodology and Use (http://www.roper.com).

[18] The measurement of newspaper and magazine circulation is notoriously difficult. For example, some indices do not count the distribution of complimentary papers, e.g., *USA Today* in hotels. Advertising agencies also complain that the indices are not provided frequently enough to be timely and relevant—often only twice a year. The Starch Reports, or those by comparable providers, such as First Magazine Marketing Reader Panels in the U.K. (http://www.fmm.co.uk), can provide more customized and tailored consumer data.

[19] For more on research from Simmons Market Research Bureau, Inc., see http://www.smrb.com.

The service conducts personal interviews to obtain measures of respondent readership of individual magazines and newspapers. Self-administered questionnaires are used to gather product purchase and usage information for over 800 product categories, which remain relatively fixed from year to year. Television-viewing behavior is ascertained by means of a personal viewing diary, whereas radio-listening behavior is gathered through telephone and personal interviews.

A large number of demographic characteristics are gathered from each respondent included in the study, which permits firms to identify the heavy purchasers of various products. Table 7.7 displays a small portion of the information provided by Simmons regarding the relationship between computer use and a household's demographic characteristics. By taking into account a purchaser's media habits, firms are better able to segment and target the most promising groups.

Simmons measures magazine readership "through-the-book"—respondents are screened to determine which magazines they might have read during the past six months. They are then shown actual issues of magazines stripped of advertising pages and recurring columns and features. Nine feature articles unique to the issue are exhibited, and respondents are asked to select the articles they personally find especially interesting. At the end, a qualifying question is asked: "Now that you have been through this magazine, could you tell me whether this is the first time you happened to look into this particular issue, or have you looked into it before?" Respondents must affirm prior exposure to the issue to qualify as readers. Simmons provides databases of usage and preference for some 865 product lines, but its focus is on media, covering 150 variables on magazine readership, cable-viewing habits, radio-listening patterns, etc.

Mediamark Research also makes available information on exposure to various media and household consumption of a number of products and services. Its annual survey of 20,000 adult respondents covers more than 250 magazines, newspapers, radio stations, and television channels and over 450 products and services.[20] Information is gathered from respondents by two methods. First, a personal interview is used to collect demographics and data pertaining to media exposure. Magazine readership is measured by a "recent reading" method that asks respondents to sort a deck of magazine logo cards according to whether they (1) are sure they have read; (2) are not sure they have read; and (3) are sure they have not read a given magazine within the previous six months.

Newspaper readership is measured using a "yesterday reading" technique in which respondents are asked which of the daily newspapers on the list of papers that circulate in the area were read or looked into within the previous seven days. For Sunday and weekend papers, a four-week time span is used. Radio listening is determined through a "yesterday" recall technique in which respondents are shown a list of five time periods and are asked how much time was spent listening to a radio during each time period on the previous day. They are then asked what stations they listened to. TV audience data are collected in a similar manner.

On completion of the interview, interviewers leave a questionnaire booklet with respondents. The booklet covers personal and household usage of approximately 3,500 product categories and services and 5,700 brands.

---

[20] More detail about Mediamark's operations and the types of analyses allowed by the media exposure and product-uses databases can be found at the company's Web site, http://www.mediamark.com.

TABLE 7.7 Sample Output from Simmons Media/Marketing Service

	Total U.S. '000	Interactive Computer Services Use or Subscribe				Personal Computer: Total Own at Home/Use at Work				Own at Home				Personally Use at Work			
		A '000 % Across	B DOWN	C %	D INDX	A '000 % Across	B DOWN	C %	D INDX	A '000 % Across	B DOWN	C %	D INDX	A '000 % Across	B DOWN	C %	D INDX
TOTAL ADULTS	187747	9973	100.0	5.3	100	58794	100.0	31.3	100	41392	100.0	22.0	100	35896	100.0	19.1	100
MALES	90070	5178	51.9	5.7	108	28652	48.7	31.8	102	20931	50.6	23.2	105	16917	47.1	18.8	98
FEMALES	97676	4795	48.1	4.9	92	30142	51.3	30.9	99	20462	49.4	20.9	95	18980	52.9	19.4	102
# SHOPPERS	115901	5596	56.1	4.8	91	33828	57.5	29.2	93	22997	55.6	19.8	90	21535	60.0	18.6	97
18-24	23951	1407	14.1	5.9	111	7535	12.8	31.5	100	5652	13.7	23.6	107	3680	10.3	15.4	80
25-34	41492	2466	24.7	5.9	112	13864	23.6	33.4	107	7931	19.2	19.1	87	9545	26.6	23.0	120
35-44	40678	3112	31.2	7.6	144	16372	27.8	40.2	129	11910	28.8	29.3	133	10649	29.7	26.2	137
45-54	29045	2124	21.3	7.3	138	11628	19.8	40.0	128	8691	21.0	29.9	136	7395	20.6	25.5	133
55-64	21263	656	6.6	3.1	58	5684	9.7	26.7	85	4041	9.8	19.0	86	3281	9.1	15.4	81
65 OR OLDER	31318	*208	2.1	0.7	13	3712	6.3	11.9	38	3168	7.7	10.1	46	1347	3.8	4.3	22
18-34	65443	3873	38.8	5.9	111	21399	36.4	32.7	104	13582	32.8	20.8	94	13225	36.8	20.2	106
18-49	122143	8176	82.0	6.7	126	44653	75.9	36.6	117	30601	73.9	25.1	114	28109	78.3	23.0	120
25-54	111215	7702	77.2	6.9	130	41864	71.2	37.6	120	28532	68.9	25.7	116	27589	76.9	24.8	130
35-49	56701	4304	43.2	7.6	143	23254	39.6	41.0	131	17019	41.1	30.0	136	14884	41.5	26.3	137
50 OR OLDER	65603	1797	18.0	2.7	52	14141	24.1	21.6	69	10791	26.1	16.4	75	7787	21.7	11.9	62
COLLEGE GRAD	37353	4261	42.7	11.4	215	19396	33.0	51.9	166	14460	34.9	38.7	176	12998	36.2	34.8	182
SOME COLLEGE	39301	3243	32.5	8.3	155	15170	25.8	38.6	123	10506	25.4	26.7	121	9358	26.1	23.8	125
H.S.	73139	2112	21.2	2.9	54	18834	32.0	25.8	82	12486	30.2	17.1	77	11037	30.7	15.1	79
SOME H.S.	37954	*357	3.6	0.9	18	5395	9.2	14.2	45	3940	9.5	10.4	47	2504	7.0	6.6	35
EMPLOYED MALES	62041	4359	43.7	7.0	132	22896	38.9	36.9	118	16191	39.1	26.1	118	14722	41.0	23.7	124
EMP FEMALES	53100	4197	42.1	7.9	149	22405	38.1	42.2	135	13920	33.6	26.2	119	16125	44.9	30.4	159
EMP FULL-TIME	99735	7571	75.9	7.6	143	39145	66.6	39.2	125	25452	61.5	25.5	116	27601	76.9	27.7	145
EMP PART-TIME	15406	985	9.9	6.4	120	6156	10.5	40.0	128	4659	11.3	30.2	137	3247	9.0	21.1	110
NOT EMPLOYED	72606	1417	14.2	2.0	37	13494	23.0	18.6	59	11281	27.3	15.5	70	5049	14.1	7.0	36
PROF'L/MANAGER	32308	3716	37.3	11.5	217	17275	29.4	53.5	171	12245	29.6	37.9	172	12575	35.0	38.9	204
TECH/CLERK/SALE	35568	3752	37.6	10.5	199	15754	26.8	44.3	141	9646	23.3	27.1	123	11142	31.0	31.3	164
PRECISION/CRAFT	12562	*430	4.3	3.4	65	3640	6.2	29.0	93	2537	6.1	20.2	92	2156	6.0	17.2	90
OTHER EMPLOYED	34704	658	6.6	1.9	36	8631	14.7	24.9	79	5684	13.7	16.4	74	4974	13.9	14.3	75
SINGLE	41125	2448	24.5	6.0	112	12533	21.3	30.5	97	8489	20.5	20.6	94	6954	19.4	16.9	88
MARRIED	111354	6208	62.3	5.6	105	39317	66.9	35.3	113	28638	69.2	25.7	117	24221	67.5	21.8	114
DIV/SEP/WDW	35268	1317	13.2	3.7	70	6944	11.8	19.7	63	4266	10.3	12.1	55	4721	13.2	13.4	70
PARENTS	61860	4511	45.2	7.3	137	23819	40.5	38.5	123	16839	40.7	27.2	123	14792	41.2	23.9	125
WHITE	159985	8666	86.9	5.4	102	52721	89.7	33.0	105	37324	90.2	23.3	106	32329	90.1	20.2	106
BLACK	21570	882	8.8	4.1	77	4266	7.3	19.8	63	2605	6.3	12.1	55	2732	7.6	12.7	66

OTHER	6191	*426	4.3	6.9	130	1808	3.1	29.2	93	1463	3.5	23.6	107	836	2.3	13.5	71
NE-CENSUS	38611	1966	19.7	5.1	96	11922	20.3	30.9	99	8163	19.7	21.1	96	7272	20.3	18.8	99
MIDWEST	45021	2576	25.8	5.7	108	15610	26.6	34.7	111	10468	25.3	23.3	105	9944	27.7	22.1	116
SOUTH	65246	3721	37.3	5.7	107	18893	32.1	29.0	92	13309	32.2	20.4	93	11449	31.9	17.5	92
WEST	38869	1710	17.2	4.4	83	12368	21.0	31.8	102	9453	22.8	24.3	110	7231	20.1	18.6	97
COUNTY SIZE A	76945	4369	43.8	5.7	107	24542	41.7	31.9	102	17476	42.2	22.7	103	14688	40.9	19.1	100
COUNTY SIZE B	55516	3229	32.4	5.8	110	18012	30.6	32.4	104	12638	30.5	22.8	103	11308	31.5	20.4	107
COUNTY SIZE C	27293	1190	11.9	4.4	82	8752	14.9	32.1	102	6254	15.1	22.9	104	5303	14.8	19.4	102
COUNTY SIZE D	27993	1184	11.9	4.2	80	7488	12.7	26.7	85	5025	12.1	17.9	81	4597	12.8	16.4	86
METRO CITY	58084	2824	28.3	4.9	92	17115	29.1	29.5	94	12005	29.0	20.7	94	10374	28.9	17.9	93
METRO SUBURB	88940	5638	56.5	6.3	119	30126	51.2	33.9	108	21543	52.0	24.2	110	18334	51.1	20.6	108
NON-METRO	40722	1512	15.2	3.7	70	11553	19.5	28.4	91	7845	19.0	19.3	87	7188	20.0	17.7	92
TOP 5 ADI'S	42410	2098	21.0	4.9	93	13209	22.5	31.1	99	9165	22.1	21.6	98	7848	21.9	18.5	97
TOP 10 ADI'S	59256	3183	31.9	5.4	101	18943	32.2	32.0	102	13219	31.9	22.3	101	11365	31.7	19.2	100
TOP 20 ADI'S	81977	4730	47.4	5.8	109	26089	44.4	31.8	102	18500	44.7	22.6	102	15985	44.5	19.5	102
HSHLD. INC. $75K+	26297	2967	29.7	11.3	212	12811	21.3	48.7	156	10029	24.2	38.1	173	7919	22.1	30.1	157
$60,000 OR MORE	43694	4393	44.1	10.1	189	20680	35.2	47.3	151	15855	38.3	36.3	165	13037	36.3	29.8	156
$50,000 OR MORE	61638	5922	59.4	9.6	181	28313	48.2	45.9	147	21123	51.0	34.3	155	17876	49.8	29.0	152
$40,000 OR MORE	83714	7345	73.6	8.8	165	36288	61.7	43.3	138	26594	64.2	31.8	144	22835	63.6	27.3	143
$30,000 OR MORE	110173	8431	84.5	7.7	144	45042	76.6	40.9	131	32011	77.3	29.1	132	28400	79.1	25.8	135
$30,000–$39,999	26459	1087	10.9	4.1	77	8753	14.9	33.1	106	5417	13.1	20.5	93	5565	15.5	21.0	110
$20,000–$29,999	28910	841	8.4	2.9	55	6755	11.5	23.4	75	4530	10.9	15.7	71	3770	10.5	13.0	68
$10,000–$19,999	29666	424	4.3	1.4	27	4575	7.8	15.4	49	3052	7.4	10.3	47	2555	7.1	8.6	45
UNDER $10,000	18998	**277	2.8	1.5	27	2423	4.1	12.3	41	1800	4.3	9.5	43	1171	3.3	6.2	32
HHOLD =1 PERSON	23989	626	6.3	2.6	49	4499	7.7	18.8	60	2458	5.9	10.2	46	3083	8.6	12.9	67
2 PEOPLE	61625	2525	25.3	4.1	77	17399	29.6	28.2	90	11972	28.9	19.4	88	11261	31.4	18.3	96
3 OR 4 PEOPLE	75459	5268	52.8	7.0	131	27736	47.2	36.8	117	20306	49.1	26.9	122	16349	45.5	21.7	113
5+	26674	1554	15.6	5.8	110	9161	15.6	34.3	110	6657	16.1	25.0	113	5203	14.5	19.5	102
#CHILDREN	113318	4693	47.1	4.1	78	31278	53.2	27.6	88	21714	52.5	19.2	87	19495	54.3	17.2	90
#<2 YEARS	13676	657	6.6	4.8	90	4461	7.6	32.6	104	2760	6.7	20.2	92	2659	7.4	19.4	102
2–5 YEARS	27475	1493	15.0	5.4	102	8887	15.1	32.3	103	5954	14.4	21.7	98	5544	15.4	20.2	106
6–11 YEARS	35656	2595	26.0	7.3	137	12916	22.0	36.2	116	9451	22.8	26.5	120	7798	21.7	21.9	114
12–17 YEARS	34050	2769	27.8	8.1	153	13431	22.8	39.4	126	10183	24.6	29.9	136	7627	21.2	22.4	117
OWN RESIDENCE	129490	7682	77.0	5.9	112	44189	75.2	34.1	109	31867	77.0	24.6	112	27007	75.2	20.9	109
VALUE: $70,000+	80885	6351	63.7	7.9	148	32555	55.4	40.2	129	24353	58.8	30.1	137	19684	54.8	24.3	127
VALUE: <$70,000	48605	1331	13.3	2.7	52	11633	19.8	23.9	76	7515	18.2	15.5	70	7323	20.4	15.1	79
RENT	52590	1781	17.9	3.4	64	12694	21.6	24.1	77	8111	19.6	15.4	70	7786	21.7	14.8	77

*Projection relatively unstable because of sample base—use with caution

** # cases too small for reliability—shown for consistency only

Source: Simmons Market Research Bureau, Inc., http://www.smrb.com.

Customized Measurements

It is true that some industries are more likely than others to compile databases on their vendors and customers. For example, consumer packaged goods have access to scanner data, which yield information about one's own product and one's competitors, and the marketing mix environment for both. Similarly, data are plentiful in the pharmaceuticals industry, e.g., physicians' scripts. In contrast, for many business and services marketing questions, secondary data are minimal, and primary marketing research dominates.

MAIL PANELS

To discuss all the suppliers of customized, primary marketing information would take us far afield, but we do want to discuss mail panels to give readers a sense of their operation. Although they are not a true source of secondary data (because the data collected using them are specifically designed to meet the client's needs), the studies are standardized, as you'll see.

NFO Research Inc. is one of the major independent research firms specializing in custom-designed consumer surveys using mail panels. NFO maintains representative panels drawn from a sampling frame of more than 550,000 U.S. households and more than 100,000 in Europe. These panels represent over one million consumers who have agreed to cooperate without compensation in completing self-administered questionnaires on a variety of topics, including specific product usage; reaction to a product or its ads; reaction to a product package; attitude toward or awareness of some issue, product, service, or ad, etc.

Parts of the national panel are continually dissolved and rebuilt (for complete turnover every two years) so that the panel is fresh and still matches current family population characteristics with respect to income, population density, age of homemaker, and family size for each of the nine geographic divisions in the census.

A current demographic profile is maintained for each family in the data bank. Included are such characteristics as size of family, education, age of family members, presence and number of children by gender, occupation of the principal wage earner, race, and so on. This information is used to generate highly refined population segments. If the user's needs require it, NFO can offer the client panels composed exclusively of mothers of infants, teenagers, elderly people, dog and cat owners, professional workers, mobile home residents, multiple car owners, or other segments. Each of these panels can be balanced to match specific quotas dictated by the client.[21]

The Consumer Mail Panel (CMP), operated as part of Market Facts Inc., also represents a sample of households that have agreed to respond to mail questionnaires and product tests. Samples of persons for each product test or use are drawn from over 655,000 households in the CMP pool. The pool is representative of the geographical divisions in the U.S. and Canada and is broken down, according to census data on total household income, population density and degree of urbanization, and age of panel member.

According to CMP, its mail panel is ideally suited for experimental studies because the samples are matched. In particular, CMP is believed to be particularly valuable when:

1. Large samples are required at low cost because the size of the subgroups is large or many subgroups are to be analyzed

---

[21] For more information on NFO Worldwide, see http://www.nfow.com.

2. Large numbers of households must be screened to find eligible respondents
3. Continuing records are to be kept by respondents to report such data as products purchased, how products are used, TV programs viewed, magazines read, etc.

CMP has recorded a number of other characteristics with respect to each participating household that allow for cross-tabulation of the client's criterion variable against such things as place of residence (state, county, standard metropolitan area), marital status, occupation and employment status, household size, age, gender, home ownership, type of dwelling, and ownership of pets, dishwashers, washing machines, dryers, PCs, and automobiles.[22]

Summary

When confronted by a new problem, the researcher's first attempts at data collection should logically focus on secondary data. Secondary data are statistics that already exist, in contrast to primary data, which are collected for the purpose at hand. Secondary data possess significant cost and time advantages, and it is only when their pursuit shows diminishing returns and the problem is not yet resolved that the researcher should proceed to primary data. The problem will typically not be resolved completely with secondary data, because secondary data rarely suit the problem perfectly. There are usually problems of appropriateness, because units of measurement, class definitions, and publication currency may be different from those required. Nevertheless, diligent pursuit of secondary data still offers the researcher a great deal of insight into the problem, the information required to resolve it, and ways in which the information can be obtained. Sometimes secondary data will completely eliminate any need to collect primary data.

Secondary data can be found in either primary or secondary sources. A primary source is the source that originated the data, whereas a secondary source is a source that secured the data from an original source. The primary source should always be used. Further, the researcher should make some judgment about the quality and accuracy of secondary data by examining the purpose of publication, the ability of the organization to collect the data, and general evidence of careful work in its presentation and collection.

Secondary data include internal company data, published external secondary data, and data supplied by commercial marketing information services. Internal sales and cost data are the least expensive source of marketing information and can be used to gain perspective on research problems. A wealth of published external secondary data is available, and it helps to follow the process listed in Figure 7.2 to focus your search.

Standardized marketing information services can be an important adjunct to the researcher's data-collection efforts. These services offer economies of scale because they serve a number of clients for a variety of purposes, and thus they are able to spread their costs of operation among clients. If they are suitable for the clients' needs, they offer substantial time and cost advantages in the collection of primary data. Some common uses of the standardized marketing databases are to profile customers, to measure product sales and market share, and to measure advertising exposure and effectiveness.

---

[22] More detail about the Market Facts mail panel and its other services can be found at http://market facts.com.

Review Questions

1. What is the difference between primary and secondary data?

2. What are the advantages and disadvantages of secondary data?

3. What criteria can be employed to judge the accuracy of secondary data?

4. What is the difference between a primary source and a secondary source of secondary data? Which is preferred? Why?

5. What distinguishes internal secondary data from external secondary data?

6. How would you search for secondary data on a particular topic?

7. How would you perform an online computer search? What types of information would you hope to find?

8. What is the basic operation of a store audit?

9. Describe how a type of business can be more successfully identified using Dun's Business Locator.

10. If you were a product manager for Smooth-n-Creamy frozen yogurt and you needed up-to-date market share information by small geographical sectors, would you prefer NPD data or Nielsen data? Why?

11. For what types of studies would you prefer NPD consumer diary data rather than BehaviorScan consumption data? Vice versa?

12. What is the advantage of using single-source data?

13. How are Starch scores determined?

14. What is the basis for the Nielsen television ratings?

15. How do the multimedia services operate?

16. For what types of studies would you use mail panels?

Applications and Problems

1. List some major secondary sources of information for the following situations:

    a. The marketing research manager of a national soft-drink manufacturer has to prepare a comprehensive report on the soft-drink industry.

    b. Mr. Baker has several ideas for instant cake mixes and is considering entering this industry. He needs to find the necessary background information to assess its potential.

    c. Ms. Smith wishes to make the tee-off times at the golf course she manages available to schedule online. She needs to collect information on the golf business and Internet penetration in her city.

    d. Mr. Wabit has heard that the profit margins in the fur business are high. The fur industry has always intrigued him, and he decides to do some research to determine if the claim is true.

    e. A recent graduate hears that condominiums are once again a good investment. She decides to collect some information on the condominium market.

2. Assume that you are interested in opening a fast-food Mexican restaurant in St. Louis, Missouri. You are unsure of its acceptance by consumers and are considering doing a marketing research study to evaluate their attitudes and opinions. In your search for information you find the following studies:

    Study A was recently conducted by a research agency for a well-known fast-food chain. To secure a copy of this study, you would be required to pay the agency $350. The study evaluated consumers' attitudes toward fast food in general based on a sample of 500 stay-at-home moms for the cities of Springfield, Illinois; St. Louis and Kansas City, Missouri; and Topeka, Kansas. The findings indicated that respondents did not view fast food favorably. The major reason for the unfavorable attitude was the low nutritional value of the food.

    Study B was completed by a group of students as a requirement for an MBA marketing course. This study would not cost anything; it is available in your university library. The study evaluated consumers' attitudes toward various ethnic fast foods. The respondents consisted of a convenience sample of 200 students from St. Louis. The findings indicated a favorable attitude toward two ethnic fast foods, Italian and Mexican. Based on these results, one of the students planned to open a pizza parlor, but instead accepted a job as sales representative for General Foods Corporation.

a. Critically evaluate the two sources of data.

b. Which do you consider to be better? Why?

c. Assume that you decide it will be profitable to become a fast-food franchisee. Identify five specific secondary sources of data and evaluate the data.

3. For many years, Home Decorating Products had been a leading producer of paint and equipment (brushes, rollers, turpentine, etc.). The company is now considering adding wallpaper to its line. At least initially, it did not intend to actually manufacture the wallpaper, but rather planned to subcontract the manufacturing. Home Decorating Products would assume the distribution and marketing functions. Before adding wallpaper to its product line, however, Home Decorating secured secondary data assessing the size of the wallpaper market. One mail survey made by a trade association showed that, on average, families in the United States wallpapered two rooms in their homes each year. Among these families, 60% did the task themselves. Another survey, which had also been done by mail by one of the major home magazines, found that 70% of the subscribers answering the questionnaire had wallpapered one complete wall or more during the last twelve months. Among the 70% of the families, 80% had done the wallpapering themselves. Home Decorating Products thus has two sets of secondary data on the same problem, but the data are not consistent.

Discuss the data in terms of the criteria one would use to determine which set, if either, is correct. Assume that you are forced to make the determination on the basis of the information in front of you. Which would you choose?

4. Assume that your school is interested in developing a marketing plan to boost sagging attendance at major athletic events, particularly home football games. As an initial step in developing the new marketing plan, the athletic department has decided that it needs demographic and lifestyle profiles of people who currently attend games on a regular (season ticket) basis. Fortunately, the ticket office maintains a listing of all season ticket purchasers (including names and addresses) from year to year. What potential sources of internal secondary data might the athletic department first investigate before considering the collection of primary data?

5. Several scenarios follow. In each case, a need exists for standardized marketing information. Recommend a service that could provide the required information. Explain your choices.

a. As part of its advertising-sales strategy, radio station KMJC wants to stress that its programming appeals to young adults between the ages of 19 and 25. The advertising salespeople need "numbers" to back up this claim.

b. Fresh Express brand managers have developed a unique coupon and TV campaign for its self-contained bags of salads. The company needs to know the following in order to evaluate the campaign:

i. Are people more likely to use the coupon if they have also seen the TV ad?

ii. What is the median size of the household using the coupon?

iii. What is the proportion of new purchasers to past purchasers among the users of the coupon?

c. A national manufacturer of a pain remedy is considering a package change to a childproof container specifically targeted to households with young children. The change will necessitate a 10% price increase. The manufacturer wants to know if its target market (parents with children under eight) will perceive the price increase as justified since the new package is childproof.

d. DLH Advertising Agency assured one of its clients that, despite the $300,000 cost of placing a half-page ad in one issue of a national magazine, the actual cost of the ad per reader would be less than two cents. DLH is preparing a report to the client and needs data to back its assurance.

e. WestTowne Shopping Center wants to know the demographic characteristics of its patrons. However, the mall's retail tenants recently voted to ban marketing research interviews in or around the mall area, due to numerous customer complaints about harassment by interviewers. Where might the mall obtain the desired information?

## CHAPTER 8

Data Collection: Primary Data

Questions to Guide Your Learning:

Q1: What are the kinds of data that marketers want (e.g., demographic, psychographic)?

Q2: What can surveys do for me? What are their limitations?

Q3: How do I write a questionnaire?

Q4: What are the options I have in terms of administering a survey (e.g., mail, phone, e-mail)?

In Chapter 7, we saw that secondary data represent fast and inexpensive research information; the researcher who gives secondary data only a cursory look is being reckless. However, it is also the case that secondary data rarely provide a complete solution to a research problem. The data may also be dated by the time of their publication. At this point, the researcher logically turns to primary data.

This chapter is an introduction to primary data. In the next two chapters, we describe data-collection forms used to obtain primary data, and we talk about how to measure consumer attitudes and behaviors. The current chapter is divided into three parts: types of primary data generally obtained from customers; communication and observation techniques; and types of questionnaires and modalities of administration for communication and observational methods.

Types of Primary Data

The varieties of primary data to be collected are nearly endless. We present the most popular categories used in marketing research.

Demographic and Socioeconomic Characteristics

One type of primary data of great interest to marketers is a consumer's demographic and socioeconomic characteristics, such as age, education, occupation, marital status, gender, income, or social class. These variables are used to cross-classify the collected data to help make sense of the consumers' responses. Suppose we are interested in people's attitudes toward ecology and pollution. We might suspect, test, and find that attitudes toward green marketing are related to the respondents' level of education. Similarly, marketers frequently ask whether the consumption of particular products (SUVs, disposable diapers, vacation golf packages) are related to a person's (or family's) age, education, income, and so on. Demographic variables may seem simple (that is, they would not capture nuances of consumer preferences), so it may seem risky to make such generalizations about people. However, consider two stable examples of the usefulness of demographics in predicting consumer preferences and behaviors: (1) 18- to 49-year-old men tend to be interested in sports, and it is this segment that makes sports TV programming highly profitable; (2) most of the disposable income in the U.S. comes from people 40 years old and older.[1] Such demographic information (age and gender) and socioeconomic characteristics (wealth and discretionary funds) are often used to delineate market segments.[2]

Demographic and socioeconomic characteristics represent attributes of people. Some of these attributes, such as a respondent's age, gender, and level of formal education, can be readily verified. Some, such as social class or cultural traditions can only be approximated because they are relative and not absolute measures of a person's standing in society.[3] Income represents an intermediate degree of difficulty in verifiability—though a person's income is an actual quantity, ascertaining the amount sometimes proves to be difficult.

Psychological and Lifestyle Characteristics

Another type of primary data of interest to marketers is the customer's psychological and lifestyle characteristics in the form of personality traits, activities, interests, and values. Personality refers to the typical patterns of behavior that an individual exhibits—the attributes, traits, and mannerisms that distinguish one person from another. We often characterize people by the personality traits they display, e.g., aggressiveness, dominance, friendliness, or sociability.[4] The argument is that personality

---

[1] http://www.census.gov/econ, e.g., Jim Mateja, "Car-Buying Life Begins at 40, Study Finds," *Chicago Tribune* (April 16, 2001), p. 6.1.

[2] Martin Koschat and William Putsis, "Audience Characteristics and Bundling," *Journal of Marketing Research* 39 (2002), pp. 262–273; Milorad Krneta, "Data Deluge," *Marketing Magazine* 108 (April 7, 2003), p. 15.

[3] John Kavaliunas, "The Aging of America," *Marketing Research* 13 (Fall 2001), p. 6; John Fetto, "An All-American Melting Pot," *American Demographics* 23 (July 2001), pp. 8–10.

[4] Two collections that are especially relevant to marketers and consumer behavior researchers are: Gordon C. Bruner, Karen James and Paul Hensel (eds.), *Marketing Scales Handbook* (AMA, 2000) and Richard Netemeyer, William Bearden and Subhash Sharma, *Scaling Procedures* (Sage, 2003).

affects a consumer's choice of stores or products (a consumer concerned with animal testing may purchase body lotions only at the Body Shop) or an individual's response to an in-store ad or point-of-purchase display (appealing to consumers who are "impulsive" or "variety seekers"), just as it is believed, say, that extroverts are successful salespeople.

Lifestyle or psychographic analysis rests on the premise that the firm can plan more effective strategies to reach its target market if it knows more about those customers in terms of how they live, what interests them, and what they like. For example, the financial services market is evolving beyond demographics (e.g., income, age) and even comfort-level with risk, to incorporate information about potential investors. This includes whether consumers take an active interest in their finances, invest whenever they can, are comfortable with borrowing, seek to interact with financial brokers via traditional channels or online, etc.[5] It's easy to imagine pitching different investment portfolios to segments of people who vary along these central properties. It's also easy to see why just knowing a client's income isn't sufficient— just because two households share an income in the bracket "50,000 to 100,000" doesn't mean they are similar in their lifestyles or psychographic profiles, and so they would find different investment packages attractive.

Much psychographic research has been focused on developing a number of statements that reflect a person's activities, interests, and opinions (AIO) and consumption behavior (see Table 8.1). The statements include such things as, "I like to watch football games on television," "I like stamp collecting," "I am very interested in national politics." For example, the NPD Group taps its ongoing panel of 65,000 to 250,000 consumers monthly with multipage surveys on category-specific purchase behaviors (apparel, food, and sporting goods) as well as omnibus trends and lifestyle patterns. The goal is to identify groups of consumers who have similar lifestyle profiles and therefore are likely to behave similarly toward the product or service. Research Realities 8.1 provides descriptions of travelers who share the goal of visiting friends or relatives, but who differ in family composition (children or not), length of trip (short or long), and the activities they seek (visiting beaches or theme parks). Segment descriptions help the marketer determine which groups may be attractive to target, and which attributes would be appealing in advertising (e.g., shots of children at theme parks, or couples on beaches).

TABLE 8.1
Lifestyle Dimensions

Activities	Interests	Opinions
Work	Family	Themselves
Hobbies	Home	Social issues
Social events	Job	Politics
Vacation	Community	Business
Entertainment	Recreation	Economics
Club membership	Fashion	Education
Community	Food	Products
Shopping	Media	Future
Sports	Achievements	Culture

[5] Suzanne Soper, "The Evolution of Segmentation Methods in Financial Services," *Journal of Financial Services Marketing* 7 (2002), pp. 67–74.

Research Realities

8.1 Lifestyle Descriptions and Qualities Sought by People Traveling to Visit Friends and Family in Australia

Beach Relaxation (38%) Major reason for trip is pleasure travel. Visiting friends and family is important along with taking advantage of warm weather and beaches. Tend to be repeat visitors, staying with friends and relatives, or in recreation vehicle parks.

Active Beach Resort (15%) Tend to be younger, traveling with children, coming longer distances. Seek weather as dominant feature. They'll visit theme parks, beaches, and other family attractions. These young families stay in suites or apartments, or with friends and relatives. This group incurs the greatest overall expenditures.

Active Nature Lovers (16%) Seek good weather, then visiting friends and family, and the Great Barrier Reef. Likely to have traveled greater distances (e.g., from Europe), and therefore spend the most on transportation. They stay the longest, often with friends and relatives.

Inactives (31%) Visiting friends and relatives is the only major activity planned; likely to have traveled shorter distances, staying the shortest duration. They spend the least.

Source: Gianna Moscardo et al., "Developing a Typology for Understanding Visiting Friends and Relatives Markets," *Journal of Travel Research* (Feb. 2000), pp. 251–259.

It is inefficient for marketers to develop new psychographics or AIO inventories for every different category, each product requiring new data collection and analysis. As an alternative, value and lifestyle research (VALS) avoids these problems by creating a more general psychographic framework that can be used for a variety of products.[6] Research Realities 8.2 shows the basic framework of VALS, and Table 8.2 illustrates an example of six international segments that have been identified by applying values surveys to teenagers.

Attitudes and Opinions

The term **attitude** is used to refer to an individual's "preference, inclination, views, or feelings toward some phenomenon," and **opinions** are "verbal expressions" of

TABLE 8.2
Segments Identified Using Values Surveys Among Teens Worldwide

Segment	%	Key Countries	Enjoy	Worry About	Own / Wear / Do
Thrills & chills (sensations)	18	Germany, U.K., Lithuania, Greece, Netherlands, South Africa, U.S.	Going out to eat, going to a bar, drinking, smoking cigarettes, going to a party, going on a date, dancing; Have most online access	Finding love, unplanned pregnancy, own attractiveness	Fast food, acne medication, perfume, would dye hair, would like tattoo or nose ring; Do NOT have a job or attend church *(continued)*

---

[6] Another value-based classification scheme is the List of Values (LOV); for an application, see Leon Schiffman, Elaine Sherman and Mary Long, "Toward a Better Understanding of the Interplay of Personal Values and the Internet," *Psychology and Marketing* 20 (2003), pp. 169–186.

TABLE 8.2
(continued)

Segment	%	Key Countries	Enjoy	Worry About	Own / Wear / Do
Upholders (family, tradition)	16	Vietnam, Indonesia, Taiwan, China, Italy, Peru, Venezuela, Puerto Rico, India, Philippines, Singapore	Reading books, spending time with family and visiting relatives; Have least online access	Not living up to others' expectations; Believe the world will improve in their lifetime	Do NOT have jobs to earn money, eat fast food, wear deodorant, have tattoos or nose rings, carry guns; Girls do NOT wear makeup
Quiet achievers (success, anonymity)	15	Thailand, China, Hong Kong, Ukraine, Korea, Lithuania, Russia, Peru	Studying, listening to music, visiting museums; Do NOT enjoy going to parties or drinking wine/beer	Not living up to others' expectations; Believe the world will improve in their lifetime; Do NOT worry about finishing education, pregnancy, AIDS, drugs	Do NOT have jobs, or backpacks, blue jeans, or athletic shoes; Girls do NOT wear makeup
Resigned (low expectations)	14	Denmark, Sweden, Korea, Japan, U.K., Norway, Germany, Belgium, France, Netherlands, Spain, Argentina, Canada, Turkey, Taiwan	Do NOT enjoy doing something artistic/creative, attending opera, play, or ballet, or visiting relatives	Do NOT worry about going to college, the economy, rain forest, global warming, living up to others' expectations	Have dyed or would dye hair; Do NOT care about access to new technology
Bootstrappers (achievement, individualism)	14	Nigeria, Mexico, U.S., India, Chile, Puerto Rico, South Africa, Venezuela, Colombia	Spending time with family and visiting relatives	Do NOT worry about not having friends or being lonely; Believe education is good preparation for future and that they will have a good life	Attend religious services; Do NOT receive allowances
World savers (environment)	12	Hungary, Brazil, Philippines, Venezuela, Spain, Colombia, Belgium, Argentina, Russia, Singapore, France, Poland, Ukraine, Italy, South Africa, Mexico, U.K.	Attending opera, plays, and ballet, doing something artistic/creative (such as taking photos), going camping/hiking, going to a bar, dancing	Racism, poverty for others, environment, AIDS, war, terrorism, being able to have children, finding love	Would NOT carry gun

For more information, see Elissa Moses, *The $100 Billion Allowance: Accessing the Global Teen Market* (Wiley, 2000), pp. 80–103.

Research Realities

8.2 The Structure of the VALS Inventory

VALS is basically a questionnaire about different aspects of consumers' lives and value systems. The survey asks the consumer to indicate the extent to which they agree or disagree with items on numerous issues, such as:

- "I like a lot of variety in my life."
- "I love to make things I can use everyday."
- "I like being in charge of a group."
- "I like trying new things."
- "I like to dress in the latest fashions."
- "I like my life to be pretty much the same from week to week."
- "I would like to spend a year or more in a foreign country."

Consumers who provide similar patterns of responses are segmented into one of eight groups, as described shortly. These values-based segments have been used in a wide variety of marketing applications, including:

- Concept formation in new product development
- Development of ads and media selection to communicate targeted messages about features and benefits of new and improved products
- Selection of the most suitable business alliance partners and distribution channel relationships

The eight segments of consumers are formed as follows. First, people are classified according to their *primary motivation*. That is, people are thought to be primarily driven by one of the following (which are you?)

- Ideals-people (people guided by knowledge and principles)
- Achievement-oriented (consumers look for products and services as signs of their success)
- Self-expression (people seeking social or physical activity, variety, and risk)

People may also be classified according to their level of resources and innovativeness. People with greater incomes and education levels have more resources to bring to expressing themselves in the marketplace, but resources are not just about money. People with high-energy and self-confidence, and people who are intelligent, seek novelty, are leaders, and somewhat vain have greater cognitive and emotional resources to bring to their expression.

The three primary motivations, and a person's level of resources determine their membership in one of six segments:

- **Thinkers:** are the people with many resources motivated by ideals.
- **Believers:** are the people with fewer resources for whom ideals are very important.
- **Achievers:** are people who care about achievement and have the resources to go after such goals.
- **Strivers:** are people with fewer resources but who are trying to achieve.
- **Experiencers:** are people who care about self-expression and have the resources to do so.
- **Makers:** are people who care about self-expression but have fewer resources at their disposal.

We said "eight" and yes, you've counted only six segments. *Innovators* are purely high on the resources/innovativeness scale, but are not distinguishable on the ideals / achievement / expression dimension. At the other extreme, the *Survivors* are doing just that—they have minimal resources and are motivated more simply by survival than more abstract motivations.

Source: SRI International now runs the proprietary VALS2; see http://www.sri-bc.com.

those attitudes. We treat the terms interchangeably as representing a person's ideas, convictions, or liking with respect to a specific object or idea.

Attitudes are pervasive because it is generally thought that they are related to behavior—when consumers like a product, they are more inclined to buy it than when they do not like it, and when they like one brand more than another, they tend to buy the preferred brand. Attitudes thus are said to be the forerunners of behavior.

Accordingly, marketers are interested in people's attitudes toward a product ("Do you like soft drinks?"), their attitudes with respect to specific brands ("Coke, Pepsi, or 7-Up?"), and their attitudes toward specific features of the brands ("Diet, caffeine-free, cherry?"). Attitude is so important in marketing that we devote Chapter 10 to various attitude measures.

Awareness and Knowledge

Awareness and knowledge refer to what respondents do and do not know about some object. For instance, an important problem in marketing is determining the effectiveness of ads in such media as TV, radio, magazine, billboard, and Web banners. One measure of effectiveness is the product awareness generated by the ad, using one of the three approaches described in Table 8.3. All three tests of memory—*unaided recall*, *aided recall*, and *recognition*—are aimed at assessing the respondent's awareness and knowledge. The three measures reflect differences in the extent to which consumers have cognitively processed (in depth and detail or just superficially) the ad, the brand name, the featured attributes, and so on. It is thought that consumers have retained more knowledge from the ad when they state the brand in an *unaided recall* test ("What products and brands do you remember seeing ads for?") compared to a *recall* test where they have been given hints ("Do you remember recently seeing ads for PCs?"), and that both of these show superior knowledge and retention over simple *recognition* ("Do you remember seeing this ad for Dell?").[7]

One of the common indices used to measure the short-term success and impact of an ad is *day-after recall* (or *DAR*), which is a phone survey, as the name implies, made the day following the airing of a new ad (e.g., the day after the Super Bowl). The DAR scores are compared to the ad agency's databank of such indices to project sales, by using other recent ads that had achieved similar DAR scores as benchmarks.

Increasingly, psychologists and advertising researchers are exploring the idea that consumers do not have to explicitly remember an ad for that ad to nevertheless have an impact on their behavior. For example, after airing an ad for Reebok, the researcher might choose to use "implicit" or indirect tests of memory.[8] Rather than asking, "Do you remember any recent ads for athletic shoes or Reeboks?" the researcher might instead ask consumers to list brand names of sneakers, their first choice set of sporting shoes, shoes affiliated with athlete spokepersons, and so on, to assess the number of times the Reebok brand name appears. Researchers have even asked questions as oblique as, "Name all the brands of any kind of product that start

TABLE 8.3 Approaches Used to Measure Awareness	**Unaided recall:** Without being given any clues, consumers are asked to recall what advertisements they have seen recently. Prompting is not used because, presumably, even if prompting for the general category were used (such as for soups), respondents would have a tendency to remember more advertisements in that product category. **Aided recall:** Consumers are prompted, typically in the form of questions about advertisements in a specific product category. Alternatively, respondents might be given a list showing the names or trademarks of advertisers that appeared recently (in the ad format being tested, such as on radio or Web), along with names or trademarks that did not appear, and would be asked to check those to which they were exposed. **Recognition:** Actual advertisements are shown or described to consumers, who are asked whether they remember seeing each one.

---

[7] Asher Koriat, Morris Goldsmith and Ainat Pansky, "Toward a Psychology of Memory Accuracy," *Annual Review of Psychology* 51 (2000), pp. 481–537.

[8] William P. Wallace, Christine P. Malone and Alison D. Spoo, "Implicit Word Activation During Prerecognition Processing," *Psychonomic Bulletin and Review* 7 (2000), pp. 149–157.

with R" to see how often Reebok would appear, along with names such as Reese's, Rolex, and Ramada. The assumption in these tests is that if Reebok appears disproportionately more than it should (based on market shares), the ad was successful in bringing the Reebok brand name to mind.

Intentions

A person's intentions refer to the individual's anticipated or planned future behavior. Marketers are primarily interested in people's intentions with regard to purchasing behavior. The Survey Research Center at the University of Michigan (see http://www.isr.umich.edu/src) regularly conducts surveys for the Federal Reserve Board to determine the financial condition of consumers. The center phones a sample of 500 households monthly, asking 50 core questions about consumer confidence and buying intentions for big-ticket items such as appliances, automobiles, and homes during the next few months.

In marketing, intentions are often gathered by asking respondents to indicate which of the following best describes their plans with respect to a new product or service:

- Definitely would buy
- Probably would buy
- Undecided
- Probably would not buy
- Definitely would not buy

The number of people who answer that they "definitely would buy" or "probably would buy" are often combined into a "top 2 box" to indicate likely reaction to the new product or service.

It is true that behavioral intentions do not predict behavior perfectly; a disparity often exists between what people say they are going to do and what they actually do. However, they are fairly correlated. See Research Realities 8.3 for a demonstration.

The prediction of behaviors by intentions is not perfect, but sometimes behavioral data are too expensive, difficult, or even impossible to obtain. For example, if Doritos were to create a new spicy salsa-flavor chip as a line extension, by definition no purchase data would exist because the snack food would not have been available yet for purchase. If the marketer had data on a household's purchases of regular Doritos and salsa and spicy foods, perhaps an inference could be drawn to predict consumption of the new salsa chip (this inference requires assumptions, of course). In the absence of these behavioral data, consumer judgments of their intentions are as close to actual behaviors as marketers can get. To help compensate for the imperfect prediction,

Ethical Dilemma 8.1

Pharmaceutical Supply Company derives its major source of revenue from physician-prescribed drugs. Until recently, Pharmaceutical Supply had maintained a dominant position in the market. A new competitor has entered the market, however, and is quickly gaining market share.

In response to competitive pressure, Pharmaceutical Supply's management decided that it needed to conduct an extensive study concerning physician decision making with regard to selection of drugs. Janice Rowland, the marketing research director, decided that the best way to gather this information was through the use of personal and telephone interviews. Ms. Rowland directed the interviewers to represent themselves as employees of a fictitious marketing research agency, as she believed that a biased response would result if the physicians were aware that Pharmaceutical Supply was conducting the study. In addition, the interviewers were instructed to tell the physicians that the research was being conducted for their own purpose and not for a particular client.

Was Ms. Rowland's decision to withhold the sponsor's true name and purpose a good one?

- Do the physicians have a right to know who is conducting the research?
- It has been argued that use of such deception prevents a respondent from making a rational choice about whether she or he wishes to participate in a study. Comment on this.
- What kind of results might have been obtained if the physicians knew the true sponsor of the study?
- What are the consequences for the research profession of using this form of deception?

Research Realities

8.3 The Relationship Between Stated Purchase Intentions and Subsequent Purchase

Market Facts conducted a study in which researchers asked consumers for their *purchase intentions*, "How likely is it you will be buying a microwave oven in the next six months?" The responses are provided in the left-most column of data in the table. Most people didn't expect to buy this product in the near future.

The consumers were tracked to study their subsequent actual *purchase behaviors*. The results were not veridical (not all of the 7% of those stating they'd be buying a microwave oven in fact did so), but the results were indeed correlated. More people bought who said they'd buy, and fewer people bought who said they wouldn't.

Stated Purchase Intentions give us information about likely future Purchase Behaviors.

Microwave ovens:		% of each who:	
	Initial response	**Bought**	**Did not buy**
Intend to buy	7%	20%	56%
Do not intend to buy	78%	3%	70%

Source: "Measuring Buying Intentions: How Valid Is the Estimate?" http://www.Synovate.com *Research on Research* 23.

In an analogous investigation, the Burke marketing research firm conducted a study in which consumers were asked to rate front-line sales representatives in a services marketing sector on a 10-point scale, measuring a number of attributes, including their rep's knowledge and friendliness.

The customers were also asked about the likelihood of repeat purchasing, that is, the probability that they would stay customers of the firm.

Plotting the means on the attributes against the means of the customer retention figures is a helpful diagnostic for the firm. In the plot of the service rep's knowledge, you can see that barely exceeding the mid-point on a 10-point scale (i.e., 5 or more) translates into a customer's likelihood of staying loyal (at least for the short term) of 75% or greater. If the service rep's level of knowledge is truly poor (a rating of 4 or less), the customer retention levels are much lower, e.g., the customers stop purchasing in the category, or they take their dollars to a competitor.

The relationship between a service rep's helpfulness and customer retention is slightly different. Here, a rating of "5" is much worse news than a "5" on the knowledge dimension because customer retention deteriorates more quickly. For a knowledge rating of 5, the retention was 75%; for a helpfulness rating of 5, retention

is about 55%. At least for this particular industry, customers are less willing to tolerate front-line service people who don't try to be helpful. You can imagine this translating into employee training—"Even if you don't know the answer to a customer's question, try to be helpful, for example, go find out." Customers won't punish the firm for a service rep's lack of knowledge, but they will for their unhelpfulness.

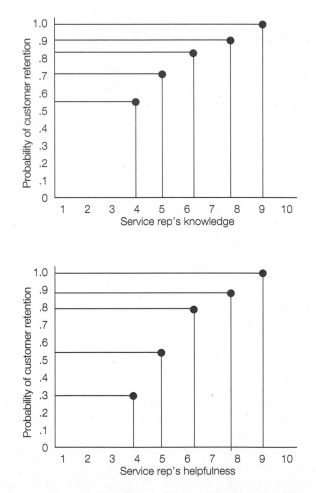

"Customer Retention as a Function of Customer Service Metrics" (http://www.Burke.com) *White Paper* series. Also see Christian Homburg, Wayne Hoyer, and Martin Fassnacht, "Service Orientation of a Retailer's Business Strategy," *Journal of Marketing* 66 (2002), pp. 86-101.

organizations that collect purchase intentions data often adjust the data for the bias that intentions data are likely to contain (based on their past experience).

Purchase intentions are most often used when studying the purchase of commodities requiring large outlays, such as an automobile for a family, or plant and equipment for a business. The general assumption is that the larger the dollar expenditure, the more planning necessary, and the greater the correlation between anticipated and actual behavior.

Motivation

The concept of motivation seems to contain some semantic confusion. Some writers insist that motives are different from drives, where the latter cover primarily basic physiological needs (hunger, thirst, shelter, and sex). Others distinguish between needs and wants, stating that needs are the basic motivating forces that translate themselves into more immediate wants that satisfy these needs (e.g., hunger *needs* give rise to *wanting* a good steak dinner). For our purposes, a motive may refer to a need, a want, a drive, an urge, a wish, a desire, an impulse, or any inner state that directs or channels behavior toward goals.

A marketing researcher's interest in motives typically involves determining why people behave as they do. If we understand the motives behind a person's behavior, we understand the behavior better and, in turn, are in a better position to influence future behavior.

Behavior

Behavior concerns what customers have done or are doing. Usually in marketing, this means purchase and usage behavior. Behavior is a physical activity that takes place under specific circumstances, at a particular time, and involves one or more participants. Table 8.4 is a checklist of the key dimensions of behavior. There are many facets to each dimension. For example, the "where of purchase" may be specified according to the kind of store, the location of the store by broad geographic area or specific address, the size of the store, or the name of the store.

Behavior data are becoming increasingly available through various technologies (e.g., scanners and the Web) and increasingly important to marketers in customer relationship management. The most prevalent behavioral data are scanner data—SKUs and other marketing information (price, coupon use) captured at purchase, stored in massive data banks, and integrated with other marketing variables (advertising exposure) to enable the marketing researcher to conduct sophisticated analyses

TABLE 8.4
Behavior Checklist

	Purchase Behavior	Use Behavior
What and how much		
Who		
When		
Where		
How		

of behavior in the marketplace. For the past 25 years, scanner data have made a great impact for consumer packaged goods marketers, but marketers responsible for pharmaceuticals, financial products, and a variety of other goods and services will also have access to these data as scanners and other technologies become more pervasive.[9] A different technology that yields behavior data is the Web, which captures personal profile data, click-stream trails, and records of response to Web advertising.[10] Many marketers feel more confident predicting customers' future behavior as a function of their past behavior, rather than from self-reports of likely future behavioral intentions; others point out that attitudinal and motivational data supplement behavioral data, giving the marketer an understanding of *why* consumers behave the way they do.[11] Clearly this information is complementary and it would enrich the marketer's understanding to have both.[12]

Basic Means of Obtaining Primary Data

Primary data can be collected in several ways (see Figure 8.1). The primary decision is whether to use communication or observation techniques. The first involves a questionnaire or survey, oral or written. Observation does not involve questioning. Rather, facts or behaviors are recorded. The observer may be a person or some mechanical device. For example, a researcher interested in the brands of canned vegetables a family buys might conduct a pantry audit in which the shelves are checked to see which brands the family has on hand.

Communication and observation each has its own advantages and disadvantages. Generally, the strengths and weaknesses of these methods can be classified according to several dimensions:

Communication:

Ask people

Observation:

Watch them

1. Versatility: "What can you do with the technique?"
2. Business logistics: "How much will a study cost, how quickly will we see the results, and what do response rates look like?"
3. Data quality: "Are the responses objective and accurate?"

The communication method of data collection has the general advantages of versatility, speed, and lower cost, whereas observational data are typically more objective and accurate.

Versatility

Versatility refers to a technique's ability to collect information on the different types of primary data of interest to marketers. A respondent's demographic/socioeconomic characteristics and lifestyle, attitudes and opinions, awareness and knowledge,

---

[9] Scanner data were discussed in our chapter on secondary data.

[10] Shira Levine, "Clicking on the Customer," *America's Network* 104 (April 1, 2000), pp. 86–92; Rick Whiting, "Click-stream Analysis Digs Deeper," *InformationWeek* 875 (Feb. 11, 2002), p. 26.

[11] Magnus Soderlund, Mats Vilgon and Jonas Gunnarsson, "Predicting Purchasing Behavior on Business-to-Business Markets," *European Journal of Marketing* 35 (2001), pp. 168–181; Lawrence Crosby, Sheree Johnson and Richard Quinn, "Is Survey Research Dead?" *Marketing Management* (2002), pp. 24–29.

[12] Dennis Bristow and Richard Sebastian, "Holy Cow! Wait 'til Next Year! A Closer Look at the Brand Loyalty of Chicago Cubs Baseball Fans," *The Journal of Consumer Marketing* 18 (2001), pp. 256–273; Brian Rainey, "Transactional Modeling for Beginners," *Catalog Age* 18 (2001), p. 67.

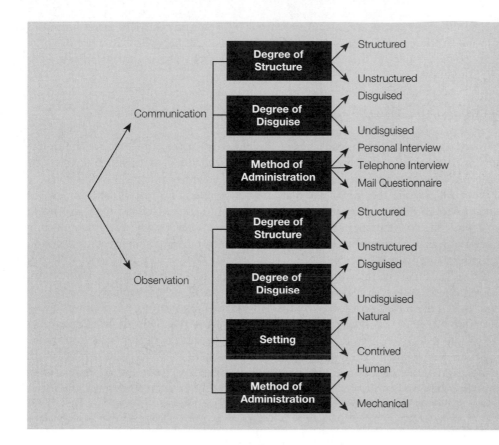

FIGURE 8.1
Choices When Collecting
Primary Data

intentions, motivations underlying actions, and even behaviors may all be obtained by the communication method. All we need to do is ask (although problems of accuracy of the replies may result, an issue we discuss later).

Observation is more limited. It is best suited for obtaining information about behavior and certain demographic/socioeconomic characteristics. Among behaviors, note that we are limited to observing present behavior; we cannot observe past behavior, nor intentions for future behavior. Among demographic/socioeconomic characteristics, some can be readily observed (e.g., gender). Others can be observed but with less accuracy. A person's age and income, for example, might be inferred by closely examining the individual, including the person's mode of dress and purchasing behavior.

Speed and Cost

The speed and cost advantages of the communication method are closely intertwined (time is money!). Communication is often a faster means of data collection, because researchers are not forced to wait for events to occur as they are with the observation method. For example, an observer checking for the brand purchased most frequently in one of several appliance categories might have to wait a long time to make any observations at all. Much of the time the observer would be idle. Such idleness is expensive, given that the worker is probably compensated on an hourly rather than a per-contact basis.

There are always exceptions. Observation is faster and costs less than communication in the purchase of consumer packaged goods. Scanners allow many more purchases to be recorded and at less cost than if purchasers were questioned about what they bought.

Objectivity and Accuracy

Balanced against these disadvantages of limited scope, time, and cost are the objectivity and accuracy of the observational method. Typically data are more accurate by observation because this method is independent of the respondent's unwillingness or inability to provide the information desired. For example, respondents are often reluctant to cooperate whenever their replies would be embarrassing or would in some way place them in an unfavorable light. Since observation allows the recording of behavior as it occurs, it does not depend on the respondent's memory or mood in reporting what occurred.

Observation typically produces more objective data than does communication. The interview represents a social interaction situation. Thus, the replies of the person being questioned are conditioned by the individual's perceptions of the interviewer. The same is true of the interviewer, although the interviewer's selection and training affords the researcher a greater degree of control over these perceptions than those of the interviewee. With observation, though, the consumer's perceptions play less of a role. Sometimes people are not even aware that they are being observed, thus removing the opportunity for them to tell the interviewer what they think the interviewer wants to hear or to give socially acceptable responses.

Communication Methods

Choosing the communication method of data collection implies several decisions. Should we administer questionnaires by mail, over the telephone, in person at a shopping mall, or by using fax, e-mail, or the Web? Should the purpose of the study be disguised? Should the answers be open-ended, or should the respondent choose from a set of alternatives? These decisions are interdependent; a decision about method of administration, say, has implications regarding the degree of structure that must be imposed on the questionnaire.

Figure 8.2 summarizes the decisions that a researcher must make when collecting data, including issues of structure and disguise. *Structure* is the degree of standardi-

FIGURE 8.2
Structure and Disguise in
Communication Methods

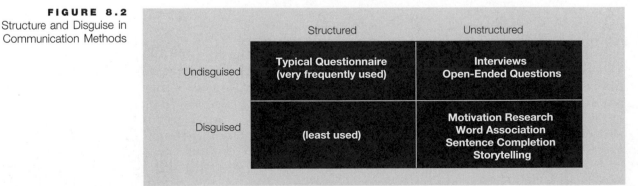

	Structured	Unstructured
Undisguised	Typical Questionnaire (very frequently used)	Interviews Open-Ended Questions
Disguised	(least used)	Motivation Research Word Association Sentence Completion Storytelling

zation imposed on the questionnaire. In a highly structured questionnaire, the questions to be asked and the responses permitted the respondents are predetermined (e.g., "Circle a number from 1 to 7"). In an unstructured questionnaire, the questions to be asked are only loosely determined, and respondents are free to answer in their own words ("Tell me how your family feels about Philadelphia Cream Cheese").

Disguise is the amount of knowledge about the purpose of a study communicated to a respondent. An undisguised questionnaire makes the purpose of the research obvious by the questions posed, whereas a disguised questionnaire attempts to hide the purpose of the study. For example, if Ford wished to determine its customers' satisfaction, they might worry that a cover letter from Ford and questions all about Ford cars and trucks would bias the respondents' answers favorably toward Ford, since the survey's purpose is clear. If Ford wanted more objective data, it might go through an outside marketing research agency, and ask its drivers about Ford, GM, and Honda cars. In this scenario, the target of the research is less clear, and it would be expected that the customer would answer more truthfully.

Structured–Undisguised Questionnaires

Structured–undisguised questionnaires are most commonly used in marketing research. Questions are presented with exactly the same wording, in the same order, to all respondents. The reason for standardizing questions is to ensure that all respondents are replying to the same question. If one interviewer asks, "Do you drink orange juice?" and another asks, "Does your family use frozen orange juice?" the replies would not be comparable.

Typically the responses are also standardized. Consider the following question regarding a person's attitude toward legislation about pollution, and note the fixed-alternative responses.

Do you feel the United States needs more or less antipollution legislation?

☐ Needs more
☐ Needs less
☐ Neither more nor less
☐ No opinion

This question is an example of a structured–undisguised question: the question's purpose is clear and respondents are limited to one of four replies.

Structured–undisguised questions are simple to administer and easy to tabulate and analyze. Respondents have little difficulty replying. Their responses should be reliable in that if they were asked the question again, they would respond in a similar fashion (assuming, of course, that their attitudes have not changed).

The fixed-alternative question is reliable for several reasons. First, the frame of reference is apparent from the alternatives. For example, if a respondent is asked, "How much do you watch television?" one person might say "every day," another might say "regularly," and still another might respond, "five hours per day." These responses would be difficult to interpret and compare. Providing responses also often helps make the question clear. The question, "What is your marital status?" is more confusing than is the question, "Are you married, single, widowed, or divorced?" The alternatives frame the reply and help ensure the reliability of the question.

Reliability can be associated with loss of validity, if the answers do not accurately reflect the true state of affairs. Fixed alternatives may force a response to a question on which the subject does not have an opinion. Even when a "no opinion" category is provided, respondents tend to keep the number of "no opinions" to a minimum. Further, the interviewer presses the respondent for a reply, and eventually the person yields. Whether the response accurately reflects the individual's attitude is another matter.

Alternatively, the respondent might have an opinion, but none of the response categories fit. The pollution example makes no allowance for distinguishing among those who feel that we definitely need a great deal more antipollution legislation ("true" environmentalists) versus those who feel not as strongly that something more should be done to clean up our air and water, and more legislation prohibiting pollution may be one answer.

Fixed-alternative responses may also lower validity when the response categories themselves introduce bias. For example, an "appropriate" response may be omitted because of an oversight. The provision of an "other" category may help, but it does not eliminate this bias altogether, because respondents are generally reluctant to respond using the "other" category. In using a fixed-alternative question, one must be reasonably certain that the alternatives are exhaustive, adequately covering the range of probable replies.

Fixed-alternative questions are best when possible replies are well known, clear-cut, and limited in number. Thus, they seem to work best when securing factual information (age, education, home ownership) and when eliciting expressions of opinion about issues on which people hold clear-cut opinions (strongly agree to strongly disagree).

Consumer research can be structured in ways other than rating scales. New technology is being explored in testing advertisements, whereby consumers watch ads and turn knobs and dials continuously through the ad to depict moments during which the ad made them feel happy or sad, or interested versus disinterested. Usually the ad is then replayed and the consumers are asked to explain their highest and lowest dial registers. Researchers find that an overall rating of an ad tends to correlate with the peak emotional experience during the ad, and the final moments in the ad. The validity and long-term viability of the method is still being determined, however; skeptics would argue that the impact of an ad is more of a gestalt, overall impression and that it might even take time to affect the consumer. Therefore the moment-by-moment judgments during the ad may not be predictive of eventual attitudes or purchase behavior.[13]

Unstructured–Undisguised Questionnaires

In unstructured–undisguised questionnaires, the purpose of the study is clear but responses to the questions are open-ended. Interviews are the primary means of unstructured and undisguised data collection. For example, the question: "How do you feel about environmental issues and the need for more antipollution legislation?" is delivered the same to every respondent but the interviewer gets the respondent to talk freely about attitudes toward pollution. After the initial question, the interview becomes very unstructured as the interviewer probes more deeply, following whatever direction the respondent leads. Figure 8.2 classifies a number of communication-based marketing research techniques by their degree of structure

---

[13] Tobi Elkin, "TiVo Introduces Service to Measure Audience Data," *Advertising Age* 74 (June 2, 2003), p. 8.

and disguise. Interviews and open-ended questions on surveys were discussed in greater detail in Chapter 4 on research design and qualitative data.

Unstructured–Disguised Questionnaires

Unstructured–disguised questionnaires lie at the heart of what has become known as motivation research. A limited experience with surveys will show you that some areas of inquiry are not amenable to exploration by direct questions. Many important motives and reasons for choice are of a kind that consumers will not describe because a truthful description would be damaging to their egos (e.g., embarrassing). Other motives are difficult to describe or the motives exist below their level of awareness. Direct questions yield replies that are either useless or misleading. Yet such motives are often of paramount importance in consumer behavior.

Projective techniques (see Chapter 4 on exploratory methods and qualitative data) were developed by researchers to circumvent respondents' reluctance to discuss their feelings. These techniques are largely independent of the respondents' self-awareness and willingness to reveal themselves. The assumption in projective methods is that an individual's reaction to a relatively unstructured stimulus is indicative of the person's basic perceptions of the phenomenon. Reactions to clear stimuli (such as a picture of a brand of toothpaste) tend to show more uniformity (though respondents can differ in whether they like or dislike the brand), whereas reactions to an ambiguous stimulus (e.g., a picture of a man seated at an office desk) allows, even requires, respondents to project their needs, motives, and values; the respondent chooses his or her own interpretation, description, and evaluation of the ambiguous stimulus.

The next research challenge in using these methods is in the analysis, or making sense of the replies. The final interpretation of what was said often reflects the interpreter's frame of reference as much as it does the respondent's. Different interpreters can reach different conclusions about the same response, which raises havoc with the coding of replies. Projective methods are thus more suited for exploratory research than for descriptive or causal research.

Structured–Disguised Questionnaires

Structured–disguised questionnaires are the least used in marketing research. They were developed in an attempt to reveal subconscious motives and attitudes yet to do so in a structured manner to facilitate coding.

One proposition holds that consumers' knowledge and memory are conditioned by their attitudes. Individuals selectively perceive and retain ideas that are consistent with their own beliefs. Thus, if we want information about people's attitudes when a direct question might produce a biased answer, we can simply ask them what they know. For example, Democratic voters would be expected to know more about Democratic candidates than those intending to vote Republican. This argument is consistent with what we know about the operation of selective cognitive processes. Thus, if we want to know someone's attitude about the environment, but we don't want them to simply respond in a socially acceptable way, we could ask people what they know rather than how they feel.

However, one ambiguity is whether a high level of awareness is indicative of a favorable or an unfavorable attitude. That is, whether this measure of knowledge can also be interpreted as a measure of the person's attitude relies on an assumption about the consumer's cognitive system.

Questionnaires Classified by Method of Administration

Questionnaires can also be classified by the method used to administer them. The main methods are personal interview, telephone, mail, fax, e-mail, and Web surveys.

A personal interview is a direct, face-to-face conversation between the interviewer and the respondent or interviewee. The interviewer asks the questions and records the respondent's answers, either while the interview is in progress or immediately afterward. The interview can take place in a home or an office, but usually is at a central location like a shopping mall, where shoppers are stopped (or intercepted, hence the term mall intercept) and asked to participate.

The telephone interview is usually a cold call with a few questions (no longer than 2–3 minutes). A mail questionnaire involves mailing the questionnaires to designated respondents with an accompanying cover letter. The respondents complete the questionnaire at their leisure and mail their replies back to the research organization. Faxed surveys operate just like mail questionnaires, except of course that they are faxed to and from the recipients. Fax surveys work much better for business-to-business research because most consumers do not have fax machines at home.

> **Means of Communication: in person, phone, mail, fax, e-mail, Web**

E-mail surveys are one of two types:

- The questions of the market research study are embedded in the text of the e-mail itself
- The questions in the survey are in an e-mail attachment file

Each has its pros and cons: Replying to embedded e-mail surveys is extremely quick. Alternatively, the attachment is likely to look more professional than the flat embedded text, and it can allow for hyperlinking, skip-patterns, artwork, and so on. However, it is one more step to open an attachment, and any additional steps that add to the hurdle of completing a survey means that response rates will drop off. Web surveys can look quite professional in that hypertext and graphics can improve both the appearance and quality control of the survey, as well as enhance the inherent appeal by, for example, requesting consumer reactions to vivid depictions of an ad or product.

A number of variations and combinations are possible. Questionnaires for a "mail" administration may be attached to products or printed in magazines. Questionnaires in a personal interview may be self-administered, perhaps in the interviewer's presence, in case the respondents seek clarification from the interviewer. Alternatively, the respondents might complete the questionnaire in private, and drop it in the mail to return to the research organization, in which case the interaction would be less like a personal interview.

Often the different modalities are mixed to enhance sample cooperation; for example, business managers may receive a letter, e-mail, or phone call asking for their help in the study, and after this pre-notification, the survey is faxed to the managers at their place of business. Web surveys are either initiated by sending an e-mail to the sample of potential respondents, with a Web address embedded in the message, or by a cooperative relationship with an Internet vendor in placing a banner on its site. The user then just clicks through to the survey.

Each of these methods of communication possesses some advantages and disadvantages which we discuss next. These include sampling control, information control, and administrative control.

Sampling Control

Sampling control concerns the researcher's ability to direct the inquiry to a designated respondent and to get the desired cooperation from that respondent.

DIRECTING THE INQUIRY

A sampling frame is the list of population elements from which the sample is drawn. With the telephone method, for example, phone books typically serve as the sampling frame, from which respondents are selected randomly. Phone book sampling frames are inadequate because they do not include households without phones or those with unlisted numbers.

Regarding phone ownership, in the U.S., the U.K., etc., 98% of households have phones, but worldwide, phone access is generally lower (e.g., 20% in Russia).[14] Differences in phone ownership by demographic factors can bias the results of a telephone survey, but phone penetration increases each year, so bias should diminish in the future, particularly with satellite services and cell phones.[15]

Approximately a third of the 90 million U.S. telephone households have unlisted numbers. Unlisted households tend to be younger, urban, nonwhite, more mobile, either very high or very low income, and the majority are in California cities.[16]

Some researchers attempt to overcome the sampling bias of unlisted numbers by using **random digit dialing (RDD)**.[17] Numbers are randomly generated and called through automatic dialing at a central interviewing facility. This procedure allows geographically wide coverage. In **plus-one sampling**, a probability sample of phone numbers is selected from the telephone directory and a single, randomly determined digit is added to each selected number.

For mail questionnaires, one or more mailing lists typically serve as the sampling frame. Again, the quality of these lists determines the sampling biases. Some firms have established panels of consumers that can be used to answer mail questionnaires and that are representative of the population. Business marketing research is usually easier in that the mailing list and lists of phone and fax numbers are more stable than those for consumers, and target businesses are fewer in number.

Suppose you run a direct-mail business that specializes in selling monogrammed baby bibs. For a fee at any given time, you can obtain a mailing list containing the names and addresses of up to one million pregnant women. And, if it suits your purposes, the list can be limited to women whose babies are expected in a certain month or who are expecting their first child. Mothers-to-be are a prime potential for relationship marketing, because "not only is she likely to buy, but she must buy" maternity clothes and skin creams during pregnancy, and baby clothes, toys, formula, and

---

[14] Census data, per http://www.worldopinion.com/the_frame; also see Andrew Beutmueller, "Stepping Out," *Communications International* (April 2000), pp. 44–47.

[15] Don't place calls to cell phones. The federal Telephone Consumer Protection Act prohibits unsolicited calls to cell phones or other machines where the recipient is charged for the call, cf. Donna Gillin, "Think Before You Dial," *Marketing Research* 14 (2002), pp. 7–11.

[16] See Survey Sampling, Inc., at http://www.ssisamples.com for statistics on listed and unlisted phone numbers, and their sampling solutions.

[17] G. Nicolaas and P. Lynn "Random-Digit Dialing in the U.K.," *Journal of the Royal Statistical Society A* 165 (2002), pp. 297–316. For concerns regarding RDD, see Allyson Holbrook, Melanie Green and Jon Krosnick, "Telephone vs. Face-to-Face Interviewing of National Probability Samples with Long Questionnaires," *Public Opinion Quarterly* 67 (2003), pp. 79–125.

so forth, upon arrival of the newborn. Lists are ultimately derived from hospital records and therefore are highly reliable. In addition, many firms continue to develop the marketing relationship by sending their representatives to deliver bedside drop-offs of gift packs, trial sizes of relevant products, and redeemable coupons at stores such as Mothercare.[18]

Sometimes the list is internally generated. Technical advances enable greater capability to target questionnaires or other mailings to specific households. For example, American Express, with its image-processing technology, can select all its cardholders who made purchases from golf pro-shops, who traveled more than once to Europe, who attended symphony concerts, or who made some other specific purchase using their American Express card. Relationship and database marketing are giving marketers many opportunities to cross-sell to customers. These databases are continually updated, so they also serve as an excellent sampling frame to survey current customers.

Beyond a good working list, it is also critical to target well. Response rates are greater for surveys on topics that the recipient cares about. Targeting is more efficient than simply increasing the sample size. That increases mailing costs, and fewer complete surveys are obtained from a mass, uncustomized effort. It is estimated that the average U.S. consumer receives some 550 unsolicited mailings per year (compared with 50–100 for Germany, the U.K., and France); direct mailing is a $1.5 trillion market in the U.S., employing 9 million people.[19]

Regarding newer technologies, fax surveys operate like phone surveys in their sampling frames. E-mail-administered questionnaires are similar to mail questionnaires when it comes to sampling control. The sample, of course, is limited to those who own or have access to a computer and an e-mail account (who tend to be more affluent and better educated). However, if an accurate, applicable, and readily available list of e-mail addresses exists, e-mail allows a geographically dispersed sample to be used.

It is conceptually difficult, but practically possible to achieve sampling control for the administration of questions using personal interviews. For some select populations (e.g., doctors, architects, businesses), a list of population members may be available in trade directories. For consumer studies, areas (e.g., zip codes) and dwelling units (apartment buildings) become the sampling units. Alternatively, consumer studies frequently use mall intercepts: interviewers stop shoppers in a mall and ask if they would be willing to participate in a research study. Those who agree are taken to the firm's interviewing facility that has been set up in the mall (a small, rented office), where the interview is conducted. Mall intercepts pose two issues: (1) most people shop at malls, but almost 20% do not; (2) a person's chances of being asked to participate depend on the frequency with which he or she shops there and the time spent in the mall.

GETTING COOPERATION

Directing the survey to a specific respondent is one thing; getting a response from that individual is quite another. In this respect, the personal interview affords the

---

[18] Lisa A. Yorgey, "Reaching Expectant and New Mums," *Target Marketing* 23 (March 2000), pp. 60–63.

[19] All those who think unsolicited mail is a bother can contact the Direct Marketing Association (http://www.the-dma.org), a trade group of over 4,600 direct-mail marketing firms (commercial and nonprofit, U.S. and 53 nations abroad), and that organization will remove the name from every member's list.

most sample control (the respondent's identity is known, and there is little opportunity for anyone else to reply). The rate of refusal-to-participate is also typically lower than with phone interviews or mail questionnaires. Usually the principle holds that the more personal the appeal, the more difficult it is for a respondent to say no: malls are face-to-face and phone solicitations are person-to-person. Mail is the least personal, most anonymous channel, and many mail surveys end up in recycling bins, unless the topic is inherently interesting to the consumer, or perhaps if some incentive is offered to complete the survey. We say more about these factors later.

Telephone methods suffer from "not-at-homes"; one-third of calls result in a no-answer, but this number is surprisingly stable even in the face of the growth of answering machines and caller ID. Research firms generally can still get through to talk to a live consumer, by being persistent (by making more contacts).[20] See Research Realities 8.4 for key ingredients to enhancing participation in phone surveys.

For mail questionnaires, the researcher has little control over whether the intended respondent is really the person who completes the survey, if anybody completes the survey at all.[21] Many persons refuse to respond. Often only those most interested in the survey topic respond. Some people are functionally illiterate (e.g., they have difficulty reading job notices or getting a driver's license).

E-mail- or Web-administered questionnaires are somewhat better in these respects. For one thing, literacy is not a problem because those owning and using computers are typically better educated. Moreover, there is much less likelihood that someone other than the intended respondents will reply, given that the questionnaires reside in personal e-mail accounts. Although fax surveys provide less control in terms of who responds, they too are less subject to literacy problems because those who have access to and use fax machines are typically better educated.

Generally, regardless of the method of survey administration, marketing researchers have noted the steady decline in sample cooperation. It has been suggested that higher compensations may be required to obtain responses. Greater incentives would drive up costs of research or tempt researchers to be frugal on sample size. Yet one consistent finding is that potential respondents are more likely to participate in the study if the research topic is inherently interesting to them—intrinsic interest exceeds extrinsic incentives in raising response rates. Enhanced databases should facilitate greater tailoring so that consumers are contacted only on topics relevant to them, and not *en masse*. Other solutions will continue to evolve. For example, it has been suggested that for e-commerce, filling out a survey may become part of the cost of an online service provider. Finally, statistical solutions are also evolving; it has been suggested that to compensate for nonrespondents, post-survey adjustments of the data may be required.[22]

---

[20] Robert Groves et al. (eds.), *Telephone Survey Methodology* (Wiley, 2001); Eve Fielder and Linda Bourque, *How to Conduct Telephone Surveys,* 2nd ed. (Sage, 2002).

[21] See Floyd Fowler, *Survey Research Methods* (Sage, 2001) or Paul Biemer and Lars Lyberg, *Introduction to Survey Quality* (Wiley, 2003) for discussions of sample control in surveys and ways to overcome respondent resistance.

[22] In business marketing surveys, the content of the survey is the clearest determinant of response rates, and, e.g., day of week had little effect; see Thomas V. Greer, Nuchai Chuchinprakam and Sudhindra Seshadri, "Likelihood of Participating in Mail Survey Research," *Industrial Marketing Management* 29 (2000), pp. 97–119; Patrick van Kenhove, Katrien Wijnen and Kristof De Wulf, "The Influence of Topic Involvement on Mail-Survey Response Behavior," *Psychology and Marketing* 19 (2002), pp. 293–303; B. Zafer Erdogan and Michael Baker, "Increasing Mail Survey Response Rates from an Industrial Population," *Industrial Marketing Management* 31 (2002), pp. 65–73. Research on consumers still find incentives effective, James Helgeson, Kevin Voss and Willbann Terpening, "Determinants of Mail-Survey Response," *Psychology & Marketing* 19 (2002), pp. 303–328.

Research Realities

8.4 Telephone Survey Practices

The Council for Marketing and Opinion Research (CMOR) is composed of four partners:

- The American Marketing Association (AMA)
- The Advertising Research Foundation (ARF)
- The Council of American Survey Research Organizations (CASRO)
- The Marketing Research Association (MRA)

CMOR conducted a study of phone survey participation. The key ingredients in a telephone interviewer's introduction that help provide the perception of a professionally conducted marketing research survey, and which in turn were helpful to enhance participant cooperation included:

- Stating the sponsoring company's name.
- Giving a brief overview about the general topic of the survey.
- Provide the first name of the interviewer.
- Assuring the interviewee that there will be no attempt to "sell anything."
- Assuring the interviewee that responses will be held confidential.
- Providing an accurate estimate as to the approximate length of the interview.

When you hire a marketing research firm, which in turn, hires a service to conduct phone interviews, it may help to understand a profile of the telephoning personnel.

- The telephone interviewers are usually working on more than one study at a time.
- Most have more than six months' experience with the particular call center facility that now employs them.
- 25% of the employees are full-time (thus, 75% are part-timers—think about that).
- In terms of compensation, the median starting hourly wages are $6.90, the top pay is around $10. Half (only!) of these employees get an annual bonus or pay raise. Half (only) get benefits (vacation time, holiday pay, health insurance, sick leave pay).
- The training received before being put into place to begin interviewing is one day.

Moral of the story: keep your survey clear and simple.

Source: http://www.cmor.org.

Information Control

The differing methods of data collection also vary in the type of questions that can be asked, and the amount and accuracy of the information that can be obtained from respondents. The personal interview can be conducted using almost any form of questionnaire: structured or unstructured, disguised or undisguised. The interaction allows the interviewer to present pictures or examples of ads, lists of words, scales, and so on. The consumer can taste new flavors of Pepperidge Farm cookies, or smell new line extensions of Michael Jordan colognes. Visual aids can be used with mail questionnaires, but not with telephone surveys.

Personal interviews allow the use of open-ended questions that require extensive probes. Written questionnaires do not lend themselves to such questions. Telephone interviews can incorporate open-ended questions, but not nearly to the same extent as in-person interviews, mostly because phone surveys need to be brief, so as not to be discontinued by an increasingly bored or irritated respondent midway through the survey.

Personal interviews also allow the automatic, contingent sequencing of questions; for example, if the answer to question 4 is positive, the interviewer may be instructed to proceed to ask questions 5 and 6, whereas if the answer had been negative, the interviewer asks questions 7 and 8. Automatic sequencing is also possible with telephone interviews, especially when the interviewer is reading from a computer screen and the question skipping is preprogrammed. Skipping questions is not advised for mail questionnaires, e-mail, or fax because respondents will get confused and make errors. Web surveys can easily be programmed to contain skip patterns.

There is also a greater danger of "sequence bias" with hard copy questionnaires; respondents can see the whole questionnaire, so their replies to any question may be conditioned by their previous responses. For example, if you present a print ad on page one, and on page three ask memory questions about the ad, the respondent could, and likely would, flip back to page one, fill in your questions dutifully, but in so doing, destroy the validity of those questions for recall. On the other hand, mail, e-mail, Web, or fax questionnaires allow respondents to work at their own pace, so their responses may be more thoughtful.

Mail questionnaires are more anonymous, so people can be more frank on sensitive issues (such as sexual behavior). Replies to e-mail can be traced to the sender, so there is less anonymity. The jury is not officially in, but early reports suggest respondents feel anonymity when answering Web surveys, and so again may answer questions more truthfully.

Personal and telephone interviews can reflect interviewer bias because of the respondent's perception of the interviewer, or because different interviewers ask questions and probe in different ways. This kind of bias does not occur for mail, e-mail, or faxed questionnaires.

With regard to length of questionnaire or amount of information to be collected, the rule of thumb is that long questionnaires can be handled best by personal interview, next best by written formats (mail, Web, fax, e-mail), and least well by telephone interview. Much depends on the topic of inquiry and the form of the questionnaire.

Computers are helpful aids in conducting surveys. From the 1970s, phone interviews were linked to minicomputers—prompts on a terminal were the questions that normally would have been on a paper questionnaire. Interviewers would read the questions as they came up on the screen and would enter respondents' answers directly on the keyboard. The early systems generated such substantial savings in time and resources that they spawned a virtual revolution in data collection. Partly because of the advantages that accrue with computer administration of questionnaires, telephone interviews have become the most popular data-collection technique (as you're probably aware, from the number of times you've been disturbed by such a call during dinner).

Currently, there are two applications of computer-aided interviewing (CAI) software:

1. Telephone surveys, in which each interviewer has a personal computer from which to ask questions (see Table 8.5 for more on Computerized Adaptive Telephone Interviewing, or CATI).
2. In-person interviews, such as mall intercepts, in which the interviewer transports a laptop computer to the interview site and uses it to interview the respondent, or places the computer in front of the respondent and lets the respondent answer questions as they appear on the screen.

One of the most important advantages of computer-assisted interviewing is its level of information control. The computer displays each question exactly as the researcher intended (and programmed). It shows only the questions and information that the respondent should see and it displays the next question only when an acceptable answer to the current one is entered on the keyboard (e.g., if a respondent says that he or she bought a brand that is not available in that particular locale, the computer can be programmed to reject the answer, which greatly simplifies skipping or

TABLE 8.5
Common Features in
Computerized Adaptive
Telephone Interviewing
(Cati) Software

Questionnaire writing system: helps the researcher create a computer-administered questionnaire. The software capabilities include the construction of complex, contingent skip patterns and logic branches, in which different answers direct respondents to different parts of the questionnaire; randomization of question alternatives; insertion of previous answers into the text of the current question; consistency checks.

Call management system: serves two functions: (1) builds sample database by manually typing in the sample or by transferring from an existing database; (2) controls the flow to interviewing stations. It ensures that: call-backs are made when scheduled, busy numbers are redialed after a preset delay, and time zones are recognized.

Call disposition monitoring system: tracks each call attempt by its disposition (no answer, busy, immediate refusal, failed to qualify, call-back, complete). Also calculates incidence of qualified respondents to compare with incidence assumed in the cost quote for study.

Interviewer system: displays the questionnaire for the interviewer, determines which call to attempt next, provides call history for the call before it is placed, dials the number, automatically reschedules a "no answer" for another attempt, automatically determines when "busy" numbers are to be redialed, and aids in scheduling call-backs.

Reporting system: generates accurate and timely reports, including quota reports, call disposition reports, incidence reports, top-line reports of respondent data, and interviewer productivity reports. Increases supervisor productivity and overall quality of the data collection (less time is spent compiling reports and more time is spent on supervising interviews).

Analysis capabilities: integrated cross-tabulation and statistical analyses.

The Latest: MCAPI stands for "mobile computer-assisted personal interviewing"; the interviewer sets up a table in a mall, intercepts a sample respondent, then either walks them through questions prompted by a laptop or has the respondent sit down in front of the computer to complete the survey at his or her own pace (cf. http://www.quirks.com).

Source: Based on "Computer-Assisted Telephone Interviewing" (http://www.sawtoothsoftware.com). Also see Pieter Willems and Paul Oosterveld, "The Best of Both Worlds," *Marketing Research* (2003), pp. 23–26.

branching procedures). Information control also manifests itself in the following ways:

1. Personalization of the questions. During the course of the interview, the computer can use answers to previous responses (name of spouse, cars owned, favorite supermarket) to customize the wording of subsequent questions, e.g., "When your wife, Ann, shops at the Acme, does she usually use the Fiat or the Buick?" Such personalized questions are thought to enhance rapport and provide for higher-quality interviews.

2. Customized questionnaires. Key information elicited early in the interview can be used to tailor the questionnaire for each respondent. For example, only product attributes previously acknowledged by respondents as determinants of their decisions are used to measure their brand perceptions, rather than using a more exhaustive list of attributes common to all respondents.

Computer-assisted interviewing speeds the data collection and processing tasks. The preliminary tabulations of the answers are available at a moment's notice, because the replies are already stored in memory. The marketing manager does not have the typical 2–3 week delay caused by coding and data entry that happens when questionnaires are completed by hand, and in turn, the data are entered by hand.

However, even computers have limitations. They cannot win over respondents with social chitchat or explain questions that are misunderstood. Computers are incapable of recognizing fuzzy or superficial answers and they cannot prod respondents to elaborate on their answers. The computer systems that ask questions by phone with mechanical voices have raised the ire of most of us; luckily these surveys seem to have declined in usage.

Administrative Control

One of the greatest advantages of Internet surveys is that they provide the marketing researcher the quickest turnaround. Half of e-mail surveys are typically completed and returned the same day they were sent. For phone surveys, a number of calls can be made from a central exchange in a short period, perhaps 15 to 20 per hour per interviewer if the questionnaire is short. It can take two weeks to achieve that same response rate using the postal service.

After a couple of weeks, during which the bulk of the replies come in, a follow-up mailing is begun. The response rates will increase, but so does the overall time required to complete the study.

In-home personal interviews are the most expensive per completed contact (followed by phone surveys); the e-mail and Web questionnaires tend to be the cheapest (followed by mail interviews). The per-contact cost of a mail questionnaire is low, but if nonresponse is substantial, the cost per return may be high. Faxing can be expensive if the destination recipients are long-distance. Telephone, mall, and in-home personal interview methods require large field staffs. The larger the field staff, the greater the problems of control. Labor and particularly good quality control costs money, so these methods are the most expensive data-collection techniques.

The targeted sample also impacts costs. A decision must be made regarding the point at which the costs of locating members of a particular population outweigh the benefits of those members' inclusion.[23]

Table 8.6 presents the results of several studies that compared the turnaround times, response rates, and costs of a variety of methods of administering questionnaires. The table shows response rates for traditional research methods (mail, phone, mall, door-to-door) as well as newer techniques (fax, e-mail, Web) as well as turnaround times and cost.

Each method of data collection has its uses, and none is superior in all situations. For example, a trial product may be sent by regular mail or picked up at a mall, with a phone or Web survey follow-up to assess consumers' reaction.

Many researchers worry that Internet samples are still peculiar, in part due to differential access to e-mail and the Web. Indeed, even as that chasm tightens, there may still be self-selection biases (see Table 8.7). Worse, the novelty of an e-mail or Web survey is starting to wear off, and response rates are beginning to plummet.

---

[23] Julien Teitler, Nancy Reichman and Susan Sprachman, "Costs and Benefits of Improving Response Rates for a Hard-to-Reach Population," *Public Opinion Quarterly* 67 (2003), pp. 126–138.

TABLE 8.6
Comparing Methods of
Administering
Questionnaires

The following table shows the comparisons among traditional techniques (door-to-door, mall, phone, mail) to newer, electronic techniques (fax, e-mail, Web) in terms of response notes, completion times, and costs.

| | **TECHNIQUE** | | | | | | |
	Door-to-Door	Mall	Phone	Mail	Fax	E-mail*	Web
Response rates	15%	29%	75%	35–63%	25%	8–37%	26%
% bad addresses				0–19%	41%	19–20%	24%
Response time in days (mean)				13–18	9	4–6	7
Days (median)				12	12	2	5
# Days to receive 45% responses				13		1	
# Days to receive 80% responses				28		9	
Fixed costs				$59	$57	$57	$57
Unit cost				$1.56	$0.56	$0.01	$0.01
Variable costs (200 surveys sent)				$312	$112	$2	$2
Total cost				$371	$169	$59	$59

*Response rates for e-mail surveys that are embedded in the text of the e-mail tend to run 20 to 25%. When the recipient must open an attached file, response rates dropped to 8%. No differences were found in the content of the responses, but attached surveys were considered more attractive and easier to fill out.

Source: The indices in this table were compiled from the following sources: *Respondent Cooperation and Industry Image Survey* (The Council for Marketing and Opinion Research, http://www.cmor.org); Duane P. Bachmann, John Elfrink and Gary Vazzana, "E-mail and Snail Mail Face Off in Rematch," *Marketing Research* 11 (2000), pp. 10–15; Curt J. Dommeyer and Eleanor Moriarty, "Comparing Two Forms of an E-Mail Survey: Embedded vs. Attached," *International Journal of Market Research* 42 (2000), pp. 39–50.

Nevertheless, at least for the near future, because e-mail surveys (embedded and attached) and Web surveys are so quick and so cheap (no real costs other than labor), and the quality of the data is consistently being compared equitably to standard techniques, e-mail and Web surveys are here to stay. Software such as surveypro is available that facilitates writing online surveys and capturing respondents' results. In addition, despite the period of "adjustment" in e-commerce, Internet shopping is here to stay, and Internet sampling and surveying seem a natural means of accessing such targeted customers.[24]

Figure 8.3 summarizes the logistics comparisons between these major methods of administering questionnaires. Table 8.8 elaborates on the overall strengths and weaknesses of these methods.

---

[24] Matthias Schonlau, Ronald Fricker and Marc Elliott, *Conducting Research Surveys via E-Mail and the Web* (Rand, 2002); Jeff Miller and Alan Hogg, "Internet vs. Telephone Data Collection" *Burke White Papers* (http://www.burke.com); Palmer Morrel-Samuels, "Web Surveys' Hidden Hazards," *Harvard Business Review* (2003), pp. 16–17; Eric Shiu and John Dawson, "Cross-National Consumer Segmentation of Internet Shopping for Britain and Taiwan," *Services Industry Journal* 22 (2002), pp. 147–166.

TABLE 8.7
Comparing Mall
and E-Panels

		Mall Tests	Internet Tests	Panel Members
Demographics are starting to look similar:	Household Size	2.8	2.9	3.0
	Average Age	40.5	39.2	37.2
	Employed	71%	72%	69%
	White	86%	88%	89%
Responses to marketing questions show:	Male	20%	21%	15%
	College	40%	43%	46%

1. Strong consistency (reliability measured as the correlation between responses over two survey occasions), and

2. Correlations between sample methodologies suggests modality is not critical and should not create bias.

	Correlation Between Responses	
	Mall vs. Internet	**Internet Test/ Retest Reliability**
Purchase Intent	.86	.94
Frequency	.94	.97
Liking	.85	.91
Price / Value	.90	.99

Other Comparative Observations

	Internet	Phone
Time Survey Took to Administer	12.5	19.4 minutes
Upon Completion, Would Respondent Participate in Future Studies?	35% yes	26% yes
More Experienced Internet Users	X	
Used Rating Scale Extreme "Endpoints" More Frequently		X

Sources: Jeff Miller and Alan Hogg, "Internet vs. Telephone Data Collection" *Burke White Paper* series 2 (4) (http://www.burke.com). Also see Ashok Ranchhod and Fan Zhou, "Comparing Respondents of E-Mail and Mail Surveys," *Marketing Intelligence & Planning* 19 (2001), p. 254.

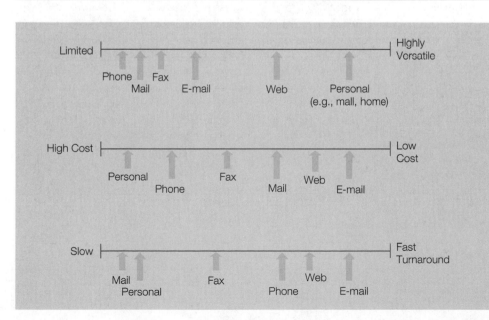

FIGURE 8.3
Comparing Methods of Survey Administration

	Sampling Control	Information Control	Administrative Control
Personal Interview (Home or Mall)	+ high response rates; best for getting response from specific, identified person – narrow distribution, difficult to identify sampling frame	+ any type of question; sequence of questions easily changed; allows probing via open-ended questions; clarification of ambiguous questions; easy use of visuals and other sensory stimuli – interviewer bias	– generally most expensive method (at home even more than at mall); relatively slow (though mall is quicker)
Written Formats (Mail, Fax, Web, E-mail)	+ only method to reach certain respondents; sampling frame easily developed with mailing lists; wide distribution – low response rates; little control in securing specific individual; cannot control speed of survey completion	+ not subject to interviewer bias; respondents work at their own pace; ensures anonymity; best for personal, sensitive questions – researcher cannot explain ambiguous questions; no probing; respondents can view entire questionnaire as they respond	+ generally least expensive; very short response time for e-mail – long response time for mail
Telephone	+ relatively strong response rates; wide distribution possible – difficult to establish representative sampling frame due to unlisted numbers	+ less interviewer bias than in person, and interviewer supervision is stronger; sequence of questions is easily changed – cannot use visual aids; more difficult to establish rapport over the phone than in person	+ relatively low cost; quick turnaround; little difficulty and cost in handling call-backs; allows easy use of computer support – interview must be brief

Structured vs. Unstructured and Disguised vs. Undisguised Observation

Like communication methods, observational data may be gathered using structured or unstructured methods that are either disguised or undisguised. Unstructured observation is used for studies in which the formulation of the problem is not specific; more flexibility is allowed the observers in terms of what they note and record. Unstructured observation is well-suited for exploratory research—just what does the customer do? For example, researchers wanted to see how women used body lotion. They thought direct observation might be too intrusive, so they videotaped the product use in action. They found two groups of women: one group "slapped on the lotion, rubbing it briskly into their skin." The other group "caressed their skin as they applied it." Querying the women, the researchers found that the first group saw the lotion as a restorative for dry skin. The second group sought the benefit of imparting softness and moisture to their skin.[25]

Structured observation is applicable when the problem is defined precisely enough to clearly specify the behaviors that will be observed and the categories that will be used to record and analyze the observations. Structured observation can be quite precise. For example, a large insurance agency began with secondary data and its compilation of accident reports, and created the list of the "10 Most Dangerous Intersections." They then sent researchers to those sites to try to piece together possible suggestions and solutions to the troublesome spots. Their work helped promote road safety and contributed to enhancing their brand equity in consumers' eyes.[26]

Disguise in observational methods refers to whether the consumers know they are being observed. A researcher acting as a mystery shopper is an example disguised observation. When a researcher interacts with the targets of their observations, e.g., "Why did you pause at the display of cashmere sweaters?" the purpose of the research becomes undisguised.

When companies capture your Web site visits unbeknownst to you, this is an example of structured, disguised recording of observations. Your behavioral data are logged in a structured manner (e.g., www addresses), and since you didn't know your behavior was being observed, the purpose of the research is disguised.[27]

Summary

Marketing researchers who cannot find secondary data to answer their marketing questions turn to primary data collection. The types of primary data of interest to marketing researchers include demographic and socioeconomic characteristics, psychological and lifestyle characteristics, attitudes and opinions, awareness and knowledge, intentions, motivation, and behavior of individuals and groups.

Communication and observation are the two basic means of obtaining primary data. Communication involves the direct questioning of respondents, whereas observation entails the systematic checking of appropriate facts or actions. Observation

---

[25] Bill Abrams, *The Observational Research Handbook* (AMA and NTC, 2000), p. 105.

[26] Faith Russell, "Dangerous Intersections," *Marketing News* (Feb. 28, 2000), p. 18.

[27] Klaus-Peter Wiedmann, Holger Buxel and Gianfranco Walsh, "Customer Profiling in E-Commerce," *Journal of Database Marketing 9* (Jan. 2002), pp. 170–184.

can be used to secure behavioral data and some demographic or socioeconomic and lifestyle characteristics, and it has the advantage of objectivity over communication methods. However, observation is not as useful for measuring those things that are not directly observable, such as attitudes, awareness, knowledge, intentions, or motivation. When these constructs are of interest, communication methods must be used.

Communication methods may be classified by their degree of structure, disguise, and method of administration. A structured questionnaire has a well-defined sequence and standardized response categories and can be used in descriptive or causal research. When the research is exploratory, unstructured questionnaires can be used. In an unstructured questionnaire, the response categories are not predetermined; respondents are allowed to answer in their own terms.

The disguised questionnaire attempts to hide the purpose of the research from the respondent. This goal is particularly important when respondents may be tempted to give socially accepted responses on sensitive issues, rather than reporting their true opinion.

Questionnaires can be administered by personal interviews in the home or at a mall, over the phone, using paper-and-pencil questionnaires by mail or fax, or by using computer-administered surveys on e-mail or the Web. Each approach has advantages and disadvantages, and the approaches vary in terms of the control they offer the researcher with respect to sample, information, and administration. The methods are not mutually exclusive and can often be used in combination.

Review Questions

1. What types of primary data interest marketing researchers most? How are they distinguished?

2. What are the general advantages and disadvantages associated with obtaining information by questioning or by observation? Which method provides more control over the sample?

3. What is a disguised questionnaire? What is a structured questionnaire?

4. What are the advantages and disadvantages of structured–undisguised questionnaires? Of unstructured–undisguised questionnaires?

5. What is the rationale for employing unstructured–disguised stimuli?

6. What operating principle or assumption underlies the use of structured–disguised questionnaires? What are the advantages and disadvantages associated with structured–disguised questionnaires?

7. How do personally administered questionnaires, telephone surveys, mail, fax, e-mail, or Web surveys differ with respect to the following?

   a. sampling control

   b. information control

   c. administrative control

Applications and Problems

1. Should the communication or observational method be used in the following situations? Justify your choice. Also specify the degree of structure and disguise for each.

   a. The Metal Products Division of Geni Ltd. devised a special metal container to store plastic garbage bags. Plastic bags posed household problems, as they gave off unpleasant odors, looked disorderly, and provided a breeding place for insects. The container overcame these problems, as it had a bag-support apparatus that held the bag open for filling and sealed the bag when the lid was closed. In addition, the storage area held at least four full bags. The product was priced at $59.99 and was sold through hardware stores. The company has done little advertising and has relied on in-store promotion and displays. The divisional manager was wondering about the effectiveness of these displays and has called on you to do the necessary research.

   b. Cardworth is a national manufacturer and distributor of greeting cards. The company recently began distributing a lower-priced line of cards that was made possible by using recycled paper. Quality differences between the higher- and lower-priced cards did not seem to be noticeable to laypeople. The company followed a policy of printing its name and the price on the back of each card. The initial acceptance of the new line of cards convinced the vice president of production that the company should use recycled paper for all its cards and increase its profit margin from 12.3% to 14.9%. The sales manager has strongly opposed this move and commented, "You know, consumers are concerned about the quality of greeting cards; a price difference of five cents on a card does not matter." The VP has called on you to undertake the study.

2. Which survey method (mail, telephone, personal interview in the home or in a mall, fax, e-mail, or Web) would you use for the following situations? Justify your choice.

   a. Administration of a questionnaire to determine the number of people who listened to the "100 Top Country Tunes of the Year!," a program that aired on December 31.

   b. Administration of a questionnaire to determine the number of households having an individual with mental health problems and a history of such problems in the family.

   c. Administration of a questionnaire by a national manufacturer of microwave ovens to test people's attitudes and opinions toward a new model.

   d. Administration of a questionnaire by a local dry cleaner who wants to determine customers' satisfaction with a recent discount scheme.

   e. Administration of a questionnaire by the management of a small hotel that wants to assess customers' opinions of its service.

3. Several objectives for marketing research projects follow. For each objective, specify the type(s) of primary data that would be of use along with a possible method of data collection.

   a. Assess "people flow" patterns inside a shopping mall.

   b. Gauge the effectiveness of a new advertisement.

   c. Gauge a salesperson's potential for success.

   d. Segment a market.

   e. Identify the shopper types that patronize a particular store.

   f. Discover how people feel about a new package design.

4. Consider each of the following research projects. In each case, identify weak areas and describe how the research might have been improved to better attain its objectives. Be specific.

   a. A local bank was interested in determining how it might better serve the needs of low-income households. It inserted a four-page survey into the monthly statement-of-account mailings of all account holders with less than $500 in their accounts. The survey was structured and undisguised; 1,200 surveys were mailed and 98 were completed and returned.

   b. The Lee-Casey Lawn and Garden Company, which recently began business in a small midwestern city, has developed a special liquid fertilizer for a certain type of shrubbery. Lee-Casey is interested in determining whether there is a market for the product among homeowners, but it is unsure whether that particular type of shrubbery is popular in that area. In order to find out, Lee-Casey conducted a telephone survey of homeowners in the area. They were eventually able to reach about 75% of the homeowners; of these, 85% participated in the survey.

c. A new business clothing shop is to open in a few months. The owners are unsure whether the new shop should be located in a shopping mall or at a downtown location. Since they think it would be best to simply ask shoppers for their preferences as to location, the owners contracted a local marketing research company to conduct a study. Using a structured, undisguised questionnaire format and the mall intercept method of administration, the research company was able to report to the owners of the new business clothing shop that most people prefer to shop for clothes in a shopping mall.

d. Quick-Stop, Inc., recently opened a new convenience store in Northglenn, Colorado. The store is open every day from 7:00 A.M. to 11:00 P.M. In order to better plan the location of other units in the Denver metro area, management is interested in determining the trading area from which this store draws its customers. How would you determine this information by questionnaire method? By observation method? Which method would be preferred? Be sure to specify in your answer how you would define "trading area."

## CHAPTER 9

Questionnaires and Data-Collection Forms

Questions to Guide Your Learning:

Q1: How do I create a questionnaire?

Q2: How do I avoid ambiguous questions, leading questions, double-barreled questions?

Q3: What's an open-ended question?

Q4: How do I implement branching?

In Chapter 8, we discussed types of questionnaires and observation forms, their methods of administration, and their pros and cons. Now we get down to the nitty-gritty—once you decide you want a survey, how do you create one? This chapter presents the procedures to follow to develop a questionnaire or observational data-collection form.

Questionnaire Design

Much progress has been made, but designing questionnaires is still an art, not a science. It is easier to embrace admonitions such as "avoid leading questions" or "avoid ambiguous questions" than it is to develop questions that are neither leading nor ambiguous.

Figure 9.1 is a procedural template to develop questionnaires.[1] The stages are presented here in sequence, but in reality, this step-by-step procedure is often modified via some iteration and looping. For example, you may read a nearly completed draft of a survey, only to find that some items are worded badly and therefore aren't likely to procure the desired information. This discovery, of course, requires a loop back to an earlier stage to make the necessary changes. Working back and forth among the stages is natural.

Nor should you take the stages too literally. They are presented as a guide or a checklist. With questionnaires, the proof of the pudding is very much in the eating.

FIGURE 9.1
Procedure for
Developing a
Questionnaire

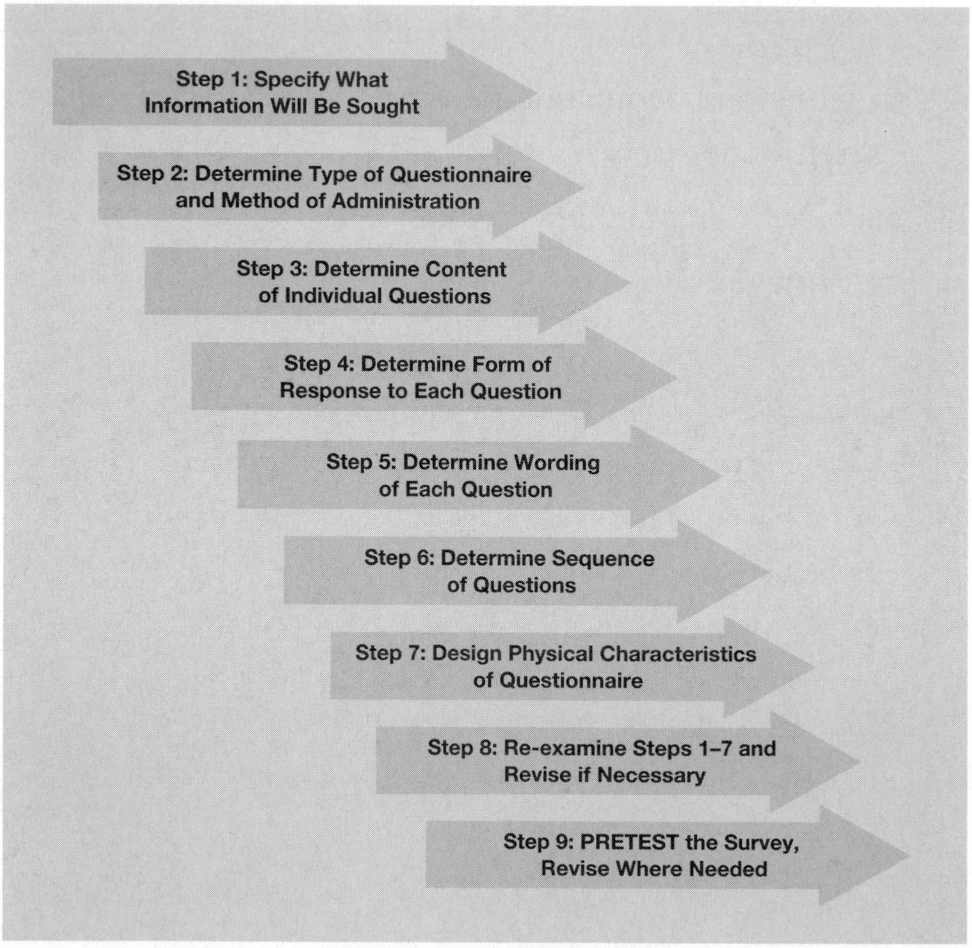

Step 1: Specify What Information Will Be Sought

Step 2: Determine Type of Questionnaire and Method of Administration

Step 3: Determine Content of Individual Questions

Step 4: Determine Form of Response to Each Question

Step 5: Determine Wording of Each Question

Step 6: Determine Sequence of Questions

Step 7: Design Physical Characteristics of Questionnaire

Step 8: Re-examine Steps 1–7 and Revise if Necessary

Step 9: PRETEST the Survey, Revise Where Needed

---

[1] Cf., Arlene Fink, *How to Design Surveys,* 2nd ed. (Sage, 2002).

Does the questionnaire produce accurate data of the kind needed? Blind adherence to procedure is no substitute for creativity in approach, nor is it any substitute for a pretest (Step 9), which can tell us whether the typical respondent will understand each question and is able and willing to supply the information sought.

Specify What Information Will Be Sought

Deciding what information will be sought is easy to the extent that researchers have been meticulous and precise at earlier stages in the research process. Both descriptive and causal research demand sufficient prior knowledge to allow the framing of specific hypotheses for investigation, which then guide the research, which in turn helps guide writing the questionnaire. The hypotheses determine what information will be sought and from whom, because they specify what relationships will be investigated. If researchers have heeded the earlier admonition to establish "dummy tables" to structure the data analysis, their job of determining what information is to be collected is essentially complete. It's just a matter of collecting information on those variables.

What information do you *want* from the survey?

It is certainly true that the preparation of the questionnaire itself may suggest further hypotheses and other relationships that might be investigated at slight additional effort and cost. If the new hypothesis is indeed vital to understanding the phenomenon, by all means include it in the questionnaire. But if it simply represents one of those potentially "interesting findings" and is not vital to the research effort, forget it. Items that are not vital simply lengthen the questionnaire, in turn lowering response rates.

The exploratory research effort is, of course, aimed at the discovery of ideas and insights and not at their systematic investigation. The questionnaire for an exploratory study is, therefore, loosely structured, with only a rough idea of the kind of information that might be sought. The research is intended to shed clarity on the priorities for hypotheses in future research.

Type of Questionnaire and Method of Administration

After specifying the basic information that will be sought, the researcher needs to specify *how* it will be gathered. This stage requires decisions about the *structure* and *disguise* to be used in the questionnaire and whether it will be administered by *mail, telephone, personal interviews, fax, e-mail,* or *Web*. These decisions are not independent—e.g., a disguised–unstructured questionnaire using a picture stimulus storytelling format precludes phone and probably mail administration. Similarly, mail is not recommended for unstructured–undisguised questionnaires with open-ended questions, particularly if they should have probes.

The type of data to be collected will have an important effect on the method of data collection. For example, the San Francisco research firm King, Brown & Partners had a client that wanted to know what proportion of Internet users had various multimedia plug-ins (e.g., Shockwave or Acrobat for downloading and playing multimedia files). From experience, King, Brown & Partners knew that one-third or more users don't accurately know which plug-ins or versions they have. It would have been a waste of time to call computer users and ask. Rather, the researchers created an online survey in which plug-in files of different formats were used to display images. For each image, survey respondents were asked whether they could see the

Research Realities

9.1 How Cultural Differences Affect Marketing Research in Different Countries

Willingness to Cooperate. Compared with people around the world, Americans tend to be unusually open, which is reflected in their general willingness to cooperate in marketing research surveys. Quite often, Americans will answer the questions of a total stranger (in the research industry, we call them "interviewers") about almost any subject—up to and including one's sex life. And Americans will agree to be interviewed anywhere: over the telephone, in a shopping mall, or at their place of business.

This climate of assumed cooperation can spoil Americans for doing research elsewhere in the world. Individual consumers in many other countries are less ready to answer any questions from an interviewer, let alone delicate or personal ones. Businesspeople in many parts of the world have a more closed attitude than Americans about taking part in surveys.

In Korea, for example, businesspeople are reluctant to answer any survey questions about their company—it is considered disloyal to divulge any type of information to "outsiders." And most Japanese businesspeople are hesitant to take part in surveys during business hours—taking time away from your work for a survey is like "stealing" from your employer.

Differences in Research Costs. The cost of doing exactly the same research can vary dramatically from country to country. Japan is generally regarded as the most expensive research market in the world; projects there usually cost several times what the same study would cost in the United States.

But even within a single region, such as the European community, costs can vary dramatically from country to country. ESOMAR, the European Society for Opinion and Marketing Research (the European equivalent of a combined American Marketing Association and Advertising Research Foundation), periodically studies differences in research costs from country to country within Europe. See http://www.esomar.org.

Differences in Administration Methods. Telephone interviews are common in the U.S., and frequent in the Netherlands, Germany, and the U.K. They are rare in Japan, where it is not culturally acceptable to answer questions from "strangers" over the telephone. For different reasons (the unreliability of the communications networks), phone surveys are rare in Mexico, Argentina, and Hungary. Door-to-door interviewing is illegal in Saudi Arabia, legal but prohibitively expensive in the U.S., and more common in Switzerland and the U.K. Finally, good mailing lists are critical to the success and frequent use of mail surveys in the U.S. and also in Sweden, where the government routinely publishes lists of every Swedish household, making mail studies feasible there.

Sources: For more on cultural research differences, see Robin Birn (ed.), *The Handbook of International Market Research Techniques,* 2nd ed. (Kogan, 2002); V. Kumar, *International Marketing Research* (Prentice Hall, 2000); Samuel Craig and Susan Douglas, *International Marketing Research,* 2nd ed. (Wiley, 1999).

image. If they clicked yes, the researchers knew, by the format used to create the image, precisely what plug-in they were using. This methodology let respondents provide data without knowing the technical details.[2]

Another influence on the data collection method is the culture of the country where the study is being done (see Research Realities 9.1). A researcher investigating the relationship between some behavior and a series of demographic characteristics in the U.S. (e.g., how dishwasher ownership is related to income, age, family size) could use mail, telephone, Web, or mall personal interviews to gather the data. (The methods would not be equally attractive because of cost and other considerations, but they all could be used.) A researcher measuring attitudes could use some of the methods, depending on issues of structure and disguise (e.g., a long scale would preclude a phone survey, many open-ended items would preclude mail, etc.).

Figure 9.2 offers another example. The research is about attitudes toward various brands of coffee. The questions are all very structured and undisguised. The survey is to be administered by mail, using part of the NFO (National Family Opinion, Inc.) panel. Given the structure, note how easily most of the responses could be tabulated.

---

[2] Chris Grecco and Hal King, "Of Browsers and Plug-Ins," *Quirk's Marketing Research Review* (http://www.quirks.com).

1. What type of coffeemaker do you usually use to prepare your ground coffee at home? (Check ONE)
   1 ☐ Automatic drip
   2 ☐ Electric percolator
   3 ☐ Stove top percolator
   4 ☐ Stove top dripolator
   ☐ Other (please specify): _____

2. a. Check all the brands of regular ground coffee that you have ever used at home. (Check ALL that apply):
   b. Check the one brand you use most often. (Check ONE):
   c. Check all the brands you currently have on hand. (Check ALL that apply):
   d. Check the one brand you will probably buy next. (Check ONE):
   e. For each brand please indicate how much you like the brand overall on a scale of 1 to 10 with "1" meaning "dislike it extremely" and "10" meaning "like it extremely." Rate each brand, whether you have used the brand or not.

	A Ever Used	B Use Most Often	C Have On Hand	D Will Buy Next	Brand Rating "1" ← Dislike It Extremely									→ "10" Like It Extremely
Folgers	1☐	1☐	1☐	1☐	1☐	2☐	3☐	4☐	5☐	6☐	7☐	8☐	9☐	10☐
Hills Brothers	1☐	1☐	1☐	1☐	1☐	2☐	3☐	4☐	5☐	6☐	7☐	8☐	9☐	10☐
Maxwell Reg.	1☐	1☐	1☐	1☐	1☐	2☐	3☐	4☐	5☐	6☐	7☐	8☐	9☐	10☐
Maxwell House Master	1☐	1☐	1☐	1☐	1☐	2☐	3☐	4☐	5☐	6☐	7☐	8☐	9☐	10☐
Yuban	1☐	1☐	1☐	1☐	1☐	2☐	3☐	4☐	5☐	6☐	7☐	8☐	9☐	10☐
Other	1☐	1☐	1☐	1☐	1☐	2☐	3☐	4☐	5☐	6☐	7☐	8☐	9☐	10☐

(please specify): _____

3. What do you usually add to the coffee you drink? (Check ALL that apply):
   1 ☐ Nothing (I drink it black)
   2 ☐ A dairy creamer, like milk, cream, or half-and-half
   3 ☐ A non-dairy creamer, powdered or liquid
   4 ☐ Sugar
   5 ☐ Artificial sweetener
   ☐ Something else (please specify): _____

4. Are you the principal coffee purchaser for your household?
   1 ☐ Yes
   2 ☐ No

5. Please indicate how important it is to you that a ground coffee have each of the following characteristics. (Check ONE box for EACH characteristic):

	Not at all Important									Extremely Important
Rich taste	1☐	2☐	3☐	4☐	5☐	6☐	7☐	8☐	9☐	10☐
Always fresh	1☐	2☐	3☐	4☐	5☐	6☐	7☐	8☐	9☐	10☐
Gets the day off to a good start	1☐	2☐	3☐	4☐	5☐	6☐	7☐	8☐	9☐	10☐
Full-bodied taste	1☐	2☐	3☐	4☐	5☐	6☐	7☐	8☐	9☐	10☐
Rich aroma in the cup	1☐	2☐	3☐	4☐	5☐	6☐	7☐	8☐	9☐	10☐
Good value for the money	1☐	2☐	3☐	4☐	5☐	6☐	7☐	8☐	9☐	10☐
The best coffee to drink in morning	1☐	2☐	3☐	4☐	5☐	6☐	7☐	8☐	9☐	10☐

(continued)

FIGURE 9.2
Mail Questionnaire for Caffeinated Ground Coffee Study

FIGURE 9.2
(continued)

	Not at all Important									**Extremely Important**
Rich aroma in the can/bag	1☐	2☐	3☐	4☐	5☐	6☐	7☐	8☐	9☐	10☐
Smooth taste	1☐	2☐	3☐	4☐	5☐	6☐	7☐	8☐	9☐	10☐
Highest quality coffee	1☐	2☐	3☐	4☐	5☐	6☐	7☐	8☐	9☐	10☐

	Not at all Important									**Extremely Important**
Premium brand	1☐	2☐	3☐	4☐	5☐	6☐	7☐	8☐	9☐	10☐
Not bitter	1☐	2☐	3☐	4☐	5☐	6☐	7☐	8☐	9☐	10☐
The coffee that brightens my day	1☐	2☐	3☐	4☐	5☐	6☐	7☐	8☐	9☐	10☐
Costs more than the other brands	1☐	2☐	3☐	4☐	5☐	6☐	7☐	8☐	9☐	10☐
Strong taste	1☐	2☐	3☐	4☐	5☐	6☐	7☐	8☐	9☐	10☐
Has no aftertaste	1☐	2☐	3☐	4☐	5☐	6☐	7☐	8☐	9☐	10☐
Economy brand	1☐	2☐	3☐	4☐	5☐	6☐	7☐	8☐	9☐	10☐
Rich aroma while brewing	1☐	2☐	3☐	4☐	5☐	6☐	7☐	8☐	9☐	10☐
Best ground coffee available	1☐	2☐	3☐	4☐	5☐	6☐	7☐	8☐	9☐	10☐
Enjoy drinking with a meal	1☐	2☐	3☐	4☐	5☐	6☐	7☐	8☐	9☐	10☐
Costs less than other brands	1☐	2☐	3☐	4☐	5☐	6☐	7☐	8☐	9☐	10☐

6. On a scale of 0 to 10 with "0" meaning "does not describe at all" and "10" meaning "describes completely," please indicate how well the following statements describe each of the coffee brands listed below. Rate each brand. Please write in the number that indicates your answer on the lines provided:

	Folgers	Hills Bros.	Maxwell Reg.	Maxwell Master	Yuban
Rich taste	_____	_____	_____	_____	_____
Always fresh	_____	_____	_____	_____	_____
Gets the day off to a good start	_____	_____	_____	_____	_____
Full-bodied taste	_____	_____	_____	_____	_____
Rich aroma in the cup	_____	_____	_____	_____	_____
Good value for the money	_____	_____	_____	_____	_____
The best coffee to drink in morning	_____	_____	_____	_____	_____
Rich aroma in the can/bag	_____	_____	_____	_____	_____
Smooth taste	_____	_____	_____	_____	_____
Highest quality coffee	_____	_____	_____	_____	_____
Premium brand	_____	_____	_____	_____	_____
Not bitter	_____	_____	_____	_____	_____
The coffee that brightens my day	_____	_____	_____	_____	_____
Costs more than the other brands	_____	_____	_____	_____	_____
Strong taste	_____	_____	_____	_____	_____
Has no aftertaste	_____	_____	_____	_____	_____
Economy brand	_____	_____	_____	_____	_____
Rich aroma while brewing	_____	_____	_____	_____	_____
Best ground coffee available	_____	_____	_____	_____	_____
Enjoy drinking with a meal	_____	_____	_____	_____	_____
Costs less than other brands	_____	_____	_____	_____	_____

7. Please indicate your gender and age: 1 ☐ Male   2 ☐ Female   Age:_____

Individual Question Content

The researcher's previous decisions (information needed, structure and disguise, method of administration) largely control the decisions regarding individual question content. But in editing the survey, the researcher should ask some additional questions.[3]

IS THE QUESTION NECESSARY?

If an issue is important and it's not been adequately covered by other questions, a new question is in order. It should be framed to yield an answer with the required detail but not more than needed. For example, family consumption behavior is often explained by "stage in the life cycle," a concept captured by a composite of variables such as marital status, presence of children, and ages of the children. The presence of children indicates a dependency relationship, particularly if the youngest child is under 6. In a study using stage of life cycle as a variable, there is no need to ask the age of each child. Rather, all that is needed is one question aimed at securing the age of the youngest child, if there are children.

ARE SEVERAL QUESTIONS NEEDED INSTEAD OF ONE?

There are often situations in which several questions are needed instead of one. Consider the question, "Why do you use Crest?" One respondent may reply, "To reduce cavities." Another may reply, "Because our dentist recommends it." Obviously two different frames of reference are being employed to answer this question. The first respondent is replying in terms of current usage, whereas the second is replying in terms of initial brand choice. It would be better to break this one question down into separate questions that reflect the possible frames of reference that could be used:

- How did you first happen to use Crest?
- What is your primary reason for using it?

DO RESPONDENTS HAVE THE NECESSARY INFORMATION?

Each item should be carefully examined to see whether the typical respondent is likely to have the information sought. Respondents will give answers, but whether the answers mean anything is another matter. Sometimes we just don't want to be embarrassed to admit we don't know something in a public opinion survey, and sometimes the question is so plausible and the interviewer so credible that we assume the question has validity. For example, you could survey people about the Consumers' Rights Act on Privacy of Internet Information, say, and, 50% or more people will report a familiarity with the Act, when in fact such an act does not exist (but it sounds plausible that it might, doesn't it?). If you ask people whether they've tried SmileBrite toothpaste, some will say they have, when the brand doesn't exist. If you ask "When is the last time you saw the Jolly Green Giant (or any of a number of brand icons) on TV?" they'll say "within the past year" when in fact the tall fellow hasn't appeared in years.

From a different perspective, consider the question, "How much does your family spend on groceries in a typical week?" Unless the respondent does the grocery shopping, he or she is unlikely to know. In a situation like this, it might be helpful to

---

[3] E.g., see Gordon Willis, *Cognitive Interviewing and Questionnaire Design* (Sage, 2003); Charles Briggs, *Learning How to Ask* (Cambridge University Press, 2002).

begin with "filter questions" to determine if the individual is indeed likely to know, e.g., "Who does the grocery shopping in your family?"[4]

Your respondents need to have the information sought, and they need to remember it. Our ability to remember various events is influenced partly by the importance of the event itself, e.g., most of us remember where we were during the attack on the World Trade Center buildings, or more pleasantly, the first car we ever owned, but many of us are unable to recall the amount of TV or the particular shows we watched last Wednesday evening, or the first brand of mouthwash we ever used, when we switched to our current brand, or why we switched. The switching information might be very important to a brand manager for mouthwashes, but it is unimportant to most individuals, a condition we have to keep in mind when designing questionnaires. We need to put ourselves in the shoes of the respondent, not those of the product manager, when deciding what information is important enough for the individual to remember.

Can the
respondent
answer?

We also need to recognize that a person's ability to remember an event is influenced by how long ago it happened. Although we might recall the television programs we watched last night, we would have more difficulty remembering what we watched last week and impossible to recall our viewing pattern of a month ago. If an event is likely to be considered relatively unimportant to most individuals, we should ask about very recent occurrences of it.

For more important events, two effects operating in opposite directions affect a respondent's ability to provide accurate answers about events that happened in some specified time period (e.g., how many times the person has seen a doctor in the last six months). **Telescoping error** refers to the fact that most people remember an event as having occurred more recently than it had. **Recall loss** means that they forget an event happened at all. The extent of the two sources of error on the accuracy of the reported information depends on the length of the reference period. For long periods, the telescoping effect is smaller whereas the recall loss effect is larger. For short periods, the reverse is true. The appropriate reference period to frame questions depends on factors such as the purchase cycle of the product category.[5]

WILL RESPONDENTS GIVE THE INFORMATION?

Even though respondents have the information, there is always a question of whether they will share it. Often respondents are flattered that they are being asked for their opinions. Participation in Nielsen television panels makes one believe that one is influencing programming choices. Rapport is quickly built in person-to-person interviewing (in the mall, on the phone), but if mail surveys and online questionnaires are at least vaguely interesting and designed well, they won't take too much of the respondents' time and most continue through the survey.

Respondents can be unable to articulate their answers, so sometimes we must design creative surveys to help them. For example, respondents might not be able to express their preferences in furniture styles, but they can certainly state which they like best when shown pictures, prototypes, hardware samples, and fabric swatches.

Sometimes the concern is that the survey question is rather sensitive, and the respondent might not wish to divulge private information. When an issue is embar-

---

[4] Janet Kelly and David Swindell, "The Case for the Inexperienced User: Rethinking Filter Questions in Citizen Satisfaction Surveys," *American Review of Public Administration* 33 (2003), pp. 91–108.

[5] Other common errors include frequent users in a category underestimating their purchases, and light users overestimating their usage, cf. Eunkyu Lee, Michael Hu and Rex Toh, "Are Consumer Survey Results Distorted?" *Journal of Marketing Research* 37 (2000), pp. 125–133.

rassing or otherwise threatening to respondents, they are likely to refuse to cooperate. Such issues should be avoided if possible. If the issue is essential to the study, the researcher needs to pay close attention to how the issue is addressed, particularly with respect to question location and question phrasing.

As we develop the questionnaire, we also need to be mindful of the amount of effort it might take respondents to give the information we seek. When the effort is excessive, we may have to settle for approximate answers, or we may be better off omitting the issue completely, since these types of questions tend to irritate respondents and damage their cooperation with the rest of the survey.

Ethical Dilemma 9.1

As a new researcher for a large research supplier, you are told to design an attitude and usage questionnaire for a new customer, an appliance manufacturer. Before starting this project, your supervisor mentions that a similar study was completed 12 months ago and may provide some useful background information. Because you have no experience in durable consumer goods, you decide to use this previous report as a good source of secondary information.

After finding a copy of the previous study's final report, you discover that the report was completed for a competing appliance company. However, the report provides valuable background and competitive information. Because a questionnaire was developed and used successfully for this project, you decide to take a copy of the questionnaire and update it for the current client.

- Is it ethical for researchers to use questionnaires developed and paid for by prior clients on competitive client projects?
- Instead of using the questionnaire, would it have been legitimate to use the previous report as a source of secondary information to provide background information for the current project?
- Would the preceding situation be different if the prior research had been completed for a long-term, contract client?

In general, it is better to address sensitive issues later rather than earlier in the survey.[6] Rapport gets established as respondents answer nonthreatening questions early in the interview, particularly when those questions that establish the legitimacy of the project.

When sensitive questions must be asked, it helps to consider ways to make them less threatening. Some helpful techniques include:

Will the respondent answer?

1. Hide the question among other, more innocuous, questions.
2. State that the behavior or attitude is *not unusual* before asking the specific questions of the respondent (e.g., "Recent studies show that one of every four households has trouble meeting monthly financial obligations"). This technique, known as the use of counterbiasing statements, makes it easier for the respondent to admit the potentially embarrassing behavior.
3. Phrase the question in terms of *others* and how they might feel or act ("Do you think most people cheat on their income tax? Why?"). Respondents might readily reveal their attitudes toward cheating when preparing income tax forms when asked about other people, but they might be very reluctant to do so if they were asked outright if they ever cheat on their taxes and why.
4. Use the **randomized response model**, a now fairly standard approach in which the respondent answers one of several paired questions. The particular question is selected at random—for example, by having the respondent flip a coin. The respondent is instructed to answer Question A if the coin comes up "heads," and Question B if the coin is "tails." The interviewer is unaware of the question being answered by the respondent, because he or she never sees the outcome of the coin flip. Under these conditions, respondents are less likely to refuse to answer or to distort their answer. A study to investigate the incidence of shoplifting might pair the sensitive question, "Have you ever shoplifted?" with the innocuous question, "Is your birthday in January?" The incidence of shoplifting can still be estimated

---

[6] Question sequence is discussed more fully later in the chapter.

by using an appropriate statistical model, because the percentage of respondents answering each question is controlled by the coin flips.

For a fair coin, the probability that the respondent will answer Question A, "Have you ever shoplifted?" is .5. The proportion of people whose birthdays fall in January is known to be .05 from census data. Suppose that the proportion who answered "yes" to either Question A or B is .20. Using the standard laws of probability, we could then estimate the proportion of the people in the sample who were responding "yes" to the sensitive question by using the formula:

$$\lambda = p\pi_s + (1-p)\pi_A$$

where

λ = the total proportion of "yes" responses to both questions,
p = the probability that the sensitive question is selected,
$1-p$ = the probability that the innocuous question is selected,
π_S = the proportion of "yes" responses to the sensitive question, and
π_A = the proportion of "yes" responses to the innocuous question.

Substituting the appropriate quantities indicates that

$$.20 = .50\,\pi_s + .50\,(.05)$$
yielding $\pi_s = .35$.

That is, 35% of the respondents had shoplifted. Note, though, that we do not know specifically which respondents have shoplifted. Thus we cannot determine, for example, if shoplifting behavior was associated with any particular demographic characteristics.

Form of Response

Once the content of the individual questions is determined, the researcher needs to decide on the particular form of the response. Will the question be open-ended or fixed-alternative? If fixed-alternative, will it be a multichotomy, a dichotomy, or perhaps a scale?

OPEN-ENDED QUESTIONS

Respondents are free to reply to open-ended questions in their own words rather than being limited to choosing from a set of alternatives. The following are examples:

How old are you?

Do you think laws limiting the amount of interest businesses can charge consumers are needed?

Can you name three sponsors of the Monday night football games?

What commercials do you remember seeing on TV last night?

Do you intend to purchase an automobile this year?

Why did you purchase a Sony brand color TV?

Do you own a DVD player?

How many long-distance telephone calls do you make on your cell phone in a typical week?

Open-ended questions are extremely versatile—we can ask questions about demographic characteristics, attitudes, intentions, and behavior.

Open-ended questions can be used to begin a questionnaire. It's thought best to proceed from general to specific topics in constructing questionnaires, so an opening question like, "When you think of TV sets, which brands come to mind?" gives a sense of the respondent's frame of reference. The open-ended question is also often used to probe for additional information. The probes "Why?" "Why do you feel that way?" and "Please explain" are often used to seek elaboration of a respondent's reply.

MULTICHOTOMOUS QUESTIONS

The multichotomous question is a fixed-alternative question; respondents are asked to choose the alternative that most closely corresponds to their position on the subject. Table 9.1, for example, contains some of the preceding open-ended questions rewritten as multichotomous questions.

Note some of the limitations when using multiple-choice questions. In the interest-ceiling legislation question, the respondent's true opinion may be more complex; e.g., he or she may believe that legislation is needed, if businesses won't reduce the amount of credit available to customers or shorten the repayment period. If the conditions can't be satisfied, the respondent may feel just the opposite. The multiple-choice question doesn't permit individuals to elaborate but requires them to condense their complex attitude into a single statement. Of course, a well-designed series of multiple-choice questions could allow for such elaborations (but an exhaustive coverage of the potential qualifiers would also increase the length of the questionnaire).

Most researchers believe that 4-point or 5-point scales provide more fine-tuned information from customers. However, even simple 2-point, binary responses allow customers to say "yay" or "nay" (see Research Realities 9.2).

TABLE 9.1
Examples of Multichotomous Questions

Age

How old are you?

☐ Less than 20

☐ 20–29

☐ 30–39

☐ 40–49

☐ 50–59

☐ 60 or over

Interest-Ceiling Legislation

Do you think laws limiting the amount of interest businesses can charge consumers are needed?

☐ Definitely needed

☐ Probably needed

☐ Probably not needed

☐ Definitely not needed

☐ No opinion

Television Purchase

Why did you purchase a Sony brand color TV?

☐ Price was lower than other alternatives

☐ Feel it represents the highest quality

☐ Availability of local service

☐ Availability of a service contract

☐ Picture is better

☐ Warranty was better

☐ Other

Telephone-Use Behavior

How many long-distance telephone calls do you make in a typical week?

☐ Fewer than 5

☐ 5–10

☐ More than 10

Research Realities
9.2 Information in Binary Scales?

Market Facts compared consumers' responses on 5-point scales vs. 2-point checklists (yes/no) for several product categories.

Figure A shows the results for pain relievers. Some consumers were asked:

> "<Branded Aspirin> lasts longer than others."
> | 1 | 2 | 3 | 4 | 5 |
> |---|---|---|---|---|
> | disagree strongly | disagree somewhat | neither agree/disagree | agree somewhat | agree strongly |

The % of these respondents who answered "4" or "5" (agree somewhat or strongly) is charted in Figure A.

Other consumers were asked to simply check:

> "<Branded Aspirin> lasts longer than others."
> | 1 | 2 |
> |---|---|
> | disagree | agree |

The % of these respondents who marked "2" (agree) is charted in Figure A.

There is some consistency in the overall favorability and perceived strengths and weaknesses of these products over the different attributes rated. Whether comparing branded aspirin to branded ibuprofen, or branded aspirin to unbranded aspirin, results are often strikingly comparable. For example, the two branded products are thought to "last longer"; the ibuprofen is thought to "not irritate the stomach" as much as the aspirins, etc.

For the beer category, some consumers were asked:

> "<Brand of Beer> is a good thirst quencher."
> | 1 | 2 | 3 | 4 | 5 | 6 | 7 |
> |---|---|---|---|---|---|---|
> | disagree strongly | | | neither agree/disagree | | | agree strongly |

The % of these respondents who answered "6" or "7" is charted in Figure B.

Other consumers were asked to:

> "Please check the beers listed below that you think are good thirst quenchers."
> _____ Budweiser
> _____ Coors
> _____ Heineken
> _____ Miller

The % of the respondents who checked each brand is charted in Figure B.

Again, there is some consistency. Bud and Coors are largely comparable, except on perceptions of "value" where Coors' profiles resembles Miller's more. Heineken is perceived as the "premium quality" beer, not a good value, and not terribly thirst-quenching.

Thus, perhaps surprisingly, 2-point scales can deliver basic customer reactions that are largely consistent with the finer 7-point scale information.

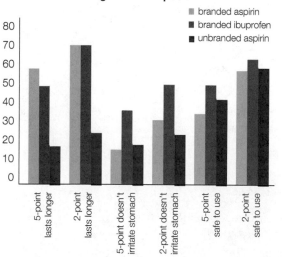

Figure A: Top 2 box % from 5-point & % agree from 2-point

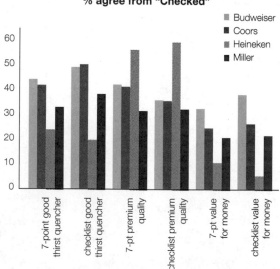

Figure B: Top 2 box % from 7-point & % agree from "Checked"

Source: http://www.Synovate.com "The Effect of the Number of Scale Points in Measuring Product Perceptions," *Research on Research* series.

The TV-set purchase question (Table 9.1) illustrates other problems associated with multiple-choice questions. First, the list of reasons cited for purchasing a Sony color TV may not be *exhaustive*. The "other" response category attempts to solve this problem. However, if many respondents check the "other" category, the study will be useless. Thus, the burden is on the researcher to make the list of alternatives comprehensive.

Unless the respondent is instructed to check all alternatives that apply, or is to rank the alternatives in order of importance, the multiple-choice question also demands that the alternatives be *mutually exclusive*. The income categories shown below violate this principle:

☐ $10,000–$20,000
☐ $20,000–$30,000

Ethical Dilemma 9.2

A financial institution has developed a new type of savings bond. The marketing director of this institution has requested that a local research supply company design a questionnaire that will help quantify target consumers' interest in this new bond. However, the marketing director is concerned about the possibility that competitors will hear about the new product concept because of the survey. He requests that the questionnaire be written in such a way that the true purpose of the study is masked.

To mask the actual purpose of the study, the questionnaire primarily asks respondents for details of their holiday plans and budgets. Because respondents are asked questions about their finances only after being asked multiple vacation-related questions, it is hoped that respondents will assume the information is for a travel company. Moreover, the marketing director of the financial institution asks that interviewers tell respondents that the information is being gathered for a travel-related company.

- Discuss the implications of deceiving respondents on a questionnaire in this way.
- If the interviewers had not been told to explicitly tell respondents that the information was for a travel-related corporation, would the deception be acceptable?
- Are there ways of acquiring this type of information without resorting to deception while still protecting the institution's new product idea?
- Discuss the validity issues associated with respondents knowing the purpose of the survey as they are completing it.

A respondent with an income of $20,000 would not know which alternative to check. When questions are about a product's features, (a TV's picture, warranty, price, etc.), you often see instructions such as, "Check the most important reason," "Check all those reasons that apply," or "Rank all the reasons that apply from most important to least important."

The list of alternative responses should be exhaus*tive*, but a long list will be exhaus*ting* to respondents! So, when designing multiple-choice questions, the researcher should remain cognizant of human beings' limited data-processing capabilities.

The fourth weakness of the TV-purchase question is that it may be susceptible to order bias. The recommended procedure for combating this order bias is to prepare several forms of the questionnaire, with several different orders. If each alternative appears early, late, and in the middle across the different forms, the researcher can feel reasonably comfortable that position bias has been neutralized.[7]

The long-distance telephone call example in Table 9.1 illustrates a problem with questions designed to get at the frequency of behaviors. The range of the categories used in the question seems to cue respondents about how they should reply. A scale with the following categories would likely produce a different picture than the one shown in Table 9.1:

☐ Fewer than 10
☐ 10–20
☐ More than 20

---

[7] David Moore, "Measuring New Types of Question-Order Effects," *Public Opinion Quarterly* 66 (2002), pp. 80–91.

Respondents seem reluctant to report behaviors that are unusual in the context of the response scale—e.g., extreme behaviors. It's thought better to just use an open-ended question to get data on behavioral frequencies.

DICHOTOMOUS QUESTIONS

The dichotomous question is also a fixed-alternative question but one in which there are only two alternatives.

> Do you think laws limiting the amount of interest businesses can charge consumers are needed?
>
> ☐ Yes
> ☐ No
>
> Do you intend to purchase an automobile this year?
>
> ☐ Yes
> ☐ No

Dichotomous questions are easy for respondents to answer and they're easy to code and tabulate. Not surprisingly, they're the most popular kind of survey question.

Question framing is critical for the dichotomous question; e.g., consider:

> Do you think that gasoline will be *more* expensive or *less* expensive next year than it is now?
>
> ☐ More expensive
> ☐ Less expensive
>
> Do you think that gasoline will be *less* expensive or *more* expensive next year than it is now?
>
> ☐ Less expensive
> ☐ More expensive

The questions appear identical, but they will elicit different responses. Which, then, is the correct wording?

One generally accepted "fix" is to use a "split ballot"—each order is used on half of the questionnaires.[8] The averaged percentages from the two forms should then cancel out any biases.

SCALES

Another fixed-alternative question is the kind that uses a scale. For instance, when inquiring about VCR use, the following question might be asked:

> How often do you tape programs for later viewing with your VCR?
>
> ☐ Never
> ☐ Occasionally
> ☐ Sometimes
> ☐ Often

In this form, the question is multichotomous. However, the responses also represent a scale, which is perhaps more obvious in a different form, such as:

Never	**Occasionally**	**Sometimes**	**Often**
├─────────────┼─────────────┼─────────────┼─────────────┤			

[8] George Bishop and Andrew Smith, "Response-Order Effects, and the Early Gallup Split-Ballots," *Public Opinion Quarterly* 65 (2001), pp. 479–505; Marco Vriens, Michel Wedel and Zsolt Sandor, "Split-Questionnaire Designs," *Marketing Research* 13 (2001), pp. 14–19.

In this format, the descriptors are usually presented at the top of the page, and types of programs could be listed along the left margin (e.g., films, sporting events, network specials). The respondent then designates the frequency of VCR usage for recording each type of show. The instruction would only need to be given once at the beginning, and a great deal of information could be obtained from the respondent in a short period of time.

Decide on Question Wording

Step 5 in the questionnaire development process involves the phrasing of each question. This task is critical—poor phrasing of a question will cause respondents to skip over the question and not answer it, or they'll answer the question incorrectly. The first condition, **item nonresponse**, can create problems during data analysis. The second condition produces *measurement error*, in that the recorded score does not equal the respondent's true opinion.

Experienced researchers know that the phrasing of a question can directly affect the responses:

A Dominican priest and a Jesuit priest are discussing whether it is a sin to smoke and pray at the same time. "After failing to reach a conclusion, each goes off to consult his respective superior. The next week they meet again. The Dominican says, 'Well, what did your superior say?' The Jesuit responds, 'He said it was all right.' 'That's funny,' the Dominican replied, 'my superior said it was a sin.' Jesuit: 'What did you ask him?' Reply: 'I asked him if it was all right to smoke while praying.' 'Oh,' says the Jesuit, 'I asked my superior if it was all right to pray while smoking.' "

Several rules of thumb are useful for enhancing the wording of questions:

USE SIMPLE WORDS

Most researchers are more highly educated than the typical respondent, so it's easy to make the mistake of writing questions with vocabulary that may be unfamiliar to the respondents. The average person in the U.S. has a high school education and many people have difficulty in coping with tasks like completing a job application form. So, keep the words simple. Research Realities 9.3 lists some problem words and explains why these words can cause difficulty.

AVOID AMBIGUOUS WORDS AND QUESTIONS

The words used should also be unambiguous. Consider again the multichotomous question:

How often do you tape programs for later viewing with your VCR?

☐ Never
☐ Occasionally
☐ Sometimes
☐ Often

For all practical purposes, the replies to this question would be worthless. The words 'occasionally,' 'sometimes,' and 'often' are ambiguous. To one respondent, the word 'often' might mean "almost every day." To another it might mean, "once a week." Thus, the question would generate little understanding of VCR usage.

Research Realities

9.3 Ambiguous Words Researchers Should Use With Caution

- **about** "About" is sometimes intended to mean "somewhere near" in the sense that both 48% and 52% are "about" half. It is also used to mean nearly or almost, in the sense that 48% is "about" half whereas 52% is "over" half. This small difference in interpretation would yield different responses.

- **all** This is a "dead giveaway" word. Your own experience with true-false tests has probably demonstrated to you that it is safe to count almost every all-inclusive statement as false.

   Would you say that all cats have four legs?
   Is the mayor doing all he can for the city?

An all-inclusive word usually produces an overstatement. Most people may go along with the idea, accepting it as a form of literary license, but the purists and quibblers may either refuse to give an opinion or may even choose the other side in protest.

- **always** Another dead giveaway word.

   Do you always observe traffic signs?
   Is your boss always friendly?

- **and** This simple conjunction in some contexts may be taken either as separating or connecting two alternatives.

   Is there much rivalry among the baseball park vendors who sell beer and soft drinks?

Some people will answer in terms of rivalry between two groups—those who sell beer and those who sell soft drinks. Others will take it as rivalry within the single group comprising both beer and soft drinks vendors.

- **any** The trouble with "any" is that it may mean "every," "some," or "one only" in the same sentence or question, depending on the way you look at it. See whether you can get both the "every" and "only one" illusions from this question and notice the difference in meaning that results.

   Do you think any word is better than the one we are discussing?

You could think, "Yes, I think just any old word (every word) is better." On the other hand, you might think, "Yes, I believe it would be possible to find a better word."

- **bad** In itself the word "bad" is not at all bad for question wording. It conveys the meaning desired and is satisfactory as an alternative in a "good or bad" two-way question.

   Experience seems to indicate, however, that people are generally less willing to criticize than they are to praise, so sometimes the critical side needs to be softened. For example, after asking, What things are good about your job?, it might seem perfectly natural to ask, What things are bad about it? But if we want to lean over backward to get as many criticisms as we can, we may be wise not to apply the "bad" stigma but to ask, What things are *not so good* about it?

- **ever** This word tends to be a dead giveaway in a very special sense. "Ever" is such a long time and so inclusive that it makes it seem plausible that some unimpressive things may have happened.

   Have you ever listened to the Song Plugger radio program? "Yes, I suppose I must have at some time or other."

- **go** "Go" is given more space in the index of The American Thesaurus of Slang than any other word—a total of about 12½ columns.

   When did you last go to town?

If the respondent takes this literally, it is a good question, but the "go to town" phrase has more than a dozen different slang meanings, including a couple that might get your face slapped.

- **less** This word is usually used as an alternative to "more," where it may cause a minor problem. The phrase "more or less" has a special meaning all its own in which some respondents do not see an alternative. Thus, they may simply answer "yes, more or less" to a question like:

   Compared with a year ago, are you more or less happy in your job?

The easy solution to this problem is to break up the "more or less" expression by introducing an extra word or so to reverse the two:

   Compared with a year ago, are you more happy or less happy in your job?
   Compared with a year ago, are you less happy or more happy in your job?

- **like** This word is sometimes used to introduce an example. The problem with bringing an example into a question is that the respondent's attention may be directed toward the particular example and away from the general issue that it is meant only to illustrate. The use of examples may sometimes be necessary, but the possible hazard should always be kept in mind. The choice of an example can affect the answers to the question—in fact, it may materially change the question, as in these two examples:

   Do you think that leafy vegetables like spinach should be in the daily diet?
   Do you think that leafy vegetables like lettuce should be in the daily diet?

- **you** The dictionary distinguishes only two or three meanings of "you"—the second person singular and plural and the substitution for the impersonal "one"—"How do you get there?" in

(continued)

place of "How does one get there?" In most questions "you" gives no trouble whatever, it being clear that we are asking the opinion of the second person singular. However, the word sometimes may have a collective meaning as in a question asked of radio repairmen:

How many radio sets did you repair last month?

This question seemed to work all right until one repairman in a large shop countered with, "Who do you mean, me or the whole shop?"

Much as we might want to, therefore, we can't give "you" an unqualified recommendation. Sometimes "you" needs the emphasis of "you yourself" and sometimes it just isn't the word to use, as in the above situation where the entire shop was meant.

Source: See the classic Stanley L. Payne, *The Art of Asking Questions* (Princeton University Press, 1979), pp. 158–176.

A better strategy would be to provide concrete alternatives for the respondent, for example:

☐ Never use
☐ Use approximately once a month
☐ Use approximately once a week
☐ Use almost every day

The question provides a consistent frame of reference for each respondent. Respondents are no longer free to superimpose their own definitions on the response categories.

An alternative way to avoid ambiguity in response categories when asking about the frequency of some behavior is to ask about the most recent instance. For example:

Did you tape any programs with your VCR in the last two days?

☐ Yes
☐ No
☐ Can't recall

The proportion responding "yes" would then be used to infer the frequency with which the VCR was used, and the follow-up question, "For what purpose?" (among those responding yes) would give insight as to how respondents are using it. Some respondents who normally use their VCR might not have used it the last two days, but the opposite would be true for others. There might be some variation compared to what they normally do, but the variation should cancel out if a large enough sample were used. Thus, the aggregate sample should provide a good indication of the VCR usage.

AVOID LEADING QUESTIONS

A leading question is one framed to give the respondent a clue about how he or she 'should' answer. Consider the question:

Do you feel that limiting taxes by law is an effective way to stop the government from picking your pocket every payday?

☐ Yes
☐ No
☐ Undecided

This was one of three questions in an unsolicited questionnaire that we received as part of a study sponsored by the National Tax Limitation Committee. The committee intended to make the results of the poll available to members of Congress and to state legislators. Given the implied purpose, it is probably not surprising to see the leading words "picking your pocket" being used in this question, or the leading word "gouge" being used in another question. What is especially unfortunate is that it is unlikely the questions themselves accompanied the report to Congress. Rather, it is more likely that the report suggested that some high percentage (e.g., 90% of those surveyed) favored laws that limited taxes. Conclusion (?): Congress should pay attention to the wishes of the people and pass such laws.

You can see instances every day in the newspaper. Without seeing the questionnaire, the public is treated to a discussion of the results of studies concerning how people feel on issues. Yet the wording of a question makes a difference and it is important for researchers to realize that. If you want accurate data, you need to avoid leading the respondent.

AVOID IMPLICIT ASSUMPTIONS

Questions are frequently framed so that there is an implied assumption about what will happen as a consequence. The question "Are you in favor of placing price controls on crude oil?" will elicit different responses from individuals, depending on their views of what that might produce in the way of rationing, long lines at the pumps, and so forth. A better way to state the question is to make explicit the consequence(s). Thus, the question would be altered to ask, "Are you in favor of placing price controls on crude oil if it would produce gas rationing?"

AVOID GENERALIZATIONS AND ESTIMATES

Questions should always be asked in specific rather than general terms. The question, "How many salespeople did you see last year?" might be asked of a purchasing agent. To answer the question, the agent would probably estimate how many salespeople call in a typical week and would multiply this estimate by 52. This burden should not be placed on the agent. Rather, a more accurate estimate would be obtained if the purchasing agent were asked, "How many representatives called last week?" and the *researcher* multiplies the answer provided by 52.

AVOID DOUBLE-BARRELED QUESTIONS

A double-barreled question is one that calls for two responses and thereby creates confusion for the respondent. The question, "What is your evaluation of the price and convenience offered by catalog showrooms?" is asking respondents to react to two separate attributes by which such showrooms could be described. The respondent might think that the prices are attractive but the location is not, and thereby has a dilemma about how to respond. One can avoid double-barreled questions by splitting the question into two.

Decide on Question Sequence

Now the items are put together into the questionnaire. The order of the questions can be crucial. Here are some useful rules of thumb.

USE SIMPLE, INTERESTING OPENING QUESTIONS

The first questions are key. If respondents cannot answer them easily, find them uninteresting, or find them threatening, they may refuse to complete the remainder of the questionnaire. Thus, it is essential that the first few questions be simple, interesting, and in no way threatening. Questions that ask respondents for their opinion on some

- **Open with interesting questions**
- **Move from general to specific**
- **Demographics and sensitive questions go last**

issue are often good openers, as most people like to think that their opinion is important. Sometimes it is helpful to use such an opener even when those responses will not be analyzed, simply to relax the respondents and get them to talk freely.

USE THE FUNNEL APPROACH

The funnel approach to question sequencing gets its name from its shape: we start with broad questions and progressively narrow the scope. If

Ethical Dilemma 9.3

A candy manufacturer tells you that he wants to raise the price of his gourmet chocolates and he needs you to establish the maximum price increase that shoppers will stand. He suggests that you interview patrons of gourmet candy shops without informing them of the sponsor or purpose of the research, describe the candy to them in general terms, and suggest prices that they might find acceptable, starting with the highest price.

- Is it ethical to ask people questions when their answer may be detrimental to their self-interest?
- Is it ethical not to reveal the purpose or sponsor of the research? If you did reveal the purpose of the research, would survey respondents give the same answer as otherwise?

respondents are to be asked, "What improvements are needed in the company's service policy?" and also "How do you like the quality of service?" the first question needs to be asked before the second. Otherwise, quality of service will be emphasized disproportionately in the responses simply because it is fresh in the respondents' minds. There should also be some logical order to the questions. Avoid making sudden changes and jumping around from topic to topic.

DESIGN BRANCHING QUESTIONS WITH CARE

Branching questions are used to direct respondents to different places in the questionnaire, based on their response to the question at hand. A respondent replying "yes" to the question of whether he or she bought a new car within the last six months would be asked for specific details about the purchase, whereas someone responding "no" would be asked other questions. Branching questions and directions are easy to program via "if-then" statements in computer-assisted interviewing for surveys administered by telephone or in person. With mail questionnaires, branching can be used (e.g., "If Yes, please go to question 37"), but it needs to be kept to a minimum and the directions need to be crystal clear. It is good practice to develop a flow chart of the logical possibilities and then prepare the branching questions and instructions to follow the flow chart.

ASK FOR CLASSIFICATION INFORMATION LAST

The typical questionnaire contains two types of information: basic information and classification information. Basic information refers to the subject of the study (e.g., intentions or attitudes of respondents). Classification information refers to the other data that we collect to classify respondents, e.g., demographic variables.

The proper questionnaire sequence is to ask questions about the basic information first and the classification information last. Why? The basic information is most critical—without it, there is no study. We cannot risk alienating the respondent by asking personal questions before getting to the heart of the study. Respondents who readily offer their attitudes toward the energy crisis may balk when asked for their income. An early question aimed at determining their income may affect the whole tenor of the interview or other communication. It is best to avoid this possibility by placing the classification information at the end.

PLACE DIFFICULT OR SENSITIVE QUESTIONS LATE IN THE QUESTIONNAIRE

The basic information itself can also present some sequence problems. If respondents feel threatened, they will leave the interview or stop filling out the questionnaire. Thus, the sensitive questions should be relegated to the body of the questionnaire, intertwined and hidden among some not-so-sensitive ones. Once respondents have become involved in the study, they are less likely to react negatively or be turned off completely when delicate questions are posed.

Determine Physical Characteristics

The physical characteristics of the questionnaire can affect the accuracy of the replies, respondents' reactions, and the ease of processing. Here are some tips.

ACCEPTANCE OF THE QUESTIONNAIRE

The physical appearance of the questionnaire can influence respondents' cooperation. If the questionnaire looks sloppy, respondents are likely to think that the study is unimportant and not bother to cooperate. If the study is important (and why conduct it if it is not?), make the questionnaire reflect that importance. It should look as sharp as your résumé.[9]

The introduction is also important. With mail questionnaires, the cover letter introduces the study. It must convince the designated respondent to cooperate (see Research Realities 9.4). With personal and telephone interviews, the introduction is quick, but it still needs to convince respondents about the importance of the research and their participation. The basics include describing how the respondents can benefit, the fact that their replies will be confidential, and the incentive, if any, that they will receive for participating.

It is a good idea to include the name of the sponsoring organization and the name of the project on the first page. Both of these lend credibility to the study. At the same time, awareness of the sponsoring firm can induce bias in respondents' answers, so many firms use fictitious names for the sponsoring organization.

FACILITATE HANDLING AND CONTROL

Questionnaire length is important. Smaller questionnaires are better than larger ones if they do not appear crowded. Smaller questionnaires seem easier to complete; they appear to take less time and are less likely to cause respondents to refuse to participate. They are easier to carry in the field and are easier to sort, count, and file in the office than larger questionnaires. But smaller size can't be gained at the expense of a cramped appearance. A crowded questionnaire has a bad appearance, leads to errors in data collection, and results in shorter and less informative replies. For example, researchers have found that the more lines left for recording the response to open-ended questions, the more extensive the reply.

Numbering the questions facilitates handling and is particularly important when using branching questions (e.g., "If the answer to Question 2 is Yes, please go to Question 5"). Arrows and other icons can also be useful.

---

[9] Richard Harbaugh, "Proven Lessons for Generating Good Mail Survey Response Rates," *Medical Marketing and Media* 37 (2002), pp. 70–76.

Research Realities

9.4 Sample Cover Letter for Mail Questionnaire

Panel A: Contents

1. Personal communication
2. Asking a favor
3. Importance of the research project and its purpose
4. Importance of the recipient, how recipient was selected
5. How the recipient may benefit from this research
6. Completing the questionnaire will take only a short time
7. The questionnaire can be answered easily
8. A stamped reply envelope is enclosed
9. Answers are anonymous or confidential
10. Offer to send report on results of survey
11. Appreciation of sender
12. Importance of sender or sender's organization
13. Description and purpose of incentive
14. Style, format, and appearance
15. Brevity

Panel B: Sample

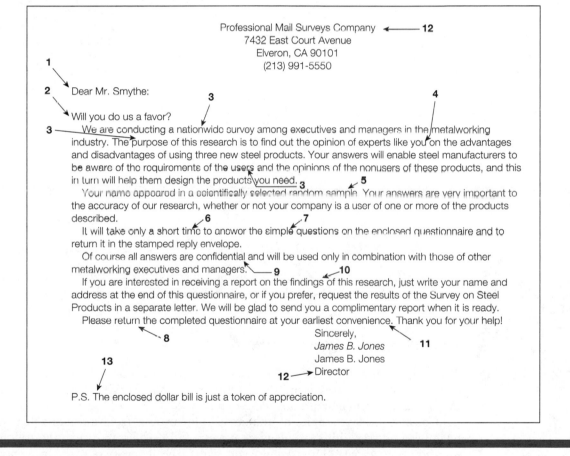

Numbering the questions makes it easier to edit, code, and tabulate the responses. If the questionnaires themselves are numbered, it is easier to keep track of them, monitor interviewer performance, etc. Mail questionnaires, however, should not be numbered—respondents interpret the presence of some number as a means by which their responses can be identified. This loss of anonymity raises refusal rates.

The guidelines are analogous for the preparation of Web surveys. See Research Realities 9.5.

Research Realities

9.5 Guidelines for Web Surveys

Here are 7 suggestions for enhancing Web survey response rates.

1. Don't look like spam (use text, not fancy html)

2. In the "subject line," include:
   a. The sponsor
   b. The topic
   c. The word "survey" (not "research," too geeky, and not "marketing," too related to pushy sales e-mails—see point #1!)

3. First sentence, you have a split second to capture the reader's attention, and this might be all of your e-mail they can see before deciding whether to open it. A suggestion: "This is an invitation to take part in a survey project. It's not a sales solicitation."

4. Key drivers to participation:
   a. Is research topic interesting?
   b. How much will I be compensated?
   c. Who is the sponsor?
   d. How much time/effort will this take? (Don't mess around—be truthful!)

5. Have a screener to identify relevant respondents. If a user is bounced out after answering just a few questions, that makes it clear that they're not the tattooed-Harley-rider-with-a-teenage-daughter-who-needs-a-prom-dress that you were looking for. Be sure to thank them anyway, e.g., "I'm sorry, you do not qualify to participate in the rest of our survey, but we thank you for your time thus far, and we will enter you into a drawing to win $100 just for trying."

6. Make it clear how the user could contact you for help or more information.

7. Make your privacy statement clear!
   a. E.g., "We are a marketing research firm that values your privacy. All of your responses will be kept strictly confidential and reported only in the aggregate. Your personal information will not be sold or traded to anyone." (And then don't!)
   b. It couldn't hurt to also have a link to a more elaborate statement of your privacy policy . . . these are paranoid times.
   c. Ditto for an opt-out opportunity (via e-mail or an 800 number).

Source: Bill MacElroy, "Persuasive E-mail Invitations," *Online Research* (http://www.quirks.com).

Re-examination and Revision of the Questionnaire

> **The most important step in survey development? PRETEST it!**

First drafts usually don't result in usable questionnaires. Rather, each question should be reviewed to ensure that it isn't confusing or ambiguous, offensive, leading, etc. Be extremely critical of the survey at this stage—it will save you grief later on.

Pretesting the Questionnaire

The real test of a questionnaire is how it performs under actual conditions of data collection. For this assessment, the questionnaire **pretest** is vital (much like the role of test marketing in new-product development).

Consider these examples of unintended implications from questions that could have been avoided with an adequate pretest. In one lifestyle study, the following question was asked: "How would you like to be living two years from now?" Though the question was intended to get at desired lifestyles, a large group of the respondents simply replied "yes." In another study, a question about "house cleaners" made some people respond with brands like "Comet" or "Ajax" and others answered "Yes, we have a service that comes once a week." Data collection should *never* begin without an adequate pretest of the instrument.

The pretest can assess individual questions as well as their sequence. It is best if there are two pretests. The first pretest should be done by personal interview (regardless of the actual mode of administration that will be used), so the interviewer can watch to see how people answer the questions, where they get confused, etc. The pretest interviews should be conducted by the firm's most experienced interviewers among respondents similar to those who will be used in the actual study.

Next, the questionnaire can be pretested using mail, telephone, or personal interviews, whichever method is going to be used for the full-scale study. This time, less-experienced interviewers should also be used to determine if typical interviewers will have any special problems. The second pretest will uncover problems unique to the mode of administration.

Finally, the responses that result from the pretest should be coded and tabulated. The code book can be used to process the incoming questionnaires. The tabulation of pretest responses into dummy tables can help us verify whether we've conceptualized the problem right, and see if we'll be getting the data to answer our questions.

The researcher who avoids a questionnaire pretest and tabulation of replies is either naïve or a fool. The pretest is the most inexpensive insurance the researcher can buy to ensure the success of the questionnaire and the research project.

Table 9.2 provides a checklist of steps to take and decisions to make in creating a questionnaire. The steps in the process are those in Figure 9.1—we've just highlighted the main points. The checklist can be used as a quick, handy reference when you're called to write a survey.

TABLE 9.2
Some Do's and Don'ts When Preparing Questionnaires

Step 1: Specify What Information Will Be Sought

1. Make sure that you have a clear understanding of the issue and what it is that you want to know (expect to learn). Frame your research questions, but refrain from writing questions for the questionnaire at this time.

2. Make a list of your research questions. Review them periodically as you are working on the questionnaire.

3. Use the "dummy tables" that were set up to guide the data analysis to suggest questions.

4. Conduct a search for existing questions on the issue.

5. Revise existing questions on the issue; prepare new questions to address your issues.

Step 2: Determine Type of Questionnaire and Method of Administration

1. Use the type of data to be collected as a basis for deciding on the type of questionnaire.

2. Use degree of structure, disguise, and cost to determine the method of administration.

3. Compare the capabilities and limitations of each method of administration and the value of the data collected from each, with the needs of the survey.

Step 3: Determine Content of Individual Questions

1. For each research question, ask yourself, "Why do I want to know this?" Answer it in terms of how it will help your research. "It would be interesting to know" is not an acceptable answer.

2. Make sure each question is specific and addresses only one important issue.

(continued)

TABLE 9.2
(continued)

3. Does the question apply to all respondents, if not, make provision for skipping it.

4. Split questions that can be answered from different frames of reference into multiple questions, one corresponding to each frame of reference.

5. Ask yourself whether respondents will be informed about and can remember the issue that the question is dealing with.

6. Make sure the time period of the question is related to the importance of the topic. Consider using aided-recall techniques like diaries, records, or bounded recall.

7. Avoid questions that require excessive effort, that have hard-to-articulate answers, and that deal with embarrassing or threatening issues.

8. If threatening questions are necessary:
   a. Hide the questions among more innocuous ones.
   b. Make use of a counterbiasing statement.
   c. Phrase the question in terms of others and how they might feel or act.
   d. Ask respondents if they have ever engaged in the undesirable activity; then ask if they are presently engaging in such an activity.
   e. Use categories or ranges rather than specific numbers.
   f. Use the randomized response model.

Step 4: Determine Form of Response to Each Question

1. Determine which type of question—open-ended, dichotomous, or multichotomous—provides data that fit the information needs of the project.

2. Use structured questions whenever possible.

3. Use open-ended questions that require short answers to begin a questionnaire.

4. Try to convert open-ended questions to closed (fixed) response questions to reduce respondent workload and coding effort for descriptive and causal studies.

5. If open-ended questions are necessary, make the questions sufficiently directed to give respondents a frame of reference when answering.

6. When using dichotomous questions, state the negative or alternative side in detail.

7. Provide for "don't know," "no opinion," and "both" answers.

8. Be aware that there may be a middle ground.

9. Be sensitive to the mildness or harshness of the alternatives.

10. When using multichotomous questions, be sure that the choices are exhaustive and mutually exclusive, and if combinations are possible, include them.

11. Be sure that the range of alternatives is clear and that all reasonable alternative answers are included.

12. If the possible responses are very numerous, consider using more than one question to reduce the potential for information overload.

13. When using dichotomous or multichotomous questions, consider the use of a split ballot procedure to reduce order bias.

14. Clearly indicate if items are to be ranked or if only one item on the list is to be chosen.

(continued)

TABLE 9.2
(*continued*)

Step 5: Determine Wording of Each Question

1. Use simple words.

2. Avoid ambiguous words and questions.

3. Avoid leading questions.

4. Avoid implicit assumptions.

5. Avoid generalizations and estimates.

6. Use simple sentences; avoid compound sentences.

7. Change long, dependent clauses to words or short phrases.

8. Avoid double-barreled questions.

9. Make sure each question is as specific as possible.

Step 6: Determine Question Sequence

1. Use simple, interesting questions for openers.

2. Use the funnel approach, first asking broad questions, then narrowing them down.

3. Ask difficult or sensitive questions late in the questionnaire when rapport is better.

4. Follow chronological order when collecting historical information.

5. Complete questions about one topic before moving on to the next.

6. Prepare a flow chart whenever filter questions are being considered.

7. Ask filter questions before asking detailed questions.

8. Ask demographic questions last; if respondent refuses, the other data are still usable.

Step 7: Determine Physical Characteristics of Questionnaire

1. Make sure that the questionnaire looks professional and is relatively easy to answer.

2. Use quality paper and print; do not photocopy the questionnaire.

3. Make the questionnaire as short as possible, but avoid a crowded appearance.

4. Use a booklet format for ease of analysis and to prevent lost pages.

5. List the name of the organization conducting the survey on the first page.

6. Number the questions to ease data processing.

7. If the respondent must skip more than one question, use a "go to."

8. If the respondent must skip an entire section, consider color coding the sections.

9. State how the responses are to be reported, e.g., check mark, number, circle, etc.

Step 8: Re-examine Steps 1–7 and Revise if Necessary

1. Examine each word of every question to ensure the question is not confusing, ambiguous, offensive, or leading.

2. Get peer evaluations of the draft questionnaire.

(*continued*)

TABLE 9.2
(continued)

Step 9: Pretest Questionnaire and Revise if Necessary

1. Pretest the questionnaire first using personal interviews among respondents similar to those to be used in the actual study.

2. Obtain comments from the interviewers and respondents to discover any problems with the questionnaire, and revise it if necessary. When the revisions are substantial, repeat steps 1 and 2 of the pretest.

3. Pretest the questionnaire by mail or telephone to uncover problems unique to the mode of administration.

4. Code and tabulate the pretest responses in dummy tables to determine if questions are providing adequate information.

5. Eliminate questions that do not provide adequate information, and revise questions that cause problems.

Observational Forms

Generally, fewer problems occur in constructing observational forms, because the researcher is no longer concerned with whether the question will affect the response. The observers will be properly trained, and their expertise means the data-collection instrument will be used consistently. Mechanical devices also measure certain behaviors quite consistently. Figure 9.3 is the observation form used by customers of a bank to evaluate its customer service.

What do you want to observe? Almost any event can be described in a number of ways. When we watch someone making a cigarette purchase, we might report that (1) the person purchased one package of cigarettes; (2) the woman purchased one package of cigarettes; (3) the woman purchased a package of Tareyton cigarettes; (4) the woman purchased a package of Tareyton 100's; (5) the woman, after asking for and finding that the store was out of Virginia Slims, purchased a package of Tareyton 100's; and so on.

The decision about what to observe requires that the researcher specify the following:

- *Who* should be observed? Anyone entering the store? Anyone making a purchase? Anyone making a cigarette purchase?
- *What* aspects of the purchase should be reported? Which brand they purchased? Which brand they asked for first? Whether the purchase was of king size or regular cigarettes? What about the purchaser? Is the person's gender to be recorded? Is the individual's age to be estimated? Does it make any difference if the person was alone or in a group?
- *When* should the observation be made? On what day of the week? At what time of the day? Should day and time be reported? Should the observation be recorded only after a purchase occurs or should a customer approaching a salesclerk also be recorded, even if it does not result in a sale?
- *Where* should the observation be made? In what kind of store? How should the store be selected? How should it be noted on the observational form—by type, by location, by name? Should vending-machine purchases also be noted?

These are the same kinds of who, what, when, and where decisions that need to be made in selecting the research design. The "why" and "how" are also implicit.

> As baseball player Yogi Berra once said, "You can observe a lot by watching."

FIGURE 9.3
Observation Form
Sample for Bank

Bank _____

Date _____   Time _____   Shopper's Name _____

Nature of Transaction: _____ In Person   _____ Telephone

Details: _____

_____

_____

_____

A. For In-person Transaction, what was Bank Employee's Name? _____
How did you obtain that information?

☐ Employee had name tag

☐ Name plate on counter or desk

☐ I had to ask for name

☐ Name provided by another employee

☐ Other: _____

B. For Telephone Transaction, what was Bank Employee's Name? _____
How did you obtain that information?

☐ Employee gave name upon answering the telephone

☐ Name provided by another employee

☐ I had to ask for name

☐ Employee gave name during conversation

☐ Other: _____

C. Customer Relations Skills	Yes	No	Does not apply
1. Did the employee notice and greet you immediately?	☐	☐	☐
2. Did the employee speak pleasantly and smile?	☐	☐	☐
3. Did the employee answer the phone within 2 rings?	☐	☐	☐
4. Did the employee find out your name?	☐	☐	☐
5. Did the employee use your name during the transaction?	☐	☐	☐
6. Did the employee ask you to be seated?	☐	☐	☐
7. Was the employee helpful?	☐	☐	☐
8. Was the employee's desk or work area neat and uncluttered?	☐	☐	☐
9. Did the employee show a genuine interest in you as a customer?	☐	☐	☐
10. Did the employee thank you for coming in?	☐	☐	☐
11. Did the employee enthusiastically support the bank and its services?	☐	☐	☐
12. Did the employee handle any interruptions effectively (phone calls, etc.)?	☐	☐	☐

(continued)

FIGURE 9.3
(continued)

Comment on any positive or negative details of the transaction that you found particularly noticeable:

_____

_____

_____

_____

D. Sales Skills

	Yes	No	Does not apply
1. Did the employee determine if you had any accounts with this bank?	☐	☐	☐
2. Did the employee use "open-ended" questions to obtain information about you?	☐	☐	☐
3. Did the employee listen to what you had to say?	☐	☐	☐
4. Did the employee sell you on bank services by showing you what the service could do for you?	☐	☐	☐
5. Did the employee ask you to open the service that you inquired about?	☐	☐	☐
6. Did the employee ask you to bank with this particular bank?	☐	☐	☐
7. Did the employee ask you to contact him/her when visiting the bank?	☐	☐	☐
8. Did the employee ask if you had any questions or if you understood the service at the end of the transaction?	☐	☐	☐
9. Did the employee give you brochures about other services?	☐	☐	☐
10. Did the employee give you his/her business card?	☐	☐	☐
11. Did the employee indicate you might be contacted by phone or letter as a means of follow-up?	☐	☐	☐
12. Did the employee ask you to open or use other services?	☐	☐	☐

Check the following if they were mentioned:

☐ Savings account   ☐ Checking account   ☐ Automatic savings

☐ Mastercharge   ☐ Master Checking   ☐ Safe deposit box

☐ Loans   ☐ Trust services   ☐ Automatic loan payment

☐ Bank hours   ☐ Other: _____

Comment on the overall effectiveness of the employee's sales skills:

_____

_____

_____

_____

The research problem should dictate the why of the observation, whereas the how involves choosing the observation device or form to use. A paper-and-pencil form should be very simple to use. It should parallel the logical sequence of the purchase act (e.g., a male approaches the clerk, asks for a package of cigarettes, and so on, whichever behaviors are relevant) and should permit the recording of observations by a simple check mark if possible.

Summary

A researcher wishing to collect primary data needs to tackle the task of designing the data-collection instrument. Typically this means designing a questionnaire, although it may mean framing an observational form.

Questionnaire design is still very much of an art rather than a science, and there are many admonitions of things to avoid when doing the designing. A nine-step procedure (Figure 9.1) was offered as a guide: What information will be sought? What type of questionnaire will be used? How will that questionnaire be administered? What will be the content of the individual questions? What will be the form of response—dichotomous, multichotomous, or open-ended—to each question? How will each question be phrased? How will the questions be sequenced? What will the questionnaire look like physically?

Researchers should not be surprised to find themselves repeating the various steps when designing a questionnaire. Further, although the temptation is sometimes great, one should never omit a pretest of the questionnaire. Regardless of how good it looks in the abstract, the pretest provides the real test of the questionnaire and its mode of administration. At least two pretests should be conducted. The first should use personal interviews, and after all the troublesome spots have been smoothed over, a second pretest using the normal mode of administration should be conducted. The data collected in the pretest should then be subjected to the analyses planned for the full data set, as this will reveal serious omissions or other shortcomings while it is still possible to correct these deficiencies.

Observational forms generally present fewer problems of construction than questionnaires, because the researcher no longer needs to be concerned with the fact that the question itself, and the way it is asked, will affect the response. Observational forms do, however, require a precise statement of who or what is to be observed, what actions or characteristics are relevant, and when and where the observations will be made.

Review Questions

1. What role do the research hypotheses play in determining the information that will be sought?

2. Suppose you were interested in determining the proportion of men in a geographic area who use hair spray. How could the necessary information be obtained by open-ended question, by multiple-choice question, and by dichotomous question? Which would be preferable?

3. How does the method of administration of a questionnaire affect the type of question to be employed?

4. What criteria can a researcher use to determine whether a specific question should be included in a questionnaire?

5. What is telescoping error? What does it suggest about the period to be used when asking respondents to recall past events?

6. What are some recommended ways by which one can ask for sensitive information?

7. What is an open-ended question? A multichotomous question? A dichotomous question? What are some of the key things researchers must be careful to avoid in framing multichotomous and dichotomous questions?

8. What is a split ballot, and why is it used?

9. What is an ambiguous question? A leading question? A question with implicit alternatives? A question with implied assumptions? A double-barreled question?

10. What is the proper sequence when asking for basic information and classification information?

11. What is the funnel approach to question sequencing?

12. What is a branching question? Why are such questions used?

13. Where should one ask for sensitive information in the questionnaire?

14. How can the physical features of a questionnaire affect its acceptance by respondents? Its handling and control by the researcher?

15. What is the overriding principle guiding questionnaire construction?

16. What decisions must the researcher make when developing an observational form for data collection?

Applications and Problems

1. Evaluate the following questions:

   a. Which of the following magazines do you read regularly?
      ☐ Time
      ☐ Newsweek
      ☐ BusinessWeek

   b. Are you a frequent purchaser of Birds Eye frozen vegetables?
      ☐ Yes   ☐ No

   c. Do you agree that the government should impose import restrictions?
      ☐ Strongly agree
      ☐ Agree
      ☐ Neither agree nor disagree
      ☐ Disagree
      ☐ Strongly disagree

   d. How often do you buy detergent?
      ☐ Once a week
      ☐ Once in two weeks
      ☐ Once in three weeks
      ☐ Once a month

   e. Rank the following in order of preference:
      ☐ Kellogg's Corn Flakes
      ☐ Quaker's Life
      ☐ Post Bran Flakes
      ☐ Kellogg's Bran Flakes
      ☐ Instant Quaker Oat Meal
      ☐ Post Rice Krinkles

   f. Where do you usually purchase your school supplies?

   g. When you are watching television, do you also watch most of the advertisements?

   h. Which of the following brands of tea are most similar?
      ☐ Lipton's Orange Pekoe
      ☐ Turnings Orange Pekoe
      ☐ Bigelow Orange Pekoe
      ☐ Salada Orange Pekoe

   i. Do you think that the present policy of cutting taxes and reducing government spending should be continued?
      ☐ Yes   ☐ No

   j. In a seven-day week, how often do you eat breakfast?
      ☐ Every day of the week
      ☐ 5–6 times a week
      ☐ 2–4 times a week
      ☐ Once a week
      ☐ Never

2. Make the necessary corrections to the preceding questions.

3. Evaluate the following multichotomous questions. Would dichotomous or open-ended questions be more appropriate?

   a. Which one of the following reasons is most important in your choice of stereo equipment?
      - ☐ Price
      - ☐ In-store service
      - ☐ Brand name
      - ☐ Level of distortion
      - ☐ Guarantee/warranty

   b. Please indicate your education level.
      - ☐ Less than high school
      - ☐ Some high school
      - ☐ High school graduate
      - ☐ Technical or vocational school
      - ☐ Some college
      - ☐ College graduate
      - ☐ Some graduate or professional school

   c. Which of the following reflects your views toward the issues raised by ecologists?
      - ☐ Have received attention
      - ☐ Have not received attention
      - ☐ Should receive more attention
      - ☐ Should receive less attention

   d. Which of the following statements do you most strongly agree with?
      - ☐ American Airlines has better service than Northwest Airlines.
      - ☐ Northwest Airlines has better service than United Airlines.
      - ☐ United Airlines has better service than American Airlines.
      - ☐ United Airlines has better service than Northwest Airlines.
      - ☐ Northwest Airlines has better service than American Airlines.
      - ☐ American Airlines has better service than United Airlines.

4. Evaluate the following open-ended questions. Rephrase them as multichotomous or dichotomous questions if you think it would be appropriate.

   a. Do you go to the movies often?

   b. Approximately how much do you spend per week on groceries?

   c. What brands of cheese did you purchase during the last week?

5. Discuss how each of the following respondent groups would influence the development of the questionnaire form.

   a. Medical doctors
   b. Welfare recipients
   c. Air Force commanders
   d. Cuban refugees

6. Your employer, a commercial marketing research firm, has contracted you to perform a study whose objective is the investigation of usage patterns and brand preferences for infant diapers among migrant farm workers in the southeastern United States. You have been assigned to develop a suitable questionnaire and method of administration to collect the desired information. What potential problems might arise in the design and administration due to the nature of the population in question? List these problems and provide solutions. What method of administration would you recommend?

7. Campus Cookery, the local burger spot, has asked you to comment on some of the questions that have been developed for a survey it is conducting on a new sandwich offering. What is wrong (if anything) with each of the following questions?

   a. Why haven't you tried our new sandwich at Campus Cookery?

   b. Don't you think that Campus Cookery's products are of the highest quality?

   c. Would you say that our new sandwich tastes good, is priced correctly, is attractive, and is healthy?
      - ☐ Yes   ☐ No

   d. Have you tried our new sandwich at Campus Cookery?

VERY INFREQUENTLY	INFREQUENTLY	AVERAGE	VERY FREQUENTLY
___	___	___	___

8. Analyze the following questions. What (if anything) is wrong with each question?

   a. How do you like the flavor of this high-quality, top-bean coffee?

   b. What do you think of the taste and texture of this Danish Treat coffee cake?

   c. We are conducting a study for "Guess?" watches. What do you think of the quality of "Guess?" watches?

   d. How far do you live from the closest mall?

   e. Who in your family shops for clothes?

   f. Where do you buy most of your clothes?

9. A small brokerage firm was concerned with the declining number of customers and decided to do a quick survey. The objective was to find out the reasons for patronizing a particular brokerage firm and to find out the importance of customer service. The following

questionnaire was to be administered by telephone. Evaluate the questionnaire.

Good Afternoon Sir/Madam:

We are doing a survey on attitudes toward brokerage firms. Could you please answer the following questions? Thank you.

1. Have you invested any money in the stock market?

   ____ Yes   ____ No

   If respondent replies Yes, continue; otherwise terminate interview.

2. Do you manage your own investments or do you go to a brokerage firm?

   ____ Manage own investments

   ____ Go to a brokerage firm

   If respondent replies "Go to a brokerage firm," continue; otherwise, terminate interview.

3. How satisfied are you with your brokerage firm?

		NEITHER SATISFIED NOR		VERY
VERY SATISFIED	SATISFIED	DISSATISFIED	DISSATISFIED	DISSATISFIED
____	____	____	____	____

4. How important is personal service to you?

VERY IMPORTANT	IMPORTANT	NOT PARTICULARLY IMPORTANT	NOT AT ALL IMPORTANT
____	____	____	____

5. Which of the following reasons is the most important in patronizing a particular firm?

   ____ The commission charged by the firm

   ____ The personal service

   ____ The return on investment

   ____ The investment counseling

6. Approximately how long have you been investing through the brokerage firm you are currently using?

   ____ about 3 months   ____ about 9 months

   ____ about 6 months   ____ about 1 year or more

7. How much capital do you have invested?

   ____ $500–$750   ____ $1,000–$1,500

   ____ $750–$1,000   ____ $1,500 or more

   Good-bye and thank you for your cooperation.

10. Suppose that the Nuclear Regulatory Commission is considering a proposal made by a California utility company to build a nuclear reactor in a small town located in southern California. According to the proposal, the new reactor could provide energy for a good portion of southern California at considerable savings over conventional sources of energy. Ultimately, substantial savings would be passed along to the consumer, according to the utility company. Opponents of the project, primarily antinuclear groups and environmental organizations, claim that such a project would needlessly put people who reside in the area, as well as the environment, at risk while the utility company makes a handsome profit. The proponents respond that no other suitable site can be found in southern California and that the benefits of less-expensive energy sources far outweigh any potential risks associated with the project—particularly for individuals and families at or below the poverty line. Both sides, citing statistics from various public opinion polls, claim to have public opinion on their side.

   a. Write a question for a public opinion survey that is likely to produce results in favor of building the nuclear reactor (that is, results that support the utility's position).

   b. Write a question for a public opinion survey that is likely to produce results showing that most people are not in favor of building the new nuclear facility (that is, results that support the opposition's viewpoint).

   c. Write an appropriate survey question that attempts to accurately measure public opinion about whether the nuclear reactor should be built.

Attitude Measurement

Questions to Guide Your Learning:

Q1: What precisely is an "attitude" and what are the psychological components of an attitude?

Q2: What are "levels of measurement" and why do they matter?

Q3: What are Likert scales, semantic differential scales, and constant sum scales?

Attitude is one of the most pervasive notions in all of marketing. It plays a pivotal role in the major models describing consumer behavior, and is included, in one form or another, in most marketing investigations. Attitude plays this central role mainly because it is believed to strongly influence behavior. Many marketers believe that attitudes directly affect purchase decisions and that purchase and usage experiences, in turn, directly affect consumers' subsequent attitudes toward the product or service.

People hold attitudes about virtually everything, and marketers study many of them. For example, Research Realities 10.1 reports on an annual poll—the *Fortune* rankings of most admired companies. The companies with the best overall reputations are listed, as are those high on particular qualities, like strengths in social responsibility, innovation, management quality, etc.

Research Realities

10.1 *Fortune* Polls on Most Admired Companies*

Overall Rankings:

1. Wal-Mart
2. Southwest Airlines
3. Berkshire Hathaway
4. Dell Computer
5. General Electric
6. Johnson & Johnson
7. Microsoft
8. FedEx
9. Starbucks
10. Procter & Gamble

Top Ten Outside the U.S.:

1. Toyota Motor, Japan
2. BMW, Germany
3. Sony, Japan
4. Nokia, Finland
5. Nestle, Switzerland
6. Singapore Airlines, Singapore
7. L'Oreal, France
8. Honda Motor, Japan
9. BP, Britain
10. Royal Dutch/Shell Group, Netherlands/Britain

*March 3, 2003.

Leaders on the Eight Key Attributes of Corporate Reputation:

Social Responsibility:

1. Alexander & Baldwin
2. Johnson & Johnson
3. American Express

Innovation:

1. PepsiCo
2. Nike
3. Medtronic

Long-Term Investment Value:

1. Medtronic
2. Cardinal Health
3. Cintas

Use of Corporate Assets:

1. Berkshire Hathaway
2. Cintas
3. Philip Morris (Altria)

Employee Talent:

1. General Electric
2. American Express
3. Philip Morris (Altria)

Financial Soundness:

1. Microsoft
2. Berkshire Hathaway
3. Philip Morris (Altria)

Quality of Products/Services:

1. Philip Morris (Altria)
2. Medtronic
3. Procter & Gamble

Quality of Management:

1. Philip Morris (Altria)
2. Berkshire Hathaway
3. General Electric

Attitude is one of the most widely used ideas in all of social psychology or consumer behavior, but it is also difficult to pin down a definition. However, there seems to be agreement about the following:

1. Attitude represents a *predisposition* to respond to an object (not yet the actual behavior toward the object). Attitude thus possesses the quality of readiness.
2. Attitude is *persistent* over time, and changing a strongly held attitude requires substantial pressure.

3. Attitude is a latent variable that produces consistency in verbal and physical behavior.
4. Attitude has a directional quality. It connotes a preference regarding the outcomes involving the object, evaluations of the object, or positive/neutral/negative feelings for the object.[1]

These consistencies lead to our definition of attitude as: *representing a person's ideas, convictions, or liking with regard to a specific object or idea.*

Scales of Measurement

We're working toward the topic of "attitude measurement." We have a beginning of an understanding of "attitude," but we also need to define measurement. Then we'll be ready to present the types of *scales* that can be used to measure attitudes. The term "scale" is used in two different contexts when discussing measurement. It can refer to the "level of measurement" (e.g., an ordinal scale) or to the particular scale or type of instrument used (e.g., a scale of customer satisfaction). We take up the level of measurement issues first.

Measurement is the assignment of numbers to objects (e.g., consumers) in a way that reflects the quantity of the attribute that the object possesses (e.g., preference for a brand). Note that we speak of measuring the attributes of objects, not the objects themselves. We do not measure a person, for example, but we measure that person's income, height, or attitudes, all of which are attributes of this person. Note also that the definition does not specify how the numbers are to be assigned. We need to discuss that numerical assignment.

Let's start simply with thinking about properties of numbers. With the numbers 1, 2, 3, and 4, let the number "1" stand for one object, "2" for two objects, and so on—a simple count. That simple scale possesses several qualities; e.g., we can say that 2 is larger than 1, we can say that the difference between 1 and 2 is the same size as that between 3 and 4, and we can say that 3 is three times greater than 1.

However, when we assign numbers to attributes of objects, these relations do not necessarily hold. For each attribute, and each scale assignment, we have to determine which properties of numbers actually apply. The four different types of scales of measurement are nominal, ordinal, interval, and ratio. Table 10.1 summarizes important features of these scales.

Nominal Scale

The simplest property of a scale is identity. A person's social security number is a **nominal scale**. The numbers simply identify the individual. In a market segmentation study, if we're coding gender or ethnicity, we have a nominal scale. Males might be coded "1" and females "2." Each individual is uniquely identified as male or female, but note that nothing is implied by the numbers other than identification of gender. We assigned women a higher number, but they are not necessarily "more" of anything than the men. We could just as easily reverse our coding procedure so that women are "1" and men, "2."

---

[1]One reason for the many definitions of attitude is the age-old scientific problem of going from construct to operational definition, a problem that is reviewed in the appendix.

TABLE 10.1
Scales of Measurement

Scale	Basic Comparisons[a]	Examples	Measures of Average[b]
Nominal	Identity	Male–female, User–nonuser, Occupations, Uniform numbers	Mode
Ordinal	Order	Preference for brands, Social class, Hardness of minerals, Graded quality of lumber	Median
Interval	Comparison of intervals	Temperature scale, Grade point average, Attitude toward brands	Mean
Ratio	Comparison of absolute magnitudes	Units sold, Number of purchasers, Probability of purchase, Weight	Geometric mean, Harmonic mean

[a] The scales are hierarchical, so all comparisons applicable to a given scale are permissible with all scales *above* it in the table. For example, the ratio scale allows the comparison of intervals and the investigation of order and identity, in addition to the comparison of absolute magnitudes.

[b] The measures of average applicable to a given scale are also appropriate for all scales *below* it in the table; that is, the mode is also a meaningful measure of the average when measurement is on an ordinal, interval, or ratio scale.

Ordinal Scale

Nominal
Ordinal
Interval
Ratio

A second property of numbers is that of order. We can say that the number 3 is greater than 2 and 1, and 4 is greater still. If this is the nature of our scale, the idea is that the larger the number, the greater the amount of the attribute we're measuring. Note that the *ordinal scale* also implies the identity quality of the nominal scale, since the same number is used for all objects that are the same. For example, say we assigned the number "1" to denote freshmen, "2" for sophomores, "3" for juniors, and "4" for seniors. We could have used the numbers "10" for freshmen, "20" for sophomores, "25" for juniors, and "32.3" for seniors. Either set of scores would indicate the class level of each student. Note also that we cannot interpret the differences between ranks. If we take the three top people in a graduating class, the fact that one person was ranked number one while the second was ranked number two tells us nothing about the difference in academic achievement between the two. Nor can we say that the difference between those two equals the difference between the 2nd- and 3rd-ranked people, even though the difference between the numbers "1" and "2" equals the difference between "2" and "3."

One reason that ranks are used in marketing is to force customers to distinguish among choices. For example, if a customer is asked "which of these attributes are important to you," many customers simply rate every attribute as fairly important. This is not great information for a company—how do you take those data and decide what features to include or improve if all are deemed important? Instead, if customers are asked to rank the attributes, the customer has to make a decision about one feature being more important than another.[2]

---

[2] E.g., John McCarty and L. J. Shrum, "The Measurement of Personal Values in Survey Research," *Public Opinion Quarterly* 64 (2000), pp. 271–298.

Interval Scale

A third property of the scale of numbers is that the intervals between the numbers are meaningful. That is, the numbers tell us how far apart the objects are with respect to the attribute being measured. The difference between "1" and "2" is equal to the difference between "2" and "3," and the difference between "2" and "4" is twice the difference that exists between "1" and "2."

A classic example of an **interval scale** is the temperature scale. If the low temperature for the day was 40°F and the high was 80°F, can we say that the high temperature was twice as hot (represented twice the heat) as the low temperature? No. If we convert these temperatures to Celsius (where C = (5°F – 160)/9), then the low was 4.4°C and the high 26.6°C, a much different ratio. Thus we cannot compare the absolute magnitude of interval scales.

What can we say about data from an interval scale? We can say that 80°F is warmer than 40°F. We can say the difference in "heat" (the attribute being measured) between 80°F and 120°F is the same as the difference between 40°F and 80°F, and that the difference between 40°F and 120°F is twice the difference between 40°F and 80°F.[3]

Ratio Scale

The **ratio scale** possesses a natural or absolute zero, one for which there is universal agreement about its location. Height and weight are obvious examples. Given the existence of a real zero, the comparison of the absolute magnitude of the numbers is legitimate. Thus, a person weighing 200 pounds is said to be twice as heavy as one weighing 100 pounds.

We say more about these scales—nominal, ordinal, interval, and ratio—when we begin to talk about data analysis. The statistics we can compute depend on these levels of measurement. For example, we'll see that we can only compute a mode on nominal data, but we could compute a mean on interval level data.

Scaling of Psychological Attributes

The attribute we're trying to measure is itself the key determinant to the level of scale that we can use to measure the characteristic. If the attribute is naturally "interval," the best we can do is get an "interval" level variable from a survey. We could end up writing a survey item that yields only an "ordinal" or "nominal" level variable, but we could not write a question that yielded a "ratio" level variable. Thus the procedure used in constructing the scale determines the type of scale actually generated, so we have to be careful in conceptualizing the attribute so as not to delude ourselves or mislead others with our interpretation of the measures. The more powerful scales (ratio, interval) allow stronger comparisons and conclusions to be made than simpler levels of measurement (ordinal or nominal).

---

[3] To check on the validity of these claims, convert the temperatures: 120°F represents 48.8°C, and the difference between 4.4°C (40°F) and 26.6°C (80°F) is the same as that between 26.6°C (80°F) and 48.8°C (120°F)—namely, 22.2°. Further, the difference of 44.4°C between 4.4°C and 48.8°C is twice as large as that between 4.4°C and 26.6°C, as it was with the Fahrenheit scale. The relationship between intervals holds regardless of the values of "a" and "b" in the transformation.

There is a great temptation to assume that our measures have the properties of at least the interval scale (to conduct the statistics that interval scales allow). Whether they do in fact is another question. We should critically ask: What is the basic nature of the attribute? Have we captured this basic nature by our measurement procedure?

Ratio scales can be more demanding on respondents. For example, Figure 10.1 asks the question of consumers' preferences for six soft drinks, framed via a nominal, ordinal, interval, and ratio scale. Try to answer those questions for yourself and see if you agree.

Attitude-Scaling Procedures

By far the most common approach to measuring attitudes is self reports, in which people are asked directly for their beliefs or feelings toward some stimulus, an object, activity, e.g., ads, brands, spokespersons, service packages, etc. **Self report scales** are so prevalent that we'll spend the next section discussing them and the varieties of forms they take. For now, we note that attitudes can also be measured in other ways, including: the observation of overt behavior, indirect techniques, performance of "objective" tasks, and physiological reactions. These other measures lend complementary insights and can help validate the self report measure. *Multiple measures* are useful to establish the convergent and discriminant validity of a measure.[4]

FIGURE 10.1
Assessment Using Nominal, Ordinal, Interval, and Ratio Scales

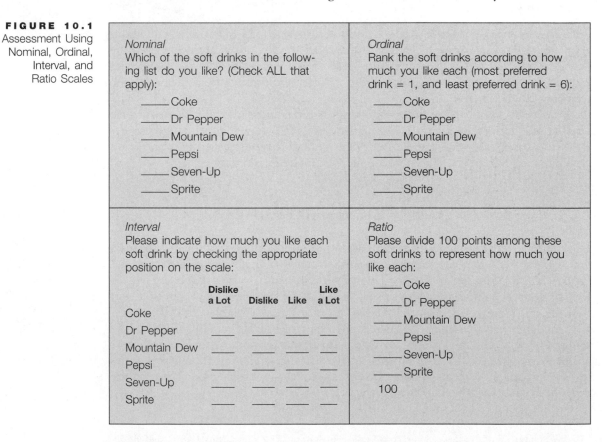

---

[4] The ideas of convergent and discriminant validity are discussed in the appendix. Convergent validity (of a measure) is the extent to which it correlates highly with other measures designed to assess the same construct. Discriminant validity is indicated by low correlations between the measure of interest and measures that are supposedly not measuring the same variable or construct.

OBSERVATION OF BEHAVIOR

The observation approach to attitude determination rests on the presumption that a person's behavior is conditioned by his or her attitudes and, thus, that we can use the observed behavior to infer these attitudes. Thus, observers inferred that consumers are *not* looking for a low-fat meal when they enter McDonald's from the fact that the McLean hamburger was a marketing flop in spite of the $50 million product launch.[5] Sometimes a researcher might create an artificial situation and observe how the individual behaves. For example, to assess people's attitude toward antipollution legislation, they might be asked to sign a "strong" petition prohibiting pollution. Their attitude toward pollution would be inferred on the basis of whether they signed. Alternatively, we might put them into a group and ask them to discuss pollution and observe their behavior—did the persons oppose or support antipollution legislation in the discussion?

INDIRECT TECHNIQUES

Indirect techniques use some unstructured or partially structured stimuli, such as word association tests, sentence completion tests, storytelling, and so on. Because the arguments concerning the use of these devices were detailed in Chapter 8 on primary data collection, they will not be repeated here.

PERFORMANCE OF "OBJECTIVE" TASK

These approaches presume that people's performance of objective tasks depends on their attitude. To assess a person's opinion about pollution, we might ask him or her to memorize a number of facts about the extent of pollution, the magnitude of the cleanup task, and pending antipollution legislation. This material would reflect both sides of the issue. The researcher would then attempt to determine what facts the person assimilated. The assumption is that they are more likely to remember the arguments most consistent with their own position.

PHYSIOLOGICAL REACTIONS

The physiological reaction approach to attitude measurement uses electrical or mechanical means, such as the galvanic skin response technique, to monitor a person's response to some stimulus. These measures provide an indication of the intensity of the individual's feelings but not an assessment of positive or negative valence.

Self Report Attitude Scales

In this section, we review types of self report scales, focusing particularly on those that have novel features or have been used extensively in marketing. We describe what each scale looks like, how it is constructed and how it is used.

Equal-Appearing Intervals

Suppose that one of the banks in town is interested in comparing its image to its competitors' and has developed a list of statements that could be used to describe each bank. Let's say a respondent describes Bank A as having "convenient hours"

---

[5] Hugh Graham, "Annals of Marketing: Don't Go Changin'," *Dow Jones Publications Library,* http://www.dowjones.com.

and "a convenient location" but "generally discourteous service" and "higher service charges on personal checking accounts." Does this customer have a favorable or unfavorable attitude toward Bank A? Suppose that the respondent describes Bank B as just the opposite. Which bank does this person like more? "Equal-appearing interval scaling" develops values for these statements so we can assess the person's attitude toward these banks.[6]

SCALE CONSTRUCTION

We first generate a large number of statements about the object of interest (the banks). The statements are edited to remove ones that are ambiguous, irrelevant, and awkward, as well as those that are simply factual rather than opinion-based. A relatively large sample of judges then sorts the statements by how favorable they are, and a scale value is determined for each statement by noting how many judges consider the statement most favorable, next most favorable, etc. The statements are then screened on the basis of two criteria: the scale values and the dispersion in judgments exhibited by a pretest of participants. A final scale is formed from those statements that span the range of scale values and that display relatively good interjudge reliability. Let's illustrate.

In the first phase, generating a large number of statements, we draw from a search of the literature, discussions with knowledgeable people, personal experience, etc., trying to be exhaustive. The following are examples.

1. The bank offers courteous service.
2. The bank has a convenient location.
3. The bank has convenient hours.
4. The bank offers low interest rates on loans.
5. The bank pays low interest on its savings accounts.
. . . etc. through to the last:
"m."   The bank's service is friendly.

Ideally, "m" (the number of items we've generated) would be in the neighborhood of 100 to 200, and each statement would be presented on a separate card.

After editing the statements, we recruit a large number of respondents to serve as judges. Each judge is instructed to sort the statements into one of 11 piles based on the "degree of favorableness" of the statement. The judges are not asked whether they agree or disagree with a statement, but simply to evaluate the positiveness of the statement. They place the most unfavorable statements in the "A" pile of Figure 10.2; the most favorable statements in K; and the neutral statements into the F pile. The

FIGURE 10.2
Thurstone Equal-Appearing Interval Continuum

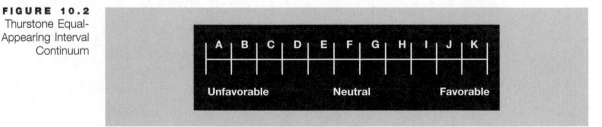

---

[6] The equal-appearing interval technique was developed by L. L. Thurstone and E. J. Chave, *The Measurement of Attitude* (University of Chicago Press, 1929), as an alternative to the paired comparison method when the number of statements was large. A reference from before your great-grandmother was born—how great and geeky is that!

TABLE 10.2
Equal-Appearing Interval
Sort of Statements into
Categories

| | **Sorting Categories** | | | | | | | | | | | | |
Statement	A 1	B 2	C 3	D 4	E 5	F 6	G 7	H 8	I 9	J 10	K 11	Scale Value	Q Value
1	0	8	10	30	60	60	14	12	6	0	0	5.4	1.7
2	0	0	0	0	0	6	16	28	44	66	40	9.6	1.8
3	0	0	0	0	10	10	14	32	84	34	16	8.9	1.5
4	0	0	8	16	36	58	48	24	10	0	0	6.2	2.0

presumption is that each judge will perceive the categories A through K as representing equal increments of favorableness, hence the name, "equal-appearing intervals."

Suppose that 200 judges sorted the m statements according to their favorableness and that Table 10.2 contains the resulting distribution for the first four statements. The right-hand columns of the table contain the scale and Q values for each statement (hence a name for this technique, the "Q sort"). The scale value represents the "average" (median) value of the statement, which places each statement on the favorability continuum in Figure 10.2. The Q value is the interquartile range, which provides a measure of dispersion.

Both the scale values and the measures of dispersion are used to select a subset of statements to serve as the final survey instrument. Typically, we'd select about 20 statements that span the scale of favorableness; some with low scale values, some intermediate, and some high. Ideally, the scale values would be equally spaced. You can see even from this small example that several of the initial statements have approximately equal scale values. We don't need all of them, so how do we choose among them? This is where the interquartile range enters. We would like to have items that will be interpreted consistently, not statements that could be seen as both positive and negative. Large values of Q indicate wider disagreement among the judges as to the favorableness of the statement, and, therefore, the statement is ambiguous. Given that two statements have approximately equal values, we choose the one that has the smaller Q. In sum, both the scale and Q values serve as filters for reducing the total stimuli to a more manageable number.

SCALE USE

Assume that some 20 to 22 statements have been selected from the larger list. The statements are placed randomly in the survey so that there is no detectable order to the scale values. The instrument is then ready to be administered to another sample of respondents.

When the instrument is administered, people are asked to indicate those statements with which they agree, e.g., "Which statements from this list best reflect your feelings toward Bank A?" The person's attitude score is computed as the average of the scale scores for the statements with which the person agrees. Thus, if someone agreed with three statements with the scale scores 8.2, 8.7, and 9.8, that person's attitude score would be 8.9. Since the scale value 6 represents a neutral attitude, we'd conclude that this person had a favorable attitude toward Bank A.

Several criticisms have been leveled at the method of scoring. For one, the method doesn't allow respondents to express the intensity of their feelings. People might "agree" with the statement that "the bank has convenient hours" when they really think, "the bank hours are *really* convenient" or they might think, "the bank hours are *okay,* but could be improved." In either case, the respondent would have agreed with the statement, yet the two attitudes are different.

The equal-appearing interval scale is time consuming to construct, but once it's been constructed, it is easy to administer and is easy for respondents to complete. It can be used to assess attitudes toward a variety of objects (e.g., each bank in town). The technique can also be used to scale other characteristics, such as the amount of perceived puffery in each of a series of advertising claims. The equal-interval technique is a valuable component in the marketing researcher's measurement arsenal.

Summated Ratings

Different kinds of self report scales:

- **Equal-appearing intervals**
- **Likert's summated ratings**
- **Semantic differential**
- **Stapel scale**

What are they? How to create them?

The Likert method of summated ratings allows an expression of intensity of feeling.[7] The method is both constructed and used in a slightly different way than equal-appearing intervals.

SCALE CONSTRUCTION

The basic format of the scale for the summated ratings method is the same in both construction and use. Respondents are asked to indicate how much they agree or disagree with every statement in the list. Figure 10.3 serves as an example.

The researcher begins, again, by developing many statements that reflect qualities about the object that might influence a person's attitude toward it. We classify each statement *a priori* as favorable or unfavorable. A screening sample, of say 200 people (representative of the subsequent target population) reduces the set of statements to a smaller, more refined instrument. They're asked to indicate how much they agree or disagree with each statement regarding the bank by checking the appropriate category. The levels of agreement are assigned scale values, e.g., –2, –1, 0, 1, 2, or 1, 2, 3, 4, 5 (either is fine). Suppose that we decide to use the values 1 through 5. These scales give us more information—a person's attitude might be positive if he or she either *agreed* with a *favorable* statement or *disagreed* with an *unfavorable* statement. We "reverse" the scaling with negative statements so that a "strongly agree" response to a favorable statement and a "strongly disagree" response to an unfavorable statement would both receive scores of 5.

FIGURE 10.3
Example of Likert Summated Rating Form

	Strongly Disagree	**Disagree**	**Neither Agree nor Disagree**	**Agree**	**Strongly Agree**
1. The bank offers courteous service.	____	____	____	____	____
2. The bank has a convenient location.	____	____	____	____	____
3. The bank has convenient hours	____	____	____	____	____
4. The bank offers low interest rate loans.	____	____	____	____	____

[7] Trivia: What's Likert's first name? The Likert scale was first proposed, in 1932, "A Technique for the Measurement of Attitudes," *Archives of Psychology* 140 by Rensis Likert.

A total attitude score is calculated for each respondent, and the distribution of total scores is used to refine the list of m statements. This procedure is known as item analysis, and it assumes that there should be consistency in the response pattern of any individual. If the individual has a very favorable attitude toward the object, he or she should basically agree with the favorable statements and disagree with the unfavorable ones and vice versa. If we have a statement that generates a very mixed response, we would question the statement on the grounds that it must be ambiguous or at the very least not discriminating of attitude.

How do we use the scale to determine the respondents' attitude, while we're developing the scale? We assume that the total score (on all m statements) serves as a proxy for the person's true attitude. We then relate each statement in turn to this total score to ascertain which statements discriminate clearly between people with positive vs. negative attitudes.

We can relate individual statement scores to total scores by several methods. One approach calculates the correlation of each item with the total score. Those items that have the highest correlation with the total are the best. Those with correlations near zero are suspect and should be eliminated. By ranking the correlations, we can use this method to devise a final scale of any length desired. We simply select those 25, 50, or however many statements having the highest correlations with the total score, although there usually is some attempt to include negative as well as positive statements.

An alternative way of performing an item analysis involves dividing the raters into groups, e.g., those with totals in the top 25% would be considered to have the most favorable attitudes, vs. those with the lowest 25% scores, who would be considered to have the least favorable attitudes. If the item is a good one, it would seem reasonable that (after correcting for the scoring direction), the mean score for each statement for the favorable attitude group should exceed the mean score for the unfavorable attitude group. The statements with mean differences near zero are poor statements and should be eliminated.[8] Table 10.3 displays a comparison of means for a sample statement, "The bank has a convenient location," and responses for the 50 people with the most favorable and the 50 with the least favorable attitudes. The

TABLE 10.3
Difference in Means for Groups with the Most Favorable and the Least Favorable Attitudes

	Scale Value	High Group		Low Group	
Response Category	x	f	fx	f	fx
Strongly agree	5	28	140	2	10
Agree	4	14	56	6	24
Neither agree nor disagree	3	6	18	18	54
Disagree	2	2	4	20	40
Strongly disagree	1	0	0	4	4
Sums		50	218	50	132

$$\bar{x}_H = \frac{218}{50} = 4.36, \quad \bar{x}_L = \frac{132}{50} = 2.64, \quad d = \bar{x}_H - \bar{x}_L = 4.36 - 2.64 = 1.72$$

[8] We could even test for the difference in mean scores for the two groups, and retain only those statements that showed a statistically significant difference—the statistical test would be the t-test for the difference in two means.

calculation indicates that the statement is a discriminating one, because the difference in mean scores is positive.

SCALE USE

The statements remaining after purification of the original list are randomly ordered on the survey to mix positive and negative ones, and people indicate their degree of agreement with each statement. One advantage of the Likert scale is that directions for its use are the same as the directions used to generate scores in screening statements. People generally find the scales easy to use, because the response categories do allow the expression of the intensity of the feeling. The respondent's total score is generated as the sum (or mean) of the scores across the statements.[9]

Interpretation can be somewhat ambiguous, e.g., what does a score of 78 on a 20-item Likert scale indicate? The maximum is $20 \times 5 = 100$, so is it safe to assume that the person's attitude toward the bank is favorable? Not really—these scores assume meaning only when compared to a standard. On the other hand, we make judgments like these every day, e.g., when we say "The man is tall," we are in effect saying that on the basis of the experience we have, the man is taller than average. In psychological scaling, this comparison is formalized somewhat by clearly specifying the standard, usually simply the average score in our sample (or averages computed for segments within the sample), i.e., the process of developing norms.

Semantic Differential

The semantic differential scale grew out of research at the University of Illinois designed to investigate the underlying structure of words.[10] The technique has been adapted, however, to measure attitudes.

The original semantic differential scale consisted of a great many bipolar adjectives, used to get people's reactions to various objects of interest. It was found that the ratings tended to be correlated and that three basic uncorrelated dimensions accounted for most of the variation in ratings: an *evaluation* dimension represented by adjective pairs such as good–bad, helpful–unhelpful; a *potency* dimension represented by bipolar items like powerful–powerless, strong–weak; and an *activity* dimension captured by pairs like fast–slow, alive–dead, noisy–quiet. The same three dimensions tended to emerge regardless of the object being evaluated.[11] The general idea in semantic differentials is to form scales that cover each of the evaluation, potency, and activity dimensions.

Semantic differentials have been adapted for marketing. First, instead of applying adjective pairs, marketers have generated items of their own. The items have not always been antonyms, nor have they been single words. Rather, marketers have used phrases to anchor the ends of the scale, such as descriptions of a product's attributes. Second, instead of worrying about scores for evaluation, potency, and

---

[9] See Gilbert A. Churchill, Jr., "A Paradigm for Developing Better Measures of Marketing Constructs," *Journal of Marketing Research* 16 (1979), pp. 64–73; Paul E. Spector, *Summated Rating Scale Construction* (Sage, 1992). For an example, see Teresa McGlone, Sonny Butler and Vernon McGlone, "Factor Influences Consumers' Selection of a Primary Care Physician," *Health Marketing Quarterly* 19 (2002), pp. 21–37.

[10] Charles E. Osgood, George J. Suci and Percy H. Tannenbaum, *The Measurement of Meaning* (University of Illinois Press, 1957).

[11] Factor analysis is the procedure we'd use to reduce a number of bipolar adjective pairs to basic dimensions.

FIGURE 10.4
Example of Semantic
Differential Scaling Form

Service is discourteous	__:__:__:__:__:__	Service is courteous
Location is convenient	__:__:__:__:__:__	Location is inconvenient
Hours are convenient	__:__:__:__:__:__	Hours are inconvenient
Loan interest rates are high	__:__:__:__:__:__	Loan interest rates are low

activity, marketers have been more interested in developing profiles (for brands, stores, companies, etc.), as well as total scores to compare competitors.[12]

Using the bank example, we'd begin by generating a large list of bipolar adjectives or phrases. Figure 10.4 lists attributes in a semantic differential format. Note that the negative phrase sometimes appears at the left side of the scale and other times at the right. This is done to prevent respondents from simply checking either the right- or left-hand sides without even bothering to read the descriptions.

The scale would then be administered to a sample. Respondents would be asked to read the set of bipolar phrases and to check the cell that best described their feelings toward the object. The end positions are usually defined in the instructions as being very closely descriptive of the object, the center position as being neutral, and the intermediate positions as slightly descriptive. For example, if someone thought that Bank A's service was courteous but only moderately so, that person would check the 6th position reading from left to right.

Respondents could be asked to evaluate two or more banks using the same scale. When several banks are rated, the different profiles can be compared. Figure 10.5 (a "snake diagram"), illustrates that Bank A is perceived as having more courteous service, a more convenient location, and lower interest rates on loans, but also less convenient hours than Bank B. Note the customary practice in constructing these profiles is to place all positive descriptors on the right. The plotted values simply represent the average score of all respondents on each descriptor.[13] The plotted profiles represent the positioning—comparative strengths and weaknesses—of Banks A and B as perceived by the sample.

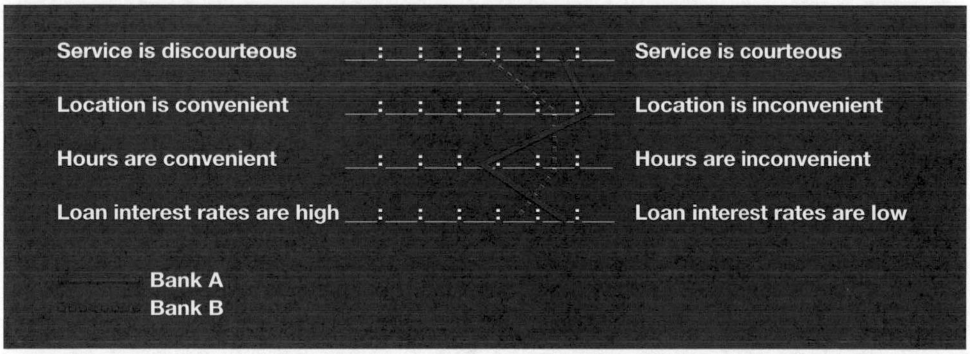

Service is discourteous	: : : : : :	Service is courteous
Location is convenient	: : : : : :	Location is inconvenient
Hours are convenient	: : : : : :	Hours are inconvenient
Loan interest rates are high	: : : : : :	Loan interest rates are low

——— Bank A
········ Bank B

FIGURE 10.5
Contrasting Profiles
of Banks A and B

---

[12] After a sample of respondents uses the scale to evaluate an object, the scale should be purified in the same manner as the summated rating scale. The total score for each person is calculated and ambiguous items eliminated by calculating item-to-total correlations or by looking at the mean scores by item of the high and low total scores.

[13] Although the mean is most often used, there is some controversy about whether the scale increments can be treated as an interval scale. If not, as critics contend, then the median scores should be used to develop the profiles.

When we want to compare objects (e.g., to choose among alternative package designs based on customer preferences), we need a total score. We compute the score by summing (or averaging) the scores, aggregating over the sample of respondents and over items. The items may be scored −3, −2, −1, 0, 1, 2, 3, or 1, 2, 3, 4, 5, 6, 7, and the procedure for an item analysis is like that for the Likert scale.

Semantic differential scales are very popular in marketing, perhaps because the scales are easy to create or the findings communicated, or perhaps because marketing managers have accumulated a lot of experience of the scales' usefulness. The technique is also clearly versatile, allowing people to express the intensity of their feelings toward company, product, package, advertisement, or whatever.

Stapel Scale

A modification of the semantic differential scale that is used in marketing is the Stapel scale. It differs from the semantic differential scale in that:

1. Adjectives or descriptive phrases are tested separately instead of simultaneously as bipolar pairs
2. Points on the scale are identified by number
3. There are 10 scale positions rather than 7

Figure 10.6 shows our four bank attributes in a Stapel scale format. Respondents are asked to rate how accurately each statement describes the object of interest (e.g., Bank A). Instructions such as the following are given to respondents:

"Select a plus number for words that you think describe Bank A accurately. The more accurately you think the word describes it, the larger the plus number you would choose. Select a minus number for words you think do not describe it accurately. The less accurately you think a word describes it, the larger the minus number you would choose. Therefore, you can select any number from +5, for words that you think are very accurate, all the way to −5, for words that you think are very inaccurate."

The advantage claimed for the Stapel scale is that it frees the researcher from the need to develop so many bipolar adjectives, which can be a formidable task.

We've talked about a number of scales, including the semantic differential, Stapel, and Likert scales. There is some controversy about whether their total scores represent interval or ordinal scaling. Marketers have been inclined to assume the posture of many psychological scaling specialists, who assume interval scaling of their constructs, not because they believe that they have necessarily measured them on an interval scale, but because interval scaling allows more powerful methods of statistical analysis. If this assumption is wrong, the construct won't have been measured as

FIGURE 10.6
Example of a
Stapel Scale

	−5	−4	−3	−2	−1	1	2	3	4	5
Service is courteous	☐	☐	☐	☐	☐	☐	☐	☐	☐	☐
Location is convenient	☐	☐	☐	☐	☐	☐	☐	☐	☐	☐
Hours are convenient	☐	☐	☐	☐	☐	☐	☐	☐	☐	☐
Loan interest rates are high	☐	☐	☐	☐	☐	☐	☐	☐	☐	☐

clearly as one would hope—that is, the assumption introduces measurement error, but all these errors do is result in the attenuation of relations among variables (e.g., weakening the strength of a correlation between such a scale and some other variable). So, the assumption of interval measurement (when the variable may be ordinal) is at least "statistically conservative," in that it will not lead to the spurious overestimation of results.

Importance Judgments

In addition to determining a person's perceptions of a bank, we might wish to assess how *important* each attribute is to that person. For example, even though someone believes that a

bank has convenient hours, if "convenience" isn't valued by that person, then it wouldn't affect his or her overall attitude toward the bank. On the other hand, if there are customers who value location and they think the bank is inconveniently located, this will have a negative, and perhaps a strong negative, effect on their overall feelings toward the bank. Researchers have tried a number of ways to capture the differing emphases people place on specific attributes.[14]

Some controversy exists about how the importance of attributes should be incorporated in determining a person's attitude toward an object. For example, we can create multiplicative indices by taking each person's rating of the importance of every attribute and multiply it by that person's rating of how positively or negatively the bank is performing on that attribute. A simple measurement problem is that when we ask people directly to rate importance, we often get data that basically say "everything" is important.[15] Such "information" isn't all that useful if we're trying to diagnose which features of our bank need improvement most urgently, or which attributes have the greatest impact on loyalty. A popular assessment tool is described in Research Realities 10.2—the importance ratings and the performance ratings aren't combined into a single index per bank, but used as axes for a perceptual map into which we plot a product or firm and its competitors.

---

[14] For empirical comparisons involving various forms of self-report scales of attribute importance, see "Measuring the Importance of Attributes," *Research on Research* 28 (http://www.marketfacts.com); "The Use of Concern Scales as an Alternative to Importance Ratings," *Research on Research*, 44; "An Analysis of Importance Ratings," *Research on Research* 60.

[15] Some researchers suggest we determine attribute importance indirectly rather than through self reports, e.g., through conjoint analysis, information display boards, or statistical derivation of them for groups of respondents.

10.2 Quadrant Analysis

A quadrant analysis combines customers' ratings of "how important" a number of attributes are with their ratings of "how well are we doing?" on those attributes. Computing means yields two coordinates for each attribute—the perceived excellence in performance of that attribute, and the importance of that attribute. These two judgments (performance and importance) become axes in a two-dimensional space, or the rows and columns of a two-way matrix. These simple data yield surprisingly impactful diagnostics for strategic competitive analysis, e.g., answering questions such as, "What are our product's strengths and weaknesses?" "What is our marketplace position vis-à-vis the competition?" "Where should we focus our attention and resources for improvement?" and so forth.

This first panel shows the basic structure. One dimension charts excellence/performance, and the other dimension represents the importance of an attribute. Attributes of a product or firm that are in the upper right quadrant are those that are important to customers, and the company is perceived to be doing a good job on these features. The lower right maps the attributes where the company is also doing well, perhaps too well, considering customers don't care that much about these qualities. The upper left are places to focus on improving, because customers care about these features, yet the company is not perceived as excelling in these areas.

Here is an example, set in the financial services sector, with the corresponding relevant attributes. Note, for example, that "flexible payment plans" are important to customers, yet this firm is not seen as providing such terrific flexibility.

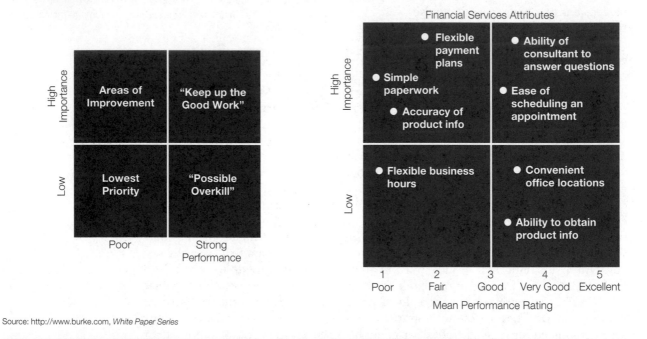

Source: http://www.burke.com, *White Paper Series*

Graphic

Graphic rating scales are becoming more important with online surveys. Individuals indicate their rating by marking the appropriate point on a line that runs from one extreme of the attribute to the other (e.g., see Figure 10.7). The line may be vertical or horizontal, ticked or unmarked.[16] Respondents mark the line, e.g., using a mouse click somewhere along the line (or just marking with an "X" if the survey is hard-

---

[16] If the graphic scale is marked, the divisions may be few or many, as in the case of a "thermometer" scale, so called because it looks like a thermometer.

This matrix is still another variant.

Note the competitive analysis is immediately apparent.

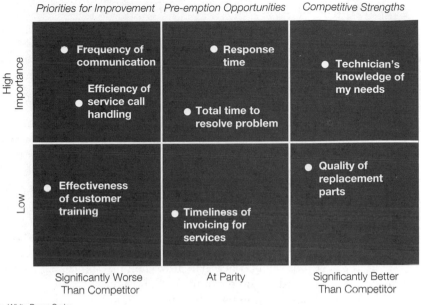

Source: http://www.burke.com, *White Paper Series*

FIGURE 10.7
Graphic Rating Scale

Please evaluate each quality in terms of how important it is to you personally by clicking the cursor at the position on the horizontal line that best reflects your feelings.

	Not Important		**Very Important**
Courteous service			
Convenient location			
Convenient hours			
Low interest rate loans			

FIGURE 10.7
Graphic Rating Scale

copy), and we infer the importance value by measuring the length of the line from the left origin to the marked position.

One of the advantages of graphic rating scales is that they are easy to construct and use. They provide an opportunity to make fine distinctions, though we wouldn't want to overinterpret the difference in someone's mouse click being at the 387th vs. 389th pixel, for example. And as for any scale, the end statements should be anchors that aren't so extreme that they are unlikely to be used.[17]

[17] Fine distinctions are possible with the graphic rating scale, but when scales have numbers, the categories of responses are clearly defined and generally produce more reliable ratings. Think of it this way, if you were to mark your satisfaction with your bank online by clicking your mouse over a line, what are the chances, if you were asked to do that again, that you'd click in exactly the same spot? Versus, if you rated your satisfaction on a 5-point scale, 1 = "extremely dissatisfied," 2 = "dissatisfied," 3 = "neither," 4 = "satisfied," and 5 = "extremely satisfied," isn't there a much better chance that you'd choose the same number?

Comparative

Comparative rating scales involve relative judgments. Raters judge each attribute with direct reference to the other attributes being evaluated.

An example of a comparative rating scale used for securing importance values is the **constant sum scaling method**. In the constant sum method, we instruct respondents to divide some given sum, e.g., 100 points, among two or more attributes on the basis of their importance. Thus, in Figure 10.8, if the respondent assigned 50 points to courteous service and 50 points to convenient location, the attributes would be judged to be equally important; if the points were 80:20, courteous service would be considered to be four times as important.[18] Note that with this method all judgments are made in comparison to other alternative attribute(s).

Comparative scales require fairly complicated judgments from the rater (e.g., if you program this in an online survey, you can build in a check that the points indeed sum to 100). But here are two strengths of the scales: first, it is not unusual for respondents to want to claim that "all" attributes are important. Yet research indicates that we tend to simplify our decision making by first reducing the number of alternatives (e.g., brands) by deciding which attributes matter—the same kind of process that these scales are trying to capture. Second, when constant sum scales are used to get judgments other than attribute importance, e.g., say the performance of brands, these scales tend to eliminate "halo effects." Halo effects occur when there is carryover from one judgment to another, e.g., if a consumer rates a movie, overall, as "7 = great!" they're likely to also rate the "storyline," "acting," "music," etc. as "7 = great!" with little or no distinction. The points assigned in these scales could be evenly distributed, but they tend not to be; evidence that raters try to choose which attributes matter more.

Which Scale to Use

It might seem overwhelming to think about choosing among all these scale types, number of scale points to use, whether to reverse some of the items, etc., but you should find comfort in the findings of an extensive study of reliability.[19] **Reliability**

FIGURE 10.8
Comparative
Rating Scale

Please divide 100 points among the following bank services in terms of relatively how important each is to you:

_____ Courteous service

_____ Convenient hours

_____ Convenient location

_____ Low interest rates

100

---

[18] If we consider all possible pairs of attributes in combination, we can construct unidimensional scale values. In "magnitude estimation," respondents are asked to judge directly the magnitude of each stimulus versus a reference stimulus.

[19] Gilbert A. Churchill, Jr. and J. Paul Peter, "Research Design Effects on the Reliability of Rating Scales: A Meta-Analysis," *Journal of Marketing Research* 21 (1984), pp. 360–375.

assesses the similarity or consistency of results provided by comparable measures of the same object or construct (and it is a necessary, but not a sufficient, condition for ensuring the validity of a measure).[20] Table 10.4 reports the study's findings and the good news is that many of the choices do not seem to materially affect the quality of the measure. The exception is that reliability increases as the number of items and number of scale points increase. For the other characteristics, though, no choices are superior in all instances, and all the scales (semantic differential, Likert, etc.) are useful at one time or another. All rightly belong in the researcher's measurement tool kit, and you're largely free to choose among them, whichever suits your research needs and interests.

The nature of the marketing problem and the mode of administration (e.g., online vs. phone) will affect the final choice. So will the characteristics of the respondents, their commitment to the task, and their experience and ability to respond. For example, the simple "happy-to-sad faces" scale in Figure 10.9 can be used for consumer research on children.

TABLE 10.4
Impact of Selected Measure Characteristics on Reliability

Measure Characteristic	Conclusion
Number of items in final scale	The hypothesis that a positive relationship exists between the number of items used in the scale and the reliability of the measure is supported.
Difficulty of items	The hypothesis that a negative relationship exists between the difficulty of the items and the reliability of the measure is not supported.
Reverse scoring	The hypothesis that scales with reverse-scored items have lower reliability than scales without them is not supported.
Type of scale	No a priori prediction was made that one of the scale types is superior, and no relationship was found between scale types and the reliability.
Number of scale points	The hypothesis that a positive relationship exists between the number of scale points and the reliability is supported.
Type of labels	No a priori prediction was made that numerical and verbal labels are superior to verbal labels only, or vice versa, and no relationship was found between type of labels and the reliability of the measure.
Extent of scale points description	The hypothesis that scales that have all points labeled have higher reliability than scales with only anchors labeled is not supported.
Respondent uncertainty or ignorance	The hypothesis that scales with neutral points have higher reliability than forced-choice scales is not supported.

Source: Adapted from Gilbert A. Churchill, Jr. and J. Paul Peter, "Research Design Effects on the Reliability of Rating Scales: A Meta-Analysis," *Journal of Marketing Research* 21 (1984), pp. 365–366.

---

[20] The issue of reliability and its relationship to the validity of a measure are discussed in the appendix.

FIGURE 10.9
Happy-to-Sad Faces
that Work with Children
(and Adults!)

Summary

This chapter reviewed methods for measuring attitudes, which were defined as representations of the person's ideas of, or liking for, a specific object or idea. Typically, marketers are concerned with objects like companies, brands, advertisements, Web sites, and packages.

Measurement was defined as the assignment of numbers to objects (e.g., consumers) to represent quantities of attributes (e.g., their brand preferences). Measurement can be done using a nominal, ordinal, interval, or ratio scale. Attitudes are measured by observing behavior, indirect questioning, performing objective tasks, and measuring physiological reactions, but direct assessment by self-report devices is the most common. The main self report techniques were reviewed, including the methods of equal-appearing intervals, summated ratings, semantic differential, Stapel scale, and Q sorts. These scales are intended to measure what individuals believe and like about specific objects (e.g., brands, companies, etc.). In addition, we might ascertain the importance of the attributes of the objects. Graphic and comparative rating scales were also reviewed.

Review Questions

1. What is an attitude?

2. What is measurement? What are the scales of measurement, and what information is provided by each?

3. What is a Thurstone equal-appearing interval scale?

4. In an equal-appearing interval scale, what is the scale value for a statement?

5. How does one construct a Likert summated rating scale?

6. How are subjects scaled with a Likert scale? What must be done to give meaning to the scales?

7. What is a semantic differential scale? How is a person's overall attitude assessed with a semantic differential scale?

8. How does a Stapel scale differ from a semantic differential scale? Which is more commonly used?

9. What is the task assigned subjects and what is the thrust or emphasis of Q-sort methodology?

10. What is a graphic rating scale? A constant sum scale?

Applications and Problems

1. Identify the type of scale (nominal, ordinal, interval, or ratio) being used in each of the following questions. Justify your answer.

   a. During which season of the year were you born?

      _____Winter _____Spring _____Summer _____Fall

   b. What is your total household income?

   c. Which are your three most preferred candy bars? Rank them from 1 to 3 according to your preference, with 1 as most preferred.

      _____ M&M plain _____ M&M peanut _____Reese's
      _____ Almond Joy _____Good 'N Plenty

   d. How much time do you spend traveling to school every day?

      _____Under 5 minutes

      _____5–10 mins

      _____11–15 mins

      _____16–20 mins

      _____21 minutes or more

   e. How satisfied are you with *Newsweek* magazine?

      _____Very satisfied

      _____Satisfied

      _____Neither satisfied nor dissatisfied

      _____Dissatisfied

      _____Very dissatisfied

   f. On an average, how many cigarettes do you smoke in a day?

      _____Over 1 pack

      _____½ to 1 pack

      _____Less than ½ pack

   g. Which of the following courses have you taken?

      _____Marketing research

      _____Sales management

      _____Advertising management

      _____Consumer behavior

   h. What is the level of education for the head of the household?

      _____Some high school _____H.S. graduate

      _____Some college _____College graduate and/or graduate work

2. The analysis for each of the preceding questions is given below. Is the analysis appropriate for the scale used? Is the conclusion appropriate?

   a. About 50% of the sample were born in the fall, 25% of the sample were born in the spring, and the remaining 25% were born in the winter. It can be concluded that the fall is twice as popular as the spring and the summer seasons.

   b. The average income is $25,000. There are twice as many individuals with an income of less than $9,999 than individuals with an income of $40,000 and over.

   c. M&M plain is the most preferred brand. The mean preference is 3.52.

   d. The median time spent traveling to school is 8.5 minutes. Three times as many respondents travel fewer than 5 minutes than respondents traveling 16–20 minutes.

   e. The average satisfaction score is 4.5, which seems to indicate a high level of satisfaction with *Newsweek* magazine.

   f. 10% of the respondents smoke less than ½ pack of cigarettes a day, whereas three times as many respondents smoke over one pack of cigarettes a day.

   g. Sales management is the most frequently taken course because the median is 3.2.

   h. The responses indicate that 40% of the sample has some high school education, 25% of the sample are high school graduates, 20% have some college education, and 10% are college graduates. The mean education level is 2.6.

3. (a) Assume that a manufacturer of a line of packaged meat products wanted to evaluate customer attitudes toward the brand. A panel of 500 regular consumers of the brand responded to a questionnaire that was sent to them and that included several attitude scales. The questionnaire produced the following results:

   (i) The average score for the sample on a 20-item Likert scale was 105.

   (ii) The average score for the sample on a 20-item semantic differential scale was 106.

   (iii) The average score for the sample on a 15-item Stapel scale was 52.

   The vice president has asked you to indicate whether these customers have a favorable or unfavorable attitude toward the brand. What would you tell him? Please be specific.

(b) Following your initial report, the vice president has provided you with more information. The following memo is given to you: "The company has been using the same attitude measures over the past eight years. The results of the previous studies are as follows:

	Likert	Semantic Differential	Stapel
1998	86	95	43
1999	93	95	48
2000	97	98	51
2001	104	101	55
2002	110	122	62
2003	106	112	57
2004	104	106	53
2005	105	106	52

We realize that there may not be any connection between attitude and behavior, but it must be pointed out that sales peaked in 2002 and since then have been gradually declining." With this information, do your results change? Can anything more be said about customer attitudes?

4. A leading manufacturer of electric guitars routinely attempts to measure consumer attitudes toward its products, generally by asking a consumer to examine a product and then to complete a brief questionnaire about several of the product's attributes. Over the years, the research manager for the company has decided that scale items related to five attributes have high correlations with total scale scores. The attributes are tone quality, appearance, durability, price, and ease of playing. The following scale is thus used to assess attitudes toward a product:

	Strongly Disagree	Disagree	Neither Agree nor Disagree	Agree	Strongly Agree
1. Tone quality is good.	___	___	___	___	X
2. The guitar is attractive.	___	___	___	X	___
3. The design is durable.	___	___	___	X	___
4. The price is appropriate.	___	X	___	___	___
5. The guitar is easy to play.	___	___	___	___	X
	(1)	(2)	(3)	(4)	(5)

a. Suppose that a consumer has examined a guitar and provided the responses shown in the table. Determine the total score. Would you say that the consumer has a favorable attitude toward the guitar?

b. The particular model of guitar that the respondent examined has been available for five years. The average total scores using this scale for each of these years are as follows:

1st year	18
2nd year	17
3rd year	18
4th year	16
5th year	17

Would you conclude that the consumer has a favorable attitude toward the guitar?

c. Assume that the respondent had also completed a comparative rating scale by dividing 100 points among the five attributes according to their importance to her. How could this information be useful in assessing the respondent's attitude toward the electric guitar?

d. Following are the results of the comparative rating task completed by the respondent:

Tone quality	10
Appearance	25
Durability	10
Price	40
Ease of playing	15

What can you now conclude about the respondent's attitude toward the guitar?

Appendix: Psychological Measurement

Questions to Guide Your Learning:

Q1: What kinds of errors arise when measuring customers' attitudes?

Q2: What is reliability? How do I write a survey to enhance reliability?

Q3: What are content, construct, and predictive validity? How do I maximize validity?

A problem that marketers have in common with scientists is how to measure the variables they want to understand. For example, marketers know that consumer spending can be affected by consumers' general feelings as to "how good things are." But how do you measure a sense of "well-being," or psychological attitudes in general? *American Demographics* considered productivity and technology, leisure, consumer attitudes, social and physical environment, income, and employment opportunities in developing its "Well-Being Index," which it uses in comparing areas and preparing forecasts.[1]

The measurement problem is depicted in Figure 10A.1. The researcher uses theories to explain phenomena. These theories or models consist of constructs (denoted by the circles), linkages among the constructs (single line connections), and data that connect the constructs with the empirical world (double lines). The single lines in Figure 10A.1 represent conceptual definitions; that is, one construct is defined in terms of its relationship to other constructs in the theorizing.

---

[1] The fabulous magazine, *American Demographics*, can be found at http://demographics.com.

FIGURE 10A.1
Schematic Diagram
Illustrating the Structure
of Science and the
Problem of Measurement

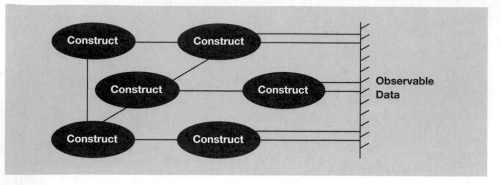

Measurement:

Mapping customer

characteristics

into Numbers

The definition may take the form of a precise equation that expresses the relationship, such as the equation in mechanics that suggests that force equals mass times acceleration, i.e., F = MA. Alternatively, the relationship may be only imprecisely stated, which is typically the case in the social sciences, e.g., brand choice = function (preference, price, availability, etc.).

The double lines in Figure 10A.1 represent operational definitions, that is, a mapping of how the constructs will be measured. The mapping specifies what the researcher must do in order to assign a value to the construct (e.g., sum the scores on the 10 Likert-type statements to generate a total score). Table 10A.1 lists some items used to assess different facets of consumer sentiment toward marketing. The measure comprises respondents' reactions to product quality, prices, advertising, and retailing and personal selling support. Conceptual definitions logically precede operational definitions and guide their development—we have to specify what a construct is before we can measure it.

The role of scientific inquiry is to establish the relationships that exist among the constructs of the model. Some of the constructs must be related to observable data so the model is testable. Otherwise, the model will be circular—with unobservable constructs being defined in terms of other unobservable constructs. A circular model cannot be supported or refuted by empirical data, so it is not legitimately considered a theory. A theory or system of explanation rests on the condition that at least some of the constructs can be operationalized sufficiently to allow measurement. We just saw in the previous chapter that measurement is defined as "rules for assigning numbers to objects to represent quantities of attributes." How rigorously these rules are defined and how skillfully they're implemented determine whether the construct has been captured adequately by the measure.

You would undoubtedly scoff at the following measurement procedure. If the claim were made, "John has blue eyes and Bill has brown eyes and, therefore, John is taller than Bill." You might reply that, "The color of a person's eyes has nothing to do with the person's height, so you have not in fact measured height. If you wanted to see who was taller, the best procedure would be to measure their heights with a ruler or stand them side-by-side and compare their heights."

The challenge with measuring attitudes is that we cannot rely on visual comparisons to either confirm or refute a measure. We cannot see an attitude, a personality characteristic, a person's knowledge about or awareness of a particular product, or other psychological characteristics, such as intelligence, anxiety, or whatever. These characteristics must be inferred from our measurements. Eye color is certainly not height, but have we captured the sales reps' job satisfaction if we just ask them how satisfied they are? Perhaps not, for reasons that will become obvious shortly.

Concept	Measurement
	Sum of responses to these items, each measured on 5-point disagree-agree scale:
Product Quality	The quality of most products I buy today is as good as can be expected.
	I am satisfied with most of the products I buy.
	Most products I buy wear out too quickly. (R)
	Products are not made as well as they used to be. (R)
	Too many of the products I buy are defective in some way. (R)
	The companies that make products I buy don't care enough about how well they perform. (R)
	The quality of products I buy has consistently improved over the years.
Price of Products	Most products I buy are overpriced. (R)
	Business could charge lower prices and still be profitable. (R)
	Most prices are reasonable considering the high cost of doing business.
	Competition between companies keeps prices reasonable.
	Companies are unjustified in charging the prices they charge. (R)
	Most prices are fair.
	In general, I am satisfied with the prices I pay.
Ads for Products	Most advertising provides consumers with essential information.
	Most advertising is annoying. (R)
	Most advertising makes false claims. (R)
	If most advertising were eliminated, consumers would be better off. (R)
	I enjoy most ads.
	Advertising should be more closely regulated.
	Most advertising is intended to deceive rather than to inform consumers. (R)
Retailing or Selling	Most retail stores serve their customers well.
	Because of the way retailers treat me, most of my shopping is unpleasant. (R)
	I find most retail salespeople to be very helpful.
	Most retail stores provide an adequate selection of merchandise.
	In general, most middlemen make excessive profits. (R)
	When I need assistance in a store, I am usually not able to get it. (R)
	Most retailers provide adequate service.

An (R) indicates scoring of the item needs to be reversed so that higher scores indicate more positive attitudes.

Source: Developed from John F. Gaski and Michael J. Etzel, "The Index of Consumer Sentiment Toward Marketing," in Gordon C. Bruner, Karen James and Paul Hensel (eds.), *Marketing Scales Handbook* (AMA, 2000).

· The problem of establishing operational definitions for measuring the constructs is not unique to the researcher interested in scientific explanation. The practitioner shares this concern. For example, a manufacturer interested in assessing customer reactions to a new product needs to know that the research has in fact measured consumer attitudes toward the new product, and that the accuracy of the data has not been influenced by the interviewers asking the questions or by some other factors. The ability to make these assessments relies heavily on an understanding of measurement, measurement error, and the concepts of reliability and validity—so, here we go!

Variations in Measured Scores

Psychological measurement usually takes place in complex situations in which many factors affect the characteristic being measured, including the process of measurement itself. For example, whenever energy prices suddenly soar, a public outcry arises, accompanied by accusations that the oil companies are deliberately creating strategies to manipulate prices. Say we develop an attitude scale to measure those feelings and administer the scale to a sample of respondents. A high score means that the respondent believed the oil companies had little to do with precipitating the crisis (a positive attitude), whereas a low score indicates the opposite, therefore reflecting a more negative attitude. Suppose that Heather had a score of 75 and Sofia had a score of 40 (where the minimum and maximum scores were 25 and 100). Conclusion: "Heather has a much more favorable attitude toward the oil companies than does Sofia." Ideally, yes; practically, maybe. It depends on the quality of the measurement. Consider some of the potential sources of differences in the scores of 75 and 40.

1. *True differences in the characteristic we're attempting to measure.* In the ideal situation, the difference in scores would reflect true differences in the attitudes of Heather and Sofia and nothing else. This situation will rarely, if ever, occur. The difference will also reflect the factors that follow.
2. *True differences in other relatively stable characteristics of the individuals that affect the score.* Perhaps the difference between Heather's and Sofia's scores is because Sofia is more willing to express her negative feelings, whereas Heather follows the adage, "If you can't say something nice, don't say anything at all." Her cooperation in the study has been requested and so she responds, but not truthfully.
3. *Differences caused by transient personal factors.* A person's mood, state of health, fatigue, and so on, may all affect the individual's responses. These factors are all temporary and can vary, e.g., Sofia's mood would be different if she had just returned from an IRS audit, vs. she had just received a sizable tax refund.
4. *Differences caused by situational factors.* The situation can affect the score. For example, researchers studying family purchase decisions find that a person's score often changes when the survey is completed in the presence of the spouse.
5. *Differences because of variations in administration.* Marketing surveys can be conducted in person, over the phone, via the Internet, etc. Interviewers can vary in the way they ask questions, so the consumer's responses also may vary as a function of the interviewer. The same interviewer may even handle two interviews differently enough to trigger variance in recorded answers, even when the respondents are similar on the characteristic.
6. *Differences resulting from sampling of items.* When we measure any construct, we tap only a sample of items relevant to the characteristic being measured. If we varied the sample of items on the survey (by adding, deleting, or changing the wording), we would undoubtedly change the absolute scores of Heather and Sofia and could conceivably even change their relative scores so that Sofia came

out with the more positive attitude. Thus, we must constantly be aware that our measurement represents a narrow conception of the construct. A person's height can serve as an indicator of "size," but so can weight, thigh circumference, length of forearm, and so on. We'd expect to have a better measure of size if we included all these items. Same with psychological measurements—other things being equal, a 1-item scale is a less adequate sample of the universe of items capturing some characteristic than a 25-item scale.

7. *Differences caused by lack of clarity of the measuring instrument.* Sometimes a difference in response to a questionnaire may represent differences in interpretation of an ambiguous or complex question. The researcher must generate items that mean the same thing to all respondents so that the observed differences in scores are "real," and not caused by differences in interpretation.

8. *Differences caused by mechanical factors.* Scores can also be affected by online surveys with bugs, inadequate space to record responses, inadvertent check marks in the wrong box (like circling the wrong "bubble" in your GMAT test), etc.

9. *Finally, differences in international respondents.* Increasingly, as the mighty multinationals seek to satisfy global customer bases, they're comparing numbers that may be a bit 'apples to oranges.' For example, customer satisfaction scores in Brazilian segments might differ from those in German, Irish, Japanese, and Canadian segments. As Research Realities 10A.1 indicates, it's difficult to tease apart whether the different numbers mean the levels of satisfaction are different or whether these groups of people use survey scales differently.

Classification and Assessment of Error

Survey researchers talk about a measure reflecting both the true attitude, as well as the kinds of errors we've just described. We'll call the measured variable, X_O, ("O" for observed), and write it as a function of several components:

$$X_O = X_T + X_S + X_R$$

X_T represents the *true* score of the characteristic being measured

X_S represents *systematic* error

X_R represents *random* error

The total error of a measurement has two components, $X_S + X_R$. **Systematic error** affects the measurement in a predictable way, e.g., measuring a person's height with a poorly calibrated wooden yardstick. Other stable characteristics of the individual are another source of systematic error. **Random error** is not systematic. It's due to transient aspects of the person or measurement situation. A random error produces inconsistency in repeated measurements. An example is the use of an elastic ruler to measure a person's height—it is unlikely that on two successive measures, the person using the elastic ruler would stretch it to the same degree of tautness, so the two measures wouldn't agree even though the person's height hadn't changed.

The distinction between systematic error and random error is critical because of the way the validity of a measure is assessed. **Validity** is synonymous with accuracy or correctness. The validity of a measuring instrument is defined as the extent to which scores reflect true individual characteristics, not systematic biases nor random errors. When a measure is valid, $X_O = X_T$ (there is no error). Our goal is to develop measures in which the score we observe actually represents the true score of the object on the

Research Realities
10A.1 Cross-Cultural Differences in Response Styles

When marketing researchers investigate "response styles," they're talking about two kinds of measurement issues. One has to do with *means,* and the other has to do with *variances.*

More positive *means,* e.g., higher ratings of customer satisfaction, tend to come from Asian and Latin American cultures. Why? These cultures are said to value acquiescence or getting along with the community. As a result, these respondents tend to yield more socially desirable responses as a simple "courtesy bias." (All of this research admittedly relies upon stereotypes and generalizations, but the idea is to start with big patterns in the data, and then make more subtle refinements as the research investigation progresses.) Americans and Western Europeans tend to be more individualistic, a crabbier lot, so their ratings appear more negative, even when they're relatively satisfied with the purchase they're evaluating.

So, if your customer satisfaction ratings in Japan exceed those in the U.K., do you have a "real" customer difference (i.e., is the product better received in Japan?) or is it a rating scale usage difference? Take the mean difference with a grain of salt, unless you learn there are marketing structural differences, such as better pricing in Japan, better service, easier access, etc.—some "real" reason for the apparent satisfaction differences.

In addition, response styles also differ in terms of *variances.* Respondents from cultures labeled "enthusiastic" (including the U.S., France, Italy, Ireland, Australia) tend to select extreme scale values more often than those from cultures expecting more reserved, conservative behavior (Japan, Germany, England). Imagine a 9-point rating scale for customer satisfaction, where 1 means "extremely dissatisfied" and a 9 means "extremely satisfied." The reported consistent cultural differences would have us predict that the Italian would more frequently say, "Oo! I *love* it!" (a rating of 9) or, "Oh, how *awful!*" (a rating of 1), whereas an English respondent says, "Well, perhaps . . ." (a rating of 6) or, "Goodness, I'm not sure" (a rating of 4).

If the differences in means and standard deviations intimidate you to think that numbers could never be compared across countries, consider your friend the correlation coefficient (which we discuss in greater detail in Chapter 17, investigating associations among variables):

$$r = \frac{\sum_{i=1}^{n}\left(X_i - \bar{x}\right)\left(Y_i - \bar{y}\right)}{ns_x s_y}$$

Say X represents respondents' ratings on a customer satisfaction measure, and Y represents their ratings on their perception of qual-

ity (or value, or price, or pleasantness of packaging, whatever). When we correlate satisfaction with quality, note that the means come out—that is, in the numerator of that equation, we take each person's X and subtract the group's $\bar{x}$, and we subtract $\bar{y}$ from each person's Y score. Similarly note that whether s_x is large or small, ditto for s_y, we divide out those numbers in the equation. The correlation coefficient r captures the relationship between X and Y when we've taken these issues into account.

So! According to the observations stated above, we'd expect a sample from Japan to yield both higher means and lower variances than data on customers from the U.S. But the correlation coefficient is standardized across means and variances. That is, in any data set, regardless of whether one group's means are higher than another's and/or one group's variance is bigger than another's, we're testing whether the relationship between satisfaction and quality is strong or weak. If the correlation between satisfaction and quality is high in the Japanese data, but lower in the U.S. data, you'd know that for Japan, quality is a clear driver of satisfaction, whereas the American customers are satisfied, or not, by other features (e.g., price, service, whatever—you'd have to look into the data). In sum, if you're dealing with international data frequently, you might make correlations your focus, given the ambiguities in interpreting mean differences or differences in standard deviations.

If you want to learn more, you also need to know that equating means is sometimes referred to as "equivalence in origins" and a difference in standard deviations is alternatively referred to as a "scaling" difference or a difference in "measurement units."

For more information, including suggestions regarding "correcting" for these response style differences, here are the experts:

- C. Samuel Craig and Susan Douglas, *International Marketing Research,* 2nd ed., Chichester, UK: Wiley, 2000 (especially Chs.10 and 11).
- Hans Baumgartner and Jan-Benedict Steenkamp, "Response Styles in Marketing Research: A Cross-National Investigation," *Journal of Marketing Research* 38 (2001), pp. 143–156.
- Eric Greenleaf, "Improving Rating Scale Measures by Detecting and Correcting Bias Components in Response Styles," *Journal of Marketing Research* 29 (1992), pp. 176–188.
- Irvine Clarke, "Extreme Response Style in Cross-Cultural Research," *International Marketing Review* 18 (2001), pp. 301–324.
- Svein Olsen and Ulf Olsson, "Multientity Scaling and the Consistency of Country-of-Origin Attitudes," *Journal of International Business Studies* 33 (2002), pp. 149–167.

characteristic we are attempting to measure. Easier said than done! This relationship between measured score and true score is inferred, based on: (1) direct assessment of validity, and (2) indirect assessment via reliability.[2] We'll consider each.

---

[2] See Mary Allen and Wendy Yen, *Introduction to Measurement Theory* (Waveland Press, 2001), Richard Netemeyer, William Bearden and Subhash Sharma, *Scaling Procedures* (Sage, 2003).

Direct Assessment of Validity

As mentioned, a measure is valid to the extent that variability in scores among objects reflects the true differences of the characteristic being measured. We don't usually know the true score—if we did, we wouldn't need a measure. But we infer the accuracy of the measure by looking for evidence of three types of validity: predictive, content, and construct.

Predictive Validity

In *predictive* or *criterion-related validity,* we assess the usefulness of the measure as a predictor of some other characteristic of the individual. For example, the GMAT is required by most business schools, in part because it is useful in predicting how well a student will do in an MBA program. The test score is used to predict the criterion of performance. Or, an example in attitude scales would be whether a job satisfaction scale was useful in predicting the sales reps most likely to resign.

For some tests, we're not as interested in predicting something in the future as we are in assessing *concurrent validity,* or the relationship between the measure and the criterion variable that occurs at the same point in time. For example, the validity of a pregnancy test is not about whether a woman will become pregnant in the future, but in determining if she is pregnant now.

This type of validity is determined by the correlation between the measure and criterion—if the correlation is high, the measure is said to have predictive validity. It is easy to assess, though it requires a reasonably valid criterion (e.g., grades in an MBA program, sales reps quitting or not).

Content Validity

Content validity focuses on the adequacy with which the domain of the characteristic is captured by the measure. Say we wished to measure spelling ability, and we used the following words: strike, shortstop, foul, inning, catcher, pitcher, ball, umpire, bullpen, dugout. You can see the nature of the objection has to do with the fact that all the words relate to the sport of baseball. Someone who is a poor speller might do well on this test simply because he or she is a baseball enthusiast. A person who is pretty good at spelling but has little interest in baseball might do worse. We'd conclude that the test lacks content validity—it doesn't properly sample the domain of all possible words that could be used—it's too selective in emphasis.

Content validity is sometimes known as "face validity" because it is assessed by looking at the measure to ascertain the domain being sampled. If the actual items look different from the possible domain, the measure is said to lack content validity. Theoretically, to capture a person's spelling ability, we should administer all words in their native language. The person who spelled the greatest number of these words correctly would be the best speller. This is, of course, unrealistic, so we sample the domain by constructing spelling tests comprising subsets of all possible words.

We can never guarantee that we've created a measure that possesses content validity because it is partly a matter of judgment. We may think our items provide good coverage, whereas a critic may argue that we have failed to sample some aspect of the characteristic. So, how can we diminish the critics' objections?

One of the most critical elements in generating a content-valid instrument is conceptually defining the domain of the characteristic. The researcher has to specify what the variable is, and what it is not. The definition is expedited by examining the literature to determine how the variable has been defined and used previously. It's unlikely that those definitions will agree, so the researcher must specify which elements are important for the current use of the term. Next, a large collection of items is written that broadly represents the variable as defined. Items must be included to represent all the relevant dimensions of the variable. For the sales rep example, the job satisfaction scale would need to include items about every component of the job (duties, fellow workers, top management, sales supervisor, customers, pay, promotion opportunities, etc.) if it is to be content valid. The number of items must be large so that after scale refinement (pretesting) the measure still contains enough items to adequately sample each of the variable's dimensions.

Construct Validity

Construct validity is concerned with the question of "Does the instrument, in fact, measure what we purport it to measure?" What construct, concept, or trait underlies the score achieved on that test? Does the measure of attitude actually measure attitude or some other characteristic of the individual? Construct validity lies at the very heart of scientific and pragmatic progress. In marketing, we speak of people's socioeconomic class, personality, attitudes, and so on. These are all constructs that we use to explain marketing behavior. And again, they are constructs that are not directly observable, only inferred, e.g., from related behaviors. We operationally define the constructs in terms of a set of observables (measured variables).

Construct validity is difficult to establish. It requires adequately sampling the domain of the construct and internal consistency among the items. This assumption means that the attitude that we're trying to measure is the underlying cause of the correlations among the items. As the correlations increase, we have greater confidence that they're measuring the same construct. A measure said to be strong on construct validity must be consistent internally, but a consistent measure isn't necessarily one that has construct validity. For example, the items might indeed be measuring the same thing, but they might be measuring something other than what you hoped they measured.

What have the steps been so far? We've specified the domain of the construct, generated a set of items relevant to the breadth of that domain, refined the items, and shown the remaining items are internally consistent. The remaining step is to see how well the measure relates to measures of other constructs that we expect to be theoretically related. Does it behave as expected? Does it fit the theory or model relating the constructs? The diagram showing the relationships among a set of constructs is often referred to as the "nomological net." Determining if the relationships among constructs are as expected is consequently referred to as establishing nomological validity.

For example, Figure 10A.2 depicts the relationship between the constructs "customer satisfaction" and "repeat purchasing." If we've developed the measure X to assess customer satisfaction, construct validity could be assessed by examining the relationship between the measure and customer turnover, measured by Y. Companies where X scores are low have less customer satisfaction, and they should experience more turnover than those with high X scores. If they do not, we'd question the construct validity of the customer satisfaction measure. Thus, the construct validity of a measure is assessed by whether the measure confirms or denies the hypothesized relationships predicted among the constructs. The difficulty, of course, is that the failure to obtain the hypothesized relationships among the observed variables may

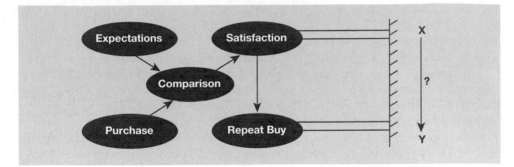

FIGURE 10A.2
The Relationship
between the Construct
"Customer Satisfaction"
and its Determinants
and Consequences

be due to a lack of construct validity, or due to incorrect theory. To prevent this ambiguity, we usually try to relate a construct to several other constructs, not just one, and we also try to use theories that are well founded, tried and true, to inspire confidence in their probable correctness.

A construct should also be measurable by several different methods, otherwise it could be considered nothing more than an artifact of the measurement procedure. In attempting to triangulate, the methods should be independent if possible. Given that the different methods are all measuring the same construct, the measures should be highly correlated, and this would provide evidence of **convergent validity**. **Discriminant validity** requires that a measure doesn't correlate too highly with measures that aren't supposed to be related.

Indirect Assessment through Reliability

The similarity of results provided by independent but comparable measures of the same object or construct is called **reliability**. Reliability is an index of consistency—we should see correlations between two measures of the same concept when we use the same measure. (For validity, we should see correlations between two measures of the same concept even when the methods are different.) If we want the goal to be consistency in comparable measures of the same concept, then we wouldn't want a measure to be one that was influenced by transitory factors. In other words, the more reliable the measure, the lower is X_R.

A measure could be reliable and still not be valid, since even if X_R equals zero, $X_O = X_T + X_S$ (i.e., the X_S can still throw off the validity). The converse is not true—if the measure is valid, $X_O = X_T$ (the measure is reflecting true scores without error). Thus, it is often said that (1) if a measure is valid, it is reliable; (2) if it is not reliable, it cannot be valid;[3] and (3) if it is reliable, then it may or may not be valid, because reliability does not account for systematic error. In sum, reliability is a necessary, but not sufficient, condition for validity. Reliability is easier to measure than validity, which is probably why researchers emphasize its measurement.

Stability

One of the more popular ways of establishing the reliability of a measure is to measure the same objects or individuals at two different points in time and to correlate

Reliability is necessary for validity

---

[3] How can we claim validity (i.e., "this test measures X") when we don't have reliability (i.e., the items measure something different each time)!

the scores. If the objects or individuals have not changed in the interim, the two scores should correlate perfectly. To the extent that they do not, random disturbances were operating in either one or both of the test situations to produce less reliable measurement. The procedure is known as test–retest reliability assessment.

A critical decision is determining how long to wait between successive administrations of the measure. If we're looking at attitudes and we wait too long, attitudes may change, producing a low correlation between the two scores. On the other hand, a short wait means people may well remember how they responded the first time and be more consistent in their responses. Two weeks seems to be the interim norm. Further, instead of administering the exact same set of items, many researchers use alternate forms with items that are not identical, but that are very similar in content.

Equivalence

The basic assumption in constructing an attitude scale is that when several items are summed into a single score, the items are measuring the same underlying attitude. Each item can be considered a measure of the attitude, and the items should be consistent (or equivalent) in what they indicate about the attitude. The equivalence measure of reliability focuses on the internal consistency or internal homogeneity of the set of items forming the scale.

The earliest measure of the internal consistency of a set of items was the split-half reliability of the scale. In assessing split-half reliability, the total set of items is divided into two equivalent halves and the total scores for the two halves are correlated to estimate the reliability. For example, the "even" numbered items form one-half and the "odd" the other half, and their scores correlated.

An even better way to assess the internal homogeneity of a set of items is to use coefficient alpha. This index uses all items simultaneously, not just half; furthermore, coefficient alpha reflects the method of domain sampling. The idea is that items tapping the domain of a construct should be correlated, and if some item is not highly correlated with the others, it is probably drawn from a different domain and its inclusion produces error and unreliability.

Alpha is calculated as:

$$\alpha = \left(\frac{k}{k-1} \right) \left(1 - \frac{\sum_{i=1}^{k} \sigma_i^2}{\sigma_t^2} \right)$$

where k = number of items in the scale

σ_i^2 = the variance of scores on item i across respondents

σ_t^2 = the variance of total scores across subjects where the total for each respondent represents the sum of the k item scores. This term includes the sum of the σ_i^2 terms (the numerator), but also includes the covariances between the pairs of items, i.e., the extent to which the items are correlated.

If all k items are measuring different concepts, the correlations among the items will be near zero, so the σ_t^2 will be close in size to σ_i^2, and the term $\sum_{i=1}^{k} \sigma_i^2 / \sigma_t^2$ will be close to one. The term in the parentheses goes to $(1-1)$ or zero, and alpha is low (e.g., 0). When the items are all highly correlated, σ_t^2 will be larger than σ_i^2, so $\sum_{i=1}^{k} \sigma_i^2 / \sigma_t^2$ will be small, close to zero. Then the parenthetical terms go to $(1-0)$ or 1, and alpha is much higher (e.g., 1).

Coefficient alpha should be calculated routinely to assess the quality of measure.[4] If alpha is low, what should the analyst do? If the item pool is large, the poor items should be eliminated. Poor items are easy to identify—we calculate the correlation of each item with the total score and plot the correlations by decreasing order of magnitude. Items with correlations near zero are then deleted.[5]

We've been talking about assessing the reliability of a measure. On occasion, we're also interested in "inter-rater reliability." For example, you might be interested in rating entertainment media for themes like product placement, or actors smoking or swearing, etc. If so, you would have several viewers code the content of an ad, TV pilot, or movie pretest for those themes. Or, if you're interested in how your supplier partners perceive the service your firm provides, you might ask each supplier to give you comments from multiple informants in their organization. Or, in observational studies, we would have greater confidence in the data if two or more independent observers made similar judgments of the consumers' behavior, etc. Inter-rater reliability is greater when the raters agree and produce consistent results.

Summary

So, altogether, how does one contend with the basic issues of reliability and validity, and how does one choose among the various coefficients that can be computed? Figure 10A.3 diagrams a sequence of steps that can be followed to develop valid measures of marketing constructs.

Step 1 involves *specifying the domain* of the construct to be measured. If you're interested in measuring customer satisfaction with recently purchased space heaters, what attributes of the product should be measured to assess the family's satisfaction? We'd create an exhaustive list of product features, e.g., cost, durability, quality, operating performance, and aesthetic features. But how far should the domain extend? Satisfaction is usually also affected by service and sales assistance. Or, what if you saw an ad for a competitor's product at a lower price? Or what if you were to learn of some negative environmental effects resulting from use of the product? You have to draw the line somewhere, of course, but it's clear that we need to be very careful about specifying what is to be included in the domain of the construct being measured and what is to be excluded.

Step 2 in the process is to *generate items* that capture the domain. Exploratory research techniques, including literature searches and experience surveys, are productive here. The literature indicates how the variable has been defined and how many dimensions it has. For the customer satisfaction example, we'd examine product

---

[4] The square root of the reliability is the estimated correlation of the k-item test with the true scores.

[5] If the construct had, say, five identifiable dimensions, coefficient alpha would be calculated for each dimension. The item-to-total correlations used to delete items would also be based on the total score for that dimension.

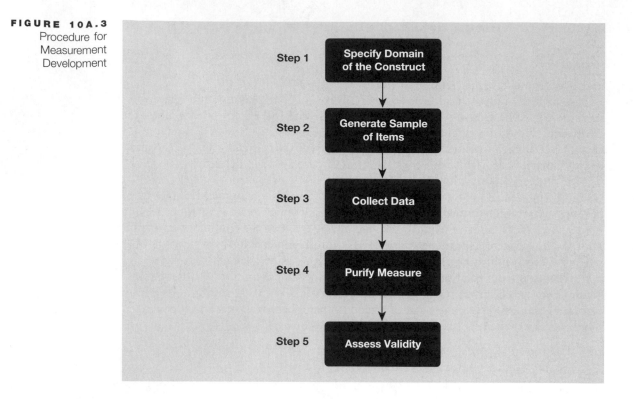

brochures, trade magazines, results of product tests like those in *Consumer Reports*.
The experience survey might include discussions with people in the product group
responsible for the product, sales reps, dealers, marketing researchers, consumers,
and outsiders who have a special expertise in heating equipment.

Step 3 involves *collecting data* from a sample of the target population, e.g., all
those who have purchased a space heater within the last six months.

Step 4 uses the data collected in Step 3 to *purify the original set of items*. We
eliminate items that are not highly correlated with the others.

Step 5 involves *determining the validity* of the purified measure. At this stage, we
assess the convergent, discriminant, and construct validity. Content validity will
have been addressed in Steps 1 through 4.

Review Questions

1. How is measuring an attitude more difficult than measuring a person's height?

2. What is a true score? A systematic error? A random error?

3. How is the quality of a measurement instrument assessed?

4. What is validity? What are the types of validity?

5. What is reliability? The types?

6. What steps should you go through to develop a measure? How many items should you have at each step?

Applications and Problems

1. Discuss the idea that a particular measure could be reliable and still not be valid. Distinguish between reliability and validity.

2. Discuss the use of IQ tests (or similar tests, such as the GMAT) in measuring intelligence, an often-used construct. Do you believe that these tests adequately measure a person's abilities? If not, what traits, abilities, or types of intelligence do the tests fail to measure?

3. You have developed a questionnaire designed to measure attitudes toward a set of TV ads for a new snack food product. The respondents, as a group, will view the ads on a TV set and then complete the questionnaire. Due to logistical circumstances beyond your control, you must split your sample of respondents into three groups and collect data on three separate days. What steps might you take in an effort to minimize possible variance in scores caused by the three separate administrations?

4. Many areas of marketing research rely heavily on measures of psychological constructs, e.g., compulsive shopping, motivation to search for information (e.g., online), etc. What characteristics inherent in these constructs make them so difficult to measure? What tools can the marketing researcher bring to bear when evaluating the goodness of the measure? In other words, what things can we do that allow us to state with some degree of confidence that we are indeed measuring the construct of interest?

5. You are the national sales manager for Perry Pharmaceutical, Inc. You have been concerned with trying to determine the most important characteristics a salesperson must possess to be successful. Much of the current research suggests that salesperson adaptiveness is a key component of success. You would like to determine if this is indeed the case. To assess this, you need to develop a scale to measure salesperson adaptiveness, collect data with your sales force, and then compare the results to each individual's sales record. At this time, you are asked only to develop a scale to measure salesperson adaptiveness. What kinds of questions would you include? Are there general areas that you think must be measured with a number of different questions?

Cases

E-Food and the Online Grocery Competition (B)

Ashley Sims is the MBA student who is considering starting her own online grocery service. Two weeks ago, she ran a focus group consisting of 12 of her classmates, some of whom use an online grocer, and some of whom do not. She kept the moderator questions broad, just trying to get a sense of what e-visitors are looking for in their online grocery trips. Figure 3.1.1 contains a sampling of the verbata from that focus group.

Those data indicate variance on satisfaction with the current system, and even for loyal users, different levels of satisfaction with different features of the system. Though people seem generally happy, there is clearly room for improvement in elements of online grocery shopping.

In addition, Sims is trying to think long-term, knowing that she wants one arm of her business to focus on grocery delivery, and one arm of her business to grow into a profitable consumer research business, offering in-depth insight into the consumer-decision processes for grocery shopping and online shopping more generally. Sims figures additional research will be required to understand how to set priorities in potentially improving the software, and the broader questions of how to understand the consumer's behavior and infer the thought processes underlying that behavior.

Sims used this textbook in her own marketing research class, so she knows there are many research methodologies to choose from. She is fresh off of her experience running the focus group that yielded the data in Figure 3.1.1. Although it was fun and she thinks she learned a lot, she doubts that she could run another focus group that could be shaped to address these fairly specific concerns. She's thought about doing a survey—just asking people, "Do you care about brands?" or "Are you price sensitive?" and so on. However, she doubts that people would admit to being overly influenced by brand or price, even though their purchases may indicate that they are. She's also rejected an observational technique—a friend had suggested that she sit down next to a person who is about to do an online grocery run and just watch what they do and take notes. She's afraid that her presence would be off-putting and the person doing the grocery shopping might behave differently from how they normally would (for example, maybe buy asparagus rather than M&M's).

Ashley's computer-geeky friend tells her that every mouse click gets stored into a user file and that she should look at what people actually do rather than what they say. Sims is intrigued by this but understandably is having difficulty in obtaining such data from current online grocery providers. She decides to invest in having a programmer create a smaller-scale simulation of an online grocer. She will ask participants to pretend they are grocery shopping online. She'll strip off each user file and analyze the clickstream data. She might run a survey, too, but with the clickstreams, she'll know just what people did, not just what they say they would do.

Questions

1. Sims has considered a number of marketing research approaches. Do you agree with her general assessment or do you feel she was hasty in dismissing any of the techniques? Which of the methods would you recommend and why? How would you modify the technique from what she has been considering?

2. What did you learn from the focus group verbatim accounts? Was the sample suitable? When would it be important to run two different focus groups, one for users, one for nonusers?

FIGURE 3.1.1 Sampling of Verbatim Accounts from Focus Group on Online Grocery Trips

- "It's great! I don't need a car!" (Current user)
- "It's difficult to just browse, like if I'm not sure what I'm in the mood for." (Had tried online shopping but is no longer a user)
- "I can't touch the fruits. I can't read the side of the box on cereals." (Current user)
- "They chose my vegetables better than I would have!" (Current user)
- "I wish they could pick up my dry cleaning too." (Not a user, intends to begin)
- "It's kind of expensive. There's a big annual fee, a delivery charge each time, and you know you've got to tip the delivery guy." (Current user)
- "This is terrific—I don't like to shop for food even if I had the time, which I certainly do not." (Current user)
- "I guess it's okay. Thing is, there's a <name of local grocery> on my way home from work, so that's just as convenient. For me." (Non-user, does not intend to begin)
- "Don't I get any, you know, frequent flyer points things?" (Non-user, getting used to the concept)

CASE 3.2

Premium Pizza Inc.[1]

The 1980s saw a sharp increase in the use of promotions (coupons, cents-off deals marked on the package, free gifts, and so on) because of their manifest success at increasing short-term purchase behavior. In fact, sales promotion is now estimated to account for over one-half of the typical promotion budget, whereas advertising accounts for less than half. In many industries, however, the initial benefit of increased sales has resulted in long-term escalation of competition. As firms are forced to "fight fire with fire," special offer follows special offer in a never-ending spiral of promotional deals.

The fast-food industry has been one of the most strongly affected by this trend. Pizzas come two for the price of one; burgers are promoted in the context of a double-deal involving cuddly toys for the kids; tacos are reduced in price some days, but not others. It is within this fiercely competitive, erratic environment that Premium Pizza Corporation has grown from a small local chain into an extensive midwestern network with national aspirations. Over the past few years, Jim Battaglia, vice president of marketing, has introduced a number of promotional offers, and Premium Pizza parlors have continued to flourish. Nevertheless, as the company contemplates further expansion, Jim is concerned that he knows very little about how his customers respond to his promotional deals. He believes that he needs a long-term strategy aimed at maximizing the effectiveness of dollars spent on promotions. And, as a first step, he thinks that it is important to assess the effectiveness of his existing offers.

SPECIFIC OBJECTIVES

In the past, Jim has favored the use of five types of coupons, and he now wishes to determine their independent appeal, together with their relation to several identifiable characteristics of fast-food consumers. The five promotional concepts are listed in Table 3.2.1. The consumer characteristics that Jim's experience tells him warrant investigation include number of children living at home, age of youngest child, propensity to eat fast food, propensity to eat Premium Pizza in particular, preference for slices over pies, propensity to use coupons, and occupation.

The specific objectives of the research study can therefore be summarized as follows:

1. To evaluate the independent appeal of the five promotional deals to determine which deals are most preferred.
2. To gain insight into the reasons that certain deals are preferred.
3. To examine the relationships between the appeal of each promotional concept and various consumer characteristics.

[1] The contributions of Jacqueline C. Hitchon to this case are gratefully acknowledged.

TABLE 3.2.1 Five Promotional Concepts

Coupon A	Get a medium soft drink for 5 cents with the purchase of any slice.
Coupon B	Buy a slice and get a second slice of comparable value free.
Coupon C	Save 50 cents on the purchase of any slice and receive one free trip to the salad bar.
Coupon D	Buy a slice and a large soft drink and get a second slice free.
Coupon E	Get a single-topping slice for only 99 cents.

PROPOSED METHODOLOGY

After much discussion, Jim's research team finally decided that the desired information could best be gathered by means of personal interviews, using a combination of open-ended and closed questions. A medium-sized shopping mall on the outskirts of a metropolitan area in the Midwest was selected as the research site. Shoppers were intercepted by professional interviewers while walking in the mall and asked to participate in a survey requiring five minutes of their time.

The sampling procedure employed a convenience sample in which interviewers were instructed to approach anyone passing by, providing that they met certain criteria (see Figure 3.2.1). In sum, the sample of respondents was restricted to adult men and women between the ages of 18 and 49 who had both purchased lunch, dinner, or carryout food at a fast-food restaurant in the past seven days and had eaten restaurant pizza within the last 30 days, either at a restaurant or delivered to the home. In addition, interviewers were warned not to exercise any bias during the selection process, as they would do, for example, if they approached only those people who looked particularly agreeable or attractive. Finally, interviewers were asked to obtain as close as possible to a 50–50 split of male and female participants.

The questionnaire was organized into three sections (see Figure 3.2.2). The first section contained the screening questions aimed at ensuring that respondents qualified for the sample. In the second section, respondents were asked to evaluate on 10-point scales the appeal of each of the five promotional concepts based on two factors: perceived value and likelihood of use. After they had evaluated a concept, interviewees were asked to give reasons for their likelihood-of-use rating. The third and final section consisted of the questions on consumer characteristics that Jim believed to be pertinent.

The questionnaire was to be completed by the interviewer based on the respondent's comments. In other words,

FIGURE 3.2.1 Interviewer Instructions

Below are suggestions for addressing each question. Please read all the instructions before you begin questioning people.

Interviewer Instructions
Approach shoppers who appear to be between 18 and 49 years of age. Since we would like equal numbers of respondents in each age category and a 50% male-female ratio, please do not select respondents based on their appeal to you. The interview should take approximately five minutes. When reading questions, read answer choices if indicated.

- Question 1: Terminate any respondent who has not eaten lunch or dinner from any fast-food restaurant in the last seven days.

- Question 2: Terminate any respondent who has not eaten pizza within the last 30 days. This includes carry-out, drive-thru, or dining in.

- Question 3: Terminate respondent if not between 18 and 49 years of age. If between 18 and 49, circle the appropriate number answer. For this question, please read the question and the answer choices.

After completing questions 1 through 3, hand respondent the coupon booklet. Make sure that the booklet and the response sheets are the same color. Also check to see that the coupon booklet number indicated on the upper right-hand corner of the response sheet matches the coupon book number.

- Question 4: Ask the respondent to open the coupon booklet and read the first coupon concept. Read the first section of Question 4 showing the respondent that the scales are provided on the page above the coupon concept. Enter his or her answer in the box provided.

- Read the second section of the question and enter respondent's answer in the second box provided.

- When asking the respondent, "Why did you respond as you did for use," please record the first reason mentioned and use the lines provided to probe and clarify the reasons.

This set of instructions applies to Questions 5 through 8. Periodically remind the respondent to look at the scales provided on the page above the coupon concept that he or she is looking at.

- Question 9: Enter number of children living at home. If none, enter the number zero and proceed to Question 11.

- Question 10: Enter age of youngest child living at home in the box provided.

- Question 11: Read the question and each answer slowly. Circle the number corresponding to the appropriate answer.

- Question 12: Read the question and each answer slowly. Circle the number corresponding to the appropriate answer. If answer is never, proceed to Question 14. Otherwise, continue to Question 13.

- Question 13: Circle the number corresponding to the appropriate answer. Do not read answer choices.

- Question 14: Circle the number corresponding to the appropriate answer. Do not read answer choices.

- Question 15: Read the question and each answer slowly. Circle the number corresponding to the appropriate answer.

- Question 16: Read the question and each answer slowly. Circle the number corresponding to the appropriate answer.

- Question 17: If an explanation is requested for occupation, please tell respondent that we are looking for a broad category or title. "No occupation" is not an acceptable answer. If this should happen, please probe to see if the person is a student, homemaker, retired, unemployed, etc.

At the end of the questionnaire, you are asked to indicate whether the respondent was male or female. Please circle the appropriate answer. This is not a question for the respondent.

Cases

FIGURE 3.2.2 Premium Pizza Inc. Questionnaire

Response Number _____

Coupon Book # _____

(Approach shoppers who appear to be between the ages of 18 and 49 and say . . .)

Hi, I'm _____ from Midwest Research Services. Many companies like to know your preferences and opinions about new products and promotions. If you have about 5 minutes, I'd like to have your opinions in this marketing research study.

(If refused, terminate)

1. *Have you eaten lunch or dinner in, or carried food away from, a fast-food restaurant in the last seven days?*
   . . . (must answer Yes to continue)

2. *Have you eaten restaurant pizza within the last 30 days, either at the restaurant or by having it delivered?*
   . . . (must answer Yes to continue)

3. *Which age group are you in?* (read answers, circle number)

   <u>1:</u> 18–24   <u>2:</u> 25–34   <u>3:</u> 35–49   <u>4:</u> other—terminate interview

I'm now going to show you five different coupon concepts and ask you 3 questions for each. Please respond to each coupon independently of the others. Look at the next coupon only when I ask you to.

4. *Please read the first coupon concept. Using a 10-point scale as shown above, how would you rate this concept if 1 represents very poor value and 10 represents very good value?* (enter value): _____

Looking at the second scale, how would you rate this concept if 1 represents "definitely would not use" and 10 represents "definitely would use"? (enter value): _____

Why did you respond as you did for use? _____
_____
_____

5. *Please turn the page and read the next coupon concept.*

Ignoring the last coupon and using the same scale, how would you rate this concept in terms of value? (enter value): _____

Referring to the second scale, how would you rate this concept in terms of your level of use? (enter value): _____

Why did you respond as you did for use? _____
_____
_____

6. *Please turn the page and read the next coupon concept. Ignoring the last coupon and using the same scale, how would you rate this concept in terms of value?* (enter value): _____

Referring to the second scale, how would you rate this concept in terms of your level of use? (enter value): _____

Why did you respond as you did for use? _____
_____
_____

7. *Please turn the page and read the next coupon concept. Ignoring the last coupon and using the same scale, how would you rate this concept in terms of value?* (enter value): _____

Referring to the second scale, how would you rate this concept in terms of your level of use? (enter value): _____

Why did you respond as you did for use? _____
_____
_____

8. *Please turn the page and read the next coupon concept. Ignoring the last coupon and using the same scale, how would you rate this concept in terms of value?* (enter value): _____

Referring to the second scale, how would you rate this concept in terms of your level of use? (enter value): _____

(continued)

FIGURE 3.2.2 *(continued)*

Why did you respond as you did for use? _____
_____

_____

Thank you. The following questions will help us classify the preceding information.

9. *How many children do you have living at home?* (enter value): _____
(if answer is none, proceed to question 11)

10. *What is the age of your youngest child?* (enter age): _____

11. *How often do you eat fast food for lunch or dinner?*
(read answers, circle number):   1) Once per month or less
                                 2) 2–3 times per month
                                 3) Once or twice a week
                                 4) More than twice a week

12. *How often do you eat at Premium Pizza?*
(read answers, circle number)   1) Never visited Premium Pizza
                                 2) Once per month or less
                                 3) 2–3 times per month
                                 4) Once a week or more
(if answer is Never, proceed to question 14)

13. *Do you yourself usually buy whole pies or slices at Premium Pizza?*
(circle one):   1) whole pies
                                 2) slices

14. *Have you used fast-food or restaurant coupons in the last 30 days?*
(circle one):   1) yes
                                 2) no

15. *Have you ever used coupons for Premium Pizzas?*
(read answers, circle number)   1) Never
                                 2) I sometimes use them when I have them.
                                 3) I always use them when I have them.

16. *What is your marital status?*
(read answers, circle number)   1) Single
                                 2) Married
                                 3) Divorced, Separated, Widowed

17. *What is your occupation?* _____

This is not a question for the respondent.
Respondent was (circle one): 1 male   2 female

Thank you for your participation. (Terminate interview at this time.)

the interviewer read the questions aloud and wrote down the answer given in each case by the interviewee. It was decided to show respondents an example of each coupon before they rated it. For this purpose, enlarged photographs of each coupon were produced. It was also thought necessary to depict the 10-point scales that consumers should use to evaluate the promotional offer. Coupons and scales were therefore assembled in a booklet so that, as the interviewer showed each double-page spread, the respondent would see the scales on the top page and the coupon in question on the bottom page (see Figure 3.2.3).

Because the researcher wished to counterbalance the order in which the coupons were viewed and rated, the five coupons were organized into booklets of six different sequences. Each sequence was subsequently bound in one of six distinctly colored binders. A total of 96 questionnaires were then printed in six different colors to match the binder. In this way, there were 16 questionnaires of each color, and the color of the respondent's questionnaire indicated the sequence that he or she had seen.

The questionnaire and procedure were pretested at a mall similar to the target mall and were found to be satisfactory.

FIGURE 3.2.3 Respondent Reference to Scale and Coupon Offer

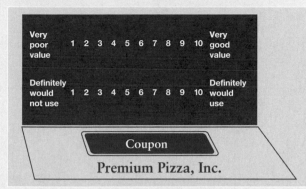

Questions

1. Is the choice of mall intercept interviews an appropriate data-collection method given the research objectives?
2. Do you think that there are any specific criteria that the choice of shopping mall should satisfy?
3. Evaluate the instructions to interviewers (Figure 3.2.1).
4. Evaluate the questionnaire (Figure 3.2.2).
5. Do you think it worthwhile to present the coupons in a binder, separate from the questionnaire? Why or why not?
6. Do you consider it advisable to rotate the order of presentation of coupons? Why or why not?

CASE 3.3
CTM PRODUCTIONS (A)[2]

CTM Productions, formerly Children's Theatre of Madison, was formed in 1965 to "produce theater of the highest quality." CTM's mission is to "ensure that our [CTM's] efforts are inclusive of all the human family, rather than parts of it." In order to measure its present and future achievement of this goal, CTM must learn who its audience actually is.

CTM's research team decided to study the audience of CTM's production *To Kill a Mockingbird*. The study had three major objectives: (1) to develop an audience profile, including demographic and media exposure data; (2) to provide a framework and data-collection instrument for future marketing research; and (3) to supply a list of potential season subscribers. CTM had never undertaken any marketing research before this study, so internal secondary information did not exist. External secondary information provided guidance as to the types of questions to be asked on this type of questionnaire and the appropriate phrasing for such questions. The questionnaire is shown in Figure 3.3.1.

[2] The contributions of Sara L. Pitterle to the development of this case are gratefully acknowledged.

CTM's volunteer ushers distributed the survey at each performance of *To Kill a Mockingbird*. The volunteers gave the survey and a pencil to all adults attending the performances (for the purpose of this survey, adults were defined as anyone 16 years or older). Respondents were instructed to complete the questionnaire and hand it back to the ushers during the intermission. In addition, collection boxes were placed next to all the exits. Although the survey was intended for all adult members of the audience, it is unclear as to whether these instructions were followed at every performance.

CTM Productions held five shows each weekend for three weekends. Surveys were distributed at each of the 15 performances; however, the number of completed surveys varied with the size of the audience for each show. A total of 1,016 usable surveys were collected during the course of the study.

Questions

1. The CTM research team used secondary data for question types and wording of specific questions. Did the research team use secondary information effectively in this study?
2. Read the questionnaire shown in Figure 3.3.1 (on page 306). Does the questionnaire provide CTM with the information necessary to meet the stated objectives? Explain.
3. Considering CTM's objectives, does the sampling plan used for the study provide the necessary information? Does the sampling plan bias the results?

CASE 3.4
Calamity-Casualty Insurance Company

Calamity-Casualty is an insurance company located in Dallas, Texas, that deals exclusively with automobile coverage. Its policy offerings include the standard features offered by most insurers, such as collision, comprehensive, emergency road service, medical, and uninsured motorist. The unique aspect of Calamity-Casualty Insurance is that all policies are sold through direct mail. Agents do not make personal calls on clients, and the company does not operate district offices. As a result, Calamity-Casualty's capital/labor requirements are greatly reduced at a substantial cost savings to the company. A great portion of these savings are passed on to the consumer in the form of lower prices (that is, 20 to 25% below the average market rate).

The company's strategy of selling automobile insurance by mail at low prices has been very successful. Calamity-Casualty has traditionally been the third largest seller of automobile insurance in the Southwest. During the past five years, the company has consistently achieved an average market share of some 14% in the four states it serves: Arizona, New Mexico, Nevada, and Texas. This compares favorably to the 19% and 17% market shares realized by

FIGURE 3.3.1 CTM Questionnaire

Introduce Yourself to CTM

Welcome to CTM's production of *To Kill a Mockingbird*. CTM Productions has been around for a long time—since 1965. And in this time we have had over 33,000 people in our audience. People to whom we have never been introduced. Real people like you that presently exist as numbers in our records. Now you have a chance to change your status. Introduce yourself to us by taking two minutes to answer the following questions to help us understand who you really are.

Let's start out with the basics. Your name is _____ *and you live at (please include mailing address with ZIP Code)* _____

How many CTM productions have you attended?   [ ] This is my first CTM production.

2002–2003 Season	2001–2002 Season	2000–2001 Season
[ ] season subscriber	[ ] season subscriber	[ ] season subscriber
[ ] *Wind in the Willows*	[ ] *Red Shoes*	[ ] *Beauty and the Beast*
[ ] *A Christmas Carol*	[ ] *A Christmas Carol*	[ ] *A Christmas Carol*
[X] *To Kill a Mockingbird*	[ ] *Anne of Green Gables*	[ ] *I Remember Mama*
[ ] *Babar II* (plan to attend)	[ ] *Narnia*	[ ] *Babar the Elephant*

Who is with you today? (check all that apply)

[ ] just myself	[ ] my spouse/partner	[ ] my kids
[ ] adult friend(s)	[ ] unrelated kids	[ ] other families

Whom have you attended with in the past? (again, check all that apply)

[ ] myself	[ ] my spouse/partner	[ ] my kids
[ ] adult friend(s)	[ ] unrelated kids	[ ] other families

Have you or any of your family participated in any of these CTM activities? (check all that apply)

[ ] after-school drama classes	[ ] auditions	[ ] have not participated
[ ] summer school	[ ] performances	[ ] did not know I could

How did you find out about our production of To Kill a Mockingbird? (again, check all that apply)

[ ] season brochure   [ ] poster

Read story in:

[ ] *State Journal*	[ ] *Capitol Times*	[ ] *Ishtmus*	[ ] other

Saw ad in:

[ ] *State Journal*	[ ] *Capitol Times*	[ ] *Ishtmus*	[ ] other
[ ] radio (which station?) _____		[ ] television (which station?) _____	
[ ] magazine (which one?) _____		[ ] word of mouth	

Did you come to this performance because you knew someone in the cast?

[ ] yes   [ ] no

What other events have you attended in the last six months? (check all that apply)
With your family or friends:

[ ] sports	[ ] movies	[ ] live musical performances
[ ] museums	[ ] lectures	[ ] other live theatrical performance

Alone:

[ ] sports	[ ] movies	[ ] live musical performances
[ ] museums	[ ] lectures	[ ] other live theatrical performance

Your answers to the following demographic questions will help us understand who you are.

Are you female or male?   [ ] female   [ ] male

Which age category do you belong to?

[ ] 16–20	[ ] 31–40	[ ] 51–60	[ ] 71–80
[ ] 21–30	[ ] 41–50	[ ] 61–70	[ ] 81–100

(continued)

FIGURE 3.3.1 *(continued)*

How did you get here today?
[ ] walked   [ ] car   [ ] bus   [ ] other

From how far away did you come?
[ ] within Madison   [ ] less than 5 miles   [ ] 6–10 miles   [ ] over 10 miles

How long have you lived in the Madison/south-central Wisconsin area?
[ ] do not live here   [ ] just arrived   [ ] 1–3 years   [ ] 4–7 years   [ ] more

What is your highest level of education?
[ ] some high school   [ ] some college   [ ] some graduate school   [ ] more
[ ] high school graduate   [ ] college graduate   [ ] graduate school degree

What is your annual household income?
[ ] below $20,000   [ ] $31–40,000   [ ] more than $50,000   [ ] do not wish to reply
[ ] $21–30,000   [ ] $41–50,000   [ ] not sure

Does this represent a dual income?
[ ] yes   [ ] no

How many people live in your household? (circle only one, include yourself)
         1   2   3   4   5   6   more

If you have children, how many are in each grade category?
[ ] not in school yet   [ ] 4th–5th grade   [ ] high school   [ ] other
[ ] kindergarten–3rd grade   [ ] 6th–8th grade   [ ] college

Would you like to be on our mailing list to keep informed of CTM activities? [ ] yes   [ ] no

Are you a CTM member? [ ] yes   [ ] no

Now here's your chance to share your thoughts with us.

I wish I had known that CTM _____

I'm glad CTM _____

I wish CTM would _____

I want CTM to know _____

It was a real pleasure meeting you. CTM looks forward to seeing you again very soon.

the two leading firms in the region. However, Calamity-Casualty has never been highly successful in Arizona. The largest market share gained by Calamity-Casualty in Arizona for any one year was 4%, which placed the company seventh among firms competing in that state.

The company's poor performance in Arizona greatly concerns Calamity-Casualty's board of executives. Demographic experts estimate that during the next six to ten years, the population in Arizona will increase 10 to 15%, the largest projected growth rate of any state in the Southwest. Thus, for Calamity-Casualty to remain a major market force in the area, the company needs to improve its sales performance in Arizona.

In response to this matter, Calamity-Casualty sponsored a study that was conducted by the Automobile Insurance Association of America (AIAA), the national association of automobile insurance executives, to determine Arizona residents' attitudes toward and perception of the various insurance companies selling policies in that state. The results of the AIAA research showed that Calamity-Casualty was favorably perceived across most categories measured. Calamity-Casualty received the highest ratings with respect to service, pricing, policy offering, and image. Although these findings were well received by the company's board of executives, they provided little strategic insight into how Calamity-Casualty might increase sales in Arizona.

Because the company was committed to obtaining information useful for developing a more effective Arizona sales campaign, the executive board sought the services of Aminbane, Pedrone, and Associates, a marketing research firm specializing in insurance consulting, to help with the matter. After many discussions between members of the research team and executives at Calamity-Casualty, it was decided that the most beneficial approach toward designing a more appropriate sales campaign would be to ascertain the psychographic profiles of nonpurchasers and direct-mail purchasers of Calamity-Casualty insurance. This would help the company better understand the personal factors influencing people's decision to respond or not to respond to direct-mail solicitation.

RESEARCH DESIGN

To learn more about which psychographic factors are important in describing purchasers of automobile insurance, some exploratory research was undertaken. In-depth interviews were held with two insurance salespersons, who offered various insights on the subject. These experience interviews were followed by a focus group meeting with Arizona residents who had received a direct-mail offer from Calamity-Casualty. Finally, the research team consulted university professors in both psychology and mass communications to uncover other determinants of buyer behavior. Output from these procedures revealed three psychographic factors that could be used to segment purchasers of insurance by mail—namely, risk aversion, powerlessness, and convenience orientation. It was believed that people who were risk averse, had a sense of powerlessness, and

were convenience-oriented would be more favorably disposed toward direct-mail marketing efforts and thus would be more likely to purchase Calamity-Casualty automobile insurance.

METHOD OF DATA COLLECTION

Given these factors of interest, the list of items contained in Table 3.4.1 was generated to form the basis of a questionnaire to be administered to Arizona residents. Two samples of subjects were to be used—one of direct-mail buyers and one of nonbuyers. The research team estimated that 175 subjects would be required from both samples to adequately assess the three constructs. Because a mail questionnaire dealing with psychographic subject matter might have a very low response rate, and because attitude toward direct mail was one of the attributes being measured, a telephone interview was believed to be best suited to the needs at hand.

Questions

1. Conceptually, what are the constructs risk aversion, convenience orientation, and powerlessness?
2. Do you think that the sample of items adequately assesses each construct? Can you think of any additional items that could or should be used?

TABLE 3.4.1 Calamity-Casualty Marketing Research Questionnaire Items(*)

Risk Aversion

1. It is always better to buy a used car from a dealer than from an individual.
2. Generally speaking, I avoid buying generic drugs at the drugstore.
3. It would be a disaster to be stranded on the road due to a breakdown.
4. It would be important to me to plan a long road trip very carefully and in great detail.
5. I would like to try parachute jumping sometime.
6. Before buying a new product, I would first discuss it with someone who had already used it.
7. Before deciding to see a new movie in a theater, it is important to read the critical reviews.
8. If my car needed even a minor repair, I would first get cost estimates from several garages.

Powerlessness

1. Persons like myself have little chance of protecting our personal interests when they conflict with those of strong pressure groups.
2. A lasting world peace can be achieved by those of us who work toward it.
3. I think each of us can do a great deal to improve world opinion of the United States.
4. This world is run by the few people in power, and there is not much the little guy can do about it.
5. People like me can change the course of world events if we make ourselves heard.
6. More and more, I feel helpless in the face of what's happening in the world today.

(continued)

TABLE 3.4.1 *(continued)*

Convenience Orientation

1. I like to buy things by mail or catalog because it saves time.
2. I think that it is not worth the extra effort to clip coupons for groceries.
3. I would rather wash my own car than pay to have it washed at a car wash.
4. I would prefer to have an automatic transmission rather than a stick shift in my car.
5. When choosing a bank, I believe that location is the most important factor.
6. When shopping for groceries, I would be willing to drive a longer distance in order to buy at lower prices.

(*) Note: Each item requires one of the following responses:

Responses	Code
S.A.—Strongly Agree	5
A.—Agree	4
N.—Neither Agree nor Disagree	3
D.—Disagree	2
S.D.—Strongly Disagree	1

CASE 3.5

MEASURING MAGAZINES

When companies decide to advertise, they have many decisions to make: how much to spend, in which media, how frequently should the ads appear, etc. Each component question is difficult.

Say your company sells pharmaceutical drugs. Magazines are a perfect fit for drug advertisements because the outlet allows the company to express in detailed ad copy the side effects and other precautions and disclaimers. The FTC prohibits explicit claims of success on television, which makes most TV ads for drugs ambiguous. For example, you've seen the types of ads in which people are moving through meadows in slow motion . . . what ailment does the drug purport to cure? Magazines are a popular medium for many industries, not just pharmaceuticals (see Figure 3.5.1).

So, say your firm decides, "Okay, we're going to run a magazine print ad." Now what? "In which magazine should we run an ad?" Well, a "good one." *Good,* as a construct, means what?

Companies decide in which magazines they advertise based on the success of the magazine. Magazines earn their money through circulation and advertising, hence, a magazine's "success" may be measured in two ways. One is advertising revenue, depicted in Figure 3.5.2. According to this monetary index, *People, Sports Illustrated,* and *Parade* are the top magazines.

The second, equally valid means of measuring a magazine's success is readership circulation. Figure 3.5.3 shows that *People* and *Sports Illustrated* are still in the top 12, but

FIGURE 3.5.1 Measuring Magazines—Magazine Spending by Category ($mm)

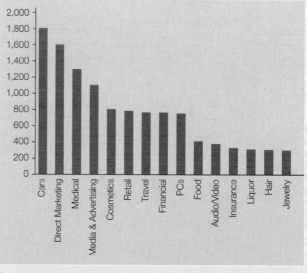

Source: adweek.com

nowhere near as prominent as their expenditure data had suggested. That is, the ranking of the magazines varies depending on how you measure the success of the magazine.

Note that we're not even trying to measure some subjective, intangible consumer attitude on some customer survey. We're simply trying to get a useful index for the success of a magazine. Yet even something as seemingly simple as the "success" of a magazine is a construct that can usually be measured in more than one manner. In this case, the

FIGURE 3.5.2 Measuring Magazines—Ad Revenue ($mm)

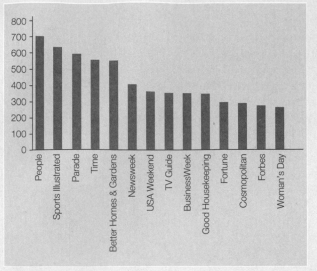

Source: adweek.com

FIGURE 3.5.3 Measuring Magazines—Magazine Circulation (mm)

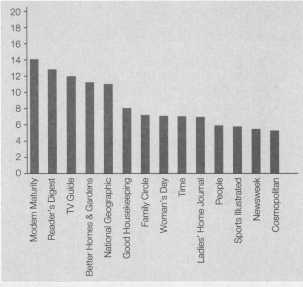

Source: adweek.com

measure of success that is adopted probably depends on the point of view taken: i.e., the magazine (ad space seller) vs. the manufacturer (buyer).

Questions

1. Which of these definitions do you think the magazine industry thinks is most important? On which index do you think the survival of any particular magazine depends?

2. Which of these indices would matter most to your firm? If you want your ad to appear before the most people, do you go after *People* magazine, or do you go for the older population (*Modern Maturity*) and middle America (*Reader's Digest*)?

3. Where do segmentation, targeting, and positioning enter in the decision making? Which kinds of drugs (or products more generally) fit best with each of these outlets? Your choice of measure of success depends on what marketing and marketing research question you want to answer. You've got to think through how you will use the index to determine which scores are most reflective of your current marketing questions.

If you think the measure of "success" was an isolated example, consider another (there are many!). A different kind of question might be, "Who are the big spenders in magazine advertising?" Instead of playing the role of a pharmaceuticals company looking to place an ad, what if you were the marketing manager in charge of soliciting ads for a magazine? Advertising expenditures per company can be measured not just in how much money is spent, but in how many pages the money buys. Thus, you could approach your quest in one of two ways: you could try to increase the ad revenue for the magazine, or you could increase the number of ads placed in the magazine. Once again, these lead to different results.

Figure 3.5.4 lists the companies who spend a lot on magazine advertising, as measured by cash-ola. Figure 3.5.5 lists the same companies, in the same order for ease of comparison, but note the change in the height of the histograms from Figure 3.5.4 to Figure 3.5.5.

Questions

1. Which companies spend the most, if the expenditure is measured in dollars? If measured by number of pages?

2. Why do these profiles differ? When is either measure most relevant?

FIGURE 3.5.4 Measuring Magazines—Magazine Spending by Company ($mm)

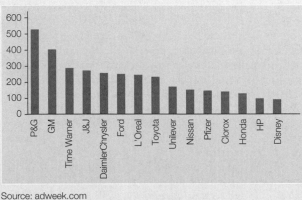

Source: adweek.com

3. Which is most relevant to show your boss that you've been successful?

Each of these illustrations offered two items that shared similarly strong "face validity" yet were rival indices. Your understanding of the marketing and managerial concerns has to distinguish which measure to use.

FIGURE 3.5.5 Measuring Magazines—Magazine Spending by Company (# pages)

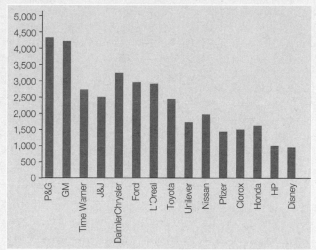

Source: adweek.com

CASE 3.6

Secondary Data on Health from CDC (Data set available on text Web site)

Monstrous amounts of secondary data exist online, for free. The government is easily the largest source of population-related and economic and business-related data (http://www. census. gov). You can also get absorbed for hours (okay, we're geeks) at http://www.cdc.org if you're interested in health data.

Table 3.6.1 is a listing, per state and per year, of the percentage of citizens estimated to be obese. Go online to see how these data were compiled (and to see precisely how obese is defined). Secondary data are free and "quick," but finding all the bits and pieces of these numbers is rather tedious and time consuming (you'll be glad to have a marketing research staff). It's also easy to make copying mistakes, so be sure to factor in quality control before using the data and basing decisions on them.

Questions

1. First, go online, and add the most recent columns of data. Table 3.6.1 currently ends at 2001, so add the years 2002, 2003, etc.
2. Second, what question do you want to answer with these masses of data?
   a. You can focus on current data, e.g., find the answer to the question: "For the most recent year, which are the top ten states with obesity problems?"
   b. You can make comparisons with older data, e.g., answer these questions: "Were the states you just

TABLE 3.6.1 CDC Data (http://www.cdc.org) on Obesity (Percentages):

STATE, YEAR:	1990	1991	1992	1993	1994	1995	1996	1997	1998	1999	2000	2001
Alabama	12.3	13.9	12.4	11	17.4	18.7	20.5	18.2	21.3	22.4	23.9	24.5
Alaska	**	13.4	12.1	13.7	13.2	19.8	17.5	19.7	21.4	20.4	21	22.1
Arkansas	**	13.2	**	16.3	17	17.5	17.8	18.1	19.8	22.7	23.3	22.4
California	9.8	10.5	11.8	13.2	13.5	15.1	14.6	16	17.3	18.7	19.9	21.9
Colorado	6.9	8.5	7.7	11.1	10.8	10.1	10.3	11.8	14.4	14.9	14.2	14.9
Connecticut	11.7	11.1	10.5	11	11.9	12.5	13.4	14.7	15.5	15.1	17.4	17.9
Delaware	14.4	15.5	13	13.5	15.1	17.1	17.7	18.8	17.2	17.5	16.6	20.8
District of Columbia	16	15.6	13.4	11.3	14.2	**	16.8	14.5	20.2	18.5	21.5	20
Florida	13.6	10.6	12.1	13	12.7	17.2	16.7	16.1	18	18.6	18.7	18.8
Georgia	10.8	9.5	11.9	13.1	14.9	13.3	11.5	14.4	19.2	21.1	21.5	22.7
Hawaii	9.1	10.7	9.7	10.3	10.6	10.8	12.9	13.6	15.5	15.7	15.7	17.9
Idaho	11.9	11.8	12.6	13.3	14.8	14.2	16.9	16.3	16.4	20	18.9	20.5
Illinois	10.9	13.1	14.2	13.5	15.7	16.7	17	17.1	18.5	20.9	21.7	21
Indiana	14.5	15.3	14.8	17	17.8	20.1	18.6	21.2	19.9	19.9	21.8	24.5
Iowa	12.8	14.5	14.4	15.4	15.6	17.5	18.7	19.4	19.8	21.5	21.5	22.5
Kansas	**	**	13.1	12.2	12.1	15.9	13.4	14.7	17.7	18.9	20.8	21.6

(continued)

TABLE 3.6.1 (continued)

STATE, YEAR:	1990	1991	1992	1993	1994	1995	1996	1997	1998	1999	2000	2001
Kentucky	12.2	13.3	15.3	16.4	16.4	16.9	19.2	21.8	20.4	21.7	23	24.6
Louisiana	12.3	16	17.6	16.7	16.8	17.7	19.7	19.6	21.8	22.3	23.6	24
Maine	12.2	12.5	12.1	13.7	15.2	14.1	16.1	16.2	17.4	19.4	20	19.5
Maryland	12	11.6	12.6	13.9	14.7	16.3	17.7	17.5	20.5	18.2	20.2	20.5
Massachusetts	10.1	9	11.5	10.3	12.7	11.7	13.1	14.8	14.3	14.7	16.8	16.6
Michigan	14.1	15.9	16.5	16.5	17	18.2	18.2	19.3	21.2	22.8	22.4	25
Minnesota	10.2	11	12.7	14.2	14.3	15.3	14.3	16.5	16.2	15.5	17.4	19.9
Mississippi	15	16	17.8	18.9	19.7	19.5	19.8	22	22.8	23.2	25	26.5
Montana	8.7	10	10.9	12.3	13.3	13.4	14.3	14.6	15	15.8	15.9	18.8
Nebraska	11.6	13.3	12	14.5	14.6	16.3	16.3	17	18.3	21	21.1	20.7
Nevada	**	**	12.5	11.9	13.8	13.3	15.5	14.1	14	15.8	17.9	19.5
New Hampshire	11.1	10.6	10.8	11.2	12.4	15.1	14.5	14.2	15.6	14.6	18.1	19.4
New Jersey	**	9.9	10.4	10	12.5	14.5	13.5	16	15.5	17	18.5	19.6
New Mexico	9.8	8.2	11	10.8	10.9	13	14.1	14.9	15.2	17.7	19.3	19.7
New York	9.8	13.4	13	14.8	14.2	13.9	14.5	16	16.3	17.4	17.7	20.3
North Carolina	12.9	13.4	13.4	15.7	16.3	16.9	18.1	18.3	19.4	21.5	21.8	22.9
North Dakota	12.1	13.1	14.1	15.2	14.2	16.4	18.4	17	19.2	21.9	20.4	20.4
Ohio	11.3	15.6	13.6	14.5	16.3	17.5	18.9	17.7	20	20.3	21.5	22.4
Oklahoma	11.6	11.9	14.1	12.1	13.2	13.5	16.8	15.1	19.5	21.1	19.7	22.6
Oregon	10.9	11.5	12.3	11.6	14.1	15.2	16.4	19.4	18.3	19.9	21.5	21.1
Pennsylvania	12.5	14.7	15.2	16.4	15.9	16.4	18.7	17.5	19.4	20.3	21.2	22.1
Rhode Island	11.1	9.7	12.3	12.3	**	13.2	14.3	13.8	16.8	16.8	17.1	17.7
South Carolina	13.6	14.2	14.3	16.8	16.3	16.7	18.4	16.9	20.6	20.6	22	22.5
South Dakota	10.7	13.1	12.8	15.2	14.4	13.9	14.7	17	15.8	19.6	19.8	21.2
Tennessee	11.8	12.8	13	15.6	14.9	18.4	17.4	17.7	19.2	20.5	22.9	23.4
Texas	12.3	13	13.6	15.6	16.4	15.9	17.2	18.7	20.2	21.6	23.1	24.6
Utah	9.3	10	11.5	11.6	11.4	13	13.7	15.2	15.9	16.7	19.1	19.1
Vermont	10.7	10.5	12.4	11.7	13.8	14.6	14.9	15.9	14.8	18	18.2	17.6
Virginia	9.9	10.6	11.7	14	13	15.7	15.9	16.4	18.7	19.3	18.2	20.9
Washington	9.4	10.5	10.6	13.9	13.9	13.9	15.6	15.2	18.1	18.2	18.8	19.3
West Virginia	15	15.7	16.9	17.7	17.1	18.3	19.9	20.6	23.9	24.6	23.2	25.1
Wisconsin	11.3	12.7	15.5	15.6	17.5	16	17.1	16.6	18.3	19.9	20	22.4
Wyoming	**	**	**	**	13.7	14.3	15.1	15	15.1	16.9	18	19.7

listed always the fattest states?" "What does such a list look like when the data began (in the table, in 1990)?"

c. Pick your state and graph the trend (e.g., in Excel). Is the increase constant and steady, or is there a jump between any years? To what might the jump(s) be attributable (e.g., more fat consumption? the end of an exercise fad? different measures of obesity?)? As a social marketer, how might you slow or reverse the trend? Have we (as a country) been successful at changing any such behaviors? (Don't be pessimistic, the answer is yes—think about smoking, condom use for AIDS prevention, etc.)

d. Do you think the trend that you just plotted for your state is typical or unusual? How would you defend your point of view? Plot the trends for add-itional states—which states would be the best comparisons? Others in your immediate area? Others with comparable population statistics (go to http://www.census.gov to find those numbers!)?

3. In these obesity data, pick either a year and select all states, or pick your state and select all years. Then return to http://www.cdc.org and pick up more data. There are tons of lifestyle-related indices. For example, there are statistics on percentage of people who smoke, percentage of people covered by health insurance, etc. Correlate these obesity figures with some of these other measures. As suggested, to keep from getting overwhelmed in the data, do the correlations within your state (and correlate different measures over years) or, better, within the year (correlating over states). Before you conduct the analyses, write down the (social)

marketing and (health) managerial questions you think you want to answer.

4. After you play with the data a bit, write down the answers you've arrived at, and compare them to the questions you had posed. Have you answered all the questions you set out to answer? If not, why not? Were they harder to answer than you thought, or did you get distracted? How many new questions arose as you began your exploration in the data? If this latter number exceeds five, there's good news and bad news. The good news is that you're now a *bona fide* "data miner." The bad news is that you're a hopeless geek. (Wear that label with pride—it will get you far in life!)

CASE 3.7

CRITIQUING QUESTIONNAIRES

Be forewarned! These exercises usually make "monsters" out of otherwise meek business school students. Once you learn to critique a questionnaire, you'll never be able to look at another survey in quite the same way. Instead of answering the marketing researcher's questions, you'll be looking at the question thinking, "I could have worded that better!" That's okay with us—it's a good measure of your knowledge!

So, to get you started, take a look at the following real surveys (these are all "real" but we've changed the brand names to protect the incompetent).

Figure 3.7.1 was a postcard-sized survey. You see the front. On the back was the address of the office for ease of the customer return (though it was not stamped).

What are the survey's strengths? It's short, and obviously so, so consumers know immediately that filling out the survey won't take too much of their time.

- Short surveys enhance response rates.
- Better response rates mean more representative samples.

In addition, a number of different attributes are assessed, to enhance the multidimensionality of the service assessment. There is an open-ended section so that the consumer may say whatever is on his/her mind, whether anticipated by the rating scales of quality, timeliness, etc.

What are the survey's weaknesses? The trade-off on length is that the survey will yield little information. Further, if any of the features is deemed weak, are any of the scales precise enough to diagnose how to remedy the service? A complaint about marketing research that you always want to avoid is, "We can't do anything on the basis of these data."

Figure 3.7.2 also has strengths and weaknesses (as does any real survey—nothing is perfect). For example, there are again ratings, and an open-ended space providing the opportunity to vent or rave about anything the consumer cares about. At the bottom of the survey, there is a means of communication should the customer wish feedback. Nice touch. On the other hand, what the heck do "Our everyday in stock" and our "Ad in stock" mean? We're marketers, we're smart, we can figure this out. But if it takes us a moment to interpret the jargon, how much longer will it take the average consumer? In the meantime, do we lose that respondent?

Figure 3.7.3 is a survey from a large network of travel agencies. Many of the questions could be improved, but if you want a chuckle, look at the last question.

Enough hints. Now you're on your own. Identify the strengths and weaknesses in the remaining surveys, depicted in Figures 3.7.4 through 3.7.7.

FIGURE 3.7.1 Questionnaires to Critique—A Campus Administration Office

Dear Valued Customer,

To assist us in maintaining the highest possible quality service to your department, please complete and return this card, rating performance on the services performed for you. Please feel free to make any other comments or suggestions. Thank you.

	Excellent	Good	Adequate	Inadequate	Unacceptable
Quality	☐	☐	☐	☐	☐
Timeliness	☐	☐	☐	☐	☐
Price	☐	☐	☐	☐	☐
Convenience	☐	☐	☐	☐	☐
Overall service	☐	☐	☐	☐	☐

Comments/Suggestions: _____

_____

_____

Job Number: _____ Date: _____ Name (optional): _____

FIGURE 3.7.2 A Big Drug Store

	Excellent	Average	Poor
Overall how would you grade this store?	☐	☐	☐
Please check one:			
Our pharmacy	☐	☐	☐
Our check-out service	☐	☐	☐
Our variety & selection	☐	☐	☐
Our everyday prices	☐	☐	☐
Our ad in stock	☐	☐	☐
Our cleanliness	☐	☐	☐
Our film processing	☐	☐	☐
Our everyday in stock	☐	☐	☐
Our people are friendly & helpful	☐	☐	☐

Date of visit: _____

Time of day: _____

Your comments and concerns: _____
_____
_____
_____
_____

☐ I would like a reply   ☐ I don't need a reply

Name _____
Address _____
City _____
State _____ Zip _____ Phone _____

FIGURE 3.7.3 A Travel Agency

Please help us maintain our high standards of quality by answering the following questions.

On this trip did we:

Provide lowest applicable airfare?	Yes	No	NA/DK
Enter frequent flyer # w reservation?	Yes	No	NA/DK
Book the hotel you requested?	Yes	No	NA/DK
Reserve the type of car requested?	Yes	No	NA/DK
Provide confirmation numbers?	Yes	No	NA/DK
Provide travel documents on time?	Yes	No	NA/DK
Handle special requests and note on tix?	Yes	No	NA/DK
Provide accurate destination information?	Yes	No	NA/DK

How would you rate each of the following?	Excellent	Good	Fair	Poor	NA
Courtesy of service?	E	G	F	P	NA
Extent to which your questions were answered?	E	G	F	P	NA
Manner in which our staff resolved any problems?	E	G	F	P	NA
Our *overall* service to you?	E	G	F	P	NA

On a scale of 0 to 100, if most travel agencies get an overall quality score of 80, what score would you give to our WorldZoom Travel Network? _____

FIGURE 3.7.4 A Big Hotel Chain

Please take a moment to share your thoughts with us. We value your business and thank you for your confidence in the *ComfyStay* Brand. Your feedback is greatly encouraged and appreciated.

Overall satisfaction with this ComfyStay	Low	1 2 3 4 5 6 7	High	n/a
Likelihood you would recommend this ComfyStay	Low	1 2 3 4 5 6 7	High	n/a
Likelihood, *if returning to the area,* you would return to this ComfyStay	Low	1 2 3 4 5 6 7	High	n/a
Overall value for the price paid	Low	1 2 3 4 5 6 7	High	n/a

Primary purpose of visit
- ☐ Individual business
- ☐ Convention/Meeting
- ☐ Pleasure

How many times have you been a guest at this ComfyStay?   1   2   3   4   5+

Did you have a problem during your stay? Y   N

If yes, did you report it to the staff?   Y   N

Was the problem resolved?   Y   N

If yes, how did our staff measure against your expectations? ☐ Exceeded   ☐ Met   ☐ Fell Below

What was the nature of the problem? _____

_____

_____

_____

Room Number _____   Your name _____

Hotel Name _____   Day phone _____

Date of Stay _____

FIGURE 3.7.5 A FancyPen Online/Catalog Company

Dear Customer,

This order comes with a string attached: your satisfaction.

Our goal is to ensure that you're 100% satisfied every time you shop with us. Would you mind taking a couple of minutes to tell us how we did? If there's additional assistance we can offer, please call or e-mail us anytime.

Thank you for your business. We hope we met (or exceeded) your expectations.

Sincerely,

Moi

Director of Customer Service (Phone, E-mail address listed here)

Customer Satisfaction Survey

1. Was the merchandise what you expected? _____ Yes _____ No Here's why: _____

_____

2. Did you buy it as a gift? _____ Yes, for this occasion _____ _____ No

3. Will you order from FancyPen again? _____ Yes _____ No Here's why: _____

_____

4. What are your three favorite stores or catalogs?

_____   _____   _____

5. Overall, how would you grade us on customer service?
   ☐ A   ☐ B   ☐ C   ☐ D   ☐ F

How can we make your experience with FancyPen more satisfying? _____

_____

Thank you. Just drop this card in the mail—we'll pay the postage.

FIGURE 3.7.6   YuppieHouseWares

Customer Service

If you ordered by phone

The Phone Representative's courtesy and
professionalism   ☐ excellent   ☐ very good   ☐ satisfactory   ☐ needs improvement

The ease and efficiency of the ordering
process   ☐ excellent   ☐ very good   ☐ satisfactory   ☐ needs improvement

If you spoke with a Product Specialist

The Product Specialist's courtesy and   ☐ excellent   ☐ very good   ☐ satisfactory   ☐ needs improvement
professionalism

The Product Specialist's promptness in   ☐ excellent   ☐ very good   ☐ satisfactory   ☐ needs improvement
answering your inquiry

The value of the Product Specialist's   ☐ excellent   ☐ very good   ☐ satisfactory   ☐ needs improvement
assistance to you

The ease and efficiency of ordering from   ☐ excellent   ☐ very good   ☐ satisfactory   ☐ needs improvement
the Product Specialist

If you ordered by mail or fax

The ease of following the instructions on   ☐ excellent   ☐ very good   ☐ satisfactory   ☐ needs improvement
the Order Form

Delivery

The arrival of your order compared with   ☐ excellent   ☐ very good   ☐ satisfactory   ☐ needs improvement
anticipated time of delivery

The appearance and condition of the   ☐ excellent   ☐ very good   ☐ satisfactory   ☐ needs improvement
packaging

The condition of the merchandise upon   ☐ excellent   ☐ very good   ☐ satisfactory   ☐ needs improvement
receipt

Merchandise

Your initial reaction to the quality of the   ☐ excellent   ☐ very good   ☐ satisfactory   ☐ needs improvement
products you ordered

Your initial perception of the value received   ☐ excellent   ☐ very good   ☐ satisfactory   ☐ needs improvement
for the money spent

Just a few more questions

Are you likely to purchase from YuppieHouseWares again?
_____

What additional services may we provide?
_____

If you could implement one change at YuppieHouseWares, what would it be?
_____

May we send our catalog to a friend? Please provide name and address:
_____

If you have a concern or question about your order, please call our Product Specialist at 1-800-etc.

FIGURE 3.7.7 A Car Dealership

I know you had a choice of where to service your vehicle and I would like to thank you for the opportunity to earn your business. I also know that if I expect to build a strong customer base, I need to make sure that you are completely satisfied with your service experience here today.

Below is a list of questions that may appear on a questionnaire from my dealership. Although some of them seem to rate our entire operation, in fact they all rate my personal performance and the scores become part of my permanent record. If you feel I have not earned all "5" or "Yes" ratings, please call and allow me the opportunity to correct any of my failures.

F A I L I N G !

	Highest				Lowest
	5	4	3	2	1
Promptness, courtesy writing your order:	☐	☐	☐	☐	☐
Communication with Service Consultant	☐	☐	☐	☐	☐
Knowledge and expertise	☐	☐	☐	☐	☐
Treated in honest, straightforward manner	☐	☐	☐	☐	☐
Amount of time spent with you	☐	☐	☐	☐	☐
Understanding your service, repair request	☐	☐	☐	☐	☐

	Yes	No
Were service items requested completed?	☐	☐
Able to schedule appointment?	☐	☐
Vehicle available when promised?	☐	☐
Car washed, clean when you picked it up?	☐	☐
Was the work explained to your satisfaction?	☐	☐

## PART 4

Sample Design for Data Collection and Sample Size

In this section, we get into the actual collection of the data needed to answer a problem:

- Chapter 11 discusses sampling plans.

- Chapter 12 answers the question, "How many respondents do I need?" (to answer the marketing research problem with precision and confidence).

- Chapter 13 presents the kinds of errors that can arise in collecting data.

Sampling Procedures

Questions to Guide Your Learning:

Q1: How do you get a sample?

Q2: What is a probability sample (vs. a nonprobability sample)?

Q3: How does sampling relate to some basic statistical concepts?

Q4: What is a stratified sample?

Q5: What is cluster sampling?

Once the researcher has clearly specified the problem and developed an appropriate research design and data-collection instrument, the next step in the research process is to select those elements from which the information will be collected. One way to do this is to collect information from each member of the population of interest by a complete canvas, or **census**, of the population. Another way is to collect information from a portion of the population by taking a **sample** of elements from the larger group, and, on the basis of the information collected from the subset, infer something about the larger group (and one's ability to make this inference depends on the method by which the sample of elements was chosen).

Incidentally, "element" in a population here refers not only to people but also to manufacturing and retail firms, organizations, markets, countries, or even inanimate objects, e.g., ads to be sampled, manufactured parts to be tested for quality control, etc. **Target population** is defined as the totality of cases that conform to some designated specifications. The specifications define the elements that belong to the target group and those that are to be excluded. A study aimed at establishing a demographic profile of frozen-pizza eaters requires specifying who is to be considered a frozen-pizza eater. Anyone who has ever eaten a frozen pizza? Those who eat at least one such pizza a month? A week? Those who eat a certain minimum number of frozen pizzas per month? Researchers need to be explicit and very precise in defining the target group, and careful to actually sample the target population rather than some other population due to an inappropriate sampling strategy.

We sample rather than canvas the entire population for several reasons: (1) complete counts on populations of moderate size are very costly, (2) a census would take so much time that the information would be obsolete by the time it was completed, (3) sometimes a census is impossible. For example, in TQM studies, imagine testing the life of electric light bulbs. A 100% inspection using all bulbs until they burned out would reveal the average bulb life but would leave no product to sell, (4) This may surprise the novice researcher, but one chooses a sample over a census for purposes of accuracy. Censuses involve larger field staffs, which, in turn, introduce greater potential for nonsampling error.[1]

Required Steps

Figure 11.1 outlines a 6-step procedure that researchers can follow when drawing a sample of a population. First, *define the target population* about which you wish to make an inference. Relevant elements thus are the objects on which measurements are taken. You must decide whether the target population consists of individuals, households, business firms, other organizations, credit-card transactions, Web pages, or some other unit. In making this specification, the researcher also has to specify what units are to be excluded, e.g., geographic boundaries, time periods, etc. For example, a target population may be defined as all consumers over 18, or females only, or those with a high school education only. A combination of respondent characteristics (age, gender, education, ethnicity, etc.) can also be used.

Specifying geographic boundaries is particularly difficult in international marketing research studies. The composition of the population can vary depending on the location within the country, e.g., northern Chile has a highly centralized Indian population, whereas the south has high concentrations of individuals of European descent.

In general, the simpler the definition of the target population, the higher the incidence and the easier and less costly it is to find the sample. **Incidence** refers to the percentage of the general population that satisfies the criteria defining the target population. Incidence has a direct bearing on the time and cost it takes to complete studies. When incidence is high (i.e., most people qualify for the study because only one or very few, easily satisfied criteria are used to screen potential respondents), the cost and time to collect data are minimized. Alternatively, as the number of criteria used to describe what constitutes eligible respondents for the study increases, so does the cost and time necessary to find them. For example, Figure 11.2 shows the percentage of adults estimated to participate in various sports. The data suggest that it would be more difficult and costly to focus a study on people who motorcycle, who are only 9% of all adults, than people who walk for health, 59% of all adults. The most important thing in defining the target population is that the researcher be precise

---

[1] This is one reason the Bureau of the Census uses sample surveys to check the accuracy of various censuses. Yep, samples are used to infer the accuracy of the census.

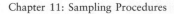

FIGURE 11.1
Six-Step Procedure for
Drawing a Sample

Step 1 — Define the Target Population

Step 2 — Identify the Sampling Frame

Step 3 — Select a Sampling Procedure

Step 4 — Determine the Sample Size

Step 5 — Select the Sample Elements

Step 6 — Collect the Data from the Designated Elements

in specifying exactly what elements are of interest and what elements are to be excluded. A clear statement of research objectives helps immeasurably in determining the appropriate elements of interest.

Common sense helps. A large restaurant chain was puzzling over whether their customers wanted 60:40 health:taste or 60:40 taste:health in their product offerings.

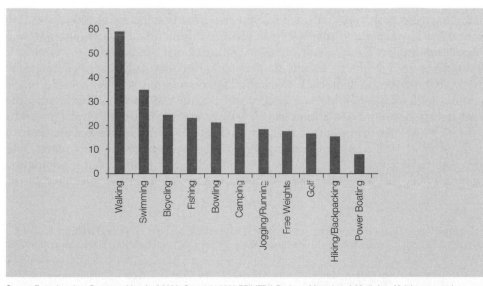

FIGURE 11.2
Percent of Adults who
Participate in Leisure
Time Sports

They'll never know whether they solved the problem because they screwed up the sampling. They conducted surveys in urban environments, concentrating on young, high-income, white-collar professionals. They then located many of their retail units in low-income, blue-collar areas. Not surprisingly, the results didn't generalize, and sales didn't take off.[2]

The second step in the sample selection process is identifying the **sampling frame**, which is the listing of the elements from which the actual sample is drawn. A telephone book is an example of a sampling frame, which also illustrates the condition that there is rarely a perfect correspondence between the sampling frame and the target population of interest. Even though the target population may be all households in a particular metropolitan area, the telephone directory provides a somewhat inaccurate listing of these households, omitting those without phones and those with unlisted numbers, and double counting others that have multiple listings.[3] One of the researcher's more creative tasks in sampling is developing an appropriate sampling frame when the list of population elements is not readily available. This may mean sampling working blocks of numbers and exchanges, as when random-digit dialing (RDD) is used with telephone surveys (see Research Realities 11.1). Or it sometimes means sampling geographic areas or organizations and then subsampling within these units when, say, the target population is individuals but a current, accurate list of appropriate individuals is not available.

The third step in selecting a *sample procedure* depends on what the researcher can develop for a sampling frame. As we describe in greater detail later in the chapter, a simple random sample requires that a complete, accurate list of population elements by name or other identification code be available.

Step 4 in the sample selection process requires the *sample size* to be determined, an issue covered in Chapter 12. Step 5 indicates that the researcher needs to *do the sampling,* i.e., choose the elements that will be included in the study, which we discuss as we present the sampling methods. Finally, the researcher needs to actually *collect data* from the designated respondents.

Population

→ **target**

   population

→ **sampling**

   frame

→ **sample**

Types of Sampling Plans

Sampling techniques can be divided into the two broad categories of probability and nonprobability samples. **Probability samples** are distinguished by the fact that each population element has a known, nonzero chance of being included in the sample. It is not necessary that the probabilities of selection be equal, only that one can specify the probability with which each element of the population will be included in the sample. With **nonprobability samples**, in contrast, there is no way of estimating the probability that any population element will be included in the sample, and thus there is no way of ensuring that the sample is representative of the population. All nonprobability samples rely on personal judgment somewhere in the process, and although these judgment samples may indeed yield good estimates of a population characteristic, they do not permit an objective evaluation of the adequacy of the

---

[2] You might think this is an avoidable, stupid error. It happens all the time, cf. James Nelems, "Follow Up Effective Marketing Research to Yield Maximum Business Success," *Nation's Restaurant News* (Oct. 28, 2002), pp. 22–24.

[3] Clyde Tucker, James Lepkowski and Linda Piekarski, "The Current Efficiency of List-Assisted Telephone Sampling Designs," *Public Opinion Quarterly* 66 (2002), pp. 321–338.

11.1 Changes in the Structure of Telephone Numbers

Since 1986, the estimated number of telephone households in the United States has increased by 14.2%, while the number of working residential exchanges has increased by 27.1% and the number of working blocks by 182.4%. See the chart below. During the same time period, the number of directory-listed households has increased by only 10.4%, causing the continuing decline in listed rates.

Technological changes, particularly the explosive growth of cellular and mobile phones, paging equipment, modems, and fax machines, have dramatically increased the demand for telephone numbers. This has not only spurred the introduction of new area codes, but has also produced a reduced density of listed numbers in the working blocks because some of the numbers are dedicated to modems and fax machines.

The new competitive telephone market is also contributing to the declining working block density. Multiple telephone companies are serving smaller markets and are assigned exclusive exchanges. More exchanges are being assigned to more telephone companies, but the working blocks are not being filled out as completely.

What's the significance for sampling? The most obvious change concerns the working phone rate (WPR) of a random-digit dialing (RDD) sample. As the number of listed phones per working block decreases, the probability of selecting a listed number in an RDD sample decreases, which may decrease the WPR. Samples that include metropolitan areas are more likely to be affected by this trend.

	1986	1996	Growth
Telephone households	80,900,000	92,366,039	14.2%
Directory-listed households	59,788,590	66,016,760	10.4%
Working residential exchanges	31,530	40,083	27.1%
Working blocks	1,391,237	3,928,200	182.4%

Definition

Block or bank:	the first two digits of the last four digits of the telephone number
Working block:	any block with at least one listed number
Exchange/prefix:	"exchange" designates the city, town, or community in which the number originates; "prefix" is the 3-digit number assigned to an exchange area. The terms are often used interchangeably.

Source: "Working Block Density Declines" (Fairfield, CT: Survey Sampling, Inc., 1996).

sample. It is only when the elements have been selected with known probabilities that one can evaluate the precision of a sample result.[4]

Samples can also be distinguished by whether they are fixed or sequential. **Fixed samples** imply an *a priori* determination of sample size and they are the most commonly employed types in marketing research (e.g., budget proposals are contingent on sample size). Nevertheless, you should be aware that sequential samples can also be taken and that they can be employed with each of the basic sampling plans to be discussed. **Sequential samples** are distinguished by the successive decisions they imply. They aim at answering the research question on the basis of accumulated evidence. If the evidence is not conclusive after a small sample is taken, more observations are made; if still inconclusive, a larger sample is drawn, and so on. The sequential sample allows trends in the data to be evaluated as the data are being collected, and this affords an opportunity to reduce costs when additional observations show diminishing usefulness.

---

[4] The National Council on Public Polls distinguishes probability, "scientific" polls from nonprobability "pseudo" polls wherein, e.g., respondents volunteer their opinions, e.g., via call-ins to 800 numbers (http://www.ncpp.org). Gallup Polls' experts concur, saying you can't have confidence in results without a random sample (http://www.gallup.com).

FIGURE 11.3
Classification of
Sampling Techniques

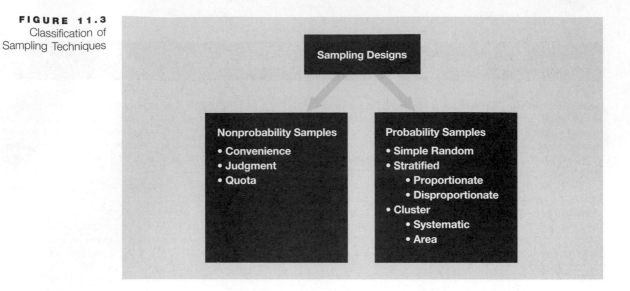

Both probability and nonprobability sampling plans can be further divided by type. Nonprobability samples, for instance, can be classified as convenience, judgment, or quota, whereas probability samples can be simple random, stratified, or cluster samples (see Figure 11.3).

Nonprobability Samples

Nonprobability samples should be used with caution for two reasons: (1) They involve personal judgment somewhere in the selection process. Sometimes this judgment is imposed by the researcher, and in other cases it is left to individual field workers. (2) Given that the sample is not probabilistic, "sampling error" cannot be assessed, which in turn means we cannot place bounds on the precision of our estimates.

Convenience Samples

Examples of convenience samples abound—we talk to a few friends, and, on the basis of their reactions, we infer the political sentiment of the country; a local radio station asks people to call in and express their reactions to some controversial issue, and the opinions expressed are interpreted as prevailing sentiment; we ask for volunteers and use those who come forward.

The problem with convenience samples, of course, is that we have no way of knowing if those included are representative of the target population. And although we might be hesitant to infer that the reactions of a few friends indicate prevailing political sentiment, there does seem to be some temptation to conclude that large samples, even though selected conveniently, are representative.

For example, it is not unusual for political parties or various rights groups to encourage their members to call in, frequently, to voice their opinions. Polls reported on the basis of volunteers calling one 900 phone number for "pro" and another number for "con" are another example of likely nonrepresentative samples. Who are the callers?

When a sample is not representative, increasing its size would not make it so. What is unfortunate is that many people believe the results of these polls are accurate.

An all-too-common use of convenience samples in international marketing research is to use transplanted ex-pats from the countries being studied who are currently residing in the country where the study is being conducted (e.g., Mainland Chinese currently residing in the United States). Even though such convenience samples can shed some light on certain country conditions, it must be recognized that these individuals typically represent the elite class, often already "westernized," and may not be in touch with current developments in their own country. Convenience samples are not recommended for descriptive or causal research. They may be used with exploratory designs in which the emphasis is on generating ideas and insights, but even here the judgment sample seems superior.

Ethical Dilemma 11.1

You are designing an experiment to compare the effectiveness of different types of commercials and need to recruit a large group of participants of varying ages to watch TV for an hour every night for a week. You approach your local church minister and tell her that you will make a donation to the church restoration fund for every member of the congregation who agrees to participate.

- When might incentives be coercive?
- Is it ethical to coerce people to participate in research?
- Will the quality of the data suffer from the coercive recruitment of participants?

Judgment Samples

Judgment samples are often called purposive samples; the sample elements are handpicked because it is expected that they can serve the research purpose. Typically, sample elements are selected because it is believed that they are representative of the population of interest. For example, this occurs every four years at presidential election time, when television viewers are treated to in-depth analyses of swing communities. These communities are handpicked because they are "representative" in that historically the winner there has been the next president. By monitoring these pivotal communities, election analysts are able to offer an early prediction of the eventual winner.

Purposive judgment samples may be useful in exploratory designs. When searching for ideas and insights, the researcher is not interested in sampling a cross section of opinion but rather in sampling those who can offer some perspective on the research question.

The **snowball sample** is a judgment sample that is sometimes used to sample special populations.[5] The researcher locates an initial set of respondents with the characteristics of the target population. These individuals then identify others with the desired characteristics. Thus, if one were doing a study among the deaf investigating the desirability of various product configurations that would allow deaf people to communicate over telephone lines, one might attempt to initially identify some key people in the deaf community and then ask them for names of others who might be used in the study. Those initially asked to participate are asked for names of others whose cooperation would be solicited, so the sample "snowballs" by getting larger as participants identify still other possible respondents.

---

[5] The technique was originally suggested by Leo A. Goodman, "Snowball Sampling," *Annals of Mathematical Statistics* 32 (1961), pp. 148–170. It's related to word-of-mouth, opinion leaders, network, and buzz marketing, cf., Edward B. Keller, Jonathan L. Berry and Douglas B. Reeves, *The Influentials: One American in Ten Tells the Other Nine How to Vote, Where to Eat, and What to Buy* (Simon & Schuster, 2004).

Judgment samples cannot be extrapolated as representative of the population. For example, most people believe the Consumer Price Index (CPI) reflects prices everywhere in the U.S. Actually, the CPI is called the Consumer Price Index for Urban Wage Earners and Clerical Workers, and it samples a little over 50 cities, selected on the bases of judgment and political pressure.

Quota Samples

A third type of nonprobability sample is the quota sample. Quota samples attempt to ensure that the sample is representative by selecting sample elements in such a way that the proportion possessing a certain characteristic is approximately the same as the proportion in the population. For example, consider an attempt to select a representative sample of a business school's students. If the eventual sample of 100 contained no marketing majors, one would have serious reservations about the representativeness of the sample and the generalizability of the conclusions beyond the immediate sample group. With a quota sample, the researcher could ensure that marketing majors would be included and in the same proportion as they occur in the entire business school.

Suppose that a researcher is interested in sampling the student body in such a way that the sample reflects the composition of the student body by major and gender. Suppose further that there are 1000 students in all and that 320 were finance majors, 260 marketing majors, 220 MIS majors, and 200 accounting majors, and further that 700 are men and 300 women. In a sample of 100, the quota sampling plan requires that 32 sample students be from finance, 26 from marketing, 22 from MIS, and 20 accountants, and further that 70 of the sampled students be male and 30 female. The researcher accomplishes this by giving each field worker a quota specifying the types of students to contact. Thus, one field worker assigned 20 interviews might be instructed to find and collect data from:

- 6 finance—5 male and 1 female
- 6 marketing—4 male and 2 female
- 4 MIS—3 male and 1 female
- 4 accounting—2 male and 2 female

Note that the specific sample elements to be used are not specified by the research plan but are left to the discretion of the individual field worker. The field worker's personal judgment governs the choice of specific students to be interviewed. The only requirement is that the interviewer diligently follow the established quota.

The quota for this field worker accurately reflects the gender composition of the student population, but it does not completely parallel the class composition; 70% (14 of 20) of the field worker's interviews are with men but only 30% (6 of 20) are with finance majors, whereas they represent 32% of the students. It is not necessary for the quotas *per field worker* to accurately mirror the distribution of the control characteristics in the population; as long as the total sample has the same proportions as the target population.

Note finally that quota samples still rely on personal, subjective judgment rather than objective procedures for the selection of sample elements. Here the personal judgment is that of the field worker rather than the designer of the research. Thus, quota samples reflect the target population proportions, but can they be considered "representative"? Consider three issues.

First, the sample could be far off with respect to some other important characteristic likely to influence the result. Thus, if the study is concerned with images of domestic brands, it may very well make a difference whether field workers interview U.S. or international students. Since a quota on country-of-origin was not specified, it is unlikely that the sample will accurately reflect this characteristic. The alternative, of course, is to specify quotas for all potentially important characteristics. The problem is that increasing the number of control characteristics makes specifications more complex and makes locating sample elements more difficult and more expensive. It is a more difficult task for a field worker to locate an upper-middle-class, Brazilian male marketing major than to locate a male student.

Second, it is difficult to verify whether a quota sample is indeed representative. Certainly one can check the distribution of characteristics in the sample not used as controls to ascertain whether the distribution parallels that of the target population. However, this type of comparison provides only negative evidence; i.e., it can indicate that the sample does not reflect the target population if the distributions on some characteristics are different, but if the sample and target population distributions are similar for each of these characteristics, it is still possible for the sample to be different from the target population on characteristics not explicitly compared.

Finally, interviewers left to their own devices are prone to follow certain practices. They tend to interview their friends in excessive proportion. Because their friends are often similar to themselves, this can introduce bias. Interviewers who fill their quotas by stopping passersby are likely to concentrate on areas where there are large numbers of potential respondents, such as business districts, airline terminals, and shopping malls. This practice tends to overrepresent the particular kinds of people that frequent these areas. When field workers concentrate their interviews at certain times of the day, working people are underrepresented, etc.

Depending on the study, all these tendencies have the potential for bias. They may or may not in fact actually bias the result, but it is difficult to correct them when analyzing the data. When the sample elements are selected objectively, on the other hand, researchers have certain tools they can rely on to make the question of whether a particular sample is representative less difficult. In these probability samples, one relies on the sampling procedure and not the composition of the specific sample to solve the problem of representation.

Probability Samples

One can calculate the likelihood that any given population element will be included in a probability sample because the final sample elements are selected objectively by a specific process, not according to the whims of the researcher or field worker. The objective selection of elements, in turn allows the objective assessment of the reliability of the sample results (something not possible with nonprobability samples regardless of the careful judgment exercised in selecting individuals).

Occasionally a nonprobability sample may indeed be representative, but what probability samples allow is an assessment of the amount of "sampling error" likely to occur. (In comparison, nonprobability samples allow the investigator no objective method for evaluating the adequacy of the sample.)

Simple Random Sampling

You are probably already familiar with simple random samples, because they are used in statistics courses. In a simple random sample, each population element has not only a *known* but an *equal* chance of being selected and every combination of n population elements is a sample possibility just as likely to occur as any other combination of n units.

PARENT POPULATION

To discuss probability sampling plans and sampling error, let's explore the notion of a sampling distribution.[6] Consider the hypothetical population of 20 individuals shown in Table 11.1. This population can be described by certain parameters. A **parameter** is a characteristic or measure of a parent or target population; it is a fixed quantity that distinguishes one population from another. We can calculate a number of parameters to describe this population (e.g., average income, dispersion in educational levels, proportion of the population subscribing to a newspaper, etc.). The quantities are fixed in value and would be known perfectly if we could conduct an entire census on the population. However, we usually select a sample and use its values to estimate population parameters.

TABLE 11.1
Hypothetical Population

#	Element	Income (Dollars)	Education (Years)	Newspaper Subscription
1	A	28,000	8	X
2	B	30,000	9	Y
3	C	32,000	11	X
4	D	34,000	11	Y
5	E	36,000	11	X
6	F	38,000	12	Y
7	G	40,000	12	X
8	H	42,000	12	Y
9	I	44,000	12	X
10	J	46,000	12	Y
11	K	48,000	13	X
12	L	50,000	13	Y
13	M	52,000	14	X
14	N	54,000	14	Y
15	O	56,000	15	X
16	P	58,000	16	Y
17	Q	60,000	16	X
18	R	62,000	17	Y
19	S	64,000	18	X
20	T	66,000	18	Y

[6] If you're not confident with statistics, refresh yourself with your intro stats text. If you are confident, skip ahead to "Stratified Samples." If you're not sure, read on!

Suppose we wanted to estimate the average income in this population. First, on this small database, let's figure out what the true parameters are. (We'll be estimating those parameters using samples shortly.) Let μ denote the mean population income (a measure of central tendency) and σ^2 the variance of incomes (a measure of spread), defined as:

$$\mu = \frac{\sum_{i=1}^{N} X_i}{N} = \frac{28,000 + 30,000 + \ldots + 66,000}{20} = 47,000$$

$$\sigma^2 = \frac{\sum_{i=1}^{N}\left(X_i - \mu\right)^2}{N} = \frac{\left(28,000 - 47,000\right)^2 + \left(30,000 - 47,000\right)^2 + \ldots + \left(66,000 - 47,000\right)^2}{20} = 133,000,000$$

where X_i is the value of the ith observation and N is the number of population elements. Thus, to compute the actual population mean, we divide the sum of all the values by the number of values making up the sum. To compute the population variance, we calculate the deviation of each value from the mean, square these deviations, sum them, and divide by the number of values making up the sum.

DERIVED POPULATION

It seems logical that our estimates of these population parameters would rest on similar calculations. A **statistic** is a characteristic or measure of a sample. We use the statistic to estimate the parameter (but different sampling plans yield different statistics that we need to adjust).

Consider the derived population of all possible unique samples that can be drawn from this parent population. Let's say we're interested in a sample of size n=2 (drawn by simple random sampling without replacement). Imagine the lottery machines that blow plastic balls around in a machine, and imagine that there are 20 balls, each with one of the incomes printed on it. Table 11.2 displays the derived population of all possible samples from following this procedure. There are 190 possible combinations of the 20 balls. For each combination, we can calculate the sample mean income. Thus, for the sample AB, the sample mean income $\bar{x}_1 = (28,000 + 30,000)/2 = 29,000$, and, in general,

$$\bar{x}_k = \frac{1}{n}\left(\sum_{i=1}^{n} X_i\right)$$

where k refers to the sample number, $\bar{x}$ to the sample average, and n to the sample size. Figure 11.4 (one page 333) displays the estimates of population mean income and the amount of error in each estimate when samples k = 25, 62, 108, 147, and 189 are drawn.

Note that in practice, we do not actually generate the derived population. All the practitioner does is draw one sample of size n. But the researcher makes use of the "derived population" concept in making inferences. (We shall see how shortly.) Also note that the derived population is defined as the population of all possible distinguishable samples that can be drawn under a given sampling plan. Change any part of the sampling plan and the derived population also changes. For example, if the researcher samples with replacement, the derived population will also include the

TABLE 11.2
Derived Population of
All Possible Samples
of Size n=2 with
Simple Random
Selection

k	Sample Identity	Mean	k	Sample Identity	Mean	k	Sample Identity	Mean	k	Sample Identity	Mean
1	AB	29,000	51	CQ	46,000	101	GI	42,000	151	KQ	54,000
2	AC	30,000	52	CR	47,000	102	GJ	43,000	152	KR	55,000
3	AD	31,000	53	CS	48,000	103	GK	44,000	153	KS	56,000
4	AE	32,000	54	CT	49,000	104	GL	45,000	154	KT	57,000
5	AF	33,000	55	DE	35,000	105	GM	46,000	155	LM	51,000
6	AG	34,000	56	DF	36,000	106	GN	47,000	156	LN	52,000
7	AH	35,000	57	DG	37,000	107	GO	48,000	157	LO	53,000
8	AI	36,000	58	DH	38,000	108	GP	49,000	158	LP	54,000
9	AJ	37,000	59	DI	39,000	109	GQ	50,000	159	LQ	55,000
10	AK	38,000	60	DJ	40,000	110	GR	51,000	160	LR	56,000
11	AL	39,000	61	DK	41,000	111	GS	52,000	161	LS	57,000
12	AM	40,000	62	DL	42,000	112	GT	53,000	162	LT	58,000
13	AN	41,000	63	DM	43,000	113	HI	43,000	163	MN	53,000
14	AO	42,000	64	DN	44,000	114	HJ	44,000	164	MO	54,000
15	AP	43,000	65	DO	45,000	115	HK	45,000	165	MP	55,000
16	AQ	44,000	66	DP	46,000	116	HL	46,000	166	MQ	56,000
17	AR	45,000	67	DQ	47,000	117	HM	47,000	167	MR	57,000
18	AS	46,000	68	DR	48,000	118	HN	48,000	168	MS	58,000
19	AT	47,000	69	DS	49,000	119	HO	49,000	169	MT	59,000
20	BC	31,000	70	DT	50,000	120	HP	50,000	170	NO	55,000
21	BD	32,000	71	EF	37,000	121	HQ	51,000	171	NP	56,000
22	BE	33,000	72	EG	38,000	122	HR	52,000	172	NQ	57,000
23	BF	34,000	73	EH	39,000	123	HS	53,000	173	NR	58,000
24	BG	35,000	74	EI	40,000	124	HT	54,000	174	NS	59,000
25	BH	36,000	75	EJ	41,000	125	IJ	45,000	175	NT	60,000
26	BI	37,000	76	EK	42,000	126	IK	46,000	176	OP	57,000
27	BJ	38,000	77	EL	43,000	127	IL	47,000	177	OQ	58,000
28	BK	39,000	78	EM	44,000	128	IM	48,000	178	OR	59,000
29	BL	40,000	79	EN	45,000	129	IN	49,000	179	OS	60,000
30	BM	41,000	80	EO	46,000	130	IO	50,000	180	OT	61,000
31	BN	42,000	81	EP	47,000	131	IP	51,000	181	PQ	59,000
32	BO	43,000	82	EQ	48,000	132	IQ	52,000	182	PR	60,000
33	BP	44,000	83	ER	49,000	133	IR	53,000	183	PS	61,000
34	BQ	45,000	84	ES	50,000	134	IS	54,000	184	PT	62,000
35	BR	46,000	85	ET	51,000	135	IT	55,000	185	QR	61,000
36	BS	47,000	86	FG	39,000	136	JK	47,000	186	QS	62,000
37	BT	48,000	87	FH	40,000	137	JL	48,000	187	QT	63,000
38	CD	33,000	88	FI	41,000	138	JM	49,000	188	RS	63,000
39	CE	34,000	89	FJ	42,000	139	JN	50,000	189	RT	64,000
40	CF	35,000	90	FK	43,000	140	JO	51,000	190	ST	65,000
41	CG	36,000	91	FL	44,000	141	JP	52,000			
42	CH	37,000	92	FM	45,000	142	JQ	53,000			
43	CI	38,000	93	FN	46,000	143	JR	10,800			
44	CJ	39,000	94	FO	47,000	144	JS	11,000			
45	CK	40,000	95	FP	48,000	145	JT	11,200			
46	CL	41,000	96	FQ	49,000	146	KL	9,800			
47	CM	42,000	97	FR	50,000	147	KM	10,000			
48	CN	43,000	98	FS	51,000	148	KN	10,200			
49	CO	44,000	99	FT	52,000	149	KO	10,400			
50	CP	45,000	100	GH	41,000	150	KP	10,600			

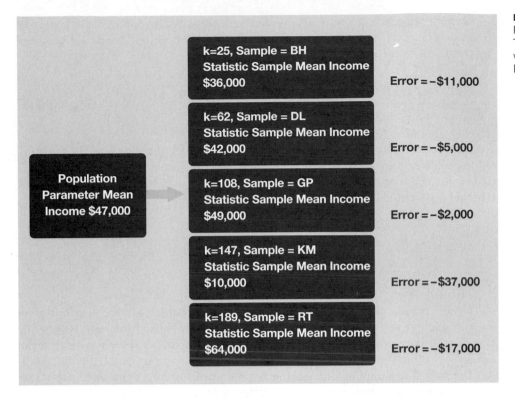

FIGURE 11.4
Possible Samples and Their Respective Errors when Estimating the Population Means

sample possibilities AA, BB, and so on. With samples of size 3 instead of 2, drawn without replacement, ABC is a sample possibility, and there are a number of additional possibilities as well—1,140 versus the 190 with samples of size 2. Finally, note that picking a sample of size n from a parent population is equivalent to picking a single element (one of the 190 possibilities) out of the derived population. We'll use this fact in making statistical inferences.

SAMPLE MEAN VERSUS POPULATION MEAN

Now consider the relationship between the sample means and the population mean. Note three things. First, if we add up all the sample means in Table 11.2 and divide by the number of samples—in other words, average the averages, this yields:

$$\frac{29,000 + 30,000 + \ldots + 65,000}{190} = 47,000$$

which is the mean of the population. This is what is meant by an unbiased statistic. A statistic is **unbiased** when its average value equals the population parameter it is supposed to estimate. The fact that it is unbiased says nothing about any particular value of the statistic. Even though the statistic overall is unbiased, a particular estimate may be far from the true population value—e.g., look at samples AB and ST. In some cases, no given sample equals the true population value, though in this example, some samples, such as AT yield a sample mean that equals the population average.

Second, consider the spread of these sample estimates and particularly the relationship between this spread of estimates and the dispersion of incomes in the population. We saw previously that the population variance $\sigma^2 = 133,000,000$. We can calculate the variance of mean incomes similarly—that is, by taking the deviation of each mean around its overall mean, squaring and summing these deviations, and then dividing by the number of cases:

$$\frac{(29,000-47,000)^2 +(30,000-47,000)^2 +\ldots+(65,000-47,000)^2}{190} = 63,000,000$$

Note the relationship between σ^2 (the variance or spread of the variable in the original population) and the spread of the estimates in the derived population (call it $\sigma_{\bar{x}}^2$ to denote the variance of means). Instead of direct calculations using the 190 sample estimates, $\sigma_{\bar{x}}^2$ could have also been calculated by the following expression:[7]

$$\sigma_{\bar{x}}^2 = \frac{(N-n)\sigma^2}{(N-1)n} = \frac{(20-2)133,000,000}{(20-1)2} = 63,000,000$$

Third, consider the distribution of the estimates in contrast to the distribution of the variable in the parent population. Figure 11.5 is the histogram representing the sampling distribution of the statistic. It is symmetrical about the population mean value of 47,000. The frequencies are those in Table 11.3.

The notion of **sampling distribution** is the single most important notion in statistics; it is the cornerstone of statistical inference procedures. If one knows the sampling distribution for the statistic in question, one is in a position to make an inference about the corresponding population parameter. If, on the other hand, one knows only that a particular sample estimate will vary with repeated sampling and

FIGURE 11.5
Distribution of Mean
Estimates in Derived
Population

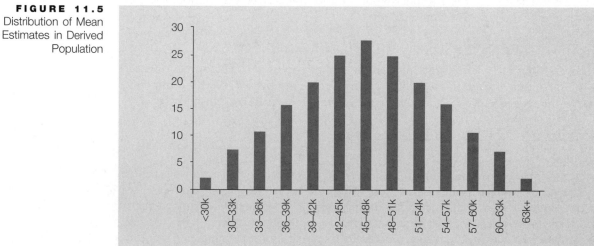

---

[7] The expression $(N-n)/(N-1)$ is known as the finite population correction factor. Whenever the sample size is less than 10% of the population size, the finite population correction factor is ignored, since $(N-n)/(N-1)$ is very close to 1 and the more complex form $\sigma_{\bar{x}}^2 = (\sigma^2/n)(N-n)/(N-1)$ reduces to $\sigma_{\bar{x}}^2 = \sigma^2/n$.

TABLE 11.3
Classification of
Estimates by Size

Sample Mean	#Samples
≤$30,000	2
$30,500–33,000	7
$33,500–36,000	11
$36,500–39,000	16
$39,500–42,000	20
$42,500–45,000	25
$45,500–48,000	28
$48,500–51,000	25
$51,500–54,000	20
$54,500–57,000	16
$57,500–60,000	11
$60,500–63,000	7
$63,500+	2

has no information about how it will vary, it will be impossible to devise a measure of the sampling error associated with that estimate. Because the sampling distribution of an estimate describes how that estimate will vary with repeated sampling, it provides a basis for determining the reliability of the sample estimate. This is why probability sampling plans are so important to statistical inference. With known probabilities of inclusion of any population element in the sample, statisticians are able to derive the sampling distribution of various statistics. Researchers then rely on these distributions—whether they are for a sample mean, sample proportion, sample variance, or some other statistic—in making their inferences from single samples to population values. Note that the distribution of sample means is mound shaped and symmetrical about the population mean with samples of size 2.

Recapitulating, we have shown that:

1. The mean of all possible sample means is equal to the population mean.
2. The variance of sample means is related to the population variance by the expression

$$\sigma_{\bar{x}}^2 = \frac{(N-n)\sigma^2}{(N-1)n}$$

3. The distribution of sample means is mound shaped, whereas the population distribution is spiked.

This first result is true in general for simple random sampling (with or without replacement, from a finite or infinite parent population). The second result is true only when sampling is from a finite population without replacement. If sampling from an infinite population or when sampling from a finite population with replacement, the simpler expression $\sigma_{\bar{x}}^2 = \sigma^2/n$ holds.

The simpler expression derives from the fact that when the size of the sample is small in comparison to the size of the population, the term $(N-n)/(N-1)$ is approximately equal to one and can be ignored. For many, if not most, problems in marketing, the simpler expression $\sigma_{\bar{x}}^2 = \sigma/n$ is used to relate the variance of sample means to the variance of the variable.

CENTRAL-LIMIT THEOREM

The third result of a mound-shaped distribution of estimates provides preliminary evidence of the operation of the Central-Limit Theorem. The Central-Limit Theorem holds that if simple random samples of size n are drawn from a parent population with mean μ and variance σ^2, then when n is large, the sample mean will be approximately normally distributed with mean equal to μ and variance equal to $\sigma_{\bar{x}}^2 = \sigma^2/n$. The approximation becomes more accurate as n becomes larger. This result is important—it means that regardless of the shape of the parent population, the distribution of sample means will be normal if the sample is large enough. How large is large enough? If the distribution of the variable in the parent population is normal, the means of samples of size n=1 will be normally distributed. If the distribution of the variable is symmetrical but not normal, samples of very small size will produce a distribution in which the means are normally distributed. If the distribution of the variable is highly skewed in the parent population, samples of a larger size will be needed.

The distribution of the sample mean statistic can be assumed to be normal only if we work with a sample of sufficient size. We do not need to rely on the assumption that the variable is normally distributed in the parent population to make inferences using the normal curve. Rather, we rely on the Central-Limit Theorem and adjust the sample size according to the population distribution so that the normal curve will hold. Fortunately, the normal distribution of the statistic occurs with samples of relatively small size, as Figure 11.6 indicates.

FIGURE 11.6
Distribution of Sample Means for Different Sample Sizes, Population Shapes

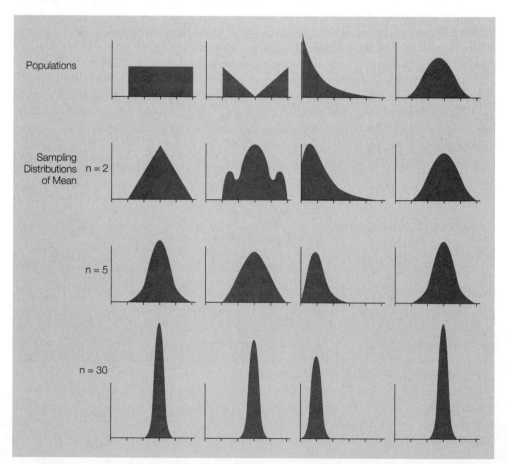

CONFIDENCE INTERVAL ESTIMATES

How does all this information help us make inferences about the parent population mean? After all, in practice we do not draw all possible samples of a given size but only one, and we use the results to infer something about the target group. It all ties together in the following way:

It is known that with any normal distribution, a specific percentage of all observations is within a certain number of standard deviations of the mean, for example, 95% of the values are within ±1.96 standard deviations of the mean. The distribution of sample means is normal if the Central-Limit Theorem holds. The mean of this sampling distribution is the population mean μ, and its standard deviation is given by the standard error of the mean, $\sigma_{\bar{x}}^2 = \sigma^2/n$. Therefore, it is true that

- 68.26% of the sample means will be within $\pm 1\sigma_{\bar{x}}$ of the population mean,

- 95.45% of the sample means will be within $\pm 2\sigma_{\bar{x}}$ of the population mean, and

- 99.73% of the sample means will be within $\pm 3\sigma_{\bar{x}}$ of the population mean,

and, in general, $\mu \pm z\sigma_{\bar{x}}$ will contain some certain proportion of all sample means, depending on the selected value of z. This expression can be rewritten as an inequality relation:

$$\mu - z\sigma_{\bar{x}} \leq \bar{x} \leq \mu + z\sigma_{\bar{x}} \tag{1}$$

which is held to be true a certain percentage of the time and which implies that the sample mean will be in the interval formed by adding and subtracting a certain number of standard deviations to the mean value of the distribution. This inequality can be transferred to the equivalent inequality,

$$\bar{x} - z\sigma_{\bar{x}} \leq \mu \leq \bar{x} + z\sigma_{\bar{x}} \tag{2}$$

If equation 1 is true, say, 95% of the time (z = 1.96), equation 2 is also true 95% of the time. When we make an inference on the basis of a single sample mean, we make use of equation 2.

It is important to note that equation 2 says nothing about the interval constructed from a particular sample as including the population mean. Rather, the interval addresses the sampling procedure. The interval around a single sample mean may or may not contain the true population mean. Our confidence in our inference rests on the property that 95% of all the intervals we could construct under that sampling plan would contain the true value. We trust or hope (or are "95% confident") that our sample is one of those 95 out of 100 that includes the true value (when z = 1.96).[8]

---

[8] This interpretation of a confidence interval is the traditional or classical statistics argument, which holds that the parameter is fixed in value. Thus, it is meaningless to interpret the statement probabilistically (i.e., "there is a 95% chance that the population mean is in our confidence interval"—wrong!), because a given interval *will* or *will not* contain the population parameter. Bayesian analysts adopt a different perspective. They hold that it is legitimate to assign personal probabilities to the values of the unknown parameter. One then combines these judgments with sample information to produce posterior probabilities regarding the value of the unknown parameter. The confidence interval formed for a population mean is the same under the two approaches if one adopts the Bayesian assumption that the initial probabilities for each of the possible values of the unknown parameter are equal. The difference in perspectives, though, allows Bayesian analysts to interpret the resulting interval as a probability statement; that is, there is a 95% probability that the confidence interval contains the true population mean.

To illustrate this point, suppose the distribution of sample means of size $n=2$ was normal. Suppose further that by chance the sampling process yielded sample AB, in which the mean income was \$29,000. The 95% confidence interval ($z = 1.96$) using equation 2 would then be $\left(\sigma_{\bar{x}} = \sqrt{\sigma_{\bar{x}}^2} = \sqrt{63{,}000{,}000} \right) = 7937.25$:

$$29{,}000 - 1.96(7937.25) \le \mu \le 29{,}000 + 1.96(7937.25) = 13{,}443 \le \mu \le 44{,}557$$

The confidence interval does not include the true (in this case, known) population value, and an inferential error would have been made. The example illustrates that after the sample has been drawn, it is a matter of fact whether the particular interval estimate covers the universe mean. Table 11.4 illustrates the outcome pictorially for the first 10 of the 190 samples. Note that only 7 of the 10 intervals contain the true population mean. Confidence in the estimate arises because of the procedure, not because of a particular estimate. The procedure is one that with, say, a 95% confidence interval, if 100 samples were to be drawn, 95 of the confidence intervals would include the true population value. The accuracy of a specific sample is evaluated only by reference to the procedure by which the sample was obtained. A sampling plan that is representative does not guarantee that a particular sample is representative. Statistical inference procedures rest on the representativeness of the sampling plan, and this is why probability samples are so critical to those procedures. Probability samples allow an estimate of the *precision* of the results in terms of how closely the estimates will tend to cluster around the true value. The greater the standard error of the statistic, the more variable, or less precise, the estimate.

If it disturbs you that the confidence level applies to the procedure and not to a particular sample result, you can take refuge in the fact that you can control the level of confidence with which the population value is estimated. Thus, if you do not wish to take the risk that you might have 1 of the 5 sample intervals in 100 that does not contain the population value, you might use a 99% confidence interval, in which the risk is that only 1 in 100 sample intervals does not contain the population mean. Further, if you are willing to increase the size of the sample, you can increase your confidence and at the same time increase the precision of the population value estimate (a topic explored in the next chapter).

POPULATION VARIANCE UNKNOWN

There is one further complication. The confidence interval estimate made use of three values: μ, z, and $\sigma_{\bar{x}}$. The mean $\bar{x}$ is computed from the sample, and z is specified

TABLE 11.4
Confidence Intervals for First 10 Samples, Assuming the Distribution of Sample Means Was Normal

Sample #	Identity	Mean	Lower Limit	Upper Limit	Confidence Interval True μ = 47,000
1	AB	29,000	13,445	44,555	(__x__) ↓
2	AC	30,000	14,445	45,555	(__x__)
3	AD	31,000	15,445	46,555	(__x__)
4	AE	32,000	16,445	47,555	(__x__)
5	AF	33,000	17,445	48,555	(__x__)
6	AG	34,000	18,445	49,555	(__x__)
7	AH	35,000	19,445	50,555	(__x__)
8	AI	36,000	20,445	51,555	(__x__)
9	AJ	37,000	21,445	52,555	(__x__)
10	AK	38,000	22,445	53,555	(__x__)

to produce the desired level of confidence. But what about $\sigma_{\bar{x}}$? It is equal to $\sigma_{\bar{x}} = \sigma^2/\sqrt{n}$ and thus to calculate it, we need to know the standard deviation of the variable in the population. What do we do if σ is unknown? No problem. We can either use the value from a previous related marketing study, or, once the sample is selected and the information gathered, we can calculate the sample variance to estimate the population variance. The unbiased sample variance $\hat{\sigma}^2 = s^2$ is calculated as

$$ s^2 = \frac{1}{n} \sum_{i=1}^{n} \left(X_i - \bar{x} \right)^2 $$

where $\bar{x}$ is the sample mean and n the sample size.[9] To compute the sample variance, then, we first calculate the sample mean. We then calculate the differences between each of our sample values and the sample mean, square them, sum them, and divide the sum by the number of sample observations minus one. The sample variance not only provides an estimate of the population variance, but it can also be used to get the estimate of the standard error of the mean. When the population variance, σ^2, is known, the standard error of the mean, $\sigma_{\bar{x}}$, is also known because $\sigma_{\bar{x}} = \sigma/\sqrt{n}$. When the population variance is unknown, the standard error of the mean can only be estimated. The estimate is given by $s_{\bar{x}}$, which equals $s/\sqrt{n}$, i.e., the sample standard deviation is substituted for the population standard deviation. Thus, if we draw sample AB, with its mean of 29,000,

> **The equation for a standard error may some day save your life:**
> $\sigma_{\bar{x}} = \sigma/\sqrt{n}$

$$ s^2 = \frac{\left(28,000 - 29,000 \right)^2 + \left(30,000 - 29,000 \right)^2}{1} = 2,000,000 $$

thus $s = 1414$ and $s_{\bar{x}} = s/\sqrt{n} = 1414/\sqrt{2} = 1000$ and the 95% confidence interval is now

$$ 29,000 - 1.96(1000) \leq \mu \leq 29,000 - 1.96(1000) - 27,040 \leq \mu < 30,960 $$

which is somewhat smaller than before.[10]

DRAWING THE SIMPLE RANDOM SAMPLE

The state of the art means of drawing a simple random sample is through the use of a table (hardcopy or in computer procedures) of random numbers.[11] Using a random number table involves the following sequence of steps. First, the elements of the parent population are numbered serially from 1 to N; for the hypothetical population,

---

[9] Division by n, the sample size, is more intuitive because it produces the normal conception of average, here, the average of the deviations squared. However, the sample variance, when defined as $s^2 = \frac{1}{n} \sum_{i=1}^{n} \left(X_i - \bar{x} \right)^2$ produces a biased estimate of the population variance. Thus it is customary to use the unbiased definition of the sample variance to generate an estimate of σ^2.

[10] Strictly speaking the t-distribution would be used when σ was unknown. We say more about this in the chapter on hypothesis testing.

[11] The national draft during the Vietnam War using a lottery serves as an example of why tables or computers are better random number generators than "mechanical" devices like the aforementioned lottery ball machines. For that war, draft priorities were determined by drawing disks with birth dates stamped on them from a large container in full view of a TV audience. Unfortunately, the dates of the year had been poured into the bowl systematically, January first and December last. The bowl was then stirred vigorously, but still, December dates tended to be chosen first and January dates last. The procedure was later revised to produce a more random selection process.

the element A numbered as 1, B as 2, and so on. Next, the numbers in the table are treated to have the same number of digits as N. With N = 20, two-digit numbers are used; if N is between 100 and 999, three-digit numbers are required, and so on. Third, a starting point is determined randomly.[12] We might simply open the table to some arbitrary place and point to a position on the page with our eyes closed. Since the numbers in a random number table are in fact random (i.e., without order), it makes little difference where we begin.[13] Finally, we proceed in some arbitrary direction (e.g., up, down, or across) and select those elements for the sample for which there is a match of serial number and random number.

To illustrate, consider the partial list of random numbers contained in Table 11.5. Since N = 20, we need work with only two digits, and therefore we can use the entries in the table as is, instead of having to combine columns to produce numbers covering the range of serial numbers. Suppose that we had previously decided to read down and that our arbitrary start was in the 11th row, 4th column, specifically the number 77. This number is too high and would be discarded (our population elements are numbered only 1 to 20). The next two numbers would also be discarded, but the fourth entry, 02, would be used, because 2 corresponds to one of the serial numbers in the list, element B. The next five numbers would also be passed over as too large, but the number 05 would designate the inclusion of element E. Elements B and E would thus represent our sample of two.

An alternative strategy is to use a computer program to generate the random numbers. These algorithms are generally called "pseudo" random number generators—after all, if a computer subroutine is generating the numbers, they are programmed, not random. But they're programmed to be as independent as possible (e.g., knowing a string of numbers does not help you predict subsequent numbers), hence appearing as random as possible.[14]

On a final note, a simple random sample requires a numbered list of population elements, which means that the identity of each member of the target population must be known. For some populations this is no problem; e.g., if the study is to be conducted among *Fortune* magazine's list of the 500 largest corporations in the U.S., the list is readily available, and a simple random sample of these firms could be selected easily. For many other target populations, the list is harder to come by (e.g., all families living in a particular city), and applied researchers often resort to other sampling schemes.

Main types of *probability sampling:*

1. **Simple probability sampling**
2. **Stratified sampling**
3. **Cluster sampling**

Stratified Sampling

A stratified sample is a probability sample that is distinguished by the following two steps:

1. The population is divided into *mutually exclusive and exhaustive* subsets.
2. A simple random sample of elements is chosen independently *from each* subset.

It is up to the marketer to choose the criterion or criteria used to create the groups. The subsets are called *strata* or subpopulations. Every population element is assigned to one and only one stratum and no population elements are omitted. To

---

[12] Computer random number generators usually use the time of day (in hours, minutes, seconds, milliseconds) as the input seed, i.e., the starting point.

[13] Note that one cannot discard a sample because it does not "look right."

[14] For example, see D. Neuenschwander and H. Zeuner, "Generating Random Numbers of Prescribed Distribution Using Physical Sources," *Statistics and Computing* 13 (2003), pp. 5–11.

TABLE 11.5
Abridged List of
Random Numbers

10 09 73 25 33	76 52 01 35 86	34 67 35 48 76	80 95 90 91 17	39 29 27 49 45
37 54 20 48 05	64 89 47 42 96	24 80 52 40 37	20 63 61 04 02	00 82 29 16 65
08 42 26 89 53	19 64 50 93 03	23 20 90 25 60	15 95 33 47 64	35 08 03 36 06
99 01 90 25 29	09 37 67 07 15	38 31 13 11 65	88 67 67 43 97	04 43 62 76 59
12 80 79 99 70	80 15 73 61 47	64 03 23 66 53	98 95 11 68 77	12 17 17 68 33
66 06 57 47 17	34 07 27 68 50	36 69 73 61 70	65 81 33 98 85	11 19 92 91 70
31 06 01 08 05	45 57 18 24 06	35 30 34 26 14	86 79 90 74 39	23 40 30 97 32
85 26 97 76 02	02 05 16 56 92	68 66 57 48 18	73 05 38 52 47	18 62 38 85 79
63 57 33 21 35	05 32 54 70 48	90 55 35 75 48	28 46 82 87 09	83 49 12 56 24
73 79 64 57 53	03 52 96 47 78	35 80 83 42 82	60 93 52 03 44	35 27 38 84 35
98 52 01 77 67	14 90 56 86 07	22 10 94 05 58	60 97 09 34 33	50 50 07 39 98
11 80 50 54 31	39 80 82 77 32	50 72 56 82 48	29 40 52 42 01	52 77 56 78 51
83 45 29 96 34	06 28 89 80 83	13 74 67 00 78	18 47 54 06 10	68 71 17 78 17
88 68 54 02 00	86 50 75 84 01	36 76 66 79 51	90 36 47 64 93	29 60 91 10 62
99 59 46 73 48	87 51 76 49 69	91 82 60 89 28	93 78 56 13 68	23 47 83 41 13
65 48 11 76 74	17 46 85 90 50	58 04 77 69 74	73 03 95 71 86	40 21 81 65 44
80 12 43 56 35	17 72 70 80 15	45 31 82 23 74	21 11 57 82 53	14 38 55 37 63
74 35 09 98 17	77 40 27 72 14	43 23 60 02 10	45 52 16 42 37	96 28 60 26 55
69 91 62 68 03	66 25 22 91 48	36 93 68 72 03	76 62 11 39 90	94 40 05 64 18
09 89 32 05 05	14 22 56 85 14	46 42 75 67 88	96 29 77 88 22	54 38 21 45 98
91 49 91 45 23	68 47 92 76 86	46 16 28 35 54	94 75 08 99 23	37 08 92 00 48
80 33 69 45 98	26 94 03 68 58	70 29 73 41 35	53 14 03 33 40	42 05 08 23 41
44 10 48 19 49	85 15 74 79 54	32 97 92 65 75	57 60 04 08 81	22 22 20 64 13
12 55 07 37 42	11 10 00 20 40	12 86 07 46 97	96 64 48 94 39	28 70 72 58 15
63 60 64 93 29	16 50 53 44 84	40 21 95 25 63	43 65 17 70 82	07 20 73 17 90
61 19 69 04 46	26 45 74 77 74	51 92 43 37 29	65 39 45 95 93	42 58 26 05 27
15 47 44 52 66	95 27 07 99 53	59 36 78 38 48	82 39 61 01 18	33 21 15 94 66
94 55 72 85 72	67 89 75 43 87	54 62 24 44 31	91 19 04 25 92	92 92 74 59 73
42 48 11 62 13	97 34 40 81 21	16 86 84 87 67	03 07 11 20 59	25 70 14 66 70
23 52 37 83 17	73 20 88 98 37	68 93 59 14 16	26 25 22 96 63	05 52 28 25 62
04 49 35 24 94	75 24 63 38 24	45 86 25 10 25	61 96 27 93 35	65 33 71 24 72
00 54 99 76 54	64 05 18 81 59	96 11 96 38 96	54 69 28 23 91	23 28 72 95 29
35 96 31 53 07	26 89 80 93 54	33 35 13 54 62	77 97 45 00 24	90 10 33 93 33
59 80 80 83 91	45 42 72 68 42	83 60 94 97 00	13 02 12 48 92	78 56 52 01 06
46 06 88 52 36	01 39 09 22 86	77 28 14 40 77	93 91 08 36 47	70 61 74 29 41
32 17 90 05 97	87 37 92 52 41	05 56 70 70 07	86 74 31 71 57	85 39 41 18 38
69 43 26 14 06	20 11 74 52 04	15 95 66 00 00	18 74 39 24 23	97 11 89 63 38
19 56 54 14 30	01 75 87 53 79	40 41 92 15 85	66 67 43 68 06	84 96 28 52 07
45 15 51 49 38	19 47 60 72 46	43 66 79 45 43	59 04 79 00 33	20 82 66 95 41
94 86 43 19 94	36 16 81 08 51	34 88 88 15 51	01 54 03 54 56	05 01 45 11 76
98 08 62 48 26	45 24 02 84 04	44 99 90 88 96	39 09 47 34 07	35 44 13 18 80
33 18 51 62 32	41 94 15 09 49	89 43 54 85 81	88 69 54 19 94	37 54 87 30 43
80 95 10 04 06	96 38 27 07 74	20 15 12 33 87	25 01 62 52 98	94 62 46 11 71
79 75 24 91 40	71 96 12 82 96	69 86 10 25 91	74 85 22 05 39	00 38 75 95 79
18 63 33 25 37	98 14 50 65 71	31 01 02 46 74	05 45 56 14 27	77 93 89 19 36
74 02 94 39 02	77 55 73 22 70	97 79 01 71 19	52 52 75 80 21	80 81 45 17 48
54 17 84 56 11	80 99 33 71 43	05 33 51 29 69	56 12 71 92 55	36 04 09 03 24
11 66 44 98 83	52 07 98 48 27	59 38 17 15 39	09 97 33 34 40	88 46 12 33 56
48 32 47 79 28	31 24 96 47 10	02 29 53 68 70	32 30 75 75 46	15 02 00 99 94
69 07 49 41 38	87 63 79 19 76	35 58 40 44 01	10 51 82 16 15	01 84 87 69 38

Source: This table is from The Rand Corporation, *A Million Random Digits with 100,000 Normal Deviates*
(http://www.rand.org). Copyright © 2002 by The Rand Corporation. Used by permission.

TABLE 11.6
Stratification of
Hypothetical
Population of
Education

Stratum I Elements	Stratum II Elements
A	K
B	L
C	M
D	N
E	O
F	P
G	Q
H	R
I	S
J	T

illustrate, assume we divide our hypothetical population in Table 11.1 into two strata on the basis of educational level. Say all those with a high school education or less are considered as one stratum and those with more education form another. Table 11.6 displays the results of this stratification procedure; elements A through J form what is labeled the first stratum and elements K through T form the second stratum. There is no magic in the choice of two strata. The parent population can be divided into any number of strata. Two were chosen for purposes of convenience in illustrating the technique.

Stage 2 in the process then requires that a simple random sample be drawn independently from each stratum. Suppose that we again work with samples of size 2, formed this time by selecting one element from each stratum. (The number of elements from each stratum does not have to be equal, but again the assumption is made simply for exposition purposes.) The procedure used to select two elements for the stratified sample now parallels that for the simple random sample. Within each stratum, the population elements are serially numbered from 1 to 10. A table of random numbers is consulted. The first number encountered between 1 and 10 designates the element from the first stratum. The element from the second stratum can be selected after another independent start or by continuing from the first randomly determined start. In either case it would again be designated by the first encounter with a number between 1 and 10.

DERIVED POPULATION

Although only one sample of size 2 is selected, let us look at this derived population of all possible samples of size 2 for this sampling plan (see Table 11.7). Note that every possible combination of sample elements is no longer a possibility, since every combination of two elements from the same stratum is precluded. There are now only 100 possible sample combinations of elements, whereas with simple random sampling there were 190 possible combinations. Note that once again every element has an equal chance of being included in the sample—1 in 10—because each can be the single element selected from the stratum (per the requirement in step 2 to obtain a simple random sample).

SAMPLING DISTRIBUTION

Table 11.8 contains the classification of sample means by size, and Figure 11.7 displays the plot of this sample statistic. Note that in relation to Figure 11.5 (for simple

TABLE 11.7
Derived Population of
All Possible Samples of
Size n=2 with Stratified
Selection

k	Sample Identity	Mean	k	Sample Identity	Mean	k	Sample Identity	Mean	k	Sample Identity	Mean
1	AK	38,000	26	CP	45,000	51	FK	43,000	76	HP	50,000
2	AL	39,000	27	CQ	46,000	52	FL	44,000	77	HQ	51,000
3	AM	40,000	28	CR	47,000	53	FM	45,000	78	HR	52,000
4	AN	41,000	29	CS	48,000	54	FN	46,000	79	HS	53,000
5	AO	42,000	30	CT	49,000	55	FO	47,000	80	HT	54,000
6	AP	43,000	31	DK	41,000	56	FP	48,000	81	IK	46,000
7	AQ	44,000	32	DL	42,000	57	FQ	49,000	82	IL	47,000
8	AR	45,000	33	DM	43,000	58	FR	50,000	83	IM	48,000
9	AS	46,000	34	DN	44,000	59	FS	51,000	84	IN	49,000
10	AT	47,000	35	DO	45,000	60	FT	52,000	85	IO	50,000
11	BK	39,000	36	DP	46,000	61	GK	44,000	86	IP	51,000
12	BL	40,000	37	DQ	47,000	62	GL	45,000	87	IQ	52,000
13	BM	41,000	38	DR	48,000	63	GM	46,000	88	IR	53,000
14	BN	42,000	39	DS	49,000	64	GN	47,000	89	IS	54,000
15	BO	43,000	40	DT	50,000	65	GO	48,000	90	IT	55,000
16	BP	44,000	41	EK	42,000	66	GP	49,000	91	JK	47,000
17	BQ	45,000	42	EL	43,000	67	GQ	50,000	92	JL	48,000
18	BR	46,000	43	EM	44,000	68	GR	51,000	93	JM	49,000
19	BS	47,000	44	EN	45,000	69	GS	52,000	94	JN	50,000
20	BT	48,000	45	EO	46,000	70	GT	53,000	95	JO	51,000
21	CK	40,000	46	EP	47,000	71	HK	45,000	96	JP	52,000
22	CL	41,000	47	EQ	48,000	72	HL	46,000	97	JQ	53,000
23	CM	42,000	48	ER	49,000	73	HM	47,000	98	JR	54,000
24	CN	43,000	49	ES	50,000	74	HN	48,000	99	JS	55,000
25	CO	44,000	50	ET	52,000	75	HO	49,000	100	JT	56,000

random sampling), stratified sampling can produce a more concentrated distribution of estimates. This suggests one reason that we might choose a stratified sample: Stratified samples can produce sample statistics that are more precise (i.e., have smaller error as a result of sampling) than simple random samples. With the stratification variable, there is a reduction in the number of sample means that deviate widely from the population mean.

A second reason for drawing a stratified sample is that stratification allows the investigation of the characteristic of interest for particular subgroups. For example, by stratifying, we can guarantee representation in our sample of both those with a

TABLE 11.8
Classification of Sample
Means by Size with
Stratified Sampling

Sample Mean	#Samples
36,500–39,000	3
39,500–42,000	12
42,500–45,000	21
45,500–48,000	28
48,500–51,000	21
51,500–54,000	12
54,500–57,000	3

FIGURE 11.7
Distribution of Sample
Means with Stratified
Sampling

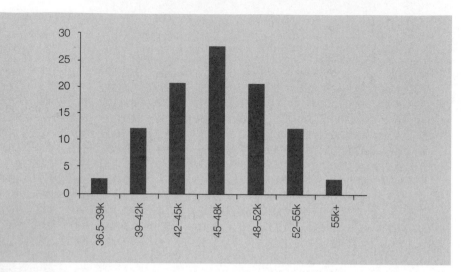

high school education or less and those with more education. This quality can be extremely important when sampling from populations with rare segments. For example, the upper class represents only 3% of the total population, yet it might be an important segment to, say, a diamond ring manufacturer. It is often true of many populations in marketing that a small subset accounts for a large proportion of the behavior of interest, e.g., consumption of the product (the so-called 80-20 rule, which is usually even more exaggerated, e.g., 10% of the population accounting for 90% of the purchases). It becomes imperative that the small but important subgroup be adequately represented in the sample. Stratified sampling is one way of ensuring adequate representation from each subgroup of interest.

CONFIDENCE INTERVAL ESTIMATE

In establishing a confidence interval with a simple random sample, we saw that we needed three things to complete the confidence interval specifications given by $\bar{x} - zs_{\bar{x}} \le \mu \le \bar{x} + zs_{\bar{x}}$:

1. The degree of confidence desired so that a z value can be selected
2. A point estimate of the population mean given by the sample mean $\bar{x}$
3. An estimate of the amount of sampling error associated with the sample mean, which was given by $s_{\bar{x}} = s/\sqrt{n}$ when the population variance was unknown

The same three quantities are required for making inferences with a stratified sample. The only difference in the procedure occurs in the way items 2 and 3 are generated. With stratified sampling, the sample estimate of the population mean and the standard error of estimate are determined by "appropriately weighting" the individual strata results.

What are the appropriate weights? They are related to the stratum population size relative to the total population size. Say two elements were sampled from each stratum, for a total sample of 4. In particular, suppose that B and E were randomly selected from the first stratum, and N and S from the second. Table 11.9 contains the sample means, sample variances, and estimated standard errors of estimate for each stratum, calculated exactly as before.

TABLE 11.9
Sample Means,
Sample Variances,
and Estimated
Standard Errors of
Estimates for Each
Stratum

Stratum I

Element	Income
B	30,000
E	36,000

Mean:

$$\bar{x}_1 = \frac{1}{n_1}\sum_{i=1}^{n_1} X_i = \frac{30{,}000 + 36{,}000}{2} = 33{,}000$$

Variance:

$$s_1^2 = \frac{1}{n_1 - 1}\sum_{i=1}^{n_1}\left(X_i - \bar{x}_1\right)^2$$

$$= \frac{\left(30{,}000 - 33{,}000\right) + \left(36{,}000 - 33{,}000\right)^2}{2-1}$$

$$= 18{,}000{,}000$$

Standard error of estimate:

$$s_{\bar{x}_1} = \frac{s_1}{\sqrt{n_1}} = \frac{\sqrt{18{,}000{,}000}}{\sqrt{2}} = 3000$$

Variance of estimate:

$$s_{\bar{x}_1}^2 = 9{,}000{,}000$$

Stratum II

Element	Income
N	54,000
S	64,000

Mean:

$$\bar{x}_2 = \frac{1}{n_2}\sum_{i=1}^{n_2} X_i = \frac{54{,}000 + 64{,}000}{2} = 59{,}000$$

Variance:

$$s_2^2 = \frac{1}{n_2 - 1}\sum_{i=1}^{n_2}\left(X_i - \bar{x}_2\right)^2$$

$$= \frac{\left(54{,}000 - 59{,}000\right) + \left(64{,}000 - 59{,}000\right)^2}{2-1}$$

$$= 50{,}000{,}000$$

Standard error of estimate:

$$s_{\bar{x}_2} = \frac{s_2}{\sqrt{n_2}} = \frac{\sqrt{50{,}000{,}000}}{\sqrt{2}} = 5000$$

Variance of estimate:

$$s_{\bar{x}_2}^2 = 25{,}000{,}000$$

We first combine the strata sample means to produce an estimate of the population mean. The weights here are the relative proportions of the population in each of the strata, that is,

$$\bar{x}_{st} = \sum_{h=1}^{L} \frac{N_h}{N}\bar{x}_h \tag{3}$$

where

N_h is the number of elements in the population in stratum h,

N is the total size of the population,

$\bar{x}_h$ is the sample mean for stratum h,

$\bar{x}_{st}$ is the sample mean for a stratified sample,

summed across all L strata. In the Table 11.9 example, $L = 2$; there are 10 elements in each stratum, 20 in all; and the overall point estimate of the population mean is

$$\bar{x}_{st} = \frac{N_1}{N}\bar{x}_1 + \frac{N_2}{N}\bar{x}_2 = \frac{10}{20}(33{,}000) + \frac{10}{20}(59{,}000) = 46{,}000$$

The relative sizes of the strata also factor into the standard error. The formula for the variance of the estimate is

$$s_{\bar{x}_{st}}^2 = \sum_{h=1}^{L}\left(\frac{N_h}{N}\right)^2 s_{\bar{x}_h}^2 \tag{4}$$

For the example

$$s_{\bar{x}_{st}}^2 = \left(\frac{N_1}{N}\right)^2 s_{\bar{x}_1}^2 + \left(\frac{N_2}{N}\right)^2 s_{\bar{x}_2}^2 = \left(\frac{10}{20}\right)^2 (9,000,000) + \left(\frac{10}{20}\right)^2 (25,000,000)$$

$$= 2,250,000 + 6,250,000 = 8,500,000$$

so that the standard error is:

$$s_{\bar{x}_{st}} = \sqrt{8,500,000} = 2915.5$$

The 95% confidence interval for this sample would then be

$$\bar{x}_{st} - zs_{\bar{x}_{st}} \leq \mu \leq \bar{x}_{st} + zs_{st}$$

$$46,000 - 1.96(2915.5) \leq \mu \leq 46,000 + 1.96(2915.5)$$

$$40,285 \leq \mu \leq 51,714$$

This interval is interpreted as before. The true mean may or may not be in the interval, but since 95 of 100 intervals constructed by this process contain the true mean, we are 95% confident that the true population mean income is between $40,285 and $51,714.

INCREASED PRECISION OF STRATIFIED SAMPLES

We had mentioned that one reason to choose a stratified sample is that it reduces sampling error, or increases precision. When estimating a mean, sampling error is given by the size of $s_{\bar{x}}$; the smaller $s_{\bar{x}}$, the less the sampling error, the more precise the estimate, as indicated by the narrower confidence interval.

Consider equation 4 again. N and N_h are fixed. The only way for total sampling error to be reduced is for the variance of the estimate within each stratum to be made smaller. The variance of the estimate by strata, in turn, depends on the variability of the characteristic within the strata, because $s_{\bar{x}_h}^2 = s_h^2 / n_h$, where s_h^2 is the sample variance within the hth stratum and n_h is the size of the sample selected from the hth stratum. Thus, the estimate of the mean can be made more precise to the extent that the population can be partitioned so that there is little variability within each stratum, i.e., to the extent the strata can be made internally homogeneous.

The investigator can do nothing about the variation *per se* because it is a fixed characteristic of the population. But the investigator can divide the population into strata so that the elements within each stratum are as similar in value as possible, and the values between any two strata are as disparate as possible. In the limit, if the investigator is successful in partitioning the population so that the elements in each stratum are exactly equal, there will be no error associated with the estimate of the population mean. Woohoo! The population mean can then be estimated without error because the between-strata variability does not enter into the calculation of the standard error of estimate.

Take a simple case. Suppose a population of 1,000 elements, 200 had the value 5, 300 had the value 10, and 500 had the value 20. The mean of this population $\mu = 14$ and the variance $\sigma^2 = 39$. If a simple random sample of size n = 3 were to be employed to estimate this mean, then the standard error of estimate would be

$$\sigma_{\bar{x}} \frac{\sigma}{\sqrt{n}} = \frac{\sqrt{39}}{\sqrt{3}} = 3.61$$

and the width of confidence interval would be ±z times this value 3.61. Suppose, on the other hand, that a researcher employed a stratified sample and was successful in partitioning the total population so that all the elements with a value of 5 on the characteristic were in one stratum, those with the value of 10 were in the second stratum, and those with the value 20 were in the third stratum. To generate a completely precise description of the mean of each stratum, the researcher would then need to take a sample of only one from each stratum. Further, when the investigator combines these individual results into a global estimate of the overall mean, the standard error of the estimate is zero, because each stratum's standard error of estimate is zero. The population mean value would be determined exactly.

BASES FOR STRATIFICATION

The investigator attempts to partition the population according to one or more criteria that are expected to be related to the characteristic of interest. Thus it was no accident that in the hypothetical example, education was employed to divide the population elements into strata. As Table 11.1 indicates, there is a relation between these variables: the more years of school, the higher the income. Newspaper subscriptions, on the other hand, would have made a poor variable for partitioning, because there is no relation between paper subscriptions and income.

In addition, the standard error of estimate provides a clue to the number of strata that should be employed. Since the estimate depends only on variability within strata, the various strata should be made as homogeneous as possible. One way of doing this is to employ many, very small strata. There are practical limits, however, to the number of strata used in actual research studies, e.g., the creation of additional strata is often expensive in terms of sample design, data collection, and analysis. Further, regardless of the criteria by which the population is segmented, a certain amount of variation is likely to remain unaccounted for, and the additional strata will serve no productive purpose.

PROPORTIONATE AND DISPROPORTIONATE STRATIFIED SAMPLING

Whether one chooses a stratified sample over a simple random sample depends in part on the trade-off between cost and precision. Stratified samples typically produce more precise estimates, but they also usually cost more. Once the decision is made to select a stratified sample, the researcher must still decide whether it should be a proportionate stratified sample or a disproportionate stratified sample.

With a **proportionate stratified sample**, the number of observations in the total sample is allocated among the strata in proportion to the relative number of elements in each stratum in the population. A stratum containing ⅓ of all the population elements would account for ⅓ of the total sample observations and so on. Proportionate sampling was used in the example; each stratum contained half of the population and thus was sampled equally.

An alternative allocation scheme can produce still more efficient estimates. Disproportionate stratified sampling involves balancing the two criteria of strata size and strata variability. With a fixed sample size, strata exhibiting more variability are sampled more. Conversely, those strata that are very homogeneous are sampled less (see Research Realities 11.2 for an ACNielsen example).

Proportionate stratified samples: proportional to population numbers

Disproportionate stratified samples: inversely proportional to population variances

Research Realities

11.2 Disproportionate Stratified Sampling Scheme Used by ACNielsen

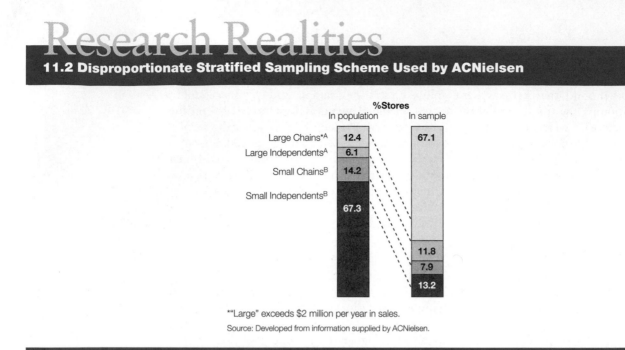

*"Large" exceeds $2 million per year in sales.

Source: Developed from information supplied by ACNielsen.

The determination of the precise sample size for each stratum is technical, but consider the rationale. At the extreme, if a stratum has zero variability, all the elements are identical in value, so a single observation tells all. In contrast, a stratum that is characterized by great variability requires a large number of observations to produce a more precise estimate of the stratum mean (recall that $s^2_{\bar{x}_h} = s^2_h / n_h$).

A disproportionate stratified sample requires more knowledge about the population of interest than does a proportionate stratified sample. To sample the strata in relation to their variability, one needs knowledge of relative variability. Sampling theory is a peculiar phenomenon in that knowledge begets more knowledge. One can sometimes anticipate the relative homogeneity likely to exist within a stratum on the basis of past studies and experience. Sometimes the investigator may have to rely on logic and intuition in establishing sample sizes for each stratum. For example, it might reasonably be expected that large retail stores would show greater variation in sales of some product than would small stores.[15]

Cluster Sampling

Cluster sampling involves the following steps: (1) The parent population is divided into mutually exclusive and exhaustive subsets. (2) A random sample of the subsets is selected. If the investigator then uses all the population elements in the selected subsets for the sample, the procedure is one-stage cluster sampling. If a sample of ele-

---

[15] Stratified samples are sometimes confused with quota samples. Both involve the division of the population into segments and the selection of elements from each segment. However, there is one huge difference: elements are sampled probabilistically with stratified samples, so we know the sampling distribution of the statistic and can create confidence intervals. There are no statistics for quota samples.

ments is selected probabilistically from the selected subsets, the procedure is known as two-stage cluster sampling.

Note the similarities and differences between cluster sampling and stratified sampling. Both involve the division of the population into mutually exclusive and exhaustive subgroups, although the criteria used are different (described shortly). Then for stratified sampling, a sample of elements is selected from each subgroup, whereas with cluster sampling, one chooses a *sample of subgroups*.

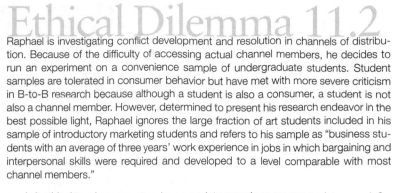

Raphael is investigating conflict development and resolution in channels of distribution. Because of the difficulty of accessing actual channel members, he decides to run an experiment on a convenience sample of undergraduate students. Student samples are tolerated in consumer behavior but have met with more severe criticism in B-to-B research because although a student is also a consumer, a student is not also a channel member. However, determined to present his research endeavor in the best possible light, Raphael ignores the large fraction of art students included in his sample of introductory marketing students and refers to his sample as "business students with an average of three years' work experience in jobs in which bargaining and interpersonal skills were required and developed to a level comparable with most channel members."

- Is it ethical to misrepresent an inappropriate sample as an appropriate sample?

Because one chooses a sample of subgroups with cluster sampling, it is important that each subgroup be a small scale model, representative of the population. At the extreme, if the distribution of the characteristic in each subgroup exactly parallels that for the population, one subgroup can tell all. Thus in cluster sampling, the subgroups ideally should be formed to be as *heterogeneous* as possible. In the hypothetical example, newspaper subscription might be a good basis for forming subgroups for a cluster sample. If all those subscribing to paper X were one subgroup and all those subscribing to paper Y a second, one could randomly select either subgroup to estimate the mean income in the population (this would work, i.e., one newspaper group would resemble the population unless newspaper subscriptions were correlated with income, e.g., wealthier people preferring a different paper compared with the newspaper choice of the less affluent). Although the distribution of incomes within each subgroup is not exactly the same as it is in the population, the range of incomes is such that there would be only a slight error if one were to estimate the mean income and variance of incomes of the population with the elements from either subset.

How does cluster sampling compare to stratified sampling or simple probability sampling? **Statistical efficiency** is a way to compare sampling plans. One sampling plan is more statistically efficient than another if, for the same size sample, it produces a smaller standard error of estimate. Cluster samples are typically less efficient than comparable stratified samples or even simple random samples. And yet, cluster sampling is probably the most widely used sampling procedure in large-scale field surveys. Why? Simply because they can be more economically efficient, even to the point that the cost allows a large enough sample size to equate the efficiencies.

SYSTEMATIC SAMPLING

The systematic sample offers one of the easiest ways of sampling many populations of interest. A systematic sample involves selecting every k^{th} element after a random start.

Consider again the hypothetical population of 20 individuals and suppose that a sample of 5 is to be selected from this population. Number the elements from 1 to 20. With 20 population elements and a sample size of 5, the sampling fraction is $n/N = 5/20 = 1/4$, meaning that one element in four will be selected, the sampling interval is 4. Thus, after a random start, every 4th element will be chosen, e.g., 1st, 5th, 9th, 13th, 17th, etc., or 2nd, 6th, 10th, 14th, 18th, etc.

Systematic sampling is one-stage cluster sampling, because all the elements in the selected cluster(s) are used. The subgroups or clusters are:

Cluster I:	A, E, I, M, Q
Cluster II:	B, F, J, N, R
Cluster III:	C, G, K, O, S
Cluster IV:	D, H, L, P, T

The random start, of course, determines which of these the clusters is used.

You can see how easy it is to draw a systematic sample. They can also be more representative than a simple random sample. With our hypothetical population, we are guaranteed representation from the low-income segment and the high-income segment given that the list had been ordered by income, whereas a simple random sample of size 5 might or might not include low-income and high-income people.

The same is true when sampling from other populations. If we are sampling retail stores, we can guarantee representation of both small and large stores by employing a systematic sample, if the stores can be arrayed from smallest to largest according to some criterion such as annual sales or square footage. A simple random sample of stores will probably contain inadequate representation from the large stores, since there are fewer large stores than small stores. Yet the fewer large stores account for a great proportion of all sales.

There is at least one danger with systematic samples. If there is a natural periodicity in the list of elements, the systematic sample can produce estimates seriously in error. For example, suppose that we have the annual ticket sales of an airline by day and that we wish to analyze these sales in terms of length of trip. To analyze all 365 days may be prohibitively costly, but perhaps the research budget allows the investigation of 52 days of sales. A systematic sample of days using a sampling interval of 7 (365/52) would obviously produce some misleading conclusions, because the day's sales will reflect all Monday trips, Friday trips, or Sunday trips, for example. Any other sampling interval is acceptable, and in general, an enlightened choice of the sampling interval can do much to eliminate the problems associated with natural periodicities in the data. The enlightened choice of sampling interval, of course, depends on knowledge of the phenomenon and nature of the periodicity.

AREA CLUSTER SAMPLING

In every probability sampling plan discussed so far, the investigator needs a list of population elements in order to draw the sample. A list identifying each population element is a necessary requirement for simple random samples, stratified samples, and systematic cluster samples. The latter two procedures also require knowledge about some other characteristic of the population if they are designed optimally. For many populations of interest, these detailed lists are unavailable or costly to construct. However, area cluster samples need only the list of population elements for the selected clusters.

Suppose that an investigator wished to measure certain characteristics of consultants, such as their earnings, attitudes toward the job, hours worked, and so on. It would be extremely difficult (if not impossible) and certainly costly to develop an up-to-date roster listing each consultant. Yet such a list would be required for a simple random sample. A stratified sample would further require the investigator to possess knowledge about some additional characteristics of each person on the list (e.g., education, employer) so that the population could be divided into mutually exclusive and exhaustive subsets. With a cluster sample, on the other hand, one could use companies as sampling units. The investigator would generate a sample of business firms from the population of firms of interest. The business firms would be primary sampling units. The marketing researcher could then get a list of people working for each of the selected firms—a much more plausible assignment.

The same principle underlies **area sampling**. Current, accurate lists of population elements are rarely available. Directories of all those living in a city at a particular moment simply do not exist for many cities, and when they do exist, they are obsolete when published; people move, others die, and new households are constantly being formed.[16] Although lists of families are nonexistent, relatively accurate lists of area divisions of the city are available. Here are the basics.

ONE-STAGE AREA SAMPLING

Suppose that the investigator is interested in estimating the amount of wine consumed per household in the city of Chicago and how consumption is related to family income. An accurate listing of all households is unavailable for the Chicago area. A phone book when published is already somewhat obsolete, in addition to the other inadequacies previously mentioned. One approach to this problem is the following:

1. Choose a simple random sample of n city blocks from the population of N blocks.
2. Determine wine consumption and income for all households in the selected blocks, and generalize the sample relationships to the larger population.

The probability of any household being included in the sample can be calculated. It is given simply as n/N, because it equals the probability that the block on which it is located will be selected. Because the probabilities are known, the procedure is probability sampling. Here, though, blocks have been substituted for households when selecting primary sampling units. The substitution is made because the list of blocks in the Chicago area can be developed from city maps. Each block can be identified, and the existence of this universe of blocks permits the calculation of the necessary probabilities.

Because each household on the selected blocks is included in the sample, the procedure is one-stage area sampling. Note that the blocks divide the parent population into mutually exclusive and exhaustive subsets. Note further that the blocks do not serve very well as ideal subsets statistically for cluster samples; households on a given block can be expected to be somewhat similar with respect to their income and wine consumption rather than heterogeneous as desired. On the other hand, the data-collection costs will be very low because of the concentration of households within each block.

TWO-STAGE AREA SAMPLING

The distinguishing feature of the one-stage area sample is that all the households in the selected blocks (or other areas) are enumerated and studied. It is not necessary to employ all items in a selected cluster; the selected areas themselves can be sampled, and it is often quite advantageous to do so. We distinguish two types of two-stage sampling:

1. Simple, two-stage area sampling
2. Probability-proportional-to-size area sampling

---

[16] R. L. Polk and Company publishes some 1,400 directories for most medium-sized cities in the range of 50,000–800,000 people. The directories contain both an alphabetical list of names and businesses and a street address directory of households; they are revised every 2–3 years.

With simple, two-stage area sampling, a certain proportion of 2nd-stage sampling units (e.g., households) is selected from each 1st-stage unit (e.g., blocks). Consider a universe of 100 blocks; suppose that there are 20 households per block; assume that a sample of 80 households is required from this total population of 2,000 households. The overall sampling fraction is thus 80/2,000 = 1/25. There are a number of ways by which the sample can be completed: by (1) selecting 10 blocks and 8 households per block; (2) selecting 8 blocks and 10 households per block; (3) selecting 20 blocks and 4 households per block; or (4) selecting 4 blocks and 20 households per block. The last alternative would, of course, be one-stage area sampling, whereas the first three would be two-stage area sampling.

The probability with which the blocks are selected is called the block or 1st-stage sampling fraction and is given as the ratio of n_B/N_B, where n_B and N_B are the number of blocks in the sample and in the population, respectively. For the first three schemes, the fractions would be, 1 in 10, 1 in 12.5, and 1 in 5. The probability with which the households are selected is the household or 2nd-stage sampling fraction. Since there must be a total of 80 households in the sample, the 2nd-stage sampling fraction differs for each alternative. The 2nd-stage sampling fraction is given as $n_{H/B}/N_{H/B}$, where $n_{H/B}$ and $N_{H/B}$ are the number of households per block in the sample and in the population. For sampling scheme 1, the household sampling fraction is calculated to be 8/20 = 2/5, for scheme 2 it is 10/20 = 1/2, and for scheme 3 it is 4/20 = 1/5. Note that the product of the 1st-stage and 2nd-stage sampling fractions in each case equals the overall sampling fraction of 1/25.

Which scheme would be preferable? Economies of data collection dictate that the second-stage sampling fraction should be high. This means that a great many households would be selected from each designated block, as with scheme 2. Statistical efficiency would dictate a small second-stage sampling fraction, because one can expect that the blocks would be relatively homogeneous, and thus it would be desirable to have very few households from any one block. Scheme 3 would be preferred on statistical grounds. Statistical sampling theory would suggest the balancing of these two criteria. There are formulas for this purpose that essentially reflect the cost of data collection and the variability of the characteristic within and between clusters.

Simple two-stage area sampling is quite effective when there are approximately the same number of 2nd-stage units per 1st-stage unit. When the 2nd-stage units are decidedly unequal, there can be bias in the estimate and probability-proportional-to-size sampling is the better choice.

Consider the data in Table 11.10, and suppose that a sample of 20 elements is to be selected from this population of 2,000 households. With **probability-proportional-to-size sampling**, a fixed number of 2nd-stage units is selected from each 1st-stage unit. After balancing economic and statistical considerations, suppose that the number of 2nd-stage units per 1st-stage unit is determined to be 10. Two 1st-stage units must be selected to produce a total sample of 20. The procedure gets its name from the way these 1st-stage units are selected. The probability of selection is variable because it depends on the size of the 1st-stage unit. In particular, a table of four-digit random numbers would be consulted. The first two numbers encountered between 1 and 2,000 are employed to indicate the blocks that will be used. All numbers between 1 and 800 indicate the inclusion of block 1, those from 801 to 1,200 indicate block 2, those from 1,201 to 1,400 indicate block 3, and so on.

The probability that any particular household will be included in the sample is equal, since the unequal 1st-stage selection probabilities are balanced by unequal 2nd-stage selection probabilities. Consider, for example, blocks 1 and 10, the two extremes. The 1st-stage selection probability for block 1 is 800/2,000 = 1/2.5, since

Block	Number of Households	Cumulative Number of Households
1	800	800
2	400	1200
3	200	1400
4	200	1600
5	100	1700
6	100	1800
7	100	1900
8	50	1950
9	25	1975
10	25	2000

TABLE 11.10
Illustration of Probability-Proportional-to-Size Sampling

800 of the permissible 2,000 random numbers correspond to block 1. In contrast, only 25 of the permissible random numbers (1,976 to 2,000) correspond to block 10, and thus the first-stage sampling fraction for block 10 is 25/2,000 = 1/80. Because 10 households are selected from each block, the second-stage sampling fraction for block 1 is 10/800 = 1/80, whereas for block 10 it is 10/25 = 1/2.5. The products of the 1st- and 2nd-stage sampling thus compensate, since

$$\frac{800}{2000} \times \frac{10}{800} = \frac{25}{2000} \times \frac{10}{25}$$

which is also true for the remaining blocks.

Probability-proportional-to-size sampling requires knowledge about the size of each 1st-stage unit but this is easily obtained from http://www.census.gov. The Census Bureau reports the number of households per block for all cities over 50,000 in population as well as for many other urbanized areas.

Sampling gets trickier when collecting international data. Decisions must be made about coverage between countries, as well as likely markets and localities within countries. Most research budgets cannot afford thorough coverage, so choices are based on managerially driven questions (i.e., theory).[17]

Summary

Sample design is a very detailed subject.[18] This chapter reviewed the basic types of samples that may be used to infer something about a population. A sample might be preferred to a census on grounds of cost or accuracy.

---

[17] N. L. Reynolds and A. C. Simintiras, "Theoretical Justification of Sampling Choices in International Marketing," *Journal of International Business Studies* 34 (2003), pp. 80–89.

[18] For more information, there are many excellent books on sampling, e.g., Leslie Kish, *Survey Sampling* (Wiley, 1995); Seymour Sudman and Brian Wansink, *Consumer Panels* (American Marketing Association, 2002); Steven K. Thompson, *Sampling* (Wiley, 2002). For information on the history of sampling, see Fritz Scheuren, "Looking Back So We Can Look Forward," *American Statistician* 57 (May 2003), pp. 94–96.

A practical procedure to use when drawing a sample includes the following steps:

1. Define the population.
2. Identify the sampling frame.
3. Select a sampling procedure.
4. Determine the sample size.
5. Select the sample elements.
6. Collect the data from the designated elements.

Probability samples are distinguished by the fact that every population element has a known, nonzero chance of being included in the sample. With nonprobability samples, the chance of inclusion is not calculable because personal judgment is involved somewhere in the actual selection process. Thus, nonprobability samples do not allow the construction of the sampling distribution of the statistic in question. As a result, traditional tools of statistical inference are not legitimately employed with nonprobability samples. The basic types of nonprobability samples are convenience, judgment, and quota samples.

Simple random samples are probability samples in which each population element has an equal chance of being included, and every combination of sample elements is just as likely as any other combination of n sample elements. Simple random samples were used to illustrate the basis of statistical inference, in which a parameter (a fixed characteristic of the population) is estimated from a statistic (a characteristic of a sample). The value of the statistic depends on the sample actually selected, since it varies from sample to sample. The derived population is the set of all possible distinguishable samples that could be drawn from a parent population under a given sampling plan, and the distribution of some sample statistic's values is the sampling distribution of the statistic. The concept of the sampling distribution is the cornerstone of statistical inference.

A stratified sample is a probability sample in which the parent population is divided into mutually exclusive and exhaustive subsets and a sample of elements is drawn from each subset. Stratified samples are typically the most statistically efficient (i.e., they have the smallest standard error of estimate for a given size), and they also allow the investigation of the characteristic of interest for particular subgroups within the population. The most statistically efficient stratified samples result when the strata are made as homogeneous as possible. Thus, variables expected to be correlated to the characteristic of interest, and whose values are known, are often employed when establishing the strata. In proportionate stratified sampling, the size of the sample taken from each stratum depends on the relative size of the stratum in the population, whereas with disproportionate stratified sampling, sample size depends on the variability within the stratum.

A cluster sample is a probability sample in which the parent population is divided into mutually exclusive and exhaustive subsets and then a random sample of subsets is selected. If each of the elements within the selected subsets is studied, it is one-stage cluster sampling; if the selected subsets are also subsampled, the procedure represents two-stage cluster sampling. Since only a sample of subsets is selected for analysis, statistical efficiency considerations suggest that the subsets be as heterogeneous as possible. A systematic sample is a form of cluster sample in which every k^{th} element is selected after a randomly determined start.

An area sample is an important type of cluster samples for large-scale studies. Area samples make use of one very desirable feature of cluster samples—one only needs the list of population elements for the selected clusters. By defining areas as clusters and then randomly selecting areas, the investigator needs to develop lists of population elements only for the selected areas. Even here the researcher can use dwelling units and select them systematically. Thus, area samples permit probability samples to be drawn when current lists of population elements are unavailable. In drawing area samples, the researcher typically attempts to balance statistical and economic considerations. Because small areas are basically homogeneous, statistical considerations suggest that a great many areas should be used. However, the economies of data collection dictate that few areas be used, and many observations collected within each area.

Review Questions

1. What is a census? What is a sample?

2. Is a sample ever preferred to a census? Why?

3. What distinguishes a probability sample from a non-probability sample?

4. What is a convenience sample?

5. What is a judgment sample?

6. Explain the operation of a quota sample. Why is a quota sample a nonprobability sample? What kinds of comparisons should one make with the data from quota samples to check their representativeness, and what kinds of conclusions can one legitimately draw?

7. What are the distinguishing features of a simple random sample?

8. What is a derived population? How is it distinguished from a parent population?

9. Consider the estimation of a population mean. What is the relationship between the mean of the parent population and the mean of the derived population? Between the variance of the parent population and the variance of the derived population?

10. What is the Central-Limit Theorem? What role does it play in making inferences about a population mean?

11. What procedure is followed in constructing a confidence interval for a population mean when the population variance is known? When the population variance is unknown? What does such an interval mean?

12. How should a simple random sample be selected? Describe the procedure.

13. What is a stratified sample? How is a stratified sample selected?

14. Is a stratified sample a probability or nonprobability sample? Why?

15. What principle should be followed in establishing the strata for a stratified sample? Why? How can this principle be implemented in practice?

16. Describe the procedure that is followed in developing a confidence interval estimate for a population mean with a stratified sample. Be specific.

17. Which sampling method typically produces more precise estimates of a population mean—simple random sampling or stratified sampling? Why?

18. What is a proportionate stratified sample? What is a disproportionate stratified sample? What must be known about the parent population to select each?

19. What is a cluster sample? How is a cluster sample selected?

20. What are the similarities and differences between a cluster sample and a stratified sample?

21. What is statistical efficiency?

22. Which sampling method is typically most statistically efficient? Which method is typically most economically efficient? Which method is typically most efficient overall? Why?

23. What is a systematic sample? How are the random start and sampling interval determined with a systematic sample?

24. What are the advantages and disadvantages associated with systematic samples?

25. What is an area sample? Why are area samples used?

26. How does a two-stage area sample differ from a one-stage area sample?

27. Illustrate the selection of a simple, two-stage area sample using hypothetical data of your own choosing.

28. Illustrate probability-proportional-to-size two-stage area sampling using an example of your own choosing.

29. What information is needed to effectively draw
    a. a simple, two-stage area sample?
    b. a probability-proportional-to-size area sample?

Applications and Problems

1. For each of the following situations, identify the appropriate target population and sampling frame.
   a. The National Head Injury Foundation Inc. wants to test the effectiveness of a brochure soliciting volunteers for its local chapter in Indianapolis, Indiana.
   b. A regional manufacturer of yogurt selling primarily in the Pacific Northwest wants to test market three new flavors of yogurt.
   c. A national manufacturer wants to assess whether adequate inventories are being held by wholesalers in order to prevent shortages by retailers.
   d. A large wholesaler dealing in electronic office products in Seattle wants to evaluate dealer reaction to a new discount policy.
   e. The Internet branch of a men's casual clothing retailer wants to assess the satisfaction with a new credit and return policy.

2. The Gap wants to determine consumer preference for several varieties of t-shirts. Respondents will participate in a touch test—they will touch several different t-shirts and then state their preferences. Some aspects of the t-shirts that will be compared are armbands, neckbands, and shirt material. The marketing researcher conducting the study has recommended that the touch tests be conducted using mall intercepts.
   a. What problems, if any, do you see in trying to use the results of this study to estimate the population of consumers who buy t-shirts?
   b. Suggest an alternative to a mall intercept study for determining consumer preferences for t-shirts. Why is this a better method?

3. A leading film and electronics company wishes to investigate the market potential for a new photo-imaging apparatus. Because this is a completely new technology, the company believes that industry leaders might offer insights into the desires of customers and consumers. However, a list of industry leaders does not exist. Discuss possible methods of generating a sampling frame for the influential people in this high-tech industry.

4. The owners of a popular bed and breakfast inn in Kauai, Hawaii, noticed a decline in the number of tourists and length of stay during the past three years. An overview of industry trends indicated that the overall tourist trade was expanding and growing rapidly. The managers decided to conduct a study to determine people's attitudes toward the particular activities that were available at and around the inn. Because they wanted to cause the minimum amount of inconvenience to their guests, the owners devised the following plan. Interview request cards, which were available at the Chamber of Commerce office, the Visitor Information Center, and three of the more popular restaurants, indicated the nature of the study and encouraged visitors to participate. Visitors were asked to report to a separate room at either the Chamber of Commerce office or the Visitor Information Center. Personal interviews, lasting 20 minutes, were conducted at these locations.
   a. What type of sampling method was used?
   b. Critically evaluate the method used.

5. The makers of Spam (the weird meat, not the annoying e-mails) were planning to enter a new Asian market. Before the final decision about launching its product, management decided to test market the products in two cities. After reviewing various cities in terms of external criteria, such as demographics, shopping characteristics, and so on, the research department settled on Yokohama and Hiroshima.
   a. What type of sampling method was used.
   b. Critically evaluate the method used.

6. A Credit Union chain in Philadelphia has witnessed a sharp increase in the number of branches it operates and in the company's gross sales and net profit margin in the past five years. Management plans to offer free retirement planning and consultation, a service for which other competing credit unions, banks, and

brokerage firms charge a substantial price. To offset the increase in operating expenses, management plans to raise the rates on other services by 7%. Before introducing this new service and increasing rates, management decides to do a survey using customers as a sample and employing the method of quota sampling. Your assistance is required in planning the study.

a. What variables would you suggest for the quotas? Why? List the variables with their respective levels.

b. Management has kept close track of the demographic characteristics of customers during the five-year period and decides that these would be most relevant in identifying the sample elements to be used.

Variable	Level	%Customers
Age	0–15 years	5%
	16–30 years	30
	31–45 years	30
	46–60 years	15
	61–75 years	15
	76 years+	5
Gender	Men	42
	Women	58
Income	$0–$9,999	10
	$10,000–$19,999	20
	$20,000–$29,999	30
	$30,000–$39,999	20
	$40,000+	20

Based on these three quota variables, indicate the characteristics of a sample of 200 subjects.

c. Discuss the possible sources of bias with the sampling method.

7. The following table lists the results of one question taken from a survey conducted for Joe's Bar and Grill. The Grill has recently undergone renovations, and with the new look, management has decided to change the menu. They are interested in knowing how well customers like the new menus.

a. Calculate the mean, standard deviation, and confidence interval for menu preference assuming simple random sampling was used.

b. Calculate the mean, standard deviation, and confidence interval for menu preference assuming stratified sampling based on the meal eaten was used (i.e., the strata being breakfast, lunch, and dinner customers). How do the results compare with those you obtained with the previous sampling plan? Why?

Respondent	Meal Eaten at Joe's Bar and Grill	Menu Preference on a Five-Point Scale
1	Breakfast	3
2	Breakfast	5
3	Breakfast	4
4	Breakfast	5
5	Breakfast	5
6	Lunch	10
7	Lunch	9
8	Lunch	8
9	Lunch	10
10	Lunch	9
11	Dinner	14
12	Dinner	15
13	Dinner	15
14	Dinner	14
15	Dinner	16

8. The Nevada National Bank, headquartered in Las Vegas, has some 400,000 users of its credit card scattered throughout the state. The application forms for the credit card ask for the usual information about name, address, phone, income, education, and so on that is typical of such applications. The bank is interested in determining if there is any relationship between the uses of the card and the socioeconomic characteristics of the user; e.g., is there a difference in the characteristics of those people who use the credit card for major purchases only (e.g., appliances) and those who use it for minor as well as major purchases?

a. Identify the population and sampling frame that would be used by the bank.

b. Indicate how you would draw a simple random sample from the sampling frame identified in part a.

c. Indicate how you would draw a stratified sample from the sampling frame.

d. Indicate how you would draw a cluster sample from the sampling frame.

e. Which method would be preferred? Why?

9. Howdy Supermarkets is considering entering the Cleveland market. However, before doing so, management wishes to estimate the average square feet of selling space among potential competitors' stores to plan better the size of the proposed new outlet. A stratified sample of supermarkets in Cleveland produced the following results:

Size	Total# in City	#This Size in Sample	Mean Size (sq.ft.)	Std.Dev. (sq.ft.)
Small supermarkets	490	24	4,000	2,000
Medium supermarkets	280	14	27,000	4,000
Large supermarkets	40	2	60,000	5,000

a. Estimate the average-size supermarket in Cleveland. Show your calculations.

b. Develop a 95% confidence interval around this estimate. Show your calculations.

c. Was a proportionate or a disproportionate stratified sample design used in determining the number of sample observations for each stratum? Explain.

10. A long-distance telephone company wants to investigate the needs of its customers. Propose a stratification scheme for the sample and discuss the benefits of your scheme.

11. The manager of a local theater is interested in assessing customer satisfaction. The manager decides to distribute a survey to every 10th ticket purchaser.

a. What type of sampling is to be used?

b. Critically evaluate this method.

## CHAPTER 12

Determining Sample Size

Questions to Guide Your Learning:

Q1: How do we determine sample size to achieve a desired level of precision confidence?

Q2: How is this done when estimating a population mean vs. a population proportion?

In Chapter 11, our discussion of sampling concentrated on sampling plans. In this chapter, we consider another important question, that of sample size. The researcher needs to determine the size of the sample needed before collecting data. Often this estimation occurs at the research proposal stage, because sample size affects the cost of the research project.

The question of sample size is complex because it depends on the type of sample; the statistic in question; the homogeneity of the population; and the time, money, and personnel available for the study. We illustrate the basic statistical principles by determining sample size for simple random samples.

Before we get into those geeky details though, let's look at the big picture. Sample size has to be big enough to satisfy two criteria—first, is it sufficient to make the results sound? Second, are the results convincing?

- For example, most of us think it's remarkable that a sample of only several hundred voters can represent the likely political sentiment of the country, but statistically it's sufficient. If voting outcomes were projected on numbers that only satisfied the statistical criterion, the samples could be even smaller, but who would "believe" a prediction based on, say, 75 citizens?

- Same with marketing research—a survey of 45 customers might, under some conditions, be statistically sufficient, but are you going to want to stake million-dollar decision, and, ahem, your job, on such a small sample?

- The practice of running small studies in the medical field, and basing future patient treatments on the results is even considered "unethical" because the study participants undergo risks, yet the results of small studies "will not produce useful findings."[1]

- *Consumer Reports* is a reputable and therefore influential source of recommendations—when it characterizes a particular automobile manufacturer's model as more or less reliable than others', it has based its judgments on sample sizes of 100 *per model*.[2]

- In transitioning from a consumer diary to the People Meter to measure television viewing, Nielsen is doubling its normal sample size, to be able to make comparisons between the two methodologies.[3]

Basic Considerations

As you might imagine, the sampling distribution of the statistic underlies the determination of sample size.[4] This distribution indicates how the sample estimates vary as a function of the particular sample selected. The spread of the sampling distribution thus indicates the error that can be associated with any estimate. For instance, the error associated with the estimation of a population mean by a sample mean is given by the standard error of the mean $\sigma_{\bar{x}} = \sigma/\sqrt{n}$ when the population variance is known, and $s_{\bar{x}} = s/\sqrt{n}$ when the population variance is unknown. The first factor to consider in estimating sample size, then, is the standard error of the estimate obtained from the known sampling distribution of the statistic.

A second consideration is the precision desired from the estimate. Precision is the size of the confidence interval around the population parameter. For example, a researcher investigating mean income might want the sample estimate to be within ±$1000 of the true population value, a more precise estimate than ±$5000.

A third factor is the desired degree of confidence associated with the estimate. There is a trade-off between degree of confidence and degree of precision with a sample of fixed size; one can specify either the degree of confidence or the degree of precision but not both. When sample size is allowed to vary, one can achieve both a

---

[1] Paul Raeburn, "Not Enough Patients? Don't Do the Study" *Business Week* (Oct. 21, 2002), p. 143.

[2] Karen Lundegaard, "GM, Hyundai Excel in Consumer Reports Survey," *Wall Street Journal* (March 11, 2003), p. D3.

[3] Louis Chunovic, "Dear Diary: Increasing Sample Size," *Electronic Media* (Feb. 24, 2003), pp. 1, 52.

[4] Kevin Murphy and Brett Myors, *Statistical Power Analysis* (Erlbaum, 2003); Helena Chmura Kraemer, *How Many Subjects?: Statistical Power Analysis in Research* (Sage, 1987); Steven Thompson, *Sampling*, 2nd ed. (Wiley, 2002).

FIGURE 12.1

Illustration of the Relationship between Sample Size, Confidence Levels, and Confidence Interval Precision (Narrowness)

Recall the equation for confidence interval: $\bar{x} \pm z_\alpha \sigma_{\bar{x}}$ where: $\sigma_{\bar{x}} = \hat{\sigma}_{\bar{x}}/\sqrt{n}$

Computation: 95% confidence, mean = 475 (say), sample standard deviation, $\hat{\sigma} = 100$:

n	95% confidence interval		interval width
5	$475 \pm 1.96\ (100/\sqrt{5})$	= 387.35 to 562.65	175.30
30	$475 \pm 1.96\ (100/\sqrt{30})$	= 439.22 to 510.78	71.56
100	$475 \pm 1.96\ (100/\sqrt{100})$	= 455.40 to 494.60	39.20
500	$475 \pm 1.96\ (100/\sqrt{500})$	= 466.23 to 483.76	17.53

What do those confidence interval widths look like? You need different levels of precision for different marketing research questions:

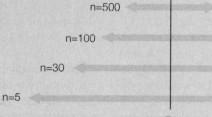

By comparison, what if you wanted a 99% confidence interval? z changes from 1.96 to 2.58:

n	95% confidence interval		interval width
5	$475 \pm 2.58\ (100/\sqrt{5})$	= 359.62 to 590.38	230.76
30	$475 \pm 2.58\ (100/\sqrt{30})$	= 427.90 to 522.10	94.20
100	$475 \pm 2.58\ (100/\sqrt{100})$	= 449.20 to 500.80	51.60
500	$475 \pm 2.58\ (100/\sqrt{500})$	= 463.46 to 486.54	23.08

old (95%)

new (99%)

specified precision and a specified degree of confidence in the result. Determining sample size involves balancing the two considerations against each other.

To illustrate the distinction between confidence and precision, consider trying to estimate mean income. We can have complete confidence in the following statement: "The population mean income is between $0 and $10 million." The statement may be accurate, but it is not particularly helpful, because it is simply too imprecise to be of any value.

In a moment, we're going to take the equation for a confidence interval, turn it inside out, and solve for sample size. To help motivate this discussion, Figure 12.1 shows you how sample size and confidence levels affect the precision of research conclusions.

Sample Size Determination When Estimating Means

The interrelation among the basic factors affecting the determination of sample size is best illustrated through example. Consider a simple random sample to estimate the mean annual expenditures of visitors at a theme park on food and souvenirs. The Central-Limit Theorem[5] suggests that the distribution of sample means will be normal for samples of reasonable size regardless of the distribution of expenditures in the population of theme park visitors. Consider, then, the sampling distribution of sample means in Figure 12.2 and distinguish two cases: Case I, in which the population variance is known, and Case II, in which the population variance is unknown.

Case I: Population Variance Known. The population variance σ might be known from past studies, even though the average expenditures might be unknown, since variation typically changes much more slowly than level. Given the relationship, $\sigma_{\bar{x}} = \sigma/\sqrt{n}$, we'd also be able to derive the standard error of estimate, $\sigma_{\bar{x}}$.

Suppose that the decision maker wanted the estimate to be within ±$25 of the true population value. Total precision is thus $50, and half precision (call it H) is $25.[6] Suppose further the decision maker wishes to be 95% confident, then z = 1.96, or say "2" to simplify the calculations.

Now we have all we need for determining sample size, because it is known that a number of standard deviations on each side of the mean include a certain proportion of all observations with a normal curve, e.g., 1.96 standard deviations include 95% of all observations. In Figure 12.2, each observation is a sample mean; the distribution of these means is centered around the population mean, and two standard devi-

FIGURE 12.2
Sampling Distribution of Sample Means

$$\sigma_{\bar{x}} = \frac{\sigma}{\sqrt{n}}$$

Standard Deviation

$E(\bar{x}) = \mu$

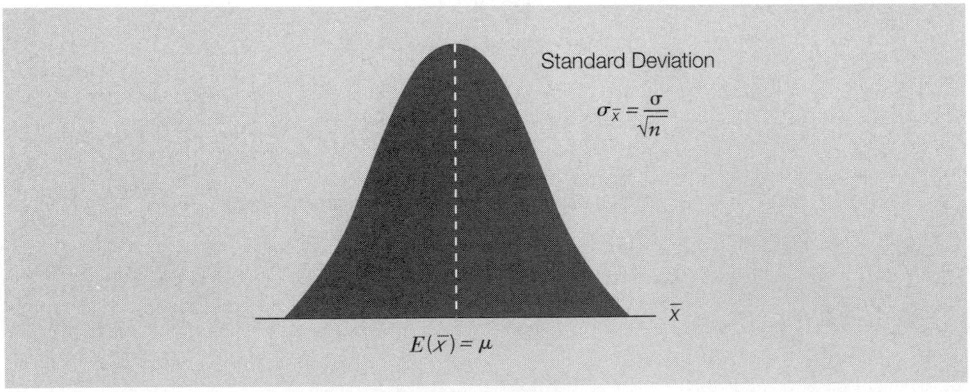

[5] Jeffrey Blume and Richard Royall, "Illustrating the Law of Large Numbers (and Confidence Intervals)," *American Statistician* 57 (2003), pp. 51–57.

[6] We work with H instead of the full length of the interval because the normal curve is symmetrical around the true population mean, and it simplifies the calculations to work with only one-half of the curve.

ations are $2\sigma_{\bar{x}}$. We want our estimate to be no more than $25 removed from the true population value, so we can simply equate the size of the specified half interval with the number of standard deviations to yield:

$$H = z\sigma_{\bar{x}} \qquad (1)$$

$$= z\frac{\sigma}{\sqrt{n}}$$

This equation can be solved for n (H and z are specified, and σ is known from past studies):

$$n = \frac{z^2}{H^2}\sigma^2 \qquad (2)$$

To illustrate, suppose that the historic variation in expenditures on food and souvenirs as measured by σ was $100. Then

$$n = \frac{(2)^2}{(25)^2}(100)^2$$

and n = 64. Thus, only a relatively small sample needs to be taken to estimate the mean expenditure level when the population standard deviation is $100 and the allowed precision is $50.

If the estimate must be twice as precise; i.e., $25 is the total width of the desired interval, so H = 12.5:

$$n = \frac{(2)^2}{(12.5)^2}(100)^2$$

and n = 256. Doubling the precision (halving the total width of the interval) increased the required sample size by a factor of four. This is the basic trade-off between precision and sample size. Whenever precision is increased by a factor c, sample size is increased by a factor c^2. Thus, if the desired precision were $10 instead of $50—in other words, the estimate must be five times more precise (c = 5)—the sample size would be 1,600 instead of 64 ($c^2 = 25$).

One also pays dearly to increase the degree of confidence. For example, if one wished to be 99% confident in one's estimate rather than 95% confident, let's plug in z = 3 instead of 2 (with H = 25 and $\sigma = 100$):

$$n = \frac{(3)^2}{(25)^2}(100)^2$$

and n = 144, whereas n = 64 when z = 2. When z was increased by a factor of d (d = 3/2 here), sample size increased by a factor of d^2 ($d^2 = 9/4$ here).

In sum, you should be aware of the price to be paid for increased precision and confidence. We constantly strive for very precise estimates in which we can have a great deal of confidence, but we can see why applied researchers often learn to live with somewhat imprecise estimates. The degree of precision and confidence that is required is a function of the consequences of the decision associated with the result—

Ethical Dilemma 12.1

Researchers in the laboratory of a regional food manufacturer recently developed a new dessert topping. This topping was more versatile than those currently on the market because it came in a variety of flavors and thus had more potential uses than a product like whipped cream, for instance. Although the manufacturer believed that the product had great promise, management also thought it would be necessary to convince the trade of its sales potential in order to get wholesalers and retailers to handle it. The manufacturer consequently decided to test market the product in a couple of areas where it had especially strong distribution. It selected several stores with which it had a long working relationship to carry the product.

During the planned two-month test period, product sales did not begin to compare to sales of other dessert toppings. Feeling that such evidence would make it very difficult to gain distribution, the manufacturer decided to do two things: (1) run the test for a longer period, and (2) increase the number of accounts handling the test product. Four months later, the results were much more convincing and management felt more comfortable in approaching the trade with the test market results.

- Is it ethical to conduct a test market in an area where a firm's distribution or reputation are especially strong?
- Is it ethical not to report this fact to the trade, thereby causing it to misinterpret the market response to the item?
- Is it ethical to increase the size of the sample until one secures a result one wants? What if the argument for increasing sample size was that the product was so novel that two months simply was not enough time for consumers to become sufficiently familiar with it?
- Would it have been more ethical to plan initially for a larger and longer test than to adjust the length and scope of the test on the basis of early results? Why or why not?

the more dire the consequences, the more precise and confident the results must be.

Case II: Population Variance Unknown. What happens when the population variance is unknown, as is typically the case? As you might anticipate, the procedure for estimating the sample size is the same except that an estimated value of σ is used in place of the previously known value of σ.

Suppose that there were no past studies on which to base an estimate of σ. You could do a pilot study, a small, quick study to get a rough estimate. Alternatively, the variance might be estimated from the conditions surrounding the approach to the problem, e.g., Research Realities 12.1 discusses the estimation of the variance when rating scales are used to measure the important variables.

Still a third possibility is to use the fact that for a normally distributed variable, the range of the variable is approximately equal to ±3 standard deviations. Thus, if you don't have an estimate of σ but you have an estimate the range of variation, you can estimate the standard deviation by dividing by six. Let us illustrate: Some theme park visitors might spend nearly nothing on souvenirs, others might visit several theme parks a year and buy a lot each time. Suppose that 5 days a year were considered typical of the upper limit, and food and souvenir expenses were calculated at $90 per day; the total dollar upper limit would be $450. The range would also be 450, and the estimated standard deviation would then be 450/6 = 75.

With desired precision of ±$25 and a 95% confidence interval, the calculation of sample size is now

$$n = \frac{z^2}{H^2}s^2 = \frac{(2)^2}{(25)^2}(75)^2 = 36$$

A sample of size 36 would then be selected and the information collected. Suppose that these observations generated a sample mean, $\bar{x} = 35$, and a sample standard deviation, $s_{\bar{x}} = 60$. The confidence interval is then, as before, $\bar{x} \pm zs_{\bar{x}}$, or[7]

$$35 \pm 2\frac{s}{\sqrt{n}} = 35 \pm 2\frac{60}{\sqrt{36}} = 35 \pm 20, \text{ or} \qquad 15 \le \mu \le 55$$

---

[7] One would more strictly use the t distribution to establish the interval, since the population variance was unknown. The example was framed using the approximate z = 2 value for a 95% confidence interval to better illustrate the consequences of a poor initial estimate of σ.

Research Realities

12.1 Guidelines for Estimating Variances When Using Rating Scales

Rating scales are doubly-bounded: on a 5-point scale, for instance, responses cannot be less than 1 or greater than 5. This constraint leads to a relationship between the mean and the variance. For example, if a sample mean is 4.6 on a 5-point scale, there must be a large proportion of responses of 5, and it follows that the variance must be relatively small. On the other hand, if the mean is near 3.0, the variance can be potentially much greater. The nature of the relationship between the mean and the variance depends on the number of scale points and on the "shape" of the distribution of responses (e.g., approximately normal or symmetrically clustered around some central scale value, or skewed, or uniformly spread among the scale values). By considering the types of distribution shapes typically encountered in practice, it is possible to estimate variances for use in calculating sample size requirements for a given number of scale points.

The table lists ranges of variances likely to be encountered for various numbers of scale points. The low end of the range is the approximate variance when data values tend to be concentrated around some middle point of the scale, as in a normal distribution. The high end of the range is the variance that would be obtained if responses were uniformly spread across the scale points. Although it is possible to encounter distributions with larger variances than those listed (such as distributions with modes at both ends of the scale), such data are rare.

In most cases, data obtained using rating scales tend to be more uniformly spread out than in a normal distribution. Hence, to arrive at conservative sample-size estimates (that is, sample sizes that are at least large enough to accomplish the stated objectives), it is advisable to use a variance estimate at or near the high end of the range.

Number of Scale Points	Typical Range of Variances
4	0.7–1.3
5	1.2–2.0
6	2.0–3.0
7	2.5–4.0
10	3.0–7.0

Source: *Research on Research* (MarketFacts.com).

Note that the desired precision was ±$25 and the obtained precision is ±$20. The interval is narrower than planned (a bonus) because we overestimated the population standard deviation as judged by the sample standard deviation. If we had underestimated the standard deviation, the situation would have been reversed, and we would have ended up with a wider confidence interval than desired.

Relative Precision

The preceding examples were all framed employing **absolute precision**. The estimates were to be within plus or minus so many units (e.g., dollars). It is also possible to frame the calculations of sample size employing **relative precision**, meaning that precision is expressed relative to "level." When level is measured by the "mean," relative precision suggests that the estimate should be within plus or minus so many percentage points of the mean regardless of its value. For example, if you require that an estimate is within ±10% of the mean, if the mean is 50, the interval will be from 45 to 55, whereas if the mean is 100, the interval will be from 90 to 110.

The calculation of sample size is no more complicated in the scenario of relative precision. The precision term H is simply replaced by the measure of relative precision:

$$H = z\frac{\sigma}{\sqrt{n}} \text{ becomes } r\,\mu = z\frac{\sigma}{\sqrt{n}}$$

where r is the measure of relative precision and μ is the population mean. Again, we simply solve for n. Divide both sides of the equation by $r\mu$ and multiply both sides by n^2 to yield

There are sample size equations for: absolute & relative estimation of means, and absolute & relative estimation of proportions

$$n = \frac{z^2 \sigma^2}{r^2 \mu^2} \qquad\qquad (3)$$

The desired level of confidence is z, so z^2 is known, and r, the expressed level of precision is also known. The right-hand term, σ^2 / μ^2, or $(\sigma / \mu)^2$, would entail making a judgment about the size of the population standard deviation relative to the size of the population mean. There might be past studies to guide the judgment. "What-if" scenarios (plugging in multiple likely values for σ and μ) are also helpful to see the range of what n is likely required to be.

Multiple Objectives

A study is rarely conducted to estimate a single parameter. It is much more typical for a study to involve multiple objectives. So, realistically, the researcher may be interested in both estimating the mean expenditures on food and souvenirs as well as the number of miles traveled in a year to the theme parks. Multiple means now need to be estimated. If each is to be estimated with 95% confidence and the desired absolute precision and estimated standard deviation are as given in Table 12.1, then you can see how the sample sizes also vary.

The different variables produce conflicting sample sizes; n could equal 36, 16, or 100, depending on the mean being estimated. The researcher must somehow reconcile these values to come up with a sample size suitable for the study as a whole. A conservative approach would be to choose n = 100, the largest value, to ensure that each variable is estimated with the required precision, assuming that the estimates of the standard deviations are accurate.

If the estimate of miles traveled were less critical than the others, then the use of a sample of size 100 would waste resources. Instead, focus on the variables that are most critical, and select a sample sufficient in size to estimate them with the required precision and confidence. The other variables would simply be estimated with a lower degree of confidence or less precision. For example, if the expenditure data were most critical, the analyst would decide on a sample size of 36. From a sample of 36, say the mean was $\bar{x} = 300$, and s = 500 for the variable that had suggested a larger necessary sample, miles traveled. The confidence interval for miles traveled is then calculated as

$$\bar{x} \pm z s_{\bar{x}} = \bar{x} \pm z \frac{s}{\sqrt{n}} = 300 \pm 2\frac{500}{\sqrt{36}} \text{ or } \left(133.3 \le \mu \le 466.7\right)$$

TABLE 12.1
Sample Size Needed
to Estimate Each of
Three Means

	Variable		
	Expenditures on Food	**Expenditures on Souvenirs**	**Miles Traveled**
Confidence Level	95% (z = 1.96)	95% (z = 1.96)	95% (z = 1.96)
Desired Precision	±$25	±$10	±100 miles
Estimated standard deviation	±$75	±$20	±500 miles
Required sample size	36	16	100

The desired precision was ±100 miles, and the obtained precision is ±166.7 miles. In order to produce an estimate with the desired precision, the degree of confidence would have to be lowered from its present 95% level.

Sample Size Determination When Estimating Proportions

The examples considered previously all concern determining sample size to estimate means. The population proportion π is often another parameter of interest in marketing. Thus, the researcher might be interested in determining the proportion of theme park visitors who are from out of state or who took at least one overnight trip, etc. This section focuses on the determination of sample size necessary to estimate a population proportion. The logic is the same, but the equations change slightly.

Absolute Precision

Let's start with what's different—the sampling distribution of the sample proportion. If the sample elements are independent, a reasonable assumption if the sample size is small relative to the population size, then the distribution of the sample proportion is the "binomial." When π is close to .5, or n is large, the binomial becomes indistinguishable from the normal,[8] thus it is convenient to use the normal approximation when estimating sample size.

The distribution of sample proportions is centered around the population proportion (Figure 12.3) and the sample proportion is an unbiased estimate of the population proportion. The standard deviation of the normal distribution of sample proportions, i.e., the standard error of the proportion is $\sigma_p = \sqrt{\pi(1-\pi)/n}$. Plugging σ_p into equation (1), we get:

$$H = z\,\sigma_p \qquad (4)$$

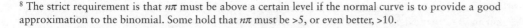

FIGURE 12.3
Approximate Sampling Distribution of the Sample Proportion

Standard Deviation

$$\sigma_p = \sqrt{\frac{\pi(1-\pi)}{n}}$$

$E(p) = \pi$

p

---

[8] The strict requirement is that $n\pi$ must be above a certain level if the normal curve is to provide a good approximation to the binomial. Some hold that $n\pi$ must be >5, or even better, >10.

Substituting $\sqrt{\pi(1-\pi)/n}$ for σ_p and solving for n yields

$$n = \frac{z^2}{H^2}\pi(1-\pi) \tag{5}$$

Let's say that the researcher is interested in estimating the proportion of all travelers who took at least one overnight trip in the past year. The researcher wants this estimate within ±2 percentage points, with 95% confidence in the result:

$$n = \frac{(2)^2}{(0.02)^2}\pi(1-\pi)$$

This equation contains two unknowns—the population proportion being estimated and the sample size—and is thus not solvable as it stands. To determine sample size, the researcher needs to estimate the population proportion. Yep! The researcher must estimate the very quantity the study is being designed to get at in order to determine sample size. Once again, you might use past studies or published data to generate an initial estimate. Alternately, you might conduct a pilot study or use informed judgment and a range of estimates about the probable approximate value of the parameter.

Another "what-if" exercise is to run a worst-case scenario. For example, if it would be unacceptable to have a wide confidence interval, you can plug $\pi = .5$ into the equations since this value maximizes the standard error.[9] If in fact the standard error is smaller (π is less than or greater than .5), the real confidence interval will be narrower and contained in the more conservative estimate, the broader confidence interval based on $\pi = .5$.

Relative Precision

The estimation of sample size for relative precision of proportions is analogous to that for relative precision of means. For example, if the relative precision were ±10% and if the sample proportion were 0.20, the interval would be 0.18 to 0.22; if the sample proportion were 0.30, the interval would be 0.27 to 0.33.

$$\text{We use } r\pi = z\sigma_p = r\pi = z\sqrt{\frac{\pi(1-\pi)}{n}},$$

where r is the specified relative precision. Solving for n, we obtain:

$$n = \frac{z^2}{r^2}\frac{(1-\pi)}{\pi} \tag{6}$$

Once again some initial estimate of the population proportion is needed. To illustrate, suppose that the population proportion was estimated to be 0.2, the level of confidence was 95% (z = 2), and the desired level of relative precision r = 0.10. Then

---

[9] Intuitively, the idea is that when $\pi = .5$, half of the population behaves one way and the other half the other way, so you would require more evidence for a valid inference than if the situation were more clear-cut and a substantial proportion all behaved in the same way.

$$n = \frac{(2)^2}{(0.10)^2} \frac{(.8)}{(.2)} = 1600$$

After the information is collected from the sample respondents, $s_p = \sqrt{p(1-p)/n}$ (not σ_p based on guesstimates of π) is used to calculate the confidence interval.

Population Size and Sample Size

Note that the size of the population does not enter into the calculation of the size of sample. Except for one slight modification to be discussed shortly, it has no direct effect on the size of the sample. Why not?

When estimating a mean, if all population elements have exactly the same value of the characteristic, then a sample of n = 1 is all that is needed to determine the mean, regardless of whether there are 1,000, 10,000, or 100,000 elements in the population. The thing that affects the size of the sample is the *variability* in the population; the more variable the characteristic, the larger the sample needed to estimate it with some specified level of precision. This makes intuitive sense, and it can be seen in the formulas for determining sample size, $n = z^2\sigma^2 / H^2$. Thus, population size affects sample size only indirectly through its impact on variability. The larger the population, the greater the potential for variation of the characteristic.

The slight modification alluded to earlier is the finite population correction. When the sample represents a large portion of the population, the assumption of independence between the sample elements may be no longer warranted, and the formulas must be altered accordingly. The formula for the standard error of the mean, $\sigma_{\bar{x}} = \sigma/\sqrt{n}$ would be adjusted to:

$$\sigma_{\bar{x}} = \frac{\sigma}{\sqrt{n}} \sqrt{\frac{N-n}{N-1}}$$

when the sample elements were not independent of one another, given this scenario of a sample size large relative to the population. The factor $(N-n)/(N-1)$ is the finite population correction factor used when the estimated sample represents more than 5% of the population.[10]

Other Probability Sampling Plans

So far, the discussions of sample size have been based on simple random samples. There are formulas for determining sample size when other probability sampling plans are used. The formulas are more complex, but the same underlying principles apply.

The issue of sample size is compounded, however, by the fact that one now has a number of strata or a number of clusters with which to work. This means that one has to deal with within-strata variability and within- and between-cluster variability in calculating sample size, whereas with simple random sampling, only total population variability entered the picture. As before, the more variable the strata or cluster, the larger the sample that needs to be taken from it, other things being equal.

---

[10] Ignoring the finite population correction results in overestimating the standard error of estimate.

Cost must also be equal. Cost did not enter directly into the calculation of sample size with simple random sampling, although it does affect sample size. Perhaps the costs of data collection with a sample of the calculated size would simply exceed the research budget, in which case cost would act to constrain sample size below that indicated by the formulas.

With stratified or cluster samples, cost exerts a direct impact. In calculating sample size, one has to allow for unequal costs per observation by strata or by cluster, and in implementing the sample size calculation, one has to have some initial estimate of these costs. The task then becomes one of balancing variability against costs and assessing the trade-off function relating the two.

Finally, there are also formulas for determining sample size for hypothesis testing (versus confidence interval estimation). The principles are the same, and now the "costs" involve the levels of Type I and Type II errors to be tolerated.

Using Anticipated Cross Classifications to Determine Sample Size

Thus far we have focused on the determination of sample size using only statistical principles, particularly the trade-off between confidence and precision. Another practical basis for determining sample size is the anticipated cross classifications of the data.

Suppose that in our problem of estimating the proportion of all theme park visitors who took at least one overnight trip in the past year, we were also interested in assessing whether the likelihood of engaging in this behavior is somehow related to an individual's age and income. Say the age categories were <20, 20–29, 30–39, 40–49, and 50+, and the income categories were <$20,000, $20,000–$39,999, $40,000–$59,999, $60,000–$79,999, and $80,000+. We would estimate the proportions for each variable, but we should also recognize that the two variables are interrelated, in that increases in income are typically related to increases in age. To allow for this interdependence, we need to consider the effect of the two variables simultaneously. The way to do this is through a cross-classification table in which age and income jointly define the cells.[11]

Table 12.2 is a cross-classification table that could be used for this example. This dummy table is complete in all respects except for the numbers that actually go in each of the cells. These would, of course, be determined by the actual data. In the table, 25 cells need estimation. It is unlikely that the decision maker is going to be

TABLE 12.2
Number and Percent of Theme Park Visitors Staying Overnight, as a Function of Age and Income

Income	<20	20–29	Age 30–39	40–49	50+
<$20,000					
$20,000–$39,999					
$40,000–$59,999					
$60,000–$79,999					
$80,000+					

[11] We say more about analyzing cross-classification tables later in the book.

comfortable with an estimate based on only a few cases. Yet even with a sample of, say, 500 travelers, there is only a potential of 20 cases per cell if the sample is evenly divided with respect to the age and income levels considered. Further, it is very unlikely that the sample would split this way, which would put the researcher in the awkward position of estimating the proportion in some cells with $n>20$, and others on the basis of fewer than 20 cases.

Conversely, we can use the table to estimate sample size. First compute the number of cells in the intended cross classifications (e.g., 25 here). Then allow for the likely distribution of the variables and estimate the sample size so that the important cells can be estimated with a sufficient number of cases to inspire confidence in the results. For example, for the most critical cells, aim for 100+ observations, and 20–50 in the remaining cells. The researcher "builds up" the sample from the size of the cross-classification table with these considerations.

If cross classification will not be the basic method used to analyze the data, but rather regression or some multivariate technique, one needs a sufficient number of cases to satisfy the requirements of the technique to inspire confidence in the results. Different techniques have different sample size requirements, often expressed by the degrees of freedom required for the analysis. (Some of these requirements become obvious when the techniques are discussed.) We reiterate the point made earlier regarding the research process—the stages are very much related and a decision about one stage can affect all the other stages, e.g., a decision about stage 5 regarding the method of analysis can have an important effect on stage 4, which precedes it, with respect to the size of the sample that should be selected. Thus, the researcher needs to think through the entire research problem, including how the data will be analyzed, before commencing the data-collection process.

Research Realities 12.2 pulls together information on sample size and sample plans. You can begin to see how the statistical questions about sampling plans and sample sizes relate to the marketing questions about target markets and audiences.

Ethical Dilemma 12.2

A recent discussion between the account manager for an independent research agency and the marketing people for the client left the account manager feeling perplexed. After numerous discussions, the account manager believed that she had a good handle on the client's problem and major concerns. On the basis of this understanding, she had developed a set of dummy tables by which the client's concerns could be investigated. During the most recent meeting, she had presented these to the client. The client had accepted the account manager's recommendation about how the data would be viewed; she closed the meeting by asking how large a sample the account manager would recommend and how much the study would cost.

The account manager's anxiety was caused by the fact that she believed from the earlier discussions and some preliminary investigation that two of the seven hypotheses were especially promising. The sample size that was needed to investigate these two hypotheses was almost 60% smaller than that needed to address some of the other hypotheses. The account manager was in a dilemma about whether she should take the safe route and recommend the larger sample size to the client and thereby ensure that all the planned cross classifications could be completed or whether she should go with her instinct and recommend the smaller sample size and save the client some money.

- What would you recommend that the account manager do?
- Is it ethical for the account manager to recommend the larger sample size when she is fairly certain that the smaller one will provide the answers the client needs? Is it ethical to do the reverse and recommend the smaller sample when there is some risk that the smaller sample will not adequately answer the problem that the firm was hired to solve?
- What are the account manager's responsibilities to the client in a case like this?

Summary

We reviewed the basic statistical principles involved in determining the size of a sample. The principles were used to develop confidence interval estimates for either a population mean or a population proportion using simple random samples. The examples demonstrated the influence of the sampling distribution of the statistic, the

Research Realities
12.2 Statistical Samples and Target Markets

Figure A contains secondary data, statistics on people who like to play golf, classifying them by their age (using the census age categories). You could use these data in a number of ways.

If you wanted golfers' opinions about a new golf shoe, you could do a "golf course intercept" with a simple probability sampling plan, and anticipate a sample with the ages of the respondents distributed much like that in Figure A. Indeed, if you were confident about the quality of the data in Figure A, you could take this to be a rough estimate of the population, to use as a benchmark. You'd then compare your sample age distribution to this one, to judge whether your sample is representative of the golfing population.

If you were hoping to get more adoption of your golf shoe by younger golfers, you would look at these data and determine that you'd have to conduct a stratified sample to increase the representation of the golfers younger than 44 years, even if your sample weren't representative as a result.

The difference is statistical representativeness versus targeting a nonrepresentative but demographically desired segment.

FIGURE A
#Rounds Played Annually by Golfer's Age

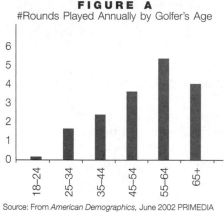

Similarly, Figure B contains data on television audiences for many stations, classifying them by three simple variables: the viewers' median age, the viewers' median income in thousands of dollars, and the percentage of the viewers who are male (each demographic presented separately per channel).

These data can also be used in a number of ways. We could estimate the sample size we would need to estimate the elusive female ESPN viewer (using the equation for proportions), or the apparently equally rare older MTV viewer (using the equation for means, as a rough approximation for these median data). We could use the equation for estimating sample size, plug in different values of "z" to represent different confidence levels, to determine the widths of the confidence intervals for, say, the age of the average ABC viewer compared with that of the CBS viewer. Are they different? The 95% confidence intervals, in both cases, are narrower than the 99% confidence intervals. Wider intervals are more likely to overlap, which in turn would lead to the conclusion that the two sta-

tions attracted roughly the same age of viewers. Is that conclusion desirable? Would we prefer narrower intervals?

FIGURE B
TV Demographics

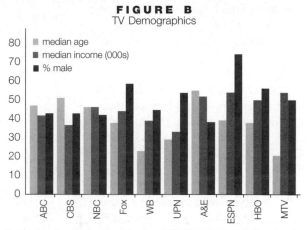

This sort of analysis certainly works for any medium. Figure C contains radio listening preferences by the teen segment. You can see where you'd put your radio advertising budget if you wanted to attract these young consumers: top hits and hip-hop/rap stations. Would you program at R&B and alternative stations? Depends on what you want, depends on what you're marketing. Would you go to all news radio stations? Unlikely, no matter what you're marketing.

All these examples show you secondary data in action. They present marketing research questions with the conjunction of marketing questions about targeted segments along with sampling questions (both the sampling schema as well as sampling size issues).

FIGURE C
Ten Radio Preferences

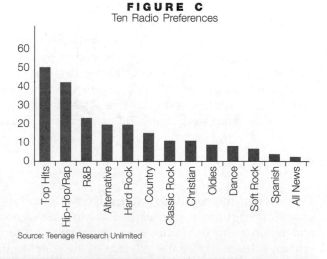

Source: Teenage Research Unlimited

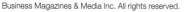

degree of confidence, and the level of precision on sample size. Both absolute and relative precision were discussed. The general conclusion is that sample size must be increased whenever population variability, degree of confidence, or the precision required of the estimate are increased.

Review Questions

1. In determining sample size, what factors must a marketing research consider?

2. When estimating a population mean, what is meant by absolute precision? What is meant by relative precision?

3. What is the difference between degree of confidence and degree of precision?

4. Suppose that the population variance is known. How does one then determine the sample size necessary to estimate a population mean with some desired degree of precision and confidence? Given that the sample has been selected, how does one generate the desired confidence interval?

5. How does the procedure in question 4 differ when the population variance is unknown?

6. What effect would relaxing the absolute precision with which a population mean is estimated by 25% have on sample size? How about decreasing the degree of confidence from 95% to 90% ($z = 1.64$)?

7. Suppose that one wants to estimate a population mean within ±10% at the 95% level of confidence. How would one proceed and what quantities would one need to estimate?

8. Suppose that one wants to estimate a population proportion within ±3 percentage points at the 95% level of confidence. How would one proceed and what quantities would one need to estimate?

9. Suppose instead that the researcher wanted the estimate to be within ±3% of the population value. What would the procedure be now and what quantities would she or he need to estimate?

10. What happens if the sample proportion is larger than the estimated population proportion used to determine sample size? If it is smaller? What value of the population proportion should be assumed if one wishes to take no chance that the generated interval will be larger than the desired interval?

11. What is the correct procedure for treating multiple study objectives when calculating sample size?

12. How does one determine sample size based on anticipated cross classifications of the data?

Applications and Problems

1. A survey was being designed by the marketing research department of Conner Peripherals, Inc., a large ($2 billion plus) manufacturer of advanced electronic data storage for laptops. The general aim was to assess customer satisfaction with the drives. As part of this general objective, management wanted to measure the average maintenance expenditure per year per computer, the average number of malfunctions or breakdowns per year, and the length of service contracts purchased with new portable computers. Management wanted to be 95% confident in the results. Further, the magnitude of the error was not to exceed ±$20 for maintenance expenditures, ±1 malfunction, and ±3 months. The research department noted that although some individuals and businesses would spend nothing on maintenance expenditures per year, others might spend as much as $400. Also, although some computers would experience no breakdowns within a year, the maximum expected would be no more than three. Finally, although some computers might not be purchased with a service contract, others might be purchased with up to a 36-month contract.

   a. How large a sample would you recommend if each of the three variables is considered separately? Show all your calculations.

   b. What size sample would you recommend overall given that management thought that accurate knowledge of the expenditure on repairs was most important and the service contract length least important?

c. The survey indicated that the average maintenance expenditure is $100 and the standard deviation is $60. Estimate the confidence interval for the population parameter μ. What can you say about the degree of precision?

2. The management of a major brewery wanted to determine the average number of ounces of beer consumed per resident in the state of Washington. Past trends indicated that the variation in beer consumption (σ) was 4 ounces. A 95% confidence level is required, and the error is not to exceed $\pm\frac{1}{2}$ ounce.

   a. What sample size would you recommend? Show your calculations.

   b. Management wanted an estimate twice as precise as the initial precision level and an increase in the level of confidence to 99%. What sample size would you recommend? Show your calculations. Comment on your results.

3. The director of a state park recreational center wanted to determine the average amount of money that each customer spent traveling to and from the park. On the basis of the findings, the director was planning on raising the entrance fee. The park director noted that visitors living near the center had no travel expenses but that visitors living in other parts of the state or out of state traveled upward of 250 miles and spent about 24 cents per mile. The director wanted to be 95% confident of the findings and did not want the error to exceed ± 50 cents.

   a. What sample size should the park director use to determine the average travel expenditure? Show your calculations.

   b. After the survey was conducted, the park director found that the average expenditure was $24.00 and the standard deviation was $15.00. Construct a 95% confidence interval. What can you say about the level of precision?

4. A large manufacturer of corrugated paper products recently came under severe criticism from various environmentalists for its disposal of industrial effluent and waste. In response, management launched a campaign to counter the bad publicity it was receiving. A study of the effectiveness of the campaign indicated that about 20% of the residents of the city were aware of the campaign and the company's position. In conducting the study, a sample of 480 was used and a 95% confidence interval was specified. Six months later, it was believed that 40% of the residents were aware of the campaign. However, management decided to do another survey and specified a 99%

confidence level and a margin of error of ± 3 percentage points.

   a. What sample size would you recommend for this study? Show all your calculations.

   b. After doing the survey, it was found that 35% of the population was aware of the campaign. Construct a 99% confidence interval for the population parameter.

5. Pac-Trac, Inc., is a large manufacturer of video games. The marketing research department is designing a survey to determine attitudes toward the products. In addition, the percentage of households owning video games and the average usage rate per week are to be determined. The research department wants to be 95% confident of the results and does not want the error to exceed ± 3 percentage points for video game ownership and ± 1 hour for average usage rate. Previous reports indicate that about 20% of the households own video games and that the average usage rate is 15 hours with a standard deviation of 5 hours.

   a. What sample size would you recommend, assuming that only the percentage of households owning video games is to be determined? Show all your calculations.

   b. What sample size would you recommend, assuming that only the average usage rate per week is to be determined? Show all your calculations.

   c. What sample size would you recommend, assuming that both of the preceding variables are to be determined? Why?

   After the survey was conducted, the results indicated that 30% of the households own video games and that the average usage rate is 13 hours with a standard deviation of 4.

   d. Compute the 95% confidence interval for the percentage of individuals owning video games. Comment on the degree of precision.

   e. Compute the 95% confidence interval for the average usage rate. Comment on the degree of precision.

6. The local mass transit company in a southwest city of the United States recently started a campaign to encourage people to increase car pooling or use public transportation. To assess the effectiveness of the campaign, management wanted to do a survey to determine the proportion of people who had adopted the recommended energy-saving measures.

   a. What sample size would you recommend if the error is not to exceed 65 percentage points and the confidence level is to be 90%? Show your calculations.

b. The survey indicated that the proportion adopting the measures was 20%. Estimate the 90% confidence interval. Comment on the level of precision. Show your calculations.

7. A manufacturer wants to assess the taste preferences of children under age seven for its new brand of hot dogs versus its competitor's brand. They also want to assess the average number of hot dogs that a child under seven eats in a month. The director of marketing research wants to be 95% confident in the results of the study and does not want the error to exceed 1% on any of the estimates. The director believes that 75% of children under seven will prefer the new brand to the competitor's leading brand. Past research has shown that children eat approximately five hot dogs each month with a standard deviation of 1.

   a. What sample size would you recommend, assuming that only the percentage of children under seven preferring the manufacturer's new brand of hot dogs is to be determined?

   b. What sample size would you recommend, assuming that the average number of hot dogs consumed by a child under seven is to be determined?

   c. The manufacturer decided to use a sample halfway between the two estimates. What is the consequence of doing so?

   d. The actual results of the survey showed that 63% of children under seven prefer the manufacturer's new brand of hot dogs to the competitor's hot dogs. Compute the 95% confidence interval for this point estimate.

   e. The actual results of the survey showed that a child under seven eats an average of seven hot dogs in a month with a sample standard deviation of 2. Compute the 95% confidence interval for this point estimate.

8. The transit system of a major metropolitan area was interested in determining the average number of miles a commuter drives to work. Past studies have shown that the variation (σ) in commuting distances was 5 miles. The managers of the transit system want to be 95% confident in the result and do not want the error to exceed 0.75 mile.

   a. What sample size would you recommend?

   b. The results of the survey showed that commuters actually drive an average of 20 miles to work with a standard deviation of 10. Compute the 95% confidence interval.

   c. Compute the 95% confidence interval if the mean was found to be 20 miles but the standard deviation was found to be 5.

9. The owner of a local record store specializing in alternative music wanted to determine the average age of his customers. He estimated a 25-year range from his youngest customer to his oldest customer. He wanted to be 95% confident in the results of the survey, and he did not want the error to exceed 9 months.

   a. What sample size would you recommend?

   b. The results of his survey indicated that the customers' average age is 35 with a standard deviation of 15. Construct a 95% confidence interval.

10. Mary Scott has just been assigned to do a customer satisfaction study for one of her firm's clients. Mary needs to estimate the sample size required for 95% confidence and error not to exceed 5%; however, Mary is missing one vital piece of information—the standard error. Suggest to Mary several possible methods of estimating the standard error.

11. Tom Johnson, the owner of a local pizzeria, wanted to conduct a survey to find out local residents' favorite pizza toppings. However, he had only enough funds to have a sample of 100 local residents. Based on the sales of toppings in his pizzeria, Tom expected 40% of the residents to like pepperoni the best.

   a. If Tom wanted to be 95% confident in the results of this survey, what corresponding level of precision would he be able to achieve?

   b. If Tom instead wanted to not exceed an error rate of 5%, what corresponding level of confidence would he be able to achieve?

   c. Relate your results in parts a and b to the concept that one cannot increase both confidence and precision with a fixed sample size.

12. Worldly Travels is a large travel agency located in Indianapolis, Indiana. Management was concerned about its declining leisure travel-tour business. It believed that the profile of those engaging in leisure travel had changed during the past few years. To determine if that was indeed the case, management decided to conduct a survey to determine the profile of the current leisure travel-tour customer. Three variables were identified that required particular attention. Before conducting the survey, the three following dummy tables were developed.

   a. How large a sample would you recommend be taken? Justify your answer.

   b. The survey produced the following incomplete table for the variables of age and education. Complete the table on the basis of the assumption that the two characteristics are independent (even though that assumption is wrong). On the basis of the completed table, do you think that an appropriate sample size was used? If yes, why? If not, why not?

13. The managing partner of a local granite marker manufacturer wants to know consumer attitudes toward
the price of cemetery headstones. He wants to be 99%
confident of the survey results and within a $30 range
of error. Customers can spend between $225 and
$1,000 on headstones, depending on their size.

a. What sample size should he use to determine the
average expenditure on markers? Show your
calculations.

b. After performing the survey, the manager found
the average expenditure to be $375, with a
standard deviation of $95. Construct the 99%
confidence interval. What can you say about the
level of precision?

c. If the manager had been willing to accept 90%
confidence in his results, what sample size would
he have needed? What is the 90% confidence
interval?

Income	Age			
	18–24	25–34	35–54	55+
0–$9,999				
$10,000–$19,999				
$20,000–$29,999				
$30,000–$39,999				
Over $40,000				

Age	Education			
	Some High School	High School Graduate	Some College	College Graduate
18–24				
25–34				
35–54				
55+				

Income	Education			
	Some High School	High School Graduate	Some College	College Graduate
0–$9,999				
$10,000–$19,999				
$20,000–$29,999				
$30,000–$39,999				
Over $40,000				

Age	Education				Total
	Some High School	High School Graduate	Some College	College Graduate	
18–24					100
25–34					200
35–54					350
55+					250
Total	200	400	300	100	1000

## CHAPTER 13

Collecting the Data: Field Procedures and Nonsampling Errors

Questions to Guide Your Learning:

Q1: What is "sampling error" versus "nonsampling error"?

Q2: How can we minimize nonsampling errors?

The research process proceeds from "sample design," which we just covered, to the actual "data collection." Data collection entails the use of some kind of field personnel operating either literally in the field or from an office, as in a phone, mail, e-mail, Web, or fax survey. The field staff must be properly selected, trained, and monitored. This chapter investigates these issues from the perspective of what can go wrong when collecting data. An understanding of the various sources of error in data collection will give you insight into the selection, training, and control questions, and should also assist you in evaluating the research information for decision making, understanding a project's limitations, caveats, etc.

Impact and Importance of Nonsampling Errors

Two basic types of errors arise in research studies: sampling errors and nonsampling errors. We've seen the first kind of errors in the chapters on sampling—there we used the concept of a sampling distribution to see whether our observed statistic (mean, proportion, etc.), was similar to or different from the many possible samples that we might have obtained using the same sampling procedures. The statistic varies from sample to sample because we draw only part of the population in each case. Sampling error can be reduced (the distribution becomes more concentrated about the population parameter), by increasing sample size, because the sample statistic is more stable (equal across samples) when it is based on a larger number of observations (each sample has more data points in common). **Sampling error**, then, is the difference between our statistic and the values we'd expect over many repetitions of sampling.

Nonsampling errors reflect the many other kinds of error that arise in research, even when the survey is not based on a sample. They can be random or nonrandom. Random errors produce estimates that vary from the true value; sometimes above, sometimes below, but the average sample estimate will equal the population value. Nonrandom errors are more troublesome—they tend to produce mistakes only in one direction, biasing the sample value away from the population parameter (and we don't usually know in which direction; i.e., too high or too low). Nonsampling errors can occur due to errors in conception, logic, interpretation of replies, statistics, or arithmetic; errors in tabulation or coding; or errors in reporting the results.[1]

Further, we can't make nonsampling errors go away by increasing our sample size. In fact, nonsampling errors can increase with larger samples (thus, making them relatively more important as sample sizes get larger, since larger samples help reduce sampling error). Whereas sampling errors can be estimated, the magnitude and even direction of nonsampling errors is often unknown, e.g., it is difficult to answer the simple question: "Is our statistic an underestimation or overestimation of the parameter?" Finally, nonsampling errors usually increase the standard error of estimates and therefore, the widths of confidence intervals. Altogether: blech!

Two common types of nonsampling errors—"no response" or poor responses—can wreak havoc with survey results. We try to reduce nonsampling errors by improving our research methods.

Types of Nonsampling Errors

Bigger samples help reduce sampling errors, but they don't fix nonsampling errors.

Figure 13.1 offers an overview of nonsampling errors—they are due to observation or nonobservation. **Nonobservation errors** means we've neglected parts of the survey population; e.g., they were accidentally not included or they did not respond. **Observation errors** occur when we get data from the sample, but the information is inaccurate, or errors are introduced when processing the data or reporting the findings. With nonobservation errors, we usually know we have a problem of noncoverage or nonresponse, but with observation errors, we may not even be aware that a problem exists.[2]

---

[1] Paul Biemer, *Introduction to Survey Quality* (Wiley, 2003).

[2] We usually trust, e.g., that data will be recorded properly. So . . . , we build in mechanisms to double-check.

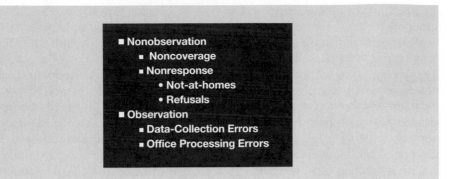

FIGURE 13.1
Overview of
Nonsampling Errors

How do we estimate (the direction and magnitude of) possible data-collection errors? Studies have:

1. Relied on available, bias-free information, which served as a validity check
2. Used split-run comparisons in which the respondent received different forms of the same questions, so that the person's consistency in responding could be measured
3. Measured the consistency of replies over time from the same respondent

These methods, while useful, cannot always be applied in marketing studies, and it becomes difficult to adjust the obtained information for response error. Instead, we usually take our data at face value. Thus, it is vital that researchers understand the sources of response bias so that they can better anticipate and prevent it.

Noncoverage Errors

"Noncoverage" means that our starting point, the sampling frame itself, doesn't include some elements of our target population. As a result, the probability that we will sample these units is zero. We can exclude a segment of the population deliberately, depending on our research question, e.g., we often survey only adults. (The target population is *usually* a portion of some broader population.) But noncoverage means we've unknowingly or accidentally excluded a segment.[3]

Noncoverage error is a sampling-frame problem. For instance, researchers realize that the telephone directory does not provide a complete sampling frame for most general surveys. For example, many people choose to have unlisted phone numbers.[4] The predictable demographics that correlate with phone ownership are exaggerated for other media, e.g., Web or fax surveys work fine for business marketing research, but these technologies are problematic for consumer surveys due to their lower penetration. In addition, the sampling frame of e-mail lists is still woefully inadequate, highly unlikely to represent the population to be studied.

---

[3] Clearly noncoverage can be a problem, whether a segment is knowingly or unknowingly overlooked. It was one of several criticisms of survey research in a legal case brought by Anheuser Busch suing a Czech brewer over brand confusion in New Zealand. Oy! Janet Hoek and Philip Gendall, "David Takes on Goliath: An Analysis of Survey Evidence in a Trademark Dispute," *International Journal of Market Research* 45 (2003), pp. 99–121.

[4] Phone penetration itself, in the U.S. and Western Europe is high, e.g., in the U.S., 98% among households making $30,000 or more, and even 85% of households with incomes of 15,000 or less (http://www.census.gov). However, in still developing economies, phone penetration can still be surprisingly low, e.g., 25% in Romania (http://www.snt.at/data/ English/ the_market/ Romania.shtml).

There are sampling-frame problems when personal interviews are conducted in shopping malls. There is no list of population elements. Only those people who shop in a particular mall have a chance of being included in the study, and their chances of being included depend on how much time they spend there. As a result, quota samples are often used in mall-intercept studies. Even so, nearly instinctively (i.e., not necessarily explicitly or consciously), interviewers typically underselect in both the high- and low-income classes. This bias is not always discovered, because interviewers have also been known to falsify characteristics to achieve the appropriate number of cases per cell. Further, the more elaborate and complex the quota sample, the more critical this "forcing" problem becomes. With three or four variables defining the individual cells, the interviewer finds it difficult to locate respondents who have all the prescribed characteristics. Thus, contrary to instructions for random or quota selection, interviewers typically select the most accessible individuals, all of which means that a portion of the intended population is underrepresented in the study, while the accessible segment is overrepresented.[5]

Noncoverage bias is *not* a problem in every survey. For some studies, clear, convenient, and complete sampling frames exist. For example, the department store wanting to conduct a study among its charge-account customers should have little trouble with frame bias. The sampling frame is simply those with charge accounts.

Nevertheless, noncoverage bias is more likely than not, so we might ask: (1) How pervasive is it? (2) What can be done to reduce it? The first question can be addressed only by comparing the sample survey results with some outside criterion; i.e., a variable that can be established through an auxiliary quality check for some respondents, or from another reliable study, such as the population census.

The second issue, trying to lessen the effect of noncoverage is addressed by trying to improve the quality of the sampling frame, e.g., by taking the time to bring available city maps up to date, taking a sample to check the quality and representativeness of a mailing list with respect to a target population. The unlisted number problem common to telephone surveys can be handled by random digit or plus-one dialing.

If you know you have an imperfect sampling frame, you can weight subsample results to account for the imperfections. For example, in a study using a list of car registrations each contacted respondent might be asked, "How many cars do you own?" The response of someone who said two might be weighted ½, and someone who said three might be weighted ⅓.

Though the precise adjustment procedures are technical, we note:

1. Noncoverage bias is a nonsampling error, so it is not dealt with in our standard statistical formulas.
2. Noncoverage bias is not likely to be eliminated by increasing the sample size.
3. It can be of considerable magnitude.
4. It can be reduced, but not necessarily eliminated, by recognizing its existence, working to improve the sampling frame, and employing a sampling specialist to help reduce (through the sampling procedure) and adjust (through analysis) the remaining frame imperfections.

> **Noncoverage? Problem due to sampling frame. Spend the $ for a good list!**

---

[5] Overcoverage error can also be a source of bias. It can arise because of duplication or multiple entries in the sampling frame. For example, families with several phone listings would have a higher probability of being included in a phone sample.

Nonresponse Errors

Another source of nonobservation bias is **nonresponse error**, which represents a failure to obtain information from the sample. It's hard to appreciate all the things that can go wrong with an attempt to contact a designated respondent. Figure 13.2 depicts the various outcomes of an attempted telephone contact. There is such a bewildering array of alternatives that even the calculation of a measure of the extent of the nonresponse problem becomes difficult. To try to assess the magnitude of nonresponse problems, a study was conducted by the Council of American Survey Research Organizations (CASRO).[6] They mailed questionnaires that displayed actual contact and response data from three phone surveys (a phone directory sample, a random-digit sample, and a list sample). Respondents (marketing researchers!) were asked to calculate the response, contact, completion, and refusal rates for each of the surveys. The difference in results was startling. Panel A of Table 13.1 displays the raw data from the phone directory sample. There was little agreement—using the same data, one organization computed the response rate as 12% whereas another suggested it was 90%. Panel B displays the three most frequently used definitions, as well as the definitions producing the minimum and maximum response rates. Thus, there are no official standards, and not much more consensus, in industrywide methods of calculation for rates of response and nonresponse.

This variation causes confusion and it becomes difficult to discern whether a seemingly low nonresponse rate in some study was truly low, or low only due to the particular computation used. To improve the practice of survey research, CASRO

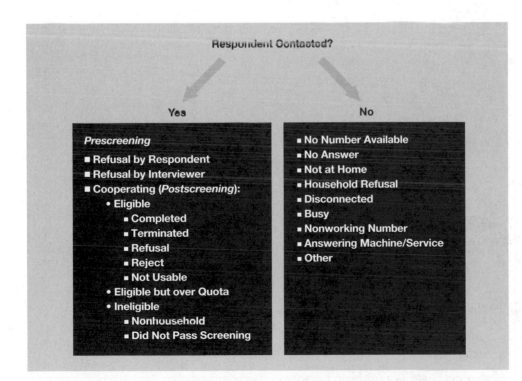

FIGURE 13.2
Outcomes in Telephone Surveys

---

[6] "On the Definition of Response Rates," http://www.casro.org. Also see Robert Groves, Don Dillman, John Eltinge and Roderick Little, *Survey Nonresponse* (Wiley, 2001).

Panel A: Outcome of Telephone Call

A = Disconnected/nonworking telephone number	426
B = Household refusal	153
C = No answer, busy, not at home	1,757
D = Interviewer reject (language barrier, hard of hearing, . . .)	187
E = Respondent refusal	711
F = Ineligible respondent	366
G = Termination by respondent	74
H = Completed interview	501
Total	4,175

Panel B: Most Frequent, Minimum, and Maximum Response Rates

Most frequent:

$$\frac{(B+D+E+F+G+H)}{All} = \frac{(153+187+711+366+74+501)}{4175} \qquad = 48\% \quad (1)$$

$$\frac{(D+E+F+G+H)}{All} = \frac{(187+711+366+74+501)}{4175} \qquad = 44\% \quad (2)$$

$$\frac{(H)}{All} = \frac{(501)}{4175} \qquad = 12\% \quad (3)$$

Minimum: $\dfrac{(H)}{All} = \dfrac{(501)}{4175}$ $\qquad = 12\%$

Maximum: $\dfrac{(E+F+G+H)}{(D+E+F+G+H)} = \dfrac{(711+366+74+501)}{(187+711+366+74+501)}$ $\qquad = 90\%$

Source: "On the Definition of Response Rates" (published in 1982) and "CASRO Guidelines for Survey Research Quality" (revised in 1998). Council of American Survey Research Organizations™ (http://www.casro.org).

developed a definition of response rate that the industry is supposed to embrace as the standard:

$$Response\ rate = \frac{number\ of\ completed\ interviews\ with\ responding\ units}{number\ of\ eligible\ responding\ units\ in\ the\ sample}$$

Nonresponse is a problem because it raises the question of whether the respondents are somehow different from those who didn't respond. Many studies have indicated that it is risky to assume that these groups are the same. The two main sources of nonresponse bias are not-at-homes and refusals.

NOT-AT-HOMES

Some respondents are inaccessible when the interviewer calls. There has been a long upward trend in this problem. The percentage of not-at-homes depends on the nature of the designated respondent and the time of the call. Given societal division of labor, married women with young children are more likely to be at home during the weekdays than are men, married women without children, or single women. Seasonal variations occur, e.g., during the holidays, as do weekday-to-weekend variations.[7] Further, it is much easier to find a "responsible adult" at home than the specified respondent, and thus the choice of the elementary sampling unit is key in the not-at-home problem.

Ethical Dilemma 13.1

During the introduction in a telephone interview, interviewers introduce themselves, provide the research company's name, and then assure potential respondents that the client will be unable to link their responses back to them. However, the interviewer notes the respondents' first names and phone numbers on the completed survey so that the supervisor can randomly select a sample of questionnaires for verification. The possibility of a verification call is explained to the respondents.

Once the fieldwork has been completed, the research supplier bundles all the questionnaires and sends them to the client for coding, entry, and analysis. The questionnaires are sent with respondents' names and phone numbers attached.

- Is there a problem with providing the names and phone numbers of respondents to the client company?
- If the client has signed a confidentiality agreement with the field company, is this problem avoided?

To reduce the problem: For busy executives, make an appointment with the respondent. For consumers, call them back. Callbacks are effective if they are made at a time different from the original call. The nonresponse problem due to not-at-homes is acute and important to the accuracy of most surveys, but the common solution these days is typically solved mechanically—computers automatically redial until the household picks up.

Inaccessibility can take other forms, some of which might also be solved by calling back, e.g., when the attempts to contact result in busy signals, such as when potential respondents are online with a nondedicated phone line, or answering machine pickups. Other variants won't be resolved by repeated calling, e.g., when numbers are really assigned to faxes and not phones, no pickups due to call-screening and other blocking mechanisms, etc.

One technique that is sometimes naïvely suggested for handling the not-at-homes is substituting the neighboring dwelling unit, or, in a phone survey, calling the next name on the list. This is a very poor way of handling the not-at-home condition. All it does is substitute more at homes for the population segment the researcher is in fact trying to reach, in effect, aggravating the problem instead of solving it.

Interviewers can be compared with respect to their contact rate. The **contact rate** (K) is defined as the percentage of eligible assignments in which the interviewer makes contact with the designated respondent; essentially a measure of the interviewer's persistence:

$$K = \frac{number\ of\ eligible\ sample\ units\ contacted}{number\ of\ eligible\ sample\ units\ approached}$$

Interviewers with low contact rates can be checked to determine why. Perhaps they are operating in traditionally high not-at-home areas, such as high-income areas. Or, time of day may be a problem, with ineffective follow-up procedures. The field supervisor can help retrain the caller.

Researchers have suggested a statistical adjustment to lessen the effect of not-at-home nonresponse bias. Essentially, the responses from each informant are weighted

---

[7] Mary Losch, Aaron Maitland and Gene Lutz, "The Effect of Time of Year of Data Collection on Sample Efficiency," *Public Opinion Quarterly* 66 (2002), pp. 594–607.

by the inverse of their likelihood of being reached. For example, people who are usually not at home tend to be underrepresented in the survey, so their data are weighted more than respondents who say they're typically home and therefore reachable.

REFUSALS

In almost every study, some respondents refuse to participate. If the first big class of problems is the inaccessibility of respondents, the second class is simply the unwillingness of respondents to participate. If contact is made, many people refuse to participate, even before the interviewers complete their introductory words, for reasons such as disinterest, inconvenient timing, concerns of privacy, and confusion between telemarketing and telephone calls for marketing research.[8] The steep decline over the last decade of response rates (from 50–60% to about 20–25%) adds to the costs of these surveys. Research Realities 13.1 provides numbers representing contact rates and refusal rates per method of administration (phone, mall, Web).

The rate of refusals depends on the nature of the respondent, the auspices of the research, the circumstances surrounding the contact, the nature of the topic, and the interviewer, etc. For example: (1) the culture can affect the refusal rate: e.g., in countries like Saudi Arabia, it is still nearly impossible to interview women.[9] (2) The method used to collect the data makes a difference: phone interviews yield slightly better response rates over mail questionnaires. (3) The research topic affects refusal rates: predictably those who respond are most interested in the topic. Nonresponse errors increase with the sensitivity of the information being sought. (4) People respond differently to different sponsors. (5) The interviewers themselves can have an important effect: their approach, their manner, and their own demographic characteristics can affect a respondent's willingness to participate.

What can be done to correct the nonresponse bias introduced when designated respondents refuse their participation? There seem to be three available strategies. One, the initial response rate can be increased. Two, the impact of refusals can be reduced through follow-up. Three, the obtained information can be extrapolated to allow for nonresponse.

INCREASING INITIAL RESPONSE RATE

The nature of the respondent is beyond the researcher's control. The marketing problem dictates the target population, and this population is likely to contain households with different educational levels, income levels, cultural backgrounds, occupations, etc. We can try to sell respondents on the value of the research and the importance of their participation. Advance notice may help. Some individuals refuse to participate because they do not wish to be identified with their responses, so a guarantee of confidentiality (if true) is often effective in calming such fears. Sometimes money or another incentive is offered.[10]

---

[8] Peter Tuckel and Harry O'Neill, "The Vanishing Respondent in Telephone Surveys," *Journal of Advertising Research* 42 (2002), pp. 26–48; James Mitchel, "Telephone Surveys," *LIMRA's MarketFacts Quarterly* 21 (2002), p. 39.

[9] Sometimes marketing researchers risk life and limb, the main strategy in a recent survey in Kashmir was, "Finish quickly!" Joanna Slater, "What the Pollster Found in Kashmir—Bold Questioners, Armed with Sharp Pencils, Faced Risks, Got Looks, Learned," *Wall Street Journal* (Aug. 14, 2002), p. A10.

[10] Michael Davern et al., "Prepaid Monetary Incentives and Data Quality" *Public Opinion Quarterly* 67 (2003), pp. 139–147; Kenneth Goldstein and M. Kent Jennings, "The Effect of Advance Letters on Cooperation in a List Sample Telephone Survey," *Public Opinion Quarterly* 66 (2002), pp. 608–617; Katy Bachman, "Consumers: Respond, S.V.P." *Mediaweek* (Jan. 6, 2003), p. 5.

Research Realities

13.1 Rates of Contact, Refusal to Participate, and Cooperation

The Marketing Research Association has tracked participation rates in research studies and has analyzed these numbers per contact method.

Note the telephone lists appear to be beneficial; contact rates suggest they're not as inaccurate as their reputation would suggest, and survey completions are strong (the RDD method probably doesn't match interests of survey taker and recipient better than the randomness of the method would suggest, and though interest levels on B2B customers may be higher, they may simply be too busy to engage in the survey call).

The Mall still serves as a workhorse for marketing research. You may be the sort of person who walks by those people with the clipboards saying, "Sorry" but many people stop. Once engaged in the interview, the completion rate is the strongest of all the techniques investigated. It's hard to walk away after agreeing to participate, and it's hard to say no to another person, in person.

The Web has strengths and weaknesses. It's quick and inexpensive, accessible to huge numbers of potential respondents, but the flip side of that same story is that it's anonymous and there is no social cost to quitting, upon seeing what the survey is about, or even in the middle of the survey.

Many marketing researchers are interested in comparing different methods of contacting potential survey respondents, to decide how to spend their (usually insufficient) marketing research budget efficiently. For example, for reasons such as the participation rates in the chart, Thomas Miller in "Make the Call," *Marketing News* (Sept. 24, 2001), pp. 30–35, compares phone and Web surveys. For telephone surveys, 95% of the population has access to the medium, 67% of those with phones opt in (they do not refuse initially), 26% of those opting in complete the survey. For online surveys, those numbers are more like: 55% have access, 43% opt in, and 34% complete the survey.

Modality of Survey	Contact Rate	Initial Refusal Rate	Survey Completion Rate
Telephone Overall	18%	33	26
Telephone RDD	10	40	13
Telephone List	29	24	45
Telephone B2B	19	29	26
Mall / Central Location	38	21	71
Internet Web Survey	34	57	34

Source: (http://www.mra-net.org).

Nonresponse attributable to the sponsor can be overcome by hiding the sponsor; e.g., by hiring a professional research organization to conduct the field study. This is one reason companies with established, sophisticated research departments outsource some of their research.

FOLLOW-UP

Because many of the circumstances surrounding a contact are temporary and changeable, this source of bias introduced through refusals can often be reduced. If a respondent declined participation because he or she was busy or sick, a callback at a different time may be sufficient to secure cooperation. Thus, one means of reducing this source of bias is in the training of the field staff.

Perhaps little can be done regarding the research topic as a source of nonresponse bias, because it is dictated by the marketing problem to be solved. A sensitive research subject or one of little interest to the respondents is likely to elicit a high rate of refusals. Thus, the researcher needs to make the study as interesting as possible, e.g., avoiding those questions that are "interesting but not vital," with implications for the design of the survey instrument.

With mail and e-mail surveys, responses are frequently obtained with a second or third mailing to those who did not respond previously. Of course, follow-up requires identification of those not responding earlier, and respondents who know that they can be identified may refuse to participate. The alternative—sending each mailing to each designated sample member, without screening those who have responded previously—can be expensive for the research organization and frustrating for the already cooperative respondents.

ADJUSTING THE RESULTS

If we could estimate the nonresponse bias, we could adjust the results accordingly. Say the problem was one of estimating the mean income for a certain population and responses were obtained from only a portion (p_r) of the designated sample. The proportion not responding would be denoted p_{nr}. If $\bar{x}_r$ is the mean income of those responding and $\bar{x}_{nr}$ the mean income of those not responding, then the overall mean would be

$$\bar{x} = p_r\bar{x}_r + p_{nr}\bar{x}_{nr}$$

This computation, of course, assumes that $\bar{x}_{nr}$ is known or at least can be estimated. An intensive follow-up of a sample of the nonrespondents is sometimes used to generate this estimate for a crude adjustment of the initial results. Ignoring the initial nonresponse is equivalent to assuming that $\bar{x}_{nr}$ is equal to $\bar{x}_r$, which is usually incorrect.

A second type of adjustment involves keeping track of those responding to the initial contact, the first follow-up, the second follow-up, and so on. The mean of the variable is then calculated, and each subgroup is compared to determine whether any statistically significant differences emerge as a function of the difficulty experienced in making contact. If not, the variable mean for the nonrespondents is assumed to be equal to the mean for those responding. If a discernible trend is evident, the trend is extrapolated to allow for nonrespondents.

The preceding discussions all deal with *total* nonresponse. **Item nonresponse**, which can also be a problem, occurs when the respondent agrees to the total interview but refuses, or is unable, to answer some specific questions because of the content, form, or the amount of work required to produce the requested information.

We can distinguish between flagrant item nonresponse and isolated or sporadic nonresponse. If too many questions are left unanswered, the entire survey or interview becomes unusable. If only a few items are left unanswered, the respondent is included in the sample, and we use whatever data they did give us. In addition, the "don't know" and "no answers" can be treated as separate categories when reporting results.[11]

Alternatively, the information from the missing item or items can sometimes be inferred from other information in the questionnaire.[12] If other questions on the questionnaire relate to the same issue, we check those data and formulate a consistent answer for the unanswered item. Regression is usually used where the missing item is treated as the criterion variable, and we attempt to predict that value from the respondent's other data. A simpler way of handling item nonresponse is to substitute

---

[11] Jon Krosnick et al., "The Impact of 'No Opinion' Response Options on Data Quality," *Public Opinion Quarterly* 66 (2001), pp. 371–403.

[12] Paul Allison, *Missing Data* (Sage, 2001); Roderick Little and Donald Rubin, *Statistical Analysis with Missing Data,* 2nd ed. (Wiley, 2002); Marco Vriens and Eric Melton, "Managing Missing Data," *Marketing Research* 14 (2002), pp. 12–17; Jun Shao and Hansheng Wang, "Sample Correlation Coefficients Based on Survey Data Under Regression Imputation," *Journal of the American Statistical Association* 97 (2002), pp. 544–564.

for the missing data the average for that variable (based on the data of those who did respond to that item). In doing so, of course, we are assuming that the nonrespondents are similar to those who answered the item.

Just as the contact rate can be used to compare and evaluate interviewers with respect to not-at-homes, at least two ratios have been suggested for comparing interviewers with respect to refusals: the **response rate R** and the **completeness rate C**. The response rate, discussed previously, equals the ratio of the {# of completed interviews with responding units} divided by the {# of eligible responding units in the sample}. The response rate reflects the interviewer's effectiveness at the door or on the phone. The completeness rate determines whether the response is complete. It is defined similarly but typically applies to the individual items in the study, such as the crucial or sensitive questions (e.g., a respondent's debt, etc.).

Ethical Dilemma 13.2

During a telephone survey, the names of respondents who refuse to answer the survey are placed in a special bin. All of these respondents are recontacted 24 hours later and asked again for their answers. The person making these follow-up calls receives special training in converting these refusals to completions. If the respondent refuses again, the interviewer attempts to "sell" the respondent on cooperating in the study. If the respondent remains unwilling to complete the survey, the interviewer terminates the call and notes this as a refusal.

- List the implications arising from increased refusals, as the number of telephone surveys increases.
- List the implications for marketing research if research companies make follow-up calls to refusals the industry standard.
- Should an initial refusal be taken as a refusal? Explain.

Field Errors

Field errors are by far the most prevalent type of observation error. They arise after the individual has agreed to participate in a study. Instead of cooperating fully, the individual refuses to answer specific questions, or provides a response that somehow differs from what is actually true or correct, errors that have been referred to as errors of omission and errors of commission. We discussed errors of omission (item nonresponse) in the last section. Now we turn to errors of commission, typically referred to as "response errors."

If you think about how complicated the response process actually is, you can see the many places where response errors can occur: respondents first need to understand what is being asked. Second, the individual needs to engage in some cognitive processing to arrive at an answer, including retrieval of the pertinent attitudes, facts, or experiences, and the formulation of these cognitions into a response. Third, the person needs to evaluate the response in terms of its accuracy. Fourth, the respondent needs to evaluate the answer in terms of other human goals, even subconscious things like preserving one's self-image or attempting to please the interviewer. Finally, the participant needs to give the response that is the result of all this mental processing. Reaching the final step is the object of the survey process. Breakdowns can occur at any of the preceding steps resulting in an inaccurate answer: a response error.

Some data-collection errors arise due to the biases that both the interviewer and the interviewee bring to the marketing research interaction, as depicted in Figure 13.3. Each person brings certain background characteristics and psychological predispositions to the interview. Although some of the characteristics are readily observable, others are not. Yet both interviewer and interviewee form attitudes toward the other person on the basis of their initial perceptions. The interview is an interactive process, and both parties are important determinants of the process, perceiving and reacting to each other.

There are many types of interviewer bias. Sometimes a good, standardized survey makes better sense.

FIGURE 13.3
Biases Brought to
Marketing Research
Interview

Interviewer	Interviewee
Background (age, education, socioeconomic status, ethnicity, religion, gender, etc.)	Background (age, education, socioeconomic status, ethnicity, religion, gender, etc.)
Psychological factors (perceptions, attitudes, expectations, motives, etc.)	Psychological factors (perceptions, attitudes, expectations, motives, etc.)
Behavioral factors (mistakes made in asking questions, probing, recording, etc.)	Behavioral factors (responses inadequate, responses inaccurate, etc.)

BACKGROUND FACTORS

Better cooperation and more information are obtained when the backgrounds of the interviewer and respondent are similar than when they are different. This is particularly true for readily observable characteristics, such as ethnicity, age, and gender, but it also applies to characteristics such as social class and income. This suggests that it is productive to match the background characteristics of the interviewer and respondent as closely as possible, to enhance the probability of successful interviews.

There are often practical constraints, e.g., the interviewing profession attracts many part-time workers, such as students or school teachers, and these people probably do not represent a balanced demographic cross section of people. To minimize biases, we might compute a measure of interviewer variability while analyzing the results. Alternatively, we can modify interviewer schedules during a specific project to improve background matches. And recruiting could well be aimed at hiring interviewers with diverse demographic backgrounds, if other things are equal.

PSYCHOLOGICAL FACTORS

The interviewers themselves are human, and their opinions, perceptions, expectations, and attitudes affect the responses they receive. The primary way to control for these psychological factors is through training. We don't want these factors to affect interviewers' behavior during the interview, thereby contaminating the response.

As a result, most surveys are conducted using a rather rigid set of procedures that interviewers must follow. The instructions should be clear and should be written. Further, they should state the purpose of the study clearly. They should describe the materials to be used, such as questionnaires, maps, time forms, and so on. They should describe how each question should be asked, the kinds of answers that are acceptable, and the kinds and timing of probes that are to be used, if any. The instructions should also specify the number and identity of respondents that interviewers need to contact and the time constraints under which they will be operating. It is also important that the instructions are well organized and unambiguous.

The instructions must be clearly articulated, and it is even more important that interviewers understand and can follow them. Practice training sessions can be necessary. It might also be necessary to actually interview the interviewers with respect to study purposes and procedures. Finally, interviewers might also be required to complete the questionnaire to see if there is a relationship between the interviewers' answers and the answers they get when administering the questionnaire.

BEHAVIORAL FACTORS

The respondents' background, attitudes, expectations, and motives are also potentially biasing. Whether they actually do introduce bias depends on how the interviewer and respondent interact. In other words, the predisposition to bias becomes operative only in behavior.

For example, even when the interviewing instructions and rules are rigid and the questionnaires relatively simple and structured, interviewers do not necessarily follow the rules. Interviewers might shorten questions or fail to follow up ambiguous answers, thereby introducing bias.

At least three interviewer behaviors lead to response bias: (1) errors in asking questions and in probing when additional information is required, (2) errors in recording the answer, and (3) errors due to cheating. The first problem is particularly acute with open-ended questions. No two inter-

Ethical Dilemma 13.3

A well-known car agency needed to make a decision about whether to import a relatively unknown line of foreign cars to complement its domestic line. To aid in its decision making, the agency contracted a research firm to conduct a study to determine potential consumer interest in and demand for this foreign car line. The results indicated that substantial awareness and interest existed, and consequently the decision was made to take on the new line.

To publicize the new line, a special preview was arranged for interested community members, such as local newspaper and radio people, executives in related automotive industries, filling station and repair shop owners, and leaders of men's and women's clubs. The agency's owners also wanted to invite the survey participants who had expressed an interest in the car; consequently, they asked the research firm to make known to them the respondents' names. The research firm refused to comply with this request, arguing that to do so would be a violation of the respondents' promised anonymity.

- Should the research firm comply with the agency's request?
- Does the car agency have the right to receive the participants' names since it has paid for the research?
- Would it have made a difference if the study had not been one to determine sales potential?
- What are some of the consequences of making the respondents' names known to the car agency?
- If the question had been anticipated before the survey was begun, could the interview structure have avoided the dilemma in which the company and the agency now find themselves?

viewers are likely to use the same probes. Differences in answers, then, may be due to the probes rather than any "true" differences in the attitudes of the respondents.

The phrasing of questions can also introduce error. Interviewers sometimes reword the question to fit their perceptions of what the respondent is capable of understanding or in a way that incorporates their own opinions of what constitutes an appropriate answer. Even multiple-choice questions have potential for interviewer bias because interviewers sometimes emphasize one of the alternatives when stating the question. Slight changes in tone can change the meaning of the entire question.

One of an interviewer's main tasks is keeping the respondent interested and motivated. At the same time, the interviewer tries to record what the respondent is saying by dutifully writing down the person's answers. These dual, sometimes incompatible, responsibilities can also be a source of error. Interviewers may not correctly "hear" what the respondent is actually saying. Perhaps the respondent is inarticulate, or perhaps the interviewer is recording what he or she wants to record. Lest we be too hard on interviewers, however, we need to recognize that their job is a difficult one. It demands a good deal of ingenuity, creativity, and dogged determination. Computer-driven surveys relieve some of these problems, but of course introduce others (e.g., a respondent cannot ask for clarification).

Finally, interviewer cheating can also be a source of response error. Cheating may range from the fabrication of a whole interview to one or two answers to make the response complete. Most commercial research firms validate 10 to 20% of the completed interviews through follow-up telephone calls or by sending postcards to a sample of "respondents" to verify that they have in fact been contacted.

Another form of cheating, which is not exactly response error but which has a strong effect on all nonsampling errors, is padding bills. The interviewer may falsify

Ethical Dilemma 13.4

"These new computer-voiced telephone surveys are wonderful!" your friend enthuses over lunch. "We don't have to pay telephone interviewers, so we can afford to have target numbers automatically redialed until someone answers. The public finds the computer's voice irritating and the whole notion of being interviewed by a machine rather humiliating, but we can overcome most people's reluctance to participate by repeatedly calling them until they give in and complete the questionnaire."

- Is it ethical to contact respondents repeatedly until they agree to participate in a research study? How many contacts are legitimate?
- If an industry is unable to constrain its members to behave ethically, should the government step in with regulations?
- If the public reacts against this kind of telephone survey, what are the results likely to be for researchers using traditional, more considerate telephone surveys?

the number of hours worked or the number of miles traveled. The problem is widespread because of the nature of the interviewing situation. The interviewer works without direct supervision in a low-paying job. Further, the supervisor's pay is normally geared to the interviewer's charges, so the higher the interviewer's bills, the higher the supervisor's compensation. Bill padding drains resources from other parts of the study and thereby decreases the efficiency and value of the information because it is obtained at higher cost.

As we've stated, it is more difficult to adjust for response errors than for nonresponse errors. Their direction and magnitude are unknown, because in order to estimate their effects, the true value must be known. The researcher's main hope lies in prevention rather than subsequent adjustment of the results. The various sources of errors themselves suggest preventives. For example, training can help reduce errors in asking questions and recording answers. Similarly, the way interviewers are selected, paid, and controlled could reduce cheating. Overall interviewer performance can be assessed by rating the quality of the work in terms of appropriate characteristics, such as costs, types of errors, ability to follow instructions, and so on. It's a beginning to recognize the existence of response errors, their sources, and their potentially devastating effect.

OFFICE ERRORS

Problems with nonsampling errors do not end with data collection. Errors arise in the editing, coding, tabulation, and analysis of the data. For the most part, these errors can be reduced, if not eliminated, through the exercise of proper controls in data processing. These questions are discussed in the next chapter.

Total Error Is Key

By now you can see that "total" error, rather than any single type of error, is key in designing good marketing research. Statistical theory indicates that large samples are much more likely to produce a statistic close to the population parameter being estimated than a small sample. However, that theory applies only to sampling error. Nonsampling error may increase because the larger sample requires more interviewers, which creates additional burdens in selection, training, and control. Further, nonsampling error is a much more insidious kind of error. We have attempted to highlight some of the more common sources of nonsampling error and suggest ways of dealing with them.

Table 13.2 summarizes the issues regarding nonsampling errors and how they can be reduced or controlled. You can use it as a checklist to evaluate the quality of research before making managerial decisions on the basis of the results.

TABLE 13.2
Overview of Nonsampling
Errors and Some Methods
for Handling Them

Type	Definition	Methods for Handling
Noncoverage	Failure to include some elements of the defined survey population in the sampling frame.	1. Improve basic sampling frame using othersources. 2. Select sample in such a way as to reduce incidence, such as by ignoring ineligibles on a list. 3. Adjust the results by appropriately weighting the subsample results.
Nonresponse	Failure to get data from some elements of the population that were selected for the sample	
Not-at-homes	Designated respondent is not home when the interviewer calls.	1. Have interviewers make advance appointments. 2. Call back at another time, preferably at a different time of day. 3. Attempt to contact the designated respondent using another approach (e.g., use a modified callback).
Refusals	Respondent refuses to cooperate in the survey.	1. Attempt to convince respondent of the value of the research and the importance of his or her participation. 2. Provide advance notice that the survey is coming. 3. Guarantee anonymity. 4. Provide an incentive for participating. 5. Hide sponsorship by using an independent research organization. 6. Try "foot in the door"; get respondent to comply with some small request before getting the survey. 7. Use personalized cover letters. 8. Use a follow-up contact at a more convenient time. 9. Avoid interesting-but-not-vital questions. 10. Adjust the results to account for the nonresponse.
Field	Although the individual participates in the study, he or she refuses to answer specific questions or provides incorrect answers to them.	1. Match interviewer-respondent background characteristics. 2. Make sure interviewer instructions are clear and written down. 3. Conduct practice training sessions with interviewers. 4. Examine interviewers' understanding of the study's purposes and procedures.

(continued)

TABLE 13.2
(continued)

Type	Definition	Methods for Handling
Field (cont.)		5. Have interviewers complete the questionnaire, examine the replies to check for relationship between these answers and their own answers.
		6. Verify a sample of each interviewer's interviews.
Office	Errors that arise when coding, tabulating, or analyzing the data	1. Use field edit to detect glaring omissions and inaccuracies in the data.
		2. Use a second edit in the office to decide how to handle data with incomplete answers, obviously wrong answers, and answers that reflect a lack of interest.
		3. Use closed questions to simplify coding, and specify the appropriate codes that will be allowed when using open-ended questions.
		4. When open-ended questions are being coded and multiple coders are used, divide the task by questions, not by data-collection forms.
		5. Have each coder code a sample of the other's work to ensure a consistent set of coding criteria is being employed.
		6. Follow established conventions; use numeric codes and not letters of the alphabet when coding the data for computer analysis.
		7. Prepare a code book that lists the codes for each variable and the categories included in each code.
		8. Use appropriate methods to analyze the data.

Summary

This chapter concentrated on the data-collection phase of the research process. Researchers and consumers of research need to be aware of the many potential sources of error so that they can better evaluate research proposals and can place research results in a proper perspective. Researchers need an understanding of error sources so they can design studies with proper controls and allowances.

The main distinction is that between sampling error and nonsampling error. Sampling error represents the difference between the observed values of a variable and the long-run average of the observed values in repetitions of the measurement. Nonsampling errors include everything else. They may arise because of errors in conception, logic, analysis, data gathering, etc. They are divided into the two major categories: errors of nonobservation, and errors of observation. Errors of nonobservation can, in turn, be divided into: errors of noncoverage, and errors of nonresponse. Errors of observation arise while collecting the data or while processing the information collected.

Noncoverage errors are essentially sampling frame problems. The list of population elements is rarely complete. Nonresponse errors reflect a failure to obtain information from certain elements of the population that were designated for inclusion in the sample. They can arise because the designated respondent was not at home or refused to participate. Empirical evidence indicates that the not-at-homes and the refusals differ from respondents, and thus a systematic bias is introduced when they are excluded.

The interviewer-interviewee interaction model was offered as a vehicle for conceptualizing the errors that can arise while collecting the data. This model presents the interview as an interactive process between interviewer and respondent. Each principal brings different background and psychological factors to the interview. These affect each person's behavior and the way he or she perceives the other's behavior.

Finally, office errors occur because of weaknesses in the procedures for editing, coding, tabulating, and analyzing the collected data. The research objective of minimization of total error was reiterated. Total error in conjunction with cost determines the value of any research effort.

Review Questions

1. Distinguish between sampling error and nonsampling error. Why is the distinction important?

2. What are noncoverage errors? Are they a problem with telephone surveys? Mail surveys? Personal interview studies? E-mail or Web questionnaires? How?

3. How can noncoverage bias be assessed? What can be done to reduce it?

4. What is nonresponse error?

5. What are the basic types of nonresponse error? Are they equally serious for mail, telephone, e-mail, Web, or personal interview studies? Explain.

6. What can be done to reduce the incidence of not-at-homes in the final sample?

7. What is the contact rate? What role does it play in evaluating the results?

8. What are the typical reasons why designated respondents refuse to participate in a study? What can be done to reduce the incidence of refusals? Do refusals generally introduce random error or systematic biases into studies?

9. What is item nonresponse? What alternatives are available to the researcher for treating item nonresponse?

10. What is the response rate? What is the completeness rate? Is there any relation between the two?

11. What are observation errors? What are the basic types of observation errors?

12. Are observation errors likely to be a more serious or less serious problem than nonobservation errors? Explain.

13. Describe the interviewer-interviewee interaction model, including its basic propositions.

14. What does the interviewer-interviewee interaction model suggest with respect to the background characteristics of interviewers? With respect to their psychological characteristics?

15. What types of interviewer behavior can lead to response bias?

16. Explain the statement, "Total error is key."

Applications and Problems

1. Discuss some of the potential problems with each of the following sampling frames. For each potential problem you list, indicate whether it would result in a noncoverage or overcoverage error.

   a. Phone book

   b. Mailing list

   c. E-mail list of students enrolled in your business school

   d. Maps

2. Sue Candleshoe, a manager of marketing research at a large over-the-counter drug manufacturer, wanted to investigate consumers' reactions to a recent poisoning scare in one of her brands. She needed the results quickly, but she was familiar with some of the faults of using a phone book for a sampling frame. Recommend another option that would allow Sue to get the results quickly by telephone but would not introduce as much bias as using a phone book. Discuss which biases, if any, your suggested solution might still have.

3. Henry Brown owns a sailboat rental yard located in Sister Bay, Wisconsin. He has been considering altering the services that his business offers to customers. He would like to offer sailboards for rental as well as add a convenience store so that customers could picnic at the state park adjacent to his rental yard. Before making these changes, he has decided to administer a short questionnaire in the store to a random sample of customers. For a period of one month, clerks have been instructed to conduct personal interviews with every fourth customer. Henry gave specific instructions that on no account were customers to be harassed or offended. Identify the major sources of noncoverage and nonresponse errors. Explain.

4. Deal-A-Wheel, a large manufacturer of radial tires located in Pittsburgh, Pennsylvania, was experiencing a problem common to tire manufacturers. The poor performance of the auto industry was having a severe negative impact on the tire industry. To maintain sales and competitive positions, the various manufacturers were offering wholesalers additional credit and discount opportunities. Deal-A-Wheel's management was particularly concerned about wholesaler reaction to a new discount policy they were considering. The first survey the company conducted to explore these reactions was unsatisfactory to top management. Management thought that it was conducted in a haphazard manner and contained numerous nonsampling errors. Deal-A-Wheel's management decided to conduct another study containing the following changes:

   a. The sampling frame was defined as a list of 1,000 of the largest wholesalers that stocked Deal-A-Wheel tires, and the sample elements were to be randomly selected from this list.

   b. A callback technique was to be employed, with the callbacks being made at times different from the original attempted contact.

   c. The sample size was to be doubled from 200 to 400 respondents.

   d. The sample elements that were ineligible or refused to cooperate were to be substituted for by the next element from the list.

   e. An incentive of a crisp dollar bill was to be offered to respondents.

   Critically evaluate the steps that were being considered to prevent the occurrence of nonsampling errors. Do you think they are appropriate? Be specific.

5. Andrew Blake is a new employee at S&S Research. He has just been instructed to write an introduction to a survey for a mail study. Andrew has been told that the survey will evaluate long-distance customers' reasons for calling long distance. He has also been told that the respondents will each receive $20 after the survey has been completed and returned to S&S. Andrew is having a difficult time remembering what he should include in an introduction in order to persuade respondents to complete the questionnaire. First, list several persuasive techniques that Andrew should include in his introduction, then write an introduction to this study that you think will increase the response rate.

6. Sharon Klein, the owner of a local furniture store chain, has recently hired you as her research analyst. Sharon has little experience in research and is expecting you to lead her in the right direction. She wants to conduct a study to determine the buying cycle for living room furniture. Sharon feels that the best approach in conducting this study is to use the largest possible sample that her budget allows. Try to convince Sharon why increasing the sample size may not be the best research strategy. Be sure to include specific strategies on which Sharon might want to spend some of her money rather than spending it all on increasing the sample size.

7. A major publisher of diverse magazines was interested in determining customer satisfaction with three of the company's leading publications: TrendSetter, BusWhiz, and CompuTech. The three magazines dealt with

women's fashions, business trends, and computer technology developments. Three sampling frames, consisting of lists of subscribers residing in New York, were formulated. Three random samples were to be chosen from these lists. Personal interviews were to be conducted. The publishing company had a regular pool of interviewers that it called on whenever interviews were to be conducted. The interviewers had varying educational backgrounds, although 95% were high school graduates and the remaining 5% had some college education. In terms of age and gender, the range varied from 18 to 45 years, with 70% female and 30% male. The majority of interviewers were stay-at-home moms and students. Before conducting a survey, the company sent the necessary information in the mail and asked interviewers to indicate whether they were interested. The questionnaires, addresses, and other detailed information were then sent to those interviewers replying affirmatively. After the interviewer completed his or her quota of interviews, the replies were sent back to the company. The company then mailed the interviewer's remuneration.

a. Using the guidelines in Table 13.2, critically evaluate the selection, training, and instructions given to the field interviewers.

b. Using the interaction model, identify the major sources of bias that would affect the interviews.

Cases

Riverside County Humane Society (B)

The demands on the Riverside County Humane Society (RCHS) had increased rather dramatically over the past several years, while the tax dollars the society received to provide services remained relatively unchanged. In an effort to halt further decline in the quality of its services and to provide better care for the pets at the center, the Membership Committee of the board of directors began making plans for a member/contributor drive. The organized drive was the first of its kind for the local chapter and the committee members wanted it to be as productive as possible.

As the plans began to evolve, the committee realized that the organization had only scattered bits and pieces of information about its current members. It did have a list of members and contributors for the last five years that had been compiled by the RCHS staff. In addition, it had access to the results of a survey that had been done by a staff member several years earlier that focused on member usage of shelter facilities and their opinions of shelter services and programs. However, the organization had only sparse knowledge of the profile of its typical member and contributor, why they belonged or contributed, how long they had been associated with the humane society, how the services of the humane society could be improved, and so on. The committee members believed information on these issues was important to the conduct of a successful membership drive, and thus they commissioned research to secure it.

Initial contacts with other humane society chapters and interviews with some RCHS staff and board members produced a number of hypotheses regarding who is likely to become a member or contributor, why, how much people are likely to give, and so on. The researchers are interested in examining these hypotheses through a mail survey sent to current members and contributors. (See Case 2.2, Riverside County Humane Society (A) for details.)

SAMPLING PLAN

For the last five years, the RCHS had maintained a master list of members and contributors. Contributors were those who had sent a donation to RCHS but had not filled out an official form making them members, which essentially entitled them to receive RCHS's newsletter. The separate list of members contained all those who had expressed interest in membership and who were receiving the newsletter. Both lists were alphabetical. The contributor list included the amount received from each person or business, but not the number of times the person or business had given during the last five years. The member list showed the number of years each organization or person had belonged.

For purposes of the study, all names of businesses or other organizations were deleted and a separate sample was taken from each list. Approximately 1,050 people were on the member list and 300 on the contributor list. The researchers decided to take 120 names from the member list and 50 from the contributor list. They identified those to be sent questionnaires by drawing two random numbers—3 and 5—using a random number table. They then sent questionnaires to the 3rd, 11th, 19th, and so on person on the member list, and the 5th, 11th, 17th, and so on, person on the contributor list.

Questions

1. What is the sampling frame and is it a good frame for the target population?
2. What type of sample is being used?
3. Can you think of some ways in which the sample could be improved?

PartyTime, Inc.[1]

Andrew Todd, chief executive officer of PartyTime, Inc., a manufacturer of specialty paper products, is preparing to make an important decision. In the 14 years since he founded the company, sales and profits have increased over tenfold to all-time highs of $7,000,000 and $1,150,000, respectively, during the current year. Industry analysts predict continued stable growth during the upcoming year. Despite his firm belief in the adage, "If it's not broken, don't fix it," Todd thinks that it might be time for the addition of a new channel of distribution, based on information he has recently received.

ABOUT THE COMPANY

PartyTime manufactures a variety of specialty paper products that can be grouped into three basic categories: gift wrap (all types), party goods (printed plates, cups, napkins, party favors, etc.), and other paper goods (e.g., specialty advertising and calendars). When Todd founded the company, he purchased and renovated an existing paper mill located in the Pacific Northwest. Today, company headquarters and production facilities remain at the original location. During the heavy production season, the company employs approximately 200 people. As shown in Table 4.2.1, gift wrap accounts for about 60% of revenues (50% of profits), and party goods amount to about 30% of sales (40% of profits). All other paper products sold by the company produce about 10% of revenues and an equivalent percentage of profits. Sales of gift wrap and other

[1] The contributions of Tom J. Brown to the development of this case are gratefully acknowledged.

TABLE 4.2.1 Current-Year Sales and Profit Breakdown by Category

Category	Sales	Percentage	Profit	Percentage
Gift wrap	$4,302,300	61	$564,700	49
Party goods	2,045,500	29	472,300	41
Other paper goods	705,200	10	115,000	10
Total	$7,053,000	100	$1,152,000	100

paper goods have been stable, increasing 3–4% per year during the previous five years. Interestingly (and as Todd is pleased to note), total sales of party goods have been increasing at about a 9% annual rate.

THE DISTRIBUTION DECISION

Given the profitability of the party-goods line and its substantial sales growth in recent years, Todd is very interested in further increasing sales of specialty party goods. A recent publication of the National Association of Paper and Party Retailers (NAPPR) indicated that industrywide sales of party goods are expected to increase some 10 to 20% during the upcoming year. Of particular interest is the projection that sales of party goods through independent party goods (IPG) shops will increase more than 25%. Currently, PartyTime party goods are distributed only through mass merchandisers and chain drugstores.

Although sales have been increasing steadily using existing channels, Todd wondered if the time was right to add the IPG channel. Any decision to include the new channel would have to be made early in the year, however, before orders for the holiday season begin arriving (a large percentage of total sales of party goods at the retail level occur during the holiday season).

INDEPENDENT PARTY GOODS (IPG) SHOPS

IPG retailers typically operate small to moderate-sized stores that are often located in malls or strip shopping centers. The label "independent" indicates that the stores are not owned or franchised by major manufacturers, such as Hallmark. In recent years, the number of IPG shops has grown tremendously, to the point where it is not unusual to have 15 to 20 shops in larger cities. Growth has been particularly strong in California, Florida, the upper Midwest, and the East.

COMPETITIVE ISSUES

Competition within traditional channels of distribution for party goods is intense. Within these channels, PartyTime must compete against major producers, such as C.A. Reed, Beach Products, Unique, Hallmark, and Ambassador. The major competitors within the IPG channel, in contrast, are fewer in number; only AMSCAM, Contempo, and Paper Art serve as primary suppliers. Competition within the IPG channel is thought to be much less intense than that in the traditional channels.

December 13 Todd is leaning strongly toward committing the resources necessary to enter the IPG channel and has called a meeting of his managers to discuss the proposed move. He believes that there is room for at least one more supplier, because the competition is less intense than in the traditional distribution channels. In addition, he regards this as an opportunity to further expand the most profitable area of PartyTime's business.

At the meeting, most of PartyTime's managers seem to agree with Todd, although Kim Shinoda, the company's chief accountant, suggests that the company should learn more about IPG retailers before a decision is made. In a memorandum distributed at the meeting, she details the following areas in which more information is needed before a decision is reached:

1. Competitive Products: Are IPG retailers satisfied with current product offerings on the market? Do they receive a satisfactory level of service from the current suppliers?
2. Purchase Criteria: In addition to price and product considerations, what other characteristics of suppliers and product lines do retailers think are important?
3. Supplier Loyalty: To what extent are retailers willing to carry product lines of more than one supplier?

Todd agrees that more information would be useful in making a decision, but he realizes that time constraints will force him to make a decision within the next few weeks. Along with his managers, he decides to bring in a marketing research team.

January 16 The marketing research team is now ready to share the results of the research project with the managers at PartyTime. To implement the research, they had developed an undisguised, semistructured telephone questionnaire designed to obtain the information that Shinoda had suggested.

Officials at PartyTime are particularly interested in the responses of retailers located in those geographic areas in which growth is expected to be strongest over the next year; therefore, a sampling frame was developed using telephone directories in the major cities within these geographic regions. Because many types of stores could conceivably be considered

IPG shops, two criteria were established for inclusion in the sampling frame: (1) the shop must devote more than 50% of its shelf space to paper and party goods, and (2) the shop must carry products from more than one supplier. A total of 110 shops were identified using the telephone directories. Although attempts were made to contact each of these shops during business hours, only 82 could be reached. Thirty-two of these met the two criteria, and 23 agreed to participate in the interview.

January 19 Based on the results of the marketing research project and the input of his managers, Todd has decided to increase production of party goods and market these products through the IPG channel.

Questions

1. Evaluate the research team's development of the sample of store owners. How would you have recommended the research team develop the sampling frame?
2. Do you think that a telephone survey was the best way to collect the needed information?

CASE 4.3
HotStuff Computer Software (B)

Simpson, Edwards and Associates, encouraged by its success with a computer software package for government agencies, is developing a second software product, Hot-Stuff, which is tailored specifically for use in the firefighting industry. In the normal course of affairs, fire departments need to handle and store a considerable amount of information: building layouts, hazardous material characteristics and locations, equipment inventories, and so on. Further, although some exploratory research has suggested that some fire departments already owned computers, it was generally recognized that the information-processing needs of the industry made additional computerization a likely probability. Based on preliminary inquiries into the composition of the industry, Simpson, Edwards and Associates decided to restrict its marketing efforts to volunteer fire departments only, at least initially, and planned a national survey to determine the market potential of HotStuff.

SAMPLING PLAN

The key issue in executing a national survey turned on sampling control: how could the research select and contract volunteer fire departments in a reliable, systematic fashion? After much deliberation and a few false starts, Craig Simpson's research staff finally presented him with two cohesive sampling plans.

Option 1 The first option that Craig and his staff considered was a mail survey based on a sample drawn from a list of volunteer fire departments nationwide. The National Fire Protection Agency, like other national fire safety organizations, had a comprehensive mailing list of all 30,000 United States fire departments, but it did not distinguish between volunteer and municipal fire departments. Fortunately, the research team discovered a firm that sells listings of population groups. Moreover, the company could provide Craig's team with an exhaustive mailing list of volunteer fire departments, organized by the state in which they are located. The total number of volunteer fire departments included on the recently updated list was almost 20,000, and the cost of sampling names from the list was $40 per 1,000 departments sampled. The names could be drawn according to whatever scheme Simpson, Edwards and Associates preferred.

The research team believed that a viable way to proceed to sample from the list would be to order the 48 states in the United States (excluding Alaska and Hawaii) according to the number of volunteer fire departments in each state. Once the states were ordered from smallest to largest in terms of incidence of volunteer fire departments, a sample could be drawn from all the departments on the list by selecting every kth department after a random beginning. If it adopted a pessimistic perspective, expected only a 20% response rate, and were satisfied with only 100 completed surveys, Simpson, Edwards and Associates calculated that it would need to mail 500 questionnaires. With 20,000 population elements and a sample of 500, every 40th volunteer fire station on the list would need to be selected, after a random start between 1 and 40.

Option 2 The second sampling plan being considered was founded on information received from the local state fire marshall and on two assumptions. The marshall informed the researchers that most volunteer fire departments were located in communities with populations under 25,000. Based on the assumption that towns with a population under 5,000 would be too small to productively use a computer, the team decided that it should concentrate on two categories of towns: those with populations between 5,000 and 15,000, and those with populations between 15,000 and 25,000. In addition, it seemed logical to assume that volunteer fire departments located near large cities would be more progressive than those in more isolated areas and thus they would be more likely to own or plan to purchase a computer. Consistent with the preceding reasoning, the research team also considered drawing a sample in the following way:

- Step 1: Randomly select two cities of over 10,000 inhabitants from every state in the continental United States.
- Step 2: Randomly select a town of population 5,000–15,000 within 20 miles of one city, and a town of population 15,000–25,000 within 20 miles of the second city.
- Step 3: Obtain telephone numbers of the volunteer fire departments in each of the two towns selected in each state from Directory Assistance.

This strategy would provide a sample size of 96 volunteer fire departments from the 48 states. After some discussion, Craig decided to adopt the second option to use in conjunction with a telephone survey.

Questions

1. What kind of sampling plan was considered for sampling from the mailing list?
2. What kind of sampling plan was actually used to sample volunteer fire departments?
3. Evaluate the sampling plans.

CASE 4.4

International Differences in the Cost of Data

A multinational bank, MNB, was interested in measuring customer satisfaction with its consumer banking services and financial products. The managers at MNB Corporate differed in their opinions regarding the form of the optimal customer satisfaction study: survey, focus group, interview, and so on. So as a starting point, MNB commissioned bids from marketing research firms in the United States to describe how they would approach studying their U.S. banking customers. In particular, they asked the bidding firms to offer cost estimates; that is, how many customers could be sampled given the proposed budget of $15,000 for this research project using different techniques.

The bids covered a variety of research methods, which differed in their costs. They considered a personal interview method in which the customer would be intercepted in the bank and asked several questions regarding service and satisfaction. They compared that method to the costs of sending out mail surveys to current customers. Finally, they explored the efficiency of placing small, postcard-sized surveys at each teller station that the banking customer might pick up and complete and return at their leisure.

MNB gathered the marketing research firms' proposals to begin to make a decision of how the bank should approach its customers. In terms of outlay expenses, more postcards could be printed less expensively than surveys sent or interviewers staffing each of the local bank branches. However, in terms of response rates, somewhat fewer people turned down the personal interview than who returned the mail survey or postcard survey. Table 4.4.1 presents the comparative estimates for the three different techniques. Clearly the table shows that in the U.S., the postcard technique appears to be the most cost effective. Thus, the bank managers are considering implementing this research tool.

MNB Corporate's second concern is with a few of its satellite locations; in particular the news from abroad is that the Indonesian banking customers are not happy, and MNB wants to understand what is going on. Its first assumption was that the bank should proceed with the postcard methodology to be able to compare the results in Indonesia to those from the States. However, they conducted some preliminary investigations and found the costs of the methods to be quite different. The bank plans to proceed with personal interviews in Indonesia. Consider Tables 4.4.1 and 4.4.2 and answer the questions that follow.

Questions

1. Under what conditions might it matter that one method is used in one country and another method is used in another?
2. What is the target population under investigation, both in the U.S. and in Indonesia? What are the differences between the sampling frames of each of the three techniques? What customers will each technique miss?
3. What other issues must the bank managers consider in addition to the cost efficiencies of the three methods?

TABLE 4.4.1 The Estimates for the U.S. Samples

	Interview	Mail Survey	Postcards
a. Research budget	$15,000	$15,000	$15,000
b. Cost per contact	$25	$2.50	$0.25
c. Prospects reached*	2400	6000	60,000
d. Response rate	5%	3%	1.5%
e. Estimated net sample size (c × d)	120	180	900
f. Effective cost per capita (a/e)	$125.00	$83.33	$16.67

* For mail and postcard, c = a/b; for interviews, cost is $25 per hour, times a five-hour day, = $125 per day, for each interviewer. Each of 12 interviewers (spread across the area local bank branches) would spend two weeks (10 bank days) approaching and interviewing customers. Each interviewer on each day would target 20 bank customers, on average.

TABLE 4.4.2 The Projections for Indonesia

	Interview	Mail Survey	Postcards
a. Research budget	$15,000	$15,000	$15,000
b. Cost per contact	$12*	$2.50	$0.25
c. Prospects reached	5000	6000	60,000
d. Response rate	20%*	1.5%*	0.5%
e. Estimated net sample size (c x d)	1000	90	300
f. Effective cost per capita (a/e)	$15.00	$166.67	$50.00

* These estimates differ from those for conducting the research in the States. Labor costs for interviewing are much less, propensities for customers to acquiesce and be interviewed are much greater, mail surveys are somewhat less efficient because CD-ROM databases on addresses are less accurate, and postcards are an unfamiliar format and are therefore rarely filled out. Given the changes in the interviewing parameters, if the project duration is still two weeks, 25 interviewers can be deployed, so 5,000 customers would be approached.

CASE 4.5

Digital Euro Music

The music industry is nearing a revolution as consumers pull digital recordings off of the Internet. Music is available online through a variety of portals, most of which use a compression software like MP3 to file music in portable sizes to download and play. A hand-held device can contain hours of personally selected favorite tunes.

A variety of devices are available for purchase to store and play back the digital, compressed music files. These hand-held jukeboxes differ on a number of attributes: price, memory storage, batteries required, whether the LCD provides information on the album title and artist, remaining battery life and storage space, and so forth. Music industry experts claim the sound is not as good as CD-quality sound, but "blind" hearing tests suggest consumers cannot distinguish between a song played directly from a CD versus one that had been compressed, stored, and replayed.

Downloading music is becoming an increasingly popular phenomenon. Currently, approximately one-third to one-half of Internet users have or shortly expect to download music. The confluence of the product sought (that is, music) and the technology by which it is obtained (the Internet) suggests that digital music players would be more popular with younger people, and indeed, teenagers are more likely to be visitors of online music sites than are older people. Internet music sites are hitting heads with traditional music providers (for example, Sony Music Entertainment) over copyrights and issues of piracy. However, even the big, established music companies acknowledge the digital music future, as all the industry players struggle to sort out what form will be attractive to consumers and yet protect the current copyrights.

A new wrinkle is that the software and playback devices are entering other markets. The hand-held devices are being "pulled" through channels by international customers who have Internet access, and therefore access to the compressed music files, but no devices for playback. Some music industry analysts think the European market will not be a large one for these portable MP3 players because Internet penetration in Europe still somewhat lags that in the States. Others worry that it might become even more popular to circumvent the European taxes. Specifically, Table 4.5.1 contains the Value Added Tax (VAT) for CDs in most of the European countries; the VATs for books are given for comparison. (The VATs for books are lower than those for CDs because a book is considered a purchase of greater cultural status.) Consider these figures and answer the questions that follow.

Questions

1. If you were determining which European countries to target first, what information would be most useful to you in the table? What information is lacking?
2. How would you sample potential customers from more than one country?
3. If the MP3 music format is newer to Europeans, what kinds of questions would you ask in those countries compared to the questions you would ask of the U.S. consumers?
4. How would you determine whether there might be market potential in Australia, Japan, or Hong Kong?

TABLE 4.5.1

Country	Population (Millions)	Expenditure per Capita (ECU)	Album Units per Capita	VAT on CDs (%)	VAT on Books (%)
Austria	8.1	38.9	2.7	20	10
Belgium	10.2	30.0	2.0	21	6
Denmark	5.3	45.5	3.4	25	25
Finland	5.1	22.0	2.1	22	0
France	58.6	33.1	2.1	21	6
Germany	81.7	30.6	2.7	16	7
Greece	10.5	9.8	0.8	18	4
Ireland	3.6	26.7	1.8	21	0
Italy	57.6	9.1	1.0	20	4
Netherlands	15.6	34.3	2.4	18	6
Norway	4.4	52.3	3.0	23	0
Portugal	9.9	14.5	1.4	17	5
Spain	39.4	13.4	1.4	16	4
Sweden	8.9	36.8	2.5	25	25
Switzerland	7.1	38.4	3.1	7	0
U.K.	60.0	40.1	3.3	18	0

CASE 4.6

Sampling Gambling

Americans spend nearly $50 billion annually on gambling. That expenditure is more than three times the amount spent on going to the movies and theme parks, as alternative means of entertainment. State-run lotteries and casino games are the most popular legal games of chance. Gambling traditionally held negative connotations, being associated with immoral or even criminal behavior. Critics worry that legalized gambling can encourage compulsive gamblers, that it may encourage people to gamble who can least afford to do so, and that casinos bring an undesirable element to the surrounding neighborhood.

Legalized gambling, however, especially in the form of state lotteries, has largely sanitized the image of gaming behavior. Among people who abstain from gambling, fewer people cite moral or religious objections, instead offering practical reasons: for example, they don't want to spend the money or they don't have the money to spend. Proponents claim casinos create jobs and provide revenue for education that would otherwise be raised by tax hikes.

Secondary data suggest that there is no particular demographic profile of a gambler—people of all walks of life (for example, age and income) enjoy casinos and lotteries. Beyond demographics, the commonly held motivations appear to be a desire to win a large amount of money, and a quick and relatively inexpensive form of entertainment.

The heterogeneity of the demographics of gamblers, and the homogeneity of the motives of gamblers have left some casino managers perplexed as to how the consumer market might be segmented. One hypothesis, based on collective wisdom, is that novice gamblers tend to prefer slot machines because they are simple, whereas more experienced gamblers prefer games like blackjack, baccarat, and craps because they are more strategic in nature. Another frequent assumption is that people who buy lottery tickets are different from people who go to casinos, and that the two types of games satisfy different needs.

The Internet introduces yet another medium in which a consumer might gamble. Although the number of gamblers online are far fewer than those who frequent casinos or lotteries, and online gambling revenues are far less than nonelectronic games (approximately only $2 billion), the online gambling industry is expected to enjoy rapid growth.

If a gaming industry representative were to come to

you and say, "I'd like to do some interviews. I want to know more about what kinds of games my casino visitors want me to provide. I want to know how much floor space to allot to slots versus blackjack tables. I want to know why they come to any casino, or my casino, rather than to the movies or something. Maybe I should just sell lottery tickets." How would you address the following issues?

Questions

1. What is the relevant population?
2. What would you recommend in terms of a sampling plan—would you intercept people in (or entering or exiting) casinos? Would you talk to people buying lottery tickets at convenience stores? Would you interview people strolling along in a shopping mall? What sampling frame does each of these locations presume?
3. If you wanted to verify the aforementioned assumptions (for example, that demographics do not matter, or that novice versus experienced gamblers have different game preferences), how would you modify your sampling plan?
4. How would you try to assess objectively whether there are moral or religious concerns against gambling? What kinds of sampling plans would you need to avoid, given the likelihood that they would shape your conclusions pro or con?

PART 5

Data Analysis and Interpretation

Once data have been collected, the research process logically turns to analysis, which amounts to the search for meaning in the data. This *translation and interpretation* of data into *information and meaning* involves many questions and several steps:

- Chapter 14 presents the idea of "preprocessing" the data—before analyses are run; e.g., from editing and wording, to "cross-tabs."
  - The Appendix to Chapter 14 presents the chi-square and log linear models.

- Chapter 15 raises the questions that help us select the proper statistical analyses to conduct on the data.
  - The Appendix to Chapter 15 presents a quick stats review, covering the logic of hypothesis testing, Type I and Type II errors, and the concept of power.

- Chapter 16 presents procedures appropriate for examining group differences.
  - The Appendix to Chapter 16 extends the tests of differences to three or more groups, in the analysis of variance.

- Chapter 17 examines associations between variables, such as correlations and regressions for forecasting.

- Chapter 18 introduces the multivariate techniques of discriminant analysis, factor analysis, cluster analysis, and multidimensional scaling.
  - The Appendix to Chapter 18 continues with more contemporary multivariate techniques.

Preprocessing the Data, and Doing Cross-Tabs

Questions to Guide Your Learning:

Q1: What are the basic steps in getting data ready for analysis?

Q2: What are coding, editing, and tabulation?

Q3: What information can we get from a *frequency table*?

Q4: What can I do with *nominal* data? What's a *chi-square* goodness-of-fit test?

Q5: What can I do with *rank order* data? What's a *Kolmogorov-Smirnov* test?

Q6: What's a *cross-tab*?

Q7: What information can I get from a *contingency table*; what does "*conditional probability*" mean?

The purpose of analysis is to obtain meaning from the data. All previous steps in the research process have been undertaken to support this search for meaning. The specific analytical procedures to be used are closely related to the preceding steps, and so should be factored in when designing the other steps. The marketing researcher should go so far as to develop dummy tables, indicating how each item of information will be used, before beginning data collection. Thorough preparatory work should reveal undesirable data gaps and should also pinpoint items that are "interesting" but that do not relate to the problem being examined.

The search for meaning can take many forms. In this chapter, we examine the preliminary analytical steps of editing, coding, and tabulation. When we create tables for the frequency distributions of variables, we also look at the chi-square statistic.

Editing

The basic purpose of editing is to impose some minimum quality standards on the raw data. Editing involves the inspection and, if necessary, correction of each questionnaire or observation form. Inspection and correction are often done in two stages: the field edit and the central office edit.

Field Edit

The **field edit** is a preliminary edit, designed to detect the most glaring omissions and inaccuracies in the data. It is also useful in helping to control the field force and to clear up its misunderstandings about procedures, specific questions, etc. For example, if the field staff is supposed to interview people, but all the questionnaires from one particular field agent have different markings, you'll know that person just gave the survey to the respondents to fill out themselves.

Ideally, the field edit is done as soon as possible after the questionnaire (or other data-collection form) has been administered, so that problems can be corrected before the interviewing or observation staff is disbanded and while the experience is still fresh in the interviewer's mind. The preliminary edit is most often conducted by a field supervisor. Some of the items that are checked are described in Research Realities 14.1.

Central Office Edit

The field edit is typically followed by a **central office edit**. This involves more complete and exacting scrutiny and correction of the completed returns. The work calls for the keen eye of a person well versed in the objectives and procedures of the study. To ensure consistency of treatment, it is best if one individual handles all completed instruments. If this is impossible because of length and time considerations, the work can be divided. However, the division should be by parts of the data-collection instruments rather than by respondents. That is, one editor would be concerned with editing "Part A," say, of all questionnaires, while the other would edit "Part B."

Unlike the field edit, the central office edit depends less on follow-up procedures and more on deciding just what to do with the data. Follow-up is now more difficult because of the time that has elapsed. In deciding what to do with the data, the editor usually has to decide how to handle incomplete answers, obviously wrong answers, and answers that reflect a lack of interest. Because such problems are more prevalent with questionnaires than with observational forms, we discuss these difficulties from that perspective, but the discussion applies to all types of data-collection forms.

It almost never happens that a study has all the returned questionnaires completely filled out. Some surveys have entire sections omitted; others reflect sporadic item nonresponse. The editor's decision on how to handle these incomplete questionnaires depends on the severity of the problem. Questionnaires that omit entire sections are obviously suspect, yet they should not automatically be thrown out. It

The preprocessing data mantra: editing, coding, tabulation!

Research Realities

14.1 Items Checked in the Field Edit

1. *Completeness:* The check for completeness involves scrutinizing the data form to ensure that no sections or pages were omitted, and checking individual items. A blank for a specific question could mean that the respondent refused to answer; alternatively, it may simply reflect an oversight on the respondent's part, or that she or he did not know the answer. It may be important for the purposes of the study to know which reason is correct. By contacting the field worker while the interview is fresh in her or his mind, the needed clarification should be provided.

2. *Legibility:* It is impossible to code a questionnaire that cannot be deciphered because the interviewer's handwriting is unintelligible or because abbreviations were used that are not understood by others. It is a simple matter to correct this now, whereas it is often extremely time consuming later.

3. *Comprehensibility:* Sometimes a recorded response is incomprehensible to all but the field interviewer. By detecting this now, the necessary clarification can be easily provided.

4. *Consistency:* Marked inconsistencies within an interview or observation schedule typically indicate errors in collecting or recording the data and may indicate ambiguity in the instrument or carelessness in its administration. For instance, if a respondent indicated that she or he saw a particular commercial on TV last night on one part of the questionnaire and later indicated that she or he did not watch TV last night, the analyst would indeed be in a dilemma. Such inconsistencies should be detected and corrected in the field edit.

5. *Uniformity:* It is very important that the responses be recorded in uniform units. For instance, if the study is aimed at determining the number of magazines read per week per individual, and the respondent indicates the number of magazines for which she or he has monthly subscriptions, the response base is not uniform, and the result could cause no small amount of confusion in the later stages of analysis. If detected now, perhaps the interviewer can recontact the respondent and get the correct answer.

might be, for example, that the omitted section is not relevant. This person's data would be usable in spite of the incomplete section. Alternatively, there might not be a logical justification for the large number of questions that went unanswered. In this case, the total reply would probably be thrown out, increasing the nonresponse rate for the study. Questionnaires containing only isolated instances of item nonresponse would be retained, although they might undergo some data cleaning after coding, a subject discussed later in this chapter.

Careful editing of the questionnaire sometimes shows that an answer to a question is obviously incorrect. For example, respondents might be asked for the type of store in which they purchased a camera in one part of the questionnaire and the name of the store in another. If the person responded "department store" whereas the name of the store indicated a discount store, one of the answers is incorrect. The editor may be able to determine which from other information in the questionnaire. Alternatively, the editor may need to establish policies concerning which answer will be treated as correct, if either, when these inconsistencies or inaccuracies arise.

Indications that the completed questionnaire reflects a lack of interest on the part of the subject are sometimes subtle and sometimes obvious. For example, a subject who checked the "5" position on a five-point scale for each of the 40 items in an attitude questionnaire in which some items were expressed negatively and some positively is obviously not taking the study very seriously. An editor would probably throw out such a response. A discerning editor might also be able to pick up more subtle indications of disinterest, such as check marks that are not within the boxes provided, scribbles, spills on the questionnaire, and so on. An editor may not want to throw out these responses, but they should be coded so that it is later possible to run separate tabulations for both questionable instruments and obviously good questionnaires, to see if that makes any difference in the results and conclusions.

Coding

Coding is the technical procedure by which raw data are transformed into symbols. Most often the symbols are numerals, because they can be tabulated and counted more easily. The transformation is not automatic, however, but involves judgment on the part of the coder.

The first step in coding is specifying the categories or classes into which the responses are to be placed. There is no magic number of categories. Rather, the number depends on the research problem being investigated and the specific items used to generate the information. Nevertheless, several rules for specifying the classes can be stated. First, the classes should be mutually exclusive and exhaustive. Every response should logically fall into one and only one category. Multiple responses are legitimate, of course, if the question is, "For what purposes do you use whipped cream?" and the responses include "a dessert item," "an evening snack," "an afternoon snack," and so on. Or, if a question focuses on the person's age, then only one age category is, of course, acceptable, and the code should indicate unequivocally one category.

Coding closed questions and most scaling devices is simple because the coding is established, for all practical purposes, when the data-collection instrument is designed (e.g., a 7-point scale results in data of 1s through 7s). Coding open-ended questions can be very difficult and time consuming, and is therefore more expensive. The coder has to determine appropriate categories on the basis of answers that are not always anticipated. Because of the freedom allowed respondents, the responses to open-ended questions are often so vague that they can be misclassified by coders in spite of the detailed instructions given them.[1]

International studies can create their own special coding problems because different labels may mean different things. For example, a conservative in Russia is someone who wishes to adhere to or return to the "old Communism," which would be coded as left wing in Western countries. Liberal Russians, in turn, are the ones who wish to introduce market perspectives into economics and politics, a perspective that would be coded as "conservative" in the West.

When using several coders, it's best to have each coder focus on one or two questions, so they can get "good" at coding those questions, and provide consistency across the respondents' questionnaires. This approach is also more efficient because coders can learn the codes for their few questions without having to consult the code book for every survey. If several people do code the same question, be sure they also code a sample of the others' work to ensure that they're all using a consistent set of coding criteria.[2]

The second step in coding involves assigning code numbers to the classes. For example, gender might be assigned the letters M for male and F for female. Alternatively, the classes could be denoted by 1 for male and 2 for female. Generally, it is better to use numbers than letters. It also is better to treat numerical data in their reported form at this stage rather than collapsing data into categories. For example, it is not advisable to code age in years as 1 = under 20, 2 = 20 to 29, 3 = 30 to 39, and so on. This would entail some unnecessary sacrifice of information in the original measurement and if need be can be done at later stages in the analysis.

---

[1] For examples of instructions for coding open-ended questions, see Carl Auerbach and Louise Silverstein, *Qualitative Data: An Introduction to Coding and Analysis* (New York University Press, 2003).

[2] For more on inter-coder reliability indices, see Kilem Gwet, *Handbook of Inter-Rater Reliability* (Stataxis, 2001).

Most data analysis is done by computer, so it is necessary to code the data so they can be read by the machine. Regardless of whether that input comes directly through a keyboard, by mouse-activated optical readers, etc., it is helpful to visualize the input in terms of a multiple-column record. Further, it is advisable to follow certain conventions when coding the data:

1. Use only one character per column. Most computer programs cannot read multiple characters per column. When the question allows multiple responses, use separate columns for each answer. Thus, the question on whipped cream usage would dictate that a separate column be provided in the coding form to indicate whether the respondent used it as a dessert item, another column for use as an evening snack, and so on.

2. Use only numeric codes and not letters of the alphabet, special characters such as @, or blanks. Most computer statistical programs have severe difficulty manipulating anything but numbers.

3. The field or portion of the record assigned to a variable should consist of as many columns as are necessary to capture the variable. Thus, if the variable is such that the 10 codes from 0 to 9 are not sufficient to exhaust the categories, then the analyst should use two columns in the record, which provides 100 codes from 00 through 99. Moreover, no more than one variable should be assigned to any field. Sometimes programs make these adjustments automatically. For instance, you type in a "100" in an Excel spreadsheet, and it captures the number as "100" not "1" and "0" and "0," and furthermore, when the data are then imported into a package like Sas or Spss, those programs usually also recognize the "100."

4. Use standard codes for "No information." Thus, all "Don't know" responses, for any question on the survey, might be coded 8, "No answers" as 9, and "Does not apply" as 0.

5. Give each respondent an identification number. This number need not, and typically does not, identify the respondent by name. The number simply ties the questionnaire to the coded data. This is often useful when data cleaning. If there are too many variables for one line, be sure to repeat the respondent ID number on each record. Column 10 in the first line might then indicate how the respondent answered Question 2, whereas Column 10 in the second record might indicate whether the person is male or female.[3]

The final step in the coding process is to prepare a codebook. The codebook contains the general instructions indicating how each item of data was coded, so that the people conducting the data analysis can see what the people who were the coders did. The codebook lists the codes for each variable and the categories included in each code. It further indicates where on the computer record the variable is located, and how the variable should be read—for example, with a decimal point or as a whole number. The latter information is provided by the format specifications.

---

[3] Raymond Kent, *Data Construction and Data Analysis for Survey Research* (Macmillan, 2001); Mark Saunders, Philip Lewis, Adrian Thornhill and Joseph Freeman, *Research Methods for Business Students* (Pearson, 2003); Robert Sommer and Barbara Baker Sommer, *Practical Guide to Behavioral Research* (Oxford University Press, 2001).

Cross-tabs come soon!

Tabulation

Tabulation consists of counting the number of cases that fall into the various categories. The tabulation may take the form of a simple tabulation or a cross-tabulation. **Simple tabulation** involves counting a single variable. It may be repeated for each of the variables in the study, but the tabulation for each variable is independent of the tabulation for the other variables. In **cross-tabulation**, two or more of the variables are treated simultaneously; the number of cases that have the joint characteristics are counted (e.g., the number of people who bought Campbell's soup at a Kroger store).

Although tabulation by hand might be useful in simple studies involving a few questions and a limited number of responses, most studies rely on computer tabulation using packaged programs. Many such programs are available, from Excel, including add-ins, Sas, Spss, etc. The input to these statistical analyses is the data array—the spreadsheet or value of each variable for each sample unit.

A number of important questions concerning the analysis of data can be illustrated using one-way tabulations. Let's work with the data in Table 14.1 as an example. The data were collected for a study focusing on car ownership; we look at one-way tabulations and cross-tabs in this chapter.

TABLE 14.1 Raw Data for Car Ownership Study

	(1)	(2)	(3)	(4)	(5)	(6)	(7)	(8)	(9)	(10)	(11)
family ID	$income	# in family	educat. (yrs) hhold	region: North South	lifestyle Liberal Conserv.	#cars	car financed?	station wagon?	economy car?	van?	other car?
1001	26,800	3	12	N	L	1	N	N	N	Y	N
1002	17,400	4	12	N	L	1	N	N	N	N	Y
1003	14,300	2	10	N	L	1	N	N	N	N	Y
1004	35,400	4	9	N	L	1	N	N	N	N	Y
1005	24,000	3	8	N	L	1	N	N	N	N	Y
1006	17,200	2	12	N	L	1	N	N	Y	N	N
1007	27,000	4	12	N	L	1	N	N	N	N	Y
1008	16,900	3	10	N	L	1	N	N	N	N	Y
1009	26,700	2	12	N	L	1	N	N	N	N	Y
1010	13,800	4	6	N	C	1	Y	N	N	N	Y
1011	34,100	3	8	N	C	1	N	N	N	N	Y
1012	16,300	3	11	N	C	1	N	N	N	N	Y
1013	14,700	2	12	N	C	1	N	N	N	N	Y
1014	25,400	4	12	N	C	1	N	N	N	N	Y
1015	15,400	4	12	N	C	1	N	N	N	N	Y
1016	25,900	3	11	N	C	1	Y	N	N	N	Y
1017	36,300	3	12	N	C	1	N	N	N	N	Y
1018	27,400	2	12	N	C	2	N	N	N	N	Y
1019	17,300	2	12	N	C	1	N	N	N	N	Y
1020	13,700	3	8	N	C	1	N	N	N	N	Y
1021	26,100	2	12	N	C	1	N	N	Y	N	N
1022	16,300	4	12	N	C	1	Y	N	N	N	Y
1023	33,800	3	6	N	C	1	N	N	N	N	Y
1024	34,400	4	8	N	C	1	N	N	N	N	Y

(continued)

TABLE 14.1 (*continued*)

	(1)	(2)	(3)	(4)	(5)	(6)	(7)	(8)	(9)	(10)	(11)
family ID	$income	# in family	educat. (yrs) hhold	region: North South	lifestyle Liberal Conserv.	#cars	car financed?	station wagon?	economy car?	van?	other car?
1025	15,300	2	9	N	C	1	Y	N	N	N	Y
1026	35,900	3	12	N	C	1	N	N	N	N	Y
1027	15,100	4	12	S	L	1	N	N	N	Y	N
1028	17,200	2	12	S	L	1	N	N	N	N	N
1029	35,400	4	10	S	L	1	N	N	N	N	Y
1030	15,600	3	12	S	L	1	N	N	N	N	Y
1031	24,900	3	12	S	L	1	N	N	N	N	Y
1032	34,800	4	11	S	C	1	N	N	N	Y	N
1033	14,600	4	12	S	C	1	N	N	N	N	Y
1034	23,100	3	9	S	C	1	N	N	N	N	Y
1035	15,900	3	12	S	C	1	N	N	N	Y	N
1036	26,700	4	12	S	C	1	N	N	N	N	Y
1037	17,300	4	12	S	C	1	N	N	N	Y	N
1038	37,100	3	12	S	C	1	N	N	N	Y	N
1039	14,000	3	10	S	C	1	N	N	N	N	Y
1040	23,600	3	10	S	C	1	N	N	N	N	Y
1041	16,200	3	12	S	C	1	N	N	N	N	Y
1042	24,100	4	10	S	C	1	N	N	N	Y	N
1043	12,700	2	8	S	C	1	N	N	N	N	Y
1044	26,000	4	13	S	L	1	N	Y	N	N	N
1045	15,400	3	16	N	L	2	N	Y	Y	N	N
1046	16,900	4	16	N	L	1	N	N	N	N	Y
1047	23,800	6	10	S	C	1	Y	Y	N	N	N
1048	37,100	8	16	N	L	2	Y	N	Y	N	Y
1049	16,800	5	15	S	C	2	Y	N	N	N	Y
1050	22,900	5	8	N	L	1	N	Y	N	N	N
1051	13,700	6	8	N	L	1	Y	Y	N	N	N
1052	26,800	8	12	S	C	2	N	Y	N	N	Y
1053	16,100	8	12	N	L	2	N	Y	N	N	Y
1054	25,700	6	12	N	C	1	N	N	N	N	Y
1055	38,200	2	12	N	L	1	N	N	N	N	Y
1056	49,800	3	12	N	L	1	Y	N	N	N	Y
1057	60,400	4	12	N	L	1	Y	N	N	N	Y
1058	39,000	2	12	N	L	1	N	N	N	N	Y
1059	57,600	4	12	N	L	1	Y	N	N	N	Y
1060	42,000	3	12	N	L	1	N	N	N	N	Y
1061	38,600	3	12	N	L	1	N	N	N	Y	N
1062	66,400	4	12	N	L	2	Y	N	Y	N	Y
1063	71,200	2	12	N	L	1	Y	N	N	N	Y
1064	49,300	4	10	N	C	1	Y	N	N	N	Y
1065	37,700	4	10	N	C	1	Y	N	N	N	Y
1066	72,400	3	12	N	C	2	N	N	Y	N	Y
1067	88,700	3	12	N	C	1	N	N	N	Y	N

(*continued*)

TABLE 14.1 (continued)

	(1)	(2)	(3)	(4)	(5)	(6)	(7)	(8)	(9)	(10)	(11)
family ID	$income	# in family	educat. (yrs) hhold	region: North South	lifestyle Liberal Conserv.	#cars	car financed?	station wagon?	economy car?	van?	other car?
1068	44,200	2	12	S	L	1	Y	N	N	N	Y
1069	55,100	3	12	S	L	2	N	N	N	Y	Y
1070	73,300	4	12	S	L	1	N	N	N	Y	N
1071	80,200	2	12	S	L	1	Y	N	N	N	Y
1072	39,300	3	10	S	C	2	N	N	N	Y	Y
1073	48,200	4	12	S	C	1	N	N	N	N	Y
1074	57,800	2	12	S	C	1	Y	N	N	N	Y
1075	38,000	3	10	S	C	1	Y	N	N	Y	N
1076	81,300	4	16	N	L	1	N	Y	N	N	N
1077	96,900	4	16	N	L	2	N	N	N	N	Y
1078	44,700	3	14	N	L	1	N	N	N	N	Y
1079	107,300	3	17	N	L	1	N	N	N	N	Y
1080	38,100	2	13	N	L	2	Y	N	N	N	Y
1081	304,200	2	14	N	L	1	N	N	N	N	Y
1082	46,100	3	16	S	L	1	N	N	N	Y	N
1083	49,300	4	13	S	L	1	N	N	N	N	Y
1084	160,800	4	16	S	L	9	N	N	N	N	Y
1085	39,100	4	16	S	L	1	N	N	N	Y	N
1086	46,400	2	14	S	C	1	N	N	N	Y	N
1087	58,300	6	10	N	L	2	Y	N	N	N	N
1088	47,800	5	10	N	L	2	Y	Y	N	N	Y
1089	58,000	7	8	N	L	2	Y	Y	N	N	Y
1090	69,600	9	12	N	L	2	Y	Y	N	N	Y
1091	44,200	11	12	N	L	2	N	N	Y	N	Y
1092	62,100	6	10	N	L	2	Y	Y	N	N	Y
1093	99,000	5	12	S	L	3	Y	N	Y	Y	Y
1094	53,300	6	12	S	L	2	N	Y	N	N	Y
1095	72,200	9	10	S	C	2	N	Y	N	Y	N
1096	64,700	7	12	S	C	2	Y	Y	N	Y	N
1097	77,300	6	16	N	L	2	Y	Y	Y	N	N
1098	116,900	10	18	N	L	3	Y	Y	Y	N	Y
1099	71,200	7	15	S	L	1	N	N	N	Y	N
1100	103,800	5	16	S	C	2	Y	Y	Y	N	N

One-Way Tabulation

One-way tabulations are useful in communicating the results of a study. In addition, they can be used for other purposes:

1. To determine the degree of item nonresponse
2. To locate blunders
3. To locate outliers or unusual observations

4. To determine the empirical distribution of the variable in question
5. To calculate summary statistics

The first three of these are often referred to as "data cleaning."

Dealing with the *nonresponse* percentages is always aggravating. In fact, the degree of item nonresponse often serves as a useful indicator of the quality of the research. When it is excessive, it calls the whole research effort into question and suggests that a critical examination of the research objectives and procedures should be undertaken. When nonresponse is less extreme, it still demands that decisions be made with respect to what to do about the missing items before analyzing the data. There are several possible strategies:

1. Leave the items blank and report the number as a separate category. Though this procedure works well for simple one-way and cross tabulations, it doesn't work well for some statistical techniques.
2. Eliminate the case with the missing item in analyses using the variable. When using this approach, the analyst must continually report the number of cases on which the analysis is based, because the sample size is not constant across analyses. This approach also ignores the fact that a significant incidence of "no information" on any item might in itself be insightful; it signals that respondents do not care very deeply about the issue being addressed by the question.
3. Substitute values for the missing items. Typically, the substitution involves some measure of central tendency, such as the mean. Alternatively, sometimes the researcher estimates the answer, e.g., predicting it using the respondent's other answers.[4]

There is no single "right" answer for how missing items should be handled. It all depends on the purposes of the study, the incidence of missing items, and the methods that will be used to analyze the data.

A *blunder* is simply an error. It can happen during editing, during coding, or when entering the data on the computer. Consider the one-way tabulation of the number of cars owned per family in Table 14.2. A check of the original questionnaire indicates that the family having nine cars had, in fact, one car. The nine is a mistake. The simple one-way tabulation has revealed the error, and it can be corrected at this very early stage in the analysis with a minimum of difficulty and it hadn't yet led to erroneous results in other analyses.

The sample size for the data displayed in Table 14.2 is 100, so the numbers are readily converted to percentages. It is good practice to indicate percentages in the table—percentages facilitate communication. A more typical presentation of the preceding result, corrected for errors, is shown in Table 14.3. Note the percentages are presented to zero decimal places. Particularly with small samples, one has to be careful not to convey a greater accuracy than the figures can support. Numbers also are

Ethical Dilemma 14.1

After collecting the data for a study that is being repeated using an updated questionnaire, an analyst is instructed to complete the analysis and report for the project. The fieldwork took longer than expected to complete, leaving the analyst with very little time to complete the analysis for the project. So that the project can be completed on time, the analyst follows the analysis plan used for the previous project. For the final report, the analyst decides simply to update the tables from the previous report to reflect the new data and to alter wording only where required by the table information.

- Is it acceptable to charge the new client for a full analysis on this project when the researcher has not completed a full analysis?
- What are the risks associated with this shortcut in data analysis?
- Under the same constraints, what would you have done in this situation?

---

[4] Sam Koslowsky, "The Case of the Missing Data," *Journal of Database Marketing* 9 (2002), pp. 312–318; MarcoVriens and Eric Melton, "Managing Missing Data," *Marketing Research* 14 (2002), pp. 12–17.

TABLE 14.2
Cars per Family

#Cars per Family	#Families
1	74
2	23
3	2
9	1

TABLE 14.3
Cars per Family, with
Percentages

#Cars per Family	#Families	%Families
1	74	74
2	23	23
3	2	2
9	1	1

easier to read when rounded off, and therefore probably have more impact to the consuming manager reading the report. Occasionally, one decimal place might be used, rarely are two used. The general rule in reporting percentages is: Unless decimals serve a special purpose, they should be omitted.

Sometimes the percentages also are presented in parentheses (see Table 14.4) immediately to the right or below the actual count entry in the table. Sometimes only the percentages are presented, and then it is imperative that the sample size (the total number of cases) is provided.

The third use of the one-way tabulation is to locate **outliers**. An outlier is not an error. It is an observation so different in magnitude from the rest of the data that the analyst chooses to treat it as a special case. This may mean eliminating the observation from the analysis or determining the specific factors that generate this unique observation.[5] Consider, for example, the tabulation of incomes contained in Table 14.4. The tabulation indicates there are only four families with incomes greater than $105,000, and Table 14.1 indicates that only one family had an annual income greater than $161,000, namely Number 1081 with an income of $304,200. This is clearly out of line with the rest of the sample and should probably be considered an outlier. In this case, it is not unreasonable for a family to have such an income, so the observation will be retained in the analysis.

The fourth use of the one-way frequency tabulation is to determine the *empirical distribution* of the variable. Some researchers ignore the shape of the distribution and just go right to calculating summary statistics, such as the mean. Ignoring the distribution of the variables can be a serious mistake. Preferences for some products are bipolar, e.g., some people like "mild" salsa, and others like "hot" salsa. If you take an average, you might think you should roll out a new product that is "medium" salsa. Dumb! It's a good idea to get a feel for a variable's distribution before performing any analysis with it.

---

[5] Peter Rousseeuw and Annick Leroy, *Robust Regression and Outlier Detection* (Wiley, 2003); Andre Lucas, Philip Franses and Dick Van Dijk, *Outlier Robust Analysis of Economic Time Series* (Oxford University Press, 2003).

TABLE 14.4
Income Distribution of
Respondents in Car
Ownership Study

Income	#Families	%Families	Cumulative # Families	Cumulative % Families
< $15,000	8	(8.0)	8	(8.0)
$15,000–$24,900	25	(25.0)	33	(33.0)
$25,000–$34,900	15	(15.0)	48	(48.0)
$35,000–$44,900	18	(18.0)	66	(66.0)
$45,000–$54,900	8	(8.0)	74	(74.0)
$55,000–$64,900	8	(8.0)	82	(82.0)
$65,000–$74,900	7	(7.0)	89	(89.0)
$75,000–$84,900	3	(3.0)	92	(92.0)
$85,000–$94,900	1	(1.0)	93	(93.0)
$95,000–$104,900	3	(3.0)	96	(96.0)
$105,000+	4	(4.0)	100	(100.0)
Total #Families	100	(100.0)		

The distribution of a variable can be visualized through a histogram. A **histogram** is a form of bar chart in which successive values of the variable are placed along the x-axis (abscissa), and the absolute frequency or relative frequency of occurrence of the values is indicated along the y-axis (ordinate). The histogram for the income data in Table 14.4 appears in Figure 14.1, with the incomes over $105,000 omitted because their inclusion would have required an undue extension of the income axis. A picture is worth a megabyte of words! It is readily apparent that the distribution of incomes is skewed to the right. The actual distribution can be compared to some theoretical distribution to determine whether the data are consistent with some *a priori* model. Further insight into the empirical distribution of income can be obtained by constructing the **frequency polygon**. The frequency polygon is derived from the histogram by connecting the midpoints of the bars with straight lines. It is superimposed in Figure 14.1.

An alternative way of gaining insight into empirical distribution is through the **cumulative distribution function**. The number of observations with a value less than

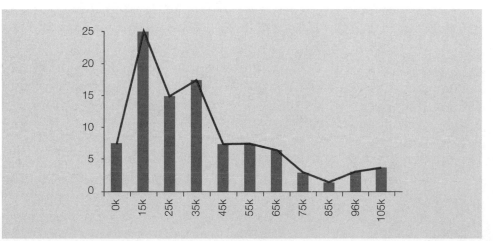

FIGURE 14.1
Histogram and
Frequency Polygon
of Incomes of Families
in Car Ownership Study

or equal to a specified quantity is determined—the cumulative frequencies are generated. Thus, in the right-hand column of Table 14.4, we see that there are eight families with incomes less than $15,000; 33 families (8 + 25) with incomes of $24,900 or less; and 48 families (8 + 25 + 15) with incomes of $34,900 or less. These cumulative frequencies are denoted along the ordinate in Figure 14.2, while the abscissa again contains incomes. The empirical cumulative distribution function is generated by connecting the points representing the given combinations of x's (values) and y's (cumulative frequencies) with straight lines.

The one-way tabulation is also useful in calculating other *summary* measures, such as the mode, mean, and standard deviation. The mode, or the most frequently occurring item, can be read directly from the one-way tabulation. Thus, Table 14.3 suggests that most families own one car. The mean, or "average" response, can be calculated from a one-way tabulation by weighting each value by its frequency of occurrence, summing these products, and dividing by the number of cases. The average number of cars per family given the data in Table 14.3 would thus be estimated to be the following:

Value	Frequency	Value x Frequency
1	75	75
2	23	46
3	2	6
	100	127

or 127/100 = 1.27 cars per family.

The standard deviation provides a measure of spread in the data. It is calculated from the one-way tabulation by taking the deviation of each value from the mean and squaring these deviations. The squared deviations are then multiplied by the frequency with which each occurs, these products are summed, and then divided by sample size minus one to yield the sample variance. The square root is then the sample standard deviation. The calculation of the standard deviation is thus very similar to that for ungrouped data, except that each value is weighted by the frequency with

FIGURE 14.2
Cumulative Distribution of Incomes of Families in Car Ownership Study

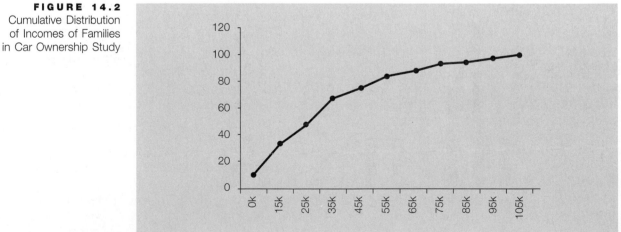

which it occurs. The standard deviation for the data in Table 14.3 is thus calculated as follows:

Value	Value-Mean	(Value-Mean)²	Frequency	Frequency Times Difference Squared
1	−0.27	0.0729	75	5.4675
2	0.73	0.5329	23	12.2567
3	1.73	2.9929	2	5.9858
				23.7100

yielding a variance of 23.7100/99 = .2395 and a standard deviation of $\sqrt{.2395}$ = .4894.

The one-way tabulation is also a communication vehicle for the results. All you have to do is look at Table 14.1 to see how much insight can be gathered about the variable and then compare that with the insight generated in the one-way tabulation contained in Table 14.4. When you realize that one-way tabulations also serve as the input to the histogram, frequency polygon, and empirical cumulative distribution function, and they are also used to calculate summary statistics, you can see it's worth the time to study the tabulations to get a good feel for your data.[6]

Goodness-of-Fit Chi-Square Test on One Variable

When we look at the distribution of income for the families in our car ownership sample, we might try to answer the question "How representative is our sample?" (at least on this one demographic variable). The *chi-square* statistic can give us the answer. Suppose through the use of secondary data, like the U.S. Census, you were able to determine the income distribution for your target market (such as your metropolitan area, your area of the country, and your particular head-of-household age focus). The car ownership income data from Table 14.4 are reproduced in the second column of Table 14.5 for convenience, and the target percentages derived from the secondary data compose the third column in Table 14.5. The question of representativeness is directly answered by comparing the data in the sample to the distribution that would be expected if the sample reflected the population.

We'll label the sample data "o" for "observed" frequency and "e" for the data you would "expect" if your sample were representative of the target population. Thus, the 2nd and 3rd columns are labeled o_i and e_i, denoting the *observed* number and *expected* number of observations that fall in the ith row for each of the r rows of income level. The chi-square is an easy spreadsheet computation. The differences between the observed and expected frequencies are computed $(o_i - e_i)$, and standardized by dividing by $\sqrt{e_i}$ (to compensate for the fact that a difference of, say, 5 is a proportionately smaller error where the base numbers are bigger, such as 22, than in the table where the numbers are smaller, e.g., 5 or 6). Square those pieces and sum them up, and the calculated χ^2 statistic is defined as follows:

$$\chi^2 = \sum_{i=1}^{r} \frac{\left(o_i - e_i\right)^2}{e_i}$$

---

[6] "Box and whisker plots" are also used to plot a distribution. They also mark the mean, median, 25th and 75th percentiles, and outliers. See "Graphic Displays of Data: Box and Whisker Plots" (MarketFacts.com).

Income	o_i #Families	e_i=Target figures	$\dfrac{(o_i - e_i)}{\sqrt{e_i}}$	$\dfrac{(o_i - e_i)^2}{e_i}$
< $15,000	8	22	−2.985	8.909
$15,000–$24,900	25	19	1.377	1.895
$25,000–$34,900	15	12	.866	.750
$35,000–$44,900	18	18	.000	.000
$45,000–$54,900	8	6	.816	.667
$55,000–$64,900	8	5	1.342	1.800
$65,000–$74,900	7	6	.408	.167
$75,000–$84,900	3	5	−.894	.800
$85,000–$94,900	1	5	−1.789	3.200
$95,000–$104,900	3	1.5	1.225	1.500
$105,000+	4	.5	4.950	24.500
Total #Families	100	100		χ^2=44.188

The chi-square for these data equals 44.188. By comparing it to a table of critical values, it can be interpreted as big (that is, the observed sample data do not follow the expected distribution) or small (the sample may be "off" from the target but the difference is attributable to sampling errors). Critical values for the χ^2 can be found in the Appendix in the back of this book at the intersection of an alpha-level and degrees of freedom, which are computed as (r−1), i.e., the number of rows in the table minus one.[7] Our income table has 11 rows, and the critical χ^2 value for 10 degrees of freedom is 18.31. Our χ^2 value exceeds the critical value, so we reject the "null hypothesis" that our sample resembles the population, and instead conclude that our sample is unlike the general population in terms of its distribution of incomes. (It is rare that a sample exactly resembles a population, and if there had been a good fit on income, another demographic variable might have been skewed. So the marketer must consider the extent to which the differences in income may affect the research questions at hand.)

Standardized Residuals

It might seem that the 4th column in Table 14.5 was merely a "computational" worksheet column, en route to the final column to be summed, but it also contains valuable information. Whereas the χ^2 indicates, overall, whether the sample reflects the population, the numbers in the 4th column are called *standardized residuals,* and they indicate, for specific income brackets, whether the sample reflects the population or differs from it. Standardized residuals are interpretable like z-scores, in that if they exceed 1.96 in magnitude, they are significant.[8]

In the income bracket of $35,000–$44,900, our sample had exactly the same number of families as would be expected by the target population data. Hence, the residual ($o_i - e_i$) is zero. Less perfect matches are found in the other rows.

Many of the standardized residuals are positive, indicating that our sample contained more families with incomes in those categories than we would have predicted

---

[7] FYI: The mean of the chi-square distribution is equal to the number of degrees of freedom v, and the variance is equal to $2v$. For large values of v, the chi-square distribution is approximately normally distributed.

just knowing the population data. Conversely, the standardized residuals that are negative indicate that our sample contained fewer families with those incomes than we would have expected.

When the standardized residuals do not exceed 1.96, those differences, positive or negative, are attributable to sampling chance. When they exceed 1.96, they are considered "real" effects in the sample. For example, the −2.985 indicates that our sample included significantly fewer families with incomes less than $15,000 than the target contains. On the high end of the income scale, the 4.950 indicates that the sample comprised significantly more families whose incomes exceed $105,000 than characterizes the target population.

In total, we learn that our sample is somewhat more affluent than the target population. This difference must be factored into any subsequent projections about the rest of the data. One-way chi-square statistics can be useful in numerous ways. This example used known population profile data as expected frequencies. The chi-square goodness-of-fit test can also help determine whether a sample seems to follow a particular form. For instance, if we want to use a statistical procedure that assumes our variable is normally distributed, we test that assumption. We would construct the sample frequency histogram to get the o_i's and compare them to the e_i's corresponding to the normally distributed counterpart to see whether we should proceed with the technique that requires normality.

There are numerous uses of the chi-square. For example, if the rows of a table represented manufacturers (e.g., General Mills, Kraft) or brands in a category (e.g., Compaq, Dell, Aerostar), the observed data may be market shares or sales in numbers of units, and the expected frequencies may be the comparable data on the previous selling quarter. Many types of "benchmark" data can be used as the expected frequencies against which to compare one's sample data.

Take another kind of example. Any time the marketer wants to know whether an observed pattern of frequencies corresponds to an "expected" pattern, the chi-square is appropriate. Say a cereal manufacturer knows that in the industry, the three standard sizes of cereal boxes—small, large, and family size—sell at different rates. For every small package, 3 large and 2 family size are also sold. Let's say the manufacturer conducts a market test to determine the relative frequencies of sales for one of their cereal lines.

Suppose that, in a test market over a one-week period, 1,200 boxes of the new cereal were sold and the distribution of sales by size was as follows:

Small	Large	Family	Total
240	575	385	1200

Are these data consistent with what is considered typical?

We'll compute the chi-square. We have the o_i, the observed number of cases falling in each of the three categories, and we need the e_i's, the expected number of cases for each category.

The null hypothesis would be that these sales would follow the typical distribution, of {small: large: family size} being {1: 3: 2}. The proportions are: $\pi_1 = 1/(1 + 3 + 2) = 1/6$, $\pi_2 = 3/6$, and $\pi_3 = 2/6$, so the expected sales would be: $e_1 = n\pi_1 = 1,200(1/6) =$

> **Chi-square** tells you, overall, if there is a pattern. **Standardized residuals** tell you, microscopically, cell-by-cell.

---

[8] Shelby J. Haberman, "The Analysis of Residuals in Cross-Classified Tables," *Biometrika* 29 (1973), pp. 205–220.

200 of the small size, $e_2 = n\pi_2 = 1,200(3/6) = 600$ of the large size, and $e_3 = n\pi_3 = 1,200(2/6) = 400$ of the family size. The χ^2 statistic is computed as:

$$\chi^2 = \frac{(240-200)^2}{200} + \frac{(575-600)^2}{600} + \frac{(385-400)^2}{400} = 9.60$$

The degrees of freedom is $v = k - 1 = 2$, and the tabled value of χ^2 for 2 df at $\alpha = .05$ is 5.99. Since the calculated value $\chi^2 = 9.60$ is larger, the conclusion is that the sample result would be unlikely to occur by chance alone. Rather, the preliminary market test results suggest that sales of this cereal line follows a different pattern than is typical. The null hypothesis of sales in the ratio of 1:3:2 is rejected.

A final application of the one-way chi-square is described in Research Realities 14.2. It's a versatile statistic.

Kolmogorov-Smirnov Test

The Kolmogorov-Smirnov test is similar to the chi-square goodness-of-fit test in that it compares observed and expected frequencies to determine whether observed results are in accord with a stated null hypothesis. But the **Kolmogorov-Smirnov test** is appropriate for ordinal variables.

Say a manufacturer of cosmetics is testing four different shades of a sparkly nail polish—pale pink, light pink, medium pink, and dark pink. The company has hired a marketing research firm to determine whether any distinct preference exists toward either extreme. If so, the company will manufacture only the preferred shades. Otherwise, it will have to market all shades. If a sample of 100 yields 50 women who prefer the "pale" shade, 30 the "light," 15 the "medium," and 5 the "dark" shade, do these results indicate some kind of preference? The shading quality has an inherent ordering of light to dark, so the Kolmogorov-Smirnov test can be used to test the preference hypothesis. We specify the cumulative distribution function that would occur under the null hypothesis and comparing that with the observed cumulative. The point at which the two functions show the maximum deviation is determined, and the value of this deviation is the test statistic.

The null hypothesis is that there is no preference, so it would be expected that 25% of the sample would like each shade. The cumulative distribution function resulting from this assumption is presented as the last column of Table 14.6.

Kolmogorov-Smirnov D is equal to the absolute value of the maximum deviation between the observed cumulative proportion and the theoretical cumulative proportion. For our data, D = .80 − .50 = .30. For $\alpha = .05$, the critical D for large samples is given by $(1.36/\sqrt{n})$, where n is the sample size. So our critical value is .136. Calculated D exceeds the critical value, and thus the null hypothesis of no preference among shades is rejected—the data indicate a statistically significant preference for the lighter shades.[9]

---

[9] The hypothesis of no preference could also have been tested with the chi-square test. When the data are ordinal, the Kolmogorov-Smirnov test is preferred—it is more powerful than chi-square in almost all cases, easier to compute, and doesn't require a minimum expected frequency in each cell as the chi-square test does. The Kolmogorov-Smirnov test can also be used to determine whether two independent samples have been drawn from the same population or from populations with the same distribution.

14.2 It's a Conspiracy![10]

Mars Candy polled children to indicate their favorite colors, whereupon Mars introduced the new M&M color, blue. Subsequent investigation has indicated, however, that the blue M&M may appear less frequently in bags of these chocolates than its nonblue counterparts.

Conduct a study for yourself. Go out and purchase some M&M's, er, data. (Perhaps your dean will offer you research funds to study this phenomenon.) Count the number of each color, and sum those counts. If you found, say, 120 M&M's in the bag, how would you expect those 120 observations to be distributed over the six color categories; that is, what are the expected frequencies?

Compute the χ^2. Overall, what does it indicate? What do the standardized residuals tell you?

Do the answers change if you select Peanut M&M's instead of Plain? Peanut Butter? Almond? What special result do you find for the latter two?[11]

	o_i: Number of M&M's	e_i: Expected Number of M&M's	$\dfrac{(o_i - e_i)}{\sqrt{e_i}}$	$\dfrac{(o_i - e_i)^2}{e_i}$
Blue				
Brown				
Green				
Orange				
Red				
Yellow				
Total:				$\chi^2 =$

TABLE 14.6
Observed and Theoretical Cumulative Distributions of Nail Polish Color Preference

Shade	Observed Number	Observed Proportion	Observed Cumulative Proportion	Theoretical Proportion	Theoretical Cumulative Proportion
Pale Pink	50	0.50	0.50	0.25	0.25
Light Pink	30	0.30	0.80	0.25	0.50
Medium Pink	15	0.15	0.95	0.25	0.75
Dark Pink	5	0.05	1.00	0.25	1.00

Cross-Tabs

We now turn to the analysis of frequencies for variables studied two at a time. One variable in our investigation forms the rows of a table, another variable forms the columns. To continue with the car ownership example, we might tabulate "family size" crossed with "numbers of cars owned." The table entries represent the number of cases in our sample that have the joint characteristics of the row variable value (e.g., small vs. larger family) and the column variable value (e.g., few vs. many cars).

A cross-tabulation, better known as a "cross-tab" is easily the most widely used data analysis technique in marketing research—the "bread and butter" of marketers. Most marketing research studies go no further, and the studies that do use more

---

[10] Ronald D. Fricker, Jr., "The Mysterious Case of the Blue M&M's," *Chance* 9 (1996), pp. 19–22.

[11] Statisticians distinguish between a "sampling zero," where you could have observations in that row, but you simply did not (e.g., your sample may have been too small), and a "structural zero," where it is not possible to obtain observations in that row. Which do you suppose the zeros are for Peanut Butter and Almond orange M&M's?

sophisticated analytical methods still contain cross-tabs as an important component. Thus, the marketing researcher (analyst) and the marketing manager (decision maker) both need to understand how cross-tabs are developed and interpreted.

Why are they so important? A cross-tab allows us to study relationships between variables. The variables for cross-tabs are either naturally nominal or ordinal, or they represent categorizations of continuous measures (e.g., categories of income or age).[12] Cross-tabs are also sometimes called "contingency tables" because we're looking at how one variable behaves contingent upon values of the other variable, e.g., are family size and car ownership independent of each other, or, instead, if you knew one (size of family), could you predict better than just guessing the other (number of cars)?

We start with a discussion of the kinds of relationships cross-tabs let us study. In the appendix, we present the chi-square test for a two-way table, and a discussion of log linear and logit models, tools often used to predict brand choices.

Cross-tabs are the heart of marketing research.

Contingent Relationships in Cross-Tabs

A number of important questions concerning the analysis of data can be illustrated using cross-tabulations. We'll work with the data on car ownership to answer the following questions:

- What characteristics distinguish families who own two or more cars from families who own one car? E.g., income?
- What are the distinguishing characteristics of those who buy station wagons? Foreign economy cars? Vans?
- Are families who financed their automobile purchase different from those who did not?

Let's see if there is any relationship between the number of cars that a family owns and family income. To keep things simple, we'll use the median income in the population of $37,500 to split the sample into two groups—those with incomes above or below the average.

Table 14.7 presents the two-way classification of the sample families by income and number of cars. Looking at the marginal totals, we see that 75 families have one car or less, whereas 25 families have two cars or more. We also see that the sample is not unrepresentative of the population, at least as far as income is concerned: 54 families fall into the lower-than-average income group using the $37,500 cutoff.

TABLE 14.7
Family Income and Number of Cars Family Owns

Income	#Cars		
	0 or 1	2+	Total
< $37,500	48	6	54
$37,500+	27	19	46
Total	75	25	100

---

[12] Relationships between pairs of continuous variables may be measured via correlations and regressions.

Does the number of cars depend on income? Table 14.7 suggests yes— 19 of the families owning two or more cars are in the upper-income group. We can shed additional light on the relationship by computing percentages. Tables 14.8 and 14.9 are mathematically equivalent to Table 14.7 but are based on percentages calculated in different directions: horizontally, or "row percentages" in Table 14.8 and vertically, or "column percentages" in Table 14.9.

Tables 14.8 and 14.9 contain quite different messages. Table 14.8 suggests that multiple-car ownership is affected by family income: 41% of the families with above-average incomes had two or more automobiles, but only 11% of the below-average-income families did. Table 14.9, on the other hand, suggests that 64% of those who owned one car had below-average incomes, whereas only 24% of those who owned two or more cars were below average in income. Does this mean that multiple-car ownership paves the way to higher income? Definitely not. Rather, it illustrates a fundamental rule of calculating percentages: Always calculate percentages in the direction of the causal factor, or across the effect factor. In this case, income is logically considered to be the cause, or independent variable, and multiple-car ownership to be the effect, or dependent variable. The percentages are correctly calculated, therefore, in the direction of income as in Table 14.8.

Ethical Dilemma 14.2

A manufacturer of aspirin had its marketing research department conduct a national survey among doctors to investigate what common household remedies doctors would be most likely to recommend when treating a patient with a cold. The question asked doctors to pick the one product they would most likely prescribe for their patients from among the choices Advil, Tylenol, aspirin, or none of the above. The distribution of responses was as follows:

Advil	100
Tylenol	100
Aspirin	200
None of the three	600
Total	1,000

The firm used the results of the survey as a basis for an extensive ad campaign that claimed: "In a national survey, doctors recommended aspirin two to one over Advil and Tylenol as the medicine they would most likely recommend to their patients suffering from colds."

- Is the firm's claim legitimate?
- Is it ethical for the firm to omit reporting the number of doctors that expressed no preference?
- What would be the fairest way to state the ad claim? Do you think stating the claim in this way would be as effective as stating it in the way the firm did?

TABLE 14.8
Percentage Family Income by Number of Cars

Income	#Cars		Total
	0 or 1	2+	
< $37,500	89%	11%	100%
$37,500+	59%	41%	100%

TABLE 14.9
Family Income by Number of Cars, Column Percentage

Income	#Cars	
	0 or 1	2+
< $37,500	64%	24%
$37,500+	36%	76%
Total	100%	100%

A useful way to think about the direction to calculate percentages is to conceptualize the problem in terms of *conditional probability;* the probability of one event occurring given that another event has occurred or will occur. Thus, the notion of the probability that the family has two or more cars given that they are high income makes sense, whereas the notion that the family is high income given that they have two or more cars does not.

This two-way cross-tab is just a start into the data. Consider the relationship between multiple-car ownership and size of family. Table 14.10 indicates the number of small and large (five or more members) families that possess two or more cars. Size of family is logically considered a cause of multiple-car ownership and not vice versa. Thus, the percentages would properly be computed in the direction of size of family or across number of cars. Table 14.11 presents these percentages and suggests that the number of cars a family owns is indeed affected by the size of the family— 77% of the large families have two or more cars, whereas only 10% of the small families do.

So, does multiple-car ownership depend on family size or, as previously suggested, on family income? We need to simultaneously examine the effects of income and family size on likelihoods of multiple-car ownership. The two-way cross-tab needs to be partitioned into forming a three-way table of income, family size, and multiple-car ownership, as in Table 14.12.

TABLE 14.10
Number of Cars and Size of Family

Size of Family	#Cars		
	0 or 1	2+	Total
4 or less	70	8	78
5+	5	17	22
Total	75	25	100

TABLE 14.11
Number of Cars and Size of Family, Row Percentages

Size of Family	#Cars		
	0 or 1	2+	Total
4 or less	90%	10%	100%
5+	23%	77%	100%

TABLE 14.12
Number of Cars by Income and Size of Family

Income	4 or fewer in family #Cars			5 or more in family #Cars			Totals #Cars		
	0–1	2+	Total	0–1	2+	Total	0–1	2+	Total
< $37,500	44	2	46	4	4	8	48	6	54
$37,500+	26	6	32	1	13	14	27	19	46
Total	70	8	78	5	17	22	75	25	100

Income	4 or fewer in family #Cars			5 or more in family #Cars			Totals #Cars		
	0–1	2+	Total	0–1	2+	Total	0–1	2+	Total
< $37,500	96%	4%	100%	50%	50%	100%	89%	11%	100%
$37,500+	81%	19%	100%	7%	93%	100%	59%	41%	100%

TABLE 14.13
Number of Cars by Income and Size of Family (Row % within Family Size)

Table 14.13 contains the percentages computed in the direction of income within each table. It looks like multiple-car ownership depends on both income and family size. For small families of four or fewer, 19% of those with above-average incomes have two or more cars, whereas only 4% of those with below-average incomes have more than one automobile. For large families, 93% of the above-average-income and 50% of the below-average-income families have more than one vehicle.

The preceding comparisons highlight the effect of income on multiple-car ownership, holding family size constant. We could also compare the effect of family size on multiple-car ownership, holding income constant. We would find that each provides a partial explanation for multiple-car ownership.

The information in Tables 14.12 and 14.13 is there to be mined, but it could have been presented in a more revealing manner. Look specifically at the first row of the first section of Table 14.13, reproducing it as Table 14.14. One figure, 4%, is the percentage of small, below-average-income families that have two or more cars. The complementary percentage, 96%, represents those that have one automobile or none.

Table 14.15 shows the rest of the data in Table 14.13 treated in the same way. The entry in each case is the percentage of families in that category that own two or more automobiles. Table 14.15 conveys the same information as Table 14.13, but it delivers the message with greater clarity. The separate effect of income on multiple-car ownership, holding family size constant, can be determined by reading down the columns, while the effect of family size, holding income constant, can be determined by reading across the rows. Cool, yes? Omitting the complementary percentages has helped reveal the structure of the data. Therefore, we'll use this format whenever we consider several explanatory variables simultaneously.

Size of Family	#Cars		
	0–1	2+	Total
< $37,500	96%	4%	100% (n=46)

TABLE 14.14
Car Ownership for Small, Below-Average-Income Families

Income	Size of Family		
	4 or fewer	5+	Total
< $37,500	4%	50%	11%
$37,500+	19%	93%	41%

TABLE 14.15
Percentage of Families Owning 2+ Cars, by Income and Size of Family

The original association between number of cars and family income reflected in Table 14.8 is called the *total* (or **zero order**) association between the variables. Table 14.15, which depicts the association between two variables within categories of family size, is called a conditional table that reveals the **conditional association** between the variables. Family size is a control variable here. Conditional tables that are developed on the basis of one control variable are called first-order conditional tables, and those developed using two control variables are called second-order conditional tables, etc.

Which variable has the greater effect on multiple-car ownership—income or family size? We can calculate the difference in proportions as a function of the level of the variable. Let's look at Table 14.8 for the effect of income on the probability of a family having multiple cars. The proportion of low-income families that have two or more cars is .11, whereas the proportion of high-income families is .41. The probability of having multiple cars is clearly different depending on the family's income, (.41 − .11); high income increases the probability of having two or more cars by .30. Similarly in Table 14.11, the probability of multiple-car ownership is different depending on family size. Whereas .10 of the small families have multiple cars, .77 of the large families do. Thus, being a large family increases the probability of having two or more cars by .67 (i.e., .77 − .10) over small families.

To determine whether income or family size has the greater impact, the factors are considered simultaneously using a similar analysis. We draw the effect of income from Table 14.15. To determine income's effect, we hold family size constant, or we "control for" family size. So we must investigate the relationship between income and car ownership for small families and then again for large families. Among small families, having high income increases the probability of having multiple cars by .15 (.19 − .04). Among large families, having high income increases the probability of having multiple cars by .43 (.93 − .50) compared to low income. The size of the associations between income and multiple-car ownership are different for different family sizes. We conclude that there is a statistical interaction between the independent variables; to generate a single estimate of the effect of income on car ownership, an average of the separate effects needs to be computed. The weighted average takes into account the sizes of the groups: 78 small families and 22 large families; so the weights are .78 and .22. The weighted average is

$$.15(.78) + .43(.22) = .21$$

which suggests that, on average, high versus low income increases the probability of owning multiple cars by .21.

To investigate the effect of family size, we do the obverse, and hold income constant. We investigate the impact of family size on car ownership for low-income families, then for high-income families, and then generate a weighted average of the two results. Among low-income families, being large increases the probability of having multiple cars by .46 (.50 − .04) compared to small families. Among high-income families, large size increases the probability by .74 (.93 − .19) versus small size. There were 54 low-income and 46 high-income families, so the weighted calculation yields:

$$.46(.54) + .74(.46) = .59$$

as the estimate of the impact of family size on multiple-car ownership.

Family size has a more pronounced effect on multiple-car ownership than does income. It increases the probability of having two or more cars by .59, whereas income increases it by .21.

Panel I: Initial Relationship Is Modified by the Introduction of a Third Variable

The previous example highlights an important application of cross-tabs—the use of an additional variable (family size) to refine an initial cross tabulation (the relationship between car ownership and income). A number of conditions can occur when additional variables are introduced, as shown in Table 14.16. As indicated in Panel IA, the two-way table may initially indicate the existence or nonexistence of a relationship between the variables, and the introduction of a third variable may refine that initial conclusion. We now offer examples in the rest of the table.

CASE IB: INITIAL RELATIONSHIP IS SPURIOUS

In the automobile purchase study, it was expected that *van* ownership would be related to lifestyle—the hypothesis was that liberals would more likely own vans than would conservatives. Table 14.17 indicates that, contrary to expectation, conservatives are more apt than liberals to own vans, 24% vs.16%.

Is there some logical explanation for this unexpected finding? Let's add a third variable, region of the country in which the family resides, to the analysis. As Table 14.18 indicates, van ownership is not related to lifestyle, but instead depends on the location of residence. When region is held constant, there is no difference in van ownership between liberals and conservatives. Families living in the South are much

Initial Conclusion	With the Additional Variable	
	Change Conclusion	**Retain Conclusion**
Some Relationship	I	II
	A: Refine Explanation	
	B: Reveal Spurious Explanation	
	C: Provide Limiting Conditions	
No Relationship	III	IV

TABLE 14.16
Conditions That Can Arise with the Introduction of an Additional Variable into a Cross-Tabulation

Lifestyle	Own Van?		
	Yes	**No**	**Total**
Liberal	9 (16%)	46 (84%)	55 (100%)
Conservative	11 (24%)	34 (76%)	45 (100%)

TABLE 14.17
Van Ownership by Lifestyle

Lifestyle	Region of Country		
	North	**South**	**Total**
Liberal	5%	41%	16%
Conservative	5%	43%	24%

TABLE 14.18
Van Ownership by Lifestyle and Region of Country

more likely to own a van than are families who live in the northern states. It just so happens that people in the South tend to be more conservative in their lifestyle than people in the North. The original relationship is, therefore, said to be spurious.

We already know that region has a big effect and lifestyle very little, but we calculate the difference in proportions for each variable anyway, to demonstrate what is meant by a "main effect" without a statistical interaction. Consider first the zero-order association between van ownership and lifestyle contained in Table 14.17. Being conservative increases the probability of van ownership by .08 (.24 − .16) compared to being liberal. Yet Table 14.18 shows that this is a spurious effect due to region of the country, since it disappears when region is held constant. Among those living in the North, the partial association between van ownership and lifestyle is .00 (.05 − .05). Among those living in the South, there is a slightly higher probability of van ownership among conservatives, namely .02 (.43 − .41). This effect is so small that it can be attributed to rounding error or sampling error. Regardless of the region of the country in which the family resides, its political leaning has no effect on whether it owns a van.

Note that the effect of region is pronounced and consistent. Among liberal families, living in the South increases the probability of van ownership by .36 (.41 − .05) compared to living in the North. Among conservative families, living in the South increases the probability by .38 (.43 − .05). Within rounding error, the effect is the same for families with both philosophies, which means that there is no interaction among the two predictor variables. Rather, there is only a main effect of region on van ownership, and the best estimate of its size is given by either of these estimates or their average.

CASE IC: LIMITING CONDITIONS ARE REVEALED

Does ownership of foreign economy cars depend on family size? Table 14.19 suggests that it does. Smaller families are less likely to own a foreign economy car than are larger families! Only 8% of the small families but 27% of the large families have such automobiles. Can this counterintuitive finding be accounted for?

Let's expand this cross classification by adding the number of cars variable. Table 14.20 presents the data, which indicate that it is only when large families have two or more cars that they own a foreign economy car. No large families with one car

TABLE 14.19
Import Economy Car Ownership by Family Size

Size of Family	Own Import Economy Car?		
	Yes	No	Total
4 or fewer	6 (8%)	72 (92%)	78 (100%)
5+	6 (27%)	16 (73%)	22 (100%)

TABLE 14.20
Import Economy Car Ownership by Family Size and Number of Cars

Size of Family	Own Import Economy Car?		
	Yes	No	Total
4 or fewer	4%	38%	8%
5+	0%	35%	27%

own such an automobile. The introduction of the third variable has revealed a condition that limits the effect of foreign economy car ownership—multiple-car ownership where large families are concerned.

Panel II: Initial Conclusion of a Relationship Is Retained

Consider now the analysis of station wagon ownership. *A priori*, it would seem to be related to family size—larger families have a greater need for station wagons than smaller families. Table 14.21 suggests that larger families do display a higher propensity to own station wagons: 68% of the large families and only 4% of the small families own wagons.

Consider, however, whether income might also affect station wagon ownership. As Table 14.22 indicates, income has an effect over and above family size. As one goes from a small to a large family, the propensity to own a station wagon increases. With larger families, though, the increase is larger. From the other angle, if one focuses solely on large families, there is an increase in station wagon ownership from below-average-income to above-average-income families. The initial conclusion is retained; large families do display a greater tendency to purchase station wagons. Further, the effect of family size on station wagon ownership is larger than the effect of income.

Panel III: A Relationship Is Established with the Introduction of a Third Variable

Table 14.23 contains the cross-tab for financing crossed with education of the head of household. There is no relationship between education and this debt; the percentage of families is 30% in each case.

Size of Family	Own Station Wagon?		
	Yes	No	Total
4 or fewer	3 (4%)	75 (96%)	78 (100%)
5+	15 (68%)	7 (32%)	22 (100%)

TABLE 14.21
Station Wagon Ownership by Family Size

Size of Family	Income		
	< $37,500	$37,500+	Total
4 or fewer	4%	3%	4%
5+	63%	71%	68%

TABLE 14.22
Station Wagon Ownership by Family Size and Income

Education Level	Car Purchase Financed?		
	Yes	No	Total
H.S. or less	24 (30%)	56 (70%)	80 (100%)
Some College +	6 (30%)	14 (70%)	20 (100%)

TABLE 14.23
Financed Car Purchase, by Education of Head of Household

Education Level	Income		
	< $37,500	$37,500+	Total
H.S. or less	12%	58%	30%
Some College +	40%	27%	30%

Table 14.24 illustrates the situation when income is added to the analysis. For below-average-income families, the likelihood of financing increases with education. For above-average-income families, the financing decreases with education. The effect of education was obscured in the first analysis (in Table 14.23) because the effects canceled each other out. When income is also considered, the relationship of installment debt to education is in fact pronounced.

Panel IV: The Conclusion of No Relationship Is Retained with the Addition of a Third Variable

Table 14.25 starts to answer the question, "Is station wagon ownership affected by region of the country in which the family lives?" It looks like, no, station wagon ownership doesn't depend on region; 18% of the sample families living in both the North and the South are owners.

Let's look at the relationship when family size is taken into account. Table 14.26 shows again the percentages are constant across regions. The minor variation is due to rounding error. Small families display a low propensity to purchase station wagons, regardless of whether they live in the North or the South. Large families have a higher propensity, and this, too, is independent of where they live. The original lack of relationship between station wagon ownership and region of residence is confirmed with the addition of the third variable, family size.

Region	Own Station Wagon?		
	Yes	No	Total
North	11 (18%)	49 (82%)	60 (100%)
South	7 (18%)	33 (82%)	40 (100%)

Region	Size of Family		
	4 or fewer	5+	Total
North	4%	69%	18%
South	3%	67%	18%

Summary Comments on Cross-Tabulation

The previous examples certainly should highlight the tremendous usefulness of cross-tabulation as a tool in analysis. We have seen an application in which a third variable helped uncover a relationship not immediately discernible, as well as applications in which a third variable triggered the modification of conclusions drawn on the basis of a two-variable classification.

Why stop with three variables? Would the conclusion change with the addition of a fourth variable? A fifth? Indeed it might. In fact, the problem is that one never knows for sure when to stop introducing variables. The conclusion is always susceptible to change with the introduction of the "right" variable or variables. The researcher is always in the position of "inferring" that a relationship exists. Later research may demonstrate that the inference was incorrect, or perhaps "more complicated" than originally thought. This is why the accumulation of studies, rather than a single study, supporting a particular relationship is so vital to the advancement of knowledge.

Table 14.27 is an overview of the dilemma that the researcher faces. The true situation is unknown—if it were known, there would be no need to research it. The analyst may conclude that there is no relationship, or that there is some relationship between two or more variables when in fact there is none or there is some. Only one of these four possibilities in Table 14.27 necessarily corresponds to a correct conclusion—when the analyst concludes that there is no relationship and in fact there is none. Two of the other possibilities are incorrect, and one contains the possibility for error. Spurious noncorrelation results when the analyst concludes that there is no relationship when, in fact, there is. Spurious correlation occurs when the true state of affairs is one of no relationship among the variables, and the analyst concludes that a relationship exists.

The opportunities for error are great, and this gives rise to a temptation to keep adding variables *ad infinitum*. Fortunately, the marketer is constrained by theory and by data. Theory is a constraint because certain tabulations simply do not make any sense. Data are a constraint in several ways. First, some variables might not have been measured. Once the analysis has begun, it's too late to say, "If only we had collected information on variable X!" (Recall our urging you to create dummy tables before collecting data.) Second, unless the sample size is huge, the cell sizes can become extremely small in multidimensional tables. In our fairly simple example, the three-way table (families either below or above average in income; small or large in size; living either in the North or in the South) had 8 cells ($2 \times 2 \times 2$), yielding on average, only 12.5 cases per cell. This is clearly a small number on which to base any kind of conclusion. The problem would have been compounded with more variables (e.g., $2 \times 2 \times 2 \times 2$) and/or more levels of a variable (e.g., $3 \times 4 \times 5$).

TABLE 14.27
The Researcher's Dilemma

Researcher's Conclusion	True Situation	
	No Relationship	Some Relationship
No Relationship	Correct decision	Spurious noncorrelation
Some Relationship	Spurious correlation	Correct decision if concluded relationship is of proper form

Presenting Tabular Data

We certainly know how to analyze categorical (nominal and ordinal) data now! A simpler question is how to present them when trying to communicate your marketing point. We've seen a variety of two-way and three-way tables. Alternatively, sometimes tabular results for commercial marketing-research studies are presented using "banners." A **banner** is a series of cross-tabulations between a criterion or dependent variable and several (sometimes many) explanatory variables in a single table on a single page. The dependent variable, or phenomenon to be explained, serves as the row variable. The predictor or explanatory variables serve as the column variables, with each category of these variables serving as a banner point. Table 14.28 shows what the banner format looks like for the car study. You can see why it is a flexible means of presentation—although only two explanatory variables are shown, income and family size, many more could be. The top line in each row of the table indicates the absolute number possessing the characteristic, whereas the second line indicates the percentage.

Banner tables have several advantages. They allow a great amount of information to be conveyed in a very limited space, and their format makes it easy for nonresearch managers to understand the data. A difficulty with these tables is that they tend to hide relationships in which it is necessary to consider several variables simultaneously (e.g., the joint effect of income and family size on multiple-car ownership), consequently making it more difficult to probe alternative explanations for what is producing the results. They are an efficient form of data presentation, but they should not be considered as a substitute for careful cross-tabulation analysis.

Summary

This chapter reviewed the common analysis functions of editing, coding, and tabulation. Editing involves the inspection and correction, if necessary, of each questionnaire or observation form. The field edit, a preliminary edit most often conducted by the field supervisor, is aimed at correcting the most glaring omissions and inaccuracies while the field staff is still intact. The central office edit follows and involves a more careful scrutiny and correction of the completed data-collection instruments. In the central office edit, particular attention is given to such matters as incomplete

TABLE 14.28
Banner Format for Car Ownership Data

	Total Sample	Income		Family Size	
		< $37,500	$37,500+	4 or fewer	5+
Total	100	54	46	78	22
	100	100	100	100	100
1	75	48	27	70	5
	75	89	59	90	23
2	23	6	17	8	15
	23	11	37	10	68
3	2	0	2	0	2
	2	0	4	0	9

answers, obviously wrong answers, and answers that reflect a lack of interest.

Coding is the procedure by which data are categorized. It involves the three-step process of (1) specifying the categories or classes into which the responses are to be placed, (2) assigning code numbers to the classes, and (3) preparing a codebook. If the data are to be analyzed by computer, a number of conventions should be followed in assigning the code numbers, including the following:

Ethical Dilemma 14.3

Sarah is very happy on the whole with the project that she has just completed for the Crumbly Cookie Company. Most of her hypotheses were supported by the survey data. Two hypotheses did not work out, but she thought that she would just leave them out of the report.

- Is it ethical to omit information that does not tally with your beliefs?
- Can valuable information be lost through the omission?

1. Use only one character per column.
2. Use only numeric codes.
3. Assign as many columns as are necessary to capture the variable.
4. Use the same standard codes throughout for "No information."
5. Code in a respondent identification number on each record.

Tabulation consists of counting the number of cases that fall into the various categories. The simple, or one-way, tabulation involves the count for a single variable, whereas cross-tabulation involves counting the number of cases that have the characteristics described by two or more variables considered simultaneously. The one-way tabulation is useful for communicating the results of a study, and it can also be employed to locate blunders or errors, to determine the degree of item nonresponse, to locate outliers (observations very different in value from the rest), and to determine the empirical distribution of the variable in question. It also serves as basic input to the calculation of measures such as the mean, median, and standard deviation, which provide a summary picture of the distribution of the variable.

The chi-square goodness-of-fit test is appropriate when a nominally scaled variable falls naturally into two or more categories and the analyst wants to determine whether the observed number of cases in each cell corresponds to the expected number. The Kolmogorov-Smirnov test is its ordinal counterpart.

Cross-tabulation is one of the more useful devices for studying the relationships among variables because the results are easily communicated. Further, cross-tabs can provide insight into the nature of a relationship, because the addition of one or more variables to a two-way cross-classification analysis is equivalent to holding each of the variables constant.

A useful method for determining the effect that one variable has on another variable in a cross-tab is to compute the difference in proportions with which the dependent variable occurs as a function of the levels of the independent variable. This can be done for zero order tables as well as conditional tables of higher order. The higher order tables are used to remove the effects of other variables that might be influencing the dependent variable.

In commercial studies, tabular results are often presented using banners. Banners succinctly represent a series of cross-tabs between a dependent variable and several explanatory variables in a single table.

Review Questions

1. Distinguish among the preliminary data analysis steps of editing, coding, and tabulation.

2. What are the differences in emphasis between a field edit and a central office edit?

3. What should an editor do with incomplete answers? Obviously wrong answers? Answers that reflect a lack of interest?

4. What are the principles that underlie the establishment of categories so that collected data may be properly coded?

5. Suppose that you have a large number of very long questionnaires, making it impossible for one person to handle the entire coding task. How should the work be divided?

6. When should you use machine tabulation? Manual tabulation?

7. What are the possible ways for treating item nonresponse? Which strategy would you recommend?

8. What is an outlier?

9. With how many digits should percentages be reported?

10. What is a histogram? A frequency polygon? What information do they provide?

11. What is the cumulative distribution function? Of what value is it?

12. How is the mean calculated from the one-way tabulation? The standard deviation?

13. What is the proper procedure for investigating the following hypotheses using cross-tabs?

   a. Consumption of Product X depends on a person's income.

   b. Consumption of Product X depends on a person's education.

   c. Consumption of Product X depends on both.

14. How would you determine whether income or education had the greater effect on the consumption of Product X?

15. Illustrate the procedure from Questions 1 and 2 with data of your own choosing: develop the tables, fill in the assumed numbers, and indicate the conclusions to be drawn from each table.

16. What is meant by the statement: The introduction of an additional variable:

   a. refined the original explanation?

   b. revealed a spurious explanation?

   c. provided limiting conditions?

17. How do you explain the condition in which a two-way cross-tabulation of Variables X and Y revealed no relationship between X and Y but the introduction of Z revealed a definite relationship between X and Y?

18. What is the researcher's dilemma with respect to cross-tabulation analysis?

19. What constraints operate on researchers that prevent them from adding variables to cross-classification tables *ad infinitum*?

20. What are banners?

Applications and Problems

1. A marketing research supplier has five employees in its coding department. The firm has just received 10,000 completed mail questionnaires. The survey contains 175 questions. How would you recommend that the company handle the editing and coding process? What would you instruct them to look for in the edit, and how would you recommend they handle each of these problems if found?

2. The WITT TV station was conducting research to develop programs that would be well received by the viewing audience and would be considered a dependable source of information. A two-part questionnaire was administered by personal interview to a panel of 3,000 respondents residing in the city of Chicago. The field and office edits were done simultaneously so that the deadline of May 1 could be met. A senior supervisor,

Mr. Z, was placed in charge of the editing tasks and was assisted by two junior supervisors and two field workers. The two field workers were instructed to discard instruments that were illegible or incomplete. Both the junior supervisors were instructed to scrutinize 1,500 of the instruments each for incomplete answers, wrong answers, and responses that indicated a lack of interest. They were instructed to discard instruments that had greater than five incomplete or wrong answers (the questionnaire contained 30 questions). In addition, they were asked to use their judgment in assessing whether the respondent showed a lack of interest, in which case they should also discard the questionnaire.

a. Critically evaluate the preceding editing tasks. Be specific.

b. Make specific recommendations to Mr. D. Witt, the owner of the WITT TV station, about how the editing should be done.

3. Establish response categories and codes for the question, "What do you like about this new brand of cereal?"

4. Code the following responses using your categories and codes.

a. "$1.50 is a reasonable price to pay for the cereal."

b. "The raisins and nuts add a nice flavor."

c. "The sizes of the packages are convenient."

d. "I like the sugar coating on the cereal."

e. "The container does not tear and fall apart easily."

f. "My kids like the cartoons on the back of the package."

g. "It is reasonably priced compared to other brands."

h. "The package is attractive and easy to spot in the store."

i. "I like the price; it is not so low that I doubt the quality and at the same time it is not so high as to be unaffordable."

j. "The crispness and lightness of the cereal improve the taste."

5. Establish response categories and codes for the following question that was asked of a sample of business executives: "In your opinion, which types of companies have not been affected by the present economic climate?"

6. Code the following responses using your categories and codes.

a. *Washington Post*
b. Colgate-Palmolive
c. Gillette
d. Hilton Hotels
e. Chase Manhattan
f. Prentice-Hall
g. Hoover
h. Fabergé
i. Marine Midlands Banks
j. Zenith Radio
k. Holiday Inns
l. Dryden Press
m. Singer
n. Saga
o. Bank of America

7. A large manufacturer of electronic components for automobiles recently conducted a study to determine the average value of electronic components per automobile. Personal interviews were conducted with a random sample of 400 respondents. The following information was secured with respect to each subject's "main" vehicle when he or she had more than one.

Average Dollar Value of Electronic Equipment per Automobile

Dollar Value of Electronic Equipment	Number of Automobiles
Less than $50	35
$51 to $100	40
$101 to $150	55
$151 to $200	65
$201 to $250	65
$251 to $300	75
$301 to $350	40
$351 to $400	20
More than $401	5
Total # of automobiles	400

a. Convert the preceding information into percentages.

b. Compute the cumulative absolute frequencies.

c. Compute the cumulative relative frequencies.

d. Prepare a histogram and frequency polygon with the average value of electronic equipment on the x-axis and the absolute frequency on the y-axis.

e. Graph the empirical cumulative distribution function with the average value on the x-axis and the relative frequency on the y-axis.

f. Locate the median, first sample quartile, and third sample quartile on the cumulative distribution function in part e.

g. Calculate the mean, standard deviation, and variance for the frequency distribution. (Hint: Use the midpoint of each class interval and multiply that by the appropriate frequency. For the interval starting at $401, assume the midpoint is 425.5.)

8. An analyst for a leading *Fortune* 500 company demanded that all percentages be reported to one decimal place on graphs being presented to upper management. Several of the cells had sample sizes of less than 30. Discuss why you feel it is or is not necessary to record all the percentages to one decimal place.

9. An office-products retailer recently conducted a study. One question asked of those interviewed was the following: "In an average month, how many times does your company purchase office supplies from an office-products retailer?" The following table lists the results of this question. Calculate the mean and standard deviation.

Value	Frequency
0	25
1	10
2	15
3	5
4	20

10. A manufacturer was interested in assessing how children ages four, five, and six play with one of the manufacturer's toys. Each child was asked 15 questions. Following the child's completed interview, the parent was asked the same 15 questions to validate the child's answers. The following table lists the number of responses to selected items from the survey. One hundred interviews were conducted with both the parent and the child. Notice that item response rates varied from question to question. For each question, state at least one method that could be used to attempt to correct for this item nonresponse bias.

Question	# Children Responding	# Parents Responding
Age of child	95	100
Location of play	80	85
How much the child liked the toy	30	50

11. A large publishing house recently conducted a survey to assess the reading habits of teenagers. The company publishes four magazines specifically tailored to suit the interests of teenagers. Management hypothesized that there were no differences in the preferences for the magazines. A sample of 1,600 teenagers interviewed in the city of Buffalo, New York, indicated the following preferences for the four magazines.

Publication	Frequency of Preference
Rock-Town	350
Rappin'	500
Teen-Tips	450
R.A.D.	300
Total	1600

Management needs your expertise to determine whether there are differences in teenager preferences for the magazines.

a. State the null and alternate hypotheses.
b. How many degrees of freedom are there?
c. What is the chi-square critical table value at the 5 percent significance level?
d. What is the calculated χ^2 value? Show all your calculations.
e. Should the null hypothesis be rejected or not? Explain.

12. Moon Shine Company is a medium-sized manufacturer of shampoo. In recent years, the company has increased the number of product variations of Moon Shine shampoo from three to five to increase its market share. Management conducted a survey to compare sales of Moon Shine shampoo with sales of Sun Shine and Star Shine, the brand's two major competitors. A sample of 1,800 consumers indicated the following frequencies with respect to most recent shampoo purchased:

Shampoo	#Buying
Moon Shine	425
Sun Shine	1175
Star Shine	200
Total	1800

Past experience indicated that three times as many households preferred Sun Shine to Moon Shine and that, in turn, twice as many households preferred Moon Shine to Star Shine. Management wants to determine if the historic tendency still holds, considering that Moon Shine Company has increased the range of shampoos available.

a. State the null and alternate hypotheses.
b. How many degrees of freedom are there?
c. What is the chi-square critical table value at the 5% level?
d. What is the calculated χ^2 value? Show all your calculations.
e. Should the null hypothesis be rejected or not? Explain.

13. A large manufacturer of healthful snacks wants to test whether the sales of a health-food snack bar follow the same pattern with respect to package size in both Los Angeles and New York. The company has equal distribution in both cities and sells the following package sizes: packages of 6 bars, packages of 8 bars, packages of 12 bars, and econo-packs of 24 bars. In

Los Angeles, sales of these package types are in the following ratio: 3:1:2:5. In New York during the same period, 4,880 bars are sold; specifically, sales for the four package types are as follows: 1500, 475, 925, 1980.

a. State the null and alternative hypotheses for the test.

b. What is the appropriate test in this situation? How many degrees of freedom are there? At $\alpha = .05$, can the null hypothesis be rejected?

14. A manufacturer of miniature recorders, the kind that executives dictate into, built to fit into a pen, is testing microchips that vary in length capacity: 30 minutes, 60 minutes, 90 minutes, and 120 minutes. The company has hired you to determine whether customers show any distinct preference toward either extreme. If there is a preference toward any extreme, the company would manufacture only chips of that length; otherwise, the company is planning to market chips for all four time capacities. A sample of 1,000 customers indicated the following preferences.

Duration Capability	Frequency of Preference
30 min.	150
60 min.	250
90 min.	425
120 min.	175
Total	1000

a. State the null and alternate hypotheses.

b. Compute Kolmogorov-Smirnov D by completing the following table.

c. Compute the critical value of D at $\alpha = .05$. Show your calculations.

d. Would you reject the null hypothesis? Explain.

e. What are the implications for management?

f. Explain why the Kolmogorov-Smirnov test would be used in this situation.

Duration Capability	Observed #	Observed Proportion	Observed Cumulative Proportion	Theoretical Proportion	Theoretical Cumulative Proportion
30 min.					
60 min.					
90 min.					
120 min.					

15. A large financial institution wanted to know which options were most important to small businesses. The financial institution hypothesized that the options that businesses found important would vary as annual sales of the businesses varied. The financial organization set up a cross-tabulation to investigate if any changes in importance were occurring between the groups of businesses. The following table lists the number of businesses that reported each of the options as most important. Calculate the percentages. Interpret your calculations.

	Annual Sales	
Option	Under $2 million	$2 to $10 million
Checking account	50	30
Mutual fund	10	70
Savings account	40	50

16. A social organization was interested in determining if there were various demographic characteristics that might be related to people's propensity to contribute to charities. The organization was particularly interested in determining whether individuals over age 40 were more likely to contribute larger amounts than individuals under age 40. The average contribution in the population was $1,500, and this figure was used to divide the individuals in the sample into two groups, those who contributed large amounts or more than average versus those who contributed less than average. Table A presents a two-way classification of the sample of individuals by contributions and age.

In addition, the social organization wanted to determine if contributions depended on income, age, or both. Table B presents the simultaneous treatment of age and income. The median income in the population was $38,200, and this figure was used to split the sample into two groups.

a. Does the amount of personal contribution depend on age? Generate the necessary tables to justify your answer.

b. Does the amount of personal contribution depend on age alone? Generate the necessary tables to justify your answer.

c. Present the percentage of contributions that are more than $1,500 by age and income in tabular form. Interpret the table.

Table A: Personal Contribution and Age

Contribution	Age ≤39	Age 40+	Total
≤ $1500	79	50	129
$1500+	11	60	71
Total	90	110	200

Table B: Personal Contributions by Age and Income

	Income < $38,200 Age ≤39	Age 40+	$38,200+ Age ≤39	Age 40+	Totals Age ≤39	Age 40+
Contribution						
≤ $1500	63	22	16	28	79	50
$1500+	7	18	4	42	11	60
Total	70	40	20	70	90	110

17. Suppose that the following exhibit was prepared to present a portion of the results of a national survey aimed at identifying demographic and socioeconomic differences between individuals with published telephone numbers and individuals with unpublished telephone numbers.

	Published Telephone Numbers	Unpublished Telephone Numbers
Sex		
Male	43%	40%
Female	57	60
Age		
Under 25	8%	6%
25–34	21	26
35–44	13	27
45–54	14	17
55–64	19	15
65+	25	9

	Published Telephone Numbers	Unpublished Telephone Numbers
Ethnic Background		
White	95%	87%
Nonwhite (including Hispanic)	5	13
Household Income		
Under $10,000	10%	12%
$10,000–14,999	16	14
$15,000–19,999	15	16
$20,000–24,999	15	16
$25,000–29,999	16	15
$30,000–44,999	18	21
$45,000+	10	6

a. Describe the type of analysis represented in the exhibit. Is this an appropriate representation of the information on which the exhibit is based? Why or why not?

b. Suppose that the exhibit is based on 4,060 responses; 3,586 respondents indicated that they had a published telephone number and 474 indicated that they did not publish their number. Complete the exhibit below.

	Published Phone #s Frequency (%)	Unpublished Phone #s Frequency (%)	Total Frequency (%)
Sex			
Male			
Female			
Age			
Under 25			
25–34			
35–44			
45–54			
55–64			
65+			
Ethnic Background			
White			
Nonwhite (including Hispanic)			
Household Income			
Under $10,000			
$10,000–14,999			
$15,000–19,999			
$20,000–24,999			
$25,000–29,999			
$30,000–44,999			
$45,000+			

Appendix: Chi-Square and Related Indices for Cross-Tabs

Questions to Guide Your Learning:

Q1: What is a chi-square for cross-tabs?

Q2: What are these indices: contingency coefficients and the index of predictive association?

Q3: What are log linear models and logit models, and when would I use them?

Q4: What are the nonparametric tests: Spearman's rank correlation coefficient and the coefficient of concordance?

Now that we have a better appreciation for the kinds of relationships that might exist between two or more variables as depicted in a cross-tab, we need to follow-up these descriptive impressions with inferential tests. In Chapter 14, the chi-square statistical test for a one-way tabulation was presented as a tool to enable the marketing researcher to determine whether the pattern observed in frequency data was a "real" pattern, or was no more than random fluctuations due to sampling variability. Here too, we can proceed beyond descriptions of proportions in cross-tabs to find out whether various results reflected sample aberrations or real conditions of relationships between variables.

Hypotheses and Statistics to Test Them

For the chi-square on a two-way table, the null hypothesis is that there is no contingency between the two variables. We usually seek to reject that hypothesis in favor of supporting evidence for a relationship between the variables. Stated precisely, the null hypothesis for a two-way chi-square is this:

H_0: the row variable is independent of the column variable

Chi-square tests whether the row and column variables are independent (unrelated).

To say two variables are "independent" is also to say they show no association (which is analogous to saying they are not correlated). For example, if the two variables in Table 14A.1 are not related, then knowing the size of a family would not help predict the number of cars accurately—there is no contingent relationship. If asked to guess the number of cars in a household, one would use the distribution in the sample as a whole—the marginal frequencies of 75 versus 25 tell us the odds of having 0 or 1 car versus 2 or more cars are 3:1. Those proportions would be used as an estimate regardless of family size (i.e., for either row). The question is whether we can improve our prediction if we take into account family size. We should be able to, if there is a relationship between family size and car ownership.

The hypothesis to be tested states that the row variable, A (to use a generic label), is independent of the column variable, B. In Table 14A.1, A would be family size and B, the number of cars the family owns. For notation purposes, let:

A_1 = family of 4 or fewer members
A_2 = family of 5 or more members
B_1 = family owns 0 or 1 car
B_2 = family owns 2 or more cars

Recall from your basic statistics class that the probability of two events occurring jointly if those events are independent is simply the product of the likelihood of either occurring: $P(AB) = P(A) \times P(B)$. In the application to contingency tables, if variables A and B are indeed independent, then the probability of occurrence of the event A_1B_1 (a family with 4 or fewer members and 0 or 1 cars) is given as the product of the separate probabilities for A_1 and B_1:

$P(A_1B_1) = P(A_1)P(B_1)$

The probability $P(A_1)$ is given by the number of cases possessing the characteristic A_1, that is, n_{A1} (or the number of small families), over the total number of cases, n:

$$P(A_1) = \frac{n_{A_1}}{n} = \left(\frac{78}{100}\right)$$

TABLE 14A.1
Frequency Data on Car Ownership

Family Size	#Cars		
	0–1	2+	Total
4 or fewer	70	8	78
5+	5	17	22
Total	75	25	100

Similarly, $P(B_1)$ is given by the number of cases having the characteristic B_1, or n_{B1} (the number of families having 0 or 1 car), over the total sample size. $P(B_1) = n_{B1}/n = 75/100$. The joint probability $P(A_1B_1)$ is:

$$P(A_1B_1) = P(A_1)P(B_1) = \left(\frac{78}{100}\right)\left(\frac{75}{100}\right)$$

Given a total of $n = 100$ cases, the number expected to fall in the cell A_1B_1, e_{11}, is given as the product of the total number of cases and the probability of any one of these cases falling into the A_1B_1 cell; that is,

$$e_{11} = nP(A_1B_1) = 100\left(\frac{78}{100}\right)\left(\frac{75}{100}\right)$$

Two of the n's cancel, so the formula for e_{11} simplifies to:

$$e_{11} = nP(A_1B_1) = nP(A_1)P(B_1) = n\frac{n_{A_1}}{n}\frac{n_{B_1}}{n} = \frac{n_{A_1}n_{B_1}}{n} = \frac{78 \times 75}{100}$$

Thus, to generate the expected frequencies for each cell, multiply the marginal frequencies and divide by the total. The expected frequencies, all calculated this way, appear in Table 14A.2.

The χ^2 value is calculated over the r rows and c columns, with o_{ij} and e_{ij} denoting the observed and expected number of observations in the $(i,j)^{th}$ cell:

$$\chi^2 = \sum_{i-1}^{r}\sum_{j=1}^{c}\frac{(o_{ij} - e_{ij})^2}{e_{ij}}$$

$$= \frac{(70 - 58.5)^2}{58.2} + \frac{(8 - 19.5)^2}{19.5} + \frac{(5 - 16.5)^2}{16.5} + \frac{(17 - 5.5)^2}{5.5}$$

$$= 2.261 + 6.782 + 8.015 + 24.046$$

$$= 41.104$$

The expected frequencies in any row sum to the marginal total so there are $(c-1)$ degrees of freedom in a row (c is the number of columns). Similarly, the expected frequencies in a column must sum to the marginal total, thus there are $(r-1)$ degrees of freedom per column (where r is the number of rows). Total degrees of freedom (df) in a two-way contingency table are $(r-1)(c-1)$.

TABLE 14A.2
Expected Frequencies on Car Ownership Data

Family Size	#Cars 0–1	#Cars 2+
4 or fewer	58.5	19.5
5+	16.5	5.5

In our problem, df $= (2-1)(2-1) = 1$. Using an $\alpha = .05$, the tabled critical value of χ^2 from the appendix in the back of the book is 3.84. The computed $\chi^2 = 41.104$ thus falls in the critical region. The null hypothesis (of independence) is rejected. Thus, we conclude that family size is a factor in determining number of cars purchased.

The chi-square test is one of the most widely used tests in marketing research. Research Realities 14A.1 summarizes its assumptions.

Contingency Coefficient

The χ^2 contingency table test indicates whether two variables are independent, but it does not measure the strength of association when they are dependent. The contingency coefficient (C) can be used for this purpose. It is directly related to the χ^2 test, so it can be generated with relatively little additional computational effort:

$$C = \sqrt{\frac{\chi^2}{n + \chi^2}}$$

Chi-square: Are the variables related?

Contingency coefficient: How strong is the relationship?

where n is the sample size and χ^2 is calculated in the normal way.

The calculated χ^2 for the data just described is 41.104. The contingency coefficient is:

$$C = \sqrt{\frac{\chi^2}{n + \chi^2}} = \sqrt{\frac{41.104}{100 + 41.104}} = .540$$

Does this value indicate strong or weak association between the variables? We need to compare this value against its limits. When there is no association, the contingency coefficient is zero. Unfortunately, the contingency coefficient does not possess the attractive property of the Pearson product-moment correlation coefficient (discussed in the chapter on correlation and regression) of being equal to 1 when the variables are completely dependent or perfectly correlated. Rather, its upper limit is a function of the number of categories. When the number of categories is the same for each variable (that is, r = c), the upper limit on the contingency coefficient for two perfectly related variables is: $\sqrt{(r-1)/r}$.

In the example at hand, r = c = 2, so the maximum possible value for the contingency coefficient is .707. The calculated value, .540, is more than halfway between the limits of zero for no association and .707 for perfect association, suggesting that there is moderately strong association between size of family and number of cars purchased.

Index of Predictive Association

If we had a correlation coefficient, r, we would square it, r^2, to see how much variance in one variable is explained by the other. The index of predictive association does this for cross-tabs.[1]

In the example of size of family vs. car ownership, there is one predictor variable, A (family size) and one criterion variable, B (number of cars in the household). Both

---

[1] James Higgins, *Introduction to Modern Nonparametric Statistics* (Duxbury, 2003).

Research Realities

14A.1 Requirements for the Chi-Square Test

1. The test deals with frequencies. Percent values need to be converted to counts of the number of cases in each cell.
2. The chi-square distribution, although continuous, is used to approximate the distribution of a discrete variable. This approximation results in the computed value being proportionately inflated if too many of the expected frequencies are small. It is generally agreed that only a few cells (fewer than 20%) should be permitted to have expected frequencies fewer than 5, and none should have expected frequencies fewer than 1. Categories may be meaningfully combined to conform to this rule.

3. Multiple answers per respondent should not be analyzed with chi-square contingency table analysis, because the normal tabled critical values of the chi-square statistic for a specified alpha error no longer apply when more than one cross-tabulation analysis is conducted with the same data. The choices for respondents' answers must be exclusive categories (a consumer is classified as one and only one type).
4. Each observation should be independent of the others. The chi-square test would not be appropriate, for example, for analyzing observations on the same individuals in a pretest-posttest experiment.

variables have two classes: A_1 and A_2, and B_1 and B_2. Say we wish to predict the B classification of a family chosen at random—should we predict they'd fall into category B_1 (0 or 1 car), or B_2 (2 or more cars). If we have no knowledge of the family's classification on A, the best guess is to predict B_1, because 75% of all the observations fall in this category. On this basis, we would make 75% of all assignments correctly, since we would assign them all to B_1. (Of course, we would be wrong 25% of the time.) Suppose we know that the family is small (A_1)—the best guess is B_1, since 70 of 78 cases possessing A_1 fall in the B_1 classification. If the A classification is A_2 (the family is large), the best guess is B_2 (17 of 22 cases).

The index of predictive association, $\lambda_{B/A}$, measures the relative decrease in the probability of error by taking account of the A classification in predicting the B classification, over the error of prediction when the A classification is unknown. In the example, $\lambda_{B/A} = .48$. The errors in predicting the B classification are reduced by 48% by taking account of the A classification. The original classification error rate is 25%; these errors drop 12% (25% times .48 equals 12%; there would have been 25 misclassifications without knowing A, but with A, only 13 would be misclassified).

The index of predictive association varies from 0 to 1. It is zero if the A variable is of no help in predicting B. It is 1 if the knowledge of the A classification allows the B classification to be predicted perfectly. The index, predicting B from A, is calculated as follows. Let

$n_{.m}$ be the largest marginal frequency among the B classes, and
n_{am} be the largest frequency in the ath row of the table.

Then

$$\lambda_{B|A} = \frac{\sum_a n_{am} - n_{.m}}{n - n_{.m}}$$

where $\sum_a n_{am}$ is taken over all the A classes. For the example, n = 100. The largest marginal frequency among the B classes, $n_{.m}$, is 75, corresponding to 0 or 1 cars. If a

Contingency coefficient is like correlation index of predictive association is like regression family has 4 or fewer members, the largest frequency in the first row of the cross-classification table, n_{1m}, is 70; similarly, $n_{2m} = 17$. Thus, the index of predictive association is:

$$\lambda_{B|A} = \frac{\left(n_{1m} + n_{2m}\right) - n_{.m}}{n - n_{.m}} = \frac{\left(70 + 17\right) - 75}{100 - 75} = .48$$

We reduced the errors in predicting B from A, from 25 to 13, a 48% improvement. The enhanced predictive accuracy is substantial. (This result, that A helps us understand B, is consistent with the chi-square test for independence on this contingency table, where we had rejected the notion of independence between the variables.)

These findings demonstrate the two important questions in association analysis. First, is there an association between the criterion and predictor variables, or are they independent? Second, if they are dependent, how much are predictions about the criterion variable improved by taking into account the important predictor variables? The chi-square test and contingency coefficient answer the first question, and the index of predictive association is used to answer the second. The distinction between these two questions is analogous to the difference between correlation and regression, which analogously seek linear association and prediction.

Log Linear Models

Log linear models extend the chi-square test to frequency tables of three or more variables.[2] For example, we might explore the relationship between family size, household income, and number of cars, as in Table 14A.3.

Recall that in the chi-square for two variables, the model of independence between A and the B was reflected in the equation for computing the expected frequencies:

$$e_{ij} = \frac{n_{A_i} n_{B_j}}{n}$$

This equation is multiplicative, which makes the calculus of optimization complicated. If we take the natural logarithm of both sides, the equation simplifies to a "linear" form (terms are added or subtracted) in the "log" scale—hence they are called "log linear" models:

$$ln(e_{ij}) = ln(n_{A_i}) + ln(n_{B_j}) - ln(n)$$

TABLE 14A.3
Car Ownership as a Function of Income and Family Size

A = family size	B = income	C = 0 or 1 car	2 or more cars
4 or fewer	< $37,500	44	2
	>$37,500	26	6
5 or more	< $37,500	4	4
	> $37,500	1	13

[2] For more details, see Colin Mills and Daniel Wright, *Introducing Log Linear Modeling* (Sage, 2003).

The first term on the right-hand side of the equation reflects the rows (Λ_i), the second term reflects the columns (B_j), and the third term, the total sample size.

To facilitate generalization to bigger tables and to more complex models, let's write the parameters simply as "u-terms":[3]

$$ln(e_{ij}) = u + u_{A(i)} + u_{B(j)}$$

where

$$u = \frac{1}{rc} \sum_i \sum_j ln(e_{ij})$$

$$u_{A(i)} = \frac{1}{c} \sum_j ln(e_{ij}) - u$$

$$u_{B(j)} = \frac{1}{r} \sum_i ln(e_{ij}) - u$$

The first term is an overall mean of the expected frequencies that looks unusual only because we are working in the natural log scale. The second two terms are also means (e.g., the sum over columns, j, divided by the number of columns) "centered around" (subtracting) the overall mean, u. The first term, u, is not typically of substantive interest, but the latter two, $u_{A(i)}$ and $u_{B(j)}$, reflect the differences among the rows (A), and those among the columns (B).

In Table 14A.2, variable A is family size, B is income, and C is the number of cars the family owns. We might wish to test whether there are significant associations between all pairs of variables, A and B, A and C, and B and C. We would write our model as follows:

$$ln(e_{ijk}) = u + u_{A(i)} + u_{B(j)} + u_{C(k)} + u_{AB(ij)} + u_{AC(ik)} + u_{BC(jk)}$$

with the first four terms estimated analogously to those in the equations above, and the last three terms, which reflect the pairwise associations estimated as follows, for example:[4]

$$u_{12(ij)} = \frac{1}{k} \sum_k ln(e_{ijk}) - u_{1(i)} - u_{2(j)} - u$$

Suppose the model fit, but, say, the BC term was not significant (i.e., no relationship existed between income and number of cars), we might fit a model that is nested within the larger model, maintaining comparable fit, yet improved parsimony, for example:[5]

$$ln(e_{ijk}) = u + u_{A(i)} + u_{B(j)} + u_{C(k)} + u_{AB(ij)} + u_{AC(ik)}$$

Log linear models: scary notation, but just an extension of cross-tabs.

---

[3] With constraints, given the df or the fact that the estimates are centered on u, that $\sum_i u_{A(i)} = \sum_j u_{B(j)} = 0$.

[4] Both $u_{A(i)}$ and $u_{B(j)}$ are expressed as deviations around the u, thus: $\sum_i u_{AB(ij)} = \sum_j u_{AB(ij)} = 0$. As tables get bigger or models more complex, they cannot all be written in analytical form; the iterative proportional fitting or Newton-Raphson algorithm estimation procedures rely upon iterative convergence to solutions.

[5] The χ^2 may be computed, but usually we compute: $G^2 = 2 \sum_{i=1}^{r} \sum_{j=1}^{c} o_{ij} ln(o_{ij} / e_{ij})$, a "badness of fit" index like χ^2 in that both get larger as the data and expected frequencies differ more, and both draw their critical values from chi-square tables, but G^2 has superior statistical properties.

In truth, in this particular example, it is not simply the case that we have three arbitrary variables, and any of them might be related to any of the others. Rather, we have come to think of C, the number of cars, as the dependent variable that might be predicted once we know the family size, A, and the household income, B. Although the log linear models help us understand relationships among the variables, a "logit" model is used for prediction purposes.

Logits are really important in marketing research. They allow us to answer central marketing questions such as, "Will that household buy my product?" (where the expected answer is yes or no) and, "Which brand will that consumer choose?" (where the expected answer is one of a number of categories).[6]

For our data, a logit model poses the question, "Are the odds of having 0 or 1 car versus 2 or more cars different depending on the size and income of the family?" Imagine the model above stated for just the families with 0 or 1 cars (C=1):

$$ln(e_{ij1}) = u + u_{A(i)} + u_{B(j)} + u_{C(1)} + u_{AB(ij)} + u_{AC(i1)} + u_{BC(j1)}$$

and comparing it to the model fit to the families that own 2 or more cars (C=2):

$$ln(e_{ij2}) = u + u_{A(i)} + u_{B(j)} + u_{C(2)} + u_{AB(ij)} + u_{AC(i2)} + u_{BC(j2)}$$

We might compare the odds directly in a ratio, e_{ij1}/e_{ij2}, or again, given that it is easier to work in the log scale, we would examine the "log odds ratio," also called the "logit," as defined here:

$$ln(e_{ij1} / e_{ij2}) = ln(e_{ij1}) - ln(e_{ij2})$$

$$= u + u_{A(i)} + u_{B(j)} + u_{C(1)} + u_{AB(ij)} + u_{AC(i1)} + u_{BC(j1)}$$

$$- \left[u + u_{A(i)} + u_{B(j)} + u_{C(2)} + u_{AB(ij)} + u_{AC(i2)} + u_{BC(j2)} \right]$$

Note that several common terms cancel, and algebraically we are left with:

$$(u_{C(1)} - u_{C(2)}) + (u_{AC(i1)} - u_{AC(i2)}) + (u_{BC(j1)} - u_{BC(j2)})$$

In logit models, there are only two levels of the dependent variable (our variable C). And recall that the estimates sum to zero: $u_{C(1)} + u_{C(2)} = 0$. Thus, if $u_{C(1)}$ is some value such as .5, then $u_{C(2)}$ will equal −.5. Thus, the term $(u_{C(1)} - u_{C(2)})$ in the equation above may be restated as $(u_{C(1)} + u_{C(1)})$, or $2u_{C(1)}$. Thus, the equation above simplifies to:

$$2(u_{C(1)} + u_{AC(i1)} + u_{BC(j1)})$$

Now instead of seven terms in the model, there are only three, all of which involve the dependent variable, C; the first is a logit intercept; the second reflects the impact of A (family size) on C; and the third reflects the impact of B (household income) on C.

If we fit this logit model to the data in Table 14A.3, using a statistical computing package such as Sas or Spss, we obtain the following estimates:

$$ln(e_{ijk}) = -2.18 + 3.56(A_i) + 1.96(B_j)$$

Log linear models // correlations

Logit models // regression

---

[6] Philip Hans Franses, "How Nobel-Worthy Economics Relates to Databases," *Marketing News* (Mar. 12, 2001), p. 14; also see Michael Lieberman, "Using Discrete Choice Models to Measure Brand Equity," http://www.quirks.com and Yilian Yuan and Gang Xu, "Discrete Choice Modeling in Pharmaceutical Marketing Research," http://www.quirks.com.

Both predictors are significant (the printouts list standard errors of .73 and .72 respectively for A and B; the parameter estimates in the equation, divided by their standard errors yield z-statistics of 4.88 and 2.72). Thus, both family size and household income are significant determinants in predicting the number of cars a family is likely to own.[7] Both parameters are positive, which indicates that as either predictor increases (larger family or greater income), the likelihood that the family owns 2 or more cars (compared with 0 or 1) increases.[8]

Nonparametric Measures of Association

We have been focusing on techniques and measures of association appropriate for nominal or ordinal data—cross-tabs, chi-square, contingency coefficient, index of predictive association, log linear, and logit models. There are also two indices that are appropriate only for the analysis of rank-order data—Spearman's rank-order correlation coefficient and the coefficient of concordance.

Spearman's Rank Correlation Coefficient

One of the best known coefficients of association for rank-order data is Spearman's rank correlation coefficient, denoted r_s. The coefficient is appropriate when both variables are measured on an ordinal scale so that the sample elements may be ranked in two ordered series.

Suppose a company wished to determine whether there was an association between the overall performance of a distributor and the distributor's level of service. The company's management defined "overall performance" as a composite of measures of sales, market share, sales growth, and profit. The marketing research department developed an index of "service provided" based on customer complaints and compliments, service turnaround records, etc.

Table 14A.4 contains the ranks of the company's 15 distributors with respect to each of these performance criteria. We start by looking at the differences in ranks on each variable. Let X_i be the rank of the ith distributor in terms of service and Y_i be the rank of the distributor with regard to overall performance. Let $d_i = X_i - Y_i$ be the difference in rankings. If the rankings on the two variables are exactly the same, each d_i will be zero. If there is some discrepancy in ranks, some of the d_i's will not be zero, and the greater the discrepancy, the larger some of the d_i's would be. The Spearman rank-order correlation coefficient is calculated as:

$$r_s = 1 - \frac{6\sum_{i=1}^{n} d_i^2}{n(n^2 - 1)}$$

---

[7] Did we "know" this from the cross-tabs previously? Sort of. But now we know it "officially" via a statistical test.

[8] The models we have considered here require both the dependent variable and the predictors to be categorical. If some predictors are continuous, models called "logistic regressions" may be fit, using similar logic.

TABLE 14A.4
Distributor Performance

Distributor	Service Ranking X_i	Overall Performance Ranking Y_i	Ranking Difference $d_i = X_i - Y_i$	Difference Squared d_i^2
1	6	8	−2	4
2	2	4	−2	4
3	13	12	+1	1
4	1	2	−1	1
5	7	10	−3	9
6	4	5	−1	1
7	11	9	+2	4
8	15	13	+2	4
9	3	1	+2	4
10	9	6	+3	9
11	12	14	−2	4
12	5	3	+2	4
13	14	15	−1	1
14	8	7	+1	1
15	10	11	−1	1
				$\Sigma d_i^2 = 52$

In the example, $\sum_i d_i^2 = 52$, and $r_s = 1 - \dfrac{6(52)}{15(15^2 - 1)} = 1 - \dfrac{312}{3360} = .907$

The null hypothesis is that there is no association between service level and overall performance, whereas the alternative hypothesis suggest there is a relationship. The null hypothesis that $\rho_s = 0$ can be tested by referring directly to tables of critical values of r_s or, when the sample size is greater than 10, by calculating the t statistic,

$$t = r_s \sqrt{\frac{n-2}{1 - r_s^2}}$$

which is referred to a t-table for $n - 2$ degrees of freedom. Calculated t is:

$$t = .907 \sqrt{\frac{15 - 2}{1 - (.907)^2}} = 7.77$$

and critical t for $\alpha = .05$ and 13 degrees of freedom is 2.16. Calculated t exceeds critical t, and the null hypothesis of no relationship is rejected. Overall distributor performance is related to service level. The upper limit for the Spearman rank correlation coefficient is 1.0, since if there were perfect agreement in the ranks, Σd_i^2 would be zero. Thus, the relationship is significant and relatively strong.

Coefficient of Concordance

In some cases, we want to analyze the association among three or more rankings of n objects or individuals. When there are k sets of rankings, we use Kendall's coefficient of concordance.

An example of the use of this index is in examining interjudge reliability. A computer equipment manufacturer was interested in evaluating its domestic sales branch managers. Many criteria could be used: sales from the branch office, sales in relation to the branch's potential, sales growth, and sales representative turnover are just a few. Management believed that different executives in the company would place different emphasis on the various criteria and that a consensus about how the criteria should be weighted would be hard to achieve. It was decided, therefore, that the VP in charge of marketing, the general sales manager, and the marketing research department should all attempt to rank the 10 branch managers from best to worst. Table 14A.5 contains these rankings. The company wished to determine whether there was agreement among these rankings.

The right-hand column of Table 14A.5 contains the sum of ranks assigned to each branch manager. If perfect agreement existed among the three rankings, the sum of ranks, R_i, for the top-rated branch manager would be $1+1+1 = k$, where $k = 3$. The second-rated branch manager would have sum of ranks $2+2+2 = 2k$, and the nth-rated branch manager would have sum of ranks $n+n+n = nk$. Thus, when there is perfect agreement among the k sets of rankings, the R_i would be k, 2k, 3k, ..., nk. If there is little agreement among the k rankings, the R_i would be roughly equal. Thus, the degree of agreement among the k rankings is measured by the variance of the n sums of ranks; the greater the agreement, the larger the variance in the n sums would be.

The **coefficient of concordance** (W) is a function of the variance in the sums of ranks. First, the sum of the R_i for each of the n rows is determined. Second, the average R_i, $\bar{R}$, is calculated by dividing the sum of the R_i by the number of objects. Third, the sum of the squared deviations is determined; call this quantity s, where

$$s - \sum_i \left(R_i - \bar{R} \right)^2$$

Branch Manager	VP, Marketing	General Sales Manager	Marketing Research Dept.	Sum of Ranks, R_i
A	4	4	5	13
B	3	2	2	7
C	9	10	10	29
D	10	9	9	28
E	2	3	3	8
F	1	1	1	3
G	6	5	4	15
H	8	7	7	22
I	5	6	6	17
J	7	8	8	23

TABLE 14A.5
Branch Manager Rankings

The coefficient of concordance finally is computed as:

$$W = \frac{s}{\frac{1}{12}k^2\left(n^3 - n\right)}$$

The denominator of the coefficient represents the maximum possible variation in sums of ranks if perfect agreement in the rankings were achieved. The numerator reflects the actual variation in ranks. The larger the ratio, the greater the agreement among the evaluations. For our data,

$$\overline{R} = \frac{\left(13 + 7 + \ldots + 23\right)}{10} = \frac{165}{10} = 16.5$$

$$s = \left(13 - 16.5\right)^2 + \left(7 - 16.5\right)^2 + \ldots + \left(23 - 16.5\right)^2 = 720.5$$

and

$$\left(\frac{1}{12}\right)k^2\left(n^3 - n\right) = \left(\frac{1}{12}\right)(3)^2\left(10^3 - 10\right) = 742.5$$

Thus,

$$W = \frac{720.5}{742.5} = .970$$

The significance of W can be examined by using special tables when the number of objects being ranked is small (when $n \leq 7$). When the sample size is larger, the coefficient of concordance is approximately chi-square distributed where $\chi^2 = k(n-1)W$ with $n-1$ degrees of freedom. The null hypothesis is that there is no agreement among the rankings, and the alternative hypothesis is that there is some agreement. For an assumed $\alpha = .05$, critical χ^2 for 9 degrees of freedom is 16.92, whereas calculated X^2 is:

$$X^2 = k(n - 1)W = 3(9)(.970) = 26.2$$

Calculated X^2 exceeds critical χ^2, the null hypothesis of no agreement is rejected—there is indeed some agreement. Further, the agreement is good—the limits of W are 0.0 with no agreement and 1.0 with perfect agreement among the ranks. The calculated value of $W = .970$ suggests that although the agreement in the ranks is not perfect, it is certainly good. The marketing VP, general sales manager, and marketing research department applied essentially the same standards in ranking the branch managers.

Kendall has suggested that the best estimate of the true ranking of n objects is provided by the order of the various sums of ranks, R_i, when W is significant. Thus, the best estimate of the true ranking of the sales managers is that F is doing the best job and B the next best job, and that C is doing the poorest job.

Summary

The chi-square statistic tests whether the associations spotted in cross-tabs are statistically reliable, or more likely the result of sampling variability. Log linear models are a natural extension of the chi-square test to three- and higher-dimensional tables. The addition of variables naturally allows for more complex modeling.

Logit models are particularly important to the marketing researcher, because they allow the modeling of categorical dependent variables. Brand choice is categorical and predicting it is typically of great importance in many marketing decision systems.

The Spearman rank correlation coefficient and the coefficient of concordance are additional indices that can shed further light on associations between rank-order data.

Review Questions

1. What is the basic question at issue in a chi-square test on a two-way contingency table? What is the null hypothesis for this test? How are the expected frequencies determined?

2. What is the contingency coefficient, and to what types of situations does it apply? How does one determine whether the association between the variables indicated by the calculated value of the contingency coefficient is "strong" or "weak"?

3. What is the index of predictive association? When is it properly used? What is meant by an index of predictive association of $\lambda_{B/A} = .75$?

4. How is a log linear model an extension of the χ^2?

5. If the data are ordinal and the analyst wishes to determine whether the observed frequencies correspond to some expected pattern, what statistical test is appropriate? What is the basic procedure to follow in implementing this test?

6. What is the Spearman rank correlation coefficient? To what types of situations does it apply? How is it calculated and interpreted?

7. What is the coefficient of concordance? When is it used? What is the rationale underlying its computation?

Applications and Problems

1. A large publishing house wants to determine if there is an association between newspaper-publication choice and the education level of the customer. A random sample of 400 customers provided the data in Table 14A.1:

   a. State the null and alternate hypotheses.

   b. Generate the expected frequencies for each cell.

   c. Is there an association between newspaper publication choice and level of education at $\alpha = .05$? Show your calculations.

   d. What is the strength of association as measured by the contingency coefficient between education level and newspaper choice? Show your calculations.

TABLE 14A.1 Education Level versus Newspaper Choice: Observed Frequencies

| Newspaper Publication | Level of Education | | | |
	H.S.	Undergrad degree	Graduate degree	Total
A	75	45	5	125
B	35	10	30	75
C	50	35	10	95
D	65	35	5	105
Total	225	125	50	400

2. A marketing researcher from the publishing company in Problem 1 stated that the best estimate of newspaper choice by a customer chosen at random would be the A publication, since 31.25% (125 of 400) customers purchased this publication. The researcher further stated that 68.75% of the time the company would be wrong and decided to discard the previous study.

   a. How could the predictive accuracy be improved? Show your calculations.

   b. The index of predictive association is "more directly interpretable" than the contingency coefficient. Discuss.

3. Katherine Martin is the newly hired marketing director for the Alpine Bottling Company (ABC). ABC produces a premium line of soft-drink products made with all-natural ingredients. ABC soft drinks are typically about 20% more expensive than other soft drinks, including the industry leaders.

   Convinced that ABC soft drinks would appeal to a large segment of the market (beyond just the health-conscious consumers) if moved into nationwide distribution, Martin decided that the best way to introduce the product is to show that it tastes better than other soft drinks. This could be accomplished by using the "blind taste test" approach and showing the results in ABC's television advertising. Before proceeding, however, she decided to conduct a very limited taste test to get a rough idea of how ABC ranked with other soft drinks. Five consumers each sampled eight brands of soft drinks, including one of the ABC products and the industry leaders. None of the soft drinks was identified. The participants then ranked the eight soft drinks according to their taste preferences (the most preferred was given a ranking of 1). The results of this limited test are as follows:

	Consumer				
Brand	**1**	**2**	**3**	**4**	**5**
ABC Brand	2	3	1	1	1
Brand A	7	8	7	6	7
Brand B	3	2	3	2	3
Brand C	5	5	5	5	6
Brand D	8	7	8	8	8
Brand E	1	1	2	3	2
Brand F	6	6	6	7	5
Brand G	4	4	4	4	4

   a. Calculate the coefficient of concordance to determine the five subjects' degree of agreement with respect to their taste preferences.

   b. Assuming $\alpha = .05$ significance level, is there evidence of agreement among the subjects?

   c. What is the best estimate of the true ranking of the soft drinks based on this analysis?

   d. What are the managerial implications for Martin?

4. When should one use the coefficient of concordance instead of Spearman's rank correlation coefficient? What is the null hypothesis for this test? What are the limits of this test and what do these limits mean?

Data Analysis— Basic Questions

Questions to Guide Your Learning:

Q1: What considerations underlie the choice of a statistical method to analyze data?

Q2: What are the main statistical methods useful for marketing researchers?

Q3: What are the implications of "levels of measurement" (nominal, ordinal, interval, ratio) for choice of statistical tools?

Q4: What is a univariate vs. multivariate analysis?

You've seen that data analysis begins with the preliminary steps of editing, coding, and tabulating. Those preprocessing procedures are important and common to almost all research studies. Some studies stop there, with tables and cross-tabs. Many involve additional analyses to answer in more detail the question, "What's going on in the data?" To extract more information and meaning from data, we need to know which statistical procedure is appropriate. This choice depends on qualities of the research problem and qualities of our particular data. This chapter highlights these considerations in the choice of methodology.

Choice of Analysis Technique: An Example

Assume that a study was completed by a consumer products firm that manufactures the dishwashing liquid Sheen.[1] The study was designed to determine consumers' perceptions of the gentleness of Sheen and its closest competitor, Glitter. Say the study used a probability sample and the data were collected by administering a rating scale to each respondent. These consumers were asked to rate each brand on a 5-point mildness scale with the following descriptors, according to how they thought the brand affected their hands:

- Very rough (VR)
- Rough (R)
- Neither rough nor gentle (N)
- Mild (M)
- Very mild (VM)

Table 15.1 contains the responses from 10 consumers. The table also contains alternative ways of analyzing the data, and not all of them are appropriate, so some of their conclusions are wrong. We'll see that the conclusion depends on the method. There is no problem in most studies in deciding, "What ways *can* the analysis be done?" But there's a big problem in deciding the question, "How *should* the analysis be done?"

The methods reported in Table 15.1 vary according to how numeric values were assigned to the scale. For instance, underlying Method A is the assumption that mildness is desirable and roughness undesirable in dishwashing liquids. Thus, if the

TABLE 15.1 Consumers' Perceptions of Dishwashing Liquids

				Respondent Scores for Each Brand under Method								
	Perception of VR R N M VM		A −2 −1 0 1 2		B 1 2 3 4 5		C 5 4 3 2 1		D −1 0 1		E: Preferred Alternative
Respondent	S	G	S	G	S	G	S	G	S	G	
1	VM	VM	2	2	5	5	1	1	1	1	T
2	M	VM	1	2	4	5	2	1	1	1	G
3	N	VM	0	2	3	5	3	1	0	1	G
4	M	VM	1	2	4	5	2	1	1	1	G
5	M	VM	1	2	4	5	2	1	1	1	G
6	M	VM	1	2	4	5	2	1	1	1	G
7	M	M	1	1	4	4	2	2	1	1	T
8	M	R	1	21	4	2	2	4	1	21	S
9	N	R	0	21	3	2	3	4	0	21	S
10	N	M	0	1	3	4	3	2	0	1	G
Sums			8	12	38	42	22	18	7	6	
Averages			.9	1.2	3.8	4.2	2.2	1.8	.7	.6	

*A "T" indicates a tie, in that both brands received the same rating.

[1] Hey, it's not "glam," but this kind of thing is the brand manager's bread-and-butter. Wait till you're the brand manager for widgets, or TP; you'll be dreaming of soapsuds!

consumer believed that the dishwashing soap was very mild, that response received a positive score of +2. A response of "very rough" received a negative score of –2, and so on. The scores are totaled and averaged at the bottom of the table.

The averages for Method A show Sheen with an average of .8, and Glitter at 1.2. Both soaps are thus "mild." If we look at the differences between these averages and convert them to a percentage difference, with Sheen as the comparative yardstick, we find:

$$\frac{\bar{x}_G - \bar{x}_S}{\bar{x}_s}(100) = \frac{1.2 - 0.8}{0.8}(100) = 50\%$$

and the conclusion is that Glitter is 50% milder on the hands. With Glitter as the basis of comparison, the result is:

$$\frac{\bar{x}_G - \bar{x}_S}{\bar{x}_s}(100) = \frac{1.2 - 0.8}{0.8}(100) = 33\%$$

and the conclusion is that Glitter is 33% milder on the hands. Similar calculations underlie each of the comparisons for Methods A through D. Methods B and C, for example, assign numbers to response categories similar to Method A, except that Method B uses all positive numbers (with "very mild" receiving a score of 5) and Method C reverses the scoring (so a score of 5 represents a "very rough" evaluation). Method D assigns negative values to "rough" evaluations and positive values to "mild" evaluations, but the "rough" and "very rough" evaluations receive the same score (–1), as do the "mild" and "very mild" evaluations (+1), so "rough" and "very rough" aren't distinguished by this approach (nor are "mild" vs. "very mild"). In contrast, Method E doesn't rely on average scores for all respondents but simply lists whichever alternative was rated higher by each respondent. The conclusions in Method E reflect the facts that Respondents 1 and 7 perceived Glitter and Sheen to be of equal mildness, 6 of 10 respondents perceived Glitter as milder, and 2 perceived Sheen as milder.

Table 15.2 offers simple analyses of each of these methods, trying to comparatively assess which of the two brands is milder. The right-hand column suggests a variety of conclusions, so now we have to figure out which of these conflicting statements is correct, and why. The answer is Method E, and the reasons are what we illustrate in this chapter. A number of factors dictate the choice of analysis method, including the type of data, the research design, and the assumptions underlying the test statistic.

Before discussing these considerations, let's finish with these data. We'll show why the last statement is correct and, in the process, start to reveal some of the issues. First, some researchers hold that the response categories reflect order, but not interval measurements. That is, although "very rough" is rougher than "rough," the difference between "very rough" and "rough" is not the same as the difference between "rough" and "neither rough nor gentle." Further, as long as the order relationships are preserved on these data, the assignment of scale values is arbitrary, but the calculation of means is misleading. Thus, these researchers would argue that Methods A to D are inappropriate because the values were averaged.

Second, even if the data had interval properties, Methods A to D would still be incorrect for two reasons. First, the comparisons in Table 15.2 involve absolute magnitudes—each difference is compared to a mean and the result is interpreted as a

TABLE 15.2
Comparison of
Dishwashing Liquids

Method	Base in Comparison	Calculations	Conclusion
A	Sheen	$\dfrac{\bar{x}_G - \bar{x}_S}{\bar{x}_s}(100) = \dfrac{1.2 - 0.8}{0.8}(100) = 50\%$	Glitter is 50% milder
	Glitter	$\dfrac{\bar{x}_G - \bar{x}_S}{\bar{x}_s}(100) = \dfrac{1.2 - 0.8}{0.8}(100) = 33\%$	Glitter is 33% milder
B	Sheen	$\dfrac{\bar{x}_G - \bar{x}_S}{\bar{x}_s}(100) = \dfrac{4.2 - 3.8}{3.8}(100) = 10.5\%$	Glitter is 11% milder
	Glitter	$\dfrac{\bar{x}_G - \bar{x}_S}{\bar{x}_s}(100) = \dfrac{4.2 - 3.8}{4.2}(100) = 9.5\%$	Glitter is 10% milder
C	Sheen	$\dfrac{\bar{x}_G - \bar{x}_S}{\bar{x}_s}(100) = \dfrac{2.2 - 1.8}{2.2}(100) = 18.2\%$	Glitter is 18% milder
	Glitter	$\dfrac{\bar{x}_G - \bar{x}_S}{\bar{x}_s}(100) = \dfrac{2.2 - 1.8}{1.8}(100) = 22.2\%$	Glitter is 22% milder
D	Sheen	$\dfrac{\bar{x}_G - \bar{x}_S}{\bar{x}_s}(100) = \dfrac{0.7 - 0.6}{0.7}(100) = 14.3\%$	Sheen is 14% milder
	Glitter	$\dfrac{\bar{x}_G - \bar{x}_S}{\bar{x}_s}(100) = \dfrac{0.7 - 0.6}{0.6}(100) = 16.7\%$	Sheen is 17% milder
E		60% of respondents thought Glitter was milder, 20% thought Sheen milder	

certain percentage of the mean. Such comparisons are inappropriate unless the variables have a natural zero. The comparisons involving Methods A through D would be meaningful, then, if the variables were on a ratio scale but not when the zero position is arbitrary, as it is in these rating scales. Further, the evaluations of Sheen and Glitter are not independent and cannot be treated as such statistically. Instead, they represent multiple responses from the same individual. They are related or dependent samples, and the appropriate procedure involves an analysis of the difference in the evaluations per individual. Method E is the only procedure that correctly deals with these differences.

Third, the conclusion was that "60% of the people thought Glitter was milder on the hands." The question has not been raised about whether this is a statistically significant result. The question of significance involves the size of the sample used to generate the percentage. With our sample of only 10, the result is not significant, but if 60 out of 100 people thought that Glitter was milder on the hands than Sheen, the result would be statistically significant, even though the percentage preferring Glitter would remain the same. Sample size is an important barometer in determining whether a research finding is due to chance or whether it represents an underlying condition in the population.

Basic Considerations

The example has highlighted some of the considerations involved in the choice of analysis method. The appropriate technique depends on the type of data, the research design, and the assumptions underlying the test statistic and its related consideration, the power of the test.

Type of Data

When we were discussing the creation of questions for surveys, we talked about the differences between the *levels of measurement*—nominal, ordinal, interval, ratio. We revisit those levels briefly here because they have clear implications for which statistics we can use on the data that arise from a survey. To understand the different implications, consider which transformations are permissible for variables measured on each of the levels.

NOMINAL

The nominal scale is used when categorizing objects. A letter or numeral is assigned to each category so that each number represents a distinct category. For instance, if we're coding gender, the numbers 1 and 2 (or 2&1, 0&1, etc.) serve equally as well as the letters M and F. The nominal scale remains undistorted with this "transformation," this substitution of the numbers. Thus, a "2" could be used to denote men and a "1" for women, or vice versa, without loss of information. With a nominal scale, the only permissible operation is counting, so the only measure of central tendency that is appropriate is the *mode*. In a sample of 60 men and 40 women, we cannot say that the "average gender is 1.4" (e.g., $.6 \times 1 + .4 \times 2$). All we can say is that there were more men in the sample than women, or that 60% of the sample was "male" regardless of whether we choose to call the category 1, 2, or M.

ORDINAL

The ordinal scale represents a higher level of measurement because the numerals assigned reflect order as well. If we were to classify students into three categories, such as good, average, and poor, we might call the categories A, B, and C, or we might use the numbers 1 = good, 2 = average, and 3 = poor, or even the reverse, in which good = 3 and poor = 1. The schemes are equally fine. The structure of an ordinal scale is undistorted by any substitution that preserves the order. The *median* and the *mode* are now both legitimate measures of central tendency. If 20 people ranked Product A 1st in comparison with Products B and C, whereas 10 ranked it 2nd and 5 ranked it 3rd, we could say that (1) the average (median) rank of Product A was one (with 35 subjects, the median is given by the 18th response when ranked from lowest to highest), and that (2) the modal rank was also one.

INTERVAL

The assignment of numerals to objects using an interval scale conveys information about the magnitude of the differences between the objects. We can determine *how much more* one category is than another. We still cannot state that "A is five times larger than B," because the interval scale contains an arbitrary (not absolute) zero. An interval scale is undistorted under linear transformations; i.e., $y = b + cx$. The effect of this transformation is to shift the origin b units (moving the numbers up or

Now you see "level of measurement" (nominal, ordinal, interval, ratio) is important because it helps determine which statistics you can use!

down) and multiply the unit of measurement by c (stretching or shrinking the range on the scale), as in going from a Fahrenheit scale to Celsius. The *mean*, the *median*, and the *mode* are all appropriate measures of central tendency.

RATIO

The ratio scale has a natural zero point, so we can sensibly say that "A is twice as heavy" or "twice as tall as B." The ratio scale is undistorted under proportionate or scalar transformations; i.e., y = cx. The conversion of inches to centimeters is an example; c in this case would equal 2.54. All statistics appropriate for the interval scale are also appropriate for a ratio scale (i.e., *mean, median,* and *mode*). It's important to interpret numerical relationships properly, reflecting the properties of the measurement scale. Consider the following ad claim, like those you see on TV and in magazines:

> New Lustre gets your clothes 20% brighter, you need 50% less detergent, and you can use water temperatures 30% lower than that required for old Lustre.

Probably the "brighter" claim in this ad was based on consumers' subjective reactions to clothes washed with old Lustre. Consumers probably gave their perceptions on a "dingy" to "bright" rating scale. Suppose that a 7-point scale was used and that old Lustre received an average score of 5 and new Lustre got a 6; the 20% brighter claim would result from the calculation:

$$\frac{\overline{x}_{new} - \overline{x}_{old}}{\overline{x}_{old}}(100) = \frac{6-5}{5}(100) = 20\%$$

There is disagreement between people who insist that most marketing measurements, like these consumer ratings, reflect ordinal measurement vs. people who argue that such scales can be treated as interval measures. There is some evidence to support each position. On the one hand, even though a researcher develops scales to try to reflect equal increments, the scales aren't necessarily interpreted that way by the respondents. On the other hand, we can hope the patterns in data are largely robust (see Research Realities 15.1), and enhanced with larger samples. It also helps when the descriptors are carefully chosen, e.g., the descriptors "remarkably good," "good," "neutral," "reasonably poor," and "extremely poor" could be used to approximate a five-point interval scale. While the debate continues, a reasonably balanced argument suggests the following:

1. It is very safe, and certainly very useful, to treat the total score summed over a number of items as an interval scale.[2]
2. It is sometimes safe to treat individual items as interval scales, such as when specific steps have been taken to ensure the interval nature of the response categories.
3. It is always legitimate to treat the scale as ordinal when neither Condition 1 nor 2 is satisfied. If this condition applied to the "dingy" to "bright" rating scale, so that the descriptors anchoring the categories did not reflect equal increments of "brightness," then the calculation of means would be suspect.

Suppose, on the other hand, that appropriate procedures were used, that the evaluation scale did reflect interval measurement, and that the calculation of means was appropriate. The "brighter" claim would still be in error, and for the same reason

---

[2] For example, if questions 4, 5, and 6 on some survey all purport to measure consumer preference, it's not unusual, and for several reasons good practice, to create a new variable for each respondent in the database, called "preference" as a subscale, which is simply the average of the respondent's scores on questions 4–6.

Research Realities

15.1 4-point? 5-point? Stability of Responses

Something that concerns marketing survey researchers is whether to offer "4 box" or "5 box" responses. The question is essentially whether respondents should be provided with a "don't know" or "no opinion" option.

Most researchers endorse that if a respondent doesn't know an answer or has no opinion, he or she should be allowed to state as much. Some researchers suggest that a neutral point, or "no opinion" answer, should not be provided because most respondents are not likely to be exactly neutral on an issue, so they should be forced to take a stand, even if their preference is slight. Researchers who argue for including a neutral or "no opinion" category argue that forcing respondents to make a choice when their preferences are fuzzy or nonexistent simply introduces response error into the results.

Market Facts ran a comparative study, asking 3000 consumer about their purchase intention, for three different time frames, for several different product categories, whether they "definitely will buy" to "definitely will not buy" the product. Half the respondents were given the 4-point scales, the other half were given the 5-point scales that included the neutral point, "might or might not buy."

Are there differences? Sort of. The 12-month chart looks remarkably stable (i.e., 4- vs. 5-point scales don't matter, the results are largely the same, except of course the middle category cannot have any data for the 4-point sample). The 30-day and 7-day charts are also largely comparable across the 4- vs. 5-point scales, within

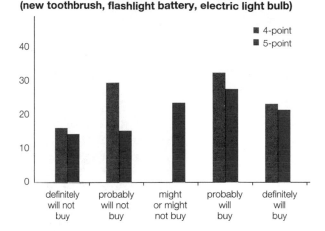

Purchase Intention in the Next 30 Days
(new toothbrush, flashlight battery, electric light bulb)

every category. The exception seems to be that in the absence of a "neutral" point (i.e., for the 4-point sample), the responses tend more negative (to "probably not buy") versus the fence-sitters in the 5-point neutral category. Results are particularly "similar" if one collapses the "top two boxes" as is frequently done to demonstrate overall positive regard, i.e., "probably" or "definitely" will buy.

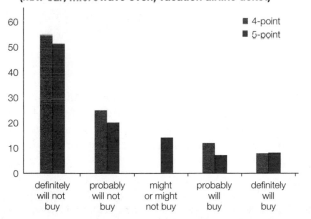

Purchase Intention in the Next 12 Months
(new car, microwave oven, vacation airline ticket)

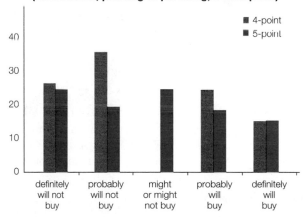

Purchase Intention in the Next 7 Days
(movie ticket, pudding or pie filling, frozen pizza)

Source: MarketFacts.com, "Measuring Purchase Intent," *Research on Research*. Also see Randall Thomas, "Not Sure About 'Don't Know,'" *Quirks Marketing Research Review* (http://www.quirks.com) and Timothy Graeff, "Uninformed Response Bias in Telephone Surveys," *Journal of Business Research* 55 (2002), pp. 261–259. There is some evidence that the extreme ratings (the 1s and 5s) would be most affected (Stephen Nowlis, Barbara Kahn and Ravi Dhar, "Coping with Ambivalence: The Effect of Removing a Neutral Opinion on Consumer Attitude and Preference Judgments," *Journal of Consumer Research* 29 (2002), pp. 319–334. However, in the charts above, the neutral data seem to get divided among the 2s and 4s (leaning toward the 2s), and the 1s and 5s appear relatively stable. Again, if the use of these data is to collapse the top 2 boxes, the results look rather consistent between the 4-point and 5-point versions of the scales.

that the temperature claim is also probably erroneous. More likely than not, the temperature claim would be based on the fact that whereas old Lustre required 200°F water to be effective, new Lustre requires only 140°F water; i.e., carrying the claim that new Lustre can operate effectively with temperatures 30% lower, because:

$$\frac{200 - 140}{200}(100) = 30\%$$

The Fahrenheit scale is an interval scale (because it possesses an arbitrary zero) so the calculation of ratios on such scales is meaningless. To see the folly in this exercise, simply convert the 200°F and 140°F temperatures to their Celsius equivalents of 93.3°C and 60.0°C. Now you can use 36% lower temperatures with new Lustre.

Thus, only one of the three ad claims is probably legitimate—the claim that 50% less detergent is needed with new Lustre. The scale here is of the ratio variety—if one uses, say, ½ cup of new Lustre vs. 1 cup of old Lustre, then indeed one needs 50% less detergent.[3]

An understanding of the level of measurement underlying data is crucial to proper interpretation.[4] Nominal, ordinal, interval or ratio help determine which methods and statistics are meaningful for your data.

Research Design

A second consideration that affects the choice of analytical technique is the research design used to generate the data. The questions involve the dependency of observations, the number of observations per object, the number of groups being analyzed, and the control exercised over the variables of interest.

SAMPLE INDEPENDENCE

Consider first the question of dependent or independent samples. Suppose that you were interested in determining the effectiveness of a recent mailing from a direct marketing campaign. Say the measure of effectiveness was attitude toward a product, measured on an interval scale, and say the research design had been:

$$X \quad O_1$$
$$O_2$$

where O_1 represents the attitudes of those who received the targeted mailing and O_2 the attitudes of those who did not. In this case, the samples are independent. The O_2 measures do not depend on the O_1 measures. An appropriate test of significance would reflect the independence of the samples. In this case, the t-test for the difference in two means would be appropriate.[5]

---

[3] These claims of temperature *could* be supported with data if measures were made on a Kelvin scale, which possesses an absolute zero, and even the brightness claim would follow if measurements were made using an integrating sphere (which measures the amount of light reflected from an object placed in the sphere—black objects do not reflect any of the light directed at them, whereas white objects reflect 100% of the light directed into the sphere). The brightness claim does not follow, though, from the aggregation of consumer perceptions.

[4] Frankly, this comment generalizes to life—for instance, meteorologists love statistics, and they'll often report dubious comparisons like, "this winter was 38% colder than normal." The statement might be based on an average winter temps of 40°F, compared to the most recent winter's 25°F, which appears 38% colder. Using the proper Kelvin scale, it was only 3% colder than normal.

[5] The t-test for the difference in means is discussed in the chapter on testing group differences.

If the research design had been:

$$O_1 \quad X \quad O_2$$

where there are again two sets of observations, O_1 and O_2, but now they're made on the same individuals, before and after receiving the mailing. The pre and post samples are composed of the same individuals, so the measurements are not independent. The focus in the analysis is on the change in attitude per individual before and after exposure to the marketing exposure. The observations must be analyzed in pre/post pairs. A paired difference test for statistical significance should be used in this case.[6]

Ethical Dilemma 15.1

A beer producer conducted a study to determine whether consumers perceive an actual or a psychological difference in the taste of beer. As part of the experiment, each consumer was asked to taste three unmarked cans of beer and to order them according to preference. Although they were led to believe that the three cans of beer were different beers, the participants discovered when the beers were unmasked that the three cans were, in fact, the same beer. A fair proportion of participants had stated that the three beers tasted quite different.

- It is argued that such an experiment may induce stress in some participants inasmuch as it may lead them to doubt their competence as shoppers. Comment on this argument.
- Should the investigator offer some sort of psychic support (such as debriefing) upon completion of the experiment to counteract any possible negative effects?
- Under what conditions might debriefing be problematic?

NUMBER OF GROUPS

Consider next the question of the number of groups being compared. Suppose that you were interested in the relative effectiveness of two different catalogs, so you run a controlled experiment in which some respondents receive one version, X_1, others get the other, X_2, and a third group receives neither. The design can be diagrammed:

$$\begin{array}{cc} X_1 & O_1 \\ X_2 & O_2 \\ & O_3 \end{array}$$

There are three groups (two experimental and one control) whereas the previous design had two groups (one experimental and one control). The appropriate procedure is the analysis of variance.[7]

NUMBER OF VARIABLES

The number of measures per object also affects the choice of analytical procedure. In the direct marketing example, we had used "attitude toward the product" as the measure of effectiveness of the mailing, and we had contrasted the attitudes of the receivers with those of the nonreceivers. Suppose that we believe that the sales impact of the catalog must also be considered. We would now wish to contrast the two groups in terms of their attitude and also in terms of each group's sales. The design is still:

$$\begin{array}{cc} X & O_1 \\ & O_2 \end{array}$$

but now O_1 and O_2 represent measures of both sales and attitudes.

One way to proceed would be to test for the differences in attitude, and then separately test for the differences in sales to the two groups. It's possible, though, for the two groups to differ only slightly on each criterion so that neither of the univariate

---

[6] The paired difference statistical test is also discussed in the chapter on testing group differences.

[7] Analysis of variance is discussed in its own appendix.

tests detects a significant difference. Would we conclude that the mailing had no impact even though the average attitude score and average sales were each slightly higher for the experimental group? Or do we conclude that the small, nonsignificant differences, taken together, indicate a real difference? It's also possible that each variable is significant but the results inconsistent; e.g., attitudes are more favorable in the control group but sales greater in the experimental group. Do we take the favorable and unfavorable results at their face value, or do we take the position that one of them represents a Type I error and in reality is attributable to chance?[8] To answer this question (and it becomes more difficult as the number of measures per object increases), we need to have some means of looking at groups on several characteristics simultaneously. This type of problem is handled using multivariate statistical procedures.[9]

VARIABLE CONTROL

Another important question in analysis involves the control of variables that can affect the result. Return to the design

$$X \quad O_1$$
$$\quad O_2$$

in which the emphasis is on the differences in attitudes between the two groups. One variable that would certainly seem to determine attitudes is previous usage of the product. If so, in the experimental design, the analyst would like to control for prior usage to minimize its effect. A good way of doing this would be to make the experimental and control groups equal with respect to prior usage by matching, randomization, or some combination of these approaches. If this control procedure is followed, the t-test for analyzing the difference in two means can legitimately be employed. If the control is not affected but attitudes do depend on prior use of the product, the conclusions produced using the t-test will be in error to the extent that the two groups differ in their previous use of the product. One way to adjust for these differences is by allowing prior use to be a covariate—that is, by regressing attitudes on use and adjusting the attitude scores represented by O_1 and O_2 by the resulting regression equation. The adjusted scores for the experimental and control groups would then be compared.

Assumptions Underlying Test Statistic

A final consideration in the choice of a statistical method is the set of assumptions supporting the various test statistics. As an example, let's look at the assumptions for the first test we saw, the t-test for the difference in two means.

Assume that the samples have been drawn independently of each other. Further, assume that the individuals composing the experimental group come from a population with unknown mean μ_1 and unknown variance σ_1^2, that those in the control group come from a population with unknown mean μ_2 and unknown variance σ_2^2, and that attitudes toward the product are normally distributed in each of these populations. Assume also that the variances of the two populations are equal—that is,

---

[8] Type I error is discussed in the "quick stats review" appendix.

[9] See the multivariate chapter for discriminant analysis, factor and cluster analysis, and multidimensional scaling.

$\sigma_1^2 = \sigma_2^2$; thus, a pooled estimator for the overall variance is used.[10] In sum, the assumptions are:

1. Independent samples
2. Normal distribution of the characteristic of interest in each population
3. Equal variances in the two populations

The t-test is more sensitive to certain violations of these assumptions than others. For example, it works fine even when the data aren't normal, but it's sensitive to violations of the equal-variance assumption. When the violation is "too severe," the conclusions drawn are inappropriate, yet it is surprising how little attention is paid to these conditions in published research. Little mention is also made of the tests used to verify that the assumptions were satisfied (e.g., the independence of samples assumption can be checked by analyzing the sampling plan, the normality assumption can be investigated through a χ^2 goodness-of-fit test or Kolmogorov-Smirnov test, and the equality of the variances can be examined through an F-test for homogeneity of variances).[11]

Our point is to illustrate the fact that statistical tests depend on certain assumptions for their validity. If the assumptions are not met, sometimes they can be satisfied through a transformation on the data (e.g., change to log units). Sometimes a different test statistic should be chosen that relies on different assumptions, e.g., a distribution-free test.[12]

Ethical Dilemma 15.2

A member of your research staff has submitted the results of an experiment to you, and you note with pleasure that all the hypotheses are fulfilled at p ≤ .05. The fact that they are all fulfilled at exactly p ≤ .05 eventually arouses your suspicions, however. When challenged, your staff member happily explains: "Oh, yes, I rounded down some .06s and .07s. Do you remember how you explained to me that measurement is by convention? And how p ≤ .05 is an arbitrary number selected to be significant by general agreement, although it is not very logical to have p ≤ .05 be significant but p ≤ .06 be insignificant? Well, I agree that it's not logical, so I decided that p-levels close to .05 could be rounded to .05 without any harm being done."

- Is your researcher's position reasonable?
- If you do not agree with a standard, does that mean that you can cheat to meet it?

Overview of Statistical Procedures

This section provides an overview of the statistical techniques discussed in later chapters. This overview will help direct you to the sections that discuss the techniques appropriate for a given problem. Figure 15.1 illustrates the questions to be asked to determine the appropriate statistical technique. The questions are one of two varieties: first, how many variables are there (how many total variables, how many of those are classified as dependent variables to be predicted, etc.); second, what is the level of measurement (remember: nominal, ordinal, interval, ratio) of the variable(s)?

---

[10] The assumption of equality of variances is not mandatory, but when it does not hold, the "proper procedure" is shrouded in controversy. There is a vast statistical literature on this condition, known as the Behrens-Fisher problem.

[11] The chi-square goodness-of-fit test and the Kolmogorov-Smirnov test are discussed in the chapter on cross-tabs. Most intro stats books discuss the F-test for the equality of variances.

[12] These "nonparametric tests" involve minimal assumptions. The parametric tests include tests like the t, z, or F and involve a greater number of and more rigorous assumptions. With nonparametric or distribution-free tests, the researcher is still trying to generate statements about population "parameters," but perhaps the median rather than the mean as a measure of central tendency. See James Higgins, *Introduction to Modern Nonparametric Statistics* (Duxbury Press, 2003); M. Desu and D. Raghavarao, *Nonparametric Statistical Methods* (CRC Press, 2003); David Sheskin, *Handbook of Parametric and Nonparametric Statistical Procedures*, 2nd ed. (CRC Press, 2000).

FIGURE 15.1
Chart for Choosing
among Statistical Tests

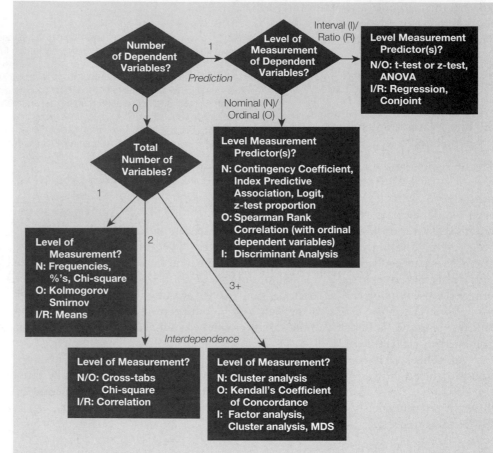

The first decision question in Figure 15.1 asks whether you're trying to predict a dependent variable or not. If yes, then if the dependent variable is continuous (interval or ratio-level scaled), you can compute a t-test, z-test, analysis of variance or regression, depending on the level of measurement of the predictor variables. If the dependent variable is categorical (nominal or ordinal), you could compute contingency coefficients, indices of predictive association, logits, or simple z-tests for proportions, if the predictor variable is nominal. When the predictor and dependent variables are both ordinal, the Spearman rank correlation coefficient is perfect. When the dependent variable is nominal, specifically group membership, and the predictors are continuous, discriminant analysis is appropriate.

If you're not trying to predict a particular variable, then the question becomes, "How many variables do you have?" If you're focusing on just one variable at a time, you can compute frequencies and percentages, chi-squares, the Kolmogorov-Smirnov test, or just straightforward means, all depending on the level of measurement of the variable. The statistics listed thus far are considered **univariate**, because you're predicting one dependent variable, or analyzing one variable.[13]

If you have two or more variables, and none of them carries the special status of a dependent variable, you're not in the realm of "prediction," but in the realm of

---

[13] Your data set probably has many observations per respondent, but the focus is on predicting or analyzing one variable at a time.

what's called the analysis of "interdependence," meaning simply, you're trying to figure out how two or more variables are somehow interrelated. If you have two variables, you can run cross-tabs and chi-squares if the variables are categorical, or correlations if the variables are continuous. If you have more than two variables, you're conducting a **multivariate** analysis. There are many useful multivariate techniques for the marketing research, most of which are discussed in later chapters.

Summary

We've discussed the basic considerations involved in choosing a statistical method to analyze the collected data. Scale of measurement, the research design, and the assumptions underlying the test statistic all affect this choice.

In terms of measurement theory, the origin of the numbers is important for the interpretation of the results. It makes a difference whether the level of measurement is nominal, ordinal, interval, or ratio.

Several questions in the research design affect choice of method, including the independence or dependence of the sample observations, the number of groups, the number of variables, and the control exercised over those variables likely to affect the results. The role of each variable in the analysis and the level of measurement reflected by each variable interact to produce a complex classification scheme of statistical analytical techniques.

Review Questions

1. What basic considerations underlie the choice of a statistical test? Explain.

2. What are the basic levels of measurement? How does the type of data affect the choice of a statistical test?

3. Discuss the difference between independent and dependent samples, and indicate how sample independence/dependence affects the choice of a statistical test.

4. Discuss the difference between 1, 2, and 3 group analyses, and indicate how the number of groups affects the choice of a statistical test.

5. Discuss the difference between a univariate analysis and a multivariate analysis.

6. Discuss the difference between dependence and interdependence analysis.

Applications and Problems

1. Evaluate the two following hypothetical advertising claims. Do you think the claims are legitimate?

   a. "Con-Air gives you twice as much satisfaction while traveling—at a price 50% lower than other major airlines."

   b. "In blind taste tests, the majority of people preferred our beer twice as much as any other major brand of beer. Is it any wonder we sell 1.5 times more beer than our nearest competitor?"

2. Discuss whether the use of adjective rating scales reflects ordinal or interval measurement.

3. The Tobacco Institute wanted to test the effectiveness of two booklets that discuss the issue of whether advertising causes children to start smoking. A random sample of 1,200 was selected from a mailing list of 10,000 people. The sample was randomly divided into three groups of size 400 each; one group received one version of the booklet, the second received the other

version, and the third group received neither booklet. One week later the attitudes of all three groups about whether advertising causes children to smoke were measured on an interval scale.

   a. Present the experimental design in diagrammatic form.

   b. What analysis technique would you recommend? Why?

4. A large national chain of department stores wanted to test the effectiveness of a promotional display for a new brand of household appliances. Fifty stores were randomly selected from a total of 263 stores. The sample of 50 stores was randomly divided into two groups of 25 stores each. Only one group used the promotional display. For three weeks, sales of the new brand of appliances were monitored for both groups.

   a. Present the experimental design in diagrammatic form.

   b. What analysis technique would you recommend? Why?

5. A medium-sized life insurance company was concerned about its poor public image resulting from a major lawsuit. The public relations department designed a 20-page bulletin that was to be mailed to all existing and prospective clients and shareholders in order to allay any negative feelings that might have resulted from the bad publicity. Prior to incurring the expenses of the complete mailing, the department randomly selected 300 clients and shareholders and mailed the 20-page bulletin to them. Attitudes toward the company were measured on an interval scale before and after sending the bulletin. However, top management was dissatisfied with this experiment and requested that another random sample of 500 clients and shareholders be generated. This sample was to be randomly divided into two groups of 250 respondents each. The bulletin was to be mailed to one group of respondents. Attitudes toward the company were to be measured for both groups on an interval scale two weeks after mailing the bulletin.

   a. Present the experimental designs in diagrammatic form.

   b. What analysis technique would you recommend for each? Why?

6. A large national automobile manufacturer wanted to relate sales of its latest models by area to the demographic composition of each area as measured by such variables as average income, average size of household, average age of head of household, and so on.

   a. Is this dependence or interdependence analysis? Why?

   b. Are there any criterion or predictor variables? If so, what are they? Identify the level of measurement of each.

   c. On the basis of the preceding information, what multivariate procedure would you recommend?

7. A medium-sized department store wanted to determine its customers' attitudes, opinions, interests, and so on using a five-point Likert scale.

   a. Is this dependence or interdependence analysis? Why?

   b. Are there any criterion or predictor variables? If so, what are they? Identify the level of measurement of each.

   c. On the basis of the preceding information, what multivariate procedure would you recommend?

8. A large soft-drink manufacturer conducted a survey to determine customers' likes and dislikes about a new diet soft drink. The "lightness" of the soft drink was perceived as being one of the three most important soft-drink attributes. The "low calorie" attribute was not ranked as high as "lightness." The company was wondering if most consumers believed that low calorie content of the soft drink was associated with lightness.

   a. Is this dependence or interdependence analysis? Why?

   b. Are there any criterion or predictor variables? If so, what are they? Identify the level of measurement of each.

   c. On the basis of the preceding information, what multivariate procedure would you recommend?

9. Discuss the advantages of Design a over Design b. Does Design a also have advantages over Design c? Explain.

   a. O_1 X_1 O_2
       O_3 O_4

   b. O_1 X_1 O_2

   c. X_1 O_1
          O_2

10. A survey asked users of a new deodorant product how satisfied they were with the product's performance using the following scale:

VERY SATISFIED	SATISFIED	NEITHER SATISFIED NOR DISSATISFIED	DISSATISFIED	VERY DISSATISFIED
1	2	3	4	5

A research analyst noticed an interesting difference between male and female respondents. The mean satisfaction score for this product was 30% higher for women than men. Given the scale, is this a valid calculation? What are valid calculations? Can any comparison between men and women be made with these data?

11. A political opinion poll was conducted concerning the performance of two presidential candidates. Two hundred respondents were asked to rate Candidates A and B on a seven-point scale. In summarizing the results, a pooled sample t-test was used to show that significant differences existed in the mean scores at $p \leq .05$ for Candidates A and B. Discuss whether the t-test is an appropriate test to use in this circumstance. Have any of the underlying assumptions of the test been violated in this example?

12. On a product-tracking survey, the following three categories were used to capture consumers' knowledge and trial of different products: "Never heard of the product," "Heard of the product but have never bought the product," and "Have bought the product." These categories were coded 1, 3, 6. The research team leader changed the codes to 1, 2, 3 so that the scores reflected equal intervals. Explain why the team leader's correction is unnecessary and unwarranted.

13. With the introduction of grocery-store scanners, elaborate marketing experiments can be run in the field. For example, a company wanting to test the effects of a new advertising campaign on its breakfast cereal sales designed the following test to determine which campaign was the most effective. Six cities were chosen for this experiment. In three cities, viewers saw the new advertisement, and in the other three cities, viewers continued to see the traditional advertising campaign.

    a. Present the experimental design in diagrammatic form.

    b. What analysis technique would you recommend? What assumptions underlie the recommended test?

    c. Given the company's research objective, discuss alternative designs.

Appendix: Quick Stats Review

Questions to Guide Your Learning:

Q1: How do I frame a null hypothesis?

Q2: What is a "significance level?

Q3: How is it related to a Type I error?

Q4: What is a Type II error? How is it related to power?

Q5: What is a one-tailed vs. a two-tailed significance test?

Many procedures discussed in the next few chapters test hypotheses, so we review some basic statistical concepts that underlie hypothesis testing in classical statistical theory. The best quantitative marketing research rests on these fundamental concepts.[1]

Lest you think hypotheses are just for geeks, look at how specifically these hypotheses were worded in a popular business press magazine:[2]

- "The most popular flight times will be 100% sold out, with more than 90% of the customers coming from the target segment."

- "Market share within the segment will exceed 80%."

- "Churn among targeted customers will decline from 11% to 3%."

- "Corporate discounts will decline from an average of $3500 to $0."

- "At least 85% of the senior executive segment will use the preflight meal service."

---

[1] Thomas Semon, "You Get What You Pay For," *Marketing News* (April 15, 2002), p. 7; William Neal, "Shortcomings Plague the Industry," *Marketing News* (Sept. 16, 2002), pp. 37–39.

[2] Larry Selden and Geoffrey Colvin, "What Customers Want," *Fortune* (July 7, 2003), pp. 122–127.

These are all extremely testable hypotheses, and upon learning of the results, immediately implementable.

Null Hypothesis

A simple fact underlies the statistical test of a hypothesis: A hypothesis may be rejected but can never be accepted except tentatively, because further evidence may prove it wrong. In other words, one rejects the hypothesis or does not reject the hypothesis on the basis of the evidence at hand. It is wrong to conclude, though, that since the hypothesis was not rejected, it can necessarily be accepted as valid.

A simple example should illustrate the issue.[3] Let's say we're testing the "hypothesis" that "John Doe is a poor man." We observe that Doe dines in cheap restaurants, lives in a poor area in a run-down building, wears worn and tattered clothes, and so on. His behavior is consistent with that of a poor man, but we cannot "accept" the hypothesis that he is poor. It is possible that Doe may, in fact, be rich but extremely tight in his spending. We can continue gathering information about him, but for the moment we must decide not to reject the hypothesis. One single observation, for example if we were to learn that he has a six-figure bank account or that he owns 100,000 shares of some blue chip stock, would allow the immediate rejection of the hypothesis, and support instead for the conclusion, "John Doe is rich."

Thus, in the absence of perfect information, which is the case when sampling, the best we can do is form hypotheses or conjectures about what is true. Further, our conclusions can be wrong, and thus there is always some probability of error in tentatively accepting any hypothesis. Statistical parlance holds that researchers commit a "Type I error" when they reject a true null hypothesis (and thereby find favor for the alternative); they commit a "Type II error" when they do not reject a false null hypothesis, which they should have, given that it is false. The null hypothesis is assumed to be true for the purpose of the statistical test. The assumption that the null is true is used to generate knowledge about the sampling distributions of estimates like means would look given the current sampling plan. It's also important to know that Type I errors can be specified to not exceed some specific amount (usually, $\leq .05$), but Type II errors are harder to control.[4]

The upshot is that we need to frame the null hypothesis in such a way that its rejection leads to the acceptance of the desired conclusion, the statement or condition that we wish to verify. For example, suppose that a firm was considering introducing a new product if it could achieve more than 10% of the market. The proper way to frame the hypotheses would be:

$$H_0 : \pi \leq .10$$
$$H_A : \pi > .10$$

If the evidence leads to the rejection of H_0, the researcher would then be able to "accept" the alternative (that the product could be expected to attract more than 10% of the market) and the product would be introduced, because statistically, such a result would have been unlikely to occur if the null were indeed true. If H_0 cannot

> **Null hypothesis: no effect, no difference between groups; hope to reject null**

---

[3] We thank Dr. B. Venkatesh of The Burke Institute for suggesting this illustration of hypotheses.

[4] We will have more to say about Type I and Type II errors shortly.

be rejected, though, the product should not be introduced unless more evidence to the contrary becomes available. This particular example involves the use of a "one-tailed" statistical test; the alternate hypothesis is expressed directionally. There are plenty of research problems that warrant a "two-tailed" test. For example, the null might be that market share achieved by a line extension of Product X is no different from that achieved by the old formula, which was 10%. A two-tailed test would be expressed as:

$$H_0 : \pi = .10$$
$$H_A : \pi \neq .10.$$

No direction (greater than or less than) is implied with the alternate hypothesis; the proportion is simply expressed as *not being equal* to .10.

The one-tailed test is preferred in marketing research when one outcome is preferred to another, e.g., greater market share, higher product quality, lower expenses, etc. In addition, when it is appropriate, the one-tailed test is more powerful statistically than the two-tailed alternative.

Types of Errors

The result of a statistical test on a null hypothesis is to reject it or not reject it. Two types of errors may occur. First, we might reject the null hypothesis when it is true. Second, we might not reject the null when we should have, i.e., it is false. These errors are termed *Type I error* and *Type II error* (or α error and β error, which are the probabilities associated with their occurrence).[5]

To illustrate each type of error, consider a legal analogy. Under U.S. criminal law, a person is innocent until proven guilty. Therefore, the judge and jury are always testing the hypothesis of innocence. The defendant may, in fact, be either innocent or guilty, but based on the evidence, the court may reach either verdict regardless of the true situation. Table 15A.1 displays the possibilities. If the defendant is innocent and the jury finds the person innocent, or if the defendant is guilty and the jury finds him or her guilty, the jury has made a correct decision. If, however, the defendant truly is innocent and the jury finds the person guilty, or if the defendant is guilty and the jury finds him or her not guilty, they have made an error. The jury must decide one way or the other, and thus the probabilities of the jury's decision must sum vertically to 1. If we let α represent the probability of incorrectly finding the person guilty when he or she is innocent, then $1 - \alpha$ must be the probability of correctly finding him or her not guilty. Similarly, β and $1 - \beta$ represent the probabilities of findings of innocence and guilt when the person is guilty. It should be clear that $\alpha + \beta$ is not equal to 1, although we'll see later that β must increase when α is reduced if other things remain the same. Because our society generally holds that finding an innocent person guilty is more serious than finding a guilty person not guilty, α error is reduced as much as possible in our legal system by requiring proof of guilt "beyond a reasonable doubt."[6]

Table 15A.2 contains the analogous research situation. Just as the defendant's true status is unknown to the jury, the true situation regarding the null hypothesis is unknown to the researcher. The researcher's dilemma parallels that of the jury in that

Type I error:
wrongly reject
the null

Type II error:
wrongly do not
reject the null

---

[5] The two types of errors are not simply complementary, in that $\alpha + \beta \neq 1$.

[6] Most professions have some form of these concerns, cf. medical diagnostic errors of "false positives" and "false negatives."

TABLE 15A.1
Legal Analogy Illustrating
Decision Error

	True Situation: Defendant Is	
Verdict	Innocent	Guilty
Not Guilty	Correct decision: probability = $1 - \alpha$	Error: probability = β
Guilty	Error: probability = α	Correct decision: probability = $1 - \beta$

he or she has limited information with which to work. Suppose that the null hypothesis is true. If the researcher concludes it is false, he or she has made a Type I error. The significance level associated with a statistical test indicates the probability with which this error may be made. Because sample information will always be somewhat incomplete, there will always be some α error. The only way it can be avoided is by never rejecting the null hypothesis (never finding anyone guilty, in the judicial analogy). The confidence level of a statistical test is $1 - \alpha$, and the more confident we want to be of a statistical result, the lower we must set α error. The power associated with a statistical test is the probability of correctly rejecting a false null hypothesis. One-tailed tests are more powerful than two-tailed tests because, for the same α error, they are simply more likely to lead to a rejection of a false null hypothesis. β error represents the probability of not rejecting a false null hypothesis. There is no unique value associated with β error.

Procedure

Research Realities 15A.1 overviews the typical sequence of steps that is followed in hypothesis testing. Say we're investigating the potential for a new product and the research involves the preferences of consumers. Perhaps, in the judgment of management, the product should not be introduced unless at least 20% of the population could be expected to prefer it. Six hundred twenty-five consumers were interviewed for their preferences.

Step 1. The null and alternate hypotheses would be:

$$H_0 : \pi \leq .20$$
$$H_A : \pi > .20$$

The hypotheses are framed so that if the null hypothesis is rejected, the product should be introduced.

Step 2. The appropriate sample statistic is the sample proportion, and the distribution of all possible sample proportions under the sampling plan is based on the assumption that the null hypothesis is true. The distribution of sample proportions is

TABLE 15A.2
Types of Errors in
Hypothesis Testing

	True Situation: Null Hypothesis Is:	
Research Conclusions	True	False
Do Not Reject H_0	Correct decision: Confidence level probability = $1 - \alpha$	Error: Type II, probability = β
Reject H_0	Error: Type I, Significance level probability = α	Correct decision: Power of test probability = $1 - \beta$

Research Realities

15A.1 Typical Hypothesis Testing Procedure

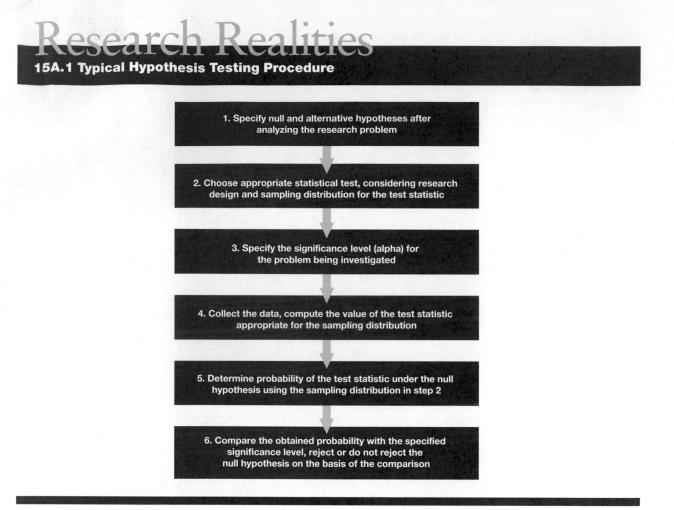

1. Specify null and alternative hypotheses after analyzing the research problem

2. Choose appropriate statistical test, considering research design and sampling distribution for the test statistic

3. Specify the significance level (alpha) for the problem being investigated

4. Collect the data, compute the value of the test statistic appropriate for the sampling distribution

5. Determine probability of the test statistic under the null hypothesis using the sampling distribution in step 2

6. Compare the obtained probability with the specified significance level, reject or do not reject the null hypothesis on the basis of the comparison

theoretically binomially distributed, but the large sample size permits the use of the normal approximation.[7] The z-test equals:

$$z = \frac{p - \pi}{\sigma_p}$$

where p is the sample proportion preferring the product and σ_p is the standard error of the proportion, or the standard deviation of the distribution of sample ps. In turn, σ_p equals

$$\sqrt{\frac{\pi 1 - \pi}{n}} = \sqrt{\frac{.20(.80)}{625}} = .016$$

---

[7] The binomial tends toward the normal distribution for a fixed π as sample size increases. The effect is fastest when $\pi = .5$. As π departs from .5 in either direction, the normal approximation becomes less adequate, although it is generally held that the normal approximation may be used safely if the smaller of $n\pi$ or $n(1-\pi)$ is 10 or more. If this condition is not satisfied, binomial probabilities can be calculated directly or found in tables. In the example, $n\pi = 625(.2) = 125$, and $n(1-\pi) = 500$, thus the normal approximation to binomial probabilities is adequate.

where n is the sample size. Note this peculiarity of proportions. As soon as we have hypothesized a population value, we have said something about the standard error of the estimate. The proportion is the most clear-cut case of "known variance," since the variance is specified automatically with an assumed π

Step 3. The researcher selects a significance level α. The α error is the probability of rejecting H_0—that is, concluding that $\pi > 0.2$, when in reality $\pi \leq .2$. This conclusion will lead the company to market the new product. However, because the venture will only be profitable if $\pi > .2$, a wrong decision to market would be financially unprofitable and possibly disastrous. The probability of Type I error should, therefore, be minimized as much as possible. The researcher recognizes, though, that the probability of a Type II error increases as α is decreased, other things being equal. Type II error implies concluding that $\pi \leq .2$ when in fact $\pi > .2$, which in turn suggests that the company would table the decision to introduce the product when it could be profitable. The opportunity loss from making such an error could also be quite serious. Although, as explained later, the researcher does not know what β would be, he or she knows that α and β are interrelated and that an extremely low value of a (say, $\alpha = .01$ or $.001$) might produce intolerable β errors. Therefore, the researcher decides on an α level of .05 as an acceptable compromise.[8]

Step 4. This step involves the computation of the test statistic, so it can be completed only after the sample is drawn and data collected. Suppose 140 of the 625 sample respondents preferred the product. The sample proportion is thus p = 140/625 = .224. The basic question is simple: "Is this value of p too large to have occurred by chance from a population with π assumed to be equal to .2?" or, in other words, "What is the probability of getting p = .224 when $\pi = .2$?"

$$z = \frac{p - \pi}{\sigma_p} = \frac{.224 - .20}{.0160} = 1.500$$

Step 5. The probability of occurrence of a z-value of 1.500 can be found from standard tabled values of areas under the normal curve. (See the appendix at the end of the book.) Figure 15A.1 shows the procedure. The shaded area between $-\infty$ and 1.500 equals .9332—this means that the area to the right of z = 1.500 is 1.000 .9332, or .0668. This is the probability of getting a z-value of 1.500 under a true situation of $\pi = .2$.

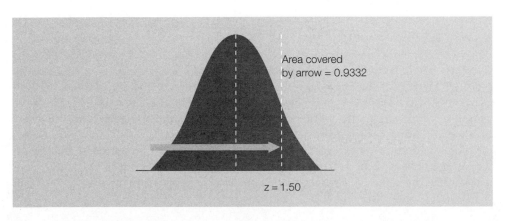

FIGURE 15A.1
Probability of z = 1.50 with a One-Tailed Test

Area covered by arrow = 0.9332

z = 1.50

---

[8] We'll say more about α and its interpretation after we have introduced the notion of power.

Step 6. Since the calculated probability of occurrence is higher than the specified significance level of $\alpha = .05$, the null hypothesis is not rejected. The product would not be introduced because, although the evidence is in the right direction, it is not sufficient to conclude beyond "any reasonable doubt" that $\pi > .2$. If the decision maker had been able to tolerate a 10% chance of committing a Type I error, the null hypothesis would have been rejected and the product marketed, since the probability of getting a sample p = .224 when the true $\pi = .2$ is, as we have seen, .0668.

Power

This example illustrates the importance of correctly specifying the risk of error. If a 10% chance of an α error were tolerable and the researcher specified $\alpha = .05$, a potentially profitable opportunity would have been lost. The choice of the proper significance level involves weighing the costs associated with the two types of error.

The β error is not a constant. It is the probability of not rejecting a false null hypothesis, so this probability depends on the size of the difference between the true, but unknown, population value and the value assumed to be true under the null hypothesis. Other things being equal, we prefer a test that minimizes such errors. And yet, since the power of a test equals $1 - \beta$, we prefer the test with the greatest power so that we have the best chance of rejecting a false null hypothesis.[9] Our ability to do this depends on how false H_0 truly is. It could be just a little bit false or way off the mark, and the probability of an incorrect conclusion would certainly be higher in the first case. The difference between the assumed value under the null hypothesis and the true, but unknown, value is known as the *effect size*. As intuition suggests, large effects are easier to distinguish than small effects.

Consider again the hypotheses

$H_0 : \pi \le .20$
$H_A : \pi > .20$

where $\sigma_p = .016$ and $\alpha = .05$, as before. Any calculated z value greater than 1.645 causes us to reject this hypothesis, since this is the z-value that cuts off 5% of the normal curve. The z-value can be equated to the critical sample proportion through the formula:

$$z = \frac{p - \pi}{\sigma_p} = \frac{p - .20}{0.160} = 1.645$$

or p = .2263. Thus, any sample proportion greater than p = .2263 will lead to the rejection of the null hypothesis that $\pi \le 0.2$. This means that if 142 or more [.2263(625) = 141.4] of the sample respondents prefer the new product, the null hypothesis will be rejected and the product introduced, whereas if 141 or less of the sample respondents prefer it, the null hypothesis will not be rejected and the new product will not be introduced.

The likelihood of a sample proportion of p = .2263 is much greater for certain values of π than for others. Suppose, for instance, that the true but unknown value of π was .22. The sampling distribution of the sample proportions is still normal, but

---

[9] Kevin Murphy and Brett Myors, *Statistical Power Analysis* (Erlbaum, 2003).

now it is centered around .22. The probability of obtaining the critical sample proportion p = .2263 under this condition is found from the normal curve table, where[10]

$$z = \frac{p - \pi}{\sigma_p} = \frac{.2263 - .22}{0.166} = .380$$

The shaded area between $-\infty$ and z = .380 is given in the appendix as .6480, and thus the area to the right of z = .380 is equal to $1 - .6480 = .3520$ (see Panel B in Figure 15A.2).

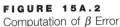

FIGURE 15A.2
Computation of β Error and Power for Several Assumed True Population Proportions for the Hypothesis, $\pi \leq .20$

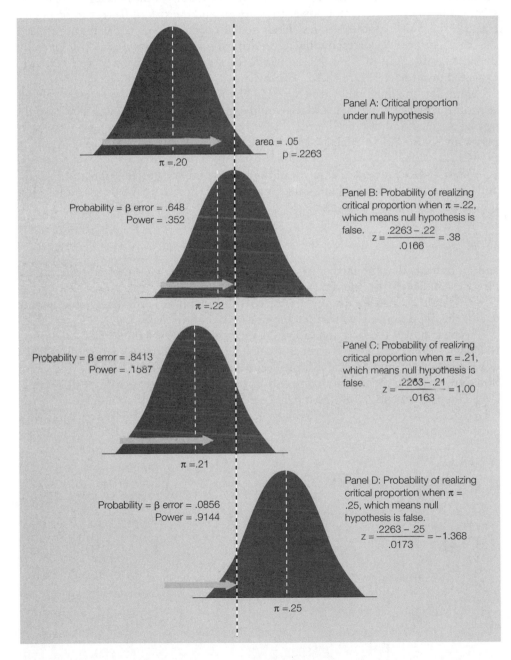

Panel A: Critical proportion under null hypothesis

area = .05
p = .2263

π = .20

Probability = β error = .648
Power = .352

Panel B: Probability of realizing critical proportion when π = .22, which means null hypothesis is false. $z = \dfrac{.2263 - .22}{.0166} = .38$

π = .22

Probability = β error = .8413
Power = .1587

Panel C: Probability of realizing critical proportion when π = .21, which means null hypothesis is false. $z = \dfrac{.2263 - .21}{.0163} = 1.00$

π = .21

Probability = β error = .0856
Power = .9144

Panel D: Probability of realizing critical proportion when π = .25, which means null hypothesis is false. $z = \dfrac{.2263 - .25}{.0173} = -1.368$

π = .25

---

[10] Note that σ_p is now $\sqrt{.22(.78)/625} = .0166$, because a different specification of p implies a different standard error of estimate.

This is the probability that a value as large or larger than p = .2263 would be obtained if the true population proportion were π = .22. It is also the power of the test in that, if π is truly equal to .22, the null hypothesis is false and .3520 is the probability that the null will be rejected. Conversely, the probability that p < .2263 equals 1 – .3520 = .6480, which is β error. The null hypothesis is false and yet the false null hypothesis is not rejected for any sample proportions p < .2263.

Suppose that the true population condition was π = .21 instead of π = .22, and the null hypothesis was again $H_0: \pi \leq .20$. Since the null hypothesis is less false in this second case, we would expect power to be lower and the risk of β error to be higher because the null hypothesis is less likely to be rejected. Let's see if that is indeed the case. The z-value corresponding to the critical p = .2263 is 1.000. Power given by the area to the right of z = 1.000 is .1587 (the β error is .8413), and so we get the expected result. (See Figure 15A.2, Panel C.)

Consider one final value, true π = .25. The null hypothesis of π = .20 would be way off the mark in this case, and we would expect only a small chance that it would not be rejected and a Type II error would be committed. The calculations are displayed in Figure 15A.2, Panel D; z = –1.368, and the area to the right of z = –1.368 is .9144. The probability of β error is .0856, and the *a priori* expectation is confirmed.

Table 15A.3 contains the power of the test for other selected population states, and Figure 15A.3 shows these values graphically. Figure 15A.3 is essentially the power curve for the hypothesis:

$$H_0 : \pi \leq .20$$
$$H_0 : \pi > .20$$

and it confirms that the farther away the true π from the hypothesized value in the direction indicated by the alternate hypothesis, the higher the power. Note that power is not defined for the hypothesized value because if the true value in fact equals the hypothesized value, a β error cannot be committed.

Because power is a function rather than a single value, the researcher attempting to balance Type I and Type II errors logically needs to ask how false the null hypothesis is likely to be and to establish the decision rule accordingly. The way to control both errors within predetermined bounds for a given size effect is to vary the sample size. The need to specify all three items—α error (or degree of confidence), β error (or power), and the size of the effect it is necessary to detect—possibly explains why

α = **Type I error**

β = **Type II error**

1 – β = power

TABLE 15A.3
β Error and Power for Different Assumed True Values of π and the Hypotheses $H_0 : \pi \leq 0.20$ and $H_A : \pi > .20$

Value of π	Probability of Type II or β Error	Power of the Test: 1 – β
.20	(.950) = 1 – α	(.05) = α
.21	.8413	.1587
.22	.6480	.3520
.23	.4133	.5867
.24	.2133	.7867
.25	.0856	.9144
.26	.0273	.9727
.27	.0069	.9931
.28	.0014	.9986
.29	.0005	.9995
.30	.0000	1.0000

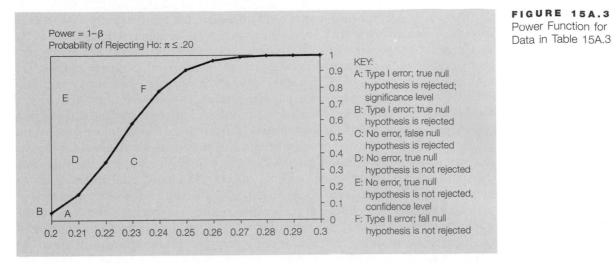

Power = 1−β
Probability of Rejecting Ho: π ≤ .20

FIGURE 15A.3
Power Function for
Data in Table 15A.3

KEY:
A: Type I error; true null
   hypothesis is rejected;
   significance level
B: Type I error; true null
   hypothesis is rejected
C: No error, false null
   hypothesis is rejected
D: No error, true null
   hypothesis is not rejected
E: No error, true null
   hypothesis is not rejected,
   confidence level
F: Type II error; fall null
   hypothesis is not rejected

so many researchers content themselves with the specification of Type I or α error and allow β error to fall where it may. The failure to even worry about, much less explicitly take into account, the power of the statistical test represents one of the fundamental problems with the classical statistics hypothesis-testing approach as it is commonly practiced in marketing research. Moreover, Type II errors are often more costly than Type I errors.

Another common problem is the misinterpretation of what a "statistically significant result" really means.[11] One of the most frequent misinterpretations is to view a p-value as representing the probability that the results occurred because of sampling error. Thus, p = .05 is taken to mean that there is a probability of only .05 that the results were caused by chance and thus there must be something fundamental causing them. In actuality, a p-value of .05 means that *if* (and this is a big if) the null hypothesis is indeed true as assumed, the odds are only 1 in 20 of getting a sample result as big or bigger than that which was observed. Unfortunately, there is no way in classical statistical significance testing to determine whether the null hypothesis is true. The p-value tells you the probability that you'd get the data you got, if the null hypothesis were true.

Another common misinterpretation is to equate statistical significance with practical significance. A difference can be of practical importance and not statistically significant if the power of the test is weak. Conversely, a result may be of no practical importance, even if highly significant, if the sample size is very large.

A third misinterpretation is to hold that the α or p-level chosen is in some way related to the probability that the research hypothesis captured in the alternative hypothesis is true. Typically, this probability is taken as the complement of the α level. Thus, a p-value of .05 is interpreted to mean that its complement, $1 - .05 = .95$, is the probability that the research hypothesis (the alternative) is true. Sometimes researchers say p < .0001 is "more significant" than p < .05, but this interpretation is incorrect. Significance is binary—a result is or is not significant.

---

[11] For excellent discussions of some common misinterpretations of significance tests and recommendations on how to surmount the problems, see Alan G. Sawyer and J. Paul Peter, "The Significance of Statistical Significance Tests in Marketing Research," *Journal of Marketing Research* 20 (1983), pp. 122–133; Jacob Cohen, "The Earth Is Round (p < .05)," *American Psychologist* 49 (1994), pp. 997–1003.

The only logical conclusion that can be drawn when a null hypothesis is rejected at some predetermined p-level is that sampling error is an unlikely explanation of the results *given* that the null hypothesis is true. In many ways that is not saying very much, because, as was argued previously, the null hypothesis is set up to be false. The null, as typically stated, holds that there is no relationship between two certain variables, say, or that the groups are equal with respect to some particular variable. Yet, we do not really believe that. Rather, we investigate the relationship between variables because we believe there is some association between them, and we contrast the groups because we believe they are different with respect to the variable. Further, we can control our ability to reject the null hypothesis simply by the power we build into the statistical test, primarily through the size of the sample used to test it. If we ramped up our sample sizes to be big "enough," we would always reject the null.

Accordingly, be careful when interpreting results of hypothesis tests to not mislead yourself or others. Keep in mind both types of possible errors. Confidence intervals help avoid misinterpretations because they give more information about the results. A test of significance is just a yes-no situation: either the sample result is statistically significant or it is not. In contrast, the confidence interval gives the yes-no answer, but also, by its width, a sense of the size of the effect in the data.

Summary

Many marketing research questions involve testing hypotheses. We took a look at the nature of the null hypothesis and its alternative. Type I and Type II errors were defined. The p-value and its proper interpretation were discussed. The power, or likelihood of finding significant results, was also presented.

Review Questions

1. Comment on the statement: "A hypothesis can never be accepted, only rejected." Is the statement true? Why or why not?

2. What is the basic scientific proposition that guides the framing of hypotheses? Illustrate the principle with a research question of your own choosing.

3. When is a two-tailed test preferred to a one-tailed test, and vice versa?

4. What is a Type I error? What is a Type II error? What is the relationship between these two types of error?

5. What is meant by the statistical notion of power?

6. Illustrate the steps involved in the statistical testing of hypotheses with your own example.

7. Explain the comment, "The farther away the true population parameter is from the hypothesized population value in the direction indicated by the alternate hypothesis, the higher the power." Is power not a constant? Why?

8. Using your own example, construct the power function.

9. What does it mean when the null hypothesis is rejected at the $\alpha = .10$ level?

Applications and Problems

1. Assume that the brand manager of a medium-sized manufacturer of consumer products decides to introduce a new brand of breakfast cereal if the company can initially acquire 1.5% of the market. The following hypotheses are to be tested:

   $$H_0 : \pi \le .015$$
   $$H_a : \pi > .015$$

   Explain and discuss the Type I and Type II errors that could occur while testing these hypotheses. What are the implications for the company?

2. Discuss the danger of specifying Type I or α error and allowing β error to fall where it may.

3. Bentley Foods, Inc., a large manufacturer of frozen foods, has developed a new line of frozen pizza. Management has agreed to begin producing and marketing the new line if at least 15% of the population would prefer the pizza over other frozen pizzas currently available. To determine preferences, a sample of 1,000 consumers was obtained; 172 indicated that they would prefer the new product over existing brands.

   a. State the null and alternative hypotheses.

   b. Compute the standard error of the proportion.

   c. Calculate the z statistic. What is the probability of obtaining this value of the z-statistic if the null hypothesis is true?

   d. The research manager for Bentley Foods is comfortable using the .05 significance level. Should the null hypothesis be rejected?

   e. At this significance level, what is the critical sample proportion?

4. A computer company is considering a nationwide introduction of a new type of personal computer. In order to test whether the product would be successful, the company is contemplating a nationwide survey to assess people's intentions to purchase the new model instead of existing models. The research team has framed the hypotheses as follows:

   $$H_0 : \pi_N \le \pi_O$$
   $$H_a : \pi_N \le \pi_O$$

   where N and O refer to the new and old models, respectively. If people do not prefer the new model, introducing it would be extremely costly for the company. Under this scenario, does the research team need to be more concerned about a Type I or Type II error? What should α be set at to minimize the company's risk?

5. A research team tested new batteries to see if they lasted significantly longer than the company's existing battery. Traditionally, all experiments have been run at $\alpha = .05$. After testing 100 old batteries as well as 100 new batteries, the mean life for the new battery was found to be greater than that of the old, at $\alpha = .05$ significance level; however, a new analyst became greatly excited when it was discovered that the difference was significant at $\alpha = .001$. He commented, "This product is much better than we thought; the difference is highly significant!"

   a. Is this a correct interpretation of the test results? Explain.

   b. Is it appropriate for the research team to announce that the difference in mean life is significant at $\alpha - .001$ instead of $\alpha = .05$?

6. Before analyzing a set of scores, a researcher decides to test whether the assumption of a normal distribution is appropriate for the data. When testing to verify assumptions, does the researcher need to be more concerned about Type I or Type II error? What should α be set at under these circumstances?

Are My Groups the Same or Different?

Questions to Guide Your Learning:

Q1: What are the key statistics for testing differences?

Q2: How do I test a hypothesis I have about a mean? Two means?

Q3: Why does it matter whether I know the population variance or not, if I'm looking at means?

Q4: How do I compare proportions?

This chapter presents statistical tests for examining differences. The difference of interest might be between your sample result and the expected population value, or it might be between two or more sample results. We focus on the parametric tests that are applicable when examining differences in means or proportions.[1]

---

[1] Previous chapters have described the χ^2 test, which is used with nominal data to compare the sample result with the expected values, and the Kolmogorov-Smirnov test, which makes analogous comparisons on ordinal data.

Hypotheses about One Mean

Many marketing research studies seek to make some statement about the population mean. The distribution of sample means is normal, with the mean equal to the population mean and the variance, $\sigma_{\bar{x}}^2$, equal to the population variance divided by the sample size ($\sigma_{\bar{x}}^2 = \sigma^2/n$). The appropriate statistic for testing a hypothesis about a mean when the *population variance is known* is:

$$z = \frac{\bar{x} - \mu}{\sigma_{\bar{x}}}$$

where $\bar{x}$ is the sample mean;

μ is the population mean; and

$\sigma_{\bar{x}} = \sigma/\sqrt{n}$ is the standard error of the mean.

The z-statistic is appropriate if the sample comes from a normal population, or if the variable is not normally distributed in the population but the sample is large enough for the Central-Limit Theorem to be operative.

When the *population variance is unknown,* the standard error of the mean, $\sigma_{\bar{x}}$, is estimated by $s_{\bar{x}} = \dfrac{s}{\sqrt{n}}$, where s is the unbiased sample standard deviation:

$$\hat{\sigma} = s = \sqrt{\frac{\sum_{i=1}^{n}\left(X_i - \bar{x}\right)^2}{n-1}}$$

The test statistic is $t = \dfrac{\left(\bar{x} - \mu\right)}{s_{\bar{x}}}$, which is t-distributed with n−1 degrees of freedom if the conditions for the t-test are satisfied. Those conditions are:

1. Is the distribution of the variable in the population normal or asymmetrical?
2. Is the sample size large or small?

If the variable of interest is normally distributed in the population, then the test statistic $\dfrac{\left(\bar{x} - \mu\right)}{s_{\bar{x}}}$ is t-distributed with n−1 degrees of freedom. This is true whether the sample size is large or small. For small samples, we actually use t with n−1 degrees of freedom when making an inference. Although t with n−1 degrees of freedom is also the theoretically correct distribution for large n, the distribution approaches and becomes indistinguishable from the normal distribution for samples of 30 or more observations. The test statistic $\dfrac{\left(\bar{x} - \mu\right)}{s_{\bar{x}}}$ is therefore referred to a z-table when making inferences with large samples. Note, though, that we do this because the theoretically correct t-distribution (since σ is unknown) has become indistinguishable from the normal curve, and the latter is somewhat easier to use.

What if the population is not normally distributed and σ is unknown? If the distribution is symmetrical or displays only moderate skew, there is no problem. The t-test is quite robust for departures from normality. However, if the variable is highly skewed in the population, the appropriate procedure depends on the sample size. If the sample is small, the t-test is inappropriate. The variable must be transformed so that it is normal, or a distribution-free test must be used. If the sample is large, the normal curve could be used for making the inference, provided that the two following assumptions are satisfied:

1. The sample size is large enough so that the sample mean $\bar{x}$ is normally distributed because of the Central-Limit Theorem. The greater the asymmetry, the larger the sample must be to satisfy this assumption.
2. The sample standard deviation, s, is a close estimate of the population standard deviation σ. The greater the variability in the population, the larger the sample must be to justify this assumption.

Research Realities 16.1 summarizes the situation for making inferences about a mean for known and unknown σ and normally distributed and asymmetrical parent population distributions.

To illustrate the application of the t-test, consider a supermarket chain investigating the desirability of adding a new product to the shelves of its stores. Suppose that 100 units must be sold per week in each store for the item to be sufficiently profitable to warrant handling it in lieu of the many other products competing for the limited shelf space. The research department decides to investigate the item's turnover by putting it in a random sample of 10 stores for a limited period of time. The average sales per store per week are as shown in Table 16.1.

The variance of sales per store is unknown and has to be estimated, so the t-test is the correct parametric test if the distribution of sales is normal. The normality assumption seems reasonable in that the little sales evidence that is available does not indicate any real asymmetry, so let's assume that the normality assumption is satisfied.

A one-tailed test is appropriate here, because it is only when the sales per store per week are at least 100 that the product will be introduced on a national scale. The null and alternate hypotheses are:

$$H_0 : \mu \leq 100$$
$$H_A : \mu > 100$$

From the data in Table 16.1,

$$\bar{x} = \frac{\sum_{i=1}^{n} X_i}{n} = 109.4$$

and

$$s = \sqrt{\frac{\sum_{i=1}^{n} (X_i - \bar{x})^2}{n-1}} = 14.40$$

TABLE 16.1
Store Sales of Trial Products per Week

Store i	Sales X_i	Store	Sales X_i
1	86	6	93
2	97	7	132
3	114	8	116
4	108	9	105
5	123	10	120

Research Realities

16.1 Testing Hypotheses about a Single Mean

Population distribution shape?	Sample size?	σ Known	σ Unknown
Distribution of variable in parent population is normal or symmetrical.	Small n	Use: $z = \dfrac{(\bar{x} - \mu)}{\sigma_{\bar{x}}}$	Use: $t = \dfrac{(\bar{x} - \mu)}{s_{\bar{x}}}$ where $s_{\bar{x}} = s/\sqrt{n}$ and $s = \sqrt{\dfrac{\sum\limits_{i=1}^{n}\left(X_i - \bar{x}\right)^2}{n-1}}$ and refer to t-table for $n-1$ degrees of freedom.
	Large n	Use: $z = \dfrac{(\bar{x} - \mu)}{\sigma_{\bar{x}}}$	Since the t-distribution approaches the normal as n increases, use: $z = \dfrac{(\bar{x} - \mu)}{s_{\bar{x}}}$ for $n > 30$.
Distribution of variable in parent population is asymmetrical.	Small n	There is no theory to support the parametric test. Either transform the variate so that it is normally distributed and then use the z-test, or use a distribution-free statistical test.	There is no theory to support the parametric test. Either transform the variate so that it is normally distributed and then use the t-test, or use a distribution-free statistical test.
	Large n	If the sample is large enough so that the Central-Limit Theorem is operative, use $z = \dfrac{(\bar{x} - \mu)}{\sigma_{\bar{x}}}$	If the sample is large enough so that the Central-Limit Theorem is operative and s is a close estimate of σ, use: $z = \dfrac{(\bar{x} - \mu)}{s_{\bar{x}}}$

The standard error of the mean $s_{\bar{x}} = \dfrac{s}{\sqrt{n}} = 4.55$. Calculations yield

$$t = \frac{(\bar{x} - \mu)}{s_{\bar{x}}} = \frac{109.4 - 100}{4.55} = 2.07$$

With a significance level of $\alpha = .05$, critical t with $= n - 1 = 9$ degrees of freedom is 1.833 (see the appendix at the end of the book). We conclude that it is unlikely that the calculated value would have occurred by chance if the sales per store in the population were indeed less than or equal to 100 units per week.

A confidence interval would give us some insight into the sales that might be expected if the product were introduced on a national scale. The formula is $\bar{x} \pm t s_{\bar{x}}$. For a 95% confidence interval and 9 degrees of freedom, t = 1.833 (as we've just seen). The 95% confidence interval is $109.4 \pm (1.833)(4.55)$, or 109.4 ± 8.3, or, alternatively, $101.1 \leq \mu \leq 117.7$.

Suppose that the product had been placed in 50 stores and that the sample mean and standard deviation were the same; that is, $\bar{x} = 109.4$ and s = 14.40. The test statistic would be z = 4.30, which we would refer to a normal table given the larger sample size. Calculated z is greater than critical z = 1.645 for $\alpha = .05$, and, as expected, the same conclusion is warranted. The evidence is stronger now because of the larger sample of stores; the product could be expected to sell at a rate greater than 100 units per store per week. The confidence interval is $109.4 \pm (1.645)(2.04)$, or 109.4 ± 3.35, or $106.1 \leq \mu \leq 112.8$, a slightly narrower interval, again, given the larger sample.

Hypotheses about Two Means

Consider testing a hypothesis about the difference between two population means. For example, when consumer expenditure surveys report that men who are 25–34 years old spend an average of $350.50 annually on clothing, vs. men who are 45–54 years old spending $461.60, are the two means are significantly different—do older men buy more in clothing, or more expensive clothing, than younger men, or is the difference not significant, and only due to sampling variability?[2]

The methodology for testing a hypothesis about two means varies according to whether the samples are independent or related. We'll do both. Let's start by assuming that the samples are independent, and look at the three possible cases:

1. The two parent population variances are known.
2. The parent population variances are unknown but can be assumed equal.
3. The parent population variances are unknown and cannot be assumed equal.

Variances Are Known

Experience has shown that the population variance usually changes much more slowly than the population mean. This means that an "old" estimate of variance can often be used as the "known" population variance for studies that are being repeated. For example, if we check annually on the per capita soft drink consumption of people living in different regions of the U.S., we could use last year's variance as the likely "known" variance for this year's study. Let's say we're trying to determine whether any differences exist between Northerners and Southerners in consumption of a new soft drink, called Spark. Past data indicate that per capita variation in the consumption of soft drinks is 10 ounces per day for Northerners and

[2] Anon., "Changes in Consumer Spending by Age," *American Demographics,* http://www.demographics.com.

14 ounces for Southerners as measured by the standard deviation, so we start with: $\sigma_N = 10$ and $\sigma_S = 14$.

The null hypothesis is that there is no difference between Northerners and Southerners in their consumption of Spark ($H_0 : \mu_N = \mu_s$), whereas the alternate hypothesis is that there is a difference ($H_a : \mu_N \neq \mu_s$). If $\bar{x}_N$ and $\bar{x}_S$, the sample means, are normally distributed random variables, their sum or difference is also normally distributed. The two sample means could be normally distributed because per capita consumption is normally distributed in each region or because the two samples are large enough that the Central-Limit Theorem helps us. In either case, the test statistic is:

$$z = \frac{(\bar{x}_1 - \bar{x}_2) - (\mu_1 - \mu_2)}{\sigma_{\bar{x}_1 - \bar{x}_2}}$$

where $\bar{x}_1$ is the sample mean for the first (Northern) sample;

$\bar{x}_2$ is the sample mean for the second (Southern) sample;

μ_1 and μ_2 are the unknown population means for the Northern and Southern samples;

and $\sigma_{\bar{x}_1 - \bar{x}_2}$ is the standard error of estimate for the difference in means and is equal to

$$\sqrt{\sigma_{\bar{x}_1}^2 + \sigma_{\bar{x}_2}^2} \text{ where, in turn, } \sigma_{\bar{x}_1}^2 = \frac{\sigma_1^2}{n_1} \text{ and } \sigma_{x_2}^2 = \frac{\sigma_2^2}{n_2}$$

The "known" population variances are $\sigma_1^2 = (10)^2 = 100$ and $\sigma_2^2 = (14)^2 = 196$. Say we took a random sample of 100 Northerners and 100 Southerners, and found $\bar{x}_1 = 20$ oz. per day and $\bar{x}_2 = 25$. Is this a real difference in consumption rates? The standard error of estimate is:

$$\sigma_{\bar{x}_1 - \bar{x}_2} = \sqrt{\frac{100}{100} + \frac{196}{100}} = \sqrt{2.96} = 1.72$$

and the calculated z is

$$z = \frac{(20 - 25) - (\mu_N - \mu_S)}{1.72} = \frac{-5 - 0}{1.72} = -2.906$$

Calculated z exceeds the critical tabled value of −1.96 for $\alpha = .05$, so we reject the null hypothesis. We conclude that there is a statistically significant difference in the per capita consumption of Spark by Northerners and Southerners.

The confidence interval for the difference in the two means is given by the formula

$$(\bar{x}_1 - \bar{x}_2) \pm z\sigma_{\bar{x}_1 - \bar{x}_2}$$

For a 95% confidence interval, z = 1.96, and the interval estimate of the difference in consumption of Spark by the two groups is −5 ± (1.96)(1.720) = −5 ± 3.4. Northerners on average are estimated to drink 1.6 to 8.4 ounces less of Spark per day than Southerners.

Variances Are Unknown

When the population variances are unknown, the standard error of the test statistic $\sigma_{\bar{x}_1-\bar{x}_2}$ is estimated. We start with:

$$s_1^2 = \frac{\sum_{i=1}^{n_1}\left(X_{i1}-\bar{x}_1\right)^2}{\left(n_1-1\right)} \quad \text{as an estimate of } \sigma_1^2$$

$$\text{and } s_2^2 = \frac{\sum_{i=1}^{n_2}\left(X_{i2}-\bar{x}_2\right)^2}{\left(n_2-1\right)} \quad \text{as an estimate of } \sigma_2^2$$

The estimates of the standard error of the means become $s_{\bar{x}_1} = \frac{s_1}{\sqrt{n_1}}$ and $s_{\bar{x}_2} = \frac{s_2}{\sqrt{n_2}}$. The general estimate of $\sigma_{\bar{x}_1-\bar{x}_2}$ is then:

$$\hat{\sigma}_{\bar{x}_1-\bar{x}_2} = s_{\bar{x}_1-\bar{x}_2} = \sqrt{\hat{\sigma}_{\bar{x}_1}^2 + \hat{\sigma}_{\bar{x}_2}^2} = \sqrt{s_{\bar{x}_1}^2 + s_{\bar{x}_2}^2} = \sqrt{\frac{\hat{\sigma}_1^2}{n_1} + \frac{\hat{\sigma}_2^2}{n_2}} = \sqrt{\frac{s_1^2}{n_1} + \frac{s_2^2}{n_2}}$$

If the two population variances *can be assumed to be equal,* a better estimate of the common population variance can be generated by *pooling* the samples to calculate:

$$s_p^2 = \frac{\sum_{i=1}^{n_1}\left(X_{i1}-\bar{x}_1\right)^2 + \sum_{i=1}^{n_2}\left(X_{i2}-\bar{x}_2\right)^2}{n_1+n_2-2}$$

where s_p^2 is the pooled sample variance used to estimate the common population variance. In this case the estimated standard error of the test statistic $s_{\bar{x}_1-\bar{x}_2}$ simplifies to

$$s_{\bar{x}_1-\bar{x}_2} = \sqrt{s_p^2\left(\frac{1}{n_1}+\frac{1}{n_2}\right)}$$

If the distribution of the variable in each population can further be assumed to be normal, the appropriate test statistic is

$$t = \frac{\left(\bar{x}_1-\bar{x}_2\right)-\left(\mu_1-\mu_2\right)}{s_{\bar{x}_1-\bar{x}_2}}$$

which is t-distributed with $v = n_1 + n_2 - 2$ degrees of freedom.

Let's say, for example, that a manufacturer of floor waxes has recently developed a new wax. The company is considering designs for two different containers for the wax, one plastic and one metal. The company decides to make the final determination on the basis of a limited sales test in which the plastic containers are introduced in a random sample of 10 stores and the metal containers are introduced in an *independent* random sample of 10 stores. The test results are contained in Table 16.2.

$$t = \frac{\left(403.0-390.3\right)-\left(0\right)}{8.15} - = 1.56$$

TABLE 16.2
Store Sales of Floor
Wax in Units

Store	Plastic Container	Metal Container	Store	Plastic Container	Metal Container
1	432	365	6	380	372
2	360	405	7	422	378
3	397	396	8	406	410
4	408	390	9	400	383
5	417	404	10	408	400

This value is referred to a t-table for $v = n_1 + n_2 - 2 = 18$ degrees of freedom. The test is two-tailed because the null hypothesis is that the containers were equal; there was no *a priori* statement that one was expected to sell better than the other. For $\alpha = .05$ and 18 degrees of freedom, critical t = 2.101. (Look in the column headed $1 - \alpha = .975$ rather than .95 in the appendix, because this is a two-tailed test.) Calculated t is less than critical t, so the null hypothesis of no difference is not rejected. The sample data do not indicate that the plastic container could be expected to outsell the metal container in the total population, even though it did so in this limited experiment.

One of the assumptions underlying the previous procedure was that the variances in sales of the plastic and metal containers were equal in the population. The assumption could be checked using an F test for the equality of variances, and indeed, the sample evidence does not contradict the assumption.[3] Suppose, though, that the assumption was not justified. Then the pooling of the variances is also no longer warranted, and the estimated standard error is:

$$s_{\bar{x}_1 - \bar{x}_2} = \sqrt{\frac{s_1^2}{n_1} + \frac{s_2^2}{n_2}}$$

If the samples are both large so that s_1^2 and s_2^2 provide good estimates of their respective population variances σ_1^2 and σ_2^2, then a normal z-statistic can be used to examine the hypothesis.[4]

The preceding discussion assumed that the samples are independent and that the variable of interest is normally distributed in each of the parent populations. The normality assumption was again necessary to justify the use of the t-distribution. What happens if the variable is not normally distributed or the samples are not independent? The second half of Research Realities 16.2 summarizes the approach for nonnormal parent distributions for known and unknown σ, and the next section treats the case of dependent samples.

Now that you know how to test whether two groups are the same, or differ statistically significantly, take a look at Research Realities 16.3. You could apply these tests for differences to see whether you detect international marketplace and demographic differences.

---

[3] See, for example, Warren Chase and Fred Brown, *General Statistics,* 4th ed. (Wiley, 2000).

[4] If not, a question arises about how to treat this problem, including its appropriate degrees of freedom. One suggested solution to this "Behrens-Fisher problem" creates df as a weighted average of the two samples' df (cf. the "Aspin-Welch test" in stats books).

Research Realities

16.2 Testing Hypotheses about the Difference in Two Means

Population shape?	Sample size?	σ Known	σ Unknown
Distribution of variable in parent population is normal or symmetrical.	Small n	Use: $$z = \frac{(\bar{X}_1 - \bar{X}_2) - (\mu_1 - \mu_2)}{\sigma_{\bar{x}_1 - \bar{x}_2}}$$ where $$\sigma_{\bar{x}_1 - \bar{x}_2} = \sqrt{\frac{\sigma_1^2}{n_1} + \frac{\sigma_2^2}{n_2}}$$	Can you assume $\sigma_1 = \sigma_2$? *If Yes:* Use pooled variance t-test where $$t = \frac{(\bar{X}_1 - \bar{X}_2) - (\mu_1 - \mu_2)}{s_{\bar{x}_1 - \bar{x}_2}}$$ and $s_{\bar{x}_1 - \bar{x}_2} =$ $$\sqrt{\frac{\sum_{i=1}^{n_1}(X_{i1} - \bar{X}_1)^2 + \sum_{i=1}^{n_2}(X_{i2} - \bar{X}_2)^2}{n_1 + n_2 - 2}\left(\frac{1}{n_1} + \frac{1}{n_2}\right)}$$ with $(n_1 + n_2 - 2)$ degrees of freedom. *If No:* Approach is shrouded in controversy. Might use Aspin-Welch test.
	Large n	Use: $$z = \frac{(\bar{X}_1 - \bar{X}_2) - (\mu_1 - \mu_2)}{\sigma_{\bar{x}_1 - \bar{x}_2}}$$	Use: $$z = \frac{(\bar{X}_1 - \bar{X}_2) - (\mu_1 - \mu_2)}{s_{\bar{x}_1 - \bar{x}_2}}$$ and use pooled variance if variances can be assumed to be equal and unpooled variance if equality assumption is not warranted.
Distribution of variable in parent population is asymmetrical.	Small n	No theory to support the parametric test. Either transform the variates so that they are normally distributed and then use the z-test, or use a distribution-free statistical test.	No theory to support the parametric test. Either transform the variates so that they are normally distributed and then use the t-test, or use a distribution-free statistical test.
	Large n	If the individual samples are large enough so that the Central-Limit Theorem is operative for each separately, it will also apply to their sum or difference. Use $$z = \frac{(\bar{X}_1 - \bar{X}_2) - (\mu_1 - \mu_2)}{\sigma_{\bar{x}_1 - \bar{x}_2}}$$	n_1 and n_2 must be large enough so that the Central-Limit Theorem applies to the sample means, so it can also be assumed to apply to their sum or difference. Use $$z = \frac{(\bar{X}_1 - \bar{X}_2) - (\mu_1 - \mu_2)}{s_{\bar{x}_1 - \bar{x}_2}}$$ using a pooled variance if the unknown parent population variances are assumed equal and unpooled variance if the equality assumption is not warranted.

Research Realities

16.3 Testing for International Marketplace Differences

These two figures depict some basic statistics on three countries: the U.S., and our northern and southern neighbors. The first panel presents a number of characteristics on which the three countries are fairly similar, compared with the second panel, which presents statistics on qualities where the countries vary more.

Tests for differences allow us to substantiate both claims. If we wanted to conclude that Canadians and Americans are similar (that is, "not statistically different") on things like education (the first set of bars), or energy consumption (the fourth set of bars), or if we sought to conclude whether the Mexican population was dispersed in urban vs. rural settings similarly to Canadians (the last set of bars), we would take the means for Canada and the U.S. on number of years of education and test via the t-test (since our standard deviation would be derived as an estimate from the sample). We'd then compare the U.S. and Canadian means on energy consumption. The Mexican-Canadian comparison involves proportions.

This panel of data includes the demographics that emphasize the countries' differences. The two-sample t-test could be use to test whether the number of tourist arrivals is the same in Canada and Mexico, and whether it is different from the numbers for the U.S. The Mexican numbers look different for youth (the first set of bars), employment of women (third set of bars), and car, phone, and television market penetration. If you have numbers like these, you're not supposed to "eyeball" them and say, "gee, looks like the Mexican phone access is less." You have to support these claims statistically. In the appendix, you'll read about a method of analyzing the three groups simultaneously. Cool, huh?☺

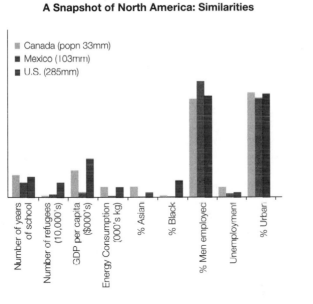

A Snapshot of North America: Similarities

- Canada (popn 33mm)
- Mexico (103mm)
- U.S. (285mm)

A Snapshot of North America: Some Differences

- Canada
- Mexico
- U.S.

Samples Are Related

A manufacturer of camping equipment wanted to study consumer color preferences for a sleeping bag it had recently developed. The bag was of medium quality and price. Traditionally, the high-quality, high-priced sleeping bags used by serious campers and backpackers came in earth colors, such as green and brown. Previous research indicated that the low-quality, low-priced sleeping bags were frequently purchased for children for use at slumber parties. The vivid colors were preferred by this market segment, with bright reds and oranges leading the way. Production capacity

New twist: Are samples independent or related?

TABLE 16.3
Store Sales of
Sleeping Bags

Store	Bright Colors	Earth Colors
1	64	56
2	72	66
3	43	39
4	22	20
5	50	45

restrictions would not allow the company to produce both sets of colors. The company ran a test by offering both types of bags in a randomly selected sample of five stores. The sales per store are indicated in Table 16.3. Do the data present sufficient evidence to indicate a difference in the average sales for the different colored bags?

The appropriate procedure to address this question is the t-test for *related samples*.[5] We define a new variable d_i, where d_i is the difference between sales of the bright-colored bags and the earth-colored bags for the ith store. Thus,

$$d_1 = 64 - 56 = 8$$
$$d_2 = 72 - 66 = 6$$
$$d_3 = 43 - 39 = 4$$
$$d_4 = 22 - 20 = 2$$
$$d_5 = 50 - 45 = 5$$

Now calculate the mean difference:

$$\bar{d} = \frac{\sum\limits_{i=1}^{n} d_i}{n} = \frac{8 + 6 + 4 + 2 + 5}{5} = 5.0$$

and the standard error of that difference:

$$s_d = \sqrt{\frac{\sum\limits_{i=1}^{n_1}\left(d_i - \bar{d}\right)^2}{(n-1)}} = \sqrt{\frac{20}{4}} = 2.24$$

The test statistic is

$$t = \frac{\bar{d} - D}{\left(\dfrac{S_d}{\sqrt{n}}\right)}$$

where D is the difference that is expected under the null hypothesis. Since there is no *a priori* reason why one color would be expected to sell better than the other,

---

[5] The t-test we've been using for the difference in means, is *not appropriate* for this problem. That test requires (assumes) that the samples are independent. These samples are not—sales of bright-colored and earth-colored bags are definitely related, since they are both found in the same stores. This example differs from the floor wax example, in which the metal containers were placed in one sample of stores and the plastic containers were located in an independent sample of stores. We need a procedure that takes into account the fact that the observations are related.

the appropriate null hypothesis is that there is no difference, whereas the alternate hypothesis is that there is:

$$H_0 : D = 0$$
$$H_0 : D \neq 0$$

Calculated t is:

$$t = \frac{50 - 0}{\left(\dfrac{2.24}{\sqrt{5}} \right)} = 5.0$$

This value is referred to a t-table for $v = $ (number of differences scores $- 1$) degrees of freedom; in this case, there are five paired differences, so $v = 4$. Critical t for $\alpha = .05$ is 2.776, and, therefore, the hypothesis of no difference is rejected. The sample evidence indicates that the bright-colored sleeping bags are likely to outsell the earth-colored ones. This conclusion is consistent with a quick eyeballing of the data: the bright-colored sleeping bags outsold the earth-colored ones in each store. Finally, the 95% confidence interval is: $d \pm t(s_d/\sqrt{n})$, or $5.0 \pm (2.776)(2.24/\sqrt{5}) = 5.0 \pm 2.8$, which suggests sales of the vivid-colored bags would be in the range of 2.2 to 7.8 bags greater per store on average.

Tests of differences on "related" samples arise frequently in marketing research. Often the setting is one of examining change. For example, do the aforementioned 45–54-year-old men spend more on their clothing now than they did 10 years ago? (Note that you'd need data from the same respondents at both points in time.[6]) Another "related" comparison would be to pose the question, "Do the 25–34-year-old men spend significantly less on their clothing (the $350.50 figure) than on electronic equipment ($662.07), alcohol ($428.40), or apartment rental ($3505.05)?," etc.

Hypotheses about Two Proportions

In this section, we illustrate the procedure for testing for the difference between two population proportions.[7] For example, there are significantly different views on the government's responsibility in health care marketing issues, such as insurance coverage and affordable prescription drugs. Comparing segments based on gender, ethnicity, education, and age yield differences: e.g., 77% of women believe the government should provide health insurance coverage for more citizens, vs. 68% of men. The numbers are 74% vs. 56% for H.S. vs. college grads.[8]

For the test of two proportions to be valid, the respective samples must be large enough so that the normal approximation (to the exact binomial distribution) can be used. This means that np and nq should be greater than 10 for each sample, where p

---

[6] An alternative is to run a "cohort" analysis, which compares today's 45–54-year-old male sample to another sample of 45–54-year-old men that was taken 10 years ago. This analysis is discussed in the chapter on descriptive research methods.

[7] The tests for population proportions are logically considered with nominal data and marketing examples abound: proportions of customers who "prefer A" vs. "prefer B"; "buy" vs. "do not buy"; are "brand loyal" vs. "not"; "sales reps meeting quota" vs. "not meeting quota." The test for the difference between two proportions uses the z-test, and an "automatic pooled sample variance" estimate.

[8] Anon., "Divergent Attitudes on Health Care," *American Demographics*, http://www.demographics.com.

Comparing two
proportions, e.g.,
% satisfied
customers in
England vs.
Ireland.

is the proportion of "successes" and q is the proportion of "failures" in the sample, and n is the sample size.

To illustrate, consider a cosmetics manufacturer that was interested in comparing male college students and nonstudents in terms of their use of hair spray. Random samples of 100 male students and 100 male nonstudents in Austin, Texas, were selected, and their use of hair spray during the last three months was determined. Suppose that 30 students and 20 nonstudents had used hair spray within this period. Does this evidence indicate that a significantly higher percentage of college students than nonstudents use hair spray?

We are interested in determining whether the two population proportions are different, so the null hypothesis is that they are the same:

$$H_0 : \pi_1 = \pi_2$$
$$H_0 : \pi_1 \neq \pi_2$$

where population 1 is the college students, and population 2 is the nonstudents. The sample proportions are $p_1 = .3$ and $p_2 = .2$, so $n_1 p_1 = 30$, $n_1 q_1 = 70$, $n_2 p_2 = 20$, $n_2 q_2 = 80$, and the normal approximation to the binomial distribution can be used. The test statistic is:

$$z = \frac{\left(p_1 - p_2\right) - \left(\pi_1 - \pi_2\right)}{\sigma_{p_1 - p_2}}$$

where σ_{p1-p2} is the standard error of the difference in the two sample proportions. What is σ_{p1-p2}? For one sample, the variance of a single proportion is $\pi(1-\pi)/n$, so the variance of the difference is:[9]

$$\sigma^2_{p_1-p_2} = \sigma^2_{p_1} + \sigma^2_{p2} = \frac{\pi_1\left(1-\pi_1\right)}{n_1} + \frac{\pi_2\left(1-\pi_2\right)}{n_2}$$

hence the standard error is the square root:

$$\sigma_{p_1-p_2} = \sqrt{\sigma^2_{p_1-p_2}} = \sqrt{\frac{\pi_1\left(1-\pi_1\right)}{n_1} + \frac{\pi_2\left(1-\pi_2\right)}{n_2}}$$

Note that this term is given in terms of the two unknown population proportions π_1 and π_2. They're unknown, but we've assumed them to be equal (check the null), so we have a "natural" case of a *pooled variance* estimate. The term $s^2_{p_1-p_2}$ is used to estimate $\sigma^2_{p_1-p_2}$:

$$s^2_{p_1-p_2} = pq\left(\frac{1}{n_1} + \frac{1}{n_2}\right)$$

where $p = \dfrac{\textit{Total number of successes in the two samples}}{\textit{Total number of observations in the two samples}}$

$$q = 1 - p$$

---

[9] The variance of the sum (or difference) of two independent random variables is equal to the sum of the individual variances. Handy, huh?

For the example,

$$p = \frac{30+20}{100+100} = \frac{50}{200} = .25$$

$$s^2_{p_1-p_2} = (.25)(.75)\left(\frac{1}{100} + \frac{1}{100}\right) = .00375$$

and $s_{p1-p2} = .061$, calculated z is found:

$$z = \frac{(.3-.2)-(0)}{.061} = \frac{.1}{.061} = 1.64$$

whereas critical $z = 1.96$ for $\alpha = .05$. The sample evidence does not indicate that there is a difference in the proportion of college students and nonstudents using hair spray.

The 95% confidence interval calculated by the formula $(p_1-p_2) \pm z(s_{p_1-p_2})$, which is $(.3-.2) \pm 1.96(.061) = .1 \pm .12$, yields a similar conclusion. The interval includes zero, suggesting that there is no difference in the proportions of guys who use hair spray in the two groups.

Comparing two proportions arises in a number of marketing research problems. Research Realities 16.4 gives you two ideas of how to apply these geeky equations to data to extract the marketing information you want.

Summary

Several statistical tests that are useful to marketing researchers for examining differences were discussed in this chapter. The "difference" might be between some sample result and some expected population value or between two sample results.

In testing a hypothesis about a single mean, the z-test is appropriate if the variance is known, whereas the t-test applies with unknown variance. A similar situation arises in the analysis of two means from independent samples. If the variances are known, the z-test is used. If the variances are unknown but assumed to be equal, a t-test using a pooled sample variance estimate applies. If unknown and probably unequal, there is controversy surrounding the correct procedure. If the samples are related instead of independent, the t-test for paired differences is appropriate.

The test of the equality of proportions from two independent samples involves a natural pooling of the sample variances. The z-test is applicable.

Research Realities

16.4 Examples of the Value in Testing Proportions

The following two figures focus on proportions, which could easily be tested using the z-test for two sample proportions presented in this chapter. In the coffee study, consumers were asked, "Do you think coffee has positive or negative health effects?" There are a number of ways to cut these data. You could compare the proportion of *coffee drinkers* who said "*positive*" to the proportion of *coffee drinkers* who said "*negative*" (the first two bars). (Even coffee drinkers acknowledge some detrimental effects of the drink.) You could compare the proportion of *coffee drinkers* who say "*positive*" (or "negative") to the proportion of people who *don't drink coffee* who said "*positive*" (or "negative"). (Hmm! More coffee drinkers think there are positive benefits, and fewer negative effects than non-coffee drinkers. Go figure!)

Gender can be tested, same with ethnicity. For age, the profiles (% who think positive vs. negative) look similar for the youngest groups (18–24 & 25–44) year olds, but around 45–54, opinions start changing, and the data are rather different among those 55 years and older.

In this chart, we have movie-going frequency. Consumers were theater-intercepted and asked, "How frequently do you go to the movies?"

___ Frequently (12 times a year or more)
___ Occasionally (2–11 times a year)
___ Infrequently (less than 2 times a year)
___ Never

You can see by this chart (and a z-test on proportions would confirm), that the most frequent moviegoer is male (versus female) and single (versus married). The less frequent moviegoers (the 3 sets of 4 bars to the right) concur, by displaying the inverse pattern.

Java Has Positive or Negative Health Effects?

Who Goes to the Movies? Or, "Wanna Meet Single Men?"

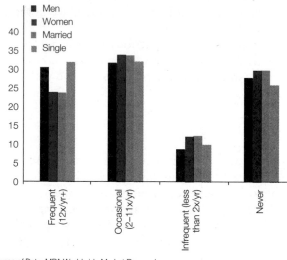

Source of Data: MPA Worldwide Market Research

Review Questions

1. What is the appropriate test statistic for making inferences about a population mean when the population variance is known? When the population variance is unknown? Suppose that the population variance is unknown, but the sample is large. What is the appropriate procedure then?

2. Suppose one is testing for the statistical significance of the observed difference between the sample means from two independent samples. What is the appropriate procedure when the two parent population variances are

a. known?

b. unknown but can be assumed to be equal?

c. unknown and cannot be assumed to be equal?

d. What conditions must occur in each case regarding the distribution of the variable?

3. Would your response to that last question change if the samples were related? Explain.

4. How do you test whether two parent population proportions differ?

Applications and Problems

1. A medium-sized manufacturer of paper products was planning to introduce a new line of tissues, hand towels, and toilet paper. However, management had stipulated that the new products should be introduced only if average monthly purchases per household were $2.50 or more. The product was market tested and the diaries of the 100 panel households living in the test market area were checked. They indicated that average monthly purchases were $3.10 per household with a standard deviation of $0.50. Management is wondering what decision it should make and has asked for your recommendation.

   a. State the null and alternate hypotheses.

   b. Is the sample size considered large or small?

   c. Which test should be used? Why?

   d. At the 5% level of significance, would you reject the null hypothesis? Support your answer with the necessary calculations.

2. The president of a chain of department stores had promised the managers of the various stores a bonus of 8% if the average monthly sales per store increased $300,000 or more. A random sample of 12 stores yielded the following sales increases:

Store	Sales Increase	Store	Sales Increase
1	$320,000	7	380,000
2	230,000	8	280,000
3	400,000	9	420,000
4	450,000	10	360,000
5	280,000	11	440,000
6	320,000	12	320,000

The president is wondering whether this random sample of stores indicates that the population of stores has reached the goal. (Assume that the distribution of the variable in the parent population is normal.)

   a. State the null and alternate hypotheses.

   b. Is the sample size considered small or large?

   c. Which test should be used? Why?

d. Would you reject the null hypothesis at the 5% level of significance? Support your conclusion with the necessary calculations.

3. Ruby Gem is the owner of two jewelry stores located in Los Angeles and San Francisco. During the past year, the San Francisco store spent a considerable amount on in-store displays compared to the Los Angeles store. Ruby Gem wants to determine if the in-store displays resulted in increased sales. The average sales for a sample of 100 days for the San Francisco and Los Angeles stores were $21.8 million and $15.3 million, respectively. (Past experience has shown that $\sigma_{SF} = 8$ and $\sigma_{LA} = 9$, the standard deviations in sales for the San Francisco and Los Angeles stores, respectively.)

   a. State the null and alternate hypotheses.

   b. What test would you use? Why?

   c. What is the calculated value of the test statistic? Show your calculations.

   d. What is the critical tabled value at the 5% significance level?

   e. Would you reject the null hypothesis? Explain.

   f. What can Ruby Gem conclude?

4. Travel Time Company, a large travel agency located in Baltimore, Maryland, wanted to study consumer preferences for its package tours to the East. For the past five years, Travel Time had offered two similarly priced package tours to the East that differed only in the places included in the tour. A random sample of five months' purchases from the past five years was selected. The number of consumers that purchased the tours during these five months is as follows:

Month	Packaged Tour I	Packaged Tour II
1	90	100
2	70	60
3	120	80
4	110	90
5	60	80

The management of Travel Time needs your assistance to determine whether there is a difference in preferences for the two tours.

  a. State the null and alternate hypotheses.

  b. What test would you use? Why?

  c. What is the calculated value of the test statistic? Show your calculations.

  d. What is the critical tabled value at the 5% significance level?

  e. Would you reject the null hypothesis? Explain.

  f. What can the management of Travel Time Company conclude about preferences for the two tours?

5. A manufacturer of exercise equipment for health clubs is interested in comparing usage of exercise equipment at health clubs by men and women. Random samples of 250 women and 250 men in Oklahoma City were selected and the usage of health club facilities was determined. The results indicated that 87 men and 51 women from the samples had been to a health club and had used exercise equipment at least once during the previous six weeks. The manufacturer is interested in determining whether this evidence indicates that a significantly higher percentage of men than women use exercise equipment at health clubs.

  a. State the null and alternate hypotheses.

  b. Which test would you use? Why?

  c. Calculate the test statistic. Show all your calculations.

  d. Assuming that $\alpha = .05$, can you conclude that a higher proportion of men use exercise equipment at health clubs? Since the discovery that a larger proportion of women than men use such equipment would be just as important a finding, use a two-tailed test.

  e. Construct a 90% confidence interval for the difference between the proportion of men and the proportion of women using exercise equipment at health clubs. What conclusions can you draw from the confidence interval?

6. A local charity wanted to run an advertisement encouraging people to donate their old winter coats to the organization to redistribute to the city's homeless people. The charity is able to obtain some free commercial time on both local TV and radio stations. However, the charity wants to use the medium that provides the greatest recall. A short pilot was conducted to test whether there was a difference in recall between spots run on the radio and those on TV. The table that follows provides the results.

Recall	Radio	TV
# People who were able to recall the charity's commercial	25	29
# People who did not recall the commercial	50	46
Total # people surveyed	75	75

  a. State the null and alternate hypotheses for the test.

  b. At $\alpha = .10$, use an appropriate test and interpret the results for the charity.

  c. If the research objective had been to determine whether TV advertisements resulted in greater recall, do the null and alternative hypotheses change? State and test the new hypotheses. Do the results change?

7. The Spazi Italian food company is considering introducing a new extra-spicy spaghetti sauce. Before introducing the new sauce, however, the company wants to test it against its major competitor's spicy sauce. In a mall test, shoppers were stopped at random and asked to taste the two sauces. Shoppers were then asked to rate the sauces on a scale of 1 to 10, with 1 being awful and 10 being excellent. The table that follows shows the ratings given to the two sauces by 10 shoppers.

Shopper	Spazi's Sauce	Other Sauce	Shopper	Spazi's Sauce	Other Sauce
1	1	7	6	8	10
2	7	10	7	10	7
3	5	7	8	2	8
4	6	10	9	3	8
5	2	9	10	9	10

  a. What is the appropriate test to use for analyzing these scores? Explain.

  b. At $\alpha = .05$, is there a significant difference in ratings for these two sauces?

  c. Is this an appropriate design to use for this situation? Explain. What are alternative designs that may be more appropriate for this situation?

  d. After looking at Spazi's scores, do you think that additional research is warranted? Why?

Appendix: Analysis of Variance

Questions to Guide Your Learning:

Q1: What is the analysis of variance, a.k.a., ANOVA?

Q2: How do these concepts enter in: between-variation vs. within-variation?

In this appendix, we turn to the analysis of variance (ANOVA). ANOVA is an extension of the t-test in two ways. First, where the t-tests enable us to compare a sample mean to a population mean, or two sample means to each other, ANOVA lets us compare means that result from three or more groups. Second, in a two-sample t-test, there is only one predictor variable that defines the group membership, e.g., men vs. women, brand A loyalists vs. those for brand B, or consider even the "plastic vs. metal containers" example that we used and to which we'll return shortly. In ANOVA, two or more factors can define the groups and help us understand the data. For example, we might divide our data into the groups: male vs. female crossed with brand A loyal vs. B loyal. We look at both of these qualities of the analysis of variance.

We begin with the example from the previous chapter, on plastic vs. metal containers, not so much because we're into packaging, but because at this point, the data are familiar to you. There are only two means (plastic, metal), so normally, we actually wouldn't conduct an ANOVA—we'd do a two-sample t-test, as we did last chapter. However, we'll work on the two-group example to present the basics, then we'll extend it.

Let's define the data point, X_{ij} = the ith observation on the jth treatment or group. There are two treatments in the example: $j = 1$ refers to plastic containers and $j = 2$ to metal containers. For each treatment there are 10 stores. Thus, for the first treatment $X_{11} = 432$, $X_{21} = 360, \ldots, X_{10,1} = 408$ and for the second treatment $X_{12} = 365$, $X_{22} = 405$, and $X_{10,2} = 400$.

n_j = the number of observations in the jth treatment; $n_1 = 10$ and $n_2 = 10$.

n = the total number of observations in all treatments combined: $n_1 + n_2 = 20$.

$\bar{x}_{.j}$ = the mean of the jth treatment $(j = 1,2)$:

$$\bar{x}_{.j} = \frac{\sum_{i=1}^{n_j} X_{ij}}{n}$$

Thus,

$$\bar{x}_{.1} = \frac{432 + 360 + \ldots + 408}{10} = 403.0$$

and

$$\bar{x}_{.2} = \frac{365 + 405 + \ldots + 400}{10} = 390.3$$

$\bar{x}_{..}$ = the grand mean of all n observations:

$$\bar{x}_{..} = \frac{\sum_{j=1}^{2}\sum_{i=1}^{n_j} X_{ij}}{n} = \frac{432 + \ldots + 408 + 365 + \ldots + 400}{20} = 396.7$$

Any given data point (sales figures, here) will likely deviate from the overall mean, $\bar{x}_{..}$, just as any data show variability. In ANOVA, we're interested in the extent to which the difference between the data point X_{ij} and the grand mean, $\bar{x}_{..}$, may be attributable to the fact that it is a plastic or metal container (i.e., $\bar{x}_{.1}$ and $\bar{x}_{.2}$ may differ somewhat from each other, and therefore from $\bar{x}_{..}$), versus the fact that there will simply be natural variation in the sales of each type of container within any given store (i.e., the X_{i1}'s will vary around, and the X_{i2}'s will vary around $\bar{x}_{.2}$). Conceptually,

$$(X_{ij} - \bar{x}_{..}) = (\bar{x}_{.j} - \bar{x}_{..}) + (X_{ij} - \bar{x}_{.j})$$

The first difference on the right-hand side is called a treatment or between-group difference, and the second is called a within-group difference.

The basic idea underlying the analysis of variance is that the population variance can be estimated from the sample in several ways, and comparisons among these estimates can tell us a great deal about the population. The null hypothesis is that the two population means are equal; $\mu_1 = \mu_2$. If the null hypothesis is true, then, except for sampling error, the following three estimates of the population variance should be equal:

Total variability = Between + Within

1. The **total variation**, computed by comparing each of the 20 sales figures with the grand mean
2. The **between-group variation**, computed by comparing each of the two treatment means with the grand mean
3. The **within-group variation**, computed by comparing each of the individual sales figures with the mean of its own group

If, however, the hypothesis is not true and there is a difference in the means, then although we expect some inevitable within-group variation (essentially sampling error), we'd expect to see a good sized between-group variation.

These three separate estimates of the population variation are computed in the following way for k groups.

1. **Total variation—sum of squares total SS_T:**

$$SS_T = \sum_{j=1}^{k} \sum_{i=1}^{n_j} \left(X_{ij} - \overline{x}_{..} \right)^2$$

$$= (432 - 396.7)^2 + \dots + (408 - 396.7)^2$$
$$+ (365 - 396.7)^2 + \dots + (400 - 396.7)^2$$

The difference between *each observation* and the *grand mean* is determined; the differences are squared and then summed.

2. **Between-group variation—sum of squares between groups SS_B:**

$$SS_B = \sum_{j=1}^{k} n_j \left(\overline{x}_{.j} - \overline{x}_{..} \right)^2$$

$$= 10(403.0 - 396.7)^2 + 10(390.3 - 396.7)^2$$

The difference between each *group mean* and the *overall mean* is determined, the difference is squared, each squared difference is weighted by the number of observations making up the group, and the results are summed.[1]

3. **Within-group variation—sum of squares within groups SS_W:**

$$SS_W = \sum_{j=1}^{k} \sum_{i=1}^{n_j} \left(X_{ij} - \overline{x}_{.j} \right)^2$$

$$= (432 - 403.0)^2 + \dots + (408 - 403.0)^2$$
$$+ (365 - 390.3)^2 + \dots + (400 - 390.3)^2$$

The difference between *each observation* and its *group mean* is determined; the differences are squared and then summed.

SS_T measures the overall variation of the n observations. The more variable the n observations, the larger the SS_T. SS_B reflects the total variability of the means. The more similar the groups are (i.e., the closer the k groups' means), the smaller SS_B becomes. If they differ a lot, SS_B will be large. SS_W measures the amount of variation within each group. If there is little variation among the observations making up a group, SS_W is small. These sources of variability sum: $SS_T = SS_B + SS_W$.

We divide each of these sums of squares by their appropriate degrees of freedom, to obtain a "mean square" (i.e., MS_B, MS_W) and these MS's are unbiased estimates of the population variance.[2] If the null hypothesis (of no difference among population means) is true, they are all estimates of the same variance and should not differ more than we'd expect by chance. If the variance between groups (MS_B) is significantly greater than the variance within groups (MS_W), then we reject the null.

----

[1] Alternatively, SS_B can be written: $SS_B = \sum_{j=1}^{k} \sum_{i=1}^{n_j} \left(\overline{x}_{.j} - \overline{x}_{..} \right)^2$

[2] J. Rick Turner, *Introduction to Analysis of Variance* (Sage, 2001).

In other words, we can view the variance within groups as a measure of the amount of variation in sales of containers that may be expected on the basis of chance. It is the *error variance* or *chance variance*. The between-group variance reflects error variance *plus* any group-to-group differences due to differences in popularity of the two containers. If the between-group variance is significantly larger than the within-group variance, the difference may be attributed to group-to-group variation, and the hypothesis of equality of means is discredited.

So we need the degrees of freedom. The total number of degrees of freedom is equal to $n-1$; we begin with n data points and there is only a single constraint $\bar{x}_{..}$ in the computation of SS_T. For the within-group sum of squares, there are n observations and k constraints, one constraint for each treatment mean. Hence, the degrees of freedom for the within-group sum of squares equals $k(n_j-1)=n-k$. There are k values, one corresponding to each treatment mean, in the calculation of SS_B, and there is one constraint imposed by $\bar{x}_{..}$; hence the degrees of freedom for the between-group sum of squares is $k-1$.

The separate estimates of the population variance, i.e., the mean squares are:

$$MS_T = \frac{SS_T}{df_T} = \frac{SS_T}{n-1}$$

$$MS_B = \frac{SS_B}{df_B} = \frac{SS_B}{k-1}$$

$$MS_W = \frac{SS_W}{df_W} = \frac{SS_W}{n-k}$$

The mean squares computed from the sample data are estimates of the true mean squares. The expected population values are:

$$E(MW_W) = \sigma^2 = \text{Error variance or chance variance}$$

and

$$E(MW_B) = \sigma^2 + \text{Treatment effect}$$

The ratio $E(MS_B)/E(MS_W)$ equals 1 if there is no treatment effect. It is greater than 1 if there is a difference in the sample means. We use the sample mean squares to estimate this ratio:

$$F = \frac{MS_B}{MS_W}$$

ANOVA goes beyond t: more than 2 groups

which follows the F-distribution. The F-distribution depends on two degrees of freedom: one corresponding to the mean square in the numerator $(k-1)$ and one corresponding to the mean square in the denominator $(n-k)$. For the plastic and metal container sales data, these degrees of freedom are 1 and 18. Using $\alpha = .05$, critical F is 4.41 (see the appendix in the back of the book).

The results are compiled in Table 16A.1 in an "analysis-of-variance table." The calculated F-value is 2.43, which is less than the critical F, so not surprisingly (we know these data), the sample evidence is not sufficient to reject the hypothesis of the equality of the two means.[3]

---

[3] A random variable that is t-distributed with v degrees of freedom, when squared corresponds to an F with 1 and v df, that is, $t^2 = F$, and if $t \sim t_v$, then $t^2 \sim F_{1,v}$. For our data, $v_1 = k-1 = 1$, $F_{1,18} = t_{18}^2 = (1.56)^2 = 2.43$.

Source of Variation	Sum of Squares	Degrees of Freedom	Mean Square	F-Ratio
Between-group	806.5	1	806.5	2.43
Within-group	5978.1	18	332.1	
Total	6784.6	19		

TABLE 16A.1
Analysis of Variance of Sales of Plastic versus Metal Containers

The plastic and metal containers example is the simplest type of what is known as a **completely randomized design**. The distinguishing feature of this design is that experimental treatments are assigned to the stores on a random basis. In this case, the container types were assigned to the stores at random, with no attempt to match stores or make them equal in any way. We assign the stores randomly to conditions to form groups that are roughly equivalent initially, so that if there are differences in sales, the sales may be attributable to the container differences.

We can make our previous model statement of "between" vs. "within" terms more precise. The model for a completely randomized design is:

$$X_{ij} = \mu + \tau_j + \varepsilon_{ij}$$

where any data point, X_{ij}, is composed of three components: the overall mean μ; the effect of the jth treatment, τ_j; and the random error associated with the ith observation in the jth treatment group, ε_{ij}. The null hypothesis of equality of population means is equivalent to the hypothesis that the treatment effects are all zero, i.e., $\mu_1 = \mu_2$ implies that $\tau_1 = \mu_1 - \mu_2 = 0$. The alternate hypothesis, when there are k treatments, is that at least one of the treatment effects is not zero; equivalent to the statement that at least one mean differs from the others:

$H_0 : \tau_j = 0$ for all j $= 1, \dots, $ k
$H_a : \tau_j \neq 0$ for at least one j where j $= 1, \dots,$ k.

The assumptions underlying the model and the test are: the samples are independent, the variable is normally distributed, and the variance is the same for each treatment.[4] The last assumption is necessary to justify the pooling of variances and, in this respect, is also similar to the t-test for two means.

ANOVA goes beyond t: more than 1 factor

Randomized Blocks

You can readily appreciate the difficulty that can arise in the preceding situation if, by chance, the stores selected to handle one type of container were, say, systematically larger than the stores chosen to distribute the other type. If a significant difference had been observed, it could have been because the plastic container was sold in the large stores, which have greater sales potential simply because they have more traffic, i.e., having nothing to do with any real preference for plastic containers.

If there is a source of extraneous variation that could potentially distort the results of an experiment, we can use a **randomized-block design**. This design involves

---

[4] Lloyd Nelson, "Did a Series of Samples Come from the Same Normal Distribution," *Journal of Quality Technology* (2002), pp. 339–341.

the grouping of "similar" test units into blocks and the random assignment of treatments to test units in each block. Similarity is determined by matching the test units on the expected extraneous source of variation (e.g., store size in the container example). The hope is that the units within each block will be more alike than units selected completely at random. Since the differences between blocks can be taken into account in the variance analysis, the error mean square should be smaller than it would be if a completely randomized design had been used. The test should be more efficient.

Say we're choosing among three possible sales training programs to enhance the effectiveness of our sales force of 500 reps. Before choosing a program and rolling it out on a big scale, management wants a trial run on a sample of 30 sales reps. We know the reps differ in sales ability, so we decide to match the sales reps in terms of their ability (using their past sales as the matching criterion). We create 10 blocks, with 3 sales reps within a block who have roughly equal sales records.

The sales by these 30 reps, who have undergone training in one of the programs—A, B, or C—are measured and presented in Table 16A.2. The randomized-block model is:[5]

$$X_{ij} = \mu + \tau_j + \beta_i + \varepsilon_{ij}$$

where X_{ij} is the ith observation (i^{th} block) on the jth treatment;

μ is the overall mean;

τ_j is the effect attributable to the jth treatment or training program, j = 1, 2,..., k;

β_i is the effect attributable to the ith block or ability level, i = 1, 2,..., r; and

ε_{ij} is the random error associated with the ith observation on the jth treatment.

The assumptions are that a random sample of Size 1 is drawn from each of the kr (k treatments times r blocks) populations; X is normally distributed in each of the kr populations; the variance of each is the same; and the block and treatment effects are additive. Except for the last assumption, these are the same assumptions that were made in the completely randomized design. But now there are kr populations, whereas there were k populations with the completely randomized design.

TABLE 16A.2
Sales Generated by Three Different Training Programs ($000s)

Block	Program A	B	C	Block	Program A	B	C
1	42	51	43	6	29	35	30
2	36	35	36	7	52	50	54
3	40	52	44	8	46	49	44
4	38	47	42	9	40	44	40
5	32	38	36	10	38	36	35

[5] The example is also an illustration of a "mixed" model, with the treatments being "fixed" (only these three programs are of interest) and the sales reps being "random."

Let j = 1 be training program A, j = 2 program B, and j = 3 program C. The average sales are:

$$\bar{x}_{.1} = \frac{\sum_{i=1}^{r} X_{i1}}{r} = \frac{42 + 36 + \ldots + 38}{10} = 39.3$$

$$\bar{x}_{.2} = \frac{\sum_{i=1}^{r} X_{i2}}{r} = \frac{51 + 35 + \ldots + 36}{10} = 43.7$$

$$\bar{x}_{.3} = \frac{\sum_{i=1}^{r} X_{i3}}{r} = \frac{43 + 36 + \ldots + 35}{10} = 40.4$$

and the overall mean is

$$\bar{x}_{..} = \frac{1}{n} \sum_{j=1}^{k} \sum_{i=1}^{r} X_{ij} = \frac{(42 + \ldots + 38) + (51 + \ldots + 36) + (43 + \ldots + 35)}{30} = 41.1$$

In addition to the total, treatment, and error sum of squares, we must now compute the sum of squares corresponding to blocks. The block means are:

$$\bar{x}_{i.} = \frac{\sum_{j=1}^{k} X_{ij}}{k}$$

for the ith block. Thus, for the first block, i = 1,

$$\bar{x}_{1.} = \frac{\sum_{j=1}^{k} X_{1j}}{k} = \frac{(42 + 51 + 43)}{3} = 45.3$$

The remaining block means, calculated similarly, follow:

$\bar{x}_{2.} = 35.7$	$\bar{x}_{5.} = 35.3$	$\bar{x}_{8.} = 46.3$
$\bar{x}_{3.} = 45.3$	$\bar{x}_{6.} = 31.3$	$\bar{x}_{9.} = 41.3$
$\bar{x}_{4.} = 42.3$	$\bar{x}_{7.} = 52.0$	$\bar{x}_{10.} = 36.3$

The sums of squares are

$$SS_T = \sum_{j=1}^{k} \sum_{i=1}^{r} \left(X_{ij} - \bar{x}_{..} \right)^2$$

$$= (42 - 41.4)^2 + (36 - 41.1)^2 + \ldots + (35 - 41.1)^2$$
$$= 1333.5$$

$$SS_{TR} = \sum_{j=1}^{k} r \left(\bar{x}_{.j} - \bar{x}_{..} \right)^2$$

$$= 10(39.3 - 41.1)^2 + 10(43.7 - 41.1)^2 + 10(40.4 - 41.1)^2$$
$$= 104.9$$

$$SS_B = \sum_{j=1}^{k} k\left(\overline{x}_{i.} - \overline{x}_{..}\right)^2$$

$$= 3(45.3 - 41.1)^2 + 3(35.7 - 41.1)^2 + \ldots + 3(36.3 - 41.1)^2$$

$$= 1093.5$$

$$SS_E = SS_T - SS_{TR} - SS_B$$

$$= 1333.5 - 104.9 - 1093.5$$

$$= 135.1$$

The randomized-block model posits any sample response as the sum of four additive factors: (1) the overall mean, (2) the effect of the jth treatment, (3) the effect of the ith block, and (4) the error term. Table 16A.3 is the analysis-of-variance table for this model. There are now two F-ratios of interest—one corresponding to blocks and one for treatments. Calculated F for the treatment mean square is 6.98; critical F for $\alpha = .05$ and $v_1 = 2$ and $v_2 = 18$ is 3.55. Calculated F exceeds critical F, and the null hypothesis of equal means is rejected. There is a difference in the effectiveness of at least one of the training programs. Program B, in particular, produces significantly better sales.[6]

Calculated F for the block effect is 16.18. Critical F for $\alpha = .05$ and $v_1 = 9$ and $v_2 = 18$ is 2.46. Since calculated F exceeds critical F, the block variation is statistically significant. This means that the grouping of sales representatives according to ability before assigning the treatment was effective, it eliminated a source of variation in the results. The randomized-block design was more efficient than a completely randomized design would have been.

The randomized block design allowed us to test the treatment factor (training program), while controlling for an extraneous factor (sales ability). There are many more kinds of experimental designs. A "Latin-Square" design allows us to test for a treatment, while controlling for two extraneous factors (e.g., sales ability *and* size of sales territory). An important and frequently used experimental design is the "factorial," discussed next.

Factorial Designs

We promised at the beginning of the chapter to show you two ways that the analysis of variance is an extension of a two-group t-test. We have now seen how the ANOVA may be used with three (or more) groups. We also stated that it can be used

TABLE 16A.3

Analysis of Variance of Randomized-Block Design Investigating Sales Programs

Source of Variation	Sum of Squares	Degrees of Freedom	Mean Square	F-Ratio
Blocks	1093.5	$(r-1) = 9$	121.50	16.18
Treatments	104.9	$(k-1) = 2$	52.45	6.98
Error	135.1	$(r-1)(k-1) = 18$	7.51	
Total	1333.5	$rk-1 = 29$		

---

[6] If the null hypothesis is rejected, "contrasts" are run to determine which means are statistically significantly different, see J. Rick Turner, *Introduction to Analysis of Variance* (Sage, 2001).

to investigate the effects of two or more factors in the same experiment. The factorial design is an experiment in which we've varied more than one factor. For instance, it might be desirable to investigate the sales impact of the shape of the packaging, in addition to whether the container is metal or plastic. Say two shapes, cylindrical and rectangular, were being considered for the containers. Package shape and package type would both be called factors, and we'd use a **factorial design**.

There are three very good reasons to use a factorial design.[7] First, we can study the interaction of the factors. The plastic container might sell better as cylinders, whereas the metal container might sell better in rectangular box shapes. An interaction can only be investigated if the factors are considered simultaneously. Second, a factorial design is efficient—if two separate experiments were conducted (one to study the effect of container type and another to study the effect of container shape), some data would yield information about either piece of the puzzle. But by combining the two factors in one experiment, all the observations bear on both factors, so factorials are said to be more "economical." Third, the conclusions reached have broader application, since each factor is studied with varying combinations of the other factors.[8] This result is much more useful (multiple factors or considerations are more like the real world) than it would be if everything else had been held constant.

The factorial design may be used with any of the single-factor designs previously discussed—completely randomized, randomized block, etc. The underlying model changes, as does the analysis-of-variance table, but the principle remains the same. Let's look at a factorial version of a completely randomized design.

Consider again our sales reps. Suppose management is thinking of the three training programs again, but also the frequency with which the sales reps contact their leads. We'll call the frequency factor "A," which takes on the values "high" and "low" (frequent and infrequent would be defined precisely depending on the particular industry, product purchase cycle rates, etc.). The three training programs are now called B_1, B_2, and B_3. We have a 2×3 factorial experiment in which each of the two levels of A occurs with each of the three levels of B to yield six treatment conditions. Suppose that the treatments were randomly assigned to each of five sales representatives. Thus, there would be five replications for each treatment.

		Training Program	
Contact Frequency	B_1	B_2	B_3
A_1	$A_1 B_1$	$A_1 B_2$	$A_1 B_3$
A_2	$A_2 B_1$	$A_2 B_2$	$A_2 B_3$

Suppose that the results were as contained in Table 16A.4. Let:

α_i = the effect of the ith level of the A factor (contact frequency), i = 1, . . . , a;

β_j = the effect of the jth level of the B factor (training received), j = 1, . . . , b;

$(\alpha\beta)_{ij}$ = the effect of the ith level of the A factor and j^{th} level of the B factor;

---

[7] The consumer behavior literature has tons of examples of factorial experiments, cf. *Journal of Consumer Research* or the *Journal of Consumer Psychology*.

[8] A subset, rather than every possible combination, can simplify the experiment, cf., Don Holcomb, Douglas Montgomery and W. Matthew Carlyle, "Analysis of Supersaturated Designs," *Journal of Quality Technology* 35 (2003), pp. 13–28.

TABLE 16A.4
Sales Generated by
Various Personal and
Telephone Call Plans

| | Personal Call Plan | | | | |
Telephone Call Plan	B_1	B_2	B_3	Total	Mean
A_1	42	51	43		
	40	52	44		
	52	50	54	691	46.1
	46	49	44		
	40	44	40		
A_2	36	35	36		
	38	47	42		
	32	38	36	543	36.2
	29	35	30		
	38	36	35		
Total	393	437	404	1234	41.1
Mean	39.3	43.7	40.4		

Cell	$A_1 B_1$	$A_1 B_2$	$A_1 B_3$	$A_2 B_1$	$A_2 B_2$	$A_2 B_3$
Total	220	246	225	173	191	179
Mean	44.0	49.2	45.0	34.6	38.2	35.8

X_{ijk} = the kth observation on the ith level of the A factor and the jth level of the B factor;

μ = the grand mean; and

ε_{ijk} = the error associated with the kth observation on the ith level of A and j^{th} level of B.

Total variability =

Contact variation

+ Training variation

+ Contact*training interaction

+ Within

The underlying model for this completely randomized design suggests that any observation X_{ijk} can be written as the sum of the grand mean, treatment effects, and an error term:

$$X_{ijk} = \mu + \alpha_i + \beta_j + (\alpha\beta)_{ij} + \varepsilon_{ijk}$$

The assumptions are the same as for a completely randomized design except there are now axb populations, whereas in the completely randomized design there were k populations—one for each treatment. Otherwise, though, we still assume that the distribution of the variable in each of the populations is normal and that the populations have the same variance.

There are three main hypotheses, all of which essentially state that the treatment effects are zero (the cell means are equal). The alternate hypotheses are that at least some of the cell means differ. The hypotheses can be written as follows:

$H_0^{(A)} : \alpha_i = 0$

$H_A^{(A)} : \alpha_i \neq 0$ for some α_i, or, not all $\alpha_i = 0$

$H_0^{(B)} : \beta_j = 0$

$H_A^{(B)} : \beta_j \neq 0$ for some β_j, or, not all $\beta_j = 0$

$H_0^{(AB)} : (\alpha\beta_{ij}) = 0$

$H_A^{(AB)} : (\alpha\beta_{ij}) \neq 0$ for some i or j (or, not all $(\alpha\beta_{ij}) = 0$)

The first two hypotheses state that there are no differences caused, respectively, by the levels of the A and B factors; the third says that the effects caused by Factors A and B are additive. To test these hypotheses, the following sums of squares are needed (n = 5 replications):

$$SS_T = \sum_{i=1}^{a} \sum_{j=1}^{b} \sum_{k=1}^{n} \left(X_{ijk} - \overline{x}_{...} \right)^2$$

$$= (42 - 41.1)^2 + (40 - 41.1)^2 + \ldots + (35 - 41.1)^2$$

$$= 1333.5$$

$$SS_{TR} = n \sum_{i=1}^{a} \sum_{j=1}^{b} \left(\overline{x}_{ij.} - \overline{x}_{...} \right)^2$$

$$= 5[(44.0 - 41.1)^2 + (49.2 - 41.1)^2 + (45.0 - 41.1)^2$$

$$(34.6 - 41.1)^2 + (38.2 - 41.1)^2 + (35.8 - 41.1)^2$$

$$= 839.9$$

$$SS_A = bn \sum_{i=1}^{a} \left(\overline{x}_{i..} - \overline{x}_{...} \right)^2$$

$$ 1 - 41.1)^2 + (36.2 - 41.1)^2] = 735.1$$

$$SS_B = an \sum_{i=1}^{b} \left(\overline{x}_{.j.} - \overline{x}_{...} \right)^2$$

$$= 2(5)[(39.3 - 41.1)^2 + (43.7 - 41.1)^2 + (40.4 - 41.1)^2] = 104.8$$

$$SS_{AB} = SS_{TR} - SS_A - SS_B$$

$$= 839.9 - 735.1 - 104.8 = 0.0$$

$$SS_E = SS_T - SS_{TR}$$

$$= 133.5 - 839.9 = 493.6$$

Table 16A.5 contains the various mean squares and F-ratios. For the interaction term, the calculated F is zero. Critical F for $\alpha = .05$ and $v_1 = 2$, $v_2 = 24$ is 3.40. Calculated

Source of Variation	Sum of Squares	Degrees of Freedom	Mean Square	F-Ratio
A (telephone)	735.1	(a−1) = 1	735.1	35.86
B (personal)	104.8	(b−1) = 2	52.4	2.56
AxB (interaction)	0.0	(a−1)(b−1) = 2	0.0	0.00
Error	493.6	ab(n−1) = 24	20.5	
Total	1333.5	abn−1 = 29		

TABLE 16A.5
Analysis of Variance Table for 2x3 Factorial Experiment of Telephone and Personal Call Plans

F is less than critical F, and the null hypothesis is not rejected—there is no special combination of frequency and training that yields better or worse sales results.

Consider next the effectiveness of the training—calculated F is again less than critical F, and the null hypothesis of equality of means is not rejected. The data do not indicate any difference in the effectiveness of the three training programs.

Consider finally the frequency of contract: calculated F is 35.86, and critical F for $v_1 = 1$, $v_2 = 24$ and $\alpha = .05$ is 4.26. Since calculated F exceeds critical F, the null hypothesis is rejected. There is a difference in effectiveness of the two frequencies. An examination of the cell means in Table 16A.4 indicates that A1 ("frequent") is much better than A2 ("infrequent"). If the company were to make a change, this would be the strategy to adopt.

If the interaction term had tested significantly, we would not have bothered to check for the significance of the A and B factors by themselves. Rather, we would have looked for the best combination of frequency and training, because a significant interaction term would have indicated that the effects were not additive; a significant interaction term would have implied that the effects of A were different for some levels of B or vice versa.

Summary

The analysis of variance, ANOVA, is the statistical extension of a t-test. The generalization is in two directions: (1) ANOVA allows us to model three or more groups simultaneously, and (2) the groups may be defined on two or more factors. There are many types of experimental designs, the completely randomized design, the randomized block design, and the factorial design being the preeminent tools of marketing researchers.

Review Questions

1. What is the basic idea underlying the analysis-of-variance procedure? In general, how are these sources of variation computed? What is the basic statistic used to test for the differences among means in analysis of variance?

2. When is a randomized-block design preferred over a completely randomized design? How does the underlying model change? How do the calculations change?

3. When is a factorial design appropriate? What is the basic model of a completely randomized factorial design? What sums of squares are calculated? What are the basic comparisons among the various mean squares?

Applications and Problems

1. Mr. LePew, the advertising manager of a medium-sized manufacturer of rug and room deodorizers, has developed three preliminary advertising campaigns for the company's line of deodorizers. The three campaigns are tested in an independent sample of 24 cities across the U.S., and the sales in each city are monitored. (Note: (1) cities are randomly assigned to each treatment or campaign, and (2) the 24 cities are comparable in terms of various socioeconomic and demographic variables.) The results of this test market are as follows:

Sales ($000s)

City	Ad 1	City	Ad 2	City	Ad 3
1	10	9	9	17	12
2	6	10	7	18	10
3	8	11	6	19	8
4	12	12	10	20	13
5	6	13	6	21	11
6	8	14	4	22	10
7	9	15	5	23	9
8	7	16	5	24	7

Mr. LePew wants to determine if there is a difference in sales as a result of the three advertising campaigns. He requires your assistance in analyzing the preceding information.

a. State the null and alternate hypotheses.

b. What statistical test is appropriate in this situation? Identify the assumptions underlying the test of the hypotheses.

c. Compute the grand mean and the mean of the jth treatment ($j = 1, 2, 3$). Show your calculations.

d. Compute the total variation (the sum of squares total). Show your calculations.

e. Compute the between-group variation (sum of squares between groups). Show your calculations.

f. Compute the within-group variation (sum of squares within groups). Show your calculations.

g. What are the degrees of freedom associated with each of these sums of squares?

h. Compute the mean squares associated with each of the sums of squares. Show your calculations.

i. Complete the following analysis-of-variance table.

j. Discuss your findings on the basis of preceding calculations. (Note: Assume that $\alpha = .05$ to find the critical F value.)

Source of Variation	Sum of Squares	Degrees of Freedom	Mean Square	F–Ratio
Between-group				
Within-group				
Total				

2. A major business school is considering different training approaches for its executive MBA students. For a particular intro course, the question is how best to offer the learning experience: the traditional lecture format vs. a group discussion format, and simultaneously a traditional text vs. online Web resource materials.

   A simple experiment is conducted using 20 new executive students. Using a factorial design, the 20 managers were randomly assigned to one of four training groups: lecture and standard text, discussion and text, lecture and Web materials, discussion and Web.

   At the conclusion of the course, the managers were given a comprehensive test to determine how much of the material each retained from the coursework. The training coordinator plans to use this information to determine how the new course should be implemented in the future. The test scores for each of the participants are as follows:

Group 1: Lecture-Textbook	Group 2: Discussion-Text	Group 3: Lecture-Web	Group 4: Discussion-Web
62	74	84	94
78	86	72	84
86	76	72	88
64	88	66	78
70	84	88	86

a. State the null and alternate hypotheses.

b. Complete the following table:

Source of Variation	Sum of Squares	Degrees of Freedom	Mean Square	F–Ratio
A (instruction format)				
B (instruction materials)				
A x B (interaction)				
Error				
Total				

c. What recommendations can you make based on the findings of the experiment? (Note: Assume that $\alpha = .05$ to find the critical F value.)

What are the underlying assumptions for the ANOVA model? Which assumption is necessary to allow the pooling of variances? What happens if this assumption is violated and the variances are still pooled?

16. A beverage company is testing different point-of-purchase displays. The marketing manager selects 12 stores in a market area and assigns them at random to the following treatment conditions: Control group (no change in display), end-of-aisle display, and store shelf flyer with tear-away coupon. The manager will measure the sales occurring in each treatment condition and analyze the figures using ANOVA. The sales for each store are shown in the following table:

Control Stores (no change)	Experimental Group 1 (end of aisle display)	Experimental Group 2 (shelf display with coupon)
6	18	7
14	11	11
19	20	18
17	23	10

a. List the sources of variation for this test. What are the corresponding degrees of freedom for each source?

b. Considering the underlying assumptions for ANOVA, which of these assumptions may be violated? Is there a more appropriate design for this experiment? Discuss the advantages and disadvantages of your proposed design.

c. Assume that all assumptions are valid for the experiment. Using the data, perform a one-way analysis of variance. What is the calculated F statistic? At $\alpha = .05$, can we reject the null hypothesis of no difference in sales between the treatment groups?

Are These Variables Related?

In the previous chapters, we focused on data analysis techniques that have the goal of testing the significance of differences obtained under various research conditions, e.g., the difference between a sample result and an assumed population condition, or between two or more samples. In many other circumstances, the marketing researcher has a different assignment: to determine whether there is any *association* between two or more variables. If there is, how strong are the relationships, and what is the specific nature of the relationship (i.e., what is the functional form)?

We try to *predict* the value of one variable, such as the consumption of a specific product by a household, on the basis of one or more other variables, such as the family's income and number of kids in the household. Prediction, or *forecasting,* is a crucial element of business planning and marketing strategy. The expectation is that some aspects of a consumer or a marketplace can serve as predictors or leading indicators of consumer or market behavior. If we can understand the antecedents (e.g., consumers' attitudes), we can understand, predict, and perhaps even change the consequences (the consumers' purchase behaviors). The variable being predicted is called the *dependent variable,* or criterion variable. The variables that form the basis of the prediction are called the *independent variables,* or predictors.

Simple Regression and Correlation Analysis

Regression and correlation analysis are terms referring to techniques for studying the relationship between two or more variables. The two terms are often used interchangeably, but the purposes are different. Correlation analysis involves measuring the closeness of the relationship or joint variation between two variables at a time. Regression analysis refers to the techniques used to derive an equation that relates the criterion variable to one or more predictor variables. Regression models the distribution of the criterion variable when one or more predictor variables are held fixed at various levels, e.g., is it the case that households with high incomes and few kids are more likely to purchase luxury vacations than households with less income and more kids?[1] It is perfectly legitimate to measure the closeness of the relationship between variables (i.e., compute a correlation) without deriving an estimating equation (i.e., conduct a regression). Similarly, one can perform a regression analysis without investigating the correlation. It is common to do both, and the body of techniques is usually referred to as either regression or correlation analysis.

We'll start with correlation analysis, first clarifying the distinction between correlation and causation. The use of the terms dependent (criterion) and independent (predictor) variables to describe the measures in correlation analysis stems from the mathematical functional relationship between the variates, not from a logic that one variable is dependent on another in a causal sense. Nothing in correlation analysis, or any other mathematical procedure, can be used to establish causality. All these procedures can do is measure the nature and degree of association or covariation between variables. Statements of causality must be based on underlying knowledge and theories about the phenomena under investigation, not the mathematics.[2]

Simple Regression

Consider an example of a national manufacturer of a sonic toothbrush, Shine. The firm is interested in investigating the effectiveness of its marketing efforts. The company uses regional wholesalers to distribute Shine and supplements its efforts with company sales representatives and spot TV advertising. It intends to use annual territory sales as its measure of effectiveness. These data and information on the number of sales reps serving a territory are readily available in company records. The other characteristics to which the company wants to relate sales—TV spots and wholesaler efficiency—are more difficult to determine. Obtaining information on TV advertising in a territory requires analysis of advertising schedules and a study of area coverage by channel to determine which areas each broadcast is reaching. Wholesaler efficiency requires rating the wholesalers on a number of criteria and aggregating the ratings into an overall measure of wholesaler efficiency, where 4 = outstanding, 3 = good, 2 = average, and 1 = poor. Because of the time and expense required to generate these advertising and distribution characteristics, the company has decided to

---

[1] The regression model theoretically applies to fixed levels of predictor variables (Xs), but it can apply when the Xs are random, assuming that certain conditions are satisfied, see Michael H. Kutner, Christopher J. Nachtschiem, William Wasserman and John Neter, *Applied Linear Statistical Models*, 5th ed. (Irwin, 2003); Terry Dielman, *Applied Regression Analysis for Business and Economics* (Duxbury Press, 2000).

[2] The chapters on causal designs, tests of mean differences, and analysis of variance are the resources for establishing causality.

carry out its analysis employing only a sample of sales territories. The data for a simple random sample of 40 territories are contained in Table 17.1.

The effect of each of the marketing-mix variables on sales can be investigated in several ways. One way is simply to plot sales as a function of each of the variables.

TABLE 17.1
Random Data Sample for Shine Toothbrush

Territory	Sales ($000s) Y	Advertising (TV spots per month) X_1	# Sales Reps X_2	Wholesaler Efficiency Index X_3
005	260.3	5	3	4
019	286.1	7	5	2
033	279.4	6	3	3
039	410.8	9	4	4
061	438.2	12	6	1
082	315.3	8	3	4
091	565.1	11	7	3
101	570.0	16	8	2
115	426.1	13	4	3
118	315.0	7	3	4
133	403.6	10	6	1
149	220.5	4	4	1
162	343.6	9	4	3
164	644.6	17	8	4
178	520.4	19	7	2
187	329.5	9	3	2
189	426.0	11	6	4
205	343.2	8	3	3
222	450.4	13	5	4
237	421.8	14	5	2
242	245.6	7	4	4
251	503.3	16	6	3
260	375.7	9	5	3
266	265.5	5	3	3
279	620.6	18	6	4
298	450.5	18	5	3
306	270.1	5	3	2
332	368.0	7	6	2
347	556.1	12	7	1
358	570.0	13	6	4
362	318.5	8	4	3
370	260.2	6	3	2
391	667.0	16	8	2
408	618.3	19	8	2
412	525.3	17	7	4
430	332.2	10	4	3
442	393.2	12	5	3
467	283.5	8	3	3
471	376.2	10	5	4
488	481.8	12	5	2

Figure 17.1 contains these "scatter diagrams." Panel A suggests that sales increase as the number of TV spots per month increases. Panel B suggests that sales increase as the number of sales reps in a territory increases. Finally, Panel C suggests little relationship exists between sales in a territory and the efficiency of the wholesaler in the territory.

Panels A and B further suggest that the relationship between sales and each of the predictor variables could be adequately captured with a straight line. One way to generate these relationships would be to "eyeball" it—draw a straight line through the points in the graphs. Such a line would represent the average value of the criterion variable, sales, for given values of either of the predictor variables: TV spots or number of sales reps. One could then enter the graph with, say, the number of TV spots in a territory and read off the average level of sales expected in the territory. The difficulty with the graphic approach is that two analysts might generate different lines to describe the relationship, which raises the question of which line is more correct or fits the data better.

An alternative approach is more objective, to mathematically fit a line to the data. The general equation of a straight line is $Y = \alpha + \beta X$, where α is the Y intercept and β is the slope coefficient. In the case of sales Y and TV spots X_1, the equation could be written as $Y = \alpha_1 + \beta_1 X_1$. For the relationship between sales Y and number of sales representatives X_2, it would be $Y = \alpha_2 + \beta_2 X_2$, where the subscripts indicate the predictor variable being considered. As written, each of these models is a deterministic model. When a value of the predictor variable is substituted in the equation with specified α and β, a unique value for Y is determined and no allowance is made for error.

When investigating customer behavior (e.g., psychological and economic variables), there is rarely, if ever, zero error. Thus, in place of the deterministic model, we substitute a probabilistic model and make some assumptions about the error. For the relationship between sales and TV spots, we build the model:

$$Y_i = \alpha_1 + \beta_1 X_{i1} + \varepsilon_i$$

FIGURE 17.1 Scatter Diagrams of Sales vs. Marketing-Mix Variables

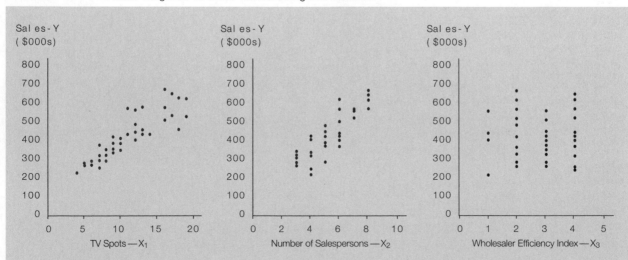

where Y_i is the level of sales in the ith territory,

X_{i1} is the level of advertising in the ith territory, and

ε_i is the error associated with the ith observation.

This is the model used for regression analysis. The error term represents a failure to include all possible determining factors of sales in the model, the fact that there is an unpredictable element in human behavior, and the condition that there are errors of measurement.[3] The probabilistic model allows for the fact that the Y value is not uniquely determined for a given X_i value. Rather, all that is determined for a given X_i value is the "average value" of Y. Individual values can be expected to fluctuate above and below this average.

The mathematical solution for finding the line of "best fit" for the probabilistic model requires that some assumptions be made about the distribution of the error term. The line of best fit could be defined in several ways. The typical way is in terms of the line that minimizes the sum of the deviations squared about the line (the least-squares solution). Consider Figure 17.2, and suppose that the line drawn in the figure is the estimated equation. Employing a caret (hat) to indicate an estimated value, the error for the ith observation is the difference between the actual Y value, Y_i, and the estimated Y value, $\hat{Y}_i$; that is, $\varepsilon_i = Y_i - \hat{Y}_i$. The least-squares solution is based on the principle that the sum of these squared errors should be made as small as possible; that is,

$$\sum_{i=1}^{n} \varepsilon_i^2$$

should be minimized. The sample estimates $\hat{\alpha}_1$ and $\hat{\beta}_1$ of the true population parameters α_1 and β_1 are determined so that this condition is satisfied.

Three simplifying assumptions are made about the error term in the least-squares solution:

1. The mean or average value of the disturbance term is zero.
2. The variance of the disturbance term is constant and is independent of the values of the predictor variable.
3. The values of the error term are independent of one another.

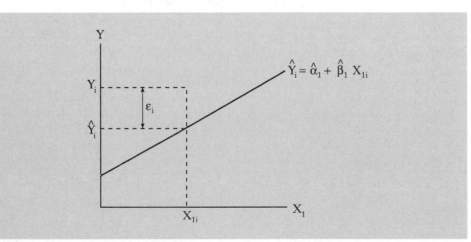

FIGURE 17.2
Relationship between Y and X_1 in the Probabilistic Model

[3] The regression model requires that errors of measurement be associated only with the criterion variable and that the predictor variables be measured without error.

Given these assumptions, the sample estimates of the intercept and slope population parameters, α and β in the general case are:[4]

$$\hat{\alpha} = \bar{y} - \hat{\beta}\bar{x}$$

$$\hat{\beta} = \frac{n\sum_{i=1}^{n}(X_i - \bar{x})(Y_i - \bar{y})}{nS_x^2} = \frac{n\sum_{i=1}^{n}X_iY_i - \left(\sum_{i=1}^{n}X_i\right)\left(\sum_{i=1}^{n}Y_i\right)}{n\left(\sum_{i=1}^{n}X_i^2\right) - \left(\sum_{i=1}^{n}X_i\right)}$$

where

$$\bar{y} = \frac{1}{n}\sum_{i=1}^{n}Y_i$$

Thus, one needs various sums, sums of squares, and sums of cross products to generate the least-squares estimates.

To predict sales Y from the number of TV spots per month X_1, use the data provided in Table 17.1 to confirm these pieces of the computations:

$$\sum_{i=1}^{40}Y_i = 260.3 + 286.1 + \ldots + 481.8 = 16,451.5$$

$$\sum_{i=1}^{40}X_{i1} = (5 + 7 + \ldots + 12) = 436.0$$

$$\sum_{i=1}^{40}X_{i1}Y_i = 5(260.3) + 7(286.1) + \ldots + 12(481.8) = 197,634$$

$$\sum_{i=1}^{40}X_{i1}^2 = (5)^2 + (7)^2 + \ldots + (12)^2 = 5476$$

$$\bar{y} = \frac{16451.5}{40} = 411.3$$

$$\bar{x} = \frac{436}{40} = 10.9$$

---

[4] For discussion of the assumptions and whether they are satisfied, see Patricia Cohen, Jacob Cohen, Stephen West and Leona Aiken, *Applied Multiple Regression: Correlation Analysis for the Behavioral Sciences,* 3rd ed. (Erlbaum, 2002); Ruth Mickey, Virginia Clark and Olive Jean Dunn, *Applied Statistics: Analysis of Variance and Regression,* 3rd ed. (Wiley, 2003).

Therefore,

$$\hat{\beta} = \frac{n\sum_{i=1}^{n} X_i Y_i - \left(\sum_{i=1}^{n} X_i\right)\left(\sum_{i=1}^{n} Y_i\right)}{n\left(\sum_{i=1}^{n} X_i^2\right) - \left(\sum_{i=1}^{n} X_i\right)} = \frac{40(197,634) - (436)(16,541.5)}{40(5476) - (436)^2} = 25.3$$

$$\hat{\alpha} = \bar{y} - \hat{\beta}_1 \bar{x}_1 = 411.3 - (25.3)(10.9) = 135.4$$

The regression equation is plotted in Figure 17.3. The slope of the line is given by β_1. The value 25.3 of $\hat{\beta}_1$ suggests that, for every unit increase in TV spots, sales increase by \$25,300. (In a moment, we'll test whether this is a statistically significant result or could it have occurred by chance.) The estimate is vital information that helps determine whether advertising expense is worth the estimated return. (The estimate of the intercept parameter is $\hat{\alpha}_1 = 135.4$; this value indicates where the line crosses the Y axis because it represents the estimated value of Y when the predictor variable equals zero.)

Standard Error of Estimate

The line seems to fit the points fairly well, but Figure 17.3 shows that some deviation still occurs in the points about the line. The size of these deviations measures the accuracy of the prediction, or the goodness of the fit of the line. We compute a numerical measure of the variation of the points about the line in much the same way as we compute the standard deviation of a frequency distribution. Just as a sample mean is the estimate of the true parent population mean, the line given by $Y_i = \hat{\alpha}_1 + \hat{\beta}_1 X_{i1} + \varepsilon_i$ is an estimate of the true regression line $Y_i = \alpha_1 + \beta_1 X_{i1} + \varepsilon_i$. Call

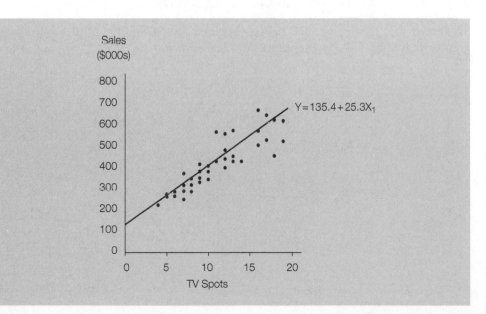

FIGURE 17.3
Plot of Equation Relating Sales to TV Spots

the variance of these random error ε_i's (around the true line of regression) σ_ε^2 or $\sigma_{Y/X}^2$. When the population variance $\sigma2$ is unknown, an unbiased estimate is given by:

$$\hat{s}^2 = \frac{\sum_{i=1}^{n}\left(X_i - \overline{x}\right)^2}{n-1}$$

Similarly, let $s_{Y/X}^2$ be an unbiased estimate of $\sigma_{Y/X}^2$:

$$s_{Y/X}^2 = \frac{\sum_{i=1}^{n} e_i^2}{n-2} = \frac{\sum_{i=1}^{n}\left(Y_i - \hat{Y}_i\right)^2}{n-2}$$

where Y_i and $\hat{Y}_i$ are the observed and estimated values of Y for the ith observation. The square root of that quantity, $s_{Y/X}$, is often called the standard error of estimate (although the term standard deviation from regression is more meaningful).

The interpretation of the standard error of estimate parallels that for any standard deviation. Consider some value for X_{i1}. The standard error of estimate means that for any such value of TV spots X_{i1}, Y_i (sales) tends to be distributed about the corresponding $\hat{Y}_i$ value—the point on the line—with a standard deviation equal to the standard error of estimate. Further, the variation about the line is the same throughout the entire length of the line. The point on the line changes as X_{i1} changes, but the distribution of Y_i values around the line does not change with changes in the number of TV spots. Figure 17.4 depicts the situation under the assumption that the error term is rectangularly distributed, for example.[5] Note that the assumption of constant $s_{Y/X}$, irrespective of the value of X_{i1}, produces parallel bands around the regression line.

The smaller the standard error of estimate, the better the line fits the data (the closer the data points lie to the line). For the line relating sales to TV spots, it is $s_{Y/X} = 59.6$ (we'll see shortly how to assess that number as large or small).

Inferences about the Slope Coefficient

To answer the question about whether the slope coefficient, $\hat{\beta}_1 = 25.3$ is significantly greater than zero (i.e., is the effect of advertising on sales "real" or just due to

FIGURE 17.4
Rectangular Distribution of Error Term

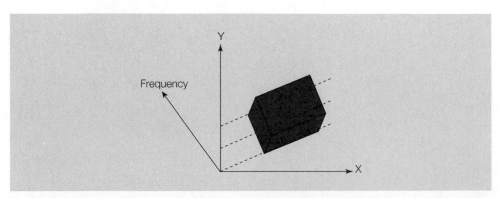

---

[5] This assumption will be modified shortly to that of normally distributed errors—an assumption necessary only if statistical inferences are to be made about the coefficients.

chance) requires an additional assumption—namely, that the errors are normally distributed.[6] If the ε_i are normally distributed, then $\hat{\beta}_1$ is also normally distributed. In other words, if we were to take repeated samples from our population of sales territories and calculate a $\hat{\beta}_1$ for each sample, the distribution of these estimates would be normal and centered on the true population parameter β_1. Further, the variance of the distribution of $\hat{\beta}_1$'s is equal to

$$\sigma^2_{\hat{\beta}_1} = \frac{\sigma^2_{Y/X}}{\sum_{i=1}^{n}\left(X_{i1} - \overline{x}_1\right)^2}$$

The population value $\sigma^2_{Y/X}$ is unknown, so $\sigma^2_{\hat{\beta}_1}$ is also unknown and has to be estimated, but the estimate is easily generated by substituting the standard error of estimate $s_{Y/X}$ for $\sigma_{Y/X}$:

$$s^2_{\hat{\beta}_1} = \frac{s^2_{Y/X}}{\sum_{i=1}^{n}\left(X_{i1} - \overline{x}_1\right)^2}$$

The null hypothesis we will test is that "no linear relationship exists between the variables," whereas the alternate hypothesis is that a linear relationship does exist:

$H_0 : \beta_1 = 0$
$H_0 : \beta_1 \neq 0$

The test statistic is $t = (\hat{\beta}_1 - \beta_1)/s_{\hat{\beta}_1}$, which is t-distributed with $n-2$ degrees of freedom. In the example,

$$s^2_{\hat{\beta}_1} = \frac{59.6}{723.6} = 4.91$$

$$s_{\hat{\beta}_1} = \sqrt{4.91} = 2.22$$

$$t = \frac{(25.3-0)}{2.22} = 11.4$$

For a .05 level of significance, the tabled t-value for $n-2 = 38$ degrees of freedom is 2.02. Our calculated t exceeds critical t, so the null hypothesis is rejected. We conclude that $\hat{\beta}_1$ is sufficiently different from zero to warrant the assumption of a linear relationship between sales and TV spots.[7]

---

[6] However, regardless of the distribution of the error term, we note that the least-squares estimators of the parent population parameters are **blue**; that is, they are the **b**est, **l**inear, **u**nbiased **e**stimators of the true population parameters. This is the remarkable result of the Gauss-Markov theorem. It is only if we wish to make statistical inferences about the regression coefficients that the assumption of normally distributed errors is required.

[7] This conclusion does not mean that the true relationship between sales and TV spots is necessarily linear, only that the evidence indicates that Y (sales) changes as X_1 (TV spots) changes and that we may obtain a better prediction of Y using X_1 and the linear equation than if we simply ignored X_1 (e.g., perhaps the relationship between X_1 and Y is linear only in the range of the number of TV sports we measured).

What if the null hypothesis is not rejected? β_1 is the slope of the line over the range of our observations and it indicates the linear change in Y for a one-unit change in X_1. If we do not reject the null hypothesis that β_1 equals zero, it does not mean that Y and X_1 are unrelated. There are two possibilities. First, we may simply be committing a Type II error by not rejecting a false null hypothesis. Second, it is possible that Y and X_1 might be strongly related in some curvilinear manner, and we have simply chosen the wrong model to describe the physical situation.

Prediction of Y

Having established that the regression is not attributable to chance, we use it to predict sales from given values of the TV spots. Two cases must be considered:

1. Predicting the average value of Y for a given X_1
2. Predicting an individual value of Y for a given X_1

For a given X_1 value, say, X_{01}, the Y value predicted by the regression equation is the average value of Y given X_1. Thus, in a territory with 10 TV spots per month, the expected sales $\hat{Y}_0$ are

$$\hat{Y}_0 = \hat{\alpha}_1 + \hat{\beta}_1 X_{01} = 135.4 + 25.3(10) = 388.4$$

This is an unbiased estimate of the true average value of expected sales when there are indeed 10 TV spots per month in a territory. Individual territories may, of course, exhibit sales above or below the average, just as there are observations above and below the prediction line. $\hat{Y}_0$ may not exactly equal Y_0, the population mean it is estimating for the given X_1 value, so it would seem useful to place bounds of error on the estimate.

To determine the bounds of error, it is necessary to know the variance of the distribution of Y_0 given X_{01}. This variance is estimated as:

$$s^2_{\hat{Y}_0/X_{01}} = s^2_{Y/X_1}\left(\frac{1}{n} + \frac{\left(X_{01} - \bar{x}_1\right)^2}{\sum\limits_{i=1}^{n}\left(X_{i1} - \bar{x}_1\right)^2} \right)$$

Note that this variance depends on the particular X_1 value in question. When X_1 equals the mean of the X_1's, the variance is smallest, because $(X_{01} - \bar{x}_1)$ then equals zero. As X_1 moves away from the mean, the variance increases. For 10 TV spots per day,

$$s^2_{\hat{Y}_0/X_{01}} = \left(59.6\right)^2\left(\frac{1}{40} + \frac{\left(10 - 10.9\right)^2}{723.6} \right) = 92.8$$

The confidence interval for the estimate is given by

$$\hat{Y}_0 \pm ts_{\hat{Y}_0/X_{01}}$$

where t is the tabled t-value for the assumed level of significance and $n - 2$ degrees of freedom. We have already mentioned that for a .05 level of significance and 38 degrees of freedom, t = 2.02. Thus, the confidence interval for the average value of sales when there are 10 TV spots per month is

$$388.4 \pm 2.02\sqrt{92.8} = 388.4 \pm 19.5$$

Although the preceding equation enables us to predict the average level of sales for all sales territories with 10 TV spots per month, we might also want to predict the sales that could be expected in some particular territory. This prediction contains an additional element of error, the amount by which the particular territory could be expected to deviate from the average. The error in predicting a specific value is larger than that for predicting the average value. Specifically, it equals:

$$s^2_{Y_0/X_{01}} = s^2_{Y/X_1}\left(1 + \frac{1}{n} + \frac{\left(X_{01} - \bar{x}_1\right)^2}{\displaystyle\sum_{i=1}^{n}\left(X_{i1} - \bar{x}_1\right)^2}\right)$$

where the caret is removed from Y_0 to indicate that we are now talking about a specific value of Y_0 rather than an average value. Note that $s^2_{Y_0/X_{01}}$ also equals $s^2_{\hat{Y}_0/X_{01}} + s^2_{Y/X_1}$. This alternate expression shows why the confidence interval is wider when the prediction involves a specific value of Y_0 instead of the average value. The second term in this expression, s^2_{Y/X_1}, represents the estimated amount by which the particular value deviates from the average value. For 10 TV spots per month,

$$s^2_{Y_0/X_{01}} = \left(59.6\right)^2\left(1 + \frac{1}{40} + \frac{\left(10 - 10.9\right)^2}{723.6}\right) = 3645$$

and the confidence interval is

$$Y_0 \pm ts_{Y_0/X_{01}} = 388.4 \pm 2.02\sqrt{3645} = 388.4 \pm 122.0$$

Note that the bounds of error are much wider when a particular Y value is being predicted.

Even though the regression equation can be used to develop predictions about the average value of Y for a given X, those doing so must be mindful of the dangers in all such predictions. It is particularly risky to predict outside of the range of values on which the equation was developed (i.e., "extrapolation"). (Check Research Realities 17.1 for Mark Twain's view on the matter!)

Correlation Coefficient

So far we have been concerned with the functional relationship of Y to X. Suppose that we were also concerned with the *strength of the linear relationship* between Y and X.

For the correlation model, we assume X_i to be a random variable also. That is, a respondent yields both an X_i and Y_i value. In addition, we assume that the observations come from a bivariate normal distribution, which implies that the X and Y variables are also univariately normally distributed.

So, let's consider the drawing of a sample of n observations from a bivariate normal distribution. Let ρ represent the strength of the linear association between the

17.1 Life on the Mississippi—742 Years from Now

Mark Twain may not have been a statistician, and he may not have had the aid of a computer, but he knew enough about the tricks numbers can play to write this little spoof for those who would predict "logical" outcomes based on past data.

"In the space of one hundred and seventy-six years the Lower Mississippi has shortened itself two hundred and forty-two miles. This is an average of a trifle over one mile and a third per year. Therefore, any calm person, who is not blind or idiotic, can see that in the Old Oölitic Silurian Period, just a million years ago next November, the Lower Mississippi River was upward of one million three hundred thousand miles long, and stuck out over the Gulf of Mexico like a fishing-rod. And by the same token any person can see that seven hundred and forty-two years from now the Lower Mississippi will be only a mile and three-quarters long, and Cairo and New Orleans will have joined their streets together, and be plodding comfortably along under a single mayor and a mutual board of aldermen. There is something fascinating about science. One gets such wholesale returns of conjecture out of such a trifling investment of fact."

Source: Mark Twain, *Life on the Mississippi*.

two variables in the parent population. Let r represent the sample estimate of ρ. Assume that the sample of n observations yielded the scatter of points shown in Figure 17.5, and consider the division of the figure into the four quadrants formed by erecting perpendicular axes at $\bar{x}$ and $\bar{y}$.

Consider the deviations from these bisectors. Take any point P with coordinates (X_i, Y_i) and define the deviations:

$$x_i = X_i - \bar{x}$$

$$y_i = Y_i - \bar{y}$$

where the small letters indicate deviations around a mean. Inspecting Figure 17.5, we see that the product $x_i y_i$ is:

- Positive for all points in Quadrant I,
- Negative for all points in Quadrant II,
- Positive for all points in Quadrant III, and
- Negative for all points in Quadrant IV.

FIGURE 17.5
Scatter of Points for
Sample of n
Observations

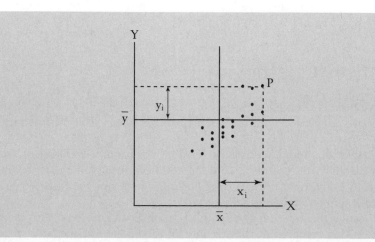

Hence, it would seem that the quantity $\sum x_i y_i$ could be used as a measure of the linear association between X and Y, because:

- If the association is positive, most of the data points will lie in Quadrants I and III, and $\sum x_i y_i$ will be positive;
- If the association is negative, most of the data points will lie in Quadrants II and IV, and $\sum x_i y_i$ will be negative; and
- If no relation exists between X and Y, the points will be scattered over all four quadrants and $\sum x_i y_i$ will be near zero.

These intuitions based on $\sum x_i y_i$ are fine, but we don't use it exactly in the calculations—it has two defects as a measure of linear association between X and Y. First, it can be increased arbitrarily by increasing the sample size. Second, it can also be arbitrarily influenced by changing the units of measurement for either X or Y or both (e.g., changing feet to meters). These defects can be removed by making the measure of the strength of linear association a dimensionless quantity and dividing by n. The result is the *Pearson product-moment correlation coefficient*:

$$r = \frac{\sum\limits_{i=1}^{n}\left(X_i - \bar{x}\right)\left(Y_i - \bar{y}\right)}{ns_x s_y} = \frac{\sum\limits_{i=1}^{n} x_i y_i}{ns_x s_y}$$

where s_X is the standard deviation of the X variable and s_Y that for Y. The correlation coefficient computed from the sample data is an estimate of the parent population parameter ρ, and part of the job of the researcher is to use r to test hypotheses about ρ. For our particular example (or any time there is only a single predictor variable), the test of the null hypothesis $H_0: \rho = 0$ is equivalent to the test of the null hypothesis $H_0: \beta_1 = 0$. (Note the identity in the numerator of this equation for r and the earlier equation for β_1.)

The product-moment coefficient of correlation may vary from −1.0 to +1.0. Perfect positive correlation, where an increase in X determines exactly an increase in Y, yields a coefficient of +1.0. Perfect negative correlation, where an increase in X determines exactly a decrease in Y, yields a coefficient of −1.0. Figure 17.6 depicts these situations and others to provide for you some appreciation of the size of the correlation coefficient associated with a particular degree of scatter.

The square of the correlation coefficient is the **coefficient of determination**. By some algebraic manipulation, it can be shown to be equal to

$$r^2 = 1 - \frac{s_{Y/X}^2}{s_Y^2}$$

Ethical Dilemma 17.1

Imagine that the analyst you recently hired for your firm's marketing research department was given the responsibility of developing a method by which market potential for the firm's products could be estimated by small geographic areas. The analyst gathered as much secondary data as he could. He then ran a series of regression analyses using the firm's sales as the criterion and the demographic factors as predictors. He realized that several of the predictors were highly correlated (e.g., average income in the area with average educational level), but he chose to ignore this fact when presenting the results to management.

- What is the consequence when the predictors in a regression equation are highly correlated?
- Is a research analyst ethically obliged to learn all he or she can about a particular technique before applying it to a problem in order to avoid incorrectly interpreting the results?
- Is a research analyst ethically obliged to advise those involved to be cautious in interpreting results because of violations of the assumptions in the method used to produce the results?
- What are the researcher's responsibilities if management has no interest in the technical details by which the results are achieved?

FIGURE 17.6
Sample Scatter Diagrams
and Their Correlation
Coefficients

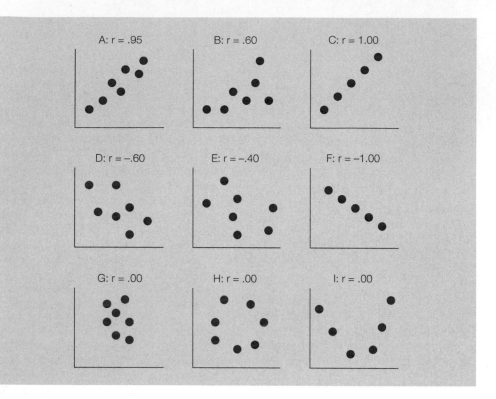

In the absence of the predictor variable, our best estimate of the criterion variable is the sample mean, $\bar{y}$. If low variability in sales from territory to territory exists, the sample mean is a good estimate of the expected sales in any territory. It is a poor estimate though, if there is high variability. Thus, the variance in sales s_Y^2 is a measure of the "badness" of such an estimating procedure. Bringing the predictor X into the model might improve the estimates (if the equation fits the data). Since the $s_{Y/X}^2$ measures the scatter of the points around the regression line, $s_{Y/X}^2$ can be considered a measure of the "badness" of an estimating procedure that takes account of X. We can compare these badness-of-fit measures to see whether our knowledge of X helps us predict Y more accurately. Specifically, if $s_{Y/X}^2$ is small relative to s_Y^2, then X can be said to have substantially improved the predictions of the criterion variable. Conversely, if $s_{Y/X}^2$ is approximately equal to s_Y^2, then X can be considered not to have helped improve the predictions of Y. Thus, the ratio $s_{Y/X}^2/s_Y^2$ can be considered to be the ratio of variation left unexplained by the regression line divided by the total variation:

$$r^2 = 1 - \frac{\left(unexplained\ variation\right)}{\left(total\ variation\right)}$$

The right side of the equation can be combined in a single fraction to yield

$$r^2 = \frac{\left(total\ variation - unexplained\ variation\right)}{\left(total\ variation\right)}$$

Total variation minus unexplained variation leaves "explained variation," or the variation in Y that is accounted for or explained by the introduction of X. Thus, the coefficient of determination is interpreted as:

$$r^2 = \frac{\left(explained\ variation\right)}{\left(total\ variation\right)}$$

where "total variation" means the variance in Y. For the sales and TV spot example, $r^2 = .77$. This means that 77% of the variation in sales from territory to territory is accounted for, or can be explained, by the variation in TV advertising across territories. Thus, we can do a (much) better job of estimating sales in a territory if we take account of TV spots than if we neglect this advertising effort.

Multiple-Regression Analysis

So far we have considered only two variables in our analysis: sales and TV advertising. We now bring in additional predictor variables and consider multiple-regression analysis. The goals are still the same; we want to construct an equation to estimate values of the criterion variable, but now we do so from several predictor variables. And we still wish to measure the closeness of the estimated relationship. Our objective in introducing additional variables is basic—to improve our predictions of the criterion variable. (See Research Realities 17.2 for an application of multiple regression to assess CEO salaries—actual vs. predicted as a function of their companies' performances.)

Revised Nomenclature

Things are getting more complicated, so we need to revise our notation. For a regression model with three predictor variables, we write:

$$Y = \alpha + \beta_1 X_1 + \beta_2 X_2 + \beta_3 X_3 + \varepsilon$$

which is a simplified statement of the more elaborate and precise equation:

$$Y_{(123)} = \alpha_{(123)} + \beta_{Y1.23} X_1 + \beta_{Y2.13} X_2 + \beta_{Y3.12} X_3 + \varepsilon_{(123)}$$

In this more precise system:

- $Y_{(123)}$ is the value of Y estimated from the regression equation, in which Y is the criterion variable and X_1, X_2, and X_3 are the predictor variables.
- $\alpha_{(123)}$ is the intercept parameter in the multiple-regression equation.
- $\beta_{Y1.23}$ is the coefficient of X_1 in the regression equation. It is called the *coefficient of partial (or net) regression*. Note the subscripts. The two subscripts to the left of the decimal point are called primary subscripts. The first identifies the criterion variable, and the second identifies the predictor variable of which this β value is the coefficient. There are always two primary subscripts. The two subscripts to the right of the decimal point are called secondary subscripts. They indicate which other predictor variables are in the regression equation. The number of secondary subscripts varies from zero for simple regression to any number $k - 1$, where there are k predictor variables in the problem. In this case, the model contains three predictor variables, so there are two secondary subscripts throughout. $\beta_{Y1.23}$ is called the **partial regression coefficient** because it reflects the impact of

Simple Regression:

y = fn (x)

Multiple Regression:

y = fn (x₁, x₂, x₃, . . .)

Easy!

Business periodicals frequently publish charts of CEO pay, along with indicators of corporate performance.

The following data were sampled from Jerry Useem's "CEO Pay," *Fortune,* April 14, 2003. (Also see "What the Boss Makes" in *Forbes,* May 12, 2003, or "Executive Pay," *BusinessWeek,* April 21, 2003, etc.)

Use the corporate performance indicators (sales in millions of dollars, and return on earnings) to predict the CEO salary and bonus package (in thousands of dollars). After obtaining the regression coefficient estimates, plug the actual company performance numbers into the equation, to obtain the predicted CEO salary figures.

- Which CEOs are overcompensated? Which are undervalued?
- If you were one of the CEOs identified as having been overcompensated, how might you argue that a regression model has limitations in this application?

Company	Total Compensation (in millions)	Shareholder Return
Apple Computer	$78.1	−34.6%
Honeywell	68.5	−27.3
Cisco Systems	54.8	−27.7
Lucent Technologies	38.2	−75.4
Tenet Healthcare	35.0	−58.1
Hancock Financial Services	34.3	−31.7
Sun Microsystems	31.7	−74.7
Abbott Laboratories	30.4	−26.7
American Intl.Group	29.2	−26.9
Alcoa	24.8	−34.6
Schering-Plough	24.4	−36.4
Wyeth	22.2	−37.9

Everybody's being rated. Here are analogous (pay and performance) statistics on baseball's "best hitters." Keep in mind possible range restrictions and regression to the mean, but again, run the predictions, and see who is a good "value" versus who is overpaid. Who should renegotiate? Who should keep quiet?

Player	At Bats	Total Bases	Salary (000s)
Bonds	403	322	$15,000
Thome	480	325	11,167
Ramirez	436	282	17,185
Giles	497	309	8,563
Rodriguez	624	389	22,000
Walker	477	287	12,667
Guerrero	614	364	11,500
Giambi	560	335	11,429
Ordonez	590	352	9,000
Helton	553	319	10,600
Sosa	556	330	16,875
Palmeiro	546	312	9,000

X_1 on Y, having partialled out, or statistically controlled for the predictors, X_2 and X_3.

- $\varepsilon_{(123)}$ is the error associated with the prediction of Y when X_1, X_2, and X_3 are the predictor variables.

It is common practice to use the simpler notation, e.g., β_2. The more elaborate notation, $\beta_{Y2.13}$, helps us remember to interpret the solution precisely.

Multicollinearity Assumption

The assumptions that we made about the error term for the simple regression model also apply to the multiple-regression equation. In addition, for multiple regression, we require another assumption—that the predictor variables not be correlated among themselves. When the data result from a survey rather than an experiment, this assumption is often violated because many variables of interest in marketing vary together (e.g., higher incomes typically correlate with higher education levels). *Multicollinearity* is said to be present in a multiple-regression problem when the predictor variables are correlated among themselves. We'll return to this issue.

Coefficients of Partial Regression

Let's say we want to model sales as a function of TV spots, as before, but also number of sales reps. We could run a simple regression using sales reps to predict sales, as we did using TV spots to predict sales. Alternatively, we could consider the simultaneous influence of TV spots and sales reps on sales using multiple-regression analysis. If we assume that that is indeed the research problem, the regression model would be written

$$Y_{(12)} = \alpha_{(12)} + \beta_{Y1.2}X_1 + \beta_{Y2.1}X_2 + \varepsilon_{(12)}$$

indicating that the criterion variable, sales in a territory, is predicted by two variables, X_1 (TV spots per month) and X_2 (number of sales reps).

The parameters are estimated from sample data using least-squares procedures via computer. For this problem, the equation turns out to be:

$$\hat{Y}_{(12)} = \hat{\alpha}_{(12)} + \hat{\beta}_{Y1.2}X_1 + \hat{\beta}_{Y2.1}X_2 = 69.3 + 14.2X_1 + 37.5X_2$$

This regression equation may be used to estimate the level of sales expected in a territory, given the number of TV spots and sales reps in the territory. Like any other least-squares equation, this line (actually it's a plane in this case because three dimensions are involved) fits the points in such a way that the sum of the deviations about the line is zero. In other words, if sales for each of the 40 sales territories were to be estimated from this equation, the positive and negative deviations about the line would exactly balance.

The level at which the plane intercepts the Y axis is given by $\hat{\alpha}_{(12)} = 69.3$. Assuming that the multicollinearity assumption is satisfied, the coefficients of partial regression $\hat{\beta}_{Y1.2}$ and $\hat{\beta}_{Y2.1}$, can be interpreted as the average change in the criterion variable associated with a unit change in the appropriate predictor variable *while holding the other predictor variable constant*. Thus, assuming that there is no multicollinearity, $\hat{\beta}_{Y1.2} = 14.2$ indicates that on the average, an increase of $14,200 in sales can be expected with each additional TV spot in the territory if the number of sales representatives is not changed. Similarly, $\hat{\beta}_{Y2.1} = 37.5$ suggests that each additional sales representative in a territory can be expected to produce $37,500 in sales, on the average, if the number of TV spots is held constant.

In simple-regression analysis, we tested the significance of the regression equation by examining the significance of the slope coefficient employing the t-test. The calculated t was 11.4 for the sales/TV spot relationship. The significance of the regression could also have been checked with an F-test. In the case of a two-variable regression, calculated F is equal to calculated t squared: $F = t^2 = (11.4)^2 = 130.6$. In general, calculated F is equal to the ratio of the "mean square due to regression" to the "mean square due to residuals." In simple regression, the calculated F value would be referred to an F-table for 1 and $n-2$ degrees of freedom. The conclusion would be exactly equivalent to that derived by testing the significance of the slope coefficient employing the t-test with $n-2$ df.

In the multiple-regression case, the significance of the overall regression is examined using an F-test. The appropriate degrees of freedom are k and $n-k-1$, where there are k predictor variables. Critical F for 2 and $40-2-1=37$ degrees of freedom and a .05 level of significance is 3.25. Calculated F for the regression we just ran, relating sales to TV spots and sales reps is 128.1. Since calculated F exceeds critical F, the null hypothesis of "no relationship" is rejected. A statistically significant linear relationship exists between sales and the predictor variables (# TV spots and # sales reps).

Now that we know the overall function is significant, the slope coefficients for each separate predictor can also be tested to see whether they significantly contribute to the prediction statistically. A t-test is used, and the validity of the procedure is highly dependent on whether there exists multicollinearity in the data. If the data are highly multicollinear, there is a tendency to commit Type II errors (i.e., many of the predictor variables will be judged as not being related to the criterion variable when in fact they are). It is even possible to have a high R^2 value and to conclude that the overall regression is statistically significant with none of the coefficients being significant. The difficulty with the t-tests for the significance of the individual slope coefficients arises because the standard error of estimate of the least-squares coefficients, s_{b_i}, increases as the dependence among the predictor variables increases. And, of course, as the denominator of calculated t gets larger, t itself decreases, occasioning the conclusion of no relationship between the criterion variable and the predictor variable in question.

Is multicollinearity a problem in our example? Consider again the simple regression of sales on TV spots; β_1 ($\hat{\beta}_{Y1}$ in our more formal notational system) was equal to 25.3. Thus, when the number of sales representatives in a territory was not considered, the average change in sales associated with an additional TV spot was $25,300. Yet when the number of sales representatives was considered, the average change in sales associated with an additional TV spot was $14,200 ($\hat{\beta}_{Y1.2} = 14.2$). Part of the sales effect that we were attributing to TV spots was in fact due to the number of sales representatives in the territory. We were thus overstating the effect of the TV advertising because of the way decisions have historically been made in the company. Specifically, those territories with the greater number of sales reps also received more TV advertising support (or vice versa). Perhaps this was logical, because they contained a larger target market. Nevertheless, the fact that the two predictor variables are not independent (the correlation between TV spots and sales reps is $r = .78$) has caused a violation of the assumption of independent predictors. Multicollinearity is present within this data set.

A multicollinear condition reduces the efficiency of the estimates for the regression parameters: the amount of information about the effect of each predictor variable on the criterion variable declines as the correlation among the predictor variables increases. The reduction in efficiency can easily be seen in the limiting case as the correlation between the predictor variables approaches 1 for a 2-predictor model. Such a situation is depicted in Figure 17.7, where it is assumed that a perfect linear relationship exists between the two predictor variables, TV spots, and number of sales reps, and also that a strong linear relationship exists between the criterion variable sales and TV spots. Consider the change in sales from $75,000 to $100,000. This change is associated with a change in the number of TV spots from three to four. This change in TV spots is also associated with a change in the number of sales reps from four to five. What is the effect of a TV spot on sales? Can we say it is $100-75 = 25$, or $25,000? No. Historically a sales representative has been added to a territory whenever the number of TV spots has been increased by one (or vice versa).

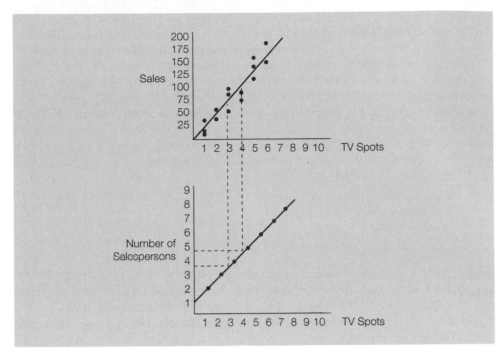

FIGURE 17.7
Hypothetical Relationship between Sales and TV Spots and between TV Spots and Number of Sales Representatives

The number of TV spots and sales representatives varies in direct proportion, and it is impossible to distinguish their separate influences on sales (their influence when the other predictor variable is truly held constant).

Very little meaning can be attached to regression coefficients when multicollinearity is present, as in our example. The "normal" interpretation of the regression coefficient as "the average change in the criterion variable associated with a unit change in the appropriate predictor variable while holding the other predictor variables constant" does not hold.[8] The equation may still be used for prediction, however, e.g., to predict sales in the various territories for given levels of TV spots and number of sales reps, assuming that conditions are stable. The partial-regression coefficients should not be used, though, as the basis for making marketing strategy decisions when significant multicollinearity is present.[9]

Coefficients of Multiple Correlation and Determination

In simple regression, the measure of the strength or closeness of the relationship between the criterion and predictor variables is very important (recall the correlation, r, and its square, the coefficient of multiple determination). In multiple regression, there are analogous coefficients.

---

[8] Aris Spanos and Anya McGuirk, "The Problem of Near-Multicollinearity Revisited," *Journal of Econometrics* (2002), pp. 365–393.

[9] Another interpretation danger is that it is reasonable to assume that both the #sales reps serving a territory and the #TV spots per month were both determined on the basis of territorial potential. If this is the case, the implied causality is reversed or at least confused; instead of the #sales reps and #TV spots determining sales, (potential) sales determine the former quantities, and they in turn could be expected to affect realized sales. If this scenario holds, the coefficient-estimating procedure needs to take into account the two-way "causation" among the variables via the estimation of simultaneous equation systems.

The coefficient of multiple correlation is formally denoted by $R_{Y.123}$, where the primary subscript identifies the criterion variable and the secondary subscripts identify the predictor variables. The **coefficient of multiple determination** is denoted by $R^2_{Y.123}$ or informally by R^2. It represents the proportion of variation in the criterion variable that is accounted for by the predictor variables. In the investigation of the relationship between sales and TV spots and number of sales reps, $R^2_{Y.12} = .874$. This means that 87.4% of the variation in sales is associated with variation in TV spots and number of sales reps. The new sales reps variable has improved the fit of the regression line; 87.4% of the variation in sales is accounted for by the two-predictor variable model, whereas only 77.5% had been accounted for previously by the one-predictor model. The square root of this quantity, $R_{Y.12} = .935$, is the coefficient of multiple correlation. (While r ranges from –1.0 to +1.0, and r² from 0.0 to 1.0, both R and R² range from 0.0 to 1.0.)

Coefficients of Partial Correlation

Two additional quantities must be considered when interpreting the results of a multiple-regression analysis that are not present in simple-regression analysis: the coefficient of partial correlation and its square, the coefficient of partial determination.

In simple regression, when we relate sales Y to TV spots X_1, we write the coefficient of simple determination as:

$$r^2_{Y.1} = 1 - \frac{\left(unexplained\ variation\right)}{\left(total\ variation\right)} = 1 - \frac{s^2_{Y.1}}{s^2_Y}$$

where the unexplained variation is given by the square of standard error of estimate, $s^2_{Y.12}$, and total variation, by the variance in the criterion variable s^2_Y.

For multiple regression with two predictor variables, X_1 and X_2, we denote the standard error of estimate by $s_{Y.12}$ and its square by $s^2_{Y.12}$. The standard error of estimate measures the variation still remaining in the criterion variable Y after the two predictor variables X_1 and X_2 have been taken into account. Since $s^2_{Y.1}$ measures the variation in the criterion variable that remains after the first predictor variable has been taken into account, the ratio $s^2_{Y.12}/s^2_{Y.1}$ can be interpreted as measuring the relative degree to which the association among the three variables Y, X_1, and X_2 provides information about Y over and above that provided by the association between the criterion variable and the first predictor variable alone. In other words, the ratio $s^2_{Y.12}/s^2_{Y.1}$ measures the relative degree to which X_2 adds to the knowledge about Y after X_1 has already been fully utilized. The ratio is the basis for the **coefficient of partial determination**, which in the sales (Y) versus TV spots (X_1) and number of sales representatives (X_2) example is

$$r^2_{Y2.1} = 1 - \frac{s^2_{Y.1}}{s^2_Y} = 1 - \frac{\left(45.2\right)^2}{\left(59.6\right)^2} = 1 - .576 = .424$$

This result means that 42.4% of the variation in sales, not associated with TV spots, is incrementally associated with the number of sales reps. Alternatively, the errors made in estimating sales from TV spots are, as measured by the variance, reduced by 42.4% when the sales reps variable X_2 is added to X_1 as an additional predictor. The square root of the coefficient of partial determination is the **coefficient of partial correlation**.

Our example had two predictors. Thus, we defined the coefficient of partial determination for the number of sales representatives X_2 as $r_{Y2.1}^2$. We could similarly define a coefficient of partial determination for TV spots. It would be denoted as $r_{Y1.2}^2$, and it would represent the percentage of the variation in sales not associated with X_2 that is incrementally associated with X_1; this latter coefficient would show the incremental contribution of X_1 after the association between Y and X_2 had already been considered.

When there are more than two predictors, we can define many more coefficients of partial determination. Each would have two primary subscripts indicating the criterion variable and the newly added predictor variable. There could be a great many secondary subscripts, as they always indicate which predictor variables have already been considered. Thus, if we had three predictor variables, we could calculate $r_{Y2.1}$, $r_{Y3.1}$, $r_{Y1.2}$, $r_{Y3.2}$, $r_{Y1.3}$, and $r_{Y2.3}$. These would all be first-order partial correlation coefficients, because they have one secondary subscript indicating that one other predictor variable is taken into account. We could also calculate $r_{Y1.23}$, $r_{Y2.13}$, and $r_{Y3.12}$. These are all second-order partial correlation coefficients. Each has two secondary subscripts, indicating that the incremental contribution of the variable is being considered after two other predictor variables have already been taken into account. Simple correlation coefficients, of course, have no secondary coefficients; they are, therefore, often referred to as zero-order partial correlation coefficients.

Summary

This chapter examined the question of association or covariation between variables when one of the variables is considered a criterion variable. Simple regression and correlation analysis is the primary statistical device for analyzing the association between a single predictor and a single criterion variable. This model allows the estimation of a functional equation relating the variables, as well as an estimate of the strength of the association between them. Some of the more useful outputs from a simple regression analysis are the following:

1. The functional equation, which allows the prediction of the criterion variable for assumed values of the predictor variable
2. The standard error of estimate, which provides an absolute measure of the lack of fit of the equation to the data
3. The coefficient of determination, which provides a relative assessment of the goodness of fit of the equation
4. The slope coefficient, which indicates how much the criterion variable changes, on the average, per unit of change in the predictor variable

The regression model is readily extended to incorporate multiple predictor variables to estimate the criterion variable. If the predictor variables are not correlated among themselves, each partial regression coefficient indicates the average change in the criterion variable per unit change in the predictor variable in question, holding the other predictor variables constant. If the predictor variables are correlated among themselves, little substantive meaning can be attached to the slope coefficients, although the regression equation often can be used successfully for prediction. The coefficient of multiple determination measures the proportion of the variation in the dependent variable explained by all the predictor variables. The coefficient of partial determination measures the relative degree to which a given variable adds to our knowledge of the criterion variable over and above the other predictor variables.

Review Questions

1. What is the basic nature of the distinction between tests for group differences and tests to investigate association?

2. What is the difference between regression analysis and correlation analysis?

3. What is the difference between a deterministic model and a probabilistic model? Which type of model underlies regression analysis? Explain.

4. What assumptions are made about the error term in the least-squares solution to the regression problem? When the analyst wishes to make an inference about a regression population parameter, what additional assumption is necessary?

5. What is the standard error of estimate?

6. Suppose that an analyst wished to make an inference about the slope coefficient in a regression model. What is the appropriate procedure? What does it mean if the null hypothesis is rejected? If it is not rejected?

7. What is the correlation coefficient, and what does it measure? What is the coefficient of determination, and what does it measure?

8. What is a coefficient of partial regression, and what does it measure? What condition must occur for the usual interpretation to apply? What happens if this condition is not satisfied?

9. What is the coefficient of multiple determination?

10. What is a coefficient of partial determination? What does it measure?

Applications and Problems

1. The quality of public school education has become a major political issue. In many states, dissatisfied parents are voting for school-choice legislation that allows them to use public money to send their children to the school they deem most appropriate. Under some school-choice legislation, parents can even choose to send their children to private schools and pay only the difference between the amount charged by the private school and the amount it would have cost to send the child to a public school.

    One local school district in which parents were calling for school-choice reform hired a marketing research company to assess customer satisfaction and relate this satisfaction to demographic variables. The school district had hypothesized that satisfaction was related to income levels, with those earning more money being more dissatisfied with the public school system. The research company found that income explained only 10% of the total variance in school satisfaction; thus, the company stated that no relationship existed between income and school satisfaction. Given the analysis described, is this a valid conclusion for the research company to make? Why?

2. A cereal manufacturer believes that there is an association between cereal sales and the number of facings the cereal has on each store's shelves. Eight stores were surveyed to test this hypothesis. The data are as follows:

Facings	Sales
5	45
6	50
6	52
7	53
5	44
7	57
6	49
8	56

a. Is there an association between shelf facings and sales?

b. Based on these data, is it appropriate to state that increased shelf facings produce additional sales? Why or why not?

c. What other variables can you think of that may help predict cereal sales?

3. The Brite-Lite Bottling Company, which provides glass bottles to various soft-drink manufacturers, has the following information pertaining to the number of cases per shipment, size of cartons, and the corresponding transportation cost:

#Cases per Shipment (00s)	Size of Carton (cubic inches)	Transportation Costs ($)
15	12	200
22	16	260
35	20	310
43	24	360
58	28	420
65	32	480
73	36	540
82	40	630
85	44	710
98	48	730

The marketing manager is interested in studying the relationship between the number of cases per shipment and the transportation costs. Your assistance is required in performing a simple regression analysis.

a. Plot the transportation costs as a function of the number of cases per shipment.

b. Interpret the scatter diagram.

c. Calculate the coefficients $\hat{\alpha}$ and $\hat{\beta}$, develop the regression equation, and interpret the coefficients.

d. Calculate the standard error of estimate and interpret it.

e. Compute the t-value with $n - 2$ degrees of freedom with the use of the following formula for the square root of the variance of the distribution of β_3:

$$s_{\hat{\beta}_1} = \sqrt{\frac{s^2_{Y/X}}{\sum\limits_{i-1}^{10}\left(X_i - \bar{x}\right)^2}}$$

$$t = \frac{\hat{\beta}_1 - \beta_1}{s_{\hat{\beta}_1}}$$

where β is assumed to be zero under the null hypothesis of no relationship; that is:

$$H_0 : \beta_1 = 0$$
$$H_0 : \beta_1 \neq 0$$

f. What is the tabled t-value at a .05 significance level?

g. What can you conclude about the relationship between transportation costs and number of cases shipped?

h. The marketing manager wants to estimate the transportation costs for 18 cases.

   i. Use the regression model to derive the average value of Y_0.

   ii. Provide a confidence interval for the estimate.

4. Using the same data, imagine the marketing manager of Brite-Lite Company wants to determine if there is an association between the size of carton and the transportation cost per shipment. (The company follows a policy of including the same-sized cartons for any particular shipment.) Refer to the previous question for information on the transportation costs per shipment and size of carton.

   a. Calculate the correlation coefficient and interpret it.

   b. Determine the coefficient of determination and interpret it.

5. Working with the Brite-Lite data, imagine the marketing manager wants to see a multiple-regression analysis with number of cartons per shipment and size of cartons as predictor variables and transportation costs as the criterion variable. The marketing researcher has devised the following regression equation:

$$\hat{Y} = \hat{\alpha}_{(12)} + \hat{\beta}_{Y1.2}X_1 + \hat{\beta}_{Y2.1}X_2 = -41.44 - 3.95X_1 + 24.44X_2$$

where X_1 is the number of cartons per shipment and X_2 is the size of the carton.

   a. Interpret $\hat{\alpha}_{(12)}$, $\hat{\beta}_{Y1.2}$, and $\hat{\beta}_{Y2.1}$.

   b. Is multiple regression appropriate in this situation? If yes, why? If no, why not?

6. An analyst for a large shoe manufacturer developed a formal linear regression model to predict sales of the firm's 122 retail stores located in different selling areas in the U.S. The model is:

$$Y_{(123)} = \alpha_{(123)} + \beta_{1.23}X_1 + \beta_{2.13}X_2 + \beta_{3.12}X_3$$

where

X_1 = population in surrounding area in thousands;

X_2 = marginal propensity to consume;

X_3 = median personal income in surrounding area in thousands of dollars;

Y = sales in thousands of dollars.

Some empirical results are as follows:

Variable	Regression Coefficient	Standard Errors
X_1	$\hat{\beta}_{1.23} = .49$	.24
X_2	$\hat{\beta}_{2.13} = -.40$	95
X_3	$\hat{\beta}_{3.12} = 225$	105
$R^2 = 0.47$	$\hat{\alpha} = -40$	225

   a. Interpret each of the regression coefficients.

   b. Are X_1, X_2, and X_3 significant at the .05 level? Show your calculations.

c. Which independent variable seems to be the most significant predictor?

d. Provide an interpretation of the R^2 value.

e. The marketing research department of the shoe manufacturer wants to include an index that indicates whether the service in each store is poor, fair, or good. The coding scheme is as follows:

1 = poor service 2 = fair service 3 = good service

   i. Indicate how you would transform this index so that it could be included in the model. Be specific.

   ii. Write out the regression model including the transformation that you developed.

   iii. Suppose that two of the parameters for the index are 4.6 and 10.3. Interpret these values in light of the scheme you adopted.

7. Carol Lynne and K. C. Lee are leaders of a popular local country and western band. Each week from late spring to early fall, the band played an outdoor concert at a different park located in the city. Advertising for the concerts consisted of handbills posted around the city on public billboards, at supermarkets, and so on. During some weeks, Carol, K. C., and the other band members were able to distribute many handbills; during other weeks, fewer were distributed. Similarly, many people attended some concerts, and only a few attended others. At the end of the summer, the band wanted to know if there were any relationship between the number of handbills that were distributed and the number of people attending its concerts. Following are the approximate number of handbills distributed each week along with the number of people attending that week's concert:

a. Develop and interpret a scatter diagram showing the number of people as a function of the number of handbills.

# Handbills	# People
900	625
550	400
750	450
300	200
600	500
1000	650
400	375
325	350
675	400
200	200
500	500
150	125
500	300
700	550
600	400

b. Calculate the coefficients $\hat{\alpha}$ and $\hat{\beta}$, and develop the regression equation using a statistical software package.

c. Interpret the coefficients and $\hat{\alpha}$ and $\hat{\beta}$. Be specific about the meaning of the terms in this situation.

d. What is the standard error of estimate, and what is its interpretation in this situation?

e. What is the t-value associated with $\hat{\beta}$? Is this value significant at the 0.05 level? If so, what can be concluded about the relationship between the number of handbills distributed and the number of people attending the concerts?

f. How much of the variance in the number of people attending the concerts can be explained by the number of handbills delivered?

g. What are some other factors that might be included in a multiple-regression model to explain the number of people attending the concerts?

Appendix: Conjoint Analysis

Questions to Guide Your Learning:

Q1: What is a variable transformation?

Q2: What's a dummy variable?

Q3: What is a conjoint analysis? How does this method help us study consumer "trade-offs"?

Q4: How do I run a conjoint analysis; specifically: What kind of data are needed, and what's the analysis procedure?

In this appendix, we focus on conjoint analysis. A number of conjoint approaches have been offered, but continuously the best-performing technique is regression-based. Hence, following our discussion of regression, we look at the machinery of a conjoint. The trick is running regressions with dummy variables. We get to dummy variables shortly, and conjoint in some detail after that, but we start with "transformations" as a more general issue.

Variable Transformations

Simple or multiple regressions should really always be called "simple linear regression" and "multiple linear regression," because each models linear relationships among variables. The scope of the regression model and its applicability may be expanded by transforming variables.

A variable transformation is simply a change in the scale in which the given variable is expressed. Consider the model

$$Y = \alpha X_1^{\beta_1} X_2^{\beta_2} X_3^{\beta_3} \varepsilon$$

in which the relationships are assumed to be multiplicative. At first glance, it would seem impossible to estimate the parameters α, β_1, β_2, β_3 using our normal least-squares procedures. However, consider the model

$$W = \ell n(Y) = \alpha' + \beta_1 Z_1 + \beta_2 Z_2 + \beta_3 Z_3 + \varepsilon'$$

This model is linear, so it can be fitted by the standard least-squares procedures, and it is exactly equivalent to our multiplicative model if we simply let:

$$W = \ell n(Y)$$
$$\alpha' = \ell n(\alpha)$$
$$Z_1 = \ell n(X_1)$$
$$Z_2 = \ell n(X_2)$$
$$Z_3 = \ell n(X_3)$$
$$\varepsilon' = \ell n(\varepsilon)$$

Thus, we have converted a nonlinear model to a linear model using variable transformations. To solve for the parameters of our multiplicative model, we simply:

1. Take the natural log of Y and each of the Xs
2. Solve the resulting equation by the normal least-squares procedures
3. Take the antilog of α' (raise ε to α' power) to derive an estimate of α; and
4. Read the values of the β_i, because they are the same in both models.

This transformation involved both the criterion and predictor variables. It is also possible to change the scale of either the criterion or predictor variables. Exponential and logarithmic transformations are some of the most useful, because they serve to relax the constraints imposed by the assumptions that the relationship between the criterion variable and the predictor variables is linear and additive, and that the errors are homoscedastic (constant for all values of the predictors).[1]

In the next section, we discuss dummy variables. They offer another form of transformation, to allow for nonlinear relationships and categorical or rank-order variables in regression problems.

Dummy Variables

The analysis of the sales data from the previous chapter is not complete. No attention was given to the effect of distribution on sales, as measured by the wholesaler

---

[1] See David Layton, "Alternative Approaches for Modeling Concave Willingness to Pay Functions in Conjoint Valuation," *American Journal of Agricultural Economics* 83 (2001), pp. 1314–1320; Dean W. Wichern and Richard A. Johnson, *Applied Multivariate Statistical Analysis,* 5th ed. (Prentice-Hall, 2002).

efficiency index. One way of considering the effect of wholesaler efficiency on sales is to introduce the index directly; i.e., the X_3 value for each observation is simply the value recorded in the last column of the data set. Letting X_3 represent the wholesaler efficiency index, the multiple-regression equation is:

$$Y = \alpha + \beta_1 X_1 + \beta_2 X_2 + \beta_3 X_3 + \varepsilon$$

The least-squares estimate of β_3 in this equation turns out to be $\hat{\beta}_3 = 11.5$. If the predictor variables are independent, this beta means that the estimated average change in sales is $11,500 for each unit change in the wholesaler efficiency index. Thus a fair distributor could be expected to sell $11,500 more on the average than a poor one; a good one could be expected to average $11,500 more than a fair one; and an excellent one could be expected to sell $11,500 more on the average than a good one. The sales increments are assumed to be constant for each change in wholesaler rating. The implication is that the wholesaler efficiency index is an interval-scaled variable and that the difference between a poor and a fair wholesaler is the same as the difference between a fair one and a good one. You might not be comfortable with this assumption for rating scales.

An alternative way of proceeding is to convert the rating index into a set of dummy variables or, more appropriately, binary variables. A binary variable is one that takes on one of two values, 0 or 1. Binary variables are very flexible; they can provide a numerical representation for attributes or characteristics that are not essentially quantitative. For example, one could introduce gender into a regression equation using the dummy variable X_i, where

$X_i = 0$ if the person is female
$X_i = 1$ if the person is male

The technique is readily extendable to handle multichotomous as well as dichotomous classifications. For instance, suppose that one wanted to introduce the variable social class into a regression equation, and there were three distinct class levels: upper, middle, and lower class. This could be handled using two dummy variables, say, X_1 and X_2, where

	X_1	X_2
• If a person belongs to the upper class	1	0
• If a person belongs to the middle class	0	1
• If a person belongs to the lower class	0	0

Given that alternative coding schemes could be used (e.g., X_1 to denote middle class and X_2 to denote lower class), it is important that the interpretation be tied back to the coding of the variables. A classification with m categories is unambiguous when represented by a set of $m-1$ binary variables; an mth dummy variable is superfluous.

Suppose that we were to employ three dummy variables to represent the four-category wholesaler efficiency index in the sales model and that

	X_3	X_4	X_5
• If a wholesaler is poor	0	0	0
• If a wholesaler is fair	1	0	0
• If a wholesaler is good	0	1	0
• If a wholesaler is excellent	0	0	1

The regression model is:

$$Y = \alpha + \beta_1 X_1 + \beta_2 X_2 + \beta_3 X_3 + \beta_4 X_4 + \beta_5 X_5 + \varepsilon$$

The least-squares estimates of the wholesaler efficiency parameters are:

$$\hat{\beta}_3 = 9.2 \qquad \hat{\beta}_4 = 20.3 \qquad \hat{\beta}_5 = 33.3$$

These coefficients indicate that on the average, a fair wholesaler could be expected to sell $9,200 more than a poor one, a good wholesaler could be expected to sell $20,300 more than a poor one, and an excellent wholesaler could sell $33,300 more than a poor one. Note that all these coefficients are interpreted with respect to the baseline which has the codes of {0, 0, 0} ("poor" in this case).[2]

The coefficient differences tell us about the difference in sales effectiveness. The estimated difference in expected sales from a good wholesaler and a fair wholesaler is: $\hat{\beta}_4 - \hat{\beta}_3 = 20.3 - 9.2 = 11.1$ (that is, $11,100). Similarly, an excellent wholesaler could be expected on the average to sell $\hat{\beta}_5 - \hat{\beta}_4 = 33.3 - 20.3 = 13.0$ (i.e., $13,000) more than a good one.

The use of dummy variables indicates that the relationship between sales and the wholesaler efficiency index is not linear as was assumed when the index was introduced as a single interval-scaled variable. Instead of an across-the-board increase of $11,500 with each rating change, the respective increases are 9.2 ($9,200) from poor to fair, 11.1 ($11,100) from fair to good, and 13.0 ($13,000) from good to excellent.

Conjoint Analysis

A very special implementation of a dummy variable regression is conjoint analysis, or conjoint measurement. Consumers make judgments about preferences among products or brands, where the products or brands they're responding to represent some systematic combinations of attributes. The goal is to determine the features that respondents most prefer. Consumers might use such attributes as miles per gallon, seating capacity, price, length of warranty, and so on in making judgments about which automobile they prefer. Yet, if asked to do so directly, many respondents find it difficult to state which attributes they were thinking about and how they were combining them to form overall judgments. Rather than trying to obtain a sense of which attributes are important directly from consumers' self reports, consumers are simply asked for their preferences and their value systems are inferred from those choices.

The word conjoint has to do with the notion that the relative values of things considered jointly can be measured when they might not be measurable if taken one at a time. Typically respondents would be asked to order the stimuli (products, brands, etc.) from most to least desirable. In doing so, the consumer implies the relative value of the features that compose the various stimuli. The conjoint analysis assigns values to the levels of each of the attributes that describe consumer's opinions. Research Realities 17A.1 offers a sampling of the questions marketing researchers have answered using conjoint techniques.

---

[2] For alternative ways of coding dummy variables and the different insights obtained, see Jacob Cohen, Patricia Cohen, Stephen West and Leona Aiken, *Applied Multiple Regression/Correlation Analysis for the Behavioral Sciences*, 3rd ed. (Erlbaum, 2002); Melissa A. Hardy, *Regression with Dummy Variables* (Sage, 1993).

Research Realities

17A.1 Applications of Conjoint Analysis in Marketing Research

Conjoint analysis is extremely popular in marketing research. The data are easy to get, and it's easy to run the analyses. The results are usually easily interpretable and they may be immediately implemented. New product design is easily the most frequent application of conjoint analysis in marketing.

- Lands' End may be the first apparel retailer to have used conjoint. They surveyed customers, presenting six pairs of outfits, asking which of each pair was preferred. From these data were derived customized combinations of features more personally tailored to each respondent's preferences, e.g., button-down, cotton vs. wool sweaters, color, price, etc. The intention clearly is to enhance the customer's satisfaction, including ease of Web transactions.[3]
- Polaroid used Web-based conjoint surveys to design its i-Zone. One of the features most valued on these sticker-photo instant cameras among the target young teen customers was the changeable face plate, to choose their own expression of cool.[4]
- Pending the possible introduction of three new types of vaccines, researchers studied parents' willingness to pay for their children to be vaccinated with one of the three new products. Product profiles varied by "type of infection covered," "duration of coverage," and "price," producing 18 combinations in all for examination.[5]

Conjoint analysis easily lends itself to studies of segmentation. Instead of segments being formed on the basis of demographic data, which often have little predictive power, consumers' preferences through the conjoint task can result in different profiles of utilities estimated for the different groups. Thus, different segments of customers can appreciate different elements of a product offering. For example:

- Companies struggling to satisfy both demanding customers and public policy issues regarding the environment have examined differences in the utilities attached to product features by their customers. Segments of "green" customers attach greater benefit to environmentally friendly products, for some purchases, to the point of being price insensitive, compared with "ordinary" customers who are not likely to value the green or energy-saving product sufficiently to pay more for it.[6]
- In a study across product categories, customers were segmented by the values and benefits they sought in their purchases:[7]
  - Customers seeking luxury cars have been segmented into groups that care about: (i) safety and service, (ii) smooth ride, (iii) safety and interior/exterior design, etc.
  - Consumers purchasing laundry detergent fall into groups that look for: (i) clothes protection and (ii) fragrance.
  - Credit card users may be segmented by the services they desire: (i) fees and interest, (ii) credit line, or (iii) both.

In addition, conjoint has been used to study:

- Pricing—it's actually very difficult to obtain data on price sensitivities via regular surveys. When asked what price we're willing to pay for some product, we all choose the lowest possibility offered. In conjoint however, whereas our preferences might begin with low prices, the advantage of studying "trade-offs" means that at some point, we must either pay more to get more, or continue to pay less but get even less.[8]
- As management increasingly demands financial indicators of success, conjoint researchers too are modeling direct and indirect links of product attributes to market value. This task is, not surprisingly, very difficult, given that it consists of tying individual conjoint responses to macro measures of the marketplace, such as potential for market expansion, heterogeneity in customer preferences and segmentation, planning for competitive pricing response, etc.[9]

---

[3] David Lipke, "Product by Design," *American Demographics* 23 (2001), pp. 38–41.

[4] Rick Whiting, "Virtual Focus Group," *Information Week* (July 30, 2001), pp. 53–58.

[5] Claudine Sapede and Isabelle Girod, "Willingness of Adults in Europe to Pay for a New Vaccine," *International Journal of Market Research* 44 (2002), pp. 463–476.

[6] Chialin Chen, "Design for the Environment," *Management Science* 47 (2001), pp. 250–263.

[7] Howard Moskowitz, Bert Krieger and Samuel Rabino, "Element Category Importance in Conjoint Analysis: Evidence for Segment Differences," *Journal of Targeting, Measurement and Analysis for Marketing* 10 (2002), pp. 366–384.

[8] David Lyon, "The Price Is Right (or Is It?)," *Marketing Research* 14 (2002), pp. 8–13; Kamel Jedidi and John Zhang, "Augmenting Conjoint Analysis to Estimate Consumer Reservation Price," *Management Science* 48 (2002), pp. 1350–1368; also see Tulin Erdem, Joffre Swait and Jordan Louviere "The Impact of Brand Credibility on Consumer Price Sensitivity," *International Journal of Research in Marketing* 19 (2002), pp. 1–19.

[9] Elie Ofek and V. Srinivasan, "How Much Does the Market Value an Improvement in a Product Attribute?" *Marketing Science* 21 (2002), pp. 398–411.

Example

Suppose that we are considering introducing a new coffee maker and wish to assess how consumers evaluate the following levels of each of these product attributes:

- Capacity—4, 8, and 10 cups
- Price—$28, $32, and $38
- Brewing time—3, 6, 9, and 12 minutes

For all three of these attributes, most consumers would probably prefer either the most or least of each property—the largest capacity maker, the shortest brewing time, at the lowest price. Unfortunately, life is not that simple. The larger coffee maker costs more to manufacture; faster brewing means a larger heating element for the same pot capacity, which also raises the cost; a larger-capacity maker with no change in the heating element requires increased brewing time. In sum, a consumer is going to have to *trade off* some of one feature to obtain more of another. The manufacturer is interested in determining how consumers value these specific attributes. Is low price most valued, or are consumers willing to pay a higher price to secure some of the other features? At what price should the coffee maker go to market, and with what other attributes?

To answer these questions, we might form all possible combinations of these product attributes, 36 combinations in all, and describe each coffee maker on an index card or a separate computer screen. We would then ask a respondent to order these product descriptions from least desirable (rank = 1) to most desirable (rank = 36), with higher numbers reflecting greater preference. Suppose that the ordering contained in Table 17A.1 resulted from this process.

Note several things about these entries. As we anticipated, the respondent preferred least the $38 maker with 4-cup capacity and 12 minutes brewing time (rank = 1) and preferred most the 10-cup maker with 3 minutes brewing time priced at $28 (rank = 36). Second, if the respondent cannot have his/her 1st choice, s/he is willing to "suffer" with a longer brewing time to get the 10-cup maker for $28 (rank = 35). The consumer is not willing to suffer too much, though, as reflected by the 3rd choice (rank = 34). Rather, the consumer is willing to pay a little more to secure the faster 3-minute brewing time rather than having to endure an even slower 9-minute brewing time, in effect, showing a willingness to trade off price for brewing time.

The type of question that conjoint analysis attempts to answer is: What are the individual's utilities for price, brewing time, and pot capacity in determining preferences and choices?

TABLE 17A.1
Respondent Ordering of
Product Descriptions

Brewing Time (minutes)	Capacity: 4 cups			8 cups			10 cups		
	Price $28	$32	$38	$28	$32	$38	$28	$32	$38
3 mins	17	15	6	30	26	24	36	34	28
6 mins	16	12	5	29	25	22	35	33	27
9 mins	9	8	3	21	20	8	32	31	23
12 mins	4	2	1	14	13	7	19	18	11

Procedure

Several analytical procedures have been used to determine an individual's utilities for each of several product attributes in a conjoint analysis. Some techniques depend on the availability of somewhat esoteric software. In these programs, the computer begins with random starting values for the utility estimates (or "part-worth functions") and iteratively converges in modifying those utility estimates until they predict the consumer's preferences within some tolerable margin of error.

However, increasingly, dummy variable regressions are being used to estimate the components of a conjoint analysis. The consumer's preferences (e.g., the judgments of 1 through 36) would form the dependent variable, and dummy variables representing the attributes (such as price) would comprise the predictors. The advantages of the dummy variable regression approach include:

- The wide availability of regression software
- The wide understanding and accessibility of regression as a model
- Demonstrable robustness and comparable results of the dummy variable approach compared to alternative, more sophisticated approaches

To demonstrate, suppose we create dummy variables for each of the attributes:

$X_1 = 1$ if brewing time = 6 minutes (otherwise, $X_1 = 0$),
$X_2 = 1$ if brewing time = 9 minutes
$X_3 = 1$ if brewing time = 12 minutes
$Y_1 = 1$ if capacity = 8 cups
$Y_2 = 1$ if capacity = 10 cups
$Z_1 = 1$ if price = \$32
$Z_2 = 1$ if price = \$38

and fit a regression model to the preference judgments:

$$\text{Predicted Preference} = \beta_1 X_1 + \beta_2 X_2 + \beta_3 X_3 + \beta_4 Y_1 + \beta_5 Y_2 + \beta_6 Z_1 + \beta_7 Z_2$$

The beta weights reflect the consumer's utilities of the attributes. If an attribute did not matter, the beta estimate would be zero (i.e., changing the feature would have no impact on the predicted preference rating). The larger the beta, the more utility the attribute has—the more the consumer cares about it.

For example, fitting a regression to the data in Table 17A.1 yields the following estimates:

$$\text{Predicted Preference} = -0/06 X_1 - 0.28 X_2 - 0.59 X_3 + 0.53 Y_1 + 0.86 Y_2 - 0.09 Z_1 - 0.36 Z_2$$

That is, we have obtained the following utilities for each level of these attributes:

Brewing Time		Capacity		Price	
3 minutes	0	4 cups	0	$28	0
6 minutes	−0.06	8 cups	0.53	$32	20.09
9 minutes	−0.28	10 cups	0.86	$38	20.36
12 minutes	−0.59				

Most often, a simple additive function is used so that the utility of any combination of features is simply the sum of the utilities of the attribute levels making up the combination. Thus, a 10-cup, 9-minute brewing time, $32 pot would have a utility of .49 (.49 = .86 − .28 − .09). The utilities for each of the other alternatives are shown in Table 17A.2.

These utilities may be plotted against the original judgments to see how well the estimated utilities anticipate the consumer's overall preferences. A measure of the goodness of prediction can be obtained by computing the correlation between the original judgments (the data in Table 17A.1) and the predicted utilities (the values in Table 17A.2). For these data, the utilities have captured the preference structure of the consumer very well, r = .99.

In addition, the utility estimates themselves may be plotted to examine whether the relationships between the levels of each attribute and the utility consumers place on the levels are linear or nonmonotonic. The utility estimates for capacity and price look approximately linear: more cups are better than fewer, and less expensive is better than more expensive. Brewing time is slightly quadratic—as waiting time increases, utility drops off faster; thus, a seemingly benign decision to go to market with a brewing time of 12 minutes versus 9 will lose more potential customers than the analogous decision of going to market with 9 minutes versus 6.

The relative importance of each of these attributes can be understood by examining the range of utilities between the highest- and lowest-rated levels of the attribute. The rationale is that, if all levels of, say, price have the same utility to an individual, then we would say that price is unimportant to the person or that the person was price insensitive. Conversely, if different levels of price produce widely differing utilities, the individual is sensitive to the levels, implying the attribute is important. In interpreting these importance values, one has to remain cognizant that they depend on the range of the attributes used to structure the stimuli. Thus, if price levels of $28, $38, and $48 were used instead of $28, $32, and $38, the differences in utilities for the various price levels would have been greater, suggesting that price was relatively more important to the individual than other attributes. Given the attribute levels used, capacity is most important and price is least important to the subject.

> Conjoint analysis tells us what *features* matter most and what *level* of each feature is most (and least) desired.

TABLE 17A.2
Utilities for Feature Combinations

Brewing Time (minutes)	Capacity: 4 cups			8 cups			10 cups		
	Price $28	$32	$38	$28	$32	$38	$28	$32	$38
3 mins	.00	−0.9	−.36	.53	.44	.17	.86	.77	.50
6 mins	−.06	−.15	−.42	.47	.38	.11	.80	.71	.44
9 mins	−.28	−.37	−.64	.25	.16	−.11	.58	.49	.22
12 mins	−.59	−.68	−.95	−.06	−.15	−.42	.27	.18	−.09

The real payoff from conjoint analysis comes from the fact that one can use the results to identify the optimal levels and importance of each attribute in structuring a new-product offering. Further, by aggregating consumers who have similar preferences or utility functions, products can be designed that come closer to satisfying particular market segments. Thus, conjoint analysis is quite useful at the concept-evaluation stage of the product-development process.

Key Decisions

The example illustrates a conjoint analysis study, but it is a simple example and does not convey a proper appreciation for the many decisions analysts typically have to make to conduct a conjoint study. Figure 17A.1 highlights the more critical decision points.

SELECT ATTRIBUTES

The first step in the process involves deciding on the attributes to be used when constructing the stimuli. When choosing, marketers should be guided by the principles that the attributes used should be both actionable and important to individuals. Actionable attributes are those that the company can do something about; that is, it has the technology or resources to make the changes that might be indicated by consumer preferences. Important attributes are those that actually affect consumer choice, as determined by managerial judgment or exploratory research. In any single conjoint study, only a handful of all the attributes that could be used are used, so it is important that they be selected with care. When the number of attributes that need to be varied exceed reasonable limits with respect to data-collection problems, a series of conjoint studies can be conducted. The number of attributes actually used in a typical conjoint analysis study averages six or seven.

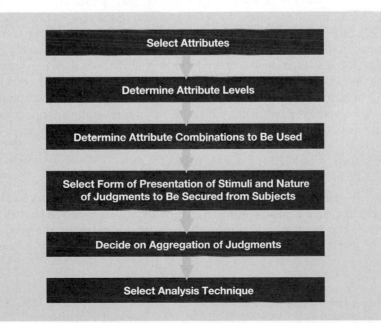

FIGURE 17A.1
Key Decisions when Conducting a Conjoint Analysis

DETERMINE ATTRIBUTE LEVELS

Step 2 involves specifying the actual levels for each attribute. The number of levels for each attribute has a direct bearing on the number of stimuli respondents will be asked to judge and consequently on the burden placed on each consumer. In general, we like to minimize that burden (both for the goodwill of interacting with that consumer as well as to try to maximize the quality of the data that the consumer gives us). At the same time, we like to end up with good estimates of the utility of each attribute level. Our ability to generate good estimates requires that the number of stimuli be relatively large versus the number of parameters that need to be estimated, and the number of parameters in turn depends on the preference model being embraced. Is the model linear in the sense that more or less of the attribute can be expected to be most desired, or is it nonlinear in a systematic way, or could there be a nonsystematic relationship between preference and attribute levels? Most subjects may prefer the lowest price or the highest quality when choosing a ballpoint pen, suggesting a linear relationship between their utilities and the attribute levels. At the same time, many may prefer a medium point to a fine or broad point, suggesting that a smooth nonlinear relationship may be appropriate. The nonlinear model requires the estimation of more parameters than the linear model, and, other things being equal, we like more stimuli when estimating it than when estimating the parameters of the linear model.

When creating stimuli for a conjoint judgment task, marketers also need to be aware that there is a relationship between the number of levels used to measure an attribute and the inferred importance of the attribute to the respondent. Specifically, the empirical evidence suggests that the more levels one uses for an attribute, the more important the attribute is going to appear in the results of the conjoint.[10] Although analysts might want to include more levels for those attributes expected to produce nonlinear versus linear utility functions, they also need to be aware of the erroneous conclusion this can produce about the importance of each of the attributes.

Another factor that affects the choice of attribute levels is their effect on consumer choice. Using levels that are similar to those in existence increases respondents' believability in the task and the validity of their preference judgments. Using attribute levels outside the range normally encountered decreases the believability of the task for respondents but can increase the accuracy by which the parameters can be estimated statistically. Similarly, decreasing the intercorrelations among the attributes being varied (such as by combining a very low price with very high quality) decreases the believability of the options for respondents but also increases the accuracy with which the parameters can be estimated. The general recommendation seems to be to make the ranges for the various attributes somewhat larger than what is normally found but not so large as to make the options unbelievable.

DETERMINE ATTRIBUTE COMBINATIONS

The third major decision is deciding on the specific combinations of attributes that will be used—that is, what the full set of stimuli will look like. In our example, only three attributes were considered, but the respondent was required to make 36 judgments. Since the number of possible combinations is given by the product of the number of levels of the attributes, one can readily appreciate what happens to the

---

[10] Dick Wittink, Joel Huber, Peter Zandan and Richard Johnson, "The Number of Levels Effect in Conjoint," *Sawtooth Software Research Paper Series,* http://www.sawtoothsoftware.com.

judgment task if the number of attributes or the number of levels for any attribute is increased. Can we reasonably expect a respondent, for example, to provide meaningful judgments if there are five attributes at three levels each (not an unusual case) requiring $3 \times 3 \times 3 \times 3 \times 3 = 3^5 = 243$ rank-order judgments? In such a situation, analysts might be tempted to reduce the number of attributes that are varied (e.g., 3^4) or the number of levels (2^5) at which attributes are set. An alternative scheme is to use only select combinations of the attributes. For example, it is possible to use orthogonal designs to select a subset of the total number of stimuli if the analyst is willing to assume that there are no interactions among the attributes (e.g., that a person's utility for various width tips on a ballpoint pen is independent of the utility for prices).[11]

The example used the "full-profile" approach to collect the judgments—all possible combinations of each of the attributes resulted in its own stimulus. One can simplify the judgment task by using a trade-off matrix to structure the stimuli instead of the full-profile approach.[12] The trade-off matrix, or pair-wise procedure, treats two attributes at a time but considers all possible pairs. Thus, in the example, the subject would be asked to indicate preference between each combination of brewing time and price, brewing time and capacity, and price and capacity by independently completing each of the matrices contained in Figure 17A.2.

It is typically easier for subjects to supply pair-wise judgments than full-profile judgments. On the other hand, typically, more pair-wise judgments are required, and one runs a danger of missing some important trade-offs among attributes when the pair-wise approach to data collection is used. There can also be a potential loss in realism when only two attributes are considered at a time, because respondents are then forced to make some implicit assumptions about the levels of the other attributes not explicitly varied. The full-profile approach tends to be more popular than the pair-wise approach in practice.

FIGURE 17A.2 Pair-wise Approach to Data Collection in Conjoint Analysis

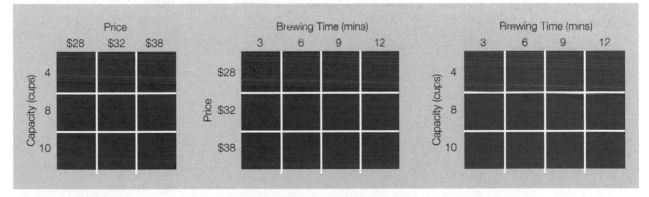

[11] Orthogonal designs of combinations can produce significant economies in the number of stimuli that respondents need to evaluate, Zsolt Sandor and Michel Wedel, "Profile Construction in Experimental Choice Designs for Mixed Logit Models," *Marketing Science* 21 (2002), pp. 455–476; Gianni Cicia, Teresa Del Giudice and Riccardo Scarpa, "Consumers' Perception of Quality in Organic Food," *British Food Journal* 104 (2002), pp. 200–213.

[12] Joel Huber, "What We Have Learned from 20 Years in Conjoint Research," *Sawtooth Software Research Paper Series,* http://www.sawtoothsoftware.com.

Another approach uses paired comparisons. An advantage of the paired-comparison approach is that it allows one to check how consistent respondents are in their judgments. Thus, unmotivated or uninterested respondents (those whose answers display a great deal of inconsistency, which suggests that the respondents are not taking the task seriously) can be removed from the analysis. Respondents simply indicate which stimulus in each pair they prefer and by how much. Figure 17A.3, for example, depicts one pair of coffee makers.

Increasingly, any of these data-collection approaches are being administered via computer, which have several advantages:

- The judgments requested from a respondent can be made individual-specific, with different attributes and attribute levels used for each consumer/segment. Thus, respondents can be interviewed in detail about only those attribute levels that would be acceptable to them and about only those attributes that they regard as relatively important.
- The number of judgments required from an individual can be reduced because the parameters can be estimated iteratively, as soon as a sufficient number of judgments are obtained. Further, the additional judgments required from a respondent can be structured to provide the most incremental information, taking into account what is already known about the respondent's utilities.
- Results can be shown to respondents immediately at the end of the exercise. They can be given the opportunity to comment on how realistically the estimates seem to mirror their preferences. The results can also be given to management more quickly.

FIGURE 17A.3
Computer-Administered
Paired-Comparison
Choice

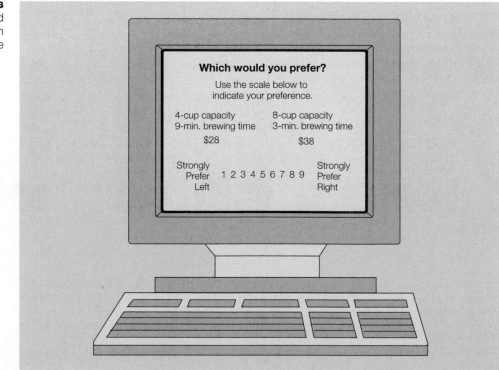

SELECT FORM OF PRESENTATION OF STIMULI AND NATURE OF JUDGMENTS

Step 4 in the process involves selecting the form of presentation of the stimuli and the nature of the judgments to be collected from subjects. The full-profile approach has used variations and combinations of three basic approaches—verbal description, paragraph description, and pictorial representation. Verbal description relies on presenting the cues in list form, typically one stimulus per screen, much as was assumed in the coffee-maker example. Paragraph description operates just as the name implies; a paragraph is used to describe each stimulus. Pictorial description relies on some kind of visual prop or three-dimensional model. When visual aids are used, they are typically used in combination with verbal descriptions.

Related to the issue of the form of presentation of the stimuli is the issue of the nature of the judgments that will be secured from respondents. The two most common approaches measure respondents' preferences for each alternative or their intention to buy each alternative. In the earliest applications of conjoint analysis, respondents were asked to rank-order the alternatives according to preference or intention to buy, but rating scales have recently become more popular. Some of the advantages of rankings are their ease of use by consumers, ease of administration, and a desire to keep the judgment task as close as possible to a consumer's behavior while actually shopping. Those using rating scales believe that they are less time consuming, more convenient for respondents to use, and easier to analyze. The nature of the task is different in the two schemes. When the rank-order method is used, consumers are asked to make relative judgments with respect to their preference for one alternative over another. When the rating method is used, the judgments are typically made independently—consumers are asked to indicate their degree of liking of each stimulus by rating their preference or intention-to-buy as each alternative is presented.

DECIDE ON AGGREGATION OF JUDGMENTS

Step 5 involves deciding if the responses from individual consumers will be aggregated and, if so, how? Although it is possible to derive the utilities for each level of each attribute at the individual level, much as we did in the example, individual-level results are very difficult for marketing managers to use for developing marketing strategy. The other extreme is to pool the results across all consumers and then to estimate one overall utility function. This option fails to recognize any heterogeneity in preference that might exist among respondents, which in turn reduces the predictive power of the model. The middle ground is to form segments or groups of respondents in such a way that the model has both predictive power and clear marketing strategy implications for managers. The question, of course, is how these groups should be formed.[13] Typically, segments are formed that are homogeneous with respect to the benefits that the respondents want from the product or service. Operationally, this goal translates into estimating utilities for the individual-level models and then clustering respondents into groups that are homogeneous with respect to the utilities assigned to the various levels of the individual attributes.

An attractive feature of conjoint analysis is that it allows market share predictions for selected product alternatives. For example, a common choice rule is the

---

[13] See Abba Krieger, Paul Green and U. Umesh, "Effect of Level of Disaggregation on Conjoint Cross Validations, *Decision Sciences* 29 (1998), pp. 1047–1058; Rick Andrews, Asim Ansari and Imran Currim, "Hierarchical Bayes vs. Finite Mixture Conjoint Analysis Models, *Journal of Marketing Research* 39 (2002), pp. 87–98.

"1st-choice rule," which assumes that, if the consumer had been shopping, he or she would choose to buy the object that he or she had rated highest in terms of preference. Given the estimated utilities for each level of each attribute, the marketer can predict which of several product options being considered is likely to appeal most to respondents and what may also be the share of preference for each of the other options. The utilities can also be linked with consumers' personal characteristics, e.g., do high-income households have a higher utility for after-sale service than low-income households? Research Realities 17A.2, for example, describes how marketing researchers used conjoint analysis to help design the EZPass system for New York and New Jersey.

SELECT ANALYSIS TECHNIQUE

Step 6 in the execution of a conjoint analysis study involves selecting the technique by which the input data will be analyzed. The choice depends in part on the type of preference model embraced and the method that was used to secure the input judgments. When linear or smooth nonlinear models are hypothesized to capture preference, a parameter estimation model like regression can be used to estimate the functions. When an irregular model is assumed, utilities need to be estimated for each level of each attribute, using dummy variables in regression, as described in the example, or a related technique like the analysis of variance. When rank-order data have been obtained, the assumption of a linear relationship may be dubious, so a nonmetric, monotonic regression model may be substituted to estimate the utilities.

GENERAL COMMENTS

It is only after the marketing researcher has made decisions about each of the steps listed in Figure 17A.1 that the data can actually be collected for a conjoint analysis study. Unfortunately, beginning researchers have a propensity to hurry into the data-collection task. Interrelationships among the many decisions need to be made, and rushing into the data-collection effort before the interrelated choices are all spelled out can only result in sub-optimizing some of the choices. For example, one technique that has become popular in recent years is obtaining conjoint responses to a limited set (usually three to nine) of full profiles drawn from a larger master set and combining that information with other information that respondents directly provide about the relative importance to them of each of the attributes and which levels of each attribute they prefer. Called hybrid models, the essential purpose is to combine the simplicity of the self-explicated approach to attribute measurement with the greater generality of conjoint models.[14]

Conjoint analysis addresses vital marketing questions in product design, and the technique is not restricted to product evaluations. It can be used whenever one is making a choice among multiattribute alternatives. With multiattribute alternatives, the consumer typically does not have the option of having more of everything that is desirable and less of everything that is not desirable. Instead, most decisions involve trading off part of something in order to get more of something else. Conjoint analysis attempts to mirror the trade-offs a consumer is willing to make. The modeling is rather straightforward, and the payoff (the results) is highly informative, making conjoint among the more popular of marketing research tools. It is most often used

---

[14] See Frenkel Ter Hofstede, Youngchan Kim and Michel Wedel, "Bayesian Prediction in Hybrid Conjoint Analysis, *Journal of Marketing Research* 39 (2002), pp. 253–261; Paul Green and Abba Krieger, "What's Right with Conjoint?" *Marketing Research* 14 (2002), pp. 24–27.

Research Realities

17A.2 Using Conjoint Analysis to Assess Consumer Response to a New Tollway Technology

A task force composed of seven transportation agencies in New York and New Jersey commissioned a study to understand their commuters' likely reaction to and adoption of "EZPass," a form of electronic toll collection. Electronic toll systems work through high frequency radio waves that are transmitted from a small "tag" or transponder mounted on a vehicle's inside windshield to an antenna in a toll booth lane as the vehicle proceeds through the lane. The information transmitted identifies the vehicle number, and the toll is debited from the owner's account.

Electronic toll collection systems have enjoyed great success in Texas, Louisiana, and Florida, where drivers extol the benefits of not needing to stop to manually pay the tolls (the vehicle can proceed through the lane up to 30 or 40 m.p.h.). As a result, traffic congestion culminating near the toll booths is alleviated. In addition, drivers need not fumble for change, and fleet operators need not advance cash to their drivers nor worry about cash reimbursements.

With such encouraging results as secondary data, the New York and New Jersey transportation groups were planning on following suit and implementing such a system. However, an electronic toll system could be designed with a variety of features, and marketing researchers were brought in to distill those features that commuters cared about the most, and determine what the optimal system might look like.

A study was designed to pretest "consumers' acceptance of and preference for a different way of paying tolls at roadways, bridges, and tunnels." A conjoint study was considered best suited to address these questions.

Different methodologies of data collection were considered for the conjoint. Providing "verbal descriptions" of the EZPass system (and then requesting ratings from the commuters) was deemed inadequate because the system was too complex and novel to express clearly in a written statement. Ideally, the researchers would have liked to set up a "demonstration toll plaza," but product trial on this scale was of course considered impractical. Researchers ultimately elected to send a videotape that contained an 11-minute "infomercial" that described the system, demonstrated its use, and explained how traffic flow would be improved, as had been experienced at other systems throughout the U.S.

After viewing the video that described the general EZPass system, commuters would be asked to judge their preferences among specific variants on the system. With much consultation, the researchers were able to whittle down the number of attributes thought to be important (by the commissioning agencies) to these seven:

1. How many facilities would the user need to open an EZPass account with, and therefore, how many periodic invoices would the user receive?
2. How and where would a user apply and pay for a new EZPass account?
3. How many lanes would be available for EZPass at a typical toll plaza and how would they be controlled?
4. Would the EZPass tag be transferable to different vehicles?
5. What would be the acquisition cost (if any) for EZPass and would there be a periodic service charge?
6. What would be the toll price be with EZPass?
7. What other uses, if any, such as parking at local airports or purchasing gasoline, would commuters find valuable for EZPass?

A subset of 49 of the possible configurations of these features formed the product descriptions used in the study. Each commuter would be asked to rate 7 of these 49 plus another "control" option (to enable comparison across the samples).

Next, sampling was considered. Each of the seven sponsoring agencies wanted data from representatives of their commuting regions. In addition, it was thought prudent to survey some commuters who regularly used several specific facilities (e.g., the George Washington Bridge, the Holland and Lincoln tunnels, and the three Staten Island bridges). Altogether, 13 sectors were delineated, and 250 commuters were sampled from each group.

Random-digit dialing was used to solicit cooperation. Households indicating that they would participate were sent a videotape and survey. The survey responses were conveyed over the phone, either to an 800-phone number printed on the survey, or by the researchers calling the commuters' home phone number again at a later date. Researchers recruited 6,500 commuters, and obtained responses from 3,369, for a rather high response rate of 52%.

Conjoint analysis indicated commuters' clear prioritization among the features, as indicated in Table 17A.A. The number of lanes and their control was the most important feature (21%). The New York and New Jersey agencies had anticipated that commuters would be concerned about the acquisition cost but were surprised to see that it was of only moderate importance (15%). Commuters did care about the price of the toll (18%), however. Commuters showed little concern for the multiple uses for the device (4%).

In addition to yielding diagnostic information as to what features are more important than others, marketing researchers were also able to provide information on which levels of each feature were deemed most desirable. For example, for the feature of acquisitions costs, the researchers had explored four levels. They derived utilities from the conjoint analysis that represented commuters' preferences for each level of this factor, as illustrated in Table 17A.B. These results indicated that the first option was most desirable, the fourth option least desirable, and commuters were indifferent between their second and third choices.

The overall conjoint results demonstrated which features should be emphasized and which could be de-emphasized in the design of the electronic toll system. System designers also studied the utilities of each of the features to provide the attribute that commuters most wanted. Finally, the marketing researchers also used the conjoint results as input to a series of simulations to forecast demand and usage of the system during its first year. Cool, huh?

(continued)

TABLE 17A.A

EZPass System Feature	Importance (in %)
How many lanes would be available and how would they be controlled?	21
Price of toll with EZPass	18
How and where a user would apply & pay for a new EZPass account	17
Acquisition cost for EZPass and periodic service charges	15
# EZPass accounts necessary / # periodic invoices received	13
Would the EZPass tag be transferable to different vehicles?	12
Other potential uses for the EZPass tag	4

TABLE 17A.B

Implementation Level of Acquisition Costs	Utility
$10 deposit + $15 yearly service charge	.68
$2 per month service charge	.48
$10 charge + $1.50 per month service charge	.43
$40 credit card charge if tag not returned + $20 annual fee	.10

Source: Terry G. Vavra, Paul E. Green and Abba M. Krieger, "Evaluating EZPass: Using Conjoint Analysis to Assess Consumer Response to a New Tollway Technology," *Marketing Research* 11 (1999), pp. 5–13; John F. Nash, Jr., "Ideal Money," *Southern Economic Journal* 69 (2002), pp. 4–12; Gail Dutton, "Updating the Pennsylvania Turnpike and Moving into the EZPass Lane," *World Trade* (2003), p. 32.

for product design and concept evaluation, in applications such as airlines, credit cards, pantyhose, pharmaceuticals, and even highway EZPass systems. Conjoint studies are also used regularly in pricing decisions, market segmentation questions, or advertising decisions. Finally conjoint analysis has been used to make distribution decisions, evaluate vendors, determine the rewards that a sales force values, and determine consumer preferences for attributes of health organizations, among other things.[15]

Summary

Variable transformations increase the scope of regression models, because they allow certain nonlinear relationships to be considered. Dummy or binary variables allow the introduction of nominal variables in the regression equation.

Conjoint analysis may be viewed as a special application of dummy variable regression, and it is an extremely powerful marketing tool for the planning of product development.

---

[15] For more on conjoint analysis, see Dick McCullough, "A User's Guide to Conjoint Analysis," *Marketing Research* 14 (2002), pp. 19–24; Pablo Marshall and Eric Bradlow "A Unified Approach to Conjoint Analysis Models," *Journal of the American Statistical Association* 97 (Sept. 2002), pp. 674–682. For more on conjoint programs (for data collection and analysis), go to http://www.sawtoothsoftware.com, http://www.spss.com, http://www.dssrearch.com/library/conjoint. Also see Bryan Orme, "Analysis of Traditional Conjoint Using Microsoft Excel, *Sawtooth Software Research Paper Series,* http://www.sawtoothsoftware.com.

Review Questions

1. What is a variable transformation? Why is it employed?

2. What is a dummy variable? When is it used? How is it interpreted?

3. What is conjoint analysis? When is it used? How do you run one?

Applications and Problems

1. The management of HotSiteTravel Company decided to introduce new vacation packages. However, management was uncertain about the price and destination to introduce. The marketing research department decided to use conjoint analysis to determine the level of each attribute that would come closest to satisfying consumers. The following levels of each of the product attributes were used:

| Price: | $499/week | $799/week | $1299/week |
| Destination: | Cancun | Miami | San Diego |

A respondent's rank ordering of the various product descriptions are noted here (1 is least preferred, 9 is most preferred):

Price	Destination		
	Cancun	Miami	San Diego
$499	4	1	2
$799	6	5	3
$1299	9	8	7

The regression assigned the following utilities:

Price	Utility	Destination	Utility
$499	0	Cancun	0.6
$799	0.43	Miami	0.2
$1299	1.03	San Diego	0.1

a. Calculate the utilities for all 9 travel package combinations.

b. Plot the original input judgments against the derived utilities from (a). Discuss your findings.

c. How might you characterize a segment that prefers the $499 price? The $1299 price?

d. Would you expect a linear utility function for price? For destination?

2. Imagine you've completed your recruiting, and you have six job offers from which to choose: Job A is on the West Coast and it pays $200,000; B is on the West Coast paying $50,000; C is in the Midwest paying $200,000; D is in the Midwest paying $50,000; E is East Coast at $200,000; F is East Coast at $50,000.

a. Which job do you prefer? If you cannot take your first choice job, what attribute are you willing to trade off for the other?

b. If you compare your answers to your friends', do you think salary preferences will tend to be linear? Will location?

Multivariate Data Analysis

Questions to Guide Your Learning:

Q1: How are multivariate statistical methods useful?

Q2: What information can a discriminant analysis provide?

Q3: How might a factor analysis help me develop surveys?

Q4: How might I use cluster analysis to assist in a market segmentation study?

Q5: How does multidimensional scaling yield perceptual maps?

In this chapter, we present the four multivariate statistical techniques that have proven to be the most popular multivariate tools for marketing researchers:

1. Discriminant analysis
2. Factor analysis
3. Cluster analysis
4. Multidimensional scaling

We introduce each technique by describing the kinds of problems the method is ideal to solve. We describe the logic underlying each analysis and how to interpret the results. In the appendix, we also give you a flavor for several additional multivariate models to illustrate further the great variety of marketing research questions that may be asked (and answered!).

Discriminant Analysis

Many marketing problems involve the investigation of group differences. Two or more groups are compared and the question is: do the groups differ, and if so, how. For example, we might be interested in determining the characteristics that differentiate the following:

- Light and heavy users of a product
- Purchasers of our brand and those of competing brands
- Customers who patronize every-day-low-pricing retail outlets vs. those who shop at high-end, service-oriented ones
- Good, mediocre, and poor sales representatives
- Good and poor loan risks

Suppose the groups were to be compared along demographic-socioeconomic lines. We might calculate the mean income, age, and education level to determine the profiles for each group. We could compare the groups on one variable at a time, to become more familiar with the data, and form hypotheses about how the groups are different. However, such a univariate analysis would not indicate the relative importance of each variable in distinguishing the groups when used in combination. Furthermore, the variables are likely to be at least somewhat correlated, so the tests of one variable to the next are not independent, and the variables' redundant information may be leveraged better jointly.

Suppose that we were investigating the characteristics that distinguish light from heavy investors of our mutual funds. If the groups differed on mean income levels, it is also likely that they would show a difference in educational level, because these two variables are fairly highly correlated. Yet if we were interested in segmenting the market using income and education, we would want to use the total effect of both variables in combination, not their separate effects. Further, we would be interested in determining which of the variables was more important or had the greater impact (e.g., like comparing the size of betas in multiple regression).

Discriminant analysis is a method of constructing a linear combination of the variables (i.e., a weighted sum) in such a way that this newly created function optimally discriminates among the groups. We can then assess how the groups differ with respect to this new linear combination score, and we can look at the relative weights assigned to each of the variables in the linear combination to understand their relative importance.

When two groups are being compared, one linear combination, or discriminant function, results. When the technique is applied to the analysis of three or more groups (e.g., light, medium, and heavy users), several discriminant functions can result.

Two-Group Case

We begin with the simpler case of two groups. Consider the following example. A pharmaceuticals firm that relied upon a large sales force conducted a "new account" sales contest among its salespeople to try to increase the number of distributors handling the firm's products. The contest ran for three months. Each salesperson was assigned a quota for the number of new accounts he or she was expected to generate in that period. The quotas were determined by the sales analysis department, which had historic data on the penetration of different industry segments and the number of accounts of each type that were not current customers in each sales territory. All

Discriminant analysis: Do groups differ? If so, how?

salespeople who had 15 or more new accounts place an order during the contest period received an all-expense-paid vacation for two to Hawaii. Salespeople who had at least five new accounts received an HDTV. Those converting fewer than five new accounts received nothing. As it turned out, 15 salespeople won the grand prize, another 15 the consolation prize, and a third of the salespeople won nothing.[1]

The sales analysis department wanted to know what salesperson activities made a difference in terms of whether a salesperson was a prizewinner or not. To demonstrate a two-group discriminant analysis, we try to determine what activities tended to have the greatest impact on whether a salesperson won a grand prize vs. a consolation prize (we'll compare all three groups later).

Table 18.1 contains the data that the sales analysis department collected on each salesperson's new account activities. Figure 18.1 contains a plot of two of the variables describing the salespeople's activities, depicting who the grand prizewinners and consolation prizewinners are. In general, the "percent calls with advance appointments" and "total number of calls" were positively related to success; the more of these activities, the more likely the salesperson was to be a grand prizewinner than a consolation prizewinner. There were exceptions, though. Some consolation prizewinners made more calls on new accounts than did grand prizewinners. Similarly, some grand prizewinners made a smaller percentage of advance appointments than did consolation prizewinners. Overall, however, the grand prizewinners made more calls, and did so with appointments.

The graphical approach is intuitively insightful, but it has its limitations. First, it is time consuming to construct all the graphs that might be useful. Even with only four variables, there are six possible pairs to graph,[2] and higher dimensional graphs become difficult to interpret. We need a mechanism to assess the effect of each factor, taking into account the factors' partially overlapping information.

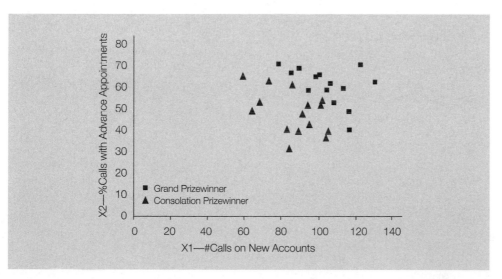

FIGURE 18.1
Scatter Plot on Sales Force Data

---

[1] See Gilbert A. Churchill, Jr., et al., *Sales Force Management*, 6th ed. (Irwin, 1999) for a discussion of sales contests.

[2] The number of possible two-way graphs for m variables is given by the standard combinatorial formula:

$$\binom{m}{2} = \frac{m!}{(m-2)!2!} = \frac{m(m-1)}{2}$$

TABLE 18.1
Sales Contest Data

Grand Prize-winner (W)		# Calls New Accounts X_1	% with Advance Appointments X_2	Calls to Prospects X_3	# New Accounts Visited X_4
1	RMB	130	62	148	42
2	ALB	122	70	186	44
3	BCC	89	68	171	32
4	JJC	104	58	135	40
5	EDC	116	40	160	36
6	WPD	100	65	151	30
7	RHH	85	66	183	42
8	BEK	113	59	130	25
9	DAK	108	52	163	41
10	JJN	116	48	154	48
11	MYS	99	57	188	32
12	PJS	78	70	190	40
13	CET	106	61	157	38
14	LLV	94	58	173	29
15	LMW	98	64	137	36
	Mean	103.9	59.9	161.7	37.0

Consolation Prizewinner (C)

1	JGB	105	39	155	45
2	RAB	86	60	140	33
3	HAF	64	48	132	36
4	PPD	104	36	119	29
5	BCE	102	53	143	41
6	ASG	73	62	128	30
7	WLH	94	51	152	36
8	LHL	59	64	130	28
9	RJL	84	31	102	32
10	WFM	91	47	96	35
11	JRP	83	40	87	30
12	EJS	95	42	114	28
13	VES	68	52	123	26
14	HMT	101	51	98	24
15	BMT	89	39	117	33
	Mean	86.5	47.7	122.4	32.4

Unsuccessful Salespeople (U)

1	RBB	80	23	69	32
2	GEB	47	42	74	33
3	ADC	26	37	132	20
4	JFC	94	24	68	26
5	LDE	57	32	94	23
6	JFH	38	41	83	28
7	JCH	29	52	96	22

(continued)

TABLE 18.1

(*continued*)

Unsuccessful Salespeople (U)	# Calls New Accounts X_1	% with Advance Appointments X_2	Calls to Prospects X_3	# New Accounts Visited X_4
8 RPF	48	24	73	26
9 APL	57	36	82	28
10 HAL	39	37	98	21
11 ERM	51	38	117	24
12 WRR	40	42	112	22
13 JTS	64	21	67	29
14 JMV	35	32	78	25
15 HEY	51	29	81	26
Mean	50.4	34.0	88.3	25.7
Overall Mean	80.3	47.2	124.1	31.7

DETERMINING THE COEFFICIENTS

To differentiate the two groups, we build an index that separates them on the basis of their measured characteristics. The index is a linear combination of four components: number of calls on new accounts X_1, percent of calls with advance appointments X_2, telephone calls made to prospects X_3, and number of new accounts visited X_4:

$$Y = v_1 X_1 + v_2 X_2 + v_3 X_3 + v_4 X_4$$

where v_1, v_2, v_3, and v_4 are the weights indicating the importance of each X in helping us distinguish the prizewinning groups. The equation form is a linear combination, or weighted sum; we're "combining" the information contained in the four X variables to create a single new score, Y. The equation is "linear" because once the Xs are multiplied by their importance weights, the terms are simply added together (or subtracted if a v is negative, but there are no such terms as $X_1 X_2$).

Given values for v_1 through v_4, we can readily calculate a Y or index score for each of the 30 prizewinners. The question is how to derive values for v_1 through v_4.

In discriminant analysis, the weights are derived so that the variation in Y scores (i.e., the new index) between the two groups is as large as possible, while the variation in Y scores within the groups is as small as possible (or, the ratio of "between-group differences" to "within-group differences" is maximized).

To keep this simple, consider for the moment only X_1 (#calls on new accounts) and X_2 (%calls with advance appointments). Given values for v_1 and v_2, we would calculate a Y score for each of the 30 prizewinners using the linear combination:

$$Y = v_1 X_1 + v_2 X_2$$

It turns out that the values for v_1 and v_2 that maximize the ratio of the between-group to within-group variation with respect to the new index scores are $v_1 = .064$ and $v_2 = .106$:

$$Y = .064 X_1 + .106 X_2$$

We can calculate each salesperson's score on the new index, and we can graph the model, because most algebraic concepts (e.g., a linear combination of variables) have geometric counterparts (e.g., a new axis in the plot). In Figure 18.1, we draw the axis from the origin to the coordinates (.064, .106), which are the v-weights.[3] Figure 18.2 contains the new axis that represents the linear combination. (Note the axis does not necessarily go through the scatterplot, as we expect for regression lines.) Take each person's data point and "project" it onto the new axis; that is, draw a line from each data point to the axis in such a way that the line drawn is perpendicular to the axis. These projections represent the Y scores that we have computed using the discriminant analysis equation. What had been a two-dimensional scatterplot (X_1 versus X_2) is now simplified to a frequency distribution of all the scores onto the one-dimensional line (Y). Once all the data points have been projected onto the discriminant axis, note that most of the consolation prizewinners would be lower on the new dimension than most of the grand prizewinners. The distinction is not perfect as we've said (some grand prizewinners overlap with some consolation prizewinners), but given that the v-weights were determined in a manner to optimally separate the groups, there are no other v-weights, or no other orientation of that axis in the two-dimensional plot, that could yield better discrimination between the groups.[4]

We can now use Y, the index score from the discriminant analysis model, to classify each salesperson as a grand prizewinner or a consolation prizewinner. If the salesperson's index score is closer to the mean of the grand prizewinners' index scores, we would classify him or her as a grand prizewinner, and vice versa.[5]

FIGURE 18.2
Discriminant Analysis
Plot with New Axis

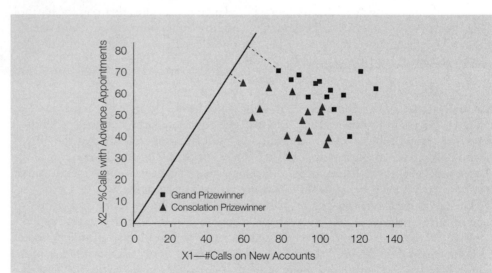

---

[3] The plot is scaled from 0 to 140 on X_1 and 0 to 80 on X_2, so it is more convenient to extend the line from the origin to a multiple of the v-weights, e.g., to the coordinates (64, 106).

[4] Once the axis is drawn, there is also a relationship between the (algebraic) *correlations* among {X_1, X_2, Y}, and the (geometric) *cosines* of angles between X_1 and X_2 and the new axis, Y. Take each weight, say v_1 for X_1 (.064), divide by the square root of the sum of the squared v-weights, and this is the cosine of the angle between X_1 and the new axis: $(.064)^2 + (.106)^2 = .015$, and $\sqrt{.015} = 0.122$. Since $.064/.122 = .525$, the angle θ between the X_1 and the new discriminant axis is given by $\cos\theta = .525$, or $\theta = 58°$. Cool, huh?

[5] The basic approach in discriminant analysis is similar to that of regression—a weighted linear combination of independent variables is used to predict a dependent variable. In regression, the dependent variable is continuous (e.g., interval scaled), whereas in discriminant analysis, it is dichotomous or multichotomous, depicting group membership. (These qualities also make the analysis similar to logit models and logistic regressions.) You can transform a two-group discriminant analysis problem into a regression problem by using a dummy code for the dependent variable (e.g., Y = 0 if consolation prize, Y = 1 if grand prize). The regression coefficients will be proportional to those obtained using discriminant analysis.

Now let's proceed to the more complex, original four-variable problem. The discriminant weights are $v_1 = .058$, $v_2 = .063$, $v_3 = .034$, and $v_4 = -.032$, so the linear combination that maximally differentiates between the groups is:[6]

$$Y = .058X_1 + .063X_2 + .034X_3 - .032X_4$$

The function presents the weights to be applied to X_1 through X_4 so that the distribution of Y scores show the largest separation (or, distinguish most clearly) between grand prizewinners and consolation prizewinners (compared to any other possible linear combination that could have been formed). These Y scores are known as discriminant scores, and they are presented for our sample in Table 18.2. You can see

TABLE 18.2

Scores for Grand Prizewinners and Consolation Prizewinners Using the Discriminant Function: $Y = 0.058X_1 + 0.063X_2 + 0.034X_3 - 0.032X_4$

Grand Prizewinner (W)		# Calls New Accounts X_1	% with Advance Appointments X_2	Calls to Prospects X_3	# New Accounts Visited X_4	Y
1	RMB	130	62	148	42	15.2
2	ALB	122	70	186	44	16.5
3	BCC	89	68	171	32	14.3
4	JJC	104	58	135	40	13.0
5	EDC	116	40	160	36	13.6
6	WPD	100	65	151	30	14.1
7	RHH	85	66	183	42	14.0
8	BEK	113	59	130	25	13.9
9	DAK	108	52	163	41	13.8
10	JJN	116	48	154	48	13.5
11	MYS	99	57	188	32	14.8
12	PJS	78	70	190	40	14.2
13	CET	106	61	157	38	14.2
14	LLV	94	58	173	29	14.1
15	LMW	98	64	137	36	13.3
	Mean	103.9	59.9	161.7	37.0	

Consolation Prizewinner (C)

1	JGB	105	39	155	45	12.4
2	RAB	86	60	140	33	12.5
3	HAF	64	48	132	36	10.1
4	PPD	104	36	119	29	11.4
5	BCE	102	53	143	41	12.8
6	ASG	73	62	128	30	11.6
7	WLH	94	51	152	36	12.7
8	LHL	59	64	130	28	11.0
9	RJL	84	31	102	32	9.3
10	WFM	91	47	96	35	10.4
11	JRP	83	40	87	30	9.4
12	EJS	95	42	114	28	11.2
13	VES	68	52	123	26	10.6
14	HMT	101	51	98	24	11.7
15	BMT	89	39	117	33	10.6
	Mean	86.5	47.7	122.4	32.4	

[6] The weights are given by the eigenvector in the solution of the equation: $(W^{-1}B - \lambda I)v = 0$, where **W** is the pooled within-sample covariance matrix and **B** is the between-group, sum-of-squares and cross-products matrix.

that the discriminant scores of grand prizewinners are similar in magnitude, as are those of consolation prizewinners, and that the two sets of scores are different from each other. The members within the groups are as much alike as possible on these generated scores, and the groups themselves are as different as possible.

With this analysis, we have taken a four-variable problem and reduced it to a much simpler, univariate problem by forming a linear combination of X_1 through X_4 to get one Y. We need to compare only the discriminant scores of the groups (Y) rather than comparing the groups on all four variables (X_1 through X_4). Further, we know that the groups are as different as possible with respect to these Ys. But how does that help us understand how grand prizewinners differ from consolation prizewinners in terms of their new account activities? Further, how does that help the sales analysis department isolate the factors that were most critical to salespeople's success? We need to:

- Interpret the discriminant function Y, and
- Use it to classify individuals in groups.

INTERPRETING THE DISCRIMINANT FUNCTION

First we must verify that the discriminant function is statistically significant, i.e., that a reliable differentiation of the groups exists. (If the function is not significant, we shouldn't interpret the function—it's meaningless because the estimates differ only due to sampling error.) Most statistical computing packages routinely print F-statistics for Mahalanobis's D^2 statistics (a squared distance measure similar to Euclidian distance that measures the distance from each salesperson to the group mean while allowing for correlated axes and different measurement units for the variables).[7] In our example, the discriminant function is statistically significant, so the interpretation of the function can proceed.

DISCRIMINANT COEFFICIENTS

Discriminant coefficients are interpreted in much the same way as regression coefficients, in that each coefficient reflects the relative contribution of a unit change of each of the independent variables on the discriminant function. A small coefficient means that a one-unit change in that particular variable produces a small change in the discriminant function score, and a larger coefficient, a larger change in Y.

Also like regression coefficients, discriminant coefficients are affected by the scale of the independent variables, i.e., the original function $Y = 0.058X_1 + 0.063X_2 + 0.034X_3 - 0.032X_4$ contains the weights to be applied to the variables in raw-score scales. This scaling means that if the unit of measurement for one of the variables changes (e.g., measure variable X_2 as a proportion rather than as a percentage), the discriminant function also changes. To remove these arbitrary scale-of-measurement effects, we standardize the discriminant weights before trying to compare the variables' contributions. We multiply each raw score weight v_k by the standard deviation of variable k. Call v_k^* the standardized weight, then:

$$v_k^* = v_k s_k$$

where s_k is the pooled (across samples) standard deviation of the kth variable. Considering our grand and consolation prizewinners, we pool over only the two prize

---

[7] See e.g., Barbara Tabachnick and Linda Fidell, *Using Multivariate Statistics*, 4th ed. (Allyn & Bacon, 2000) for details.

groups, to obtain the pooled sample standard deviations for the four variables: $s_1 = 16.76$, $s_2 = 10.89$, $s_3 = 28.16$, and $s_4 = 6.33$. Therefore:

$$v_1^* = v_1 s_1 = 058(16.76) = .972$$

$$v_2^* = v_2 s_2 = .063(10.89) = .686$$

$$v_3^* = v_3 s_3 = .034(28.16) = .957$$

$$v_4^* = v_4 s_4 = .032(6.33) = -.203$$

With the standardized weights all being on the same "scale," we can compare their sizes to determine the relative contribution of the variables. They indicate that the variables "number of calls on new accounts" (X_1) and "telephone calls made to prospects" (X_3) are the most important and that "number of new accounts visited" (X_4) is the least important in differentiating grand prizewinners from consolation prizewinners. Further, variables X_1 through X_3 exert a positive effect (>#calls, >%calls with appointments, and >#calls to prospects all mean the more likely it is the salesperson was a grand prizewinner instead of a consolation prizewinner). In contrast, the number of new accounts the salesperson visited (X_4) has a negative impact on the likelihood that the representative was a grand prizewinner.

The standardized weights agree with what intuition might suggest about the importance of the variables (when there is relatively little correlation among the predictors). For example, we can see from Table 18.2 that the largest differences between the groups occur on the means for X_1 and X_3, an observation consistent with the largest discriminant weights being v_1 and v_3. When there are correlations among the predictors (the problem of multicollinearity), the weights aren't likely to map so simply onto differences between means. In general, the coefficients need to be interpreted with more caution—just as in regression, a small standardized weight may mean either that the variable is irrelevant in discriminating between the groups or, alternatively, that its effect has been partialed out of the relationship because of the multicollinearity.

> **Standardize the weights before interpreting the relative importance of variables.**

DISCRIMINANT LOADINGS

A third method for assessing the importance of the variables in discriminating between groups is to study the discriminant loadings.[8] These values are the correlations between each variable (X_1 through X_4) in turn with the discriminant score (Y). These correlations follow:

Between Y and X_1: .627
Between Y and X_2: .679
Between Y and X_3: .847
Between Y and X_4: .441

The loadings suggest that variable X_3 (telephone calls made to prospects), is now the most important, and variable X_4 (# new accounts visited), is still the least important in discriminating between grand and consolation prizewinners. (The difference in the ordering of the variables, compared to the standardized weights, is due to the correlations among the predictors.) As with any correlation coefficient, the squared discriminant loadings (r^2) indicate the amount of variance that the discriminant score (Y) shares with the variable (X).

---

[8] We have more to say about loadings in the discussion on factor analysis.

In sum, three quantities are typically used to assess the relative importance of variables in discriminating between groups:

1. The mean differences of the groups on each variable,
2. The standardized discriminant function coefficients, and
3. The discriminant loadings.

All three produce similar conclusions when little correlation exists among the predictors. When multicollinearity is a problem, their conclusions will differ, and the same caveats that apply when interpreting coefficients in regression apply here.

CLASSIFYING INDIVIDUALS USING THE DISCRIMINANT FUNCTION

To assist in interpretation, we could also calculate the discriminant score for each group. To do this, we insert the mean values of the variables for each group into the discriminant function equation. For the grand prizewinners, the means were: $\bar{x}_1 = 103.9, \bar{x}_2 = 59.9, \bar{x}_3 = 161.7$, and $\bar{x}_4 = 37.0$, so the mean discriminant score for grand prizewinners, $\bar{Y}_w$, is:

$$\bar{Y}_w = v_1\bar{x}_1 + v_2\bar{x}_2 + v_3\bar{x}_3 + v_4\bar{x}_4$$
$$= .058(103.9) + .063(59.9) + .034(161.7) - .032(37.0) = 14.2.$$

For consolation prizewinners, $\bar{x}_1 = 86.5, \bar{x}_2 = 47.7, \bar{x}_3 = 122.4$, and $\bar{x}_4 = 32.4$, and the mean discriminant score, $\bar{Y}_c$, is calculated to be:

$$\bar{Y}_c = .058(86.5) + .063(47.7) + .034(122.4) - .032(32.4) = 11.2$$

On average, grand prizewinners have higher discriminant scores on Y than consolation prizewinners. (The same result is obtained if the discriminant scores in Table 18.2 are averaged in each group.)

We have established that the discriminant function provides statistically reliable differentiation for these data. Now let's see whether it provides meaningful and practical differentiation between the two groups. We use the discriminant function to classify each salesperson into the "grand prize" or "consolation prize" groups (as if we didn't know their actual group membership). We then compare the prediction with the individual's known actual classification to see if the function provides meaningful discrimination to accurately guess each individual's prize status. We use the simple decision rule: If a salesperson's discriminant score is closer to the mean score for grand prizewinners than for consolation prizewinners, we will classify the salesperson as a grand prizewinner.

An alternative equivalent procedure is to compute the score that divides the mean discriminant scores. This "cutting score" is then used to assign objects to groups in the following way: If the individual's score is above the cutting score, classify the salesperson as a grand prizewinner; if it is below, classify the salesperson as a consolation prizewinner. When the groups are equal in size, the cutting score, Y_{cs}, is given as the simple average of the mean discriminant scores for the groups; i.e., by the calculation $Y_{cs} = (\bar{Y}_w + \bar{Y}_c)/2 = (14.2 + 11.2)/2 = 12.7$. When the groups are not equal, the formula needs to be modified to take the size of each group into account.

The appropriate formula is then $Y_{cs} = \dfrac{\left(n_2\bar{Y}_1 + n_1\bar{Y}_2\right)}{\left(n_1 + n_2\right)}$ = where $\bar{Y}_1$ and $\bar{Y}_2$ are the mean

discriminant scores and n_1 and n_2 the sizes of Groups 1 and 2, respectively.

Either decision rule essentially finds the group most similar to the individual. The resulting predicted classifications are presented in the right-hand column of Table 18.3.

See if the model works—use the scores to predict classifications.

		Differences from Mean of		
Grand Prize-winners (W)	Discriminant Score Y_i	First Group $Y_i - \bar{Y}_w =$ $Y_i - 14.2$	Second Group $Y_i - \bar{Y}_c = Y_i - 11.2$	Predicted Group Membership
1	15.2	1.0	4.0	W
2	16.5	2.3	5.3	W
3	14.3	0.1	3.1	W
4	13.0	21.2	1.8	W
5	13.6	20.6	2.4	W
6	14.1	20.1	2.9	W
7	14.0	20.2	2.8	W
8	13.9	20.3	2.7	W
9	13.8	20.4	2.6	W
10	13.5	20.7	2.3	W
11	14.8	0.6	3.6	W
12	14.2	0.0	3.0	W
13	14.2	0.0	3.0	W
14	14.1	20.1	2.9	W
15	13.3	20.9	2.1	W
Consolation Prizewinners (C)				
1	12.4	21.8	1.2	C
2	12.5	21.7	1.3	C
3	10.1	24.1	21.1	C
4	11.4	22.8	0.2	C
5	12.8	21.4	1.6	W
6	11.6	22.6	0.4	C
7	12.7	21.5	1.5	W*
8	11.0	23.2	20.2	C
9	9.3	24.9	21.9	C
10	10.4	23.8	20.8	C
11	9.4	24.8	21.8	C
12	11.2	23.0	0.0	C
13	10.6	23.6	20.6	C
14	11.7	22.5	0.5	C
15	10.6	23.6	20.6	C

*The assignments were actually carried out using more significant digits in the calculations of discriminant scores. While the calculations to one decimal place suggest this case is equidistant from the two group means, it actually is slightly closer to the mean for the grand prizewinners.

Table 18.4 contains the predicted classifications as the columns, and the known, actual classifications as the rows. We can use this table to assess the accuracy of the predictive classification decision rule. The entries on the diagonal represent the hit rate, or the proportion of people who have been correctly classified, P_{cc}:

$$P_{cc} = (15 + 13) / (30) = 28/30 = .933$$

Actual Classification	Predicted Classification		
	Grand Prizewinner	**Consolation Prizewinner**	**Total**
Grand Prizewinner	15	0	15
Consolation Prizewinner	2	13	15

Approximately 93% of the salespeople are correctly classified as grand prizewinners or consolation prizewinners on the basis of their new account activities.

ASSESSING CLASSIFICATION ACCURACY

How good is that hit rate? The sample sizes were equal, thus chance would be 50%, so 93% sounds very good. What if the two groups were not equal in size—suppose that in a sample of 100 salespeople, 20 won grand prizes and 80 won consolation prizes (perhaps the sales contest requirements were changed). Useful criteria to evaluate hit rates include the maximum chance criterion and the proportional chance criterion.

The maximum chance criterion holds that any object chosen at random should be classified as belonging to the larger group, because that will maximize the proportion of cases correctly classified. In the 80-20 example, we would classify everybody as a consolation prizewinner, because that would make 80% of the classifications correct.

This classification rule is not very helpful from a marketing viewpoint, though, because we wish to identify the two types of winners. We would like to classify some salespeople as grand prizewinners and thereby improve upon the *a priori* odds. In such instances, we use the proportional chance criterion, C_{pro}, as the standard of evaluation:

$$C_{pro} = \alpha^2 + (1 - \alpha)^2$$

where

α = the proportion of individuals in Group 1
$(1 - \alpha)$ = the proportion of individuals in Group 2

For 20 grand prizewinners (Group 1) and 80 consolation prizewinners (Group 2), this index equals $C_{pro} = .2^2 + (8)^2 = .68$. If we use a discriminant function and get a classification accuracy of, say, 85%, that hit rate would look good compared to chance alone ($C_{pro} = .68$), but not so impressive against the maximum chance criterion (.80).[9]

Before leaving the "two-group discriminant" case . . . a couple of comments. First, given that the same data used to develop the discriminant model are also used to test the model, there is an upward bias—the hit rate is somewhat overstated. The criterion used to fit the model generates an equation that is derived to be statistically optimal, so ideally, the actual predictive accuracy of the model should be tested on a

---

[9] When the two groups are equal in size, as they are in the original example, the proportional chance criterion equals the maximum chance criterion (that is, $C_{pro} = .5^2 + (1 - .5)^2 = 0.25 + 0.25 = 0.5$).

new sample of data. However, it is costly and time consuming to collect more data, so usually what is done is to split the original sample of observations into two subsamples. One subsample, called the "analysis sample," is used to develop the equation, while the other, called the "holdout sample," is employed to examine how well the equation predicts group membership.[10]

Second, the particular decision rule we used to classify grand prizewinners and consolation prizewinners minimizes the costs of misclassification (that is, it will be optimal) when: (1) the costs of misclassifying a grand prizewinner as a consolation prizewinner, and vice versa, are equal; (2) the *a priori* probabilities of winning each prize are equal; and (3) the distribution of the variables in the two populations is multivariate normal with equal and known covariance matrices.

Three-Group Case

Ethical Dilemma 18.1

Clark was feeling very smug. He had just completed the analysis and writeup of a study that involved respondents' completing a lengthy attitude scale about such things as their need for security, their attitudes toward life insurance, their willingness to assume risk, how vulnerable they feel to life's unexpected events, and similar constructs. The purpose of the investigation was to determine if those people purchasing his firm's products could somehow be differentiated from those purchasing competitors' products on the basis of the attitude profiles.

Clark used factor analysis to purify the items. When he felt comfortable with the results, he formed a total score for each construct for each respondent by summing the responses to the items making up that construct. He used the total scores thus generated as independent variables in a discriminant analysis in which "brand purchased" served as the criterion. The results clearly indicated that the attitude profile of those purchasing his firm's insurance differed from that of people purchasing competitors' products and some of the differences lent themselves to actionable strategies by which the firm might increase its share.

Clark's smugness began to dissipate, however, when a chance conversation with one of his old college buddies caused him to wonder if he had not made a mistake. His college friend pointed out that, according to the accepted rules of thumb for factor analysis, Clark did not have a large enough sample and consequently, his factor analysis results might be quite unstable.

- What should Clark do? If he admits his error now to his boss, his boss might think less highly of him, particularly since Clark was hired into the marketing research department partially on the basis of his statistical skills. However, not reporting it could cause those in his firm to place more confidence in the results than they should.
- What are Clark's ethical responsibilities?
- Would the ethical problem be different if Clark knew of the requirement and intentionally overlooked it, knew it but inadvertently forgot it, or never learned it in the first place?

Let's now consider discriminant analysis for k ≥ 3 groups. The biggest change that occurs when we move beyond two groups is that there can be more than one discriminant function.[11] When there are k groups and p variables, the maximum number of discriminant functions are given by the following rules:

- If there are more variables p than groups k (the typical case), there will be at most k − 1 discriminant functions.
- If the number of variables p is less than the number of groups k, there will be no more than p discriminant functions.

In either case, the number of statistically significant discriminant functions is usually less than the maximum number possible. It depends on whether the extracted functions provide "meaningful differentiation" among the objects forming the groups.

---

[10] With small samples, one cannot afford the luxury of setting aside some of the observations for later use because all the data are needed to develop the equation. In such instances, one systematically deletes one case in turn and fits the equation to each of the remaining n − 1 observations. The process is repeated n times with each observation left out in turn, and provides useful estimates of the coefficients and prediction accuracy of the equation, e.g., Fu-Kwun Wang and Eldon Li, "Confidence Intervals in Repeatability and Reproducibility Using the Bootstrap Method, *Total Quality Management & Business Excellence* 14 (2003), pp. 341–355.

[11] There are two variations when there are more than two groups: the *classical* approach generates one classification function for each group that maximizes the likelihood of correct classifications of the members of the group. It produces g(g − 1)/2 discriminant functions (where g is the number of groups) to separate each pair of groups. The *simultaneous* approach (also known as the canonical approach) is emphasized here.

Consider again the example of salespeople, but this time, let's look at all three groups (grand prizewinners, consolation prizewinners, and salespeople who won nothing). The number of groups (k = 3) is less than the number of variables (p = 4), so the number of discriminant functions that can be derived is k − 1 = 2.

The two discriminant functions turn out to be

$$Y_1 = .064X_1 + .079X_2 + .027X_3 − .002X_4$$

$$Y_2 = 2.036X_1 − .037X_2 + .041X_3 − .003X_4$$

The functions have the following interpretation: Of all the linear combinations of the four variables that could be developed, the linear combination given by the first function provides maximum separation among the three groups. Maximum separation is defined, once again, on the basis of discriminant scores; the salespeople within a group are very similar with respect to their Y_1 scores, whereas the salespeople in different groups have different Y_1 scores. Given the first linear combination, the second function provides maximum separation among all possible linear combinations that were uncorrelated with (i.e., so as not to be redundant) the first set of scores ($r_{Y1,Y2} = 0$).

CLASSIFYING RESPONDENTS

We check the statistical significance of these functions before trying to use them to classify salespeople, and find that only the first function is significant. Thus, we develop a classification rule that depends only on it. The rule is an extension of the one previously described; we assign salespeople to the group closest to their discriminant score. To do so, we need to know the mean discriminant scores for each group. They are generated by substituting the means of the four variables for each group in the discriminant function:

Grand prizewinner:
$$\bar{Y}_w = .064(103.9) + .079(59.9) + .027(161.7) − .002(37.0) = 15.67$$

Consolation prizewinner:
$$\bar{Y}_c = .064(86.5) + .079(47.7) + .027(122.4) − .002(32.4) = 12.54$$

Unsuccessful salesperson:
$$\bar{Y}_u = .064(50.4) + .079(34.0) + .027(88.3) − .002(25.7) = 9.58$$

The cutting scores (15.67 + 12.54)/2 = 14.11 and (12.54 + 9.58)/2 = 11.06 bisect the difference in mean scores between grand and consolation prizewinners, and between consolation prizewinners and unsuccessful salespeople. Thus, any salesperson with a score less than 11.06 would be considered an unsuccessful contest competitor, those with discriminant scores greater than 14.11 would be considered grand prizewinners. Those with scores between 11.06 and 14.11 would be considered consolation prizewinners. The scores and predicted classifications are contained in Table 18.5. Table 18.6 contains the matrix of predicted versus actual classifications. The performance of this procedure is quite good; the hit rate says 91.1% of the salespeople are predicted correctly, against the chance criterion of 33%. The incorrect predictions involve consolation prizewinners (two of whom are predicted to be grand prizewinners and two of whom are predicted to be unsuccessful in the sales contest), so we might say that, perhaps not surprisingly, the function is particularly effective in discriminating between the extremes: the grand prizewinners and those who did not win anything.

Person	Score	Prediction*	Person	Score	Prediction	Person	Score	Prediction
1 RMB	17.25	W	1 JGB	14.00	C	1 RBB	8.80	U
2 ALB	18.40	W	2 RAB	14.06	C	2 GEB	8.32	U
3 BCC	15.73	W	3 HAF	11.47	C	3 ADC	8.18	U
4 JJC	14.91	W	4 PPD	12.74	C	4 JFC	9.76	U
5 EDC	14.94	W	5 BCE	14.60	W	5 LDE	8.73	U
6 WPD	15.66	W	6 ASG	13.06	C	6 JFH	7.92	U
7 RHH	15.63	W	7 WLH	14.18	W	7 JCH	8.58	U
8 BEK	15.45	W	8 LHL	12.38	C	8 RPF	6.94	U
9 DAK	15.45	W	9 RJL	10.59	U	9 APL	8.71	U
10 JJN	15.39	W	10 WFM	12.14	C	10 HAL	8.08	U
11 MYS	15.97	W	11 JRP	10.83	U	11 ERM	9.45	U
12 PJS	15.69	W	12 EJS	12.50	C	12 WRR	8.93	U
13 CET	15.88	W	13 VES	11.81	C	13 JTS	7.56	U
14 LLV	15.32	W	14 HMT	13.17	C	14 JMV	6.88	U
15 LMW	15.06	W	15 BMT	11.95	C	15 HEY	7.75	U

*W, grand prizewinners; C, consolation prizewinners; U, unsuccessful salespeople

TABLE 18.5
Discriminant Scores for Each Salesperson and Predicted Group Membership Using the Function $Y = 0.064X_1 + 0.079X_2 + 0.027X_3 - 0.002X_4$

Actual Classification	Predicted Classification			
	Grand Prizewinner	Consolation Prizewinner	Unsuccessful Salesperson	Total
Grand Prizewinner	15	0	0	15
Consolation Prizewinner	2	11	2	15
Unsuccessful Salesperson	0	0	15	15

TABLE 18.6
Discriminant Analysis Example: Matrix of Actual versus Predicted Group Membership

KEY VARIABLES

To determine the key new-account activities that differentiated salespeople's performance, we transform the v_k coefficients to their standardized counterparts, to equate the "units" so we can compare the impact of the variables. The standardized weights are:

$$v_1^* = v_1 s_1 = .064(15.91) = 1.018$$

$$v_2^* = v_2 s_2 = .079(8.97) = .709$$

$$v_3^* = v_3 s_3 = .027(19.99) = .540$$

$$v_4^* = v_4 s_4 = -.002(5.37) = -.011$$

Number of calls on new accounts, X_1, is the most important variable in differentiating among the levels of success in the sales contest, whereas the number of new accounts visited, X_4, is the least important. However, there is some correlation among the predictors so the relative importance of each predictor should be interpreted with a degree of caution.

Marketing Applications of Discriminant Analysis

Discriminant analysis has been used for a variety of marketing problems. It has been used to:

- Determine those characteristics that distinguish the listening audiences of radio stations
- Differentiate among segments of automobile buyers
- Predict adopters and nonadopters of new products
- Relate purchase behavior to advertising exposure
- Determine the relationship between personality variables and consumer decisions
- Understand the differences between households that save their money at commercial banks versus those who choose savings and loan institutions
- Assess the differences in importance of various attributes where the same products are being purchased in different countries
- Determine the factors that supermarket buyers use in deciding whether to stock a new product

See Research Realities 18.1 for some in-depth examples. The main "take away" on "When do I use discriminant analysis?" is this: Discriminant analysis is applicable when the marketing researcher has data on customers who fall into groups, and the information on the customers can be used to understand how the members in one group differ from those in another.

Factor Analysis

Factor analysis (and cluster analysis and multidimensional scaling, discussed next) is different from discriminant analysis in that it doesn't pose a research question in which we try to predict one variable (such as group membership in discriminant analysis) by other variables. Techniques like factor analysis are referred to as tools for "interdependence analysis." All the variables have equal status, and none is singled out for special treatment as a dependent variable. These models pose different variations on the question, "How are these p variables interrelated?"

Factor analysis addresses a number of goals. It is one of the more popular "analysis of interdependence" techniques because one of its goals is usually referred to as "data reduction." Factor analysis simplifies data analysis by taking advantage of the correlations among p variables—extracting that overlapping information and reducing the problem down to just a few core "factors." For example, Table 18.7 shows two sets of correlations among p = 9 variables. The correlations in Panel A suggest that the 9 variables might be reduced down to 2 factors. Variables 1–4 seem to go together, as do variables 5–9 (the pair-wise correlations between the variables in each set are relatively high). The two sets seem to behave differently, though, because the correlations between 1–4 and 5–9 are rather low. (If all the correlations were high, we would use only one factor.) In contrast, Panel B suggests that three factors underlie the nine variables; i.e., variables 1–3, 4–6, and 7–9 covary.

To conduct a factor analysis, we need to translate that conceptual understanding of factor analysis into a mathematical model. Mathematically, a factor is a linear combination of variables, chosen to capture the "essence" of the data. This goal may be achieved in various ways, so the term "factor analysis" applies to a body of tech-

Research Realities

18.1 More Applications of Discriminant Analysis

1. Why do some international firms enjoy success in the U.S. whereas others do not? Marketing researchers conducted a telephone survey of nearly 100 marketing vice presidents or presidents of international (European or Japanese) industrial products firms that had established a manufacturing presence in the U.S. during the last 30 years.

   Firms were considered "successful" if they had achieved at least 5% market share in the U.S., and were classified as "underachieving" with less. The results of a discriminant analysis revealed the main ingredients of the successful firms to be:

   - A larger percentage of senior managers in the U.S. firm who were U.S. nationals
   - A greater commitment to research and development
   - A willingness to tailor product design to local taste

   Other factors that were tested did not matter; neither mode of entry into the U.S. (acquiring or building a facility) nor competitive pricing were predictive in discriminating between successful firms and unsuccessful ones.

2. Dining is a big part of the tourism experience. Researchers have identified segments of travelers who seek different qualities when dining far away from home. Discriminant analysis verified that these were significantly different groups (and the model correctly classified 96% of the sample):

   - "Value seekers" care about getting good food for their money. They care about food quality and hygiene but not about the location of the restaurant, healthy or nutritious menus, or the local flavor.
   - "Service seekers" want to be treated well, they appreciate value, and healthy choices and location matter. However, food quality, interestingly, is less important to this group.
   - "Adventurous food seekers" place greatest importance on trying the local dishes. They don't care so much about health or prices.

Sources: Zoher E. Shipchandler and James S. Moore, "Factors Influencing Foreign Firm Performance in the U.S. Market," *American Business Review* 18 (2000), pp. 62–68; Atila Yuksel and Fisen Yuksel, "Measurement of Tourist Satisfaction with Restaurant Services," *Journal of Vacation Marketing* 9 (2002), pp. 52–68.

niques, which are differentiated in terms of how the weights in the linear combinations are determined.[12]

Consider a company with a large sales force (pharmaceuticals, insurance, cosmetics, machine parts suppliers, automobile dealerships, etc.). Suppose the company is interested in isolating the personality traits that lead to successful sales. There are

TABLE 18.7

Factor Analysis Example: Two Hypothetical Sets of Correlations among Nine Variables

	Panel A (Probably Two Factors):								
Variable	**1**	**2**	**3**	**4**	**5**	**6**	**7**	**8**	**9**
1	1.00								
2	.96	1.00							
3	.94	.88	1.00						
4	.91	.95	.89	1.00					
5	.05	.09	.08	.10	1.00				
6	.12	.04	.03	.11	.92	1.00			
7	.07	.14	.06	.03	.86	.91	1.00		
8	.10	.12	.08	.04	.94	.95	.88	1.00	
9	.08	.11	.06	.13	.97	.87	.91	.90	1.00
									(continued)

[12] See the two succinct volumes by J. Kim and C. W. Mueller, *Introduction to Factor Analysis* and *Factor Analysis* (Sage, 1978).

TABLE 18.7
(continued)

Variable	1	2	3	4	5	6	7	8	9
Panel B (Probably Three Factors):									
1	1.00								
2	.92	1.00							
3	.95	.98	1.00						
4	.07	.13	.02	1.00					
5	.09	.05	.11	.95	1.00				
6	.06	.09	.07	.90	.89	1.00			
7	.10	.08	.10	.08	.14	.10	1.00		
8	.05	.07	.09	.09	.06	.12	.94	1.00	
9	.13	.04	.08	.13	.09	.06	.91	.92	1.00

many ways to measure the performance of a salesperson, e.g., sales growth, profitability of sales, new account sales, etc. The company wants its salespeople to be good at all these things, not just one, so looking at any single measure would seem inadequate. On the other hand, salespeople who are good at generating sales of one kind are often also good at generating sales of another; i.e., we'd expect these three performance measures to be correlated. Table 18.8 contains data for a sample of 50 sales reps. (To compensate for differences in sales territory, these measures were converted to an index where 100 indicates "average.")

Summarizing Data

If the first purpose of factor analysis is to summarize the important information contained in the data by a fewer number of factors, the question is, "What is 'important information'?" Two kinds of information are typically highlighted: the variance of each variable (variability across customers), and the correlation between variables (covariation of variables across customers).[13]

Table 18.9 contains the pairs of correlations among the variables, and Table 18.10 is the "loadings" matrix that results from performing a principal components analysis (PCA) on the data. The loadings matrix is one of the key outputs in factor analyses, so let's interpret those.

FACTOR LOADINGS

The individual entries are the correlations between the variables (rows) and the factors (columns). For example, .976 (the entry in the 1st row and 1st column), represents the correlation between the 1st variable and the 1st factor; .083 is the

---

[13] Most factor analyses are implemented using standardized variables because in many problems, the raw variables reflect different units of measurement. By standardizing the variables (to mean zero and unit standard deviation), the effect of measurement is removed. The researcher need not actually standardize the variables—the first step of a factor analysis in statistical computing packages, e.g., SAS, SPSS, is to compute the matrix of intercorrelations among the variables you specify. Recall the equation for a correlation between two variables X and Y: $r_{xy} = \sum_{i=1}^{n} \frac{(X_i - \bar{x})(Y_i - \bar{y})}{ns_x s_y}$. In this equation, the data X_i and Y_i are adjusted to standard scores when the means are subtracted and the standard deviations divided.

TABLE 18.8
Example: Sales
Performance Data
for Sample of Sales
Representatives

Sales Rep	Sales Growth X_1	Sales Profitability X_2	New Account Sales X_3
1	93.0	96.0	97.8
2	88.8	91.8	96.8
3	95.0	100.3	99.0
4	101.3	103.8	106.8
5	102.0	107.8	103.0
6	95.8	97.5	99.3
7	95.5	99.5	99.0
8	110.8	122.0	115.3
9	102.8	108.3	103.8
10	106.8	120.5	102.0
11	103.3	109.8	104.0
12	99.5	111.8	100.3
13	103.5	112.5	107.0
14	99.5	105.5	102.3
15	100.0	107.0	102.8
16	81.5	93.5	95.0
17	101.3	105.3	102.8
18	103.3	110.8	103.5
19	95.3	104.3	103.0
20	99.5	105.3	106.3
21	88.5	95.3	95.8
22	99.3	115.0	104.3
23	87.5	92.5	95.8
24	105.3	114.0	105.3
25	107.0	121.0	109.0
26	93.3	102.0	97.8
27	106.8	118.0	107.3
28	106.8	120.0	104.8
29	92.3	90.8	99.8
30	106.3	121.0	104.5
31	106.0	119.5	110.5
32	88.3	92.8	96.8
33	96.0	103.3	100.5
34	94.3	94.5	99.0
35	106.5	121.5	110.5
36	106.5	115.5	107.0
37	92.0	99.5	103.5
38	102.0	99.8	103.3
39	108.3	122.3	108.5
40	106.8	119.0	106.8
41	102.5	109.3	103.8
42	92.5	102.5	99.3
43	102.8	113.8	106.8
44	83.3	87.3	96.3
45	94.8	101.8	99.8
46	103.5	112.0	110.8
47	89.5	96.0	97.3
48	84.3	89.8	94.3
49	104.3	109.5	106.5
50	106.0	118.5	105.0

TABLE 18.9
Factor Analysis:
Simple Pair-Wise
Correlations among
the Performance
Measures

	X_1	X_2	X_3
X_1	1.000		
X_2	.926	1.000	
X_3	.884	.843	1.000

TABLE 18.10
Factor Analysis: Factor
Loading Matrix

	Factor		
Variable	F_1	F_2	F_3
X_1	.976	.083	−.203
X_2	.961	.232	.151
X_3	.945	−.321	.056
Sum of Squares	2.769	.164	.067

correlation between the 1st variable and the 2nd factor; .961 the correlation between the 2nd variable and 1st factor, and so on. These correlations are called factor loadings. When we examine the table of loadings, we find that all three variables correlate highly with (we'd say "load heavily on") Factor F_1.

These numbers are correlations, so if we square them, we obtain the proportion of variation in the variable that is accounted for by the factor. Thus,

$.976^2 = .952$

$.961^2 = .924$

$.945^2 = .894$

are the proportions of variance in variables 1, 2, and 3, respectively, accounted for by the first factor. Thus, with just a single factor, we have very nearly represented the entire variance of each of the three variables (the 1's on the diagonal in the correlation matrix in Table 18.9).

We might also check to see how well our single factor captures the correlations among the three variables. To represent the covariability of two variables, we multiply the factor loadings of the two variables (two different rows), one factor at a time, and then sum up the products over the factors. Say we wanted to see how well the model predicted the value for the correlation between variables 1 and 2, r_{12}. We multiply the respective column entries of rows 1 and 2 of Table 18.10 and add the products:

$(.976)(.961) + (.083)(.232) + (−.203)(.151) = .926.$

In this case, we reproduce exactly the original correlation, r_{12}, between variables 1 and 2 displayed in Table 18.9. The general formula is

$$r_{jt} = \sum_{k=1}^{3} a_{jk} a_{tk}$$

where j and t denote the original variables, k denotes the factor, and a_{jk} is the loading or correlation between the jth variable and k^{th} factor (the jth row and k^{th} column of

Table 18.10). Although we have fit our data well, note that in doing so, we have not achieved the parsimonious goal of "data reduction"—we began with three variables, and we now have three factors.[14] We usually extract fewer factors than we had variables to begin with.

What happens when fewer factors are used? The model no longer reproduces the pair-wise correlations exactly; rather, they are only estimated, however, the estimates are often quite good. The estimate is given by the same formula, but now we sum from 1 to m, where m denotes the number of factors being considered (m < p). For one-factor (m = 1), the estimated correlation between variables 1 and 2 (j = 1, t = 2) is

$$\hat{r}_{12} = \sum_{k=1}^{m} a_{1k}a_{2k} = (.976)(.961) = .937$$

This estimate is actually quite close to the true value of .926. The other estimates are also quite good: $\hat{r}_{13} = (.973)(.945) = .922$ and $\hat{r}_{23} = (.961)(.945) = .908$, compared to the actual values of .884 and .843.

COMMUNALITIES

This example, showing the results for the extremes of one versus three factors, demonstrates the natural tension in factor analysis—the more factors that are extracted, the better the data are represented. However, the fewer the factors extracted, the easier it is to work with the results, interpret them, and communicate them.[15] Is one factor sufficient, or is more than one factor needed to summarize the data adequately? To answer this question, it is helpful to realize that in a principal components solution, the m newly formed components are uncorrelated. This means that the proportion of variance accounted for by m factors is simply the sum of the proportions accounted for by each factor. Take two factors, for example. The proportion of the variation in each variable accounted for by a two-factor solution is

Variable 1: $(0.976)^2 + (0.083)^2 = 0.959$
Variable 2: $(0.961)^2 + (0.232)^2 = 0.977$
Variable 3: $(0.945)^2 + (20.321)^2 = 0.997$

These values, which express the proportion of the variance of the variables extracted by m factors, are called the **communalities** of the variables and are typically denoted as h_j^2 (for variable j). Thus, we see that two factors account for 95.9% $(= h_1^2)$ of the variation in X_1, 97.7% $(= h_2^2)$ of the variation in X_2, and 99.7% $(= h_3^2)$ of the variation in X_3. The two-factor model does a remarkable job in accounting for the variability within the data. Variable 1 is most poorly captured, but even for it, 95.9% of its total variability is captured by the first two principal components. How do we know what percentage is enough? How many factors should we retain?

The column totals in Table 18.10 can assist the analyst in making a decision. Given that the row/column entries represent the correlations between the variables

---

[14] Any set of correlations can be reproduced exactly if the number of factors extracted equals the number of original variables input.

[15] The trade-off is found in most statistical modeling. For example, in multiple regression, prediction is better—the R^2 higher—with more predictors. However, the model is easier to understand, and easier to express to marketing research clients, with fewer predictors.

and the factors, and their squares represent the proportions of variation in each variable explained by the factor, the sum of the squares in a column provides a measure of the amount of variation accounted for by that factor. Take factor/column 1, for example:

$$(0.976)^2 + (0.961)^2 + (0.945)^2 = 2.769$$

the column total. The three variables are all standardized to unit variance (recall we started with a correlation matrix, 1's on the diagonal, in Table 18.9), so the total variance equals 3. Thus, the proportion of total variance that is accounted for by the first factor is 2.769/3 = 92.3%. The first two factors account for (2.769 + .164)/3 = .978, or 97.8% of the total variance. The second factor accounts for 5.5% of the total variance in the three variables. In the interest of scientific parsimony, it would seem that a one-factor solution would suffice; the addition of the second factor provides only a small gain in explained variation. (The argument is one of diminishing returns—does the second factor explain enough additional variance that it is worth retaining it?)

CONCEPTUAL BASIS OF PRINCIPAL COMPONENTS ANALYSIS (PCA)

The objective of a PCA is to transform a set of interrelated variables into a set of uncorrelated linear combinations of these variables. Each linear combination (or component) accounts for a decreasing proportion of the variance in the original variables, subject to the condition that each linear combination is uncorrelated (geometrically at right angles) to all previous linear combinations.

The physical analogy of a watermelon should help in understanding the conceptual basis of PCA. The watermelon has three basic dimensions; call them length, width, and height, and conceive of them as being at right angles to one another. Further, let length always refer to the longest dimension, width to the next longest dimension that is perpendicular to the length axis, and height to the axis perpendicular to the length and width axes. Now, the total size of the watermelon can be indicated by specifying its length, width, and height. Would fewer dimensions provide a reasonably accurate estimate of its size? It all depends on the shape of the watermelon. Suppose that the watermelon was raised near a nuclear reactor (!) and it grew to be very long and narrow, much like a cigar. Then its size would be fairly accurately indicated by simply specifying only its length (you wouldn't need the other dimensions really). If the melon were long and wide but rather flat, like a somewhat deflated football, two dimensions would be needed to accurately portray its size. Finally, if it were your good old-fashioned, normal watermelon—long, wide, and high—all three dimensions would be needed to describe its size.

The principal components correspond to the axes of the watermelon in this three-dimensional problem. Now return to the sales performance data. Each sales rep has three scores, one for each of the performance criteria. The scores could thus be plotted in 3D space (the coordinates being the reported values for X_1, X_2, and X_3). The task in PCA is to produce a set of uncorrelated composite scores that measure what the variables have in common, trying to do so getting as much "bang for the buck" (accounting for the most variance in the first extracted components). The 1st component corresponds to the principal axis of the ellipsoid in three space (the length of the watermelon). Of all the linear combinations that could be formed, it explains the maximum variation contained in all the original variables. Whether it adequately captures the important information contained in the data depends on the shape of the concentration of the swarm of points. If the 3D scatterplot of the data results in a cigar-shaped figure, one factor is enough. If not, more than one factor is needed to summarize the data. The 2nd principal component would be chosen so that it accounts for the maximum variation left unexplained (i.e., uncorrelated with the 1st, or the width of the watermelon begins at a right angle to the length). Thus, a PCA reveals how several measures can be combined and reduced down to a single measure. If the variation accounted for by each additional component is substantial, that indicates several components are needed to adequately model the data.

Ethical Dilemma 18.2

A marketing research consultant was asked to address a local business group to discuss some of the research methods currently being used in the field. To make the presentation more meaningful, the consultant recounted the details of some recent studies undertaken by her firm. The consultant was particularly explicit in recounting how her company had used cluster analysis to identify clients' customer segments. As a consequence of such detail, most of the audience had sufficient information with which to identify the clients for whom the research was conducted.

- What are the clients' rights?
- Is there a tacit agreement between the researcher and clients to uphold the confidentiality of the clients' studies?
- Should the consultant have obtained the clients' consent before revealing the nature of their studies?
- What are the consequences of such a presentation for the client?
- What might be some of the consequences for the researcher and her firm?

DETERMINING THE NUMBER OF FACTORS

One of the more important decisions in factor analysis is determining the number of factors necessary to account for the variation in the data. For the sales performance data, the determination is fairly straightforward. Recall the 1st component explains 92% of the variance, and the 2nd, only 5% more. Thus, we conclude that one component effectively summarizes the data.

Sometimes more components are required. To illustrate, let's look at some data from a study conducted to compare the images of various department stores. The data were collected using the semantic differential scales in Figure 18.3.[16] Table 18.11 shows the correlations among these items. A PCA was conducted, and the amount of variation accounted for by each factor is presented in Table 18.12.

FIGURE 18.3 Items Used to Measure Department Store Image

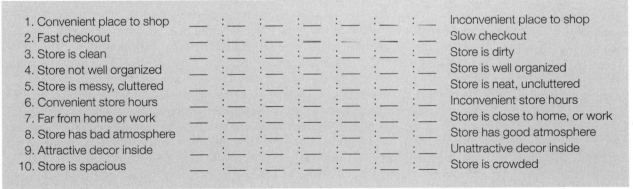

1. Convenient place to shop	__ : __ : __ : __ : __ : __ : __	Inconvenient place to shop
2. Fast checkout	__ : __ : __ : __ : __ : __ : __	Slow checkout
3. Store is clean	__ : __ : __ : __ : __ : __ : __	Store is dirty
4. Store not well organized	__ : __ : __ : __ : __ : __ : __	Store is well organized
5. Store is messy, cluttered	__ : __ : __ : __ : __ : __ : __	Store is neat, uncluttered
6. Convenient store hours	__ : __ : __ : __ : __ : __ : __	Inconvenient store hours
7. Far from home or work	__ : __ : __ : __ : __ : __ : __	Store is close to home, or work
8. Store has bad atmosphere	__ : __ : __ : __ : __ : __ : __	Store has good atmosphere
9. Attractive decor inside	__ : __ : __ : __ : __ : __ : __	Unattractive decor inside
10. Store is spacious	__ : __ : __ : __ : __ : __ : __	Store is crowded

---

[16] The negative or undesirable descriptor sometimes appears on the left and sometimes on the right, so the scoring was reversed for those variables where the negative descriptor appeared on the right so that higher scores consistently reflect more desirable amounts of the property. For a 7-point scale, you can just create a newitem = 8-olditem to get the reversal.

TABLE 18.11
Factor Analysis:
Correlations among
Items in Department
Store Image Survey

	X_1	X_2	X_3	X_4	X_5	X_6	X_7	X_8	X_9	X_{10}
X_1	1.000									
X_2	.79	1.000								
X_3	.41	.32	1.000							
X_4	.26	.21	.80	1.000						
X_5	.12	.20	.76	.75	1.000					
X_6	.89	.90	.34	.30	.11	1.000				
X_7	.87	.83	.40	.28	.23	.78	1.000			
X_8	.37	.31	.82	.78	.74	.30	.29	1.000		
X_9	.32	.35	.78	.81	.77	.39	.26	.82	1.000	
X_{10}	.18	.23	.72	.80	.83	.16	.17	.78	.77	1.000

TABLE 18.12
Factor Analysis:
Amount of Variance
Explained per Factor

Factor	Variance Explained
1	5.725
2	2.761
3	.366
4	.357
5	.243
6	.212
7	.132
8	.123
9	.079
10	.001

A number of rules have been advanced for deciding how many factors to retain for a factor analytic solution. Two of the most popular are:[17]

1. The latent roots criterion
2. The scree test

The latent roots criterion holds that the amount of variation explained by each factor must be greater than 1. The rationale is that the variation in each variable is 1.0 after the variable has been standardized, and a factor should account for at least that much variation to be considered useful from a data summarization perspective. Since there are two factors with latent roots greater than 1, the latent roots criterion would suggest a two-factor solution for the department-store image data.

The scree test plots the latent roots against the number of factors, in their order of extraction, as in Figure 18.4. Note how the curve drops sharply at first and then levels off as it approaches the horizontal axis. This is often the case in such plots, and the method actually gets its name because of the resemblance of the plot to a side view of a mountain. The high value(s) at the left-top represents the peak of the

---

[17] If the data can be assumed to be multivariate normal in distribution, maximum likelihood estimation procedures may be used to test hypotheses about the number of appropriate factors; e.g., Alexander Basilevsky, *Statistical Factor Analysis and Related Methods: Theory and Applications* (Wiley, 1994).

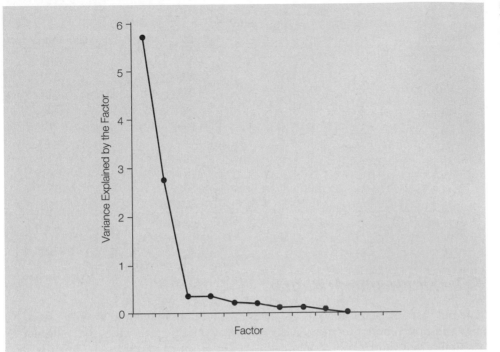

FIGURE 18.4
Variance Explained
by Each Factor
(Eigenvalue or
Latent Root)

mountain, the drop in values represents the mountain face, and at the foot of the mountain, there is a fairly straight line approaching horizontal, where rocks that have fallen off the mountain have piled up. The pile of rocks are called scree. The last "real" factor is considered to be that point before the scree begins. In the example, the scree or straight line begins at Factor 3, thus the scree plot criterion suggests that a two-factor solution is sufficient to capture the store image data.

How much of the total variation in the data is explained by the two-factor solution? The total variance of the 10 variables when standardized is 10. The first component accounts for $5.725/10 = 57.3\%$, and the second component accounts for $2.761/10 = 27.6\%$. The two components together account for 84.9% of the total variation in the 10 variables. (Note that the potential third factor would explain only an additional 3.66% of the variance, an amount not deemed worthy to pursue—it is just noise, or scree.)

In addition to examining how much variance among the 10 variables is explained by the 2 factors, we can also investigate the communalities of each of the separate variables, as we did for the previous example; i.e., how much of the variation in each variable is accounted for by the two-factor solution? The loadings matrix is contained in Table 18.13, and the communalities are in the right-hand column (recall, square each loading and add the results across factors). Thus, for variable 1, the communality is $(.633)^2 + (.707)^2 = .900$, etc. for the other variables. The information contained in each of the variables is captured rather nicely by the two-factor solution. Variable 5 is most poorly captured, but even so, 81.8% of its variation is reflected by the first two components.[18]

---

[18] Taking p = 10 variables down to 2 factors is a good example of the idea of "data reduction" or making the data analysis problem more parsimonious. It's even more impressive when 20 or 100 variables are simplified down to 2 or 3 or 5 factors. Oh boy!

TABLE 18.13
Unrotated Principal
Components Matrix
for Department Store
Image Data

Variable	Factor 1	Factor 2	Communality
1	.633	.707	.900
2	.621	.695	.869
3	.872	−.241	.819
4	.833	−.366	.828
5	.774	−.469	.818
6	.626	.719	.908
7	.619	.683	.850
8	.859	−.303	.829
9	.865	−.293	.835
10	.790	−.454	.831
Eigenvalue	5.725	2.761	

Substantive Interpretation

> Factor analysis
> is extremely
> useful in survey
> development.

The purposes of factor analysis are actually two: data reduction, as we've seen, but also substantive interpretation. After we find a small set of factors that summarizes the important information contained in a larger set of variables, we then wish to understand the nature of those factors.

In our principal components examples, we've seen the utility of data reduction, but we haven't said much yet about interpretation. For interpretation, we wish to identify the construct(s) that underlie the observed variables. Figure 18.5 depicts the model where two factors are assumed to have given rise to the five measures. Recall from your basic statistics class that "correlation does not imply causation": X_1 and X_2 may be correlated because X_1 causes X_2, X_2 causes X_1, or some other cause is common to both X_1 and X_2. The factor analysis model posits the last scenario—that

FIGURE 18.5
Search for Substantive
Interpretation in a Factor
Analysis Solution

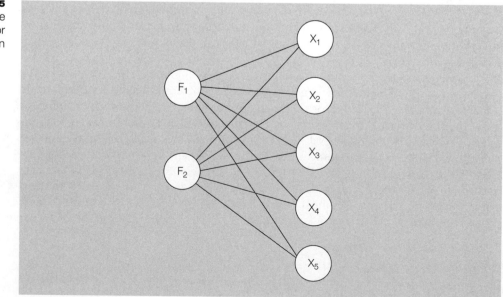

a common factor gives rise to both X_1 and X_2, thereby producing the observed correlation between the variables. The idea is that these variables share a factor in common that reflects some underlying, unobserved construct(s).

For the sales performance data, where one factor effectively summarizes the data, the substantive interpretation is straightforward. A factor score can be calculated for each sales representative using this "general performance" factor, and the sales representatives can then be ranked according to these factor scores. The "best" performing sales representative will have the highest score and the "worst" sales representative the lowest score.

Rarely is a factor solution so tidy—even the store image data are slightly more complex. In these more complicated situations (when there are two or more factors), it is useful to "rotate" the initial factor solution to facilitate substantive interpretation.

ROTATING THE FACTORS

What are the factors in the store image data? An interpretation based on the loadings in Table 18.13 is somewhat obscure. All 10 variables load on the first factor. Variables 1, 2, 6, and 7 also have high positive loadings on the second factor. Figure 18.6 shows a plot of the loadings (using the two factors as the axes and the loadings as coordinates), which suggests that the variables cluster somewhat. Variables 1, 2, 6, and 7 occupy the same general location, and variables 3, 4, 5, 8, 9, and 10 also occupy the same general two-space location. If we rotate the original factor axes to a new orientation, it may facilitate interpretation of the factors.[19]

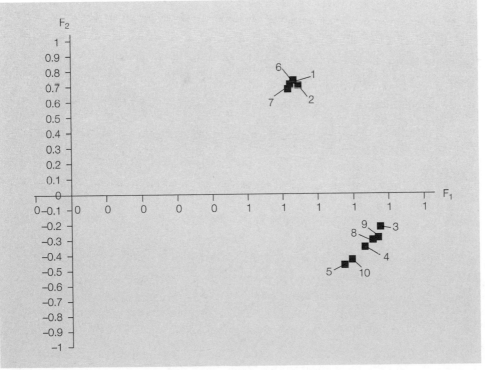

FIGURE 18.6
Scatter Diagram Using Correlations between Variables and Factors as Coordinates

---

[19] Mathematically, it's okay for axes to be rotated. An axis rotation simply amounts to forming linear combinations of the factors, essentially a new linear combination of the original variables.

Several alternatives have been proposed by which the new linear combinations can be formed. Just about all these methods attempt to produce loadings that are close to either 0 or 1, because such loadings show more clearly what things go together and, in this sense, are more interpretable. When a variable is uncorrelated with a factor (that is, the loading is near zero, or less than .3 in magnitude), we can dismiss the variable as not being useful in interpreting the factor. Conversely, when a variable is more highly correlated (the loading is nearer 1, or, say, greater than .5), we rely on that variable to help us interpret and understand the factor. Different rotation methods differ in the criterion that is satisfied when these modified loadings are produced. For example, both orthogonal and oblique rotations have been proposed. Orthogonal rotations are also called rigid or angle-preserving rotations, because they preserve the right angles that exist among the factor axes. Oblique rotations do not, which means that the factors themselves can be correlated.[20]

Figure 18.7 displays the "varimax" orthogonal rotation of the original axes. Varimax attempts to simplify the factor loadings by forcing them to be near 0 or 1. Varimax is a robust and simple procedure that typically enhances the interpretability of factors, and it is consequently the most popular orthogonal rotation scheme. In the figure, the original axes are labeled F_1 and F_2, and the rotated axes are labeled F_1' and F_2'.

Note that each of the new axes seems to be purer than the original axes. That is, whereas the variables had high loadings—as represented by the magnitude of the vertical projections—on both of the original factor axes, they seem to have high loadings on either one or the other of the new axes but not both. Table 18.14 presents

FIGURE 18.7
Scatter Diagram after
Orthogonal Rotation
of Axes

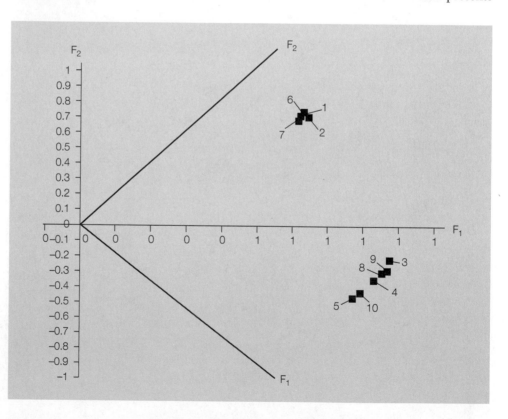

---

[20] Among oblique rotations, the algorithm "promax" programmed in Proc Factor in SAS performs best, and "direct oblimin" in SPSS is next best. Oblique rotations pass axes through groups of points where the angles between axes can be greater or less than 90 degrees.

Variable	Factor 1	Factor 2	Communality
1	.150	.937	.900
2	.147	.920	.869
3	.864	.269	.819
4	.899	.142	.828
5	.904	.024	.818
6	.138	.943	.908
7	.151	.909	.850
8	.886	.209	.829
9	.887	.221	.835
10	.910	.045	.831
Eigenvalue	4.859	3.628	

TABLE 18.14
Factor-Loading Matrix for Department Store Image Data after Orthogonal Rotation of 2 Principal Components Using Varimax

the "rotated factor loadings," which are the magnitudes of these vertical projections, or the correlations of the variables with the new factors.

NAMING THE FACTORS

What are these factors? We'll name the factors according to which variables go with each factor.

1. Begin with the first variable and first factor in the rotated factor-loading matrix and move horizontally from left to right looking for the highest loading. Circle that loading. Repeat this procedure for each of the other variables in turn.
2. Examine each of the circled loadings and assess its "significance." The significance of any loading can be judged using either statistical or practical criteria. Statistical criteria mean that the loading is statistically significant at some specified alpha level, typically .05. This means that for samples of fewer than 100, the loading would have to be greater than .30 to be considered statistically significant (and means that the factor accounts for at least 9% of the variation in the variable).
3. Underline the other significant loadings using the criteria decided on in Step 2.
4. Examine the loading matrix and identify all those variables that do not have significant loadings on any factor. Every variable is expected to load on some factor, but if there is a variable that does not, you can either (1) interpret the solution as it is and simply ignore those variables without any large loading, or (2) critically evaluate each of the variables that do not load significantly on any factor; specifically, if a variable is of minor importance to the study's objective and it has a low communality index, you might eliminate the variable and derive a new factor solution.
5. Focus on the significant loadings, and attempt to name the factors on the basis of what the variables that load on a given factor seem to have in common. Variables that have significant loadings on more than one factor complicate the naming task and are also candidates for elimination, depending on the purpose of the study as well as on whether the mixed pattern of loadings makes sense or indicates there are fundamental problems with the variable or item.[21]

---

[21] There are psychometric criteria and processes for judging whether an item is "bad," see Gilbert A. Churchill, Jr., "A Paradigm for Developing Better Measures of Marketing Constructs," *Journal of Marketing Research* 16 (1979), pp. 64–73; Anne Anastasi and Susana Urbina, *Psychological Testing,* 7th ed. (Prentice-Hall, 1996).

It turns out that when these steps are applied to the loadings in Table 18.14, each variable loads significantly on one and only one factor: variables 3, 4, 5, 8, 9, and 10 load only on Factor 1, and variables 1, 2, 6, and 7 load only on Factor 2. If you read the survey items, their content suggests that Factor 1 is a "store atmosphere" factor; e.g., is the store clean, organized, spacious, and in general has a nice atmosphere. Factor 2 reflects whether the store is a convenient place to shop because of its hours, its location, and the speed of the checkouts. Therefore, we would probably want to call it a "convenience" factor. Instead of describing differences in department stores using the 10 original variables, considerable economy is gained by describing these differences in terms of the two derived factors. For these data, we have achieved "data reduction" and "substantive interpretation"!

Note that the rotation of a factor solution is conducted for one reason only—to facilitate the isolation and identification of the factors underlying a set of observed variables. The rotation does not help explain additional variance. If two factors were originally needed to capture the important information in the data, two factors will also be needed after the rotation, if information is not to be discarded. To see this, one simply has to compare Tables 18.13 and 18.14. The communalities for each variable are the same before or after rotation. The contribution of each factor in accounting for the variation in each variable has changed, but the total explained variation has not. For variable 1, the communality before rotation was $(.633)^2 + (.707)^2 = 0.900$, and after rotation it is $(.150)^2 + (.937)^2 = .900$, but before rotation the 2nd factor accounted for 50.0% and after rotation it accounts for 87.8%. The contributions of the factors have been altered, but no additional variation has been accounted for (nor has any been lost). The same holds true for the contribution of factors to total explained variation (i.e., not just variable-by-variable). The total variance explained remains constant, but the contribution of variance explained is reapportioned across factors. Initially, the contribution of the 1st factor was $5.725/10 = 57.3\%$ and the 2nd was $2.761/10 = 27.6\%$, for a total of 84.9%. After rotation, the contribution of the 1st factor is $4.859/10 = 48.6\%$ and the 2nd is $3.628/10 = 36.3\%$.

The Key Decisions

We stated that factor analysis represents a body of techniques for studying the inter-relation among a set of variables. The method used to analyze both the sales performance data and the store image data was based on the "principal components model," which posits:

$$z_j = W_{j1} F_1 + W_{j2} F_2 + \ldots + W_{jm} F_m, \; j = 1, 2, \ldots, p$$

This model assumes that any of the p performance variables could be perfectly described by a set of m common components. Many factor analysts argue that this model can be enhanced. In particular, we might suspect that it is unreasonable to expect all the variance of a variable to be summarized by common factors only; a fraction may be "unique." For example, although income and assets are both manifestations of the underlying trait of "being rich," they are not one and the same.

What are the differences and implications? The classic factor model is:

$$z_1 = W_{11}F_1 + W_{12}F_2 + \ldots + W_{1m}F_m + d_1 V_1$$
$$z_2 = W_{21}F_1 + W_{22}F_2 + \ldots + W_{2m}F_m + d_2 V_2$$
$$\ldots$$
$$z_p = W_{p1}F_1 + W_{p2}F_2 + \ldots + W_{pm}F_m + d_p V_p$$

This model looks similar to the principal components model, except for the additional $d_j V_j$ terms. In this model, each variable is described linearly in terms of m common factors and a factor unique to the particular observed variable.

The distinction between the classical factor analysis model and the principal components model can be best appreciated by again referring to the sales performance data. We saw that if we had used all three principal components and their loadings, we were able to reproduce exactly the correlation matrix, including the 1's in the diagonal. By comparison, for the classical factor model, we care more about the correlations between variables (the off-diagonal elements in a correlation matrix) than any variable's variance (the diagonal values). The correlations between variables are reproduced by means of the common factors alone (i.e., what do the variables have in "common"). The variances for each variable (the 1's in the diagonal of the correlation matrix) are achieved using the common factors and the unique factors together. Another way to think about it is to replace the 1's in the correlation matrix with numbers approximating the communalities (what the variable has in common with other variables). Of course, this raises the question of how these communalities are to be estimated.

GENERATING COMMUNALITY ESTIMATES

The most popular approach to estimating communalities uses multiple regression. Each variable is regressed on all of the other variables in the analysis, in turn, to get the resulting R^2's. The diagonal of the correlation matrix is replaced by these squared multiple correlations before the correlation matrix is factor analyzed. This technique has been demonstrated to work well; it is widely available and often the default in the major statistical computing packages.

DECISION ITEMS

A number of decisions enter into a factor analysis. Figure 18.8 outlines the sequence of issues that arise. We have already discussed the content of some of these decisions, but let's briefly review the essential questions that need to be addressed at each stage in the process.

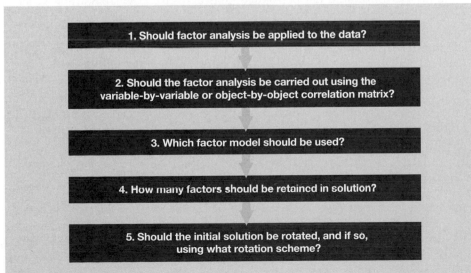

FIGURE 18.8
Key Decisions When
Factor Analyzing Data

1. Should factor analysis be applied to the data?

2. Should the factor analysis be carried out using the variable-by-variable or object-by-object correlation matrix?

3. Which factor model should be used?

4. How many factors should be retained in solution?

5. Should the initial solution be rotated, and if so, using what rotation scheme?

1. Should factor analysis be applied to the data?
   a. Factor analysis does not work well if any, or certainly if many, of the variables are binary. Rating scales generally work fine.
   b. One might examine the correlation matrix to determine whether a factor analysis is likely to prove fruitful. Factor analysis is concerned with the homogeneity of items, which means that some of the values in the correlation matrix should be large, i.e., they go together. A pattern of low correlations throughout the matrix indicates a heterogeneous set of items, probably inappropriate for factoring. A related diagnostic involves plotting the eigenvalues. The plot should indicate a sharp break. If the plot results in a continuous, unbroken line, factoring may be inappropriate. (These conditions often go together.)
2. Typically, a factor analysis is carried out on a variable-by-variable correlation matrix because most studies aim at determining which variables go together. However, the object-by-object (e.g., consumer-by-consumer) matrix can also be analyzed.
3. Which factor model would be used? We discussed the principal components model and the factor model, in which 1's and communalities are placed in the diagonal of the correlation matrix before it is analyzed. There are numerous choices available in most statistical packages.
4. How many factors should be retained in the solution? We discussed the latent roots and scree criteria, which generally work well.
   a. When too few factors are retained and rotated, the output can be difficult to interpret—the variance in each variable is forced on too few factors, resulting in a number of midsize loadings rather than loadings near 0 and 1.
   b. When too many factors are retained and rotated, some factors come out capturing the variance of a single variable or, at most, two variables. This result is counter to the whole notion underlying factor analysis, which suggests that a factor is a latent construct reflecting what a number of observed variables have in *common* (a "factor" with a single variable loading on it seems not to have identified variables with anything in common).
   c. In general, the empirical evidence suggests that over-factoring by extracting one or two extra factors has fewer severe consequences than does taking too few factors.
5. Should the initial solution be rotated, and if so, using what rotation scheme? Often different rotation schemes largely converge in what they reflect about the data. However, even if they highlight slightly different properties in the data, it is useful to keep in mind that all rotations are equivalent from a statistical point of view. They differ only in how they distribute the variation accounted for across the factors, which, of course, is what is used to name the factors. Thus, performing several rotations and examining the results to see which rotation produced the "most interpretable" structure is often a productive analysis strategy. The right rotation can be very revealing of the underlying structure in the data.

Marketing Applications of Factor Analysis

In marketing, factor analysis historically has been used to name the factors captured by the measures, as we've illustrated, as well as to "purify" scale items in survey refinement by isolating and then eliminating those items that do not seem to belong with the rest of the items. Factor analysis has also been used in lifestyle and psychographic research problems to:

- Develop consumer profiles reflecting people's attitudes, activities, interests, opinions, perceptions, and preferences to better predict their consumption and purchase behavior
- Ascertain key attributes that determine customer preferences for products (e.g., brand equity studies), or organizations
- Assess a company's image
- Isolate the dimensions of print ads that most affect readership
- Develop measure of job satisfaction in B-to-B contexts
- Screen variables before running regressions to reduce the problem of multi-collinearity

Research Realities 18.2 has more in-depth examples. The bottom line on when to use factor analysis is this: Factor analysis is useful when a survey contains multiple correlated measures that may be measuring a common underlying construct. Factor analysis extracts few factors from many variables and yet retains most of the "important information." As a result, it helps the marketing researcher simplify the task at hand.

Cluster Analysis

There are lots of marketing questions that revolve around classifying objects. Very often the objects to be classified are customers—if you hear "segmentation," you should think "cluster analysis." A firm segmenting its market is seeking to group potential customers into homogeneous groups that are large enough to be profitably cultivated. The segmentation base could involve many characteristics, including socioeconomic, psychological, and buyer behavior variables. Cluster analysis helps the marketing researcher identify natural groupings of the customers even with complex multivariate data. To segment customers using only one or two variables would be an oversimplification, but how should the multiple variables be combined? Cluster analysis techniques assign objects to groups so that there is as much similarity within groups, and difference between groups, as possible.[22]

An important use of cluster analysis is identifying aggregates of consumers who behave similarly. By determining the areas where they live and the demographics of those areas from census data, geodemographic segments of the population can be formed. Research Realities 18.3, for example, lists the 12 major groups, the subgroups forming each group, and a few features of some selected subgroups in the Claritas Prizm system. We tend to live near people who are similar to us, and at the same time, our clusters can be found in several geographic locations. For example, the "Towns and Gowns" lifestyle, which includes disproportionately high rentals of foreign videos and use of online services, and low usage of coupons and dry cleaners, is similar whether the clustered customers are in Berkeley, Boulder, or Gainesville. Even internationally, the "hip singles in America's 'Bohemian Mix' lifestyle have more in common with their counterparts in England's 'Studio Singles' cluster than with working class neighborhoods down the street. Both groups tend to buy imported food, hang out at bars and coffee shops, and dislike fast-food chains." The rich people living in "Blue-Blood Estates" in the U.S. are like the Canadian "Establishment" in that residents "live in sprawling mansions, drive luxury imports, belong

Segmentation? Probably was a cluster analysis!

---

[22] Recall that for discriminant analysis, there were *a priori* groups, and we were trying to understand the group differences using variables measured on the individuals in those groups. For cluster analysis, we have the obverse problem; we are trying to use information on consumers to form groups.

Research Realities

18.2 More Applications of Factor Analysis

1. Tens of billions of dollars are spent annually by corporations sponsoring sporting events—are they getting their money's worth? Does sponsorship enhance the sports fans' attitude to the company and its products?

   200 Australians completed 7-point scales measuring these attitudes. Using factor analysis, six factors resulted from the initial 25 items:

   - Personal liking for the event, e.g., measured by ratings scales like: "I am a strong supporter of this event"; "I enjoy following coverage of this event";
   - Perceived status of the sponsored event: "This is a significant sporting event"; "This event is important for where I live";
   - Sponsor-event fit: "There is a logical connection between the event and the sponsor"; "The image of the event and the sponsor are similar";
   - Attitude toward the sponsor: "good-bad"; "like-dislike";
   - Sincerity of the sponsor: "This sponsor would likely have the best interests of the sport at heart";
   - Ubiquity of the sponsor: "It is very common to see this company sponsoring sports events"; "This company sponsors many different sports."

   These six factors were then used in two multiple regressions to predict (1) ratings of favorability toward the sponsor and (2) the willingness to consider using the sponsor's products. A positive attitude toward the sponsor, a good sponsor-event fit, and a perception of the sincerity of the sponsor all enhanced both the favorability toward the sponsor and the likelihood of purchasing the sponsor's products. In addition, personal liking for the event enhanced likelihood of purchase, and perceived ubiquity of the sponsor decreased likelihood of purchase. The status of the event helped enhance favorability judgments.

2. Factor analysis has been used to identify the expectations customers bring to banking online. Researchers used focus groups and then quantitative surveys on young adult Internet users to inquire about what they're seeking in an online banker. Items were written to capture both the core service provision, that is, qualities about the financial service (e.g., interest, charges) as well as the supplemental service provision, namely, the Web interaction itself (e.g., ease of use). Both of these categories of features were identified, along with other benefits sought, such as customer service and the ability of a user to initiate interactions with the bank.

   For example, see these three factors identified from 13 items:

   - The 1st factor looked like *transaction-technical* qualities: "bank charges" and "when do bank charges apply"; "how to transfer money between accounts"; "policies on overdrafts"; and "how to pay money in."
   - The 2nd factor resembled *decision-making-convenience* qualities: "easy to use"; "easy to download"; "details on current interest rates"; "special packages for students."
   - The 3rd factor involved *customer service:* "contact details for complaints"; "ability to send questions via e-mail"; "a frequently asked questions page"; and "ability to order brochures and more information online."

Sources: Richard Speed and Peter Thompson, "Determinants of Sports Sponsorship Response," *Journal of the Academy of Marketing Science* 28 (2000), pp. 226–238; Kathryn Waite and Tina Harrison, "Consumer Expectation of Online Information Provided by Bank Website," *Journal of Financial Services Marketing* 6 (2002), pp. 309–322.

to nearby country clubs, . . . and hire outsiders to do everything from cooking and gardening to interior decorating and child care."[23]

Another application for cluster analysis is test markets. Test markets for products, prices, promotional campaigns, etc., require two cities (or two groups of cities), one to serve as the test market, the other to serve as a control. We need to start with cities that are similar before assigning them to be the test or control market, so if there are differences, we'd know they were related to the product being tested, not previously existing market differences. But how do you determine which cities are alike? To keep things simple, say we cared about only two city characteristics—population and median income. We standardize the variables to equate their scales of measurement, such as in Table 18.15.

---

[23] Michael J. Weiss, *The Clustered World: How We Live, What We Buy, and What It All Means About Who We Are* (Little, Brown and Co., 2000), pp. 240, 305–306.

Research Realities

18.3 Characteristics of Selected Subgroups in Prizm Lifestyle Clusters

Major Group	Subgroups	Demographic Description	Lifestyle, Media, Financial Preferences
Suburban Elite	• Blue-Blood Estates • Money and Brains • **Furs & Station**	New-money families in suburbs, upwardly mobile white collar, college grads, age 35–54	Own family laptop(s) All-news radio 31 stock transactions/yr
Affluentials	• **Pools & Patios** • Two More Rungs • Young Influentials	Upper-middle income, two-income empty nesters, age 45–64, in upscale suburbs	Foreign cruise Epicurean magazines $5,000+ mutual funds
Greenbelt Families	• Young Suburbia • **Blue-Chip Blues**	Upper-middle income, traditional suburban families, age 25–44, mixed white/blue collar, single-family houses	Go fishing Watch headline news Interest-bearing checking accounts
Urban Gentry	• Urban Gold Coast • Bohemian Mix • Black Enterprise • **New Beginnings**	Lower-middle income families and singles, age 25–34, low-level white collar and clerical	Jog/run Have first mortgage
Exurban Boom	• God's Country • **New Homesteader** • Towns & Gowns	Lower-middle income, town-dwelling, young families, age 18–34, some college, blue/white collar	Ride motorcycles Nostalgia radio Veterans' life insurance
Suburban Elders	• **Levittown, USA** • Gray Power • Rank & File	Middle-income, suburban, (older couples) age 55–65, tract housing, two income, high school education	Belong to a union Golden oldies radio Christmas Club account
Satellite Blues	• Blue-Collar Nursery • **Middle America** • Coalburg & Corntown	Lower-middle income, mid-size town families, age 45–64, blue collar, single-unit housing	Woodworking Fishing/hunt magazines Christmas Club account
Mid-City Mix	• New Melting Pot • Old Yankee Rows • Emergent Minorities • **Single City Blues**	Low income, urban singles, age 18–34, some college, mixed blue/white collar	Contribute to public radio Jazz radio Non-interest-bearing checking accounts

The **bold** subgroup is the largest subgroup in its major group. For more information, see Prizm Lifestyle Cluster System (Claritas.com).

TABLE 18.15
Cluster Analysis Example:
Key Characteristics of
Cities to Be Grouped
(in Standardized Units)

City	Income X_1	Population X_2
A	1.14	1.72
B	−1.25	−1.17
C	1.62	.89
D	1.64	1.35
E	.55	.10
F	−.94	−1.25
G	.89	1.32
H	−.87	−.63
I	−.44	−.07
J	.08	−.55
K	−.18	.62
L	−1.29	−.86
M	−1.07	−1.38
N	−.09	.02
O	.21	−.11

A simple, subjective way of grouping objects is to plot the results and make a visual assignment. Figure 18.9 uses the variables of income and population as axes. The scatterplot suggests that there are three distinct clusters in the data:

- Cluster 1, consisting of Cities {A, C, D, G}
- Cluster 2, consisting of Cities {E, I, J, K, N, O}
- Cluster 3, consisting of Cities {B, F, H, L, M}

The visual assignment procedure worked in this example because there were only two variables and the natural groupings were pretty clear. However, the cities might be grouped on potentially many characteristics, and graphical display becomes more

FIGURE 18.9
Cluster Analysis Example:
Two-Dimensional Plot
of City Characteristics

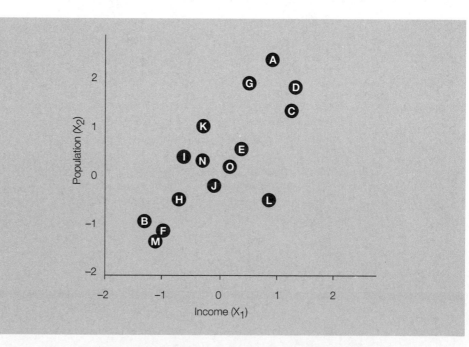

difficult as the number of dimensions increases. It would be useful to have a way of incorporating the higher dimensionality. Further, it would be useful to have a more objective means of forming the clusters, using indices of "similarity" or "likeness."

Euclidean Distance to Measure Similarity

One measure that captures the closeness of two objects in a scatterplot is the *Euclidean distance* between the points. In the 2-D figure, the distance between cities A and C is calculated:

$$d_{A,C} = \sqrt{\left(X_{C1} - X_{A1}\right)^2 + \left(X_{C2} - X_{A2}\right)^2}$$

where X_{C1} represents the coordinate of city C on the 1st dimension, median income. This distance is

$$d_{A,C} = \sqrt{(1.62-1.14)^2 + (.89-1.72)^2} = .959$$

If, in addition to having income and population variables on the cities, we also had a variable that captured, say, literacy rates, we would effectively have a 3-dimensional problem. The Euclidian distance is easily extended:

$$d_{A,C} = \sqrt{\left(X_{C1} - X_{A1}\right)^2 + \left(X_{C2} - X_{A2}\right)^2 + \left(X_{C3} - X_{A3}\right)^2}$$

and generally, for any two objects, i and j:

$$d_{ij} = \sqrt{\sum_{k=1}^{3} \left(X_{ik} - X_{jk}\right)^2}$$

(The generalization to n dimensions to account for n characteristics would mean the sum goes from k=1 to n.)

The "distance" between all 15 cities is presented in Table 18.16. (These Euclidean distances capture psychological dissimilarity or distance; they are not geographical

TABLE 18.16 Distance between Cities I and J in 2 Dimensions

j= i=	1 A	2 B	3 C	4 D	5 E	6 F	7 G	8 H	9 I	10 J	11 K	12 L	13 M	14 N	15 O
1 A	0.000														
2 B	3.750	0.000													
3 C	0.959	3.533	0.000												
4 D	0.622	3.834	0.460	0.000											
5 E	1.724	2.203	1.330	1.658	0.000										
6 F	3.626	0.320	3.337	3.663	2.011	0.000									
7 G	0.472	3.283	0.847	0.751	1.266	3.155	0.000								
8 H	3.092	0.660	2.917	3.197	1.597	0.624	2.627	0.000							
9 I	2.388	1.066	2.273	2.518	1.004	1.282	1.924	0.706	0.000						
10 J	2.505	1.467	2.108	2.458	0.802	1.237	2.038	0.953	0.708	0.000					
11 K	1.718	2.085	1.820	1.961	0.896	2.019	1.279	1.428	0.737	1.199	0.000				
12 L	3.544	0.313	3.396	3.670	2.075	0.524	3.083	0.479	1.160	1.405	1.850	0.000			
13 M	3.807	0.277	3.520	3.847	2.194	0.184	3.336	0.776	1.454	1.418	2.189	0.565	0.000		
14 N	2.098	1.662	1.919	2.182	0.645	1.528	1.628	1.015	0.361	0.595	0.607	1.488	1.709	0.000	
15 O	2.053	1.804	1.729	2.044	0.400	1.619	1.583	1.199	0.651	0.459	0.828	1.677	1.803	0.327	0.000

"distances" between cities.) Note that distance is an inverse measure of similarity because the larger the distance, the farther apart the objects. For these 15 cities, there are $15(14)/2 = 105$ distances in the matrix; in general for n objects, there would be $n(n-1)/2$ distances. How can we use these distances to find clusters of cities?

Clustering Methods

A number of clustering methods exist for forming groups of objects.[24] There are "linkage" and "nodal" procedures, and variations within each method. The objective underlying each method is the same—to assign objects to groups so that there will be as much similarity within groups and as much difference between groups as possible. The different methods can produce widely divergent results for the same data, and none of the methods is as yet accepted as the "best" under all circumstances. The marketing researcher must, therefore, be familiar with the various methods to choose the one that is most compatible with the research project's goals.

SINGLE LINKAGE

Single-linkage computer programs operate in the following way: First, the similarity values are arrayed from most to least similar. Then, those objects with the highest similarity (or smallest distance) are clustered together. Two objects might come together to form a cluster, or an object might join an already formed cluster. Then the next most similar items are clustered, etc. The threshold of how similar two objects must be before being joined is systematically lowered, and the union of objects at each similarity value is recorded. The union of two objects (i.e., the admission of an object into a cluster, or the merging of two clusters) is by the criterion of a "single linkage." This means that if the similarity level in question is, say, .20, a single link of an object at that level with any member of a cluster would enable the object to join the cluster. Similarly, any pair of objects (one in each of two clusters) related at the criterion level will make their clusters join.

Let's begin, for example, with all the similarity values less than 1.000 in Table 18.16. When arrayed from most similar to least similar, the tabulation in Table 18.17 results. The highest reported similarity value (or the smallest distance) is .184, the distance between F and M. Starting at a distance of zero, the first computer iteration would be to this value, and objects F and M would be joined to form a cluster. The next table entry is .277, the distance between objects B and M. Consider what happens at this second computer iteration value.

Since M has already been joined to F at the first iteration, the situation can be diagrammed as follows:

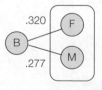

[24] See Chris Fraley and Adrian Raftery, "Model-Based Clustering, Discriminant Analysis, and Density Estimation," *Journal of the American Statistical Association* 97 (2002), pp. 611–631; Brian S. Everitt, Sabine Landau and Morven Leese, *Cluster Analysis* (Edward Arnould, 2001); Henk Kiers (ed.), *Data Analysis, Classification, and Related Methods* (Springer-Verlag, 2000); even Michael Berry and Janette Turner Hospital, *Survey of Text Mining: Clustering, Classification, and Retrieval* (Springer-Verlag, 2003).

TABLE 18.17
All Distances Less
than 1.000 Arrayed
in Increasing Order
of Dissimilarity

Distance Level	City Pairs	Distance Level	City Pairs	Distance Level	City Pairs
0.184	FM	0.524	FL	0.737	IK
0.277	BM	0.565	LM	0.751	DG
0.313	BL	0.595	JN	0.776	HM
0.320	BF	0.607	KN	0.802	EJ
0.327	NO	0.622	AD	0.828	KO
0.361	IN	0.624	FH	0.847	CG
0.400	EO	0.645	EN	0.896	EK
0.459	JO	0.651	IO	0.953	HJ
0.460	CD	0.660	BH	0.959	AC
0.472	AG	0.706	HI		
0.479	HL	0.708	IJ		

Will B be allowed to join the cluster consisting of the elements F and M? The answer is yes under the criterion of single linkage. Even though the distance from B to F is higher than the cutoff threshold of .2 (it's .320), that doesn't matter under the criterion of single linkage. Rather, the one link between B and M that satisfies the criterion value is sufficient to allow B to join F and M to form the larger group BFM.

The next iteration would be to the similarity value .313, representing the distance between B and L. Would L be allowed to join the group BFM at this iteration value? Again, the answer would be yes under the criterion of single linkage (even though the distances between F and L (.524), and L and M (.565) are both greater than the criterion value at this iteration (.313)).

Next, since BFL and M are already joined, nothing further happens at the similarity value .320 (for B and F). At the value .327, N joins O, and I joins this new pair at the iteration value .361 to form the larger group INO. E and J are subsequently admitted to this cluster of objects at the iteration values .400 and .459, respectively.

The process continues to cluster together objects until, after the 15th iteration corresponding to a distance of .607, the situation looks like this:

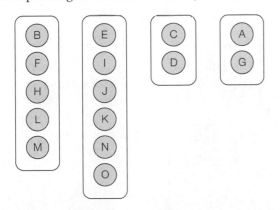

At this point, none of the variables is still in a cluster by itself.

When do the clusters themselves join to form larger groupings? According to the criterion of single linkage, the clusters join when the distance between any pair of objects in the distinct clusters equals the iteration distance value. Consider, for example, the situation between Clusters 3 and 4, which can be diagrammed as follows:

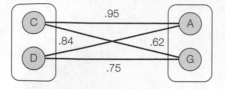

At an iteration value of .622, Cluster 3 will be joined with Cluster 4, because the single bond between A and D satisfies the criterion.

Note that although the clusters are joined because of the single link between two members of the respective clusters, some of the members within the newly formed cluster are much farther removed (or very different) from one another; e.g., the distance from A to C is .959 and the distance from C to G is .847, approximately 1.5 times larger than the merging distance. Single linkage thus frequently produces *chaining,* that is, long, straggling groups, yielding solutions that are not particularly helpful to the researcher.

Cluster analysis results are often presented in the form of a dendrogram, a "tree" figure that indicates the groups of objects formed at various similarity (distance) levels. The dendrogram for the city data employing the single linkage method is shown in Figure 18.10.

Objects A through O are shown at the top. As we saw, the class FM forms first (d_{FM} .184); B is admitted to this cluster at a distance iteration value of .277; and so on. These unions and the values at which they occur (called the "fusion coefficients") are shown on the horizontal axis in the figure. What are the natural groupings in the data? It depends on what similarity level you're using. At a distance level of .50, there are five separate classes, reading from left to right:

- Group 1—CD
- Group 2—AG
- Group 3—INOEJ
- Group 4—K
- Group 5—FMBLH

FIGURE 18.10
Dendrogram of City
Data Using Single
Linkage Clustering

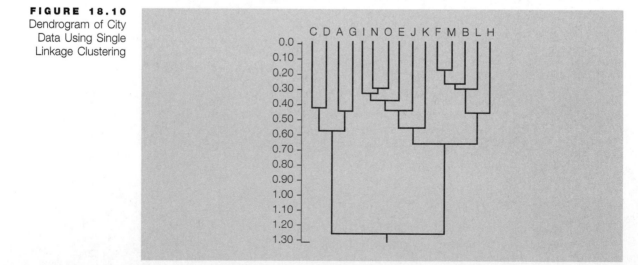

If instead a distance level of .65 is to be used, there are three clusters:

- Group 1—CDAG
- Group 2—INOEJK
- Group 3—FMBLH

Finally, if one selects a distance level of .80, there are only two groups:

- Group 1—CDAG
- Group 2—INOEJKFMBLH

Many researchers would probably select a cutoff distance of .65, because the 2-D portrayal of the data suggests that there are three natural groupings. With p variables, the decision concerning the proper cutoff value must be made without such a visual referent, making the decision much more difficult.

If the researcher simply needed two cities that were very much alike, he or she might use a stringent criterion level, such as .35 to obtain groups with quite homogeneous cities (in this example, one group consisting of the cities N and O and the other group consisting of F, M, B, and L). If a larger number of test-market cities were necessary, he or she would relax the requirement on the similarity coefficient, e.g., .65, which would produce the three groups listed above: {CDAG}, {INOEJK}, {FMBLH}.

An alternative way of deciding the number of clusters is to plot the number of clusters against the fusion coefficients. Note, for example, that at a value of .184 in the figure, where objects F and M join, there are 14 groups. At the value of .277, where objects F, M, and B join, there are 13 groups, and so on. These fusion values and number of groups serve as the coordinates for the two points farthest to the left in Figure 18.11.

The idea is to use a fusion plot in much the same way as the plot of eigenvalues is used in factor analysis. The researcher looks for large jumps in the fusion coefficient, indicating that two relatively dissimilar clusters have been merged, which suggests that the number of clusters before the merger is the most probable solution. Alternatively, the researcher can look to see where the curve flattens out, which suggests that

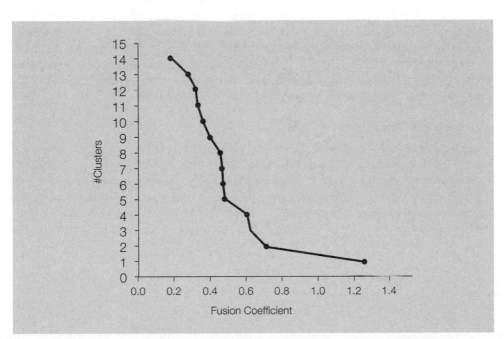

FIGURE 18.11
Plot of Number of Clusters versus Fusion Coefficient

no new information is portrayed by the subsequent mergers of the clusters that would follow. Note that in Figure 18.11 the curve flattens at two points, once when going from five to four clusters and once when going from two clusters to one, implying that five or two clusters exist in the data. The incremental change in the fusion coefficient also suggests either five or two clusters are in the data, since there is a substantial jump in the value of the coefficient between five and four and between two and one clusters. As the example indicates, these rules of thumb for determining the number of clusters can be helpful, but they sometimes produce ambiguous results.

COMPLETE LINKAGE

In the complete linkage clustering method, an object joining a cluster at a certain similarity coefficient must be that close or closer to every member of the cluster. Thus, unlike the previous technique, a single bond with just one member of the cluster would not be sufficient to effect the juncture. This condition is rigorous, with groups forming only when the criterion level is lowered considerably. As a result, complete linkage has a tendency to produce very tight, compact clusters. The clusters are so well defined that complete link clustering is one of the more useful and popular of clustering techniques.

Consider the group of cities ADGC. This group will eventually form under the complete linkage criterion, but consider how. The respective distances are:

	A	C	D	G
A	0.000			
C	0.959	0.000		
D	0.622	0.460	0.000	
G	0.472	0.847	0.751	0.000

At a value of .460, objects C and D join, and at .472, A and G join. When will the two groups join? Under the criterion of complete linkage, they will come together only when all the linkages among the objects in the two groups satisfy the criterion level. In other words, the largest distance (or most dissimilar) among the objects in the groups controls the union. This means that the two groups will not join to form the larger cluster until the iteration distance value .959 is reached. This largest distance, between object A in the one group and object C in the other, ensures that all the other distances also satisfy the criterion (that is, if .959 is "close enough," then surely so are .622, .847, and .751), and the clustered objects are "completely linked."

AVERAGE LINKAGE

The average-linkage method is an approach intermediate to single and complete linkage. As the name implies, an object will join a cluster when the average of all similarities between the object and the members of the cluster surpass the given level for linkage to occur. The average-linkage method involves some simple calculations: as soon as a new cluster forms, these average distances or similarities must be calculated and updated for the next iteration. For example, once C joins with D at the level .460, the matrix above is recalculated to reflect the cluster:

	A	CD	G
A	.000		
CD	.7905	.000	
G	.472	.799	.000

where .7905 = (.959 + .622)/2 and .799 = (.847 + .751)/2, the average of A with C and D, and the average of G with C and D. You can see from this smaller 3×3 matrix, in the next step, A would join G at the .472 level. The matrix of similarities is again updated:

	AG	CD
AG	.000	
CD	.7948	.000

where .7948 = (.7905 + .7990)/2, the average of CD with A and with G. These computations may not seem like much, especially for our small example of 15 (and here, 4) objects, but remember that cluster analysis is frequently used to segment customers—sometimes hundreds of thousands of them.

Although more computer-intensive in terms of calculations, empirical evidence indicates that the average-linkage method generally works well. For example, in simulation studies where there are known cluster configurations, average link recovers the results cleanly. It seems to exhibit the advantage of complete link (fairly tight clusters) without the disadvantage of the very rigorous criterion that all objects must be sufficiently similar. Because it performs so well empirically, it is probably the most popular of the cluster linkage techniques.

The linkage methods are all considered hierarchical clustering methods; if objects C and D cluster together when there are five clusters, they will also be together in the same cluster, perhaps with additional objects, when there are four clusters, and so on. The dendrogram captures the resulting hierarchy—an object cannot break out of a cluster once it has been subsumed into the cluster.

NODAL METHODS

Another class of clustering method involves selecting an object that serves as the focal object, or "node" for a cluster. The remaining objects are then allocated to each cluster on the basis of their similarity to the focal object(s). The basic operation of the nodal methods is illustrated by the following scheme:

- Choose as nodes those objects that have the least similarity or greatest distance between each other.
- Consider these two objects as extreme nodes, and allocate all remaining objects to one or the other cluster based on their similarity to those extreme nodes.
- Split the two resulting clusters in the same way. Continue the process until the collection of objects is split into its original members.

In the city example, Cities D and M are most dissimilar ($d_{DM} = 3.847$), and thus they would be considered as the nodes for the two clusters. Each of the remaining objects would then be allocated to each cluster on the basis of the shortest distance to either D or M. Thus, the first iteration would form these clusters:

- Group 1—DACEGK
- Group 2—MBFHIJLNO

Next, in Group 1, the least similar cities are D and K ($d_{DK} = 1.961$), so they would be considered new nodes, and the remaining objects in Group 1 would be allocated to each of the new clusters on the basis of their distances to these new nodes. Those new groups would be:

- Group 1A—DACG
- Group 1B—KE

Similarly, Group 2 would be divided (using B and J as new nodes) to yield:

- Group 2A—BFHLM
- Group 2B—JINO

At each stage, the cluster analyst could check to see if the resulting subgroups should be retained, or combined back together, based on, say, some average measure of similarity between the objects within and among subgroups.

An alternative nodal clustering method employs a "prime" node. The prime node is the most "prototypical" object—the object that has characteristics closest to the average for all the objects. Because the data have been standardized, the average median income and average population for the 15 cities are zero. City N is most typical (its values on both variables are closest to zero, the standardized mean), so it would be considered the prime node, and the clustering begins around it. Cities are added to this cluster one at a time. After each addition, a measure of the resulting homogeneity of the cluster is determined. When the measure of homogeneity (e.g., the average-within-cluster distance) takes a large jump in value, the "natural" limits of the cluster are considered to have been exceeded, and the last object added to the cluster is removed. The proper solution would be the previous stage in the iterative clustering.

After this primary cluster is determined, it is removed from the analysis. A new prototype object is determined from the remaining objects, and the process is repeated. The procedure continues until all the objects have joined clusters or until only a few isolated objects remain. (They could be left alone, or they could be attached to whatever clusters that they seemed to fit best.) The nodal methods are also known as "iterative partitioning methods" because of the way they work; they begin with some initial partition of the data and subsequently change these assignments.

The use of polar nodes or a prime node represents just two of the many alternatives that have been proposed for effecting an initial partition of the objects. Two other alternatives are to specify "seed points" by picking certain objects to serve as group centroids or even to randomly assign objects to one of a prespecified number of clusters (e.g., three). Regardless of how the initial assignment of objects to groups is determined, the next step is to calculate the centroids (group means) of each cluster and then to reallocate each data point to the nearest cluster. After all reassignments are made, the centroids of the new clusters are computed, and the process is repeated until no reassignments occur. Thus, iterative partitioning methods make more than one pass through the data, which usually results in good solutions, even if the initial partition was poor.

Currently, the most popular partitioning method is the "k-means" approach, which requires that the number of clusters, k, be specified in advance and that k starting points be determined by selecting certain objects to serve as nodes purposively or randomly. In the first pass through the data, each object is assigned to one of the k starting points according to which starting point it is most similar or closest to. Then (1) the mean or centroid for each group is calculated and (2) the objects are reassigned on the basis of the mean to which they are closest. These two steps are repeated until no objects are reclassified. Research Realities 18.4 visually demonstrates the operation of the k-means approach.

Key Decisions

The discussion so far may suggest that to use cluster analysis, there is only one decision to be made: namely, which clustering method to use. *Au contraire*. A cluster analysis requires making decisions at each of the four stages depicted in Figure 18.12.

Research Realities

18.4 Operation of k-Means Cluster Analysis

Suppose that the two swarms of data depicted as circles in Figure 18.A were two clusters of points in a two-dimensional plot awaiting discovery. If we want to find the two-cluster solution, we first pick two starting points. As a random choice, suppose that the starting points are at the A and B in the point swarm on the right.

Figure 18.A

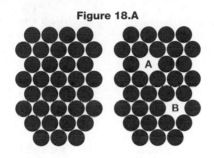

We measure the distance of each point to the starting points A and B, classifying each data point into the group associated with the closer of those two. In Figure 18.B, each point is identified with a circle or triangle, depending on whether it is closer to A or B.

Figure 18.B

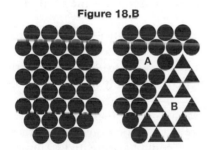

Only the lower right side of the right-hand swarm in Figure 18.C is closer to B than A. Now we compute the averages, or "centers of gravity" of all the circle data points and all the triangle data points. We indicate those by labels A and B in Figure 18.C.

Figure 18.C

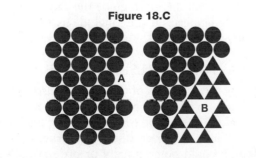

In Figure 18.D we have reclassified each point according to whether it is closer to the new A or to the B.

Figure 18.D

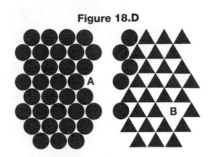

Notice that only a few points in the right-hand swarm are still closer to the A than to the B. Again, we compute the averages of the points now classified as circles and those classified as triangles, indicating those positions by A and B in Figure 18.E.

Figure 18.E

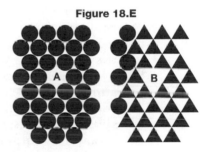

With one more iteration through the data, all points on the left would be identified as circles and all on the right as triangles, so the continuation of this process would result in no further reclassification of points. In real data, this process would have converged even more quickly if our starting points had not been chosen so poorly. For example, if one point had been in the swarm on the left and the other in the swarm on the right, convergence might have been immediate. On the other hand, whereas the example suggests k-means can recover quickly from a poor specification of starting points, that is not always true—it depends on how clearly separated the groups are.

Source: "Convergent Cluster Analysis System (CCA)," *Sawtooth Software Technical Paper Series* (http://www.sawtoothsoftware.com).

FIGURE 18.12
Key Decisions When
Cluster Analyzing Data

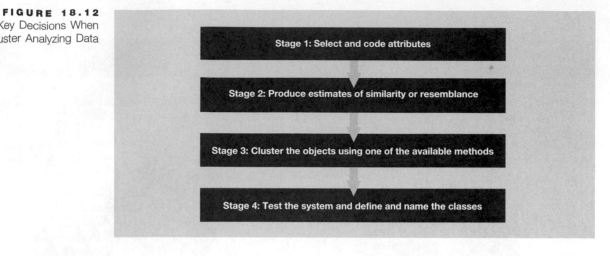

Stage 1: Select and code attributes

Stage 2: Produce estimates of similarity or resemblance

Stage 3: Cluster the objects using one of the available methods

Stage 4: Test the system and define and name the classes

SELECT AND CODE ATTRIBUTES

Stage 1 focuses on the related questions, "Which attributes will we use to generate the clusters?" and "How will these attributes be coded?" The example assumed that income and population were the most important variables in finding similar cities. These variables are both ratio-scaled, and no additional coding (other than standardization) was necessary before generating Euclidean distances to assess similarity. However, had we changed the city characteristics used to define similarity, the clusters might well have changed.

The literature does not provide a great deal of guidance with regard to selecting attributes. Yet the choice of variables used to cluster the objects is one of the most critical decisions analysts make. The best advice seems to be to choose those variables that make sense conceptually rather than using any and all variables simply because they are available.

When coding the attributes, it is necessary to keep their basic nature in mind. Some of them may be continuous in nature (e.g., income), whereas others may be categorical (e.g., geography). For example, we could have created a dummy variable to represent whether a city was in the southern or northern U.S.

The basic problem is to select the variables that best represent the concept of similarity for the given study. Ideally, some explicitly stated theory or assumptions based on prior brand-account knowledge would provide the basis for a rational choice of the variables to be used. The importance of using theory to guide the choice of variables should not be underestimated. Naïve empiricism (i.e., include as many variables as possible and see what comes out), always produces muddy results.

PRODUCE ESTIMATES OF SIMILARITY OR RESEMBLANCE

The estimates of similarity (used to specify the closeness of the objects) also depend on the level of measurement of the attributes. In our example, both income and population were ratio scaled, so it was natural to define similarity computing Euclidean distance. But say you wish to cluster people into similar groups for a market segmentation study, where a number of variables would be nominally or ordinally scaled (e.g., marital status, ethnic background, religious preference, stage in the life cycle). What kind of similarity index should be used as input to the cluster algorithm? Are they to be binary (0 = absence, 1 = presence of an attribute), or matching coefficients (e.g., two customers are more similar if they both subscribe to *Sports Illustrated*), or are the coefficients to reflect categories (e.g., someone in the household subscribes to theater, opera, or orchestra series performances), and so on?

If the input measures reflect cardinal measurement (i.e., whole numbers), the basic decision is whether to use a distance function or a correlation coefficient to capture resemblance. If the researcher chooses a distance function, should it be Euclidean distance, as in the example, or should it be city-block distance, or Mahalanobis distance? Euclidean distance is the most popular, yet it is not "scale invariant." That is, the relative ordering of the objects in terms of their similarity can be affected by a simple change in the scale by which one or more of the variables are measured. For example, we could measure income in dollars or in thousands of dollars and that can affect the ordering of the similarity coefficients if the data are not first standardized (to mean zero and standard deviation one). In general, we want similarity coefficients that are not sensitive to the units of measurement. Standardization is one way to equate units, but it carries its own costs, e.g., it can reduce the differences between groups on the variables that may well be the best discriminators of group differences. The best advice seems to be: If the variables' measurement scales are roughly of the same magnitude, it might be best not to standardize them. If the variables are measured on widely differing units, standardization is needed to prevent the variables measured in larger units from dominating the cluster solution.

What if the data are dichotomous or multichotomous (>2 categories)? Rather than using distance or correlations to measure similarity, a "matching coefficient" is used. A matching coefficient represents the number of qualities that two objects share. However, this simple notion begs the question of what kind of matches should count: Positive matches? Negative matches? Both kinds?

To illustrate the dilemma, consider the data for three objects contained in Panel A of Table 18.18. Each object has been measured on 10 attributes; a 1 indicates that the object possesses the attribute and a 0 indicates that it does not. The attributes could represent any number of features of the objects. Suppose that the attributes indicate which of 10 magazines these three people read, and we wish to calculate the similarity of reading habits for each of the people-pairs AB, AC, and BC. A 1–1 indicates that both people read the magazine—a positive match; a 0 0 indicates that neither person reads that particular magazine—that's a negative match; a 1–0 means that the first person reads it but the second does not, whereas a 0–1 indicates the opposite, implying a mismatch in reading habits. Panel B of Table 18.18 summarizes the information contained in Panel A concerning the number of positive matches, negative matches, and mismatches for each of the three pairs.

Panel C of Table 18.18 illustrates the computation of several popular similarity coefficients. Formula C1 expresses similarity as a function of the ratio of {# positive matches} versus {the total # of attributes on which the objects were measured}. Formula C2 also emphasizes positive matches, but it is based on the ratio of {# positive matches} to {# of total matches, both positive and negative}. Mismatches do not explicitly count in C2. Formula C3 compares {# positive matches} to {# positive matches plus # mismatches}; it explicitly deemphasizes negative matches while considering mismatches. Formula C4 also explicitly considers mismatches; it compares {# positive matches plus # mismatches} to {the total # comparisons made between the objects}. Formula C5 looks at {# features on which the objects are different} versus {# on which they are the same}.

The essential difference among the formulas is how they handle the different kinds of matches and the mismatches. A case could be made for any one of them when deciding which people have more similar reading habits. We could argue that it's the

TABLE 18.18
Some Alternative
Similarity Coefficients

A. Attributes Possessed by Each Object

					Attributes					
Object	1	2	3	4	5	6	7	8	9	10
A	1	0	0	0	1	0	0	1	1	1
B	0	1	0	0	1	0	0	1	0	0
C	0	0	1	0	0	1	0	1	1	0

B. Summary of the Number of Positive Matches, Negative Matches, and Mismatches

	Object Pairs		
	AB	AC	BC
# positive matches (a)	2	2	1
# negative matches (b)	4	3	4
# mismatches (c)	4	5	5

C. Similarity of the Various Pairs Using Alternative Similarity Coefficients

Coefficient	Object Pair	Value
C1. $\dfrac{a}{(a+b+c)}$	AB	.200
	AC	.200
	BC	.100
C2. $\dfrac{a}{(a+b)}$	AB	.333
	AC	.400
	BC	.250
C3. $\dfrac{a}{(a+c)}$	AB	.333
	AC	.286
	BC	.167
C4. $\dfrac{(a+c)}{(a+b+c)}$	AB	.600
	AC	.700
	BC	.600
C5. $\dfrac{c}{(a+b)}$	AB	.667
	AC	1.000
	BC	1.000

magazines that two people both read that determines whether they have similar reading habits, so we should choose a coefficient that emphasizes positive matches. Alternatively, we could argue that it's important to note that neither one reads, say, *Sports Illustrated,* whereas means we should choose an index that emphasizes negative matches as well. Or, we could argue that because one of the respondents reads *Sports Illustrated* while the other doesn't indicates something important about the similarity of their reading habits, and we would therefore want to give some weight to mismatches, though perhaps not as much as to positive or negative matches.

The important thing to note about these five coefficients is that they produce different orderings in terms of the similarity of the three objects. Coefficient C1 indicates that object pairs AB and AC are the most similar. Coefficient C2 suggests that object pair AC is more similar than AB, and that, in turn, is more similar than BC. A different ordering of similarity is produced by coefficient C3, etc. There is no answer as to which emphasis is inherently correct—it depends on the objectives of the marketing research study.

The most popular of the five coefficients highlighted in Table 18.18 are coefficients C1 and C3. Coefficient C1 is known as the *simple matching coefficient,* and C3 is called *Jaccards' coefficient.* Both emphasize the importance of positive matches.

A different kind of measurement problem arises if some variables are interval- or ratio-scaled whereas others are categorical. Should the continuous variables be converted to categorical variables so that a matching coefficient can be calculated? If they aren't categorized, how are the two types of measures to be combined?

Gower's coefficient of similarity to the rescue! It's capable of handling binary (e.g., gender), multicategory (e.g., religious preference), and quantitative (e.g., age) characteristics:

$$s_{ij} = \frac{\sum_{k=1}^{m} w_k s_{ijk}}{\sum_{k=1}^{m} w_k}$$

where S_{ij} is the similarity of objects i and j, s_{ijk} is the similarity of objects i and j on the kth characteristic, with m characteristics in all. The value s_{ijk} must be ≥ 0 and ≤ 1. With qualitative characters, it is 1 when there is a match and 0 with a mismatch. With quantitative characters $s_{ijk} = (|X_{ik} - X_{jk}|/R_k)$, where X_{ik} and X_{jk} are the values of attribute k for the ith and j^{th} objects, and R_k is the range of character k in the sample, w_k is the weight attached to the kth attribute.

The coefficient allows you to specify which of the two types of matches count with respect to any attribute. You simply set w_k to 1 if the comparison counts and 0 if not. Further, the coefficient allows you to weight some attributes more than others. For example, in Panel A of Table 18.18, say the first five attributes represent readership of business magazines and the last five refer to general-interest magazines such as *Time* and *Newsweek.* If we are trying to cluster executives in terms of their reading of business literature, we might want to weight the positive matches more than the negative ones. The situation can be diagrammed as follows:

Attribute

Object	1	2	3	4	5	6	7	8	9	10
A	1	0	0	0	1	0	0	1	1	1
B	0	1	0	0	1	0	0	1	0	0
S_{ijk}	0	0	1	1	1	1	1	1	0	0
w_k	2	2	2	2	2	1	1	1	1	1

The overall similarity of executives A and B is:

$$S_{AB} = \frac{2(0) + 2(0) + 2(1) + 2(1) + 2(1) + 1(1) + 1(1) + 1(0) + 1(0)}{2 + 2 + 2 + 2 + 2 + 1 + 1 + 1 + 1 + 1} = \frac{9}{15} = .600$$

To illustrate the computation of Gower's coefficient for quantitative characteristics, consider the city data again. For City A, income has a value of 1.14 and population a value of 1.72. For City E, income has a value of .55 and population a value of .10. The range of population values across all cases is 3.10, and the range for income values is 2.93. The similarity of objects $A(i = 1)$ and $E(j = 5)$ in terms of income $(k = 1)$ would be $s_{151} = (|1.14 - .55|/2.93) = .201$, whereas in terms of population $(k = 2)$ it would be $s_{152} = (|1.72 - .10|/3.10) = .526$. Assuming that we wanted to weight income and population equally, the overall similarity of objects A and E would be:

$$S_{AE} = \frac{1(.201) + 1(.526)}{1 + 1} = .364$$

As these two examples illustrate, Gower's coefficient offers a great deal of flexibility in generating similarity values, which is one of the primary reasons for its popularity.

CLUSTER THE OBJECTS USING ONE OF THE AVAILABLE METHODS

Computer simulations have been used to compare the "performance" of different clustering methods—each is tested to see how well it can recover known configurations. The hierarchical methods work fairly well, but tend to have problems when the data contain a high level of error. One problem with them is that what appear to be trivial decisions made early in the clustering tend to have large effects on the final outcome because only one pass is made through the data. The multiple-pass partitioning methods work best, particularly k-means. However, this method's performance depends on the use of fairly accurate starting points. Thus, be careful when basing decisions on interpretations of cluster analysis output.

Recognize that the different methods are variants but share the same aim. Thus, they're not mutually exclusive alternatives but complementary procedures to get at the same objective, and sometimes they can be productively used in combination. For example, one way of getting the seed points for a k-means approach is to use average linkage and the resulting dendrogram to determine both the number of clusters and which objects to use as the starting points for each cluster.

TEST THE SYSTEM AND DEFINE AND NAME THE CLUSTERS

Say we've derived a set of clusters. Now the question is: What do they mean?

First we test whether the results offer a reasonable summary of the data—is the solution consistent with the input similarities (whether correlation or distance matrix)? Suppose we got a dendrogram from one of the linkage cluster methods. For each pair of objects, we could read the fusion coefficient (also known as the *cophenetic value*, or the *amalgamation coefficient*) from the dendrogram. If the dendrogram represented perfectly all the information in the similarity matrix, the fusion value for each pair of objects would exactly equal the input similarity value. Compare the actual distances between objects F, M, and H (from the distance matrix in Table 18.16) with the distances where the objects joined the cluster (read from the dendrogram, Figure 18.10):

Object Pair	Actual Distance	Distance When Joined
FM	.184	.184
FH	.624	.479
MH	.776	.479

A similar comparison can be made for each of the other 225 pairs of objects, and then some measure of goodness-of-fit (e.g., a correlation) between the actual values with the obtained values can be calculated.

Methodologists also recommend a cross-validation test of the reliability of the cluster solution across data sets. That is, the data are split into at least two subsets, and the question is whether the same clusters are produced when the different portions of the data set are analyzed.

Still another test of the usefulness of the cluster solution is to perform significance tests comparing the clusters on variables that were not used to generate the cluster solution. For example, we could compare our 15 cities in terms of the average age of the population. Those cities in the same cluster should be similar, or approximately equal in terms of average age, whereas those cities in different clusters should be different.

If the resulting clusters are acceptable, the marketing research must then describe and name them. The cluster's description typically centers on those variables that determine membership in a given class vs. membership in other classes. The task of naming clusters is often a fun, creative one for marketers (recall the labels in Research Realities 18.3, e.g., "Pools & Patios," "Young Suburbia," "New Homesteaders," etc.).

Marketing Applications of Cluster Analysis

We've emphasized two pervasive and important marketing problems that cluster analysis is frequently called upon to address: (1) segmenting customers and (2) forming homogeneous groups of cities in preparation for test marketing.

The number of applications of cluster analysis in marketing continues to increase. For example, it has been used to:

- Sort households' demand patterns for electricity
- Group TV programs into similar types on the basis of viewers' reports
- Group other media in terms of the similarity of their audience appeal
- Develop homogeneous configurations of census tracts, e.g., for consumer and political purposes
- Group brands and products on the basis of how similar to competitors' products they are perceived to be, thus how likely they are to serve as substitutes
- Determine spheres of opinion leadership in word-of-mouth networks
- Assess the similarity of countries and cultures in world markets

For more examples, see Research Realities 18.5. The question of, "When do I use cluster analysis?" is easily answered. Cluster analysis is an extremely useful statistical tool to help the marketing researcher identify groups of similar things; e.g., brands, products, and, most frequently, people in segmentation studies.

Multidimensional Scaling and Perceptual Mapping

If factor analysis has mostly been used to help refine the questions on a survey, and cluster analysis has been mostly used to segment the consumers who respond to the survey, multidimensional scaling has been used primarily to capture consumers' perceptions of brands through the creation of perceptual maps. Multidimensional scaling (MDS) is a technique to measure and represent people's perceptions about various objects—products, brands, stores, etc. In its constant quest for a differential

18.5 More Applications of Cluster Analysis

1. Managers of Real Estate Investment Trusts and other investors are increasingly comparing their property returns against the benchmark measure of revenue per available room (revpar) because this index combines changes in occupancy and average daily rates:

   revpar = [avg. daily rate] x [# occupied rooms] / [total # available rooms]

   In a recent study, nearly 60 metropolitan areas in the U.S. were cluster analyzed on the basis of their revpar scores. The clusters were interpreted as a function both of these scores (e.g., large or small scores, fast or slow growth determined as change from last year, and so on), as well as other known qualities of the cities in each cluster.

   Cluster 1 consisted of large, mature business centers primarily on the east or west coasts, mostly served by major airport hubs (e.g., Boston; Charlotte, NC; Chicago; Newark; Philadelphia; Los Angeles; San Francisco). Cluster 2 consisted of smaller markets that were growing faster, many of which depended on port (ship or plane) and international trade (e.g., Greensboro, NC; Indianapolis; Miami; Norfolk, VA; Oakland and Sacramento, CA; St. Louis; Washington, D.C.). Cluster 3 contained several top tourist destinations whose growth can be weak in the presence of global (such as U.S. or recent Asian and Latin American) financial crises (e.g., New York; Las Vegas; Orlando, West Palm, and Fort Lauderdale, FL; Honolulu). Cluster 4 was composed of several fast-growing markets that are emerging as important high-tech and information-technology business centers (e.g., Atlanta; Austin, TX; Dallas; Raleigh, NC; Phoenix; San Diego).

2. A booming application area for cluster analysis is the problem of "recommendation agents" on the Internet. When you visit Amazon.com (among many other providers), a list of books or other products are suggested to you. These recommendations are a function of cluster analyses.

   Internet providers store huge matrices (hundreds of thousands of customers as rows and their inventory of SKUs as columns). When consumer j purchases book k, the jth, k^{th} element in the matrix becomes a "1" rather than the previous "0." Two consumers are indexed as similar if they have purchased a number of books in common. Once a consumer has been identified as similar to a segment of other customers, the segment's portfolio of purchase histories become sources of recommendations (e.g., "Purchasers of this book also tended to buy these books. . . .").

3. Segmentation studies use cluster analyses to yield precise profiles of motivations for Web site visits. Some people use the Internet in a very focused manner: (1) just e-mail access (33% of online sessions, usually via brief, 30-minute sessions), (2) just entertainment, and (3) just news. Other Internet visitors log on for multipurpose sessions, such as (4) serious searching (product information, online databases, online for almost three hours).

Sources: Mark Gallagher and Asieh Mansour, "An Analysis of Hotel Real Estate Market Dynamics," *Journal of Real Estate Research* 19 (2000), pp. 133–164; Dawn Iacobucci, Phipps Arabie and Anand Bodapati, "Recommendation Agents on the Internet," *Journal of Interactive Marketing* 14 (2000), pp. 2–11; Kim Sheehan, "Of Surfing, Searching, and Newshounds," *Journal of Advertising Research* 42 (2002), pp. 62–71.

advantage, an organization must correctly position its products against competitive offerings. To do this, managers need to identify the following:

- The number of dimensions consumers use to distinguish products and the competition
- The names of these dimensions
- The positioning of existing products along these dimensions
- The location where consumers prefer a product to be on the dimensions

One way managers can grasp the positioning of their brand versus competing brands is through the study of perceptual maps. In a perceptual map, each product or brand occupies a specific point on the map. Brands that are similar lie close together, and those that are different are farther apart. Research Realities 18.6 depicts the perceived competitive situation between Hallmark and Wal-Mart as they ready themselves for the big Christmas shopping season. Consumers' perceptions of different retailers' Christmas themes are mapped, e.g., some stores emphasize convenience, others a more religious tone. The first dimension was labeled "formal/serious" and the second dimension captured the variability of the stores' "religious" appeal.

Research Realities

18.6 Perceptual Map of Christmas Season Themes for Retailers

Source: Reprinted with permission from *Marketing Research,* published by the American Marketing Association, R. Kenneth Teas and Terry A. Grapentine, Spring 2002, vol. 14, 34–35.

Perceptual maps can be created in several ways. As Figure 18.13 indicates, they can be created using *attribute-based* or *nonattribute-based* approaches. The attribute-based approach works with data obtained from the popular sort of survey item where a consumer rates an object (e.g., their satisfaction with their stay at a hotel) on several attributes (e.g., value, friendliness of staff, ease of check-in/out, room ambience, etc.). We discuss the attribute-based MDS approach shortly; we begin with the nonattribute-based approach.

The "nonattribute-based" approach to MDS requires different data. Customers are asked to make judgments about the *similarities* among objects (e.g., Marriott vs. Hyatt vs. Four Seasons). Are the objects all alike? All dissimilar? Just how close are they perceived to be in psychological space? The notion of psychological proximity

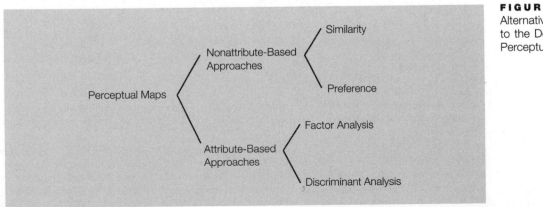

FIGURE 18.13
Alternative Approaches to the Development of Perceptual Maps

plays a central role in the technique of multidimensional scaling, and the technique is sometimes referred to as the analysis of proximities data.[25]

When making these similarity judgments, people are free to use the characteristics that matter most to them. The marketer uses the MDS model to place the brands in a multidimensional space in which the number of dimensions corresponds to the number of characteristics the individual used in forming the judgments.

Example Problem

Say we want to develop a perceptual map for cameras. Label the brands or camera models A through J. We would ask consumers to report their perceptions of the similarities among the 10 cameras by asking them to judge all possible pairs of cameras—45 pairs in all. There are a number of ways we can collect the data; say we conduct a mall intercept, bringing volunteers into our lab (a small office space rented in the mall). We would have prepared a set of 45 cards, where each card has a picture or a description of each pair of cameras. We ask the consumer to rank the cards by increasing dissimilarity of the camera pairs using whatever criteria he or she normally uses to distinguish cameras. The individual could be instructed to sort the cards into four piles with the piles labeled extremely similar, somewhat similar, somewhat dissimilar, and extremely dissimilar. After placing each of the 45 cards in one of the piles, the individual is then asked to order those within each pile from most similar to least similar. Alternatively, we might send participants to our Web site where we display on screen the ten cameras, one at a time. Then we cycle through presenting the 45 pairs, asking the consumer to judge the similarity of each pair on a 9-point scale (1 = "very similar cameras" to 9 = "very different cameras").[26] Either route, suppose Table 18.19 resulted from this process. The table indicates that the

TABLE 18.19
Respondent Similarity Judgments for Cameras

Camera	A	B	C	D	E	F	G	H	I	J
A										
B	28									
C	5	29								
D	24	21	17							
E	32	1	26	18						
F	37	3	34	25	4					
G	31	36	22	7	35	41				
H	27	43	20	13	42	45	9			
I	16	40	23	12	39	44	10	6		
J	7	30	2	15	33	38	19	14	11	

[25] Psychological proximity is defined as the psychological distance between the perceptions of two objects (or between a person's preference for an object), resulting in the scaling of similarities and preferences, respectively.

[26] "Nonmetric" MDS takes ordinal input data (the ranks) and, using monotonic regressions, derives the dimensionality and shape of the configuration (i.e., the map) to model or represent the perceived proximities among the objects. "Metric" models of MDS take rating scale data as input (interval-level, like the rating scale) and relate the model-derived distances to the input dissimilarity judgments through a more restrictive, linear relationship.

respondent perceived Cameras B and E as the most similar, Cameras C and J as the next most similar, and Cameras F and H as the least similar.

Given the data in the table, at least three questions arise:

1. How many dimensions underlie this respondent's judgments about the similarity-dissimilarity of the 10 cameras?
2. What does the configuration—the map—look like? Which cameras are perceived as most similar and which are perceived as most dissimilar when they are all considered simultaneously?
3. What attributes are being used by this consumer in making his or her judgments?

MDS can answer these questions.

Conceptual Operation of Computer Programs

Many computer programs can perform a multidimensional scaling analysis. The programs operate by finding the best "fit" in several dimensions, where quality of fit is determined by how well the distance between the points matches the input judgments. Thus, if the distances between the points in a 2-D configuration, say, when ordered for smallest to largest perfectly matched the order of the input judgments of similarity, the fit would be perfect. To the extent the ordering of the distances is inconsistent with the judged similarities, the fit is imperfect.

The computer programs operate by starting with an arbitrary configuration in each of several dimensions (1-D, 2-D, 3-D, etc.). Given the arbitrary configuration, they move the points around in systematic fashion using a series of iterations to improve the fit until that is no longer possible, at which time they stop and report how good or bad the fit is.

The number of dimensions that are appropriate for one's data and that should be interpreted and communicated, is determined by looking at the quality of fit in each dimension, and recognizing that it is easier to get a better fit in more dimensions because there is more latitude in how the points can be moved.[27] The basic aim is to find the lowest dimensionality in which the fit is good, that is, where the ordered distances between the objects "closely match" the similarity judgments.

Example Solution

Figure 18.14 displays the computer-determined two-space solution for the rank-order data of Table 18.19. As the figure shows, the cameras are fairly heterogeneous, although Cameras B, E, and F appear similar to the respondent, and Cameras A, C, and J seem to form another cluster. One can immediately see how a picture like this could help a firm or product manager quickly identify the company's or product's major competitors, as well as how the picture could be used to formulate a repositioning strategy.

Why two dimensions? The basic objective in MDS is to find the lowest dimensional space solution in which there is good correspondence between the input judgments and the distances between the objects. As suggested, the lower space solutions

---

[27] When the number of objects is small (<7 or 8), it is easy to get a "good fit" in 3-D (or fewer), but when the number of objects gets beyond 10, one will not get a "good fit" in a few dimensions unless the model has validity.

FIGURE 18.14
Multidimensional Scaling
Map of Similarity
Judgments

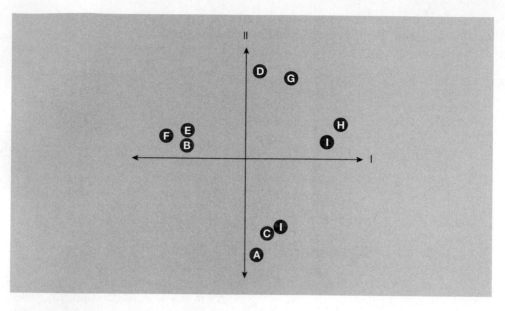

rarely provide a perfect fit—some differences will exist between the rank orders of the plotted distances and the rank orders of the judged similarities. Thus, one can compute a measure of the lack of fit for each dimension. The lower the lack-of-fit index, the better the computer configuration matches the original configuration.

Different MDS programs report different lack-of-fit indices. The particular configuration displayed in Figure 18.14 was developed using Kruskal's "stress" for its lack-of-fit index.[28] Figure 18.15 displays the plot of the stress value as a function of

FIGURE 18.15
Stress Index for Camera
Similarity Judgments

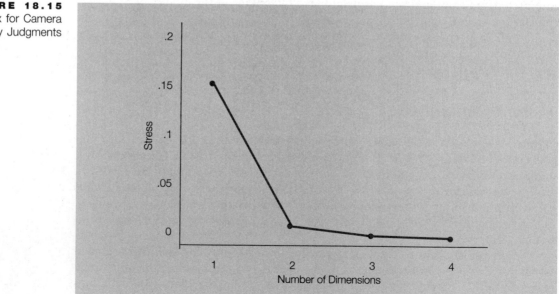

---

[28] Kruskal's "stress" is the most commonly used measure for lack of fit. See J. B. Kruskal, "Multidimensional Scaling by Optimizing Goodness of Fit to a Nonmetric Hypothesis," *Psychometrika* 29 (1964), pp. 1–27.

the number of dimensions that represent the solution. The fit in 1-D is fair-to-poor using Kruskal's evaluations:

Stress	Goodness of Fit
.200	Poor
.100	Fair
.050	Good
.025	Excellent
.000	Perfect

The fit in 2-D appears adequate enough to conclude that the two-space solution is appropriate. The stress value of .019 is excellent, and there is an elbow in the stress function. The elbow indicates that goodness of fit substantially improves with an increase in the number of dimensions from 1 to 2, but only improves slightly as the number of dimensions is increased to 3 or even to 4. Thus, the 2-D solution is parsimonious (the objective of simplicity and minimum dimensionality), and it reproduces the original rankings just as efficiently as do the 3- and 4-space solutions.[29]

Once we have the dimensions, our next task is to name them.[30] Several approaches can be used. First, the individual can be asked to evaluate the objects (here, the cameras) in terms of several attributes, such as digital, brand name, value, automatic focus, and so on. The researcher correlates the attributes for each object with the coordinates for each object. Another approach is to have the manager interpret the dimensions using his or her own experience and the visual configuration of points. Still a third approach is to attempt to relate the dimensions to physical characteristics of the cameras, such as physical size or price.

Suppose that the dimensions were named using one of these schemes, and that dimension 1 turned out to be a "good value" dimension whereas dimension 2 turned out to be an "easy to use" dimension. Suppose also that you are the manager for Brand J. The perceptual map in Figure 18.14 indicates that your brand is perceived as being difficult to use and only an average value by our single respondent. If a large enough number of respondents felt this way, and you are suffering market share problems, it might behoove you to examine how value, and especially ease-of-use, can be increased.

Although we have been focusing (cameras, get it?) on the placement of the objects on the map, we can also put consumers' preferences into the same geometric space. An individual's "ideal" camera is a hypothetical camera possessing just the perfect combination of the two attributes, ease of use and value. Consumers' ideal

---

[29] The stress plot should remind you of the scree plot in factor analysis, or the fusion coefficient plot in cluster analysis. These plots are used to help determine the number of dimensions to retain in the model. The diagnostic sought is the "break" or "elbow" in the curve. In factor analysis, a "variance explained" (or "goodness" of fit) index is being plotted, hence the number of factors to retain is the number that precede the break (1 in this case), because the next small number indicates that little is improved with the additional factor. In contrast, for MDS, "stress" (a badness-of-fit index) is plotted, so the number of dimensions to keep is the number that follows the break (2 in the figure), because that additional dimension reduces the badness of fit to something reasonable.

[30] This task is analogous to naming factors in factor analysis. In factor analysis, we examine the variables that load (correlate) high on a factor to infer what that factor is capturing. In MDS, we compare the brands at the left-most and right-most of the map (and then, top versus bottom, and so on) to try to determine what they have in common and how they differ, in order to deduce a sensible name for the dimension.

points are located from the preference data that they supply. For preferences, the objective is to locate the ideal point so that the distance between the customer's ideal and each of the objects corresponds as closely as possible to the stated preferences for the objects.[31]

Key Decisions

We have presented the conceptual underpinnings of MDS; let's review the analytical decisions that must be made (see Figure 18.16). First, specify the set of products or brands that will be considered. Although they will be partly determined by the purpose of the study, they will not be completely specified by it, and analysts will have some discretion in choosing products or brands to use. When exercising this discretion, analysts need to recognize that the dimensions that appear in the perceptual map are a direct function of the stimulus set that was used to collect the judgments. For example, suppose that a study was being conducted to determine respondents' perceptions of various soft drinks. If no diet soft drinks were included in the stimulus set, this very important dimension would not appear in the results. Thus, in designing an MDS, it is important to consider the range of perceived similarity of the objects in the set. To avoid missing an important dimension, marketers may be tempted to include every conceivable product or brand in the stimulus set. This strategy, though, can place such a burden on respondents (task tedium) that their answers may become errorful and meaningless.

The burden on respondents depends partly on the number of judgments each has to make and partly on the difficulty of each judgment. Both of these issues, in turn,

FIGURE 18.16
Key Decisions
When Conducting a
Multidimensional
Scaling Analysis

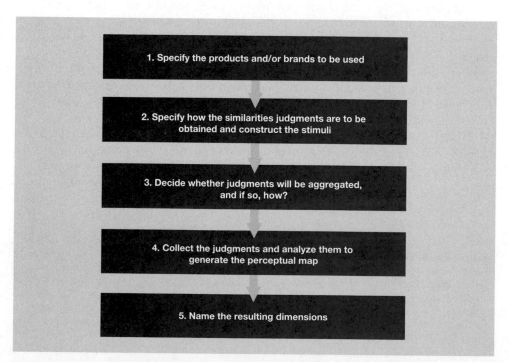

1. Specify the products and/or brands to be used

2. Specify how the similarities judgments are to be obtained and construct the stimuli

3. Decide whether judgments will be aggregated, and if so, how?

4. Collect the judgments and analyze them to generate the perceptual map

5. Name the resulting dimensions

---

[31] Wayne DeSarbo et al., "A Gravity-Based Multidimensional Scaling Model for Deriving Spatial Structures Underlying Consumer Preference/Choice Judgments," *Journal of Consumer Research* 29 (2002), pp. 91–101.

depend on how the similarity judgments are obtained. Under each alternative are two main alternatives and a number of options. The two major options are "direct" or "indirect" similarity judgments, two terms that are relatively self-explanatory. The direct methods rely on data-collection mechanisms in which respondents compare stimuli using whatever criteria they desire and, on the basis of that comparison, state which of the stimuli are most similar, least similar, and so on (as we have been discussing). The indirect methods operate differently—these are the "attribute-based" approaches that we describe in the section that follows.

The third decision to make is whether the judgments of individual respondents will be aggregated so that group perceptual maps or individual maps will be generated. The problem with individual maps is that they would be numerous, even for a modest sample size (e.g., 100 MDS maps, one for each sample member), so it becomes difficult for the marketing manager to use to develop marketing strategy. Managers typically look at marketing planning questions in terms of segments, not individuals. Yet, as soon as the segment issue is raised, the question becomes one of deciding how the individual judgments will be aggregated. Is it likely that individuals used the same number of criteria when evaluating the various brands? Even if they used the same number, are the criteria themselves likely to be the same? If they are not, what criteria should be used to group respondents? One popular algorithm allows everyone to weight the dimensions differently when forming their judgments.[32] So, in the cameras example, "value" would be weighted more for some people, and "ease of use" would be more important to others.

Step 4 involves the actual collection of the judgments and their processing. The last decision involves labeling the dimensions, a task that needs to be done rigorously and objectively to be persuasive to management.

Attribute-Based Approaches

The attribute-based approaches obtain "indirect" measures of customers' perceptions of similarities between objects. Instead of asking for a direct rating of similarity, for which respondents select their own criteria to compare the alternatives, they are asked to make the standard ratings of brands on a number of attributes (or check which brands possess which attributes, etc.). The attributes rating scales (e.g., semantic differential or Likert scales) are chosen by the marketers, prespecifying the features or criteria for the respondents. For example, rather than asking, "How similar are cameras A and B?" we would ask, for example, "How easy to use is camera A?" "How easy to use is camera B?" "How good is the value of camera A?" and "How good is the value of camera B?" A measure of similarity is then calculated for each pair of brands (usually the correlation between the ratings of the brands). These derived similarity indices are subsequently analyzed to get the map. One advantage of the attribute-based approaches to the development of perceptual maps is that they do make the naming of dimensions easier. They also seem to be easier for respondents to use.

---

[32] See Tammo Bijmolt and Michel Wedel, "A Comparison of Multidimensional Scaling Methods for Perceptual Mapping," *Journal of Marketing Research* 36 (1999), pp. 277–285; J. Douglas Carroll and Paul E. Green, "Psychometric Methods in Marketing Research: Part II, Multidimensional Scaling," *Journal of Marketing Research* 34 (1997), pp. 193–204; Trevor Cox and Michael Cox, *Multidimensional Scaling*, 2nd ed. (CRC Press, 2002).

Comparison of Approaches

The advantages of the attribute-based versus the nonattribute-based approaches to multidimensional scaling analysis are summarized in Table 18.20. Most of the nonattribute-based applications in marketing use similarity judgments. Similarity measurement has the advantage of not depending on a predefined attribute set. This is a two-edged sword. Although it allows respondents to use only those dimensions that they normally use in making judgments among objects, it creates difficulties in naming the dimensions. Further, different consumers can use different dimensions, and one then has to grapple with how best to combine consumers when forming maps. Constructing a separate map for each individual is prohibitively costly. Aggregating all the responses and then developing one map distorts reality because it implies a homogeneity in perceptions that probably does not exist. The middle ground of grouping consumers into segments raises the whole issue of how the aggregation should be effected. Even individual consumers have been known to vary the criteria they are using when making a series of judgments, indicating that the criteria depend on the products or brands in the immediate stimulus set. The fact that

TABLE 18.20
Comparison of the Nonattribute- and Attribute-Based Approaches for Developing Perceptual Maps

Technique	Respondent Measures	Advantages	Disadvantages
Nonattribute-based similarity judgments	Judged similarity of products or brands	+Doesn't depend on predefined attribute set +Allows respondents to use their normal criteria when judging objects +Perception of whole may not be simply the sum of the perception of the parts	–Difficult to name dimensions –Difficult to determine if, and how, judgments of individuals should be combined –Criteria respondents use depend on stimuli being compared –Requires special programs –Provides oversimplified view of perceptions when few objects are used
Attribute-based discriminant or factor analysis	Ratings on products or brands on pre-specified attributes	+Facilitates naming the dimensions +Easier to cluster respondents into groups with similar perceptions +Easy to use +Programs readily available	–Requires a relatively complete set of attributes –Rests on assumption that overall perception of a stimulus brand is made of the individuals' reactions to the attributed being rated

the criteria can change as a series of similarity judgments are made makes an already difficult problem of naming the dimensions even harder. One has to be especially careful when using the similarity-based programs if the number of objects being judged is fewer than eight, as it is then very easy to secure an oversimplified picture of the competitive environment.

In contrast, the attribute-based approaches presume that the list of attributes the consumers rated is relatively complete. They assume that a person's perception or evaluation of a stimulus is some combination of the individual's reactions to the attributes being rated. Yet people may not perceive or evaluate objects in terms of underlying attributes, but holistically, not decomposable in terms of separate attributes. Or, the marketer may simply overlook the inclusion of an attribute that the customer considers important.

Regardless of the approach taken, the appeal of multidimensional scaling analysis lies in the maps produced by the technique. MDS is well suited for:

- Strategic competitive analysis
- Vendor evaluation
- The evaluation of advertisements
- Test marketing
- Store image research
- Brand-switching research

In sum, the answer to the question, "When do I use multidimensional scaling?" is basically: Whenever you wish to obtain a map of customer perceptions and preferences. These maps can be used to provide insight into some very basic questions about markets, including the following:[33]

1. The salient product attributes perceived by buyers in the market
2. The combination of attributes buyers most prefer
3. The products that are viewed as substitutes and those that are differentiated from one another
4. The viable segments that exist in a market
5. The opportunities and unserved segments in a market that can support a new-product venture

Summary

Multivariate techniques are those that involve the analysis of multiple p measures. They're particularly useful in marketing research because every consumption decision is based on many variables.

Discriminant analysis treats p measures in a dependency relationship (some variables are used to predict another). Discriminant analysis shows the relationship between a dichotomous or multichotomous criterion variable and a set of p predictor variables. The emphasis is on determining the variables that are most important in discriminating among the objects falling into the various classes of the criterion variable. With a number of predictor variables and a multichotomous criterion variable, several discriminant functions may be derived. The discriminant function or functions can also be used to predict the classification of new objects.

---

[33] For more on MDS, see J. Douglas Carroll and Phipps Arabie, "Multidimensional Scaling," in Michael Birnbaum (ed.), *Measurement, Judgment, and Decision Making* (Academic Press, 1998), pp. 179–250.

Factor analysis examines the interdependence among all p variables. The emphasis is on isolating the factors that are common to the interrelated observed variables to summarize the important information in the data and assist in interpreting it. The initial factor solution and the choice of the number of factors to be retained are key in accomplishing the first task, whereas the rotation of the initial solution is important for accomplishing the latter.

Cluster analysis searches for the natural groupings among objects described by p variables. It places together the objects that are similar in terms of the p variables. Their similarity is properly captured with a coefficient reflecting the scale of measurement that underlies the variables. The analyst has many choices in this regard, as well as with respect to the clustering algorithm that will be used to generate the groupings.

Multidimensional scaling is a technique to obtain perceptual maps. The input data are typically direct similarity judgments that reflect comparisons between pairs of objects like brands. The MDS model seeks to represent the objects as points in a map so that similar objects are close in space, and different objects are farther apart in space. The number of dimensions is determined by examining stress indices, and the labeling of the dimensions can be subjective or can be assisted through the use of additional ratings data and regression.

Review Questions

1. What basic criterion is satisfied in determining the weights for a discriminant function?

2. Just as in regression analysis, discriminant analysis has two basic purposes: prediction or classification and structural interpretation. How are both of these purposes achieved with the discriminant model?

3. Suppose that more than two groups are to be discriminated. How many discriminant functions will there be?

4. Describe the basic purpose of factor analysis. What is meant by good estimates of variability and covariability?

5. What is a factor-loadings matrix? What do the individual entries measure? How does the table help determine the "appropriate" number of factors?

6. What is the "substantive interpretation" question in factor analysis? How is interpretation typically facilitated?

7. What is the essence of the communality question in factor analysis?

8. What is the basic purpose of cluster analysis?

9. Explain the differences among the linkage procedures and nodal procedures in cluster analysis. Between complete link and average link?

10. What is a dendrogram? How might its fusion coefficients be used?

11. What is MDS used for? What kind of data are required to do an MDS analysis?

12. How does one determine the number of dimensions that are optimal for a given data set? How are the dimensions interpreted?

Applications and Problems

1. The management of a large chain of grocery stores is thinking about opening several chains, "south of the border," in Mexico. The manager wants to determine how national-brand shoppers and private-label shoppers differ with respect to income and the size of household. Personal interviews with a random sample of national-brand shoppers and private-label shoppers generated the following data:

National-Brand Shoppers	Annual Income ($000s) X_1	Household size (# persons) X_2	Private-Label Shoppers	Annual Income ($000s) X_1	Household size (# persons) X_2
1	16.8	3	1	17.3	4
2	21.4	2	2	15.4	3
3	17.3	4	3	14.3	4
4	18.4	1	4	14.5	5
5	23.2	2	5	17.4	2
6	21.1	5	6	16.7	6
7	14.5	4	7	13.9	7
8	18.9	1	8	12.4	7
9	17.8	2	9	15.3	6
10	19.3	1	10	13.3	4

A discriminant analysis of the data resulted in the following discriminant function:

$$Y = .333X_1 - .315X_2$$

a. What criterion was satisfied in deriving these weights?

b. Use the discriminant function to derive the discriminant scores (Y) for each shopper.

c. What do the discriminant scores indicate?

d. Compute the pooled standard deviation for X_1 and X_2.

e. Convert the original weights of the discriminant function to standardized weights.

f. Interpret the discriminant function by evaluating the standardized weights.

g. Compute the mean values of the variables for each group.

h. Compute the mean discriminant scores for each group. Interpret them.

i. Compute the cutting score.

j. For each shopper (i), next to the discriminant score (Y_i), compute $Y_i - \bar{Y}_1$ and $Y_i - \bar{Y}_2$. Determine which difference is smaller for each shopper, and in so doing, predict their group membership.

k. Create the table of predicted versus actual classifications. Compute the hit rate or the proportion correctly classified. Assess the goodness of the hit rate by computing the proportional chance criterion. Interpret your results.

l. Suppose that management wanted to classify two individuals according to whether they were national-brand shoppers or private-label shoppers. The characteristics are as follows:

    i. Individual I

    ii. X_1—annual income, $18,300

    iii. X_2—household size, 4 persons

    Individual II

    X_1—annual income, $21,000

    X_2—household size, 7 persons

m. How should management classify these individuals? Show your calculations.

2. When is factor analysis an appropriate technique? What do the eigenvalues (or latent roots) tell you about the amount of variance explained by each factor? How can this be used to determine the number of factors retained in the final solution? Explain.

3. What is the purpose behind rotating the factors?

4. Prefertronics, Inc., is a medium-sized manufacturer of electronic toys. The vice president of sales has asked Bill Jurkowski, a product manager, to conduct a marketing research study to determine the key attributes that contribute to consumer preferences for the firm's products. Jurkowski had interviewers conduct personal interviews with a random sample of 100 customers. The respondents were asked to rate Prefertronics' toys on four attributes (expensive–inexpensive, safe–unsafe, educational–uneducational, and good quality–poor quality) using a seven-point semantic differential scale. Jurkowski conducted a principal components analysis with the standardized scores, which resulted in the following factor-loading matrix. Jurkowski needs your help in analyzing this information.

The factor-loading matrix was as follows:

Variable	Factors 1	2	3	4
X_1	0.812	0.567	0.121	0.070
X_2	0.532	-0.743	0.321	0.249
X_3	0.708	-0.640	0.205	0.217
X_4	0.773	0.630	0.018	0.078

where

X_1 = expensive–inexpensive
X_2 = safe–unsafe
X_3 = educational–uneducational
X_4 = good quality–poor quality

a. What are the individual row/column entries called, and what do they indicate?

b. What does the entry in the 2nd row and 1st column indicate?

c. What is the proportion of variation in each of the four variables that is accounted for by Factor 1? Show your calculations.

d. What is the proportion of variation in each of the four variables that is accounted for by Factor 2? Show your calculations.

e. The following table is a partially completed correlation matrix derived from the preceding factor-loading matrix. Complete the original correlation matrix using all four of the factors.

Hint: Use the formula: $r_{jt} = \sum_k a_{jk}a_{ik}$.

Simple Pair-Wise Correlations
among the Attributes
(computed from four factors)

	X_1	X_2	X_3	X_4
X_1	1.000			
X_2	.067	1.000		
X_3			1.000	
X_4			.165	1.000

f. For comparison, complete the following correlation matrix using only the first and second factors to estimate the correlations. Comment on your results.

Simple Pair-Wise Correlations
among the Attributes
(computed from two factors)

	X_1	X_2	X_3	X_4
X_1	1.000			
X_2		1.000		
X_3			1.000	
X_4				1.000

g. Compute the proportion of the total variation in the data that is accounted for by each of the four factors. Show your calculations. Comment on your results.

h. On the basis of the preceding computations, discuss how well the variability and covariability of the variables was reproduced by two factors compared to four factors.

i. Construct a scatter diagram using the correlations between the variables and the first and second factors as coordinates of the points.

j. On the basis of the scatter diagram, would you recommend that the factors be rotated? If yes, why? If no, why not?

k. Assume that the factors were rotated. Provide an interpretation of the factors.

l. Assume that the original factor solution was rotated. Explain the following statement: "The contribution of each factor in accounting for the variation in the respective variables has changed; however, the total variation accounted for by the factors has remained constant."

5. Kay Sealey is the news director for KASI-TV, the local NBC affiliate for a large southwestern city. Sealey believes that the most important quality of an on-air news broadcaster is credibility in the eyes of the viewer. Accordingly, surveys are taken every six months that attempt to evaluate the credibility of the news broadcasters who appear on the local news programs. The following figure shows one of the survey instruments used by the station to measure the credibility of a newscaster:

Evaluate the anchorperson on the news broadcast that you reviewed by completing the following scales. Place a check mark in the box that most closely matches your feelings about this anchorperson. For example, if you thought that this anchor was extremely likeable, you would place a check in the box nearest "likeable" (in this case, the far left box).

a.   Likeable ☐ ☐ ☐ ☐ ☐ ☐ ☐ Unlikeable
b.   Knowledgeable ☐ ☐ ☐ ☐ ☐ ☐ ☐ Unknowledgeable
c.   Unattractive ☐ ☐ ☐ ☐ ☐ ☐ ☐ Attractive
d.   Intelligent ☐ ☐ ☐ ☐ ☐ ☐ ☐ Unintelligent
e.   Not similar to you ☐ ☐ ☐ ☐ ☐ ☐ ☐ Similar to you
f.   Good looking ☐ ☐ ☐ ☐ ☐ ☐ ☐ Not good looking
g.   Unexciting ☐ ☐ ☐ ☐ ☐ ☐ ☐ Exciting
h.   Confident ☐ ☐ ☐ ☐ ☐ ☐ ☐ Not confident
i.   Friendly ☐ ☐ ☐ ☐ ☐ ☐ ☐ Not friendly
j.   Not believable ☐ ☐ ☐ ☐ ☐ ☐ ☐ Believable
k.   Expert ☐ ☐ ☐ ☐ ☐ ☐ ☐ Not expert
l.   Ugly ☐ ☐ ☐ ☐ ☐ ☐ ☐ Beautiful
m. Don't identify with ☐ ☐ ☐ ☐ ☐ ☐ ☐ Identify with
n.   Competent ☐ ☐ ☐ ☐ ☐ ☐ ☐ Incompetent
o.   Active ☐ ☐ ☐ ☐ ☐ ☐ ☐ Passive
p.   Irritating ☐ ☐ ☐ ☐ ☐ ☐ ☐ Not irritating
q.   Not trustworthy ☐ ☐ ☐ ☐ ☐ ☐ ☐ Trustworthy
r.   Dull ☐ ☐ ☐ ☐ ☐ ☐ ☐ Interesting
s.   Not sincere ☐ ☐ ☐ ☐ ☐ ☐ ☐ Sincere

Suppose that this questionnaire was administered to a sample of 50 people after they had watched a videotape of a nightly news broadcast that featured the specific broadcaster. The following table contains their responses:

a	b	c	d	e	f	g	h	i	j	k	l	m	n	o	p	q	r	s
1	2	5	3	3	3	4	3	3	6	3	4	4	3	3	6	6	5	6
1	4	6	3	1	2	4	2	2	6	2	5	7	1	3	5	6	5	5
5	6	5	5	5	5	6	3	3	5	6	4	3	6	2	1	2	2	2
2	2	5	2	4	3	4	3	3	5	3	5	5	3	3	3	5	5	5
2	2	6	2	1	2	6	1	1	6	1	6	5	2	1	7	6	5	6
4	5	3	3	2	5	2	2	2	4	5	4	4	3	2	3	5	2	6
3	3	5	5	2	3	5	2	2	4	3	5	2	3	3	5	5	5	6
1	1	6	1	5	2	5	1	2	7	2	5	6	1	1	7	7	6	7
5	4	3	3	1	5	4	2	2	6	3	4	3	3	6	6	6	4	6
3	3	5	1	4	2	4	1	1	7	4	4	6	1	1	7	7	7	7
3	3	5	4	3	3	4	2	4	5	4	5	4	4	3	3	4	4	5
2	5	6	4	4	3	3	5	2	1	6	5	4	5	3	3	2	4	1
3	5	2	4	1	6	3	3	4	4	5	3	3	4	3	5	4	2	3
3	3	6	2	4	2	4	2	4	5	2	5	4	3	2	6	5	4	4
2	3	6	3	4	3	6	2	2	6	4	5	4	2	2	6	5	5	5
5	4	4	3	2	4	2	3	3	4	5	4	2	4	4	1	4	3	4
3	3	4	4	3	4	4	3	3	4	4	4	3	4	3	4	5	3	4
5	3	3	6	1	3	4	1	1	2	2	4	2	2	2	3	5	3	6
2	3	6	2	1	3	5	1	1	3	5	4	2	1	1	6	5	5	3
2	2	5	2	3	4	2	3	6	4	4	4	2	2	3	5	3	4	
3	6	1	5	1	7	2	4	1	7	7	2	1	5	4	1	4	1	6
2	2	6	2	4	3	6	2	3	6	4	5	4	2	2	5	6	6	6
2	2	6	3	6	2	5	2	2	6	3	6	6	2	2	6	6	6	6
2	2	4	2	4	4	6	1	1	6	2	4	4	2	4	6	6	6	6
3	3	1	3	4	4	3	4	2	6	4	4	4	2	3	4	5	5	5
3	3	6	3	5	2	6	4	2	4	3	5	4	3	1	3	4	5	4
5	4	5	3	3	3	2	3	4	2	5	5	2	4	4	3	4	2	1
2	4	5	4	4	3	4	4	3	4	5	5	4	3	3	6	5	4	4
3	5	7	5	2	2	2	2	3	2	6	6	1	5	5	4	2	3	1
2	3	2	3	4	2	5	2	2	6	3	5	5	3	2	6	6	5	6
3	3	5	4	3	4	4	3	3	4	5	4	4	4	3	5	5	4	5
2	2	6	2	4	2	7	1	1	5	2	6	4	2	1	6	5	6	6
1	1	6	1	6	1	6	1	1	7	4	5	6	1	1	7	6	6	7
2	3	6	5	5	2	4	6	2	6	4	5	5	2	2	6	5	4	6
2	3	5	2	1	2	1	3	2	4	6	5	2	2	6	2	4	2	5
2	3	5	4	2	4	6	6	2	6	4	5	4	2	3	6	6	5	5
4	4	4	4	2	3	3	2	3	4	4	5	4	3	2	3	4	3	2
4	5	4	4	2	4	3	3	4	3	4	4	2	3	5	3	3	4	2
3	2	3	2	3	2	4	1	3	7	1	5	4	6	3	3	7	4	5
4	5	7	5	3	2	4	2	2	6	4	4	5	3	4	4	4	3	4
3	3	4	3	1	4	5	2	2	6	4	4	3	2	2	4	6	4	6
2	4	5	5	4	5	3	3	3	5	5	5	4	3	3	5	4	5	5
4	3	4	3	4	4	4	3	2	5	4	4	4	2	3	5	5	4	5
3	2	4	2	2	4	3	1	1	5	6	4	3	2	2	5	4	4	5
2	2	6	3	4	2	4	2	2	6	4	6	4	2	2	6	4	6	6
4	3	3	3	2	4	4	1	2	5	4	4	2	3	5	4	4	3	4
2	3	6	3	4	2	6	2	2	5	4	5	5	3	2	5	5	5	3
5	4	5	4	3	3	3	3	2	4	6	4	3	5	2	2	4	4	3
2	2	5	2	4	3	5	1	1	6	2	5	7	1	2	6	7	6	7
2	2	6	2	4	2	4	1	1	7	2	5	4	1	4	7	7	6	6

position. Items a, b, d, f, h, i, k, n, and o must be reverse-scaled before any analysis is attempted.

a. Discuss the possible reasons for the use of factor analysis with these data.

b. Produce a correlation matrix for the 19 variables (scale items). Does it appear that factor analysis would be appropriate for these data?

c. Do a principal components analysis (with rotation if necessary for interpretation) using these data. How many factors should be retained? What is the percentage of variance accounted for by each factor?

d. Interpret the factors.

6. A company has decided to cluster respondents based on the four product characteristics that customers have chosen as most important from a list of 18 characteristics. If the research analyst finds that a particular product characteristic is important for all customers, how should the analyst proceed? Justify your answer. How should the research team proceed if cluster membership changes substantially based on the algorithm being used?

7. Adstar, Inc., is a large advertising agency located in New York City. The marketing research manager wants to identify the market segments for one of the agency's clients, a manufacturer of caffeine-free soft drinks, so that an effective advertising campaign can be developed. The manufacturer believes that the product would appeal to high-income families with large households. The marketing research manager has collected information from a probability sample of 500 regular purchasers of the caffeine-free soft drink. The manager has decided to use cluster analysis but is not familiar with the technique. Information pertaining to a sample of 10 regular purchasers is given to you. The following table contains the standardized scores for income and household size for the sample of 10 respondents.

Average Ratings on Attributes (in standardized units)

Respondents	Income X_1	Household Size X_2
1	−2.75	−2.50
2	3.00	3.00
3	2.50	2.75
4	−1.75	−2.25
5	4.00	3.50
6	−3.50	−2.75
7	2.75	3.25
8	−2.25	−2.50
9	3.50	2.50
10	−3.00	−3.25

a. Plot the individual scores in two dimensions using the two variables as axes. What does the plot suggest?

b. Determine the similarity of each pair of respondents by computing the Euclidean distance between them.

c. Use the single linkage clustering method to develop the clusters. Consider the similarity values less than 1.00 (from part b), and array the distances from most similar to least similar.

d. What clusters exist after the 4th iteration (distance levels of approximately .70)?

e. What clusters exist after the 8th iteration (distance levels of approx. 1.12)?

f. Construct a dendrogram for similarity values up to approx. .56. Interpret the dendrogram.

g. Suppose that the complete linkage method of clustering is used; indicate at what distance level the results will be the same as part e.

8. Assume that you are a marketing researcher for a manufacturer of three nationally branded breakfast cereals. The R&D department has formulated a new type of cereal that the company has decided to introduce under a new brand name. The product manager for the breakfast cereal line has expressed concern that the new brand, unless it is carefully positioned, may cannibalize sales of the firm's current brands. You have been assigned to provide research-based information that will assist management in properly positioning the new brand to minimize the possibility of cannibalization. What method of analysis should you use and why? Given your choice of method, what are some fundamental decisions that you must make?

9. Crystal Clear Beverage Company, a medium-sized manufacturer of bottled water, wanted to expand its line of clear beverages with the introduction of a clear cola. Five major brands served the market. The marketing research department decided to use multidimensional scaling to determine the viable opportunities in the market. Perceptions of the similarities among the five brands resulted in the following similarity judgments.

Respondent Similarity Judgments

Brand	A	B	C	D	E
A					
B	5				
C	9	1			
D	10	2	6		
E	8	7	4	3	

The coordinates of the brands (determined by the computer model) in two-space for the preceding rank-order data follow:

	Dimension 1	Dimension 2
A	−.80	.30
B	−.60	.25
C	−.75	−.20
D	−.50	−.18
E	−.60	−.39
Ideal	−.55	.50

a. Plot the brands and the ideal point.

b. How are the distances between the objects ordered? The stress value, as a function of the number of dimensions employed, is shown in the following table:

#Dimensions	Stress
1	.110
2	.105
3	.100
4	.095

c. Plot the stress values.

d. Do you think that the similarity judgments between the brands can be captured by one dimension? Give three reasons to support your decision.

e. The marketing research department has identified dimension 2 as "price." How would you advise management to position its brand?

10. Refer back to Figure 18.14. Suppose that objects A–J represent 10 fast-food restaurants in a city, each of which is attempting to attract the same market segment. Dimension 1 represents the perceived price of a meal, and Dimension 2 represents the perceived quality of service. Further suppose that an ideal fast-food restaurant would feature very high-quality service and moderate to moderately high prices and that restaurant G is in exactly such a position on the map.

a. Using this information, briefly describe restaurants F and E and give managerial implications for these restaurants.

b. Briefly describe and provide managerial implications for restaurant J.

c. Briefly describe and provide managerial implications for restaurant D.

Appendix: More Multivariate Statistical Techniques

Questions to Guide Your Learning:

Q1: What is correspondence analysis? When should I use one?

Q2: What are structural equations models? What kinds of questions can they answer?

Q3: What are neural networks?

Q4: What are social networks?

Multivariate models are constantly proliferating—some methods come and go whereas others prove to be sufficiently useful to the marketing researcher that they are adopted and demonstrate staying power. In this appendix, we describe four techniques—correspondence analysis, structural equations modeling, neural networks, and social networks—that are relatively more recent developments, but are so useful that they should be added to the marketing researcher's ever-expanding analytical repertoire.

Correspondence Analysis

Correspondence Analysis (CA) produces results that look much like MDS. A perceptual map is obtained in which the interpoint distances are interpreted to represent the similarities between the objects (e.g., brands). CA differs from MDS in two ways: First, the data requirements are flexible: the data can be rating scales (as in MDS) or frequencies (e.g., number of consumers who checked a brand as their favorite from a list). Second, in addition to the map containing points representing objects, CA also allows points to represent attributes of those objects and attributes of the respondents.

For example, Figure 18A.1 contains the results of a correspondence analysis in which marketing researchers were studying the character of Web sites as a marketing tool, compared to traditional media. The various media (e.g., Web, radio, telemarketing) were the objects; they are plotted close together if they were perceived to be similar, as per MDS. In addition, there are attributes of the media plotted (do they stimulate emotions, is there strong audience involvement), as well as attributes of the respondents (segment age groups, favorite beers).

The points representing the attributes of the media help interpret the configuration and the dimensions; the closer one of the media is to one of the attribute ratings, the more that attribute is descriptive of that medium. For example, Web sites share two qualities of telemarketing: both cost relatively little to reach their target markets, and both involve interactions with the target audience members. Both of these media are different from TV and radio in being more about conveying information and less about stimulating emotions, creating awareness, or attempting to change attitudes.

The points representing the attributes of people can help segment consumers, and illustrate more richly their lifestyles and the images that are likely to appeal to them when trying to reach them. For example, the youngest segment enjoys the Web, and drinks Foster's, Guinness, and Red Dog. The oldest segment in the sample enjoys radio and magazines and prefers Coors.

The essential objective of correspondence analysis is to represent everything as a Euclidean distance—the similarities between the objects, the extent to which differ-

FIGURE 18A.1
Correspondence
Analysis of the Web
and other Media

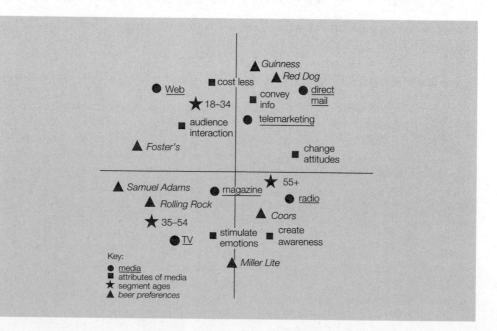

ent attributes describe those objects, and the segments of consumers that prefer those objects. The same distance formula is used as in cluster analysis or MDS (for $k = 2$ dimensions):

$$d_{ij} = \sqrt{\sum_{k=1}^{2} \left(X_{ik} - X_{jk} \right)^2}$$

where d_{ij} represents the distances between any two points in the map. For MDS, the distances would be computed among 6 objects—the 6 media. For CA, the distances are computed among 22 entities: the 6 media, the 6 attributes, the 3 segment age groups, and the 7 beer brands. References to learn more about correspondence analysis abound, and procedures for fitting the CA model are increasingly accessible in statistical computing packages (e.g., SAS, SPSS).[1]

Structural Equations Models

A structural equations model (SEM) is somewhat like a multiple regression in that several variables are used to predict another variable. SEMs are more complex than regressions, however, in that they may comprise many layers of variables and their interrelationships. Thus, a variable that is predicted by one set of variables may in turn help predict yet another. Variables that are predicted are known as dependent variables (as in regression) or endogenous variables. Variables that are not predicted, but that predict others are referred to as exogenous variables.

A structural equations model for customer loyalty is depicted in Figure 18A.2. Ultimately, the marketing researchers wish to understand loyalty, which they posit as

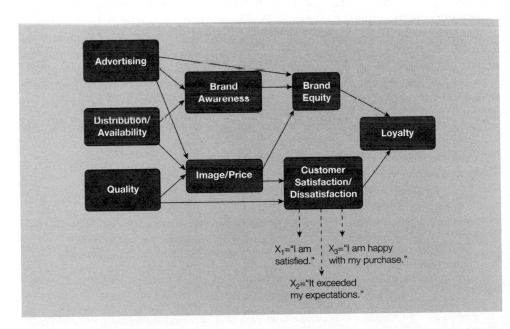

FIGURE 18A.2
Structural Equations Model of Customer Loyalty

[1] Anna Torres and Michael Greenacre, "Dual Scaling and Correspondence Analysis of Preferences, Paired Comparisons and Ratings," *International Journal of Research in Marketing* 19 (2002), pp. 401–405; Hyokjin Kwak, Richard Fox and George Zinkhan, "What Products Can Be Successfully Promoted and Sold via the Internet?" *Journal of Advertising Research* 42 (2002), pp. 23–38.

a direct function of brand equity and customer satisfaction. They expect brand equity to be a function, in turn, of advertising, brand awareness, and image or price. In an indirect manner, then, loyalty is a function of advertising, brand awareness, and image—through brand equity. If we were to try to fit the model in Figure 18A.2 via regression, we would state the following direct relationships and run five regressions:

loyalty $= b_1$ brand equity $+ b_2$ customer satisfaction
brand equity $= c_1$ advertising $+ c_2$ brand awareness $+ c_3$ image/price
customer satisfaction $= d_1$ image/price $+ d_2$ quality
brand awareness $= e_1$ advertising $+ e_2$ distribution
image/price $= f_1$ advertising $+ f_2$ distribution $+ f_3$ quality

The advantage of SEM over running a series of regressions is that these components of the larger model are fit simultaneously, so the researcher can test at once all the interrelationships, and direct and indirect paths, statistically controlling for all the others.

In the example, as these equations indicate, no variables are used to predict advertising, distribution, or quality, so they compose the set of exogenous variables. The others are endogenous. Brand awareness, brand equity, image/price, and customer satisfaction may also be referred to as mediators, in that they establish indirect links from some variables to others.

Another advantage of SEM over regression is that it incorporates factor analysis to take advantage of the correlations among variables tapping a common construct. In the figure, this element of SEM is depicted only for the construct of customer satisfaction (to keep the figure simple). There it is noted that customer satisfaction was measured by three indicator variables, X_1 ("I am satisfied"), X_2 ("It exceeded my expectations"), and X_3 ("I am happy with my purchase"). If these three variables had been used to predict loyalty, without first acknowledging that they share an underlying construct, their intercorrelations would have caused problematic multicollinearity. In SEM, their intercorrelations are first leveraged advantageously to identify the underlying factors, then the factors are used to predict the other endogenous constructs. There are many good references on structural equations models[2] and many examples of their usefulness to marketing researchers.[3] The software to fit these models is beginning to be incorporated into the larger statistical packages (e.g., SAS), but the stand-alone packages (such as Lisrel and Eqs) are readily available.[4]

---

[2] For more on SEMs, see David Kaplan, *Structural Equation Modeling* (Sage, 2000); Jan-Benedict Steenkamp and Hans Baumgartner, "On the Use of Structural Equations Models for Marketing Modeling," *International Journal of Research in Marketing* 17 (2000), pp. 195–202.

[3] For more examples of SEM, see Kalidas Ashok, William R. Dillon and Sophie Yuan, "Extending Discrete Choice Models to Incorporate Attitudinal and Other Latent Variables," *Journal of Marketing Research* 39 (2002), pp. 31–46; Kathleen Kelly, Michael Slater and David Karan, "Image Advertisements' Influence on Adolescents' Perceptions of the Desirability of Beer and Cigarettes," *Journal of Public Policy & Marketing* 21 (2002), pp. 295–304.; Carlos Rodriguez, "Relationship Bonding and Trust as a Foundation for Commitment in U.S.-Mexican Strategic Alliances," *Journal of International Marketing* 10 (2002), pp. 53–76; Soyeon Shim, Mary Ann Eastlick, Sherry Lotz and Patricia Warrington, "An Online Prepurchase Intentions Model," *Journal of Retailing* 77 (2001), pp. 397–416.

[4] The two leading software packages for SEMs are Lisrel, available from Scientific Software International (http://www.ssicentral.com) and Eqs, from Multivariate Software, Inc. (http://www.mvsoft.com).

Neural Networks

Neural networks derive from models of expert systems, where the "neural" descriptor captures the idea that these models are rough analogs of the brain. Each neuron in the brain receives inputs from other neurons, which it combines in some manner to create a resulting output signal that it subsequently passes along to other neurons. Regardless of the model's origin, or whether researchers currently believe that a network model truly describes neural functioning, network techniques have exploded as powerful and flexible analytical tools.

In their use as statistical tools, neural networks are composed of three types of layers: an input layer, an output layer, and a hidden layer. To explain neural networks in terms of familiar models—regression, or, now, structural equations—we would say the input layer consists of the predictor variables and the output layer, the dependent variable. Neural networks modelers call the variables, nodes.

As an example, consider the network model depicted in Figure 18A.3. In this figure, the marketing researchers are using neural nets to assist them in their go/no-go decision in launching a product line in China. There are three input nodes: how the product did locally in concept testing, how it fared at in-home use testing, and the marketing research department's forecasts of likely market share.

The hidden layer is also composed of nodes. These nodes are functions that translate the inputs into the output. The inputs to one hidden node are weighted and combined and then sent along to the next layer. Note that the neural net in Figure 18.A3 would be functioning like a regression if the following conditions were true: (1) there was no second, hidden node (labeled "function 2"); (2) there were no links to or from it; and (3) the weights going from the three input layer nodes to the hidden layer node were betas and the combination was linear. This neural net is more complicated than a regression because of that second hidden node. Furthermore, neural nets are different from regressions, in general, in that weights may be selected to optimize other criteria, and the inputs may be combined in a function that is nonlinear. For example, an input variable of market share is continuous, more is better, and it may well contribute to the go/no-go decision. However, coupled with that, many firms operate with the criterion that the achieved market share would have to

FIGURE 18A.3
Neural Networks Model
of Product Introduction

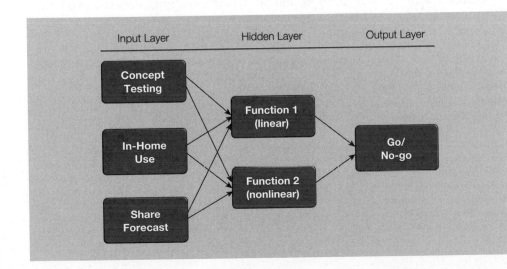

be "at least" some number to deem going to market worthwhile. Hence, a threshold or step function might be useful supplemental information in this go/no-go model.

In addition, neural network modelers speak of a network model learning the relationship among the variables. What learning means for an algorithm is convergence and cross-validation. Specifically, a "training" data set is introduced to the neural network model, which seeks to optimize the model predictions to fit the data by trying weights and functions, and updating iteratively to improve the fit. Then, when the weights and nodal functions have been estimated on the training data, the hold-out sample of data is input to see how well the model fits in the cross-validation, which is used to further refine the model parameters and specifications.

Many introductions to neural networks exist.[5] They are gaining popularity because they are so flexible; e.g., the functions at the nodes need not be so restrictive as "linear," and very few assumptions are made about the data (such as ordinal or interval) or distributions (e.g., data do not need to be multivariate normally distributed). As a result of this flexibility, the models are also quite robust—there are no distributional assumptions to be violated, and the data can be relatively messy. The only major drawback is that these techniques, like many nonparametric methods, require large databases. Increasingly, of course, many applications include large databases, e.g., CRM studies. Thus, these tools seem to be a good answer to many contemporary database problems. In particular, neural networks have been used in business applications like credit approval, predicting bankruptcy, and stock market simulations, to name a few. Marketers are currently exploring their usefulness in data-mining and other applications with large databases.[6]

Social Networks

Though "social networks" might sound like "neural networks," the two methods have little in common. A social network is a body of techniques that facilitates the description of relationships. The relationships exist between actors. In marketing, actors can be organizations, departments within organizations, or people. Perhaps the most frequent applications of networks in marketing have been to study the flow of word-of-mouth.[7] Other applications in marketing have included the study of power conflicts among distribution channel members, communication links between departments within an organization, and the dynamic exchange between two people

---

[5] See Michael Vine, Kate Smith and Jatinder Gupta (eds.), *Neural Networks in Business* (Edito Idea Group, 2003); Paulo Lisboa (ed.) *Business Applications of Neural Networks* (World Scientific, 2000); Tony Schellinck and Kent Groves, "How Low Can You Go? The Value of Sparse Data in Retail Databases," *Journal of Database Marketing* 9 (2002), pp. 143–149.

[6] For more examples of neural nets, see Derrick Boone and Michelle Roehm, "Retail Segmentation Using Artificial Neural Networks," *International Journal of Research in Marketing* 19 (2002), pp. 287–301; C. P. Rao and Jafar Ali, "Neural Network Model for Database Marketing in the New Global Economy," *Marketing Intelligence and Planning* 20 (2002), pp. 35–43.

[7] E.g., Douglas Bowman and Das Narayandas, "Managing Customer-Initiated Contacts with Manufacturers: The Impact on Share of Category Requirements and Word-of-Mouth Behavior," *Journal of Marketing Research* 38 (2001), pp. 281–297; Edward Keller, Jonathan Berry and Douglas Reeves, *The Influentials: One American in Ten Tells the Other Nine How to Vote, Where to Eat, and What to Buy* (Simon & Schuster, 2004); Aric Rindfleisch and Christine Moorman, "The Acquisition and Utilization of Information in New Product Alliances: A Strength-of-Ties Perspective," *Journal of Marketing* 65 (2001), pp. 1–18; Scott Swanson and Scott Kelley, "Service Recovery Attributions and Word-of-Mouth Intentions," *European Journal of Marketing* 35 (2001), pp. 194–211.

negotiating, such as a buyer and seller in a market exchange, or a husband and wife in a consumer purchase.[8]

As an example, consider the network depicted in Figure 18A.4. This network shows the flow of information among four marketing representatives of a high-tech firm, three engineers, and two computer scientists. The actors in the network are depicted by the labels, "M1" (1st marketer), M2 (2nd marketer), E1 (1st engineer), and so on.

The communication relationships that exist among these nine actors are depicted by the arrows linking them. Note that most of the communications are represented by bidirectional arrows, meaning that the flow of information goes in both directions. However, a few arrows are unidirectional, representing that CS1 (or CS2) shares information with CS2 (or M3), but information is not returned reciprocally. These asymmetric ties may be sensible if, say, CS2 worked for CS1, and CS1 was merely keeping CS2 informed of the firm's developments. Note also that the "strength of ties" can be captured with, say, the bold lines between M2 and M4, and between E2 and E3. These bold lines indicate that the communication ties in these two dyads are even stronger than those among the other people in the network.

Network data may be collected in a variety of ways. Each of these nine people might be asked, "How often do you talk with employee X about your work projects?" where each of the eight remaining network members' names would appear as "X" in turn. The relation might be asked more specifically, "How often do you ask for advice from X?" or "How often do you share data with X?" The relation might convey content beyond communication, for example, "How much do you respect X?" "Would your position in the company be enhanced if X were laid off in a downsizing?" or "Do you and your family socialize with X and X's family?" and so forth. Data might also be observational, for example, noting the number of e-mails in the company system that are sent from M1 to M2 and back again. Network researchers have also clocked social interaction time (e.g., around the water cooler, or visits by one person to another's office).

FIGURE 18A.4
Social Networks Model of a High-Tech Marketing Organization

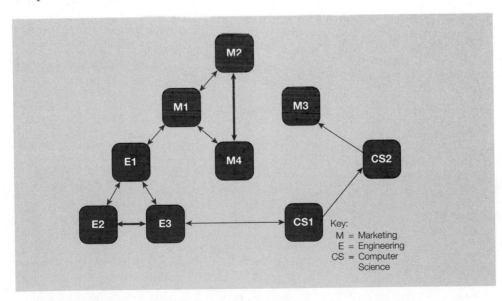

Key:
M = Marketing
E = Engineering
CS = Computer Science

[8] E.g., Kersi Antia and Gary Frazier, "The Severity of Contract Enforcement in Interfirm Channel Relationships" *Journal of Marketing* 65 (2001), pp. 67-81; Andy Serwer, "The Matrix" *Fortune* (March 31, 2003), pp. 108–109.

The diagrams of network connections are often enlightening in themselves. For example, this particular figure might indicate some problem for person M3, a marketing person who gets information only through the CS2 person, and not as a function of communication with others in the marketing department.

Beyond graphing the relationships, it is also important to analyze them more systematically. The relationship between actors i and j are recorded in a matrix, where the (i^{th}, j^{th}) element is a "1" if actor i sends an e-mail, say, to j, and "0" if not, and the (j^{th}, i^{th}) element in the matrix is a "1" if actor j sends an e-mail to actor i, and "0" if not. These matrices are then analyzed to identify certain qualities of the relationship structures. For example, actors E3 and CS1, and E1 and M1 would be considered actors with high "centrality," because if their respective links were broken, communication would not flow throughout the entire network. For information to pass from M4 to M3, say, these two particular links must remain intact. The centrality of an actor is one indication of the actor's importance in the network—without these key actors, the structure of the network would change substantially. If, on the other hand, actor M2 or E2 were removed from the network, the flow of communication would remain largely unchanged in the organization—other actors would make up for their loss, so these "less central" actors are less important to the network.

Subgroups are also a focus of network analysis. The members M1, M2, and M4, and the engineers, form two "cliques," groups of actors who are all interconnected amongst themselves. Cliques can be beneficial, as in this setting of sharing information. Cliques in other applications can be troublesome, for example, as in coalition formation and negotiation disputes. Whether a quality of a network (centrality, cliques, etc.) is good or bad depends on the setting and the content of the relationships being represented in the network.

More information about network data and their analyses can be found in several good sources. Modeling social networks will continue to increase in importance as marketers come to realize their full potential.

Cases

CTM Productions (B)[1]

CTM Productions, formerly Children's Theatre of Madison, was formed in 1965 to "produce theater of the highest quality." CTM's mission is to ensure that the theatre's efforts are inclusive of the entire family. For CTM to fulfill its role in the community, the organization must identify its present audience in terms of demographic, psychographic, and media-exposure characteristics.

The research team decided to study the audience of CTM's production *To Kill a Mockingbird*. The study had three major objectives: (1) to develop an audience profile, including demographic and media-exposure data; (2) to provide a framework and data-collection instrument for future marketing research; and (3) to supply a list of potential season subscribers.

CTM had never undertaken marketing research prior to this study, so internal secondary information about previous audiences did not exist. External secondary information provided guidance as to the types of questions to be asked in a survey and the appropriate phrasing of these questions. The questionnaire is shown in Figure 3.7.1 of CTM Productions (A) in Case 3.7.

CTM's volunteer ushers distributed the survey at each of the 15 performances of *To Kill a Mockingbird*. The number of completed surveys for each show varied with the size of the audience for that show. A total of 1,016 usable surveys were collected during the course of the study. The research team wants to analyze the data to understand the profile of CTM audiences in general as well as how the audience profiles vary among different performances of the same production.

Questions

1. Discuss the implications for CTM's marketing team if there are significant differences in the demographic profiles of those people attending the afternoon versus the evening shows.
2. Generate *a priori* hypotheses about the demographic profiles for the *To Kill a Mockingbird* performances. Identify the cross-tabulations necessary to test your hypotheses. Explain why these particular cross-tabulations are necessary.
3. Using the data, run one-way tabulations on these data. Discuss the general findings from these tabulations.
4. Run the cross-tabulations that you chose. What recommendations would you make to CTM based on these tables? Are the recommendations actionable? Explain.
5. What are the limitations of these profiles? Explain.

---

[1] The contributions of Sara L. Pitterle to this case are gratefully acknowledged.

E-Food and the Online Grocery Competition (C) (Data set available on text Web site)

Ashley Sims, the MBA student who is thinking about starting an online grocery, has some click-stream data to analyze. She recruited 10 volunteers for her study as they left a local grocery retail store. At a mutually convenient time, each participant came to the local library and sat before Sims's computer, where they were told to try using the system as if they were really going to shop for groceries. Upon completion, Sims asked them what they thought of the whole process. Figure 5.2.1 contains click-streams from four of these consumers.

Questions

1. What do you learn upon examination of the click-streams? How does consumer 1 think? 2? 3? What do you suppose is going on with consumer 4?
2. Could you reproduce the layout of the screens—where the various buttons (for example, "sort by price," "sort by nutritional value") are located, using these data? (Keep in mind that a boxed area on which a user clicks takes up several spaces in all directions, and that most users' clicks are not precisely in the center of the buttons.)
3. What do you suppose long time intervals between clicks mean? What assumptions are you making?
4. What recommendations would you make to Sims about designing her online grocery software, based on what these click-stream data suggest?

Internet Advertising and Your Brain (B)

Recall your responsibilities as the key marketing person for a relatively new Internet company that offers travel packages for "extreme sports." Given that the majority of customers are young men, and that young men are disproportionately online, it was thought that purchasing Internet banner ads at popular sites would be a cost-efficient way of encouraging these thrill-seekers and potential buyers to click through your banner ad at the host site, sending them onto your site to, it was hoped, learn about and eventually purchase an extreme sports vacation adventure.

As marketing guru, you had created two ads, a "beauty" ad (colorful and big on graphics) and an "info" ad (less splashy, more writing and detail). You tested both of these ads in a left-screen position and a right-screen position.

FIGURE 5.2.1　Click-Stream Data from Online Grocery Consumers*

Consumer 1: ,11:29:42:03; 50:49; welcome scrn. ,11:31:05:23; 50:19; search scrn. ,11:31:48:10; 49:47; i5 'coke'. ,11:32:
52:00; 85:31; sort-by-size. ,11:34:02:03; 84:61; sort-by-nutrition. ,11:37:12:59; 83:77; sort-by-price. ,11:37:44:09; 83:76;
sort-by-price. ,11:38:29:42; 85:44; sort-by-brand. ,11:40:33:13; 90:81; buy-2,cocacola, 6-12zcans,$2.99,notonsale. ,11:41:
47:53; 10:13; returntosearch. ,11:42:42:52; 50:49; i5 'pretzzels'. ,11:42:57:12; 50:50; o5 'notfound'. ,11:43:14:51; 50:49;
i5'pretzels'. ,11:43:22:33; 84:49; noinput. ,11:43:42:03; 84:45; sort-by-brand. ,11:44:12:15; 92:67; buy-1,roldgold, 15oz,
$1.99,onsale. ,11:44:47:13; 10:15; returntosearch. ,11:46:02:02; 50:51; i5'snickers'. ,11:46:24:03; 85:31; sort-by-size.
,11:46:54:12; 89:85; buy-3,bigsnickers,3.7oz,$.95,notonsale. ,11:47:41:42; 95:05; checkout.

Consumer 2: ,14:39:12:13; 50:47 welcome scrn. ,14:39:28:23; 50:42; personal-list. ,14:40:10:49; 10:89; i5'2'. ,14:40:52:38;
90:88; buy-2,lettuce,head,$1.39,notonsale. ,14:41:22:53; 11:86; i5'1'. ,14:41:42:07; 89:86; buy-1,deanskimmilk,.5gal,$2.09,
notonsale. ,14:42:09:10; 11:82; i5'3'. ,14:42:29:42; 90:81; buy-3,lrgdelicapples,$1.29/lb,notonsale. ,14:43:13:13; 10:60; i5'1'.
,14:43:19:53; 91:61; buy-1,ryebread,slcd,1lb,$2.29,notonsale. ,14:44:14:42; 94:06; checkout.

Consumer 3: ,08:23:09:42; 50:49; welcome scrn. ,08:23:17:43; 50:20; search scrn. ,08:23:58:10; 50:49; i5'mustard'.
,08:24:11:01; 85:75; sort-by-price. ,08:24:52:53; 89:61; buy-1,smlFrnchylwmustard,8oz.,$.95,onsale. ,08:25:27:23; 09:10;
returntosearch. ,08:26:32:00; 50:48; i5 'buns'. ,08:27:11:12; 10:15; returntosearch. ,08:27:49:21; 49:50; i5'hotdog buns'.
,08:29:18:51; 90:05; buy-1,htdgbuns,8ct,$2.19,onsale. ,08:33:11:12; 94:05; checkout.

Consumer 4: ,16:53:22:01; 50:50; welcome scrn. ,16:55:31:55; 50:49; welcome scrn. ,16:57:44:19; 50:62; browse.
,17:02:22:50; 95:95; helpscroll. ,17:13:42:33; 14:75; browse-frozen. ,17:17:59:22; 35:65; browse-icecream. ,17:23:45:49;
94:91; noinput. ,17:24:18:09:42; 94:95; helpscroll. ,17:30:10:27; 76:15; browse-icespecialties. ,17:32:41:03; 94:96;
helpscroll. ,17:35:12:02; 50:90; i5 'buy 1 icecream'. ,17:37:07:42; 50:10; o5 'cannotexec'. ,17:39:50:15; 95:06; checkout.

*Click-stream data can be stored in different formats. This format contains the essential information: each click is stored between , and . .
The first piece of information depicted in the click-stream data unit is the PC internal time recorder in hours, minutes, seconds, and 60ths
of seconds. The second piece of information is the location on the screen upon which the user clicked. The pixel coordinates offer the most
precise measurement of location, but for ease of interpretation, those coordinates have been translated to units ranging from 0 to 100, with
the first coordinate denoting the relative placement of the click from left (0) to right (100), and the second coordinate denoting bottom (0) to
top (100) of the screen. The final piece of information is the http, the exact location in Internet space of where the click sends the user. For
the purposes of this analysis, the data have already been preprocessed, so as to interpret those Internet locations. For example, rather than
an apparently meaningless-looking location of http://www.onlinefood.com/1445.html, the data are represented as: softdrink/CocaCola/sort-size-
by-value (that is, the "onlinefood.com" is constant since all these clicks are in its subdomain, and the content of the html is provided). In the
content stream, o = output (something the computer displays) and i = input (something the user enters).

Your research led you to expect that the beauty ad might do better at the left, so as to be processed by the right-brain hemisphere, which handles pictures better. Analogously, the info ad might do better at the right, to be processed by the left brain, which deals with verbal, detailed information better.

You've obtained the click-through data from your banner advertisement Web hosts, in proportion to the traffic to their site who did not click through your banner onto your site. The results are presented below in an analysis of variance table format. Some of the information is missing—you need to fill it in before answering the questions that follow. (The critical F-value for each test is 4.00.)

The incomplete analysis of variance table of results follows:

Source	SS	df	MS	F
Banner Type	18.4	1	?	?
Banner Placement	13.3	1	?	?
Type x Placement	?	1	?	?
Error	670.1	?	?	?
Total	756.0	99	?	?

The mean number of click-throughs for each combination of ad banner type (beauty or info) and ad banner placement (left or right) follow:

	Banner Type		
Banner Placement	Beauty	Info	Marginal Means
Right	152.5	175.4	163.9
Left	182.5	144.6	163.5
Marginal Means	167.5	160.0	

Questions

1. Fill in the analysis of variance table of results.
2. What effects are "significant" (that is, can you reject the null hypothesis)? What is going on in these data?
3. Which banner type (beauty/info) and which banner location (left/right) would you choose? Why? Can you make the choices (type and location) independently?
4. Were your initial guesses about the beauty/info and left/right combinations correct?
5. What strategic questions might supplement your interpretation of the data?

CASE 5.4

A Picture Is Worth a Megabyte of Words: Census Data and Trends in Lifestyle Purchases (Data set available on text Web site)

Although it is always dangerous to make generalizations about people and their consumption behaviors, it is helpful to the marketer to have an aggregate sense of what people tend to buy as a function of some of their demographic characteristics. For example, household expenditures on furniture might be higher for younger people as they begin to set up house, and decline as the house is established. With a fact like this in hand, and extrapolations of the likely sizes, and timing, of baby-booms and baby-busts, a furniture manufacturer could use this trend information to project market sizes, and to modify the product line (for example, bean bag chairs for college students, finer wood and upholstered furniture for older, wealthier consumers).

The data that follow were extracted from the Bureau of Labor Statistics and reflect expenditures on various goods and services categories, broken down by the census age groups. Within each purchase category (the columns), the data have been calibrated so that a score of "100" means the age group (the row) spends about the average on that category. Numbers that exceed 100 mean that the age group spends more on that category of purchases than the other age groups, and numbers that are less than 100 mean that age group spends less than other age groups. For example, people younger than 25 years old and those 65 years old or older spend less on food; people between the ages of 35–44 and 45–54 spend more. People aged 25–34 and 55–64 spend about the "average." Use these data to answer the questions that follow.

Questions

1. If you wanted to know whether expenditures on furniture and computers were correlated, why might the actual computation of a correlation coefficient be inappropriate, or at least not very compelling?
2. Plot these data with the age categories as the horizontal axis, and the different columns as profiles depicting the peaks and valleys of expenditures with age.
   a. Plot total spending by age and overlay that plot with the plots of food by age and women's apparel by age. What is the pattern of spending on these apparent basic necessities?
   b. Overlay the plots for furniture, computers, and health care by age. Generally speaking, what are your target age groups if you are Scandinavian Design? Dell? A hospital network or health and life insurance company?
   c. Overlay the plot for entertainment expenditures by age with the plot for travel by age. How do we tend to amuse ourselves as younger versus older people?
   d. Finally, use whichever variables interest you and whatever plotting format you think will lend insight to creatively discover any other phenomenon in the data.

Age (in years)	Total Spending	Food	Women's Apparel	Furniture	Computers	Health Care	Entertainment	Travel
<25	59	74	62	55	60	30	62	47
25–34	99	101	85	105	98	67	109	81
35–44	129	134	119	147	119	96	141	98
45–54	130	128	145	126	161	111	123	143
55–64	105	101	120	107	103	122	95	136
65–74	77	69	87	64	55	149	73	102
75+	50	39	49	19	15	141	26	53

CASE 5.5

CountryCable: Customer Satisfaction Survey Data (Data set available on text Web site)

CountryCable is a television cable service that focuses on people who live in small towns. The ability to provide good cable service is more challenging when the technology infrastructure is more basic in the outlying areas. Basically, these companies provide 'cable' through an electronic combination of actual cable and satellite dishes. The company wants to know how their customers think they're doing, and what are the most important areas for improvement.

Two months ago, the survey shown in Figure 5.5.1 was enclosed with the cable subscriber's bill. The particular market sampled was thought to be representative of any other small town segment that the company serves. This particular market composes 12,500 subscribers.

Within one month to 6 weeks, the data came back from 75 subscribers, and these data are shown in Figure 5.5.2. Surveys came back from 23 other subscribing households, but the surveys were unusable, e.g., they were filled out incorrectly (more than one number circled, or no numbers circled, but the customer vented his or her feelings by writing all over the survey, etc.).

The coding of these data is straightforward. Questions 1–6 and 8 are 7-point rating scales, and these correspond to the numbers in the database. Question 7 is gender, and the codes are "1" for the men and "2" for the women.

FIGURE 5.5.1 Customer Satisfaction Survey

Please tell us how satisfied you are with your CABLE TELEVISION SERVICE:

1) My cable TV service is priced reasonably.

   Strongly Disagree 1 2 3 4 5 6 7 Strongly Agree

2) I get good value for the TV shows I can watch for the price I pay.

   Strongly Disagree 1 2 3 4 5 6 7 Strongly Agree

3) The variety of programs is _____.

   Very Poor 1 2 3 4 5 6 7 Really Great

4) There are ___ kinds of TV shows I can watch.

   Not many 1 2 3 4 5 6 7 Very many

5) My service has been reliable.

   Strongly Disagree 1 2 3 4 5 6 7 Strongly Agree

6) The cable's always working.

   Strongly Disagree 1 2 3 4 5 6 7 Strongly Agree

7) I am: ___ Male ___ Female

8) Overall, I'm satisfied with my cable TV service.

   Strongly Disagree 1 2 3 4 5 6 7 Strongly Agree

FIGURE 5.5.2 Customer Satisfaction Survey Data

Obs	q1	q2	q3	q4	q5	q6	q7	q8
1	3	4	7	6	6	5	1	6
2	7	6	5	5	6	6	2	5
3	4	3	4	4	4	5	1	2
4	1	4	6	5	5	2	2	5
5	6	4	1	4	3	4	1	4
6	4	4	6	7	5	5	2	5
7	4	4	3	2	5	5	2	3
8	3	3	2	5	4	2	1	4
9	5	5	3	2	3	3	1	2
10	3	4	5	3	6	6	1	6
11	7	6	7	6	5	3	2	5
12	5	7	4	7	6	4	2	7
13	5	7	2	7	7	5	1	6
14	4	1	4	3	3	5	2	6
15	4	5	6	6	4	5	1	5
16	4	5	4	1	2	3	2	1
17	4	6	6	7	4	3	2	6
18	3	7	7	5	5	5	2	7
19	5	4	3	5	4	7	1	4
20	3	1	4	6	2	2	2	1
21	4	5	6	6	4	5	1	7
22	6	5	3	4	4	3	2	5
23	2	5	7	6	4	5	1	6
24	4	3	1	1	4	4	1	3
25	4	5	7	1	1	3	1	3
26	3	3	3	2	3	5	1	4
27	2	5	5	4	3	3	1	3
28	5	5	5	6	5	4	2	5
29	4	5	6	6	6	5	1	5
30	7	7	5	3	7	7	2	3
31	6	6	2	1	1	1	1	2
32	4	6	4	1	6	7	1	5
33	2	4	4	1	5	5	2	2
34	4	5	2	6	5	4	2	5
35	5	4	2	4	5	6	2	3
36	4	6	6	3	5	5	2	7
37	4	5	6	5	4	3	2	5
38	5	5	2	4	4	4	1	7

(continued)

FIGURE 5.5.2 (continued)

Obs	q1	q2	q3	q4	q5	q6	q7	q8
39	5	2	7	4	4	4	1	1
40	4	5	4	4	6	4	1	4
41	4	3	4	4	3	5	2	4
42	6	5	1	3	3	4	2	2
43	1	1	5	5	3	3	1	3
44	4	6	1	1	3	2	1	4
45	4	5	3	6	7	6	2	7
46	5	7	7	7	6	5	1	7
47	2	2	4	4	3	3	1	2
48	5	2	3	2	2	1	2	1
49	3	5	6	2	3	4	1	7
50	1	2	4	4	5	6	1	1
51	7	6	5	4	5	5	2	6
52	1	1	2	4	2	4	1	3
53	5	5	4	4	6	6	1	7
54	6	5	7	6	4	7	1	5
55	6	4	4	6	6	5	2	4
56	7	6	6	6	7	7	2	5
57	6	6	6	7	6	4	2	6
58	2	2	4	2	7	7	2	4
59	2	4	7	5	3	4	2	7
60	2	3	5	2	1	3	1	4
61	4	5	5	4	6	5	1	4
62	3	4	3	3	4	1	2	3
63	5	6	5	2	5	5	1	6
64	4	6	1	4	4	2	1	5
65	3	3	7	6	3	2	2	4
66	2	1	5	5	5	6	1	2
67	4	5	7	5	4	5	2	3
68	5	6	6	5	7	5	2	5
69	7	6	4	5	3	2	1	5
70	7	6	4	6	7	6	1	5
71	4	4	5	4	4	5	1	6
72	5	5	7	6	4	4	2	4
73	2	1	5	6	4	3	1	3
74	5	4	5	7	7	7	2	6
75	2	5	3	4	5	4	1	6

Questions

1. What are the marketing questions for CountryCable? What are CountryCable's research questions? What do CountryCable's hypotheses appear to be?
2. According to the data, how satisfied are these customers?
3. According to the data, what attributes appear to drive satisfaction?
4. Conceptually, are there any questions that appear to be reliability checks for any other question? What are the correlations between such pairs of items?
5. If you try to use Q1–Q7 to predict the overall judgment of satisfaction, Q8, what problems might you encounter? For example, is multicollinearity likely going to be a problem? (Check the correlations among the variables. Is there an R^2 that is significant but the individual predictors are not? Does one survey item predict significantly when another survey item that looks highly related does not?) Could you form scales, say, by averaging the two "variety" questions, and using that average as a single predictor, replacing the two individual items? (Would those two items have to be correlated?) Could you apply this strategy anywhere else? Does this help clarify the data analyses?
6. The cable company thinks it has to communicate differently to men and women. What do the data say on this point?
7. If the company is concerned with weak performance on satisfaction, what do these data suggest it should focus on to regain customers' loyalty, or do the data suggest the customers are already happy?
8. Do you think CountryCable would have addressed all their questions? If you were to (re)design this study, what would you do differently? Sampling? Questionnaire design?

CASE 5.6

Teeth-Whitening Conjoint Study

A new product entry to service our collective vanity is the whitening agents we may apply to our teeth. Colgate and Crest have their paints and strips available already in the marketplace. A large pharmaceuticals firm knows it would be trivial to develop a competitor product. Further, it has channels of distribution available for ready access to consumers. In addition, it is confident of its own image to assure a high-quality perception that should contribute to immediate positive brand equity.

Thus, it is considering variants on such a teeth-whitening agent to offer to the market. To finalize the product's attributes, it conducted a conjoint study. The firm put the current products in the middle of a focus group table and ran 6 focus groups, composed of 8–12 members of the general consumer public, 2 in Atlanta (1 was for "heavy coffee drinkers" in particular), 1 in Denver, 1 in L.A., 1 in Minneapolis, and 1 in Tampa. The participants passed the products around, opened them up, smelled them, and tasted and felt them. Blow-ups of several recent print ads were displayed on the walls around the table.

After discussing the merits of such products, the experience with or possible interest in trying these products, the moderator passed around a 7-page survey. The first 6 pages were the conjoint task. The 7th page asked participants to answer questions about themselves (age, gender, frequency of dental visits, etc.). The conjoint task is where we focus our attention.

Figure 5.6.1 has two pages of the 6-page survey. The marketing researchers are investigating the following experimental conjoint design: the form of the whitening agent application (gel, strips, or paint); the price point ($3.49, $2.19, $1.99); and the taste (regular, mint, or cherry). Finally, the last consideration is whether a celebrity spokesperson is featured in the advertisement, or just a picture of the product's packaging (which features a big white tooth, a toothbrush, etc.). This design is a 3 (form) $\times$ 3 (price) $\times$ 3 (taste) $\times$ 2 (ad) factorial. Hence, there are $3 \times 3 \times 3 \times 2 = 54$ possible combinations that the participants had to rate. Each page of the survey contained 9 of the combinations. The pages that are not featured in Figure 5.6.1 are those for the "regular" and "cherry" taste, but otherwise those pages look the same as the ones you see for "mint."

Each profile of feature combinations has a rating scale at the very bottom, and the participants are supposed to indicate the extent to which they like that particular bundle of attributes. The ratings for each person were analyzed via conjoint, using dummy variables:

$$\hat{Y}_{preference-rating} = \hat{b}_0 + \hat{b}_1 D_{strips} + \hat{b}_2 D_{paint} + \hat{b}_3 D_{med-price} +$$

$$\hat{b}_4 D_{low-price} + \hat{b}_5 D_{min\,t} + \hat{b}_6 D_{cherry} + \hat{b}_7 D_{no-spokesperson}$$

FIGURE 5.6.1 Part of the Conjoint Survey on Teeth-Whitening Agents

Figure 5.6.2 contains the results of this conjoint. Compared to gel, paint is a bit preferred, and strips are greatly preferred. The medium price is considered better than the high price, but the cheapest price isn't better still (perhaps people were concerned that quality would fall off if the product were priced too cheaply). The mint taste is thought to be better than the regular taste, and the cherry taste is even better than the mint. The ads were preferred when they didn't have a celebrity in them.

Questions
1. What should the firm do? Do you have all the data you need to answer this question?
   a. If not, what else do you wish to know?
   b. If these data are faulty, how would you rerun any part of the study?
   c. If so, what should the firm do?
2. Perhaps you don't have all the data you'd like. Nevertheless, in the real world, sometimes this is all you have. No more time or money to conduct more research. What would you do? Launch? Not launch? Why? Any other options?

FIGURE 5.6.2 Teeth-Whitening Conjoint Results

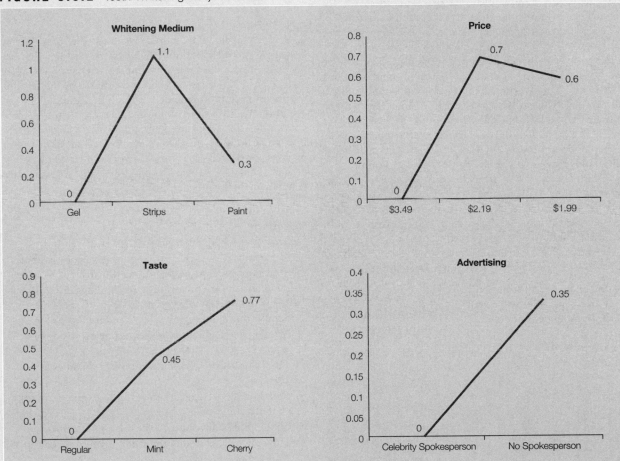

CASE 5.7

Sports Marketing and Television Programming

When you sit down to watch TV, how do you decide what channel to watch? ESPN has conducted some media research that suggests 75% of TV viewers just flip on their "favorite channel" first. The next most popular strategies are: "turn to the specific show you are tuning in to watch" (40%), and "check the listings" (40%). There are some people who "randomly surf" (30%) and some whose entertainment destiny is determined by another ("someone else decides" gets 15%).

The first choice, a favorite station, dominates the others. This finding suggests that people are more "station-loyal" than "specific TV show-loyal." It also suggests that a TV channel needs to be concerned with its brand popularity.

ESPN knows its primary segment is men (any guy over 18). Sports and News are the only two genres where 50% of men say "they watch as often as possible." Figure 5.7.1 shows simple descriptive statistics on top-of-mind mentions of favorite TV networks. ESPN clearly dominates, and it is followed by NBC, ABC, the History Channel, and others. Figure 5.7.2 shows that the strong popularity of ESPN is stable. The figure lists only the top 3, and the "popularity" is even more impressive when you factor in that most households receive on average more than 85 stations.

To get a sense of the "strengths and weaknesses" or relative positioning of the popular stations, a sample of viewers were asked to rate a selection of networks on characteristics such as: informative, helps me relax, likeable, talks to me, witty, high quality, trustworthy, respects its audience, unique, etc. These attribute ratings were factor analyzed and the factors described the channels as providing:

- Integrity and information
- Relevance and involvement
- Entertainment and fun

FIGURE 5.7.1 Favorite TV Show?

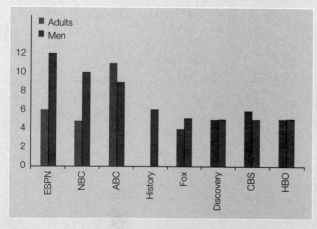

FIGURE 5.7.2 Stability of Popularity of ESPN among Men

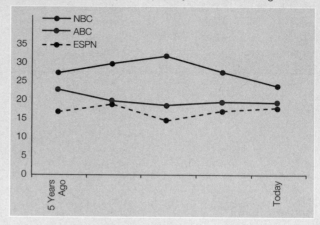

TV channels that scored well on the first factor, "integrity and information," included the History Channel and Discovery. The "relevant and involvement" channels included ESPN, Discovery, History, HBO. The "entertaining and fun" stations included HBO, NBC, and ESPN.

Now what? We're coming to the close of the book—you know a lot about marketing and marketing research. You know how to translate a marketing question into a marketing research one. You know about sampling, study design, and data analysis. You should be able to easily contemplate the following questions.

Questions

1. How could ESPN use this information?
2. What was learned (e.g., you could have guessed that men composed the likely target audience)?
3. Would your interpretation of the findings differ if you knew that the sample was a stratified "ESPN viewers" sample or a simple probability random sample?
4. Would you characterize ESPN as having strong brand equity?
5. How does this research inform other channels as brands?
6. Should ESPN be concerned with these other strongly branded stations?
7. Should ESPN advertise on the History Channel?
8. How might you modify the study if you were to run a similar one?
9. Were the attributes that were selected somehow loaded in ESPN's favor?
10. Where should you draw a sample?
11. To what population of customers could you generalize the findings?

Source: Based loosely on Artie Bulgrin, "Television Network Branding in a Digital Environment," ESPN, Inc., Research Report.

CASE 5.8

Repositioning a Brand

A small, regional airline carrier, we'll call it East-2-West, was looking to reposition its brand. The philosophy of this company had been as a high-end service provider, with no distinction between business and coach classes, offering good food and complimentary beverages of any kind. The airline's target customer was mostly men, based locally, 25–50 years old.

The airline had a 90:10 business to leisure ratio of travelers as its current customer base. It had greater than 75% of its customers satisfied, or at least reporting on surveys that they would "probably" or "definitely" fly East-2-West again. Over the years, customers told the airline they wanted convenient schedules, nonstop flights, good prices, and a frequent flyer program as their main criteria to stay with this airline rather than flying with a competitor.

The airlines industry is a notoriously tough business, and when the economy softens, it only gets tougher. Margins are narrow, the service provision is seen as a commodity, etc.

In this environment, East-2-West was looking into whether it could create a new, low-fare carrier for the growing customer segment seeking value. In particular, it wondered whether it could create such a service repositioning that would still be consistent with its image.

East-2-West commissioned some marketing research. The marketing researchers interviewed both customers who were loyal to the airline and those who had flown on the airline but preferred other airlines. The qualitative results are summarized here.

East-2-West was described in the interview data as:

- Comfortable, Roomy
- Excellent Service
- Business Oriented
- Attentive
- Convenient

The customers who were loyal to East-2-West also characterized the airline as friendly and reliable. The interviewers also asked the two segments for words that did not describe the airline. These included:

- Competitive
- Elegant
- Warm

- Classic
- On Time
- Efficient

To supplement these qualitative data, the perceptual map in Figure 5.8.1 was also drawn. This map was the result of

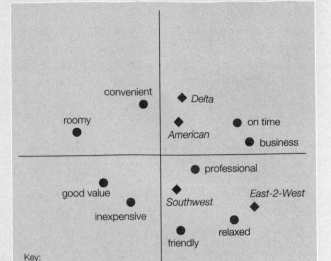

FIGURE 5.8.1 Perceptual Map of East-2-West Airlines

customer surveys. In the surveys, customers were asked to describe both East-2-West, as well as other carriers.

Questions

Discuss East-2-West's goals and results, covering topics such as:

1. Are the company's goals good ones for the economic and competitive environment?
2. Are the goals consistent with the company's traditional strengths?
3. Will there be customer confusion with this repositioning?
4. What problems do you foresee that East-2-West apparently didn't in terms of its new positioning?
5. Can you use the qualitative or perceptual map data to substantiate your answers to any of these questions?
6. Turning to the perceptual map, how would you characterize the dimensions? Are the results consistent with the qualitative data? According to the map, if East-2-West is successful in its repositioning, what competition might it confront?
7. What additional data would you want before repositioning an airline?

PART 6
The Research Report

This closing section of the book consists of one chapter and an epilogue. Chapter 19 discusses one of the most important parts of the entire research process, the research report. The research report often becomes the standard by which the research effort is assessed. The epilogue ties together the parts of the research process, reinforcing the points made earlier: that the steps in the research process are highly interrelated and that a decision made at one stage has implications for the others as well.

CHAPTER 19

The Research Report

Questions to Guide Your Learning:

Q1: What should a research report look like?

Q2: How can I improve my writing and my presentation skills?

Q3: What different purposes might different kinds of graphs serve?

Creating useful reports requires considerable skill and attention to detail. Regardless of the sophistication displayed in other portions of the research process, the project is a failure if the research report fails. The research steps determine the content, and the research report provides the form. Given that the report is all that many executives see of the project, it becomes the yardstick for evaluation. The writer must ensure that the report informs without misinforming.

The report must tell readers what they need and wish to know. Typically, executives are interested in results and must be convinced of the usefulness of the findings. They wish to act on the report, but they must also recognize the caveats entailed in the results. Thus the researcher must convey these limitations and details of the methods.

To enhance this communication, we discuss four concepts: (1) the criteria by which research reports are evaluated, (2) the parts and forms of the written research report, (3) the oral report, and (4) some graphic means of presenting the results.

Criteria of Research Reports

Research reports are evaluated by one fundamental criterion—communication with the reader. The reader is the reason that the report is prepared, so it must be tailor-made for the reader(s), keeping in mind their technical sophistication, interest in the subject area, and the use they will make of it.

The technical sophistication of the readers determines their capacity for understanding methodological decisions, such as experimental design, measures, sampling plan, analysis technique, etc. Readers with little technical sophistication will probably be overwhelmed (and annoyed) by the use of unexplained technical jargon. Researchers must be particularly sensitive to this, because, being technical people and taking much jargon for granted, they may fail to realize that they are using technical language and terms. Executives higher in the organization usually want only the proverbial "executive summary," results, but not a discussion of how the results were obtained. Other executives want considerable information on the research methods used in the study and the statistical results, but not the researcher's conclusions and recommendations.

The report writer's difficulties in tailoring the report are often compounded by the existence of several audiences. The marketing vice president might have a different technical capacity and level of interest than the manager responsible for the product discussed in the report. This problem sometimes requires the preparation of several reports, although usually the conflicting demands are satisfied with one report that contains both technical and nontechnical sections for different readers.

> **Give details if readers are technical, otherwise, keep it simple.**

Writing Criteria

To be effective, a report should be complete, accurate, clear, and concise:[1]

1. A report is *complete* when it provides all the information readers need in language they understand. This means that the writer must continually ask whether every question in the original assignment has been addressed. What alternatives were examined? What was found? The report must include necessary definitions and explanations but they must be succinct. The length of a report should be proportional to its contribution. Report writers tend not to waste collected information, but too much information may be distracting. If the report is big, it may discourage readers from even attempting to digest its contents. In general, the amount of detail should be proportionate to the amount of direct control users can exercise over the areas under discussion.
2. A report must be **accurate**, avoiding carelessness in discussing the data, illogical reasoning, or inept phrasing. Table 19.1 illustrates some examples of sources of inaccuracy in reports.
3. **Clarity** is probably violated more than any other principle of good writing. Clear and logical thinking and precise expression produce clarity. When the underlying logic is fuzzy or the presentation imprecise, readers have difficulty understanding what they read. To be *clear*, the organization of the report should follow an out-

> **Reading your draft aloud helps identify sections that should be pruned or rewritten.**

---

[1] There are many good books on business writing and summarizing research results, cf., Joseph Gibaldi and Phyllis Franklin, *MLA Handbook for Writers of Research Papers* (Modern Language Association of America, 2003).

Research Realities

19.1 Some Suggestions When Choosing Words for Marketing Research Reports

- Use short words, not long words that mean the same thing, e.g., "use" not "utilize."
- Avoid jargon, e.g., "provide incentives" not "incentivize," and "conclusion" not "net net."
- Write simply and naturally—the way you talk, e.g., "The impor-

tant point is" not "Importantly," and "There are four reasons" not "The reasons are fourfold."
- Cut redundancies, e.g., "study" not "study in depth," or "The plan" not "The advance plan."

line of major points. Tell the reader where you are going and then do what you said you were going to do. Use short paragraphs and short sentences. Don't mumble; once you have decided what to say, come out and say it. Choose your words carefully. (See Research Realities 19.1 for some specific suggestions when choosing words.) Don't expect to get it right the first time; expect to rewrite it

TABLE 19.1
Examples of Inaccuracy in Report Writing

1. **Simple Errors in Addition or Subtraction**
   "In the United States, 14% of the population has an elementary school education or less, 51% has attended or graduated from high school, and 16% has attended college."
   - An oversight such as this (14 + 51 + 16 do not equal 100%) can be easily corrected by the author, but not so easily by the reader because he or she may not know if one or more of the percentage values is incorrect or if a category might have been left out of the tally (e.g., grad school).

2. **Confusion between Percentages and Percentage Points**
   "The company's profits as a percentage of sales were 6.0% in 1995 and 8.0% in 2000. Therefore, they increased only 2.0% in five years."
   - In this example, the increase is, of course, 2.0 percentage points, or 33%.

3. **Inaccuracy Caused by Grammatical Errors**
   "The reduction in the government's price supports for dairy products has reduced farm income $600 million to $800 million per year."
   - To express a range, the author should have written: "The reduction in the government's price supports for dairy products has reduced farm income by between $600 million and $800 million per year."

4. **Confused Terminology Resulting in Fallacious Conclusion**
   "The Jones's household and annual income increased from $30,000 to $60,000 over the past ten years, thereby doubling the family's purchasing power."
   - Although the Jones's household annual income may have doubled in the 10 years, the family's purchasing power probably did not. It may have declined, given that the cost of living, as measured by the consumer price index, increased over the same period. It may have increased, given that discretionary income from 60K is much greater than that from 30K once basic needs are paid.

For more examples, see Gordon Bell, "Never Trust the Numbers," *Target Marketing* 25 (2002), pp. 93–94.

several times. When rewriting, try to reduce the length by half. That forces you to simplify and remove the clutter. Constantly ask yourself, "What am I trying to say?" (you'll be surprised at how often you don't know). Write simple declarative sentences—think what you want to say. Write your sentence. Strip it of all adverbs and adjectives. Reduce the sentence to its skeleton. Let the verbs and nouns do the work.

4. A report must also be *concise*. The writer must be selective about what is included, and avoid trying to impress the reader with all that has been found. If something does not pertain directly to the subject, it should be omitted. Concise writing is effective because it makes maximum use of every word—no word or phrase can be removed without destroying the whole composition.[2]

Form of the Report

There is no single, acceptable organization for a report, but the following format is fairly standard, yet flexible. We discuss each element in turn.

TITLE PAGE

The title page indicates the subject of the report, the name of the organization for which the report is made, the name of the organization submitting it, and the date.

TABLE OF CONTENTS

The table of contents lists, in order of appearance, the divisions and subdivisions of the report with page references. In short reports, the table of contents may simply contain the main headings. It should include lists of tables and figures and their page numbers.

EXECUTIVE SUMMARY

The executive summary is the heart and core of the report. It is its heart and core. Many executives read only this summary. Others read more, but they use the summary as a guide to see what else they'll read.

The true summary is not an abstract of the whole report in which everything is restated in condensed form; neither is it a simple restatement of the subject, nor a brief statement of the significant results and conclusions. A true summary gives the high points of the entire body of the report. Properly written, the summary saves busy executives' time without sacrificing their understanding.

The introduction in the summary provides the reader with minimal background to appreciate the study's results, conclusions, and recommendations. It should state who authorized the research and for what purpose. It should explicitly outline the problem(s) or hypotheses that guided the research. The key findings should be presented here. It is useful to include 1–3 findings to each problem or objective.

Conclusions and recommendations are not the same. A conclusion is an opinion based on the results. A recommendation is a suggestion for appropriate future action. Conclusions should be included in the summary section. The writer is in a better position to base conclusions on the evidence than are the readers, being more

---

[2] In the movie, *Amadeus,* a patron king with a short attention span asked Mozart to take out a "few notes." Mozart was incredulous, asking, "Which notes?" Fair enough, but do you want to go out on a limb and compare your writing to Mozart's compositions?

familiar with the methods used to generate and analyze the data. The writer is at fault if conclusions are omitted and readers are allowed to draw their own.

Recommendations, though, are another matter. Some managers simply prefer to determine the appropriate courses of action themselves and do not want the writer to offer recommendations. Others hold that the writer, being closest to the research, is in the best position to suggest a course of action. Increasingly, marketing researchers are being asked to interpret the findings in terms of what they mean to the business and to make recommendations as to appropriate courses of action. You will probably know what is expected of you (or ask). If in doubt, provide your recommendations. The reader can always ignore them.

INTRODUCTION

The introduction provides background information that readers need in order to appreciate the discussion in the body of the report. Its length and detail depend on the readers' familiarity with the subject, the approach to it, and the treatment of it. As a rule, a report with wide distribution requires a more extensive introduction than a report for a narrow audience.

The introduction defines terms. For instance, in a study of market penetration of a new product, the introduction might be used to define the market and discuss which products and companies were considered "competitors" in projecting the new product's market share.

The introduction may provide pertinent history. What similar studies have been conducted? What findings did they produce? What circumstances precipitated the present study? How were its scope and emphasis determined?

The introduction should state the specific objectives of the research. If the project is part of a larger, overall project, this should be mentioned. Each of the subproblems or hypotheses should be explicitly stated. After reading the introduction, readers should know exactly what the report concerns and what it omits.

BODY

The details of the research are contained in the body of the report. This includes details of method, results, and limitations.

A challenge in report writing is knowing how much detail to go into when presenting the research methods. Sufficient information must be presented so that readers can appreciate the research design, data-collection methods, sample procedures, and analysis techniques that were used without being bored or overwhelmed. However, technical jargon, which is often a succinct way of communicating a complex idea, should be omitted, because many in the audience do not understand it.

Readers must be told whether the design was exploratory, descriptive, or causal as well as why the particular design was chosen. What are its merits in terms of the problem at hand? Readers should also be told whether the results are based on secondary or primary data. If primary, were they based on observation or questionnaire? And if the latter, were the questionnaires administered in person or by mail, e-mail, or telephone? Again, it is important to mention why the particular method was chosen. What were its perceived advantages over alternative schemes? This may mean briefly discussing the perceived weaknesses of the other data-collection schemes that were considered.

Sampling is a technical subject, and the writer cannot hope to convey all the nuances. A reader needs to understand at least three things pertaining to the sample: What was done? How was it done? Why was it done? For example:

> A good test of a summary is self-sufficiency—can it stand on its own, or does it collapse without the full report?

1. How was the population defined? What were the geographical, age, gender, or other bounds?
2. What sampling units were used? Business organizations or business executives? Dwelling units, households, or individuals within a household? Why were these sampling units chosen?
3. How was the list of sampling units generated? Did this produce any weaknesses? Why was this method used?
4. Were any difficulties experienced in contacting designated sample elements? How were these difficulties overcome, and was bias introduced in the process?
5. How was the sample actually selected? How large a sample was selected?

It is useful to discuss the method in general before detailing the results. Thus, if statistical significance was established through chi-square analysis, the writer might provide the general rationale and calculation procedure for the chi-square statistic, as well as the assumptions surrounding this test and how well the data supported the assumptions.

The findings of the study consume the bulk of the report, with supporting tables and figures. The results need to address the specific problems posed, and they must be presented with some logical structure. The first requirement suggests that information that is interesting but irrelevant to the specific problems guiding the research be omitted. The second requirement suggests that the tables and figures should not be a random collection but should reflect some sensible ordering, e.g., perhaps organized by subproblem, geographic region, time, or other criterion that structured the investigation. Tables and figures should be used liberally when presenting the results. Tables in the appendix are complex and detailed, but the tables in the body of the report should be simple summaries of focused information. Brief verbal summaries of each table show the reader to the main patterns and exceptions.

There is no such thing as a "perfect" study; every study has its limitations. The researcher knows the limitations and does not hide them from the readers. A frank admission of the study's limitations can actually increase rather than diminish (as is sometimes feared) the readers' opinion of the quality of the research. If some limitations are not stated and readers discover them, they may begin to question the whole report and assume a much more skeptical, critical posture than they would if the limitations were explicitly stated. Stating them also allows the writer to discuss whether the limitations might bias the results.

For example, the sources of nonsampling error and the suspected direction of their biases should be discussed. Readers should be informed about how far the results can be generalized. To what populations can they be expected to apply? If the study was done in Miami, readers should be warned not to generalize the results to the southern states or to all the states. The writer should provide the proper caveats for readers, but maintain a balanced perspective and not overstate the limitations.

CONCLUSIONS AND RECOMMENDATIONS

The results precipitate the conclusions and recommendations. There should be a conclusion for each study objective. Researchers need to be careful that the conclusions drawn reflect an unbiased interpretation of the data.

Researchers' recommendations should follow the conclusions. In developing recommendations, focus on the value of the information that has been gathered, and interpret this information in terms of what it means for the business. One of the best ways to do this is by offering specific recommendations as to the appropriate courses of action, and reasons why. Although not all managers want the researcher's recommendations, many do, and the researcher needs to be prepared to offer and support them.

APPENDIX

The appendix contains material that is too complex, detailed, specialized, or not absolutely necessary for the text. The appendix typically contains as an exhibit a copy of the questionnaire used to collect the data. It may also contain maps used to draw the sample, or detailed calculations used to determine sample size. The appendix may include calculations of test statistics and often includes detailed tables from which the summary tables in the body of the report are generated. The appendix is read by only the most technically competent and interested reader, so material shouldn't appear in the appendix if its omission from the body of the report would create gaps in the presentation. Table 19.2 serves as a checklist of items to include in reports.

Ethical Dilemma 19.1

As a member of an independent research team, it is your job to write the final report for a client. One of your colleagues whispers to you in passing, "Make it sound very technical. Lots of long words and jargon—you know the sort of thing. We want to make it clear that we earned our money on this one."

- Is it ethical to obscure the substance of a report beneath complex language?
- Will some clients be impressed by words that they do not fully understand?

TABLE 19.2
Checklist for Evaluating Research Reports

A. **Origin: What Is Behind the Research**
- Does the report identify the organizations or departments that initiated and paid for the research?
- Is there a statement of the research purpose that says clearly what it was meant to accomplish?
- Are the organizations that designed and conducted the research identified?

B. **Design: The Concept and the Plan**
- Is there a full, nontechnical description of the research design?
- Is the design consistent with the stated purpose for which the research was conducted?
- Is the design evenhanded, free of leading questions and other biases?
- Does it address questions that respondents are capable of answering?
- Is there a precise statement of the population represented?
- Does the sampling frame represent the population under study?
- Does the report clearly describe the method of sample selection?
- Does the report describe the plan for the analysis of the data?
- Are copies of all questionnaire forms, field and sampling instructions, and other study materials available in the appendix?

C. **Execution: Collecting and Handling the Information**
- Does the report describe the data-collection and data-processing procedures?
- What procedures were used to minimize bias and ensure the quality of the data?

D. **Stability: Sample Size and Reliability**
- Was the sample large enough to provide stable findings?
- Are sampling error limits shown if they can be computed?
- Are methods of calculating the sampling error described, or, if the error cannot be computed, is this stated and explained?
- Are any possible nonsampling errors described?

(continued)

TABLE 19.2
(continued)

E. **Applicability: Generalizing the Findings**
  - Does the report specify when the data were collected?
  - Is it clear who is underrepresented by the research, or not represented at all?
  - If the research has limited application, is there a statement covering who or what it represents and the times or conditions under which it applies?

F. **Meaning: Interpretations and Conclusions**
  - Are the measurements described in simple and direct language?
  - Are the actual findings differentiated from the interpretation of the findings?
  - Have the research findings been interpreted rigorously and objectively?

G. **Candor: Open Reporting and Disclosure**
  - Is there a full disclosure of how the research was done?
  - Has the research been fairly presented?

The Oral Report

In addition to the written report, most marketing research investigations require one or more oral reports. They may also require interim progress reports. They almost always require a formal oral report at the conclusion of the study. The principles surrounding the preparation and delivery of the oral report parallel those for the written report. Presenters need to realize that many listeners will not truly understand the technical ramifications involved in research and will not be able to judge whether the research done is "quality research." However, they can judge whether the research was presented in a professional, confidence-inspiring manner or in a disorganized, uninformed one. A quality presentation can disguise poor research, but quality research cannot improve a poor presentation.

Preparing the Oral Report

The first imperative is to know the audience: its technical level of sophistication and members' involvement in the project. In general, it is better to err on the side of too little technical detail than too much. Executives want to hear and see what the information means to them as marketing managers, e.g., what do the data suggest in terms of marketing actions? They can ask for the necessary clarification about the technical details if they want it.

The flow of the presentation usually follows one of two popular forms. Both begin by stating the general purpose of the study and its specific objectives. They differ in terms of when the conclusions are introduced. In the most popular structure, the conclusions are introduced after all the evidence supporting a particular course of action is presented. By progressively disclosing the facts, the presenter is building a logical case in sequential fashion.

The alternative structure involves presenting the conclusions immediately after the purpose and main objectives. The structure tends to involve managers immediately in the findings. It not only gets them thinking about what actions are called for given the results but also sensitizes them to paying attention to the evidence supporting the conclusions. It places them in the desirable position of wanting to evaluate the strength of the evidence supporting an action, because they know beforehand the conclusions that were drawn from it.

> If you're presenting using technology, don't count on it. Bring backups (e.g., simple transparencies).

The structure used depends on the corporate culture as well as the presenter's own comfort level. In either case, the evidence supporting the conclusions must be presented systematically, and the conclusions drawn must be consistent with the evidence.

A third important consideration for effective delivery of the oral report is the use of appropriate visual aids. Powerpoint presentations, flip charts, transparencies, slides, and even chalkboards can all be used, depending on the size of the group and the physical facilities of the meeting room. Finally, make sure your visuals can be read easily by those in the back of the room (see Table 19.3).

Ethical Dilemma 19.2

A colleague confides in you: "I've just run a survey for a restaurant owner who is planning to open a catering service for parties, weddings, and the like. He wanted to know the best way to advertise the new service. In the questionnaire, I asked respondents where they would expect to see advertisements for catering facilities, and the most common source was the newspaper. I now realize that my question only established where people are usually exposed to relevant ads, not where they would like to see relevant ads or where they could most productively be exposed to an ad. All we know is where other caterers advertise! Yet I'm sure my client will interpret my findings as meaning that the newspaper is the most effective media vehicle. Should I make the limitations of the research explicit?"

- What are the costs of making the limitations of the research explicit?
- What are the costs of not doing so?
- Isn't promoting the correct use of the research one of the researcher's prime obligations?

Delivering the Oral Report

Honor the time limit set for the meeting. Use only a portion of the time set aside for the formal presentation, no more than a third to a half. At the same time, don't rush the presentation of the information, so plan not to present too many slides (details can be prepared on "back-up slides" anticipating certain questions). Remember that the audience is hearing it for the first time. Reserve the remaining time for questions and discussion. One of the unique benefits of the oral presentation is that it allows interaction. Use this benefit to advantage to clear up points of confusion and to highlight points deserving special emphasis.

Keep the presentation simple and uncluttered so that the audience does not have to mentally backtrack to think about what has been said. When writing out the presentation, choose simple words and sentences that are naturally spoken and expressed in your usual vocabulary.[3]

Graphic Presentation of the Results

The old adage that "a picture is worth a thousand words" is equally true for business reports. Text and tables can be used to present quantitative information, but

TABLE 19.3
Tips for Preparing Effective Presentation Visuals

1. Keep it simple.
2. One minute per visual. One main point. Few words.
3. Bring copies of slides to hand out to the audience before your presentation.
4. Number your pages to facilitate questions and discussion.
5. BIG font!
6. Build complexity. If you have a complicated concept to communicate, start with the ground level and use three or four slides to complete the picture.

---

[3] A number of excellent books are available on making effective oral presentations, cf., Steve Mandel, *Effective Presentation Skills: A Practical Guide for Better Speaking*, 3rd ed. (Crisp, 2000).

Ethical Dilemma 19.3

You are writing the final report for top management to make the case that your new advertising campaign has increased sales dramatically in trial areas. Your conceptual arguments on behalf of the new campaign are very convincing, but although there has been a consistent rise in sales in trial areas, the bar charts look rather disappointing: 61,500 units the first month, 61,670 units the next, 61,820 the next . . . the increase is barely visible! Then you notice how much more exciting your results would look if the y-axis were broken above the origin so that the plots started at 50,000 units.

• Where does salesmanship stop and deception start?

graphs can often serve that purpose better.[4] There are three basic kinds of graphics: charts that show *how much*, maps that show *where*, and diagrams that show *how*. Charts are generally the most useful of the three types for research reports, and diagrams the least. The following sections discuss a few of the more common chart types and maps.

Pie Chart

Probably one of the more familiar charts—the **pie chart** is simply a circle divided into sections, with each section representing a portion of the total. The sections are presented as part of a whole, so the pie chart is particularly effective for depicting relative size or emphasizing comparisons. Figure 19.1 uses the data from Table 19.4, for instance, to show the breakdown of personal consumption expenditures by major category for 2005. The conclusion is obvious: expenditures for services account for the largest proportion of total consumption expenditures. Further, expenditures for services and nondurable goods completely dwarf expenditures for durable goods.

Figure 19.1 has three slices, and the interpretation is obvious. With finer consumption classes, a greater number of sections would have been required, and although more information would have been conveyed, emphasis would have been lost. As a rule of thumb, no more than six slices should be generated; the division of the pie should start at the 12 o'clock position; and the sections should be arrayed clockwise in decreasing order of magnitude.

Line Chart

The line chart is a two-dimensional chart that is particularly useful in depicting dynamic relationships, such as time-series fluctuations of one or more series. For example, Figure 19.2, produced from the data in Table 19.5, shows the fluctuations in retail sales of domestic and imported cars during the period 1992–2005.

The line chart is probably the most commonly used chart. It is typically constructed with the x-axis representing time and the y-axis representing values of the

FIGURE 19.1
Pie Chart Showing Personal Consumption Expenditures by Major Category for 2005

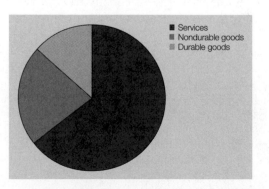

Services
Nondurable goods
Durable goods

[4] See Howard Wainer, *Visual Revelations* (Erlbaum, 2000); Robert Harris, *Information Graphics* (Oxford University Press, 2000); Gene Zelazny, *Say It With Charts: The Executive's Guide to Visual Communication*, 4th ed. (McGraw-Hill, 2001).

Total Year	Personal Consumption	Durable Expenditures	Nondurable Goods	Services
1992	2892.7	398.7	957.2	1536.8
1993	3094.5	416.7	1014.0	1663.8
1994	3349.7	451.0	1081.1	1817.6
1995	3954.8	472.8	1163.8	1958.1
1996	3839.3	476.5	1245.3	2117.5
1997	3975.1	455.2	1277.6	2242.3
1998	4219.8	488.5	1321.8	2409.4
1999	4459.2	530.2	1370.7	2558.4
2000	4717.0	579.5	1428.4	2709.1
2001	4953.9	611.0	1473.6	2869.2
2002	5215.7	643.3	1539.2	3033.2
2003	5493.7	673.0	1600.6	3220.1
2004	5848.6	698.2	1708.9	3441.5
2005	6257.3	758.6	1843.1	3655.6

TABLE 19.4
Personal Consumption
Expenditures for
1992–2005
(billions of dollars)

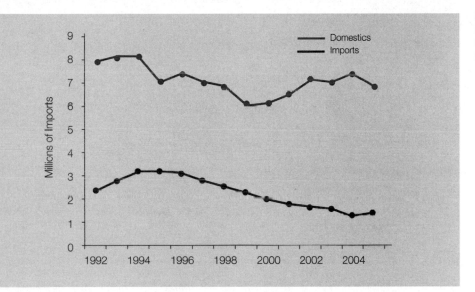

FIGURE 19.2
Line Chart Showing
Retail Sales of New
Passenger Cars

variables. Each line representing different variables should be distinctive in color or form (e.g., dots and dashes in suitable combinations) and explained in a legend.

Bar Chart

The bar chart has many variations, which probably accounts for its wide use. Figure 19.3 is a bar chart that shows personal consumption expenditures by major category at a single point in time. It expresses the same relative information as Figure 19.1 but also reveals the magnitudes. Figure 19.4 shows a "grouped" bar chart for the automobile sales data, where one set of bars represents the domestic sales, and the other set of bars, the imports. Both are represented per year.

One of the trickiest things to know is how to represent the data you've got. Research Realities 19.2 takes some data that looks overwhelming at first, then breaks it down into informative and understandable chunks of information.

TABLE 19.5
Retail Sales of New
Cars for 1992–2005
(millions of units)

Year	Total	Domestics	Imports
1992	10.4	8.0	2.4
1993	11.0	8.2	2.8
1994	11.4	8.2	3.2
1995	10.3	7.1	3.2
1996	10.6	7.5	3.1
1997	9.9	7.1	2.8
1998	9.5	6.9	2.6
1999	8.4	6.1	2.3
2000	8.2	6.2	2.0
2001	8.4	6.6	1.8
2002	8.9	7.2	1.7
2003	8.7	7.1	1.6
2004	8.7	7.4	1.3
2005	8.3	6.9	1.4

FIGURE 19.3
Bar Chart Showing
Personal Consumption
Expenditures

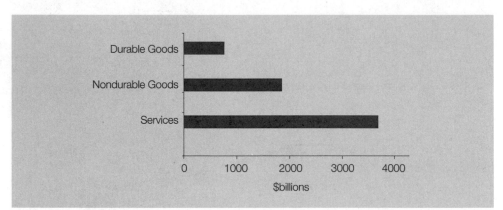

FIGURE 19.4
Grouped Bar Chart
Showing Automobile
Sales, by Type, by Year

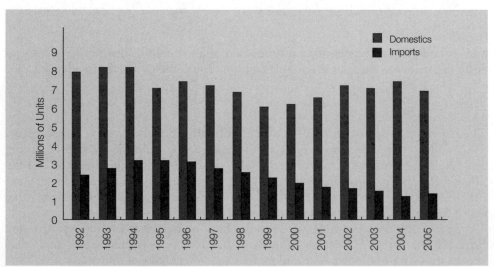

19.2 Demographic Profile of TV Viewers

Television ratings and their breakdown per audience characteristics are extremely critical, e.g., to advertisers who seek to ensure their budgets are being spent against their targeted customers. The following data show basic demographic data on viewers for the three traditional major networks (ABC, CBS, and NBC) and Fox, as well as reporting the national statistics for a basis of comparison.

If this chart were to appear in a marketing research report or in a business magazine, it would not be effective. It is too complicated to digest, and therefore it would have no impact on the reader.

Some levels of the variables seem superfluous. If we know the percentage of male viewers, can we not figure out the percentage of female viewers? If income is divided only into two rough categories (less than and greater than $50,000), can't we delete one of

these categories and focus on the other? We even selected out two levels of education. This simplification is done for the chart below. However, ethnicity and household size cannot be further simplified (unless we knew the particular focus of the marketing research). Thus, while improved, this chart has only four fewer bars, and it's still overwhelming.

Why must we view all demographics simultaneously? This chart focuses on race and is easier to read. The large number for the White category dominates however, and overwhelms the differences among the other categories.

So, let's temporarily set aside the numbers for the White category, to allow the slight, but discernible patterns among the minority ethnicities to come through. This chart is the first that allows us to

FIGURE A: All Data

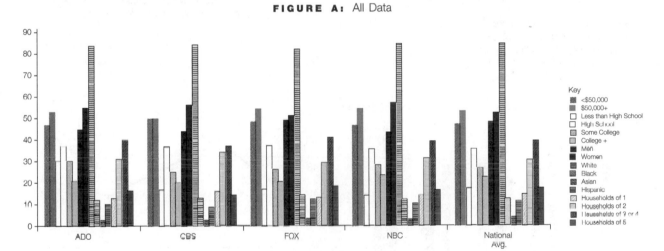

Source: Simmons Market Research Bureau, *American Demographics,* http://www.demographics.com

FIGURE B: Selectivity on Variable Level

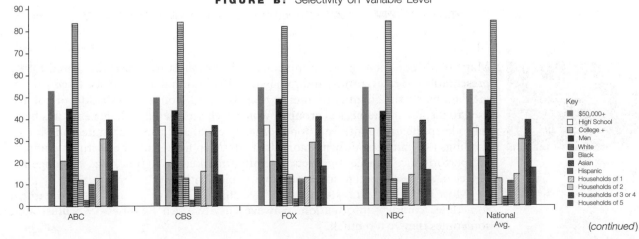

(continued)

translate "data" into "information." We can see that Blacks gravitate more toward Fox and CBS. Asians aren't served well by any of

FIGURE C1: Focus on Demographic: Ethnicity

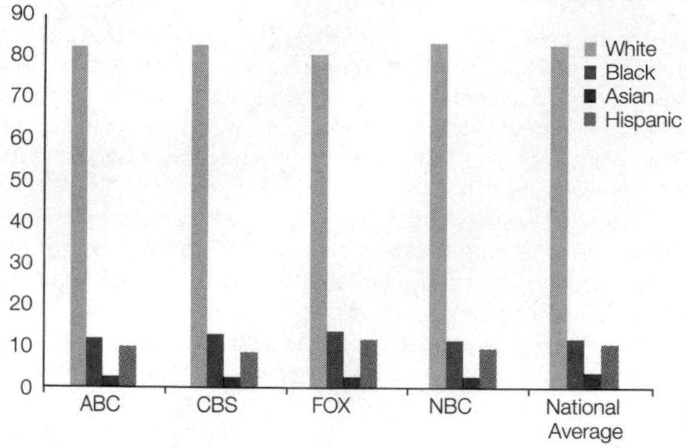

these TV stations. Hispanics are like Blacks in preferring Fox, but unlike Blacks in not preferring CBS.

So, use the information. If your products are targeted toward Blacks, where do you spend your TV advertising dollars? Hispanics? Asians?

FIGURE C2: Focus on Demographic: Minority Ethnicity

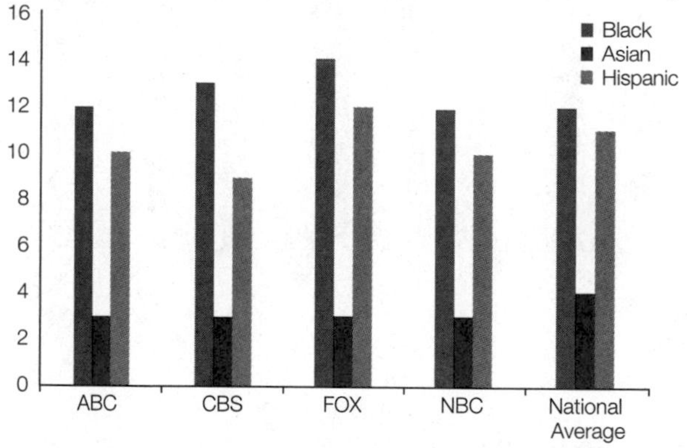

Which network is winning the hearts and minds of the male or female viewers? What pattern would be desirable?

FIGURE C3: Focus on Demographic: Gender

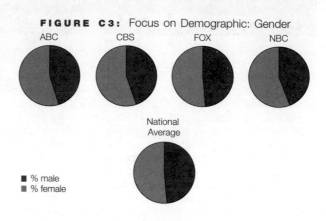

You're an EDLP retailer: which stations get your ad dollars? You're selling Beemers: where does your ad $ go?

FIGURE C4: Focus on Demographic: Income

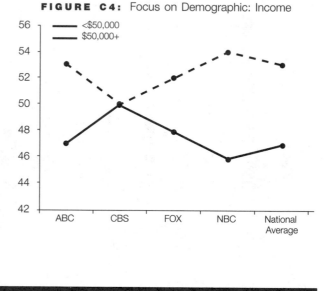

MAPS

Maps focus attention on geographic areas. Data maps are especially suited to the presentation of rates, ratios, and frequency-distribution data by areas. In constructing data maps, the quantity of interest is broken into groups, and shading or color is used to display the numerical group in which each area belongs. In general, it is helpful to keep the group intervals approximately equal and to use a limited number of shadings (4–7 and certainly no more than 10). Map figures can be useful in comparing performance between markets, or within markets over time, e.g., to gauge the degree of success of recent marketing mix implementation.

Most popular business magazines love charts. They're a quick way to express sometimes complex information. However, as Research Realities 19.3 illustrates, sometimes they're too quick.

A picture is worth a megabyte of words.

Research Realities

19.3 Be Careful Interpreting Published Charts

In a cover study on the Nasdaq, *Businessweek* analysts were trying to make the case that "Nasdaq has been losing ground to the NYSE . . ." It offered several charts of data as evidence: "Average Daily Trading, " "# of Listed Companies," and "# of IPOs." Look at the data. Do you agree? Will you take the authors' interpretation on face value? (Hint: Your answer should be no! Else, have we taught you nothing?) Think!

Some critical questions should spring to mind.

1. Are these trends? Hard to tell with only four years' worth of data.
2. What's up with '00? Why is it so big for Nasdaq?
3. If Nasdaq were losing ground to the NYSE, shouldn't the NYSE numbers be growing? These numbers are also declining, though perhaps not at as rapid a rate.
4. If the argument of "losing ground" is a relative one, why not compute a ratio or difference index to explicitly capture (model) the comparison?
5. If we were to extrapolate, in any of these graphs, what will '06 or '07 look like? (Can we extrapolate?)
6. What's the explanation? What's your "financial markets" theory? Why do these numbers look like they do?
7. Whatever your interpretation of the numbers, what implications do they have for your industry for employment (or hoped-for employment)?

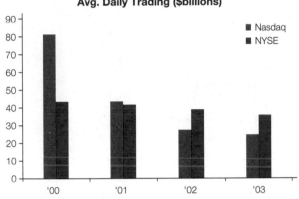

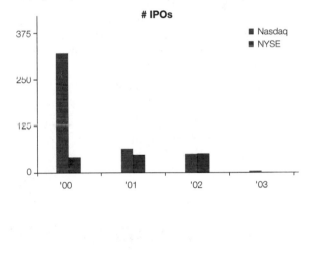

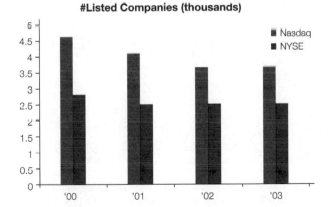

Source: Paula Dwyer and Amy Borrus, "The Crisis at Nasdaq," *Businessweek*, August 11, 2003, p. 66. We don't mean to pick on these authors, nor on this particular magazine. These particular three graphs aren't even as bad an example as can be found—they were just a random choice for the purposes of illustration.

Summary

The research report was discussed in this chapter. Four points were emphasized: the criteria for evaluating research reports, the elements of a written research report, the delivery of an oral report, and the graphic presentation of results.

The fundamental criterion for the development of every research report is communication with the audience. The readers' interests, capabilities, and circumstances determine what goes in the report, what is left out, and how the information included in the report is presented. The other criteria that need to be kept in mind in preparing the report include: completeness, accuracy, clarity, and conciseness.

A report includes: title page, table of contents, summary, introduction, body, conclusions and recommendations, and appendix. An oral report begins by stating the general purpose of the study and the specific objectives. The remainder of the presentation needs to systematically build on the evidence so that logical conclusions are drawn.

Graphic presentation is often the best way to communicate those findings that require emphasis. Three main forms are the pie chart, the line chart, and the bar chart.

Review Questions

1. What is the fundamental report criterion? Explain.

2. What is meant by the report criteria of completeness, accuracy, clarity, and conciseness?

3. On the one hand, it is argued that the research report must be complete and, on the other, that it must be concise. Are these two objectives incompatible? If so, how do you reconcile them?

4. What is the essential content of each of the following parts of the research report?
   a. Title page
   b. Table of contents
   c. Executive summary
   d. Introduction
   e. Body
   f. Conclusions and recommendations
   g. Appendix

5. What are the key considerations in preparing an oral report?

6. What is a pie chart? For what kinds of information is it particularly effective?

7. What is a line chart? For what kinds of information is it generally employed?

8. What is a bar chart? For what kinds of problems is it effective?

Applications and Problems

1. Many marketing research professionals would argue that the summary is the most important part of the research report. Describe the information that should be contained in the summary and why it is so important.

2. The owner of a medium-sized home building center specializing in custom-designed and do-it-yourself kitchen supplies asked the I & J Consulting firm to prepare a customer profile report for the kitchen design segment of the home improvement market. Evaluate the following sections of the report.

   The customer market for the company can be defined as the do-it-yourself and kitchen design segments. A brief profile of each follows.

   The do-it-yourself (DIY) market consists of individuals in the 25–45 age group living in a single dwelling. DIY customers are predominantly male, although an increasing number of females are becoming active DIY customers. The typical DIY customer has an income in excess of $40,000 and the median income is $44,100 with a standard deviation of 86. The DIY customer has an increasing amount of leisure time, is strongly value and convenience conscious, and displays an increasing desire for self-gratification.

   The mean age of the custom-kitchen design customer segment is 41.26, and the annual income is in the range of $45,000 to $55,000. The median income is $49,000 with a standard deviation of 73. Custom-kitchen design customers usually live in a single dwelling. The wife is more influential and is the prime decision maker about kitchen designs and cabinets.

3. The executive director of the Cortland Chamber of Commerce asked the marketing research class of the community college located nearby to prepare a research report on members' attitudes toward the service offerings of the chamber. Evaluate the completeness of the executive summary portion of their report, which follows.

> To provide a foundation for a comprehensive marketing plan, the Cortland Chamber of Commerce (CCC) undertook a membership survey in November 2005. Eighty-four usable surveys were returned from a stratified proportionate sampling plan of 172 CCC members.
>
> Results showed that members were familiar with all of the services except National Safety Council materials and employers' manuals. Newsletters were found to be the most often used as well as the most important service offered by CCC. Government regulation and mandated employee benefits were thought to be the most threatening issues facing businesses, according to the survey results. Over half of all members responding felt favorably toward 11 statements about CCC services.

4. Discuss the difference between conclusions and recommendations in research reports.

5. Your marketing research firm is preparing the final written report on a research project commissioned by

a major manufacturer of water ski equipment. One objective of the project was to investigate seasonal variations in sales, both on an aggregate basis and by each of the company's sales regions individually. Your client is particularly interested in the width of the range between maximum and minimum seasonal sales. The following table was submitted by one of your junior analysts. Critique the table and prepare a revision suitable for inclusion in your report.

Seasonal Variations in Sales ($000s)

Sales Region	Spring	Summer	Fall	Winter
Northeast	120.10	140.59	50.90	30.00
East-Central	118.80	142.70	61.70	25.20
Southeast	142.00	151.80	134.20	100.10
Midwest	100.20	139.42	42.90	20.00
South-Central	80.77	101.00	90.42	78.20
Plains	95.60	120.60	38.50	19.90
Southwest	105.40	110.50	101.60	92.10
Pacific	180.70	202.41	171.54	145.60

6. The management of the Canco Company, a manufacturer of metal cans, presents you with the following information.

The Canco Company Comparative Profit and Loss Statement, Fiscal Years 2001–2005

	2001	2002	2003	2004	2005
Net sales	$40,000,000	$45,000,000	$48,000,000	$53,000,000	$55,000,000
Costs and expenses					
Cost of goods sold (COGS)	$28,000,000	$32,850,000	$33,600,000	$39,750,000	$40,150,000
Selling and administrative expenses	4,000,000	4,500,000	4,800,000	5,300,000	5,500,000
Depreciation	1,200,000	1,350,000	1,440,000	1,590,000	1,650,000
Interest	800,000	900,000	960,000	1,060,000	1,100,000
	$34,000,000	$39,600,000	$40,800,000	$47,700,000	$48,400,000
Profits from operations	6,000,000	5,400,000	7,200,000	5,300,000	6,600,000
Estimated taxes	$ 2,400,000	$ 2,160,000	$ 2,880,000	$ 2,120,000	$ 2,640,000
Net profits	$ 3,600,000	$ 3,240,000	$ 4,320,000	$ 3,180,000	$ 3,960,000

a. Management has asked that you develop a visual aid to present the company's distribution of sales revenues in 2005.

b. Develop a visual aid that compares the change in the net profit level to the change in the net sales level.

c. The management of Canco Company wants you to develop a visual aid that presents the following expenses (excluding COGS) over the five-year period: selling and administrative expenses, depreciation, and interest expenses.

d. Management has the following sales data relating to the company's two major competitors:

	2001	2002	2003	2004	2005
The We-Can Co.	$35,000,000	$40,000,000	$42,000,000	$45,000,000	$48,000,000
The You-Can Co.	$41,000,000	$43,000,000	$45,000,000	$46,000,000	$48,000,000

Prepare a visual aid to facilitate the comparison of Canco Company's sales performance with that of its major competitors.

Epilogue

The topic of marketing research can be approached in several ways. The perspective used in this book is primarily a project emphasis. We focused on the definition of a problem and the research needed to answer it. We separated each step of the research process into logical components so that we could highlight the research design issues that arise at each stage. Yet, as we've stated all along, the steps in the research process are highly interrelated, and a decision made at one stage has implications for the others as well. To remind us how this integration functions, the research process and some of the key decisions that must be made are reviewed in this epilogue.

A research project should not be conceived as the end in itself. Projects arise because managerial problems need solving. The problems themselves may concern the identification of market opportunities, the evaluation of alternative courses of action, or control of marketing operations. These activities are the essence of the managerial function, so the research activity can also be viewed from the broader perspective of the firm's marketing intelligence system.

Marketing research was defined as the function that links the consumer, customer, and public to the marketer through information—information used to identify and define marketing opportunities and problems; to generate, refine, and evaluate marketing actions; to monitor marketing performance; and to improve our understanding of marketing as a process. Addressing these issues involves the systematic gathering, recording, and analyzing of data. These tasks are logically viewed as a sequence called the research process, consisting of the following steps:

1. Formulate the problem.
2. Determine the research design.
3. Design data-collection methods and forms.
4. Design the sample and collect the data.
5. Analyze and interpret the data.
6. Prepare the research report.

The decision problem logically comes first. It dictates the research problem and the design of the project. However, the transition from *problem* to *project* is not an automatic one. There is a good deal of iteration from problem specification to tentative research design to problem respecification to modified research design and back again. This is natural, and one of the researcher's more important roles involves helping define and redefine the problem so that it can be researched and so that it answers the decision maker's problem. This task can be formidable, because it requires a clear specification of objectives, alternatives, and environmental constraints and influences. The decision maker may not readily provide these, and it is up to the researcher to dig them out in order to design effective research.

Sometimes research is not necessary. If the decision maker's views are so strongly held that no amount of information might change them, the research will be wasted.

It is up to the researcher to determine this before, rather than after, conducting the research. Asking "what-if" questions can be diagnostic: What if consumer reaction to the product concept is overwhelmingly favorable? What if it is unfavorable? What if it is only slightly favorable? If the decision maker indicates that the same decision will be made in each case, there are other objectives that have not been explicitly stated. Every research project should have one or more objectives, and one should not proceed to other steps in the process until these can be explicitly stated.

It is also important to ask whether the contemplated benefits of the research exceed the expected costs. It is a mistake to assume that simply because something might change as a result of the research, the research is called for. It may be that the likelihood of finding something that might warrant a change in the decision is so remote that the research still would be wasted. Researchers constantly need to ask: Why should this research be conducted? What could we possibly find out that we do not already know? Will the expected benefits from the research exceed its costs? If the answers indicate research, then the question logically turns to: What kind?

If the problem cannot be formulated as some specific "if-then" relationship, exploratory research is in order. The primary purpose of exploratory research is to gather ideas and insights. The output of an exploratory study will not be answers but more specific questions or statements of tentative relationships. The search for insights demands a flexible research design. Structured questionnaires or probability sampling plans are not used in exploratory research, because the emphasis is not on gathering summary statistics. The personal interview is much more appropriate than the telephone interview, and that, in turn, is more appropriate than a mail survey, to allow for unstructured questions. Interviewees are chosen because they can provide the desired information; thus, a convenience or judgment sample is acceptable here, whereas it would be completely out of place in descriptive or causal research. Focus groups are an extremely useful and popular means for gaining important insights.

When the exploratory effort has generated one or more specific hypotheses to be investigated, the next research thrust would logically be descriptive or causal research. The design actually selected depends on the conviction with which the tentative explanation is held to be the explanation, and the feasibility and cost of conducting an experiment. Though experiments typically provide more convincing proof of causal relationships, they also usually cost more than descriptive designs. This is one reason descriptive designs are the most commonly employed type in marketing research.

Whereas exploratory designs are flexible, descriptive designs are structured. Descriptive designs demand a clear specification of the who, what, when, where, how, and why of the research before data collection begins. They generally employ structured questionnaires or scales because these forms provide advantages in coding and tabulating. In descriptive designs, the emphasis is on generating an accurate picture of the relationships among variables. Probability sampling plans are optimal if one seeks to generalize back to the broader population. Descriptive studies typically rely heavily on cross-tabulation analysis or other means of investigating the association among variables, such as regression analysis, although the emphasis can also be on the search for differences. The great majority of descriptive studies are cross-sectional, although some do use longitudinal information.

Experiments are the best means we have for making inferences about cause-and-effect relationships, because, if designed properly, they provide the most compelling evidence about concomitant variation, time order of occurrence of variables, and elimination of other factors. A key feature of the experiment is that the researcher is able to control who will be exposed to the experimental stimulus (the presumed cause). This assignment of participants to conditions allows the researcher to establish the prior equality of groups by randomization, either with or without matching, which in turn allows the adjustment of the results to eliminate many contaminating influences.

The emphasis in experiments is on testing a specific relationship, so causal designs demand a clear specification of what is to be measured and how it is to be measured. Structured data-collection instruments should be used, and, though structured questionnaires and scales are often employed, experiments can also be used to collect observational data, with the result of typically more objective, accurate information. The major thrust in the analysis of experimental results is a test for differences between those exposed to the experimental stimulus and those not exposed; t-tests and the analysis of variance procedures are most often used.

This brief summary should remind the reader how intimately the marketing research steps are interrelated. Note how the basic nature of the research design implies a number of choices in terms of the structure of the data-collection form, design of the sample, and collection and analysis of the data. A decision about appropriate research design does not completely determine the latter considerations, of course, but definitely suggests their basic qualities. The marketing researcher still has to determine the specific format, e.g., is the structured questionnaire to be disguised or undisguised; is the probability sample to be simple, stratified, or cluster; how large a sample is needed, etc. The marketing researcher has to balance the various sources of error so that the overall total error can be diminished.

Marketing research can be quite complicated. When done well, it is extremely useful and valuable to the manager intent upon making important decisions. Marketing research can also be fun! We hope this text has given you sufficient overview that whether your career takes you close to marketing research questions or you work with marketing research results in a broader managerial scope, you'll understand how to obtain the information you need. We also sincerely hope that in addition to your having a greater appreciation for marketing research information, the text provides sufficient details to serve as a resource throughout your career. Best wishes!

Appendix A

Cumulative Probabilities for the Standard Normal Distribution

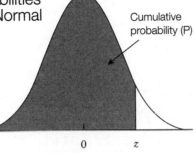

Cumulative probability (P)

0   z

Entries in the table give the area under the curve to the left of the z value. For example, for $z = 1.25$ the cumulative probability is .8944.

z	.00	.01	.02	.03	.04	.05	.06	.07	.08	.09
.0	.5000	.5040	.5080	.5120	.5160	.5199	.5239	.5279	.5319	.5359
.1	.5398	.5438	.5478	.5517	.5557	.5596	.5636	.5675	.5714	.5753
.2	.5793	.5832	.5871	.5910	.5948	.5987	.6026	.6064	.6103	.6141
.3	.6179	.6217	.6255	.6293	.6331	.6368	.6406	.6443	.6480	.6517
.4	.6554	.6591	.6628	.6664	.6700	.6736	.6772	.6808	.6844	.6879
.5	.6915	.6950	.6985	.7019	.7054	.7088	.7123	.7157	.7190	.7224
.6	.7257	.7291	.7324	.7357	.7389	.7422	.7454	.7486	.7517	.7549
.7	.7580	.7611	.7642	.7673	.7704	.7734	.7764	.7794	.7823	.7852
.8	.7881	.7910	.7939	.7967	.7995	.8023	.8051	.8078	.8106	.8133
.9	.8159	.8186	.8212	.8238	.8264	.8289	.8315	.8340	.8365	.8389
1.0	.8413	.8438	.8461	.8485	.8508	.8531	.8554	.8577	.8599	.8621
1.1	.8643	.8665	.8686	.8708	.8729	.8749	.8770	.8790	.8810	.8830
1.2	.8849	.8869	.8888	.8907	.8925	.8944	.8962	.8980	.8997	.9015
1.3	.9032	.9049	.9066	.9082	.9099	.9115	.9131	.9147	.9162	.9177
1.4	.9192	.9207	.9222	.9236	.9251	.9265	.9279	.9292	.9306	.9319
1.5	.9332	.9345	.9357	.9370	.9382	.9394	.9406	.9418	.9429	.9441
1.6	.9452	.9463	.9474	.9484	.9495	.9505	.9515	.9525	.9535	.9545
1.7	.9554	.9564	.9573	.9582	.9591	.9599	.9608	.9616	.9625	.9633
1.8	.9641	.9649	.9656	.9664	.9671	.9678	.9686	.9693	.9699	.9706
1.9	.9713	.9719	.9726	.9732	.9738	.9744	.9750	.9756	.9761	.9767
2.0	.9772	.9778	.9783	.9788	.9793	.9798	.9803	.9808	.9812	.9817
2.1	.9821	.9826	.9830	.9834	.9838	.9842	.9846	.9850	.9854	.9857
2.2	.9861	.9864	.9868	.9871	.9875	.9878	.9881	.9884	.9887	.9890
2.3	.9893	.9896	.9898	.9901	.9904	.9906	.9909	.9911	.9913	.9913
2.4	.9918	.9920	.9922	.9925	.9927	.9929	.9931	.9932	.9934	.9936
2.5	.9938	.9940	.9941	.9943	.9945	.9946	.9948	.9949	.9951	.9952
2.6	.9953	.9955	.9956	.9957	.9959	.9960	.9961	.9962	.9963	.9964
2.7	.9965	.9966	.9967	.9968	.9969	.9970	.9971	.9972	.9973	.9974
2.8	.9974	.9975	.9976	.9977	.9977	.9978	.9979	.9979	.9980	.9981
2.9	.9981	.9982	.9982	.9983	.9984	.9984	.9985	.9985	.9986	.9986
3.0	.9986	.9987	.9987	.9988	.9988	.9989	.9989	.9989	.9990	.9990

Appendix B

Critical Values of χ^2

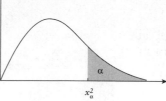

Degrees of Freedom	$\chi^2_{.995}$	$\chi^2_{.990}$	$\chi^2_{.975}$	$\chi^2_{.950}$	$\chi^2_{.900}$
1	0.0000	0.0002	0.0010	0.0039	0.0158
2	0.0100	0.0201	0.0506	0.1026	0.2107
3	0.0717	0.1148	0.2158	0.3518	0.5844
4	0.2070	0.2971	0.4844	0.7107	1.0636
5	0.4117	0.5543	0.8312	1.1455	1.6103
6	0.6757	0.8721	1.2373	1.6354	2.2041
7	0.9893	1.2390	1.6899	2.1673	2.8331
8	1.3444	1.6465	2.1797	2.7326	3.4895
9	1.7349	2.0879	2.7004	3.3251	4.1682
10	2.1559	2.5582	3.2470	3.9403	4.8652
11	2.6032	3.0535	3.8157	4.5748	5.5778
12	3.0738	3.5706	4.4038	5.2260	6.3038
13	3.5650	4.1069	5.0088	5.8919	7.0415
14	4.0747	4.6604	5.6287	6.5706	7.7895
15	4.6009	5.2293	6.2621	7.2609	8.5468
16	5.1422	5.8122	6.9077	7.9616	9.3122
17	5.6972	6.4078	7.5642	8.6718	10.0852
18	6.2648	7.0149	8.2307	9.3905	10.8649
19	6.8440	7.6327	8.9065	10.1170	11.6509
20	7.4338	8.2604	9.5908	10.8508	12.4426
21	8.0337	8.8972	10.2829	11.5913	13.2396
22	8.6427	9.5425	10.9823	12.3380	14.0415
23	9.2604	10.1957	11.6886	13.0905	14.8480
24	9.8862	10.8564	12.4012	13.8484	15.6587
25	10.5197	11.5240	13.1197	14.6114	16.4734
26	11.1602	12.1981	13.8439	15.3792	17.2919
27	11.8076	12.8785	14.5734	16.1514	18.1139
28	12.4613	13.5647	15.3079	16.9279	18.9392
29	13.1211	14.2565	16.0471	17.7084	19.7677
30	13.7867	14.9535	16.7908	18.4927	20.5992
40	20.7065	22.1643	24.4330	26.5093	29.0505
50	27.9907	29.7067	32.3574	34.7643	37.6886
60	35.5345	37.4849	40.4817	43.1880	46.4589
70	43.2752	45.4417	48.7576	51.7393	55.3289
80	51.1719	53.5401	57.1532	60.3915	64.2778
90	59.1963	61.7541	65.6466	69.1260	73.2911
100	67.3276	70.0649	74.2219	77.9295	82.3581

(continued)

Critical Values of χ^2 (continued)

Degrees of Freedom	$\chi^2_{.100}$	$\chi^2_{0.50}$	$\chi^2_{.025}$	$\chi^2_{.010}$	$\chi^2_{.005}$
1	2.7055	3.8415	5.0239	6.6349	7.8794
2	4.6052	5.9915	7.3778	9.2103	10.5966
3	6.2514	7.8147	9.3484	11.3449	12.8382
4	7.7794	9.4877	11.1433	13.2767	14.8603
5	9.2364	11.0705	12.8325	15.0863	16.7496
6	10.6446	12.5916	14.4494	16.8119	18.5476
7	12.0170	14.0671	16.0128	18.4753	20.2777
8	13.3616	15.5073	17.5345	20.0902	21.9550
9	14.6837	16.9190	19.0228	21.6660	23.5894
10	15.9872	18.3070	20.4832	23.2093	25.1882
11	17.2750	19.6751	21.9200	24.7250	26.7568
12	18.5493	21.0261	23.3367	26.2170	28.2995
13	19.8119	22.3620	24.7356	27.6882	29.8195
14	21.0641	23.6848	26.1189	29.1412	31.3193
15	22.3071	24.9958	27.4884	30.5779	32.8013
16	23.5418	26.2962	28.8454	31.9999	34.2672
17	24.7690	27.5871	30.1910	33.4087	35.7185
18	25.9894	28.8693	31.5264	34.8053	37.1565
19	27.2036	30.1435	32.8523	36.1909	38.5823
20	28.4120	31.4104	34.1696	37.5662	39.9968
21	29.6151	32.6706	35.4789	38.9322	41.4011
22	30.8133	33.9244	36.7807	40.2894	42.7957
23	32.0069	35.1725	38.0756	41.6384	44.1813
24	33.1962	36.4150	39.3641	42.9798	45.5585
25	34.3816	37.6525	40.6465	44.3141	46.9279
26	35.5632	38.8851	41.9232	45.6417	48.2899
27	36.7412	40.1133	43.1945	46.9629	49.6449
28	37.9159	41.3371	44.4608	48.2782	50.9934
29	39.0875	42.5570	45.7223	49.5879	52.3356
30	40.2560	43.7730	46.9792	50.8922	53.6720
40	51.8051	55.7585	59.3417	63.6907	66.7660
50	63.1671	67.5048	71.4202	76.1539	79.4900
60	74.3970	79.0819	83.2977	88.3794	91.9517
70	85.5270	90.5312	95.0232	100.4252	04.2149
80	96.5782	101.8795	106.6286	112.3288	116.3211
90	107.5650	113.1453	118.1359	124.1163	128.2989
100	118.4980	124.3421	129.5612	135.8067	140.1695

Appendix C

Critical Values of t

Degrees of Freedom	$t_{.100}$	$t_{.050}$	$t_{.025}$	$t_{.010}$	$t_{.005}$
1	3.078	6.314	12.706	31.821	63.657
2	1.886	2.920	4.303	6.965	9.925
3	1.638	2.353	3.182	4.541	5.841
4	1.533	2.132	2.776	3.747	4.604
5	1.476	2.015	2.571	3.365	4.032
6	1.440	1.943	2.447	3.143	3.707
7	1.415	1.895	2.365	2.998	3.499
8	1.397	1.860	2.306	2.896	3.355
9	1.383	1.833	2.262	2.821	3.250
10	1.372	1.812	2.228	2.764	3.169
11	1.363	1.796	2.201	2.718	3.106
12	1.356	1.782	2.179	2.681	3.055
13	1.350	1.771	2.160	2.650	3.012
14	1.345	1.761	2.145	2.624	2.977
15	1.341	1.753	2.131	2.602	2.947
16	1.337	1.746	2.120	2.583	2.921
17	1.333	1.740	2.110	2.567	2.898
18	1.330	1.734	2.101	2.552	2.878
19	1.328	1.729	2.093	2.539	2.861
20	1.325	1.725	2.086	2.528	2.845
21	1.323	1.721	2.080	2.518	2.831
22	1.321	1.717	2.074	2.508	2.819
23	1.319	1.714	2.069	2.500	2.807
24	1.318	1.711	2.064	2.492	2.797
25	1.316	1.708	2.060	2.485	2.787
26	1.315	1.706	2.056	2.479	2.779
27	1.314	1.703	2.052	2.473	2.771
28	1.313	1.701	2.048	2.467	2.763
29	1.311	1.699	2.045	2.462	2.756
30	1.310	1.697	2.042	2.457	2.750
35	1.306	1.690	2.030	2.438	2.724
40	1.303	1.684	2.021	2.423	2.704
50	1.299	1.676	2.009	2.403	2.678
60	1.296	1.671	2.000	2.390	2.660
120	1.289	1.658	1.980	2.358	2.617
∞	1.282	1.645	1.960	2.326	2.576

Appendix D

Percentage Points of the F Distribution. $\alpha = .05$

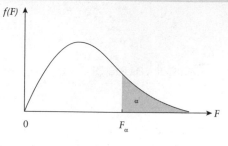

Numerator Degrees of Freedom

v_2 \ v_1	1	2	3	4	5	6	7	8	9
1	161.4	199.5	215.7	224.6	230.2	234.0	236.8	238.9	240.5
2	18.51	19.00	19.16	19.25	19.30	19.33	19.35	19.37	19.38
3	10.13	9.55	9.28	9.12	9.01	8.94	8.89	8.85	8.81
4	7.71	6.94	6.59	6.39	6.26	6.16	6.09	6.04	6.00
5	6.61	5.79	5.41	5.19	5.05	4.95	4.88	4.82	4.77
6	5.99	5.14	4.76	4.53	4.39	4.28	4.21	4.15	4.10
7	5.59	4.74	4.35	4.12	3.97	3.87	3.79	3.73	3.68
8	5.32	4.46	4.07	3.84	3.69	3.58	3.50	3.44	3.39
9	5.12	4.26	3.86	3.63	3.48	3.37	3.29	3.23	3.18
10	4.96	4.10	3.71	3.48	3.33	3.22	3.14	3.07	3.02
11	4.84	3.98	3.59	3.36	3.20	3.09	3.01	2.95	2.90
12	4.75	3.89	3.49	3.26	3.11	3.00	2.91	2.85	2.80
13	4.67	3.81	3.41	3.18	3.03	2.92	2.83	2.77	2.71
14	4.60	3.74	3.34	3.11	2.96	2.85	2.76	2.70	2.65
15	4.54	3.68	3.29	3.06	2.90	2.79	2.71	2.64	2.59
16	4.49	3.63	3.24	3.01	2.85	2.74	2.66	2.59	2.54
17	4.45	3.59	3.20	2.96	2.81	2.70	2.61	2.55	2.49
18	4.41	3.55	3.16	2.93	2.77	2.66	2.58	2.51	2.46
19	4.38	3.52	3.13	2.90	2.74	2.63	2.54	2.48	2.42
20	4.35	3.49	3.10	2.87	2.71	2.60	2.51	2.45	2.39
21	4.32	3.47	3.07	2.84	2.68	2.57	2.49	2.42	2.37
22	4.30	3.44	3.05	2.82	2.66	2.55	2.46	2.40	2.34
23	4.28	3.42	3.03	2.80	2.64	2.53	2.44	2.37	2.32
24	4.26	3.40	3.01	2.78	2.62	2.51	2.42	2.36	2.30
25	4.24	3.39	2.99	2.76	2.60	2.49	2.40	2.34	2.28
26	4.23	3.37	2.98	2.74	2.59	2.47	2.39	2.32	2.27
27	4.21	3.35	2.96	2.73	2.57	2.46	2.37	2.31	2.25
28	4.20	3.34	2.95	2.71	2.56	2.45	2.36	2.29	2.24
29	4.18	3.33	2.93	2.70	2.55	2.43	2.35	2.28	2.22
30	4.17	3.32	2.92	2.69	2.53	2.42	2.33	2.27	2.21
40	4.08	3.23	2.84	2.61	2.45	2.34	2.25	2.18	2.12
60	4.00	3.15	2.76	2.53	2.37	2.25	2.17	2.10	2.04
120	3.92	3.07	2.68	2.45	2.29	2.18	2.09	2.02	1.96
∞	3.84	3.00	2.60	2.37	2.21	2.10	2.01	1.94	1.88

(Denominator Degrees of Freedom)

(continued)

Percentage Points of the F Distribution. α = .05 (continued)

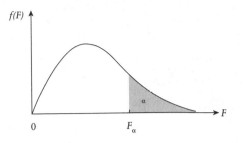

Numerator Degrees of Freedom

v_2 \ v_1	10	12	15	20	24	30	40	60	120	∞
1	241.9	243.9	245.9	248.0	249.1	250.1	251.1	252.2	253.3	254.3
2	19.40	19.41	19.43	19.45	19.45	19.46	19.47	19.48	19.49	19.50
3	8.79	8.74	8.70	8.66	8.64	8.62	8.59	8.57	8.55	8.53
4	5.96	5.91	5.86	5.80	5.77	5.75	5.72	5.69	5.66	5.63
5	4.74	4.68	4.62	4.56	4.53	4.50	4.46	4.43	4.40	4.37
6	4.06	4.00	3.94	3.87	3.84	3.81	3.77	3.74	3.70	3.67
7	3.64	3.57	3.51	3.44	3.41	3.38	3.34	3.30	3.27	3.23
8	3.35	3.28	3.22	3.15	3.12	3.08	3.04	3.01	2.97	2.93
9	3.14	3.07	3.01	2.94	2.90	2.86	2.83	2.79	2.75	2.71
10	2.98	2.91	2.85	2.77	2.74	2.70	2.66	2.62	2.58	2.54
11	2.85	2.79	2.72	2.65	2.61	2.57	2.53	2.49	2.45	2.40
12	2.75	2.69	2.62	2.54	2.51	2.47	2.43	2.38	2.34	2.30
13	2.67	2.60	2.53	2.46	2.42	2.38	2.34	2.30	2.25	2.21
14	2.60	2.53	2.46	2.39	2.35	2.31	2.27	2.22	2.18	2.13
15	2.54	2.48	2.40	2.33	2.29	2.25	2.20	2.16	2.11	2.07
16	2.49	2.42	2.35	2.28	2.24	2.19	2.15	2.11	2.06	2.01
17	2.45	2.38	2.31	2.23	2.19	2.15	2.10	2.06	2.01	1.96
18	2.41	2.34	2.27	2.19	2.15	2.11	2.00	2.02	1.97	1.92
19	2.38	2.31	2.23	2.16	2.11	2.07	2.03	1.98	1.93	1.88
20	2.35	2.28	2.20	2.12	2.08	2.04	1.99	1.95	1.90	1.84
21	2.32	2.25	2.18	2.10	2.05	2.01	1.96	1.92	1.87	1.81
22	2.30	2.23	2.15	2.07	2.03	1.98	1.94	1.89	1.84	1.78
23	2.27	2.20	2.13	2.05	2.01	1.96	1.91	1.86	1.81	1.76
24	2.25	2.18	2.11	2.03	1.98	1.94	1.89	1.84	1.79	1.73
25	2.24	2.16	2.09	2.01	1.96	1.92	1.87	1.82	1.77	1.71
26	2.22	2.15	2.07	1.99	1.95	1.90	1.85	1.80	1.75	1.69
27	2.20	2.13	2.06	1.97	1.93	1.88	1.84	1.79	1.73	1.67
28	2.19	2.12	2.04	1.96	1.91	1.87	1.82	1.77	1.71	1.65
29	2.18	2.10	2.03	1.94	1.90	1.85	1.81	1.75	1.70	1.64
30	2.16	2.09	2.01	1.93	1.89	1.84	1.79	1.74	1.68	1.62
40	2.08	2.00	1.92	1.84	1.79	1.74	1.69	1.64	1.58	1.51
60	1.99	1.92	1.84	1.75	1.70	1.65	1.59	1.53	1.47	1.39
120	1.91	1.83	1.75	1.66	1.61	1.55	1.50	1.43	1.35	1.25
∞	1.83	1.75	1.67	1.57	1.52	1.46	1.39	1.32	1.22	1.00

Denominator Degrees of Freedom

Percentage Points of the F Distribution. $\alpha = .01$

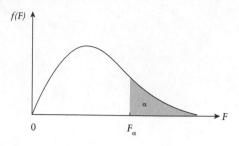

Numerator Degrees of Freedom

ν_2 \ ν_1	1	2	3	4	5	6	7	8	9
1	4052	4999	5404	5624	5764	5859	5928	5981	6022
2	98.50	99.00	99.16	99.25	99.30	99.33	99.36	99.38	99.39
3	34.12	30.82	29.46	28.71	28.24	27.91	27.67	27.49	27.34
4	21.20	18.00	16.69	15.98	15.52	15.21	14.98	14.80	14.66
5	16.26	13.27	12.06	11.39	10.97	10.67	10.46	10.29	10.16
6	13.75	10.92	9.78	9.15	8.75	8.47	8.26	8.10	7.98
7	12.25	9.55	8.45	7.85	7.46	7.19	6.99	6.84	6.72
8	11.26	8.65	7.59	7.01	6.63	6.37	6.18	6.03	5.91
9	10.56	8.02	6.99	6.42	6.06	5.80	5.61	5.47	5.35
10	10.04	7.56	6.55	5.99	5.64	5.39	5.20	5.06	4.94
11	9.65	7.21	6.22	5.67	5.32	5.07	4.89	4.74	4.63
12	9.33	6.93	5.95	5.41	5.06	4.82	4.64	4.50	4.39
13	9.07	6.70	5.74	5.21	4.86	4.62	4.44	4.30	4.19
14	8.86	6.51	5.56	5.04	4.69	4.46	4.28	4.14	4.03
15	8.68	6.36	5.42	4.89	4.56	4.32	4.14	4.00	3.89
16	8.53	6.23	5.29	4.77	4.44	4.20	4.03	3.89	3.78
17	8.40	6.11	5.19	4.67	4.34	4.10	3.93	3.79	3.68
18	8.29	6.01	5.09	4.58	4.25	4.01	3.84	3.71	3.60
19	8.18	5.93	5.01	4.50	4.17	3.94	3.77	3.63	3.52
20	8.10	5.85	4.94	4.43	4.10	3.87	3.70	3.56	3.46
21	8.02	5.78	4.87	4.37	4.04	3.81	3.64	3.51	3.40
22	7.95	5.72	4.82	4.31	3.99	3.76	3.59	3.45	3.35
23	7.88	5.66	4.76	4.26	3.94	3.71	3.54	3.41	3.30
24	7.82	5.61	4.72	4.22	3.90	3.67	3.50	3.36	3.26
25	7.77	5.57	4.68	4.18	3.85	3.63	3.46	3.32	3.22
26	7.72	5.53	4.64	4.14	3.82	3.59	3.42	3.29	3.18
27	7.68	5.49	4.60	4.11	3.78	3.56	3.39	3.26	3.15
28	7.64	5.45	4.57	4.07	3.75	3.53	3.36	3.23	3.12
29	7.60	5.42	4.54	4.04	3.73	3.50	3.33	3.20	3.09
30	7.56	5.39	4.51	4.02	3.70	3.47	3.30	3.17	3.07
40	7.31	5.18	4.31	3.83	3.51	3.29	3.12	2.99	2.89
60	7.08	4.98	4.13	3.65	3.34	3.12	2.95	2.82	2.72
120	6.85	4.79	3.95	3.48	3.17	2.96	2.79	2.66	2.56
∞	6.63	4.61	3.78	3.32	3.02	2.80	2.64	2.51	2.41

(continued)

Percentage Points of the *F* Distribution. $\alpha = .01$ (continued)

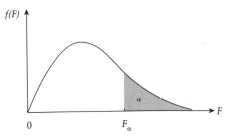

Numerator Degrees of Freedom

v_2 \ v_1	10	12	15	20	24	30	40	60	120	∞
1	6056.	6107.	6157.	6209.	6234.	6260.	6286.	6313.	6340.	6366.
2	99.40	99.42	99.43	99.45	99.46	99.47	99.48	99.48	99.49	99.50
3	27.23	27.05	26.87	26.69	26.60	26.50	26.41	26.32	26.22	26.13
4	14.55	14.37	14.20	14.02	13.93	13.84	13.75	13.65	13.56	13.46
5	10.05	9.89	9.72	9.55	9.47	9.38	9.29	9.20	9.11	9.02
6	7.87	7.72	7.56	7.40	7.31	7.23	7.14	7.06	6.97	6.88
7	6.62	6.47	6.31	6.16	6.07	5.99	5.91	5.82	5.74	5.65
8	5.81	5.67	5.52	5.36	5.28	5.20	5.12	5.03	4.95	4.86
9	5.26	5.11	4.96	4.81	4.73	4.65	4.57	4.48	4.40	4.31
10	4.85	4.71	4.56	4.41	4.33	4.25	4.17	4.08	4.00	3.91
11	4.54	4.40	4.25	4.10	4.02	3.94	3.86	3.78	3.69	3.60
12	4.30	4.16	4.01	3.86	3.78	3.70	3.62	3.54	3.45	3.36
13	4.10	3.96	3.82	3.66	3.59	3.51	3.43	3.34	3.25	3.17
14	3.94	3.80	3.66	3.51	3.43	3.35	3.27	3.18	3.09	3.00
15	3.80	3.67	3.52	3.37	3.29	3.21	3.13	3.05	2.96	2.87
16	3.69	3.55	3.41	3.26	3.18	3.10	3.02	2.93	2.84	2.75
17	3.59	3.46	3.31	3.16	3.08	3.00	2.92	2.83	2.75	2.65
18	3.51	3.37	3.23	3.08	3.00	2.92	2.84	2.75	2.66	2.57
19	3.43	3.30	3.15	3.00	2.92	2.84	2.76	2.67	2.58	2.49
20	3.37	3.23	3.09	2.94	2.86	2.78	2.69	2.61	2.52	2.42
21	3.31	3.17	3.03	2.88	2.80	2.72	2.64	2.55	2.46	2.36
22	3.26	3.12	2.98	2.83	2.75	2.67	2.58	2.50	2.40	2.31
23	3.21	3.07	2.93	2.78	2.70	2.62	2.54	2.45	2.35	2.26
24	3.17	3.03	2.89	2.74	2.66	2.58	2.49	2.40	2.31	2.21
25	3.13	2.99	2.85	2.70	2.62	2.54	2.45	2.36	2.27	2.17
26	3.09	2.96	2.81	2.66	2.58	2.50	2.42	2.33	2.23	2.13
27	3.06	2.93	2.78	2.63	2.55	2.47	2.38	2.29	2.20	2.10
28	3.03	2.90	2.75	2.60	2.52	2.44	2.35	2.26	2.17	2.06
29	3.00	2.87	2.73	2.57	2.49	2.41	2.33	2.23	2.14	2.03
30	2.98	2.84	2.70	2.55	2.47	2.39	2.30	2.21	2.11	2.01
40	2.80	2.66	2.52	2.37	2.29	2.20	2.11	2.02	1.92	1.80
60	2.63	2.50	2.35	2.20	2.12	2.03	1.94	1.84	1.73	1.60
120	2.47	2.34	2.19	2.03	1.95	1.86	1.76	1.66	1.53	1.38
∞	2.32	2.18	2.04	1.88	1.79	1.70	1.59	1.47	1.32	1.00

Denominator Degrees of Freedom

Glossary

A

absolute precision Degree of precision in an estimate of a parameter expressed as within plus or minus so many units.

accuracy Criterion used to evaluate a research report according to whether the reasoning in the report is logical and the information correct.

administrative control Term applied to studies relying on questionnaires and referring to the speed, cost, and control of the replies afforded by the mode of administration.

analysis of cases Intensive study of selected examples of the phenomenon of interest.

analysis of variance (ANOVA) Statistical test used with interval data to determine if two or more samples came from populations with equal means.

area sampling Form of cluster sampling in which areas (e.g., census tracts, blocks) serve as the primary sampling units. The population is divided into mutually exclusive and exhaustive areas using maps, and a random sample of areas is selected. If all the households in the selected areas are used in the study, it is one-stage area sampling. If the areas themselves are subsampled with respect to households, the procedure is two-stage area sampling.

attitudes/opinions Some preference, liking, or conviction regarding a specific object or idea; a predisposition to act.

awareness/knowledge Insight into or understanding of facts about some object or phenomenon.

B

banner A series of cross-tabulations between a criterion, or dependent, variable and several explanatory variables in a single table.

bar chart Chart in which the lengths of the bars show relative amounts of variables or objects.

Bayes' rule Formal mechanism for revising prior probabilities in the light of new information.

Bayesian probability Probability based on a person's subjective or personal judgments and experience.

behavior What respondents have done or are doing.

benchmarking The comparison of one's data (e.g., customers' reception of service quality) to an industry standard, or best-practices.

brain wave research Research technique that assesses the stimuli that participants find arousing or interesting by using electrodes fitted to their head to monitor the electrical impulses emitted by the brain.

branching questions A technique used to direct respondents to different places in a questionnaire based on their response to the question at hand.

brand-switching matrix Two-way table that indicates which brands a sample of people purchased in one period and which brands they purchased in a subsequent period, thus highlighting the switches occurring between brands as well as the number of persons that purchased the same brand in both periods.

C

causal research Research design in which the major emphasis is on determining a cause-and-effect relationship.

census A complete canvass of a population.

Central-Limit Theorem Theorem that holds that if simple random samples of size n are drawn from a parent population with mean μ and variance σ^2, then when n is large, the sample mean will be approximately normally distributed with the mean equal to μ and variance equal to σ^2/n. The approximation becomes more accurate as n becomes larger.

central office edit Thorough and exacting scrutiny and correction of completed data-collection forms, including a decision about what to do with the data.

chi-square goodness-of-fit test Statistical test to determine whether some observed pattern of frequencies corresponds to an expected pattern.

clarity Criterion used to evaluate a research report: is the phrasing in the report precise?

classical probability Probability determined by the relative frequency with which an event occurs when an experiment is repeated under controlled conditions.

cluster analysis Body of techniques concerned with developing natural groupings of objects based on the relationships of the p variables describing the objects.

cluster sample A probability sample distinguished by a two-step procedure in which (1) the parent population is divided into mutually exclusive and exhaustive subsets, and (2) a random sample of subsets is selected. If the investigator then uses all population elements in the selected subsets for the sample, the procedure is one-stage cluster sampling; if a sample of elements is selected probabilistically from the subsets, the procedure is two-stage cluster sampling.

codebook A document that describes each variable, gives it a code name, and identifies its location in the record.

coding Technical procedure by which data are categorized; it involves specifying the alternative categories or classes into which the responses are to be placed and assigning code numbers to the classes.

coefficient alpha A statistic that summarizes the extent to which a set of items making up a measure intercorrelate or go together.

coefficient of concordance Statistic used with ordinal data to measure the extent of association among two or more variables.

coefficient of determination Term used in regression analysis to refer to the relative proportion of the total variation in the criterion variable that can be explained or accounted for by the fitted regression equation.

coefficient of multiple correlation In multiple-regression analysis, the square root of the coefficient of multiple determination.

coefficient of multiple determination In multiple-regression analysis, the proportion of variation in the criterion variable that is accounted for by the covariation in the predictor variables.

coefficient of partial correlation In multiple-regression analysis, the square root of the coefficient of partial determination.

coefficient of partial determination Quantity that results from a multiple-regression analysis that indicates the proportion of variation in the criterion variable not accounted for by the earlier variables that is accounted for by adding a new variable into the regression equation.

coefficient of partial (or net) regression Quantity resulting from a regression that indicates the average change in the criterion variable per unit change in a predictor variable, *holding all other predictor variables constant;* the interpretation applies only when the predictor variables are independent, as required for a valid application of the multiple-regression model.

cohort The aggregate of individuals who experience the same event within the same time interval.

communality Quantity resulting from a factor analysis that expresses the proportion of the variance of a variable extracted by m factors, where m can vary from one to the total number of variables; the communalities help determine how many factors should be retained in a solution.

communication Method of data collection involving questioning of respondents to secure the desired information using a data-collection instrument called a questionnaire.

comparative rating scale Scale requiring participants to make their ratings as a series of relative judgments or comparisons rather than as independent assessments.

completely randomized design Experimental design in which the experimental treatments are assigned to the test units completely at random.

completeness Criterion used to evaluate a research report: does the report provide all the information readers need in a language they understand?

completeness rate (C) Measure used to evaluate and compare interviewers in terms of their ability to obtain needed information from contacted respondents; the completeness rate measures the proportion of complete contacts by an interviewer.

computer-assisted interviewing (CAI) The conducting of surveys using computers to manage the sequence of questions in which the answers are recorded electronically through the use of a keyboard.

conciseness Criterion used to evaluate a research report: is the writing in the report crisp and direct?

conditional association Association existing between two variables when the levels of one or more other variables are considered in the analysis; other variables are called control variables.

conditional probability Probability that Event A will occur when it is known whether another Event B has occurred.

confusion matrix Device used in discriminant analysis to assess the adequacy of the discriminant function; it's a cross-classification table, in which the variables of cross classification are the actual group membership categories and the predicted group membership categories, and the entries are the number of observations falling into each cell.

conjoint analysis Technique in which respondents' utilities or valuations of attributes are inferred from the preferences they express for various combinations of these attributes.

constant sum method A type of comparative rating scale in which an individual is instructed to divide a sum (e.g., 100 points) among two or more attributes on the basis of their importance to him or her.

Construct, or constitutive or conceptual definition Definition in which a given construct is defined in terms of other constructs in the set, sometimes in the form of an equation that expresses the relationship among them.

construct validity Approach to validating a measure by determining what construct, concept, or trait the instrument is in fact measuring.

contact rate (K) Measure used to evaluate and compare the effectiveness of interviewers in making contact with designated respondents. K = number of sample units contacted/total number of sample units approached.

content validity Approach to validating a measure by determining the adequacy with which the domain of the characteristic is captured by the measure; sometimes called face validity.

contingency coefficient Statistic used to measure the extent of association between two nominally scaled attributes.

contingency table Statistical test employing the X^2 statistic that is used to determine whether the variables in a cross-classification analysis are independent.

controlled test market A market in which an entire marketing test program is conducted by an outside service; also called a forced distribution test market.

convenience sample Nonprobability sample, sometimes called an accidental sample, because those included in the sample enter by accident, in that they just happen to be where the study is being conducted when it is being conducted.

convergent validity Confirmation of the existence of a construct determined by the correlations exhibited by independent measures of the construct.

cophenetic value Level at which a pair of objects or classes are linked in cluster analyses.

correlation analysis Statistical technique used to measure the closeness of the linear relationship between two or more interval scaled variables.

cross-sectional study Investigation involving a sample of elements selected from the population of interest at a single point in time.

cross-tabulation Count of the number of cases that fall into each of several categories when the categories are based on two or more variables considered simultaneously.

cumulative distribution function Function that shows the number of cases having a value less than or equal to a specified quantity; the function is generated by connecting the points representing the combinations of Xs (values) and Ys (cumulative frequencies) with straight lines.

cutting score Term used in discriminant analysis to indicate the score that divides the groups; if the object's score is above the cutting score, the object is assigned to one group, whereas if its score is below the cutting score, it is assigned to the other group.

D

data system The part of a decision support system that includes the processes used to capture and the methods used to store data coming from a number of external and internal sources.

decision support system (DSS) A coordinated collection of data, system tools, and techniques with supporting software and hardware by which an organization gathers and interprets relevant information from business and the environment and turns it into a basis for marketing action.

decision tree Decision flow diagram in which the problem is structured in chronological order, typically with small squares indicating decision forks and small circles indicating chance forks.

dendrogram Treelike device employed to interpret the output of a cluster analysis that indicates the groups of objects forming at various similarity levels.

deontology An ethical or moral reasoning framework that focuses on the welfare of the individual and that uses means, intentions, and features of the act itself in judging its ethicality; sometimes referred to as the rights or entitlements model.

depth interview Unstructured personal interview in which the interviewer attempts to get respondents to talk freely and to express their true feelings.

derived population Population of all possible distinguishable samples that could be drawn from a parent population under a specific sampling plan.

descriptive research Research design in which the major emphasis is on determining the frequency with which something occurs or the extent to which two variables covary.

dialog system The part of a decision support system that permits users to explore the databases by employing the system models to produce reports that satisfy their particular information needs; also called language systems.

dichotomous question Fixed-alternative question in which respondents are asked to indicate which of two alternative responses most closely corresponds to their position on a topic.

discriminant analysis Statistical technique employed to model the relationship between a dichotomous or multichotomous criterion variable and a set of p predictor variables.

discriminant validity Criterion imposed on a measure of a construct requiring that it not correlate too highly with measures from which it is supposed to differ.

disguise Amount of knowledge about the purpose of a study communicated to the respondent by the data-collection method. An undisguised questionnaire is one in which the purpose of the research is obvious from the questions posed, whereas a disguised questionnaire attempts to hide the purpose of the study.

disproportionate stratified sampling Stratified sample in which the individual strata or subsets are sampled in relation to both their size and their variability; strata exhibiting more variability are sampled more than proportionately to their relative size, whereas those that are very homogeneous are sampled less than proportionately.

domain sampling model A measurement model that holds that the true score of a characteristic is obtained when all the items in the domain are used to capture it. Only a sample of items is typically used, so a primary source of measurement error is the inadequate sampling of the domain of relevant items; to the extent that the sample of items correlates with true scores, it is good.

double-barreled question A question that calls for two responses and thereby creates confusion for the respondent.

dummy table Table that contains a title and headings to denote the categories to be used for each variable making up the table to categorize the data when they are collected.

dummy (or binary) variable Variable that is given one of two values, 0 or 1, and that is used to provide a numerical representation for attributes or characteristics that are not essentially quantitative.

E

editing Inspection and correction, if necessary, of each questionnaire or observation form.

electronic test market Market or geographic area in which a firm tracks purchases made by specific households that are part of its panel, using identification cards held by panel members and the electronic recording (using scanners) of the products they purchase.

element Term used in sampling to refer to the objects on which measurements are to be taken, such as individuals, households, business firms, or other institutions.

equal-appearing intervals Self-report technique for attitude measurement in which consumers are asked to indicate those statements in a larger list of statements (typically 20 to 22) with which they agree and disagree; their attitude scores are the average score of the scale values of the statements with which they agree.

equivalence Measure of reliability applied to both single instruments and measurement situations. When applied to instruments, the equivalence measure of reliability is the internal consistency or internal homogeneity of the set of items forming the scale; when applied to measurement situations, the equivalence measure of reliability focuses on whether different observers or different instruments used to measure the same individuals or objects at the same point in time yield consistent results.

ethics A concern with the development of moral standards by which situations can be judged; applies to all situations in which there can be actual or potential harm of any kind (e.g., economic, physical, or mental) to an individual or group.

expected value Value resulting from multiplying each consequence by the probability of that consequence occurring and summing the products.

expected value of perfect information Difference between the expected value under certainty and the expected value of the optimal act under uncertainty.

expected value of a research procedure Value determined by multiplying the probability of obtaining the kth research result by the expected value of the preferred decision given the kth research result and summing the products.

expected value under certainty Value derived by multiplying the consequence associated with the optimal act under each possible state of nature by the probability associated with that state of nature and summing the products.

experience survey Interviews with people knowledgeable about the general topic being investigated.

experiment Scientific investigation in which an investigator manipulates and controls one or more independent variables and observes the dependent variable for variation concomitant to the manipulation of the independent variables.

experimental design Research investigation in which the investigator has direct control over at least one independent variable and manipulates at least one independent variable.

experimental mortality Experimental condition in which test units are lost during the course of an experiment.

exploratory research Research design in which the major emphasis is on gaining ideas and insights; particularly helpful in breaking broad, vague problem statements into smaller, more precise subproblem statements.

external data Data that originate outside the organization for which the research is being done.

external validity One criterion by which an experiment is evaluated; the extent to which the observed experimental effect can be generalized to other populations and settings.

eye camera Camera used to study eye movements while the participant reads advertising copy.

F

factor Linear combination of variables.

factor analysis Body of techniques concerned with the study of interrelationships among a set of variables, none of which is given the special status of a criterion variable.

factor loading Quantity that results from a factor analysis and that indicates the correlation between a variable and a factor.

factorial design Experimental design used when the effects of two or more variables are being studied simultaneously; each level of each factor is used with each level of each other factor.

field edit Preliminary edit, typically conducted by a field supervisor, designed to detect the most glaring omissions and inaccuracies in a completed data-collection instrument.

field error Nonsampling error that arises during the actual collection of the data.

field experiment Research study in a realistic situation in which one or more independent variables are manipulated by the experimenter under as carefully controlled conditions as the situation will permit.

field survey Survey research conducted in realistic situations (e.g., shopping mall, home).

fixed-alternative questions Questions in which the responses are limited to stated alternatives.

fixed sample Sample for which size is determined *a priori* and needed information is collected from the designated elements.

focus group Personal interview conducted among a small number of individuals simultaneously; the interview relies more on group discussion than on directed questions to generate data.

frequency polygon Figure obtained from a histogram by connecting the midpoints of the bars of the histogram with straight lines.

full profile An approach to collecting respondents' judgments in a conjoint analysis in which each stimulus is made up of a combination of each of the attributes.

funnel approach An approach to question sequencing that gets its name from its shape, starting with broad questions and progressively narrowing the scope.

fusion coefficients In linkage cluster analysis, the numerical values at which various cases merge to form clusters; also called amalgamation coefficients, can be read from dendrograms.

G

galvanometer Device used to measure the emotion induced by exposure to a particular stimulus by recording changes in the electrical resistance of the skin associated with the minute degree of sweating that accompanies emotional arousal; in marketing research, the stimulus is often specific advertising copy.

geodemography The availability of demographic consumer behavior and lifestyle data by arbitrary geographic boundaries that are typically quite small.

goodness of fit Statistical test employing X^2 to determine whether some observed pattern of frequencies corresponds to an expected pattern. See also chi-square goodness of fit.

graphic rating scale Scale in which individuals indicate their ratings of an attribute by placing a check at the appropriate point on a line that runs from one extreme of the attribute to the other.

H

halo effect Problem arising in data collection when there is carryover from one judgment to another.

histogram Form of bar chart on which the values of the variable are placed along the X axis, or abscissa, and the absolute frequency or relative frequency of occurrence of the values is indicated along the Y axis, or ordinate.

history Specific events external to an experiment but occurring at the same time that may affect the criterion or response variable.

hit rate Measure used to assess the results of a discriminant analysis by measuring the proportion of the objects that were correctly classified by the discriminant function(s) in the group to which they actually belong.

hypothesis A statement that specifies how two or more measurable variables are related.

I

implicit alternative An alternative answer to a question that is not expressed in the options.

implied assumption A problem that occurs when a question is not framed to explicitly state the consequences; thus, it elicits different responses from individuals who assume different consequences.

incidence The percentage of the general population that satisfies the criteria defining the target population.

index of predictive association A statistic used to measure the extent of association between two nominally scaled attributes.

information control Term applied to studies using questionnaires and concerning the amount and accuracy of the information that can be obtained from respondents.

instrument variation Any and all changes in the measuring device used in an experiment that might account for differences in two or more measurements.

intention Anticipated or planned future behavior.

interdependence analysis Problem in multivariate analysis to determine the relationship of a set of variables among themselves; no one variate is selected as special in the sense of the dependent variable.

internal data Data that originate within the organization for which the research is being done.

internal validity One criterion by which an experiment is evaluated; the criterion focuses on obtaining evidence demonstrating that the variation in the criterion variable was the result of exposure to the treatment or experimental variable.

interval scale Measurement in which the assigned numbers legitimately allow the comparison of the size of the differences among and between members.

interviewer-interviewee interaction model Model that attempts to describe how an interviewer and a respondent could be expected to respond to each other during the course of an interview; it is helpful in suggesting techniques by which response errors can be potentially reduced.

item nonresponse Source of nonsampling error that arises when a respondent agrees to an interview but refuses or is unable to answer specific questions.

itemized rating scale Scale in which individuals must indicate their ratings of an attribute or object by selecting one from among a limited number of categories that best describes their attitude toward the attribute or object.

J

judgment sample Nonprobability sample that is often called a purposive sample; the sample elements are handpicked because they are expected to serve the research purpose.

K

k-means One of the nodal or partitioning methods for cluster analysis; the technique revolves around the selection of k starting points and the assignment of each element to the starting point to which it is most similar. After all points are assigned, the mean or centroid for each group is determined. Then the objects are reassigned on the basis of which mean they are closest to, and the process of computing new centroids and reassigning points is repeated until no objects are reclassified.

Kolmogorov-Smirnov test Statistical test employed with ordinal data to determine whether some observed pattern of frequencies corresponds to some expected pattern; also tests whether two independent samples have been drawn from the same population or from populations with the same distribution.

L

laboratory experiment Research investigation in which investigators create a situation with exact conditions in order to control some variables and manipulate others.

Latin-square design Experimental design in which (1) the number of categories for each extraneous variable we wish to control is equal to the number of treatments, and (2) each treatment is randomly assigned to categories according to a specific pattern. The Latin-square design is appropriate when two extraneous factors are to be explicitly controlled.

leading question A question framed to give the respondent a clue about how he or she should answer.

line chart Two-dimensional chart constructed on graph paper in which the X axis represents one variable (typically time) and the Y axis represents another variable.

literature search Search of statistics, trade journal articles, other articles, magazines, newspapers, and books for data or insight into the problem at hand.

longitudinal study Investigation involving a fixed sample of elements that is measured repeatedly through time.

M

mail questionnaire Questionnaire administered by mail to designated respondents with an accompanying cover letter to be returned by mail by the participant to the research organization.

mall intercept A method of data collection in which interviewers in a shopping mall stop a sample of those passing by to ask them if they would be willing to participate in a research study; those who agree are typically taken to any interviewing facility that has been set up in the mall, where the interview is conducted.

market test Controlled experiment, done in a limited but carefully selected sector of the marketplace; its aim is to predict the sales or profit consequences, either in absolute or relative terms, of one or more proposed marketing actions.

marketing information system (MIS) Set of procedures and methods for the regular, planned collection, analysis, and presentation of information for use in making marketing decisions.

marketing research Function linking the consumer to the marketer through information used to identify and define marketing opportunities and problems; to generate, refine, and evaluate marketing actions; to monitor marketing performance; and to improve understanding of marketing as a process.

maturation Processes operating within the test units in an experiment as a function of the passage of time *per se*.

maximum chance criterion Decision rule used in discriminant analysis to develop a comparison yardstick for assessing the predictive accuracy of the discriminant function: the maximum chance criterion holds that an object chosen at random should be classified as belonging to the largest size group.

MDS See multidimensional scaling (MDS)

measurement Rules for assigning numbers to objects to represent quantities of attributes.

method variance The variation in scores attributable to the method of data collection.

model system The part of a decision support system that includes all the routines that allow the user to manipulate the data in order to conduct the kind of analysis the individual desires.

motive Need, want, drive, wish, desire, or impulse, or any inner state that energizes, activates, or moves and that directs or channels behavior toward goals.

multichotomous question Fixed-alternative question in which respondents are asked to choose the alternative that most closely corresponds to their position on the topic.

multicollinearity Condition said to be present in a multiple-regression analysis when the predictor variables are not independent as required but are correlated among themselves.

multidimensional scaling (MDS) Approach to measurement in which people's perceptions of the similarity of objects and their preferences among the objects are measured, and these relationships are plotted in a multidimensional space.

multivariate Problem of analysis in which there are two or more measures of each of n sample objects, and the variables are to be analyzed simultaneously.

N

nominal scale Measurement in which numbers are simply assigned to objects or classes of objects solely for the purpose of identification.

noncoverage error Nonsampling error that arises because of a failure to include some units or entire sections of the defined survey population in the actual sampling frame.

nonobservation error Nonsampling error that arises because of nonresponse from some elements designated for inclusion in the sample.

nonparametric tests Class of statistical tests, also known as distribution-free tests, that are applicable when the data reflect nominal or ordinal measurement or when the data reflect interval measurement but the assumptions required for the appropriate parametric test are not satisfied.

nonprobability sample Sample that relies on personal judgment somewhere in the element-selection process and therefore prohibits estimating the probability that any population element will be included in the sample. See also quota sample.

nonresponse error Nonsampling error that represents a failure to obtain information from some elements of the population that were selected and designated for the sample.

nonsampling errors Errors that arise in research that are not due to sampling; nonsampling errors can occur because of errors in conception, logic, misinterpretation of replies, statistics, and arithmetic; errors in tabulating or coding; or errors in reporting the results.

not-at-home Source of nonsampling error that arises when replies are not obtained from some designated sampling units because the respondents are not at home when the interviewer calls.

O

observation Method of data collection in which the situation of interest is watched and the relevant facts, actions, or behaviors are recorded.

observation error Nonsampling error that arises because inaccurate information is obtained from the sample elements or because errors are introduced in processing the data or in reporting the findings.

office error Nonsampling error that arises in the processing of the data because of errors in editing, coding, entering, tabulating, or some other part of the analysis.

omnibus panel Panel in which the information collected from the participating panel members varies from study to study.

open-ended question Question characterized by the condition that respondents are free to reply in their own words rather than being limited to choosing from among a set of alternatives.

operational definition Definition of a construct that describes the operations to be carried out in order for the construct to be measured empirically.

ordinal scale Measurement in which numbers are assigned to data on the basis of some order (e.g., more than, greater than) of the objects.

outlier Observation so different in magnitude from the rest of the observations that the analyst chooses to treat it as a special case.

overcoverage error Nonsampling error that arises because of the duplication of elements in the list of sampling units.

P

paired comparison A data-collection procedure in which respondents indicate which item in each pair of items is preferred; when used in conjoint analysis, the items in each pair represent predetermined combinations of attributes.

pair-wise procedure Method by which pairs of stimuli (e.g., print ads, brands) are presented to be compared, as when asking consumers, "Which do you prefer?"

panel (omnibus) Fixed sample of respondents who are measured repeatedly over time but on variables that change from measurement to measurement.

panel (true) Fixed sample of respondents who are measured repeatedly over time with respect to the same variables.

parameter Fixed characteristic or measure of a parent or target population.

parametric tests Class of statistical tests used when the variable(s) is (are) measured on at least an interval scale.

part-worth function Function that describes the relationship between the perceived utilities associated with various levels of an attribute and the objective or physical levels of the attributes (e.g., utilities associated with various prices).

payoff table Table containing three elements: alternatives, states of nature, and consequences of each alternative under each state of nature.

people meter A device used to measure when a TV is on, to what channel it is tuned, and who in the household is watching it. Each member in a household is assigned a viewing number, which the individual is supposed to enter into the people meter whenever the set is turned on, the channel is switched, or the person enters or leaves the room.

performance of objective tasks Method of assessing attitudes that rests on the presumption that a person's performance of a specific assigned task (e.g., memorizing a number of facts) depends on the person's attitude.

personal interview Direct, face-to-face conversation between a representative of the research organization (the interviewer) and a respondent, or interviewee.

personal (or subjective) probability See Bayesian probability.

personality Normal patterns of behavior exhibited by an individual; the attributes, traits, and mannerisms that distinguish one individual from another.

physiological reaction technique Method of assessing attitudes in which the researcher, by electrical or mechanical means, monitors the individual's response to the controlled introduction of some stimuli.

pictogram Bar chart in which pictures represent amounts, say, piles of dollars for income, pictures of cars for automobile production, people in a row for population.

pie chart Circle, representing a total quantity, divided into sectors, with each sector showing the size of the segment in relation to that total.

plus-one sampling Technique used in studies employing telephone interviews in which a single randomly determined digit is added to numbers selected from the telephone directory.

population See target population.

power Function associated with a statistical test indicating the probability of correctly rejecting a false null hypothesis.

pragmatic validity Approach to validation of a measure based on the usefulness of the measuring instrument as a predictor of some other characteristic or behavior of the individual; it is sometimes called predictive validity or criterion-related validity.

precision Desired size of the estimating interval when the problem is one of estimating a population parameter; the notion of degree of precision is useful in determining sample size.

pretest Use of a questionnaire (or observation form) on a trial basis in a small pilot study to determine how well the questionnaire (observation form) works.

primary data Information collected specifically for the purpose of the investigation at hand.

primary source Originating source of secondary data.

probability-proportional-to-size sampling Form of cluster sampling in which a fixed number of second-stage units is selected from each first-stage cluster. The probabilities associated with the selection of each cluster are variable because they are related to the relative sizes of each cluster.

probability sample Sample in which each population element has a known, nonzero chance of being included in the sample.

projective technique A method of questioning respondents using a vague stimulus that respondents are asked to describe, expand on, or build a structure around; the basic assumption is that an individual's organization of the relatively unstructured stimulus is indicative of the person's basic perceptions of the phenomenon and reactions to it.

proportional chance criterion Decision rule used in discriminant analysis to develop a comparison yardstick for assessing the predictive accuracy of the discriminant function; the proportional chance criterion compares the percentage of objects likely to be classified correctly by chance alone to the model's algorithm.

proportionate stratified sampling Stratified sample in which the number of observations in the total sample is allocated among the strata in proportion to the relative number of elements in each stratum in the population.

psychographic analysis Technique that investigates how people live, what interests them, and what they like; it is also called lifestyle or *AIO* analysis, because it relies on a number of statements about a person's Activities, Interests, and Opinions.

Q

Q-sort technique General methodology for gathering data and processing the collected information. The participants are assigned the task of sorting various statements by placing a specific number of statements in each sorting category; the emphases are on determining the relative ranking of stimuli by individuals and deriving clusters of individuals who display similar preference orderings of stimuli.

quota sample Nonprobability sample chosen in such a way that the proportion of sample elements possessing a certain characteristic is approximately the same as the proportion of the elements with the characteristic in the population; each field worker is assigned a quota that specifies the characteristics of the people he or she is to contact.

R

random-digit dialing (RDD) Technique used in studies employing telephone interviews in which the numbers to be called are randomly generated.

random error Error in measurement due to the transient aspects of the person or measurement situation.

randomized-block design Experimental design in which (1) the test units are divided into blocks or homogeneous groups using some external criterion, and (2) the objects in each block are randomly assigned to treatment conditions. The randomized-block design is typically employed when there is one extraneous influence to be explicitly controlled.

randomized-response model Interviewing technique in which potentially embarrassing and relatively innocuous questions are paired, and the question the respondent answers is randomly determined.

ratio scale Measurement that has a natural or absolute zero and that therefore allows the comparison of absolute magnitudes of the numbers.

recall loss A type of error caused by a respondent forgetting that an event happened at all.

refusals Nonsampling error that arises because some designated respondents refuse to participate in the study.

regression analysis Statistical technique used to derive an equation that relates a single criterion variable to one or more predictor variables.

relative precision Degree of precision desired in an estimate of a parameter as expressed relative to the level of the estimate of the parameter.

reliability Similarity of results provided by independent but comparable measures of the same object, trait, or construct.

research design Framework or plan for a study that guides the collection and analysis of the data.

research process Sequence of steps in the design and implementation of a research study, including problem formulation, determination of sources of information and research design, determination of data-collection method and design of data-collection forms, design of the sample and collection of the data, analysis and interpretation of the data, and the research report.

response latency The amount of time a respondent deliberates before answering a question.

response rate (R) Measure used to evaluate and compare interviewers in terms of their ability to induce contacted respondents to participate in the study; R = number of interviews/number of contacts.

S

sample Selection of a subset of elements from a larger group of objects.

sample survey Cross-sectional study in which the sample is selected to be representative of the target population and in which the emphasis is on the generation of summary statistics such as averages and percentages; also called a field survey.

sampling control Term applied to studies relying on questionnaires and concerning the researcher's dual abilities to direct the inquiry to a designated respondent and to secure the desired cooperation from that respondent.

sampling distribution Distribution of values of some statistic calculated for each possible distinguishable sample that could be drawn from a parent population under a specific sampling plan.

sampling error Difference between the observed values of a variable and the long-run average of the observed values in repetitions of the measurement.

sampling frame List of sampling units from which a sample will be drawn; the list could consist of geographic areas, institutions, individuals, or other units.

sampling units Nonoverlapping collections of elements from the population.

scanner Electronic device that automatically reads imprinted Universal Product Codes (UPC) as the product is pulled across the scanner, looks up the price in an attached computer, and instantly prints the price of the item on the cash register tape.

secondary data Statistics not gathered for the immediate study at hand but for some other purpose.

secondary source Source of secondary data that did not originate the data but secured them from another source.

selection bias Contaminating influence in an experiment occurring when there is no way of certifying that groups of test units were equivalent at some previous time.

self report Method of assessing attitudes in which individuals are asked directly for their beliefs about or feelings toward an object or class of objects.

semantic differential Self-report technique for attitude measurement in which people are asked to check which cell between a set of bipolar adjectives or phrases best describes their feelings toward the object.

sentence completion Questionnaire containing a number of sentences that consumers are directed to complete with the first words that come to mind.

sequence bias Distortion in the answers to some questions on a questionnaire because the replies are not independently arrived at but are conditioned by responses to other questions; problem is particularly acute in mail questionnaires because the respondent can see the whole questionnaire.

sequential sample Sample formed on the basis of a series of successive decisions. If the evidence is not conclusive after a small sample is taken, more observations are taken; if still inconclusive after these additional observations, still more observations are taken. At each stage, a decision is made about whether more information should be collected or whether the evidence is sufficient to draw a conclusion.

simple random sample Probability sample in which each population element has a known and equal chance of being included in the sample and in which every combination of n population elements is a sample possibility and is just as likely to occur as any other combination of n units.

simple tabulation Count of the number of cases that fall into each category when the categories are based on one variable.

simulated test marketing Test marketing done by firms in shopping malls or consumers' homes as a prelude to a full-scale marketing test for the product.

snake diagram Diagram (so called because of its shape) that connects with straight lines the average responses to a series of semantic differential statements, thereby depicting the profile of the object or objects being evaluated; also called profile plot.

snowball sample Judgment sample that relies on the researcher's ability to locate an initial set of respondents with the desired characteristics; these individuals are then used as informants to identify still others with the desired characteristics.

Spearman's rank correlation coefficient (r_s) A statistic employed with ordinal data to measure the extent of association between two variables.

split ballot A technique used to combat response bias in which one phrasing is used for a question in one-half of the questionnaires whereas an alternative phrasing is used in the other one-half of the questionnaires.

spurious correlation Condition that arises when there is no relationship between two variables but the analyst concludes that a relationship exists.

spurious noncorrelation Condition that arises when the analyst concludes that there is no relationship between two variables but, in fact, there is.

stability A technique for assessing the reliability of a measure by measuring the same objects or individuals at two different points in time and then correlating the scores; the procedure is known as test–retest reliability assessment.

standard error of estimate Term used in regression analysis to refer to the absolute amount of variation in the criterion variable that is left unexplained or unaccounted for by the fitted regression equation.

standard test market A market in which companies sell their products through normal distribution channels.

Stapel scale Self-report technique for attitude measurement in which respondents are asked to indicate how accurately each of a number of statements describes the object of interest.

statistic Characteristic or measure of a sample.

statistical efficiency Measure used to compare sampling plans; one sampling plan is said to be superior (more statistically efficient) to another if, for the same size sample, it produces a smaller standard error of estimate.

statistical regression Tendency of extreme cases of a phenomenon to move toward a more central position during the course of an experiment.

storytelling Questionnaire method of data collection relying on a picture stimulus such as a cartoon, photograph, or drawing, about which the consumer is asked to tell a story.

stratified sample Probability sample that is distinguished by the two-step procedure in which (1) the parent population is divided into mutually exclusive and exhaustive subsets, and (2) a simple random sample of elements is chosen independently from each group or subset.

stratum chart Set of line charts in which quantities are aggregated or a total is disaggregated so that the distance between two lines represents the amount of some variable.

stress Measure of the "badness of fit" of a configuration determined by multidimensional scaling analysis when compared to the original input data.

structure Degree of standardization imposed on the data-collection instrument. A highly structured questionnaire is one in which the questions asked and the responses permitted are completely predetermined; a highly unstructured questionnaire is one in which the questions are only loosely predetermined and respondents are free to respond in their own words and in any way they see fit.

summated ratings Self-report technique for attitude measurement in which people are asked to indicate their degree of agreement or disagreement with each of a number of statements; a person's attitude score is the total obtained by summing the scale values assigned to each category checked.

syndicated research Information collected on a regular basis that is then sold to interested clients (e.g., Nielsen Retail Index).

systematic error Error in measurement that is also known as constant error, since it affects the measurement in a systematic way.

systematic sample Probability sample in which every 8th element in the population is designated for inclusion in the sample after a random start.

T

tabulation Procedure by which the number of cases that fall into each of a number of categories are counted.

tachistoscope Device that provides the researcher timing control over a visual stimulus; in marketing research, the visual stimulus is often a specific advertisement.

target population Totality of cases that conforms to some designated specifications.

teleology An ethical or moral reasoning framework that focuses on the net consequences that an action may have. If the net benefits minus all costs are positive, the act is morally acceptable; if the net result is negative, the act is not morally acceptable.

telephone interview Telephone conversation between a representative of the research organization, the interviewer, and a respondent or interviewee.

telescoping error A type of error resulting from the fact that most people remember an event as having occurred more recently than in fact is the case.

testing effect Contaminating effect in an experiment occurring because the process of experimentation itself affected the observed response. The main testing effect refers to the impact of a prior observation on a later observation, whereas the interactive testing effect refers to the condition when a prior measurement affects the test unit's response to the experimental variable.

Thematic Apperception Test (TAT) Copyrighted series of pictures about which the consumer is asked to tell stories.

total association Association existing between the variables without regard to the levels of any other variables; also called the zero-order association between the variables.

trade-off matrix A method of structuring the stimuli that respondents evaluate in a conjoint analysis that treats two attributes at a time but considers all possible pairs; also known as the pair-wise procedure.

turnover table See brand-switching matrix.

Type I error Rejection of a null hypothesis when it is true; also known as α error.

Type II error Failure to reject a null hypothesis when it is false; also known as β error.

U

unbiased Used to describe a statistic when the average value of the statistic equals the population parameter it is supposed to estimate.

univariate Problem of analysis in which there is a single measurement on each of n sample objects or there are several measurements on each of the n observations, but each variable is to be analyzed in isolation.

utilitarianism The most well-known branch of teleological ethics; the utilitarian perspective holds that the correct course of action is the one that promotes the greatest good for the greatest number and that all acts for which the net benefits exceed the net costs are morally acceptable.

V

validity Term applied to measuring instruments reflecting the extent to which differences in scores on the measurement reflect true differences among individuals, groups, or situations in the characteristic that it seeks to measure, or reflect true differences in the same individual, group, or situation from one occasion to another, rather than constant or random errors.

variable transformation Change in scale in which a variable is expressed.

varimax Angle-preserving rotation of a factor-analytic solution done to facilitate substantive interpretation of the factors.

voice-pitch analysis Type of analysis that examines changes in the relative frequency of the human voice that accompany emotional arousal.

W

word association Questionnaire containing a list of words to which respondents are instructed to reply with the first word that comes to mind.

Z

zero-order association See total association.

Subject Index

Author Index